W9-AGA-431

The Study of Second Language Acquisition

Rod Ellis

Oxford University Press

Oxford University Press
Great Clarendon Street, Oxford, OX2 6DP

Oxford New York
Athens Auckland Bangkok Bogota Bombay Buenos Aires
Calcutta Cape Town Dar es Salaam Delhi Florence Hong Kong
Istanbul Karachi Kuala Lumpur Madras Madrid Melbourne
Mexico City Nairobi Paris Singapore Taipei Tokyo Toronto Warsaw

and associated companies in
Berlin Ibadan

Oxford and *Oxford English* are trade marks of
Oxford University Press.

ISBN 0 19 437189 1

© Rod Ellis 1994

First published 1994
Fifth impression 1997

No unauthorized photocopying

All rights reserved. No part of this publication may be reproduced,
stored in a retrieval system, or transmitted, in any form or by any
means, electronic, mechanical, photocopying, recording or otherwise,
without the prior written permission of Oxford University Press.

This book is sold subject to the condition that it shall not, by way of
trade or otherwise, be lent, resold, hired out, or otherwise circulated
without the publisher's prior consent in any form of binding or cover
other than that in which it is published and without a similar
condition including this condition being imposed on the subsequent
purchaser.

Set by Tradespools Ltd., Frome, Somerset

Printed in Hong Kong

Contents

Acknowledgements

Many people have assisted me in the preparation of this book, but, of course, I alone am responsible for any shortcomings. I would like to give special thanks to Henry Widdowson and Gaby Kasper, both for their support and their critical acumen. Others who have commented on individual chapters are Leslie Beebe, Kevin Gregg, Eric Kellerman, Patsy Lightbown, Barry McLaughlin, Teresa Pica, Peter Skehan, Elaine Tarone, Leo van Lier, Lydia White, and Julia Sallabank of Oxford University Press. Above all I am grateful for the support provided by Temple University Japan: both its students, who have been instrumental in shaping the contents of the book, and Ken Schaefer for helping me to maintain belief in its value and for ensuring that I had the time to write it. A special word of thanks is due to Andrew Jones for helping me to prepare the manuscript for publication and for providing a final—and crucial—'test' of its contents.

The author and publisher are grateful to the following for permission to reproduce extracts and figures from copyright material:

Ablex Publishing Corporation: extract from Blum-Kulka, S., House, J., and Kasper, G.: *Cross Cultural Pragmatics* (1989), and table from Pica, T. and Doughty C., 'Variations in classroom interaction as a function of participation pattern and task' in Fine, J. (ed.): *Second Language Discourse: A Textbook of Current Research* (1988);

Academic Press Inc: table from Givón, T.: *On Understanding Grammar* (1979), and a figure from Wenk, B. and Wioland, F., 'Is French really syllable-timed?' in *Journal of Phonetics: 10* (1982);

John Benjamins Publishing Company, Amsterdam/Philadelphia: figures from Lydia White: *Universal Grammar and Second Language Acquisition* (1989), and table from Susan Gass and Josh Ard, 'Second Language acquisition and the ontology of language universals' in William E. Rutherford (ed.): *Typological Universals and Second Language Acquisition* (1984);

Blackwell Publishers and the author: figure from Preston, D.R.: *Sociolinguistics and Second Language Acquisition* (1989);

Cambridge University Press and the authors: table from Bickerton, D.: *Dynamics of a Creole System* (1975), table from Stern, H., 'Analysis and experience as variables in second language pedagogy' in Harley, B. et al.: *The Development of Second Language Proficiency* (1990), figure from Allwright, D. and Bailey, K.: *Focus on the Language Classroom: An Introduc-*

tion to Classroom Research for Language Teachers (1991), table from Young, R., 'Variation and the interlanguage hypothesis' in *Studies in Second Language Acquisition 10* (1988), table from Kellerman, E., 'Transfer and non-transfer: Where are we now?' in *Studies in Second Language Acquisition 2* (1979), table from Gardner, R. and McIntyre, P., 'An instrumental motivation in language study: Who says it isn't effective?' in *Studies in Second Language Acquisition 13* (1991), and adapted figure from White, L., 'Argument structure in second language acquisition' in *Journal of French Language Studies* (1991);

Edinburgh University Press: table from Long, M. and Sato, C., 'Methodological issues in interlanguage studies: an interactionist perspective' in Davies, A. et al.: *Interlanguage* (1984);

Professor Robert C. Gardner: figure from Gardner, R.: *Social Psychology and Second Language Learning: The Role of Attitude and Motivation* (Edward-Arnold, 1985);

Heinle and Heinle Publishers: table from Gass, S. and Varonis, E., 'Task variation and nonnative/nonnative negotiation of meaning', and extract from Olshtain, E. and Blum-Kulka, S., 'Degree of approximation: nonnative reactions to native speech act behavior', both in Gass, S. and Madden, C. (eds.): *Input in Second Language Acquisition* (Newbury House, 1985), and figure from Oxford, R.: *Language Learning Strategies: What Every Teacher Should Know* (Newbury House, 1990);

ICG Publication: figure from Chomsky, N.: *Lectures on Government and Binding* (Foris, 1981);

A. Jones: table from unpublished paper, 'Review of studies on the acquisition of relative clauses in English' (1991);

Professor G. Kasper: diagram from Kasper, G., 'Perspectives on language transfer' in *BAAL Newsletter* 24 (1984);

The Macmillan Press Ltd: table from Nunan, D., 'The teacher as researcher' in Brumfit, C. and Mitchell, R. (eds.): *Research in the Language Classroom*, ELT Documents No. 133 (Modern English Publications, in association with the British Council, 1990);

Oxford University Press: figure from Pit Corder, S.: *Error Analysis and Interlanguage* (1981), 2 tables from Ellis, R.: *Understanding Second Language Acquisition* (1985), figure from Tarone, E., 'On the variability of interlanguage systems' in *Applied Linguistics* 4 (1983), figure from Bialystok, E. and Sharwood Smith, M., 'Interlanguage is not a state of mind: an evaluation of the construct for second language acquisition' in *Applied Linguistics* 6 (1985), and table from Mangubhai, F., 'The processing behaviours of adult second language learners and their relationship to second language proficiency' in *Applied Linguistics* 12 (1991);

Prentice-Hall Inc., Englewood Cliffs, New Jersey: table from Chamot, A., 'The learning strategies of ESL students' in Wenden, A. and Rubin, J. (eds.): *Learner Strategies in Language Learning* © 1987;

The Research Club in Language Learning and the authors: table from Schachter, J., 'An error in error analysis' (1974), in *Language Learning* 27, extract from Eckman, F., 'Markedness and the contrastive analysis hypothesis' (1977), in *Language Learning* 27, figure from Bialystok, E., 'A theoretical model of second language learning' (1978), in *Language Learning* 29, figure from Zobl, H., 'Markedness and the projection problem' (1983) in *Language Learning* 33;

Sage Publications Inc.: figure from Gass, S. and Varonis, E., 'Miscommunication in nonnative speaker discourse' in Coupland, N., Giles, H., and Wiemann, J. (eds.): *Miscommunication and Problematic Talk* (1991);

Teachers of English to Speakers of Other Languages Inc. (TESOL) and the authors: figure from Krashen, S., 'Some issues relating to the monitor model' (1977) and table from Tarone, E., 'Typology of communication strategies in interlanguage: a progress report' (1977), both in Brown, H., Yorio, C. and Crymes, R. (eds.): *On TESOL '77*, table from Allen, J.P.B., Fröhlich, M. and Spada, N., 'The communicative orientation of language teaching: an observation scheme' (1984) in Handscome, J., Orem, R., and Taylor, B. (eds.): *On TESOL '83: The Question of Control*, and table from Long, M., 'Does second language instruction make a difference? A review of the research' (1983) in *TESOL Quarterly* 17.

Despite every effort to trace and contact copyright holders before publication, this has not always been possible. If notified, the publisher will be pleased to rectify any errors or omissions at the earliest opportunity.

For Takayo

Introduction

Second language acquisition research: some developments

Although it is not possible to set a precise date on when second language acquisition (SLA) research first established itself as a field of enquiry, there is general agreement that it took place around the end of the 1960s. At this time, some of the first studies of second language (L2) learners were published (for example, Ravem 1968; Huang 1970). At the same time a theoretical case for examining L2 acquisition was advanced (for example, Corder 1967). From that point SLA research developed rapidly and continues to do so. There has been an enormous amount of empirical research directed at describing the characteristics of L2 learner language and how these change as acquisition takes place. There has also been a growing interest in theory construction, as reflected in the plethora of frameworks, models and theories now available.

The developments in SLA research over the years have been of several kinds. One development concerns the scope of the field of enquiry. Whereas much of the earlier work focused on the linguistic—and, in particular, the grammatical—properties of learner language and was psycholinguistic in orientation, later work has also attended to the pragmatic aspects of learner language and, increasingly, has adopted a sociolinguistic perspective. Thus, whereas many researchers continue to focus their attention on how L2 learners develop grammatical competence, many others are concerned with how learners develop the ability to perform speech acts such as requests or apologies appropriately. Similarly, whereas many researchers continue the long-standing attempt to explain the psycholinguistic processes that underlie L2 acquisition and use, others have given attention to the social factors that influence development. The result is that the scope of SLA research is now much wider than in the 1970s or even early 1980s.

A second development concerns the increasing attention paid by SLA research to linguistic theory. This is most evident in the studies based on Chomsky's model of grammar (Universal Grammar), but is also apparent in work based on functional models of language (for example, Givón 1979a; 1995) and language typology (for example, Comrie 1984). Thus, whereas much of the earlier work made use of fairly simple grammatical concepts, derived from descriptive grammars, the later work makes greater use of technical concepts derived from a particular theory of grammar. The relationship between SLA research and linguistics is increasingly symbiotic, in the sense that L2 researchers and linguists both draw on each others' work. SLA research, therefore, is no longer a consumer of linguistics, but also a contributor to it.

Another significant development in SLA research has been the increase in theory-led research, which, in part, is a reflection of its relationship with linguistics. Much of the earlier research was of the 'research-then-theory' kind. Typically, it involved the collection of samples of learner language, their analysis, and the description of their main characteristics. Explanations of the main features were a matter of *post hoc* interpretation. This was both inevitable and desirable given the lack of hard information about what learners do when they acquire an L2. However, as theories have been developed, researchers have increasingly sought to confirm them by identifying and testing specific hypotheses, often experimentally. A brief examination of some of the current journals that publish L2 acquisition research (for example, *Language Learning, Studies in Second Language Acquisition, Second Language Research*) will reveal the current primacy of theory-led, experimental-type research. However, although there has been a general increase in confirmatory research, many studies of the interpretative kind continue to be published.

The main thrust of SLA research in the early years addressed the universal properties of L2 acquisition—looking for commonalities across learners of different ages, in different settings and with different L1s. There was, however, an alternative tradition that pre-dated the early studies of learner language—the study of how individuals differ. The 1950s and early 1960s, for example, had witnessed intensive research on language aptitude, one of the main factors contributing to individual differences, while the late 1960s and 1970s also saw a substantial body of work on motivation. This tradition, which for a while was partially submerged as SLA research established itself, has now reasserted itself and is viewed as part of the total field of enquiry. However, the study of L2 acquisition as a phenomenon with universal properties and the study of individual differences in L2 learners have not been fully integrated; the study of 'learning' and of 'learners', somewhat surprisingly, exist as separate areas within SLA research.

It is also possible to detect the emergence of another fairly distinct sub-field of SLA research devoted to investigating classroom L2 acquisition. Classroom studies of L2 learners date back to the inception of SLA research. However, many of the early studies deliberately focused on learners in natural settings. Subsequently, studies of classroom learners, either in actual classrooms or in settings that simulate classroom conditions, have proliferated. Some of these studies were designed to investigate issues important to language pedagogy but many were explicitly concerned with theoretical issues related to L2 acquisition.

As a result of these developments, SLA research has become a rather amorphous field of study with elastic boundaries. This makes the task of surveying the field a difficult one, and only a few few attempts have been made to do so: for example, Ellis 1985a, McLaughlin 1987, Spolsky 1989, and Larsen-Freeman and Long 1991. Instead, scholars have usually preferred to identify specific areas of SLA research. Thus, books on such topics as learner errors, vocabulary acquisition, Universal Grammar and L2 acquisition, L2 pragmatics, variability, the role of input, the role of social factors, attitudes and motivation, learner strategies, and classroom L2 acquisition are more common. In a sense, SLA research stands at the cross-roads. It may continue as a coherent field of enquiry with its own recognized research community, or it may splinter into a series of sub-fields, and, in some cases, perhaps become submerged in the 'mother' disciplines that inform these sub-fields.

The aims of the book

The extent to which SLA research can claim to constitute a discipline in its own right depends on whether it is possible to identify a defined field of enquiry and a body of knowledge relating to it. The main aim of this book, therefore, is to develop a framework for describing the field as it currently exists and to use this framework to provide an extensive account of what is currently known about L2 acquisition and L2 learners. It is intended to tackle this 'descriptively'—to avoid taking up any particular position regarding what constitutes the most legitimate approach to SLA research. The account offered, therefore, aims to be balanced and objective, as far as this is possible. Inevitably, though, the personal views of the author will colour the picture provided. Also, although the emphasis will be on 'describing' what has been discovered, attention will also be given to the evaluation of the methodologies that have been used to conduct research, of the significance of the information that has been unearthed, and of the theories that have been developed to explain the findings. Again, though, as far as possible, these evaluations will strive for objectivity by reflecting a range of opinion.

The book's audience

This book has been written for three kinds of reader. One is students of SLA research—those who are beginning their study of L2 acquisition and wish to obtain an understanding of the principal issues that have been addressed, the methods used to research them, the main findings and the theories that have been developed to explain them. It is hoped that the book will provide an accessible introduction to the field.

The second kind of reader is the SLA researcher who feels the need for a reference book that provides an overview of the main work accomplished in the different areas of SLA research. Such readers are likely to be experts in one or more areas of SLA research and, therefore, may have little need for the chapters that deal with their areas of specialism, but may wish to benefit from a survey of the work undertaken in other areas with which they have less familiarity. As has already been pointed out, the scope of the field is now very large and the amount of published research enormous, with the result that few researchers are able to keep themselves up to date in work undertaken in all areas.

The third, and probably the principal kind of reader for which this book is intended, is second/foreign language teachers, many of whom may be completing a post-service programme of teacher education (for example, an MA or Diploma in TESOL or Applied Linguistics). It is pertinent, therefore, to consider why teachers should make the effort to read about L2 acquisition.

Second language acquisition research and language pedagogy

The main reason why language teachers need to be familiar with SLA research was stated in my earlier book (Ellis 1985a) as follows:

> ... unless we know for certain that the teacher's scheme of things really does match the learner's way of going about things, we cannot be sure that the teaching content will contribute directly to language learning (Ellis 1985a: 1).

The study of SLA provides a body of knowledge which teachers can use to evaluate their own pedagogic practices. It affords a learning- and learner-centred view of language pedagogy, enabling teachers to examine critically the principles upon which the selection and organization of teaching have been based and also the metholodogical procedures they have chosen to employ. Every time teachers make a pedagogic decision about content or methodology, they are, in fact, making assumptions about how learners learn. The study of SLA may help teachers in two ways. First, it will enable them to make their assumptions about learning explicit, so that they can examine them critically. In this way, it will help them to develop their own explicit ideas of how the kind of learners they are teaching acquire an L2. Second, it will provide them information that they can use when they make future pedagogic decisions.

Of course, SLA research is not the only source of information of relevance to language teachers. There are other areas of enquiry—some with much longer histories than SLA research—which are important. Stern (1983) identifies five areas that language pedagogy draws on for its 'fundamental concepts'—the history of language teaching, linguistics, sociology, psychology, and education. SLA research, as we have seen, is, like language pedagogy itself, a hybrid discipline, drawing on a range of other disciplines for its own constructs. However, it would be a mistake to treat SLA research as a mediating discipline that takes concepts from other disciplines and moulds them into a form applicable to language pedagogy. SLA research has its own agenda and is best treated as another source discipline. Language pedagogy will draw on SLA research in the same way as it draws on other areas of enquiry. If it is given privileged status, then, this will only be because its aims—the description and explanation of how L2 learning takes place—are of obvious relevance to the practice of language teaching.

The information provided by SLA research, then, needs to be 'applied' in the same way as that from other sources. Indeed, caution needs to be exercised when it comes to making use of the information it supplies. SLA research is not capable of providing teachers with recipes for successful practice. As will become clear later, there is no comprehensive theory of SLA, nor even any single theory that is widely accepted. Researchers do not even agree completely over what constitutes the descriptive 'facts' of L2 acquisition. There is much disagreement and controversy—a reflection of the highly complex nature of L2 acquisition and the relative immaturity of the field. For these reasons, SLA research should be treated as providing teachers with 'insights' which they can use to build their own explicit theory. It is on the basis of this theory—not on the basis of SLA research itself or any theory it has proposed—that teaching practice should proceed.

The structure and contents of the book

The contents of this book have been organized in accordance with a general conceptual framework that takes account of (1) a general distinction between the 'description' and 'explanation' of L2 acquisition, and (2) the various subfields that have developed over the years. The following are the main Parts with a brief summary of their contents:

Part 1: Background

This section contains one chapter that outlines the conceptual framework of the whole book.

Part 2: The description of learner language

This section reports some of the main findings regarding the nature of learner language. It considers learner errors, developmental patterns, variability, and pragmatic features.

Part 3: Explaining second language acquisition: external factors

This section begins the task of explaining L2 acquisition by considering external influences—the role of social factors and of input/interaction.

Part 4: Explaining second language acquisition: internal factors

This section continues the work of explaining L2 acquisition by examining various theories of the mental processing that learners engage in.

Three perspectives on these processes are offered—language transfer, cognitive accounts of L2 acquisition, and linguistic universals.

Part 5: Explaining individual differences in second language acquisition

In this section the focus of attention switches from 'learning' to 'the learner'. Individual differences are considered from the point of view of general psychological factors (for example, motivation) and learner strategies.

Part 6: Classroom second language acquisition

This Part examines classroom-based and classroom-orientated research, from the point of view of both interaction and formal instruction.

Part 7: Conclusion

The book concludes with a critical look at the 'state of the art' of SLA research from the point of view of the data it works with, theory construction, and its applications.

There is no separate chapter on research methodology in SLA research, mainly because the methods used vary considerably according to the particular aspect of SLA being studied. However, where appropriate, information about the methods used to investigate specific areas is provided in the individual chapters.

A note on terminology

The term 'second language acquisition research' (SLA research) is used to refer to the general field of enquiry. It labels the discipline that is the focus of this book. The term 'L2 acquisition' serves as an abbreviation for 'the acquisition of a second language'. This is what learners try to do and is the object of study in SLA research.

For reasons explained later no distinction is made between 'acquisition' and 'learning', the two terms being used interchangeably.

Throughout the book, words explained in the Glossary are in italic type.

PART ONE
Background

Introduction

As was noted in the Introduction to this book, second language acquisition research (SLA research) has developed into a wide-reaching and somewhat amorphous field of enquiry, drawing on and contributing to a number of distinct disciplines—linguistics, cognitive psychology, psycholinguistics, sociolinguistics, and education. The extent to which it is still justifiable to treat SLA research as a coherent field, with identifiable goals and methods of enquiry, depends on whether it is possible to provide a clear definition of the object of enquiry (second language acquisition) and to delineate a framework that gives some structure to the issues it seeks to address.

The purpose of the chapter in this section (Chapter 1) is to attempt such a definition and to outline a framework that can serve as a means for examining the key issues. It asserts that the study of second language acquisition entails both the description of learner language, as it develops over time, and the explanation of its characteristics. While a strict separation of these twin goals—description and explanation—is not possible, it provides a way into the study of a highly complex field. It also accords with the way the field has developed historically, for whereas much of the earlier work concentrated on description, the later work has been more concerned, perhaps, with the search for a theory of second language acquisition.

1 Second language acquisition research: An overview

Introduction

The main purpose of this chapter is to set the scene for the rest of the book. In order to do this the chapter will (1) examine what is meant by the term Second Language Acquisition, (2) identify a number of central questions which second language acquisition research has addressed, and (3) present a framework for examining four major areas of enquiry and provide a brief survey of work done in each.

What is second language acquisition?

The obvious first step in the exploration of SLA research is to establish a clear understanding of what the object of the field of study is—second language acquisition. This is particularly important because, as will become evident in subsequent chapters, the nature of this object is far from clear, and different researchers have given very different interpretations of it. We will begin by examining a number of points relating to the meaning of the term 'second language acquisition'.

'Second' v. 'third' language acquisition

Many learners are multilingual in the sense that in addition to their first language they have acquired some competence in more than one non-primary language. *Multilingualism* is the norm in many African and Asian countries. Sometimes a distinction is made between a 'second' and a 'third' or even 'fourth' language. However, the term 'second' is generally used to refer to any language other than the first language. In one respect this is unfortunate, as the term 'second' when applied to some learning settings, such as those in South Africa involving black learners of English, may be perceived as opprobrious. In such settings, the term 'additional language' may be both more appropriate and more acceptable.

Second v. foreign language acquisition

A distinction between *second* and *foreign* language acquisition is sometimes made. In the case of second language acquisition, the language plays an institutional and social role in the community (i.e. it functions as a recognized means of communication among members who speak some other language as their mother tongue). For example, English as a second language is learnt in the United States, the United Kingdom, and countries in Africa such as Nigeria and Zambia. In contrast, foreign language learning takes place in settings where the language plays no major role in the community and is primarily learnt only in the classroom. Examples of foreign language learning are English learnt in France or Japan.

The distinction between second and foreign language learning settings may be significant in that it is possible that there will be radical differences in both what is learnt and how it is learnt. However, for the time being the extent to which the sociolinguistic conditions of learning determine learning outcomes or learning processes must remain an open question—to be answered as a result of our exploration of SLA research. This is addressed in greater depth in Chapter 6. There is a need for a neutral and superordinate term to cover both types of learning. Somewhat confusingly, but in line with common usage, the term 'second language acquisition' will be used for this purpose.

Naturalistic v. instructed second language acquisition

A distinction will be made between *naturalistic* and *instructed* second language acquisition, according to whether the language is learnt through communication that takes place in naturally occurring social situations or through study, with the help of 'guidance' from reference books or classroom instruction.

Klein (1986) similarly distinguishes 'spontaneous' and 'guided' acquisition, treating the distinction as a psycholinguistic one. He argues that the learner focuses on communication in naturalistic second language acquisition and thus learns incidentally, whereas in instructed second language acquisition the learner typically focuses on some aspect of the language system. It may be better, however, to view the distinction as only a sociolinguistic one—i.e. reflecting the settings and activities in which learners typically participate. It would certainly be wrong to assume that naturalistic learning is subconscious and instructed learning conscious. It remains an open question as to whether the process of acquisition is the same or different in naturalistic or classroom settings. In this book, therefore, the distinction will be used only in its sociolinguistic sense.

Competence v. performance

A distinction is often made between *linguistic competence* and *performance* when studying language. According to Chomsky (1965), competence consists of the mental representations of linguistic rules that constitute the speaker-hearer's internal grammar. This grammar is implicit rather than explicit and is evident in the intuitions which the speaker-hearer has about the grammaticality of sentences. Performance consists of the use of this grammar in the comprehension and production of language. The distinction between competence and performance has been extended to cover communicative aspects of language (see Hymes 1971a; Canale and Swain 1980). *Communicative competence* includes knowledge the speaker-hearer has of what constitutes appropriate as well as correct language behaviour and also of what constitutes effective language behaviour in relation to particular communicative goals. That is, it includes both linguistic and pragmatic knowledge. Communicative performance consists of the actual use of these two types of knowledge in understanding and producing discourse.

The main goal of SLA research is to characterize learners' underlying knowledge of the L2, i.e. to describe and explain their competence. However, learners' mental knowledge is not open to direct inspection; it can only be inferred by examining samples of their performance. SLA researchers have used different kinds of performance to try to investigate competence. Many analyse the actual utterances that learners produce in speech or writing (for example, Larsen-Freeman 1975). Some try to tap learners' intuitions about what is correct or appropriate by means of judgement tasks (for example, White 1985), while others rely on the introspective and retrospective reports that learners provide about their own learning (for example, Cohen 1984). Needless to say none of these provide a direct window into competence. Also, not surprisingly, very different results can be obtained depending on the kind of performance data the researcher studies.

Usage v. use

The distinction between *usage* and *use* was first proposed by Widdowson (1978) to facilitate a discussion of language pedagogy but it is equally applicable to language acquisition. Usage is 'that aspect of performance which makes evident the extent to which the language user demonstrates his knowledge of linguistic rules' (p. 3). We study usage if we focus attention on the extent to which the learner has mastered the formal properties of the phonological, lexical, and grammatical systems. Use is that aspect of performance which 'makes evident the extent to which the language user demonstrates his ability to use his knowledge of linguistic rules for effective communication'. We study use if we examine how learners convey meaning through the process of constructing discourse. One way in which this can be undertaken is by studying pragmatic aspects of language, such as how learners learn to perform speech acts like requests and apologizing.

SLA research has been primarily concerned with studying usage, although it is now paying more attention to use. It has become apparent that even if the aim is to find out how learners acquire purely formal features (such as verb + *-ing* or copula 'be'), it is often necessary to examine how they use these features to express meaning. Thus, analyses based on 'form' only have increasingly given way to analyses of 'form–function' and 'function–form' correspondences. Many researchers are no longer content to ask whether learners provide evidence of the correct usage of a form such as the present progressive tense in contexts that call for it. They also want to know what meanings learners use the form to perform and, in particular, whether they use it to perform meanings other than those it serves in the target language. For example, learners who say 'Sharpening please' when they want someone to sharpen their pencil are using verb + -*ing* to perform a function (commanding) which it does not usually have in the target language. Other researchers, particularly those interested in pragmatic characteristics of learner language, take 'function' as their starting point and investigate the different forms that learners use to perform specific functions.

Precisely what should be the object of enquiry in SLA research is a matter of controversy, however. On the one hand, there are researchers who argue that many properties of language are purely formal in nature.[1] On the other, there are those who emphasize the importance of studying the functional uses of language. SLA research currently employs both types of enquiry.

'Acquisition'

In order to study how learners acquire a second language, a clear, operational definition of what is meant by the term 'acquisition' is needed. Unfortunately, researchers have been unable to agree on such a definition. 'Acquisition' can mean several things.

First, some researchers (for example, Krashen 1981) distinguish between 'acquisition' and 'learning'. The former refers to the subconscious process of 'picking up' a language through exposure and the latter to the conscious process of studying it. According to this view, it is possible for learners to 'acquire' or to 'learn' rules independently and at separate times. Although such a distinction can have strong face validity—particularly for teachers—it is problematic, not least because of the difficulty of demonstrating whether the knowledge learners possess is of the 'acquired' or 'learnt' kind.[2] In this book the terms 'acquisition' and 'learning' will be used interchangeably. They will be placed inside inverted commas if used in their distinctive senses.

Second, researchers disagree about what kind of performance they think provides the best evidence of acquisition. We have already noted that some researchers work with production data, some study learners' intuitions about the L2, while others access learners' introspections. Also, some researchers (for example, Bickerton 1981) consider a feature has been acquired when it appears for the first time, while others (for example, Dulay and Burt 1980) require the learner to use it to some predetermined criterion level of accuracy, usually 90 per cent. Thus, a distinction can be made between acquisition as 'emergence' or 'onset' and acquisition as 'accurate use'.

Clearly 'acquisition' can mean several very different things. This makes it very difficult to compare the results of one study with those of another. Conflicting results can be obtained depending on whether the data used consist of learners' productions, introspections, or intuitions, or whether emergence or accuracy serves as the criterion of acquisition. It is for this reason that it is important to examine carefully the nature of the data used and the way in which acquisition has been measured, when reading reports of actual studies.

Summary

There is no simple answer to the question 'What is second language acquisition?' It can take place in either a naturalistic or an instructional setting, but may not necessarily differ according to the setting. The goal of SLA is the description and explanation of the learner's linguistic or communicative competence. To this end, the researcher must examine aspects of the learner's usage or use of the L2 in actual performance, by collecting and analysing either samples of learner language, reports of learners' introspections, or records of their intuitions regarding what is correct or appropriate L2 behaviour. The acquisition of an L2 feature may be considered to have taken place either when it is used for the first time or only when it can be used to a high level of accuracy.

Second language acquisition is a complex, multifaceted phenomenon and it is not surprising that it has come to mean different things to different people.

General questions in second language acquisition research

The study of how learners learn a second language does not have a very long history. The surge of empirical work that informs current thinking did not begin until the late 1960s. Although there have been several developments in SLA since its inception, it is still possible to identify a set of general questions for which researchers have sought answers.

1 What do second language learners acquire?

The first question, which guided much of the early research in the late sixties and seventies, concerned what it was that learners actually acquired when they tried to learn an L2. This question was motivated by the recognition that learners often failed initially to produce correct sentences and instead displayed language that was markedly deviant from target language norms.

In order to answer this question, researchers collected samples of learner language and tried to describe their main features. For example, the language samples that learners produced were inspected for errors and these were then classified. Alternatively, recordings of learners communicating with native speakers or other learners were transcribed, specific grammatical features such as negatives or interrogatives were identified in the data, and descriptions of the 'rules' which could account for the learners' productions were developed. The aim of this research, then, was essentially descriptive—to document what kind of language learners produced, to try to establish whether it manifested regularities of some kind or other, and to find out how it changed over time.

2 How do learners acquire a second language?

Not surprisingly, researchers were not content just to describe learner language; they also sought to explain it. That is, they wanted to account for why learners made errors, why their language displayed marked regularities, and why it changed systematically over time.

The answers were sought by formulating two further questions. The first was 'What contribution do external factors make to L2 acquisition?' This involved considering the role played by the social situation in which learning took place and how the language the learner was exposed to (i.e. the input) accounted for acquisition as evident in the language the learner produced (i.e. the output). Researchers seeking external explanations of learner language made extensive use of ideas and methods from the sociolinguistic study of language.

The second question was 'What contribution do internal factors make to L2 acquisition?' In this case, explanations were sought in the mental processes that the learner used to convert input into knowledge. Various processes have been identified. Some account for how the learner makes use of existing knowledge (of the mother tongue, of general learning strategies, or of the universal properties of language) to internalize knowledge of the L2. These processes can be thought of as learning processes. They serve as the means by which the learner constructs an *interlanguage* (a transitional system reflecting the learner's current L2 knowledge). Other processes account for how the learner makes use of existing knowledge to cope with communication difficulties. For example, sometimes the learner does not know the word needed to communicate an idea clearly and has to resort to paraphrase or word coinage. These processes are known as *communication strategies*. Internal explanations have made extensive use of ideas drawn from both cognitive psychology and linguistics.

A full explanation of L2 acquisition will need to take account of both external and internal factors and how the two interrelate. We are still a long way from such an explanation, however.

3 What differences are there in the way in which individual learners acquire a second language?

In the case of questions (l) and (2) the focus is on learning. In question (3) the focus is on the individual language learner. While much of the work that has taken place in SLA research is based on the assumption that learner language provides evidence of universal learning processes, there is also a long tradition of research that has recognized that learners vary enormously in their rate of learning, their approach to learning, and in their actual achievements. The study of *individual learner differences* seeks to document the factors that contribute to these kinds of variation.

4 What effects does instruction have on second language acquisition?

Much of the early research investigated naturalistic L2 learners,[3] motivated in part by claims that classroom learning would proceed most smoothly if teachers stopped interfering in the learning process and left learners to learn in the same way as children acquired their mother tongue (see Newmark 1966). Increasingly, though, researchers have turned to studying the effects that instruction of various kinds has on L2 acquisition. This research has been motivated in part by a desire to address issues of general theoretical interest to SLA research and also by a desire to improve the efficacy of language pedagogy. The classroom affords an opportunity to control very precisely the nature of the input that learners are exposed to. This in turn allows the researcher to formulate and test very specific hypotheses regarding how particular features of an L2 are acquired.

These four questions serve as a heuristic for exploring SLA research. They have helped researchers to identify a number of key issues.

A framework for exploring second language acquisition

It is possible to identify a number of different areas of SLA that have been investigated. These are shown in Table 1.1.

The first area of work concerns the description of the characteristics of learner language. This provides the researcher with the main source of information about how acquisition takes place. Four aspects of learner language have received attention: (1) errors, (2) acquisition orders and developmental sequences, (3) variability, and, more recently, (4) pragmatic features relating to the way language is used in context for communicative purposes. As we have already noted, one of the goals of SLA research is to describe learner language and to show how it works as a system.

The second area concerns learner-external factors relating to the social context of acquisition and to the input and interaction which the learner experiences.

The third area, learner-internal mechanisms, concerns how acquisition takes place and how learners use their resources in communication. These mechanisms are mental and largely hidden from view, although not necessarily completely unconscious. They relate to (1) the transfer of knowledge from the learner's L1, (2) the universal processes involved in converting input into intake and restructuring existing L2 knowledge systems, (3) the utilization of innate knowledge of *linguistic universals*, and (4) the processes for using L2 knowledge in performance, in particular those involved in dealing with problems of communication. The study of learner-external factors and learner-internal mechanisms constitutes an attempt to explain how L2 acquisition takes place.

Finally, there is the question of individual learner differences and what causes them. Learners set about the task of acquiring an L2 in different ways. They differ with regard to such general factors as motivation and aptitude, and also in the use of various strategies such as inferencing and self-monitoring for obtaining input and for learning from it.[4] The study of these general factors and learner strategies helps to explain why some learners learn more rapidly than others and why they reach higher levels of proficiency.

It is not always clear where specific lines of enquiry fit best. For example, the study of the communication processes involved in using L2 knowledge is viewed by some researchers as an aspect of interaction (area 2), by others as an aspect of mental processing (area 3) and by yet others as one type of learner strategy (area 4). They have been included in area 3 in this book as a recognition of the primacy of psycholinguistic accounts of communication processes in recent research (see Bialystok 1990a).

Also, the four areas all interrelate, so not surprisingly many investigations have covered more than one. For example, the errors that learners make (area

Focus on learning			Focus on the learner
Description		Explanation	
Area 1	Area 2	Area 3	Area 4
Characteristics of learner language	Learner-external factors	Learner-internal mechanisms	The language learner
errors	social context	L1 transfer	general factors e.g. motivation
acquisition orders and developmental sequences	input and interaction	learning processes	learner strategies
variability		communication strategies	
pragmatic features		knowledge of linguistic universals	

Table 1.1:   A framework for investigating L2 acquisition

1) reflect the operation of internal processing mechanisms (area 3) and may also be influenced by the social context in which learning takes place (area 2) and the learner's preferred learning style (area 4). One of the goals of this book will be to explore the interactions between the four areas.

Learner language

The starting point of our exploration of L2 acquisition will be the study of learner language. This area of SLA is central because it provides the data for constructing and testing theories of L2 acquisition.

Errors

One of the first ways in which researchers tried to investigate L2 acquisition was through the analysis of learner errors. The field of *Error Analysis* is closely associated with the work of Corder, who published a number of seminal articles in the 1960s/1970s, (for example, Corder 1967 and 1971a) in which he made out a case for examining errors as a way of investigating learning processes. He also helped to develop a methodology for carrying out an error analysis.

Much of the early work on learner errors focused on determining the extent to which L2 acquisition was the result of L1 *transfer* or of *creative construction* (the construction of unique rules similar to those which children form in the course of acquiring their mother tongue). The presence of errors that mirrored L1 structures was taken as evidence of transfer, while the presence of errors similar to those observed in L1 acquisition was indicative of creative construction (i.e. intralingual). In a series of studies, Dulay and Burt analysed errors produced by Spanish learners of English in order to determine which errors were interlingual (indicative of transfer), and which ones were intralingual (indicative of creative construction). (See Dulay and Burt 1973, 1974a, and 1974b.)

The results of error analyses were used to refute behaviourist views of L2 learning, which were dominant at the time. According to these, L2 learning took place in the same way as any other kind of learning—it involved procedures such as imitation, repetition, and reinforcement, which enabled learners to develop 'habits' of the L2. The study of learner errors showed that although many errors were caused by transferring L1 'habits', many more were not; learners often contributed creatively to the process of learning. They also indicated that learners appeared to go through stages of acquisition, as the nature of the errors they made varied according to their level of development.

Error analysis, however, as practised in the sixties and seventies, was an imperfect research tool. It could not show when learners resorted to avoidance (Schachter 1974) and, as it ignored what learners could do correctly, it only looked at part of learner language. Also, the methodology of error analysis was suspect in a number of respects. For example, it was not entirely clear what constituted an 'error' and it proved difficult to prepare rigorous descriptions of errors. As a result, many studies were unreliable and difficult to replicate. It is not surprising, perhaps, that error analysis has fallen out of favour with many researchers. However, the study of learner errors can still serve as a useful tool and is still undertaken, often as a means of investigating a specific research question. For example, Bardovi-Harlig and Bofman (1989) employed error analysis techniques to investigate the linguistic differences between advanced learners who were successful on a university placement test and those who were unsuccessful. Also, error analysis can prove illuminative when employed in the detailed, qualitative analysis of learner language (see Taylor 1986).

Work on errors in learner language is discussed in Chapter 2.

Acquisition orders and developmental sequences

The language that learners produce provides evidence that they acquire different morphological features in a fixed *order* and also that they pass through a *sequence* of developmental stages in the acquisition of specific syntactical features. Early evidence for this came from studies of learners' errors, but more convincing evidence was provided by a series of cross-sectional and longitudinal studies carried out in the seventies and eighties.

There is also evidence to support the existence of a general *pattern of development*. This general pattern may begin with a *silent period*, particularly in children. Many of the initial utterances that learners produce are *formulas*—ready-made chunks like 'I don't know' and 'What's this?' Gradually learners begin to produce more creative utterances, although to begin with these are often propositionally reduced and morphologically simple (for example, 'Kick' for 'He kicked me'). It has been suggested that learners work on the formulas they have learnt by substituting elements in them and joining them together to form complex structures (Wong-Fillmore 1976; Ellis 1984a). Slowly learners master the basic syntax of the L2, learning the major permutations in word order found in the target language. At this stage some morphological features are also acquired, but many do not appear until much later, if at all.

Evidence for a definite order in the acquisition of specific grammatical features was provided by the *morpheme studies*. These investigated a set of grammatical functors in English (for example, plural -s, past tense -ed, verb -ing, articles) and claimed to show that there was a natural order of acquisition (see Krashen 1977 for a review of these studies) that was not influenced by the learner's age or first language. Major variation in the order was only found when the learner had the opportunity to monitor output (i.e. make use of conscious or 'learnt' knowledge of grammatical rules). Most of these studies were cross-sectional in design. The claims they made about an order of acquisition were based on the rank order of accuracy with which learners performed the different functors in output collected at a single point in time. The assumption was that learners must have acquired those features they performed more accurately before those they performed less accurately. The morpheme studies have been criticized on the grounds that this assumption is not justified (see Hatch 1978d and 1983a). Other problems have also been identified.

Longitudinal studies of learner language afforded evidence of *developmental sequences*. Early work, based on case studies of individual learners (for example, Ravem 1968; Huang 1970; Wode 1976 and 1978) demonstrated that learners with different language backgrounds followed a remarkably similar path of development when trying to produce structures such as English negatives and interrogatives. The learners appeared to construct a series of transitional rules before they mastered the target language rules. Furthermore, the developmental route they followed seemed to closely follow that reported for the acquisition of the same structures by children learning English as their first language.

Some of the most powerful evidence for developmental sequences has come from studies of the L2 acquisition of German, such as the Zweitspracherwerb Italienischer, Spanischer und Portugiesischer Arbeiter (ZISA) project (Meisel, Clahsen, and Pienemann 1981). This project, which studied adult and child learners with romance language backgrounds, found that some grammatical features of German were not acquired in any definite sequence, but that others were. Word order rules were clearly developmental. Learners—children and adults—passed through a well-defined sequence. Other features such as copula 'sein' were subject to considerable inter-learner variation. Subsequent work in Australia (for example, Johnston 1985) has demonstrated a similar sequence for word order features of English and similar variation in features such as copula 'be'.

The existence of developmental sequences is one of the most important findings of SLA research to date. There is now general acceptance in the SLA research community that the acquisition of an L2 grammar, like the acquisition of an L1 grammar, occurs in stages. However, it should be noted that although general developmental sequences have been attested in learners in different situations and with differing backgrounds, variations in the specific order in which particular features occur have also been found. Lightbown (1984) claims that for every study that supports the idea of a universal sequence, there is another study that provides counter-evidence.

An important issue—for both theory building and for language pedagogy—concerns the effect that *formal instruction* has on the acquisition of grammatical features. A number of studies have investigated whether teaching specific grammatical features results in their acquisition (Pienemann 1984; White, Spada, Lightbown, and Ranta 1991), while others have investigated the effects of formal instruction by comparing the language produced by naturalistic and instructed learners (for example, Pica 1983; Ellis 1984c). The results of these studies are not easy to interpret, partly because the concept of what 'instruction' means has varied greatly (see Ellis 1990a) and partly because researchers have worked with very different operational definitions of acquisition. However, there is growing evidence to indicate that grammar instruction does work, providing learners are ready to assimilate the new target rule into their mental grammars, although instruction does not appear to enable learners to 'beat' a developmental sequence.

The evidence for a general pattern of development, acquisition orders and developmental sequences is examined in Chapter 3. The effect of formal instruction on the learning of grammatical features, including those that are developmental, is considered in Chapter 14.

Variability

Learner language, like the language of native speakers, appears to be inherently variable. Learners frequently use one structure on one occasion and a different structure on another. Teachers are very familiar with learners who use a feature such as 3rd person -s correctly at one time only to omit it at another. Researchers who have investigated learner language frequently comment on the 'constant development and concomitant variation' (Cancino, Rosansky, and Schumann 1978: 209) in their subjects' use of the L2. This variation is, of course, not confined to learners, as native speakers have also been shown to vary in their choice of linguistic features (Labov 1970). However, language learners seem particularly prone to variability.

A key issue is the extent to which this variability is systematic. Much of it undoubtedly is. Learners alternate their use of linguistic forms according to *linguistic context*. For example, they are less likely to omit copula 'be' if it is preceded by a pronoun subject than if it is preceded by a noun subject (Ellis 1988a). Learners also vary according to *situational context*, in particular according to who they are speaking to (Beebe 1980). A similar *stylistic continuum* has been found in learner language as in native speaker speech (see Tarone 1982). Learners are more likely to use correct target language forms in situations and tasks that call for a *careful style* (i.e. formal language use) and more likely to use transitional, learner forms in their *vernacular style* (i.e. in informal, everyday language use). Variability is also systematic in another way. Learners may make deliberate use of whatever linguistic knowledge they possess in order to distinguish different functional or semantic meanings that are important to them. Again, in this they are no different from native speakers. However, they often create unique form-function correspondences of a kind not found in the target language. For example, at a certain stage of development learners may decide to use one negative rule for making statements (for example, 'No making noise' = 'I'm not making a noise') and another for commands (for example, 'Don't make a noise').

There is less agreement as to whether some of the variability in learner language is non-systematic. In Ellis 1985c and 1989c, I argue that when learners acquire new forms they are likely to first use these in free variation with existing forms. Later they will either drop an 'old' form or use the two forms systematically in some way. Other researchers (for example, Schachter 1986a) consider non-systematic variability of little significance, however.

There is also no agreement as to how important variability is for understanding learning processes. Whereas Tarone and I see it as providing crucial evidence about the ways learners set about constructing an L2 grammar, Gregg (1990) argues that it is an uninteresting and trivial phenomenon because it only reflects performance and sheds no light on the learner's competence. The nature of variability in learner language is explored in Chapter 4, while the major theoretical positions are outlined in Chapter 9.

Pragmatic features

Pragmatics is the study of how language is used in communication. It covers a wide range of phenomena including deixis (i.e. the ways in which language encodes features of the context of utterance), conversational implicature and presupposition (i.e. the way language is used to convey meanings that are not actually encoded linguistically), illocutionary acts (i.e. the use of language to perform speech acts such as stating, questioning, and directing), conversational structure (i.e. the way in which conversations are organized across turns), and repair (i.e. the conversational work undertaken to deal with miscommunications of various kinds). Pragmatics is particularly concerned with appropriateness, both with regard to what is said in a particular context and how it is said.

Early work in SLA research did not entirely neglect pragmatic aspects of learner language. However, they were attended to only in so far as they helped to explain how learners acquired grammatical competence. Hatch (1978b), for instance, examined the ways in which learners develop topics as a way of exploring why certain grammatical features are acquired before others. Only recently, however, have researchers considered the acquisition of pragmatic competence in its own right. The bulk of the work to date has focused on specific *illocutionary acts*. Kasper and Dahl (1991) provide a useful overview of work on interlanguage pragmatics.

Learners have to learn when it is appropriate to perform a particular language function and also how to encode it. They frequently experience problems with both. Thomas (1983) distinguishes *sociopragmatic failure*, which occurs when learners produce socially inappropriate behaviour and *pragmalinguistic failure*, which occurs when learners do not express themselves in a linguistically appropriate manner. A number of studies have demonstrated the difficulties that learners experience. Beebe and Takahashi (1989a), for instance, report on the way in which Japanese and native speakers of English differed in their performance of disagreements and giving embarrassing information. Blum-Kulka, House and Kasper (1989a) report on the difficulties that even advanced L2 learners have in encoding requests and apologies in socially appropriate ways.

Chapter 5 looks at the research which has investigated how speech acts are encoded.

Learner-external factors

External factors relate to the environment in which learning takes place. What exactly their role in acquisition is and how important they are remain controversial issues. Behaviourist theories of learning view external factors as of central importance. Mentalist theories, however, emphasize the role played by learner internal factors, crediting learners with a *Language Acquisition Device* that enables them to work on what they hear and to extract the abstract 'rules' that account for how the language is organized. Cognitive theories of language acquisition tend to be interactional in the sense that they emphasize the joint contribution of external and internal factors.

Social factors

Social factors probably have an indirect rather than a direct effect on L2 learning. In particular, they are likely to be mediated by the attitudes that the learners hold. Social factors shape learners' attitudes, which, in turn, determine learning outcomes.

The impact of social factors on learning outcomes has been studied in relation to L2 proficiency rather than developmental patterns, as it has been generally assumed that social factors do not directly influence the process of L2 acquisition. There are alternative models of L2 proficiency (see Bachman 1990) but two have figured strongly in SLA research. Cummins (1983) distinguishes *basic interpersonal communication skills* (BICS) from *cognitive academic language proficiency* (CALP). Canale and Swain (1980) distinguish four 'modules' of ability relating to different types of language knowledge—grammar, sociolinguistic, discourse and strategic. The principal question that has been addressed is 'To what extent and in what ways do social factors affect the L2 proficiency attained by different groups of learners?'

The social factors that influence L2 acquisition are likely to differ according to social context. A key distinction is that between a natural and an educational setting. A general assumption is that the learning that takes place in these two types of setting is very different (see d'Anglejan 1978), but the extent to which this is the case may well depend on the nature of the more specific settings in which learners find themselves. *Natural settings* can be distinguished according to whether the L2 serves as a native language for the majority (for example, learners of L2 English in the United States), whether it serves as an official language when the majority speaks some other language (for example, L2 English in Nigeria or India), or whether it is used by linguistically heterogeneous groups in international settings (for example, the use of L2 English during a business meeting in Japan). *Educational settings* can be distinguished according to whether they involve segregation (i.e. the learners are taught the L2 or taught through the medium of the L2 separately from the majority group), mother tongue maintenance (i.e. an attempt is made to ensure that a minority group's L1 is taught and used in the educational setting), *submersion* (i.e. the L2 learner is taught in classes where L1 speakers are dominant), *immersion* (i.e. learners with a high-status L1 are taught through the medium of the L2 in classes containing only such learners, usually by bilingual teachers), or foreign language classrooms (for example, English language classrooms in Japan). Different types and levels of L2 proficiency are typically associated with each type of setting, although, of course, there can be considerable variation among learners within each setting.

One way in which the social context affects learning outcomes in these different settings is by influencing the learners' choice of *reference group*. Beebe (1985: 404) has argued that learners are 'active participants in choosing the target language models they prefer' in majority language settings. She distinguishes 'unmarked' and 'marked' choices depending on whether the choice is the expected one given the learners' social position or an unexpected one. In official language settings, the preferred model is often some indigenized variety of the L2, while in foreign language settings it is likely to be a standard native-speaker variety.

There has been relatively little research which has investigated the effects of particular social factors on L2 proficiency. However, a few studies relating to key *sociolinguistic variables* such as age, sex, social class, and ethnic membership have been carried out. The general findings are that younger learners do better than older learners (although this may also reflect psycholinguistic factors), females outperform males, middle class learners achieve higher levels of academic language proficiency than working class learners, and learners from an ethnic group that is culturally similar to the target language group tend to be more successful than learners from an ethnic group that is culturally distant. There are some interesting exceptions to these unsurprising findings, however. For example, working class children do as well as middle class children in immersion settings (Holobrow, Genesee, and Lambert 1991).

A number of theories have been developed to explain the relationship between social factors and L2 acquisition. Schumann (1978a) suggests that learners vary in the extent to which they acculturate (i.e. adapt to the target language culture). Some learners remain at a social distance from the target language community and as a result tend to pidginize (i.e. develop only a very basic competence in the L2). Other learners assimilate and develop a high level of proficiency in the L2. According to Schumann's model, social factors determine how much contact individual learners have with the L2. Giles and

Byrne (1982) have developed a similar theory to account for the effect of various social factors on L2 acquisition. They argue that the learner must be prepared to 'converge' towards the norms of the target language and that this only takes place if certain positive social factors come into play. For example, learners are more likely to converge if they perceive their culture to be equal or superior in status to that of target language speakers. This inter-group model of L2 acquisition emphasizes the role that social factors play in determining the kinds of interactions learners participate in. According to Gardner's *Socio-educational Model of L2 Learning* (Gardner 1985), the social and cultural milieu in which learners grow up determines the attitudes and motivational orientation that learners hold towards the target language, its speakers, and its culture—which in turn influence the sorts of learning behaviours learners engage in, and thereby learning outcomes.

The relationship between setting and L2 learning, the learner's choice of preference model, the impact of individual social factors such as social class and ethnic membership on learning and the different social theories of L2 acquisition are examined in Chapter 6.

Input and interaction

It is self-evident that L2 acquisition can only take place when the learner has access to input in the L2. This input may come in written or spoken form. In the case of spoken input, it may occur in the context of interaction (i.e. the learner's attempts to converse with a native speaker, a teacher, or another learner) or in the context of non-reciprocal discourse (for example, listening to the radio or watching a film). The study of input and interaction has involved the description of the adjustments which are found in language addressed to learners (i.e. *foreigner talk* and *teacher talk*) and also the analysis of discourse involving L2 learners.

There is little agreement about the role that input plays in L2 acquisition. Behaviourist theories emphasize its importance, claiming that the whole process of acquisition can be controlled by presenting learners with input in the right-sized doses and then reinforcing their attempts to practise them. According to this view of learning there is little room for any active processing by the learner. In the 1960s, however, behaviourist accounts of learning were challenged, most notably by Chomsky. It was pointed out that in many cases there was a very poor match between the kind of language found in the input learners received and the kind of language they themselves produced. It was argued that this could be best explained by hypothesizing a set of mental processes which took place inside the mind of the learner and which converted the language in the input into a form that the learner could store and handle in production. This mentalist view of input has itself been challenged by researchers on a number of grounds. For example, it has been shown that interaction can provide learners with 'scaffolding' that enables them to produce structures that would be beyond them, if left to their own resources. Researchers who emphasize the importance of input and interaction suggest that learners acquire a language through the process of learning how to communicate in it (see Hatch 1978b). There is currently little support for behaviourist views of language acquisition, but the debate continues between those who argue that input serves only as a trigger that sets off some internal language acquisition device (for example, White 1987a) and those who argue that input shaped through interaction contributes directly and powerfully to acquisition (for example, Long 1981a).

The relationship between input and acquisition has been explored in a number of ways. Several studies (for example, Snow and Hoefnagel-Höhle 1982) have examined the relationship between the frequency with which different linguistic items occur in the input and the order of acquisition of the same features. These studies have produced mixed results and are of limited value as they are all correlational in nature, thus making it difficult to make statements about cause and effect. More important are studies which have investigated the role of *comprehensible input*. Krashen (1985) has proposed the *Input Hypothesis*, according to which learners acquire morphological features in a natural order as a result of comprehending input addressed to them. Long (1981a) has argued that input which is made comprehensible by means of the conversational adjustments that occur when there is a comprehension problem is especially important for acquisition. Krashen's and Long's proposals have led to several studies that have investigated what factors are involved in making input comprehensible (for example, Parker and Chaudron 1987; Pica, Young, and Doughty 1987). However, relatively few studies to date have attempted to show that comprehensible input actually leads to the acquisition of new linguistic features. Also, there are theoretical objections to the position adopted by Krashen and Long; it has been pointed out, for example, that the processes of comprehension and of acquisition are not the same, nor are they necessarily related (Sharwood Smith 1986).

Other researchers have emphasized the role of learner output in promoting acquisition. Swain (1985), for instance, has put forward the *comprehensible output hypothesis*, which states that learners need opportunities for 'pushed output' (i.e. speech or writing that makes demands on them for correct and appropriate use of the L2) in order to develop certain grammatical features that do not appear to be acquired purely on the basis of comprehending input. Swain's case rests on the different psycholinguistic requirements of comprehension and production; whereas successful comprehension is possible without a full linguistic analysis of the input, correct production requires learners to construct sentence plans for their messages. Again, however, there is little direct evidence to support Swain's hypothesis. Finally, other researchers (for example, Hatch 1978b) have tried to show how the process of constructing discourse collaboratively with an interlocutor helps learners to develop new syntactic structures.

There has also been considerable interest in classroom interaction on the grounds that the opportunities for learning which it affords constitute the major determinant of acquisition in this setting (Allwright 1984). Much of the research has been based on Krashen's and Long's views about the importance of comprehensible input. In particular, researchers have sought to establish what classroom conditions result in the kinds of conversational adjustments that Long hypothesizes are important for acquisition. To this end, they have compared the interaction that takes place in small-group work with that occurring in teacher-led lessons (for example, Pica and Doughty 1985a and 1985b). They have also investigated the effect of task design on interaction. Certain kinds of tasks appear to result in more modified interaction than others. For example, tasks that involve a two-way exchange of information—such as when learners each hold part of the information which they need to solve a problem jointly—have been shown promote extensive meaning negotiation.

The role of input in L2 acquisition has proved to be a controversial issue. It is probably true to say that there has been too much theorizing and not enough empirical research. Very few studies have actually sought to demonstrate if and how input affects acquisition. Much of the research has been descriptive in nature—describing the kinds of linguistic modifications that occur in foreigner talk, or the devices used to negotiate meaning, or the interactions that result from asking learners to perform tasks in different conditions.

The role of input and interaction is considered in Chapter 7. Chapter 13 focuses on interaction in the L2 classroom.

Learner-internal factors

Any theory of SLA needs to provide an account of learner-internal factors. These factors are, of course, not directly observable. They are covert and can only be inferred by studying learner output and, to some extent, learners' reports of how they learn.

Language transfer

L1 transfer usually refers to the incorporation of features of the L1 into the knowledge systems of the L2 which the learner is trying to build. It is important to distinguish this learning process from other processes which involve the use of the L1 for purposes of communication (see below). Both translation and borrowing (Corder 1983)—the use of the L1 to deal with some communication problem—are examples of communication transfer, as are code-mixing (the use of both the L1 and L2 in the construction of the same sentence) and code-switching (the alternative use of the L1 and L2 within a discourse). It is, of course, not easy to distinguish empirically the process of transfer in L2 learning and the use of the L1 as a communication process.

Views about language transfer have undergone considerable change. Initially, transfer was understood within a behaviourist framework of learning. It was assumed that the 'habits' of the L1 would be carried over into the L2. In cases where the target language differed from the L1 this would result in *interference* or *ŋegative transfer*. In cases where the patterns of the L1 and the target language were similar, *positive transfer* would occur. Thus, the L1 could both impede and facilitate the acquisition of the L2. In order to try to predict when interference would take place linguists carried out elaborate contrastive analyses of the native and target languages. It was not until the late 1960s, however, that the claims of the contrastive analysis hypothesis were investigated empirically. The results of error analysis studies (for example, Dulay and Burt 1974a) cast doubts on the validity as these claims. Transfer often did not take place when there were differences between the target and native languages. Also, many of the errors that learners made appeared to reflect intralingual processes (i.e. they were the result of processes based on the learner's existing knowledge of the L2) rather than interference. This led to the advancement of a minimalist position regarding L1 influence (see Dulay and Burt 1974a).

More recently the importance of transfer has once again been acknowledged. Odlin (1989), reflecting a consensus that grew throughout the 1980s, comments:

> Despite the counterarguments ... there is a large and growing body of research that indicates that transfer is indeed a very important factor in second language acquisition (1989:4).

Evidence for transfer in all aspects of language—phonology, syntax, semantics, and pragmatics—is now abundant. Furthermore, there is recognition of the fact that transfer may not always manifest itself as errors (the focus of early studies), but also as avoidance, overuse, and facilitation. It is now generally acknowledged that transfer works in complex ways and that it constitutes only one of several processes involved in L2 acquisition (see Zobl 1980a). Much effort has gone into identifying the conditions under which transfer is likely to occur. Various factors have been identified which influence transfer. For example, Kellerman (1978) has shown that learners' perception of the distance between their native language and the target language (i.e. their *psychotypology*) affects whether they transfer or not. Other studies (for example, Wode 1976) have shown that transfer may be a developmental phenomenon in that it occurs only when the learner reaches a 'natural' stage of acquisition which bears a crucial similarity to some native language structure. Transfer may also be affected by *markedness*. According to one definition of markedness, a marked linguistic structure is one that can be used with fewer constraints than a related unmarked one. For example, the adjective 'old' is considered less marked than 'young' because it can be used in both questions (for example, 'How old are you?') and statements (for example, 'He is very old.'), whereas 'young' cannot be similarly used in questions (for example, *'How young are you?'). Learners seem more likely to transfer unmarked native language features than marked ones, particularly if the corresponding feature in their target language is marked (Zobl 1984). These and other factors determine whether transfer takes place.

Transfer as a learning process and as an aid to communication is considered in Chapter 8.

Cognitive accounts of second language acquisition

We have just noted that learners may use their L1 as both a means of learning an L2 (when we speak of transfer) and as a means of communicating. This is an example of a broad distinction between learning processes and communication processes. The former consist of the mechanisms that learners use to (1) notice features in the input, (2) compare these features with those that are currently part of their mental grammars or interlanguages, and (3) integrate the new features into their interlanguages. The latter consist of conscious or potentially conscious attempts on the part of the learner to employ their available linguistic resources, for example by developing their ability to use the L2 fluently or by compensating for inadequate knowledge when communicating a particular message.

In addition to transfer, learners use a variety of processes to learn an L2. A number of different theories of SLA have provided accounts of them. These theories are cognitive in nature, i.e. they attempt to account for the mental processes that enable learners to work on input, and for the knowledge-systems which they construct and manifest in output.

Perhaps the best known is interlanguage theory. The term interlanguage was coined by Selinker (1972) to refer to the interim grammars which learners build on their way to full target language competence. As McLaughlin (1987) observes, interlanguage theory has undergone almost constant development, but one common theme is the notion of hypothesis testing, i.e. the idea that learners form hypotheses about what the rules of the target language are and then set about testing them, confirming them if they find supportive evidence in the input and rejecting them if they receive negative evidence. This process takes place largely on a subconscious level. Interlanguage theory has also identified a number of other, more specific processes such as overgeneralization (i.e. the extension of an L2 rule to a context in which it does not apply in the target language) and simplification (i.e. the reduction of the target language system to a simpler form). Early work on learner errors, acquisition orders, and developmental sequences was closely related to interlanguage theory.

Parallel to interlanguage theory, and influenced by it, are a number of theories which seek to account for the observed characteristics of learner language, and in particular for developmental patterns. Several theories rest on the distinction between *implicit* (i.e. intuitive and unconscious) and *explicit* (i.e. metalingual and conscious) L2 knowledge, differing in whether these are seen as entirely distinct and unconnected, as in Krashen's Monitor Theory (Krashen 1981), or whether they are hypothesized to interface, as in Bialystok's Model of Second Language Learning (Bialystok 1978). More recent discussion of the implicit/explicit distinction has focused on the role of consciousness in L2 learning (see Schmidt 1990).

Other theories have been based on research that shows learner language to be highly variable. Tarone (1979, 1982, 1983) has argued that learners construct variable interlanguage grammars consisting of different styles. The learners' vernacular style develops both as a result of directly processing input, and as a result of the spread of forms from their careful style. In Ellis 1985c and 1989a, I suggest that interlanguage development entails three concurrent phases, involving: (1) innovation (i.e. the acquisition of new forms), (2) elaboration (i.e. the complexification that takes place as the learner discovers the contextual uses of a form), and (3) revision (i.e. the adjustments that are made to the entire system as a result of innovation and elaboration).

Closely related to variationist accounts of interlanguage are *functionalist models* (see Tomlin 1990; Dittmar 1992). These suggest that variability is a reflex of different modes of language use. Givón (1979), for instance, suggests that L2 development occurs as learners move from processing language in pragmatic terms (for example, as topic-comment structures) to processing it in grammatical terms (for example, as subject-predicate structures). Functionalist accounts also emphasize the importance of the form–function networks that learners are believed to construct. According to the *Competition Model* (Bates and MacWhinney 1982), language acquisition involves the learner attending to both form and function. There are inherent human tendencies that induce learners to perceive and process some forms before others but also a form is more likely to be acquired if it realizes a meaning that is transparent and important to the learner. According to this model, learners assign 'weights' to different form–function mappings and the process of acquisition involves adjusting these weights until they match those found in the input. For example, the learner of L2 English may initially work on the assumption that the semantic function 'agent' is invariably designated by word order (i.e. any noun occurring before a verb is an agent). This may lead the learner to misconstrue sentences like 'The dog was chased by the cat'. Subsequently, the 'weight' connecting word order to agency will be weakened as the learner recognizes the validity of other formal cues in the input (for example, the presence of 'by + noun' after the verb) and establishes new form-function mappings which compete with the original.

In another approach, researchers have sought to identify the *operating principles* which learners use to convert input into a form which they can store. Slobin (1973, 1985b) has identified a number of operating principles which make up the 'Language Making Capacity' of children acquiring their L1. Examples are 'pay attention to the ends of words' and 'avoid interruption and rearrangement of linguistic units'. These principles have shown to be present in the L1 acquisition of very different languages. Andersen (1984a; 1990) has built on Slobin's work and identified a number of macro-principles found in L2 acquisition. The one-to-one principle, for example, states that 'an interlanguage system should be constructed in such a way that the intended underlying meaning is expressed with one clear invariant surface form or construction' (Andersen 1984a: 79).

An adequate theory of L2 acquisition needs to account for why some linguistic features are acquired before others and why learners manifest developmental sequences when acquiring specific features. Perhaps the theory that comes closest to satisfying this requirement is Johnston and Pienemann's (1986) model of L2 acquisition. This model is a development of the *Multidimensional Model* advanced by Meisel, Clahsen, and Pienemann (1981). It accounts for the developmental properties of interlanguage in terms of a number of processing operations, which are organized hierarchically according to the order in which they are evident in learners' production. Thus, initially learners rely on non-linguistic processing devices (for example, formulas and lexical items that are not assigned to grammatical categories) and then move through a series of stages until they are able to carry out more complex grammatical operations. This model also recognizes and provides an explanation for individual learner variation.

Other cognitive models have attempted to explain L2 acquisition in terms of a general theory of skill learning. Andersen's *Adaptive Control of Thought (ACT) Model* sees language acquisition, like all other kinds of learning, as a process of proceduralizing 'declarative knowledge' (i.e. knowledge stored as facts). This takes place through 'practice'. McLaughlin (1987) proposes a Cognitive Theory based on information processing. Learners routinize linguistic information that is initially only available for use through controlled processing and this frees them to attend to new information in the input. Also, learners restructure their rule-based representations of the L2 at certain critical points in the learning process. As in the case of Andersen, McLaughlin sets considerable store on 'practice' as the mechanism of change.

All these theories are based on the assumption that learners form mental representations of 'rules' and that these rules guide the learner in using the L2 in performance. A 'rule' consists of some form of abstract generalization of a linguistic property—the fact that past tense forms in English consist of a verb stem + -*ed*, for example. However, another approach to explaining language acquisition dispenses altogether with the idea of rules. According to a *Parallel Distributed Processing Model* (Rumelhart and McClelland 1986;

Rumelhart, McClelland, and the PDP Research Group 1986), knowledge takes the form of a network of interconnections between 'units' that do not correspond to any particular linguistic construct.[5] Learning consists of the modification of the strengths of these connections as a response to input stimuli and is complete when the network corresponds to that found in native speakers. Researchers construct mathematical models of the kinds of networks that they think can account for learning and then test them in computer simulations. The criterion of success is whether the model produces similar stages of development to those that have been observed in natural language acquisition. As yet, however, there have been few PDP models specifically designed to examine L2 acquisition (see Gasser 1990).

In addition to acquiring knowledge of the L2, learners also need to develop control over existing knowledge, as suggested by Anderson's account of proceduralization and McLaughlin's views on controlled/automatic processing. The acquisition of 'control' is specifically considered in work on L2 *speech planning* by researchers at the University of Kassel in Germany (see Dechert, Möhle, and Raupach 1984) and also in the extensive work on learners' communication strategies (see Bialystok 1990a for an overview). Speech planning has been considered in terms of temporal variables, such as speech rate and pause length, and hesitation phenomena. A number of frameworks for classifying communication strategies have been developed. Færch and Kasper (1980) propose a basic distinction between reduction strategies (i.e. strategies that attempt to do away with the communication problem) and achievement strategies (i.e. strategies designed to achieve the original goal). Poulisse (1990a) proposes a distinction between conceptual strategies (i.e. strategies that attempt to get round a problem by referring to a concept obliquely in some way) and linguistic strategies (i.e. an attempt to get round a problem by exploiting L1 or L2 linguistic knowledge). Much of the work on communication strategies has focused on trying to identify instances of their use and on developing a reliable typology, although there is now some work that has examined their comparative effectiveness in facilitating communication. There is still very little known about how the use of communication strategies contributes to L2 learning. One interesting possibility is that the acquisition of knowledge and of control occur independently, with learners differing in the emphasis they give to each aspect.

Learning and communication processes are examined in detail in Chapter 9.

Linguistic universals and second language acquisition

Mentalist theories of L2 acquisition emphasize the role of innate knowledge. This takes the form of a language acquisition device which helps the learner to discover the rules of the target language grammar. This device contains knowledge of linguistic universals.

There have been two approaches to the study of the role of linguistic universals in L2 acquisition. A number of linguists have set about identifying *typological universals* through the study of a large number of languages drawn from different language families. They have then gone on to advance a number of possible explanations (including mentalist ones) for the existence of these universals. Other linguists—those belonging to the generative school associated with Chomsky—have studied individual languages in great depth in order to identify the principles of grammar which underlie and govern specific rules (i.e. *Universal Grammar*). For example, the Phrase Structure Principle states that all languages are made up of phrases consisting of a head and a complement (see Cook 1988 for an account of this and other principles). Thus, in the English prepositional phrase 'in the classroom' 'in' constitutes the head and 'the classroom', the complement. Principles are often parameterized—that is, they allow for various options. Thus in the case of the Phrase Structure Principle, one option is that the head precedes the complement (as in English), while another is that the head follows the complement (as in Japanese). Principles such as the Phrase Structure Principle can govern clusters of features. Thus, if a language manifests head initial verb phrases (for example, verb + direct object) it is also likely to manifest prepositions, while if a language has head final verb phrases (for example, direct object + verb) it will probably also have postpositions. In this way, the presence of one feature in a language implies the presence of other, related features.

One of the key arguments advanced by those claiming a role for linguistic universals is that of the *logical problem of acquisition* (see White 1989a). According to this, the input to which the learner is exposed underdetermines linguistic competence, i.e. learners are unable to discover some of the rules of the target language purely on the basis of input because it does not supply them with all the information they need. It follows that they must rely on other sources of information. These sources are knowledge of linguistic universals and in the case of L2 learners, knowledge of their L1.

A second key argument concerns the 'unlearning' of a wrongly formulated rule. It is claimed that in certain cases unlearning can only take place if the learner is supplied with negative feedback in the form of overt corrections, such as those that occur in many language classrooms. In the case of L1 acquisition such feedback is rare. It is argued that children are prevented from forming rules which they cannot unlearn without negative feedback by their knowledge of linguistic universals. It is not clear, however, whether this argument applies to L2 acquisition. For a start, L2 learners may be more prepared to abandon previously learnt rules than L1 learners (Rutherford 1989). Also, it is not yet clear whether L2 learners have continued access to Universal Grammar, or whether they rely on other methods of learning that involve general learning processes and access to negative feedback (see Bley-Vroman 1989) or, of course, whether they rely on both.

Knowledge of linguistic universals may help to shape L2 acquisition in a number of ways. First, it can provide an explanation for developmental sequences. Learners may acquire rules that reflect universal principles before they acquire rules that do not. Or they may opt for parameters that are less marked before those that are more marked.[6] Second, knowledge of linguistic universals may enable the learner to go beyond the input. This can happen in the case of clusters of features where an implicational relationship holds. Thus, once learners of L2 Japanese have discovered that the verb comes at the end of the clause in Japanese, they may be able to infer that it also has postpositions rather than prepositions. Knowledge of linguistic universals may provide the learner with a *projection capacity* (Zobl 1983b). Third, knowledge of linguistic universals may also be involved in transfer. Learners may be more prepared to transfer L1 features if these conform to universal principles.

The study of linguistic universals in L2 acquisition has attracted considerable attention in recent years. It has served as one of the ways in which the interests of linguists and SLA researchers can be brought together. Chapter 10 considers the role of linguistic universals in L2 acquisition.

The language learner

Whereas the bulk of SLA research has addressed the universal characteristics of L2 acquisition, there is also a growing body of research on individual learner differences (see Skehan 1989). It is convenient to draw a distinction between research that has investigated how general factors, such as motivation, contribute to individual learner differences and research based on the strategies that learners deliberately employ to enhance their learning of the L2.

General factors and individual differences

Learners differ in a number of ways which affect L2 acquisition, in particular their rate of development and their ultimate level of achievement. The ways in which learners differ are potentially infinite as they reflect the whole range of variables relating to the cognitive, affective, and social aspects of a human being. The factors can be divided into those that are fixed and immutable and those that are variable, influenced by social setting and by the actual course of L2 development. This distinction is, perhaps, best viewed as a continuum with specific factors treated as more or less immutable/mutable.

Age is an example of a fixed factor, in the sense that it is beyond external control. Like many other issues, the role of age in L2 acquisition is controversial. The controversy centres around whether there is a *critical period* for L2 acquisition and, if so, when it ends. Long (1990a) has presented evidence to suggest that the acquisition of a native-like accent is not possible by learners who begin learning after 6 years of age. He also argues that it is very difficult for learners who begin at puberty to acquire native-like grammatical competence. However, Scovel (1988) has presented somewhat different evidence to argue that the critical period for a native-like pronunciation is around 12 years old. He claims that the evidence in favour of a critical period for grammar is equivocal ('a potential maybe to a probable no'). There is general agreement, however, that older learners enjoy an initial advantage in rate of acquisition. A key theoretical issue relating to the age issue and the reason why it has attracted considerable attention is whether adult L2 learners have continued access to the innate knowledge of linguistic universals (see above) which guide children's acquisition of their mother tongue.

It has also been claimed that *language learning aptitude* constitutes a relatively immutable factor (Carroll 1981). This refers to the specific ability for language learning which learners are hypothesized to possess. Much of the early work on aptitude focused on developing tests to measure it. Carroll and Sapon (1959) developed the Modern Language Aptitude Test (MLAT) and Pimsleur (1966) developed the Pimsleur Language Aptitude Battery. These tests conceptualized aptitude in modular form. Different modules measured such skills as the learner's ability to perceive and memorize new sounds, to identify syntactic patterns in a new language, to detect similarities and differences in form and meaning, and to relate sounds to written symbols. The empirical work involved in developing these tests was very rigorous and it is a pity that it has not been followed up more extensively in recent years. A recent study by Skehan (1990) indicates the importance of aptitude as an explanatory factor for both L1 and L2 learning.

Motivation is an example of a factor that is clearly variable. The strength of an individual learner's motivation can change over time and is influenced by external factors. There is widespread recognition that motivation is of great importance for successful L2 acquisition, but there is less agreement about what motivation actually consists of. Motivation can be causative (i.e. have an effect on learning) and it can be resultative (i.e. be influenced by learning). It can be intrinsic (i.e. derive from the personal interests and inner needs of the learner) and it can be extrinsic (i.e. derive from external sources such as material rewards). There is a rich literature on motivation in general psychology, which has not been fully exploited in SLA. The main body of work in SLA research is that associated with Gardner, Lambert, and their associates (see Gardner 1985 for a summary). This is based on the assumption that the main determinants of motivation are the learners' attitudes to the target language community and their need to learn the L2. Motivation, so measured, affects the extent to which individual learners persevere in learning the L2, the kinds of learning behaviours they employ (for example, their level of participation in the classroom), and their actual achievement. Recent discussions of motivation (for example, Crookes and Schmidt 1990), however, have emphasized the need for investigating other aspects of motivation in L2 learning such as intrinsic motivation.

Other individual learner factors lie somewhere between the two poles of the continuum. One such factor that has attracted considerable attention, although with rather uncertain outcomes, is *cognitive style*. This is the term used to refer to the way people perceive, conceptualize, organize, and recall information. Various dimensions of cognitive style have been identified in psychology but the one that has attracted the most attention in SLA is *field dependence/independence*. Field-dependent learners operate holistically, whereas field-independent learners are analytic. The main research hypothesis is that field-independent learners will be more successful at formal, classroom learning, but the studies completed to date provide only limited support for this hypothesis (see Griffiths and Sheen 1992).

Chapter 11 will consider individual learner differences, concentrating on the above factors, but also dealing briefly with a number of others.

Learner strategies

Learner strategies are conscious or potentially conscious; they represent the learner's deliberate attempts to learn. Oxford (1989) defines them as 'behaviors or actions which learners use to make language learning more successful, self-directed and enjoyable'. The vagueness of this and other definitions points to a major problem in this area of SLA research—how to identify, describe, and classify the 'behaviors and actions' that constitute learners' attempts to learn. Nevertheless, the study of learner strategies has been one of the main areas of growth in SLA research (see O'Malley and Chamot 1989 and Oxford 1990).

A distinction is often drawn between learner strategies that are cognitive (for example, relating new concepts to other information in memory), those that are *metacognitive* (for example, organizing a personal timetable to facilitate effective study of the L2) and those that are social (for example, seeking out opportunities to converse with native speakers).

There have been a number of attempts to establish which learner strategies facilitate L2 acquisition. Studies of the *good language learner* (for example, Naiman, Fröhlich, Stern, and Todesco 1978) have tried to identify the strategies which successful learners use. Experimental studies (for example, Politzer and McGroarty 1985) have tried to establish whether the use of 'good learning behaviors' does lead to gains in learning. There have also been attempts to train learners to use effective strategies (for example, O'Malley 1987).

Learner strategies are examined in Chapter 12, while attempts to train strategy use are considered in Chapter 14.

Summary and conclusion

This chapter began by defining the term Second Language Acquisition, point-ing out the diversity of phenomena which have been investigated under its banner. It then went on to identify four general questions which SLA research has addressed. A framework for reviewing SLA research was then proposed. This consisted of four major areas: (1) learner language, (2) learner-external factors, (3) learner-internal factors, and (4) the language learner as an indi-vidual. A brief survey of some of the main issues relating to each of these areas was then provided.

It is useful to distinguish two branches of enquiry within SLA research. One has as its focus learning and the other the language learner. In the case of the former the emphasis is on identifying the universal characteristics of L2 ac-quisition. In the case of the latter the aim is to account for differences in ways in which individual learners learn an L2. These two branches have tended to work independently of each other. A complete theory of SLA must account for and interrelate the findings from both branches.

It is also useful to distinguish two main goals of SLA research: description and explanation. In the case of description, the goal is to provide a clear and accurate account of the learner's competence and, in particular, to uncover the regularities and systematicities in the learner's development and control of L2 knowledge. In the case of explanation, one goal is to reveal how learners are able to develop knowledge of an L2 from the available input and how they use this knowledge in communication. A second goal is to specify the factors that cause variation in individual learners' accomplishment of this task. A complete theory of SLA must provide an explanation for what is currently known about learner language and about language learners.

Notes

1 The claim that there are some properties of a language that are entirely for-mal in nature is not uncontroversial. However, it is an assumption of lin- · guists working within the generative tradition of Chomsky that the nature of many syntactical rules is determined by highly abstract principles of a purely formal kind (see Chapter 10).

2 A less problematic distinction than 'acquisition/learning' is that between 'implicit' and 'explicit' knowledge. This is because this distinction does not rest on how the knowledge was internalized but on how L2 knowledge is represented and used by learners. The implicit/explicit distinction is exam-ined in Chapter 9.

3 The focus on naturalistic learners came about because early research exam-ined 'second' rather than 'foreign' language learners—L2 learners of Eng-lish in the United States or the United Kingdom and L2 learners of German in Germany, for example. It should be noted, however, that many of these

'natural' learners were also receiving some instruction. A better label, therefore, might be 'mixed'.

4 A distinction is generally drawn between those cognitive processes responsible for the general pattern of L2 acquisition (i.e. its universal characteristics) and those strategies that are employed, often consciously, by learners to improve their learning. The terminological distinction between 'processes' and 'strategies' is not always adhered to, however. 'Strategies' are often invoked to account for developmental regularities. The problems of definition are dealt with in Chapter 12.

5 The claims made on behalf of Parallel Distributed Processing are not incompatible with a number of other theoretical positions. The notion of 'connection strengths', for example, is compatible with the idea of 'weights' found in the Competition Model and also relates closely to work done in variability in learner language.

6 It has been suggested that in the case of principles with multiple parameters, learners first choose an unmarked parameter which can be subsequently abandoned solely on the basis of the positive evidence available to them in the input. They do not initially choose a marked parameter which can only be abandoned with the help of negative evidence (for example, formal corrections), as this is generally not available to them in the input. They resort to a marked setting only when unmarked settings have been tried and dismissed (see White 1989a, Chapter 6, for a detailed discussion).

Further reading

Increasingly, work in SLA research deals with highly specific issues, or alternatively presents a particular view of the process of acquisition. There are few overviews written from an objective standpoint and the task of writing such overviews becomes more difficult as the field grows more complex.

R. Ellis, *Understanding Second Language Acquisition* (Oxford University Press, 1985) provides an account of much of the earlier research and theorizing.

L. Beebe (ed.), *Issues in Second Language Acquisition: Multiple Perspectives* (Newbury House, 1988), contains papers surveying a number of the key areas, including one not dealt with in this book—the neurolinguistic perspective.

D. Larsen-Freeman and M. Long, *An Introduction to Second Language Acquisition Research* (Longman, 1991), provides a more comprehensive and up-to-date account of most of the areas mentioned in this chapter. It also provides an extremely useful account of methodology in SLA research.

The *Annual Review of Applied Linguistics*, Volume 9, contains a number of articles surveying many of the areas of SLA research referred to in this chapter.

For readers who do not have the time to consult full-length books two articles provide short and accessible accounts of some of the areas:

C. James, 'Learner language', *Language Teaching Abstracts* (1990) 23: 205-213.

D. Larsen-Freeman (1991), 'Second language acquisition research: Staking out the territory', *TESOL Quarterly* (1992) 25: 315-50.

One way of starting the study of SLA, however, is by reading some of the early case studies:

E. Hatch (ed.), *Second Language Acquisition*, (Newbury House, 1978a), includes a number of such studies (see in particular the papers by Huang and Hatch, Cancino et al., and Butterworth and Hatch).

Schmidt's study of one adult learner called Wes is perhaps the best known and most rewarding of the case studies. See:

R. Schmidt, 'Interaction, acculturation, and the acquisition of communicative competence: A case study' in N. Wolfson and E. Judd (eds.), *Sociolinguistics and Language Acquisition* (Newbury House, 1983).

PART TWO
The description of learner language

Introduction

An obvious starting point in the study of second language (L2) acquisition is the study of the language that learners produce at different stages of their development. Learner language can provide the researcher with insights into the process of acquisition. For many researchers—although not all[1]—it constitutes the most important source of information about how learners learn an L2. This section, therefore, focuses on the description of learner language. Its purpose is to provide an overview of the principal ways in which it has been studied and to describe its main characteristics.

A number of different approaches to the description of learner language can be identified:

1 the study of learners' errors
2 the study of developmental patterns
3 the study of variability
4 the study of pragmatic features.

In the relatively short history of SLA research, it is possible to see a progression in the way enquiry has proceeded. Thus, initially the main approach was the study of learners' errors, but this was rapidly superseded by the study of developmental patterns and, a little later, variability. The study of L2 pragmatic features is a more recent phenomenon. This section follows this historical progression, beginning with (1) and concluding with (4). The opening chapters, therefore, focus on the early research, while the later chapters give more attention to more current research. However, as all these approaches have continued to figure in SLA research at least to some extent, each chapter, including the early ones, will also examine relevant recent research.

As we noted in the Introduction to this book, prior to the late 1960s there was almost no empirical study of L2 acquisition. Why, then, did researchers suddenly become interested in it? There appear to have been two principal reasons. One concerned the need to investigate the claims of competing theories. The other concerned the desire to improve L2 pedagogy.

According to the Contrastive Analysis Hypothesis, learners were strongly influenced by their L1. Where the L1 matched the L2, learning was facilitated; where it differed, learning was impeded. In the view of some (for example, Lado 1957), errors were mainly, if not entirely, the result of transfer of L1 'habits'. This theory of learning was challenged both by Chomsky's attack on behaviourism (see his famous review of B. Skinner's *Verbal Learning* in 1958) and also by research on L1 acquisition, which showed that children did not seem to learn their mother tongue as a set of 'habits' but rather seemed to construct mental 'rules', which often bore no resemblance to those manifest in their caretakers' speech. This challenge to the received opinion of the day created the necessary climate for the empirical study of L2 acquisition. Were learners' errors the result of L1 transfer? Did L2 learners, like L1 learners, construct unique mental 'rules'? These were questions that could only be answered by looking at learner language.

Second, many L2 researchers were directly concerned with language pedagogy. The prevailing methods of the day were the audiolingual method and the oral/situational approach (see Richards and Rogers 1986). Both of these emphasized tightly structuring the input to the learner and controlling output in order to minimize errors. It was noted, however, that children were successful in acquiring their mother tongue without such a structured learning environment. Also, many L2 learners, children and adults, seemed to be very successful in learning an L2 in natural settings. Newmark (1966), in a seminal paper, argued that L2 learning in the classroom would proceed more efficiently if teachers stopped 'interfering' in the learning process. But how did L2 learners learn in natural settings? What strategies did they use? What made some learners more successful than others? Again, these were questions that invited empirical enquiry. Many of the early studies in SLA research investigated L2 learners in untutored settings, motivated in part by the desire to find what experiences worked for them, so that suitable copies could be introduced into the language classroom.

This, then, constitutes the background to the study of learner language. It should be clear that although the empirical studies were primarily descriptive in nature, they were not atheoretical. In the late 1960s and 1970s a growing consensus was reached that behaviourist theories of L2 learning were inadequate. L2 learners, like L1 learners, were credited with a 'built-in-syllabus' (Corder 1967), which guided their progress. Selinker (1969, 1972) coined the term 'interlanguage' to refer to the special mental grammars that learners constructed during the course of their development. Interlanguage theory credited learners with playing an active role in constructing these grammars. It treated their behaviour, including their errors, as rule-governed. The language they produced, therefore, reflected the strategies they used to construct provisional grammatical rules (i.e. rules which they subsequently revised). The research that we will now consider helped to shape interlanguage theory and, in many cases, was influenced by it. Thus, although the main concern of this section is the description of learner language, some attention to theory is inevitable. Interlanguage theory is considered more fully in Chapter 9.

The research reported in these chapters was often conducted by researchers whose primary concern was L2 acquisition and L2 pedagogy. Inevitably, however, these researchers drew on various fields to help them in their enquiry. The fields of most obvious importance were linguistics (which provided researchers with well-defined linguistic categories to investigate), first language acquisition research (which provided them with useful procedures for collecting and analysing learner language), sociolinguistics (which provided both theories and methodologies for examining variability), and pragmatics/discourse analysis (which facilitated the study of learner language in a wider social and textual context). The account of learner language that follows, therefore, reflects one of the prevailing characteristics of SLA research—the utilization of a wide range of concepts and methods that have been borrowed from different fields and adapted to the particular needs of L2 researchers.

Notes

1 Some researchers prefer to work with intuitional data, obtained by asking learners to judge the grammaticality of sentences. However, as this introduction to Section 2 makes clear, the primary data in SLA research—both historically speaking and in terms of importance—has been learner language.

2 Learner errors and error analysis

Introduction

Learners make errors in both comprehension and production. An example of a comprehension error is when a learner misunderstands the sentence[1] 'Pass me the paper' as 'Pass me the pepper', because of an inability to discriminate the sounds /eɪ/ and /e/. However, comprehension errors have received scant attention, for, as Corder (1974: 125) has pointed out, although we can test comprehension in general terms, 'it is very difficult to assign the cause of failures of comprehension to an inadequate knowledge of a particular syntactic feature of a misunderstood utterance'. There is, in fact, a fundamental difference between comprehension and production in processing terms, a point that will be taken up later in Chapter 7. In this chapter, in accordance with the main focus in second language acquisition research, we will concentrate on production errors.

L2 learners are not alone in making errors. Children learning their first language (L1) also make 'errors' (for example, Bloom 1970). They regularly produce utterances like the following:

*I goes see Auntie May. (= I went to see Auntie May.)
*Eating ice cream. (= I want to eat an ice cream.)
*No writing in book. (= Don't write in the book.)

Also, even adult native speakers sometimes make 'errors'.[2] For example, they may sometimes omit a grammatical morpheme as in:

*My father live in Gloucester. (= My father lives in Gloucester.)

But it is probably true to say that these 'errors' are not generally thought of as errors in the same sense as those produced by L2 learners. Whereas L2 learners' errors are generally viewed as 'unwanted forms' (George 1972), children's 'errors' are seen as 'transitional forms' and adult native speakers' errors as 'slips of the tongue'.

The study of errors is carried out by means of *Error Analysis* (EA). In the 1970s, EA supplanted *Contrastive Analysis* (CA), which sought to predict the errors that learners make by identifying the linguistic differences between their L1 and the target language.[3] The underlying assumption of CA was that errors occurred primarily as a result of *interference* when the learner transferred native language 'habits' into the L2. Interference was believed to take place whenever the 'habits' of the native languages differed from those of the target language. CA gave way to EA as this assumption came to be challenged. Whereas CA looked at only the learner's native language and the target language (i.e. fully-formed languages), EA provided a methodology for investigating learner language. For this reason EA constitutes an appropriate starting point for the study of learner language and L2 acquisition.

EA was, of course, not a new development. The analysis of learner errors had long been a part of language pedagogy. French (1949), for example, provides a comprehensive account of common learner errors. Lee (1957) reports on an analysis of some 2,000 errors in the written work of Czechoslovakian learners, which were 'hurriedly grouped into categories' (wrong punctuation, misuse, or omission of articles, misspellings, non-English constructions, and wrong use of tenses). Lee argued that such an analysis put the teacher in 'a better position to decide how teaching time should be spent.' But such traditional analyses lacked both a rigorous methodology and a theoretical framework for explaining the role played by errors in the process of L2 acquisition. It was not until the 1970s that EA became a recognised part of applied linguistics, a development that owed much to the work of Corder (see Corder 1981a for a collection of his papers).

In an early, seminal article, Corder (1967) noted that errors could be significant in three ways: (1) they provided the teacher with information about how much the learner had learnt, (2) they provided the researcher with evidence of how language was learnt, and (3) they served as devices by which the learner discovered the rules of the target language. Whereas (1) reflects the traditional role of EA, (2) provides a new role that is of primary interest to the L2 researcher because it could shed light on (3)—the process of L2 acquisition. It should be noted, though, that many of the researchers who carried out error analyses in the 1970s continued to be concerned with language teaching. Indeed, the attempt to discover more about L2 acquisition through the study of errors was itself motivated by a desire to improve pedagogy.

Corder (1974) suggests the following steps in EA research:

1 Collection of a sample of learner language
2 Identification of errors
3 Description of errors
4 Explanation of errors
5 Evaluation of errors.

However, many studies do not include Step 5 and, in fact, the evaluation of learner errors has generally been handled as a separate issue, with its own methods of enquiry. Error evaluation studies are considered in this chapter as they represent one of the ways in which EA developed in the 1970s and 1980s.

This chapter will consider the procedures involved in each of these steps. In so doing, it will examine some of the research carried out in the 1970s and, where appropriate, the methodological problems. A general critique of EA follows. Finally, it will look at some more recent research which has made use of the techniques of error analysis.

Collection of a sample of learner language

The starting point in EA is deciding what samples of learner language to use for the analysis and how to collect these samples.

We can identify three broad types of EA according to the size of the sample. A massive sample involves collecting several samples of language use from a large number of learners in order to compile a comprehensive list of errors, representative of the entire population. A specific sample consists of one sample of language use collected from a limited number of learners, while an incidental sample involves only one sample of language use produced by a single learner. Clearly an EA based on a massive sample is a major undertaking and it is not surprising that most published EAs have employed specific or incidental samples.[4]

The errors that learners make can be influenced by a variety of factors. For example, they may make errors in speaking, but not in writing, as a result of the different processing conditions involved. Learners with one L1 may make a particular error which learners with a different L1 do not. This points to the importance of collecting well-defined samples of learner language so that clear statements can be made regarding what kinds of errors the learners produce and under what conditions. Table 2.1 lists some of the factors that need to be considered to ensure this. Unfortunately, many EA studies have not paid sufficient attention to these factors, with the result that they are difficult to interpret and almost impossible to replicate. Table 2.1 is not complete; the factors that can bring about variation in learner output are numerous, perhaps

Factors	Description
A Language	
Medium	Learner production can be oral or written
Genre	Learner production may take the form of a conversation, a lecture, an essay, a letter, etc.
Content	The topic the learner is communicating about
B Learner	
Level	Elementary, intermediate, or advanced
Mother tongue	The learner's L1
Language learning experience	This may be classroom or naturalistic or a mixture of the two

Table 2.1: Factors to consider when collecting samples of learner language

infinite. Little attention was paid to them in the early 1970s (see Chapter 4), though they were taken up in later work.

Decisions also need to be made regarding the manner in which the samples are to be collected. An important distinction is whether the learner language reflects natural, spontaneous language use, or is elicited in some way. Natural samples are generally preferred. A drawback, however, is that learners often do not produce much spontaneous data, which led Corder (1973) to argue the case for elicited data. Elicitation, however, is not to be confused with testing, which is concerned with measuring the learner's knowledge for purposes of evaluating rather than describing competence. Corder identifies two kinds of elicitation. Clinical elicitation involves getting the informant to produce data of any sort, for example, by means of a general interview or by asking learners to write a composition. Experimental methods involve the use of special instruments designed to elicit data containing the linguistic features which the researcher wishes to investigate. An example of such an elicitation instrument is the Bilingual Syntax Measure (Burt, Dulay, and Hernandez 1973). This consisted of a series of pictures which had been devised to elicit specific features and which the learners were asked to describe. The authors claimed that the resulting corpus of language reflected natural speech. The method of data collection can have a marked effect on the results obtained, as a result of the different production processes which they typically involve. Lococo (1976) found differences in the number and type of errors in samples of learner language collected by means of free composition, translation, and picture composition. For example, errors reflecting L1 influence were, not surprisingly, more common in the translation task. Again, the effects of task on learner language are considered in detail in Chapter 4.

Another issue is whether the samples of learner language are collected cross-sectionally (i.e. at a single point in time) or longitudinally (i.e. at successive points over a period of time). The majority of EAs have been cross-sectional, thus making it difficult to determine accurately the different errors that learners produce at different stages of their development.

The limitations of EA, as practised in the late 1960s and 1970s, are evident in the samples of learner language collected. Svartvik, for instance, notes that 'most error analyses use regular examination papers (composition, translations, etc.) for material' (1973b: 12). There were few studies of learner speech. Also, as we have noted, insufficient attention was paid to identifying and controlling the factors that might potentially influence the errors that learners produced.

Identification of errors

Once a corpus of learner language has been collected, the errors in the corpus have to be identified. It is necessary to decide, therefore, what constitutes an 'error' and to establish a procedure for recognizing one.

An error can be defined as a deviation from the norms of the target language. This definition raises a number of questions, however. First, there is the question regarding which variety of the target language should serve as the norm. The general practice, especially where classroom learners are concerned, is to select the standard written dialect as the norm. This, of course, is fundamentally wrong if the goal is to describe learners' oral production. Nor is it always possible to adopt the standard spoken variety as the norm. Some learners are exposed to varieties of the language which differ from the standard dialect. For example, in comparison with the norms of British or American standard written English the utterance

*She coped up with her problem very well.

is erroneous, but in comparison with norms of educated Zambian English such an utterance can be considered correct.[5]

A second question concerns the distinction between *errors* and *mistakes* (Corder 1967). An error (in this technical sense) takes place when the deviation arises as a result of lack of knowledge. It represents a lack of competence (see Chapter 1, page 12). A mistake occurs when learners fail to perform their competence. That is, it is the result of processing problems that prevent learners from accessing their knowledge of a target language rule and cause them to fall back on some alternative, non-standard rule that they find easier to access. Mistakes, then, are performance phenomena and are, of course, regular features of native-speaker speech, reflecting processing failures that arise as a result of competing plans, memory limitations, and lack of automaticity. Corder argues that the EA should be restricted to the study of errors (i.e. mistakes should be eliminated from the analysis). However, apart from the problems of identification that this distinction raises, it also assumes that competence is homogeneous rather than variable. Thus, if learners sometimes use a correct target form and sometimes an incorrect, non-target form, it cannot necessarily be concluded that the learner 'knows' the target form and that the use of the non-target form represents a mistake. It is possible that the learner's knowledge of the target form is only partial; the learner may not have learnt all the contexts in which the form in question can be used. For example, a learner may have no difficulty in using the target language form in some linguistic contexts:

My sisters are older than me.

but produce an error in others:

*My three sister are older than me.

In this early period, the study of learner errors largely ignored the problem of variability in learner language (see Chapter 4).

A third question concerns whether the error is overt or covert (Corder 1971a). An overt error is easy to identify because there is a clear deviation in form, as when a learner says:

   *I runned all the way.

A covert error occurs in utterances that are superficially well-formed but which do not mean what the learner intended them to mean. For example, the utterance (from Corder 1971a):

   *It was stopped.

is apparently grammatical until it becomes clear that 'it' refers to 'the wind'. Furthermore, a superficially correct utterance may only be correct by chance. For example, the learner may manifest target-like control of negative constructions in ready-made chunks such as 'I don't know' but fail to do so in 'created' utterances (i.e. utterances that are constructed on the basis of rules the learner has internalized). The existence of covert errors led Corder to argue that 'every sentence is to be regarded as idiosyncratic until shown to be otherwise' (page 21).

A fourth question concerns whether the analysis should examine only deviations in correctness or also deviations in appropriateness. The former involves rules of usage and is illustrated in the two examples above. The latter involves rules of language use. For example, a learner who invites a relative stranger by saying 'I want you to come to the cinema with me' has succeeded in using the code correctly but has failed to use it appropriately. In general, EA has attended to 'breaches of the code' and ignored 'misuse of the code' (Corder 1974: 124), but more recently attention has been paid to the latter (Thomas 1983). Errors of this pragmatic kind will be considered in Chapter 5.

These various distinctions are indicative of the kinds of problems which analysts face in recognizing errors. To overcome them, Corder (1971a; 1974) proposes an elaborate procedure for identifying errors, which is shown in Figure 2.1. This procedure acknowledges the importance of 'interpretation' and distinguishes three types: normal, authoritative, and plausible. A normal interpretation occurs when the analyst is able to assign a meaning to an utterance on the basis of the rules of the target language. In such cases, the utterance is 'not apparently erroneous', although it may still only be right 'by chance'. An authoritative interpretation involves asking the learner (if available) to say what the utterance means and, by so doing, to make an 'authoritative reconstruction'. A plausible interpretation can be obtained by referring to the context in which the utterance was produced or by translating the sentence literally into the learner's L1.

There are a number of major methodological problems with the procedures used in error identification, some of which we have already noted. Corder's (1967) distinction between errors and mistakes is not easy to put

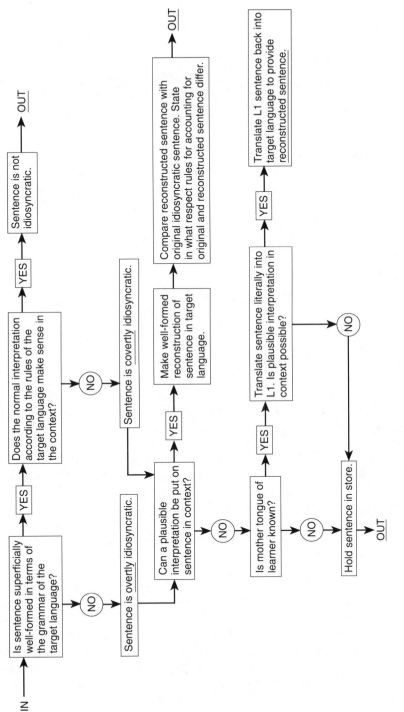

Figure 2.1:   Algorithm for providing for description of idiosyncratic dialects (from Corder 1981a)

into practice, even if the learner is available to provide an 'authoritative interpretation'. In addition, the distinction does not take account of the possibility
that learners' knowledge is variable. Also, it is not at all clear whether
Corder's suggestions for identifying covert errors will work. Reliance on the
learner as an informant has been criticized on the grounds that retrospective
accounts of intended meaning are often not reliable (Van Els et al. 1984). Also,
such a procedure assumes that learners possess the necessary *metalingual
knowledge* to talk about their own performance—an assumption that may
not be justified in the case of children and some adult learners. Not all researchers have found problems with identifying errors, however. Duskova
(1969), in a study considered in the next section, discusses it at some length
and concludes that 'the number of cases in which it was hard to decide
whether an error had been made ... did not exceed 4 per cent of all the errors
examined'. Unfortunately, Duskova does not provide inter-rater reliability
measures for the errors identified in her sample—a failing common to most of
the early studies.[6]

Description of errors

The description of learner errors involves a comparison of the learner's idiosyncratic utterances with a reconstruction of those utterances in the target
language. It requires, therefore, attention to the surface properties of the
learners' utterances (i.e. it does not attempt, at this stage, to identify the
sources of the errors). Some researchers have felt the need to maintain a clear
distinction between the description and explanation of errors. Dulay, Burt,
and Krashen (1982), for example, argue the need for descriptive taxonomies
of errors that focus only on observable, surface features of errors, as a basis
for subsequent explanation.

Perhaps the simplest type of descriptive taxonomy is one based on linguistic categories. This type is closely associated with a traditional EA undertaken for pedagogic purposes, as the linguistic categories can be chosen to
correspond closely to those found in structural syllabuses and language text
books. An example can be found in Burt and Kiparsky's *The Gooficon: A Repair Manual for English* (1972). This identifies a number of general linguistic
categories (for example, the skeleton of English clauses, the auxiliary system,
passive sentences, temporal conjunctions, and sentential complements). Each
general category is then broken down into further levels of subcategories. For
example, the auxiliary system is subdivided into 'do', 'have and be', modals,
and mismatching auxiliaries in tag questions, while errors in the use of 'do'
are classified according to whether they involve over-use in questions and
negatives, underuse in questions or overuse in affirmative sentences. Politzer
and Ramirez (1973) begin with even more general categories: morphology,
syntax, and vocabulary. Such taxonomies allow for both a detailed description of specific errors and also for a quantification of a corpus of errors.

The 1960s saw a number of studies which provided descriptions of the different kinds of linguistic errors produced by learners. Richards (1971b), in a paper designed to challenge the widely held belief that learner errors were the result of L1 interference, provided a taxonomy of different categories of linguistic error based on a number of previous studies. He examined errors made by learners from different language backgrounds (Japanese, Chinese, Burmese, French, Czech, Polish, Tagalog, Maori, Maltese, and the major Indian and West African languages) and illustrated the different kinds of errors relating to the production and distribution of verb groups, prepositions, articles, and the use of questions. However, he made no attempt to quantify the errors. Nor do we know to what extent his linguistic categories accounted for all the errors he examined. Duskova (1969)—one of the studies Richards drew on—is better in this respect. She identified a total of 1007 errors in the written work of 50 Czech learners of English, who were postgraduate students studying science. She found 756 'recurrent systemic errors' and 251 'nonce errors' (i.e. errors that occurred once only). Errors in articles were most common (260), followed by errors in lexis (233) and morphology (180). In comparison, there were only 54 errors in syntax and 31 in word order. Duskova noted, however, that the frequency of the errors did not necessarily reflect the level of difficulty the learners experienced with different linguistic features, as some features (such as articles) were attempted more often than others (for example, adverbs). Duskova also noted that although she had few difficulties in assigning errors to general linguistic categories such as 'word order', it often proved very difficult to classify them accurately into subcategories.

These studies were cross-sectional in design. Of greater interest for SLA research are longitudinal studies of learners' errors as these can show in what areas of language errors persist over time. Chamot's (1978; 1979) study of the acquisition of English by a bilingual French/Spanish boy is interesting in this respect. She found that the main linguistic problem areas were omission of constituents, verb forms, sentence formation, articles, and prepositions. In some of these (for example, omission of constituents) the number of errors reduced sharply over a 44-month period, while in others (for example, question formation) little improvement was evident. In all the areas, however, there was considerable fluctuation in error frequency throughout the period. Chamot's study suggests that it may be difficult to provide a satisfactory description of learners' L2 development by quantifying the types of errors they make.

An alternative to a linguistic classification of errors is to use a surface strategy taxonomy. This 'highlights the ways surface structures are altered' (Dulay, Burt, and Krashen 1982: 150) by means of such operations as omissions, additions and regularizations. Table 2.2 provides a part of the total taxonomy together with examples of the categories. Dulay, Burt, and Krashen claim that such an approach is promising because it provides an indication of the cognitive processes that underlie the learner's reconstruction of the L2. This seems a doubtful claim, however, as it presupposes that learners operate on the surface structures of the target language rather than create their own, unique structures. If a surface strategy taxonomy does not represent mental processes, it is not clear what value it has. This may account for why there have been few attempts to describe learner errors using such a taxonomy.

Category	Description	Example
Omissions	The absence of an item that must appear in a well-formed utterance.	She sleeping.
Additions	The presence of an item that must not appear in well-formed utterances.	We didn't went there.
Misinformations	The use of the wrong form of the morpheme or structure.	The dog ated the chicken.
Misorderings	The incorrect placement of a morpheme or group of morphemes in an utterance.	What daddy is doing?

Table 2.2:   A surface strategy taxonomy of errors (categories and examples taken from Dulay, Burt, and Krashen 1982)

Although linguistic and surface strategy taxonomies of errors may have a pedagogic application (for example, by demonstrating which errors are the most frequent and, therefore, most in need of attention), in general they shed little light on how learners learn an L2. Corder's (1974) framework for describing errors is more promising in this respect. He distinguishes three types of error according to their systematicity:

1 Presystematic errors occur when the learner is unaware of the existence of a particular rule in the target language. These are random.
2 Systematic errors occur when the learner has discovered a rule but it is the wrong one.
3 Postsystematic errors occur when the learner knows the correct target language rule but uses it inconsistently (i.e. makes a mistake).

In order to identify these different kinds of errors, however, it is necessary to interview the learner. Thus, type (1) occurs when the learner cannot give any account of why a particular form is chosen, type (2) occurs when the learner is unable to correct the errors but can explain the mistaken rule used, and type (3) occurs when the learner can explain the target-language rule that is normally used. Such a taxonomy, therefore, requires that the researcher has access to the learners and that the learners are capable of providing explanations for their L2 behaviour. For this reason it may prove difficult to operate.

The description of errors, like their identification, is problematic. Even if the error itself can be easily identified, it is often problematic to determine what the error consists of. If a learner produces the following sentence:

*My name Alberto.

there is no difficulty in reconstructing the target-language version:

My name is Alberto.

and so establishing that copula 'is' has been omitted. But in many cases—even with sentences that are overtly idiosyncratic—the reconstruction of the target language version—and, therefore, its description—is problematic. For example, if a learner produces the following sentence:

*I am worried in my mind.

it is not clear what constitutes the best reconstruction. One possibility is 'I am feeling worried.' Another is 'I have a problem on my mind.'

Even if the learner is available for consultation, it may not be possible to choose between these two reconstructions. But the description of the error will obviously vary according to which reconstruction is finally chosen. The reconstruction of covertly idiosyncratic sentences will prove even more difficult.

Another problem concerns the failure to quantify the different types of errors that have been identified and described. Many of the EA studies that have been conducted have been very informal—perhaps as a result of the kinds of problems discussed above. In some studies error frequencies are not given at all (for example, Jain 1974; Richards 1971b), while in others only absolute frequencies are given (for example, Duskova 1969). But as Schachter and Celce-Murcia (1977) point out, to say anything worthwhile about error frequency we need to know the number of times it would be possible for learners to have committed different errors. In other words, relative rather than absolute frequencies are needed.

Explanation of errors

Assuming that it is possible to identify and describe errors, the next step is to try to explain them. Explanation is concerned with establishing the source of the error, i.e. accounting for why it was made. This stage is the most important for SLA research as it involves an attempt to establish the processes responsible for L2 acquisition.

As Taylor (1986) points out, the error source may be psycholinguistic, sociolinguistic, epistemic, or may reside in the discourse structure. Psycholinguistic sources concern the nature of the L2 knowledge system and the difficulties learners have in using it in production. Sociolinguistic sources involve such matters as the learners' ability to adjust their language in accordance with the social context. Epistemic sources concern the learners' lack of world knowledge, while discourse sources involve problems in the organization of information into a coherent 'text'. In general, however, SLA research has attended only to the first of these. As Abbott puts it: 'The aim of any EA is to provide a psychological explanation' (1980: 124). Figure 2.2 plots the different psycholinguistic sources to be discussed.

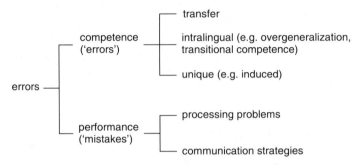

Figure 2.2:   Psycholinguistic sources of errors

The distinction between 'errors' and 'mistakes', which has already been discussed with regard to the identification stage of EA, is also relevant in explaining deviations—demonstrating the interdependence of these two steps in EA. Any deviation from target-language norms may reflect either a problem in performance or in competence.[7] It is helpful to recognize two different kinds of performance mistake: those that result from processing problems of various kinds, and those that result from such strategies as circumlocution and paraphrase, which a learner uses to overcome lack of knowledge. The latter are known as communication strategies and will be discussed in some detail in Chapter 9. As we have already seen, it is competence errors that have been considered central to the study of L2 acquisition.

A number of different sources or causes of competence errors have been identified. Richards (1971b) distinguishes three:

1 Interference errors occur as a result of 'the use of elements from one language while speaking another.' An example might be when a German learner of L2 English says *'I go not' because the equivalent sentence in German is 'Ich gehe nicht'.
2 Intralingual errors 'reflect the general characteristics of rule learning such as faulty generalization, incomplete application of rules and failure to learn conditions under which rules apply'.
3 Developmental errors occur when the learner attempts to build up hypotheses about the target language on the basis of limited experience.

However, Schachter and Celce-Murcia (1977) find the distinction between intralingual and developmental errors 'curious', and most researchers have operated with a general distinction between transfer errors (Richards' category (1)) and intralingual errors (an amalgam of Richards' (2) and (3)).

Transfer errors can be further subdivided. Lott (1983), for instance, distinguishes three categories:

1 'Overextension of analogy' occurs when the learner misuses an item because it shares features with an item in the L1 (for example, Italian learners use 'process' to mean 'trial' because Italian 'processo' has this meaning).
2 'Transfer of structure' arises when the learner utilizes some L1 feature (phonological, lexical, grammatical, or pragmatic) rather than that of the target language. This is what is generally understood as 'transfer'.
3 'Interlingual/intralingual errors' arise when a particular distinction does not exist in the L1 (for example, the use of 'make' instead of 'do' by Italian learners because the 'make/do' distinction is non-existent in Italian).

It is this third category that has caused so many of the problems in determining whether an error is transfer or intralingual.

Intralingual errors are also often further subdivided. Thus, Richards (1971b) distinguishes the following:

1 Overgeneralization errors arise when the learner creates a deviant structure on the basis of other structures in the target language. It generally involves the creation of one deviant structure in place of two target language structures (for example, *'He can sings' where English allows 'He can sing' and 'He sings').
2 Ignorance of rule restrictions involves the application of rules to contexts where they do not apply. An example is *'He made me to rest' through extension of the pattern found with the majority of verbs that take infinitival complements (for example, 'He asked/wanted/invited me to go').
3 Incomplete application of rules involves a failure to fully develop a structure. Thus learners of L2 English have been observed to use declarative word order in questions (for example, *'You like to sing?') in place of interrogative word order (for example, 'Do you like to sing?'). This type of intralingual error corresponds to what is often referred to as an error of transitional competence (Richards 1971a).
4 False concepts hypothesized (i.e. the learner fails to comprehend fully) arise when the learner does not fully comprehend a distinction in the target language—for example, the use of 'was' as a marker of past tense in *'One day it was happened'.

It is not easy to distinguish transfer and intralingual errors, and even more difficult to identify the different types of intralingual errors that Richards describes. In an attempt to deal with the problem of identifying sources, Dulay and Burt (1974b) classified the errors they collected into three broad categories:

1 Developmental (i.e. those errors that are similar to L1 acquisition)
2 Interference (i.e. those errors that reflect the structure of the L1)
3 Unique (i.e. those errors that are neither developmental nor interference).

Dulay and Burt's research has often been criticized on the grounds that reliable classification of errors in terms of these categories is still not possible. However, it might be argued that by using L1 acquisition errors as a baseline they at least provide an operational procedure for establishing which errors are intralingual.

It is customary to distinguish another general source of errors. *Induced errors* occur when learners are led to make errors by the nature of the instruction they have received. Stenson (1974) provides a number of examples of such errors in the classroom speech of Tunisian learners of English. Faulty explanation of grammatical points can give rise to errors (for example, the use of 'any' to mean 'none' when the students were told that 'any' has a negative meaning). Drills performed without consideration for meaning can also result in error. Svartvik (1973b) suggests that overdrilling may be one of the reasons why Swedish learners of L2 English overuse infinitival complements (for example, *'He proposed her to stay'). Stenson argues that such errors are not systematic and therefore do not reflect competence. However, there are probably cases when learners do internalize faulty rules derived from instruction and in such cases the resulting errors will reflect their competence. Instruction may constitute one source of what Dulay and Burt call 'unique errors'.

The bulk of the empirical work in SLA has focused on determining what proportion of the total errors in a corpus are transfer as opposed to intralingual. This is what motivated such studies as Richards (1971b) and Dulay and Burt (1974b). The issue that these researchers tackled was the competing claims of a behaviourist, habit-formation account of L2 acquisition and a mentalist, creative-construction account. According to behaviourist accounts, errors were viewed as the result of the negative transfer of L1 habits. According to mentalist accounts, errors were predicted to be similar to those found in L1 acquisition because learners actively construct the grammar of an L2 as they progress (i.e. they are intralingual). This issue dominated early work in SLA. It should be noted, however, that subsequently researchers have come to recognize that the correlation between behaviourism and transfer errors on the one hand and mentalism and intralingual errors on the other is simplistic and misleading. Transfer is now treated as a mental process in its own right (see Chapter 8).

A good example of the kind of 'proportion study' that investigated this behaviourist/mentalist question is Dulay and Burt (1974b). Five hundred and thirteen unambiguous errors produced by Spanish children acquiring L2

English were extracted from a corpus of speech collected by means of the Bilingual Syntax Measure (see page 50 in this chapter). These errors occurred in six syntactic structures which differed in English and Spanish. The errors were classified as 'developmental', 'interference', or 'unique', and detailed results for each structure were provided. In each case the developmental errors far outweighed the interference errors. For example, for the structure NP + V + Pronoun (for example, 'The dog ate it'), which is realized as NP + Pronoun + V in Spanish (for example, 'El perro se lo comio'), there were 93 developmental errors and no interference errors. Overall less than 5 per cent of the total errors were attributed to interference. This led Dulay and Burt to propose that L1 and L2 acquisition were very similar (the L2=L1 Hypothesis). It should be noted, however, that other studies (for example, George 1972 and Flick 1980) found a much higher proportion of transfer errors (see Chapter 8).

One reason for the discrepancy in research findings has been the problem of error classification. As Flick notes:

> The assignment of a particular error to such categories as 'transfer', 'overgeneralization' or 'ambiguous' has been largely an arbitrary matter, subject to the individual biases and point of view of the researcher (Flick 1979: 60).

To solve this problem, Flick proposed the use of factor analysis. This is a statistical procedure which uses the patterns of correlation that exist among scores on different variables to identify underlying factors. Flick reported on the preliminary use of this procedure to identify clusters of errors in the speech elicited from 20 adult Spanish learners of L2 English by means of an oral translation task. Five factors emerged from the analysis:

1 transfer accounted for 34 per cent of the variance in the scores assigned to each learner
2 performance (i.e. constraints imposed by processing load) for 23 per cent
3 simplifications of function words, such as errors of omission, for 17 per cent
4 overgeneralization for 16 per cent
5 pronominal reference (for example, wrong choice of pronoun) for 11 per cent.

Flick's study represents an interesting attempt to increase the rigour of error explanation, but it is open to a number of objections. For example, the five categories identified constitute a very mixed bag: while some are explanatory in nature, others seem more descriptive.

It is difficult to synthesize the results of attempts to explain errors in learner language, but the following appear to be some of the main findings:

1 A large number—and in some cases perhaps most—of the errors that learners produce are intralingual in origin rather than transfer.

However, the precise proportion of the kinds of error varies considerably from study to study.

2 According to Taylor (1975), learners at an elementary level produced more transfer errors than learners at an intermediate or advanced level. Conversely, he found that learners at an intermediate or advanced level produced more intralingual errors (for example, overgeneralization) than learners at an elementary level. However, as we will see in Chapter 8, other researchers (for example, Kellerman 1983) have challenged the view that transfer is more prevalent in beginners.

3 The proportion of transfer and intralingual errors varies in accordance with the task used to elicit samples of learner language. Thus, translation tasks tend to result in more transfer errors than tasks that call for free composition (Lococo 1976).

4 Transfer errors are more common in the phonological and lexical levels of language than in the grammatical level. Also some areas of grammar acquisition are more likely to be influenced by the learners' L1 than others. Grauberg (1971) found that interference accounted for 25 per cent of the lexical errors produced by adult German learners of L2 English, 10 per cent of their syntactic errors, and none of their morphological errors.

5 Transfer errors are more common in adult learners than in child learners. For example, White (1977) found that 21 per cent of the errors made by adult Spanish learners of English were transfer. White used the same instrument to collect data as in the Dulay and Burt (1974b) study of Spanish children referred to above, so this study is directly comparable.

6 Errors can have more than one source. For example, the 'no' + verb error (as in *'No look my card') is universal, suggesting an intralingual explanation, but Spanish learners of L2 English have been noted to make this error more frequently and for a longer period of time, suggesting that the L1 pattern for negatives (*no* + verb) is also having an influence.

Again, it is important to recognize that the concept of 'transfer', upon which many of the early EA studies were based, was simplistic. Transfer is, in fact, a very complex notion which is best understood in terms of cognitive rather than behaviourist models of learning.

It should be clear from this account of the explanation stage of EA that problems abound. In particular, the concepts of transfer and intralingual error were often not operationalized with sufficient rigour. Where one researcher identified the source of an error as transfer, another researcher identified the source of the same error as intralingual. For example, Duskova (1969) interpreted article deletion in Czech learners of English as interference, while Dulay and Burt (1974b) interpreted the same error in Spanish children learning English as intralingual. Schachter and Celce-Murcia (1977) argue that a large number of learners' errors are ambiguous with regard to source and that 'one must be extremely cautious when claiming to have identified the cause of any given error type'. Such caution has not always been exercised, however. If clear explanatory statements about errors are often not possible, the value of EA as a tool for investigating L2 acquisition is thrown into question.

Evaluating errors

Whereas all the preceding stages of EA have involved an examination of errors from the point of view of the learner who makes them, *error evaluation* involves a consideration of the effect that errors have on the person(s) addressed. This effect can be gauged either in terms of the addressee's comprehension of the learner's meaning or in terms of the addressee's affective response to the errors. Error evaluation studies proliferated in the late 1970s and in the 1980s, motivated quite explicitly by a desire to improve language pedagogy.[8] The studies surveyed in Table 2.3 constitute only a part of the total. Ludwig (1982) provides a survey of twelve early studies.

The design of error evaluation studies involves decisions on who the addressees (i.e. the judges) will be, what errors they will be asked to judge, and how they will be asked to judge them. The judges can vary according to whether they are native speakers (NS) or non-native speakers (NNS), and also according to whether they are 'expert' (i.e. language teachers) or 'non-expert'. The errors they have been asked to judge cover semantic or lexical aspects of English, different grammatical features, and spelling. The instruments used to elicit judgements vary in a number of ways. In most cases they consist of decontextualized lists of sentences containing either one or several errors. These sentences are usually taken from actual samples of learner language (mainly written compositions) but they are sometimes contrived. In some studies the sentences are contextualized. The errors can be presented orally but are usually presented in writing. The judges may be asked to evaluate the 'comprehensibility' of the sentences containing the errors, the 'seriousness' or the 'naturalness' of errors, or the degree of 'irritation' they arouse. Sometimes they may be asked to correct the errors and to give reasons for why they judged some errors as especially problematic. In some studies the judges' comprehension of the erroneous sentences is also tested.

Error evaluation studies have addressed three main research questions: (1) Are some errors judged to be more problematic than others? (2) Are there differences in the evaluations made by NS and NNS? and (3) What criteria do judges use in evaluating learners' errors? We will briefly consider the main findings on each of these issues.

NS judges tend to judge lexical errors as more serious than grammatical errors (for example, Burt 1975; Tomiyana 1980; Khalil 1985). They also tend to judge global grammatical errors as more likely to interfere with comprehension than local errors, although as Santos (1987) points out, there have been conflicting results on this point. Burt defines *global errors* as errors that

Study	Subjects	Measures	Procedure	Main Results
Burt 1975	Non-expert NS.	Partially corrected versions of 300 sentences containing multiple errors.	Subjects were asked to judge comprehensibility of different corrected versions.	Subjects found versions in which 'global' errors had been corrected more comprehensible than versions in which 'local' errors had been corrected.
Albrechtsen, Henriksen, and Faerch 1980	120 non-expert adult NSs (e.g. hotel workers in UK; 180 British sixth-formers).	Samples of oral language taken from Grade 10 Danish learners of L2 English; the samples varied with regard to error density.	Subjects listened to tapes and rated each sample using bi-polar adjective scales (e.g. easy to understand-difficult to understand).	The oral texts containing few errors (syntactic as well as lexical) and few communication strategies (CSs) received positive evaluations. Frequent use of CSs had greater negative effect than number of errors.
Tomiyana 1980	NS graduates in Education and Language departments	2 constructed passages (200 words in length), designed to include 7 instances of six kinds of errors involving articles and sentence connectors.	Subjects were asked to read the passages and correct the errors and to rate likely academic achievement of the writer of the passage.	Subjects corrected insertion errors more accurately than omission or wrong choice errors and article errors more accurately than connector errors. Errors in articles not perceived as so damaging to academic success as errors in connectors.
Chastain 1981	27 native Spanish speakers: undergraduates at university in Spain.	10 paragraphs written by American university students of Spanish.	Subjects were asked to read the passages, underline each error, and then evaluate it as comprehensible and acceptable, comprehensible but not acceptable, or not comprehensible.	The overall seriousness of the different errors was (1) word errors in noun phrases (most serious); (2) form errors in verb phrases; (3) word errors in verb phrases; and (4) form errors in noun phrases (least serious).
Hughes and Lascaratou 1982	10 Greek-speaking teachers; 10 NS teachers; 10 non-expert NS.	32 sentences containing errors in 8 categories (vocabulary, grammar, and spelling) taken from learners' compositions; 10 error-free sentences.	Subjects were asked to underline errors, write correct versions, and judge their seriousness. Also asked to give reason if error judged 'very serious'.	NNS judged errors overall as more serious than NS. NNS more lenient on spelling errors. NS judged according to whether error constituted infringement of 'basic' rule; NS judged according to intelligibility. Evaluation of specific errors inconsistent.

Study	Subjects	Measures	Procedure	Main Results
Davies 1983	43 Moroccan teachers of English; 43 non-expert NS.	82 contrived sentences (some correct) containing typical errors of Moroccan secondary school students.	Subjects were asked to rate seriousness of the errors and to add comments.	NS more lenient than NNS. NNS very hard on morphological and tense choice errors, but NNS less hard on obvious transfer errors and 'global' errors.
Vann et al. 1984	319 faculty members of US university.	24 sentences containing multiple errors and 12 containing single errors; errors in 12 error categories.	Subjects were asked to judge acceptability of sentences.	Subjects more prepared to accept errors of kind made by NS students (e.g. in spelling), but less likely to accept 'global' errors (e.g. word order).
Khalil 1985	240 American undergraduate NS.	20 gramatically deviant and 12 semantically deviant sentences taken from compositions by Arab 1st year students, some contextualized and some not.	Subjects were asked to judge intelligibility and naturalness of sentences. They were also tested on the ability to understand the sentences' meaning.	Semantic errors were judged less intelligible and found less comprehensible than grammatical errors. Contextualization of sentences did not improve intelligibility.
Sheorey 1986	64 NS teachers and 34 NNS (Indian) teachers.	20 sentences reflecting 8 categories of error taken from compositions written by foreign students at university in USA.	Subjects were asked to judge seriousness of errors.	NNS judged errors overall more serious than NS. NS judged lexical errors more serious than NNS. NNS judged errors in tense, agreement, prepositions, question formation, and spelling more serious than NS.
Santos 1987	40 university professors in physical sciences.	4 written compositions; in 2 of them 5 errors of the marked-to-unmarked kind (e.g. 'a' instead of 'an') were inserted and in the other 2, 5 errors of the unmarked-to-marked kind (e.g. 'an' instead of 'a') were inserted.	Subjects were asked to rank each composition and to underline each error and to assess the degree of irritation it aroused.	No significant difference in rankings of the compositions. Overall, unmarked-to-marked errors were found to be more irritating than marked-to-unmarked errors. Syntactic errors were also found more irritating than morphological errors.

Table 2.3:   A summary of selected error evaluation studies

affect overall sentence organization. Examples are wrong word order, missing or wrongly placed sentence connectors, and syntactic overgeneralizations. *Local errors* are errors that affect single elements in a sentence (for example, errors in morphology or grammatical functors). NS judges may also be influenced by markedness factors. Santos' study, for example, lends some credence to the idea that errors involving the substitution of marked for unmarked forms (for example, 'an book' for 'a book') are judged more severely than errors in which unmarked forms replace marked forms (for example, 'a apple' for 'an apple'). NS judges also find it easier to deal with insertion than with omission or wrong choice errors (Tomiyana 1980). It should be noted, though, that there can be considerable variation in the judgements of native speakers. Thus Vann, Meyer, and Lorenz (1984) found that some academic faculty members were inclined to view all errors as equally serious—'an error is an error'. Also, attempts to identify a hierarchy of errors according to their effect on intelligibility have not proved successful.

There are clear differences in the judgements made by NS and NNS. Overall, NNS are much more severe (James 1977; Hughes and Lascaratou 1982; Davies 1983; Sheorey 1986). NNS judges seem to be especially hard on morphological and functor errors in comparison to NS judges. However, they tend to evaluate lexical and global errors less severely than NS judges.

Judges appear to use different criteria in assessing *error gravity*. Khalil (1985) identifies three general criteria: intelligibility, acceptability, and irritation. Intelligibility concerns the extent to which sentences containing different kinds of error can be comprehended. Acceptability is a rather vague criterion, involving judgements of the seriousness of an error. Irritation concerns the emotional response of an addressee but is also related to the frequency of errors. Albrechtsen, Henriksen, and Færch (1980), who had NS judges rate the errors made by Danish learners of English in oral interviews, found that 'all errors are equally irritating . . . irritation is directly predictable from the number of errors regardless of the error type or other linguistic aspects' (1980: 394).

Obviously NS and NNS judges vary in the criteria they use. NS judges appear to be more concerned with the effect that an error has on their comprehension, whereas NNS judges are more influenced by their ideas of what constitute the 'basic' rules of the target language (Hughes and Lascaratou 1982). However, Davies (1983) points out that NNS judgements will be influenced by a number of factors relating to the particular context in which they operate. Thus NNS teachers will be influenced by their background knowledge of the syllabus and text book the learners are following and by explicit knowledge of their L1. Transfer errors are viewed leniently, but errors in grammatical structures that have already been taught will be seen as more serious. Davies makes the general point that 'any evaluation will be coloured by the particular viewpoint from which it was carried out, and this may not be consistent with evaluations made from other viewpoints' (1983: 310).

As we noted in the introduction to this chapter, EA studies have often been pedagogically motivated. They have sought to identify criteria for establishing error gravity so that teachers can be guided in what errors to pay more attention to. The general conclusion is that teachers should attend most carefully to errors that interfere with communication (i.e. semantic and global grammatical errors).[9] Johansson (1973) suggests that errors should be evaluated by first asking whether they are comprehensible, and second whether they cause irritation. Other, secondary factors—the frequency and generality of the feature involved—also need to be considered. In this way, Johansson constructs a hierarchy of errors. However, he acknowledges that 'it is not possible to illustrate the scale of errors at the present time since there is no available information concerning the degree of comprehensibility/irritation caused by different errors' (1973: 109). Although there has been considerable research since, there is still insufficient evidence to support a definite scale for evaluating errors.

Like other aspects of EA, the evaluation of learner error poses a number of problems. It is not at all clear what criteria judges use when asked to assess the 'seriousness', 'intelligibility', or 'acceptability' of an error. As we have seen, error evaluation is influenced by the context in which the errors occurred. Thus, the same error may be evaluated very differently depending on who made it and where, when and how it was made. The experimental studies which have been conducted to date, however, take no account of these contextual factors, often presenting errors for evaluation in isolated sentences. It is perhaps not surprising that these studies have produced conflicting results (see Santos 1987). The appearance of rigour given by the use of descriptive and qualitative statistics may therefore be spurious.

The limitations of error analysis

There have been a number of critiques of EA (Bell 1974; Schachter and Celce-Murcia 1977; Long and Sato 1984; Van Els et al. 1984). Bell goes so far as to call EA a 'pseudo procedure'. The criticisms levelled at EA fall into two main categories: (1) weaknesses in methodological procedures, and (2) limitations in scope. The first type have already been considered in the previous sections, so we focus on the second here.

A frequently mentioned limitation is that EA fails to provide a complete picture of learner language. We need to know what learners do correctly as well as what they do wrongly. This problem has been overstated, however. First, Corder (1971b) explicitly recognized the importance of examining the totality of the learner's production. Second, there is nothing to prevent the researcher doing this. At the very least, EA can be considered to have a place 'as a partial and preliminary source of information at an initial stage of investigation (Hammarberg 1973: 34). Indeed, EA continues to be used as a means of investigating learner language with due attention paid to non-errors as well as to errors.

EA is limited in a second way. Most of the studies are cross-sectional in nature, affording only a very static view of L2 acquisition. In many cases little care has been taken to separate out the errors made by learners at different stages of development. As a result, EA has not proved very effective in helping us understand how learners develop a knowledge of an L2 over time. This weakness is, again, not a necessary one. EA can be used in longitudinal studies of L2 learners as in the Chamot (1978, 1979) study referred to earlier. A study of how learners' errors change from one stage to another can shed light on the process of L2 acquisition.

The third problem is more substantive, however. Schachter (1974) conducted an analysis of the relative clause errors produced by two sets of learners (one Arabic and Iranian, and the other Chinese and Japanese). She found that the first group of learners made more errors than the second group, despite the fact that relative clause structures existed in their L1s and did not exist in Japanese and Chinese. However, she also discovered that the Arabic and Iranian learners made many more attempts to use relative clauses than did the Japanese and Chinese learners. She concluded that learners may resort to avoidance if they find a structure difficult. Subsequent studies by Kleinmann (1978), Kellerman (1977), Dagut and Laufer (1985), and Hulstijn and Marchena (1989) testify to the prevalence of avoidance in L2 acquisition. EA, which focuses exclusively on what learners do, has no way of investigating avoidance and is, therefore, seriously limited. Avoidance is clearly an important issue for SLA research; it is examined more fully in Chapter 8.

Summary

Error analysis (EA) was one of the first methods used to investigate learner language. It achieved considerable popularity in the 1970s, replacing contrastive analysis. The first step in carrying out an EA was to collect a massive, specific, or incidental sample of learner language. The sample could consist of natural language use or be elicited either clinically or experimentally. It could also be collected cross-sectionally or longitudinally. The second stage involved identifying the errors in the sample. Corder distinguished errors of competence from mistakes in performance and argued that EA should investigate only errors. Corder also proposed a procedure for identifying errors by reference to normal, authoritative, and plausible interpretations. The third stage consisted of description. Two types of descriptive taxonomies have been used: linguistic and surface strategy. The former provides an indication of the number and proportion of errors in either different levels of language (i.e. lexis, morphology, and syntax) or in specific grammatical categories (for example, articles, prepositions, or word order). The latter classifies errors according to whether they involve omissions, additions, misinformations, or misorderings. The fourth stage involves an attempt to explain the errors psycholinguistically. Competence errors can result from transfer, intralingual, or unique processes. They can also be induced through instruction. EA studies have produced widely differing results regarding the proportion of errors that are the result of L1 transfer, but most studies concur that the majority of errors are intralingual. The precise proportion varies as a product of such factors as the learners' level, the type of language sampled, the language level (for example, lexis v. grammar) and the learners' ages. Also, errors can have more than one cause. Finally, evaluation studies entail establishing the effect that different errors have on the person addressed—either in terms of comprehension or affective response. They have produced evidence to show that global errors affect comprehension more than local errors, that non-native speakers are inclined to be harsher judges of errors than native speakers, and that different criteria involving intelligibility, acceptability, and irritation are used to make judgements.

EA has lost popularity as a result of its perceived weaknesses. These weaknesses include methodological problems involving all stages of analysis and, also, limitations in the scope of EA. Focusing solely on the errors which learners produce at a single point in time—as most of the studies have done—can only provide a partial picture. It takes no account of what learners do correctly, of development over time, and of avoidance phenomena.

Conclusion: a reassessment of EA

EA constituted the first serious attempt to investigate learner language in order to discover how learners acquire an L2. Its heyday was in the 1960s and 1970s. It then went out of fashion, as a result of the perceived weaknesses in procedure and scope discussed above. Currently, it is showing signs of making a come-back (see, for example, Taylor 1986 and Lennon 1991).

As we have already noted, some of the weaknesses are not inherent in EA. Taylor (1986) outlines a number of principles that he believes should guide the practice of EA. These principles are based on the general claims that 'what constitutes significant error is not strictly quantifiable' and that we should 'conceive our analytical aims to lie rather more in the interpretative traditions of a humanistic discipline than has recently been customary' (1986: 162). Taylor demonstrates, through the detailed analysis of a piece of writing produced by a native speaker, how the study of errors should be located in the 'whole text' and how it can afford valuable insights into the process of language use. Lennon (1991) remains more committed to the quantification of errors and seeks to show how some of the problems of error identification can be overcome. He points out that most 'erroneous forms are, in fact, in themselves not erroneous at all, but become erroneous only in the context of the larger linguistic unit in which they occur' (1991: 189). To take account of this in error identification he proposes two new dimensions of error: domain and extent. Domain refers to the breadth of the context (word, phrase, clause, previous sentence, or discourse) which needs to be considered for determining whether an error has occurred. Extent refers to the size of the unit (morpheme, word, phrase, clause, sentence) that requires deleting, replacing, reordering, or supplying in order to repair an erroneous production. For example, in an error like *'a scissors', the domain is the phrase and the extent is the word, while in an error like *'well, it's a great hurry around', both domain and extent are the whole sentence.[10] Lennon illustrates how the concepts of domain and extent can help to distinguish different kinds of lexical error. The qualitative approach that Taylor recommends and the improved quantitative approach proposed by Lennon have much to offer SLA.

EA, in fact, continues to be practised, although now it is more likely to serve as a means for investigating a specific research question rather than for providing a comprehensive account of learners' idiosyncratic forms. For example, Felix (1981) and Pavesi (1986) use error analysis to compare the language produced by instructed and naturalistic learners. Bardovi-Harlig and Bofman (1989) wished to investigate the differences between a group of learners who successfully passed the Indiana University Placement exam and a group who failed to do so. They examined the nature of the errors which the two groups produced in one part of the examination—written compositions—and found, unremarkably, that the pass group made fewer overall errors than the non-pass group and, more interestingly, that the major differences were in the number of lexical and morphological rather than syntactical errors. Santos (1987), in the study already referred to, carried out an error evaluation in order to investigate linguistic claims regarding markedness. Clearly EA is still alive, often used alongside other analytical techniques. It is interesting to note, however, that in these recent studies there is no mention of any of the methodological problems involved in EA.

EA has made a substantial contribution to SLA research. It served as a tool for providing empirical evidence for the behaviourist/mentalist debates of the 1970s, showing that many of the errors that learners make cannot be put down to interference. It helped, therefore, to support the claims made by Corder, Dulay and Burt, and others regarding the 'creativeness' of much learner language. Perhaps, above all, it helped to make errors respectable—to force recognition that errors were not something to be avoided but were an inevitable feature of the learning process. Indeed, the very concept of 'error' came to be challenged on the grounds that learners act systematically in accordance with the mental grammars they have constructed and that their utterances are well-formed in terms of these grammars. As Corder put it, 'everything the learner utters is by definition a grammatical utterance in his dialect' (1971a: 32).

Notes

1 This example of a sentence containing an error—and others in this chapter—is intended to reflect the kind of errors that are often made. In cases where attested sentences are used to illustrate a point their source will be indicated.

2 The study of production errors in native speakers has received explicit attention by Fromkin (1971), among others. As Crookes (1991) points out, speech errors serve as the primary data for the construction of models of language production. In retrospect, it is somewhat surprising that the L2 researchers who developed and made use of error analysis techniques made so little reference to work on L1 production.

3 Contrastive analysis is considered in greater detail in Chapter 9, where we examine the role of language transfer in L2 acquisition.

4 Although most studies have employed either specific or incidental samples, this need not be seen as a limiting factor, as it is possible to compare and aggregate the results of relatively small-scale studies in order to construct a general picture. Richards (1971b) did just that.

5 Learners' 'model preferences' (Beebe 1985) are a reflection of their reference group, a point discussed in Chapter 6.

6 Some errors are likely to be easier to identify than others. Pragmatic 'errors', for example, are particularly difficult, partly because of the problem of establishing which target language norms should serve as the point of reference but mainly because it is essential to know what the learners' exact meaning intentions were.

7 The distinction between competence and performance in an L2, which here is discussed in terms of 'errors' and 'mistakes', has more recently been considered in terms of the general distinction between 'knowledge' and 'control' (for example, Bialystok and Sharwood Smith 1985). This distinction is discussed in the Introduction to Section 4.

8 Svartvik (1973b) refers to error evaluation as 'therapy'.

9 The claim that greater attention should be paid to errors that affect comprehension does not mean that no attention should be paid to local errors in morphology or the use of grammatical functors. Indeed, the fact that such structures do not have much communicative value may be one reason why they are often not acquired and why an instructional focus on them may be necessary (see Chapter 10).

10 Lennon (1991: 192) claims that 'for any given error, domain will be at higher rank than or equal rank to extent, but never at a lower rank'.

Further Reading

There have been a number of collections of articles on error analysis. One of the earliest is:

J. Svartvik (ed.), *Errata: Papers in Error Analysis* (CWK Gleerup, 1973).

More accessible, and also one of the best, is:

J. Richards (ed.), *Error Analysis* (Longman, 1974). This contains key articles by Corder and Richards.

Another useful collection is:

B. Robinett and J. Schachter (eds.), *Second Language Learning* (University of Michigan Press, 1983). In addition to articles by Corder and Richards, this contains Duskova's study, Stenson's article on induced errors, and Schachter and Celce-Murcia's critique of error analysis.

Finally, there is a collection of Corder's papers published in 1981 by Oxford University Press (*Error Analysis and Interlanguage*).

Dulay and Burt's work on errors has been subject to heavy criticism but is worthy of consideration. Chapter 7, 'Errors', of the following provides a good overview:

H. Dulay, N. Burt, and S. Krashen, *Language Two* (Oxford University Press, 1982).

There are numerous error evaluation studies. One of the most thought-provoking is:

E. Davies, 'Error evaluation: the importance of viewpoint.' *English Language Teaching Journal* (1983) 37: 304–11.

Finally, the following are strongly recommended for those who are thinking of carrying out an error analysis of their own:

G. Taylor, 'Errors and explanations.' *Applied Linguistics* (1986) 7: 144–66;
P. Lennon, 'Error: some problems of definition, identification, and distinction.' *Applied Linguistics* (1991) 12: 180–95).

3 Developmental patterns: order and sequence in second language acquisition

Introduction

The previous chapter began the study of learner language by focusing on error analysis. A number of methodological and theoretical problems with this type of investigation were identified. In particular, it was noted that error analysis did not provide a complete picture of how learners acquire an L2 because it described learner language as a collection of errors. Increasingly, researchers have recognized the need to consider the entirety of learner language in order to uncover the systems of rules or interlanguages that learners construct at different stages of development. Central to this enterprise is the description of how learner language develops over time.

One of the most powerful ideas to have emerged from this work was that L2 acquisition proceeds in a regular, systematic fashion. In this chapter we will examine the descriptive evidence that lends support to the existence of regular developmental patterns in L2 acquisition, reserving theoretical and pedagogical considerations until later.

In this chapter, a distinction will be made between the idea of an *order* and a *sequence* of acquisition. One question we can ask is 'Do learners acquire some target-language (TL) features before others?' This is a question about the order of acquisition. We can answer it by showing that one feature, say plural -*s* in English, is acquired before another. A second and entirely different question is 'How do learners acquire a particular TL linguistic feature?' To answer this question we need to investigate some specific feature (such as negation) in detail and, preferably, over time, in order to show how learners gradually arrive at the TL. Showing that learners pass through stages on route to the TL rule provides evidence for a sequence of acquisition. *Developmental pattern* will be used as a cover term for the general regularities evident in language acquisition. As such, it subsumes the ideas of order and sequence.

The starting point for this chapter will be an account of the main methods that have been used to study developmental patterns in language acquisition. A brief examination of developmental patterns in L1 acquisition follows, setting the scene for a more thorough account of L2 acquisition. The emphasis will be on description (explanation being handled in later chapters) and on research carried out primarily with naturalistic L2 learners.[1] The survey will begin with a description of three aspects of early L2 acquisition: (1) the silent period, (2) the use of formulas, and (3) structural/semantic simplification. It continues with an account of research which has investigated the acquisition of grammatical morphemes. There is a review of the morpheme studies, which investigated whether the acquisition of a set of grammatical morphemes (mainly in English) follows a fixed order, and there is also a detailed account of acquisition in one group of morphemes (those belonging to the pronoun system of a language) in order to show the stages of development evident in these features. Next comes an examination of research which has produced evidence to show that the acquisition of certain syntactic structures follows a defined sequence, with learners manifesting various *transitional constructions* in the process of acquiring TL rules. A brief discussion of the *L2 = L1 Hypothesis* follows. Finally, there will be a general evaluation of the claims regarding developmental patterns.

Methods for investigating developmental patterns

There are a number of different ways in which researchers can set about trying to identify developmental patterns. One way is to examine whether learners' errors change over time. There is some evidence to show that this does happen, but as we saw in the last chapter, error analysis has not succeeded in providing clear and conclusive evidence of developmental patterns. A second way is to examine samples of learner language collected over a period of time in order to identify when specific linguistic features emerge. According to this approach, 'acquisition' is defined as 'first occurrence'. It has been used extensively in first language acquisition research (for example, Wells 1985) but is less common in SLA research. However, a number of L2 researchers (for example, Bickerton 1981 and Pienemann 1984) have recommended the use of emergence as the criterion of acquisition in SLA research.

One common method for identifying and describing developmental patterns is *obligatory occasion analysis*. This has been widely used by L2 acquisition researchers and is clearly described in Brown (1973). The basic procedure is as follows. First, samples of naturally occurring learner language are collected. Second, obligatory occasions for the use of specific TL features are identified in the data. In the course of using the L2, learners produce utterances which create obligatory occasions for the use of specific target-language features, although they may not always supply the features in question. Thus, if a learner says: 'My sister visited us yesterday' or '*My father arrive yesterday', obligatory occasions for the use of past *-ed* have been created in both utterances. Third, the percentage of accurate use of the feature is then calculated by establishing whether the feature in question has been supplied in all the contexts in which it is required. A criterion level of accuracy can then be determined in order to provide an operational definition of whether a feature has been 'acquired'. Usually, the level is set at 80–90 per cent, below 100 per cent, to take account of the fact that even adult native speakers may not achieve complete accuracy. Brown (1973) considered a feature to be 'acquired' if it was performed at the 90 per cent level on three consecutive data collection points—a very rigorous definition.

One problem with obligatory occasion analysis is that it takes no account of when a learner uses a feature in a context for which it is not obligatory in the TL. For example, the learner who says '*I studied last night and now I understood better' has overgeneralized the past tense, using it where the TL requires the present tense. Clearly, acquisition of a feature such as past tense requires mastering not only when to use it but also when not to use it. To take account of over-uses as well as misuses a number of researchers (for example, Pica 1983) have suggested a procedure known as *target-like use analysis*. Pica (1984) has shown that substantial differences in estimates of learners' abilities arise depending on whether obligatory occasion or target-like use analysis is employed.

Both obligatory occasion and target-like use analysis are target-language-based—that is, like error analysis, they seek to compare learner language and the TL. Bley-Vroman (1983) has pointed out the dangers of what he calls the 'comparative fallacy'. The main one is that it ignores the fact that learners create their own unique rule systems in the process of learning an L2. Target-language-based analyses cannot be used to describe these systems as they only provide information about the extent to which the learner's language approximates to the TL.[2] One way of overcoming this objection, which some researchers adopt (for example, Cazden et al. 1975), is to catalogue the various linguistic devices that learners use to express a particular grammatical structure (such as negatives) and then to calculate the frequency with which each device is used at different points in the learners' development. This method has no commonly recognized name but might usefully be called *frequency analysis*. It is able to show the 'vertical variation' in learners' development (i.e. how different devices become prominent at different stages) and serves as one of the best ways of examining developmental sequences.

Many of the studies considered in this chapter are longitudinal, involving data collection over a period of many months and, in some cases (for example, Schmidt 1983) several years. Such studies provide the strongest evidence in support of developmental patterns. In addition, there were a number of studies that were cross-sectional in design (i.e. data were collected only at a single point in time). In order to make claims about the order of acquisition on the basis of cross-sectional data, researchers resorted to a number of statistical procedures. For example, some researchers argued that the accuracy order with which different features were performed corresponded to their acquisition order (for example, Dulay and Burt 1973 and 1974c). Thus, for example, if the data showed that short plural -s (as in 'boys') was performed more accurately than long plural -es (as in 'churches'), then this indicated that the short plural form was acquired before the long plural form. An alternative procedure for establishing order of acquisition from cross-sectional data involves *implicational scaling*. This technique was first used in Creole studies (Decamp 1971). It seeks to exploit the inter-learner variability that exists in a corpus of learner language in order to establish which features different learners have acquired and whether the features can be arranged into a hierarchy according to whether the acquisition of one feature implies the acquisition of one or more other features for each learner. For interested readers, Hatch and Farhady (1982: chapter 14) provide a clear explanation of how implicational scaling is carried out. An example can be found in Figure 4.1 on on page 126 of this book. The extent to which cross-sectional data, so processed, can provide valid information about developmental sequences is a matter of some dispute.

The existence of developmental patterns can be investigated in different areas of language: linguistic (phonological, lexical, and grammatical), semantic, and functional. This chapter will deal more or less exclusively with the acquisition of grammatical systems—mainly because this reflects the general emphasis on grammar in SLA research, and serves as the primary evidence for theory construction. However, limited attention will also be given to phonological and lexical aspects of learner language, while Chapter 5 will examine the acquisition of pragmatic features.

Developmental patterns in L1 acquisition

The study of developmental patterns in L1 acquisition research is a good starting point in our investigation of L2 developmental patterns for two reasons. First, it has provided L2 researchers with useful methodological procedures for investigating developmental patterns in learner language. Second, L1 acquisition orders and sequences provide a baseline for considering L2 acquisition orders and sequences. An important issue is whether the patterns in the two types of acquisition are the same or different.

Early work on L1 acquisition in the 1960s and 1970s consisted of detailed case studies of individual learners based on the speech they produced (for example, McNeill 1970; Slobin 1970; Brown 1973), of cross-sectional studies of larger numbers of learners (for example, de Villiers and de Villiers 1973), and of some experimental studies of children's production and comprehension of specific linguistic features (for example, Berko 1958; C. Chomsky 1969). These early studies, which attempted to identify the general pattern of children's language development, began what Atkinson (1986) has referred to as the SHARP tradition in first language acquisition research (i.e. the empirical study of L1 acquisition).[3] This tradition has continued into the 1980s and 1990s, spawning an enormous amount of research in a great range of languages. Notable recent projects include the Bristol Study, 'Language at Home and at School' (Wells 1985), which involved the longitudinal study of more than 60 children and the enormous cross-linguistic project initiated by Slobin (see Slobin 1985a). Inevitably in this span of time there have been shifts in emphasis, but in this tradition researchers largely continue to follow a research-then-theory approach, emphasizing the description of children's language as a basis for theory building. An alternative tradition, referred to as FLAT (First Language Acquisition Theories) by Atkinson, grew up in the 1980s. This eschews empirical enquiry and instead seeks to examine L1 acquisition from the point of view of learnability theory and Universal Grammar. In this chapter we will be concerned exclusively with the SHARP tradition, although we will also briefly consider some of the theoretical issues with which this tradition is concerned. Learnability theory and Universal Grammar will be considered in detail in Chapter 10.

One of the pervasive findings in first language acquisition research is that children appear to follow a fairly well-defined pattern of development. This pattern is evident in the way in which all linguistic systems are acquired. Children typically begin with one-word utterances which function as holophrases (i.e. express whole propositions). They gradually extend the length of their utterances, passing through stages when the bulk of their speech consists of first two-word, then three- and four-word utterances. At the same time, they systematically acquire the various syntactical and morphological rules of the language. The result is that remarkable regularities are evident in both the overall pattern of development and in the acquisition of specific linguistic systems (for example, tense markings or negatives). These regularities are often described with reference to mean length of utterance as a general measure of development. Crystal (1976), for example, describes the specific grammatical features that are evident in children's language when the mean length of their utterances is one word, two words, three words, etc.

In one of the most influential studies of L1 acquisition—the Harvard Study—Brown (1973) found evidence for the fixed order of acquisition of various English morphological features in three children. The same order was obtained in de Villiers and de Villiers' (1973) cross-sectional study of twenty children. Table 3.1 gives the order. The acquisition of individual morphemes also involves stages. For example, the acquisition of English past tense forms involves an initial stage in which there is little or no use followed by sporadic use of some irregular forms, then use of the regular -*ed* form including overgeneralization to irregular verbs, and finally target-like use of regular and irregular forms. Thus, the acquisition of forms such as 'went' follows a U-shaped pattern of development, with children first using it correctly (for example, 'went') and then incorrectly (for example, 'goed') before they finally once again produce the correct form ('went').

Clear examples of developmental sequences in L1 acquisition are those found in the acquisition of English negatives and interrogatives. Klima and Bellugi (1966), for example, identified three stages in the acquisition of negatives, which are summarized in Table 3.2. Bloom (1970) found evidence of the

Morpheme	Example
1 Present progressive *-ing*	He is sitting down.
2 Preposition 'in'	The mouse is in the box.
3 Preposition 'on'	The book is on the table.
4 Plural *-s*	The dogs ran away.
5 Past irregular	The boy went home.
6 Possessive *-'s*	The girl's dog is big.
7 Uncontractible copula 'be'	Are they boys or girls?
8 Articles 'a'/'the'	He has a book.
9 Past regular *-ed*	He jumped the stream.
10 Third person regular *-s*	She runs very fast.
11 Third person irregular e.g. has/does	Does the dog bark?
12 Uncontractible auxiliary 'be'	Is he running?
13 Contractible copula 'be'	That's a spaniel.
14 Contractible auxiliary 'be'	They're running very slowly.

Table 3.1:   Order of L1 acquisition in English morphemes (abridged from Clark and Clark 1977: 345)

systematic acquisition of the semantic functions which negatives can realize in English. The children she studied first used 'no' and 'not' to refer to non-presence (for example, 'No cookie'), then to refer to rejection of an offer or suggestion (for example, 'No car' = 'I don't want the car'), and finally to denial. Similar regularities are evident in the acquisition of the formal and semantic aspects of English interrogatives (see Klima and Bellugi 1966 and Cazden 1972).

Stage	Description	Examples
1	Negative utterances consist of a 'nucleus' (i.e. the positive proposition) either preceded or followed by a negator.	Wear mitten no. Not a teddy bear.
2	Negators are now incorporated into the affirmative clauses. Negators at this stage include 'don't' and 'can't', used as unitary items. Negative commands appear.	There no squirrels. You can't dance. Don't bite me yet.
3	Negators are now always incorporated into affirmative clauses. The 'auxillary + not' rule has been acquired, as 'don't', 'can't', etc. are now analysed. But some mistakes still occur (e.g. copula 'be' is omitted from negative utterances and double negatives occur),	I don't have a book. Paul can't have one. I not crying. No one didn't come.

Table 3.2:   The L1 acquisition of English negatives (examples from Klima and Bellugi 1966)

These regularities in grammatical development are the product of the acquisition task which the child faces. Clark and Clark (1977) describe this task as follows:

> From the outset children are faced with two general problems. First of all, they have to figure out how to map their ideas and general knowledge onto propositions[4] ... Second, they have to find out how to communicate speech acts and thematic information along with the propositional content of their utterances (Clark and Clark 1977: 296).

They emphasize that the two tasks of mapping and communicating go hand in hand. This claim is supported by the fact that regularities are also evident in the way in which the different pragmatic and textual functions of the TL are mastered. Thus, for example, Clark and Clark illustrate how initially children learn to perform assertions and requests and only later develop the ability to express directives (for example, asking, ordering, forbidding, and permitting) and commissives (such as promising). Expressives (for example, thanking) and declarations follow even later. A full account of the developmental path, therefore, must describe how children master the formal, functional, and semantic properties of a language. A good example of such an account is that provided by Wells (1986a) and summarized in Table 3.3. It is important to recognize, however, that although certain stages of acquisition can be identified, development is, in fact, continuous. Children do not usually jump from one stage to the next but rather progress gradually with the result that 'new' and 'old' patterns of language use exist side by side at any one point in time.

It is also important to acknowledge the inter-learner variability that exists in L1 acquisition. This is most evident in the rate of acquisition. Some children learn their L1 with great rapidity while others do so much more slowly. Wells (1986b), for instance, notes that the difference between the most and least advanced children when they were three and a half years old was equivalent to almost 36 months—an enormous discrepancy. It is for this reason that it is not possible to describe the sequence of development in terms of age. The individual differences go further than rate, however. They concern the overall strategy that children appear to follow. For example, although many children use an *analytical strategy* and show evidence of the developmental progression described above, other children use a *gestalt strategy*, typically remaining silent for a longer period before producing full sentences when they first start talking (Peters 1977). All children make use of unanalysed units (formulas) but some seem to rely on them much more extensively than others (Nelson 1973). There is a considerable body of research into L1 acquisition that has sought to identify the factors responsible for inter-learner variation. The variables studied include sex, intelligence, personality and learning style, social background, and experience of linguistic interaction (Wells 1986b).

The results of the empirical studies of L1 acquisition have been used to

Stage	Functions	Meanings	Forms
1	3 functions signalled initially: (1) calling attention, (2) ostension, and (3) expressing wants; 2 other functions emerge later: (4) statements and (5) requests.	Child typically names objects initially; later, meaning relationships connected with location appear.	Early utterances very limited with regard to form. Utterances consist of 'operator' (e.g. 'there', 'look', 'more', 'all gone') or 'operator + object' (e.g. 'There Mark').
2	Questions appear: initially 'where' and 'what' and yes/no questions.	The child is obsessed with naming and classification. Change of location and simple attributes (e.g. 'hot' and 'big') appear at this stage.	Questions lack auxiliary verb – yes/no questions make use of rising intonation. Two constituent utterances emerge (e.g. Verb + Object and Subject + Object/Complement). Also two-word noun phrases appear (e.g. article + noun and preposition + noun.
3	Questions firmly established and more complex expression of wants.	Change-in-state expressed (e.g. 'You dry hands'); also mental states (e.g. 'listen' and 'know'), non-present time reference, aspectual state of an action, and ongoing activity.	Questions still signalled with rising intonation; three constituent utterances (e.g. Subject + Verb + Object) and three-word noun phrases (e.g. Preposition + Article + Noun).
4	Full expression of questions and negatives takes place. Several new functions appear: (1) requesting permission, (2) indirect requests, (3) explanation, and (4) requesting an explanation (i.e. 'Why?').	Various modal meanings appear associated with futurity, ability, and permission. Complements of psychological verbs (e.g. 'I know that you are there') and qualification of noun phrases (e.g. 'Where's the pen what papa gave me?') appear.	Auxiliary verb is integrated into structure of the clause. 'Do' appears early, followed by 'can' and 'will'. Principle of recursion (one grammatical clause is embedded within the structure of another) is learnt.
5	New functions are (1) hypothetical statements, (2) threats, and (3) formulations (i.e. offering an alternative way of getting an action performed).	More differentiated expression of time frame: reference to particular times as points of reference (e.g. 'before dinner') and different aspectual distinctions (habitual, repetitive, and inceptive).	Child finally sorts out the structure of wh-questions (i.e. subject-verb inversion now mastered). Variety of two-clause sentences increases. Development of various cohesive devices (pro-verb 'do', anaphorical pronoun reference, and ellipsis).

Table 3.3:   General outline of the development of English as an L1 (based on Wells 1986a)

evaluate different theoretical positions. Although our concern in this chapter is primarily with the description of developmental patterns in learner language, it is helpful to understand the nature of these positions in broad outline, particularly as they also figure in SLA research. The key debate in the 1960s and 1970s revolved around the rival claims of behaviourist and mentalist models of acquisition. According to the former, children acquired their L1 by trying to imitate utterances produced by their parents and by receiving negative or positive reinforcement of their attempts to do so. Language acquisition, therefore, was considered to be environmentally determined. Such a model does not accord with the empirical facts, however. For example, children receive remarkably little formal feedback on the correctness of their utterances, many of which are uniquely created rather than imitated. Indeed, the behaviourist model was advanced not on the basis of studies of child language but through extrapolation from studies of animals in laboratory settings.

A mentalist model makes the following claims (see Ellis 1985a: 44):

1 Language is a human-specific faculty.
2 Language exists as an independent faculty in the human mind (i.e. it is separate from the general cognitive mechanisms responsible for intellectual development).
3 The primary determinant of acquisition is the child's 'language acquisition device', which is genetically endowed and provides the child with a general set of principles about language which can be used to discover the rules of a particular TL.
4 Input data are required to trigger the process by which the 'language acquisition device' discovers the rules of the TL.

This model is closely associated with the work of Chomsky (for example, 1965 and 1980a) in linguistics and Lenneberg (1967) in the biological prerequisites of language. Precisely how the 'language acquisition device' works is a matter of some controversy, however. Some L1 acquisition researchers (for example, McNeill 1966) have argued that children form hypotheses about the rules to be found in the TL and then test them out against input data and modify them accordingly. Other researchers (for example, Braine 1971) have challenged this view on the grounds that hypothesis-testing is too inefficient. They seek to explain acquisition in terms of discovery procedures which are used to scan input data and to store noticed features.

Although much of the early discussion centred on the behaviourist/ mentalist debate, considerable attention has been given also to a third type of model: a cognitive processing model. Proponents of such a model (for example, Sinclair-de-Zwart 1973) agree with the mentalists that children must make use of innate knowledge, but disagree about its nature. Whereas mentalists consider that it takes the form of a specific language faculty, cognitive psychologists argue that it consists of a general learning mechanism responsible for all forms of cognitive development, not just language. They point to the non-linguistic origins of language acquisition (i.e. the sensory motor stage that precedes the onset of speech in children) and to the concurrent development of linguistic and cognitive knowledge. One of the clearest accounts of the kinds of cognitive processing involved in L1 acquisition is to be found in Slobin's (1973 and 1985b) description of the operating principles that children learning a variety of L1s resort to in order to learn from input. These are discussed in some detail in Chapter 9.

The debate between the behaviourists and the mentalists was a poor contest, easily won by the mentalists. However, the arguments regarding the nature of the internal mechanisms responsible for L1 acquisition continue to find current expression in the rival claims of cognitive and linguistic theories of L2 acquisition (such as the Competition Model (MacWhinney and Bates 1989) and Universal Grammar (White 1989a)), discussions of which can be found in Chapters 9 and 10 respectively.

In the sections that follow we will see a number of parallels between work on developmental patterns in L1 and L2 acquisition research.

Developmental patterns in second language acquisition

The research that we shall be reviewing has investigated learners in naturalistic settings and has been based on what might roughly be called 'unplanned language use' (i.e. the learner language that results from attempts by learners to express their meaning intentions more or less spontaneously). L2 learners, particularly adults, have the capacity to engage in 'planned language use' by paying deliberate attention to the language forms they choose (for example, by using explicit knowledge of grammatical rules or by translating). Unplanned and planned language use display markedly different features, as we shall see in the next chapter. The idea of 'developmental patterns' is based on unplanned language use and it is not at all clear to what extent it is applicable to planned language use.

The early stages

The early stages of L2 acquisition in naturalistic settings are often characterized by a *silent period*, by the use of *formulaic speech*, and by *structural* and *semantic simplification*.

The silent period

In the case of L1 acquisition, children go through a lengthy period of listening to people talk to them before they produce their first words. This silent period is necessary, for the young child needs to discover what language is and what it does. In the case of L2 acquisition, the silent period is not obligatory, as the learner already knows about language, having already acquired one. Yet many learners—especially children—opt for a silent period. Itoh and Hatch (1978), for instance, describe how their subject, Takahiro—a two-and-a-half-year-old Japanese boy—refused to speak English at an American nursery school and also to the researcher in his own home for the first three months. Hakuta (1976) reports the difficulty he had in obtaining any data from his subject, Uguisu—a 5-year-old Japanese girl—for the first three months, but then comments that her English suddenly 'blossomed'. Saville-Troike (1988) reports that six out of the nine children learning L2 English that she studied opted for a silent period. Hanania and Gradman's (1977) study of the acquisition of English in the USA by Fatmah, a 19-year-old Saudi woman, also indicates that some adults go through a silent period. Krashen (1985) cites Rodriguez (1982) as another example of an adult learner who began with an extensive silent period. Rodriguez describes his own case history of learning L2 English, noting that he said nothing in class in the American school he attended for the first six months.

Of course, not all learners go through a silent period, as Saville-Troike's study shows. Many learners—particularly classroom learners—are obliged to speak from the beginning. But even when production is not required, some learners opt for it. Paul, a 5-year-old Taiwanese boy studied by Huang and Hatch (1978), appears to have begun talking in English almost immediately, although most of his early utterances involved imitation. Studies of 'good language learners' report that many adult learners (82 per cent in a study carried out by Naiman et al. 1978) claim they begin to speak right from the start. Gibbons (1985) reviewed the evidence in favour of a silent period in both children and adults and found it inconclusive. His own survey of 47 children learning English as an L2 in Sydney primary schools revealed considerable individual variation, with a mean length of just two weeks' silence. It is also interesting to note that in many of the studies which Krashen cites as providing evidence of a silent period, the learners were not, in fact, completely silent, but often produced some formulaic expressions right from the beginning.[5]

The question arises as to why some learners opt for a silent period while others do not. Saville-Troike (1988) suggests that the reason may lie in differences in the learners' social and cognitive orientation. She distinguishes *other-directed* and *inner-directed* learners. The former 'approach language as an interpersonal, social task, with a predominant focus on the message they wish to convey', while the latter 'approach language learning as an intrapersonal task, with a predominant focus on the language code' (page 568). She suggests that while other-directed learners do not typically go through a silent period, inner-directed learners do.

There is some disagreement regarding the contribution that the silent period makes to language learning. Krashen (1982) argues that it provides an opportunity for the learner to build up competence via listening. According to this view, speaking ability emerges naturally after enough competence has been developed through listening. Itoh and Hatch (1978), however, take a different view, referring to Takahiro's silent period as a 'rejection stage', during which he tried to avoid learning English. Rodriguez (1982), cited by Krashen 1982, claims that he only began to learn English when he started to speak it at home with his parents. Gibbons (1985) concludes that the initial silent period is in many cases a period of incomprehension that does little or nothing to promote acquisition and that if the silent period is a prolonged one it may reflect psychological withdrawal.

One possibility is that the silent period provides learners with opportunities to prepare themselves for social use of the L2 by means of *private speech,* which they engage in while they are 'silent'. Saville-Troike, in the study of child L2 learners referred to above, defines silent speech as speech that is produced at a very low volume so as to be inaudible to anyone present and with no apparent expectation of a response. She used a radio-microphone hung round the neck of the children to record it. Five of the children who went through a silent period manifested private speech, using a variety of intrapersonal strategies. These included repeating other speakers' utterances, recalling and practising English words and phrases, creating new linguistic forms, substituting items in utterances, and expanding them and rehearsing utterances for overt social performance. All five learners eventually began to speak using first single words, memorized chunks, and repetitions of other children's L2 utterances. A sixth child who manifested a silent period, however, did not engage in silent speech and, unlike the others, remained silent throughout the study (approximately 18 weeks), apparently not learning any English. Saville-Troike's study suggests that while some child learners may use silence as a strategy for avoiding learning, many make active use of it to prepare for the time they begin speaking the L2. However, as Saville-Troike acknowledges, her study does not show whether the learning strategies some learners employ during their silent period are related to long-range L2 development.

Formulaic speech

Formulaic speech consists of 'expressions which are learnt as unanalysable wholes and employed on particular occasions' (Lyons 1968: 177). Hakuta (1976) and Krashen and Scarcella (1978) distinguish *routines* and *patterns* to refer respectively to whole utterances learnt as memorized chunks (for example, 'I don't know') and to utterances that are only partially unanalysed and have one or more open slots (for example, 'Can I have a ____?'). In Ellis 1984b, I too suggested that formulaic speech can consist of entire scripts, such as greeting sequences, which the learner can memorize because they are fixed and predictable.

Formulaic speech can be observed in the speech of native speakers. Nattinger and DeCarrico (1992:1) suggest that what they call 'lexical phrases' (defined as 'multi-word lexical phenomena that exist somewhere between the traditional poles of lexicon and syntax') are commonly used by native speakers, reflecting the ritualization of language behaviour. Pawley and Syder (1983) argue that achieving native-like control involves not only learning a rule system that will generate an infinite number of sentences, but also 'memorized sequences' and 'lexicalized sentence stems'. They state that 'the number of memorized complete clauses and sentences known to the mature English speaker is probably many thousands' (1983: 205). Some examples are 'Can I come in?', 'What's for dinner?' and 'Speak for yourself'. Sequences longer than simple, single clauses also exist. In addition, native speakers internalize sentence stems in which the structure is fully specified together with a nucleus of lexical and grammatical morphemes. An example is:

NP be-*tense* sorry to keep-*tense* you waiting

which can be realized in a number of forms:

I'm sorry to keep you waiting.
I'm so sorry to have kept you waiting.
Mr X was sorry to keep you waiting the other day.

Pawley and Syder characterize the task facing the language learner as to discover precisely what permutations of a sentence stem are possible—a view of learning which bears a strong resemblance to that which underlies some current models of language use and acquisition, such as Parallel Distributed Processing (see Chapter 9). Formulaic expressions frequently embody the societal knowledge which a given speech community shares and, according to Coulmas, 'are essential in the handling of day-to-day situations' (1981: 4). They enable the speaker to say the right thing at the right time in the right place. They also perform a psycholinguistic function in speech production. Dechert (1983) suggests that fixed expressions serve as 'islands of reliability' that help speakers to construct and execute production plans, a point explored more fully in Chapter 9.

   Formulaic speech has been observed to be very common in L2 acquisition, particularly in the early stages. It figures frequently in the speech of all learners, irrespective of their age. Itoh and Hatch note two very common patterns in the speech of Takahiro, once he began talking—'I get . . .' and 'I wanna . . .'. Ervin-Tripp (1974) notes that one of the first utterances produced by young English-speaking learners of L2 French was 'Peut-je jouer avec Corinne?' and notes that 'the size of the unit stored is impressive'. Hakuta (1986) discusses three patterns in the speech of his subject, Uguisu—those using copula, 'do you' in questions, and 'how to' in embedded 'how' questions. Rescorla and Okuda (1987) report similar patterns in their subject, Atsuko, a six-year-old Japanese child. Hanania and Gradman (1977) observe that at the start of their study, Fatmah relied almost entirely on 'memorized items'. They note that 'the use of these expressions does not imply that she recognized the individual words within them, or that she was able to use the words in new combinations' (page 78). Initially, Fatmah seemed to resist segmentation of expressions such as 'Thank you, I can't . . .' and 'Do you like . . . ?' There are, in fact, few case studies based on naturally occurring learner language that do not make some mention of the prevalence of formulas.

What sets these formulas off from other samples of learner language is their well-formedness. Thus, routines and patterns typically manifest TL morphology and syntax. 'I don't know', for example, makes correct use of the auxiliary verb 'do' and has post-verbal negation. In this respect learners' formulaic speech contrasts markedly with their early creative utterances, which frequently show little evidence of any knowledge of inflectional morphology or grammatical functors (for example, 'No like it' = 'I don't like it'). It is this that enables researchers to distinguish formulaic from creative speech in a corpus of learner language.

The particular formulas learnt by individual learners are likely to vary, but some seem to figure in just about every learner (for example, 'I don't know' and 'What's this?'). Each formula is closely tied to the performance of a particular language function which is communicatively important to the learner. Hakuta (1986) notes that Uguisu's formulas enabled her to express functions which would have been beyond her if she had relied on her rule-governed knowledge. In Ellis (1984b), I observed that the three classroom learners I studied learnt formulas to enable them to meet their basic communicative needs in an ESL classroom, where English functioned as the medium of instruction. Krashen (1982) claims that formulaic speech occurs when learners are forced to speak before they are ready and that, left to their own devices, they will remain silent. But Krashen's view seems to ignore the fact that it is perfectly natural for any language user to seek to simplify the burden of processing language—by using formulas to establish 'islands of reliability', for example. Learners, like native speakers, learn formulas because it reduces the learning burden while maximizing communicative ability.

It is not surprising, therefore, to find that learners sometimes use the formulas they have acquired in unique ways. For example, they do not always use them to perform the same functions as native speakers. Huebner (1980) provides a detailed account of how an adult Vietnamese learner of L2 English used two formulas 'waduyu' (= 'what d'you') and 'isa' (= 'is a'). 'Waduyu' served initially as a general question marker. It was used ubiquitously where native speakers would employ a variety of *wh*-question words ('what', 'how', 'why', and 'when'). Over time the learner gradually and systematically replaced 'waduyu' with these target forms. 'Isa' functions initially as a topic marker, but it was only used when the topic was not an agent or object and was not identical to the topic of the immediately preceding sentence. The general point that Huebner makes is that the acquisition of the functions performed by formulas may be an evolutionary process.

A key question is that posed by Hakuta (1976): 'To what extent do these routines and patterns facilitate or hinder the acquisition of TL grammar?' A number of researchers have suggested that formulaic speech serves as the basis for subsequent creative speech when the learner comes to realize that utterances initially understood and used as wholes consist of discrete constituents which can be combined with other constituents in a variety of rule-bound ways. Clark (1974) illustrates how in first language acquisition new structures can result from the juxtaposition of two routines or from the embedding of one within another. Wong-Fillmore (1976), in a study of five Spanish-speaking learners of English, suggests that in L2 acquisition, formulas are slowly analysed, releasing constituent elements for use in 'slots' other than those they initially occupied. For example, to begin with, Nora (the fastest of Wong-Fillmore's learners) used two formulas:

I wanna play wi' dese.
I don' wanna do dese.

and then discovered that the constituents following 'wanna' were interchangeable:

I don' wanna play dese.
I wanna do dese.

She comments that this 'formula-based analytical process ... was repeated in case after case' (1976: 645). In Ellis 1984b, I too found evidence to support the view that formulas are worked on systematically by learners. I demonstrated how the 'I don't know' formula was built on by combining it with other formulas:

That one I don't know.
I don't know what's this.

It was also broken down, so that 'don't' came to be used in similar but different expressions:

I don't understand.
I don't like.

'Know' was eventually used without 'don't':

I know this.

and with subjects other than 'I':

You don't know where it is.

It is possible, therefore, that formulas are slowly unpackaged, releasing valuable information, which is fed into the knowledge system the learner uses to produce and understand creative speech.

A rather different view is taken by Krashen and Scarcella (1978). They argue that formulaic speech and rule-created speech are unrelated. According to this view, learners do not unpackage the linguistic information contained in formulas, but internalize L2 rules independently through attending to input. Their conclusion is that 'the use of routines and patterns is certainly part of language, but it is probably not a very large part'. This view is supported by Bohn (1986), who analysed data that Wode (1981) collected from four German children learning English in the United States. This study found that these child learners relied on formulaic speech very little in most situations, although Bohn admits that they may not have been subject to the same communicative pressures as other L2 learners. Formulaic-like speech was evident when the children were involved in playing games, leading Bohn to suggest that the prevalence of formulas in Wong-Fillmore's subjects' speech was an artefact of the fact that she collected most of her spontaneous data during games. Bohn concludes that formulas serve only 'short-term production tactics' and play no role in acquisition.

It is not easy to choose between these two interpretations of the role played by formulas. McLaughlin (1985), in a lengthy discussion of formulas, comes down on the side of Wong-Fillmore, at least where children are concerned. In considering this controversy, we should note that it is not easy to make a clear distinction between formulaic and creative speech. In many instances, learners seem to make use of patterns which are varied to a greater or lesser extent through lexical substitutions. Such speech has both formulaic and creative elements, suggesting that 'we should move beyond misleading dichotomies such as prefabricated formulas versus creative constructions' (Rescorla and Okuda 1987: 293). Even if Krashen and Scarcella are right and formulaic frames do not evolve into productive rules, they almost certainly underestimate the importance of formulas for L2 learners. As Pawley and Syder have shown, the task facing the learner is not just that of acquiring a rule system but also of mastering a set of lexicalized sentence stems that will enable them to process language efficiently. The development of target-like L2 ability, then, requires the memorization of a large set of formulaic chunks and patterns.

Structural and semantic simplification

In comparison with formulaic speech, the learner's early creative utterances are typically truncated, consisting of just one or two words, with both grammatical functors and content words missing. Hanania and Gradman (1977) give the following examples produced by their adult subject, Fatmah:

> library (= He is in the library)
> clean floor (= Give me something for cleaning floors)
> come back (= He is coming back).

Pienemann (1980) gives similar examples from the speech of children learning L2 German:

> ein junge ball weg (= Ein Junge wirft den Ball weg)

ein mädchen bier (= Ein Mädchen kauft Bier)
zwei kinder (= Es gibt zwei Kinder).

In Ellis 1984a, I found further evidence of simplified speech in the speech of three children learning English in a classroom setting:

me no blue (= I don't have a blue crayon)
eating at school (= She eats meat at school).

Such speech, therefore, is very common in the unplanned speech of both child and adult learners.

These utterances, which bear a strong resemblance to those found in pidgin languages, indicate that both structural and semantic simplification are taking place. Structural simplification is evident in the omission of grammatical functors such as auxiliary verbs, articles and bound morphemes like plural -s and past tense -ed. Semantic simplification involves the omission of content words—nouns, verbs, adjectives and adverbs—which would normally occur in native-speaker speech (see Ellis 1982). Both structural and semantic simplification may occur either because learners have not yet acquired the necessary linguistic forms or because they are unable to access them in the production of specific utterances. In other words, they may reflect processes of language acquisition or of language production.[6]

Corder (1981b) argues that it may be misleading to talk of 'simplification' in such utterances:

... if in the process of first or second language acquisition the learner demonstrates that he is using a simple grammar or code, as is well attested, then he has not arrived at that code or grammar by a process of simplification of the target code. In other words, you cannot simplify what you do not possess (1981b: 149).

According to this view, it is appropriate to refer to learner language descriptively as 'simple', but is not appropriate to talk of 'simplification' by the learner. There are, however, a number of problems with Corder's position. First, when the learner produces an utterance like 'hitting' (= 'He hit me'), it is possible that the learner is simplifying for purposes of production (i.e. does have the necessary knowledge to say 'He hit me' but does not do so because it is too difficult in the particular communicative circumstances). Second, it is also possible that an utterance like 'hitting' is indicative of an acquisitional process. The learner may have acquired this particular form because it is easy to perceive in the input, in a sense, 'simplifying' the input by attending to and internalizing a feature early on because it is more salient. It would seem appropriate, therefore, to continue to talk of structural and semantic simplification.

Structural simplification can be described by means of the traditional categories of a descriptive grammar. Semantic simplification is best accounted for in terms of the descriptive categories provided by a case grammar (Fillmore

1968; Greenfield and Dent 1980). For example, if a learner wishes to encode the proposition:

He is hitting me

which involves these semantic categories:

(Agent) (Action process) (Patient)

the message can be conveyed by producing any one of these abridged versions:

Hitting (= Action process)
He hitting (= Agent + Action process)
Hitting me (= Action process + Patient)
He me (= Agent + Patient).

Which version the learner chooses will reflect: (1) the linguistic resources available or readily accessible, and (2) which constituents will be maximally informative in context.

There is some evidence to suggest that learners, particularly children, tend to begin speaking first in single-word utterances and then in increasingly longer utterances, many of which are novel (see Saville-Troike 1988). However, the nature of this progression is not as well-defined as in L1 acquisition, perhaps because L2 learners have more developed processing capacities. Often, utterances that manifest structural and semantic simplification are used along with others that display little or even none.

One interesting possibility in the case of semantic simplification is that learners follow some kind of order in acquiring the various semantic roles described by the case categories—as has been shown to occur in L1 acquisition. But to date there is little evidence to support such a claim, as few studies have attempted to use case grammar to describe learner language (see Ellis 1982 and 1984a for one such attempt). The question of the order of acquisition of structural features is considered in the sections that follow.

The acquisition of morphemes: order and sequence

As we have already noted, it is possible to consider acquisition in terms of both the order in which different features are acquired and also the sequence of stages evident in the acquisition of a single feature. Much of the early research focused on the order of acquisition. Subsequent research has increasingly paid attention to sequence.

The morpheme studies

In the 1970s a number of studies, commonly referred to as the *morpheme studies*, were carried out to investigate the order of acquisition of grammatical functors such as articles and inflectional features such as plural -*s*. These studies were motivated by similar studies in L1 acquisition (see the previous section on L1 acquisition). In particular, they sought to establish whether, as in L1 acquisition, there was an invariant order of acquisition. There were both cross-sectional and longitudinal studies, although the former predominated.

The studies employed obligatory occasion analysis in order to establish the accuracy with which learners of L2 English performed a range of morphemes. In the case of cross-sectional studies, an accuracy order was calculated and this was equated with acquisition order by some researchers, on the grounds that the more accurately a morpheme was used, the earlier it must have been acquired.

In two early studies, Dulay and Burt (1973; 1974c) investigated Spanish and Chinese children, eliciting 'natural' spoken data by means of the Bilingual Syntax Measure (BSM—see Chapter 2, page 50 for a description of this instrument). They found that the 'acquisition order' for a group of English morphemes remained the same irrespective of the learners' L1 or of the methods they used to score the accuracy of the morphemes. Bailey, Madden, and Krashen (1974) replicated these studies with adult subjects, again using the BSM. They found an 'acquisition order' that correlated significantly with those obtained by Dulay and Burt. Larsen-Freeman (1976b) extended these studies in two ways. First, she used learners with a wider range of L1s (Arabic, Spanish, Japanese, and Farsi) and second she used five tasks to collect data: the BSM, a picture-cued sentence repetition test, a listening comprehension task, a multiple-choice reading cloze test, and a writing test involving filling in blanks. She found that the learners' L1s made little difference to the accuracy orders she obtained. However, there were some differences in the orders for the different tasks. The most notable was that between the speaking/imitation tasks and the reading/writing tasks. Some morphemes (for example, plural -*s* and third person -*s*) rose in the rank order in the reading and writing tasks. One possibility, then, is that different orders exist for oral and written learner language. This finding is not problematic where production is concerned, as speaking and writing are influenced by different sociolinguistic and psycholinguistic conditions. It becomes problematic if the goal is to determine a single, invariant order of acquisition that is distinct from actual use. However, Krashen, Butler, Birnbaum, and Robertson (1978) found that the accuracy orders obtained from written data did correlate significantly with those reported by Dulay and Burt for oral data. In this study, two kinds of writing task were used—one requiring 'fast' writing and the other 'careful' writing—but neither encouraged attention to discrete items as was the case with Larsen-Freeman's writing task. The distinction between 'free' and 'careful' writing did not affect the morpheme orders. These studies are summarized in Table 3.4. They constitute only a small selection of the total morpheme studies that were undertaken.

Study	Subjects	Data collection	Results	Conclusions
Dulay and Burt 1973	3 separate groups of 6–8 yr. old Spanish-speaking children; total 151.	Oral data from Bilingual Syntax Measure.	1 85% of errors were developmental. 2 The 'acquisition orders' for the three groups were strikingly similar, but different from L1 orders. 8 morphemes investigated.	1 There may be 'a universal or natural order' in which L2 children acquire certain morphemes. 2 Exposing a child to a natural communication situation is sufficient for L2 acquisition to take place.
Dulay and Burt 1974b	60 Spanish-speaking children; 55 Chinese-speaking children; both groups 6–8 years.	Oral data from Bilingual Syntax Measure.	1 The 'acquisition orders' for both groups of children were basically the same. 11 morphemes investigated. 2 The orders obtained by different scoring methods were the same.	1 The learner's L1 does not affect the order of development in child L2 acquisition. 2 'Universal cognitive mechanisms' are the basis for the child's organization of the target language.
Bailey, Madden, and Krashen 1974	73 adults aged 17–55 yrs; classified as Spanish and non-Spanish-speaking; members of 8 ESL classes.	Oral data from Bilingual Syntax Measure.	1 The 'acquisition orders' for both Spanish and non-Spanish groups were very similar. 2 The adult orders of this study were very similar to those reported for all but one of Dulay and Burt's (1973) groups. 3 The adult orders were different from L1 order.	1 Adults use common strategies independent of L1 for L2 acquisition. 2 Adults process linguistic data in similar ways to children. 3 The most effective instruction is that which follows observed order of difficulty.

Study	Subjects	Data collection	Results	Conclusions
Larsen-Freeman 1976b	24 adults (L1s = Arabic, Japanese, Persian, Spanish); learning English at University of Michigan.	Battery of 5 different tests of reading, writing, listening, speaking, and imitating.	1 L1 did not have a significant effect on way adults learn English morphemes. 2 Differences in morpheme orders occurred on different tasks but orders on production tasks (speech and imitation) agreed with Dulay and Burt's order. 3 Accuracy orders correlate with frequency orders for production of morphemes.	1 There is a standard morpheme order for production tasks. 2 The frequency counts for morphemes on speaking task reflect the actual occurrence in real communication. Frequency in native-speaker speech is main determinant of accuracy orders.
Krashen, Butler, Birnbaum, and Robertson 1978	70 adult students from 4 language backgrounds; at University of Southern California.	Free compositions, with (1) time limit; (2) no time limit and chance for self-correction.	1 The 'acquisition' order for the 'fast' writing was the same as that for the 'careful'. 2 The orders obtained in both written tasks were very similar to those reported for adults in the Bailey, Madden, and Krashen study.	1 The students were focused on communication in both tasks, hence a 'natural order' was obtained. 2 The processes involved in L2 acquisition underlie both the oral and the written mode.

Table 3.4:   A summary of key morpheme studies (from Ellis 1985a)

One of the problems of rank orders is that they disguise the difference in accuracy between various morphemes. Thus a morpheme that is just 1 per cent lower than another morpheme is given a different ranking in just the same way as a morpheme that is 30 per cent lower. To overcome this problem, Dulay and Burt (1975) and later Krashen (1977) proposed a grouping of morphemes. They argued that each group constituted a clear developmental stage in that the morphemes within it were 'acquired' at more or less the same time. Figure 3.1 presents Krashen's 'natural order' of morpheme acquisition.

The picture that emerges from these studies is of a standard 'acquisition order' that is not rigidly invariant but is remarkably similar irrespective of the learners' language backgrounds, of their age, and of whether the medium is speech or writing. A different order occurs only when the learners are able to focus on the form rather than the meaning of their utterances. As Krashen (1977: 148) put it, whenever the data reflects a focus on meaning there is 'an amazing amount of uniformity across all studies'.

A number of later cross-sectional morpheme studies have been carried out, including some of languages other than English (for example, Van Naerssen's (1980) study of L2 Spanish). One of the best is Pica's (1983) study of the morpheme orders of three separate groups of L2 learners—a 'naturalistic' group, an instructed group, and a mixed group. We will consider this study in some detail in Chapter 14. Here we simply note that Pica—who was careful to claim only an 'accuracy order'—found the same 'natural order' even when she took account of learners' over-use of morphemes in her scoring procedure (i.e. used target-like use analysis rather than obligatory occasion analysis). This is important because it helps counter one of the main criticisms levelled

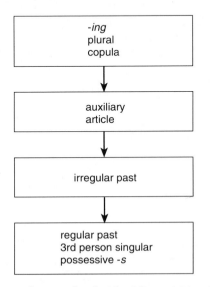

Figure 3.1:   Proposed 'natural order' for L2 acquisition (Krashen 1977)

at the morpheme studies, namely that they have failed to consider inappropriate morpheme use in non-obligatory contexts.

There have been fewer longitudinal morpheme studies. Rosansky (1976) examined the order of acquisition of the same morphemes investigated by Dulay and Burt in the speech of Jorge, a Spanish learner of English, over a period of 10 months. She concluded that the order of acquisition of this individual learner did not conform to the 'natural order' reported for groups of learners. Also, when she carried out cross-sectional analyses with data collected at different points in time she found varying orders. Hakuta (1974) collected spoken data from a five-year-old Japanese girl, Uguisu, over several months. The acquisition order he obtained did not match that of Dulay and Burt. Articles, for instance, which have a high ranking in the cross-sectional accuracy orders, had a low ranking in the acquisition order for Uguisu. Schmidt's (1983) study of Wes, a Japanese painter living in Hawaii, also found some discrepancies with the cross-sectional order (plural, article, and past regular having lower ranks). One possible explanation for the difference in results between the cross-sectional and longitudinal studies is that the results of the latter were misleading because accuracy levels were sometimes calculated using fewer than ten obligatory occasions, a point that Krashen (1977) emphasizes. Nevertheless, the differences do cast some doubt on the validity of equating cross-sectional accuracy with acquisition orders.

The morpheme studies have been subject to some stringent criticisms in addition to the doubts about using accuracy order as a basis for discussing acquisition (see Hatch 1978d and 1983a; Long and Sato 1984). One criticism is that the method of scoring morphemes does not take account of misuse in inappropriate contexts. But, as we have seen, Pica's (1983) study suggests that even when overuse is taken into account it does not affect the order. Another criticism is that the use of rank order statistics hides meaningful differences, but Krashen's grouping of features into a 'natural order' (see Figure 3.1) goes some way to overcoming that objection. Other objections are that the research has been restricted to a small set of morphemes, that the morphemes studied constitute a rag-bag of disparate features (the acquisition of 'articles' and '3rd person -*s*', for instance, pose the learner very different tasks, as one involves semantic considerations and the other is a purely formal feature), and that the research has lacked theoretical motivation. These criticisms are generally acknowledged, with the result that morpheme studies have now been discontinued. However, Larsen-Freeman and Long (1991) conclude their own survey of these studies with the claim that they provide strong evidence of a developmental order:

> Contrary to what some critics have alleged, there is in our view too many studies conducted with sufficient methodological rigor and showing sufficiently consistent general findings for the commonalities to be ignored (1991: 92).

Such a conclusion, however, appears overly charitable, as it fails to recognize the most serious limitation in the morpheme studies—the conceptualization of acquisition in terms of what Rutherford (1988) calls 'accumulated entities', i.e. the mastery of grammatical items one at a time. The inadequacy of this view will become clear when we take a closer look at how learners acquire individual morphemes.

The acquisition of individual morphemes: pronouns

A close look at individual morphemes shows that they are acquired gradually and systematically. Learners do not progress from a state of non-acquisition to a state of acquisition, but rather pass through a series of stages. In Chapter 4 we shall discuss the extensive research that has looked at individual morphemes; here, we will consider just one grammatical feature—pronouns—drawing on research which has investigated the acquisition of this feature in several languages.[7]

In the pronoun system of a language, a number of semantic distinctions are to be found. For example, English distinguishes gender (for example, 'he' and 'she'), person (for example, 'I' and 'you'), number (for example, 'he' and 'they'), and case (for example, 'I' and 'me'). A further distinction between personal pronouns and possessives (for example, 'him/her' v. 'his/her') can also be made. Learners also have to discover when pronouns can be omitted and when it is obligatory to use them. Not surprisingly, pronouns present the learner with a challenge that can only be met over time. Felix and Hahn (1985) note that nearly all studies of naturalistic acquisition provide evidence of frequent omission of pronouns and overgeneralization of individual pronouns during the early stages. This is evident in all the languages which have been studied.

In the case of English—an example of a language where pronouns are obligatory in many contexts—learners are initially still likely to produce utterances with no pronouns:

Kicking (= He kicked me)

Felix and Hahn (1985) suggest that the various semantic features are then systematically acquired and propose a tentative ordering. Learners begin by distinguishing just one feature, usually person. During this stage, they may distinguish only first person from all other persons. Thus 'I' or 'me', or sometimes both interchangeably, are used to realize first person, while a single pronoun (such as 'you' or 'he') refers to all other persons. Later, they distinguish pronouns according to number. Third person pronouns are added next, but no gender distinction is made. This is acquired last. A similar sequence of acquisition is evident for possessives by French learners of English (see Table 3.5). Butterworth and Hatch (1978) illustrate the kind of substitutions and overgeneralizations which result from this process of acquisition in their

Stage	Description	Examples
1	The use of definite articles in place of possessives.	*She reads the book.
2	The use of a generalized possessive for all persons, genders, and numbers.	*She reads your book.
3	The use of a single third person possessive, which is overgeneralized.	*She reads his book.
4	Differentiated use of possessives with some possessed nouns but continued errors with human nouns.	*She reads her book to her brother.
5	Correct use of possessives with all nouns.	She reads her book to her brother.

Table 3.5:   The acquisition of possessive pronouns by francophone learners of English (table based on information provided in Lightbown and Spada 1990)

subject, Ricardo, an adolescent learner of English. When they first started studying him he used both 'me' and 'I' for subject pronoun. He failed to distinguish personal and possessive pronouns, producing errors like:

*You girlfriend (= Your girlfriend)
*He car (= His car).

Ricardo used 'he' and 'she' infrequently, often substituting them with a noun, perhaps because he found it easier to simply repeat a noun than to substitute it with a pronoun. 'We', 'it', and 'they' were also omitted or replaced with 'he'.

Further evidence of developmental regularities in pronoun acquisition comes from a study by Gundel and Tarone (1983). This investigated five adult learners of L2 English (three with Spanish as their L1 and two with Chinese) and utilized data from a variety of sources (tape-recorded conversations, a recorded picture description task, and two kinds of *grammaticality judgement* tasks). It also reports an analysis of data collected from grade 1 learners of L2 French in an immersion program in Canada. The main focus of the study was the learners' omission of object pronouns in obligatory contexts: for example, '*He didn't take'.

In the case of the Chinese learners, the lack of use of object pronouns is attributable to transfer, as object pronouns are not obligatory in Chinese. However, the Spanish learners of English and the English learners of French made more such errors than did the Chinese ones, despite the fact that object pronouns are obligatory in their L1s. Gundel and Tarone suggest that these learners begin with a transfer hypothesis (i.e. that the TL will have object pronouns in the same position as the L1), but reject this when they find that the L2 input is not consistent with it. This leads them to construct a second hypothesis, that the L2 has no object pronoun forms at all. As the L2 input also belies this hypothesis, they abandon it and form a third hypothesis: that the L2 does have object pronouns but not in the same positions as in their L1s. Once again, then, we see evidence of the systematic acquisition of a particular feature—in this case the use of object pronouns.

Similar patterns of pronoun acquisition are evident in other languages. Klein and Rieck (1982, cited in Klein 1986) used data from a sentence repetition task administered to Spanish and Italian migrant workers to investigate the acquisition of pronouns in L2 German, where, as in English, they are obligatory in many contexts. They note that the first/second person singular distinction is acquired early and the number distinction later. Nominative case forms (for example, 'ich') are acquired before accusative and dative case forms (for example, 'mich' and 'mir'). For example, when asked to repeat the sentence 'Vielleicht hat sie ihn zu Hause bei ihren Eltern vergessen' (= 'Perhaps has she it at home with her parents forgotten') the least advanced learners omitted both 'sie' and 'ihn' while the most advanced learners included 'sie' (= subject) but omitted 'ihn' (= object). This occurred despite the fact that the learners' L1s permit deletion of subject pronoun but require retention of object pronoun. Klein also notes the tendency for the learners to replace pronouns with nouns.

The acquisition of pronouns in Dutch has been investigated by Broeder, Extra, and van Hout (1989) in a study of four adults that was part of a large international project directed at investigating untutored L2 acquisition by adult immigrants in a number of European countries (the European Science Foundation Second Language Project on Adult Second Language Acquisition). The main findings were that subject pronoun forms were acquired first, followed by object forms, and then possessive forms. Also, singular pronoun forms were acquired before plural forms. This study found no clear evidence of L1 influence, leading the researchers to conclude that 'target language related principles were ... more influential determiners of acquisition than source language related principles' (1989: 104).

Finally, we consider pronoun acquisition in Spanish. Andersen (1983a) provides a detailed discussion of the acquisition of clitic pronouns (i.e. pronouns like 'lo', 'me', and 'se', which function as direct objects, indirect objects, or as reflexives) by one native speaker of English, Anthony. The following are some of his findings. Anthony tended to use nouns in place of clitic pronouns. He showed greater control of first person 'me' and 'nos' than of third person singular pronominal forms ('lo' and 'la'). He omitted plural third person forms ('los' and 'las'). He was able to position first person 'me' correctly before the verb but experienced difficulty with the third person pronouns in this position. He had no difficulty in positioning pronouns after the verb.

The commonalities in these accounts of pronoun acquisition are striking. They suggest that learners of different languages (English, French, German, Dutch, and Spanish) experience similar problems with pronouns and solve them in similar ways. In many studies, there is evidence that the learner's L1 is a factor—in Anthony's preference for post- rather than pre-verbal pronoun positioning, for instance. But there is also strong evidence of 'universal' patterns of acquisition, at least where these five Indo-European languages are concerned. To substantiate claims regarding universality, of course, it will be necessary to obtain evidence from a wider range of languages.

The acquisition of syntactic structures

We will look at three sets of syntactic structures to see to what extent they provide support for the existence of developmental patterns in second language acquisition. First, we will review a number of early studies which examined the acquisition of negatives in English and German and which provide evidence of a clear sequence of development. Second, we will consider relative clauses, which provide evidence of an order of acquisition. Third, we will look at the acquisition of word order rules in L2 German. This provides evidence of both an acquisition order (as different TL rules are acquired one after another) and also of a developmental sequence (as learners also manifest transitional structures which differ from the TL norms). Finally, we will look at an attempt to characterize general grammatical development in an L2.

The acquisition of negatives in English and German

The development of negatives in English outlined below is based on several early studies (Ravem 1968; Milon 1974; Cazden et al. 1975; Wode 1976 and 1981; Adams 1978; Butterworth and Hatch 1978). These studies cover learners of English with Japanese, Spanish, German, and Norwegian as their L1, and also children, adolescents, and adults. Schumann (1979) provides an excellent overview of a number of studies involving Spanish learners of English.

Negation is an example of a transitional structure (see Dulay, Burt, and Krashen 1982). That is, it involves a series of forms or structures which learners use en route to mastering the TL form. These interim forms are indicative of the developmental stages that learners pass through on the way to TL competence. Initially, negative utterances are characterized by external negation. That is, the negative particle (usually 'no' but sometimes 'not') is attached to a declarative nucleus:

No very good.
No you playing here.

A little later, internal negation develops; that is, the negative particle is moved inside the utterance. This often coincides with the use of 'not' and/or 'don't', which is used variably with 'no' as the negative particle. 'Don't' at this stage is formulaic as it has not been analysed into its separate components 'do' and 'not'.

Mariana not coming today.
I no can swim.
I don't see nothing mop.

A third step involves negative attachment to modal verbs, although this may again occur in unanalysed units initially:

I can't play this one.
I won't go.

In the final stage, the TL rule is acquired. The learner has developed an auxiliary system and uses 'not' regularly as the negative particle (i.e. the use of 'no' with verb is eliminated). Negative utterances are now marked for tense and number, although not always correctly:

He doesn't know anything.
He didn't said it.
She didn't believe me.

This sequence is summarized in Table 3.6.

Stage	Description	Example
1	External negation (i.e. 'no' or 'not' is placed at the beginning of the utterance).	No you are playing here.
2	Internal negation (i.e. the negator – 'no', 'not' or 'don't' is placed between the subject and the main verb).	Mariana not coming today.
3	Negative attachment to modal verbs.	I can't play that one.
4	Negative attachment to auxiliary verb as in target language rule.	She didn't believe me. He didn't said it.

Table 3.6:   Summary of general stages in the sequence of acquisition in L2 English negation

The way along this route is a gradual one. Some learners can take longer than two years and some never travel the whole distance. The stages are not clearly defined but overlap considerably. Development does not consist of sudden jumps, but of the gradual reordering of early rules in favour of later ones. There are also some differences among learners, reflecting their L1. These are discussed in Chapter 8. Individual learners display different preferences in the choice of negative particle—'no' is the most common, but 'not' and unanalysed 'don't' have also been attested.

German negation differs from English in a number of respects. Like English, German places the negative particle after the finite verb:

Ich kann nicht kochen (= I can not cook).
Ich habe nicht gekocht (= I have not cooked).

but unlike English, German does not have a dummy auxiliary, so 'nicht' follows the main verb in sentences like:

Ich koche nicht (= I cook not).

Also, when there is a direct object and a 'free' adverb, 'nicht' follows them as in:

Ich habe den Wagen gestern nicht gefahren.
(= I have the car yesterday not driven).

Studies of the naturalistic acquisition of sentential negation in L2 German include those by Felix (1978), Lange (1979), Pienemann (1981), and Clahsen (1982). Weinert (1987) and Eubank (1990) provide summaries of the general pattern of development. The first stage involves sentence external negation, using 'nein' usually in sentence-initial position:

nein helfen (= no help)
nein spielen Katze (= no play cat).

Learners then move on to internal negation, placing the negator in both preverbal or postverbal position. Main verbs tend to be negated preverbally and other verb types postverbally:

ich das nicht mach (= I that not do)
ich kann das nicht (= I can that not).

As learners master internal negation, they eliminate preverbal negation, positioning the negative particle after the verb even with main verbs:

ich fallst nicht runter (= I fall not down)

In the final stage, learners master the position of negator after direct objects and free adverbials (i.e. they are able to separate 'nicht' from the verb). Thus, despite the differences in the 'final states' towards which learners of English and German are targeted, marked similarities in the sequence of acquisition of negatives in the two languages can be seen.

The acquisition of relative clauses in English and Swedish

The acquisition of relative clauses presents learners with two tasks. In the case of English, they must first learn that relative clauses can modify noun phrases that occur both before the verb (i.e. as subject of the main clause) and after the verb (i.e. as object or in a prepositional phrase):

The man who lives next door is getting married.
We met the man who lives next door.

Second, they must learn the various functions that the relative pronoun can serve. English permits a range of functions, as shown in Table 3.7. These two tasks amount to a substantial learning burden. How do learners tackle it?

Function	Example
Subject	The man who lives next door . . .
Direct object	The man whom I saw . . .
Indirect object	The man to whom I gave a present . . .
Oblique (object of preposition)	The man about whom we spoke . . .
Genitive	The man whose wife had an accident . . .
Object of comparative	The man that I am richer than . . .

Table 3.7:　Relative pronoun functions in English

Studies which have investigated the acquisition of relative clauses in L2 English include those by Cook (1973), Schachter (1974), Ioup (1977), Gass (1979), Schumann (1980), Chiang (1980), Gass and Ard (1980), Hyltenstam (1984), Pavesi (1986), and Hansen-Strain and Strain (1989). The learners in these studies again come from a variety of language backgrounds.

With regard to the first task, Schumann found that the five Spanish-speaking learners he investigated began by attaching a relative clause to a noun phrase that follows the verb. Often learners include a pronominal copy:[8]

I know the man who he coming.

in which case the relative pronoun may be functioning in a similar way to the co-ordinator 'and', joining two main clauses. Only when learners omit the pronominal copy can they be said to have acquired the use of relative clauses:

Joshua's a boy who is silly.

Relative clauses modifying the subject of the main clause appear later:

The boys who doesn't have anybody to live they take care of the dogs.

Gass and Ard (1980) provide evidence for a different sequence of acquisition. Where the data Schumann used consisted of naturally occurring speech, their data came from a sentence joining task, which may explain the differences.

With regard to the second task, learners may begin by omitting the relative pronoun (see Schumann 1980):

I got a friend speaks Spanish.

Next, they may use an ordinary personal pronoun:

I got a friend he speaks Spanish.

and finally the relative pronoun proper is used:

I got a friend who speaks Spanish.

The first function to be mastered is that of subject. The order of acquisition then proceeds as shown in Table 3.7. Two studies, one of L2 Swedish

(Hylstenstam 1984) and the other of L2 English (Pavesi 1986), both of which used implicational scaling, could find no clear evidence for differentiating the order of acquisition of indirect object/oblique and genitive/object of comparison, however.

The retention of pronominal copies is also linked to the acquisition of the functions of the relative pronouns. Hyltenstam's study indicates that the extent to which learners retain copies is influenced by their L1. Thus, Persian learners, whose L1 permits copies, are much more likely to retain them than Finnish learners, whose L1 does not. However, all learners use at least some copies and, interestingly, are more likely to use them with the relative pronoun functions that are difficult to acquire. Hylstenstam and Pavesi provide evidence to suggest that copies disappear from learners' language in the same order as the relative pronoun functions are acquired.

The study of the acquisition of relative clauses is an important area of work in SLA research because it has been used to test predictions based on markedness. We will return to it in Chapters 8 and 10. Also, we will examine several studies which have investigated the effects of instruction on the acquisition of relative clauses in Chapter 14.

The acquisition of German word order rules

A large number of studies have investigated the acquisition of German word order rules in naturalistic L2 acquisition. One of the most important was the Zweitspracherwerb Italienischer und Spanischer Arbeiter (ZISA) project, which focused on learners with a romance language background. This has been reported in a series of articles by Meisel, Clahsen, and Pienemann (for example, Meisel, Clahsen, and Pienemann 1981; Clahsen 1980; Clahsen 1984; Clahsen, Meisel, and Pienemann 1983; Pienemann 1980). Subsequent work has also examined Turkish learners (for example, Clahsen and Muysken 1986). Jordens (1988) provides a helpful survey of the relevant research.

A clear developmental pattern of the acquisition of German word order rules emerges from this research. This is summarized in Table 3.8. Pienemann, Johnston, and Brindley (1988: 222) claim that this pattern 'is now probably one of the most robust empirical findings in SLA research, because the same sequence has been found with a considerable number of further informants in studies carried out independently of each other.' The pattern does allow for some variation, however. Thus, stage 1 (canonical order) may not necessarily consist of subject-verb-object (SVO) for all learners. Whereas learners with romance language backgrounds begin with SVO, other learners (for example, Turkish) begin with different basic word orders that reflect their L1. Also, learners vary in how they progress through the sequence. Some learners appear to move slowly, consolidating each new stage before they move on to the next, whereas others move on to a new stage very

Stage	Name	Description	Examples
1	Canonical order	Romance learners begin with SVO as their initial hypothesis about German word order. Adverbials appear in sentence-final position.	die kinder spielen mim ball (= the children play with the ball).
2	Adverb preposing	Learners are now able to move an adverbial into sentence-initial position. However, they do not yet invert the subject and verb as is required when a sentence begins with an adverbial. This is not acquired until stage 4.	da kinder spielen (= there children play).
3	Verb separation	Learners move non-finite verbal elements into clause-final position, as required in the target language.	alle kinder muss die pause machen (= all the children must the pause make).
4	Inversion	Learners learn that in certain contexts such as sentence-initial adverbials and interrogatives, the verb must precede the subject.	dann hat sie wieder die knocht gebringt (= then has she again the bone bringed).
5	verb-end	Learners learn that the finite verb in subordinate clauses goes in clause-final position.	er sagte dass er nach hause kommt (= he said that he to home comes).

Table 3.8:   Sequence of acquisition of German word order rules (based on Pienemann, Johnston, and Brindley 1988)

rapidly, not bothering if they have not achieved a high level of accuracy in the structure belonging to the prior stage. For example, in stage 4 (inversion) some learners acquire the rule in one linguistic context (for example, with sentence initial adverbials) and then move on to stage 5 (verb-end) before acquiring inversion in other linguistic contexts (such as interrogatives). Other learners take time to acquire the rule in all its contexts before they progress to verb-end. Differences among learners also exist with regard to their ultimate level of achievement. Many of the learners in the ZISA project failed to reach stages 4 and 5.

A general pattern of L2 grammatical development

In subsequent work, an attempt has been made to explain the developmental pattern in the acquisition of German word order rules by means of a set of cognitive processing operations that underlie the production of sentences manifesting each word order rule. These will be described in Chapter 9 when

Stage	Main features	Example
1	Single words; formulas	My name is ___ .
2	SVO; plural marking	I eat rice.
3	'Do'-fronting; adverb preposing; neg. + V	Do you understand me? Yesterday I go to school. She no coming today.
4	Pseudo-inversion; yes/no inversion; V + to + V	Where is my purse? Have you car? I want to go.
5	3rd pers. -s; do-2nd	He works in a factory. He did not understand.
6	Question-tag; adverb-VP	He's Polish, isn't he? I can always go.

Table 3.9: Generalized pattern of acquisition for L2 English (based on information provided in Johnston and Pienemann 1986)

we examine the Multidimensional Model. They are mentioned here because the operations which have been identified provide a basis for predicting the development of word order rules (and indeed other kinds of rules) in languages other than German. Johnston and Pienemann (1986), for instance, tested the predictions afforded by the model on the acquisition of English by migrant workers in Australia and found evidence to support it. They used implicational scaling on data collected cross-sectionally to establish the hierarchy of stages shown in Table 3.9. This constitutes one of the most successful attempts to date to identify a general pattern of development.

Finally, the work on L2 German and English suggests that not all features are developmental in the sense that their acquisition occurs at a particular stage of learners' overall development. Some are variational, i.e. they may or may not be acquired by individual learners and can be acquired at any stage of development. Meisel, Clahsen, and Pienemann (1981) give copula as an example of a variational feature, pointing out that learners vary enormously regarding both whether and when they acquire it.[9]

The L2 = L1 hypothesis

We have now reviewed some of the major features of L1 and L2 acquisition and so can turn to consider the *L1=L2 hypothesis* (also referred to as the *identity hypothesis*). This has received considerable attention in SLA research as it raises a number of important theoretical issues (see Clahsen 1990). These concern whether the fundamental principles that underlie L1 and L2 are the same, and whether the language acquisition device which mentalists claim is responsible for L1 acquisition is available to L2 learners. A number of studies have sought to compare learner language resulting from the two types of acquisition (for example, McNamara 1973; Dulay and Burt 1974c; Ervin-Tripp 1974; Cook 1977; McLaughlin 1978a and 1985; Felix 1978; Ellis 1985b; Bley-Vroman 1988).

The similarities in learner language in L1 and L2 acquisition are perhaps most pronounced in the early stages of development. There is evidence of a silent period, of the use of formulas, and of structural and semantic simplification in both types of acquisition. However, there are also obvious differences. Whereas all L1 learners necessarily pass through a silent period, many L2 learners—especially adults—do not. Many L2 learners appear to make greater use of formulas than L1 learners. Also, L2 learners are able to produce longer and less propositionally reduced utterances from the beginning. A correct characterization of early L1 and L2 acquisition might be to say that L2 learner language displays many of the features of L1 learner language plus some additional ones. Felix (1978) points to a number of differences in a comparison of sentence types in the acquisition of German. He found that the L2 children he studied produced only three different multi-word utterance types, and argues that this contrasts with L1 acquisition, where learners have been shown to produce a multitude of different structures from the two-word stage.

The morpheme order acquisition is not the same in the two types of acquisition. Dulay and Burt (1974c) compared the 'acquisition order' they obtained for nine English morphemes with the acquisition order for the same morphemes obtained in both longitudinal studies (for example, Brown 1973) and cross-sectional studies (for example, de Villiers and de Villiers 1973) of L1 English. They found that the orders were different. Articles, copula, and auxiliary 'be' were acquired earlier by L2 learners, while irregular past tense was acquired later. However, the L2 order they obtained did correlate with the L1 order obtained by Porter (1977), who used the same data collection instrument—the Bilingual Syntax Measure (BSM). This has led some researchers (for example, Rosansky 1976; Hakuta and Cancino 1977) to suggest that Dulay and Burt's acquisition order is an artefact of the BSM.

The process by which individual morphemes are acquired displays both similarities and differences. For example, both L1 and L2 learners omit pronouns and they both overgeneralize individual pronouns. The substitution of nouns for pronouns also occurs in both types of acquisition. However, L1 learners commonly substitute their own name in place of the first person singular pronoun for example, 'Lwindi eating' (= I am eating), which has not been attested in L2 acquisition, except by very young children.

The similarities between L1 and L2 acquisition are strongest in syntactical structures. The evidence from studies of negation (and also interrogatives) suggests that learners pass through a remarkably similar sequence of acquisition for these structures. Readers are invited to compare the order of L1 acquisition for English negatives shown in Tables 3.2 and 3.6. The similarities are truly striking. However, once again, the sequences in the two types of acquisition are not identical. For example, children acquiring German as an L1 begin with the verb in final position (Clahsen 1988):

wurs hier schnitt (= sausages here cut)

whereas, as we have seen, L2 learners begin with a canonical order derived from their L1, which in the case of romance language learners results in an SVO word order.

Given the mixed results available from comparative studies of L1 and L2 acquisition, it is perhaps not surprising to find widely diverging conclusions regarding the L2=L1 hypothesis. Bley-Vroman (1988) emphasizes the differences between L1 and adult foreign language learning (see Table 3.10) and ends up with the following claim:

Feature	L1 acquisition	L2 (foreign language) acquisition
Overall success	Children normally achieve perfect mastery of their L1.	Adult L2 learners are very unlikely to achieve perfect mastery.
General failure	Success is guaranteed.	Complete success is very rare.
Variation	There is little variation among L1 learners with regard to overall success or the path they follow.	L2 learners vary in both their degree of success and the path they follow.
Goals	The goal is target language competence.	L2 learners may be content with less than target language competence and may also be more concerned with fluency than accuracy.
Fossilization	Fossilization is unknown in child language development.	L2 learners often cease to develop and also backslide (i.e. return to earlier stages of development).
Intuitions	Children develop clear intuitions regarding what is a correct and incorrect sentence.	L2 learners are often unable to form clear grammaticality judgements.
Instruction	Children do not need formal lessons to learn their L1.	There is a wide belief that instruction helps L2 learners.
Negative evidence	Children's 'errors' are not typically corrected; correction not necessary for acquisition.	Correction generally viewed as helpful and, by some, as necessary.
Affective factors	Success is not influenced by personality, motivation, attitudes, etc.	Affective factors play a major role in determining proficiency.

Table 3.10:   Differences between L1 and L2 acquisition (based on Bley-Vroman 1988)

These general characteristics of foreign language learning tend to the conclusions that the domain-specific language acquisition of children ceases to
operate in adults, and in addition, that foreign language acquisition resembles general adult learning in fields for which no domain-specific learning system is believed to exist. (page 25)

Ervin-Tripp (1974), however, emphasizes the similarities she found in naturalistic child learners of L2 French and L1 learners:

We found that the functions of early sentences, and their form, their semantic redundancy, their reliance on ease of short-term memory, their
overgeneralization of lexical forms, their use of simple order strategies
were similar to processes we have seen in first language acquisition. In
broad outlines, then, the conclusion is tenable that first and second language learning is similar in natural situations (cited in Hatch 1978a: 205).

These two quotations reveal why researchers have reached such different
conclusions. Whereas Bley-Vroman concentrates on the product of acquisition, Ervin-Tripp focuses on the process. Whereas Bley-Vroman talks about
foreign language learners, Ervin-Tripp refers to naturalistic learners.

L2 learners appear to tackle the problem of learning a language in similar
ways to L1 learners. These similarities are most clearly evident in informal
learning situations when learners are attempting to engage in unplanned language use. But there are also differences in the ways in which L2 learners go
about 'cracking the code', and these become most evident in formal learning
situations. The differences between the kinds of learning involved in these
two settings are described by McNamara (1973) and d'Anglejan (1978). For
example, informal learning typically takes place in contexts where the input is
not consciously structured and the primary focus is on message conveyance,
while formal learning occurs in contexts where the input is usually carefully
organized and the primary focus is on form. Informal learning involves implicit knowledge, while formal learning is likely to involve at least some explicit
knowledge of L2 rules.

Formal and informal learning can also be differentiated in the kind of memory learners rely on. Adult L2 learners have access to a more developed memory capacity than L1 learners and when they can use it (or are required to use
it, as in many pedagogic learning activities), differences between the language
they produce and that produced by L1 learners occur. However, when they
are not able to use it, they will produce language that resembles young children's. Cook (1977) found that when adults were unable to utilize their memory capacity to process relative clauses they behaved in the same way as L1
learners. In another experiment designed to establish the number of digits
adult learners could remember in the L2, Cook found that they behaved like
native-speaking adults. This led Cook to conclude that when the memory
process depends on features of syntax, the same restrictions apply to the L1

and adult L2 learner, but where the memory process is minimally dependent on language, the adult L2 learner exploits his or her general memory capacity. In other words, when L2 learners make use of their special language-learning faculties, the identity hypothesis receives support, but when they rely on cognitive learning procedures of a general kind it does not.

Another obvious source of difference between L1 and L2 acquisition lies in the fact that L2 learners have access to a previously acquired language, in some cases to several. There is clear evidence to show that this results in differences between L2 and L1 acquisition—for example, in the case of the acquisition of German word order rules. Chapter 8 considers the various ways in which the learner's L1 influences L2 acquisition.

The L2 = L1 acquisition hypothesis is important because it raises so many key issues. The evidence that we have considered here suggests that the hypothesis is partially supported. Given the immense cognitive and affective differences between very young children and adults, the similarities in the language they produce are striking. However, there are also significant differences which have been shown to exist and, as we will see in Chapter 10, when we consider whether L2 learners have continued access to Universal Grammar and, also in Chapter 11, when we examine the role of age in L2 learning, these differences have implications for theory-building.

Summary

The investigation of developmental patterns in learner language was motivated by the desire to describe learner language in its own right, as a system of rules that learners constructed and repeatedly revised. It has proceeded by means of cross-sectional, longitudinal, and more recently experimental research. It has employed a number of methodological procedures, including obligatory occasion analysis, target-like use analysis, frequency analysis, and implicational scaling.

First language acquisition researchers sought evidence with which to test the rival behaviourist and mentalist accounts of language learning. They provided evidence of (1) an order of acquisition for morphemes, (2) sequences of development in the acquisition of specific structures such as negatives, (3) an overall pattern of development embracing grammatical, semantic, and pragmatic features of the TL, and (4) cross-linguistic similarities.

In L2 acquisition, early learner language is characterized by (1) a silent period (although not in all learners), (2) extensive use of formulas and (3) structural and semantic simplification, particularly in unplanned language use. Early studies of the order of acquisition of grammatical morphemes such as plural -s and articles produced mixed results. The cross-sectional studies reported a consistent accuracy order when the learner was focused on communicating meaning, which some researchers equated with acquisition order. Krashen (1977) proposed a 'natural order' of acquisition based on these studies. However, longitudinal studies did not always confirm this order. A major criticism of the morpheme studies is that acquisition is viewed as one of 'accumulated entities', and insufficient attention is paid to the ways in which learners achieve gradual mastery over specific linguistic features. However, studies of individual morphemes such as pronouns, and syntactical structures such as negation, lend strong support to the existence of developmental sequences. Learners of different L2s manifest similar patterns of development when acquiring pronouns. For example, they all omit pronouns and/or replace them with nouns, and they all overgeneralize individual pronouns. Also, certain semantic features (for example, person) appear to be acquired before others (for example, gender). In the case of syntactic structures the regularities are even more evident. The acquisition of English and German negation involves a series of transitional stages in which learners gradually switch from external to internal negation and from pre-verbal to post-verbal negation. Relative clauses constitute a complex learning task. There is evidence to suggest that learners solve it piecemeal by learning first to modify noun phrases before the verb, and then noun phrases that follow the verb. Also, learners acquire the functions that relative pronouns can perform in a fairly well-defined order. Finally, the ZISA project has provided some impressive evidence to show that learners acquire German word order rules in a clear sequence. This work has since been further extended to cover the acquisition of a range of features in L2 English. ZISA researchers have also distinguished developmental and variational features.

A comparison of the developmental patterns found in L1 and L2 acquisition lends partial support to the identity hypothesis. Some striking similarities have been found in syntactic structures such as negatives, but there are also differences. It has been suggested that adult L2 learners are more likely to manifest similar patterns of acquisition to children acquiring their native language when they engage in informal learning, but that they also have access to formal learning strategies, which result in differences.

Conclusion

In the Introduction to an influential collection of papers, Hatch (1978a) wrote:

> Nothing can be certain until second language acquisition has been studied in tangible case histories or until empirical evidence has been obtained (1978: 10).[10]

A considerable amount of empirical evidence is now available. This chapter has reviewed a selection of it in order to examine to what extent there are testifiable developmental patterns (orders and sequences) in L2 acquisition of the kind that have been observed in L1 acquisition.

What constitutes evidence for a developmental pattern? This question has rarely been addressed in an explicit manner, but the following would seem to be the criteria that researchers have applied:

1 Developmental patterns can be established by looking at either the order in which different target structures are acquired, or the sequence of stages through which a learner passes en route to mastery of a single TL structure.
2 In the case of transitional structures, a 'stage' consists of a period during which learners use a particular form or structure in a systematic manner, although not necessarily to the exclusion of other forms and structures.
3 The forms and structures that a learner produces at different points during the process of L2 acquisition can be ordered such that one form or structure always precedes another.
4 Learners progress step-by-step along an order or a sequence, mastering one particular structure—target-language or transitional—before another.
5 Strong evidence for developmental patterns occurs when it can be shown that an order or a sequence is universal (i.e. applies to different L2s and to all learners). Weaker evidence is found if it is shown that an order or a sequence applies only to specific L2s and/or to specific groups of learners.

These criteria raise many questions to do with the definition of such key terms as 'form', 'structure', 'systematic use', and 'master'. Different researchers have worked with rather different operational definitions, with the result that it is not easy to compare results across studies. Inevitably, then, the picture is often a fuzzy one, suggesting that it may be better in many cases to talk of 'regularities' than of 'definite patterns'.

The strongest evidence for developmental patterns undoubtedly comes from studies of syntactic structures. We have seen that the morpheme studies, on which great store was once set, are of doubtful validity, because their view of acquisition as one of 'accumulated entities' is seriously flawed. But in the case of negatives, relative clauses, and word order rules (as well as other areas of syntax such as interrogatives), there is evidence to support at least the 'weak' definition of developmental patterns referred to in (5) above. The acquisition of these structures in a particular L2 shows surprising uniformity, and in some cases the regularities hold across different L2s. For example, learners of all L2s so far investigated appear to go through an initial stage of preverbal negation.

There is also plenty of evidence that acquisitional sequences are not completely rigid. For example, in the case of pronouns all learners seem to go through a stage when they overgeneralize one pronominal form, but they may vary in the form they choose to overgeneralize. A sequence can also be influenced by the learner's L1. Thus, the starting point for the acquisition of

German word order rules seems to vary according to the basic word order of the learner's L1. Also, the L1 may result in an additional stage, as when German and Norwegian learners of L2 English add a negator after the main verb at a certain developmental point.

It is also necessary to recognize the limitations of the research which has investigated developmental patterns.

1   Focus on grammar

As was pointed out in Chapter 1, a major limiting factor in SLA research has been its preoccupation with grammar. This chapter has concerned itself only with research into the acquisition of grammar. It is worth briefly noting, however, that the idea of developmental sequences has also been explored in L2 phonology. It has been claimed, for example, that learners have a marked preference for open syllables (i.e. syllables that end in a vowel) as opposed to closed syllables (i.e. syllables that end in a consonant) in the early stages (Tarone 1978). This is reflected in a universal tendency towards epenthesis (the insertion of a vowel where it is not required in the TL) and consonant deletion.[11] It also appears to be the case that whereas learners often substitute L1 sounds for TL sounds, this does not always happen. Wode (1977), for instance, found that the German children he studied followed the same developmental sequence for /r/ as that observed in native, English-speaking children. However, as Ioup and Weinberger (1987) note, it is still not clear why developmental processes sometimes occur and sometimes do not in L2 phonology.[12]

There has also been some work on developmental patterns in L2 lexis, which led Meara (1984) to speculate that learners go through transitional stages. Meara's own work on learners' word associations concentrated on showing the qualitative differences in the networks of word associations between learners and native speakers. Learners' responses tend to be very varied and unpredictable when they are given a stimulus word and asked to produce an association, which 'makes it very difficult to use word associations as an index of development, or to link change in association patterns with progress in other areas' (1984: 232). Even allowing for Sharwood Smith's (1984) rejoinder that Meara underestimates what his own research shows, it is probably premature to speak of anything so defined as an 'order' or a 'sequence' in the L2 acquisition of lexis.

Ideally, the study of L2 vocabulary acquisition requires longitudinal studies, but there have been very few of these, most researchers preferring, like Meara, to conduct experimental, cross-sectional studies. Two exceptions to this generalization are Yoshida (1978) and Wode et al. (1992). Yoshida investigated the acquisition of English by a young Japanese child. One finding was that this child showed a marked propensity for nouns over verbs in the early stages of development. Wode et al. report the results of their study of the

English vocabulary acquired by four German children in a natural setting. They point to three differences between L1 and L2 vocabulary acquisition. Whereas vocabulary growth is slow in L1 acquisition up to the first fifty words and then rapidly accelerates, it is initially much more rapid but soon decelerates in L2 acquisition. The kind of overgeneralizations evident in L1 acquisition (for example, 'cat' is used to refer to a variety of four-legged animals) is not apparent in L2 acquisition. Closed-class items like prepositions, articles and pronouns are acquired late in L1 children, while L2 learners manifest a high percentage of such items early on. Wode et al. explain these differences in terms of the cognitive abilities and background knowledge of the two types of learner.

Clearly, it is not yet possible to say much about developmental patterns in L2 vocabulary acquisition. The research to date, however, suggests that such patterns may exist.

2 Lack of a general index of second language acquisition

We noted that in L1 acquisition research, mean length of utterance (MLU) served as a reliable measure of a child's development, at least until the later stages. However, as Larsen-Freeman (1978) observes, MLU cannot be used in SLA research because so many of the learners' early utterances are formulaic. Various alternative devices have been suggested, but none has become widely accepted. The result is that it is difficult to make reliable comparisons between learners.

3 Inter-learner variability

If the variability between learners becomes too great, it makes little sense to continue to talk of a standard developmental route, a point raised by Lightbown (1984). She claims that for every study that reports an order or a sequence, there is another study which has produced counter-evidence and argues that the learners' L1, the input they experience, and their socio-psychological attitudes can all result in variant patterns. But Lightbown's conclusion is not that clear patterns do not exist, merely that we need to examine how these variables interact with universal tendencies. Again, this raises the whole question as to what constitutes a 'definite pattern' of L2 acquisition, a question partly but not completely answered by the criteria listed above.

4 Intra-learner variability

The learner language produced by a single learner is likely to display marked variability. Thus, at any one stage of development, a learner is likely to produce utterances reflecting different stages of development. How then can we speak of a clear developmental pattern? The answer that researchers like Cancino et al. (1978) have given is to show that it is possible to identify sequences in terms of gradual shifts in the frequencies of the varied structures a learner employs at different stages. However, if the variability becomes too great it makes little sense to talk of a 'stage' of development.

Intra-learner variability also poses problems of description. Bley-Vroman (1983) has pointed out that nobody to date has succeeded in writing a 'systematic grammar' of learner language—even for L2 English, the most studied language. The descriptions that do exist are piecemeal. The closest to an overall account of the developmental path is that provided by Johnston and Pienemann (1987), but this still only accounts for a small proportion of the total grammar of a language.

5 Methodological problems

It is easy to find methodological flaws with many of the studies. Lightbown (1984) lists a number of them. Some studies have been carried out in a manner that makes replication of them difficult and yet, clearly, replication is essential if claims about the universality of sequences are to be substantiated. Another problem is that researchers have tended to base their claims on data collected by means of a single instrument and, thus, have ignored the variability in learner language produced in different contexts. Lightbown also suggests that some researchers have used inappropriate data collection procedures for their subjects, while others have presented the results anecdotally rather than quantitatively. The need for quantification is not something that all researchers would acknowledge, however.[13]

Despite all these problems, the work on developmental patterns has been substantial and in many cases convincing. But how significant is this work? In the opinion of some, it is not very important. Sharwood Smith (1984) argues that searching for developmental sequences is less important than revealing the qualitative ways in which the system a learner builds at a given time differs from that of the native speaker. Others, like Bley-Vroman (1983), have argued that learner language must be described in its own right without reference to the TL. This latter view has underscored some of the best descriptive work in SLA research.

The discovery that learners do follow identifiable routes has generated immense interest. Any theory of L2 acquisition will need to account for developmental patterns. The theory that has been dominant in SLA—interlanguage theory (Selinker 1972)—was initially formulated to provide such an account. It claimed that learners construct a series of interlanguages (i.e. mental grammars that are drawn upon in producing and comprehending sentences in the L2) and that they revise these grammars in systematic and predictable ways as they pass along an interlanguage continuum. It has also proposed that this continuum involves both recreation and restructuring (Corder 1978a). Learners create unique rules not to be found in either the L1 or the TL and then gradually complexify these rules in the direction of those in the TL, particularly in the case of syntax learnt in informal environments. They also make use of their L1, gradually restructuring it as they discover how it differs from the TL, a process that Corder suggests is more prevalent in the case of phonology learnt in formal environments, a point taken up in Chapter 8. Thus, both universal principles and the learner's L1 are involved in the process of acquiring an L2. How these work and interact is of crucial importance for understanding L2 acquisition and is the main subject of Section Three of this book.

Notes

1 In fact, though, many of the subjects of the studies reported in this chapter were of the 'mixed' kind. That is, although they had opportunities for exposure in non-instructional settings they were also receiving some classroom instruction. This is particularly true of children learning the L2 in a country where it functions as an official language (see, for example, Dulay and Burt 1973; Pienemann 1980).

2 A second problem with target-language based analyses is that of deciding which set of TL norms to use as the basis for the comparison with learner language. These norms vary somewhat in different dialects of the TL and it cannot be assumed that all L2 learners are targeted on the standard dialect. This problem is further discussed in Chapters 5 and 6.

3 The label SHARP is not an acronym, in fact. Atkinson chose it as an antonym to FLAT, the other tradition followed by L1 researchers. This *is* an acronym, referring to 'First Language Acquisition Theories'.

4 According to one view of L2 acquisition, children begin with a nonlinguistic system of representing objects and their relationships (for example, a sensory motor representation) and then learn how this system 'maps' on to the linguistic system (see Sinclair-de-Zwart 1973).

5 There is also the general problem of determining exactly what a learner's 'silence' signifies. Silence can be used as a conversational strategy—a means of indicating disagreement, disapproval of someone's behaviour, or plain uncooperativeness, for example.

6 The fact that structural/semantic simplification can reflect the processes either of acquisition or production raises an epistemological and methodological problem in SLA research. What actually counts as 'acquisition'? To what extent is it possible to distinguish between what learners 'know' and what they 'do', given that the primary evidence for what they know rests in what they do? This issue raises its head at various points throughout this book and is discussed in some detail in Chapter 15.

7 The acquisition of pronouns is further considered in Chapter 10 when studies working within the framework of Universal Grammar are discussed.

8 The retention of pronominal copies may be a manifestation of the same psycholinguistic mechanism underlying the choice of nouns over pronouns—the learner's attempt to be transparent by ensuring that all meanings map on to overt forms.

9 The claim that *variational* features like copula are not acquired in a fixed order does not preclude their acquisition involving a sequence of stages. Indeed, there is some evidence to suggest that the acquisition of copula 'be' does involve transitional stages (see Ellis 1988a and Chapter 4). Thus, copula may first appear in learner language at any time; its mastery, however, takes time and involves stages of development.

10 It is assumed that Hatch's use of 'or' is not meant to suggest that 'case studies' do not constitute 'empirical research'. They clearly do.

11 Not all researchers agree with Tarone that there is a universal tendency towards open syllables in interlanguage. Sato (1987), for example, found negligible use of epenthesis in her Vietnamese learners of English, which she saw as 'evidence against the hypothesized universal preference for the CV (i.e. open) syllable' (1987: 260). Riney (1990) provides evidence to suggest that the crucial factor may be the age the learner began learning the L2 (see Chapter 11).

12 Much of the work on L2 phonology focuses on the influence of the learner's L1 and for this reason is considered in greater detail in Chapter 8, when language transfer is considered. Useful overviews of L2 phonology research can be found in Leather and James (1991).

13 There is a rich ethnographic and descriptive tradition in SLA research which eschews quantification in favour of rich, illustrative accounts of L2 learners (see Johnson 1992, in particular Chapters 4 and 6, for an account of these).

Further Reading

A good account of the methodological procedures used in the description of learner language can be found in:

M. Long and C. Sato, 'Methodological issues in interlanguage studies: an interactionist perspective' in A. Davies et al. (eds.), *Interlanguage* (Edinburgh University Press, 1984).

A very readable general account of the acquisition of English as an L1 is Chapter 2 of G. Wells, *The Meaning Makers* (Hodder and Stoughton, 1986).

More detail is available in the articles in P. Fletcher and M. Garman (eds.) *Language Acquisition* (Cambridge University Press, 1986).

An interesting study of the role of the silent period in L2 acquisition can be found in M. Saville-Troike, 'Private speech: evidence for second language learning strategies during the 'silent' period.' *Journal of Child Language* (1988)15: 567–90.

An informative study of formulaic speech in L2 acquisition is

L. Rescorla and S. Okuda, 'Modular patterns in second language acquisition', *Applied Psycholinguistics* (1987) 8: 281-308.

There is now a wealth of descriptive studies of L2 acquisition to draw on, which makes selection very difficult. Key volumes providing collections of some of the most important papers are:

E. Hatch (ed.), *Second Language Acquisition* (Newbury House, 1978).

R. Andersen (ed.), *The Acquisition and Use of Spanish and English as First and Second Languages* (TESOL, 1979).

S. Felix (ed.), *Second Language Development* (Gunter Narr, 1980).

R. Scarcella and S. Krashen (eds.), *Research in Second Language Acquisition* (Newbury House, 1980).

R. Andersen (ed.), *Second languages: A Cross-linguistic Perspective* (Newbury House, 1984).

G. Ioup and S. Weinberger (eds.), *Interlanguage Phonology: The Acquisition of a Second Language Sound System* (Newbury House, 1987).

Articles by E. Hatch and S. Corder in J. Richards (ed.), *Understanding Second and Foreign Language Learning* (Newbury House, 1978), provide useful general accounts of learner language.

Many of the key articles have appeared in journals—in particular, *Interlanguage Studies Bulletin, Working Papers on Bilingualism, Language Learning, TESOL Quarterly,* and *Studies in Second Language Acquisition.* The first two are no longer published, but are available in many university libraries.

4   Variability in learner language

Introduction

In Chapters 2 and 3, evidence was provided to suggest that learner language displays significant systematicity. However, we also noted that a pervasive feature of learner language is its variability. We have seen that learners sometimes make an error in the use of a specific target-language structure, and sometimes do not. Also, we saw that the identification of a 'stage' of development in the sequence of acquisition does not mean that learners consistently make use of a single form or pattern, but rather that they show a preference for the use of one form among others that they use during the same period. Any researcher who has grappled with L2 data has had to recognize and find a way of dealing with variation.

There are, in fact, three approaches to resolving the apparent contradiction between variation and systematicity in learner language. The first approach is that practised by linguists in the Chomskyan tradition (for example, White 1989a and Gregg 1989), who adopt what Tarone (1983) has called 'a homogeneous competence model'. In this approach variation is seen as a feature of performance rather than of the learner's underlying knowledge system. The general claim is that in order to study language it is necessary to abstract what learners 'know' from what they 'do'. This involves various kinds of idealization. Lyons (1972) proposes three ways in which abstract 'sentences' can be derived from actual 'utterances': (1) regularization, the elimination of variation related to the speech disfluencies that occur in natural language use, (2) standardization, the elimination of the variation found in different dialects of a language, and (3) decontextualization, the elimination of the variation associated with the use of language in different social situations. As a result of these idealizing processes, the linguist gains access to data that are invariable and so can be used to investigate the learner's linguistic competence. The type of data often preferred by researchers who operate within the homogeneous competence paradigm consist of speakers' intuitions regarding what they think is correct in the L2 rather than actual instances of language use.[1] The problem of variability, therefore, is solved by distinguishing 'competence' and 'performance', and by establishing the description and explanation of linguistic competence as the main goals of enquiry. In effect, then, variability is ignored in this paradigm.

The second approach is a sociolinguistic one; its goal is to study language in relation to social context. There are a number of sociolinguistic models that have informed SLA research (see Beebe 1988b). These seek to account for the variation evident in different varieties of English (for example, from one dialect to another), the variation which occurs among speakers who differ in terms of general social factors such as class and ethnicity, and also the variation which arises within the speech of a single speaker as a result of changes in situational context. Researchers in this tradition (for example, Beebe 1980; Dickerson 1975) aim to describe both the learner's linguistic and sociolinguistic competence. They are concerned, therefore, both with what learners know about the L2 system and with what they know about how it is used in communication. Not surprisingly, they prefer to work with data that reflect actual instances of language use rather than with intuitions. In this approach, the problem of variability is solved by demonstrating that it is patterned—in other words, that language use can be both variable and systematic.

The third approach is psycholinguistic. Psycholinguistic processing models seek to account for the variation that results from factors that influence the learner's ability to process L2 knowledge under different conditions of use. For example, systematic differences in performance have been found to exist in learner language depending on whether it is planned or unplanned (Ellis 1987b; Crookes 1989). Researchers in this tradition also make use of data reflecting natural language use. They seek to show that planning variability is systematic and to explain it in terms of mental processing.

Thus, whereas the linguistic approach ignores variability, the sociolinguistic and the psycholinguistic approaches try to describe and explain it. Sociolinguistic approaches treat social factors as primary, although, as we will see, they may also refer to psycholinguistic mechanisms to explain how situational factors result in variability. Psycholinguistic approaches are concerned with identifying the internal mechanisms responsible for variable performance and pay little attention to the social factors that motivate them. Sociolinguistic and psycholinguistic approaches, therefore, are complementary and a full account of variability in learner language requires both.

L2 variability has attracted increasing attention in SLA research, drawing on a range of different theoretical perspectives. Wolfram (1991: 104), in a review of a number of books on L2 variability, finds the 'range of models and perspectives almost overwhelming in its inclusiveness' and considers the 'search for a unitary model of SLA variation very elusive'. Similarly, Zuengler argues that 'it is misguided to search for one comprehensive theory, since one theory will most likely be insufficient in explaining the complexity of performance variation . . .' (1989: 66). The aim of this chapter is not to provide a 'unitary model' but rather to concentrate on the descriptive information which has been uncovered.

Finally, it needs to be pointed out that because learner language is a natural language, the types of variability that it manifests are not unique. All natural languages will manifest *variable forms* that have two or more *variants*. A variable form is a feature (phonological, lexical or grammatical) that is realized linguistically in more than one way. Variants are the linguistic devices that realize a variable form. For example, in native speaker English, copula 'be' constitutes a variable form; it has two variants (full copula and contracted copula). Of course, the variants found in learner language will not necessarily be the same as those found in the target language. Thus, learners' interlanguages have been found to manifest three rather than two variants for copula 'be' (zero, full, and contracted). Also, as we have already noted, variability seems especially prevalent in learner language. However, the types of variability and their sources are the same as those observed in natural languages.

The starting point for this chapter is a fuller discussion of the sociolinguistic and psycholinguistic theories that have informed variability research in SLA research. A taxonomy of the different types of variability in learner language follows. This provides a basis for an examination of the empirical research into L2 acquisition. Finally, further consideration will be given to the contradictory views regarding the significance of variability phenomena in L2 acquisition.

Some theoretical perspectives

A number of different lines of primarily sociolinguistic enquiry have informed the study of variability in learner language. These include (1) the Labovian paradigm, (2) the dynamic paradigm, and (3) the social psychological perspective of Accommodation Theory. This section will also examine psycholinguistic models of language production and, in particular, the distinction between planned and unplanned discourse, as this has also been used to account for L2 variation. These models are presented, in the first instance, without reference to how they have been exploited in SLA research.

Sociolinguistic models

The Labovian paradigm

The Labovian paradigm has exerted the greatest influence on the study of variability in SLA research, particularly in much of the earlier work. Two constructs are of particular importance: speech styles and variable rules.

Labov distinguishes social factors (responsible for inter-speaker variation) and stylistic factors (responsible for intra-speaker variation). Social factors such as social class, age, and gender can account for differences among speakers. The variable forms in which these individual differences are evident are called *indicators*. An example of such an indicator is *-ing*, which may be pronounced [ɪn] in a number of dialects in accordance with such social factors as sex and social class (see Fischer 1958). According to Labov and other sociolinguists, some sociolinguistic variables—such as *-ing*—are 'more highly developed' in the sense that they are both 'social' and 'stylistic' (i.e. manifest both inter-speaker and intra-speaker or stylistic variation). They are referred to as *markers*. Bell (1984), in fact, has argued that there is no clear distinction to be made between social and stylistic variation.

Labov (1970) lists five axioms relating to the study of speech styles (i.e. markers):

1 '... there are no single style speakers'. All speakers vary their language to some degree when the social context or topic changes.
2 'Styles can be ranged along a single dimension, measured by the amount of attention paid to speech'. Language users vary in the degree to which they monitor their speech in different situations.
3 The vernacular style is the style in which minimum attention is given to monitoring speech. It is the style associated with informal, everyday speech and it provides 'the most systematic data' for linguistic study.
4 It is not possible to tap the vernacular style of users by systematic observation of how they perform in a formal context (such as an experiment).
5 The only way to obtain good data on the speech of language users is through systematic observation.

The conflict between the fourth and the fifth axioms leads to what Labov calls the *Observer's Paradox*. Good data require systematic observation, but this prevents access to the user's vernacular style.

As an example of how Labov set about examining speech styles, let us consider one of his studies. Labov (1970) examined the speech patterns of New Yorkers. He collected data using a variety of tasks in order to sample a range of speech styles, which he classified as (1) casual speech (i.e. the relaxed speech found in the street and in bars), (2) careful speech (for example, the speech found in interviews), (3) reading, (4) word lists, and (5) minimal pairs. These styles were spread along a continuum according to the amount of attention paid by the speakers to their own speech, the least attention being paid in (1) and the most in (5). Thus, attention is seen as the mechanism through which other factors can affect style. Labov's model, therefore, although primarily sociolinguistic, also incorporates a psycholinguistic factor—attention. Attention serves as the mechanism through which causative social factors such as verbal task (in particular), topic, interlocutor, setting, or the roles of the participants influence actual performance.

Labov investigated a number of pronunciation features and was able to show that the use of sounds like /θ/ (i.e. the first sound in 'thing') and their variants (for example, /t/) functioned as markers. Speakers used the prestige /θ/ more frequently in styles where they were able to pay attention and the less prestigious sounds such as /t/ in styles where little or no attention to speech was paid. Labov referred to these changes in speech as *style shifting*.

Labov's work indicated that style shifting was systematic and, therefore, predictable. This systematicity can be of two kinds: categorical and probabilistic. Categorical systematicity is evident when it can be shown that speakers always use one particular feature (such as /θ/) in one style and another (such as /t/) in a different style. In such cases it is possible to write a categorical rule to describe the speech behaviour. Such a rule has this form:

$$X \rightarrow Y / \underline{\quad} A$$

where X refers to the variable itself, Y to its actual realization, and A the particular context or style (for example, the first sound of 'thing' is realized as /t/ in a casual style). The actual behaviour of Labov's subjects, however, was not usually categorical in this way. They tended to use one variant in one style and another variant in another style to a greater or lesser extent. In other words, their behaviour was probabilistic. To account for this, Labov proposed the use of variable rules. These have a much more complex form to account for the probability of occurrence of a specific feature in a given style or context. Færch (1980) provides the following example:[2]

Y with the probability of .6   in context/style A
Z with the probability of .4
X
Y with the probability of .9   in context/style B
Z with the probability of .1

This states that a given variable feature, X, is manifest as either Y or Z with differing levels of probability depending on the context/style. Such a rule can account for the patterns of variability in the choice of /θ/ and /t/ which Labov found in the speech of New Yorkers. It can show that speakers are much more likely to use the prestige feature, Y, in a careful style, B, than in a more casual style, A, and, conversely, that they are less likely to use the less socially prestigious feature, Z, in B than in A.

Variable rules have been used to describe the extent of the systematic variation that occurs in relation to situational factors (i.e. in style shifting) and also that which arises as a result of linguistic context. For example, Labov (1969a) was also able to show that the use of variants of copula 'be' (full, contracted, and zero copula) in Black English Vernacular (BEV) was influenced by the preceding and following elements in the sentence. Thus, zero copula was most likely to occur when the preceding word ended in a vowel and 'gonna' followed:

He gon' try to get up. (+ vowel/+ verb)

and least likely to occur when the preceding word ended in a consonant and a noun phrase followed:

Bud is my friend. (+ consonant/+ noun phrase)

A variable rule can express the probability of a particular form being used in a particular linguistic context.

More recently, powerful statistical programmes such as VARBRUL have been developed to account for the effects that various factors relating to both situational and linguistic context can have on speakers' choice of language forms (see Preston 1989: 14ff for an account of this procedure). VARBRUL provides a means of determining the differential effect of a number of factors and, also, how they interact.

A question of considerable theoretical importance is the status of variable rules. Labov argues that the variation described through variable rules is 'an inherent and regular property of the system' (1970: 225) and that it cannot be accounted for in terms of dialect mixing and switching. Furthermore, Labov dismisses claims that variable rules reflect 'performance' rather than 'competence', even though he accepts that they are rules of production rather than reception. He argues that there is 'a deep asymmetry between perception and production' (1970: 226). For Labov, then, variable rules are an aspect of that competence that underlies production. He claims that it can be studied only through examining language in use, as speakers have no intuitive awareness of such rules.

The Labovian paradigm has come in for considerable criticism in recent years (for example, Wolfson 1976; Beebe 1982; Bell 1984; Rampton 1987). One of the main problems consists of Labov's use of 'attention to speech' as a causative factor in style shifting. As Wolfson points out, very little is known about the relationship between audio-monitoring and speech style and it is difficult to obtain independent measures of attention. Thus we cannot be sure that a speaker really does attend to speech more in a 'careful' than in a 'casual' style. Sometimes speakers may pay close attention to a feature in an informal setting, for example, if the feature in question is important for communicating in this kind of language use or, as Hulstijn (1989a) suggests, simply because the learner lacks full control of a feature. A further serious criticism, advanced by Bell (1984), is that the attention-to-speech model ignores the effect that the addressee has on the interaction. It cannot account for the role played by such factors as feelings of ethnic identity and solidarity with one's in-group. Beebe argues that 'attention to speech is inadequate as an explanation for style' (1982: 13) and points to a number of studies (for example, Bourhis and Giles 1977) where style shifting does not appear to involve attention on the part of speakers. Beebe also criticizes Labov's preoccupation with the standardness dimension of style shifting (i.e. whether speakers use a standard or non-standard linguistic norm), pointing out that 'shifts have been found in amount of talk, degree of elaboration, speech rate, duration, vocal intensity, pause and utterance length, stress, pitch, intonation, content expressed and even complete code switches' (page 15). Variable rules have also been attacked. In particular, doubts have been expressed as to whether the probabilities expressed in a variable rule can be seen as part of the native speaker's competence, as Labov claims. As we will see in the next section, Bickerton (1975) has shown how variability can be accounted for entirely through categorical rules. Variable rules, therefore, may be unnecessary. Wolfram (1991), in fact, dismisses them as 'passé'. However, other sociolinguists such as Preston (1989) continue to see value in them and, more especially, in VARBRUL.[3]

The Labovian paradigm has had a profound impact on the study of variability in learner language. It provided the methodology for a number of early studies (for example, Dickerson 1975 and Beebe 1980) and also served as the basis for theories of L2 acquisition (for example, Tarone 1982; 1983).

The dynamic paradigm

Whereas Labov sought to account for variability in groups of speakers by means of variable rules, Bailey (1973) and, in particular, Bickerton (1975), developed alternative means, based on a view of how language change takes place.

Bailey sought to show how a theory of language change can account for synchronic variability in language use. According to his *Wave Theory*, linguistic innovation is first introduced by one group of speakers. By the time it is taken up by a second group, the first group has introduced a second innovation. And so as old rules spread, new rules arise. The spread, or diffusion, of new rules also takes place in another way. Initially, a rule may be restricted to a specific linguistic environment and then gradually come to be used in an increasing range of environments. Linguistic environments can be distinguished according to their weight. Change originates in 'heavy environments' (i.e. those environments that favour the use of a particular variant) and then spreads through intermediate to 'light environments' (i.e. those environments that do not favour the use of the variant). For example, for zero copula, the heaviest context in Black English Vernacular is + vowel/ + gonna and the lightest + consonant/ + noun phrase (see pages 123–4 for examples). Thus, like Labov's variable rule, the wave theory accounts for the systematic effects of both social and linguistic factors.

The relationship between language change and synchronic variation (i.e. the variation evident in speakers at a single point in time) is clearly evident in *creoles*—languages that began as pidgins but then developed rapidly when they came to be used and learnt as first languages. A creole generally has several varieties, or 'lects' as they are called: (1) the basilect manifests the 'deepest' creole features, (2) the mesolect contains middle-level features, and (3) the acrolect is the variety closest to the standard language. Together the lects constitute a creole continuum, going from the simplest, most basic variety to the most complex. In a study of Guyanese Creole, Bickerton (1975) was able to show how different speakers could be located at different points on the continuum by using implicational scaling (see Table 4.1). Thus, speakers 1 and 2 (whose speech provided evidence of only one of the four grammatical features Bickerton examined) were basilectal speakers, while speakers 3 and 4 (who provided evidence of two or three of the features) were mesolectal, and speakers 5 and 6 (who used all four features) were acrolectal. Table 4.1 constitutes an implicational scale because it can be shown that the presence of a feature to the left in the horizontal list of features entails the presence of all features to the right. For example, an acrolectal speaker who has acquired Ving will also have acquired Ning, doz, and a. Bickerton claims that it is possible to write separate grammars consisting only of categorical rules to account for each lect. The resulting description is called a polylectal grammar.

Speaker	Linguistic features			
	Ving	Ning	doz	a
1	0	0	0	X
2	0	0	0	X
3	0	0	X	X
4	0	X	X	X
5	X	X	X	X
6	X	X	X	X

X = occurs; 0 = does not occur

Table 4.1:   Varieties of Guyanese Creole in the speech of six speakers (simplified table from Bickerton 1975: 79)

Different types of variability can be accounted for using Bickerton's model. First, there is *inter-speaker variation*. Some speakers may have access to one variety and others to other varieties, although the full continuum of varieties will only be evident in the 'langue' of the speech community as a whole (see page 130 for a definition of langue). Second, there is *intra-speaker variation*. This occurs when speakers who have access to more than one lect engage in *code-switching*. In accordance with situational factors such as the topic of the discourse, its purpose, and the addressee, a speaker may choose to use one lect sometimes and another at other times. Code-switching works in much the same way as style shifting, the difference being that in the dynamic paradigm it can be accounted for in terms of a polylectal grammar rather than variable rules. Third, there is *free variation*. When a speaker first acquires a new feature, this is likely to exist alongside an existing feature and to be used to realize the same meanings. Bickerton claims that this occurs only in those speakers whose language systems are still unstable—a relatively small set of the total population. He also claims that free variation is short-lived.

Free variation becomes evident only when a *form-function analysis* is undertaken. In this kind of analysis, a specific form is chosen for study. All instances of this form are then identified in the data and the different meanings which it realizes described. Free variation is held to occur when it can be shown that two or more forms are used randomly to perform the same set of functions. This kind of analysis is important in SLA research because it provides a means of showing what Tarone (1988: 11) refers to as 'internal variation' (i.e. variation in the learner's L2 system that is independent of the target language). In this respect it contrasts with error analysis and performance analysis, which describe learner language in relation to how it differs from the target language and, therefore, can only show 'external variation'.

The dynamic paradigm offers the SLA researcher some powerful theoretical constructs (for example, the notion of environmental weight, of distinct lects, and of code-switching), together with some useful tools for investigating L2 variability (such as implicational scaling and form-function analysis). However, it is not without its problems. It is not clear, for instance, to what extent it is possible to identify distinct varieties in learner language as Bickerton was able to do for Guyanese Creole. L2 acquisition involves even more rapid change than creolization, with the result that the stages of development are not sharply defined. The idea of a polylectal grammar, while attractive, may not be applicable to L2 acquisition. Also, as Preston (1989) notes, Bickerton's dismissal of variable rules may not be warranted, given that at least some creole speakers manifest a variable grammar—a point that may be even more relevant in the case of L2 learners.

The dynamic paradigm has influenced a number of SLA researchers. Gatbonton's (1978) *gradual diffusion model* owes much to Bailey's work. Huebner (1979; 1983) and Tarone in her later work (for example, Tarone 1985) have found form-function analysis revealing.

Social psychological models

Social psychological models seek to relate the language attitudes of speakers to their actual language use. In other words, they attempt to explain variation in language use by reference to the speakers' views about the social, institutional, and ethnic status of their own in-group, and also that of out-groups with whom they come into contact. A number of social psychological models have been used in SLA research (see Gardner 1985 and Beebe 1988b). However, one model in particular has been used as a basis for examining L2 variability—Giles' *Speech Accommodation Theory*—and so we will focus on this, reserving a more thorough consideration of social psychological accounts of L2 acquisition for Chapter 6, when we look in detail at the role played by social factors.

Speech accommodation theory identifies three principal types of variation, according to the nature of the adjustments which speakers make to their speech during interaction. Convergence occurs when speakers adjust their normal speech to make it more similar to their interlocutor's speech or to a stereotype of it (i.e. the speaker converges towards some prestige norm that they believe their interlocutor values). Divergence occurs when the opposite takes place—speakers seek to make their speech dissimilar from that of their addressee. Speech maintenance occurs when speakers do not make any changes. However, Giles views this as a failure to converge (the expected type of behaviour) and therefore considers it a subtype of divergence. Both convergence and divergence can take place upwards or downwards. Upward convergence takes place when speakers adjust their speech in the direction of the speech norms of persons of higher social status. It is the most common type because it is based on the universal human desire for approval. Downward convergence involves adjustments in the direction of the speech norms of persons of lower social status. Downward divergence involves speakers emphasizing the non-standard features in their repertoire, while upward divergence involves emphasizing the standard features.

Accommodation can take place at any level of language use—in the choice of language used in a bilingual situation, or in terms of volume, speed, pronunciation, choice of vocabulary, and grammatical structures, and also in discourse features such as length of turn and choice of topic in monolingual situations.

An example (based on Giles 1971) will make this clear. Let us imagine that a shop assistant who normally speaks standard English is communicating with a customer who speaks a non-standard variety. If the shop assistant adopts some of the non-prestige forms used by the customer, downward convergence takes place. If the customer adopts some of the prestige forms of the shop assistant, upward convergence takes place. This is what we might normally expect to happen. But let us now imagine that the customer is trying to return some article she bought yesterday and the shop assistant is refusing to refund her the money it cost. The shop assistant may gradually diverge upwards by emphasizing the standardness of her language, while the customer may diverge downwards by resorting to the 'vernacular' forms of her dialect.

Giles and his associates have carried out a number of studies to test the claims of speech accommodation theory. A good example is Thakerar, Giles, and Cheshire (1982). They studied conversations between British nurses of unequal ranks and found that higher-status nurses tended to decrease their speech rate and become less standard in their speech (for example, they used the glottal stop /ʔ/ in place of /t/ more frequently), while the lower status nurses increased their speech rate and used a higher proportion of standard forms. The researchers argued that this study indicated that the nurses were converging towards a stereotype of their interlocutors' speech.

Speech accommodation is motivated by the attitudes that speakers hold towards their audience. The variation occurs on a moment-by-moment basis during an interaction. It constitutes a kind of style-shifting that is audience-designed. According to Bell (1984), speakers respond to three aspects of their addressees in deciding what adjustments to make: (1) their personal characteristics, (2) the general style of their speech, and (3) their use of specific linguistic features. Bell also suggests that the pressures on speakers to accommodate increase when speakers address large audiences and take part in service encounters (for example, interactions in shops and restaurants).

One of the strengths of speech accommodation theory is that it recognizes the central importance of the addressee in accounting for variation. It can also account for the shifting patterns of variation which occur within a single interaction—more easily, perhaps, than is possible in the Labovian or dynamic paradigms. Speakers can switch from convergence to divergence as they reassess their addressee during the course of an interaction. One disadvantage of the model, claimed by Bell (1984), is that it rests on the concept of 'response matching', and therefore provides only a responsive dimension. Bell argues that stylistic variation also needs to take into consideration an initiative dimension (i.e. where stylistic choice is used dynamically to redefine an existing situation). Finally, speech accommodation theory cannot account for all patterned variability. Beebe (1982: 22) recognizes that there is also 'extravergence' (i.e. 'variation which cannot or should not be described as converging towards or diverging from an interlocutor') and lists several kinds including the interlanguage variation that results from learning, communication or performance strategies, and systematic variation according to the linguistic environment.

Speech accommodation theory has been used in SLA research by Beebe (1981), Beebe and Zuengler (1983), and Zuengler (1989) among others.

Sociolinguistic models: some final comments

The sociolinguistic models belonging to the Labovian, dynamic, and social psychological paradigms, which have been discussed in this section, offer the L2 acquisition researcher a number of tools for investigating learner language. Each paradigm has contributed in different ways. The Labovian paradigm has provided an excellent means for examining stylistic variation in learner language. The dynamic paradigm has served as a basis for exploring how the learner's interlanguage develops in terms of shifting form-function relationships. Speech accommodation theory has contributed to the study of how learners vary in the way they use their L2 repertoire according to addressee factors operating in a particular interactional context.

There is, however, one important caveat regarding the use of sociolinguistic models in the study of L2 acquisition, in particular the Labovian and dynamic paradigms. Sociolinguists like Labov, Bailey, and Bickerton are concerned with variability in the speech of social groups. Labov, for instance, sees the regular patterns of variability that he found in the speech of New Yorkers or BEV as part of their 'langue'. This concept, which comes from the work of de Saussure, is a social one. It recognizes that the values that comprise a particular language may not be reflected exactly in the speech of an individual speaker. Bickerton (1975) also sees variability as a group phenomenon, arguing that most of the individual Guyanese Creole speakers he studied had relatively non-variable systems. As Preston (1989) has pointed out, such a view of language does not fit easily with the goal of SLA research, which is to describe and explain the acquisition of L2s by *individual* learners. Nor is it clear whether the notion of 'social group' is applicable to many language learners. For example, it does not seem appropriate to suggest that the L2 learners in a classroom in Spain or Japan make up a social group in the same way as street gangs in New York City do. Thus, while it may be possible to transfer the techniques used by sociolinguists such as Labov and Bickerton to the study of individual learners, there are obvious problems regarding the applicability of the 'social' explanations that sociolinguists have provided.

Psycholinguistic models

Whereas the models discussed above come from the fields of sociolinguistics and social psychology, the ones we will consider in this section are psycholinguistic in nature. They concern the way in which speech is planned and monitored by speakers.

Planning models

The concept of planning has been widely used in models of language production. As Crookes (1991: 115) points out, most models subdivide planning into macro- and micro-planning. The former 'concerns the long range semantic and syntactic organization of a sizeable chunk of speech', whereas the latter 'is concerned with purely local functions, like marking clause boundaries and selecting words' (Butterworth 1980b: 159, cited in Crookes 1991).

If, as de Bot argues, 'many aspects of speaking are the same for monolingual and bilingual speakers' (1992: 2), it should be possible to make use of a general model of speech production, such as that proposed by Levelt (1989)—the model de Bot favours. Such a model suggests a number of possible psycholinguistic sources of variability, in accordance with different stages of speech production:

1 In the 'conceptualizer', where decisions are taken regarding which variety of language to use, in accordance with situational factors, and also which specific communicative intentions are to be realized in the spoken message.

2 In the 'formulator', where the 'pre-verbal message' provided by the conceptualizer is converted into a speech plan by selecting the appropriate words from the lexicon and by applying grammatical and phonological rules.

3 In the 'articulator', which converts the speech plan into actual speech.

4 In the 'speech comprehension system', which provides the speaker with feedback regarding the presence of possible mistakes in the phonetic plan or in overt speech and which also enables the speaker to make adjustments in the 'conceptualizer'.

De Bot emphasizes that in the Levelt model 'the different components are at work simultaneously' (1992: 6) and 'that various parts of the same sentence will be at different processing stages'.

L2 variability research has focused somewhat narrowly on the effect of 'planning time' on this production process, influenced no doubt by the fact that, whereas L1 production is largely automatic, L2 production is often not, so that the amount of time a learner has to plan the different processing stages is likely to affect output. Ochs (1979), again discussing production in the L1, distinguishes *planned* and *unplanned* discourse. The former is 'discourse that lacks forethought and organizational preparation', while the latter is 'discourse that has been thought out and organized prior to its expression' (1979: 55). The distinction constitutes a continuum, and Ochs emphasizes that most of the discourse encountered in day-to-day communication falls at neither end but somewhere in the middle. Ochs also notes that some types of discourse are more plannable than others. Thus conversations are usually not planned ahead, but more ritualistic speech events (such as sermons) are.

There are linguistic differences in the two types of discourse. In unplanned discourse, Ochs found that speakers rely more on the immediate context to help them convey their message, make use of syntactic structures that tend to emerge early during acquisition (for example, demonstrative modifiers, active voice and present rather than past tenses) and make extensive use of repetition and word replacement. Danielewicz (1984) found that there were clear differences in the unplanned spoken language taken from dinner table conversations and the planned spoken language produced by the same speakers in lectures. The differences were both global in nature (for example, the way evidence was used to construct an argument) and specific (for example, in the complexity of clause and sentence construction and the use of attributive adjectives and participles). Danielewicz's study is important because it shows that the distinction between planned and unplanned discourse is independent of that between speech and writing.

Monitoring

Speakers may *monitor* their output (i.e. pay conscious attention to specific elements of the utterance in order to correct or improve them). Morrison and

Low (1983) make use of a similar production model to that of Levelt to distinguish post-articulatory monitoring, which operates on overt speech, and pre-articulatory monitoring, which occurs prior to the implementation of the phonetic plan. Levelt (1983), cited in Crookes (1991: 116), similarly distinguishes a 'production theory of monitoring', according to which learners respond to 'alarm signals' during the course of implementing a plan and make appropriate adjustments, and a 'perceptual theory of monitoring', according to which users compare the final result of the production process with their original intention. Macro- and micro-monitoring can also be distinguished. The former involves adjustments to the communicative goal of discourse and sentence plans. The latter takes place as the speaker/writer begins the process of filling out constituent plans with linguistic forms and involves the substitution of one selected form with another, preferred form. Micro-monitoring can be carried out on lexis, syntax, morphology, and the phonetic realization of the utterance.

Psycholinguistic models: a final comment

The conditions under which speech has to be produced will vary, and lead to differences in the actual language that is used. A speech production model such as Levelt's enables us to recognize that whereas some variability is socially motivated (for example, in message generation in the 'conceptualizer'), some (such as the construction of a phonetic plan in the 'formulator') is not. Instead, it reflects the tension between the amount of effort needed to access words from the lexicon, execute a grammatical encoding, and then assign a phonological coding, and the availability of planning time. Some items in the lexicon are likely to be more readily accessible than others. Production involves a constant trade-off of the competing demands on memory and control mechanisms. The result will be systematic differences in language use in accordance with opportunities available for planning.

Like sociolinguistic and social psychological models, psycholinguistic models of L2 variability have their limitations. The psycholinguistic aspects of language production that figure in L2 variability research draw heavily on the notion of 'attention'—with regard to both what is attended to, and the extent to which the attention is conscious or not. In this respect, they do not differ from the Labovian paradigm, which, as we saw, treats attention as the psycholinguistic mechanism through which social and stylistic factors affect performance, and are subject to the same criticisms as this construct. Also, the concepts of planning time and monitoring cannot easily account for the kind of within-conversation shifting identified in speech accommodation models and, in particular, for the influence the addressee exerts on performance. Clearly, the study of L2 variability requires both a sociolinguistic and a psycholinguistic perspective.

The effects of planning time on L2 use have been investigated by myself (Ellis 1987b) and Crookes (1989). Monitoring plays a key role in Krashen's Monitor Model (see Krashen 1981) and in a study by Hulstijn and Hulstijn (1984).

Type of model	Main constructs	Methods	Key SLA studies
Sociolinguistic: Labovian paradigm	Inter- and intra-learner variation; style shifting occurs as a result of varying attention to speech.	Tasks designed to elicit varying attention to speech; variable rules; VARBRUL statistical models.	Dickerson 1975; Beebe 1980; Tarone 1985; Young 1988
Dynamic paradigm	Language change as a source of variability; environmental weight; lectal variation; code-switching; grammar-internal variation; free variation.	Implicational scaling; form-function analysis.	Huebner 1983 and 1985; Ellis 1985c
Social psychological paradigm	Speech shifts involving convergence and divergence; importance of addressee and of speaker's attitudes to addressee's social group.	Experimental investigation of factors that induce convergence and divergence.	Beebe 1981; Beebe and Zuengler 1983
Psycholinguistic: Speech planning models	Planned and unplanned discourse; demands of short term memory.	Experimental manipulation of discourse planning conditions.	Ellis 1987b; Crookes 1989
Speech monitoring models	Macro- and micro-monitoring; pre- and post articulation monitoring; production-based and perception-based monitoring.	Experimental manipulation of conditions that affect monitoring.	Hulstijn and Hulstijn 1984

Table 4.2:   Summary of different types of models used to explain variability in language production

A typology of variability in learner language

This section draws on many of the constructs that have already been introduced (and which are summarized in Table 4.2) to present a typology of the different kinds of formal variation that can be found in the use of natural languages—including learner language. The outline of the typology is shown in Figure 4.1. The typology addresses variation in choice of linguistic form. It excludes functional variation (i.e. variation in the choice of language function), which is considered in the next chapter.

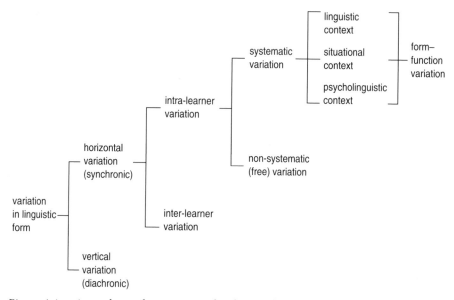

Figure 4.1:   A typology of variation in the choice of linguistic form found in learner language

A basic distinction is made between *horizontal* and *vertical* variation. Horizontal variation refers to the variation evident in learner language at any single time, while vertical variation refers to variation over time and is, therefore, coterminous with 'order/sequence of development'. There is some evidence to suggest that horizontal variation mirrors vertical variation for, as Widdowson puts it, 'change is only the temporal consequence of current variation' (1979a: 195), a view that accords with the role of change in the dynamic paradigm.

   Horizontal variation can be further subdivided into inter- and intra-learner variation. Inter-learner variability reflects individual learner factors such as motivation and personality, but it also arises as a result of social factors such as social class and ethnic grouping, as the Labovian paradigm has demonstrated. As these same social factors are also involved in intra-learner variation, there is clearly an interaction between individual learner factors such as sex and social class and the situational factors involved in style-shifting; as we noted earlier, the markers involved in stylistic variation also function as social indicators. In this chapter the focus is on intra-learner variation; Chapters 6 and 8 examine the social and psychological sources of inter-learner variation.

Intra-learner variation can be both systematic and non-systematic (alternatively called free variation). This distinction is, however, somewhat controversial, as many sociolinguists consider that free variation does not exist or that it occurs for only a very short period of time and is of minor interest.[4] Gatbonton (1978) and I (Ellis 1985c; 1989c) have, however, argued that free variation constitutes an important mechanism of development.

Systematic variability arises as a result of external factors to do with the linguistic context, the situational context, and the psycholinguistic context. The linguistic context concerns the elements that precede and follow the variable structure in question. The situational context covers a whole host of factors. Brown and Fraser (1979) classify 'situation' into 'scene' and 'participants'. Scene involves 'setting' and 'purpose', which can in turn be further subdivided. Participants can be considered in terms of their individual or social characteristics and in terms of the relationships that exist between them. Preston (1989) also offers a detailed breakdown of situational factors (for example, time, topic, purpose, and tone). It is probably true to say that to date SLA research has examined only a few of these situational factors. The psycholinguistic context refers to the extent to which the type of language use affords time for planning and encourages or discourages monitoring.

Form–function variation is also systematic and is contextually induced. All three types of context—linguistic, situational, and psycholinguistic—may influence which forms learners employ to perform specific language functions. Form–function variation is identified by means of a form-function analysis. Learners construct networks of form-function relationships, and the description of these networks provides clues about the nature of the learner's internal system.

Finally, we can also talk of *task-induced variation.* This is best considered as a blanket term to cover the variability evident when learners perform different tasks, and is ultimately traceable to one of the other sources (the linguistic, situational, or psycholinguistic context). We include it here because in some studies no attempt has been made to identify the specific sources of variability induced by different tasks.

Young (1989) suggests that the description of variability in learner language involves two processes. The first is to describe how changes in one sociolinguistic variable influence variation in form. The second is to evaluate the relative impact on variation of different sociolinguistic variables. However, as Young points out, relatively few studies have addressed the second question, so we will be concerned primarily with the first question.

The review of the research that now follows begins by looking at free variation. This leads into a discussion of form-function variation. A detailed examination of systematic variation in relation to context follows. This starts with an account of studies which have reported general task-induced differences in learner output, and then moves on to examine form-function relationships and the effects of specific contextual variables on learner output. Finally, a multi-factor approach is outlined.

Free variation in learner language

In Ellis 1985c, I reasoned that free variation can be considered to occur when two or more forms occur randomly in (1) the same situational context, (2) the same linguistic context, (3) the same discourse context, (4) perform the same language function, and (5) are performed in tasks with the same processing constraints. In other words, in order to claim that forms are in free variation, it is necessary to demonstrate that there is no feature of the linguistic, situational, or psycholinguistic context that exerts any probabilistic pull on the use of one form in preference to another.

As an example, I referred to data from my study of three classroom learners. One of the learners, 'J'—a 10-year-old Portuguese boy—produced the following two utterances in close proximity to each other during a game of word bingo:

> No look my card.
> Don't look my card.

I noted that the 'don't' negative was the single instance out of 18 spontaneous negative utterances produced during the first month of the study and was used in an identical way to the predominant 'no' + V form of this period. A further example from the same data can be found in one of the other learners' use of copula 'be'. 'R'—a 10-year-old Punjabi-speaking boy—used the zero and contracted copula in successive utterances, produced while pointing at a map:

> There church.
> There's church.

I was able to detect regularities in the overall use of copula according to linguistic context (see the section on page 143 in this chapter), but specific instances of apparent free variation such as the one above were conspicuous in the data.

A number of longitudinal studies testify to apparent free variation in the use of two or more forms in learner language. Cancino, Rosansky, and Schumann (1978) found that their subjects made use of a variety of forms to express negation at each stage of their development. Jorge (one of the five learners they investigated), for instance, used two forms initially ('no' + V and 'don't' + V). From the second month of the study, Jorge began to use four forms (the previous two plus an auxiliary negative and analysed 'don't'), and continued to do so for the remaining eight months of the study. Cancino et al. were unable to write 'rules' to account for the use of the different forms, suggesting that they were in free variation.

Another possible area in which free variation appears to occur is in the use of English simple and progressive verb forms in early learner language. Wagner-Gough (1975), in a longitudinal study of Homer, a Persian boy, reports that he used both verb forms for an identical range of functions over an extended period of time. Eisenstein, Bailey, and Madden (1982) also found that their beginner learners used the two verb forms indiscriminately, while their more advanced learners used them more systematically. Vogel and Bahns (1989) report on the general pattern of acquisition of the two verb forms, based on data collected by Wode in his longitudinal study of the naturalistic acquisition of English by five German children (see Wode 1981). They also found evidence of free variation. One verb after another appeared in its inflected (*-ing*) form and its simple form before the learners distinguished the use of the two forms functionally.

Free variation can also occur in learners' use of pronoun forms. Nicholas (1986) found that his subject, Cindy—a 3-year-old learner of L2 German—rapidly acquired three first person pronoun forms (ich, mich, and mir) but used them variably to perform the same functions. Nicholas claims that Cindy set about diversifying her L2 system by incorporating as many features into it as possible. She recognized that the same function could be expressed by a range of related forms and this motivated her to explore the potential of variation.

A general finding of these studies is that free variation occurs during an early stage of development and then disappears as learners develop better organized L2 systems, a view of acquisition first put forward by Gatbonton (1978).[5] According to her gradual diffusion model, there are two broad stages of L2 development: an 'acquisition phase' and a 'replacement phase'. In the former, the learner first uses one form in a variety of situations and contexts, and then introduces another form which is used in free variation with the first in all contexts. In the replacement phase, each form is restricted to its own contexts through the gradual elimination of the other in first one context and then another. Gatbonton developed this model to account for the patterns of variation which she found in the production of three phonological features (/θ/, /ð/, and /h/) in the speech of 27 French-Canadian learners of English elicited by means of reading-aloud and spontaneous-speaking tasks. In Ellis 1985c, I extended Gatbonton's model to account for the elimination of free variation as learners come to use each form to perform specific functions.

It is important to recognize that this account of free variation refers to the early stage of acquisition, when a feature first appears in a learner's language. It can be tested effectively only by longitudinal studies that provide information about what learners do when they first acquire a new feature. It is not possible to argue, as has Young (1993: 86), that the apparent absence of free variation in data collected cross-sectionally from learners designated 'low level' on a general proficiency test constitutes evidence against free variation, as such data does not show us how learners handle the acquisition of specific linguistic features from one time to the next. It is crucial to do this to test my claims about free variation.

Nevertheless, care needs to be exercised in making claims about free variation. As Tarone (1988: 113) and Preston (1989) have pointed out, it is always possible that what appears to be free variation is, in fact, systematic and that the researcher has simply failed to uncover the factors that make it systematic. In the last analysis, it is not possible to know all the factors (in particular the psychological ones) that influence language use. Also, even if it does exist it may not be of much significance for understanding how learners develop their L2 competence. Whereas Gatbonton and I see free variation as an important step in the acquisition process, Schachter (1986a) considers it of little interest on the grounds that it occurs before the onset of the productive use of a new feature. She comments: 'Those isolated occurrences of a structure prior to onset remind me of the puts-puts of a motor just before it catches on with a roar.' For her, acquisition begins 'where the structure/form occurs across different lexical items with some (unquantified) regularity' (1986a: 127).

Systematic variation

We begin by considering task-induced variability and form-function variability. In both cases, the variability is context-induced. A particular task creates specific contexts of use which influence the forms a learner chooses to use. Similarly, the choice of a particular form to realize a particular function is influenced by linguistic, situational, and even psychological contexts. However, the research which we will consider first has not sought to identify the effect of specific contextual factors on L2 use and, therefore, is best considered apart from that which has. The bulk of this section, however, will consider research that has examined the effect of these specific factors.

Task-induced variation

A number of studies have made use of two or more instruments to collect data. These studies testify to the general effect that context has on learner output but they do not tell us anything about the specific causes of variability. Tarone (1988: 61) provides a comprehensive list of such studies, compiled to refute the claim by Swan (1987) that variation in learner language was less common than she (and others) have claimed.

Two such studies have been mentioned in previous chapters. Larsen-Freeman (1976b) used five different tasks—speaking, listening, reading, writing, and elicited imitation—in her study of grammatical morphemes. She found different accuracy orders, in particular between those tasks involving speaking of some kind and the reading/writing tasks (see Chapter 3, page 91). Lococo's (1976) error analysis study also found that the number of errors made by adult elementary learners of L2 Spanish varied according to task. For example, preposition errors were more common and adjective and determiner errors less common in the translation task than in the free composition and picture description tasks. Lococo suggested that the learners' perception of the task might be one factor influencing the results. Thus, the learners might have focused on accuracy in the translation task and on expressing ideas clearly in the picture description task.

The results of several studies lend support to the claim that differences in learner language will occur according to whether the task requires something approximating to normal communicative language use, as, for example, in a recorded conversation, or less conventional language behaviour, as, for example, that elicited by a grammaticality judgement task. Schmidt (1980) investigated second-verb ellipsis in sentences like 'Mary is eating an apple and Sue a pear', and found that learners from a variety of language backgrounds always included the second verb in free oral production, but increasingly omitted it in proportion to the degree of monitoring that different tasks (imitation, written sentence-combining, and grammaticality judgements) were hypothesized to permit. Bahns and Wode (1980) reported differences in two German children's use of English negative constructions in naturally occurring speech and structured interviews (which involved translation). They found evidence of clear form-function distributions for 'don't' and 'didn't' in the spontaneous data but not in the elicited data. Finally, Hyltenstam (1984) investigated pronoun copies in relative clauses and negatives in the L2 Swedish of learners from different language backgrounds (see Chapter 3 for an account of pronoun copies). Hyltenstam found that some tasks (for example, written composition) failed to elicit the use of these structures, other tasks (for example, written grammaticality judgements) produced data that 'lacked patterning', while yet other tasks (for example, an oral picture description task) produced patterned data that showed a definite acquisition sequence. Hyltenstam speculated that different tasks resulted in both quantitative differences (i.e. more or less target-like behaviour) and qualitative differences (i.e. different, even contradicting rules).

Task-induced variability of the kind reported in these studies makes it difficult to decide whether a learner can be said to 'know' or 'not know' a particular linguistic form. It raises the whole question of what is meant by 'knowledge' of an L2—a question we will address in the concluding section of this chapter. It also makes it difficult to plot developmental patterns. Some researchers interested in linguistic universals have preferred to work with data derived from a single task, often a grammaticality judgement task, to avoid these problems. Chaudron (1983a), in a review of this kind of task, has argued that the data it elicits mirror those obtained from natural language use. However, the studies considered above, and others reviewed below, suggest that this claim is not justified. Substantial differences arise depending on whether the task permits or encourages the use of metalingual knowledge, or whether it taps 'communicative' behaviour. It is precisely this kind of variation which researchers such as Tarone have set out to explore and to account for.

Form–function relationships in learner language

Tarone (1988) suggests that the study of the way learners use particular forms to express particular functions is relevant to the study of interlanguage variation because 'it provides a method of analysis which can reveal the linguistic system hidden in a learner's apparently unsystematic use' (1988: 54). A good example of this can be found in the study by Schachter (1986a), already briefly referred to.

Schachter set out to re-examine the data for one of Cancino, Rosansky, and Schuman's learners (Jorge) in order to establish whether his use of negative forms was as random as the original authors suggested. She argued that the variability was not explicable in terms of different situation requirements, as the data collection took place on a regular basis with the same situational constraints throughout. However, Schachter was able to find evidence of 'a rich system, complex from the very beginning, which became even more so as time progressed' (1986a: 123–4). The main basis for this claim was a form-functional analysis. Schachter identified seven functions performed by Jorge's productive negative utterances and found surprising regularity in his pairing of forms and functions. For example, the formula 'I don't know' was always used to perform the same function of 'no information' (i.e. to indicate that the speaker is not in a position to confirm or deny whether something is the case), while 'no + V' with one exception carried the 'denial' function (i.e. to assert that an actual, supposed, or proposed state of affairs does not hold for the speaker). Only 'no' by itself was functionally ubiquitous. Schachter's study is important because it shows how essential it is to investigate form-function relationships in learner language in order to understand the kind of internal systems that learners build.

Even more powerful evidence of systematicity in the way a learner uses language to realize different functions is to be found in Huebner's (1979; 1983) longitudinal study of Ge, a Hmong learner of English. Huebner was able to show that although Ge did not use forms to perform the same set of functions that they performed in the target language, he did nevertheless establish systematic form–function relationships. Huebner began by identifying a number of linguistic forms for analysis, one of which was Ge's use of articles ('da' and zero article). He analysed these in terms of two binary categories of semantic function:

+/– information assumed to be known by the hearer (HK)
+/– specific referent (SR)

which, when combined, yield four categories of noun phrases, as shown in Table 4.3.

Type	Standard English forms	Examples
1 – SR/+ HK	'the', 'a', or zero	Lions are beautiful.
2 + SR/+ HK	'the'	Ask the man over there.
3 + SR/– HK	'a' or zero	She gave me a present.
4 – SR/– HK	'a' or zero	He's a nice man.

Table 4.3:   Noun phrase types

Initially, Ge used 'da' mainly for (2), unless the noun phrase in question functioned as a topic of the sentence, in which case he used zero article. Later he used 'da' for all four types of noun phrase. Later still, he dropped 'da' for type (4) and finally for type (3). In a subsequent paper, Huebner (1985) also shows how Ge introduced 'a' with type (3) noun phrases. Huebner's main point is that what appears to be random use of articles in an obligatory occasion analysis, turns out to be highly systematic in a form–function analysis.

The same functional analysis of the use of articles was also employed in another study (Tarone and Parrish 1988). They reanalysed data which Tarone (1985) had collected using three different tasks: (1) a grammaticality judgement test, (2) an oral interview, and (3) an oral narration task. Tarone and Parrish re-examined the data from the two oral tasks. The accuracy level of the (ten Japanese and ten Arabic-speaking) learners' use of articles varied according to task. Tarone and Parrish were able to show that the different tasks elicited different types of noun phrases to a different extent, and that this went a long way to explaining the overall pattern of task variation. For example, both accuracy and use of Type 2 articles was greater on the narrative than on the interview task. It was this combination that accounted for the overall difference in performance on the two tasks. The point here is that the different tasks favoured the use of different noun phrase types because they required the performance of different functions involving articles. Again, this study demonstrates that the communicative function of particular forms must be taken into account if we are to understand the underlying systematicity of learner language.

There have been several other studies that have investigated form-function relationships in learner language. Pfaff (1987a) studied oral narratives produced by seventh grade Turkish learners of L2 German and found clear evidence of form–function mapping. For example, the learners referred to protagonists in their narratives using pronouns, but used article + noun to refer to other participants. Several studies (for example, Godfrey 1980; Veronique 1987) show that learners vary their use of syntactic devices according to whether information is foregrounded or backgrounded. Williams (1989) found that standard English speakers, speakers of Singaporean English, and L2 learners from a variety of language backgrounds used subject pronouns in very similar ways. They were likely to drop them if the identity of the subject was clear from the ongoing discourse and to use them when it was not. The general conclusion to be drawn from these studies is that learners will express what is important to them, sometimes realizing a function linguistically and sometimes leaving it to be inferred with the help of various non-linguistic clues.

The following are the main conclusions that can be drawn from the research to date:

1 A form–function analysis can identify systematic patterns of variability where a target-based analysis has failed.
2 Learners construct form–function systems in the process of learning and using an L2. These systems are likely to differ from the form–function systems found in the target language.
3 The learner's form–function systems evolve over time. Thus at any stage of development different form–function systems are likely to be observed.
4 Learners will seek to use their linguistic resources to perform those functions that are communicatively important for accomplishing specific tasks.

Form–function analyses of learner language are very promising because they seem to afford a window through which to view how learners construct their L2 systems. One problem, as Tarone (1988) has observed, is that the term 'function' has been interpreted very loosely. It includes 'pragmatic function' (for example, requests and denials), 'discourse function' (for example, topic and cohesion), 'semantic function' (for example, specific and non-specific information), and even 'grammatical function' (for example, subject and object). Clearly these are very different aspects of language. Ultimately, it will be necessary to show how learners use the forms they have acquired to perform all these functions, and also how the different kinds of function interact in determining linguistic choice—a potentially huge undertaking.

Context-induced variation

The studies of task-induced variability and of form–function relationships discussed in the previous section demonstrate that much of the variability in learner language is systematic. Learners make use of their L2 resources in accordance with context. We now turn to research which has examined the effects of different aspects of context: linguistic, sociolinguistic, and psycholinguistic.

The effects of linguistic context

Irrespective of the kinds of data used to study learner language, variability induced by the linguistic context occurs. This kind of variability, therefore, does not appear to be strongly task-induced. The effects of the linguistic environment are evident at the phonological, morphological, and syntactic levels of language.

One of the earliest studies to investigate the effects of linguistic context on learners' production was Dickerson's (1975) study of ten Japanese learners' production of English /z/. Dickerson examined four different phonological environments and found that in a dialogue reading task, the learners used the correct target-language form whenever /z/ was followed by a vowel, but were progressively less accurate in the other environments (+ consonants such as /m/ and /b/, + silence, and + consonants such as /θ/ and /t/). Dickerson collected data at three different points in time and found that the same pattern occurred at each. Although the learners improved in their ability to use target-language /z/ in the more difficult contexts over time, the environmental effects observed at time 1 were also evident at time 3.

The form of a word can affect the learners' use of specific grammatical features. Thus, Wolfram (1989) reports that Vietnamese learners of L2 English in the United States were more likely to manifest past tense marking on suppletive forms (for example, 'go/went') than on replacive forms (for example, 'make/made'). Wolfram suggests that this may reflect a 'principle of perceptual saliency', according to which the more distant the past tense form is phonetically from the present tense form, the more likely it is to be more marked for past tense. Whereas Wolfram's study demonstrates an effect for the phonetic form of a word, Saunders' (1987) study indicates that the grammatical form is also influential. He studied Japanese learners' production of the -s morpheme in consonant clusters (-ps, -ts, and -ks) in nouns and verbs. He found that they were more likely to omit or shorten the -s in verbs than in nouns. Saunders suggests that this may be due to the 'amount of information contained in the morpheme; the third person singular is almost always redundant while the plural usually gives some information not available in the rest of the sentence' (1987: 261).

Saunders' explanation accords with what Young (1993) has referred to as the functional hypothesis. This predicts that 'the grammar of a language will contain a constraint which prevents the deletion of elements when their absence would result in loss of semantic information' (page 78). Thus, a feature like plural -s can be expected to be deleted in contexts where plurality is marked by some other means (such as a quantifier such as 'many'), but utilized when there is no such marker. Young's review of studies that have examined this hypothesis shows very mixed results, while his own study of plural marking in Chinese and Czech/Slovak learners of English, however, produced little support for the hypothesis.

Another issue of considerable interest is the relationship between linguistic context and acquisition over time. One possibility is that learners begin with a single feature which they use in all environments (i.e. initially learners display categorical use of a language form), then manifest free variation as they acquire new variants for the form before progressing to a stage when they distribute the variants systematically according to context. Dickerson's study, however, found no support for this. Systematic variation was evident at time 1 in her study, although it should be noted that her subjects were not complete beginners. However, Gatbonton's (1978) study of English /θ/, /ð/, and /h/ in the speech of 27 French-Canadians does support a diffusion model (see the discussion on page 137). Gatbonton obtained independent measures of the subjects' proficiency and found that in the least proficient (those in the 'acquisition stage') a single variant or free variation was evident, whereas in the more proficient (those in the 'replacement phase') systematic variation in accordance with linguistic context occurred. However, as Tarone (1988) points out, Gatbonton's study is cross-sectional in design and thus does not constitute totally convincing evidence for acquisition as a process of gradual diffusion.

Unfortunately, there have been few longitudinal studies that have investigated the influence of the linguistic environment. In Ellis 1988a, I investigated the effects of linguistic context on two morphological features (3rd person -*s* and copula -*s*) in the English speech of three classroom learners (one Portuguese and two Punjabi-speaking) over a two year period. For purposes of space, only results for copula -*s* (which is a variable form in native speaker use) will be considered here. The main findings were:

1 Three variants of copula -*s* were identified (zero, full, and contracted).
2 These variants emerged in the same order for all three learners. The learners first used the zero form, then the full form, and finally the contracted copula.
3 The target-language variants (full and contracted copula) were used more consistently when the preceding subject was a pronoun than when the preceding subject was a noun. Conversely, the non-target-language variant (zero copula) occurred more frequently when the subject was a noun.
4 Some pronoun environments also favoured the use of the target-language variants more than others.
5 The acquisition of the target-language variants took place initially in 'easy' environments (i.e. those involving a closed class of items), and then appeared to spread to more 'difficult' environments (i.e. those involving an open class).
6 None of the learners achieved the pattern of variability for copula use which has been reported for native-speaker speech (i.e. they did not acquire the target-language variable rule).

This study, therefore, suggests that the acquisition of target-language forms may be closely linked to their use in specific linguistic environments. It provides some support for the diffusion model.

Finally, linguistic context affects the choice of syntactical features. Hyltenstam (1977) showed that two environmental factors had an effect on where learners of L2 Swedish placed the negator; whether the negative clause was a main or subordinate clause and whether the finite verb was an auxiliary or a lexical verb. Using implicational scaling he showed that the learners went through several stages of development, mastering the placement of the negative in first one environment and then another. This study, then, also indicates that the acquisition of syntactic forms proceeds from one context to another.

There have been several other studies that have investigated linguistic context (for example, Carlisle 1991; Bailey 1989; Veronique 1987), providing fairly conclusive evidence that it plays a major role in determining the process by which phonological, morphological, and syntactic features are acquired. A number of issues remain unclear, however. First, it is still not certain what the learner's starting point is. Is it categorical use of a single form followed by free variation, as Gatbonton and I propose? Or do learners begin with the systematic use of two or more variants in accordance with linguistic context, a view Dickerson and Tarone favour? Second, there is some controversy as to whether patterns of variability can best be explained in terms of form-function relationships or in terms of linguistic context. For example, Kumpf (1984) suggests that the variable use of past tense forms is governed by whether the information is foregrounded or backgrounded, whereas Wolfram (1985) claims that the main factor is linguistic context. The position that has been adopted in this chapter is that both factors exert an influence and, in fact, may not easily be separated. Ideally, information regarding how the two factors interact is desirable, but this is not yet available. Thirdly, it is not clear to what extent the idea of systematic 'diffusion' is applicable to all learners. Meisel, Clahsen, and Pienemann argue that 'learners differ greatly with respect to which context is most suitable for the application of a new rule' (1981: 126). But several studies (such as Carlisle's study of epenthesis in initial consonant clusters) have been able to show that at least some of the effects of linguistic context hold good across learners.

The effects of situational context

The basis for many of the studies considered in this section was Labov's notion of style shifting. Tarone (1982) suggests that L2 learners possess a continuum of styles, ranging from the *superordinate* (or *careful*) to the *vernacular*. The former reflects the kind of language found in formal situations that require careful language use, while the latter is evident in informal situations that permit more spontaneous language use. Each style has its own linguistic norms. Learners style shift between the two styles in accordance with the demands of the situation. Tarone argues that both the superordinate and vernacular norms constitute part of the learners' overall language competence or, as she later calls it, their *capability* (Tarone 1983). It follows that in order to investigate this it is necessary to collect data that reflect different sets of norms.

To study style shifting, Tarone adapts Labov's methodology. She accepts that the psycholinguistic mechanism responsible for style shifting is attention to speech and suggests that different styles can be elicited using tasks that require different degrees of attention to speech. Figure 4.2 demonstrates the relationships between task, attention, and style that Tarone recognizes. Thus, to examine learners' vernacular style it is necessary to collect 'unattended speech data', while to investigate their careful style, data from grammaticality judgement tasks can be used. Various other kinds of task elicit intermediate styles.

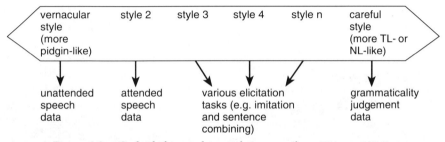

Figure 4.2:   Style shifting in learner language (from Tarone 1983)

A number of studies have used this methodological framework for investigating variability. For example, Dickerson (1975), in the study already referred to, used three different tasks to elicit data and found that the use of the target-language variant of /z/ was used least frequently in free speech, and most consistently when her subjects were reading word lists aloud; performance on a task that required learners to read dialogues aloud was intermediate. The learners increased their use of the target-language variant over time, but manifested the same order of accuracy in the three tasks on each occasion. Dickerson also found that her subjects were more likely use those non-target-language variants that were closest to the target-language variant in tasks that allowed them to attend more closely to their speech.

In early discussions of the stylistic continuum (for example, Dickerson 1974; Tarone 1979), it was assumed that the careful style had more correct, target-like variants than the vernacular style. However, learners do not always manifest the target-language variant in careful language use. Sometimes they transfer forms from their L1, particularly if these forms have prestige value in their speech community. Beebe (1980) found that her subjects (adult Thai learners of English) produced fewer instances of the target sound, /r/, in formal language use than in informal language use. This was because they used a prestige Thai variant of /r/, which they associated with formal language use in their own language. Beebe's study and similar studies by Schmidt (1977) and Major (1987) provide evidence of the complex nature of style shifting in learner language. They show that the careful style may not always be the most target-like. To accommodate this, Tarone (1983) revised her view of the careful style to allow for use of either a target-language or L1 variant. It is this view that is reflected in Figure 4.2. This raises the important, but apparently unanswered question, as to precisely when learners choose an L1 variant and a target-language variant as the norm for the superordinate style.

A later study by Tarone (1985) also testifies to the complexity of style shifting. She investigated three grammatical morphemes (third person -*s*, the article, plural -*s*) and one grammatical structure (direct object pronouns) using data collected from three tasks. In the case of third person -*s*, the results demonstrated the expected pattern of style shifting. That is, the learners were most accurate in the test and least accurate in the oral narrative. However, the pattern was reversed for the article and direct object pronouns—the learners were most accurate in the task that had been designed to require the least attention to form. Tarone attempted to explain these results by suggesting that the narrative task led the learners to attend to discourse cohesiveness to a greater extent than the other two tasks, the article and object pronouns serving as important markers of discourse cohesiveness. In other words, the functional demands of the task imposed unexpected demands on the learner's attention. It was this that led Tarone and Parrish (1988) to investigate form-function relations in the use of the article (see the discussion on page 141).

The non-occurrence of style shifting is demonstrated by Sato's (1985) study of a 12-year-old Vietnamese boy's acquisition of English. Sato collected data over a ten-month period using three different tasks (free conversation, oral reading of a continuous text, and elicited imitation of words and short phrases). She looked at target final consonants and consonant clusters. The accuracy rankings of the first of these on the three tasks changed from one time to the next. Greater consistency was evident for the second feature. Sato concluded that not all variables yield the same pattern of variation.

Sato's findings should not be considered inconsistent with those of Tarone or, indeed, Labov. Both Tarone and Labov have made it clear that not all linguistic features function as markers and, therefore, not all will style-shift. In the case of Labov's work, it is possible to predict which features are likely to style-shift on the basis of whether they display sensitivity to social factors (function as indicators). However, social factors may not affect many L2 learners (for example, foreign language learners in a classroom setting). This raises the important question as to why some L2 features style-shift and others do not. Sato suggested that one factor may be linguistic difficulty. Features that are particularly difficult may not be subject to much variation for the simple reason that learners cannot alter their performance whatever the task.

These studies—and others—indicate that style-shifting is influenced by a number of different factors (for example, the learner's L1, the learner's stage of development, and the difficulty of the target-language feature). Although the studies were informed by a sociolinguistic model designed to account for how situational factors affect language use, they have not shed much light on the relationship between the situational context and learners' use of the L2. This is because the nature of the link between attention and social factors—the primary causative variables—is particularly unclear in the case of L2 learners. In fact, as we have already noted, L2 researchers have used the stylistic continuum to address the psycholinguistic causes of variability rather than the sociolinguistic ones. Tarone (1988), in fact, treats L2 models based on Labov as exemplars of 'psychological processing theories'. This is understandable given the problematicity of applying the concept of 'social group' to many L2 learners, which we discussed earlier. In effect, then, Tarone has chosen to ignore what is central to the Labovian model, namely social organization, with the result that the difference between sociolinguistic and psycholinguistic models has been blurred.

Other studies have taken place within the social-psychological perspective of Accommodation Theory, and these have proven more illuminative of the relationship between social/situational factors and L2 use in so far as they have examined what social factors motivate the use of psycholinguistic factors such as attention. Studies by Beebe (1977) and Beebe and Zuengler (1983) demonstrate that learners are sensitive to their interlocutor. The subjects (adults in the first study and children in the second) were Chinese-Thai bilinguals who were interviewed twice on the same topics, once by a Chinese interviewer and once by a Thai. Both interviewers, however, were fluent in Thai. The bilinguals adapted their speech to their interlocutor by using more Thai phonological variants with the Thai interviewer and more Chinese variants with the Chinese interviewer. Beebe and Zuengler (1983) also report a similar study involving Puerto Rican learners in English in New York, who were interviewed in English by a monolingual native English speaker, an English-dominant Hispanic, and a Spanish-dominant Hispanic. They found that the learners used more dependent clauses with the monolingual English speaker than with the English-dominant Hispanic. They suggest that learners have difficulty in identifying with members of their own ethnic group when speaking in the L2 and, therefore, do not converge. This idea receives some support from Takahashi's (1989) study of the effects of Japanese and non-Japanese listeners on the speech patterns of Japanese learners of L2 English. She found that the learners became more hesitant and briefer when addressing a listener with the same native language background, and also were less prepared to negotiate any communication problem. They also reported feeling more uncomfortable.[6] Dowd, Zuengler, and Berkowitz (1990) review the L2 research that has investigated 'social marking' by learners and conclude that it can occur even during the early stages of learning, despite the learners' obvious limitations in repertoire, and that learners seem to be aware of specific linguistic features that 'stereotype' native speakers of a language.

Learners also seem to be aware of their own identity as learners and, at times, to exploit it. Rampton (1987), in a study considered in more detail in the next chapter, noted that intermediate learners of L2 English sometimes resorted to 'me no' constructions (for example, 'me too clever' and 'me no do it'), even though they clearly possessed the competence to produce target-like utterances. He suggests that the learners used this primitive negative construction as a means of impression management—to tone down the force of their speech acts by drawing attention to their insignificant status as learners. Once again, then, we see the importance of a form-function analysis.

Another aspect of the situation which learners have been shown to be sensitive to is topic. Selinker and Douglas (1985) found that a Polish learner of L2 English varied markedly on a number of linguistic features according to whether the 'discourse domain' concerned an everyday topic (telling your life-story) or a specialized, technical topic (critical path schedules). Zuengler (1989) also refers to evidence that shows that the attitude learners have towards a topic—whether they see themselves as experts or non-experts on it relative to their native speaker interlocutors—will affect their language behaviour, making them more or less likely to interrupt, for example.

It is clear that learners, like native speakers, are influenced by situational factors and, in particular, by their addressee. Learners exploit their linguistic resources in order to behave in sociolinguistically appropriate ways. Sometimes this results in more target-like behaviour and sometimes in less, depending on who their addressee is, the particular language functions they wish to perform, the topic of the discourse, and their perceptions of their own expertise on a subject. In general, however, the research to date has been disappointing in its failure to tease out the contributions that different situational factors make to overall variation in learner language.

The effects of psycholinguistic context

We have already seen that learners seem to vary in their use of linguistic forms depending on where their attention is focused. The studies of style-shifting considered in the previous section were based on the assumption that learners will pay more or less attention to form in different tasks and that this will be reflected in systematic variability. Thus, although these studies afforded little insight into the role of situational factors, they do testify to the importance of language processing factors. Unfortunately, however, 'attention to speech' remains a vague concept and cannot be easily demonstrated independently of language performance (see the criticisms of the Labovian paradigm earlier in this chapter).

Other studies have specifically set out to examine the effects of psycholinguistic processing factors. In one such study, Hulstijn and Hulstijn (1984) investigated the effects of time pressure, focus of attention (i.e. whether on information or on linguistic form), and metalingual knowledge on the accuracy with which two Dutch word order rules (Inversion and Verb-end) were performed in a story-retelling task in L2 Dutch. These rules operate in very similar ways to the same rules in L2 German (see Chapter 3 for a description). The results indicated that neither time pressure nor metalingual knowledge by themselves had any effect, but that focusing attention on form increased accuracy in both structures. It should be noted, however, that the time factor did influence two other aspects of the learners' performance, response duration and speech rate.

Two other studies have examined the effects of planning time on L2 production. In Ellis (1987b), I asked 17 adult learners of English to perform three narrative tasks. Task 1 consisted of a written composition for which one hour was allowed; Task 2 was an oral reproduction of the same composition (without recourse to the written version); Task 3 consisted of a different composition which the subjects were asked to relate orally without any advance planning. I compared the accuracy with which the learners used three past tense morphemes (regular *-ed*, irregular, and copula). In the case of the regular past tense, a clear pattern emerged. The learners were most accurate in Task 1 and least accurate in Task 3, with Task 2 intermediate. This study suggests, contrary to Hulstijn and Hulstijn's study, that the availability of planning time systematically affects the accuracy with which at least some target variants are performed.[7]

The contradiction in the results of these two studies is apparent rather than real. Clearly, it is what learners do with planning time that is important. If they use it to focus on form (as opposed to other aspects of the speech production process), the result is likely to be increased accuracy. However, if they use it to plan and organize the informational content of their output, an increase in accuracy is less likely. This suggests, as Hulstijn points out, that 'it is necessary to distinguish between task and task requirement' (1989a: 29), as in fact his own study did by distinguishing task in terms of time-pressure and task requirement in terms of attention to form.[8] It must also be acknowledged that not all linguistic forms are affected by planning. Those forms that conform to some regular underlying pattern (like past tense *-ed*) are more likely to respond than those that do not.

Further evidence of substantial effects on L2 production resulting from planning time comes from Crookes (1989). Forty intermediate and advanced Japanese learners of L2 English were asked to complete tasks involving a description of how to construct a Lego model and an explanation for the siting of a set of buildings on a map. Some of the tasks were performed under a 'minimal planning condition' (no planning time allowed) and others under a 'planning condition' (ten minutes was provided to plan words, phrases, and ideas). The tasks performed under the planning condition resulted in more complex language as measured, for instance, by the number of subordinate clauses per utterance. However there were no statistically significant differences in general measures of accuracy, although the trend was in the direction of the planning condition. The article 'the' was used more accurately in the planning condition, but other grammatical morphemes (plural -s and article 'a') were not. The results of this study, like my own, were mixed; the accuracy of some linguistic features increased as a result of planning time while that of others did not.

The psycholinguistic context—like the linguistic and situational context—influences learner production, accounting for some of the overall variability. Planned discourse is likely to manifest more frequent use of target-language variants and also greater overall complexity than unplanned discourse. However, the availability of planning time does not guarantee increased accuracy, as production involves learners in an intricate series of interlocking acts of planning, which compete for their attention. Thus, for example, the effort required to plan the propositional content or to produce complex sentences may inhibit the learner from attending to specific linguistic forms. What is becoming clear, however, is that L2 production is characterized by predictable patterns.

A multi-factor approach

In the preceding sections we have been able to identify a number of factors that induce variability in learner language. However, because most of the studies we considered focused on single factors (for example, linguistic context, audience design, or form-function relationships), it has not been possible to establish the differential contribution of particular factors, nor how they interact. Clearly, though, to account for the complexity and multidimensionality of learner language, such a multi-factor approach is needed. In this respect, a study by Young (1988a; 1991) is of considerable importance. Young investigated one linguistic variable—marking plural -s on English nouns—in the speech of twelve Chinese learners, who were interviewed in English twice, once by a native English speaker and the second time by a fellow Chinese speaker. Data relating to four general factors were obtained: (1) the context of the situation (in particular the extent to which each learner converged with the interviewers in terms of general social factors such as ethnicity, sex, education, and occupation), (2) the subjects' proficiency in English (whether 'high' or 'low'), (3) the linguistic context (whether the plural nouns were definite or animate, the syntactic function of the noun phrase, and the phonological environment), and (4) redundancy in plural marking (whether plural -s was omitted because plurality was indicated by some other linguistic device such as a numeral or verb-subject agreement).

Young reports that the learners marked 65 per cent of nouns correctly for plural -*s*. Using the VARBRUL computerized statistical procedure, Young was able to calculate the effect that each factor had on the learners' use of plural -*s*. Table 4.4 summarizes the main results. As predicted, Young found that all four general factors accounted for the variability present in the data. One of the most interesting findings was that different factors influenced the performance of low- and high-proficiency learners. Thus, for instance, the phonological environment of -*s* had a significant impact on variation only during the early stages of acquisition, while social convergence with an interlocutor had a significant effect only during the later stages. Another interesting discovery was that the presence of some other marker of plurality (for example, a numeral) seemed to trigger -*s*. One reason for this was that the learners, particularly those of low proficiency, made frequent use of a closed set of 'measure expressions' (for example, numeral + years, days, hours,

Factor	Low proficiency	High proficiency	Combined proficiency
1 Social convergence with an interlocutor	–	+	+
2 Definiteness	–	–	–
3 Animacy	+	+	–
4 Position of noun within noun phrase	+	+	+
5 Syntactic function of noun phrase	+	+	+
6 Phonological context (preceding segment)	+	–	+
7 Phonological context (following segment)	–	–	+
8 -s marked irrespective of existence of other + markers of plurality in noun phrase	+	+	+
9 Noun–verb concord	–	–	–

+ = factor accounts significantly for observed variability
– = factor does not account significantly for observed variability

Table 4.4:　The contribution of different factors to the variable production of plural -s (simplified from Young 1988a: 293)

dollars). These expressions were formula-like; the nouns in them were more or less invariably marked with -*s*.

Another study that employs a multi-factor approach, again using VARBRUL, is Adamson and Regan (1991). This investigates the acquisition of variable -*ing*, which occurs in a number of English grammatical structures including tenses, participles, and nouns and has two phonetic forms, [ɪn] and [ɪŋ], the latter constituting the prestige target-language variant. The subjects included both native speakers and Vietnamese and Cambodian learners of English. Hypothesizing that the learners would begin with [ɪŋ] as a result of transfer from their L1, Adamson and Regan investigated the factors that contributed to the appearance of the non-prestige [ɪn], arguing that this would signal the learners' integration into the speech community. Data were collected using interviews designed to control for shifts of formality. The results showed that the learners' sex, the opportunity to monitor production by attending to speech, and the grammatical category of -*ing* all had a significant effect on the variant used. Thus, males favoured the non-standard [ɪn] to a greater extent than females and, when monitoring, were more likely to use it. The authors suggest that this reflected the males' desire to match male native-speaker norms. The results for the different grammatical categories suggest that the spread of [ɪn] from one category to another was influenced partly by its frequency in the input, but also by whether the category in question was open or closed (for example, [ɪn] appeared early in words like 'something' and 'nothing', both of which of are members of a closed grammatical class).

These two studies provide some of the most convincing evidence to date that variability in learner language is systematic. They testify to its enormous complexity but also show that it is possible to account for it.

Summary

The research reported in the previous sections has focused on variability in linguistic form (i.e. the starting point has been a specific linguistic form or forms) in the output of individual learners. In accordance with the overall goal of this section of the book, the main aim has been to describe rather than to explain the variability. For this reason, there has been no in-depth discussion of theories of L2 acquisition based on variability. These are considered in Chapter 9. The main characteristics of learner language variability are summarized below.

First, somewhat controversially, a number of researchers have claimed to have observed instances of free variation (i.e. the unsystematic use of two or more forms). In most cases evidence for this kind of variability is only found in the rich data available in longitudinal case studies of individual learners. It appears to be most common in the early stages of development and may rapidly disappear. It has been suggested that learners go through an 'acquisition phase', involving free variation as new features are acquired, and then a 'replacement' phase, during which variability becomes systematic as the learner sorts out when to use the new features.

Form-function analyses have shown that what appears to unsystematic may in fact be systematic. A number of studies—again mainly longitudinal—indicate that learners construct form-function networks in which individual forms are used to perform specific functions. These networks may not be target-like, and they evolve over time. They provide some of the strongest evidence of the 'creativity' of the L2 learning process and indicate the importance of going beyond a target-language-based analysis of learner language.

Third, as the form-function analyses show, much of the variability in learner language is highly systematic. This systematicity is context-induced. The effects of context are evident globally as task-induced variation. Quantitative and qualitative differences in learner language can occur according to whether the data come from tasks designed to tap natural language use, or tasks intended to elicit knowledge of specific linguistic forms.

Specific effects for the linguistic, situational, and psycholinguistic context have also been identified. Linguistic context has been shown to have an effect on phonological, morphological, and syntactic features. Some environments favour target-language variants, while others favour interlanguage variants, suggesting that learners find it easier to use the target-language form in particular environments to begin with. As they progress, so they master the use of the form in the more difficult environments. There may be considerable interlearner differences in the way linguistic context affects acquisition, however.

Situational context, which has figured so strongly in variability studies in general, has received rather scant attention in SLA research. A number of studies have demonstrated that style-shifting occurs in learner performance, but, as has now become clear, learners do not always use the target-language variant in tasks requiring formal language use and interlanguage variants in tasks requiring informal language use. The learners' stage of development, their L1, and the linguistic feature under study all influence whether and in what direction style shifting occurs. More promising is the research that indicates that learners are sensitive to both their audience and the discourse topic, but to date the research in these areas has been limited.

Although the L2 studies undertaken within the Labovian paradigm shed little light on how situational variables affect learner performance, they did demonstrate conclusively that attention (a psycholinguistic construct) is an important factor. Other studies undertaken within a more explicit psycholinguistic framework also show that planning time affects both the accuracy with which specific forms are performed in different tasks, and also the overall complexity of the language used. The attention that learners pay to different aspects of language is influenced by various factors, one of which is clearly planning time.

A multi-factor approach to identifying sources of variability has been described. This suggests that the patterns of variability in the use of a single linguistic variable (such as plural -*s*) can only be fully identified and accounted for if a range of possible factors that affect learner language are taken into account. This approach also suggests that different factors may be important at different stages of the learner's development.

The research to date suggests that horizontal and vertical variability are inextricably intertwined. This is most clearly evident in the studies that have investigated linguistic context, form-function relationships, and planning variability. Initially learners begin with 'simple' systems, characterized by the use of a given form in 'heavy' environments only (often in closed classes) and in planned discourse, and also by unique form-function mappings. Over time they learn to use the form in a target-like way by extending its use to increasingly 'lighter' contexts and to unplanned discourse and by reorganizing form-function networks so that they correspond more closely to those of native speakers.

Conclusion

In this chapter we have explored the nature of variability in learner language and have seen that there is ample evidence to show that variability is systematic, traceable to particular causes. It remains for us to consider whether variability is a significant phenomenon—whether it constitutes, as Tarone has argued, 'a phenomenon that must be accounted for by any theory of second language acquisition' (1988: 142). Here we find conflicting opinions, depending on whether the approach is a linguistic one following the Chomskyan tradition or a sociolinguistic/psycholinguistic one.

As we saw in the introduction to this chapter, researchers in the Chomskyan tradition argue that the primary goal of SLA research is to build a theory of L2 competence, and that in this respect variability is of no interest. As Gregg (1990) puts it:

> The variabilist is committed to the unprincipled collection of an uncontrolled mass of data, running the real risk that the object of study will become as Roger Brown once put it, 'cognitively . . . repellent.'

Although Gregg acknowledges that variability is 'a fascinating and puzzling phenomenon', he believes that variable features are the exception rather than the rule in learner language. In this he is surely mistaken, as the studies reported in this chapter provide indisputable evidence of extensive variability in learner language. Gregg argues that although the study of variability might contribute to a theory of performance, it will tell us nothing about competence. Variability studies, he argues, describe, but Gregg seeks to explain. For Gregg, knowledge is categorical—we either know a rule or we do not. He is unable to accept the notion of a fuzzy, probabilistic knowledge and is particularly dismissive of variable rules.

On the other hand, researchers in the functionalist tradition see the study of language in its social context as necessary for theory-building. In responding to Gregg's arguments, Tarone (1990) quotes Romaine (1984: 78–9), who takes a very different view of what knowledge of a language involves:

> Rule acquisition is not an all or nothing affair . . . There may be a number of aspects of the internal workings of a rule, some of which may be acquired before others. There are also social dimensions of a rule relating to its use.

Here knowledge itself is seen as containing variability. Tarone argues that a theory of L2 acquisition must account for the learner's capability—the actual ability to use particular rules that a learner has—and not just knowledge about what is grammatically correct. For Tarone it is this capability rather than competence that underlies actual performance. In Ellis 1990c I make a similar point in arguing that even if competence (narrowly defined) is itself not variable, the learner's proficiency is. I used this term with the meaning assigned to it by Taylor (1988)—the ability to use knowledge in specific contexts.[9] I argued that for many researchers—especially those interested in educational issues—it is not the learners' competence that is important but their proficiency. Both Tarone and I also maintain that the study of the systematicity evident in learner language variability can help explain how learners organize their L2, although we both accept that work in the Chomskyan tradition that Gregg favours can also contribute to theory development.

This debate is an old one and is likely to continue into the future. It rests on how competence is defined, in particular on whether it is to be viewed narrowly in terms of 'knowledge' or more broadly in terms of 'ability to use knowledge', both of which are seen as distinct from 'performance'.[10] As Widdowson has pointed out in a discussion of these distinctions, 'as soon as you talk about competence as *ability*, or what people can actually *do* with language, you get into all kinds of difficulty' (1989: 134) . This is because it necessarily involves consideration of a multitude of interacting factors, as indeed the discussion of variability in this chapter has demonstrated. Whereas 'universalists' see this as a reason for treating competence as 'knowledge' and so avoiding the 'difficulty' that Widdowson talks about, variabilists are prepared to accept it in order to undertake what they see as the essential task—to account for competence as 'ability'.

Notes

1 While many linguists—including those who work with L2 data—continue to make use of data based on speakers' intuitions regarding what is grammatical, many now recognize the need to work with other kinds of data, including those derived from natural language use.

2 The example of a variable rule is taken from Færch (1980) rather than Labov because it is presented in a form that is easy to understand. Readers who would like to see examples of Labov's variable rules can do so (Labov 1972: 229, 240).

3 Preston (1989: 20) comments: 'the psycholinguistic possibility for a variable rule does not seem to be arcane'.

4 Fischer (1958) states the position adopted by many sociolinguists on free variation as follows:

'Free variation' is of course a label, not an explanation. It does not tell us where the variants come from nor why the speakers use them in differing proportions, but is rather a way of excluding such questions from the scope of immediate inquiry.

5 Beebe (1982) puts forward a similar view to that of Gatbonton. She argues that deviations in interlanguage phonology are relatively few initially but then increase markedly as more variants are acquired and compete in the learner's interlanguage system before diminishing in the later stages.

6 The claim that the difficulty L2 learners experience communicating with members of their own ethnic group in the L2 is arguable. It may be that this difficulty simply reflects the fact that they find using the L2 with native speakers of their own L1 bizarre.

7 Planning variability cannot account for all the variability evident in learners' use of the past tense, as Wolfram's (1989) review of studies that have investigated systematic variability in L2 tense marking demonstrates. In particular, Wolfson draws attention to a 'lexical variable' in the early stages of acquisition. That is, learners vary in their ability to mark for past tense according to the particular verb they are using.

8 One of the main differences between the Hulstijn and Hulstijn (1984) and Ellis (1987b) studies and the style-shifting studies of Dickerson (1975) and Tarone (1985) is that the former clearly do distinguish 'task' and 'task requirement' whereas the latter do not. The style-shifting studies use different tasks to elicit what they presume to be differences in attention. The psycholinguistic studies use the *same* task and vary the conditions under which it is performed.

9 Widdowson (1983: 8) uses the term 'capacity' to refer to 'the ability to produce and understand utterances by using the resources of the grammar in association with features of context to make meaning'. It is clear that 'capability', 'capacity', and 'proficiency' have much in common.

10 This distinction between competence as abstract knowledge and competence as ability to use knowledge was first discussed in Hymes (1971). Hymes took the view that the latter definition was to be preferred. However, other theorists, including those working in the field of education, have adopted different viewpoints. Canale and Swain (1980), for example, opt for the narrower definition. It should also be noted that this

distinction is separate from and cuts across the other frequently discussed distinction in the literature—that between 'linguistic competence' and 'communicative competence'. Thus, although Canale and Swain prefer to exclude 'ability to use' from their definition of 'competence', they argue in favour of including sociolinguistic, discourse, and strategic knowledge within its compass.

Further reading

It is probably useful to begin your further reading with some background information about sociolinguistics.
D. Preston, *Sociolinguistics and Second Language Acquisition* (Basil Black-well, 1989), provides a thorough introduction. A somewhat more readable, shorter but less comprehensive account is available in
R. Fasold, 'Variation theory and language learning' in P. Trudgill (ed.), *Applied Sociolinguistics* (Academic Press, 1984).

Variability in learner language has attracted considerable attention. There are a number of full length books devoted to it. The following are collections of papers:
R. Ellis (ed.), *Second Language Acquisition in Context* (Prentice Hall International, 1987).
S. Gass et al. (eds.), *Variation in Second Language Acquisition: Volumes 1 and 2* (Multilingual Matters, 1989).
M. Eisenstein (ed.), *The Dynamic Interlanguage: Empirical Studies in Second Language Variation* (Plenum Press, 1989).

A survey of much of the research together with a clear account of the main theoretical positions can be found in:
E. Tarone, *Variation in Interlanguage* (Edward Arnold, 1988).

For readers less concerned with detailed research reports and more interested in the general approaches to L2 variability, two excellent sources are:
E. Tarone, 'On the variability of interlanguage systems'. *Applied Linguistics* (1983) 4: 143–163.
L. Beebe's chapter in L. Beebe (ed.), *Issues in Second Language Acquisition* (Newbury House, 1988).

Readers may also wish to read more about different views regarding 'competence'. Two sources are useful here:
Applied Linguistics, 10: 2 (This issue is devoted to a reconsideration of 'communicative competence'.)
Applied Linguistics, 11: 4 (This issue contains Gregg's attack on 'variabilists' and responses by Tarone and myself.)

5   Pragmatic aspects of learner language

Introduction

The focus of enquiry in the preceding chapters has been the formal linguistic properties of learners' interlanguages. As was made clear in Chapter 1, mainstream second language acquisition research has been primarily concerned with these aspects of second language (L2) learning. Increasingly, however, researchers are giving attention to pragmatic aspects of learner language. This has been motivated in part by the belief that a full understanding of how formal properties are learnt will not be achieved without examining the way in which these properties are used in actual communication (hence the form-functional analyses discussed in the last chapter). It has also been motivated by the belief that the study of learner language requires a consideration of pragmatic aspects in their own right. According to this view the goal of SLA research is to describe and explain not only learners' *linguistic competence*, but also their *pragmatic competence*. The growing interest in interlanguage pragmatics reflects the enormous developments in the theoretical and empirical study of pragmatics over the last two decades (see Levinson 1983; Coulthard 1985; Hatch 1992, for surveys of the field).

Pragmatics is the term used to refer to the field of study where linguistic features are considered in relation to users of the language (Levinson 1983). When speakers perform utterances in context they accomplish two things: (1) *interactional acts* and (2) *speech acts*. The former impose structure on the discourse by ensuring that one utterance leads smoothly to another; they concern how speakers manage the process of exchanging turns, how they open and close conversations, and how they sequence acts to ensure a coherent conversation. Speech acts constitute attempts by language users to perform specific actions, in particular interpersonal functions such as compliments, apologies, requests or complaints.[1] They are considered in greater detail in the following section.

This chapter will not attempt to provide a comprehensive overview of the work undertaken in interlanguage pragmatics to date. Instead, we will adopt what Kasper and Dahl (1991) refer to as the 'narrow sense' of 'interlanguage pragmatics—the performance and acquisition of speech acts by L2 learners.[2] The justification for this decision lies in the fact that it is this aspect of pragmatics which has received the greatest attention in SLA research and that, although there is some work on how L2 learners *perform* interactional acts, there has been relatively little on how they *acquire* the ability to do so. However, we will give some attention to *impression management*—the way learners make use of their L2 resources in interaction to create social meanings favourable to themselves—as this relates closely to work on speech acts. Also, we will concentrate on the pragmatic aspects of learners' spoken rather than written language.

Speech acts and illocutionary meaning

According to speech act theory (Austin 1962; Searle 1969) the performance of a speech act involves the performance of three types of act: a locutionary act (the conveyance of propositional meaning), an illocutionary act (the performance of a particular language function), and a perlocutionary act (the achieving of some kind of effect on the addressee). Searle (1975) distinguished 'direct' and 'indirect' speech acts. In a direct speech act, there is a transparent relationship between form and function as when an imperative is used to perform a request (for example, 'Pass me the salt.'). In an indirect speech act, the illocutionary force of the act is not derivable from the surface structure, as when an interrogative form serves as a request (for example, 'Can you pass me the salt?').

The successful performance of an illocutionary act is achieved when the speaker meets a number of conditions associated with that particular act. Searle (1969) distinguishes three types of conditions: preparatory conditions, sincerity conditions, and essential conditions. For example, the illocutionary act of 'ordering' is successfully performed when both the speaker and hearer recognize that the speaker is in a position of authority over the hearer (preparatory condition), that the speaker wants the ordered act to be done (sincerity condition), and that the speaker intends the utterance as an attempt to get the hearer to do the act (essential condition). If any one of these conditions is not met or is challenged by the hearer, the act may not be successfully performed. For this reason, they are seen as of primary importance in a theory of speech acts.

Other considerations of a secondary nature also enter into speech act performance—in particular, politeness (see Leech 1983 and Kasper 1990). Speakers have to take account of their relationship with the addressee and the degree of imposition on the addressee in order to ensure that harmonious social relations between the speakers are not endangered. In so doing they give recognition to the need to signal solidarity with and/or power over their hearers, both of which determine the nature of their relations with them. Brown and Levinson (1978) have developed a model of politeness, in which they distinguish a number of options or 'strategies' available to the speaker (see Figure 5.1). First, the speaker can choose to perform the act or not to perform it. If the act is performed it can be 'off-record' (i.e. performed in such a way that it can be ignored by the addressee) or 'on-record'. On-record acts can be 'baldly on record' (i.e. performed by means of a direct speech act) or can in-volve 'face-saving activity'. The latter can take the form of a 'positive strat-egy' or a 'negative strategy'. The former involves some kind of attempt to establish solidarity with the addressee by emphasizing commonality. It is likely to occur when there is minimal social distance and little power differ-ence between the participants. A 'negative strategy' involves performing the act in such a way that deference is shown to the hearer—the aim is to give the hearer a way out of compliance with the act. It is used when the power differ-ence between the participants is considerable. Brown and Levinson, and also Scollon and Scollon (1983), argue that the strategies shown in Figure 5.1 are universal, but subsequent research (see Kasper 1990 for a review) suggests that this may not be the case. As we will see, how L2 learners handle polite-ness has attracted the attention of a number of researchers.

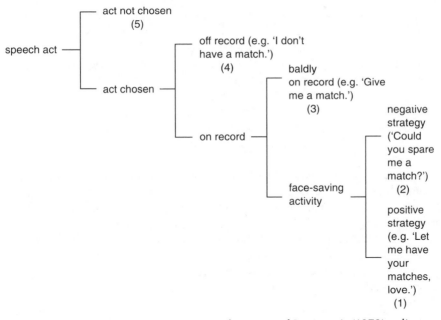

Figure 5.1: A schematic representation of Brown and Levinson's (1978) politeness model

The study of speech acts in interlanguage has concentrated on illocutionary meanings, or language functions as they are commonly known. The questions that have been addressed are: (1) To what extent and in what ways do learn-ers perform illocutionary acts in the L2 differently from native speakers of the target language? and (2) How do learners learn to perform different illocu-tionary acts? The bulk of the research has been cross-sectional, so little is cur-rently known about the second question. However, a few longitudinal and pseudo-longitudinal studies cast some light on the process by which learners gradually master the performance of specific illocutionary acts.

We will begin by considering the research methods that have been used to investigate illocutionary acts in learner language. A survey of the research that has studied a number of L2 illocutionary acts follows, with a focus on three particular acts: requests, apologies, and refusals. A number of general features of learners' attempts to perform and to acquire illocutionary acts is then discussed. Finally, although the focus of this chapter is on description, a number of explanatory factors will be considered.

Research methods for studying illocutionary acts in learner language

Ideally, the study of illocutionary acts in learner language should involve the collection of three sets of data: (1) samples of the illocutionary act performed in the target language by L2 learners, (2) samples performed by native speakers of the target language[3], and (3) samples of the same illocutionary act performed by the learners in their L1. Only in this way is it possible to determine to what extent learner performance differs from native-speaker performance and whether the differences are traceable to transfer from the L1. Relatively few L2 studies, however, have provided such a base of data.

Kasper and Dahl (1991) distinguish data collection methods according to the modality of the data elicited (perception/comprehension/intuition versus production) and the degree of control over learners' speech (elicited versus observational). They also point out that some of the most successful studies have employed combined methods of data collection.

A number of researchers have used questionnaires to elicit learners' intuitions about how to perform specific acts appropriately in different situations. Olshtain and Blum-Kulka (1985), for example, investigated learners' intuitions of politeness in Hebrew by means of a questionnaire consisting of descriptions of situations calling for apologies and requests followed by lists of possible strategies for performing these acts in each situation. The learners were asked to rate each strategy for politeness on a three-point scale. Here is an example:

> A friend of yours at the university comes up to you after class and tells you that she has finally found an apartment to rent. The only problem is that she has to pay $200 immediately and at present she only has $100. She turns to you and says:
> a Say, could you lend me $100 until next week?
> b You can lend me $100 until next week, right?
> c Lend me the money, please.
> d Could you lend me $100 until next week?
> e Do you think you could lend me $100 until next week?
> f Maybe you have a little money to give me so that I could take the apartment?
> (Olshtain and Blum-Kulka 1985: 324)

Observational performance data have also been used to investigate the comprehension of illocutionary acts. Carrell (1981), for example, had learners listen and react to requests, while Kasper (1984a) gauged learners' comprehension on the basis of the kinds of responses that they provided to their interlocutor's previous turn.

The study of learners' production of illocutionary acts has made use of (1) discourse completion tasks, (2) role play, and (3) naturally occurring speech. Discourse completion tasks have been extensively used. In the Cross-Cultural Speech Act Realization Project (Blum-Kulka, House, and Kasper 1989a) a series of studies involving subjects from a variety of language backgrounds (for example, American, British, and Australian English, Canadian French, Hebrew, German, and Danish) made use of a questionnaire consisting of eight request and eight apology contexts. Each context was briefly described and was then followed by a short dialogue with an empty slot which the learners were asked to fill in by writing down the request or apology they would make. Here is an example, designed to elicit an apology:

A student has borrowed a book from her teacher, which she promises to return today. When meeting her teacher, however, she realizes that she forgot to bring it along.

Teacher: Miriam, I hope you brought the book I lent you.
Miriam: _____
Teacher: OK, but please remember it next week.
(Blum-Kulka, House, and Kasper 1989b: 14).

Similar questionnaires have been used by Beebe and her colleagues (for example, Beebe, Takahashi, and Uliss-Weltz 1990), and by a number of other researchers.

Role plays also provide the learners with a description of a context calling for the performance of a particular illocutionary act. But in this case the learners are asked to respond orally. The role plays may be performed with the help of puppets (for example, Walters 1980), or by the learners interacting with other learners (for example, Kasper 1981), or with the researcher. The data collected from role plays provide information about learners' ability to construct a discourse context for the specific act under investigation.

The use of naturally occurring speech as a basis for studying interlanguage pragmatics has been less common, partly because of the difficulty of assembling a sufficient corpus of data. Wolfson (1989b), however, used this approach to investigate learners' complimenting behaviour (compliments together with compliment responses). Bardovi-Harlig and Hartford (1990) used data collected from academic advising sessions to investigate differences between native speakers' and L2 learners' suggestions.

Each of these methods has its advantages and disadvantages. Controlled methods such as the *discourse completion questionnaire* allow for large amounts of data to be collected quickly, provide information about the kinds of semantic formulas that learners use to realize different illocutionary acts, and reveal the social factors that learners think are important for speech act performance. However, a number of studies which have compared data obtained from discourse completion questionnaires with that from observational studies (for example, Beebe and Cummins 1985; Rintell and Mitchell 1989; Wolfson, Marmor, and Jones 1989) have found differences with regard to the actual wording used, the semantic formulas employed, the length of learners' responses, and the size of the discourse context created. These differences raise questions about the extent to which the elicited data can serve as evidence of learners' pragmatic competence, as they may not accurately reflect actual language use. Also, as Bonikowska (1988) has pointed out, in naturally occurring contexts speakers always have the option of 'opting out', whereas discourse completion questionnaires oblige learners to perform linguistically even when they would normally keep quiet. Wolfson (1989a) has also argued strongly that learners' intuitions about what they would say in a particular situation are not reliable, as the sociolinguistic knowledge they draw on in performing illocutionary acts lies beneath the threshold of consciousness. On the other hand, it is difficult to obtain a sufficient corpus of data from ethnographic observation. There is also a danger of the data being unrepresentative of the population under investigation. For example, work by Wolfson (1983) and Holmes (1986) on the compliments produced by native speakers of English in America and New Zealand was based on data collected from predominantly female, graduate students. Also, if a pen-and-paper approach is used, as in some of Wolfson's early work, it is difficult to obtain reliable information about the full discourse context of specific illocutionary acts. Kasper and Dahl (1991) conclude that researchers are 'caught between a rock and a hard place'.

The study of pragmatics in learner language, then, faces an additional problem—the matter of target-language norms. In order to decide in what way the learner's performance differs from the native speaker's, it is necessary to determine what is normative in the latter. We need to know, for example, how native speakers handle compliments. The difficulty is that native speakers are likely to vary considerably in this respect. For example, middle-class Americans have different norms for complimenting from those of middle-class white South Africans (Herbert 1989). Similarly, females do not compliment in exactly the same way as males (see Holmes 1988). As Kasper (1992) points out, the obvious solution to this problem is to choose those norms found in whatever variety the learner is typically exposed to as the 'target'. However, as Kasper also points out, many learners are exposed to more than one variety. Kasper's conclusion is that 'investigators might want to give more attention to "choosing the right stuff" as an L2 norm in interlanguage pragmatics' and that this is 'largely a matter of logistics' (1992: 225). In many learning situations, however, the 'logistics' may be very complicated.

Illocutionary acts in learner language

The knowledge required to perform illocutionary acts constitutes part of communicative competence. Canale includes it in sociolinguistic competence, which he defines as 'the extent to which utterances are produced and understood appropriately in different sociolinguistic contexts' (1983: 7). He goes on to point out that appropriateness involves both appropriateness of meaning (i.e. when it is proper to perform a particular illocutionary act) and appropriateness of form (i.e. the extent to which a given act is realized in a verbal or non-verbal form proper for a given situation). A similar distinction is to be found in discussions of pragmatic errors in learner language. Thomas (1983) distinguishes *sociopragmatic failure*, which takes place when a learner fails to perform the illocutionary act required by the situation (i.e. deviates with regard to appropriateness of meaning), and *pragmalinguistic failure*, which occurs when a learner tries to perform the right speech act but uses the wrong linguistic means (i.e. deviates with regard to appropriateness of form).

A good example of sociopragmatic error can be found in Wolfson's (1989a) account of how L2 learners typically respond to compliments. Wolfson argues that compliments are used by native speakers of American English as a means of establishing and maintaining solidarity. It is for this reason that they are most common among status-equal acquaintances and co-workers rather than among intimates; the former involve more uncertain relationships which have to be negotiated. Compliments serve as one of the ways in which Americans (particularly women) undertake this negotiation. Wolfson points out that many negotiating sequences involving native speakers are long and elaborate. In comparison, those involving non-native speakers are typically short, because learners often fail to take up a compliment, preferring instead to give no response at all:

> NS: You have such a lovely accent.
> NNS: (No response).

Wolfson argues that by failing to conform to native-speaker complimenting norms, learners deprive themselves of the opportunities to establish relationships with native speakers and, thereby, of the input that they need to develop both their linguistic and sociolinguistic competence.

Not all of Wolfson's learners manifested sociopragmatic failure through failing to respond to a compliment. Many displayed pragmalinguistic failure—that is, they responded to a native-speaker compliment but in linguistically inappropriate ways. Middle-class, white Americans are likely to respond by giving unfavourable comments about the object that is the target of a compliment:

NS: I like your sweater.
NS: It's so old. My sister bought it for me from Italy a long time ago.

In contrast, learners often tried to refuse the compliment or to downgrade themselves. They also tended to respond with a simple 'thank you'. Such responses also served to act as dampeners on the conversation.

Pragmalinguistic failure by learners is widely reported in the literature. Another good example comes from Eisenstein and Bodman's (1986) study of expressions of gratitude. This made use of a discourse completion questionnaire administered to 67 learners with different L1 backgrounds. Baseline data were collected from native speakers of English. Eisenstein and Bodman report that the learners performed very differently from the native speakers—in fact, their responses were similar only 30 per cent of the time. They experienced difficulty with both syntax and vocabulary, and also in identifying the formulas and conventionalized routines that characterized native-speaker thanking. In a subsequent study (Bodman and Eisenstein 1988), learners were asked to role play situations calling for expressions of gratitude. Lower-proficiency learners often translated expressions from their L1. For example, in thanking someone for a loan they might say 'May God increase your bounty'. More advanced learners avoided this kind of pragmalinguistic error, but instead displayed considerable hesitation and awkwardness. Pragmalinguistic difficulty, therefore, can also be manifested in the failure to conform to the temporal norms of native-speaker speech.[4]

The distinction between sociopragmatic and pragmalinguistic errors, however, is not as clear-cut as these examples may have suggested. Kasper points out that 'the distinction becomes fuzzy in the case of indirectness' (1992: 210). For example, the decision regarding whether to provide an explanation for having committed some offence can be seen as a sociopragmatic one, but if providing an explanation is seen as one of several possible strategies for performing the act of apologizing (as in Olshtain and Cohen's 1983 framework discussed later), its inclusion or omission constitutes more of a pragmalinguistic decision. Nevertheless, Kasper acknowledges that the distinction is 'analytically useful'.

Research into the use and acquisition of illocutionary acts has been somewhat limited. It has tended to make use of rough and ready categories of sociocultural reality—the problem of norms referred to earlier. It has also tended to concentrate on a fairly small set of speech acts. Complaints have been investigated by Olshtain and Weinbach (1987) and Bonikowska (1988), thanking by Eisenstein and Bodman (1986), invitations by Scarcella (1979), suggestions by Bardovi-Harlig and Hartford (1990) and Rintell (1981), compliments by Wolfson (1989b) and Billmyer (1990), and arguing by Adger (1987). Many of these acts have two points in common. First, they constitute 'relatively well-defined' acts (De Beaugrande and Dressler 1981: 117) in the sense that they are realized by means of a small set of easily recognizable linguistic elements (many formulaic). For example, Wolfson (1983) has shown that nine syntactic patterns account for 95 per cent of the compliments in her native-speaker corpus. Second, these acts are face-threatening in nature and, therefore, provide a means of studying to what extent L2 learners with different L1 backgrounds are able to use native-like politeness strategies. We will focus on three acts (requests, apologies, and refusals) which are among those which have received the most attention from researchers.

Requests

Requests are attempts on the part of a speaker to get the hearer to perform or to stop performing some kind of action. A number of general interactional, illocutionary, and sociolinguistic features of requests can be identified:

Interactional features

1 They tend to serve an initiating function in discourse.
2 They can be performed in a single turn or, if they involve some kind of preparatory act or pre-request, over several turns, for example:
   T: Have you finished your work?
   S: Yes.
   T: Read your book then.

Illocutionary aspects

3 The speaker wishes the hearer to perform the request, believes the hearer is able to perform the act, and does not believe the act will be performed in the absence of the request (Fraser 1983).
4 A request can be more or less direct (Searle 1976). Blum-Kulka, House, and Kasper (1989b) identify eight 'strategy types', which they order according to directness (see Table 5.1).
5 Requests are also subject to internal and external modification. Internal modification takes the form of downgraders, which are intended to mitigate the force of the act, and upgraders, which are intended to increase the degree of coerciveness of the act. External modification consists of moves that occur either before or after the head act (i.e. the act that actually performs the request); these moves can also be classified according to whether the purpose is to downgrade or upgrade the force of the act.
6 Requests can be encoded from the speaker's perspective (for example, 'Give me the book'), from the hearer's perspective (for example, 'Could you give me the book?'), from a joint perspective ('Let's read a book') or from an impersonal perspective ('It would be nice to read a book').

Sociolinguistic aspects

7 Requests are 'inherently imposing' (Blum-Kulka, House, and Kasper 1989b). For this reason they call for considerable 'face-work'. The choice of linguistic realization depends on a variety of social factors to do with the relationship between the speaker and the addressee, and the perceived degree of imposition which a particular request makes on the hearer (i.e. it involves a choice of politeness strategy).

8 Although the main sociopragmatic categories of requests can be found in different languages, there are pragmalinguistic differences relating to the preferred form of a request that is used in a particular situation. Also, cross-linguistic differences exist in the choice of other linguistic features such as internal and external modification devices.

Level of directness	Strategy	Example
Direct	1 Mood-derivable	You shut up.
	2 Performative	I am telling you to shut up.
	3 Hedged performative	I would like to ask you to shut up.
	4 Locution-derivable	I want you to shut up.
Conventionally indirect	5 Suggestory formula	Let's play a game.
	6 Query-preparatory	Can you draw a horse for me?
Non-conventionally indirect	7 Strong hint	This game is boring.
	8 Mild hint	We've been playing this game for over an hour now.

Table 5.1:   Request strategies (summarized from Blum-Kulka, House, and Kasper 1989b)

Requests have received considerable attention in SLA research for a number of reasons. They are face-threatening and, therefore, call for considerable linguistic expertise on the part of the learner, they differ cross-linguistically in interesting ways and they are often realized by means of clearly identifiable formulas. Table 5.2 summarizes the main studies.

A number of studies have investigated learners' intuitions about what constitutes an appropriate request. A focus of enquiry is whether L2 learners are able to recognize the distinctions between polite and less polite forms. Advanced learners appear to have few problems. Olshtain and Blum-Kulka (1985) found that learners of L2 Hebrew, who had been resident in Israel for over 10 years, showed the same high level of tolerance for direct and positive politeness strategies as native speakers of Hebrew. Walters (1979) and Carrell and Konneker (1981) also report that the advanced learners they

Study	Type	Modality studied	Subjects	Data collection instruments	Main results
Scarcella 1979	Cross-sectional	Production	10 beginners & 10 advanced learners (L1 Arabic); 6 NSs	Role play involving different addressees	Some politeness forms (e.g. 'please' acquired early; others (e.g. inclusive 'we') acquired late. Learners acquire forms before their social meanings. L2 learners use a limited range of politeness features.
Walters 1979	Cross-sectional	Perception	75 advanced ESL learners (mixed L1s); 60 NSs of English	Judgement tasks involving paired comparisons.	Learners performed like NS females in making clearer distinctions between polite and impolite forms than NS males.
Fraser, Rintell, and Walters 1980	Cross-sectional	Perception	Adult ESL learners (L1 Spanish); NS controls	Ratings of speech produced in role-playing situations on a deference scale of 1–5.	Learners perceived deference to older and female addressees in a similar way to NSs. (i.e. they did not transfer L1 pragmatic rules).
Carrell and Konneker 1981	Cross-sectional	Perception	73 advanced and intermediate ESL learners (mixed L1s); 42 NSs	Sorting task, requiring subjects to rank strategies according to politeness.	Learners performed like NSs but tended to perceive more distinctive levels of politeness i.e. they were oversensitive to syntactic/form distinctions.
Tanaka and Kawade 1982	Cross-sectional	Perception	ESL learners (L1 Japanese) NS controls	M/C questionnaire; subjects select strategy most appropriate to situation.	Both learners and NSs choose more polite strategies with increased social distance but learners chose less polite strategies overall.
Schmidt 1983	Longitudinal (3 yrs)	Production	One adult ESL learner (L1 Japanese)	Audio recordings in different natural settings	Learner showed initial reliance on small set of formulas and lexical clues ('please'); by end he had control of wide range of request formulas but could not always use them appropriately.

(*continued overleaf*)

Study	Type	Modality studied	Subjects	Data collection instruments	Main results
Olshtain and Blum-Kulka 1985	Cross-sectional	Perception	172 NSs of English; 160 NSs of Hebrew; 124 learners of Hebrew	M/C questionnaire in English and Hebrew; subjects asked to rate each of 6 strategies for politeness on a 3-point scale	Learners showed increased preference for direct request strategies and positive politeness (i.e. NS norms) according to length of stay in target community; learners capable of achieving NS acceptability patterns.
Cathcart 1986	Cross-sectional	Production	8 ESL learners (children; L1 Spanish) in bilingual classroom	Audio-recordings of classroom speech	Children used longer and more complex requests addressed to adults than to other children. Requests also longer and more complex with other children in tasks with joint goals.
Blum-Kulka and Olshtain 1986	Cross-sectional	Production	Learners of L2 Hebrew; (mixed proficiency); NS controls	Discourse completion questionnaire	High-intermediate learners used longer requests than low-intermediate or advanced learners.
Ervin-Tripp et al. 1987	Cross-sectional	Comprehension	Learners of French (3 age groups 3–9); NSs of English and French	Subjects asked to explain implicit requests based on narratives; also to carry out implicit requests.	The child learners relied on situational rather than linguistic clues to interpret requests; accuracy of interpretation increased with age.
House and Kasper 1987	Cross-sectional	Production	Advanced learners of L2 English (L1 = Danish and German)	Discourse completion questionnaire	Learners showed similar choice of directness levels but used less varied syntactic and lexical down-graders less frequently. Also, learners produced longer requests.
Tanaka 1988	Cross-sectional	Production	8 Japanese ESL learners in Australia; NS controls	Role play involving two hearers (friend and lecturer)	The learners were more direct and used politeness strategies inappropriately.

Study	Type	Modality studied	Subjects	Data collection instruments	Main results
Færch and Kasper 1989	Cross-sectional	Production	200 learners of English & 200 learners of German; (L1 = Danish) NS of Danish, British English and German	Discourse completion questionnaire	Learners tend to be more verbose e.g. tend to use double markings ('Could you possibly...?') 'Please' is over-used, but 'possibly' is underused.
Rintell and Mitchell 1989	Cross-sectional	Production	34 ESL learners (low-advanced level, mixed L1s); 37 NSs	Discourse completion questionnaire; role play	Learners' requests longer than NSs'; no major differences in choice of forms/ strategies.
Ellis 1992a	Longitudinal (2 yrs)	Production	2 ESL learners (10/11 yrs old; L1s Portuguese and Punjabi) classroom setting	Pencil and paper records and audio recordings	Clear evidence of developmental progression but learners did not make elaborated requests and were limited in their ability to use requests in a number of ways (e.g. used few hints and little modification).

Table 5.2:   Survey of studies of interlanguage requests

studied perceived the politeness level of different requests in accordance with native-speaker norms. However, there is also evidence of some differences. In particular, advanced learners appear to develop a greater sensitivity to the use of politeness strategies in requesting than is evident in native speakers. Walters notes that there was greater unanimity between his learners and native-speaker females, who tended to distinguish polite and impolite forms more sharply than native-speaker males. Carrell and Konneker found that their advanced learners tended to perceive more distinct levels of politeness than native speakers. A tentative conclusion, therefore, is that with sufficient exposure to the L2, learners are able to perceive the sociolinguistic distinctions encoded by native speakers in requests, but that they may become over-sensitive to them.

There is less information available about how low-level (as distinct from advanced or intermediate) learners understand different kinds of requests. One possibility is that such learners rely more on situational than linguistic clues as a means of comprehending requests, as Ervin-Tripp et al.'s (1987) study of child learners of L2 French suggests. Low-level learners are likely to have problems selecting request strategies that are appropriate to different situations. Thus, Tanaka and Kawade (1982) found that Japanese ESL learners (who had probably had little exposure to the sociolinguistic norms of native speakers) tended to opt for less polite strategies overall. Further evidence of the problems that learners face in their choice of request strategy is to be found in Olshtain and Blum-Kulka (1985). They noted that learners of L2 Hebrew who had spent less than two years in Israel were reluctant to accept the informal, positive-orientated request strategy or the direct request strategy found in native-speaker speech. For example, learners were inclined to reject the Hebrew equivalent of 'I hope you can take me back to town' when asking for a ride, whereas native speakers were more likely to accept it. The learners may have responded in accordance with the politeness norms for requesting of their L1.

Most of the research has focused on the production of requests elicited in the form of written responses to a discourse completion questionnaire or oral responses to role play tasks. Many of the studies have investigated high-intermediate or advanced learners. One of the strongest findings from these studies is that even these learners do not acquire fully native-like ways of requesting. In particular, they tend to produce longer requests than native speakers—the 'waffle phenomenon' (see Blum-Kulka and Olshtain 1986; House and Kasper 1987; Færch and Kasper 1989; Rintell and Mitchell 1989; Edmondson and House 1991). This is the result of the over-suppliance of politeness markers, of syntactic downgraders, and, in particular, of supportive moves. This verbosity is more evident in high-intermediate than in advanced learners (Blum-Kulka and Olshtain 1986). A number of explanations have been suggested for this phenomenon. It may reflect a desire to 'play it safe' by making propositional and pragmatic meanings as transparent as possible. The need to 'play it safe' may in turn derive from the fact that although advanced learners have access to the standardized routines needed to perform requests, they make less use of them than native speakers because they are not sure about the range and appropriateness of their application in particular situations (Edmondson and House 1991: 285). Verbosity may also reflect a desire on the part of such learners to display their linguistic competence or, conversely, it may be indicative of the learners' awareness of their own status as second language users—an acknowledgement of the diminished identity they feel in certain situations. Again, though, conclusions about learners' pragmatic competence on the basis of their elicited performance can only be tentative.

Other differences between high-level learners and native speakers have been noted. For example, they tend to overuse the politeness marker 'please', to employ more double-markings (for example, '*Could* you *possibly* present your paper this week?') and to make more extensive use of external (as opposed to internal) modification (Færch and Kasper 1989). These high-level learners, however, show control over a wide range of forms and strategies for performing requests.

In contrast, lower-level learners display only a limited range of politeness features. Scarcella (1979), for instance, reports that 'low level L2 speakers showed much less variety in the politeness strategies they used and lacked any apparent distribution of politeness features' (page 287). For example, they used imperative requests to all addressees irrespective of social distance and power differences, and deployed hedges in totally inappropriate ways. Tanaka (1988) found that Japanese students at an Australian university differed markedly from native English speakers in their requesting behaviour. They failed to give concrete reasons for their requests and also showed less uncertainty regarding whether the conditions for a request were met. In general, they were less indirect and tentative. Thus, whereas Australians were likely to say 'Do you think I could have . . .?' when requesting a book from a lecturer, the Japanese used 'Can I . . .?' They also differed in their choice of strategies, using negative politeness strategies (for example, 'If you don't mind . . .') where the native speakers did not, and failing to use them in other situations where the native speakers employed them. They avoided positive politeness strategies (for example, mention of first name). These lower-level learners had no difficulty in performing the illocutionary meaning of requesting, but they were unable to do so in socially appropriate ways. They made an attempt to vary their request in accordance with social factors such as addressee—as Cathcart (1986) also found in a study of the communicative behaviour of children in a bilingual kindergarten—but could not do so very effectively.

Ideally, detailed information is needed about how individual learners with different L1 backgrounds gradually develop the ability to perform requests over time. Unfortunately, there have been few longitudinal studies so far. Schmidt's (1983) study of Wes examined his acquisition of directives (a general class of speech acts that includes requests) over a three-year period. Initially, Wes relied on a small set of formulas (for example, 'Can I have a . . .?'). On occasions he used V + -*ing* in place of the imperative form, and he tended to rely heavily on lexical clues such as 'please' (a phenomenon that Scarcella also noted in beginner learners). Wes also made substantial use of hints, which Schmidt says native speakers often had difficulty in interpreting. Over three years considerable development took place so that 'by the end of the period gross errors in the performance of directives had largely been eliminated' (1983: 154). Wes could use request formulas productively, he had abandoned V + -*ing* in commands, he had increased the range of request patterns at his disposal (for example, 'Let's . . .' and 'Shall we . . .?' had appeared), and in general gave evidence of much greater elaboration in his requesting behaviour. However, Schmidt notes that Wes was still limited in his ability to vary the use of directive type in accordance with situational factors, and also sometimes used a particular pattern in inappropriate ways.

The second longitudinal study indicates a similar pattern of development to that of Wes, although in this case the two learners were children acquiring L2 English in a classroom context in London. In Ellis 1992a, I claimed that there was clear evidence of a developmental progression. For example, requests for goods were first performed by means of verbless utterances (such as

'Pencil please?'). Next, mood derivable requests with an imperative verb appeared (such as 'Give me a paper') and only a short time afterwards query preparatory requests using 'Can I have . . .?' This formula was frequently used and alternative ways of requesting goods did not appear until much later. It also took time for 'Can I . . .?' to appear in a range of syntactic frames (for example, 'Can I take a book with me?' and 'Can you pass me the pencil?'). I also identified a number of general areas of development. For example, the overall range of request types expanded, the range of exponents of a specific request type increased, and requests that encoded the hearer's perspective (as opposed to the speaker's) emerged. However, the learners' requests were still limited in a number of ways by the end of the two-year period. The majority of their requests were still of the direct kind. There were few examples of non-conventional requests. Certain types of requests (performatives and hedged performatives) did not occur at all. The range of formal devices was still very limited. There was little attempt to employ either internal or external modification. The learners failed to modify their choice of request strategy systematically according to addressee (teacher or another pupil). I suggested two possible explanations for these developmental limitations. One was that the learners were still in the process of acquiring the linguistic and pragmatic knowledge needed to perform requests. According to this explanation, many features of requests are acquired late. The other explanation was that the classroom setting did not afford the appropriate communicative conditions for full acquisition of request forms and strategies, a point taken up later in Chapter 13.

What general conclusions can we come to regarding L2 learners' use and acquisition of requests? Learners—even relative beginners—appear to have few problems in understanding the illocutionary force of a request, probably because they are able to make use of situational cues. Later on they are able to perceive the sociolinguistic meanings encoded by different request types, although they tend to be oversensitive to these. With regard to production, learners begin with very simple requests and then slowly build up their repertoire, learning not only an increasing number of formal devices for performing them, but also the social meanings attached to these devices. There is considerable evidence, however, to suggest that even very advanced learners fall short of native-speaker competence. Although they eventually master native-speaker politeness strategies, they show a tendency to verbosity, perhaps because they are aware of the dangers that are inherent in making requests.

Apologies

Like requests, apologies are face-threatening acts. However, they differ from requests in that they impose on the speaker rather than the hearer. An apology requires the speaker to admit responsibility for some behaviour (or failure to carry out some behaviour) that has proved costly to the hearer. Apologies also differ from requests in that they refer to past rather than future events.

Apologies may also differ from requests in another important way. Whereas there are substantial cross-cultural differences in the way requests are realized in different situations, this does not appear to be the case with apologies. Olshtain (1989), in a study that was part of the Cross-cultural Speech Act Realization Project, investigated the strategies used to realize apologies by speakers of four different languages: Hebrew, Australian English, Canadian French, and German. As in most of the other studies in this project, data were collected by means of a discourse completion task. Olshtain reached the following conclusion:

> ... we have good reason to expect that, given the same social factors, the same contextual factors, and the same level of offence, different languages will realize apologies in very similar ways (1989: 171).

In other words, the strategies used to perform apologies are largely universal.[5] As such, it might be expected that this speech act will pose L2 learners few problems, as they will be able to make use of L1 strategies. However, as we will see, learners do experience difficulty in apologizing in an L2.

The principal strategies for apologizing have been described by Olshtain and Cohen (1983). They point out that when a speaker is confronted with a situation in which the interests or rights of a hearer have been violated, one of two things can happen: the speaker can reject the need for an apology, or can accept responsibility for the violation and apologize. In the case of the former, the speaker may deny that there is a need to apologize or deny responsibility for the violation. In the case of the latter, there are a number of strategies which the speaker can choose from and perform with different levels of intensity.

The basic strategies, together with examples of the semantic formulas that realize them, are shown in Table 5.3. Following Fraser (1981), a 'semantic formula' is defined as 'a word, phrase or sentence which meets a particular semantic criterion or strategy' (cited in Olshtain and Cohen 1983: 20). The strategies and formulas shown in Table 5.3, which comprise the speech act set for apologies, have been confirmed in subsequent studies. Blum-Kulka, House, and Kasper (1989b), for instance, provide a similar list. The strategies vary in their directness. The first ('an expression of an apology'), which is realized by an explicit illocutionary force indicating device of a formulaic nature, constitutes a direct strategy, whereas the other strategies are more indirect. An apology can be performed with different levels of intensity. For example, the speaker can say 'I'm sorry' or 'I'm very sorry', or can use multiple strategies to increase the intensity. There are also strategies for downgrading apologies, such as when the speaker says 'Sorry, but you shouldn't be so sensitive' (Blum-Kulka, House, and Kasper 1989b: 21). It should also be noted that paralinguistic features such as tone of voice are likely to be important in apologizing. However, these have not been systematically investigated.

Strategy	Example
1 An expression of an apology	
a expression of regret	I'm sorry.
b an offer of apology	I apologize.
c a request for forgiveness	Excuse me.
2 An explanation or account of the situation	The bus was late.
3 An acknowledgement of responsibility	
a accepting the blame	It's my fault.
b expressing self-deficiency	I wasn't thinking.
c recognizing the other person as deserving apology	You are right.
d Expressing lack of intent	I didn't mean to.
4 An offer of repair	I'll pay for the broken vase.
5 A promise of forbearance	It won't happen again.

Table 5.3:   The speech act set for apologies (information and examples taken from Olshtain and Cohen 1983)

Apologies in an L2 have been studied by Cohen and Olshtain (1981), Olshtain and Cohen (1983), Fraser (1981), Olshtain (1983), Blum-Kulka and Olshtain (1984), Olshtain and Cohen (1989), and Rintell and Mitchell (1989). All these studies made use of data elicited by means of either a written discourse completion or oral role play task. The subjects of these studies came from a variety of language backgrounds. In most of them baseline data from the learners' L1 and from native speakers of the target languages were also collected. The studies suggest that L2 learners' performance of apologies is influenced by a number of factors: (1) the learners' level of linguistic proficiency, (2) their L1, (3) their perception of the universality or language specificity of how to apologize, and (4) the nature of the specific apology situation.

Evidence that the learners' level of linguistic proficiency influences how they apologize is forthcoming when it can be shown that subjects' L1 apologies and those of native speakers of the target language are very similar, but differ from the subjects' L2 apologies. In such cases L1 transfer is possible but does not actually occur, presumably because the learners lack the necessary L2 proficiency to do so. Cohen and Olshtain (1981) provide several examples in a study of Hebrew learners of L2 English. They found situations where the learners did not seem to be familiar with the semantic formulas needed for the apology. For example, they were less likely to offer repair when they had backed into someone's car, and less likely to acknowledge responsibility when they had bumped into and shaken up an old lady than when they performed the same apologies in their L1. Lack of linguistic proficiency was in this case reflected in the use of general formulas and saying too little.

In a later paper, Olshtain and Cohen (1989) distinguish three types of deviation resulting from gaps in linguistic competence. Overt errors occur when the learner is evidently trying to apologize but produces a linguistic error as in this example:

> Situation: bumping into a woman in the way. 'I'm very sorry but what can I do? It can't be stopped'.

where the speaker uses 'stopped' instead of 'avoided'. Covert errors occur when the learner's apology is linguistically correct but is inappropriate. For example, a Hebrew learner of L2 English apologized for failing to keep a meeting with a friend with 'I really very sorry. I just forgot. I fell asleep. Understand'. Faulty realization of a semantic formula occurs when the learner has chosen an appropriate formula but phrases it incorrectly, as when one learner wanted to offer repair for forgetting a meeting with someone by using this formula: 'I think I can make another meeting with you'.

Despite the fact that all languages share the same set of basic strategies for apologizing, negative transfer is evident in a number of respects. For example, the learner's L1 may have an effect on the intensity with which apologies are performed. Cohen and Olshtain (1981), for example, note that Hebrew speakers of English were less likely to accept responsibility for an offence or to make offers of repair than native English speakers. Also, they did not intensify their expressions of regret as much. Olshtain and Cohen (1983) refer to an unpublished study by Wu (1981) which found that Chinese learners of English intensified regret much more than native English speakers. These differences corresponded to differences in the learners' L1s. Olshtain and Cohen comment 'while Hebrew L2 speakers may appear somewhat rude to native English speakers when expressing regret, Chinese L2 speakers may appear overly polite, even obsequious' (1983: 30). The Chinese learners also tended to offer explanations, where native English speakers did not. This resulted in the same phenomenon observed in studies of L2 requests—a tendency to say too much.

However, it may not be the actual differences between languages, but rather the learners' attitudes about how apologies should be performed cross-linguistically, that matter. Olshtain (1983) found that the overall frequency of semantic formulas was higher in native English speakers than in native Hebrew speakers, with native Russian speakers intermediate:

English > Russian > Hebrew

She hypothesized that 'transfer from Russian or English into Hebrew as the target L2 might therefore be expected as an increase in the overall frequency of use of semantic formulas' (1983: 245). However, this was not quite what she found. Whereas the English learners decreased the frequency of their use of semantic formulas to a level approximating to that of native Hebrew speakers, the Russian learners maintained the same level as in their native Russian. Olshtain suggests that this reflects the different perceptions of the English and Russian learners. Whereas the former perceived Hebrew speakers as apologizing less than native English speakers, the latter viewed apologizing as a universal phenomenon, 'claiming that people needed to apologize according to their feelings of responsibility, regardless of the language which they happen to be speaking . . .' (op. cit.: 246). Thus, transfer was governed by whether the learners saw apologies as language-specific or universal in nature. However, as Kasper (1992) notes, the Russian learners in fact supplied apology strategies in three out of five situations more frequently in L2 Hebrew than in their native Russian, despite their perceptions of universality. This suggests that learners' attitudes can be overridden by other factors.

Olshtain (1983) also argues that transfer effects can only be accurately identified if attention is given to the specific situation that leads to an apology. She suggests that transfer might be more likely in situations where the learners' culturally-determined perceptions of the importance of status and distance and of the severity of the offence are different from those of native speakers of the target language. For example, in the case of a situation involving backing into someone's car and causing damage, English speakers of L2 Hebrew apologize in much the same way as they do in their L1, whereas in the situation where they have insulted someone at a meeting, they do not transfer their L1 strategies but rather behave in a similar way to native Hebrew speakers. The extent to which learners acquire the sociocultural rules of the L2 is, therefore, situation-dependent.

To sum up, the study of L2 apologies bears out many of the findings of the research on L2 requests. Both the learners' general level of linguistic proficiency and the socio-cultural norms of their L1 influence how they apologize in an L2. Learners may be too concise or they may be verbose. The extent to which transfer takes place can be influenced by the learners' perceptions of the universality of how to apologize, transfer being *less* likely if learners recognize the language-specificity of apologies. Transfer is also more likely in situations where learners feel the need to act in accordance with the sociocultural norms of the native culture. The research to date has not examined how learners of different levels of proficiency perform apologies, or how apologies are learnt over time.

Refusals

Refusals constitute another face-threatening act; in this case they threaten the hearer more than the speaker. They require a high level of pragmatic competence. L2 learners' refusals have been studied in a series of investigations involving Beebe and her co-researchers (Beebe and Takahashi 1989a and 1989b; Takahashi and Beebe 1987; Beebe, Takahashi, and Uliss-Weltz

1990). These studies relied primarily on data collected from a written discourse completion questionnaire, but some specific examples of naturally occurring refusals are also discussed.

Refusals occur in the form of responses to a variety of illocutionary acts (for example, invitations, offers, requests, and suggestions). On the basis of an analysis of native-speaker refusals, Beebe and Takahashi were able to show that they are performed by means of a fairly limited set of direct and indirect 'semantic formulas', which are shown in Table 5.4. Individual refusals are made up of different selections from these formulas in accordance with the status and power relationships holding between speaker and hearer. The analysis of learners' refusals considered (1) the order of semantic formulas, (2) the frequency of formulas, and (3) the content of individual semantic formulas in relation to native-speaker use.

Type	Semantic formula	Example
Direct	1 Performative	I refuse.
	2 Non-performative statement	I can't.
Indirect[6]	3 Statement of regret	I'm sorry.
	4 Wish	I wish I could help you.
	5 Excuse, reason, explanation	I have a headache.
	6 Statement of alternative	I'd prefer to ...
	7 Set condition for past or future acceptance	If you'd asked me earlier I'd have ...
	8 Promise of future acceptance	I'll do it next time.
	9 Statement of principle	I never do business with friends.
	10 Statement of philosophy	One can't be too careful.
	11 Attempt to dissuade interlocutor	I won't be any fun tonight.
	12 Acceptance that functions as refusal	Well, maybe.
	13 Avoidance (e.g. silence or hedging)	I'm not sure.

Table 5.4:   Semantic formulas used in refusals (based on information provided in Beebe, Takahashi, and Uliss-Weltz 1990)

The subjects of the various studies were Japanese learners of English. Beebe and Takahashi are at pains to point out that there are certain stereotypes regarding Japanese people. Japanese people are supposed to apologize a lot, to be less direct and less explicit than Americans, to avoid making critical remarks to someone's face, to avoid disagreement, and to avoid telling people things that they do not want to hear. The results of their research indicate that these stereotypes are not warranted. Frequently, for instance, the learners were more direct than the native speakers and in certain situations they showed no reluctance to impart unpleasant information. There were, however, a number of differences between the way Japanese learners and Americans performed refusals.

One type of pragmalinguistic error concerned the order of semantic formulas. Beebe, Takahashi, and Uliss-Weltz (1990) found that although even proficient Japanese speakers of English in the United States employed the same range of semantic formulas as Americans, they differed in the order in which they were typically used. For example, the Japanese speakers omitted expressions of apology or regret in refusing invitations made by people lower in status than themselves. They reacted differently according to whether the invitation originated from a higher- or lower-status person, whereas the native speakers responded according to how familiar they were with their interlocutors. The same difference was evident in the frequency with which semantic formulas were used. The Japanese English speakers increased the number of formulas they used when refusing a higher-status interlocutor, while the American English speakers did so when addressing familiar equals. In other words, where Americans adopted strategies consonant with solidarity, the Japanese preferred power-orientated strategies. A similar difference is evident in the content of semantic formulas, the Japanese excuses tending to be less specific than American excuses (except when refusing food) and sounding more formal in tone. This was particularly evident in the frequent use of lofty-sounding appeals to principle and philosophy. For example, refusing the offer of a new diet, one Japanese learner responded 'I make it a rule to be temperate in eating'.

The main focus of Beebe and Takahashi's research is pragmatic transfer—the extent to which learners transfer the 'rules of speaking' of their native language into the L2. A key question is to what extent transfer is influenced by the learners' level of L2 proficiency. Takahashi and Beebe (1987) hypothesized that Japanese learners (EFL and ESL) with higher proficiency would display more Japanese communicative characteristics in their English than less proficient learners. They based this hypothesis on the argument that lower-level learners lack the linguistic resources to encode socio-culturally appropriate Japanese patterns and so resort to a simplification strategy, whereas the higher-level learners have acquired the linguistic means to make socio-cultural transfer possible. The results of an analysis of the refusals produced by Japanese ESL learners gave support to this hypothesis. The more proficient learners (defined in this study as those who had been resident longer in the United States) made more frequent use of native-language patterns—in particular, the high level of formality in the tone and content of refusals (for example, 'I am very delighted and honoured to be asked to attend the party, but . . .'). However, the results for the EFL learners (i.e. those studying English at college level in Japan) failed to support the hypothesis, there being no difference in the refusals of undergraduates and graduates. Takahashi and Beebe suggest that this was because 'pragmatic competence is not affected by just a few years' difference in school in the EFL context' (page 149). Again, this study suggests that the development of pragmatic competence depends on whether the learners experience any sociolinguistic need to vary their performance of specific acts.

The study of L2 refusals is more limited than the study of requests or apologies. There have been fewer studies, none of them longitudinal, and a narrow range of subjects (only adult Japanese). However, the work done raises a number of interesting points. First, L2 learners' pragmatic behaviour is not always in accordance with stereotypical views. Second, although advanced L2 learners have no difficulty in performing refusals, they do not always do so in the same way as native speakers. One possible reason for this is pragmatic transfer. Thus, highly proficient Japanese learners respond to the status of their interlocutors, rather than to how familiar with them they are. Third, learners may need to reach a threshold level of linguistic proficiency before pragmatic transfer can take place.

Some generalizations regarding the performance of illocutionary acts in learner language

Although the study of interlanguage pragmatics is still in its infancy (there being an unfortunate lack of longitudinal studies), it is possible to identify a number of general characteristics:

1 Just as learners make linguistic errors, so too they make pragmatic errors. These are of two kinds: sociopragmatic and pragmalinguistic (Thomas 1983).
2 Following and building on Blum-Kulka (1991), three broad phases of development of pragmatic competence can be identified:

Phase 1: Message-orientated and unsystematic:
During this stage learners rely on situational clues to interpret the illocutionary force of different acts and on simplification strategies to produce them (for example, the use of formulas and the over-use of simple politeness markers such as 'please'[7]). The learner uses 'any linguistic and non-linguistic means at his or her disposal to achieve a communicative end' (1991: 270).

Phase 2: Interlanguage-orientated and potentially systematic:
During this stage learners are able to differentiate the social meanings performed by alternative realizations of an illocutionary act. They are also able to use a variety of strategies in their own production. However, their performance will differ from that of native speakers in two major ways: it is more verbose and it shows evidence of pragmatic transfer from the native language. Thus 'the learners' speech acts will be pragmatically and socially acceptable in part and in part unacceptable' (1991: 270).

Phase 3:   Interculturally-orientated and potentially systematic:
During this stage learners approximate closely to native-speaker performance. Thus, they use the same range of politeness strategies as native speakers. However, they may continue to display residual transfer of 'deep' cultural elements (for example, the importance attached to status differences), to use too many words, to manifest a different distribution of linguistic devices used to realize speech acts, and, generally, to display oversensitivity and hesitancy in comprehending and performing face-threatening acts.

3 It probably takes a large number of years of exposure to the L2, and also a setting that creates a need for learners to vary their performance of illocutionary acts in accordance with the addressee and other factors, before learners reach Phase 3. Many learners will probably never do so.

A number of different factors have been proposed to explain this pattern of development. Obviously, the learner's linguistic proficiency is a key one. Learners with little lexical or grammatical knowledge of the L2 will be restricted not only in what illocutionary acts they can perform, but also in how they perform them. In the previous chapter, it was suggested that learners first acquire forms and later learn what functions they can use them to perform, a view supported by Scarcella's (1979) study of requests. For example, she found instances of forms used at least ten times by individual learners but without variation according to addressee.

Transfer is the other major factor identified. Learners perform speech acts such as requests, apologies, and refusals in accordance with the sociolinguistic rules of their native language. However, as discussed above, transfer can only take place when learners have achieved sufficient L2 resources to make it possible. Also, the extent to which transfer takes place may be governed by the learners' perceptions about transferability, as Olshtain's (1983) study of English- and Russian-speaking learners of L2 Hebrew showed.

There are also other explanatory factors that may be involved. Beebe and Takahashi (1989a) invoke accommodation theory (see Chapter 4) to suggest that Japanese learners' directness may reflect 'psychological convergence'. That is, they may attempt to converge towards a stereotypical norm of native-speaker behaviour, but overshoot the mark, thus diverging. Such convergence can be teacher-induced, as when Japanese teachers advise their students to be direct when in the United States, resulting in learners producing such refusals as 'Hell no!'. Another possibility is found in Preston's (1989) observation that learners may sometimes wish to appear 'learner-like' as this brings communicative advantages in certain situations, a point we will take up later when we consider impression management. Preston suggests that this may account for the greater verbosity of advanced learners' speech acts. It is possible that learners vary in their style of speaking, sometimes opting to perform in accordance with their stereotypes of native speakers and sometimes emphasizing their status as learners.

Yet another possibility, which can explain the greater verbosity observed in advanced learners, is that learners prefer a more transparent communicative style because it is safer. Kasper (1989) suggests that learners may be conscious of their foreigner role and, as a result, feel a stronger need to establish, rather than presuppose, common ground than do native speakers. This leads learners to try to make their reasons for imposing on interlocutors as explicit as possible when performing illocutionary acts such as requests.

Three other explanatory factors are worth mentioning. As in the case of linguistic errors, pragmatic errors may be the result of overgeneralization. Learners may overextend a realization strategy from a situation in which it is appropriate to one in which it is not. Also, the extent to which learners are able to encode illocutionary acts in socially appropriate ways may depend on whether their attention is focused on simply getting the propositional content of their utterance across or also on its modality. Kasper (1984a) found that when learners were under communicative pressure they tended to engage in *modality reduction*.[8] That is, they omitted grammatical features such as modal verbs and adverbials associated with the expression of modal meanings like possibility and tentativeness.

This account of pragmatic development tends to assume that learners are targeted on some set of native-speaker norms. As Blum-Kulka (1991) has noted, such an assumption is questionable, however. Learners may prefer to maintain their own ethnic identity or they may wish to establish a separate identity as an L2 learner/user. In such cases, behaving in accordance with native-speaker norms will be perceived as inappropriate. The distinctive pragmatic features evident in the language of even very advanced L2 learners may reflect not so much a failure to achieve target-language norms as the attainment of a mode of behaviour compatible with the learners' chosen sense of identity (see Chapter 6 for further discussion of this aspect of L2 acquisition). This observation may apply more to sociopragmatic than pragmalinguistic choices, for, as Thomas points out, 'sociopragmatic decisions are *social* before they are linguistic, and while foreign learners are fairly amenable to corrections they regard as linguistic, they are justifiably sensitive about having their social . . . judgement called into question' (1983: 104).

Impression management

The study of language functions such as requests, apologies, and refusals has taken place within the framework provided by speech act theorists such as Austin and Searle. The study of impression management, however, has been informed by interactional sociolinguistics (Erickson and Schultz 1982; Gumperz 1982; Scollon and Scollon 1983). This examines how speakers achieve communicative effects by manipulating their linguistic and non-linguistic resources.

The choices that individual speakers make from the repertoire of signs available to them serve as one of the ways in which they seek to form and change the attitudes that other speakers have towards them. Speakers exploit contextualization cues (i.e. the signals that trigger how speakers view the context they are attempting to build through interaction) to channel the listeners' interpretations of what is being said. In particular, cues that are in some way unexpected serve as devices for managing the listener's impressions of a speaker. The study of these cues has involved the qualitative analysis of social encounters in which potential problems of communication arise because the speakers do not share the same cues or because they attribute different values to those cues they do share (see Gumperz 1982).

Conversations between L2 speakers and native speakers constitute a good example of the 'unequal' encounters that have attracted the attention of researchers in the field of interactional sociolinguistics. Learners are likely to find themselves in an unequal position for two reasons. First, they are unequal in terms of their knowledge of the language they are trying to communicate in. Second, many L2 learners find themselves trying to communicate with native speakers who hold positions of power and so can affect their future (for example, in terms of employment or access to social amenities).

A simple example of how impression management works in such encounters is provided by Ellis and Roberts (1987). An Asian applicant in Britain is being interviewed by white managers for a job. They are discussing how the Asian obtained a previous job:

> NS: So you eventually did get a job with the assistance of a friend. Did he recommend you to the employment centre or to the manager ...?
> NNS: No—well, he brought me a form ...

The Asian's comment that his friend assisted him by bringing him an application form constitutes a device for amending the interviewer's preconception that Asians obtain jobs illicitly by having their friends help them get round the system. The comment constitutes a contextualization cue because it is unexpected in relation to the interviewer's preceding comment. In this case, the Asian possesses the L2 resources to successfully redefine the context in a way more favourable to himself.

Not all learners are so successful in impression management. Chick (1985, cited in Wolfson 1989a) found that black students in South Africa were unable to overcome the negative cultural stereotypes held by their white professors in discussions of their examination results despite the fact that they were fluent L2 speakers. Chick argues that this failure arose from 'a mismatch of contextualization cues'. Roberts and Simonot (1987) report on a study of minority ethnic workers in encounters with an estate agent and in more informal conversations with a researcher. They describe the interactional style of one worker who was content to play a subservient role in the estate agent encounter. He never offered information, he developed only those themes which the estate agent had explicitly sanctioned and he omitted affective responses that might have conveyed to the estate agent that his wishes were not satisfied. Roberts and Simonot suggest that this learner's repeated failure to negotiate a context in which he could participate as an equal resulted in his failure to acquire the interactional knowledge needed to escape from his disadvantaged social position. They note that this learner was typical of their subjects.

Learners are likely to experience difficulties in identifying the right contextualization cues to deal with problems that arise in interaction. Fiksdal (1989) used the techniques developed by Erickson and Schultz (1982) to investigate how Chinese speakers of English handled uncomfortable moments during academic advisory sessions with native-speaker advisers. In this kind of situation, problems arise when the learners need to reject the advice offered by the native speaker. Fiksdal found that, unlike native-speaker students, the Chinese students either delayed or omitted offering verbal repair of uncomfortable moments and, in the case of delayed repair, showed a preference for an implicit rather than an explicit statement. She suggests that this may reflect their wish to avoid forcing the advisers to lose face by indicating that their advice is not acceptable.

Sometimes learners may be able to substitute alternative contextualization cues, by drawing creatively on their interlanguage resources. Rampton's (1987) study of ESL learners in a London language unit indicates one way in which this might take place. He observed these learners using primitive interlanguage forms such as 'me no like' and 'me too clever', even though they clearly possessed the competence to produce more target-like forms. A form-function analysis revealed that the 'broken English' forms were used to perform potentially face-threatening acts such as rejection/refusal and boasting. Rampton suggests that the learners made deliberate use of 'me' constructions to symbolize their cultural and social incompetence as a way of mitigating the force of these face-threatening speech acts. By emphasizing their learner status, they were able to challenge the teacher or play down their attempt to claim superiority over their peers.

To sum up, when learners participate in conversations with native speakers and other learners—particularly if the encounters are of the unequal kind—they need to negotiate the impression they wish to create. Frequently, they lack knowledge of the relevant contextualization cues. One solution is to accept the social role allocated to them—a kind of avoidance strategy. Another is to substitute cues from their native language—a form of transfer. A third solution is to make creative use of their interlanguage resources to exploit their status as language learners. Little is currently known about how learners' use of contextualization cues develops over time and how they learn to manage impressions in a manner compatible with target-language norms.

Summary

The focus of research on interlanguage pragmatics to date has been a relatively small set of well-defined illocutionary acts. The research has made use of spoken data collected in natural settings and also data elicited by means of discourse completion tasks. Learners have been found to make both sociopragmatic errors (as when they fail to respond to a native-speaker compliment) and pragmalinguistic errors (as when they resort to formulas and conventionalized routines borrowed from their L1 in order to express gratitude).

Requests, apologies, and refusals are three acts which have received considerable attention. The perception/understanding of requests poses few problems for learners, but production is more problematic. Low-proficiency learners tend to make use of a limited range of formulas, employ non-target-like politeness strategies, and have difficulty in adjusting their strategy in accordance with situational requirements. Advanced learners manifest knowledge of a broad range of linguistic realization devices which they are able to use with native-like appropriateness. However, their requests differ from those of native speakers in that they tend to be verbose. In the case of L2 apologies, both linguistic proficiency and L1 transfer are also factors. Interestingly, learners differ from native speakers by both failing to say enough on some occasions and saying too much on others. The learners' perception of the universality of speech act realization also influences performance. The study of refusals by Japanese learners of English shows that they are not always stereotypically indirect and that, when a threshold level of L2 proficiency has been achieved, pragmatic transfer is more likely to occur. As with requests, the classroom setting may not afford learners the range of situations needed to develop full sociolinguistic competence.

Impression management is also problematic to learners, as they may not have access to the contextualization cues they need to construct a context favourable to themselves. Sometimes they make no effort to do so, sometimes they borrow cues from their L1 and at other times they may even deliberately employ interlanguage forms to exploit their identity as language learners when performing face-threatening language functions.

Conclusion

Studies of interlanguage pragmatics have concentrated on describing the differences between the way in which L2 learners and native speakers perform the same speech acts. They have also focused on the pragmatic problems that learners experience. Less attention has been given to how learners' pragmatic competence develops over time. As a result, although quite a lot is now known about how learners *use* an L2, very little is known about how 'rules of speaking' are acquired. For this, longitudinal studies are needed.

The studies to date suggest that three factors are of major importance in the acquisition of pragmatic competence. The first is the level of the learners' linguistic competence. Learners cannot construct native-speaker-type discourse unless they possess the linguistic means to do so. Learners with limited L2 proficiency find few problems in performing the speech acts that are communicatively important to them but considerable difficulty in performing them in native-like ways. The need to achieve this may be one of the prime factors motivating continued L2 linguistic development.[9]

The second factor of obvious importance is transfer. There is ample evidence that learners transfer 'rules of speaking' from their L1 to their L2. As Riley (1989: 247) emphasizes, cultural transfer is evident in the types of communicative events that learners expect to occur in a given situation, the manner of their participation in them, the specific types of acts they perform and the way they realize them, the way topics are nominated and developed, and the way discourse is regulated. Yet it is important not to overstate the role of the non-native speaker's L1 and culture. First, as we saw in the case of requests, learners have to develop a satisfactory level of linguistic competence before transfer of complicated L1 strategies and routines becomes possible. While acknowledging the importance of transfer, we also need to recognize that other factors are involved. Second, as Kasper and Dahl (1991) point out, researchers of interlanguage pragmatics have tended to take a very product-orientated view of transfer, which has been rejected in current process-orientated accounts. Transfer needs to be viewed as a complex process, constrained by other factors such as the learner's stage of development (see Chapter 8). They comment: 'Clarifying the concept of pragmatic transfer should have high priority on the research agenda in IL pragmatics' (1991: 225).

The third factor is the status of the learner. Learners do not usually participate in communicative events as equals—at least when their interlocutors are native speakers. One reason for the lack of equality may be the learner's overall social status in the native-speaker community. This is reflected in the discourse which has been observed to take place in 'gate-keeping encounters'. But learners also have a reduced status simply because they are learners. As Harder (1980: 268) puts it, 'the learner is a coarse and primitive character from an interactional point of view'. Learners are, in a sense, 'clients', and this status determines the kind of discourse they typically take part in and the role they play in it. For example, adult learners in conversations with native speakers are likely to have few opportunities to nominate topics and tend not to compete for turns. This restricts the range of speech acts they will need to perform. It is not yet clear what the repercussions of this are for the acquisition of both linguistic and pragmatic competence, but there is sufficient evidence to suggest that learners may benefit from opportunities for a more equal discourse role, such as occurs in communication with other learners.

Finally, it is should be pointed out that the study of interlanguage pragmatics acts in L2 acquisition has focused on the spoken medium and has paid little attention to writing. This is particularly the case with illocutionary acts. In effect, therefore, although we know something about how 'contextualized' acts such requests, apologies, and refusals are acquired, we know little about how learners acquire the ability to perform acts found in decontextualized, written language. Snow's (1987) study of the acquisition of definitions by French/English bilingual children indicates that 'formal definitional knowledge' constitutes an area of learning that is independent of 'communicative adequacy'. This suggests that the ability to perform speech acts like requests, apologies and refusals in face-to-face interaction may be distinct from the ability needed to perform speech acts like definitions in writing.[10] Clearly, if the study of interlanguage pragmatics is to progress it will need to examine written as well as spoken learner language.

Notes

1 Levinson (1983) points out the term 'speech act' is generally used to refer exclusively to 'illocutionary act'.
2 Kasper and Dahl (1991: 216) specifically exclude the following aspects from their review of research methods in interlanguage pragmatics: '... conversational management, discourse organization ... sociolinguistic aspects of language use such as choice of address forms'.
3 Native-speaker norms will vary according to the native-speaker variety that is sampled. The pragmatic rules that govern the performance of specific illocutionary acts may vary from one group of native speakers to another.
4 It should also be noted that learners may prefer to retain the patterns of pragmatic behaviour of their L1, i.e. refuse to conform to native-speaker norms. This may be because they wish to maintain their own identity or may be done for strategic reasons (see the section on 'impression management' in this chapter).
5 Olshtain (1989) adds a caveat to her claim that apology strategies are universal. She notes that it may be 'an artefact of our data collection instrument—the seven apology-inducing situations were selected intentionally to create contexts that were cross-culturally very similar' (1989: 171). It remains a possibility, therefore, that there are cross-cultural differences regarding *when* speakers apologize. It can be noted that Japanese speakers of L2 English sometimes apologize in contexts that call for thanking—on leaving someone's house where they have been given dinner, for instance.
6 The semantic formulas that Beebe classifies as 'indirect' appear to be of two kinds, which perhaps should be distinguished. Some of the formulas, for example, (4) 'Wish', are likely to be used alongside direct refusals—for example, by preparing for them—while others, for example, (5) 'Excuse, reason, or explanation' can be used in place of a direct refusal.

7 In some cases, learners may continue to overuse politeness markers such
   as 'please' even when they develop alternative linguistic means. Examples
   of such learners are the Japanese subjects studied by Beebe and
   Takahashi.
8 Learners are not alone in ignoring modality under certain conditions.
   Native speakers are also likely to forsake politeness markers if the context
   does not favour the explicit indication of social positions.
9 An issue of considerable interest is whether learners first acquire linguistic
   forms and then learn how to use them in appropriate ways, as variabilists
   like myself propose (Ellis 1989c), or whether the linguistic forms are acquired as a product of learning how to communicate, as discourse analysts such as Hatch (1978b) propose. It is likely that both processes are
   involved, although classroom learners in particular are likely to acquire
   form before function.
10 There is, of course, a substantial amount of work on the performance of
   decontextualized speech acts by native speakers (see, for example,
   Flowerdew's (1992) study of definitions in science lectures).

Further Reading

The available literature on interlanguage pragmatics tends to assume a gen-
eral familiarity with descriptive and theoretical frameworks employed in the
study of pragmatics. Information about these frameworks can be found in:
M. Coulthard, *An Introduction to Discourse Analysis* (Longman, 1985) and,
in a shorter form, in:
E. Hatch and M. Long, 'Discourse analysis, what's that?' in D. Larsen-
Freeman (ed.), *Discourse Analysis in Second Language Research* (Newbury
House, 1980).
N. Wolfson, 'Rules of speaking' in J. Richards and R. Schmidt (eds.), *Lan-
guage and Communication* (Longman, 1983), also provides a very readable
introduction.
   The field of interlanguage pragmatics is somewhat disparate and there is no
comprehensive overview available.
Kasper, G. and M. Dahl, 'Research methods in interlanguage pragmatics.'
Studies in Second Language Acquisition (1991) 13, focuses on the research
methods used to investigate L2 illocutionary acts, but in the process provides
an excellent account of the research in this area.
N. Wolfson, *Perspectives: Sociolinguistics and TESOL* (Newbury House,
1989), also provides a good overview.
G. Kasper, 'Pragmatic transfer.' *Second Language Research* (1992) 8, offers a
sound overview of L2 speech act research and a solid discussion of the role of
transfer.

In general, though, the reader should turn to the original reports of the research. The following reflect the range of work undertaken and are fairly easy to read:

1 Pragmatic errors

P. Riley, 'Well don't blame me! On the interpretation of pragmatic errors' in W. Oleksy (ed.), *Contrastive Pragmatics* (John Benjamins, 1989).

2 Requests

R. Scarcella, 'On speaking politely in a second language' in C. Yorio, K. Perkins, and J. Schachter (eds.), *On TESOL '79* (TESOL, 1979).

3 Apologies

E. Olshtain and A. Cohen, 'Apology: A speech-act set' in N. Wolfson and E. Judd (eds.), *Sociolinguistics and Second Language Acquisition* (Newbury House, 1983).

4 Refusals

L. Beebe, T. Takahashi, and R. Uliss-Weltz, 'Pragmatic transfer in ESL refusals' in. R. Scarcella, E. Andersen, and S. Krashen (eds.), *Developing Communicative Competence in a Second Language* (Newbury House, 1990).

5 Impression management

B. Rampton, 'Stylistic variation and not speaking "Normal English"' in R. Ellis (ed.), *Second Language Acquisition in Context* (Prentice Hall, 1987).

Readers interested in more technical accounts might like to look at some of the publications that have come out of the Cross-Cultural Speech Act Realization Project, for example:
S. Blum-Kulka, J. House, and G. Kasper (eds.), *Cross-cultural Pragmatics: Requests and Apologies* (Ablex, 1989).

There are also a number of relevant articles in:
S. Gass et al. (eds.), *Variation in Second Language Acquisition, Volume I: Sociolinguistic Issues* (Multilingual Matters, 1989).

PART THREE

Explaining second language acquisition: External factors

Introduction

The chapters in the previous section concentrated on the description of learner language. The chapters in the next three sections will attempt to explain learner language by addressing three major questions:

1 How do learners learn a second language?

To answer this question it is necessary to explain how learners obtain information about the L2 and how they process this information in order to develop their interlanguages.

2 Why do learners vary in how fast they learn a second language?

Learners vary in the speed with which they acquire an L2. What factors account for this inter-learner variation?

3 Why do most learners fail to achieve full target-language competence?

As we have already seen in Chapter 3, learners vary in the ultimate level of proficiency they achieve, with most of them failing to reach target-language competence. A full explanation of L2 acquisition must account for this phenomenon.

To answer these questions we will need to consider three aspects of L2 acquisition: (1) the external environment, (2) the 'black box' (i.e. the learner's existing knowledge and the internal mechanisms that guide L2 acquisition), and (3) individual learner factors, such as age and motivation.

Our search for explanations will be guided by the framework shown in the figure below. There are three principal components in this framework: (1) social factors/settings, (2) language processing mechanisms, and (3) individual learner factors. These are interrelated in a number of ways. Social factors (for example, a learner's ethnic background) may influence individual learner factors (for example, a learner's motivation to learn a particular language). It is also possible, of course, that individual learner factors (for example, a learner's personality) may have an effect on the social conditions of learning, for example by influencing the nature of the social settings experienced. Social factors/settings serve as the major determinant of the input that learners receive. For example, they influence what variety of the target language the learners will be exposed to and also the amount of exposure. Input provides the data for the language processing mechanisms. These are also, potentially at least, influenced by individual learner factors and also by the learner's 'other knowledge' (including the L1). The language processing mechanisms account for changes in the learner's L2 knowledge (the interlanguage system). This knowledge is used in both the comprehension and production of utterances in the L2 (i.e. output). Output also helps to shape subsequent input, as, for example, when what learners say influences what is said to them.

The process of L2 acquisition is very complex, and this framework simplifies it somewhat. Also, some of the relationships shown are more controversial than others. For example, as we will see in Chapter 11, not all researchers agree that individual learner factors have a direct impact on language processing. However, the framework serves as a heuristic in our search for explanations.

This section will focus on the components that lie outside the 'black box': Chapter 6 will consider social factors and settings while Chapter 7 will examine the nature of the input and interaction that learners experience and how this influences L2 acquisition. As in subsequent sections, we will be searching for explanations by looking for answers to all the three questions mentioned at the beginning of this Introduction. However, it will also be necessary to review research of a descriptive nature. We need to know, for example, what are the main characteristics of different social settings as well as how these influence learning outcomes. Similarly, we need to understand what is the nature of the input and interaction learners experience, as well as how these affect language processing.

The categorization of explanations in terms of external factors, internal factors, and individual learner differences is justified because it reflects identifiable orientations in SLA research and because it provides a means of organizing the information provided by research. However, it should be emphasized that there is no single and no simple explanation of L2 acquisition. A complete explanation will need to consider all the three components

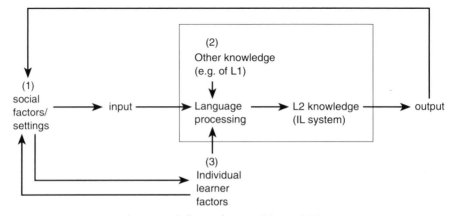

A framework for explaining L2 acquisition

and how they interact. Social factors/settings and input/interaction cannot be considered in total isolation from individual learner factors or language processing. In the two chapters in this section, therefore, while focusing attention on external factors, we will also need to give some consideration to the other two components shown in the framework.

6 Social factors and second language acquisition

Introduction

This chapter examines the relationship between society and second language (L2) learning. It considers the role of social factors in L2 proficiency. Learners differ enormously in how quickly they learn an L2, in the type of proficiency they acquire (for example, conversational ability as opposed to literacy in the L2) and the ultimate level of proficiency they reach. In part, these differences can be explained by reference to psychological factors such as language aptitude, learning style and personality (see Chapter 11) but in part they are socially determined.

This chapter will also consider the relationship between different learning contexts and L2 proficiency. 'Context' here refers to the different settings in which L2 learning can take place—whether the setting is a 'natural' or an 'educational' one, and various subdivisions of these, such as *submersion* and *immersion*. It is, perhaps, a matter of debate as to whether such distinctions are to be viewed as 'social', but the view taken here is that, in essence, they are. Each setting can be seen as a context in which constellations of social factors typically figure to influence learning outcomes.

Social factors have a major impact on L2 proficiency but probably do not influence it directly. Rather, their effect is mediated by a number of variables. One set of variables which have been found to be of major importance is learner attitudes. Social factors help to shape learners' attitudes which, in turn, influence learning outcomes. Social factors also influence L2 learning in-directly in another way. They determine the learning opportunities which in-dividual learners experience. For example, the learners' socio-economic class and ethnic background may affect the nature and the extent of the input to which they are exposed.

Social accounts of L2 learning have been primarily concerned with *L2 proficiency*. In this respect, they differ from other branches of SLA research, which, as we saw in Part Two of this book, have focused on specific linguistic and pragmatic properties of learner language. L2 proficiency has been con-ceptualized in different ways, none of which, according to Stern (1983: 356), provides 'a completely satisfactory expression'. It has been measured by means of rating scales, where the assumption is that learners range from zero to full native-like proficiency, standardized tests such as the TOEFL examination, and performance on a range of different tasks designed to tap different components of proficiency.

One model of L2 proficiency that has figured significantly in socially-oriented SLA research is that of Cummins. In his early work, Cummins distinguished two types of proficiency. Basic interpersonal communication skills (BICS) are the skills required for oral fluency and sociolinguistic appropriateness. They are 'basic' in the sense that they develop naturally as a result of exposure to a language through communication. Cognitive/academic language proficiency (CALP) consists of the linguistic knowledge and literacy skills required for academic work. In his later work (for example, Cummins 1983; Cummins and Swain 1986), Cummins has proposed that language proficiency be conceptualized along two interacting continua. One continuum relates to the extent of the contextual support available for expressing or receiving meaning. At one extreme, a task might require context-embedded language where communication derives from 'inter-personal involvement in a shared reality', while at the other the task might require context-reduced language, where 'shared reality cannot be assumed' (Cummins and Swain 1986: 153). The other continuum concerns the extent to which a task is cognitively demanding. This reflects 'the amount of information that must be processed simultaneously or in close succession' and also the extent to which the information needed to perform the task has become automatized.

This chapter will begin with a brief discussion of learner attitudes and how they have been studied. It will then address three broad questions:

1 To what extent do specific social factors (age, sex, social class, and ethnic identity) affect L2 proficiency?
2 To what extent do social factors influence the learner's choice of target language variety?
3 How can we characterize the different social contexts in which L2 acquisition takes place, and what effect does the type of context have on learning outcomes?

The chapter also provides an account of a number of social models of L2 acquisition.

Learner attitudes

Learners manifest different attitudes towards (1) the target language, (2) target language speakers, (3) the target-language culture, (4) the social value of learning the L2, (5) particular uses of the target language, and (6) themselves as members of their own culture. These attitudes are likely to reflect the particular social settings in which learners find themselves. Learner attitudes have an impact on the level of L2 proficiency achieved by individual learners and are themselves influenced by this success. Thus, learners with positive attitudes, who experience success, will have these attitudes reinforced. Similarly, learners' negative attitudes may be strengthened by lack of success. We will also find cases of learners who begin with positive attitudes but who, for one reason or another, experience inadequate learning opportunities, fail to progress as they expected, and, consequently, become more negative in their outlook.

Baker (1988) discusses the main characteristics of attitudes:

1 Attitudes are cognitive (i.e. are capable of being thought about) and affective (i.e. have feelings and emotions attached to them)—see Triandis 1971.
2 Attitudes are dimensional rather than bipolar—they vary in degree of favourability/unfavourability.
3 Attitudes predispose a person to act in a certain way, but the relationship between attitudes and actions is not a strong one.
4 Attitudes are learnt, not inherited or genetically endowed.
5 Attitudes tend to persist but they can be modified by experience.

Attitudes have been measured both indirectly and directly. An example of indirect measurement is the Semantic Differential Technique. This presents learners with a series of antonyms (for example, useful–useless; ugly–beautiful) and asks them evaluate a given phenomenon (for example, a language or a speaker's accent) on each dimension. It has been used in Matched Guise studies (see Lambert, Hodgson, Gardner, and Fillenbaum 1960), in which the same speaker, who is bilingual, reads a passage in two languages. Learners are then asked to make judgements about the readers (i.e. they are not told that it is one person). In this way, they inadvertently reveal their attitudes towards the two languages. Spolsky's Identity Scale (Spolsky 1969) also measures attitudes indirectly. Subjects are given a list of adjectives and asked to say how well each adjective describes themselves, their ideal selves, people whose native language is the same as theirs, and native speakers of the target language.

Direct measurement of attitudes usually involves self-report questionnaires. These often take the form of a series of statements to which the learners respond on a five-point scale (for example, from 'strongly agree' to 'strongly disagree'). Gardner and Lambert (1972) used this kind of question extensively in their studies of attitudes among American students learning L2 French in the United States. Questions were devised to investigate learners' reasons for learning French, their degree of *anomie* (dissatisfaction with their place and role in society), their ethnocentrism, their preference for America over France, and their attitudes towards French Americans. An example of an item used to measure ethnocentrism is:

The worst danger to real Americanism during the last fifty years has come from foreign ideas and agitators. Certain people who refuse to salute the flag should be forced to conform to such patriotic action, or else be imprisoned.

There is some disagreement regarding the validity and reliability of these measures of learner attitudes. Oller has argued that people will 'self-flatter' by responding to an attitude test in a way that makes them appear more prestigious than is the case, or else will seek to give socially desirable answers (see Oller 1977 and 1981) and that they are, therefore, unreliable. Gardner (1980; 1985), however, rejects Oller's criticisms on the grounds that it is possible to safeguard against such responses by giving careful thought to the way the questionnaire is designed (for example, by ensuring that there are multiple measures of each attitude).

Learners' attitudes may predispose them to make efforts to learn the L2 or not to do so. In some cases, learners may be subject to conflicting attitudes. On the one hand they wish to learn the L2 because it is seen as a way of assimilating into the majority culture, while on the other they wish to maintain their L1 as a way of affirming their own identities. A good example of this kind of conflict can be seen in Irish people's attitudes towards learning Gaelic. The 5 year study by the Committee on Irish Language Attitudes Research (1975) found that there was general agreement that Gaelic was necessary for ethnic and cultural integrity, but at the same time there was only low or lukewarm commitment to its actual use. Edwards (1984) concluded that the Irish like their Irish, but that they like it dead!

In general, positive attitudes towards the L2, its speakers, and its culture can be expected to enhance learning and negative attitudes to impede learning. This need not necessarily be so, however. Negative attitudes may have a positive effect on L2 learning if the learners have a strong reason for learning. Lanoue (1991) provides a fascinating account of the Sekani's linguistic development in British Columbia, Canada. This remote Indian tribe rejected its own mother tongue in favour of L2 English for even inter-ethnic communication not because they felt positively disposed towards Anglo-Canadian culture (in fact, they held negative attitudes) and not because of the socio-economic advantages of English, but because English had become a symbol of pan-Indianism, which was seen as the only way ensuring the tribe's identity in the future.

Lanoue's study testifies to the enormous complexity of the relationship between attitudes and L2 learning. Given that much of the research has been correlational in design (i.e. has used statistical procedures to correlate attitude measures with proficiency measures) and, therefore, does not address cause-and-effect directly, considerable caution needs to be exercised in interpreting the results.

Social factors and second language acquisition

We will now consider a number of specific social factors which influence the attitudes held by different groups of learners and which lead to different levels of L2 proficiency. Discussion will be restricted to the four variables which have received the most attention in SLA research: (1) age, (2) sex, (3) social class, and (4) ethnic identity. Although each variable will be considered separately, it should be recognized that they interact in complex ways, thus making it difficult to determine the precise ways in which each variable contributes to L2 learning.

Age

The age factor is considered in some detail in Chapter 11, where psycho-linguistic aspects of age and L2 acquisition are examined. The discussion here is restricted to sociolinguistic aspects.

Age has received considerable attention from sociolinguists. Chambers and Trudgill (1980), for instance, document variants of /ŋ/ in the speech of different generations of speakers in Norwich (England). The younger generation (10–19 years) used non-standard variants, while middle-aged speakers (30–60 years) preferred the standard variant. Older speakers (70+ years) demonstrated use of non-standard variants, although not to the same extent as the younger generation. Chambers and Trudgill seek to explain this pattern by suggesting that younger speakers are subject to social pressures from their peer group, while middle-aged speakers have less cohesive social networks and are more influenced by mainstream societal values. In older, retired people, social pressures lessen and social networks again become narrow.

The general pattern of social influence which Chambers and Trudgill document may help to explain age-related factors in L2 acquisition. Learners who commence learning an L2 after the onset of puberty (and possibly earlier) are unlikely to acquire a native-speaker accent, while those who begin after the age of about 15 years are less likely to develop as much grammatical ability as those who begin before (see Chapter 11). Preston (1989) suggests that children may be more prepared to share external norms because they are not subject to peer pressure and have not formed stereotypes of their own identities. He argues that the threat to identity in older learners occurs even in 'short-term, restricted' L2 acquisition, which may account for why many adolescents are resistant to L2 learning in foreign language settings. This explanation is not entirely convincing, however. It does not explain why adolescent learners progress more rapidly than younger learners to begin with. Nor does it explain why adolescents tend to do better than middle-aged learners, who ought to outperform the younger generation given their greater acceptance of prestige social norms. As Preston recognizes, a social explanation of age-related effects in L2 acquisition is, at best, only a partial explanation.

Sex

A distinction is often made between 'sex' and 'gender'. The former constitutes a biological distinction, while the latter is a social one. A number of socio-linguists currently prefer the term 'gender' because it places the emphasis on the social construction of 'male' and 'female' (see Kramarae 1990). As Labov notes, 'there is little reason to think that sex is an appropriate category to explain linguistic behavior' (1991: 206), and so it is necessary to posit some intervening variable (i.e. the distinct roles assumed by the different sexes). The term 'sex' is used here to reflect the way in which the variable has been typic-ally measured in SLA research (i.e. as a bipolar opposite).

Sociolinguistic research has identified two distinct and apparently contra-dictory principles relating to sex differentiation in native-speaker speech (see Labov 1991: 206–7):

1 In stable sociolinguistic stratification, men use a higher frequency of non-standard forms than women.
2 In the majority of linguistic changes, women use a higher frequency of the incoming forms than men.

Women, therefore, nearly always outstrip males in the standardness of their speech and use of prestige forms, and yet they also tend to be in the forefront of linguistic change. This can be explained by positing that women are more sensitive to new forms and more likely to incorporate them into their speech, but, when they become aware of the change, they are inclined to reject them. Men, on the other hand, may be less sensitive to new forms but once they have started to use them are less likely to reject them, perhaps because they are less likely to notice them. Both principles suggest that women might be better at L2 learning than men; they are likely to be more open to new linguistic forms in the L2 input and they will be more likely to rid themselves of interlanguage forms that deviate from target-language norms.

These predictions based on sociolinguistic theory are borne out by several studies. Female learners generally do better than male. Burstall (1975), for example, investigated sex differentiation in her longitudinal study of some 6,000 children beginning L2 French at eight years old in English primary schools. She reports that the girls scored significantly higher than the boys on all tests measuring achievement in French throughout the period of the study. Boyle (1987) reports on a study of 490 (257 male and 233 female) Chinese university students in Hong Kong. The female students achieved higher over-all means on ten tests of general L2 English proficiency and in many cases the differences were significant.

Other studies, however, have produced conflicting results. Boyle (1987) reports that the male students in his study performed better on two tests of listening vocabulary, lending support to L1 research that boys are superior in this particular aspect of language proficiency. However, Nyikos (1990) reports that women outperformed men in a German vocabulary memorization task. Also, some studies have reported no or few differences between males and females. Bacon (1992), for instance, found no difference between the sexes in two authentic listening tasks.

A number of studies suggest that females have more positive attitudes to learning an L2 than males. Burstall, in the study referred to above, notes that low-achieving boys tended to drop French to a significantly greater extent than low-achieving girls from the age of 13 onwards. Furthermore, the girls displayed consistently more favourable attitudes towards learning French than did the boys. Gardner and Lambert (1972) also report that female learners of L2 French in Canada were more motivated than male learners and also had more positive attitudes towards speakers of the target language. Spolsky (1989) found that girls learning L2 Hebrew in Israel (a majority language setting) demonstrated more favourable attitudes to Hebrew, Israel, and Israelis than boys. One study (Ludwig 1983) found that male learners were more instrumentally motivated (i.e. more motivated to learn the L2 for purely functional reasons), while another (Bacon and Finnemann 1992) reported that female learners of L2 Spanish at university level had the stronger instrumental motivation.

Other studies suggest that women tackle the task of learning an L2 differently from men. Gass and Varonis' (1986) research on sex differences in interactions involving learners concluded that men use the opportunities to interact to produce more output, whereas women use it to obtain more input. However, Pica et al. (1991) failed to find much evidence to support sex differences in interactions involving adult male and female Japanese learners of L2 English. Clearer evidence for sex differences comes from self-report studies of the strategies learners use. Bacon (1992) found that men reported using translation strategies more than women, while the women reported monitoring their comprehension more. Bacon and Finnemann (1992) found that women reported greater use of a 'private/non-oral mode' in language learning than men (for example, they relied on their L1 to make the L2 meaningful, rehearsing in their heads before they spoke and guessing at what might be going on). It is not clear, however, whether such questionnaires reflect the actual practices learners follow or their ideas about what constitutes socially appropriate answers.

It is not easy to find clear-cut explanations for these results, nor, perhaps, should any be attempted at the present time. The explanations that follow are speculative in nature. One obvious explanation for females' greater success in L2 learning in classroom settings is that they generally have more positive attitudes. This, in turn, may reflect their employment expectations. Girls may perceive a foreign language as having significant vocational value for them, whereas boys do not. These beliefs may derive from the students' parents. However, although this explanation is convincing for 'foreign' languages learnt in Europe or the United States, it is less clearly applicable for 'second' language learning in situations such as the United States or Hong Kong. It is possible that general differences associated with male and female 'culture' are also involved. Maltz and Borker (1982) suggest that girls are more likely to stress co-operation and that they learn to deal sensitively with relationships, whereas boys emphasize establishing and maintaining hierarchical relations and asserting their identity. The female 'culture' seems to lend itself more readily to dealing with the inherent threat imposed to identity by L2 learning. Another possible explanation is that females benefit from more and better input as a result of their superior listening comprehension skills, which some, but not all, studies have reported. There is some evidence to suggest that females are more sensitive to input (for example, the Gass and Varonis study). Eisenstein (1982) found that females consistently and significantly outperformed males in discriminating among different American English accents. Female learners may also be more active strategy users.

A number of puzzles remain. Why, for instance, do males have a wider listening vocabulary? Boyle offers a number of explanations, none of which are very convincing (for example, he cites Carroll (1969), who suggests that boys in a male culture interact over a wider range of subjects and thus develop a broader recognition vocabulary). It is particularly puzzling given the evidence that women are better at vocabulary learning. Perhaps it is necessary to consider sex differences in language learning in relation to both what learners *know* (where women are generally superior) and how they *use* this knowledge under varying performance conditions (where men may sometimes prove superior).

Sex (or gender) is, of course, likely to interact with other variables in determining L2 proficiency. It will not always be the case, therefore, that females outperform males. Asian men in Britain generally attain higher levels of proficiency in L2 English than do Asian women for the simple reason that their jobs bring them into contact with the majority English-speaking group, while women are often 'enclosed' in the home. Sex interacts with such factors as age, ethnicity, and, in particular, social class.

Social class

An individual's social class is typically determined by means of a composite measure that takes account of income, level of education and occupation. It is customary to distinguish four groups: lower class, working class, lower middle class, and upper middle class.

As Preston (1989: 117) points out, there is a clear parallel between sociolinguistic phenomena associated with social class and language change and interlanguage development. Preston compares a number of sociolinguistic and interlanguage features. *Hypercorrection* (for example, the overextension of a feature like /h/ to words such as 'hour'), which occurs when lower-middle-class speakers seek to incorporate a prestige feature into their careful speech, parallels *overgeneralization* in learner language. *Hypocorrection* (the retention of an old norm which has covert prestige in the speech of the working class) is like *negative transfer*. An *indicator* (defined by Preston as 'a form not involved in change') is similar to *fossilization* (the persistence of a non-standard form in interlanguage). *Change from above* can be compared to *monitoring* (Krashen 1981—see Chapter 9), in so far as both involve conscious attention to linguistic form. However, as Preston recognizes, although these processes seem very similar, it does not follow that they are motivated by the same social factors. Indeed, there is no reason to expect any relationship between social class and overgeneralization, negative transfer, etc. The similarity may rest more in the psychological processes which underlie both linguistic change and L2 learning.

There is evidence of a relationship between social class and L2 achievement, however. Burstall (1975; 1979) found that for both male and female primary and secondary school learners of L2 French there was a strong correlation between socio-economic status and achievement. Children from middle-class homes regularly outperformed those from lower- and working-class homes. There were also class-related differences in the learners' attitudes. Working-class children tended to drop French after their second year in secondary school, while middle-class children were likely to continue. Olshtain, Shohamy, Kemp, and Chatow (1990) investigated the levels of proficiency in L2 English reached by 196 grade 7 learners in Israel. The learners were divided into an 'advantaged' and a 'disadvantaged' group on the basis of socio-economic status. Olshtain et al. found that the two groups differed significantly in L1 (Hebrew) cognitive academic level proficiency (CALP) and that a number of measures of this correlated significantly with L2 English achievement. One interpretation of this result was that the 'advantaged' children were better at learning English in a classroom setting because they had a more developed L1 CALP. Interestingly, variance in the 'advantaged' group was not attributable to differences in self-reported attitudes and motivation, whereas in the 'disadvantaged' group it was. Overall, though, L1 CALP explained much more of the variance in L2 achievement than did motivation and attitudes. Finally, Skehan (1990) also reports moderate correlations between the family background of 23 secondary school children in Bristol and both language learning aptitude and foreign language achievement in French and German, with middle-class children again outperforming lower-class. Skehan suggests that these relationships may reflect the learners' underlying ability to deal with context-disembedded language, thus bearing out Olshtain and her colleagues' main conclusion.

All these studies examined L2 achievement in foreign language classrooms. Their results mirror the general finding that children from lower socio-economic groups are less successful educationally than those from higher groups. Another study, however, suggests that the disadvantage in language learning shown by lower-status groups is not inevitable. Holobrow, Genesee, and Lambert (1991) report on a study of partial immersion involving kindergarten and grade 1 pupils in Cincinnati (USA). They found no difference in either French listening comprehension or oral production in children from different socio-economic and ethnic groups:

> ... the working-class and black students were able to benefit from the second language experience as much as middle-class and white students. In other words, the disadvantaged students were not disadvantaged when it came to second language learning (1991: 194).

One possible reason for this is that the immersion programme placed greater emphasis on BICS. The researchers suggest that 'the development of oral/aural interpersonal communication skills in a second language do not appear to be dependent on individual differences of a cognitive, linguistic and ... social nature.' In other words, where BICS are concerned, social differences in learners have no effect.

There have been few studies investigating social class and L2 learning. The results to date suggest that middle-class children achieve higher levels of L2 proficiency and more positive attitudes than working-class children when the programme emphasizes formal language learning. This may be because they are better able to deal with decontextualized language. However, when the programme emphasizes communicative language skills, the social class of the learners has no effect.

It is important to recognize, however, that it is not socio-economic class per se that produces these effects, but rather the experiences of the world which members of the different social classes are likely to have. Heath's (1983) ethnographic study of children in two neighbouring communities demonstrates how contrasting life experiences eventually lead to different levels of school achievement. Heath shows how the types of language use working class black children experience at home differs from that found in the classroom and thus puts them at an immediate disadvantage in comparison to white children, where there is greater congruity between language use at home and at school. For example, 'no one lifts labels and features out of their contexts' and 'no one requests repetitions' (1983: 353) in the black children's homes, whereas this is common in the classroom. Conversely, the black children are encouraged to create 'highly imaginative stories' at home, but not in the classroom. Heath's detailed analysis supports Labov's (1969) earlier contention that it is 'difference' and not 'deficit' that is at the root of many of the language problems black children face at school. Although neither Labov nor Heath were concerned with L2 learning, their arguments are of obvious relevance.

Ethnic identity

Gudykunst and Ting-Toomey (1990) inform us that 'ethnicity is a slippery concept'. This is partly because there is tension between 'objective' and 'subjective' definitions of the term. Objective definitions predominated in early anthropological studies, in which researchers imposed external categorizations on their subjects. Subjective definitions see ethnicity as a process whereby individuals use labels to define themselves in communication with others and are now generally favoured. Gudykunst and Ting-Toomey point out that both self- and other categorizations of ethnic identity may influence the way language is used in inter-ethnic communication.

There is a general consensus that ethnic identity can exert a profound influence on L2 learning. This influence can take three possible forms, corresponding to normative, socio-psychological, and socio-structural views of the relationship. As these perspectives (and the theories that derive from them) are considered in depth later (see page 230), we will focus here on representative samples of the kinds of research to which each has given rise.

Research based on a normative view of the relationship between ethnic identity and L2 learning seeks to establish to what extent membership of a particular ethnic group affects L2 achievement. A key concept here is that of the 'distance' between the cultures of the native and target languages, the idea being that the more distant the two cultures are, the more difficult L2 learning is and, therefore, the lower the achievement levels.

Svanes (1988) investigated the acquisition of L2 Norwegian by three ethnic groups in Norway. One group (the 'near' group) consisted of learners from Europe and America who shared a common 'western' culture. The second group (the 'intermediate' group) consisted of learners from the Middle East and Africa, all of whom had contact with western culture. The third group (the 'distant' group) contained students from Asian countries (for example, India and Vietnam). Svanes found a clear relationship between cultural distance and L2 achievement, measured by an examination that tested a wide variety of knowledge and skills. The Western students had the best grades, the Middle Eastern and African students the next best, and the Asians the poorest results. It should be noted, however, that there is no way of knowing whether the difference in the grades obtained by the three groups was a reflection of cultural distance or linguistic difference (see Chapter 8 for a discussion of the role of linguistic difference).

A socio-psychological view of the relationship between ethnic identity and L2 proficiency emphasizes the role of attitudes. The attitudes that learners hold towards the learning of a particular L2 reflect the intersection of their views about their own ethnic identity and those about the target-language culture. These views will influence both L2 and L1 learning, as shown in Table 6.1.

Lambert (1974) distinguishes *additive* and *subtractive bilingualism*. In the former learners maintain their L1, adding the L2 to their linguistic repertoire. In such cases, learners may become *balanced bilinguals*. This is likely to occur when learners have a positive view of their own ethnic identity and of the target-language culture. In the case of subtractive bilingualism learners replace their L1 with the L2, failing to develop full competence in their mother tongue or, in some cases, actually losing competence that has already been acquired. This arises when learners have a low estimation of their own ethnic identity and wish to assimilate into the target-language culture. When learners have negative attitudes towards both their own culture and that of the target language, *semilingualism* may result. That is, the learners may fail to develop full proficiency in either language. It should be noted, however, that semilingualism (so defined) is a controversial notion, as it runs the danger of depicting as deficit what is in fact only difference, and that the native L1 language competencies of poor minority language children may be fully functional in the out-of-school contexts in which they are used. This point has already been made with reference to Heath's work on black and white children and is further discussed in Edelsky et al. 1983. *Monolingualism* (i.e. failure to acquire the L2) is associated with a strong ethnic identity and negative attitudes towards the target-language culture. Of course, the relationship between ethnic attitudes and the different kinds of 'lingualism' is not as absolute as shown in Table 6.1. It does not follow, for instance, that learners with negative attitudes towards the target-language culture will invariably fail to learn the L2, as other factors (such as instrumental need) can affect the outcomes.

| | Attitudes towards | |
	Native culture	Target culture
Additive bilingualism	+	+
Subtractive bilingualism	−	+
Semilingualism	−	−
Monolingualism	+	−

Key: + = positive attitudes
     − = negative attitudes

Table 6.1:   Attitudes and L2 learning

The role of attitudes in L2 learning has been extensively researched by Lambert and Gardner and their associates (for example, Gardner and Lambert 1972; Gardner 1985), primarily in Canada but also in other settings (for example, the United States and the Philippines). The theoretical framework which has informed these studies is described in the final section of this chapter, so here we will focus on some of the research it has led to.

A number of studies have supported Gardner and Lambert's original claim that a socially based motivation involving a 'willingness to be valued members of the (second) language community' (Gardner and Lambert 1959: 271) results in high levels of L2 proficiency (see Gardner and Clement 1990). Learners' attitudes also affect language attrition. Gardner, Lalonde, and McPherson (1985) found that learners of L2 French with favourable attitudes showed little decline, while those with less favourable ones showed significant loss in self-rated proficiency six months after an intensive course. However, other studies suggest that the relationship between positive attitudes and L2 proficiency is less clear-cut. In some cases no significant relationship has been found and in others there have been negative correlations. For example, Oller (1977) found that Chinese students with high levels of L2 English rated Americans lower on traits such as cleverness and happiness than did those with lower levels. Svanes, in the study referred to on page 207, found that the Asian group, which had the lowest level of achievement, displayed the most positive attitudes towards Norwegians. In this study, too, there was a negative correlation between attitudes and language proficiency. Svanes suggests that 'for groups of adult students living in a foreign country, it is more important to have a balanced and critical attitude to the host people than to admire it uncritically' (1988: 365–6). It is also possible, of course, that learners of a non-international language like Norwegian may respond positively to Norwegian *people* and their culture while showing little interest in their *language*.

The setting is likely to affect the nature of the relationship. There is an obvious difference between Mexicans learning English in California and native speakers of English learning French in Canada, for example. Whereas the former may well feel their ethnic identity is under threat from the majority culture, the latter are likely to feel secure as members of the majority culture. Also, as Okamura-Bichard's (1985) study of Japanese children temporarily residing in the United States showed, socially determined attitudes interact with learners' personal views. Okamura-Bichard argues that the 'personal translation of social factors is ... critical in motivating individual learners to make efforts in their learning attempts' (1985: 85). She suggests that what she calls the 'happiness' factor may be more important than interest in or attitudes towards the target language when the learner is a young child. It is not surprising, perhaps, that conflicting results have been obtained.

A socio-structural view of the relationship between attitudes and L2 learning is evident in work which has examined the effect that ethnic identity has on the interactions between members of different ethnic groups. This view has been explored within the general theoretical framework of interpersonal accommodation discussed in Chapter 4. According to ethnolinguistic identity theory (Giles and Johnson 1981), members of an in-group may or may not adopt positive linguistic distinctiveness strategies when communicating with members of an out-group. Giles and Ryan (1982) suggest that speakers evaluate a situation and then decide whether to adopt status or solidarity, and person-centred or group-centred strategies. In situations where people emphasize solidarity with their own in-group, linguistic divergence from the out-group is likely, whereas in situations where they are more concerned with status and are person-centred, convergence is likely. Language attitudes play an important role in this model, too, but whereas Gardner and Lambert see attitudes as affecting learning outcomes via motivation, Giles and his associates see them as influencing learning via the nature of the inter-ethnic communication that takes place. Successful L2 learning is held to occur when learners engage in frequent and long-term convergence.

There have been no longitudinal studies of learners who tend towards divergence or convergence. Sato (1981) showed that ethnicity affects the communication styles found in ESL classroom discourse. Asian learners participated in fewer self-selected and teacher-allocated turns than did non-Asian learners. She suggests that this reflected the Asian learners' reluctance to accommodate to American ways of speaking in the classroom. Sato did not investigate the effect of these different patterns of interaction on L2 learning, although she speculates that the Asians might be disadvantaged.

Giles and Byrne (1982) have drawn on ethnolinguistic identity theory to propose a theory of L2 learning known as the *Inter-group Theory*. This is discussed on page 234.

Summary

In this section we have examined in what ways specific social factors affect L2 learning. With regard to age, it has been found that younger learners are generally more successful than older learners, possibly because their identity is less threatened by target-language norms. In the case of sex, mixed results have been obtained, but female learners generally outperform male learners in language classroom settings and also display more positive attitudes. Male learners do better in listening vocabulary, however. The effects of social class may depend crucially on the setting; in language classrooms that emphasize formal language learning, working-class children are often less successful than middle-class children, whereas there is some evidence to suggest that in immersion settings they do just as well. The central factor, and the one that has attracted the most attention, is ethnic identity. A normative view emphasizes the effect of 'cultural distance' on L2 learning; learners who are close to the target-language culture are likely to outperform those who are more distant. A socio-psychological model emphasizes the role of attitudes. The relationship between attitudes and L2 learning is almost certainly bi-directional and dynamic, and is likely to vary according to setting. In general, learners with positive attitudes towards their own ethnic identity and towards the target culture can be expected to develop a strong motivation and high levels of L2 proficiency while also maintaining their own L1. Successful L2 learning is also possible, however, in learners with non-integrative attitudes towards the target culture. Attitudes based on learners' sense of ethnic identity can also affect the nature of the interactions in which learners participate. Learners who are status- and person-centred are more likely to converge on L2 norms and therefore more likely to be successful learners than those whose solidarity with their own in-group encourages divergence.

It is clear that the relationships between these four factors and L2 learning is extremely complex. It should be recognized that it is not age, sex, social class, or ethnic identity that determine L2 proficiency, but rather the social conditions and attitudes associated with these variables. Also, the factors interact among themselves, and their effect on learning depends to a large extent on the setting. Any conclusions, therefore, need to be cautious.

Learners' choice of target language variety

One way in which social factors of the kind considered in the previous section impact on L2 learning is in terms of the influence they exert on the learners' choice of target variety. Much of SLA research has been predicated on the assumption that learners are targeted on the standard dialect of the L2. Such an assumption, however, is not warranted in the case of many learners. As Beebe (1985: 404) observes, learners may be 'active participants in choosing the target-language models they prefer'. They do not just learn 'a language' but rather 'adopt a variety or varieties of that language'. Some deviations from standard English, therefore, may not be 'errors', but may simply reflect the dialect which the learner has targeted. For example, learners who display copula deletion may do so because they are targeted on Black English Vernacular, in which this feature is the norm.

The choice of *reference group* depends crucially on the social context and how this shapes learners' attitudes towards the different varieties with which they come into contact. L2 learners in settings where the target language serves as a medium of communication appear to be sensitive to differences in the dialects to which they are exposed. Eisenstein (1982) found adult ESL learners in the New York metropolitan area were able to recognize dialect differences early on in the learning process, but that their ability to categorize the specific varieties developed more slowly. The same study also found that dialect sensitivity and attitude formation develop in parallel and that the advanced-level learners had assimilated the attitudes associated with native speakers of English. Goldstein (1987) also found evidence of learners' awareness of the sociolinguistic rules of dialect use. One of her learners commented:

> I think we should learn to talk different ways ... when you outside, they talk different ways, so to the right people you talk the right English (1987: 429).

Learners also seem to find some dialects more intelligible than others. Eisenstein and Verdi (1985) report that 113 adult working-class ESL learners of mixed proficiency levels and with different L1 backgrounds found black American more difficult to understand than either the regional standard or

New Yorkese (a non-standard English spoken in metropolitan New York). This was considered 'surprising' because the learners had considerable exposure to black English and, in some cases, actually exhibited black features in their interlanguage production. One explanation for this may lie in the learners' recognition of the low prestige of black American English. Eisenstein and Verdi found that the learners' attitudes to the dialects mirrored their ability to comprehend them.

Other studies have set out to investigate which social variables influence a learner's 'preference model'. Beebe (1985) reviews the sociolinguistic literature dealing (mainly) with native speakers' preference models, and concludes that both 'unmarked' and 'marked' choices are evident. The unmarked choices reflect what is 'frequent, basic or expected'. Unmarked choices can be seen in learners' preferences for the variety used by peers over teachers, peers over parents, own social group over other social group, friends over non-friends, high-contact over low-contact group, and high-prestige over low-prestige group. Marked choices constitute a 'secondary type of preference'. Beebe emphasizes that they are just as principled and systematic as the unmarked choices. To explain the choice an individual learner makes Beebe suggests that learners decide whether to give precedence to solidarity or status. Learners with a solidarity orientation are likely to manifest unmarked choices, while those with a prestige orientation will make a marked choice.

There have been few empirical studies of L2 learners' (as opposed to native speakers') preferences, however. An exception is Goldstein's (1987) study of the preferred variety of 28 advanced Hispanic ESL learners from urban high schools in the New York metropolitan area, and what factors could account for this preference. Two linguistic variables associated with black English were examined; negative concord and distributive 'be'. Samples of the learners' speech were collected by means of an interview and a role-play. Goldstein found significant correlations between the amount of reported contact with black Americans and presence of both variables in the learners' speech. However, reported identification with black Americans did not prove to be significantly related to the two variables, although Goldstein queries whether the measures of identification she obtained were valid. Goldstein concludes by suggesting a number of other variables that may affect learners' preference model: covert prestige of the target-language group, the status of the target-language group vis-à-vis one's own or one's desired status, the difficulty or ease of establishing and maintaining relationships with members of the target-language group, the attitudes of one's own ethnic group to the target-language group and vice versa, and the instrumental value of using the target language. However, little is currently known about the effect these variables have.

In language settings where the L2 serves an as official language (for example, India or Nigeria), the reference group for many learners is not a native speaker but rather educated users of the L2 in the learners' own country. This is one of the main reasons for the emergence of local standards. As Kachru points out, 'the concept "native speaker" is not always a valid yardstick for the global uses of English' (1986: 17). He points out, however, that there may be 'schizophrenia about the perceived model and actual behaviour'. Thus, learners may claim to be learning standard British or American English, both of which are seen as prestige varieties, while, in fact, they are learning a local standard. Concern over the development of local standards has been expressed by some (see, for example, Prator's (1968) critique of 'the British heresy') on the grounds that they may become unintelligible to speakers of other varieties, but such worries have probably been overstated and, in any case, little can be done to change the situation, as in most cases learners have no opportunity for contact with speakers of what Kachru calls the 'inner circle' (i.e. countries where English is learnt as a native language).

In foreign-language settings the preference model is nearly always a standard variety of the inner circle. Whether the British or American variety is preferred will largely reflect areas of geographical influence (for example, British in Europe and American in the Philippines and Japan). In a sense, though, it is doubtful whether learners in these settings seriously aspire to native-speaker levels. To do so would constitute a threat to the learners' own ethnic identities and also might not be favourably received by native speakers. Janicki (1985) comments:

> It has been noticed that non-natives are likely to face social consequences when their linguistic behaviour complies with sociolinguistic rules saved (by some norm) for the natives. Examples are the usage of obscenities, slang expressions, or very formal pronunciation. It seems that there exists a set of as yet unidentified norms which proscribe the use of some forms on the part of the non-native speaker.

Such constraints seem to operate more stringently when learners are identified as belonging to a foreign-language setting than when they are seen as part of a setting where the target language is widely spoken, although even here, resistance to learners adopting native-speaker norms has been observed. (See Eisenstein 1983 for a review of native-speaker reactions to non-native speech.) Preston (1981) suggests that an appropriate model for the L2 learner is that of 'competent bilingual' rather than a native-speaker model. This may well be the implicit model of many learners in foreign-language settings.

Figure 6.1 schematizes the factors involved in learners' choice of language variety. Social context and learner attitudes interact with each other to determine the learners' preference model. This influences the L2 input learners are exposed to and, thereby, the linguistic characteristics of the developing interlanguage system.

Figure 6.1:   The learner's preference model and developing interlanguage system

The social contexts of L2 learning

This discussion of the learner's reference group has inevitably involved a consideration of the type of context or setting in which learning takes place. We have seen that learners' choices are constrained by the contexts they find themselves in. In this section we adopt a macro-social approach by identifying a number of general contexts of learning that have been shaped by social, economic, and political forces of various kinds. We consider to what extent successful language learning is likely in each. As Tollefson (1991) has noted, most models of L2 acquisition, including those examined in the final section of this chapter, are based on a neo-classical view of language learning, according to which individual learners make choices by weighing up the personal benefits and costs of learning the language. There is a need, however, to also consider how structural factors shape these choices.

Natural versus educational settings

A general distinction can be made between 'natural' and 'educational' settings. The former arise in the course of the learners' contact with other speakers of the L2 in a variety of situations—in the workplace, at home, through the media, at international conferences, in business meetings, etc. There will be some learners who experience the L2 entirely in natural settings and others whose only contact with it is in educational settings. However, many learners will be exposed to the L2 in both natural and educational settings.

A general assumption is that the learning that takes place in natural and educational settings is very different in nature. In natural settings informal learning occurs. That is, learning is considered to result from direct participation and observation without any articulation of the underlying principles or rules (see Scribner and Cole 1973). Also, there is an emphasis on the social significance of what is being learnt rather than on the mastery of subject matter. In contrast, formal learning is held to take place through conscious attention to rules and principles and greater emphasis is placed on mastery of 'subject matter' treated as a decontextualized body of knowledge. Krashen (1976) distinguishes two ways in which knowledge of an L2 can be developed; *acquisition* and *learning* (this distinction is discussed more fully in Chapter 9). The former takes place subconsciously as a result of understanding what has been said (or written) in communication, and clearly corresponds to informal learning. The latter, which involves conscious attention to linguistic forms, corresponds to formal learning.

The correlation between informal learning and natural settings on the one hand, and formal learning and educational settings on the other, is at best only a crude one (see Krashen 1976). Learners in natural settings often resort to conscious learning and may deliberately seek out opportunities to practise specific linguistic items they have studied, as Lennon's (1989) study of advanced German learners of English in Britain demonstrates. Conversely, learners in classrooms may not be required to treat the language as 'subject matter', but instead be given opportunities for acquisition. As d'Anglejan (1978) has noted, the correlation between educational settings and formal language learning depends on the pedagogic approach. In the case of the 'traditional' approach (characterized by the explicit teaching of the language), there may be few opportunities for informal learning. But in the case of 'innovative' approaches (as illustrated by the immersion bilingual programmes to be discussed below), informal learning is not only possible but is actively encouraged. There is, therefore, no *necessary* connection between setting and type of learning. However, the social conditions that prevail in natural and educational contexts may predispose learners to engage in informal or formal learning strategies. For example, as McNamara (1973) has observed, it is rare that teachers and learners participate in the spontaneous, meaningful interchanges that are characteristic of 'street' learning.

Another common assumption is that natural settings lead to higher levels of L2 proficiency than educational settings. Schinke-Llano (1990: 216), for instance, claims that 'second' language acquisition results in native-like use of the target language, while 'foreign' language acquisition does not. This assumption is also evident in the 'year-abroad' built into university level foreign language education in many European countries, and the growing popularity of 'home-stay' programmes among Japanese learners. The aim of these is to provide foreign language learners with opportunities for informal learning, so that they can reach higher levels of oral proficiency.

There is some support for this position. D'Anglejan (1978) reports that Canadian civil servants freed from their jobs for as long as a year to improve their L2 proficiency in intensive language classes did not generally become fluent in the L2, despite a strong motivation to learn. D'Anglejan suggests that one reason for this was the absence of any opportunities for contact with native speakers. In contrast, Vietnamese immigrants in California who were placed in occupational settings after a short training programme proved highly successful. Fathman (1978) found that 12- to 14-year-old ESL learners in the United States achieved a higher level of oral proficiency than EFL learners of similar ages in Germany, and also displayed greater strategic competence. The ESL learners' speech was rated higher in fluency than in grammaticality, while the opposite was true of the EFL learners. Interestingly, however, the ESL learners were much less certain about their ability to speak English than the EFL learners, perhaps because they were using a different yardstick to measure themselves against. Gass (1987) conducted a comparative study of ESL/EFL learners and also of Italian as a second language (ISL) and as a foreign language (IFL). Focusing on sentence interpretation strategies, she found no difference between the EFL/ESL groups, but a significant difference in the case of the IFL/ISL. Gass notes that sentence interpretation in English is unproblematic because it rests primarily on one type of cue (word order), whereas in Italian it is more problematic because several cue types (word order, inflectional, and pragmatic) are utilized. Thus, 'foreign' and 'second' language learners will manifest no differences where relatively simple learning targets are involved, but will differ when the targets are more complex. Complex rules cannot easily be taught, and classrooms do not offer sufficient input for them to be learnt naturally.

It is by no means certain, however, that naturalistic settings lead to high levels of proficiency—even oral proficiency. Fathman (1978) observes that there was considerable variation in the levels achieved by the ESL learners in her study, suggesting that some at least were not so successful. Schinke-Llano's claim that 'second' language learning is characterized by native-speaker levels of ability is very doubtful. Gass observes that 'most learners, be it classroom or non-classroom learners, do not attain complete mastery of an L2' (1990: 37), and queries whether native-language proficiency is ever possible for adults—a point taken up in Chapter 11 when the role of age in L2 acquisition is examined. Longitudinal studies, such as those reported by Schumann (1978b), Schmidt (1983), Klein and Dittmar (1979), and Meisel (1983) also show that learners in natural settings often fall far short of native-language proficiency.

Nor is it possible to conclude that learning in natural settings results in higher levels of grammatical competence than learning in educational settings. Indeed, as we shall see in Chapter 14, there is growing evidence to suggest that learners who receive formal instruction become more grammatically accurate than those who do not.

The notions of 'natural' and 'educational' settings are inevitably somewhat crude. The differences within each setting regarding both quality and quantity of learning opportunities are likely to exceed the differences between them. As a result, comparisons of the learning outcomes associated with each setting are of doubtful value. A more useful approach, perhaps, is to examine what factors within each setting are important for successful L2 learning. We will do this by identifying and discussing more specific learning contexts.

Natural contexts

Following Judd (1978), three broad types of context in natural L2 learning settings can be identified. The type that has been most thoroughly researched is found in situations where the target language serves as the native language (or one of the native languages) of the country—as is the case for L2 learners of English in the United States or Canada or L2 learners of French in France or Belgium. The second type is found in the decolonized countries of Africa and Asia, where the L2 functions as an official language. In such contexts it is not learnt as a mother tongue by more than a few people. The third type occurs when the L2 is used for interpersonal communications (usually of fairly specific kinds) in countries where it is neither learnt as a mother tongue nor used as an official language (for example, the use of L2 English for business communication in Japan). In all three types of context, situations may arise where the L2 learner communicates with either native speakers of the language or with other L2 users, but clearly the former is more likely in the first type of setting and the latter in the other two types.

Second language learning in majority language contexts

Second language learners in majority language contexts are typically members of ethnic minorities: immigrants (as in the case of Vietnamese immigrants to the United States), migrant workers (as in the case of Turkish workers in Germany or Mexican migrants in the United States), or the children of such groups. These learners vary enormously in the extent to which they approximate to the language norms of the majority language. In some cases a stable 'immigrant interlanguage' (Richards 1972) develops of the kind documented by Fishman, Cooper, and Conrad (1968) for the Puerto Rican community in New Jersey, as in this example where the speaker is talking about shopping:

> No make any difference, but I like when I go because I don't have too many time for buy and the little time we buy have to go some place and I find everything there.

Such varieties are the product of the social conditions in which the learners live. The Heidelberger Forschungsprojekt 'Pidgin-Deutsch' (1978) refers to the 'miserable social situation' of the foreign migrant worker population in West Germany which is due 'not only to economic factors, such as insecurity of employment, low-prestige work, and so on, but also in large measure to a rather thorough exclusion from the local social and political life' (page 2). One of the main findings of this project is that the length of residence in Germany functioned as a major explanatory factor in the workers' acquisition of L2 German for only the first two years of their stay. After that, it was overridden by other social factors such as contact with Germans during leisure time, age at time of immigration, contact with Germans at work, professional training in the country of origin, and number of years of formal education.

Some groups of learners develop varieties much closer to the target language (for example, Norwegian and Swedish groups in the United States). How can this be explained? Taylor (1980) identifies three stages in the social mobility of immigrant groups. Initially there are rewards for maintaining the

L1, as individuals compete for position from within the minority group. Next, rapid learning of the L2 takes place as individuals identify with the majority group and seek to improve their social status. This may lead to what Lambert (1974) called subtractive bilingualism (see the discussion on page 208 above). Finally, conscious attempts to maintain the L1 (the minority language) may be made as individuals react to discrimination by members of the majority group, whom they perceive as responsible for their lack of social advancement. Learners who reach this final stage are likely to achieve *additive bilingualism*. How far different groups of learners progress will depend on the kinds of social factors that the Heidelberger Forschungsprojekt 'Pidgin-Deutsch' identified. These factors govern the degree of contact that takes place between learners and target language speakers, how useful it is for an individual learner to make the effort needed to learn the L2, and, in some cases, the extent to which the interlanguage variety becomes a symbol of ethnic pride.

A somewhat different majority setting arises in countries like Canada and Belgium where large numbers of the indigenous population learn the language of the majority. In Canada, native French speakers learn English as an L2, while in Belgium, Flemish speakers learn L2 French (and vice versa). These settings are of considerable interest because they enable us to compare the differential levels of proficiency achieved by minority community members learning the language of the majority and, vice-versa, majority members learning the language of the minority. In both Canada and Belgium, minority learners of the majority language tend to reach higher levels of proficiency than majority learners of the minority language. Edwards (1977) found that French-speaking learners of English in Ottawa maintained their English language skills, whereas English-speaking learners of French tended to lose their French. Edwards suggests that long-term retention of linguistic and communicative competence is a function of successful prior learning, opportunity to use the skills acquired and interest in using them. The French-speaking learners reported both more opportunities for using their L2 and greater interest in doing so than the English speaking ones. Lambert (1974) has claimed that subtractive bilingualism characterizes many French Canadians learning L2 English, whereas additive bilingualism is more characteristic of English Canadians learning L2 French.

L2 learning in official language contexts

Under colonial rule the languages of Europe (predominantly English, French, Portuguese, Spanish, and Dutch) were introduced to a substantial number of African, American, and Asian countries. The use of these European languages served to centralize power in the hands of the colonial rulers, who constituted a social and linguistic elite.[1] Independence led some countries to search for an alternative official language (for example, Hindi in India and Bahasa

Indonesia in Indonesia), but many countries adopted the language of the ex-colonial power and maintained it in most of its previous social and official functions (for example, Nigeria chose English and Zaire chose French, while India also felt the need to maintain English alongside Hindi). Whether an indigenous or foreign language was chosen as the official language, it constituted an L2 for the vast majority of the population. Social and economic advancement depended to a large extent on its successful mastery—a fact that constituted a powerful motivation for acquiring it. Official language settings are often characterized at the national level by the rapid spread of the L2 and at the individual level by rapid acquisition in at least some sections of the population. In many instances, however, the level of proficiency attained is limited, as learners fail to develop adequate cognitive academic language proficiency (see, for example, Africa's (1980) account of L2 English proficiency in the population of Zambia).

Learner communities in official language settings differ from those found in majority language settings where, as we have seen, some social groups may resist learning the L2 and seek to maintain their native language as an expression of their ethnic vitality. In official language settings there is often less individual resistance to the acquisition of the 'foreign' official language, although there may be considerable group resistance, as in the anti-English movement in India. Less resistance occurs when the L2 is perceived as an *additional language* (Fishman, Cooper, and Conrad 1977) rather than a replacement language. In the multilingual situations that are characteristic of newly independent countries, the foreignness of the L2 is often perceived as desirable, in that it is not associated with any one indigenous group. The choice of a colonial language as the official language after independence was often politically motivated by the desire to unite a linguistically and tribally heterogeneous population. For individual learners in countries such as Zambia or Nigeria, for example, the foreign L2 constitutes a 'neutral' language that could be learnt without any obvious threat to tribal identities.

The choice of national language is, however, a controversial issue. As we will see when we discuss the different educational contexts of L2 learning, the choice of an L2 as the medium of instruction in countries such as Zambia can have a detrimental effect on children's cognitive and social development. Also, the use of a foreign language effectively excludes those sections of the population who do not have access to it (for example, those living in rural areas with no or few educational facilities) from socio-economic advancement and, in the eyes of some, it does threaten cultural values. These arguments have led a number of researchers and educationalists (for example, Mateene and Kalema 1980; Mateene, Kalema, and Chomba 1985) to propose that a vernacular language be used as the official language, either exclusively or alongside a non-indigenous language.

One the characteristics of L2 learning in official language contexts is the emergence of new varieties of the target language. Simple varieties analogous to pidgins (i.e. languages that developed in certain trade and plantation situations) appear in certain circumstances, as when the L2 functions as a lingua franca serving only a limited set of communicative purposes for a group of speakers. These varieties are similar in form to the 'immigrant varieties' discussed above. Other varieties can also emerge. Widdowson (1977) suggests that the opposite of a pidginized variety is 'babu', an over-elaborate form of language that emphasizes *how* something is said (i.e. expression) over *what* is said (i.e. content). He informs us that the term 'babu' derives from the name of the junior Indian clerk whose use of English was 'characterized by self-conscious elaboration of phrase which, before the days of the typewriter, was often conveyed in written form by means of copper-plate handwriting'.

Official language contexts can also give rise to new local standard varieties for example, 'New Englishes' (Kachru 1989). Such varieties are likely to reflect structural features of the speakers' mother tongue(s) and also overgeneralization of rules. However, as Sridhar and Sridhar (1986) and Lowenberg (1986) argue, it is doubtful whether 'nativization' and second language acquisition involve identical processes. There are differences both with regard to the linguistic contexts in which apparently similar strategies are employed, and also in the motivations underlying their use. For example, Lowenberg (1986: 6) claims that the use of prefixes to coin new lexical items as in 'outstation' (meaning 'out of town' in Singaporean English) resembles the kind of productive process found in established varieties of English rather than a transitional L2 rule.[2] Also, whereas L2 learners view their interlanguage grammars as transitional and imperfect, users of the new Englishes treat their grammars as fully developed and display positive attitudes towards them. For this reason alone, the new standard varieties should not be considered 'interlanguages' in the sense in which this term is generally used.

Second language learning in international contexts

A number of languages—in particular English—are now widely used as international languages. That is, they serve as a means of communication between speakers of different languages in a wide range of contexts: business and trade, academic and scientific, media and the arts, travel and tourism, and literature. The speakers may or may not be native speakers of the language and the speech events may or may not take place inside a country where the language is spoken as a mother tongue. Crystal (1988) claims that there are over 700 million users of English, of whom the majority (400 million) are non-native speakers. Many of these will use English primarily for international communication. Not surprisingly, the use of English as an international language has attracted considerable attention in recent years (see Strevens 1980; Quirk 1982 and 1985; Kachru 1982; Smith 1983).

Much of the work on international settings has focused on either describing the varieties of language associated with particular contexts of use (for example, the use of English for air traffic control) or on arguing the merits of some form of 'basic' language which will facilitate communication, teaching and learning (for example, Quirk's (1982) Nuclear English and Wong's (1934) Utilitarian English). There has been little work on how target-language varieties associated with international use are mastered by L2 learners, or to what extent international use promotes or restricts interlanguage development. Davies (1989) makes the point that although both international varieties and interlanguages can be described as 'simplified', they are in fact different, as the former involve functional simplification and the latter formal. Thus, whereas an interlanguage manifests formal reduction—as when functors are omitted or overgeneralized—and then gradually gets more complex, international varieties employ standard language forms and are 'simplified' only in the sense that they are used to perform a restricted set of functions. We can speculate that where international varieties are of the very restricted kind (for example, 'Seaspeak' or 'Airspeak'), they can be mastered by learning to understand and use a small set of formulas and a limited lexicon, which, as we saw in Chapter 3, are well within the compass of a beginner learner. In a sense, then, these varieties are both sociolinguistically and psycholinguistically 'simple'. We can also speculate that learners who define their learning task as the mastery of these restricted varieties will achieve only a limited proficiency. In contrast, learners who engage in international communication that involves the full resources of the standard language (for example, the preparation of academic papers for publication) are more likely to develop a higher level of proficiency.

The use of an L2 in an international setting is characterized by both non-native speaker–non-native speaker interaction and non-native speaker–native speaker interaction, but, as Kachru (1986: 16) points out, the former is more common. This has implications for acquisition (see Chapter 7). For example, Kachru argues that in non-native speaker–non-native speaker interactions:

> the *British* English or *American* English conventions of language use are not only not relevant, but may even be considered inappropriate by interlocutors. The culture bound localized strategies of, for example, politeness, persuasion and phatic communion 'transcreated' in English are more effective and culturally significant.

In such situations, then, the learners' reference group is not speakers of standard British or American English but, instead, a prestige local group. Also, in these situations, we can expect to see creative use made of interlanguage resources for impression management (see Chapter 5).

Educational contexts

Skuttnab-Kangas (1986; 1988) distinguishes four broad types of educational contexts: (1) segregation, (2) mother tongue maintenance (language shelter), (3) submersion, and (4) immersion. These types are all found in multilingual situations of one kind or another. Here we will also consider a fifth type, foreign language classrooms, as an additional context found in monolingual situations. The focus of our discussion will be the likely implications of each context for successful L2 development.

Skuttnab-Kangas identifies a number of factors that she believes will contribute to educational success in these different settings, grouping them under four broad headings: (1) organizational, (2) learner-related affective factors, (3) L1-related factors, and (4) L2-related factors. Her concern is not specifically with L2 development but with overall education provision. The factors that she identifies, however, are all of potential significance for L2 learning.

Segregation

Segregation occurs where the L2 learner is educated separately from the majority or a politically powerful minority, who speak the target language as their mother tongue. Immigrants or migrant workers who are educated in special schools, centres, or units designed to cater for their language needs constitute an example of segregation in a majority setting. 'Bantu education' in Namibia prior to independence is an example of segregation in a setting where a powerful minority spoke the official language (Afrikaans) as a mother tongue.

Skuttnab-Kangas (1988) claims that segregation settings produce poor results. She argues that the overall aim of education in these settings is the development of a limited L2 proficiency—sufficient to meet the needs of the majority or powerful minority and to ensure their continued political and economic control. She sees segregation education as characterized by inadequate organization (for example, no attempt is made to provide alternative programmes, and the cultural content of teaching materials may be inappropriate for the pupils) and negative learner-affective factors (for example, a high level of anxiety and low self-confidence). Although some support for L1 development is provided, this is also usually limited. Negative L2-related factors identified by Skuttnab-Kangas include the poor quality of L2 instruction and the lack of opportunity to practise the L2 in peer-group contexts.

However, the case against segregation is not as clear-cut as Skuttnab-Kangas makes out. In certain situations, the provision of separate educational facilities may have beneficial effects. For example, short-term programmes for refugee populations newly arrived in the United States or European countries can help them adjust socially, affectively, and linguistically to the demands of their new country. It can also be argued that the maintenance of minority languages requires at least some segregation. Magnet (1990), for example, draws on the Canadian experience to argue that a minority language will only be viable if its speakers enjoy a 'degree of autonomy and segregation in order to develop in their own way' (1990: 295). The advantages of segregation are also recognized by minority communities themselves, as illustrated by their attempts to set up separate schools for their children.

Segregation also has some advantages where L2 learning is concerned. In particular, because the learners are likely to be at the same level of development, it is possible to tailor input to their level. Where the learners have different L1s, the L2 is likely to serve as a language of classroom communication and not just as a learning target. This is likely to broaden the functions that it typically serves. For these reasons, segregation may facilitate the development of 'survival skills' in the L2.

In judging segregation it is obviously necessary to consider particular contexts. Skuttnab-Kangas is clearly right to reject segregation when its purpose is to ensure that learners' L2 development is restricted, as was the case in Namibia. However, segregated language education that is designed to meet the needs of a minority language group and is requested by them may help them both develop basic L2 skills quickly and also maintain their own L1.

Mother tongue maintenance

Skuttnab-Kangas points out that mother tongue maintenance can take two forms. In the weaker form, pupils are given classes in their mother tongue, directed at developing formal language skills, including full literacy. In the stronger form, pupils are educated through the medium of their mother tongue. Examples of the former are the programmes for Punjabi established in Bradford, UK (Fitzpatrick 1987) and for Italian in Bedford (Tosi 1984) for ethnic minority children living in those cities. Examples of the latter are the programmes for the seven main language groups in Uzbekistan, and the Finnish-medium classes for Finnish migrant workers in Sweden (Skuttnab-Kangas 1988). Mother tongue maintenance programmes are based on enrichment theory, according to which high levels of bilingualism are seen as a cognitive and social advantage. This contrasts with deficit theory, which views bilingualism as a burden and as likely to result in cognitive disadvantage. The results of research strongly suggest that additive bilingualism (the goal of mother tongue maintenance) confers linguistic, perceptual, and intellectual advantages (see Swain and Cummins 1979 for a review).

There is also evidence that mother tongue maintenance settings, particularly those of the strong kind, result in considerable educational success (Skuttnab-Kangas 1988). They are characterized by positive organizational factors (for example, appropriate cultural content in teaching materials), positive affective factors (for example, low anxiety, high internal motivation, and self-confidence in the learners), success in developing full control of the L1, and a high level of proficiency in the L2.

Mother tongue maintenance provides support for L2 learning in two main ways. First, ensuring that the L2 is an additional rather than a replacement language results in learners developing a positive self-identity. As Spolsky notes, learning an L2 is intimately tied up with one's personality and being forced to learn an L2 as a replacement for the L1 is a 'direct assault on identity' (1986: 188). Mother tongue maintenance, then, is more likely to result in the positive attitudes needed for successful L2 development.

The second way involves a consideration of Cummins' *interdependency principle* (Cummins 1981). This claims that whereas BICS develops separately in the L1 and L2, CALP is common across languages.[3] Cummins notes that whereas L2 communicative skills are typically mastered by immigrant learners in about two years, it can take from five to seven years for the same learners to approach grade norms for L2 academic skills. The interdependency principle has been demonstrated in a number of studies (for example, Cummins et al. 1984; Verhoeven 1991). Studies of the Portuguese-Canadian community in Toronto (Cummins et al. 1990), of Japanese immigrant children in Canada (Cummins and Nakajima 1987), and of Turkish immigrant children in Holland (Verhoeven 1991) support the importance of L1 academic skills as a basis for successful development of L2 CALP. The notion of interdependency is an important one because it suggests that the development of full L1 proficiency confers not only cognitive and social advantages attendant on mother tongue use but also benefits the acquisition of L2 proficiency.

Submersion

Skuttnab-Kangas defines a submersion programme as:

> a programme where linguistic minority children with a low-status mother tongue are forced to accept instruction through the medium of a foreign majority language with high status, in classes where some children are native speakers of the language of the instruction, where the teacher does not understand the mother tongue of the minority children, and where the majority language constitutes a threat to their mother tongue—a subtractive language learning situation (1988: 40).

Submersion is common in Britain and the United States, where ethnic minority children are educated in mainstream classrooms.

These characteristics of submersion settings are discussed by Cohen and Swain (1979). Right from the beginning L2 learners are taught with native speakers. This can create communication problems and insecurity in the learners. If L1 support is provided, it is of the 'pull-out' kind, which stigmatizes the L2 child and also deprives learners of the opportunity to progress in content subjects. Both the content and language teachers are typically monolingual and thus unable to communicate with the learners in their L1. In some cases, the learners are actively discouraged from speaking in their L1. The students' low academic performance may reflect the low expectations that teachers often have of the students, particularly those from certain ethnic groups (for example, Mexican American students in the United States). Reading material and subject-matter instruction in the L1 are not available, resulting in increased insecurity in the learners. Parental involvement in the school programme is usually limited.

For many learners, the disjunction between L1 use in the home and L2 use at school constitutes a painful experience, as Rodriguez' (1982) autobiography illustrates. Rodriguez was the son of a Mexican immigrant who settled in a mainly white locality of California. At school he was required to use English exclusively. At home Spanish was spoken, until his parents accepted the advice of the Catholic nun teachers at his school to speak English. Gradually, Rodriguez lost the ability to communicate in Spanish, signalling his rejection of his Spanish-Mexican identity. Although Rodriguez was ultimately successful in developing a high level of L2 proficiency, this was achieved at considerable personal and social cost. Rodriguez himself, however, while acknowledging the discomfort he experienced at both school and home, did not question the subtractive model of bilingualism to which he was exposed.

Although submersion contexts do not invariably result in lack of success in learning an L2 (as the Rodriguez' example demonstrates), in general they do not facilitate it. Cummins (1988) identifies three characteristics that are important for L2 acquisition; (1) a bilingual teacher who can understand students when they speak in their L1, (2) input that has been modified to make it comprehensible (see Chapter 7 for a discussion of comprehensible input), and (3) effective promotion of L1 literacy skills. Submersion contexts have none of these. As Cummins notes:

> L2 submersion programs for minority students involve virtually no concessions to the child's language or culture and have well-documented negative effects for many children (1988: 161).

Immersion

The term 'immersion' has come to refer to a number of different contexts, which need to be clearly distinguished. Initially, the term was used in the context of Canadian French immersion programmes, where members of a majority group (native speakers of English) were educated through the medium of French, the language of a minority group. There are a number of variants of these programmes, depending on whether the programme begins early (for example, in kindergarten) or late (for example, in Grades 4 or 7), and whether it is full (more or less all instruction is conducted in the L2) or partial (only part of the curriculum is taught through the L2).

As Cummins (1988) points out, the term 'immersion' has also come to be used to refer to a variety of programmes for minority students. He distinguishes 'L2 monolingual immersion programs for minority students' which provide English-only instruction directed at classes consisting entirely of L2 learners; 'L1 bilingual immersion programs for minority students', which begin with L1-medium instruction, introducing L2-medium instruction some time later; 'L2 bilingual immersion programs for minority students', which emphasize instruction in and on the L2 but which also promote L1 skills. He also notes that, misleadingly, even submersion programmes have been referred to as 'immersion'.

The Canadian French immersion programmes have met with considerable success. Genesee (1984; 1987) and Swain and Lapkin (1982) review the various programmes, reaching similar conclusions. Immersion students acquire normal English language proficiency and show the same or better level of general academic development. Furthermore, immersion students tend to have less rigid ethnolinguistic stereotypes of the target-language community, and place greater value on the importance of inter-ethnic contact. These advantages are evident in 'disadvantaged' as well as 'advantaged' children. Evaluation of the different kinds of programmes shows that in general, total immersion produces better results than partial immersion, and also that early immersion does better than late.

The Canadian French immersion settings also lead to a high level of L2 French proficiency, particularly with regard to discourse and strategic competence, where learners achieve near-native-speaker levels (see Swain 1985). However, such levels are not usually reached in grammatical proficiency and, as Hammerley (1987; 1989) has pointed out, in some cases a kind of 'classroom pidgin' can develop.[4] Nevertheless, there is now general agreement that immersion programmes are very effective in promoting L2 development in an educational setting.

There are many reasons for the success of these majority immersion programmes. One undoubtedly has to do with the fact that immersion settings ensure a plentiful supply of input that has been tailored to the learners' level and is therefore comprehensible. There are also social reasons. The learners' L1 and their ethnic identity is not threatened, so it is easy for the learners to adjust to the immersion setting (see Swain and Lapkin 1985: chapter 6). Furthermore, the immersion programmes are optional and, therefore, are supported by those parents who elect to send their children to them.

Bilingual minority immersion programmes of the kind found in the United States have been more controversial (see, for example, Epstein 1977 and Danoff et al. 1978, cited in Cummins 1988). In the United States there has been considerable opposition to bilingual programmes for linguistic minorities, as reflected in the Official English Movement (the attempt to have English designated as the official language of the United States and to ensure that educational resources are directed towards teaching English rather than some other language—see Bingaman 1990). Cummins (1988) points out that the debate has centred on two arguments, both of which are mistaken. Supporters of minority bilingual programmes have advanced the 'linguistic-mismatch' argument, according to which minority children will be retarded academically if they are required to learn exclusively through the L2. This is mistaken because the French Canadian immersion programmes have shown conclusively that early instruction through the medium of the L2 has no negative effects. Critics of bilingual immersion programs have advanced the 'maximum exposure' argument, according to which bilingual education is detrimental because it deprives learners of the exposure to the L2 necessary for successful acquisition. This is refuted by programs which show that minority children who spend less time on English while they are developing L1 literacy skills ultimately do just as well in L2 academic skills as those who are educated exclusively through the L2. Cummins argues that minority programmes that are designed in such a way that they reflect the interdependency principle and the comprehensible input hypothesis have been shown to be successful. Genesee, however, suggests that the success of minority immersion programmes also depends on 'changing the sociocultural fabric of the school' (1987: 168–9). He notes that ways are needed to upgrade the status and power attached to the minority language and to teachers and support personnel who speak it as an L1. Genesee's comment points to the need to consider social as well as organizational factors in immersion education.

The language classroom

Whereas the previous educational contexts have all involved L2 learners in multilingual settings, the final context we will consider involves 'the language classroom', defined here as a setting where the target language is taught as a subject only and is not commonly used as a medium of communication outside the classroom. In this sense it includes both 'foreign' language classrooms (for example, Japanese classes in the United States or English classes in China) and 'second' language classrooms where the learners have no contact with the target language outside the language classroom (for example, 'ESL' classes in a francophone area of Canada).

Two contextual aspects are of potential importance in language classroom settings according to Gardner and Clement (1990). One concerns the learning situation to be found in the classroom. The other is the level of support which parents give to the foreign/second language programme.

With regard to the classroom learning situation, the role relationships between teacher and student are likely to be crucial. In the case of traditional approaches to language teaching, where the target language is perceived primarily as an 'object' to be mastered by learning about its formal properties (see the discussion of 'formal learning' on page 214), the teacher typically acts as a 'knower/informer' and the learner as an 'information seeker' (Corder

1977b). In the case of innovative approaches where the emphasis is on the use of the target language in 'social behaviour' a number of different role relationships are possible, depending on whether the participants are 'playing at talk', as in role play activities, or have a real-life purpose for communicating, as in information gap activities; the teacher can be 'producer' or 'referee' and the learner 'actor' or 'player'. Corder notes, however, that in real-life situations outside the classroom, a somewhat different role relationship arises ('mentor' and 'apprentice'). Thus, even 'informal learning' inside the classroom may differ from that found in natural settings.[5]

The nature of these classroom roles is likely to influence the level and type of proficiency that develops. As we noted earlier, classroom learners often fail to develop much functional language ability. In part this reflects the predominance of the knower/information seeker role set in classrooms, although other factors also play a part (for example, overall contact with the target language). Lessons in French as a second language (FSL) in Canada have been shown to result in lower levels of L2 proficiency than immersion settings (see, for example, Lambert and Tucker 1972), although such comparisons are always problematic given the difficulty of controlling for intervening variables. D'Anglejan, Painchaud, and Renaud (1986) also provide evidence of the limited success of FSL lessons taught to groups of immigrants, commenting that 'it is both disappointing yet challenging to discover that after 900 hours of formal instruction, the vast majority of the subjects have attained proficiency levels which at best can be described as minimal' (page 199).

Parents may play an active role by monitoring their children's curricular activities. They may also play a more indirect role by modelling attitudes conducive to successful language learning. A number of studies have found a positive relationship between parental encouragement and achievement in L2 learning (for example, Burstall 1975; Gardner and Smythe 1975). Gardner (1985) argues that parents' influence on proficiency is mediated through the students' motivation.

L2 learning in classroom settings is discussed in detail in Chapters 13 and 14.

Summary

In this section, we have considered the relationship between social context and L2 learning. The aim has been to identify what are the potential learning outcomes associated with different types of social contexts, defined in very broad terms. A basic distinction between 'natural' and 'educational' settings has been proposed. There is some evidence to suggest that learners who have access to natural settings achieve greater functional proficiency than those who are limited to educational settings. Various types of natural and educational settings have been examined. Table 6.2 lists them and provides a summary of the potential learning outcomes associated with each. It must be emphasized once again, however, that the relationship between setting and learning outcomes is an indeterminate one, as considerable variation is evident in each setting, reflecting the interplay of different social factors. Clearly, there is a need to tease out how these social factors work in much greater detail than has been possible in this chapter.

Setting	Examples	Potential learning outcomes
Natural contexts		
Majority language settings		Considerable variation in L2 proficiency:
monolingual	L2 English learnt in USA or UK	– immigrant interlanguages (stable and unstable) – subtractive bilingualism – additive bilingualism.
bilingual	L2 English learnt by Francophones in Canada	Subtractive bilingualism likely.
Official language settings	L2 English in Nigeria; Bahasa Indonesian in Indonesia	L2 learnt as additional language; Different levels of proficiency: – pidginized varieties – 'babu' – local standards (e.g. 'New Englishes').
International settings	Use of L2 English for tourism, business, media etc.	Functionally simplified varieties (e.g. Airspeak); Transfer of culture-bound strategies for impression management.
Educational contexts		
Segregation	Special migrant worker programmes in Germany; 'Bantu education programmes'[1] in Namibia.	L2 proficiency may be restricted to development of 'survival skills'; CALP likely to be underdeveloped.
Mother tongue maintenance	Finnish-medium education for Finnish minority in Sweden.	High levels of L2 proficiency in both BICS and CALP.
Submersion	Education in mainstream classrooms for ethnic minority students in UK and USA; withdrawal for L2 instruction.	Low academic performance resulting from many learners' failure to develop CALP; subtractive bilingualism.
Immersion		
majority language	Bilingual education programmes for English-speaking students in Canada.	High level of functional L2 proficiency but grammatical proficiency fails to reach NS levels.
minority language	Bilingual education programmes for Hispanic-speaking students in the United States.	High level of L2 proficiency achieved if programme attends to L1 literacy and provides plenty of comprehensible input.
Language classroom	Foreign language classes in monolingual countries (e.g. Japan); Second language ESL classes for Francophone students in Canada.	Many learners fail to develop functional oral L2 proficiency; L2 proficiency higher in reading and writing skills.

Table 6.2:   Social contexts and potential L2 learning outcomes

Social models of L2 acquisition

We will now examine three models of L2 acquisition which seek to account for the role of social factors. The three models reflect the primary research interests of their progenitors and the contexts in which they have worked. Two of the models—Schumann's *Acculturation Model* and Giles and Byrne's Inter-group Model—have been designed to explain L2 learning in natural settings, in particular those where members of an ethnic minority are learning the language of a powerful majority group. The third model—Gardner's Socio-educational Model—was derived mainly from studies of L2 learning in language classrooms, although Gardner argues that it is also applicable to L2 learning in natural settings.

The Acculturation Model

Schumann's Acculturation Model was established to account for the acquisition of an L2 by immigrants in majority language settings. It specifically excludes learners who receive formal instruction. Acculturation, which can be defined generally as 'the process of becoming adapted to a new culture' (Brown 1980: 129), is seen by Schumann as governing the extent to which learners achieve target-language norms. As Schumann puts it:

> ... second language acquisition is just one aspect of acculturation and the degree to which a learner acculturates to the target-language group will control the degree to which he acquires the second language (1978a: 34).

In fact, Schumann (1986) distinguishes two kinds of acculturation, depending on whether the learner views the second language group as a reference group or not. Both types involve social integration and therefore contact with the second language group, but the first type of learners wish to assimilate fully into its way of life, whereas the second do not. Schumann argues that both types of acculturation are equally effective in promoting L2 acquisition.

The model recognizes the developmental nature of L2 acquisition (as discussed in Chapter 3) and seeks to explain differences in learners' rate of development and also in their ultimate level of achievement in terms of the extent to which they adapt to the target-language culture.

Schumann proposed the Acculturation Model as a means of accounting for the failure to progress of one of the six learners studied by Cazden, Cancino, Rosansky, and Schumann (1975). Whereas the other five manifested considerable development over the ten-month period of the study, Alberto did not advance in most of the structural areas investigated, for example, negatives, interrogatives, use of copula 'be', and verb auxiliaries (Schumann 1978b). Alberto's lack of development could not be satisfactorily explained by either cognitive development, as he demonstrated normal intelligence, or age, as many older learners achieve satisfactory levels of L2 proficiency. Schumann noticed that Alberto's speech manifested very similar properties to those found in pidgins, leading Schumann to argue that similar processes of pidginization were at work. Just as pidgins have been noted to develop in contact situations that call for functionally restricted communication, so learners like Alberto appear to fossilize because they too have a limited need to communicate in the L2. According to this view, learners fail to progress beyond the early stages of acquisition because they require the L2 for only the communicative function of language (basic information exchange), and not for the integrative function (social identification) or the expressive function (the realization of personal attitudes)—see Smith 1972. It was the similarity between Alberto's learner language and pidgins that led Schumann to propose acculturation as the primary causative factor.

The extent to which learners acculturate depends on two sets of factors which determine their levels of *social distance* and *psychological distance* (Schumann 1978a; 1978b; 1978c). Social distance concerns the extent to which individual learners become members of the target-language group and, therefore, achieve contact with them. Psychological distance concerns the extent to which individual learners are comfortable with the learning task and constitutes, therefore, a *personal* rather than a *group* dimension. The various social and psychological factors which Schumann identifies as important are described in Table 6.3. The social factors are primary. The psychological factors mainly come into play where social distance is indeterminate (i.e. where social factors constitute neither a clearly positive nor a negative influence on acculturation).

A learning situation can be 'bad' or 'good' (Schumann 1978c). An example of a 'good' learning situation is when (1) the L2 and TL groups view each other as socially equal, (2) both groups are desirous that the L2 group assimilate, (3) there is low enclosure, (4) the L2 group lacks cohesion, (5) the group is small, (6) both groups display positive attitudes towards each other, and (7) the L2 group envisages staying in the TL area for an extended period. Several 'bad' learning situations are possible, as many of the social variables permit three-way alternatives. Also, different learning situations manifest degrees of 'badness' in accordance with the extent of the overall social distance.

In his early writings, Schumann suggested that acculturation affects L2 acquisition by its effect on the amount of contact learners have with TL speakers. The greater the contact, the more acquisition takes place. Subsequently, Schumann (1986) suggests that acculturation may also affect the nature of the verbal interactions that learners take part in and thus the quality as well as the quantity of L2 input. The Acculturation Model, however, does not specify the internal processes that are involved in acquisition. As we will see in Chapter 9, Andersen (1983b) has added a psycholinguistic dimension to the model to try to account for these, while Schumann (1990) has also added a cognitive dimension.

Factor		Description
Social distance		
1	Social dominance	The L2 group can be politically, culturally, technically, or economically superior (dominant), inferior (subordinate), or equal.
2	Integration pattern	The L2 group may assimilate (i.e. give up its own lifestyle and values in favour of those of TL group), seek to preserve its lifestyle and values, or acculturate (i.e. adopt lifestyle and values of TL group while maintaining its own for intra-group use).
3	Enclosure	The L2 group may share the same social facilities (low enclosure) or may have different social facilities (high enclosure).
4	Cohesiveness	The L2 group is characterized by intra-group contacts (cohesive) or inter-group contacts (non-cohesive).
5	Size	The L2 group may constitute a numerically large or small group.
6	Cultural congruence	The culture of the L2 group may be similar or different to that of the TL group.
7	Attitude	The L2 group and TL group may hold positive or negative attitudes towards each other.
8	Intended length of residence	The L2 group may intend to stay for a long time or a short time.
Psychological distance		
1	Language shock	The extent to which L2 learners fear they will look comic in speaking the L2.
2	Culture shock	The extent to which L2 learners feel anxious and disorientated upon entering a new culture.
3	Motivation	The extent to which L2 learners are integratively (most important) or instrumentally motivated to learn the L2.
4	Ego permeability	The extent to which L2 learners perceive their L1 to have fixed and rigid or permeable and flexible boundaries and therefore the extent to which they are inhibited.

Table 6.3:   Factors affecting social and psychological distance (based on Schumann 1978b)

The test of any model is whether it is supported by the results of empirical research. The Acculturation Model has received only limited support, as Schumann (1986) acknowledges. Maple's (1982) study of 190 Spanish-speaking students enrolled in an ESL programme at the University of Texas found a strong relationship between social distance and measures of L2 English proficiency. Seven out of the eight social factors shown in Table 6.3 were negatively correlated with proficiency. The social factors in descending area of importance that were found to have a significant effect were: attitudes, social class, cohesiveness, intended length of residence, size of L2 group, enclosure, and perceived status. Maple's study might be taken as support for the model except for the fact that the subjects were receiving L2 instruction, and, therefore strictly speaking, lay outside the model's frame of reference. Other studies have failed to support the model either because they found that psychological distance correlated with advanced proficiency in situations where social distance was high (for example, Stauble 1978; Kelley 1982), or simply because no relationship between social distance and development was found when one might have been expected (for example, Stauble 1984; Schmidt 1983). One of the reasons for these mixed results is the difficulty of measuring acculturation. Apart from the problem of obtaining reliable measures of each social factor, there is no principled way of weighting the different variables.

A number of theoretical objections have also been lodged against the model. Several concern Schumann's pidginization analogy (see Larsen-Freeman and Long 1991: 258–9). For example, pidginization is a group phenomenon while L2 acquisition is an individual one. Pidginization reflects the incorporation of features from languages other than the target language, whereas L2 acquisition is always modelled on the target language. However, these criticisms do not really invalidate the model, as the central construct of acculturation is not really dependent on the pidginization analogy.

A more serious criticism is that advanced by Spolsky (1989), namely that Schumann presupposes social factors to have a direct effect on L2 acquisition, whereas they are more likely to have an indirect one. However, this criticism, too, is not really justified, as Schumann makes it clear that the effect of the different social factors is mediated in terms of the amount of contact with target language speakers that is likely to ensue under different social conditions. This presupposes that the amount of contact is positively correlated with L2 proficiency. It is not clear, however, to what extent such an assumption is justified. The Heidelberger Forschungsprojekt 'Pidgin-Deutsch' (1978) reports a strong relationship between the contact that migrant workers in West Germany had with native Germans and their syntactic development in the L2. Similarly, the ZISA Project, also based in West Germany (see Chapter 3) found clear evidence of a relationship between contact and *restrictive simplification* (the continued use of simplified structures, such as deletion of function words, by learners who had developed the ability to use the corresponding non-simplified structures). In this case both interactive contact with native speakers at work and in the local neighbourhood, and non-interactive contact with the German mass media, were related to more target-like language use. However, Swain (1981) and Day (1985) both failed to find a significant relationship between contact with native speakers and L2 proficiency in studies they carried out in Canada and Hawaii respectively. Freed (1990), in a study of the effects of contact on the L2 proficiency of 40 undergraduate learners of French during a six-week study abroad program, found that the lower-level students who reported more interactive contact showed greater gains in grammatical accuracy than those with less. Interactive contact had no effect or a reverse effect on the grammatical accuracy of advanced-level students, however. Non-interactive contact (for example, listening to the radio, watching television, reading French books and newspapers) worked the opposite way; it benefited the advanced but not the lower level learners. These results testify to the problems inherent in assuming that 'more contact' results in 'more acquisition'. The greatest failing of the Acculturation Model is that it has nothing to say about how social factors influence the quality of contact that learners experience. In this respect the Inter-group Model is superior.

The Inter-group Model

We have already seen that Giles and his associates have been primarily concerned with exploring how inter-group uses of language reflect the social and psychological attitudes of their speakers. Giles and Byrne (1982), Beebe and Giles (1984), Ball, Giles, and Hewstone (1984), and Hall and Gudykunst (1986) have extended this approach to account for L2 acquisition. The inter-group theory has become more complex over time in an effort to incorporate the results of ongoing research about what factors influence inter-group linguistic behaviour. The account below is based primarily on Giles and Byrne's original formulation.

The key construct is that of ethnolinguistic vitality. Giles and Byrne identify a number of factors that contribute to a group's ethnolinguistic vitality (see Table 6.4). They then discuss the conditions under which subordinate group members (for example, immigrants or members of an ethnic minority) are most likely to acquire native-like proficiency in the dominant group's language. These are: (1) when in-group identification is weak or the L1 does not function as a salient dimension of ethnic group membership, (2) when inter-ethnic comparisons are quiescent, (3) when perceived in-group vitality is low, (4) when perceived in-group boundaries are soft and open, and (5) when the learners identify strongly with other groups and so develop adequate group identity and intra-group status. When these conditions prevail, learners experience low ethnolinguistic vitality but without insecurity, as they are not aware of the options open to them regarding their status *vis-à-vis* native-speaker groups. These five conditions are associated with a desire to integrate into the dominant out-group (an integrative orientation), additive bilingualism, low situational anxiety, and the effective use of informal contexts of acquisition. The end result is that learners will achieve high levels of social and communicative proficiency in the L2.

Learners from minority groups will be unlikely to achieve native-speaker proficiency when their ethnolinguistic vitality is high. This occurs if (1) they identify strongly with their own in-group, (2) they see their in-group as inferior to the dominant out-group, (3) their perception of their ethno-linguistic vitality is high, (4) they perceive in-group boundaries as hard and closed, and (5) they do not identify with other social groups and so have an inadequate group status. In such cases, learners are likely to be aware of 'cognitive alternatives' and, as a result, emphasize the importance of their own culture and language and, possibly, engage in competition with the out-group. They will achieve low levels of communicative proficiency in the L2 because this would be seen to detract from their ethnic identity, although they may achieve knowledge of the formal aspects of the L2 through classroom study.

	Variable	Description
1	Identification with own ethnic group	This concerns the extent to which learners see themselves as members of a specific group that is separate from the out-group, and also consider their L1 an important dimension of their identity.
2	Inter-ethnic comparison	This concerns the extent to which learners make favourable or unfavourable comparisons with the out-group. Learners may or may not be aware of 'cognitive alternatives'.
3	Perception of ethnolinguistic vitality	This concerns the extent to which learners see their in-group as having low or high status and as sharing or being excluded from institutional power.
4	Perception of in-group boundaries	This concerns the extent to which learners see their group as culturally and linguistically separate from the out-group (hard boundaries), or as culturally and linguistically related (soft boundaries).
5	Identification with other social groups	This concerns the extent to which learners identify with other social groups (occupational, religious, gender) and, as a consequence, whether they hold an adequate or inadequate status within their in-group.

Table 6.4:   Variables affecting L2 acquisition according to the Inter-group Model

So far the Inter-group Model is very similar to the Acculturation Model; both were designed to account for L2 acquisition in majority language settings, both attempt to specify a set of socio-psychological factors that govern how successful individual learners will be, and both use these factors to describe 'good' and 'bad' learning situations. However, whereas Schumann's model emphasizes 'contact' as the variable that mediates between social factors and L2 acquisition, Giles and Byrne see 'interaction' as crucial. The factors they identify determine to what extent learners engage in upward convergence, and they define L2 learning as 'long-term convergence'. As we saw in Chapter 4, much of the work in SLA research based on Giles' accommodation framework has been directed at discovering which linguistic features are subject to convergence or divergence, and under which interactional conditions they operate. As such, the Inter-group Model integrates a macro- and microlinguistic approach to the study of L2 acquisition.

However, the model represents a big leap from Giles' work on variation to acquisition, seen as variation over time. The published work has focused only on the description and explanation of local phenomena in learner language (for example, Beebe and Zuengler's (1983) study of Puerto Rican and Chinese-Thai learners' use of specific linguistic phenomena in one-to-one interviews[6]). As such, there has not really been any real test of the Inter-group Model. What are needed now are longitudinal studies documenting the social factors that influence style shifting in L2 learners, the extent to which style shifting is related to acquisition, and, in particular, whether learners who regularly converge towards target-language norms in their interactions with native speakers ultimately achieve high levels of L2 proficiency.

The Socio-educational Model

Gardner's Socio-educational Model reflects the results of work begun at McGill University in Montreal in the 1950s and still carried on today. Unlike the other two models, which were designed to account for the role that social factors play in natural settings, in particular majority language contexts, Gardner's model was developed to explain L2 learning in classroom settings, in particular the foreign language classroom. It exists in several versions (Gardner 1979; 1983; and 1985). The following account is derived from the 1985 version.

The model, which is shown schematically in Figure 6.2, seeks to interrelate four aspects of L2 learning: (1) the social and cultural milieu, (2) individual learner differences, (3) the setting, and (4) learning outcomes. As such it goes beyond purely social factors and is more comprehensive than either of the other two models. The basis of the model is that L2 learning—even in a classroom setting—is not just a matter of learning new information but of 'acquiring symbolic elements of a different ethnolinguistic community' (Gardner 1979: 193).

The social and cultural milieu in which learners grow up determines their beliefs about language and culture. In monolingual settings such as Britain and the United States, the prevailing beliefs are likely to be that bilingualism is unnecessary and that assimilation of minority cultures and languages is desirable. In bilingual settings such as Canada both bilingualism and biculturalism may be encouraged. Gardner identifies a number of variables that result in individual difference. The two shown in Figure 6.2 are *motivation* and *language aptitude*. As both of these are discussed in detail in Chapter 11, we will say little about them here. The learners' social and cultural milieu determine the extent to which they wish to identify with the target-language culture (their integrative motivation) and also the extent to which they hold positive attitudes towards the learning situation (for example, the teacher and the instructional programme). Both contribute to the learners' motivation, influencing both its nature (how integrative it is) and its strength. Motivation is seen as independent of language aptitude (the special ability for learning languages). Whereas motivation has a major impact on learning in both formal and informal learning contexts, aptitude is considered to be important only in the former, although it can play a secondary role in the latter. These two variables (together with intelligence and situational anxiety) determine the learning behaviours seen in different learners in the two contexts and, thereby, learning outcomes. These can be linguistic (L2 proficiency) and non-linguistic (attitudes, self-concept, cultural values, and beliefs). Learners who are motivated to integrate develop both a high level of L2 proficiency andbetter attitudes. The model is dynamic and cyclical.

One of the predictions of the socio-educational model is that the relationship between the social/cultural milieu and L2 proficiency and also between learners' attitudes and their proficiency is an indirect one, whereas that between integrative motivation and proficiency is more direct and, therefore, stronger. Gardner, Lalonde, and Pierson (1983) and Lalonde and Gardner (1985) have investigated this using a statistical technique known as Linear Structural Analysis, which claims to be able to identify causal paths and not merely correlations among variables. These studies provide support for the view that factors in the social and cultural milieu are causally related to attitudes (integrativeness) which in turn are causally related to motivation and via this to achievement. Other studies have suggested that there may be further intervening variables between setting and L2 achievement. Clement (1980), for instance, has proposed that there is a 'secondary motivational process' connected with self-confidence. This has led to recent work by Gardner and his associates on the role of situational anxiety (see Chapter 11).

As we noted earlier, the results of studies that have investigated the relationship between integrative motivation and L2 proficiency have been very mixed. Au (1988) reviews 14 studies carried out by Gardner and his associates. Out of these, seven found a nil relationship and four found a negative relationship between at least some integrative motive measures and L2 achievement. Out of 13 studies conducted by other researchers, only a minority produced evidence of even a modest positive relationship. Au argues that 'there is little evidence that integrative motive is a unitary concept' (1988: 82) and criticizes Gardner for failing to address why some components are found to relate to L2 achievement, while others are not. Gardner's (1988) response to Au's criticisms is to claim that it is 'simplistic' to assume that the measures of the different components that make up an integrative motive will be equivalent to each other and refers to other studies not mentioned by Au (reviewed in Gardner 1980 and Lalonde and Gardner 1985), which show that a

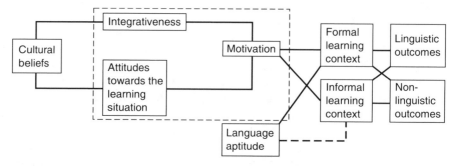

Figure 6.2:   Gardner's (1985) Socio-educational Model

composite index of motivation predicts L2 achievement. Gardner also emphasizes the importance of paying careful attention to a number of design and data analysis factors (for example, the use of valid and reliable measures of attitudinal and motivational characteristics), with the implication that studies that have produced nil or negative correlations failed to do this.

The strength of Gardner's model is that is it explains how setting is related to proficiency—one of the primary goals of any social theory of L2 acquisition—by positing a series of intervening variables (attitudes, motivation, self-confidence) and by trying to plot how these are interrelated and how they affect learning. In this respect, it provides the most detailed account of how social factors influence proficiency currently available. Missing from the model is any account of how particular settings highlight different factors that influence attitudes, motivation, and achievement, although Gardner recognizes the need to pay close attention to the social milieu in order to identify alternative factors. Also missing from the model is any reference to the concept of 'interlanguage development' and how this takes place through the process of social interaction. Gardner's model, unlike both Schumann's and Giles and Byrne's, only considers ultimate proficiency, measured mainly by language tests of various kinds. It does not consider the kinds of developmental patterns documented in Chapter 3. Nor does it consider the social aspects of variability in learner language. The model, therefore, cannot explain why learners develop in the way they do.

A historical–structural perspective

Finally, we should note that all three models can be criticized from a historical–structural viewpoint. This emphasizes the historical background of the social, political, and economic forces that determine individual choices. Tollefson (1991) embarks on a lengthy critique of speech accommodation theory, including Giles and Byrne's Inter-group Model. His main point is that it rests on the idea of 'natural law' (i.e. that human choice is essentially free and structures society) and, in so doing, fails to consider the various historical and structural variables that explain why learners from minority language backgrounds make the choices they do. According to Tollefson, the concepts of ethnolinguistic vitality and ethnolinguistic group can only be properly understood by considering issues of power and domination in the majority and minority groups involved. He also argues that by emphasizing the role of convergence in language learning, the Inter-group Model suggests that 'learners who identify with their mother tongue cannot also be fully bilingual' and thus, inadvertently, 'provides a theoretical justification for language education programmes that seek to weaken learners' ties to their mother tongue and their community' (1991: 76). Although Tollefson does not consider the Acculturation Model and the Socio-educational Model it is clear that they too are vulnerable to a historical-structural critique.

Conclusion

In this chapter we have explored how social factors affect L2 outcomes. We have considered the somewhat limited research that has investigated the relationship between specific social factors (age, sex, social class, and ethnicity/ attitudes) and L2 proficiency. We have seen that social factors govern the learners' choice of reference group, which affects the variety of the target language they choose as their model. We have also examined the different kinds of social contexts, natural and educational, and how these constrain learning outcomes. Finally, we have looked at three models of L2 acquisition that emphasize the importance of social factors.

The following are some of the major conclusions to be drawn from this exploration:

1 Social factors have a general impact on the kind of learning that takes place, whether informal or formal. Both types can occur in natural and educational settings but there is a tendency for informal learning to occur in natural settings and formal in educational settings (particularly in foreign language classrooms).

2 There is no evidence that social factors influence the nature of the processes responsible for interlanguage development in informal learning. There is ample evidence to suggest that they affect ultimate L2 proficiency, whether this is measured in terms of BICS or CALP.

3 The relationship between social factors and L2 achievement is an indirect rather than a direct one. That is, their effect is mediated by variables of a psychological nature (in particular attitudes towards to the target language, its culture and its speakers) that determine the amount of contact with the L2, the nature of the interpersonal interactions learners engage in and their motivation.

4 Regarding the role of specific social factors, few definite conclusions are currently possible. There is some evidence to suggest that greater success

in L2 learning will be observed in younger rather than older learners, females rather than males, middle class rather than working class people and in learners whose ethnolinguistic vitality is such that learning the L2 is not perceived as a threat to their ethnic identity. In each case, however, exceptions have been reported.

5 Many learners may not be targeted on the standard dialect of the target language. This suggests that measuring progress in terms of learners' approximation to the norms of the standard dialect—the normal procedure in SLA research—may be misleading. Learners may display a degree of schizophrenia regarding their 'preference choice', declaring it to be the standard variety while actually targeting on some other variety.

6 Some contexts are more likely to result in successful L2 learning than others (see Table 6.2, page 229).

7 A social model of L2 acquisition will need to consider factors that account for both the amount and the quality of the contact that learners have with other speakers of the L2, and for the attitudes that they hold towards the target language, its culture, and the specific learning situation they find themselves in.

8 A social theory of L2 acquisition will also need to consider how historical-structural factors shape individual learner choices.

It is probably true to say that although quite a lot is known about the *general* impact of social factors on L2 achievement, it is not yet possible to make accurate predictions. One reason for this is that social factors interact with other factors of a psychological nature that contribute to individual differences (for example, language aptitude, learning style, and personality). The nature of these interactions is only understood in the broadest terms.

Notes

1 Guy (1988) provides a clear account of how colonial rulers utilized language to establish and maintain their position as social elites.

2 This claim, however, can be challenged. L2 learners make use of a similar set of *communication strategies* to native speakers, including word-coinage (see Chapter 9). A new coinage such as 'outstation' might figure in learner language in the same way it figures in native-speaker speech. Perhaps the difference lies not so much in the 'process' involved, as Lowenberg suggests, as in the permanence of the item. In learner language, 'outstation' constitutes a temporary solution to a communication problem, with little chance of it becoming a fixed element in the learner's lexicon, whereas new coinages in native-speaker varieties often become fixtures.

3 Contrary to Cummins' claim, there is also some evidence that BICS is interdependent. Both Snow (1987) and Verhoeven (1991) show that children's ability to produce context-embedded language in an L2 matches their ability to do so in their L1.

4 Hammerley's attack on the Canadian French immersion programmes has come in for considerable criticism. Collier (1992: 87), for example, characterizes his 1989 book as an 'emotional, polemical, one-sided account of his personal views ... with scant research evidence cited to undergird his opinions'.

5 This discussion of roles focuses on the interactional roles adopted by teachers and learners in the classroom. Such roles reflect the status of the participants as teachers and students. They reflect the positions which educational institutions expect them to adopt. These are socially and culturally determined. This may be why teachers in some African and Asian countries seem to find it especially difficult to abandon the traditional role of 'knower'.

6 In fact, the research reported by Beebe and Zuengler (1983) was completed before Giles and Byrne (1982) proposed the Inter-group Model. It constituted an attempt to reinterpret earlier work by Beebe (see Beebe 1974) in terms of speech accommodation theory.

Further Reading

A good start is to read C. Baker, *Key Issues in Bilingualism and Bilingual Education* (Multilingual Matters, 1988). This has a particularly good section on attitudes.

Given that much of the literature draws on Cummins' model of L2 proficiency, it may also help to read:
J. Cummins, 'Language proficiency and academic achievement' in J. Oller (ed.), *Issues in Language Testing Research* (Newbury House, 1983).

A good general article providing a social perspective on L2 acquisition is:
J. Richards, 'Social factors, interlanguage and language learning.' *Language Learning* (1972) 22.

The following are representative articles dealing with the effect of various social factors on L2 acquisition:
J. Boyle, 'Sex differences in listening vocabulary' *Language Learning* (1987) 37: 273–84.
N. Holobrow, F. Genesee, and W. Lambert, 'The effectiveness of a foreign language immersion program for children from different ethnic and social class backgrounds: Report 2' *Applied Psycholinguistics* (1991) 12: 179–98.
B. Svanes, 'Attitudes and "cultural distance" in second language acquisition.' *Applied Linguistics* (1988) 9: 357–71.

Two important articles dealing with the learner's choice of target language variety are:
L. Beebe, 'Input: choosing the right stuff' in S. Gass and C. Madden (eds.), *Input in Second Language Acquisition* (Newbury House, 1985).
L. Goldstein, 'Standard English: the only target for nonnative speakers of English?' *TESOL Quarterly* (1987) 21: 417–36.

The following are some of the articles mentioned in this chapter dealing with the relationship between different types of social contexts and L2 acquisition:

T. Skuttnab-Kangas, 'Multilingualism and the education of minority children' in T. Skuttnab-Kangas and J. Cummins (eds.), *Minority Education* (Multilingual Matters, 1988).
J. Cummins, 'Second language acquisition within bilingual education programs' in L. Beebe (ed.), *Issues in Second Language Acquisition: Multiple Perspectives* (Newbury House, 1978).
A. d'Anglejan, 'Language learning in and out of classrooms' in Richards, J. (ed.), *Understanding Second and Foreign Language Learning: Issues and Approaches* (Newbury House, 1978).
A. Davies, 'Is international English an interlanguage?' *TESOL Quarterly* (1989) 23: 447–67.

These are the key books and articles dealing with the three social models of L2 acquisition discussed in this chapter:

J. Schumann, 'The acculturation model for second language acquisition' in R. Gingras (ed.), *Second Language Acquisition and Foreign Language Teaching* (Center for Applied Linguistics, 1978).
H. Giles and J. Byrne, 'An intergroup approach to second language acquisition.' *Journal of Multilingual and Multicultural Development* (1982) 3: 17–40.
R. Gardner, *Social Psychology and Second Language Learning: The Role of Attitudes and Motivation* (Edward Arnold, 1985).

Finally, for those interested in a historical-structural account of the relationship between social factors and L2 acquisition, the following is recommended:

J. Tollefson, *Planning Language, Planning Inequality* (Longman, 1991).

7 Input and interaction and second language acquisition

Introduction

Although all theories of L2 acquisition acknowledge the need for input, they differ greatly in the importance that is attached to it; the role of input in language acquisition is a controversial question. In my previous review of SLA research (Ellis 1985a: 127ff), I distinguished three different views about its role: the *behaviourist*, the *mentalist*, and the *interactionist*.

Behaviourist accounts of L2 acquisition propose a direct relationship between input and output. Because they reject the idea of 'mind' as an object for inquiry, they ignore the internal processing that takes place inside the learner. Input is comprised of stimuli and feedback. With stimuli, the person speaking to the learner models specific linguistic forms and patterns which the learner internalizes by imitating them. Feedback takes the form of positive reinforcement or correction, depending on whether the learner's output is perceived to be target-like. Behaviourist models of learning emphasize the possibility of shaping L2 acquisition by manipulating the input to provide appropriate stimuli and by ensuring that adequate feedback is always available. Acquisition is thus controlled by external factors, and the learner is viewed as a passive medium.

Mentalist theories emphasize the importance of the learner's 'black box'. Although input is still seen as essential for L2 acquisition, it is seen as only a 'trigger' that sets off internal language processing (see Cook 1989). Learners are equipped with innate knowledge of the possible forms that any single language can take, and use the information supplied by the input to arrive at the forms that apply in the case of the L2 they are trying to learn. As we will see later, a common assertion of mentalist theories is that the input is 'indeterminate' i.e. the information that it supplies is, by itself, insufficient to enable learners to arrive at the rules of the target language.

The third type of theory is the interactionist one. This label has been applied to two rather different types of theory. According to cognitive interactionist theories, acquisition is seen as a product of the complex interaction of the linguistic environment and the learner's internal mechanisms, with neither viewed as primary. Cognitive interactionist models of L2 acquisition have been drawn from contemporary cognitive psychology and, not surprisingly perhaps, vary considerably. Despite the differences, however, a common assumption can be seen to underlie them, namely that input does have a determining function in language acquisition, but only within the constraints imposed by the learner's internal mechanisms.

The second type of interactionist theory is more social in orientation. The principle that informs these theories is that verbal interaction is of crucial importance for language learning as it helps to make the 'facts' of the L2 salient to the learner. We will be concerned primarily with social interactionist theories in this chapter, delaying consideration of the cognitive kind until Chapter 9. We should note, however, that many cognitive interactionist theories also see social interaction as the primary mechanism of mental reorganization.

This chapter begins with a brief discussion of the main methods used to investigate input and interaction. Subsequently it focuses on two major questions:

1 What are the characteristics of the input that L2 learners typically receive?
2 How does the input influence L2 acquisition?

Question (1) leads us to consider research that has sought to *describe* L2 input, while (2) leads us to examine research that has sought to *explain* how input affects acquisition. Because much of the work on input in second language acquisition research has followed in the footsteps of work in first language acquisition research, attention will be given to the latter whenever this seems appropriate. As there is a separate chapter dealing with input and interaction in classroom settings (Chapter 13), this chapter will concentrate on input and interaction in non-instructional settings, although some reference to classroom research will be made when this is of particular relevance to the issue under discussion.

Methods for investigating input and interaction

Many of the earlier input studies (for example, Hatch and Wagner-Gough 1976; Hatch 1978b and 1978c; Peck 1978) used data that had been collected to study learner language. Because these data consisted of transcriptions of the interactions in which the learners took part, it was a relatively easy task to transfer attention from what the learners said to what was said to them. The data were submitted to both detailed linguistic analyses (for example, to discover the frequency with which specific morphemes occurred in the input or the complexity of input addressed to learners at different stages of development) and discourse and conversational analysis (for example, to describe the ways in which topics were nominated and developed or the strategies used to deal with communication breakdown). Discourse and conversational
analysis rapidly became the favoured method of analysis, as it provided researchers with the tools they needed to investigate the nature of the learning opportunities made available to learners through interaction.

Later, experimental and pseudo-experimental studies were designed to investigate the effect of specific variables on input and interaction. Studies carried out by Long (1980a), Gass and Varonis (1985a), and Pica and Doughty (1985a), among others, have made use of input/interaction data elicited for the purpose of the enquiry. Long, for instance, in one of the most frequently cited input studies, asked sixteen pairs of subjects (consisting of American native speakers of English, and Japanese non-native speakers) to perform six different tasks, three of them involving one-way information exchange (giving instructions, vicarious narrative, and discussing the supposed purpose of the research) and three involving two-way information exchange (conversation and playing two communication games). The advantage of such studies is that they enable the researcher to manipulate individual variables deemed likely to influence the quantity or quality of the input provided or to investigate the effects of the learners' stage of development on the input provided. The disadvantage is that it is difficult to determine to what extent the data collected are representative of the kind of communication the learners typically take part in. In many cases, as in Long's study, the interlocutors had no prior knowledge of each other - a factor which may influence the nature of the interactions which take place (see the discussion of addressee effects in Chapter 4).

One major advantage of experimental studies is that they make possible the collection of baseline data, which provide the researcher with some kind of normative point of reference. Usually these consist of conversations between native speakers performing the same tasks. Such data enable the researcher to identify what is special about the input addressed to the learners. However, as Long (1980a) points out, many studies have failed to collect baseline data.

Not surprisingly, perhaps, introspective techniques have not been widely used in input research, as neither learners nor native speakers are likely to be able to comment accurately or reliably on detailed features of the input. However, Ferguson (1975) collected data on foreigner-talk by asking students at Stanford University to rewrite standard English sentences in the way they thought they would say them to illiterate non-Europeans with no English. This method suffers from the same drawbacks we noted with discourse completion questionnaires in Chapter 5. We cannot be sure that what people think they would say is what they would actually say.

Another source of introspective information is diary studies. Brown (1985) used diaries to investigate the kinds of requests for input expressed by L2 learners. She analysed the comments the diarists made in 'any reference to input desired, to amount of input given, to type, complexity or meaningfulness of input' (page 275). Schmidt and Frota (1986) also made use of a diary study as a means of investigating what one learner *noticed* in the input. This study shows that introspection is an important tool for the input researcher, as it provides one of the best ways of discovering what it is in the input that learners attend to. It is probably not 'raw' input but 'heeded' input that works for language acquisition (see Chapter 9).

The characteristics of input to language learners

Input studies have focused on two issues. A number of studies have examined what might be called 'input text' by trying to establish what native speakers actually say or write (as opposed to what reference books claim native speaker usage consists of). Second, there are studies of 'input discourse', the special kind of 'register' that is used when speakers address language learners.[1] Studies of input discourse have been recently extended to include an examination of the ways in which interaction shapes the input that learners receive.

Input text: native-speaker usage

A number of researchers have warned of the dangers of making assumptions about the nature of the input that is addressed to language learners on the basis of descriptions of the abstract system of the target language. Lightbown and d'Anglejan (1985) argue the case for detailed empirical studies of actual usage, pointing out that such studies are particularly important before any claims can be made about universals of language acquisition.

A good example of the kind of problem that can arise in SLA research when the input is assumed rather than attested is found in interrogative structures. Research reviewed in Chapter 3 provided evidence that learners' early interrogatives take the form of declarative word order with rising intonation (for example, 'You speak English?'). The question arises as to whether this reflects a transitional construction typical of interlanguage development, indicative of the process of the learner's *creative construction* of L2 rules (Dulay and Burt 1977). Studies of native-speaker usage suggest that this may not be the case. Vander Brook, Schlue, and Campbell (1980) and Williams (1990) point out that many native-speaker questions in English are also non-inverted, particularly when there is a high presupposition of a 'yes' answer:

A: I'm studying poetry this year.
B: You're studying poetry this term?

Vander Brook et al. re-examined some of the data from Cancino et al.'s (1978) study of Spanish learners' acquisition of English interrogatives and concluded that in many cases it was not possible to judge the appropriateness of the learners' question forms because it was impossible to gauge the amount of presupposition they were making. In other words, no conclusion regarding the use of transitional constructions by the learners was possible. Williams' study of yes/no questions in Singapore English shows how difficult it is to judge when learners have achieved a level of target-like production without detailed information on what constitutes target-like use. Her advanced level subjects displayed an ability to produce 'fully formed questions' but often did not do so—certainly to a lesser extent than native speakers of American English.[2]

Lightbown and d'Anglejan (1985) found discrepancies between the declared norms for three French structures (interrogatives, negatives, and word order) and the use of these structures in everyday spoken French. They found that uninverted interrogative forms and questions with 'est-ce-que' (which also adhere to declarative word order) are predominant in native-speaker input, contrary to the claims of the formal descriptions of linguists and grammarians and also to native-speaker intuitions. In the case of negation, 'ne' is often deleted in rapid informal speech (for example, 'Elle vient pas avec vous.'), making French a post-negation rather than double-negation language. They also note that although French is considered to be a subject-verb-object (SVO) language typologically, spoken French provides copious examples of alternative orders (VOS, VS and even OSV). This study further demonstrates the importance of ensuring that learner language is examined together with accurate information about the input language.

An additional problem facing the researcher is determining which kind of input to consider when evaluating the learner's interlanguage. We have already seen in Chapter 6 that learners vary in their choice of reference group. Valdman (1992) talks of the 'illusive ideal native speaker', pointing out that even in cases where there is a single norm (for example, Metropolitan Standard French), 'the norm allows considerable leeway' (page 84). Valdman goes on to argue that 'an invariant TL norm, based on the planned discourse of educated and cultivated speakers, is an illusory target for learners' (page 94). Valdman is more concerned with the problem this poses in choosing appropriate pedagogical norms, but it is also equally problematic for the researcher concerned with examining the role of input in interlanguage development.

Even assuming that accurate information regarding target-language norms is available, the problem is not overcome, as in many cases native speakers do not adhere to these norms when communicating with non-native speakers. Frequently they modify their input in a number of ways. We will now examine the nature of these modifications in input discourse.

Input discourse: the description of modified input

When caretakers speak to young children who are in the process of acquiring their L1, they typically adjust their speech in a number of ways. The register that results has been referred to variously as 'baby-talk', 'motherese', 'care-taker talk' (the term used in this chapter), and 'child-directed language'. Similarly, when native speakers talk to L2 learners they also modify their speech; the resulting register is known as *foreigner talk*. It is also possible to talk about *interlanguage talk* (see Krashen 1981: 121), the language that learners address to each other. We will now examine the formal and interactional characteristics of these registers.

Caretaker talk

Partly as a response to mentalist claims that the input that children receive from their caretakers is 'degenerate' (see Miller and Chomsky 1963), in the 1970s researchers into L1 acquisition set out to examine the nature of caretaker talk empirically. Important collections of papers were published by Snow and Ferguson (1977) and Waterson and Snow (1978). Other studies have continued to be published since, particularly in the *Journal of Child Language*. We will concentrate on the main findings of this research.

A number of studies have shown that caretakers adjust their speech formally so that the input that children receive is both clearer and linguistically simpler than the speech they address to other adults. Broen (1972) found that speech addressed to two year-olds has only half the speed used with other adults. Garnica (1975) showed that adults use a higher pitch when talking to children. Sachs (1977) found that mothers tune the pitch, intonation, and rhythm of their speech to the perceptive sensitivity of their children. Such modifications are often linked with additional clues provided by gesture and gaze.

Comparative studies of the speech adults address to other adults and the speech they address to children have shown that caretakers also make adjustments in lexis and syntax (Snow 1976; 1977). They use a higher ratio of content words to functors and also restrict the range of vocabulary items employed (i.e. they manifest a low type-token ratio). Modifications in syntax are evident in a lower mean length of utterance (MLU), a measure that reflects both the length and the overall linguistic complexity of utterances. Caretakers use fewer subordinate and coordinate constructions, and correspondingly more simple sentences. They avoid sentence embeddings and they produce sentences which express a limited range of syntactical and semantic relations.

It has been suggested, however, that these characteristics are not necessarily found in the talk of all caretakers and, in particular, that they may reflect the particular child-rearing practices of middle-class, English-speaking parents. Harkness (1977) and Ochs (1982) respectively provide evidence to suggest that formal simplifications are not the norm in caretaker talk in Kenya and Western Samoa. Ochs and Schieffelin (1984) argue that many of the characteristics of talk observed in white, middle-class American caretakers are a reflection of a cultural predisposition for experts to assist novices and that this may not be evident in other cultures. Crago (1992) documents how Inuit children in Arctic Quebec are traditionally expected to learn language through observing and listening to others rather than through participating in conversations shaped by questions from adult caretakers.

Irrespective of cultural differences, adults' speech to children has been shown to be remarkably well-formed, thus refuting the mentalist claim that the input children receive is degenerate. For example, Cross (1977) found few examples of speech which was not fluent or intelligible, or of run-on sentences (in each case, less than 10 per cent of the mothers' total utterances). Newport, Gleitman, and Gleitman (1977) reported that only one out of 1,500 utterances was disfluent.

Another rather different type of adjustment concerns the kinds of topics that get talked about. Parents tend to follow the here-and-now principle by talking about topics which can be understood in terms of objects physically present and actions that are taking place at the time. They avoid talking about activities that are displaced in time and space until the child has developed the necessary concepts to understand them. Parents have also been found to prefer topics that are familiar to their children. Ferrier (1978) has pointed out that much of the communication with young children centres on routine activities: eating, having a bath, getting dressed, looking at picture books, playing games, etc. These activities involve caretaker and child in joint attention on a common set of objects and actions.

Caretaker speech is also characterized by *interactional modifications*. Both child and adult caretakers make plentiful use of attention-getters (for example, 'Look!' or 'Hey!'). Adult caretakers make special efforts to ensure that what they say is understood by their children by frequently checking comprehension and repeating all or parts of their utterances, as in this example from Snow (1972):

Pick up the red one. Find the red one. Not the green one.
I want the red one. Can you find the red one?

They are also ready to allow the child to initiate and control the development of topics. Some caretakers appear to be particularly skilful in the strategies they use to sustain and extend a conversation which their children have started. Frequently, however, their attempts to communicate are not successful, either because the caretaker fails to understand what the child has said or because the child cannot understand the caretaker. In the case of the former the caretaker is likely to probe further by means of requests for clarification (such as 'Mm?') or requests for confirmation which often take the form of an expansion of what the caretaker thinks the child has tried to say. When the child does not understand the caretaker, the caretaker uses repetitions and paraphrases to sort out the problem. These features, of course, are not unique to caretaker talk but they have been shown to be especially frequent in comparison to discourse involving adult addressees. As we will see later, the availability of semantically contingent input (i.e. input that is closely linked in meaning to something that the child has already said) has been found to be an excellent predictor of the child's rate of progress.

Of considerable interest to researchers is the extent to which the adjust-ments are 'fine-' or 'rough-tuned'. Krashen (1980) defines fine-tuning as the provision of the specific linguistic features which the child is ready to acquire next and claims that caretaker-talk is characterized only by rough-tuning. As evidence he cites the positive but 'not strikingly high' correlations between linguistic input complexity and linguistic competence in children found by Newport, Gleitman, and Gleitman (1977). Krashen is surely right in claiming that caretakers do not aim their input at specific linguistic structures, but he probably underestimates the extent to which adult caretakers are sensitive to their children's progress. As we will see when we discuss the relationship be-tween input frequency and acquisition, Wells (1985) provides evidence to suggest that adults step up the frequency of specific linguistic features in their input shortly *before* their children first use them in their own speech. Cer-tainly, there is plenty of evidence to show that adjustments in caretaker talk occur on a continuous scale; that is, they are responsive to the development evident in individual children at different stages of acquisition. Cross (1977) considers that this justifies claiming that the input is fine-tuned.[3]

Researchers have also considered the purposes served by caretaker talk. Ferguson (1977) suggests three possible functions: (1) to aid communication, (2) to teach language, and (3) to socialize the child. It is the first of these that seems to be the most important. Caretakers seek to communicate with their child and this leads them to modify their speech in order to facilitate the ex-change of meanings. As Brown (1977: 26) put it, the primary motivation is to communicate, to understand and to be understood, and to keep two minds focused on the same topic. Brown and Hanlon (1970) have shown that moth-ers do correct children to ensure that what they say is true.[4] Thus, if a child mislabels an object (for example, refers to a horse as 'doggie'), the mother is likely to respond with either an explicit correction (such as 'No, it's a horsie') or an implicit correction (for example, 'Yes, the horsie is jumping'). Mothers also pay attention to their children's pronunciation of words and draw their attention to politeness formulae (for example, when to say 'thank you'). However, they pay little attention to the grammatical correctness of their children's speech, allowing even blatant errors to go uncorrected. In general, then, if caretaker talk serves to teach syntax and to socialize the child into the adult's culture it does so only indirectly, as offshoots of the attempt to communicate.[5]

How do caretakers determine the nature and the extent of the modifica-tions that need to be made? Gleason and Weintraub (1978) suggest that they must form a general idea of children's linguistic ability, particularly their abil-ity to understand. They argue that they do not have an accurate knowledge of the specific linguistic features the children have mastered. Of crucial import-ance is the extent to which children *comprehend* what is said to them and the extent to which they signal their comprehension or lack of it to their care-takers. Children tend to become inattentive when they do not understand, causing their caretakers to modify their speech until attention is restored. Cross (1977; 1978) found little evidence that the mothers in her study were able to monitor their own or their children's syntactic levels, but she did find that they evaluated the extent to which the children were able to demonstrate an understanding of their previous utterances. The fact that caretaker modifications have been observed in the speech that even four-year-old children address to their younger siblings (see Shatz and Gelman 1973), also suggests that they must be based on a very general assessment of the learner's communicative abilities.

In summary, there is now plentiful evidence to show that the speech that caretakers address to children is well-adapted to their linguistic abilities, particularly comprehension. Three main features of caretaker talk stand out: (1) it is more grammatical than speech addressed to adults, (2) it is simpler, and (3) it is more redundant. However, as Snow (1986) has pointed out, it cannot be concluded on the basis of these findings that there is no innate component in L1 acquisition, as the studies do not enable us to determine the relative importance of innate and input factors. The studies show only that the claim that children receive degenerate input is unwarranted.

Foreigner talk

The foreigner talk (FT)[6] used by native speakers when communicating with non-native speakers displays many of the characteristics of caretaker talk. There are also some differences, however, particularly when the non-native speakers are adults. Freed (1980; 1981) compared the speech of fifteen mothers studied by Newport (1976) with that of native speakers of American English to eleven adult non-native speakers. She found no differences in the degree of well-formedness and syntactic complexity (although instances of ungrammatical FT are not uncommon—see page 253), but she did find some in the distribution of sentence types and the interpersonal functions they encoded. In particular, declaratives were much more common in the foreigner talk, and yes/no questions and imperatives less common. Freed suggests that this reflects a general difference in purpose: whereas the main functional intent of caretaker talk is that of directing the child's behaviour, that of foreigner talk is the exchange of information. It should be noted, however, that when FT is addressed to young children, it appears to resemble caretaker talk fairly closely. Hatch, Peck, and Wagner-Gough (1979) analysed the input in Huang's (1970) study of a five-year-old learner and found that imperatives and questions far outweighed declaratives. The crucial factor, therefore, may be age.

A detailed study of foreigner talk necessitates a consideration of a number of issues: (1) the extent to which FT is grammatical and ungrammatical, (2) the nature of the formal modifications found in FT, (3) the nature of the interactional modifications found in FT, (4) discourse structure in FT, and (5) the functions served by FT.

1 Ungrammatical input modifications

In one of the earliest discussions of FT, Ferguson (1971) noted that in languages where native speakers employ a copula in equational clauses in normal communication (for example, 'Mary *is* a doctor') they often omit it in talk directed at foreigners. Ferguson suggests that this is because the absence of the copula is considered simpler than its presence. The omission of copula is a clear example of ungrammatical FT. In subsequent publications (Ferguson 1975; Ferguson and Debose 1977), Ferguson suggests that ungrammaticality is evident in three ways: (1) omission of grammatical functors such as copula, articles, conjunctions, subject pronouns, and inflectional morphology, (2) expansion, as when 'you' is inserted before an imperative verb (for example, 'You give me money.'), (3) replacement/rearrangement, as when post-verbal negation is replaced by pre-verbal negation in English FT (for example, 'No want play'). Frequently utterances will manifest all three types of ungrammaticality. As Ferguson (1971) notes, many of the features found in FT are also evident in pidgins.

A number of studies provide evidence of ungrammatical FT (see Long 1980a and Larsen-Freeman and Long 1991 for reviews). It is particularly likely in what Ferguson and Debose (1977) refer to as 'talking down' situations. Thus, Clyne (1978) reports finding examples in the speech that Australian factory foremen use to address foreign workers. Germans have been found to address guest workers in the same way (Heidelberger Forschungsprojekt 1978). However, it is also been found in situations of a more neutral kind, as when passers-by give directions to tourists (Walter-Goldberg 1982, cited in Larsen-Freeman and Long 1991) and even in conversations between friends (Hatch, Shapira, and Wagner-Gough 1978).

There are striking similarities between ungrammatical FT and learner language. Table 7.1 compares the speech of an adult learner (Zoila) with that of a native-speaker friend (Rina) in the same conversation. It shows that Rina's input matched Zoila's output in a number of ways. Hatch, Shapira, and Wagner-Gough (1978) observe that Rina felt unable to stop herself producing ungrammatical utterances but they also point out that her speech was not an exact copy of Zoila's. The similarity between FT and learner language should not be taken as evidence in favour of the matching hypothesis (i.e. that the source of learners' 'errors' is ungrammatical FT), for, as both Long (1983a) and Meisel (1983) have noted, it may reflect a common set of cognitive processes (see the discussion on page 265 later in this section). However, native speakers may well introduce ungrammatical forms of the kind they observe in learner language into their speech as part of the process of

Grammatical structure	Learner language	Foreigner talk
Copula	Regularly deleted – but does occur in some contexts.	Only deleted in 5 out of 43 instances.
Pronoun 'it'	Pervasive deletion	Also pervasively deleted.
Verb tense	Uninflected verb form used for all time reference; also V *-ing* used in apparent free distribution. No aux-do.	V *-ing* used grammatically. Aux-do regularly deleted.
Negatives	'no + V' and 'I don't know' used.	Mixed 'no + V' and grammatical negatives used; 'no + V *-ing*' negatives most common.
Possessives	No possessive *'s*.	Nouns consistently marked with possessive *'s*.
'For'	'For' used in expressions like 'Is upset for you?'	Similar use of 'for' found in 3 out of 15 instances.

Table 7.1:   A comparison of learner language and foreigner talk (based on data from Hatch, Shapira, and Wagner-Gough 1978)

accommodating to their addressee (see Chapters 4 and 6 for a discussion of accommodation theory).

Non-standard forms are also evident in other levels of language: pronunciation and lexis, for instance. Epenthesis (the insertion of an additional vowel), the replacement of reduced vowels by full vowels, and exaggerated intonation similar to the kind observed in caretaker talk have all been noted in FT pronunciation. Interestingly, though, native speakers practising FT do not seem to follow caretakers in using a higher pitch. In lexis, 'ungrammatical' adaptations include the use of names in place of pronouns, a special lexicon of quantifiers, intensifiers and modal particles and, in highly marked forms of FT, the use of foreign or foreign-sounding words such as 'amigo', 'capito', and 'compris', which Meisel (1980) reports observing in German FT.

A number of factors appear to induce ungrammatical FT. Long (1983a) suggests that four factors may be involved:

1 The learner's level of proficiency in L2—ungrammatical FT is more likely when the learner's proficiency is low.
2 The status of the native speaker—ungrammatical FT is more likely when the native speaker is or thinks he or she is of higher status.
3 The native speaker has prior experience of using FT but only of the 'limited kind' used to address non-native speakers of low proficiency.
4 The extent to which the conversation is spontaneous—ungrammatical FT is less likely in planned, formal discourse or in experimental situations.

However, ungrammatical FT can occur both with interlocutors who are familiars (as in the conversations between Rina and Zoila) and with strangers, suggesting that factors other than those listed by Long are at work. It is, in fact, not yet possible to identify the exact conditions that will result in ungrammatical FT, perhaps because native speakers vary both culturally and individually in the kind of FT they prefer to use.

As Meisel (1980) points out, ungrammatical FT is generally felt to imply a lack of respect. Meisel reports that Italian and Spanish workers in Germany reacted negatively when played recordings of speech samples containing ungrammatical FT, claiming that it showed contempt on the part of the native speakers. However, it may not be the presence of ungrammatical modifications *per se* that arouses negative responses in learners, but their awareness of being addressed in a special manner. Lynch (1988) found that some learners objected to the speech of a teacher because they perceived it as 'talking down', even though it did not contain obvious ungrammatical modifications. Also, in cases of very close relationships (as that between Rina and Zoila) ungrammatical adjustments do not appear to be objected to.

2 Grammatical input modifications

Ungrammatical FT is highly marked. In many situations it does not occur, suggesting that it constitutes a particular discourse type. Arthur et al. (1980) recorded sixty telephone conversations between adult non-native speakers of English and airline ticket agents and reported no instance of ungrammatical input modifications. Studies of teacher talk (for example, Henzl 1973 and 1979; Gaies 1977; Hakansson 1986) also, not surprisingly, report an absence of ungrammatical modifications, although other studies (for example, Hatch, Shapira, and Wagner-Gough 1978) did find instances in the language that teachers use to organize and manage classroom activities. Grammatical FT is the norm in most classrooms, however.

Grammatical FT is characterized by modifications indicative of three general processes: (1) simplification, (2) regularization, and (3) elaboration. To illustrate the differences in the FT that results from these three processes, contrived examples are provided in Table 7.2. It should be noted that whereas (1) involves an attempt on the part of native speakers to simplify the language forms they use, (2) and (3) are directed at simplifying the learners' task of processing the input and can, in fact, result in the use of language that is not always simple in itself. This is important because it means that FT provides not only simple input, corresponding perhaps to what learners already know, but also input containing linguistic features that they have not yet learnt.

The account of FT that follows draws on a number of studies: Gaies 1977; Arthur et al. 1980; Long 1981a and 1981b; Scarcella and Higa 1981; Hatch 1980 and 1983b; Chaudron 1982; Kleifgen 1985; Hakansson 1986; Wesche and Ready 1985; Griffiths 1990 and 1991a.

Type of speech	Example
Baseline (i.e. speech addressed to native speakers)	The 747 is a large-sized jet manufactured by Boeing, an American company, with a seating capacity of over 500, arranged on two decks.
Simplified FT	Well, er, ... the 747's a big jet. And er ... er ... it's a Boeing, an American plane. Er ... there's over 500 seats with er ... some on top and er ... some down below.
Regularized FT	The 747, it is a big jet. It is made by Boeing which is an American company. The seats, they are on two levels. There is a top level and a bottom level.
Elaborated FT	The Boeing 747 or jumbo, as it is called, is a very large jet, manufactured or made by an American company, a firm in Seattle USA. It has the capacity or space to seat a large number of passengers, over 500 people. The seats are on two decks or levels, some up on top and some down below.

Table 7.2:   Contrived examples of FT illustrating the processes of simplification, regularization, and elaboration

Table 7.3 summarizes the main linguistic modifications that have been claimed to contribute to simplification. One way of simplifying is by adjusting temporal variables such as speech rate (measured usually in syllables per second), articulation rate (measured by calculating the ratio of the total number of syllables to the total articulation time) and silent pause phenomena (pause duration, pause distribution, and pause frequency). Griffiths (1991a) summarizes the research in this area of FT. His survey shows that although temporal variables have been frequently commented on in the literature (for example, Freed 1981; Dudley-Evans and Johns 1981; Hatch 1983b; Klein 1986), these comments are not accompanied by reports of detailed empirical results. Henzl's (1973; 1979) study of the teacher talk in three different languages (Czech, English, and German) addressed to advanced and beginner L2 learners and native speakers, does give results, however. The study shows that the teachers adjusted their speech rate in accordance with the listeners' proficiency, as does Hakansson's (1986) study of Swedish teachers' classroom talk. Griffiths points out a number of methodological flaws in both studies (for example, failure to control for the sequence of audiences and to account for classroom activity silences) and also draws attention to the fact that in Henzl's study there was enormous variability from one language to another and, in both studies, from one teacher to another within the same language. In the case of syntactic and lexical modifications, simplification is achieved both by avoiding difficult items in the target language and also by reduced use of them.

Regularization entails the selection of forms that are in some way 'basic' or 'explicit'. Examples include: fewer false starts, the preference for full forms

Type of simplification	Comment
1 Temporal variables	Speech to NNSs is often slower than that addressed to NSs – mainly as a result of longer pauses.
2 Length	FT makes use of shorter sentences (fewer words per T-unit).
3 Syntactic complexity	FT is generally less syntactically and propositionally complex, i.e. fewer subordinate clauses of all kinds (adjectival, noun, and adverbial), greater use of parataxis (e.g. simple coordinate constructions), and less preverb modification.
4 Vocabulary	FT manifests a low type–token ratio and a preference for high frequency lexical items.

Table 7.3:   Simplification in grammatical foreigner talk

over contracted forms; the preference for canonical word order noted by Long, Gambhiar, Ghambiar, and Nishimura (1982) in English, Hindi, and Japanese; the use of explicit markers of grammatical relations (for example, 'He asked if he could go' rather than 'He asked to go'); the movement of topics to the front of sentences (for example, 'John, I like him'); the avoidance of forms associated with a formal style (for example, 'tu' is preferred to 'vous' in French FT); and the avoidance of idiomatic expressions and the use of lexical items with a wide coverage (for example, 'flower' rather than 'rose'). Hatch (1983b: 66–7) suggests a number of ways learners might benefit from regularizations of these kinds. For example, they help to make the meanings of utterances more transparent. This may be achieved by increasing the processing time available to learners or by making key structural elements more salient, thereby helping them to identify constituent boundaries in utterances.

Elaboration is the opposite of simplification, but to claim that FT evidences both is not contradictory, as both processes can occur at different times. Elaboration often involves lengthening sentences in an attempt to make the meaning clear. Native speakers often use analytic paraphrases of lexical items they consider difficult. Chaudron (1983b) provides a number of examples in the speech used by a university lecturer to a class of ESL learners ('hold on tightly' is used in place of 'cling'; 'there's still this feeling. . .' instead of 'we have this myth'). Native speakers also sometimes offer synonyms ('funds or money') and they define items. They may add information that helps to contextualize an item (for example,'If you go for a job in a factory. . .' where 'in a factory' is redundant). Chaudron suggests that such elaborations are designed to make the message more 'cognitively simple', but he also makes the point that they can result in too much redundant and confusing information. The lecturer he studied sometimes over-elaborated, making the interconnections between ideas difficult to comprehend.

As in caretaker talk, these different kinds of adjustments are continuous in nature; speakers make more or less of them depending on their perception of the learner's ability to understand. Hakansson (1986), for instance, found that the input provided by a teacher to learners of L2 Swedish increased in length over time as a result of an increased use of subordinations and an expansion of nominal phrases through increased modification. Kleifgen (1985) found that a kindergarten teacher's input became more complex over time to children who showed improvement, but remained static for those who did not.

The learners' proficiency is not the only factor that determines the extent of modification. Age has an effect as well. Scarcella and Higa (1981) suggest that linguistic simplification is in fact triggered more by age than linguistic competence, on the grounds that they found much more to occur in FT addressed to children aged between eight and ten years than in FT to adults.

The linguistic modifications that have been observed to occur in FT correspond closely to the language found in simplified texts of the kind found in graded readers. As such, the input is often considered 'non-authentic' (see Vincent 1986). It is worth noting, however, that in FT the modifications occur quite spontaneously as part of the process of trying to communicate with learners of limited competence.

3 Interactional modifications

Increasingly, studies of foreigner talk have switched their attention from linguistic to interactional modifications. This has been motivated in part by the finding that interactional modifications occur even when input modifications do not (Long 1980a) and also by theoretical claims regarding the importance of this type of modification for comprehension and acquisition (see following sections in this chapter).

A useful distinction can be made between those interactional modifications that involve *discourse management* and those that involve *discourse repair*.[7] The former are motivated by the attempt to simplify the discourse so as to avoid communication problems, while the latter occur when some form of communication breakdown has taken place or in response to a learner utterance that contains an error of some kind (factual, linguistic, or discourse).[7] These distinctions are shown diagrammatically in Figure 7.1 on page 258.

Discourse management

One of the most effective ways of managing discourse with native speakers is to ensure that the topic of the conversation is understood. Long (1983a) identifies a number of strategies which native speakers use to achieve this end: selecting salient topics, treating topics simply and briefly, making new topics salient, and, when necessary, relinquishing topic control, although this last strategy seems to relate more to discourse repair than discourse management.

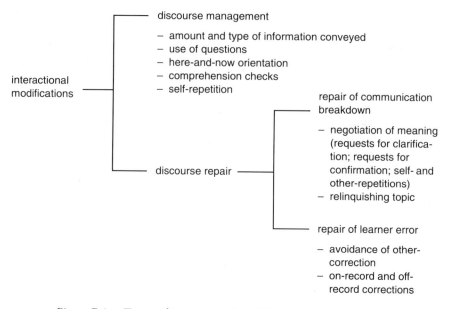

Figure 7.1:   Types of interactional modifications in foreigner talk

One method used by native speakers to control topic concerns the amount and type of information that is communicated. Arthur et al. (1980) compared the number of 'information bits' that native speaker airline agents included in their answers to a specific telephone enquiry from native speakers and non-native speakers ('What kind of plane is a ___?'). A distinction was made between 'simple' information (such as 'size' and 'jet') and 'complex' information (for example, 'seating capacity', 'name of manufacturer', and 'seating arrangement'). There was no difference in the amount of simple information given to native speaker and non-native speaker callers, but significant differences were found in the amount of complex information, the non-native speakers receiving far less. Derwing (1989) found that native speakers adjusted the information they provided about a film they had seen when speaking to low-proficiency L2 learners. The information contained in the speakers' propositions was classified as belonging to one of three categories: (1) crucial information, (2) non-essential major information, and (3) minor information, consisting of background or irrelevant information. There was no difference in the amount of crucial information which the native speaker and non-native speaker addressees received, but differences were evident in the relative proportions of major and minor information. Overall the narrators included less major information and more minor information in speech to the learners. There were considerable individual differences, however, which, as we will see later, had a significant effect on the non-native speakers' comprehension. Ehrlich, Avery, and Yorio (1989) also found evidence of variation in the amount of information supplied by individual native speakers in a problem-solving task. They distinguish 'skeletonizing', where the barest details are provided, from 'embroidering', where the information is expanded and embellished. Interestingly, they found both strategies present in interactions with both native speakers and non-native speakers, suggesting that individual native speakers may have preferred interactional styles which they use irrespective of their interlocutors. It is clear, though, that often native speakers do seek to manage discourse with non-native speakers by regulating the amount and type of information they provide.

Native speakers also make use of questions to establish and control topics. We have already noted that questions appear to be more frequent in FT than in caretaker talk. Long (1981b) found that in conversations between native English speakers and elementary level Japanese learners, the native speakers initiated most of the topics, typically making use of questions to do so. Ninety six per cent of all topic initiations were questions, whereas in native speaker–native speaker conversations only 62 per cent were. Long suggests a number of reasons why questions were favoured: they compel answers, they signal to the non-native speaker that a turn is approaching, and they lighten the learner's conversation burden because they encode part (and sometimes all) of the propositional content required to respond. Long also found differences in the types of questions used. In conversations with the learners, the native speakers made greater use of yes/no and 'or' type questions. One possibility is that the use of questions in Long's study reflected, in part at least, the lack of familiarity between the participants who made up the pairs. However, Gaies (1982) obtained similar results, suggesting that this was not the case. In this study, unlike Long's study, the native speakers and non-native speakers were already acquainted with each other, but the native speakers still used more questions when talking with the non-native speakers. It should be noted, though, that in all these studies the native speakers were adults; child native speakers seem less inclined to establish and develop topics through questioning (see Hatch 1978b; Peck 1978).

A third strategy of discourse management is to select topics that have a here-and-now orientation (see the discussion of this feature of caretaker talk on page 249). Long (1980a) and Gaies (1982) both report significantly more present-tense verbs in native speaker speech addressed to non-native speakers than in speech addressed to other native speakers, suggesting such an orientation. The here-and-now orientation allows learners to make use of the immediate context to interpret the meaning of utterances.

Finally, native speakers have been noted to try to manage discourse by frequently checking whether the learner has understood. Comprehension checks (for example, 'You understand?', 'Okay?') have been found to occur more frequently in native speaker–non-native speaker discourse than in native speaker–native speaker discourse (Long 1981a; Scarcella and Higa 1981). Teacher talk, in particular, seems to be rich in comprehension checks.

Pica and Long (1986) found that ESL teachers were much more likely than native speakers to check comprehension in informal conversations.

Discourse repair

The need for discourse repair arises in certain types of problematic communication. Gass and Varonis (1991) present a taxonomy of problematic communication types (see Figure 7.2). An initial distinction is made between 'non-engagement' and 'miscommunication'. The former occurs either when there is 'non-communication' (for example, when a non-native speaker avoids talking to a native speaker) or when there is 'communication breakoff' (for example, when a native speaker stops communicating as soon as they discover they are talking to a non-native speaker). 'Miscommunication' occurs when some message other than that intended by the speaker is understood. It can take the form a 'misunderstanding' or an 'incomplete understanding' (either 'non-understanding' or 'partial understanding'), depending on whether or not the participants overtly recognize a problem and undertake repair. In the case of an 'incomplete understanding' remediation occurs, but in the case of a 'misunderstanding' no repair occurs and the speakers are likely to lapse into silence. Gass and Varonis also note that miscommunication can occur both as a result of cross-cultural differences in the way language is interpreted and because of purely linguistic difficulties.

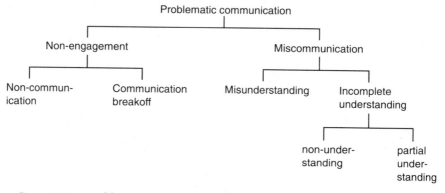

Figure 7.2:   Problematic communication types (from Gass and Varonis 1991)

Repair, then, occurs when there is an 'incomplete understanding'. It takes the form of *negotiation of meaning* - the collaborative work which speakers undertake to achieve mutual understanding. Native speakers typically use requests for clarification ('Sorry?', 'Huh?', 'I beg your pardon') and requests for confirmation, which often make use of intonation or tag questions:

NNS: Mexican food have a lot of ulcers.
  NS: Mexicans have a lot of ulcers?
(Young and Doughty 1987).

Other conversational modifications that help to repair discourse are self- and other-repetitions, which can be exact or semantic (i.e. paraphrases) and complete or partial. It should be noted that not all repetitions have a repairing function; as Pica and Doughty (1988) point out, native speakers also use them to manage discourse (i.e. to try to prevent a communication problem arising). Native speakers may also abandon the attempt to negotiate meaning by giving up a topic and allowing the non-native speaker to nominate an alternative one.

A considerable amount of research has been undertaken to establish the conditions that promote the negotiation of meaning, motivated by the claim that the comprehensible input that can result from it is of particular benefit to L2 acquisition (see the section on input and acquisition in this chapter). Pica (1987) argues that the most important factors concern the social relationships between the interactants. Interaction involving participants of equal status ensures that 'learners and their interlocutors share a need and desire to understand each other.' Conversely, unequal status makes it difficult and even unnecessary for participants to restructure interaction. This claim mirrors that made by Wells and Montgomery (1981) for caretaker interaction. When mothers act as conversational partners plentiful negotiation takes place, but when they adopt a tutorial role it is inhibited.

The distribution of power among the participants helps to explain a number of other findings, such as the influence that the non-native speaker's age has on FT. Scarcella and Higa (1981) found that adult native speakers assumed much greater responsibility for conversations when speaking with non-native speaker children than with non-native speaker adults. With children they tended to dominate conversations so that less negotiation took place. Pica and Long (1986) found interactional modifications more frequent outside than inside the classroom, a finding that can also be explained by the fact that roles are unequally distributed in the classroom, with the teacher assigned many more discourse rights than the learners. Overall, these studies suggest that when role relationships are asymmetrical, meaning negotiation is inhibited. Other kinds of non-negotiated input may still be available in such situations, however. Cathcart (1986), for instance, found that adult native speakers were more likely to respond to requests for information from child non-native speakers than were child native speakers.

A number of other factors have been found to influence negotiation: for example, the nature of the task, the characteristics of the participants, and participant structure. Much of the research that has investigated these factors has involved classroom learners or has been conducted for a clear pedagogic purpose (for example, to compare interaction in group and lockstep settings). For this reason it will be considered in Chapter 13.

The presence of higher frequencies of discourse repair functions such as requests for clarification and confirmation has been taken as evidence that higher levels of negotiation of meaning are occurring. This is, however, questionable. Aston (1986) has pointed out that these discourse acts do not unambiguously indicate negotiation of meaning, as the same procedures can be used in non-problematic conversation. He argues that they are often used 'to achieve a formal display of convergence of the participants' worlds' by allowing them to perform 'a ritual of understanding or agreement'. In other words, negotiation can be motivated by the interactants' need to display satisfactory outcomes rather than to overcome trouble sources.

In addition to repair work directed at solving problems of understanding, there is also the repair of learners' errors. Schwartz (1980) reports a general preference for self-correction over other-correction in non-native speaker–non-native speaker discourse. The same seems to be the case in native speaker–non-native speaker discourse. Gaskill (1980) examined the types of repair which an Iranian learner of English experienced in both elicited and naturally-occurring conversations with native speakers. He found only seventeen examples of other-correction in 50 pages of transcript. It would appear, then, that native speakers typically ignore learners' errors, a conclusion supported by Chun, Day, Chenoweth, and Luppescu's (1982) study of 28 ESL learners of mixed proficiency in Hawaii. In this case, less than 9 per cent of the total errors were corrected. Also, it was 'factual' errors and 'discourse errors' (for example, inappropriate openings, closings, and refusals) rather than lexical or syntactic errors that were more likely to attract repair from native speakers. Chun et al. suggest that the low level of repair reflects the native speakers' desire not to impair the cohesion of the discourse.

In the case of other-correction, a distinction can be made between *on-record* and *off-record* feedback. Day, Chenoweth, Chun, and Luppescu (1984) define the former as feedback which occurs when the native speaker responds to the source of a learner's language problems directly and unambiguously, by means of a statement with declarative intonation. Off-record repair is ambiguous and can have more than one interpretation; it can consist of a question in the form of a confirmation check (although not all confirmation checks are corrective) or a statement. They found that adult ESL learners received significantly more on-record than off-record feedback, perhaps because as friends of the learners, the native speakers felt they could overtly correct without threat to face.

In the case of linguistic modifications, there is substantial evidence that their extent in native speaker speech varies according to the learners' level of development. Somewhat surprisingly, there have been few studies that have investigated whether this is also true for interactional modifications. My study (Ellis 1985d) suggests that some, but perhaps not all, of these modifications are sensitive to the learner's level. It was found that a teacher used significantly fewer self-repetitions, but more expansions, in interactions with two learners when they had progressed beyond the stage of absolute beginners. Also, the teacher switched from topics that required object identification to topics that required the learners to make some kind of comment about an object. However, no change was observed in other interactional features such as comprehension checks, requests for clarification and confirmation, types of questions, and overall response to communication breakdown. Day et al., in the study referred to above, found that during game-like activities beginner and intermediate learners received significantly more on-record repair than did advanced learners. However, no differences were noted in conversations. The effect of the learners' proficiency on interactional modifications is clearly an area in need of further study.

The study of interactional modifications in FT has blossomed and there is now a rich literature to draw on. It is probably true to say, however, that the research has focused on a rather narrow set of interactional phenomena associated with the negotiation of meaning. The categories themselves are less watertight than researchers sometimes admit—the function of a self- or other-repetition, for example, is not always clear.[8] Also, the research has been somewhat restricted in the discourse types that it has studied—many of the studies have examined data obtained in interview-type situations or by means of information-gap activities.

4 Discourse structure

The study of interactional modifications involves examining the speech of both participants in a conversation. As Long (1983a) has pointed out, acts such as requests for clarification and confirmation take place within a discourse context—they have life across utterances and speakers. However, the study of individual discourse acts does not show how sequences of discourse are constructed. For this it is necessary to examine the structure of FT discourse.

Gass and Varonis (1985a; Varonis and Gass 1985) have developed a model to describe the structure of 'non-understanding routines' where meaning negotiation takes place. It consists of a 'trigger' (i.e. the utterance or part of an utterance that creates a problem of understanding), an 'indicator' which indicates that something in a previous utterance was not understood, a 'response' to the indicator, and finally a 'reaction to the response', which is optional. The 'indicator–response–reaction to the response' portion of a non-understanding sequence is called a 'pushdown', because it has the effect of pushing the conversation down rather than allowing it to proceed in a forward manner. The model is recursive in that it allows for the 'response' element itself to act as a 'trigger' for a further non-understanding routine. Table 7.4 provides a simple illustration of the model.

Other models exist. Ehrlich, Avery, and Yorio (1989) claim that the highly specific nature of the problem-solving task they used yielded discourse with a 'hierarchical constituent structure'. The task required the speaker (the native speaker in native speaker–non-native speaker pairs) to give instructions

Utterance	Function
NNS1: My father now is retire.	Trigger
NNS2: Retire?	Indicator
NNS1: Yes.	Response
NNS2: Oh yeah.	Reaction to Response

Table 7.4: A simple discourse model of the negotiation of meaning (example from Gass and Varonis 1985a)

about how to fill in a matrix of 16 blank squares with different objects. All the speakers proceeded through the task in the same manner beginning with an 'orientation', then moving on to the 'identification' of an object, before providing a 'description' of it. The information provided in the 'description' was also hierarchically organized, as some items of information depended on others having been previously communicated. The model was used to distinguish speakers who adopted a 'skeletonizing' strategy (i.e. provided only the basic information needed to perform a task) from those who adopted an 'embroidering' strategy (i.e. providing information that expands and embellishes beyond what is required to perform the task).

The models that have been developed are essentially data-led models; that is, they have been devised to describe the particular tokens of FT discourse elicited by the tasks used in the studies. Although there are now a number of models of FT discourse structure currently available (such as those proposed by Gass and Varonis and Ehrlich, Avery, and Yorio), it is not clear whether these are sufficiently powerful to describe different discourse types and thus to permit generalizations across studies. Nevertheless, the use of models that account for discourse structure rather than taxonomies of discrete discourse functions constitutes a definite advance, as it enables researchers to examine the 'pouring back and forth' which Brown (1968: 127) considers essential for investigating how learners acquire language.

5 The functions of foreigner talk

Overall, three functions of foreigner talk can be identified: (1) to promote communication, (2) to signal, implicitly or explicitly, speakers' attitudes towards their interlocutors, and (3) to teach the target language implicitly. Hatch (1983b) argues correctly that (1) is primary in that most adjustments are geared to simplifying utterances to make them easier to process or to clarify what has been said by either the native speaker or the non-native speaker. Hatch characterizes (2) in terms of the special kind of affective bond that FT can create between the native speaker and non-native speaker, but it is also manifest in FT whose purpose is 'talking down' (Ferguson and Debose

1977). In fact, it can reflect either downward divergence (such as when a native speaker deliberately employs ungrammatical forms with a competent native speaker to signal lack of respect), or downward convergence (such as when a native speaker approximates the interlanguage forms used by the native speaker as a way of signalling solidarity) . This double function of (2) may help to explain why ungrammatical FT can occur between non-familiar interlocutors in service or workplace encounters and between familiar interlocutors in ordinary conversation. (3) is only 'implicit' because native speakers do not usually have any pedagogic intent, although Naro (1983) in a response to Hatch argues that FT can occur with an explicit teaching function (i.e. with the intention of helping a learner learn).

Many of the formal characteristics of FT are very similar to those found in other simplified registers such as learner language, caretaker talk, and pidgins. This suggests that it reflects universal processes of simplification, knowledge of which constitutes part of a speaker's linguistic competence. However, as Meisel (1980) has pointed out, there are differences between the simplification found in FT and that observed in learner language. Whereas both manifest *restrictive simplification* (for example, the use of an infinitive in place of inflected verb forms), only learner language manifests *elaborative simplification* (for example, the use of novel verb forms through processes such as overgeneralization). Meisel suggests that restrictive simplification in both registers serves 'the purpose of achieving an optimal result in communication' (1980: 36), but elaborative simplification occurs when learners are trying to complexify their interlanguage system.

An interesting question is how native speakers come to be able to adjust the level of their FT to suit the level of individual learners. Hatch (1983b) considers three ways; (1) regression (native speakers move back through the stages of development that characterized their own acquisition of language until they find an appropriate level), (2) matching (native speakers assess a learner's current interlanguage state and then imitate the forms they observe in it), and (3) negotiation (native speakers simplify and clarify in accordance with the feedback they obtain from learners in communication with them). The second is the explanation offered by Bloomfield (1933), but it seems unlikely, as it is probably asking too much of learners' interlocutors to measure simultaneously the learners' phonology, lexicon, syntax, and discourse with sufficient accuracy to adjust their own language output. The most likely explanation is (3), although (1) is also possible.

Interlanguage talk

Interlanguage talk (ILT) consists of the language that learners receive as input when addressed by other learners. In Chapter 6 we noted that ILT constitutes the primary source of input for many learners. The treatment will be brief because there is a more extended discussion of the research in Chapter 13.

Two issues have figured prominently. The first concerns the extent to which ILT provides learners with adequate access to the grammatical proper-ties of the target language. Not surprisingly, ILT has been found to be less grammatical overall than FT or teacher talk (Pica and Doughty 1985a and 1985b; Wong-Fillmore 1992). Porter (1986) in a detailed study of the ILT produced by intermediate and advanced L2 learners in pairwork and com-parable FT found that whereas only 6 per cent of FT was 'faulty', 20 per cent of ILT proved to be so. Porter also found ILT to be sociolinguistically defi-cient. She looked at a number of speech acts such as expressing opinions, agreement, and disagreement and found that the learners failed to use polite-ness strategies to the same extent as native speakers. In general they did not generate the kind of sociocultural input needed for language learning. On the plus side, however, both Pica and Doughty and Porter found that the learners in their studies repeated only a very small amount of the faulty input they heard.

The second major issue concerns whether ILT provides learners with the same opportunities for negotiating meaning as occur in FT. Gass and Varonis (1985a), in the study referred to above, reported an average of 0.50 'push-down routines' in native speaker–native speaker pairs, 2.75 in native speaker–non-native speaker pairs, and a massive 10.29 in non-native speaker–non-native speaker pairs. Porter (1986) found that learners prompted each other five times more than the native speakers prompted non-native speakers, while repair frequencies were similar. Overall, these studies provide evidence that meaning negotiation is very extensive in ILT, more so than in comparable FT discourse.

The quality of interlanguage talk is of considerable importance given the current emphasis placed on small group work in communicative language teaching (see Brumfit 1984). It is clear that ILT differs in some respects from FT, but, if the theoretical arguments relating to the importance of meaning negotiation for acquisition are accepted, a good psycholinguistic case can be made for it (see Long and Porter 1985, and Chapter 13 of this book).

Summary

This section has examined three simple registers of language addressed to learners. First, in studies of caretaker talk, it has been shown that the input that children receive when learning their L1 is well-formed and well-adjusted linguistically to their level of development. Also, some caretakers seem adept at helping children to establish and develop topics that they want to talk about.

Foreigner talk resembles caretaker talk in some respects, but also differs from it in others (for example, there are fewer yes/no questions). Both ungrammatical and grammatical FT occur, although it is not yet possible to identify the precise social conditions that favour one over the other. In the case of grammatical FT, three processes are evident: simplification, regularization, and elaboration. The modifications are continuous, influenced by the learner's stage of development and age. FT also displays interactional modifications directed at both managing and repairing discourse when either communication breakdown or learner error occurs. Figure 7.1 on page 258 summarizes the interactional modifications associated with these broad functions. Much of the research on FT discourse has been concerned with the negotiation of meaning—the attempt to remedy mis- or non-understanding. A number of models aimed at describing FT discourse have also been developed, but no general model is available yet. Foreigner talk, like caretaker talk, seems to be primarily motivated by the desire to achieve communicative success.

Finally, we looked at interlanguage talk. This, not surprisingly, tends to be less grammatical than FT, but it is characterized by more interactional modifications associated with the negotiation of meaning.

The effect of input and interaction on acquisition

We now turn to consider what effect input and interaction have on acquisition. We will begin by considering L1 acquisition research before moving on to input studies in L2 acquisition.

Input and interaction in first language acquisition

A number of studies have investigated to what extent there is a relationship between the language that caretakers address to children and acquisition. The results have been somewhat contradictory, leading to controversy regarding the role of input in L1 acquisition. In an early study, Newport, Gleitman, and Gleitman (1977) found little evidence of a close relationship between the frequency of specific linguistic features in mothers' speech and the growth of the same features in their children. They concluded that most aspects of language structure in L1 acquisition were insensitive to individual differences in the input, although the rate of growth of certain language-specific features (such as auxiliary verbs and noun inflections) was sensitive. Furrow, Nelson, and Benedict (1979) found much greater evidence of an effect for input. In this study, four aspects of L1 development (mean length of utterance, verbs per utterance, noun phrases per utterance, and auxiliaries per verb phrase) were related to a number of input measures. Barnes, Guttfreund, Satterly, and Wells (1983) also produced evidence to suggest that input influenced language development. They reported significant correlations between the frequency of polar interrogatives and subject–verb inversion in the input, and general semantic and syntactic development in the children and also between intonation and auxiliary meanings and pragmatic functions. However, Gleit-man, Newport, and Gleitman (1984), after reanalysing the data used in their 1977 study, reaffirmed their original results, finding few correlations between input and language development measures.

As is often the case in acquisition research, these differences are difficult to interpret or to reconcile. In part, they can be accounted for methodologically, as Schwartz and Camarata (1975) and Bennett-Kastor (1988) point out. For example, most of the studies used correlational statistics, which are difficult to interpret because they do not provide any indication of the directionality of a relationship. The studies also varied in whether and how they took account of the children's age and stage of development, both of which have been shown to influence caretaker input. Snow (1986: 76) advances the argument that 'the task of learning a language is quite different in different stages of ac-quisition' and that, consequently, it is reasonable to presume that different as-pects of caretaker talk may be important at different stages. It is worth noting that *all* the studies report some relationships involving input and acquisition. *Fragile features* [9] such as auxiliary verbs seem to be sensitive to input. Wells (1985), for instance, found that caretakers increased the frequency of specific auxiliary verbs in their input just before the same verbs appeared for the first time in their children's speech. The argument, therefore, is not whether input has an effect, but rather what the extent of its effect is.

A somewhat more convincing case has been made out for the facilitative ef-fect of interactional features in caretaker talk. Wells (1985) has shown that caretakers do not vary much in the extent to which they modify their speech linguistically, but do vary considerably in the way they interact with their children. This suggests that is the interactional rather than input features that may be crucial in accounting for differences in children's rate of acquisition.

One way in which interaction may help children learn language is by pro-viding them with opportunities to form *vertical constructions*. A vertical con-struction is built up gradually over several turns. Scollon (1976) provides a number of examples of mother–child discourse, where the child produces a meaningful statement over two or more turns:

Brenda: Hiding
Adult: What's hiding?
Brenda: Balloon.

He suggests that vertical constructions prepare the child for the subsequent production of horizontal constructions (the production of a meaningful state-ment within a single turn).

Other researchers point to the contribution that specific discourse acts make to acquisition. Interaction rich in directives appears to foster rapid lan-guage acquisition, at least in the early stages (Ellis and Wells 1980), perhaps because children are equipped with an 'action strategy' (Shatz 1978) that makes them particularly receptive to directives, perhaps because directives are frequently related to the here-and-now and perhaps because they are often linguistically very simple.

Expansions also appear to promote development. These are full, correct versions of telegraphic child utterances, which often occur in the form of acknowledgements or requests for confirmation:

Child: Pancakes away
           Duh Duh stomach.
Mother: Pancakes away in the stomach, yes, that's right.

Snow (1986) cites a number of studies that provide evidence of the positive effect of expansions (for example, Malouf and Dodd 1972; Nelson 1977; Cross 1978; Wells 1980), perhaps because they provide crucial bits of information about syntax and morphology, although, as Snow notes, the same information may also be made available to children in other kinds of input.

Children also seem to benefit from assistance in building conversations about topics in which they are interested. Wells (1986a) and Snow (1986) both emphasize the importance of 'collaborative meaning making' and discuss some of the ways in which this is achieved. Successful conversations are achieved when caretakers regularly check their understanding of what their children have said, when they work hard to negotiate misunderstanding, when they help to sustain and extend topics that their children have initiated, when they give children opportunities to contribute to the conversation, no matter how minimally, and when they are responsive to feedback cues. The result is what Snow calls 'semantically contingent speech'. However, although the provision of such speech is considered to be advantageous for language acquisition, it has not yet been shown that access to it is crucial for success.

Input and interaction in second language acquisition

It is useful to distinguish four broad approaches in studies that have investigated the relationship between input/interaction and L2 acquisition. The first simply seeks to establish whether the frequency of linguistic features in the input is related to the frequency of the same features in the learner language. The second emphasizes the importance of input that is comprehensible to learners. The third emphasizes the role of learner output in interaction. The fourth looks more holistically at discourse by asking how the process of collaborative discourse construction aids acquisition.

Input frequency and second language acquisition

The *frequency hypothesis* states that the order of L2 acquisition is determined by the frequency with which different linguistic items occur in the input. The hypothesis deals with the relationship between input and accuracy rather than that between input and acquisition. The justification for considering it here rests on the claim that the accuracy order mirrors the acquisition order (see Chapter 3). The hypothesis was first advanced by Hatch and Wagner-Gough (1976), who suggested that the limited range of topics about which learners (particularly children) typically talk results in certain grammatical features occurring with great frequency in the input. The more frequently occurring items, they claimed, were among those that emerged early in the learners' output. Input frequency, however, was only one of several explanations for the morpheme order which Hatch and Wagner-Gough considered. Frequency, structural complexity, and cognitive learning difficulty overlap and may together influence acquisition. Also, it should be remembered that variations in the morpheme accuracy order were reported, reflecting the different tasks learners were asked to perform (see the discussion on pages 90–6 in Chapter 3). This raises the thorny question of which order should be used in correlational studies involving input frequency.

Table 7.5 summarizes some of the studies that have investigated the input–accuracy–acquisition relationship. The limitations of these studies need to be recognized. First, they are all correlational in nature, thus making it impossible to make any statement about cause and effect. A statistically significant correlation might simply indicate that learners and their interlocutors have a similar communicative need to use the same grammatical features. Second, some of the studies did not obtain measures of input frequency from the same data sets used to examine learner accuracy (for example, Larsen-Freeman 1976a; Long 1981b), thus making the correlations they report additionally difficult to interpret. Third, as Snow and Hoefnagel-Höhle point out, 'it may be that quantity has a threshold rather than a graded effect' (1982: 424). If this is the case, the use of correlational statistics is inappropriate, as these can only be used if the two sets are both evenly spread throughout the total range. Fourth, it can be argued that it makes little sense to investigate input–output relationships in data collected at the same time, as any effect for frequency will not be immediately apparent. It is unfortunate that there have been no L2 studies of the kind conducted in L1 acquisition where input frequencies were correlated with measures of language development (i.e. gains from one time to another). Only Lightbown's (1983) study of grade 6 ESL learners in Canada provides some indication of how input available at one time can affect acquisition that becomes apparent at a later time. In this study, the learners manifested over-use of V+-*ing* after having received massive classroom exposure to this feature at the end of Grade 5.

Table 7.5 shows that the results have been very mixed. Whereas Larsen-Freeman (1976a and 1976b), Lightbown (1980), Hamayan and Tucker (1980), and Long (1981b) all found significant positive correlations between input frequency and accuracy, Snow and Hoefnagel-Höhle (1982), Long and Sato (1983), and Lightbown (1983) did not find any direct relationship. It is perhaps premature on the basis of such mixed results to propose that 'there

Study	Design	Main results
Larsen-Freeman 1976a	L2 accuracy orders of grammatical morphemes correlated with input frequency orders of same morphemes in the classroom speech of 2 ESL teachers.	Spearman rank order correlations generally positive and significant.
Larsen-Freeman 1976b	L2 accuracy orders of grammatical morphemes correlated with frequency order of same morphemes in parental speech to children (based on Brown 1973).	Spearman rank order correlations were positive and significant except for imitation task.
Hamayan and Tucker 1980	The accuracy order of 9 French syntactic structures in speech elicited from L1 and L2 learners correlated with frequency order of same structures in teacher classroom input.	Significant rank order correlations reported for both L1 and L2. The frequency order reported for two classrooms differed but was significantly related to accuracy orders in both cases.
Lightbown 1980	Order of appearance of L2 French question words in speech of 2 children correlated with frequency order of same question words in speech addressed to the children by a French research assistant.	Frequency with which question words appeared in NS's speech matched closely the sequence of question word development in L2 learners' speech.
Long 1981b	Krashen's average order of acquisition of grammatical morphemes correlated with the frequency order of same morphemes in the speech that NSs addressed to 36 elementary Japanese ESL students.	Spearman rank order correlation positive and significant.
Snow and Hoefnagel-Höhle 1982	Achievement and gain scores of American children acquiring L2 Dutch in Holland correlated with (1) quantity of Dutch heard in the classroom, (2) percentage of speech directed specifically at learners, and (3) amount of speech directed at individual learners.	No significant relationships found.
Long and Sato 1983	Krashen's average order of acquisition of grammatical morphemes correlated with the frequency order of the same morphemes in ESL teachers' speech.	No significant relationship found. However, teachers' frequency order did correlate significantly with NSs' frequency order, which in turn correlated significantly with Krashen's average order.
Lightbown 1983	Grade 6 ESL students' accuracy order of -s morphemes in oral communication activity correlated with frequency order of same features in samples of one teacher's speech and in textbook used by students.	No direct relationship between accuracy and input frequencies found, but some evidence that high level of frequency of V + -ing in input at earlier period (Grade 5) led to over-use by the students.

Table 7.5:   Input frequency–output accuracy studies in SLA research

exist preliminary data supporting a frequency effect' (Larsen-Freeman and Long 1991: 133). It is possible that frequency may be more important at some stages of acquisition (for example, elementary) than others, but no clear conclusion is possible on the basis of these studies. All that can be said is that the frequency hypothesis has not yet been properly tested.

Two other sets of studies, however, do lend support to the claim that input frequency influences acquisition: (1) studies that have investigated the effects of ungrammatical input, and (2) studies of the formulaic speech that many learners produce.

Ungrammatical input

Evidence that ungrammatical input has a direct effect on acquisition comes from a study by Gass and Lakshmanan (1991). They reanalysed data from two of the learners investigated by Cazden et al. (1975)—Alberto and Cheo—and found a striking correlation between the presence of subjectless utterances in the input and in the production of the two learners. Again, the correlations were derived from measures of input and output based on data collected at the same time, but this study is more interesting than those reviewed in Table 7.5 because of its longitudinal design. Gass and Lakshmanan were able to show a strong and consistent relationship between input and output over time (i.e. the presence of subjectless sentences in the input closely matched those in the learners' output from one time to the next). They were also able to demonstrate that in the case of Alberto deviant input in a grammaticality judgement test was followed by a jump in this learner's production of subjectless sentences shortly afterwards. It should be noted, however, that the learners' L1 (Spanish) permits subjectless sentences. It is possible, therefore, that input and transfer work jointly to shape interlanguage development. As Gass and Lakshmanan put it, 'the learner initially searches for correspondences or matches in form between the native and the second language'.[10]

Formulaic speech

The prevalence of formulaic speech in learner language was commented on in Chapter 3. How do learners learn formulas? One possibility is that they respond to the high frequency of certain patterns and routines in the input. In Ellis 1984b, for instance, I suggested that the formulas learnt by the three classroom learners investigated reflected frequently occurring social and organizational contexts that arose during the course of communicating in a classroom environment. The prevalence of formulaic copula utterances with subjects such as 'I', 'this', 'that', and 'what', which a number of researchers have noted in learner language (Hakuta 1974; Rescorla and Okuda 1987; Ellis 1988a), may also reflect input frequency. However, although it seems reasonable to assume that frequency is a major determinant of the acquisition of formulas, there is no research that clearly demonstrates that this is so. Also, other factors are likely to be important—in particular, learners' communicative need to perform the language functions encoded by the formulas with ease and fluency.

Overall, there is little evidence to support the claim that input frequency affects L2 acquisition, but there is also little evidence to refute it. Perhaps the safest conclusion is that input frequency serves as *one* of the factors influencing development, often combining with other factors such as L1 transfer and communicative need.

Comprehensible input and second language acquisition

A number of researchers see comprehensible input as a major causative factor in L2 acquisition. The most influential theoretical positions are those advanced by Krashen and Long.

Krashen's *Input Hypothesis* (Krashen 1981; 1985; 1989) makes the following claims:

1 Learners progress along the natural order by understanding input that contains structures a little bit beyond their current level of competence.
2 Although comprehensible input is necessary for acquisition to take place, it is not sufficient, as learners also need to be affectively disposed to 'let in' the input they comprehend.
3 Input becomes comprehensible as a result of simplification and with the help of contextual and extralinguistic clues; 'fine-tuning' (i.e. ensuring that learners receive input rich in the specific linguistic property they are due to acquire next) is not necessary.
4 Speaking is the result of acquisition, not its cause; learner production does not contribute directly to acquisition.[11]

Long differs from Krashen primarily with regard to (3). While acknowledging that simplified input and context can play a role in making input comprehensible, Long stresses the importance of the interactional modifications that occur in negotiating meaning when a communication problem arises. In other words, Long's argument is that interactive input is more important than non-interactive input.

These theoretical claims have led to research into two aspects of input: (1) the relationship between input (both interactive and non-interactive) and comprehension, and (2) the relationship between linguistic/conversational adjustments and acquisition. To date, there has been far more research directed at (1), mainly because of the difficulties of designing studies to investigate (2). In recognition of these difficulties, Long (1985a: 378) suggested the following three steps as a way of gaining insight into how input/interaction affects acquisition:

Step 1: Show that (a) linguistic/conversational adjustments promote (b) comprehension of input.
Step 2: Show that (b) comprehensible input promotes (c) acquisition.

Step 3: Deduce that (a) linguistic/conversational adjustments promote (c) acquisition.

Young (1988b) points out that although a number of studies have demonstrated step (1) there have been few which have tackled (2), which is, in fact, the crucial step.

1 The relationship between interactive and non-interactive input and comprehension

What evidence is there that linguistic/conversational adjustments promote comprehension of input, and do some kinds of adjustments work better than others? To answer these questions, it is helpful to separate out research which has investigated non-interactive input from that into interactive input.

One type of non-interactive adjustment concerns speech rate. A number of studies (for example, Long 1985a; Kelch 1985; Mannon 1986; Fujimoto, Lubin, Sasaki, and Long 1986) provide evidence to suggest that a slower rate aids comprehension, but in many cases speech rate was investigated alongside other variables, making it difficult to assess the effect of speech rate *per se*. Other methodological problems also make interpretation of the results difficult. For example, Kelch (1985) claimed to present dictation passages at two different speeds (191 and 124 words per minute) but in fact allowed 45 seconds between each sentence dictated, thus introducing another variable (pause duration) into the study.

However, two other, better-designed studies indicate that rate of speech is a significant factor. Conrad (1989) asked 29 native speakers, 17 high-level non-native speakers, and 11 medium-level non-native speakers to recall five time-compressed recordings of 16 English sentences. Each sentence was presented five times at different speeds: 450, 320, 253, 216, and 196 words per minute. The native speakers managed nearly complete recall of all the sentences by the second trial (320 words per minute), but the non-native speakers of both proficiency levels experienced considerable difficulty even with the slowest rate after the fifth hearing. Griffiths (1990) investigated the effects of varying the speech rate in three 350–400 word passages on the comprehension of 15 lower-intermediate level adult non-native speakers. The speeds varied from 94–107 wpm (slow) to 143–54 (medium) and 191–206 (fast). The subjects manifested significantly reduced comprehension, measured by means of true/false questions, at fast rates, but there was no difference between the 'normal' and 'slow' rates. These studies suggest that there may be a threshold level – around 200 wpm – below which intermediate and advanced level learners experience little difficulty in comprehending and above which they might.

Of particular interest to researchers is the nature of the modifications that are most effective in promoting comprehension. Parker and Chaudron (1987) review 12 experimental studies (including Johnson 1981; Blau 1982;

Cervantes 1983; R. Brown 1987; Chaudron and Richards 1986) of the effects of input modifications on comprehension and conclude that although linguistic modifications (for example, simpler syntax and vocabulary) helped comprehension they did not do so consistently. In contrast, what they call 'elaborative modifications' had a consistent effect on comprehension. They distinguish two types of elaborative modifications: those that contribute to redundancy (such as repetition of constituents, paraphrase, use of synonyms, use of left dislocation, and slower speech), and those that help to make the thematic structure explicit (such as extraposition and cleft constructions).

However, Parker and Chaudron's own study of 43 undergraduate and graduate ESL learners, who read one of two reading passages which differed according to whether they had been modified by incorporating linguistic or elaborative modifications, failed to find any significant differences in comprehension. They explain this unexpected result by suggesting that the overall lexical and syntactic difficulty of both passages may have been so great as to negate the effects of the elaborative modifications. If this is right, it suggests that elaborative modifications will only benefit comprehension if the level of linguistic difficulty of the input does not exceed a certain threshold.

Issidorides and Hulstijn (1992) also failed to find that linguistic modifications had any effect on comprehension. This study examined the effects of simplifying Dutch AdvVSO sentences by replacing them with the ungrammatical AdvSVO and AdvSOV sentences. These 'simplifications' were motivated by the fact that learners of L2 Dutch and L2 German have been found to experience production difficulties with verb-subject inversion after initial adverbs (see Chapter 3). In an experimental study that required three groups of subjects (Dutch native speakers, English and Turkish learners of L2 Dutch) to state what the subject or agent of a series of sentences was, AdvVSO sentences were found to be no more difficult to understand than modified, ungrammatical sentences (providing that the messages conveyed by the sentences were semantically plausible). Issidorides and Hulstijn conclude that 'the fact that non-native speakers have difficulties in producing a certain grammatical structure ... does not imply that such a structure is also more difficult to understand in the speech of others' (1992: 167).

Another question of interest concerns the role of the learners' L1 in L2 comprehension. Holobrow, Lambert, and Sayegh (1984) found that 10-year-old Canadian children comprehended better when they heard an oral text in their L1 and at the same time read an L2 version of the text than when they simultaneously heard and read texts in the L2 or when they just read L2 texts. However, when Hawkins (1988) replicated this study with British undergraduate students of L2 French, he found that the bimodal condition (i.e. listening to and reading texts in the L2) worked best. No conclusions are possible on the basis of these studies, but they raise the issue of the role of the L1 in helping to make input comprehensible.

In the case of interactive discourse, two variables have been found to influence comprehension: the amount and type of information, and the extent to which the participants engage in negotiation of meaning. Derwing (1989) found that some native speakers attempted to include much more information than they used with native speaker interlocutors about a film they had seen, with the result that their non-native speaker interlocutors failed to understand their narratives. The native speakers who were successful in communicating did not differ in the kinds of information (crucial, major, and minor) that they used when talking to native speakers and non-native speakers. This study suggests that redundancy involving increased use of background detail is not helpful to comprehension, although, as Derwing notes, this does not mean that other kinds of redundancy (such as repetition) are not helpful. Ehrlich, Avery, and Yorio (1989) also report that their 'embroiderers' created problems for the non-native speakers by making it difficult for them to identify essential information and the source of communication problems.

Comprehension also appears to benefit from opportunities for negotiation of meaning. Pica, Young, and Doughty (1987) compared the effect of three types of input on the ability of sixteen low-intermediate ESL learners to comprehend oral instructions. The three types were (1) unmodified input (i.e. input of the kind that native speakers use when addressing each other), (2) premodified input (i.e. input that had been simplified and made more redundant), and (3) interactionally modified input (i.e. the subjects listened to unmodified instructions but were given the opportunity to seek clarification). The results showed that (3) resulted in the highest levels of comprehension. Subsequent studies by Loschky (1989), Tanaka (1991), and Yamazaki (1991) confirm these results. However, it should be noted that in all these studies the opportunity for negotiation led to considerable repetition and rephrasings with the result that (3) provided the learners with much more input than was available in (1) and (2). It is not clear, therefore, whether the advantage found for the interactionally modified input arises from greater *quantity* of input or better *quality* (i.e. input made relevant through the negotiation of meaning). A subsequent study by Pica (1992) found that when the extent of the input adjustments was carefully controlled in the premodified and interactionally modified conditions no difference in comprehension was found,[12] although a *post-hoc* analysis suggested that those learners rated as having lower comprehension ability by their teachers benefited from the opportunity to interact. Pica's study also found no significant differences in the comprehension of learners who observed negotiation taking place but did not actually negotiate themselves, and those who actively participated.

To sum up, there is mixed evidence regarding the value of linguistically simplified input for promoting comprehension. Whereas speech rate does have a clear effect, grammatical modifications do not always result in improved comprehension. Firmer support exists for the beneficial effect of interactionally modified input on comprehension. We should note, however, that the presence of interactional modification is no guarantee that comprehension has taken place. As both Aston (1986) and Hawkins (1985) point out, learners may choose to feign comprehension after negotiation rather than continue to demonstrate to their interlocutors that they have not understood. We will now consider to what extent comprehensible input promotes acquisition (step (2) in Long's suggested procedure).

Source of evidence	Brief explanation
Caretaker speech	Caretaker speech to young children is roughly tuned to the children's receptive abilities and is motivated by the need to aid comprehension.
Foreigner talk	Foreigner talk to NNSs is also roughly tuned and functions as an aid to comprehension.
Silent period	Some young children go through a silent period in L2 acquisition. During this period they do not produce but nevertheless learn the L2.
Age difference	Krashen (1985: 12) argues that 'older learners obtain more comprehensible input' and that this may explain why they learn more quickly initially than younger learners.
Comparative method studies	The studies show that methods that supply plenty of comprehensible input (e.g. Total Physical Response) are more successful than methods that supply little (e.g. audiolingualism).
Immersion programmes	Immersion programmes have generally been found superior to foreign/second language programmes – again because they supply plenty of comprehensible input.
Bilingual programmes	The success of different kinds of bilingual programmes is related to the extent to which they supply comprehensible input.
Delayed L1 and L2 acquisition	Studies of children in both L1 and L2 acquisition who are deprived of comprehensible input (e.g. because their parents are deaf) show that acquisition is delayed or non-existent.
Reading and vocabulary acquisition	Studies indicate that children are able to increase their L1 vocabulary and also develop a 'deep' understanding of new words through pleasure reading.
Reading and spelling acquisition	Studies indicate that spelling can be most effectively acquired through exposure to the written word in extensive reading undertaken for pleasure.

Table 7.6: Indirect evidence in support of the input hypothesis

2 The relationship between comprehensible input and acquisition

The evidence is primarily indirect. Together Long (1983b), Larsen-Freeman and Long (1991), and Krashen (1985; 1989) cite literature relating to ten sources that they claim support the claim that comprehensible input contributes to acquisition. These sources are described in Table 7.6.

Overall, this evidence supports the commonsense assumption that learners need to understand input in order to learn from it. It is less clear, however, whether this evidence warrants the claim that comprehensible input is a causative factor in L2 acquisition. A careful examination of each source of evidence reveals various doubts. In many cases, the evidence is correlational in nature: for example, caretaker and foreigner talk co-occur with successful acquisition; extensive reading is associated with vocabulary development and improved spelling; older learners learn faster and engage in more meaning negotiation. Therefore, it cannot be said to demonstrate that comprehensible input *causes* acquisition. In other cases, the validity of the evidence is in doubt. For example, the comparative method studies have problematic designs and have produced very mixed results; and many learners do not go through an extended silent period (see Chapter 3). In yet other cases, the available evidence lends less than complete support (for example, learners in long-term immersion programmes do not develop full target-language proficiency). Long (1983b) considers the fact that deprivation of comprehensible input results in delayed acquisition the strongest evidence, but Larsen-Freeman (1983) argues quite convincingly that learners can assimilate useful information about an L2 without understanding input (for example, information relating to the phonology of an L2). She also makes the point that learners can work by themselves on unmodified input—such as that found in TV programmes—and so gain input that helps them learn. Thus, at least some L2 learning may take place without comprehensible input and, more importantly, comprehending input may not result in acquisition.

There have been a number of critiques of the input hypothesis (Gregg 1984; Færch and Kasper 1986a; Sharwood Smith 1986; White 1987a; Gass 1988; Ellis 1990a and 1991a). Gass (1988) makes the point that it is not comprehensible input but rather *comprehended* input that is important, but the research reported above does not provide an account of how comprehending input is supposed to result in acquisition. In fact, little attention has been paid to what 'comprehension' entails. Rost defines listening comprehension as 'essentially an inferential process based on the perception of cues rather than straightforward matching of sound to meaning' (1990: 33). This suggests that understanding does not necessitate close attention to linguistic form. Færch and Kasper (1986) also recognize the importance of 'top-down processes', in which learners utilize contextual information and existing knowledge to understand what is said, but they also point out that they may sometimes make use of 'bottom-up processes', where they pay closer attention to the linguistic forms in the message. The question that remains unanswered, then, is what type of comprehension processes are needed for acquisition to take place. If learners can rely extensively on top-down processing they may pay little attention to the form of the input and may therefore not acquire anything new. Færch and Kasper argue that only when there is a 'gap' between the input and the learner's current interlanguage and, crucially, when the learner perceives the gap as a gap in knowledge, will acquisition take place. Sharwood Smith (1986) argues similarly that the processes of comprehension and acquisition are not the same, and suggests that input has a 'dual relevance'—there is input that helps learners to interpret meaning, and there is input that learners use to advance their interlanguages.

A second major criticism focuses on the claim that comprehensible input is *necessary* for acquisition.[13] White (1987a) has argued that a considerable part of acquisition is 'input-free'. As we will see in Chapter 10, she claims that certain types of overgeneralizations which learners make cannot be unlearnt simply by understanding input. They require negative evidence (for example, in the form of corrective feedback) which in naturalistic acquisition may not be available to the learner. She also claims that learners are able to go beyond the evidence available in the input, and develop knowledge of target-language rules by projecting from their existing knowledge (a point also discussed more fully in Chapter 10). Finally, she argues that in the case of some structures (for example, English passive constructions), it may be the failure to understand input that leads to learning. As she puts it 'the driving force for grammar change is that input is *incomprehensible*, rather than comprehensible ...' (1987a: 95). White's idea is that failure to understand a sentence may force the learner to pay closer attention to its syntactical properties in order to obtain clues about its meaning and, as such, reflects the views of Færch and Kasper (1986) and Sharwood Smith (1986) about comprehension and learning discussed above.

These criticisms can be accommodated if the hypothesis is modified in the following way:

> Comprehensible input can facilitate acquisition but (1) is not a necessary condition of acquisition, and (2) does not guarantee that acquisition will take place.

The question arises as to whether such a modified hypothesis has much explanatory value. Arguably, what is needed is a hypothesis that explains how learners' attempts to comprehend input can lead to acquisition.

3 The relationship between input/interactional modifications and acquisition

Finally, we will consider the few studies which have attempted to establish a more direct relationship between input/interactional modifications and acquisition. Pica (1992) illustrates how the negotiation of meaning provides learners with information about the semantic and structural properties of the target language (English). Native speakers (NS) responded to non-native speakers' (NNS) triggers by modifying their utterances semantically and/or formally through the segmentation and movement of input constituents, as in this example:

NNS: Ok, you have a house which has third floor.
  NS: Three floors right.
NNS: Three floors.

However, as Pica admits, it is not clear from such data whether learners use the information supplied by such exchanges to adjust their interlanguage systems.

A number of experimental studies, however, have been carried out to discover whether negotiation leads to interlanguage development. Although the results of these studies have been mixed, they give some support to the claim that FT modifications help acquisition, at least where vocabulary is concerned. The studies are summarized in Table 7.7.

These studies give support to two general conclusions. First, Li's (1989) study suggests that providing learners with contextual cues that help them to understand the meanings of words results not only in better comprehension but also in better retention of the words. Second, Tanaka's (1991) and Yamazaki's (1991) studies indicate that providing learners with opportunities to modify input interactionally improves comprehension and enables them to learn more new words than simply providing them with unmodified or premodified input. These findings augur well for Long's claims regarding the importance of interactionally adjusted input. In contrast, Loschky's (1989) study failed to find any advantage for interactionally-modified input over baseline or presimplified input where vocabulary retention was concerned. It should be noted, however, that this study, unlike the studies by Tanaka and Yamazaki, had a grammatical focus (locative particles in Japanese), so it is possible that the learners' attention was directed at this rather than at the new vocabulary items. To date there has been no empirical test of the claim that negotiation of meaning aids the acquisition of new grammatical features.

Learner output and acquisition

Interaction also provides learners with the opportunity to talk in the L2. According to Krashen (1985), this has no direct effect on acquisition. However, other researchers have argued differently, viewing learner output as contributing to interlanguage development.

Following Krashen (1989), two different hypotheses that allocate a role to output can be identified. The *skill-building hypothesis* states that we first learn rules or items consciously and then gradually automatize them through practice. We will consider this when we examine cognitive theories of L2

Study	Design	Main results
Li (1989)	Advanced Chinese ESL learners exposed to sentences under two conditions: (1) cue-adequate (meaning made clear by context) and (2) cue-inadequate.	Cue-adequate sentences were better understood and led to better retention of difficult words.
Loschky (1989)	Three groups of learners of Japanese as a second language were given lessons on locative expressions under three different conditions: (1) baseline input, (2) premodified input, and (3) interactionally modified input.	Learners receiving interactionally modified input had higher comprehension scores than learners receiving premodified input, who had higher scores than learners receiving baseline input. No differences in the three groups for retention of the new vocabulary items introduced in the lessons.
Tanaka (1991)	Three groups of Japanese high school ESL students were asked to respond to instructions given under three conditions: (1) baseline input, (2) pre-modified input, and (3) interactionally modified input. Instructions contained a number of new words. Pre-, post- and follow-up vocabulary tests were administered.	Interactionally modified input resulted in better comprehension of the instructions. It also resulted in more words being learnt and retained over time.
Yamazaki (1991)	Same design as for Tanaka's study.	Interactionally modified input resulted in better comprehension and also in more words being learnt (as evident in post-test scores), but learning advantage was not retained over time (as evident in follow-up test scores).[14]

Table 7.7:   Studies investigating the direct effects of input/interaction modifications on L2 acquisition

acquisition in Chapter 9 and the utility of formal practice in Chapter 14. Here we will focus on the second hypothesis Krashen considers, the *output hypothesis*.

This comes in two forms, according to Krashen. First, there is 'output plus correction'. According to this, learners try out rules or items in production and then use the corrections they receive from other speakers to confirm or disconfirm them. Schachter (1986b) points out that metalinguistic information relating to the correctness of learners' production is available both directly (through corrections) and indirectly (through confirmation checks, clarification requests, and failure to understand).

The second form of the output hypothesis involves the idea of *comprehensible output*. Swain (1985) argues that learners need the opportunity for meaningful use of their linguistic resources to achieve full grammatical competence. She argues that when learners experience communicative failure, they are pushed into making their output more precise, coherent, and appropriate. She also argues that production may encourage learners to move from semantic (top-down) to syntactic (bottom-up) processing. Whereas comprehension of a message can take place with little syntactic analysis of the input, production forces learners to pay attention to the means of expression.

The evidence indicating that comprehensible output is important for acquisition is largely indirect. A number of studies (Harley and Swain 1978; Harley 1988; Harley, Allen, Cummins, and Swain 1990) have shown that although immersion learners achieve considerable confidence in using the L2 and considerable discourse skills, they fail to develop more marked grammatical distinctions, such as that between French passé composé and imparfait, and full sociolinguistic competence. Swain argues that this be cannot be explained by a lack of comprehensible input, as immersion classrooms are rich in this. She speculates that it might be because the learners had limited opportunity to talk in the classroom and were not 'pushed' in the output they did produce. Allen, Swain, Harley, and Cummins (1990) conducted an observational study of interaction in French immersion classrooms in nine grade 3 and ten grade 6 classrooms and found that the students' responses were typically 'minimal'. Less than 15 per cent of students' utterances in French were more than a clause in length. Also, there was little evidence of any systematic correction of the errors learners made in their output. Only 19 per cent of overall grammatical errors were corrected and often in 'a confusing and unsystematic way'. They conclude that 'there was little indication that students were being pushed towards a more coherent and accurate use of the target language' (1990: 67).

It is important to recognize that Swain's claim is that production will aid acquisition *only when the learner is pushed*. Thus plentiful opportunities to speak, such as those that Wes undoubtedly had in Hawaii (see Schmidt 1983 and Chapter 6 of this book), will not in themselves guarantee acquisition. Learners like Wes who develop high levels of strategic competence may be able to communicate efficiently without much grammatical competence, and so may never experience the need to improve their output in order to make themselves understood.

Both versions of the output hypothesis attribute considerable importance to feedback, both direct and indirect. In the case of 'output plus correction', feedback is necessary to supply learners with metalinguistic information, while in the case of 'comprehensible output' it is necessary to push learners to improve the accuracy of their production in order to make themselves understood. We have already seen that foreigner talk provides learners with little direct feedback[15] but with plenty of indirect feedback in the form of clarification requests, confirmation requests. etc. It would seem, therefore, that it is indirect feedback that is crucial. Three questions arise: (1) Does indirect feedback actually lead to more accurate learner output? (2) Do certain types of indirect feedback work better than others in this respect? and (3) Do learners actually learn as a result of pushed output?

A series of studies by Pica have addressed the first two questions. Pica (1988) examined the interactions between a native speaker and ten non-native speakers of English in order to discover whether indirect feedback led to improved output. She found that the learners did produce more grammatical output when the native speakers requested confirmation or clarification, but in less than half of their total responses. In a subsequent study, however, Pica, Holliday, Lewis, and Morgenthaler (1989) found that the crucial factor was the nature of the feedback signals the native speaker provided. The learners (10 Japanese adults) were much more likely to produce output modifications in response to clarification requests than to confirmation requests and repetitions. This was because clarification requests constitute an 'open signal', leaving it up to the learners how to resolve the comprehension problems, whereas confirmation requests and repetitions, where the native speaker models what the learner intended to mean, remove the need for improved output. Interestingly, this study also showed that many of the modifications that learners made were grammatical and not just semantic in nature.

Evidence that learners improve the grammaticality of their utterances when pushed does not of course constitute evidence that acquisition takes place. In an exploratory study involving just six learners (three experimental and three control), Nobuyoshi and Ellis (1993) sought to establish whether pushed output resulted in improved performance over time. In two-way information gap tasks, which each learner performed with the researcher, the experimental subjects experienced 'focused meaning negotiation', where they received a clarification request every time they produced an utterance containing a past tense error.[16] The control subjects experienced 'unfocused meaning negotiation' (i.e. negotiation only took place when there was a genuine communication problem). Both sets of learners believed they were communicating rather than practising language. Nobuyoshi repeated the information-gap task with both groups one week later, this time without a special focus on past tense. Two out of three experimental learners improved the accuracy of their use of the past tense as a result of the requests for clarification and maintained this improvement one week later. The control subjects showed no improvement on either occasion. This study intriguingly suggests that pushing learners to produce more comprehensible output may have a long-term effect, but not necessarily for all learners.[17]

There is also another sense in which learners may benefit from being 'pushed'. The studies reported above examined the effect of clarification requests on the subsequent accuracy of learners' output. Some learners, however, may have achieved a high level of accuracy but only with a restricted set of 'simple' constructions. Such learners need to experience situations that call for more complex output, as, for example, when they are called on to demonstrate mastery of the forms required to communicate in a sociolinguistically appropriate manner with different addressees (see Chapter 5).

So far, there is little hard evidence to support the output hypothesis, although there is sufficient to suggest that it is worth pursuing. It is possible that when learners produce pushed output they are able to develop greater control over the features they have already acquired, as demonstrated in Nobuyoshi and Ellis's study. It is not clear whether pushed output can result in the acquisition of *new* linguistic features.

Collaborative discourse and second language acquisition

We saw that L1 researchers have produced evidence that suggests that children may acquire syntactical structures as a result of learning how to participate in conversations. Similar claims have been made by L2 researchers. Hatch, for instance, proposes:

> One learns how to do conversations, one learns how to interact verbally, and out of this interaction syntactic structures are developed (1978b: 404).

Researchers have documented a number of ways in which this might happen.

One way is through the use of an *incorporation strategy*. Wagner-Gough (1975) investigated the conversations which an Iranian boy, Homer, had with native speakers and showed how he put together utterances by 'borrowing' a chunk from the preceding discourse and then extending it by affixing an element to the beginning or end, as in these examples:

1 Mark: Come here.
   Homer: No come here.
2 Judy: Where's Mark?
   Homer: Where's Mark is school. (= Mark is at school.)

This strategy may explain why 'no + verb' constructions are so common in early L2 acquisition (see Chapter 3), although other explanations also exist.

Peck (1978) gives examples of a related but slightly different strategy which she calls 'functions' (a term borrowed from Keenan's (1974) study of L1 acquisition). These occurred frequently in child–child discourse involving Angel, a 7-year-old Mexican boy. Functions involve repeating with or without some modification part or all of the previous utterance. There are different types. A 'substitution function', for example, involves replacing a constituent in the previous utterance, as in this example:

Joe: You know what?
Angel: You know why?

Peck suggests that this kind of discourse enables learners to practise syntax and pronunciation.

Vertical constructions of the kind reported by Scollon (1976) in L1 acquisition have also been found in L2 acquisition. Hatch (1978b: 407) provides this example in an interaction involving Paul, Huang's (1970) subject:

Paul: Oh-oh!
J: What?
Paul: This (points at an ant)
J: It's an ant.
Paul: Ant.

The construction that Paul builds over three utterances is 'Oh-oh, this ant'.

Of course, these studies are not able to show that 'scaffolding' of the kind illustrated in these examples results in acquisition as opposed to just aiding production. In Ellis (1985d), however, I found evidence to suggest that this might indeed be the case. Interactions between two learners and a teacher were examined in order to identify learner utterances which featured 'new' syntactic patterns (for example, the first occurrence of two constituent utterances consisting of noun + noun). I then studied what was going on interactionally that might have helped the learner to produce them. It was found that 'new' structures emerged when the learners were allowed to initiate a topic (if necessary by the teacher abandoning his own topic) and when the teacher helped the learners by supplying crucial chunks of language at the right moment.

Collaborative discourse may also work against acquisition, however. A number of studies suggest that learners can sometimes exploit discourse strategies to compensate for morphological features they have not acquired. Studies of L2 German by Dittmar (1981), Klein (1981), and Meisel (1987) and of L2 French by Trevise and Porquier (1986) show how learners are able to refer to time and space without recourse to target-language inflections. They rely instead on adverbials, implicit reference, order of mention, and interlocutor scaffolding. This research relates to the question of how learners move from the pragmatic to the grammatical mode (how they *grammaticalize* their speech) and is considered in greater detail in Chapter 9. What is important here is to note that collaborative discourse may be so successful that it inhibits grammatical acquisition.

It would seem, then, that collaborative discourse can both facilitate the acquisition of L2 syntax and restrict it. The contradiction may be more apparent than real, however. Where basic syntax is concerned, it appears to help, particularly in the early stages of acquisition. Where morphological features such as tense markers are concerned, it may obviate the need for development.

Summary

In this section we have looked at some of the research that has investigated the relationship between input/interaction and acquisition.

First language acquisition research has shown that the frequency of linguistic forms in caretakers' speech is associated with developmental gains in children, particularly where fragile features (for example, auxiliary verbs) are concerned. However, the claim that input frequency determines acquisition is controversial. More important for rapid language development are the interactional features of caretaker talk (for example, directives, expansions, 'collaborative meaning making', and the negotiation of misunderstandings).

The relationship between input/interaction and second language acquisition has been examined in four major ways:

1 Input frequency–output accuracy studies

These have produced mixed results and suffer from methodological problems, but the positive correlations between the frequency in input of specific grammatical morphemes reported by a number of studies have received confirmation from studies of the effects of ungrammatical input on learner output.

2 Comprehensible input studies

The input hypothesis and Long's claims about the role of interaction have motivated a substantial amount of research, although they have also been subject to considerable criticism on the grounds that they fail to specify how comprehending input leads to acquisition and that they overstate the importance of comprehensible input by claiming that it is *necessary* for acquisition. Much of the research has concentrated on identifying the features that help to make non-interactive and interactive input comprehensible. In the case of non-interactive input, speech rate, elaborative modifications, and bimodal input (i.e. both oral and written) have been found to aid comprehension. In the case of interactive input, the amount of information and the extent to which meaning is negotiated through interactional adjustments have been shown to be significant variables. There is substantial indirect evidence linking comprehensible input to acquisition, but much of it is controversial. There is little in the way of direct evidence and what there is relates to the acquisition of vocabulary rather than syntax or morphology.

3 Learner output and acquisition

Swain has argued that comprehensible output contributes to acquisition in that learners need to be pushed into producing output that is concise, coherent, and appropriate in order to develop full grammatical competence. There is evidence to show that indirect feedback in the form of clarification requests pushes learners to improve their output, but little evidence as yet to show that this then leads to acquisition.

4 *Collaborative discourse and acquisition*

Illustrative evidence has been provided to show that the joint efforts of native speakers and non-native speakers to construct discourse promotes acquisition in a number of ways: for example, through the use of an incorporation strategy (the construction of utterances by borrowing from and extending elements from the preceding discourse), functions (repeating with or without modification some previous utterance), and vertical constructions (building up an utterance over several turns). However, collaborative discourse may remove the need for learners to acquire certain morphological features.

Conclusion

Young (1988b: 128) concludes his own survey of input and interaction research with the comment that 'there is still a great deal of beating about the bush', by which he means that relatively few studies have tried to investigate to what extent and in what ways input and interaction influence acquisition. One reason for this is the methodological problems that input researchers face. In L1 acquisition research it is not clear how potentially confounding variables such as the child's age and stage of development can be controlled so as to investigate the effects of input on acquisition. In L2 acquisition research, this problem is exacerbated by the difficulty of obtaining representative samples of the input that individual learners receive, for where the L1 learner is situationally restricted to interacting with a few identifiable interlocutors, the L2 learner, especially when an adult, is not. Second, whereas a number of input studies on L1 acquisition have been longitudinal, nearly all those into L2 acquisition have been cross-sectional. Third, there has been an over-reliance on correlational studies at the expense of experimental studies, making it difficult to determine what is cause and what is effect. Progress requires studies that (1) reliably sample the input data, (2) are longitudinal, and (3) are experimental.

Despite these methodological problems, a number of insights regarding the role of input and interaction have been gained. We have some understanding of how interactional modifications affect the comprehensibility of texts. It is also becoming apparent that different kinds of input and interaction are needed to facilitate acquisition at different stages of learners' development, and that input and interaction may or may not affect acquisition depending on the nature of the linguistic feature involved (consider the distinction between *resilient* and *fragile* features, for example). We are still a long way from explaining how input interacts with the learner's internal cognitive mechanisms to shape the course of language acquisition, and even further from being able to assign any weighting to external as opposed to internal factors. In all likelihood, input combines with other factors such as the learner's L1, the learner's communicative need to express certain meanings and the learner's internal processing mechanisms. No explanation of L2 acquisition will be complete unless it includes an account of the role of input, but, as Sharwood Smith (1985: 402) has noted input should be seen as just one in a 'conspiracy of factors'.

Notes

1 The distinction between 'input text' and 'input discourse' has been borrowed from Widdowson's (1974) more general distinction between 'text' and 'discourse'.

2 In Ellis 1988a, I also made the point that much of native-speaker usage is variable (for example, English copula has a full and contracted form) and the learner's target, therefore, is to achieve the same pattern of variability as that found in native-speaker usage. However, much of SLA research has been based on the assumption that the learner's target consists solely of categorical rules (such as the 3rd person -*s* rule in English) that specify the conditions requiring the obligatory use of a single linguistic form.

3 Snow (1986) makes the point that in order to consider to what extent there is 'fine-tuning' it is essential to examine correlations between child variables and complexity of caretaker talk at the right stage of development. She also discusses a number of other factors that may attenuate the relationship (for example, fine-tuning may be situation-specific).

4 The claim that children receive no corrective feedback directed at their grammatical errors is based on only one study, Brown and Hanlon (1970). As Snow (1986) notes, this study used a very narrow definition of corrective feedback (i.e. explicit corrections). Children may be able to use other clues in the caretaker's speech, such as caretaker responses that indicate the need for negotiation.

5 It should be noted, however, that in some cultures adult caretakers do seem to give something resembling 'language lessons'. Ochs and Schieffelin (1984) give examples of how Kaluli mothers in Papua-New Guinea require their children to engage in imitation exercises without any attention to the meaning of utterances being imitated.

6 The term 'foreigner talk' was initially used by Ferguson (1971) to refer solely to the kind of ungrammatical talk that native speakers sometimes address to non-native speakers. Arthur et al. (1980) use the term 'foreigner register' to refer to grammatical FT while the term 'foreigner talk discourse' has been used to refer to interactionally modified FT. Increasingly, though, 'foreigner talk' is used as a general cover term for the

modified language native speakers use with non-native speakers, and this is how the term is used in this chapter.

7 The distinction between discourse management and discourse repair of communication breakdowns mirrors Long's (1983a) distinction between 'strategies' for avoiding trouble and 'tactics' for dealing with trouble when it occurs.

8 This problem is acknowledged by Larsen-Freeman and Long (1991), who point out that the discourse moves that perform functions such as clarification requests often have 'multiple functions and also multiple realizations' (1991: 129). The need for 'finer grained analyses', therefore, is recognized by at least one researcher (Long) who has been actively involved in researching the negotiation of meaning.

9 Goldin-Meadow (1982) distinguished *resilient* and *fragile* properties in the sign language of deaf children. The former are those properties such as recursion and word order that appear to develop irrespective of environmental conditions, whereas the latter (for example, plural and verb tense) need special care.

10 Another purpose of Gass and Lakshmanan's study was to show the dangers of conducting studies based on descriptions of language which assume that the input to the learner is target-like. They comment: 'considering principles of UG, or any other principles, devoid of context is insufficient and often misleading in accounting for how L2 grammars develop'.

11 Although Krashen claims that speaking does not contribute directly to acquisition, he does allow for an indirect contribution. He writes:

> ... output aids acquisition indirectly by encouraging CI (comprehensible input), via conversation. When you speak it invites others to talk to you. Moreover, as you speak your output provides your conversational partner with information about your competence and whether he or she is communicating successfully. This information helps your conversational partner adjust the input to make it more comprehensible. (Krashen 1989: 456)

12 The premodified input was based on negotiated input and was designed to incorporate the main features of it.

13 Although both Long and Krashen claim that comprehensible input is necessary for acquisition, both acknowledge that it is not sufficient. Learners not only need access to input they can understand; they also need to be affectively disposed to 'let it in' (for example, to be motivated to learn).

14 The main difference in the results obtained by Tanaka and Yamazaki is that whereas Tanaka's subjects in the interactionally modified input group maintained their gains in vocabulary in the follow-up test, Yamazaki's subjects did not. The explanation for this difference may lie in the attitudes of the subjects. Tanaka's subjects were not highly motivated to

learn English, whereas Yamazaki's were—largely because they needed to do well in English to gain entry to the universities of their choice. Yamazaki was able to show that many of her subjects took efforts to learn the new vocabulary in their own time between the post-test and the follow-up test.

15 Formal correction does, of course, occur in classroom language learning. Chapter 14 reviews the research that has investigated the effect it has on learning.

16 This kind of 'focused meaning negotiation' can be distinguished from a more traditional grammar exercise by the fact that the learners treat the activity as one calling for 'use' rather than 'usage'; that is, they concentrate on conveying a message and not on performing a particular grammatical feature accurately.

17 Nobuyoshi and I noted that the one experimental learner who failed to improve past tense accuracy was adept at making himself understood in other ways. He manifested what Meisel, Clahsen, and Pienemann (1981) refer to as a 'communicative orientation'.

Further Reading

There is a rich literature dealing with input/interaction and L2 acquisition. A good starting point is to read one or two surveys of this literature:
R. Young, 'Input and interaction.' *Annual Review of Applied Linguistics* (1989) 9: 122–34.
D. Larsen-Freeman, and M. Long, *An Introduction to Second Language Acquisition Research*, Chapter 5 (Longman, 1991).
    The role of input and interaction in L1 acquisition is considered in:
C. Snow and C. Ferguson (eds.), *Talking to Children: Language Input and Acquisition* (Cambridge University Press, 1977).
G. Wells, *Language Development in the Pre-school Years* (Cambridge University Press, 1985).
C. Snow, 'Conversations with children' in P. Fletcher and M. Garman (eds.), *Language Acquisition*, 2nd edition (Cambridge University Press, 1986).
    For descriptive studies of FT see:
M. Clyne (ed.), Special issue on 'Foreigner Talk' of *International Journal of Sociology of language* (1981) 28.
D. Larsen-Freeman (ed.), *Discourse Analysis in Second Language Research* (see articles by Vander Brook, Schlue and Campbell, Arthur et al., and Gaskill) (Newbury House, 1980).
S. Gass and C. Madden (eds.), *Input in Second Language Acquisition* (see articles by Kleifgen, Ellis, Wesche and Ready, Hirvonen, Gass and Varonis, Long, and Lightbown and d'Anglejan) (Newbury House, 1985).
M. Long, 'Native-speaker/non native-speaker conversation and the negotiation of meaning.' *Applied Linguistics* (1983) 4: 126–41.

For the effects of input/interaction on comprehension and acquisition see:
S. Krashen, *The Input Hypothesis* (Longman, 1985).
K. Parker and C. Chaudron, 'The effects of linguistic simplifications and elaborative modifications on L2 comprehension.' *University of Hawaii Working Papers in ESL* (1987) 6: 107–33.
M. Long, 'Native-speaker/non-native-speaker conversation in the second language classroom' in M. Clarke and J. Handscombe (eds.), *On TESOL '82: Pacific Perspectives on Language Learning and Teaching* (TESOL, 1983).
T. Pica, 'The textual outcomes of native speaker–non-native speaker negotiation: What do they reveal about second language learning' in C. Kramsch and S. McConnell-Ginet (eds.), *Text and Context: Cross-Disciplinary Perspectives on Language Study* (D. C. Heath and Company, 1992).
L. White, 'Against comprehensible input: the Input Hypothesis and the development of second-language competence.' *Applied Linguistics* (1987) 8: 95–110.

PART FOUR

Explaining second language acquisition: internal factors

Introduction

Whereas the chapters in the last section endeavoured to explain how learners learn a second language, why learners vary in the speed with which they learn, and why most learners fail to achieve full target-language competence in terms of external factors, the chapters in Part Three will examine how an account of learner-internal mechanisms can increase our understanding of these issues. We will attempt to go inside the 'black box' of the learner's mind.

Basic to our study of learner-internal mechanisms is the distinction between cognitive and mentalist explanations of L2 acquisition.[1] This distinction concerns the nature of the internal mechanisms responsible for interlanguage development. A 'cognitive' view considers the mechanisms to be general in nature. It sees the process of learning a language—whether a first or a second one—as essentially the same as any other kind of learning. Language learning engages the same cognitive systems—perception, memory, problem solving, information processing, etc.—as learning other types of knowledge. In a cognitive view, language learning is treated as 'skill learning', analogous to learning how to ride a bicycle or play a violin, although probably more complex.

Key terms in a cognitive account of L2 acquisition are 'process' and 'strategy'. These are sometimes used interchangeably in the literature, but it is useful to distinguish between them. The term 'process' can be found in such phrases as the 'learning process', the 'comprehension process', and the 'production process'. Following Klaus and Buhr (1976: 990), cited in Færch and Kasper (1983b), we will use 'process' in this sense to refer 'the dynamic sequence of different stages of an object or system'. Implicit in this definition is that (1) L2 learning and L2 use both involve a series of steps which are systematic in that they occur whenever learners try to learn or use the L2, and (2) these steps are, to some extent at least, common to all learners and users. The term 'strategy' is more difficult to tie down, as it is used with somewhat different meanings. In general, the term is used to refer to some form of activity, mental or behavioural, that may occur at a specific stage in the overall process of learning and communicating. In Færch and Kasper's framework, strategies are 'plans' for accomplishing some part of the process. Other aspects of strategies are more controversial, however. Bialystok (1978) treats strategies as 'optional mental activities', in contrast to processes which are 'obligatory', but this distinction has not always been followed. Færch and Kasper consider 'problem orientedness' and 'consciousness' to be the two defining criteria of 'communication strategies', but others treat strategies as not necessarily related to problems (in learning or communication) and, at least sometimes, as subconscious.

A mentalist account of L2 acquisition is based on the distinction between 'competence' and 'performance', a distinction that we have already considered in various parts of this book (see Chapter 1, in particular). Bialystok and Sharwood Smith (1985) present a closely argued application of this distinction to L2 acquisition in their 'knowledge' and 'control' model (see the diagram below). Knowledge refers to 'the way in which the language system is represented in the mind of the learner' and control to 'the processing system for controlling knowledge during actual performance' (1985: 104). The knowledge dimension is further divided into *linguistic competence* and *pragmatic competence* (knowledge of how to use linguistic knowledge for communicating). The disparity between native-speaker and learner proficiency can reflect (1) differences in knowledge (linguistic or pragmatic), (2) differences in control, or (3) both. Similarly, L2 development can consist of changes in the learner's knowledge systems, an increase in control of this knowledge system, or both. This model allows for the possibility of studying learners' grammatical systems (i.e. 'knowledge') independently of their use in communication (i.e. 'control').

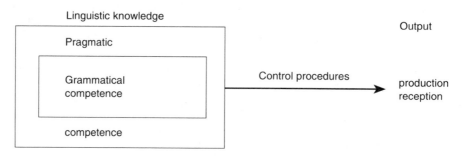

The relationship between control procedures and two aspects of linguistic knowledge (Bialystok and Sharwood Smith 1985: 106)

The main difference between cognitive and mentalist accounts of language learning lies in how they view the relationship between 'knowledge' and 'control'. In a cognitive account, knowledge is not seen as distinct from control. There is no clear dividing line between what learners know and what they can do with their knowledge, as the way linguistic knowledge is represented in the mind of the learner is influenced by the uses to which this knowledge is put. In contrast, a mentalist account of L2 acquisition treats 'knowledge' and 'control' as separate, and also sees the mechanisms responsible for the development of each as distinct. The central claim of a mentalist theory of language acquisition is that linguistic knowledge constitutes a separate cognitive faculty, independent of the other cognitive systems involved in the use of this knowledge.

The study of *L1 transfer* is the starting point for this section, mainly because, historically speaking, it constituted the first attempt to provide an explanation for L2 acquisition. Initially, transfer was viewed in behaviourist terms, but increasingly it has been treated as a cognitive strategy. The following chapter examines a number of cognitive accounts of L2 acquisition. These are varied in nature but they have in common the assumption that L2 learning constitutes a 'process', governed by mechanisms of a general cognitive nature. In the final chapter in this section we will adopt a mentalist stance by examining how theories of language have contributed to the study of L2 acquisition.

Notes

1 This distinction is similar but not identical to Bialystok's (1990b) distinction between 'processing' and 'competence' theories. Bialystok defines the former as 'descriptions of methods of storage and means of accessing rules' and the latter as 'descriptions of knowledge of rules for linguistic structure' (1990b: 637). In fact, however, both cognitive and mentalist explanations of L2 acquisition make reference to 'rules'. The difference lies in the nature of the mechanisms that are proposed to describe the rules.

8 Language transfer

Introduction

This chapter begins the study of the cognitive structures involved in second language acquisition by considering how the learner's existing linguistic knowledge influences the course of L2 development. This constitutes a suitable starting point, not so much because the learner's existing linguistic knowledge is the major factor, but because, historically speaking, it was the first factor to receive serious attention.

Behaviourist views of language learning and of language teaching were predominant in the two decades following the second world war. These views drew on general theories of learning propounded by psychologists such as Watson (1924), Thorndike (1932), and Skinner (1957). Dakin (1973) identifies three general principles of language learning derived from these theories. According to the law of exercise, language learning is promoted when the learner makes active and repeated responses to stimuli. The law of effect emphasizes the importance of reinforcing the learners' responses by rewarding target-like responses and correcting non-target-like ones. The principle of shaping claims that learning will proceed most smoothly and rapidly if complex behaviours are broken down into their component parts and learnt bit by bit. Underlying these principles was the assumption that language learning, like any other kind of learning, took the form of habit formation, a 'habit' consisting of an automatic response elicited by a given stimulus. As Brooks (1960) put it:

> The single paramount fact about language learning is that it concerns, not problem solving, but the formation and performance of habits (1960: 49).

Learning was seen to take place inductively through 'analogy' rather than 'analysis'.

According to behaviourist theories, the main impediment to learning was interference from prior knowledge. *Proactive inhibition* occurred when old habits got in the way of attempts to learn new ones. In such cases, the old habits had to be 'unlearnt' so that they could be replaced by new ones. In the case of L2 learning, however, the notion of 'unlearning' made little sense, as learners clearly did not need to forget their L1 in order to acquire an L2, although in some cases loss of the native language might take place eventually. For this reason, behaviourist theories of L2 learning emphasized the idea of 'difficulty', defined as the amount of effort required to learn an L2 pattern. The degree of difficulty was believed to depend primarily in the extent to which the target language pattern was similar to or different from a native-language pattern. Where the two were identical, learning could take place easily through *positive transfer* of the native-language pattern, but where they were different, learning difficulty arose and errors resulting from *negative transfer* were likely to occur. Such errors or 'bad habits' were considered damaging to successful language learning because they prevented the formation of the correct target-language habits. The commonly held view was that 'like sin, error is to be avoided and its influence overcome, but its presence to be expected' (Brooks 1960).

These behaviourist views have now been discredited. Chomsky's (1959) review of Skinner's *Verbal Behaviour* set in motion a re-evaluation of many of the central claims. The dangers of extrapolating from laboratory studies of animal behaviour to the language behaviour of humans were pointed out. The terms 'stimulus' and 'response' were exposed as vacuous where language behaviour was concerned. 'Analogy' could not account for the language user's ability to generate totally novel utterances. Furthermore, studies of children acquiring their L1 showed that parents rarely corrected their children's linguistic errors, thus casting doubt on the importance of 'reinforcement' in language learning (see Chapter 7). These studies suggested that language acquisition was developmental in nature, driven as much, if not more, from the inside as from the outside. As we shall see, the demise of behaviourist accounts of language learning led to a reconsideration of the role of the L1 in L2 learning.

This chapter is primarily concerned with the cognitive accounts of language transfer that have now superseded the behaviourist views outlined above. It begins with a discussion of terminological issues, the term 'transfer' itself being somewhat controversial, and then goes on to describe a number of different ways in which transfer manifests itself. The chapter then examines the *Contrastive Analysis Hypothesis*, the problems identified with it, and its current status in SLA research. There follows a brief consideration of the minimalist position regarding the role of the L1, with particular reference to the views of Dulay, Burt, and Krashen. The main section of the chapter examines various constraints on transfer in order to account for the fact that transfer is sometimes apparent and sometimes not—the 'now you see it, now you don't' nature of language transfer (Kellerman 1983). This provides the basis for a general framework to account for the role of prior linguistic knowledge. The chapter concludes with a discussion of some of the problems inherent in the study of transfer.

In subsequent chapters we will need to return to the issue of L1 transfer, as no theory of L2 acquisition that ignores the learner's prior linguistic knowledge can be considered complete. In particular, the section dealing with the

Competition Model in Chapter 9 and that dealing with UG-based empirical studies of L2 acquisition in Chapter 10 will further address the role of the L1.

Terminological issues

As we have seen, the terms 'interference' and 'transfer' are closely associated with behaviourist theories of L2 learning. However, it is now widely accepted that the influence of the learner's native language cannot be adequately accounted for in terms of habit formation. Nor is transfer simply a matter of interference or of falling back on the native language. Nor is it just a question of the influence of the learner's native language, as other previously acquired 'second' languages can also have an effect. This suggests that the term 'L1 transfer' itself is inadequate. Sharwood Smith and Kellerman (1986) have argued that a superordinate term that is theory-neutral is needed and suggest *crosslinguistic influence*. They comment:

> ... the term 'crosslinguistic influence' ... is theory-neutral, allowing one to subsume under one heading such phenomena as 'transfer', 'interference', 'avoidance', 'borrowing' and L2-related aspects of language loss and thus permitting discussion of the similarities and differences between these phenomena (1986: 1).

There is much to be said for this proposal, not least the precise definition of 'transfer' that it permits. Kellerman (1987) has suggested that the term be restricted to 'those processes that lead to the incorporation of elements from one language into another' (1987: 3). However, as is often the case in terminological disputes, usage does not always conform to reason, and the term 'transfer' has persisted, although its definition has now been considerably broadened to include most of the crosslinguistic phenomena that Kellerman and Sharwood Smith consider to be in need of attention. Odlin (1989) offers this 'working definition' of transfer as a basis for his own thoughtful treatment of such phenomena:

> Transfer is the influence resulting from the similarities and differences between the target language and any other language that has been previously (and perhaps imperfectly) acquired (1989: 27).

Transfer viewed in this way is, of course, far removed from the original use of the term in behaviourist theories of language learning. This definition, although somewhat vague (as Odlin admits), provides an adequate basis for the material to be considered in this chapter.

The manifestations of transfer

In traditional accounts of language transfer, the research focus was placed on the *errors* that learners produce. Errors occurred as a result of the negative transfer of mother tongue patterns into the learner's L2. It is possible to identify a number of other manifestations of transfer, however, three of which will be considered here: facilitation, *avoidance* (or underproduction), and *over-use*.

Errors (negative transfer)

Learners' errors were considered in detail in Chapter 2, where the procedure for conducting an error analysis was described. We noted that a substantial amount of empirical work in SLA research has been devoted to establishing to what extent errors are the result of transfer (i.e. interference) or are *intralingual* in nature (i.e. the result of general processes of language development similar to those observed in L1 acquisition). Table 8.1, from Ellis 1985a, illustrates the considerable variance in the proportion of transfer errors reported by different investigators. Whereas Dulay and Burt (1973) report that transfer accounted for only 3 per cent of the errors in their corpus of Spanish-speaking learners' L2 English, Tran-Chi-Chau (1975) reports 51 per cent in adult, Chinese-speaking learners' English. As we saw in Chapter 3, one of the main reasons for this variation is the difficulty in determining whether an error is the result of transfer or intralingual processes.

Study	% of interference errors	Type of learner
Grauberg 1971	36	First language German—adult, advanced
George 1972	33 (approx)	Mixed first languages—adult, graduate
Dulay and Burt 1973	3	First language Spanish—children, mixed level
Tran-Chi-Chau 1975	51	First language Chinese—adult, mixed level
Mukkatesh 1977	23	First language Arabic—adult
Flick 1980	31	First language Spanish—adult, mixed level
Lott 1983	50 (approx)	First language Italian—adult, university

Table 8.1:   Percentage of interference errors reported by various studies of L2 English grammar (from Ellis 1985a: 29)

Facilitation (positive transfer)

The learner's L1 can also facilitate L2 learning. Odlin (1989) points out that the facilitative effects can only be observed when learners with different native languages are studied and learner comparisons are carried out. Facilitation is evident not so much in the total absence of certain errors—as would be expected on the basis of behaviourist notions of positive transfer—but rather in a reduced number of errors and, also, in the rate of learning.

The facilitative effect of the L1 can also be adduced by certain types of *U-shaped behaviour*[1] (see Kellerman 1985a). Learners may sometimes pass through an early stage of development where they manifest correct use of a target-language feature if this feature corresponds to an L1 feature and then, subsequently, replace it with a developmental L2 feature before finally returning to the correct target-language feature. In such a case, the facilitative effect is evident in the early stages of acquisition, before the learner is 'ready' to construct a developmental rule. The 're-learning' of the correct target-language rule occurs when learners abandon the developmental rule as they come to notice that it is incompatible with the input. Evidence for such a facilitative effect, of course, can best be obtained through the longitudinal study of individual learners.

Two studies of relative clauses illustrate how transfer can have a facilitative effect. Gass (1979; 1983) investigated 17 adult learners of L2 English with diverse language backgrounds. Data relating to a number of structural aspects of relative clauses were collected, but only one—pronoun retention—provided clear evidence of transfer effects. Gass divided her subjects into two groups according to whether their L1 allowed pronoun retention (for example, Persian and Arabic) or did not allow it (for example, French and Italian). She found that learners in the first group were much more likely to accept sentences like:

* The woman that I gave a book to *her* is my sister.

as grammatical than learners in the second group. Those learners in the second group, whose languages resembled English in not permitting pronoun retention, also made fewer errors in a sentence-joining task. Interestingly, though, facilitative transfer effects were not evident in all relative clause types, there being no difference between the two groups in the case of clauses where the pronoun functioned as subject, genitive, or object of comparison in the sentence-joining task. This led Gass to claim that transfer interacts with other, universal factors—an important point which we will take up later.

The second study (Hyltenstam 1984) investigated relative clauses in L2 Swedish, a language that does not permit pronoun retention. The subjects were 45 adult learners from five language groups. These languages differed in the extent to which they manifested pronominal copies in relative clauses. Hyltenstam used pictures to elicit oral sentences for each relativizable function. The results showed that pronominal copies occurred in the speech produced by all the language groups irrespective of whether their L1 permitted retention or not, but that the frequency of the copies varied according to language group. The Persian learners produced the most copies, followed by the

Greek, with the Spanish and Finnish learners producing the fewest. This order corresponded exactly to that predicted on the basis of the structural properties of the learners' native languages.

The facilitative effect of the L1 is evident in other aspects of L2 acquisition. In many cases, this is obvious, as when two languages share a large number of cognates (for example, English and French), thus giving the learners a head start in vocabulary. Chinese learners of L2 Japanese have an enormous advantage over English learners because of the similarity of the Chinese and Japanese writing systems. They are able to make use of written as well as spoken input straight away. The positive contribution of the L1 has been ignored by some researchers who, in staking out a minimalist transfer position, have chosen to attend only to learner errors.

Avoidance

Learners also avoid using linguistic structures which they find difficult because of differences between their native language and the target language. In such cases, the effects of the L1 are evident not in what learners do (errors) but in what they do not do (omissions). The classic study of avoidance, which we considered briefly in Chapter 3, is Schachter (1974). Schachter found that Chinese and Japanese learners of L2 English made fewer errors in the use of relative clauses than Persian or Arabic learners because they produced far fewer clauses overall (see Table 8.2). In Levenston's (1971) terms, 'under-representation' occurs, which, as Levenston (1979) points out, is best characterized as an aspect of 'use' rather than 'acquisition'.

	Correct	Error	Total	Percentage of Errors
Persian	131	43	174	25
Arab	123	31	154	20
Chinese	67	9	76	12
Japanese	58	5	63	8
American	173	0	173	0

Table 8.2:   Relative clause production in five languages (Schachter 1974: 209)

The difficulty for the Chinese and Japanese learners may lie in the fact that while their mother tongues are left-branching (i.e. nouns are pre-modified):

Aki ga kinoo honya de kat-ta hon ...
(Aki NOM yesterday bookstore LOC buy-PAST) book ... [2]

English is primarily right-branching (i.e. nouns are post-modified):

The book which Aki bought yesterday at the bookstore ....

Persian and Arabic are also right-branching. Schachter hypthesizes that it is this factor which leads Chinese and Japanese learners of L2 English to avoid using relative clauses.

The identification of avoidance is not an easy task. Seliger (1989) points out that it is only possible to claim that avoidance has taken place if the learner has demonstrated knowledge of the form in question, and if there is evidence available that native speakers of the L2 would use the form in the context under consideration. In other words, it only makes sense to talk of avoidance if the learners *know* what they are avoiding. Kamimoto, Shimura, and Kellerman (1992) argue that even demonstrating knowledge of a structure is not sufficient. Hebrew speakers of English may know how to use the passive, but their infrequent use of it in the L2 may simply reflect the general preference for active over passive in L1 Hebrew rather than avoidance (i.e. negative transfer). Thus, it is also necessary to demonstrate that the structure is not under-used simply because the equivalent structure is rare in the L1.

Avoidance is a complex phenomenon. Kellerman (1992) attempts to sort out the complexity by distinguishing three types. Avoidance (1) occurs when learners know or anticipate that there is a problem and have at least some, sketchy idea of what the target form is like. This is the minimum condition for avoidance. Avoidance (2) arises when learners know what the target is but find it too difficult to use in the particular circumstances (for example, in the context of free-flowing conversation). Avoidance (3) is evident when learners know what to say and how to say it but are unwilling to actually say it because it will result in them flouting their own norms of behaviour. In all three cases it is clear that much more is involved than the learner's L1. The extent of learners' knowledge of the L2 and the attitudes learners hold toward their own and the target-language cultures act as factors that interact with L1 knowledge to determine avoidance behaviour.

Over-use

The over-use or 'over-indulgence' (Levenston 1971) of certain grammatical forms in L2 acquisition can occur as a result of intralingual processes such as overgeneralization (see Chapter 2). For example, L2 learners have often been observed to overgeneralize the regular past tense inflection to irregular verbs in L2 English (for example, 'costed'). Similarly, learners may demonstrate a preference for words which can be generalized to a large number of contexts (Levenston 1979). Over-use can also result from transfer—often as a consequence of the avoidance or underproduction of some 'difficult' structure. Japanese learners of English, for example, may overproduce simple sentences and may even be encouraged to do so, as this professional advice from a Japanese translator shows:

Translate a main clause with a relative clause in English into two main clauses and connect them with conjunctions. (Kamimoto, Shimura, and Kellerman 1992: 268).

Over-use as a result of transfer is also evident at the discourse level. Olshtain (1983) examined the apologies offered by 63 American college students learning L2 Hebrew in Israel. She was able to show that the native speakers of English used more direct expressions of apology than native speakers of Hebrew and that they tended to transfer this into L2 Hebrew. This tendency was evident across situations (see Chapter 5 for a fuller discussion of the research on apologies).

Over-use of linguistic and discourse features as a result of L1 influence is probably more common than generally acknowledged. As in the case of avoidance, it can only be detected by comparing groups of learners with different L1s.

Summary and final comment

Current discussions of transfer emphasize the necessity of considering the multiple ways in which L1 influence can exert itself. It is clearly insufficient to focus exclusively on production errors, as many of the subtle manifestations of transfer will be missed. Transfer scholars, therefore, also look for evidence of facilitation (positive transfer), avoidance, and over-use. They recognize, however, that all these aspects of L2 use are likely to demonstrate a variety of factors at work, only one of which is transfer. Thus, they emphasize the importance of looking for how L1 knowledge interacts with other factors.

Difference and difficulty: the role of contrastive analysis

Although behaviourist views of transfer are largely defunct, the central notions that they gave rise to—'difference' and 'difficulty'—are still very much alive. We will begin this section with a consideration of early formulations of the *Contrastive Analysis Hypothesis*, consider some of the problems it gave rise to and then offer a reconsideration of the 'difference = difficulty' equation and of the role of *contrastive analysis*.

The Contrastive Analysis Hypothesis (CAH) as formulated by Lado (1957) was based on this assumption:

> ... the student who comes into contact with a foreign language will find some features of it quite easy and others extremely difficult. Those elements that are similar to his native language will be simple for him, and those elements that are different will be difficult. (1957: 2)

Lado began his book, *Linguistics Across Cultures*, by referring to the work of Haugen (1956) and Weinreich (1953). This provided evidence that when languages come into contact in bilingual situations, many of the 'distortions' that arise are traceable to differences in the languages involved. Lado's book not only laid out the theoretical bases of the CAH but also described the technical procedures needed to carry out the detailed contrastive analyses that were considered necessary for the preparation of 'scientific' teaching materials.

The 1960s saw a spate of contrastive analyses involving the major European languages (for example, Stockwell and Bowen 1965; Stockwell, Bowen, and Martin 1965). They were designed to provide course developers with information regarding where the differences and hence the difficulties lay for learners of different language backgrounds. The analyses were based on surface 'structuralist' descriptions of the two languages concerned. The procedure followed involved (1) description (i.e. a formal description of the two languages was made), (2) selection (i.e. certain areas or items of the two languages were chosen for detailed comparison), (3) comparison (i.e. the identification of areas of difference and similarity), and (4) prediction (i.e. determining which areas were likely to cause errors).

The scholars of the 1960s recognized different kinds of 'difference' and also attributed to them different degrees of 'difficulty'. Table 8.3 below provides a simplified version of the hierarchy of difficulty produced by Stockwell, Bowen, and Martin (1965). It shows that 'difficulty' will be greatest when there is a split and least in the case of coalesced forms. No difficulty arises when there is a complete correspondence of items in the two languages.

Type of difficulty	L1: English L2: Spanish	Example
1 Split	x → x / y	'for' is either *por* or *para*
2 New	o ------ o	grammatical gender
3 Absent	x ------ o	'do' as a tense carrier
4 Coalesced	x \ / x ... y	'his/her' is realized as a single form *su*
5 Correspondence	x ——— x	*-ing*, *-ndo* as complement with verbs of perception, e.g. 'I saw the men running'; *vi a los hombres corriendo*.

Table 8.3:   Simplified version of the hierarchy of difficulty (based on information given in Stockwell, Bowen, and Martin 1965)

In its strongest form, the CAH claimed that all L2 errors could be predicted by identifying the differences between the learners' native language and the target language. Lee (1968: 180), for instance, stated that 'the prime cause, or even the sole cause, of difficulty and error in foreign language learning is interference coming from the learner's native language'. However, given the empirical evidence that soon became available suggesting that many errors were not the result of transfer (see Table 8.1), a weaker form of the hypothesis was proposed (Wardhaugh 1970). According to this, only some errors were traceable to transfer, and contrastive analysis could be used only *a posteriori* to *explain* rather than predict. In other words, contrastive analysis needed to be used hand in hand with error analysis.

The CAH had its heyday in the 1960s, but gradually fell out of favour in the 1970s. There were several reasons for this. The strong form became untenable when it was shown that many errors were not caused by transfer (see Dulay and Burt 1974a) and that many errors predicted by contrastive analysis did not actually occur (see Jackson and Whitnam 1971). However, the weak form is also problematic. First, an *a posteriori* contrastive analysis is something of a 'pseudo procedure' (James 1980) in the sense that it makes little sense to undertake a lengthy comparison of two languages simply to confirm that errors suspected of being caused by transfer are indeed so. James argued that a contrastive analysis was only worthwhile if it was predictive. Schachter (1974) also argued that an *a priori* contrastive analysis was needed in order to identify those areas of the L2 system which learners might try to avoid. Neither version of the CAH was convincing, therefore; the strong version was theoretically untenable and the weak version was impractical and inadequate. It was not surprising to see contrastive analysis lose ground to error analysis in the 1970s.

Despite these problems, transfer continued to be of interest to SLA researchers. To explain how researchers accommodated to the growing evidence that transfer was, at best, only a partial explanation of learning difficulty, we need to reconsider the two basic claims of the CAH:

(1) The level of difficulty experienced by the learner will be directly related to the degree of linguistic difference between the L1 and L2.
(2) Difficulty will manifest itself in errors; the greater the difficulty, the more frequent the errors.

Kellerman (1987) has argued that the only viable definition of a 'difficult' structure is one that learners fail to learn despite plentiful evidence for the existence of the structure in the input. There are many possible explanations for a structure being 'difficult'—for example, its saliency, its communicative value to the learner, the extent to which it is marked or unmarked, or the ease with which it can be processed in production or comprehension (see Chapter 9). Included in these possible explanations is the extent to which the structure is similar to or different from a comparable structure in the learner's L1 or another previously learnt L2. The problem with the CAH was its failure to acknowledge sources of difficulty other than the learner's L1. While it has been shown to be clearly incorrect to claim that L1/L2 differences *will* lead to difficulty, it has also become clear that they *might* do. The trick is to show when they do and when they do not. As Kellerman (1987) puts it, there is a need to establish the 'potential for transfer' of a given structure and to identify the nature of the constraints that govern its transferability. The second claim of the CAH is, in fact, not a necessary one—'errors' are but one aspect of the learning process and, as we saw in the previous section, difficulty can manifest itself in other forms.

In short, the problem with the CAH is that it is too simplistic and too restrictive. The solution, as many researchers have come to recognize, lies not in its abandonment but in careful revision and extension. These researchers continue to make use of contrastive analysis, but only as a tool for identifying potential areas of difficulty (Fisiak 1981a). It was generally recognized that the claims of a contrastive analysis needed to be subjected to careful empirical inquiry. As Selinker (1969) pointed out, 'experimentation in language research' is needed 'whenever it becomes clear that extrapolation from pure linguistic research is improper'. Similarly, Nemser (1971) saw the 'direct and systematic examination of learner speech' as a 'prerequisite for the validation of both the strong and weak claims of the contrastive approach'. Thus, the difficulties with the CAH set the scene for the detailed investigation of learner language, as in Selinker's study of Hebrew learners of English. Subsequently, researchers undertook the kind of learner comparisons which, as we have seen, are necessary to provide unambiguous evidence of transfer in all its manifestations.

The minimalist position

The empirical research in the late 1960s and 1970s, which we considered in Chapters 2 and 3, led to two rather different ways of accounting for the role of the L1. In one, transfer was treated as one of several processes involved in L2 acquisition. This was the approach of Selinker (1969; 1972), Nemser (1971), and James (1971). Selinker (1972) saw 'language transfer' as one of the five processes responsible for fossilization, placing it, in fact, at the top of his list. Nemser (1971) claimed that learner speech was 'structurally organized' in the sense that it constituted a system in its own right. However, like Selinker, he saw the learner's native language as one of the major determinants of these 'approximative systems'. James (1971) pointed out that contrastive analysts had never claimed that L1 interference was the sole source of error. He also noted, prophetically, that 'it will probably turn out that many of the errors which are now not traceable to the L1, and are therefore attributed to L2 overgeneralization, will ... be recognized as errors of interference' (1971: 56). As we will see later, it was such a view of transfer that came to dominate and to lead researchers to investigate how transfer interacted with other, non-L1 based strategies. In this section, however, we will focus on the second way of dealing with transfer—the minimalist approach.

The minimalist position sought to play down the importance of the L1 and to emphasize the contribution of universal processes of language learning, such as hypothesis-testing. It found expression in three ways: the dismissal of evidence of the pervasiveness of interference which came from studies of language contact situations, the conduct of empirical studies designed to test the CAH, and the development of alternative theoretical arguments.

Interference in language contact situations and second language acquisition

Although the experience of many teachers testified to the existence of transfer errors, there were, in fact, hardly any empirical studies of transfer in L2 learning. Consequently, the CAH relied for supportive evidence on the work of Weinreich (1953) and Haugen (1956) in bilingual contact situations. This showed that many of the 'linguistic distortions' observed in the speech of bilinguals corresponded to differences in the languages involved. However, Dulay and Burt (1972) claimed that the concepts of 'interference' and 'linguistic borrowing' used by Weinreich and Haugen were distinct from that of 'interference' in the CAH and that scholars such as Lado were not justified in citing Weinreich's and Haugen's research in its support. Interference in bilinguals, they argued, was motivated by social factors, was bi-directional, and increased with proficiency in the two languages; interference in language learning was not socially motivated, was unidirectional, and decreased as the learner became more proficient. It is not at all clear that the two uses of 'interference' are as distinct as Dulay and Burt claim.[3] Indeed, current definitions of the term 'transfer' (see page 301) allow for both sociolinguistic and psycholinguistic L1 effects. Although the two phenomena are not identical, they are now seen to be related. Even the frequently made distinction between *borrowing transfer* (where the L2 influences the L1) and *substratum transfer* (where the L1 influences the L2) is not always clear-cut (see Thomason and Kaufman's (1988) study of language learning in Ethiopia, cited in Odlin 1989: 12). It is no longer possible to dismiss the evidence of transfer effects in bilinguals as irrelevant to L2 acquisition.

Empirical research and the CAH

A number of studies of learner language carried out in the late 1960s and early 1970s indicated that the influence of the L1 was much less than that claimed by the CAH. These studies were based on attempts to quantify the number of transfer errors. For example, in the most frequently cited study, Dulay and Burt (1974b) examined six structures in the L2 speech of Spanish learners of English. They selected only those structures that could provide unambiguous evidence of transfer. For example, negative constructions such as the following:

* I not have a bike.

were not included in the study, because although similar constructions are present in Spanish:

Yo no tengo bicicleta.

they are also found in the L1 acquisition of English, thus making it impossible to decide whether they constitute examples of interference or developmental errors. In contrast, the presence of a preclitic in sentences like:

* The dog it ate.

constitutes clear evidence of interference because, while the same construction is found in Spanish:

El perro se lo comió.

it is not evident in the L1 acquisition of English. The study showed that less than 5 per cent of the total errors in the corpus were of the 'interference' type, the rest being either 'developmental' or 'unique' (see page 60 for a definition of these categories). Other studies have also claimed to show that the learners' L1 plays only an insignificant role. For example, Felix (1980b) examined three syntactic structures in English-speaking children's acquisition of L2 German and concluded that 'interference does not constitute a major strategy' (1980b: 107).

There are reasons for believing, however, that studies like those of Dulay and Burt and Felix seriously underestimate the role of the L1. First, it is not always easy to decide whether an error is interference or developmental, and this can result in estimations of transfer errors that are too conservative. As we have seen, it can be argued that 'no' + verb constructions produced by Spanish learners of English do not constitute a transfer error because the same error is evident in the L1 acquisition of English. It is possible, however, that 'no' + verb constructions reflect transfer and developmental processes working in conjunction. The point is that by eliminating structures with a potential for transfer (for example, negative constructions) and by investigating constructions, such as preclitics, where transfer is theoretically possible but unlikely—for reasons to be considered later—Dulay and Burt have contrived to ensure that they find few interference errors. The assumption that errors must be either the result of interference or intralingual is unwarranted. Also, before transfer can be dismissed, it is necessary to demonstrate through learner comparisons that the L1 is indeed having no effect.

As Kellerman (1987) has pointed out, researchers tend to reflect their theoretical biases in what they interpret as transfer effects. He notes that Arabski (1979) made the somewhat surprising assertion that the 974 article errors in his Polish-English corpus were not transfer errors on the grounds that, because Polish does not have articles, there is nothing to transfer. Clearly, though, the absence of a structural feature in the L1 may have as much impact on the L2 as the presence of a different feature. Kellerman points out that if Arabski had included the article errors in his corpus, the total percentage attributable to transfer would have exceeded 70 per cent (as opposed to the 50 per cent Arabski actually reported).

Another point made by Kellerman is that the contribution of the L1 can also be underestimated if insistence is placed on quantification in terms of error tokens rather than error types. As the number of error tokens will depend on the number of obligatory occasions for the use of a particular structure, it is obvious that wide fluctuations can occur. Kellerman gives the example of article errors, which are likely to be more common than passive errors for the simple reason that there is greater opportunity for their commission. Obviously, the true effect of the L1 can only be established if researchers examine error types (i.e. the number of different structures in which L1 influence is evident). The minimalist positions of Dulay and Burt and Felix are based on counting error tokens and consider very few error types.

Word order studies of transfer

A good example of the kind of problems that can arise in trying to determine the extent of L1 influence is found in studies of basic word order. Languages vary in (1) their basic word order (the majority of languages being VSO, SVO, or SOV) and (2) the extent to which their basic word order is rigid or flexible (for example, English has a rigid word order, while Russian is flexible).

Odlin (1989; 1990) provides a review of the research that has investigated to what extent word order in interlanguage is affected by the L1. He refers to the 'universalist position' advanced by Rutherford and Zobl, namely that there is little negative transfer where basic word order is concerned. He cites Rutherford (1983), for instance, as claiming that 'Japanese learners of English do not at any time produce writing in which the verb is wrongly placed sentence finally' (1983: 367). Given that Japanese is rigidly SOV and English SVO, transfer might have been expected. Zobl (1986) similarly argues that L2 learners do not make recourse to L1 knowledge where basic word order is concerned, except where the target language has more than one basic word order, as in the case of Dutch and German, which have SVO (and other patterns) in main clauses and SOV in subordinate clauses. Rutherford and Zobl's universalist position is in direct opposition to a transfer position.

Minimalist accounts of transfer seek to explain away apparent instances of L1 effects on word order. For example, Turkish learners of German have been observed to sometimes manifest constructions where the verb appears at the end of a sentence, suggesting that L1 transfer is taking place. However, Clahsen and Muysken (1986) argue that what appears to be transfer is in fact a discourse strategy. Odlin (1989: 89), too, accepts that there is 'detailed evidence for the heavy reliance of some learners on topic-comment patterning in the early stages of acquisition'. He cites these examples from Huebner's (1983) study of a Hmong refugee in Hawaii:

mii wok (As for me, I walked)
hos, ai reis (As for horses, I raced).

Learners of German, irrespective of their L1, have been found to produce similar utterances (see Klein 1986; Clahsen and Muysken 1986).

These studies, then, suggest that the learner's L1 has little influence on basic word order and that, even when transfer is apparent, it can be better explained in terms of a discourse strategy. They lend support to the minimalist position. However, Odlin (1990) goes on to muster substantial and convincing evidence of L1 transfer where basic word order is concerned.

He provides evidence from 11 studies of substratum transfer (i.e. from the L1 to the L2) and borrowing transfer (i.e. from the L2 to the L1) of word order rules. For example, Nagara (1972) reports that Japanese speakers of Hawaiian pidgin produce sentences like:

Mi: cu: stoa gecc (me two store get = I got two stores)
hawai kam (Hawaii came = I came to Hawaii).

It is possible that such utterances reflect a topic-comment patterning. However, Bickerton and Givón (1976) have demonstrated that Japanese and Filipino speakers of Hawaiian Pidgin English manifest a word order that differs in accordance with their L1. Givón (1984) provides further evidence against a discourse explanation. He showed that Filipino and Korean speakers of Hawaiian pidgin displayed a preference for different word order patterns which directly reflected their L1s. Odlin also argues convincingly that Lujan, Minaya, and Dankoff's (1984) study of Spanish spoken in Peru and Ecuador provides evidence of influence from the L1 word order of local Indian languages, again dismissing Muysken's (1984) claim that the observed OV patterns are the result of 'stylistic considerations'. Further examples of substratum transfer cited by Odlin are in Korean Bamboo English, a pidgin used in contacts between American soldiers and Japanese and Korean civilians in the 1940s and 1950s, and Pidgin Fijian.

Odlin concludes that 'there is no universal constraint on the transfer of basic word order' (1990: 107), contradicting the claim of Rutherford and Zobl. Again, then, the minimalist position is not supported—even in the case of a structure that might be considered to be highly amenable to a universalist explanation.

However, Odlin (1990) does admit that there are relatively few instances of basic word order transfer in the literature and suggests two principal reasons why this might be so. First, he points out the relative lack of research on beginner learners, in whom word order transfer is most likely. Second, learners are likely to be highly conscious of word order as it involves the arrangement of semantically important elements. He notes that learners are very successful in identifying word order errors and, also, adept at imitating the word order patterns of other languages. He reports that Korean-English and Spanish-English bilinguals were much more consistent in judging word order errors than article errors. Teachers are also likely to pay attention to word order violations. The high level of awareness that word order seems to arouse may help learners to monitor their production in order to eliminate the effects of transfer. This might explain why Rutherford's Japanese learners displayed no evidence of the L1 order in their written compositions.

Minimalist theoretical positions on transfer

Minimalist theoretical positions on transfer have tended to emphasize the similarity between L2 and L1 acquisition. Newmark (1966), for instance, drew extensively on research in L1 acquisition in dismissing behaviourist accounts of L2 learning. He was primarily concerned with rejecting the view of language as an incremental process, according to which learners were supposed to acquire a language structure by structure, proceeding from the simplest to the most complex. He acknowledged 'interference' but saw it as of little importance, arguing that it simply reflected ignorance. Newmark and Reibel (1968) produce the following description of what has become known as the *Ignorance Hypothesis*:

> ... a person knows how to speak one language, say his native one; but in the early stages of learning his new one, there are many things that he has not yet learned to do ... What can he do other than use what he already knows to make up for what he does not know? To an observer who knows the target language, the learner will be seen to be stubbornly substituting the native habits for target habits. But from the learner's point of view, all he is doing is the best he can: to fill in his gaps of training he refers for help to what he already knows (1968: 159).

Krashen (1983) adopts a similar position, drawing directly on Newmark's ideas. He views transfer as 'padding', the result of falling back on old knowledge when new knowledge is lacking. The cure is 'comprehensible input' (see Chapter 7). In effect, Newmark and Reibel and Krashen treat L1 transfer as a kind of *communication strategy* (i.e. a means of overcoming a communication problem) rather than as a *learning strategy* (i.e. a device for developing interlanguage). This distinction between communication and learning transfer will be considered in greater detail later.

In place of the behaviourist notions of 'habit formation' and 'interference', researchers such as Dulay and Burt (1972) have posited the existence of 'general processing strategies', which were seen as universal in the sense that they were used by all language learners, first and second. They identified a number of general production strategies to account for the various types of errors they observed. For example, the absence of grammatical functors was explained in terms of 'the pervasiveness of a syntactic generalization' while the use of intonation to signal questions in the early stages of learning was the result of 'using a minimal number of cues to signal the speaker's intentions'. Occasional instances of transfer errors were explained away as the result of the pressure to perform in the L2 (Newmark's idea), of the nature of the learning environment (for example, Ervin-Tripp (1974)) claimed that interference was more likely in contexts where the L2 was not part of the learner's larger social milieu [4]), and of the use of tasks, such as translation, that predisposed learners to refer to their L1.

In retrospect, there can be little doubt that some scholars were too ready to reject transfer as a major factor in L2 acquisition. This over-reaction was caused by the close connection between the ideas of transfer and behaviourism, which, as we have seen, had become discredited. In clambering on to the mentalist bandwagon, however, researchers like Dulay and Burt mistakenly dismissed transfer, often on the basis of flimsy evidence. Subsequently, researchers have sought to relocate transfer within a cognitive framework and have focused their endeavours on identifying the precise conditions that lead to it.

Constraints on transfer

We have seen that a minimalist position on the role of transfer is not justified; transfer constitutes an important factor in L2 acquisition. However, we have also seen that behaviourist accounts of transfer, as reflected in the CAH in particular, overpredict both the transferability of specific items (that is, they fail to explain when they are transferred and when they are not), and transfer load (how much is transferred). Increasingly, researchers have sought to identify the conditions that promote and inhibit transfer. In this section we will consider a number of differing constraints on transfer that incorporate linguistic, psycholinguistic, and sociolinguistic factors. These constraints are: (1) language level (phonology, lexis, grammar, and discourse), (2) social factors (the effect of the addressee and of different learning contexts on transfer), (3) markedness (the extent to which specific linguistic features are 'special' in some way), (4) prototypicality (the extent to which a specific meaning of a word is considered 'core' or 'basic' in relation to other meanings of the same word), (5) language distance and psychotypology (the perceptions that speakers have regarding the similarity and difference between languages), and (6) developmental factors (constraints relating to the natural processes of interlanguage development). It should be noted that these are not the only constraining factors. Non-structural factors such as individual learner differences (such as personality and age), and the nature of the tasks a learner is performing, also constrain L1 transfer. However, as these are considered in some detail elsewhere (see Chapters 11 and 5) they are not dealt with here.

1 Language level

There is widespread recognition that transfer is more pronounced at the level of the sound system than at the level of syntax. The existence of 'foreign accents' in L2 learning is so well attested that it hardly requires documenting. In general, native speakers have little difficulty in distinguishing the language background of different learners. Furthermore, as Purcell and Suter (1980) have shown, the L1 of learners serves as the best predictor of native speakers' evaluations of their speech. In this study, the native speakers were asked to judge the pronunciation accuracy of L2 learners of English with different L1s (Thai, Japanese, Arabic, and Persian). The greater the difference between the L1 and the L2, the lower the rating. Thus, Thai and Japanese learners were rated as less accurate than Arabic and Persian. However, the obvious effects of the L1 on pronunciation, while indicative of the importance of transfer at this level, do not warrant uncritical acceptance of the 'difference = difficulty' hypothesis. As we shall soon see, learners do not invariably transfer the phonological features of their L1. As is the case with syntax, phonological transfer is governed in part by universal developmental tendencies (see Major 1986).

Similar evidence exists regarding the prevalence of transfer of L1 lexis. Kellerman comments 'there are enormous quantities of evidence for the influence of the L1 on IL (interlanguage) when it comes to lexis' (1987: 42). For example, Ringbom (1978) found that the majority of lexical errors made by Swedish and Finnish learners of L2 English could be attributed to the transfer of partial translation equivalents. Also, the acquisition of lexis appears to be facilitated if the L1 and L2 are related languages. Thus, Sjoholm (1976) reports that Swedish learners of L2 English did better in vocabulary learning than Finnish learners, Swedish being closer than Finnish to English.

There is also general acceptance that transfer is a major factor at the level of discourse. In a frequently cited paper, Schachter and Rutherford (1979) argue that what might at first sight appear to be transfer-induced syntactic errors are, in fact, transfer-induced discourse errors. They examined errors of the following type produced by Chinese and Japanese learners of L2 English:

> Most of food which is served in such restaurant have cooked already.
> Irrational emotions are bad but rational emotions must use for judging.

which were judged by native speakers to reflect a confusion between active and passive. Schachter and Rutherford, however, claim that these sentences reflect the transfer of the topic-comment structure found in Chinese and Japanese. They suggest that learners learn a particular target language form and then hypothesize that the form is used to express a particular discourse function. The topic-comment structure is, in fact, a universal feature of early interlanguage (see Chapter 9, page 371), but where the L1 supports its use—as in the case of the Japanese and Chinese learners—it is more prevalent. In a subsequent paper, Rutherford (1983) argues that whereas there is clear evidence of transfer involving topic prominence and pragmatic word-order in Japanese learners of English, there is no evidence of transfer involving grammatical word order. He comments: 'I take these observations as evidence that it is therefore discourse and not syntax that gives gross overall shape to interlanguage' (1983: 368). However, as we have seen in the previous section, Rutherford's rejection of word order transfer is open to criticism. Thus, while there can be few objections to his claim that discourse and pragmatic transfer is common (see Kasper 1992 and Chapter 5 for evidence supporting this), his assertion that it is more prevalent than syntactical transfer needs to be treated with circumspection. It is not even clear how the relative occurrences of transfer in discourse and syntax should be measured.[5]

It is, in fact, very difficult to quantify the extent of transfer in the different language levels. There is, however, a theoretical reason for expecting the influence of the L1 to be felt more strongly in pronunciation, lexis, and discourse than in syntax. In the previous section we noted Odlin's (1990) arguments that metalingual awareness may inhibit transfer in the case of word order. It is probably true to say that most learners have a much more highly developed metalingual awareness of grammatical properties than of phonological or discourse/pragmatic properties. This awareness may enable learners to control their choice of linguistic form at the level of grammar to a greater extent than at the other language levels and this may inhibit transfer.

2 Sociolinguistic factors

Sociolinguistic factors have also been shown to influence when and to what extent transfer takes place. We will consider the effects of (1) the social context and (2) the relationship between the speaker and the addressee on transfer.

The social context can influence the extent to which transfer occurs. Odlin (1989; 1990) has suggested that negative transfer is less likely in focused contexts, where there is concern to maintain the standardness of languages, than in unfocused contexts. This distinction between focused and unfocused contexts is taken from Le Page and Tabouret-Keller (1985), who claim that whereas some communities have a very clear idea of what constitutes a language, others do not, mixing languages without much concern for what is 'grammatical' or 'ungrammatical'. Odlin suggests that negative transfer is less common in classroom settings than in natural settings because in the former, learners constitute a 'focused' community and as a consequence treat L1 forms as intrusive and even stigmatized. In natural settings learners may comprise either a 'focused' or an 'unfocused' community; where they are unfocused, language mixing will be freely permitted, thus encouraging negative transfer to take place.[6] In addition, classroom learners are often explicitly warned when interference might occur through the contrastive presentation of items.

However, as we noted in Chapter 4, it may be misleading to talk of 'communities' where many L2 learners are concerned. It is likely that when learners are in a classroom setting, they will adhere to target-language norms and thus try to avoid negative transfer. However, when the same learners are outside the classroom, they may show much less regard for target-language forms and transfer quite freely.[7] Thus, where L2 learners are concerned, rather than talk of 'communities', it may be better to consider the effect of social context in relation to the kind of norm—external or internal—that learners have in mind. If the context requires attention to external norms (as manifested in textbooks, reference books, and the teacher), negative transfer is inhibited; if, however, the context encourages attention to internal norms (as in free conversation involving speakers with shared languages), learners may resort more freely to the L1 if this helps comprehensibility and promotes positive affective responses. Such variable transfer behaviour is most likely in official language settings (see Chapter 6), where the L2 is used both inside and outside of the classroom, but it may also be found in other settings as well. Of course, learners with access to only one type of setting (such as the classroom) may behave more like a 'community' where transfer is concerned.

Generalizations regarding the effect of macro contexts or settings on L1 transfer are dangerous, however, as they overlook the influence that specific social factors can have on learners' use of their L1. Studies by Beebe (1977) and Beebe and Zuengler (1983) examined the effect of addressee factors on transfer. Bilingual Thai/Chinese learners of English drew variably on their two L1s depending on whether their interlocutor was Thai or Chinese. Beebe (1980) found that Thai learners of English made use of a native variant of /r/ to a greater extent in a formal than in an informal context. Drawing on these and other studies of variability, Tarone (1982) has argued that L1 transfer is likely to be more evident in learners' *careful style* than in their *vernacular style*, on the grounds that when learners are paying greater attention to how they speak, they are more likely to make use of all their potential resources, including L1 knowledge. This variable use of the L1 was considered in more detail in Chapter 4.

It is interesting to note that the conclusion reached by Odlin on the basis of a macro-sociolinguistic perspective is very different from that reached by Tarone on a basis of a micro-sociolinguistic perspective. Given that 'focused' classroom learners are likely to make extensive use of a 'careful style', it seems contradictory to claim that transfer is inhibited in such learners and yet also prevalent in the careful style. This contradiction may be more apparent than real, however. Classroom learners may indeed seek to avoid transfer in general recognition of the importance of external norms, but in cases where the use of an L1 norm appears socially appropriate (because, for example, it gives prestige) they may still resort to transfer. Clearly, though, much work needs to be done to sort out such apparent contradictions.

3 Markedness

One of the strongest claims in recent research on transfer is that the transferability of different features depends on their degree of *markedness*. The term 'marked' has been defined in different ways, but underlying all of the definitions is the notion that some linguistic features are 'special' in relation to others, which are more 'basic'. Thus, for example, the adjectives 'old' and 'young' can be considered unmarked and marked respectively, because whereas 'old' can be used to ask about a person's age:

How old is she? (= what is her age?)

'young' cannot, except in some very special sense:

How young is she? (= is she as young as she makes out?).

More technical definitions of 'markedness' can be found in different linguistic traditions. These are discussed in some detail in Chapter 10, so here we will provide only a brief account to enable us to examine the hypothesized relationship between markedness and transfer. One definition of 'markedness' derives from Chomsky's theory of *Universal Grammar*. This distinguishes the rules of a language that are core and periphery, as shown in Figure 8.1. Core rules are those that can be arrived at through the application of general, abstract principles of language structure, which Chomsky and other generative linguists have held to be innate. Basic word order, for example, is considered part of the core. Peripheral rules are rules that are not governed by universal principles; they are idiosyncratic, reflecting their unique historical origins. The structure 'the more ... the more' is an example of a peripheral rule in English. Peripheral rules are marked. Core rules, as we will see in Chapter 10, can be both unmarked and marked.

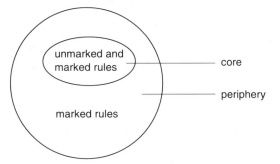

Figure 8.1:   Markedness in core and peripheral grammar

Another definition of markedness is found in language typology (the study of different types of language carried out in order to identify those properties that are universal). The identification of *typological universals* has been used to make claims about which features are marked and which ones are unmarked. The broad claim is that those features that are universal or present in most languages are unmarked, while those that are specific to a particular language or found in only a few languages are marked. Drawing on language typology, Zobl (1984) offers three senses in which rules can be marked. The first is typological specialization. For example, whereas English adheres to the universal tendency of languages to avoid non-extractable 'how' in 'how' + adjective phrases:

> I didn't realize how comfortable I was.
> *I didn't realize how I was comfortable.

French permits extraction of 'combien' in equivalent sentences. The structural properties of a language may also be marked as a result of typological inconsistency. Zobl cites the example of German and Dutch, which permit two different word orders, one in main clauses (SVO) and the other in subordinate clauses (SOV). Thus, German and Dutch word order can be considered marked in relation to English word order, which displays a high level of consistency. Finally, typological indeterminacy occurs when a structure predicted on the basis of a language's overall typology is not found. For example, English, as a SVO language, might be expected to manifest a noun + adjective ordering, but does not do so. Also, some linguistic properties—such as adverbial position—are not stringently controlled by overall typology and so can be considered 'fuzzy'. Typologically indeterminate features are seen as marked.

There is somewhat mixed evidence regarding the effects of markedness on the transferability of L1 features. Two general hypotheses have been investigated: (1) learners will transfer unmarked forms when the corresponding TL form is marked, and (2) learners will resist transferring marked forms, especially when the corresponding TL form is unmarked. As Hyltenstam (1984) puts it:

> Unmarked categories from the native language are substituted for corresponding marked categories in the target language ... Marked structures are seldom transferred, and if they are transferred, they are much more easily eradicated from the target language (1984: 43).

Zobl has provided several examples of how learners tend to fall back on their L1 if the corresponding L2 rule is obscure because it is typologically inconsistent or indeterminate. For example, Zobl (1983a) notes that the following errors are common in French learners of L2 English:

> * They have policeman for stop the bus.
> * He do that for to help the Indians.

The 'for' + infinitive error corresponds closely to the L1 structure ('pour' + infinitive). Zobl points out that there are dialects of English where 'for to' occurs, that transformation grammar posits 'for to' as the deep structure and that it appears in Old and Middle English. He suggests that this creates a 'structural predisposition' for transfer. In other words, 'for to' can be considered unmarked in relation to the modern English structure. Zobl's basic point—reiterated in a number of papers (Zobl 1980a; 1980b; 1982; 1983a and 1984)—is that an L1 rule must meet certain conditions before it will be transferred; it must be productive in the L1 (not some kind of exception), it must be used frequently, and it must not be 'on the way out' historically speaking.

Evidence for the second hypothesis comes from Zobl (1984). On the grounds that extraction is typologically specified (i.e. marked), Zobl predicts that French learners of English will not accept ungrammatical English sentences such as the following:

* How many do you want oranges? (1984: 86),

even though such extraction is permitted in L1 French. The results of a study in which a grammaticality judgement task was administered to mixed proficiency learners lent broad support to this hypothesis. Interestingly, though, the low-intermediate learners were more inclined to accept extraction than either the beginner or advanced level learners (i.e. there was evidence of U-shaped development involving transfer). Zobl suggests that this may reflect the intermediate learners having noticed that English is tolerant of extraction in other grammatical areas (for example, *preposition stranding*, as in 'Who did he give it to?'). This study suggests that (1) learners do resist transferring marked forms when the corresponding TL structure is unmarked, but that (2) this resistance can be overcome if learners obtain evidence that transfer is possible. There is counter-evidence relating to (1), however. A study by Liceras (1985) suggests that learners may be prepared to accept transfer of a marked structure manifesting extraction. Liceras investigated preposition stranding by English-speaking learners of L2 Spanish. English permits extraction of the preposition in sentences like:

Who did John give the book to?

whereas Spanish does not. In this study, 43 per cent of the beginners accepted stranding in Spanish. Liceras' results, therefore, contradict Zobl's.

Indeed, not all researchers take the view that learners will resist transferring marked L1 forms. White (1987b: 266–7) argues forcefully that 'transfer is not confined to unmarked forms, that L2 learners may transfer marked forms from the L1 to the interlanguage, and that such transfer is compatible with the theory of markedness currently invoked in generative grammar'. She points out that the crucial test of the markedness hypothesis occurs only in situations where the L1 has a marked structure but the L2 does not. Such a situation arises for English learners of L2 French in the case of double object constructions, as in:

John gave Fred the book.

and preposition stranding, as in:

Who(m) did John give the book to?

neither of which occur in French. White found that whereas the English learners she investigated provided evidence of resisting the transfer of the marked preposition stranding construction in their grammaticality judgements, they showed a readiness to transfer the marked double object construction. Interestingly, another group of learners with different L1 backgrounds but with a knowledge of English as their first L2, were prepared to transfer both structures. The learners with L1 English, therefore, behaved anomalously, in that they alone resisted transferring one of the marked structures. White suggests that one possible explanation for this exceptional behaviour could be the influence of prescriptive English mother-tongue teaching, where stranding is often presented as stylistically undesirable. White concludes that overall her study supports the view that marked forms are transferred and refers to other studies that show the same (for example, Selinker, Swain, and Dumas 1975 and Tarallo and Myhill 1983).

Some of the most convincing evidence of markedness effects on transfer can be found in studies that have examined asymmetrical patterns. A straight contrastive analysis is unable to cope with evidence that shows that a given feature (z) is transferred in one direction (i.e. transfer of z occurs from language x to language y) but not in the other (i.e. transfer of z does not occur from language y to language x). A theory of transfer that incorporates markedness, however, can provide an explanation for such phenomena.

The study that is most commonly cited to illustrate asymmetrical patterns is Eckman (1977). Eckman investigated transfer in English learners of L2 German and German learners of L2 English, focusing on voice contrast in pairs of phonemes such as /t/ and /d/. In English this contrast exists word initially (for example, 'tin' v. 'din'), medially (for example, 'betting' v. 'bedding'), and finally (for example, 'wed' v. 'wet'). In German, however, the distinction only exists word initially and word medially; in word-final position, only voiceless stops occur. Both the German and the English L2 learners, therefore, are faced with learning to make a known distinction (i.e. voiced/voiceless stops) in a new position. Eckman argues that typologically, voice contrast in word-final position is more marked than in the other two positions. He provides evidence to show that English learners have no difficulty in learning that German has no voicing in word-final stops, but that German learners experience considerable problems in learning that English does. In other words, no transfer effects are evident when the L1 position is marked and the L2 position marked, but they appear when the L1 position is unmarked and the L2 marked.

In a subsequent study, Eckman (1981) provides evidence to show that devoicing of English stops in the most marked position (i.e. word finally) occurs in learners whose L1s, like English, include voicing. Cantonese learners, for instance, sometimes say 'pick' for 'pig'. This suggests, as Eckman acknowledges, that the devoicing of final stops is a 'natural' phenomenon. In the case of the German learners, therefore, the transfer may be reinforcing what is a universal tendency—a point we take up later when we consider developmental constraints on transfer.

In order to explain how markedness affects transfer, Eckman advances the *Markedness Differential Hypothesis*:

> Those areas of difficulty that a second language learner will have can be predicted on the basis of a comparison of the native language (NL) and the target language (TL) such that:
> (a) those areas of the TL that are different from the NL and are relatively more marked than in the NL will be difficult;
> (b) the degree of difficulty associated with those aspects of the TL that are different and more marked than in the NL corresponds to the relative degree of markedness associated with those aspects;
> (c) those areas of the TL that are different from the NL but are not relatively more marked than the NL will not be difficult.
> (Eckman 1977: 321)

The notion of 'markedness' is defined typologically; that is, an area (X) is to be considered relatively more marked than some other area (Y), if cross-linguistically X implies the presence of Y, but Y does not imply the presence of X. An example is found in the comparison of voiced and voiceless stops in English and German discussed above. The Markedness Differential Hypothesis constitutes an attempt to reformulate the CAH to take account of markedness factors. As Eckman (1985) points out, it differs from the CAH in a number of important ways: it seeks to explain (1) not only where learning difficulty will occur, but also the relative degree of difficulty; (2) where differences between the native and target languages will not result in difficulty; and (3) why certain structures are typically acquired before other structures. As such it constitutes a much more powerful theory.

One problem with work involving markedness is the vagueness of the concept. Eckman (1985: 306) acknowledges this by admitting that 'one area in which more research is needed is in defining markedness relations'. The concept is characterized by a fuzziness that sometimes makes it difficult to determine which features are marked in relation to others. This is, in part, the result of differences in the linguistic descriptions and shifts in the linguistic theories upon which claims regarding the degree of markedness of specific linguistic properties rest. One way in which greater precision can be given to the concept is by defining it with reference to 'native speakers' own perceptions of the structure of their language' (Kellerman 1977). Thus, instead of determining markedness through reference to some linguistic description or theory, as was the case in the studies discussed in this section, it can be determined by asking native speakers whether they perceive specific features as 'infrequent, irregular, semantically or structurally opaque, or in any other way exceptional' (Kellerman 1983: 117). We now turn to Kellerman's work on markedness, or, as he calls it, *prototypicality*.

4 Prototypicality

In a series of papers, Kellerman (1977; 1978; 1979; 1986; 1989) sought to demonstrate that learners have perceptions of the structure of their own language, treating some structures as potentially non-transferable and others as potentially transferable, and that these perceptions influence what they actually transfer. The majority of the studies that Kellerman carried out to test this hypothesis have examined lexico-semantics. Unlike the research reported in the previous section, which was based on analyses of learner language, Kellerman's studies make use of native speakers' intuitions regarding their L1.

The best known of Kellerman's studies is the 'breken' study (Kellerman 1978). This study had two stages. In the first stage, native speakers of Dutch were asked to sort seventeen sentences containing the verb 'breken' (see Table 8.4) into groups so that the sentences in each group were similar in meaning. Kellerman then examined the number of times a given pair of sentences were placed in the same group. A multidimensional scaling analysis was carried out to investigate the 'dimensions' of the 'semantic space' occupied by 'breken'. Kellerman (1979) reports two major dimensions, which he labelled 'core/non-core' and 'concrete/abstract'. In the second stage of the study, Kellerman asked 81 Dutch students of English in their first and third years at university to say which of the 17 sentences containing 'breken' they would translate using the English verb 'break'. There were clear differences in the percentage of students prepared to translate each sentence. For example, whereas 81 per cent considered 'hij brak zijn been' (= he broke his leg) translatable only 9 per cent identified 'sommige arbeiders hebben de staking gebroken' (= some workers have broken the strike) as translatable. Kellerman found that the rank order for the 'transferability' of the 17 sentences correlated poorly with the 'concrete/abstract' rank order derived from native speaker intuitions. However, it correlated strongly and significantly with the 'core/non-core' order. This led Kellerman (1979: 51) to conclude that native speakers' intuitions about semantic space can be used to predict transferability, at least for the meanings of 'breken' and also that 'the most important factor is "coreness".' It should be noted that Kellerman's results could not have been predicted on the basis of a contrastive analysis, as the learners clearly resisted transferring 'brekens' that had exact equivalents in English.

	Dutch	English
1	Hij brak zijn been.	He broke his leg.
2	't Kopje brak.	The cup broke.
3	Na't ongeluk is hij 'n gebroken man geworden.	After the accident, he became a broken man.
4	Zij brak zijn hart.	She broke his heart.
5	De golven braken op de rotsen.	The waves broke on the rocks.
6	De lichtstralen breken in het water.	The light rays refract in the water.
7	Dankzij 'n paar grapjes, was 't ijs eindelijk gebroken.	Thanks to a couple of jokes, the ice was finally broken.
8	Hij brak zijn woord.	He broke his word.
9	De man brak zijn eed.	The man broke his oath.
10	'Nood breekt wet.'	'Necessity breaks law' (a saying).
11	Zij brak 't wereldrecord.	She broke the world record.
12	Zijn val werd door 'n boom gebroken.	His fall was broken by a tree.
13	Zijn stem brak toen hij 13 was.	His voice broke when he was 13.
14	Sommige arbeiders hebben de staking gebroken.	Some workers have broken the strike.
15	Welk land heeft de wapenstilstand gebroken?	Which country has broken the ceasefire?
16	Het ondergrondse verzet werd gebroken.	The underground resistance was broken.
17	n' spelletje zou de middag enigszins breken.	A game would break up the afternoon a bit.

Table 8.4:   Sentences with 'breken' ranked according to coreness (prototypicality) (adapted from Kellerman 1979: 49)

In an extension of the 'breken' study, Kellerman (1979) asked 291 learners of English (including the 81 subjects in the study described above), who ranged from twelve-year-olds in their second year of English to third year university students, to assess the translatability of nine of the 17 'breken' sentences. He found that the rank orders for the different groups of learners were 'remarkably consistent' and concluded that 'the effects of teaching, learning and growing older do not significantly alter learners' beliefs about the *relative* transferability of the "brekens"' (1979: 52). Kellerman's study, therefore, suggests that learners' perceptions of what is transferable are not influenced by their L2 proficiency, but clearly this needs further investigation.

The concepts of 'coreness' and 'markedness' are obviously related, which Kellerman (1983) acknowledges. In this later paper, he refers to 'psycholinguistic markedness' in recognition of the importance he attaches to native speakers' *perceptions* of the structure of their own language. In a further terminological switch, Kellerman (1986) refers to prototypicality to label the same basic idea. He draws on work on 'semantic prototypes' in cognitive psychology, citing Coleman and Kay (1981):

> a semantic prototype associates a word or phrase with a prelinguistic cognitive schema or image ... speakers are equipped with an ability to judge the degree with which an object (or ... the internal representation thereof) matches this prototype schema or image.

Kellerman suggests that the prototypical meaning of a lexical item, such as 'breken', is that which a dictionary gives as the primary meaning of the item.

The bulk of Kellerman's empirical work has concerned lexico-semantics—the early 'breken' study and the later 'eye' study (Kellerman 1986), for example. However, one study has also examined a syntactical structure, conditionals. Kellerman (1989) provides evidence to show that advanced Dutch learners of L2 English are likely to produce errors of this kind:

> * If it would rain, they would cancel the concert in Damrosch Park (= If it rained they would cancel the concert in Damrosch Park).

despite the fact that Dutch makes use of equivalent verb forms in main and subordinate clauses to English. Kellerman suggests that the failure to transfer the Dutch verb forms is the result of two tendencies. One is the learners' resistance to transferring a marked form. In this case, markedness is associated with the idea of a 'semantically transparent grammar'. It is more transparent to say 'would rain' than 'rained' because the verb is explicitly marked for future time. The second tendency is that of symmetry—the attempt to match the verb forms in the main and subordinate clauses. Kellerman points out that the same tendencies are also evident in both standard and non-standard varieties of the target language (English), suggesting that there is 'an interaction between natural tendencies and the native language' (1989: 111). This, he speculates, may explain why fossilization occurs.

A number of points emerge from Kellerman's work on prototypicality. The first is that it is possible to provide a clear operational definition of 'markedness' or 'prototypicality' by making use of native speakers' judgements of 'similarity'. The second is that learners have perceptions about what is transferable from their L1 and act in accordance with these perceptions. The third is that these perceptions reflect learners' ideas about what is prototypical or semantically transparent in their L1. Kellerman (1983) suggests that learners prize 'reasonableness in language' and 'attempt to keep their L2s transparent' (1983: 129). L1 structures that they perceive to be working against this principle—such as idioms that are highly metaphorical or grammatical structures where meanings are not overtly encoded—are not transferred. Finally, Kellerman has shown that learners' perceptions regarding the translatability of L1 items is not influenced by their experience with the L2.

While Kellerman's work has gone a long way to teasing out the nature of the constraints on positive transfer, a few words of caution are in order. With the exception of the study on conditionals, Kellerman's research has been based on the elicitation of native speakers' intuitions regarding the similarity and translatability of decontextualized sentences. Kellerman (1986) justifies this by pointing out that corpora of spontaneous speech are unlikely to supply the crucial data needed to test hypotheses. The weakness of such an approach, which Kellerman acknowledges, is that we do not know to what extent learners' judgements about what can be done accurately reflect what they actually do when using the L2. It is perhaps also wise to exercise caution about equating 'translatability' with 'transferability'. In Chapter 4 we examined a number of studies which show that differences in L1 transfer occur depending on whether the task requires translation or some other kind of performance. It does not follow that learners are prepared to make the same use of their L1 in natural speech as they are in translation.

Kellerman's research raises an important question; what kind and how much evidence do learners need before they will accept non-prototypical elements, present in their L1, into their interlanguages? This is a crucial question because it concerns how learners overcome the kind of constraints on positive transfer that Kellerman has identified. However, as Kellerman (1986) notes there are, as yet, no clear answers.

5 Language distance and psychotypology

We now turn to consider another constraint on L1 transfer—the 'distance' between the native and the target languages. Distance can be viewed as both a linguistic phenomenon (i.e. by establishing the degree of actual linguistic difference between two languages) or a psycholinguistic phenomenon (i.e. by determining what learners *think* is the degree of difference between their native language and the target language). Kellerman (1977) used the term *psychotypology* to refer to learners' perceptions about language distance.

There is substantial evidence to indicate that the actual distance between the native and the target languages acts as a constraint on transfer. The importance of this factor is reflected in the different amounts of time which the Foreign Service Institute in the United States allocates to courses aimed at achieving a high level of proficiency in different languages (for example, 20 weeks for French as opposed to 44 for Serbo-Croatian). Similarly, the British Foreign Service pays different rates of language proficiency allowance according to a scale of difficulty in learning different groups of languages.

Language distance can affect L2 learning either through positive transfer or through negative transfer. Corder (1978b; 1981a: 101) chooses to emphasize positive transfer, arguing:

> ... other things being equal (e.g. motivation and access to data etc.), the mother tongue acts differentially as a facilitating agency. Where the mother tongue is formally similar to the target language the learner will pass more

rapidly along the developmental continuum (or some parts of it), than where it differs.

It is likely, however, that language distance is a factor in both positive and negative transfer.

Evidence for this claim comes from the research conducted in Finland on the acquisition of English by Swedish-speaking and Finnish-speaking Finns (see Sjoholm 1979; Ringbom 1976; 1978; and 1987). Finland constitutes an ideal setting for testing the effects of language distance. Whereas 93 per cent of the population speak Finnish as their mother tongue, a language distant from English, 6 to 7 per cent speak Swedish, a language much closer to English. Both groups consider themselves to belong to the same culture, however. Sjoholm, Ringbom, and their co-researchers have been able to show that Swedish-speaking Finns enjoy a substantial learning advantage over Finnish-speaking Finns. For example, Sundquist (1986) found that Swedish-speaking Finns did as well in reading comprehension tests after one and a half years as Finnish-speaking Finns did after three and a half. Interestingly, however, there is evidence to suggest that, contrary to the predictions of the CAH, the Finnish-speaking Finns often make fewer errors, i.e. they manifest less negative transfer. Sjoholm (1976), for instance, found fewer L1-based errors in Finnish-speaking university students than in the Swedish speakers. Furthermore, Ringbom (1978) was able to show that both the Swedish- and Finnish-speaking groups (both of whom are bilingual in the two languages) were much more likely to transfer word morphology from Swedish than from Finnish. Language switch was entirely from Swedish and word blends were almost always Swedish-English. In other words, whereas the Finnish speakers avoided transferring elements from their L1, preferring instead to fall back on their first L2 (Swedish), the Swedish speakers did transfer elements from their L1 but avoided doing so from their first L2 (Finnish).

Kellerman (1977) has claimed that learners possess a psychotypology (a set of perceptions about language distance), and that it is this—rather than actual distance—that triggers or constrains transfer. Learners form 'projections' about what can be transferred on the basis of their beliefs as to whether the native and target languages are the 'same'—either in terms of 'linguistic detail' or 'in very general terms'. On the basis of these projections, learning decisions, or 'conversions', are made.

An extension of the 'breken' study reported in the previous section provides support for the idea of a psychotypology. Kellerman compared Dutch learners' judgements regarding the translatability of the 'brekens' into L2 German (a language close to Dutch) with their judgements regarding their translatability into L2 English (a language more distant from Dutch). The results showed that, in general, whereas they accepted the sentences in German, they sometimes rejected them in English. These results demonstrate a clear effect for perceived language distance.

Further evidence for the role of pyschotypology comes from Singleton's (1987) case study of Philip, an English-speaking learner of French. Philip displayed a high level of communicative efficiency in French, despite the fact that he had minimal opportunities to learn it. Singleton provides evidence to show that he borrowed extensively from his known languages (Latin, Spanish, and Irish, as well as English). Philip utilized Romance sources (i.e. those that were close to French) and, furthermore, was often able to attribute the forms he borrowed to a particular language. He demonstrated well-informed notions about which languages would assist him most in learning French. It would seem, then, that learners do have clearly defined perceptions regarding the similarities and differences between languages.

Kellerman (1979) argues that learners' psychotypology is not fixed. Rather, it is revised as they obtain more information about the target language. Thus, Dutch learners of German may start out with the assumption that the target language is very similar to their mother tongue, but later on come to adjust this perception as they recognize the many differences. Kellerman comments:

> Thus experience affects the provisional typology the learner is building up. This means that at any given moment certain NL (native language) features will be available for transfer to the given TL (target language), and others will not be (1979: 40).

It follows that L1 items are not perceived as inherently 'neutral' (and so available for transfer) or 'specific' (and so not available for transfer).

According to Kellerman, learners' psychotypologies interact with their intuitive feel for prototypicality, which, it should be remembered, does not appear to change with developing proficiency. Prototypicality determines what learners are prepared to risk transferring. Their psychotypology determines what is actually transferred in performance. On the basis of the perceived distance between the native and target languages, learners decide whether to go ahead and transfer those items that they perceive to be prototypical and, therefore, potentially transferable. This interaction between psychotypology and prototypicality results in an extremely complex process, especially as learners' psychotypologies change with experience.

6 Developmental factors

The constraints that developmental factors impose on L1 transfer will be considered with reference to (1) the extent to which transfer is evident at different levels of development, and (2) the complex interplay between natural principles of L2 acquisition and transfer.

The learner's general level of development

One way of looking at interlanguage is as a *restructuring continuum* (Corder 1978a). That is, the starting point of L2 acquisition is the learner's L1, which is gradually replaced by the target language as acquisition proceeds. Such a view suggests that transfer will be more evident in the early than the later stages of development. This is what Taylor (1975) found when he compared the proportions of transfer errors and developmental errors (such as overgeneralization) produced by Spanish-speaking students of L2 English. The students in less advanced classes were more likely to make translation errors that reflected their L1 than were students in more advanced classes, who produced more overgeneralization errors.

Further support for a relationship between the learner's general level of development and the presence or absence of transfer comes from studies of L2 phonology. Major (1986), for instance, found that phonological transfer was especially evident in the earlier stages of development. Wenk's (1986) study of French learners' acquisition of L2 English rhythm also lends support to a restructuring view of interlanguage. Wenk characterizes French rhythm as 'trailer-timed' and English as 'leader-timed'. In the former, the accented syllable is towards the end of a rhythmic group, it is lengthened, and there is no increase in loudness; unaccented syllables are relatively tense and vowels are only weakly centralized. In the latter, the accented syllable is towards the beginning of a rhythmic group, it manifests only variable lengthening, but there is an increase in loudness; in accented syllables the vowels are lax but strongly centralized. Figure 8.2 shows the three stages of development that Wenk found in French-English interlanguage. Beginner learners simply transfer trailer-timed rhythm into English. Intermediate learners seem to produce a kind of hybrid rhythm, with features of both trailer-timing and leader-timing. Advanced learners exhibit standard English leader-timed rhythm. Wenk points out the crucial items are cognates like 'Japan', 'command', and 'police', where the accent falls on the final syllable in both the L1 and L2. Such items would seem to lend themselves to transfer, but Wenk found that they were among the items judged least 'native' in a group of intermediate learners and argues that this reflects the 'transitional rhythmic grouping' found at stage 2.

However, although such evidence strongly suggests that learners gradually restructure their interlanguage by replacing L1 features with L2 features, caution is needed. Not all errors in early interlanguage are traceable to transfer—many are intralingual and resemble those found in L1 acquisition. This is as true for phonology as it is for grammar (see Wode's (1980) account of the acquisition of L2 English phonology by four German children discussed below).

Also, some errors, clearly attributable to L1 influence, only emerge at later stages of development. Kellerman (1983), for example, points out that trans-

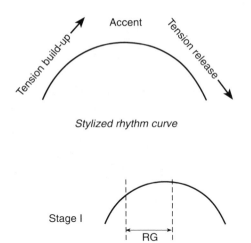

Stylized rhythm curve

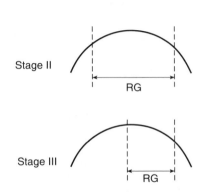

Figure 8.2: *Three stages of development in the acquisition of L2 English rhythm by French learners (Wenk 1986)*

fer errors involving pronominal copies in relative clauses can only occur when the learner is at a sufficiently advanced stage of development to produce relative clauses. Klein (1986: 27) also argues that 'the possibilities of transfer increase as knowledge of the second language increases'. Bhardwaj (1986) illustrates this in a detailed study of an adult learner of L2 English. This learner was unable to express his Punjabi conception of location until he had acquired some idea of the meaning of words like 'up', 'down' and 'on', and had also developed the linguistic means to make these elements the head of definite noun phrases. Only then did the influence of L1 Punjabi appear in phrases like 'the up', 'the down', etc.

Nor can it be assumed that transfer errors which appear at an early stage of development are subsequently eliminated. Some transfer errors that appear at an initial stage continue to manifest themselves in advanced learners. Bohn and Flege (1992), for instance, found that German learners of L2 English failed to develop target-like categories for vowels that were similar but not identical to vowels in their L1, perhaps because 'category formation is blocked by equivalence classification' (1992: 156). Finally, as Odlin (1989) points out in his discussion of Taylor's study, it is necessary to consider the facilitating effects of transfer as well as negative transfer. It seems reasonable to assume that advanced learners will be in a better position to take advantage of similar L1 material—such as cognate vocabulary—than beginners.

Interlanguage is clearly not a restructuring continuum. Although some aspects of L2 development, such as rhythm, may reflect the gradual replacement of L1 by target-language features, other aspects do not. In some cases, transfer is only evident in the later stages of development, while in others early transfer is never eliminated.

Natural principles of language acquisition

There is growing evidence to suggest that the L1 and developmental factors work together in determining the course of interlanguage—or, to put it another way, 'transfer is selective along the developmental axis' (Zobl 1980a). This selectivity is evident in a number of ways: (1) the effects of the L1 only become evident when the learner has reached a stage of development that makes transfer possible, (2) development may be retarded when a universal transitional structure arising naturally in early interlanguage corresponds to an L1 structure, and (3) development may be accelerated when an early transitional structure is not reinforced by the corresponding L2 structure.

A number of studies show that the influence of the L1 is developmentally constrained in the sense that it only occurs when the learner has reached a stage of development that provides a 'crucial similarity measure' (Wode 1976). Wode (1976; 1978; 1980) illustrates how this works. In the case of negation, for instance, the children that he studied initially manifested the universal pattern of development (see Chapter 3), but when they learnt that the negative particle could follow the verb 'be' or an auxiliary/modal verb in English, as in German, they assumed that it could also follow a main verb, as it does in German but not in English. In other words, when confronted with evidence that L2 negation worked in the same way as L1 negation, they assumed that the two languages were completely identical in this structure. A similar pattern of development has been observed in the acquisition of L2 English by other learners whose L1 possesses post-verbal negation (for example, Norwegian—see Ravem 1968), but has not been observed in learners whose L1s have other ways of conveying negation—for example, Japanese (Milon 1974), Chinese (Huang 1970), or Spanish (Cazden et al. 1975). Wode (1978) found further evidence for developmentally constrained L1 transfer in interrogatives. He concluded that L2 learners make use of L1 syntactical knowledge in systematic ways, depending on the formal properties of the structures involved. He admits, though, that the exact nature of the 'crucial similarity measure' is not clear.

The notion of 'developmental transfer' is also applicable to L2 phonology. Wode (1980) found that L2 phonological systems are acquired 'through the grid of the learner's L1 system' (1980: 129). Thus, elements of the L2 that are sufficiently similar to elements in the learner's L1 repertoire will be substituted by L1 elements to begin with. However, L2 elements that fall outside these 'crucial similarity measures' are not replaced with L1 elements, but instead undergo autonomous development, similar to that observed in L1 acquisition. Wode also notes that some elements appear to pose no learning difficulty even when there is no equivalent L1 element. What is missing is precise information about the conditions under which L1 transfer is activated. As Leather and James (1991) conclude in their detailed survey of studies of L2 speech acquisition, only 'preliminary results' are available.

There is also the possibility that errors can be doubly determined—that is, reflect both 'naturalness' factors and L1 influence. Hatch (1983a) identifies a number of 'naturalness' factors that are independent of the L1, such as how salient a feature is to the L2 learner and how transparent the relationship between a particular form and meaning is. In a similar vein, Andersen (1983a) also advances the view that:

> Transfer can only function in conjunction with operating principles that guide language learners and users in their choice of linguistic forms to express the intended meaning (1983a: 180).

These principles (considered in greater detail in the next chapter) affect learning difficulty and, thereby, the order and sequence of development in both L1 and L2 acquisition.

Hatch argues that both naturalness and L1 transfer are at work in phonology and morphology, but that at higher levels of language—syntax and discourse—naturalness factors may predominate. Some of the clearest examples of 'doubly-determined' errors, however, are to be found in L2 syntax. Cazden et al. (1975) noted that the early 'no + verb' negatives observed in the speech of their Spanish-speaking learners cannot be attributed to L1 transfer, even though Spanish has the same negative pattern. This is because such negatives are found in all learners, irrespective of the pattern in their L1. Cazden et al. also noted that the 'no + verb' pattern persisted in the interlanguage of their learners longer than was the case with other learners whose L1s did not have this pattern. They concluded that when a developmental pattern coincides with an L1 pattern, progress may be hindered.

Finally, the L1 has also been shown to have a facilitative effect when there is a lack of correspondence between the L1 pattern and a natural developmental pattern. Hammarberg (1979) re-analyses the data from Hyltenstam (1977) to show that, although the original conclusion (i.e. learners with different language backgrounds go through the same stages of development in acquiring Swedish negation) holds true, some learners progressed through these stages more rapidly than others and that this could be explained by their language background. Thus, English-speaking learners, whose L1 has post-verb negation, appeared to miss out the first stage (pre-verb negation). As Kellerman (1987) puts it, the L1 can provide 'a leg-up along the developmental ladder'.

It is clear that an acceptable theory of transfer must take account of how learners' previous L1 knowledge interacts with the linguistic and cognitive principles responsible for the universal properties of interlanguage development. The relative strength of contributions from these two sources also needs to be determined. It is probably true to say that current work in transfer treats the linguistic and cognitive principles as primary and L1 knowledge as secondary. Gass (1983), for instance, concludes her study of pronoun retention (see page 303) by stating that 'in considering the relationship between NL facts and language universals, the latter were found to play the leading role' (1983: 79). However, such a conclusion may not be valid for all levels of language, nor even for all aspects of syntax. Certainly, where phonology is concerned, there are grounds for considering L1 knowledge as primary, as suggested by Wode's and Wenk's studies.

A theory of transfer must also specify in precise terms how and when the two sources interact. One attempt to do this is Andersen (1983a). Using data from a number of earlier studies, he tests out a number of constraints on transfer, including all those considered above. He concludes that although it is clear that transfer interacts with natural acquisitional principles, there is still 'leakage' (i.e. it is not possible to fully predict when, how, and to what extent transfer will take place). We are still a long way from a fully 'developmental' theory of transfer.

Summary

We have now examined six general constraints on L1 transfer:

1 Language level

Although it is difficult to quantify the extent of transfer in the different language levels, there are some grounds for claiming that transfer is more conspicuous at the levels of phonology, lexis, and discourse than grammar, possibly because learners have a more developed metalingual awareness of grammar.

2 Sociolinguistic factors

It has been suggested that when learners attend to external norms, as they are likely to in classroom settings, transfer will be impeded. However, learners may also make use of L1 forms in their careful style if they have a strong social motivation to do so.

3 *Markedness*

There is some evidence to suggest that learners are ready to transfer unmarked L1 forms, but resist transferring L1 marked forms; however, not all the research points clearly in this direction. Eckman's Markedness Differential Hypothesis constitutes an improvement on the Contrastive Analysis Hypothesis by indicating how markedness interacts with linguistic difference to determine when transfer will and will not take place. Markedness, however, remains a somewhat ill-defined concept.

4 *Prototypicality*

Kellerman tapped native speakers' intuitions to determine which meanings of a lexical item are unmarked or 'prototypical'. Learners resist transferring non-prototypical meanings.

5 *Language distance and psychotypology*

The actual distance between languages affects positive transfer; learners find it easier to learn an L2 that is similar to their own language. However, perceived distance may be more important than actual distance. Kellerman suggests that whereas prototypicality influences what learners are prepared to risk transferring, their psychotypology (which changes as their proficiency develops) governs what they actually transfer.

6 *Developmental factors*

Whereas some researchers (for example, Taylor 1975) have claimed that negative transfer is more evident in beginners, other researchers have argued that learners may need to reach a certain stage of development before transfer of some L1 properties becomes possible. In general, except possibly where phonology is concerned, the evidence does not support the claim that interlanguage constitutes a restructuring continuum. Transfer interacts with natural principles of L2 acquisition, sometimes occurring early on and sometimes later. It can both retard and accelerate natural development.

The research that has investigated these constraints has helped us to understand what is transferred and what is not and also when transfer takes place and when it does not. However, as yet there is no overall theory of transfer that can account for how these various constraints interact.

Towards a theory of first language transfer

It should be clear from the preceding section that a theory of transfer is likely to also be a general theory of L2 acquisition, in that the role of the L1 cannot easily be separated from other factors that influence development. The theory, then, must account for how L1 knowledge interacts with input in shaping the learner's interlanguage system and also how both L1 and interlanguage knowledge are drawn on in L2 production.

An important distinction—not always made in discussions of transfer—is between transfer in L2 communication and transfer in L2 learning. This distinction mirrors the distinction we made in Chapter 7 between the role that input plays in comprehension and the role it plays in acquisition. There we noted that input that works for comprehension may not always work for acquisition. According to Kasper (1984b) and Færch and Kasper (1986b), transfer in communication involves the use of the L1 to either receive incoming messages (reception) or to process output (production). Transfer in learning occurs when the learner uses the L1 in the attempt to develop hypotheses about L2 rules. There are, therefore, a number of possibilities; one is that transfer is primarily a characteristic of communication, a second is that it is primarily a feature of learning (i.e. learners draw directly on their L1 in constructing their interlanguages), while a third is that both communication and learning transfer are significant and inter-related aspects of L2 acquisition.

Communication transfer

There is general acceptance that transfer in communication is common. Minimalist accounts of transfer acknowledge the role played by the L1 in communication while denying any role or any substantial role for the L1 in interlanguage hypothesis construction (i.e. in learning). Corder's (1983) view of transfer is that it is primarily a communication strategy, which he terms *borrowing*. He emphasizes that borrowing is 'a *performance* phenomenon, not a *learning* process, a feature, therefore, of language use and not of language structure' (1983: 92). It is invoked in order to compensate for deficiencies in the interlanguage system. He suggests that the term 'transfer' is, in fact, inappropriate for this use of the L1 as 'nothing is being transferred from anywhere to anywhere'. Corder acknowledges that the occurrence of borrowing is not the same for all learners, but is rather 'a feature of the perception of the relationship between first and second languages' (1983: 93).

It should be noted, however, that not all communication transfer need be strategic in nature. Færch and Kasper (1986b; 1989) distinguish three types of production transfer.[8] In the case of strategic transfer, the learner gives focal attention to a planning problem and to its solution, which may involve the use of the L1. This is Corder's 'borrowing'. Subsidiary transfer occurs when there is no focal awareness of either the production problem or of the transferred L1 knowledge, although awareness may develop later as a result of monitoring. Automatic transfer takes place when the learner makes use of a highly automatized L1 subroutine. In this case, attention is completely diverted to other aspects in the production process. Færch and Kasper (1989) illustrate how these different types of production transfer can be distinguished by studying 'signals of uncertainty' (for example, pausing, sighing, laughing).

Communication transfer involves both production and comprehension transfer. The former has received more attention than the latter, perhaps because it is easier to identify in learner performance. However, Ringbom (1992) has pointed out that 'transfer is at least as important in comprehension as it is in production' (1992: 88). He provides evidence from Swedish-speaking Finns and Finnish-speaking Finns to show that the advantage which the former derive from the closer proximity of their L1 to English enables them to outperform the latter in both reading and listening comprehension. He suggests that the L1 constitutes 'potential knowledge' that can be drawn on more easily in decoding, which involves form-to-function mapping, than in encoding, which involves function-to-form mapping. Ringbom also acknowledges constraints on transfer in both comprehension and production, arguing that in both 'the closer the perceived distance, the more (positive) the transfer is' (1992: 106).

Transfer in communication is motivated by the learner's desire to comprehend or produce messages, but it may also have an effect on the process of hypothesis construction and testing, which many scholars see as central to interlanguage development. In other words, transfer in communication may lead to transfer in learning. Corder (1983) explains how this can happen:

> ... persistent communicatively successful borrowing works backwards, as it were, and the successfully borrowed forms are eventually incorporated into the interlanguage grammar, both the correct and the incorrect (1983: 94).

Ringbom (1992) suggests that it is transfer in comprehension that is most likely to induce a change in the learner's mental grammar. Such a view accords with theories that give centrality to comprehensible input in L2 acquisition. While acknowledging the legitimacy of Ringbom's claim, we should also recognize, as claimed by the comprehensible output hypothesis (see Chapter 7), that L2 output and, therefore, transfer in production can also contribute significantly to interlanguage development.

Learning transfer

Researchers like Corder seek to explain transfer entirely in terms of communication; it is either a performance phenomenon or it is learnt as a product of repeated performance. They reject the idea that learners transfer directly from their L1 into their interlanguages. Such a position is difficult to maintain, however. For one thing, there is evidence that particular transfer errors occur in whole populations with the same L1. It is far-fetched to suggest that all these learners engaged persistently in borrowing and as a result learnt the L1 structure. It is also not clear how communication transfer can account for the fossilization of certain L1 influenced structures in learners' interlanguages of the kind that Kellerman (1989) identified in advanced Dutch learners of English.[9]

Thus, whereas some instances of transfer can be put down to the use of a communication strategy, it is also necessary to recognize a more direct role for the L1 in L2 acquisition (i.e. transfer in learning). The general view, well represented by Schachter's (1983) 'new account of transfer', is that direct learning transfer regularly occurs and that it can best be explained within a cognitive rather than in a behaviourist framework. Transfer is conceptualized as one 'strategy' operating within a general process of hypothesis construction and testing.

Schachter argues that learners construct and reconstruct hypotheses by means of inductive inferencing (scanning data, observing regularities, and generalizing) and deductive inferencing (testing hypotheses by looking in the first instance for confirming evidence and subsequently for disconfirming evidence). She suggests that the learner begins with the concept of a 'universe of hypotheses' (i.e. the hypotheses that might be worth testing). One source which the learner draws on is the L1. Schachter also notes that the universe expands and contracts during the course of learning, thus allowing for the utilization of the L1 at different stages of development. The hypotheses in a universe fall into natural groupings, called domains, which Schachter suggests correspond to abstract linguistic categories such as clause and phrase types. Domains can vary in size; for example, the general domain of 'main verbs' can be broken down into the narrower domains of 'main verbs with complements' and 'main verbs without complements'. Learning takes place when the learner chooses a domain and samples hypotheses within it, testing them out against the input. The L1, as part of the learner's existing knowledge, influences both the choice of domain and the specific hypothesis to be tested; it can contribute to both correct and incorrect hypotheses. Schachter also acknowledges that constraints, such as the distance between the native and target languages, affect both how and how much the L1 is drawn on.

A framework for explaining first language transfer

Figure 8.3 provides a framework that incorporates both communication and learning transfer.[10] It proposes the following:

1 The L1 system is utilized by both comprehension and production mechanisms. In both cases, there are constraints that govern when transfer takes place.

2 The interlanguage system is also utilized in the processes of comprehending and receiving messages.

3 The L1 system is utilized in the hypothesis construction responsible for interlanguage development. Again, constraints exist on when transfer takes place.

4 Comprehensible input, including that input which has been made comprehensible with the help of L1 knowledge, serves as a major source of
information for hypothesis construction.
5 L2 output, including that output which has been made comprehensible
with the help of L1 knowledge, may be used for hypothesis construction.

The 'constraints' referred to in Figure 8.3 are those discussed in the previous
section of this chapter. As we have already noted, the precise ways in which
they delimit the use of the L1 in comprehension, production, and hypothesis
construction are not yet fully understood.

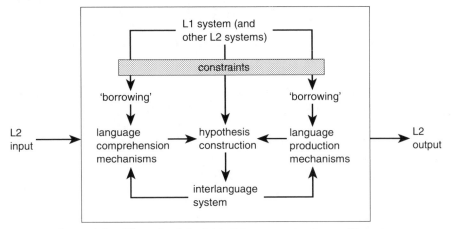

Figure 8.3:   The role of the L1 in L2 communication and learning

Conclusion: problems in the study of transfer

Over the last twenty or so years there have been considerable advances made
in the study of L1 transfer, not least in the methods used to investigate it. In
early studies, there was a tendency to claim that any L2 error that showed a
similarity to an L1 feature was the result of transfer. Jackson (1981), for instance, argued that non-inverted *wh-* questions (such as 'How I do this?')
were indicative of the L1 influence in Punjabi-speaking learners of English. As
we have seen, such conclusions are not warranted unless it can be shown that
these errors are not 'developmental' (i.e. do not occur in the interlanguages of
all learners). There is plenty of evidence that non-inverted *wh-* questions are
universal features of L2 acquisition. More recent studies have avoided such
misjudgements by carrying out learner comparisons (comparing the output
of learners with L1s that differ with regard to the presence or absence of particular linguistic features). Another promising approach, illustrated in Eckman (1977) and Gass (1987), involves the bi-directional study of transfer (i.e.
in the case of two languages, x and y, investigating whether a specific feature,
z, is transferred from x to y and also from y to x). Both the crosslinguistic and
the bi-directional approaches not only result in more reliable research but

also provide insights not readily available from the more traditional contrastive approach.

There are still a number of problems faced by transfer researchers, however. We will consider two: (1) the problem of how to distinguish communication and learning transfer, and (2) the problem of how to compare two languages. Neither problem is specific to the study of transfer, of course. All L2 acquisition researchers face the general problem of distinguishing what is strategic—the product of some compensatory strategy—and what is evidence of the learner's L2 knowledge system. Also, comparative linguists and writers of pedagogical grammars have to cope with the theoretical and practical difficulties involved in comparing two languages. Both problems, however, seem quite central to the work of transfer researchers.

In the last section, we saw that it is possible to make a clear theoretical distinction between communication and learning transfer. It is less clear, however, whether these two types of transfer can be distinguished empirically, given that the main data for the study of transfer come from language performance. The problem is acute because, as Kasper points out, 'learners sometimes transfer in want of a better solution even though they consider a given concept non-transferable' (1984b: 20). Thus, not all L1 features found in communication transfer will find their way into the learner's interlanguage. Not surprisingly, most researchers ignore this problem and assume that evidence of transfer in performance (usually production) is also evidence of transfer in learning. One solution lies in collecting introspective data from the learner, as in Poulisse's (1990a) study of communication strategies, which we will consider more fully in the next chapter. In this study, the subjects were invited to comment retrospectively on the strategies they used to describe referents for which they had no available L2 word. They frequently commented on their L1-based strategies without being prompted. Introspective data may also be helpful in identifying instances of avoidance.

Many of the problems that arise in comparing two languages were evident in the early days of contrastive analysis. One was that contrastive analyses generally failed to meet the criteria of descriptive and explanatory adequacy that any description of language must meet. They faced the same challenges found in the study of single languages—how to develop comprehensive descriptions, to what extent the linguistic data should be idealized, and how to cater for the interaction of linguistic subsystems (the influence that one system, say discourse, has on other systems). There was the problem of equivalence—whether it was possible to find a theoretically sound basis for comparing two languages. Sajavaara (1981a) listed the procedures that could be followed: (1) identify linguistic categories common to the two languages and compare how they are realized in each language, (2) search for equivalents of a given category in one language in the other, (3) compare rules or hierarchies of rules in the two languages, (4) examine how a given semantic category is realized in the two languages, and (5) investigate how a given language function is performed in both languages. All of these procedures were used, but there was little agreement about which constituted the optimal method. These problems are perhaps less acute now than earlier, given that less emphasis is placed on preparing comprehensive contrastive analyses and more on the detailed examination of specific linguistic elements. However, even the more focused studies found in current transfer research necessitate some kind of contrastive analysis, so many of the earlier problems continue to arise. It is worth noting, though, that transfer studies can also contribute to linguistic description, Kellerman's (1989) study of conditionals in the L2 English of advanced Dutch learners being a case in point.[11]

As well as the difficulty of quantifying transfer, there is the problem of determining just how significant it is in L2 acquisition. It is now generally accepted that although transfer is an important factor in L2 acquisition, it is not the only factor and often works together with other factors, such as natural principles of language acquisition. For this reason it may not be inappropriate to attempt a precise specification of its contribution or to try to compare its contribution with that of other factors, which was the concern of the early research in the 1970s. More important, perhaps, is to work towards a fuller theoretical understanding of how and when learners draw on their L1. The continued interest in the study of transfer, evident in such publications as Kellerman and Sharwood Smith (1986), Ringbom (1987), Dechert and Raupach (1989), and Odlin (1989), testifies to its importance in L2 acquisition and has contributed substantially to our understanding of how it operates.

No theory of L2 acquisition is complete without an account of L1 transfer. This will become apparent in the next two chapters when we consider a variety of cognitive theories, such as the Competition Model in which the L1 constitutes a major factor, and also theories based on *linguistic universals*. In both, the learner's L1 is a central factor.

Summary

Definitions of transfer

'Transfer' is to be seen as a general cover term for a number of different kinds of influence from languages other than the L2. The study of transfer involves the study of errors (negative transfer), facilitation (positive transfer), avoidance of target language forms, and their over-use.

Contrastive analysis and behaviourism

According to behaviourist theories of learning, the L1 facilitates learning where native- and target-language structures are the same, and results in errors where they are different. The strong form of the contrastive analysis hypothesis (CAH) claims that it is possible to predict when difficulty will occur on the basis of the differences between the native and target languages. Behaviourist views and the strong form of the CAH are no longer considered tenable on the grounds that many errors are not caused by transfer and that many predicted errors do not occur. However, contrastive analysis is still an essential tool in transfer research, particularly if it is supplemented by comparisons of learners with different language backgrounds.

Minimalist positions

The rejection of the CAH led to the advancement of 'minimalist positions' regarding the L1, as reflected in the work of Dulay and Burt, and also to the *Ignorance Hypothesis*, according to which the L1 functions primarily as a communication strategy for filling in gaps in the learner's competence. Minimalist positions underestimate the role of the L1. Even in structural areas such as basic word order, where it has been claimed transfer is almost non-existent, clear evidence for transfer can be found. The ignorance hypothesis is not tenable given the weight of evidence which suggests that direct learning transfer does occur.

Current research

Current research is directed at explaining why target–native language differences sometimes result in transfer and sometimes do not. To this end, a number of constraints on the transferability of items have been identified; the language level, sociolinguistic factors of both a macro and micro nature, linguistic markedness, prototypicality, language distance and the learner's psychotypology, and developmental factors involving universal principles or tendencies in language acquisition. However, although there is clear evidence that these constraints influence when transfer takes place and also what is transferred, little is yet known about how the various factors interact.

Transfer in communication

Current theorizing about transfer takes place within a cognitive framework. It has been suggested that both transfer in communication and transfer in learning take place and, furthermore, that the former can contribute to the latter. However, the L1 can have a direct effect on interlanguage development by influencing the hypotheses that learners construct.

Like any other area of SLA research, work on transfer faces a number of problems, the major one being the difficulty in distinguishing empirically between instances of communication and learning transfer.

Conclusion

Despite these problems, there is now clear evidence that the L1 acts as a major factor in L2 acquisition. One clear advance in transfer research has been the reconceptualization of the influence of the L1; whereas in behaviourist accounts it was seen as an impediment (a cause of errors), in cognitive accounts it is viewed as a resource which the learner actively draws in interlanguage development.

Notes

1 U-shaped behaviour involving transfer in an early stage can also be investigated by means of pseudo-longitudinal studies. These involve the cross-sectional examination of groups of learners with the same L1 but different stages of L2 development. The developmental pattern is evident in the differences between the groups. One difficulty with this approach, however, concerns how to determine what stage of development each learner in the sample has reached. Given that learners can produce the same correct feature at both an early and a late stage of development, this is obviously not an easy task.

2 This example of left-branching in Japanese is taken from Kamimoto et al. (1992: 268).

3 Kellerman (1987) also points out that Dulay and Burt were wrong in their claim that the meanings of 'interference' as used in the work of Haugen and Weinreich on the one hand and in that of the contrastive analysts on the other were distinct. He provides quotations from Haugen (1956) to show that, in fact, Haugen's idea of 'interference' was more or less identical to that of Lado.

4 Ervin-Tripp's claim amounts to the assertion that transfer will be more common in classroom than in naturalistic language learning. This claim is not supported by research, which in fact suggests the opposite, as is clear in the discussion of transfer in relation to social setting on page 317.

5 I am grateful to Kellerman for pointing out to me the problems of measuring the frequency of transfer effects at different language levels.

6 Odlin (1989) also argues that focused learning situations are likely to favour positive transfer.

7 I am grateful to Kellerman for helping to clarify the role of social context in language transfer and, in particular, for pointing out that learners can behave very differently, where transfer is concerned, inside and outside of the classroom.

8 It is also possible to distinguish a number of different types of communication (production) transfer according to 'transfer load'; code-shifting (i.e. the use of an L1 word, phrase or sentence in L2 discourse); foreignizing (i.e. the use of an L1 word in accordance with the L2 sound

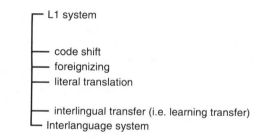

Figure 8.4:   Types of production transfer (Kasper 1984b)

system) and literal translation. Kasper (1984b) suggests that these different types, which seem to apply especially to lexis, can be ordered according to their transfer load as shown in Figure 8.4.

9   Again, I am grateful to Kellerman for pointing out these problems with a communication-based account of transfer.

10   The model suggests that L1 knowledge and interlanguage knowledge are separate. However, Færch and Kasper (1989: 178) rightly point out that 'different linguistic levels may have different types of cognitive representation'. Thus, L1/L2 knowledge may have a co-ordinate representation in the mind of the learner (as is likely for at least part of the lexicon and, perhaps also for phonology) or a compound representation (likely in the case of grammar). The type of representation may also be influenced by the learner's psychotypology.

11   Kellerman (1989) points out that whereas descriptions of English typically insist that 'would' does not appear in the subordinate clause of conditional sentences, there are clear instances of intrusive 'would', as for instance in 'By the time you'd have noticed it, it'd have been too late' (from Wong-Fillmore 1985). Thus, the tendency evident in Dutch learners' English interlanguages is also reflected in at least some (generally unacknowledged) L1 sentences.

Further reading

The best general account of L1 transfer, both because of its extensive coverage of the research and its readability, is T. Odlin, *Language Transfer* (Cambridge University Press, 1989).

A balanced and readable account of the contrastive analysis hypothesis can be found in C. James, *Contrastive Analysis* (Longman, 1980).

H. Ringbom, *The Role of the First Language in Foreign Language Learning* (Multilingual Matters, 1987) provides a good account of the important work carried out with Swedish- and Finnish-speaking Finns.

There are several useful collections of papers on transfer, the most important of which are:

S. Gass and L. Selinker (eds.), *Language Transfer in Language Learning* (Newbury House, 1983).

Kellerman, E. and M. Sharwood Smith (eds.), *Crosslinguistic Influence in Second Language Acquisition* (Pergamon, 1986).

Dechert, H. and M. Raupach (eds.) *Transfer in Production* (Ablex, 1989).

The first of these is particularly valuable to readers beginning their study of transfer, because it includes papers that reflect behaviourist, minimalist, and cognitivist positions.

Of the many papers that have been published in journals, the following is a representative sample, reflecting the key issues discussed in this chapter:

F. Eckman, 'Markedness and the contrastive analysis hypothesis.' *Language Learning* (1977) 27: 315–30.

S. Gass, 'Language transfer and universal grammatical relations.' *Language Learning* (1979) 29: 327–44.

K. Hyltenstam, 'Implicational patterns in interlanguage syntax variation.' *Language Learning* (1977) 27: 383–411.

E. Kellerman, 'Transfer and non-transfer: where are we now.' *Studies in Second Language Acquisition* (1979) 2: 37–57.

J. Schachter, 'An error in error analysis.' *Language Learning* (1974) 24: 205–14.

D. Singleton, 'Mother and other tongue influence on learner French.' *Studies in Second Language Acquisition* (1987) 9: 327–46.

L. White, 'Markedness and second language acquisition.' *Studies in Second Language Acquisition* (1987) 9: 261–86.

H. Zobl, 'Developmental and transfer errors: their common base and (possibly) differential effects on subsequent learning.' *TESOL Quarterly* (1980) 14: 469–79.

In addition, there is a rich literature dealing with pragmatic transfer (see the suggestions for further reading at the end of Chapter 5).

9 Cognitive accounts of second language acquisition

Introduction

In the last chapter we noted that language transfer has been increasingly understood as a cognitive process; that is, L2 learners make strategic use of their L1 in the process of learning the L2, and in the process of understanding and producing messages in the L2. In this chapter, we will examine a number of other accounts of L2 acquisition which adopt a broadly 'cognitivist' stance in the sense that they see language acquisition as a mental process involving the use of strategies that explain how the L2 knowledge system is developed and used in communication.

As we noted in the Introduction to Part Four, a cognitive theory of language acquisition sees linguistic knowledge as no different in kind from other types of knowledge, and views the strategies responsible for its development as general in nature, related to and involved in other kinds of learning. This perspective contrasts with a linguistic theory of L2 acquisition, which treats linguistic knowledge as unique and separate from other knowledge systems, and acquisition as guided by mechanisms that are (in part at least) specifically linguistic in nature. It is, of course, not always possible to classify particular theories of L2 acquisition as exclusively 'cognitive' or 'linguistic', as often both perspectives are drawn on. In fact, the two perspectives are not mutually exclusive, and in all probability, a comprehensive theory of L2 acquisition will need to incorporate elements from both. It is useful to distinguish the two perspectives, however, as they reflect clear epistemological differences (see, for example, the debate between Piaget and Chomsky in Piatelli-Palmarini 1980). This chapter focuses on accounts of L2 acquisition that are broadly cognitive in nature, while the following chapter examines those that are linguistic in orientation.

The bulk of this chapter is organized into two major sections, one dealing with cognitive accounts of L2 learning, and the other with L2 communication. In other words, a distinction is made between theories that explain how learners construct their mental representations of the L2 (i.e. how knowledge of the rules and items that comprise the L2 is developed) and theories that explain how learners employ their knowledge in actual language use (i.e. how L2 comprehension and production is accomplished). This distinction between 'acquisition' and 'procedural ability' is theoretically clear, but as we will see, it becomes blurred in theories that view 'acquisition' as the concomitant of 'use'. Nevertheless, it is a useful tool for surveying the wealth of theorizing that has taken place. Accordingly, we will focus first on how rules and items are acquired before examining aspects of L2 procedural ability.

Linguistic knowledge is traditionally described in terms of rules and items, whether the theory is a cognitive or a linguistic one. However, one school of cognitive psychology has challenged this assumption, arguing that language knowledge is best seen as a network, involving a complex set of interconnections between various units (see McClelland, Rumelhart, and the PDP Research Group 1986). In this theory, therefore, the distinction between 'learning' and 'procedural ability' no longer seems appropriate, as L2 knowledge and use are accounted for together in terms of 'connection strength' rather than separately as rules, items, and processes of language comprehension or production. *Parallel Distributed Processing*, as it is applied to language acquisition, is examined in the final section of this chapter.

The theoretical positions outlined in this chapter should be seen as affording multiple perspectives on what are enormously complex phenomena. The positions often overlap, but not always in ways that can be clearly specified.

Cognitive accounts of second language acquisition

Linguistic accounts of interlanguage are directed at describing learners' competence, conceptualized as an abstract system of rules and items that underlie actual performance. They are concerned with what learners 'know', not with what they 'do'. In contrast, although the cognitive accounts to be considered in this section are still concerned with what the learner 'knows', knowledge is considered to be inseparable from actual use. The focus, therefore, is not on abstract linguistic knowledge, but on the extent to which the learner has achieved mastery over the formal and functional properties of language and the mental processes involved. An assumption of all the theories considered in this section is that 'mastery' is gradable and that there are degrees of 'knowing'—that learners can, for example, *partially* know the rule for subject relativization in English. It is with regard to this notion of 'mastery' that the theories can be seen as cognitive in nature.

A general theoretical framework

A complete synthesis of the various theories and models considered in this section is not possible, as they reflect widely diverging positions regarding both which phenomena are in need of an explanation, and how this can best be provided. However, to give some shape and order to the exposition that follows, a general framework for investigating L2 acquisition will be outlined and an indication given of which parts of this framework the various models might help us to understand.

The theoretical framework, which is shown diagrammatically in Figure 9.1, is a development of Gass (1988). Gass distinguishes (1) apperceived (or noticed) input, (2) comprehended input, (3) intake, and (4) integration. Apperceived input is the first stage of acquisition—a 'passing through of the initial data' (1988: 201). It consists of 'noticing' features in the input as a result of the saliency of the features themselves and of the learner's existing L2 knowledge. Not all apperceived input is comprehended (or contributes to the learner's understanding of message content). Similarly, not all comprehended input becomes intake. As Gass puts it, 'what is comprehended can either feed into the intake component or, alternatively, it may be not used by the learner for anything beyond communication' (1988: 205). Intake, following Chaudron (1985), is seen as 'a *process* which mediates between target language input and the learner's internalized set of rules' (1988: 206). It does not become part of the learner's implicit knowledge system until it has been 'integrated'.

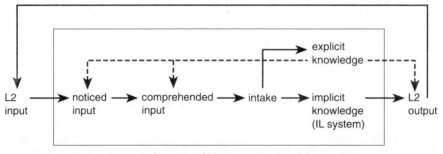

Figure 9.1:   A framework for investigating L2 acquisition

These distinctions have been maintained in Figure 9.1. One additional component is proposed—explicit knowledge. In fact, Gass seems to acknowledge the existence of this when she suggests that some input may be processed and 'put into storage' if it is not yet possible to integrate it into the interlanguage system (1988: 207). This 'storage', it is suggested, takes the form of some kind of explicit representation of L2 items and rules. Explicit knowledge, as we will see later, can contribute to output through monitoring, and also may aid the processes that contribute to intake. Output can influence input through interaction, as suggested in Chapter 7.

The different theoretical positions considered in this chapter address different aspects of this framework. Interlanguage theory (Selinker 1972), with which we will begin, is primarily concerned with implicit L2 knowledge and the strategies that contribute to its development. Models based on the explicit/implicit distinction (for example, Krashen's Monitor Theory), which we turn to next, are primarily concerned with identifying the relationship between these two types of knowledge and how they are used in L2 output.

Variability theories (such as those of Tarone 1983 and Ellis 1985c) provide an account of L2 knowledge in relation to observed L2 output. Variability is seen as the product of both the differential use of explicit and implicit knowledge, and also the heterogeneous nature of implicit knowledge itself. Variability theories that see implicit knowledge in terms of form-function networks (for example, Ellis 1985c) also shed light on the way learners organize their implicit knowledge, as do functionalist grammar accounts of L2 learning (such as those of Klein and Sato). An assumption of both types of theory is that qualitative as well as quantitative changes take place over time, and that the introduction of a new item or rule has repercussions for the whole system. Both the Competition Model (Bates and MacWhinney) and Operating Principles (Andersen) constitute an attempt to specify how input is noticed and interpreted at different stages of development and how this information is then organized as implicit knowledge. The Multidimensional Model (Meisel, Clahsen, and Pienemann) focuses on the relationship between implicit knowledge and output by indicating the strategies which have to be mastered in order to produce different structures. Finally, skill-learning models (Anderson and McLaughlin) consider the changes in the way knowledge is represented as a result of the need to use the L2 efficiently in a range of tasks that place different demands on the learner's processing abilities. Some of the models (for example, the Multidimensional Model) also account for variation in the success of individual learners.

What is common to all the theories and models we will examine in this section is that they attempt to explain the learner's representation of L2 knowledge and how this changes over time. The models differ in terms of whether their primary focus is (1) the relationship between input and implicit knowledge, (2) the relationship between explicit and implicit knowledge, (3) the relationship between L2 knowledge (implicit or explicit) and output, and (4) whether they try to account for individual learner differences.

Interlanguage theory

The starting point for any discussion of the mental processes responsible for L2 acquisition is the concept of *interlanguage*, a term coined by Selinker (1972).[1] It is used to refer to both the internal system that a learner has constructed at a single point in time ('an interlanguage') and to the series of interconnected systems that characterize the learner's progress over time ('interlanguage' or 'the interlanguage continuum'). This construct has been subject to both cognitive and linguistic interpretations, but we will be concerned with only the former here.

Interlanguage theory is an appropriate starting point because it was the first major attempt to provide an explanation of L2 acquisition, and many later theories (such as my and Tarone's variability models) were developments of it. Like all theories, it is dynamic, constantly adapting to new information. Early interlanguage theory was informed by the research that investigated learners' errors and the general pattern of L2 development (see Chapters 2 and 3). What follows is a general account of its main premises, considered from a cognitive perspective.

The key questions addressed by interlanguage theory are: (1) What processes are responsible for interlanguage construction? (2) What is the nature of the interlanguage continuum? and (3) What explanation is there for the fact that most learners do not achieve full target language competence?

Processes of interlanguage construction

In the article that first introduced the term 'interlanguage', Selinker (1972) identifies five principal cognitive processes responsible for L2 acquisition:

1 Language transfer (some, but certainly not all, items, rules and subsystems of a learner's interlanguage may be transferred from the first language).
2 Transfer of training (some interlanguage elements may derive from the way in which the learners were taught).
3 Strategies of second language learning (Selinker talks about an 'identifiable approach by the learner to the material to be learned', 1972: 37).
4 Strategies of second language communication ('an identifiable approach by the learner to communication with native speakers of the TL', 1972: 37).
5 Overgeneralization of the target language material (some interlanguage elements are the result of a 'clear overgeneralization' of target language rules and semantic features).

In retrospect, a number of problems with Selinker's list are apparent. It is not clear, for instance, why 'language transfer' and 'overgeneralization' are listed separately from 'learning strategies', as they would both appear to be examples of these. However, the list was a valuable one. It constituted one of the first attempts to specify the mental processes responsible for L2 acquisition, and also served to introduce a number of key distinctions, such as that between 'learning' and 'communication strategies'.

Subsequent work has focused on 'learning strategies', defined more broadly than in Selinker's initial formulation. Selinker, Swain, and Dumas (1975), for instance, identify three central strategies: language transfer, overgeneralization, and simplification on the basis of errors found in the speech of children in a French immersion classroom. These strategies have already received attention; overgeneralization was considered in Chapter 2, simplification in Chapter 3, and transfer in Chapter 8.

At a more general level, interlanguage processes have been discussed in terms of *hypothesis-testing*. Corder (1976), for instance, suggested that learners form hypotheses about the structural properties of the target language on the basis of the input data they are exposed to. In this way, they build a 'hypothetical grammar' which is then tested receptively and productively. Hypotheses are confirmed if learners' interpretations are plausible and their productions accepted without comment or misunderstanding. They are disconfirmed if their understanding is defective and if their output fails to communicate and is corrected. In such cases, learners may restructure their hypotheses, providing they are sufficiently motivated to do so. One of the main problems of such accounts is that it is not clear how learners obtain the linguistic information they need to modify hypotheses during communicative exchanges (see Chapter 7). As we will see in Chapter 10, linguistic theories of interlanguage maintain that hypothesis-testing cannot provide an adequate account of interlanguage development.

The nature of the interlanguage continuum

Cognitive theories of interlanguage postulate that, with the assistance of learning strategies, learners build mental grammars of the L2. These grammars account for performance in the same way as a native-speaker grammar; that is, learners draw on the 'rules' they have constructed to interpret and produce utterances. Interlanguage is said to be systematic because learners behave 'grammatically' in the sense that they draw on the rules they have internalized—a view that casts doubt on the use of the term 'error' itself (Jakobovits 1970; Cook 1971), as learners' utterances are only erroneous with reference to target-language norms, not to the norms of their own grammars.

These mental grammars are perceived as dynamic and subject to rapid change. Thus, the interlanguage continuum consists of a series of overlapping 'grammars'. Each grammar shares some rules with the previously constructed grammar, but also contains some new or revised rules. A rule has the status of a 'hypothesis'. Each grammar or interlanguage is likely to be characterized by competing rules, or, as Corder (1976) puts it, there will be 'several concurrent hypotheses, leading to a set of coexistent approximative systems'. It is this that accounts for systematic variability in learner performance.

One of the outcomes of this view of the interlanguage continuum is that L2 acquisition is characterized not by 'simplification' but by 'complexification'. Each grammar the learner builds is more complex than the one that preceded it. Corder (1977a) has suggested that the learner's starting point is the same as in L1 acquisition: a 'basic' system consisting of lexical items and a few simple rules for sequencing them. This system constitutes the 'initial hypothesis' and may be universal (i.e. all languages, when stripped down, result in the same basic system). It follows that L2 acquisition involves a *recreation* rather than a *restructuring continuum*; that is, the starting point is not the full L1 which is gradually replaced by L2 rules and items, but a simple, reduced system of the L1, which is gradually complexified. Corder suggests that this explains why interlanguage systems manifest universal properties, particularly in the early stages of development (see Chapter 3).

As we will see later, the nature of the learner's 'initial hypothesis' is controversial. If, as Corder suggests, the starting point is the same as in L1 acquisition—a claim that is in itself controversial—then the question arises as to whether this starting point is some remembered early version of the L1, which is complexified through the general process of hypothesis-testing (Corder's position and one that is essentially cognitive), or whether it is the innate knowledge of language which all children bring to the task of learning their L1, as proposed by Chomsky (1965). In essence, this is an argument between a cognitivist and a linguistic explanation of L2 acquisition. In addition, as we saw in Chapter 8, there are grounds for believing that in some aspects of language (for example, phonology) the starting point may be the L1 and that interlanguage may be, in part at least, a restructuring continuum.

Fossilization

One point on which there is broad agreement is that L2 learners, unlike L1 learners, generally do not reach the same level of competence as native speakers; their 'final state' grammar is not the target-language grammar (see Chapter 3). Thus, certain rules and items 'fossilize'. As Selinker (1972) puts it:

> Fossilizable linguistic phenomena are linguistic items, rules and subsystems which speakers of a particular NL will tend to keep in their IL relative to a particular TL, no matter what the age of the learner or amount of explanation and instruction he receives in the TL.

Fossilized forms may sometimes seem to disappear but are always likely to reappear in productive language use, a phenomenon known as *backsliding*. Selinker talks of an 'interlanguage norm' that learners will gravitate towards, especially when under some kind of pressure. He suggests that there is a psychological mechanism, which he calls 'fossilization', which underlies the production of fossilized items. More commonly, however, the term *fossilization* has been used to label the process by which non-target forms become fixed in interlanguage.[2]

A number of studies give support to the prevalence of fossilization. Mukkatesh (1986), for example, identified a number of persistent errors in the written production of 80 students at a Jordanian university who had an average of eleven years' instruction in English. Examples of such errors were the use of simple past instead of simple present, the deletion of 'be', and the retention of pronominal reflexes in relative clauses. Mukkatesh found that neither error correction nor explicit grammatical explanation had any effect on these errors, thus reinforcing the view that certain error types are not susceptible to de-fossilization. More general evidence of fossilization comes from Higgs and Clifford (1982), discussed in Chapter 13.

A number of possible causes of fossilization have been identified. These are summarized in Table 9.1. As Selinker and Lamendella (1978) conclude, there is probably no single cause; both internal and external factors play a role. Ideally we need to specify the differential contribution of the various factors and how they interact, but we are a long way from being able to do so.

Factors	Description	Reference
Internal		
1 Age	When learners reach a critical age their brains lose plasticity, with the result that certain linguistic features cannot be mastered.	Scovel 1988 (see also Chapter 11).
2 Lack of desire to acculturate	As a result of various social and psychological factors, learners make no efforts to adopt TL cultural norms.	Schumann 1978a (see also Chapter 6).
External		
1 Communicative pressure	Persistent pressure to communicate ideas that require the use of language that exceeds the learner's linguistic competence leads to fossilization.	Higgs and Clifford 1982
2 Lack of learning opportunity	Learners lack opportunities for receiving input and also for using the L2.	Bickerton 1975
3 The nature of the feedback on learner's use of L2	Positive cognitive feedback (signalling 'I understand you') results in fossilization; negative feedback (signalling 'I don't understand you') helps avoid fossilization.	Vigil and Oller 1976

Table 9.1:   Factors hypothesized to influence fossilization

Subsequent developments in interlanguage theory

Interlanguage theory has helped to shape the development of SLA research by advancing the notion that learners possess a separate mental grammar that they draw on in L2 performance. The term 'interlanguage' is now used by theorists of very different persuasions and has become almost theory-neutral. It can be glossed as the 'system of implicit L2 knowledge that the learner develops and systematically amends over time'. The idea of 'fossilization' has also stuck. However, with the obvious exception of 'transfer', Selinker's 'strategies'—the specifically cognitive dimension of the initial theory—have not been taken up by theorists. Selinker's (1992) 'rediscovery' of interlanguage does list 'training and learning strategies' and 'simplification and complexification strategies' as components of the 'interlanguage hypothesis' (1992: 247), but offers little elucidation of them. Instead, as we will see in Chapter 10, subsequent developments have concentrated on the role of linguistic universals in interlanguage construction.

Implicit and explicit second language knowledge; the role of consciousness

Early interlanguage theory did not make a clear distinction between different types of L2 knowledge, but two other early theories did. Both Krashen's Monitor Model and Bialystok's Theory of L2 Learning owed much to early interlanguage theory and to the research that it spawned. Krashen and Bialystok were concerned with the role of formal instruction in L2 development and it was this that led them to distinguish *implicit* and *explicit knowledge*. It should be noted, though, that whereas Bialystok saw her theory as clearly 'cognitive' in nature, Krashen drew more directly on linguistic concepts, in particular Chomsky's notion of innate linguistic knowledge. However, the distinction between implicit and explicit knowledge, which is central to Krashen's thinking, is a cognitive one. This section will begin with a brief definition of implicit and explicit knowledge. There follows an account of Krashen's and Bialystok's theories. Finally, the role of consciousness in L2 acquisition is discussed.

A definition of implicit and explicit knowledge

Explicit knowledge has been defined in different ways, but in SLA research it is generally used to refer to knowledge that is available to the learner as a conscious representation. It is not the same as 'metalingual knowledge' (knowledge of the special terminology for labelling linguistic concepts), although it is often developed hand in hand with such knowledge. Learners may make their knowledge explicit either in everyday language or with the help of specially learnt 'technical' language. They may, for example, be able to explain the error in sentences like:

* The London is my favourite city.

by saying ' "the" is not used with the names of cities' or they may do so with the help of grammatical terminology, as in 'proper nouns like "London" do not take a definite article'.

There are two types of implicit knowledge, formulaic knowledge and rule-based knowledge. The former consists of ready-made chunks of language (see

Chapter 3). Rule-based implicit knowledge consists of generalized and abstract structures which have been internalized. In both cases, the knowledge is intuitive and, therefore, largely hidden; learners are not conscious of what they know. It becomes manifest only in actual performance.

Krashen's Monitor Theory

The distinction between these two types of knowledge underlies Krashen's Monitor Theory, which is the first and, in many ways, the most central of his five hypotheses.[3] Krashen (1981; 1982) claims that learners possess an 'acquired system' and a 'learned system' which are totally separate. The former is developed by means of *acquisition*, a subconscious process which arises when learners are using language for communication. The latter is the result of *learning*, the process of paying conscious attention to language in an effort to understand and memorize rules. It is clear that the acquisition/learning distinction mirrors the implicit/explicit distinction, a point that Krashen himself acknowledges (1982: 10).

Whereas the claim that there are two types of knowledge is not controversial, Krashen's insistence that 'learned' knowledge is completely separate and cannot be converted into 'acquired' knowledge is. This position has become known as the *non-interface position*. Krashen argues that 'acquired knowledge' can *only* be developed when the learner's attention is focused on message conveyance, and that neither practice nor error correction enables 'learned knowledge' to become 'acquired'. Furthermore, he claims that utterances are initiated by the 'acquired' system, and that the 'learned' system only comes into play when learners *monitor* the output from it. Monitoring is possible when learners are focused on form rather than meaning and have sufficient time to access their 'learned' knowledge. Learners can also modify their output by means of 'feel', using 'acquired' knowledge. Krashen has continued to maintain a non-interface position despite considerable criticism from McLaughlin (1978b; 1987), Sharwood Smith (1981), and Gregg (1984), among others. He argues that an *interface position* does not account for cases such as 'P', an advanced L2 learner who consciously knows rules like 3rd person -*s* and yet cannot use them in free speech, nor for other cases of learners who have 'acquired' rules without ever having learned them (Krashen 1985: 39–40).

Bialystok's view of second language learning

Bialystok's (1978) theory of L2 learning, which is modelled on Figure 9.2, does allow for an interface between explicit and implicit knowledge. According to this theory, implicit knowledge is developed through exposure to communicative language use and is facilitated by the strategy of 'functional practising' (attempts by the learner to maximize exposure to language through communication). Explicit knowledge arises when learners focus on the language code, and is facilitated by 'formal practising', which involves either conscious study of the L2 or attempts to automatize already learnt explicit knowledge. In these respects, Bialystok's theory is the same as Krashen's. It differs, however, in allowing for an interaction between the two types of knowledge. Formal practising enables explicit knowledge to become implicit, while inferencing allows explicit knowledge to be derived from implicit. The model also distinguishes two types of output. Type I output is 'spontaneous and immediate', while Type II is 'deliberate and occurs after a delay' (Bialystok 1978: 74). As might be expected, Type I relies entirely on implicit knowledge, whereas Type II involves both implicit and explicit. A feedback loop from both types allows for continual modification of a response.

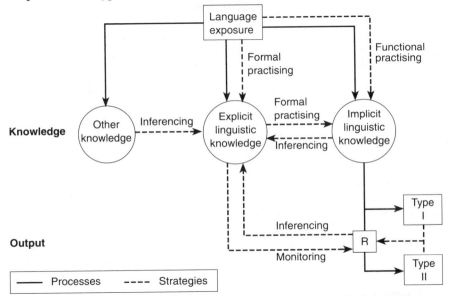

Figure 9.2:   Model of Second Language Learning (from Bialystok 1978)

Whereas Krashen's position has remained more or less immutable over the years, Bialystok's has undergone considerable revision (see Bialystok 1981a; 1982; 1990a; 1991; and also Hulstijn 1990). The development that concerns us most here is the reconceptualization of L2 knowledge. In the early model this was represented as a dichotomy—knowledge was either implicit or explicit—but in subsequent formulations it is represented in terms of two intersecting continua reflecting the extent to which rules and items are 'controlled' or 'analysed'. Again, Bialystok's definition of 'control' has shifted somewhat. Whereas initially (for example, in Bialystok 1982), it concerned the ease and rapidity with which the knowledge can be accessed in differing types of language use, in later formulations (for example, Bialystok and Ryan 1985) it refers to three different functions: the selection of items of knowledge, their co-ordination, and the extent to which selection and co-ordination can be carried out automatically.

By 'analysis', Bialystok refers to the extent to which the learner has abstracted an account of some linguistic phenomenon:

> Analysis of knowledge is the process by which mental representations of this knowledge are built up, structured, and made explicit for the learner. (Bialystok 1991: 65)

One way in which this can take place is by analysing formulas (i.e. discovering the parts that make them up). It is tempting to see this 'analysis' dimension as equivalent to the explicit/implicit distinction, with analysed knowledge corresponding to explicit knowledge and unanalysed to implicit. Bialystok, in fact, does equate analysis with the development of an explicit representation of knowledge, but she emphasizes that analysed knowledge need not involve consciousness. As she puts it 'a criterion of consciousness seriously underestimates the level of analysis with which linguistic knowledge is represented (1991: 68).

In explaining how analysed knowledge is developed, Bialystok (1991) draws on the work of Karmiloff-Smith's (1986) three phases of skill development. The first phase is called 'Implicit'. Here knowledge of a linguistic item is closely associated with procedures for using it in communication and is not represented independently. For example, the learner may supply linguistic determiners with a variety of nouns and yet not have organized them into a system of determiners. The second phase is called 'Explicit 1', during which learners examine, analyse, and organize their performances in order to construct explicit and independent representations of linguistic knowledge. In the final phase—Explicit 2—linguistic knowledge is available for conscious consideration. This model was intended to account for language development in children, and thus progress is reflected in movement from Implicit to Explicit 1 and finally to Explicit 2. It is not clear how—or whether—this model can be applied to L2 acquisition, nor does Bialystok consider this in her later work.

The goal of much of Bialystok's later work is to show the relationship between different types of knowledge and different types of language use (conversations, tests, reading, studying, etc.). Hulstijn (1990: 38), in fact, characterizes it as 'a functional model, aimed at explaining language use in terms of task demands' rather than a theory of acquisition. The primary effect of analysing knowledge is to increase the potential for use in cognitively demanding tasks. Unanalysed knowledge also has its use—in conversation, for example. This aspect of Bialystok's research mirrors Cummins' work on language proficiency (see Chapter 6).

There are a number of problems with Bialystok's views of language acquisition (see Hulstijn 1990). In particular, the claim that language must begin with unanalysed knowledge seems unwarranted in the case of L2 acquisition. Many instructed L2 learners begin with explicit knowledge. Hulstijn comes out strongly in favour of the kind of skill-learning theory of L2 acquisition that we will consider later (see page 388).

The legitimacy of the explicit/implicit distinction

Not all L2 acquisition researchers have been happy with the implicit/explicit distinction. McLaughlin (1987: 21) has argued that Krashen's acquired/learnt distinction is not tenable because it cannot be falsified; Krashen has failed to provide adequate definitions of what he means by 'subconscious' and 'conscious', and 'he has provided no way of independently determining whether a given process involves acquisition or learning'. McLaughlin's criticisms, however, appear to be levelled primarily at Krashen's attempt to distinguish 'acquired' and 'learnt' knowledge at the level of process, but as Bialystok (1981a) has noted, the existence of two types of knowledge is widely recognized in cognitive psychology. The distinction is not especially problematic at the level of product, therefore. Furthermore, there have been a number of successful attempts to operationalize the distinction between 'implicit' and 'explicit' learning (for example, Reber 1976).

Examples of studies that have sought to examine learners' implicit and explicit knowledge of grammatical rules are Seliger (1979), Tucker, Lambert and Rigault (1977), Hulstijn and Hulstijn (1984), Sorace (1985) and Green and Hecht (1992). In all of these studies explicit knowledge was equated with learners' oral or written explanations of grammatical rules, while implicit knowledge was determined by examining the learners' use of the same grammatical features in some kind of performance. The main question the studies sought to answer was 'What is the relationship, if any, between learners' explicit and implicit knowledge?' We will focus on the Green and Hecht (1992) study here, as it provides a comprehensive examination of this question.

The subjects were 300 German learners of English with between three and twelve years' exposure to formal teaching, and, also, 50 native English speakers. The subjects were shown sentences containing different kinds of grammatical errors and asked to correct each sentence and in each case to state the rule that had been violated. The native speakers were able to correct 96 per cent of the errors, while the German learners corrected 78 per cent overall. The most advanced group of learners, however, corrected 97 per cent. Green and Hecht found that the German learners could only state the correct explicit rule in less than half the cases (46 per cent). Again, the more experienced learners showed higher levels of explicit knowledge, the university students with the most experience formulating correct rules in 85 per cent of the cases. Although the learners nearly always produced an accurate correction when they had produced a correct rule (97 per cent of such cases), they were able to make successful corrections without recourse to explicit knowledge in 43 per cent of the cases. This study suggests that the learners relied primarily on

implicit knowledge, but that the availability of accurate explicit rules facilitated performance of the correction task. Explicit rules obviously constitute
only a subset—and a fairly small one at that—of available implicit knowledge, a point which Krashen has emphasized (see Krashen 1982).

Whereas the Green and Hecht study examined the implicit/explicit distinction at the level of product (the way knowledge is represented in the mind of
the learner), other studies have tried to investigate it in terms of process (how
the two types of knowledge are internalized). N. Ellis (1991), for instance,
draws on earlier studies in cognitive psychology (for example, Reber 1976;
Reber, Kassin, Lewis, and Cantor 1980) as well as SLA theorizing. Interestingly, Ellis produces definitions of the two types of learning that are very similar to Krashen's definitions of acquisition and learning:

> Implicit learning is coming to learn the underlying structure of a complex
> stimulus environment by a process which takes place naturally, simply and
> without conscious operations. Explicit learning is a more conscious opera-
> tion where the individual makes and tests hypotheses.

The results obtained by this and other studies are considered in some detail in
Chapter 14.

There would seem to be a reasonable basis in both theory and research for
the distinction at both the level of product and process. In this respect, therefore, Krashen's acquisition/learning hypothesis is vindicated. It should be
noted, however, that in a number of respects Krashen appears to have been
mistaken. First, there is evidence from the Green and Hecht study that learners are capable of learning a substantial number of explicit rules. Krashen's
(1982: 98ff.) claim, therefore, that 'learning' is limited to a few 'simple' rules
is not warranted. Second, there is evidence that 'learning' through an explicit
presentation of a rule can sometimes work more effectively than 'acquiring' a
rule implicitly.

Accepting the acquisition/learning distinction, however, does not entail accepting the non-interface position. Krashen bases this on descriptive work in
SLA research which shows that learners follow a 'natural order' of development (see Chapter 3) and some early studies of the effects of formal instruction which indicate that instructed learners follow the same order and make
the same kinds of errors, irrespective of the instruction they receive (see Turner 1979; Felix 1981; Pica 1983). However, as we saw in Chapter 3, the
whole notion of 'natural order' is suspect. Also, more recent studies (for example, Pienemann 1989; White, Spada, Lightbown, and Ranta 1991) have
shown that learners, with certain constraints, can learn what they are taught.
Again, the evidence for these claims is considered in detail in Chapter 14. The
important point here is to note that these studies suggest that 'learning' can
sometimes turn into 'acquisition'.

What then is the nature of the relationship between explicit and implicit
knowledge? Does explicit knowledge convert into implicit knowledge

through practice, as claimed by Bialystok and argued by Sharwood Smith (1981), or does it, in the main, only facilitate the acquisition of implicit knowledge, as suggested by Terrell (1991), and myself in Ellis 1993a? These two alternatives are considered in Chapter 14 under the headings the *interface hypothesis* and the *selective attention hypothesis*.

'Consciousness' and 'noticing'

Underlying the whole question of the relationship between explicit and implicit knowledge and how they are internalized is the question of 'consciousness' in language learning. As Schmidt (1990) points out, this is a controversial issue. He distinguishes three senses of 'conscious'. First there is 'consciousness as awareness'. Here there are degrees or levels of awareness. 'Perception' is not necessarily conscious, but 'noticing', which Schmidt defines as 'availability for verbal report', requires focal awareness, while 'understanding' involves conscious analysis and comparison with what has been noticed on previous occasions. Second, there is 'consciousness as intention'. Schmidt accepts that not all intentions are conscious. Finally, there is 'consciousness as knowledge'. Schmidt suggests that the explicit/implicit contrast represents a continuum, but notes that there is no consensus on where to draw the line to demarcate conscious knowledge.

The general position that Schmidt adopts is that the role of unconscious learning has been exaggerated. He emphasizes that 'subliminal language learning' is impossible and that some degree of consciousness is necessary for 'noticing' to take place. Schmidt and Frota (1986) examined one learner's (R's) diary to establish which features in the input R had consciously attended to. They also examined R's output to see to what extent the noticed forms turned up in communicative speech. In nearly every case the forms that R produced were those that he noticed people saying to him. Conversely, forms that were present in comprehensible input did not show up until they had been noticed.

Noticing is of considerable theoretical importance because it accounts for which features in the input are attended to and so become *intake* (information stored in temporary memory which may or may not be subsequently accommodated in the interlanguage system). Schmidt and Frota suggest that for noticed input to become intake, learners have to carry out a comparison of what they have observed in the input and what they themselves are typically producing on the basis of their current interlanguage system. They refer to this as 'noticing the gap', and argue that this too is a conscious process.

Other research relevant to the role of 'noticing' is Hulstijn's (1989b) study of implicit and incidental L2 learning. In two studies involving a natural language (L2 Dutch) and an artificial language, learners were presented with word order structures implicitly (i.e. the structures were not explained to them) and incidentally (i.e. they did not know they would be tested for recall of the structures). They were assigned to one of three treatments involving exposure to sentences containing the target structures. One group (the form-focused group) had to perform an anagram task that directed their attention to the structure without any need to consider its meaning. The second group (the meaning-focused group) were shown the same sentences on a screen and asked to respond meaningfully to them by saying 'yes', 'perhaps' or 'I don't know'. The third group (the form- and meaning-focused group) were simply told to pay attention to both form and meaning but were given no special task to perform. The results showed that the form-focused group outperformed the other two groups in terms of gains in scores on a sentence-copying task and a task requiring cued recall of the sentences used in the learning tasks. Hulstijn interprets the results as showing that attention to form when encoding input is a 'sufficient condition' for implicit and incidental learning. However, as the meaning-focused group also produced significant gains, the hypothesis that exclusive attention to meaning will inhibit acquisition was not supported. It is possible, though, that the learners in this group engaged in some degree of 'noticing' of the target structures. As Hulstijn points out, meaning may be the learner's first priority, but attention to form occurs as a 'backup procedure' in case meaning fails to provide an adequate interpretation.

This discussion of consciousness in L2 acquisition suggests that the distinction between conscious 'learning' and subconscious 'acquisition' is overly simplistic. It is clear that 'acquisition', in the sense intended by Krashen, can involve at least some degree of consciousness (in noticing and noticing the gap). But it is also clear, if the evidence from studies of implicit learning is to be accepted, that learning can take place without learners being aware of it. [4] At the level of product the explicit/implicit distinction seems less problematic. Clearly, learners may know a rule, or know about it, or both.

The relationship between explicit and implicit knowledge, then, continues to be a key issue. One possibility, suggested by both Schmidt and Frota (1986) and myself (Ellis 1993a), is that explicit knowledge functions as a facilitator, helping learners to notice features in the input which they would otherwise miss and also to compare what they notice with what they produce. In a sense, then, explicit knowledge may contribute to 'intake enhancement', but it will only be one of several factors that does this (see Chapter 7 for a fuller discussion of this point).

Summary

The explicit/implicit distinction is controversial, as it depends on the idea of 'consciousness', which for some researchers remains too elusive a concept to be criterial (see McLaughlin 1990c). The following are the main claims that have been made:

1 Learners possess two kinds of knowledge, explicit and implicit. This claim is widely accepted.

2 Learners can internalize L2 knowledge both explicitly (Krashen's 'learning') and implicitly ('acquisition'). This claim is less widely accepted, although a number of studies suggest that the distinction between implicit and explicit is valid at the level of process (for example, N. Ellis 1991)

3 An alternative to the explicit/implicit distinction is to view knowledge as more or less 'analysed' and more or less 'controlled' (as in Bialystok's view of language learning).

4 Neither a non-interface nor a strong interface model satisfactorily accounts for the relationship between explicit and implicit knowledge.

5 Increasingly, explicit knowledge is being viewed as a facilitator of implicit knowledge, by enabling learners to notice features in the input and compare them with their own interlanguage representations (Schmidt 1990)

6 Different types of language use typically require different kinds of knowledge (Bialystok 1982).

One possible way of resolving some of the problems of the explicit/implicit distinction can be found in the information-processing accounts of L2 acquisition considered in a later section of this chapter (see page 389).

Variability theories of second language acquisition

The theories based on the implicit/explicit distinction provided a means for explaining the variability that many researchers observed in learner-language: learners varied because they sometimes drew on their implicit knowledge and sometimes on their explicit. A number of other researchers (such as Tarone and myself), who were also influenced by early interlanguage theory, were unconvinced by this explanation and developed alternative theories to account for variability. Although these theories drew extensively on concepts from sociolinguistics, they were essentially cognitive in nature as they sought to account for the way in which learners organized their L2 knowledge and the strategies they deployed for both learning and using it.

Whereas in Chapter 4 we concentrated on identifying different types of variability and the factors that have been found to induce variability in interlanguage use, here we address the question 'How is variability related to L2 acquisition?' We will examine my and Tarone's theoretical positions, and also consider Preston's more explicitly sociolinguistic theory.

Tarone's 'Capability Continuum'

Tarone (1983) considers three paradigms for studying interlanguage. According to the 'Homogeneous Competence Paradigm', as reflected in Adjemian (1976):

learners have grammatical intuitions which the linguist may use as data in modelling that competence. Variation is a phenomenon which occurs in speech performance and not in the grammatical intuitions on the basis of which the 'grammar itself' is written (1976: 150).

This paradigm, which is the one that informs the linguistic theories to be considered in the following chapter, is inadequate according to Tarone, because it does not satisfactorily account for the results of variability research, which show that the *careful style* is more permeable to invasion from the target language than the *vernacular style*. The Homogeneous Competence Paradigm predicts the opposite.

Krashen's Monitor Model is illustrative of the 'Dual Knowledge Paradigm', according to which there are two knowledge systems, both of which are homogeneous. Variability is explained by 'monitoring', the process by which learners modify utterances generated by 'acquired' knowledge. There is no recognition of variability within 'acquired' knowledge itself.[5] Tarone's main criticism of this paradigm is that the research findings show more than just two dichotomous styles in learner language. Thus the Monitor Model does not account for the 'inherent variability in the system on any observed occasion' (1983: 159).

Tarone's own model, the Capability Continuum, is based on the Labovian paradigm, which was described in some detail in Chapter 4. 'Capability' is preferred to 'competence' because she needs a term that refers broadly to the linguistic knowledge that underlies '*all* regular language behaviour' (1983: 151). The learner's capability, therefore, is evident in the regularities observed in production and perception, writing and reading, and making judgements on grammaticality. Tarone suggests that it is composed of 'regularities' (defined as 'patterns which underlie phenomena in observed behaviour') rather than 'rules' (defined as 'normative standards of behaviour'), but still constitutes 'an abstract linguistic system' which exists apart from its use (1983: 151–2). Capability consists of a continuum of styles, ranged from the 'careful' to the 'vernacular', and is, therefore, heterogeneous (see Figure 4.2). The vernacular style is considered to be 'primary' in the sense that it is the most stable and consistent.

Tarone's theory is more than just an attempt to model the kind of L2 knowledge that learners internalize. It also provides an explanation of how knowledge is acquired and, importantly for any theory of L2 acquisition, how changes in the learner's interlanguage take place. It posits that new forms enter interlanguage in two ways: (1) directly into the learner's vernacular style, in which case they may subsequently 'spread' to more formal styles over time, and (2) initially into the learner's most formal style, manifest only when the learner is paying close attention to speech production, and subsequently by 'spreading' into the less formal styles where they replace those forms that entered these styles earlier. In the case of (1), there may be a tendency for the new forms to appear in a 'universal order'.

Whereas Tarone's 1983 paper does not offer much detail about the key notion of 'spreading', her 1988 book does, drawing on the work of Dickerson (1975) and Gatbonton (1978). Dickerson's work suggests that learners initiate change in one linguistic environment, which then spreads to other linguistic environments in a clear order. Thus, learners move systematically towards target-language norms over time. Whereas Dickerson's view of 'spreading' allows for variation at the beginning of the acquisition process, Gatbonton's sees acquisition as proceeding in two phases: in the acquisition phase and the replacement phase. Tarone does not offer any views as to which of these interpretations of 'spreading' is the preferred one.

Ellis' Variable Competence Model

In my account of L2 variability, I have assumed that the way language is learnt is a reflection of the way it is used. There are two strands to this position. One draws on the idea of a relationship between a differentiated knowledge store and different types of language use, and the other on the idea of form-function networks.

Like Bialystok, I see L2 knowledge as represented differently in the mind of the learner according to how analysed and how automatic it is (Ellis 1984a). The unanalysed/analysed and the non-automatic/automatic distinctions constitute intersecting continua in which any L2 item or rule is located. In the case of native-speaker competence, the most usual form of representation is unanalysed/automatic, although as the discussion of Bialystok's model in the previous section made clear, native speakers also have access to analysed knowledge. Language use is differentiated according to the amount of planning that takes place. Thus, following Ochs (1979), it can be planned or unplanned. Planned discourse is discourse that is thought out prior to expression, whereas unplanned discourse lacks forethought and preparation. Unplanned discourse can be considered primary in that it is the type found in everyday communication and spontaneous conversation.

Knowledge is activated for use by means of 'processes', which, again, are distinguished according to whether they are primary or secondary. Primary processes are utilized when learners wish to engage in unplanned discourse. They draw on knowledge that is relatively unanalysed and automatic—semantic simplification (see Chapter 3 and Ellis 1984a) is an example. Secondary processes are utilized in planned discourse and draw on knowledge towards the analysed end of the continuum—*monitoring* (the conscious editing of language performance) is an example.

I also suggest that the processes that the learner calls on in order to participate in discourse are developmental, that is, their prominence in L2 acquisition coincides with the general stages of development discussed in Chapter 3. Thus, early on, learners make heavy use of semantic simplification because this process requires little L2 knowledge. Also, L2 knowledge that to begin

with can only be used via secondary processes because it exists only in analysed form, can eventually be accessed through primary processes and so becomes available for use in unplanned as well as planned discourse.

According to this *Variable Competence Model*, L2 development takes two
forms. Learners learn how to activate items and rules that are available initially only in planned discourse for use in unplanned discourse. In this respect,
my position is similar to that of Tarone. Also, learners acquire new L2 rules
through participating in different types of discourse. In other words, as Widdowson (1979b: 62) has suggested, 'we create discourse and commonly bring
new rules into existence by so doing'. It is this latter type of development that I
explored in my subsequent work on variability by drawing on the idea of
form-function networks.

The starting point for my ideas on how learners construct variable interlanguage systems as a result of participating in discourse is free variation
(see Chapter 5 for an account of this). In Ellis 1985c, I suggest that the learner's interlanguage is composed of competing rules at any stage of its development. In some cases, these competing rules are systematic, as they relate to
situational and contextual factors. In other cases, the competing forms are
used arbitrarily, in free variation. I argue that new linguistic forms emerge in
all natural languages 'quite spontaneously', and that interlanguage is no different. However, it is inefficient to operate a system in which two forms have
total identity of function, so learners seek to remove free variation by (1) eliminating forms that are deemed non-standard or unnecessary, and (2) building
form-function networks in which different forms are used to perform different functions. Like Tarone, I draw on Gatbonton's (1978) ideas of 'diffusion'
to explain how form-function networks are constructed. L2 acquisition involves a first stage (the 'acquisition phase'), where new forms are acquired
and used in free variation, and subsequent stages (the 'reorganization phase')
where learners sort these forms into functional pigeon-holes. The initial
form-function correlations that learners establish are not likely to correspond
to those found in the target language. This requires several sortings and may
never be achieved.

I have not fully drawn together the two strands of my theorizing relating to
(1) the knowledge types and processes involved in different kinds of discourse, and (2) the construction of form-function networks about variability.
Whereas my earlier work drew on psycholinguistic models of L2 acquisition,
the later work was strongly influenced by Huebner's 'dynamic paradigm'
(Huebner 1979 and 1983; see Chapter 4) and belongs to a functional account
of interlanguage.

Preston's Sociolinguistic Model

Both Tarone's and my models are based on the psycholinguistic notions of
'attention' and 'planning'. However, there is a clear need to incorporate an

interactional/social dimension to account fully for interlanguage variability. It was this that led me to examine form-function networks. Preston's Sociolinguistic Model includes both dimensions and constitutes the most comprehensive variability theory to date.

Preston (1989) envisages interlanguage development, like other kinds of language change, as involving both 'change from above' and 'change from below'. In the case of general language change, the former 'involves linguistic responses to straightforward social pressures' and is accompanied by awareness of features that are prestigious or stigmatized, while the latter involves changes that are not conscious and which usually arise spontaneously in the speech of members of the working class. In the case of interlanguage, the vernacular style can be influenced both from above (when forms enter through the learner's careful style) and from below (when they enter directly into the vernacular style). Forms that enter from above are 'odd' and 'require more effort and attention to maintain'. Examples are English third person singular -s and noun plurals. The distinction between these two types of change is necessary to account for the finding that the direction of stylistic shifting varies, with some features (such as articles) showing greater accuracy in the vernacular and others (like third person -s) greater accuracy in the careful style (see Tarone 1985 and Chapter 4).

Preston's model, which is shown in Figure 9.3, rests on the idea of the learner's knowledge of the L2 as 'a complex variation space' (1989: 265), which can be accounted for in terms of (1) planning, (2) depth, and (3) stability. The concept of planning is envisaged as a continuum, as in my model. Preston, however, sees 'planning' not just as something that learners do when using their knowledge, but as actually reflected in the knowledge system itself. He talks of the 'planned and unplanned sides of learner systems' in a distinction that seems very close to Bialystok's ideas of 'analysed' and 'unanalysed' knowledge. Learners will vary as to which side—or type of knowledge—is most fully represented in their interlanguage systems.

The 'depth' dimension of the model is an attempt to take account of the social uses that learners make of their variable systems. Thus, there are likely to be different frequencies of use that reflect gender, class, age, genres, relationships, etc. These differences reflect the attempts of learners to use their knowledge functionally for social purposes. Learners, like native speakers, will use forms symbolically for these purposes.

'Stability' is a characteristic of both the surface structure of the learner's interlanguage system and also of the way this system is used to convey social meanings. In the case of the former, a stable system is one where there is an absence of variation because no new forms are entering the system and existing forms have become categorical. In the case of the latter, 'stability' is evident when continued association of a given feature with a given social meaning halts or slows the development of that feature. When this kind of stability is found, fossilization may occur.

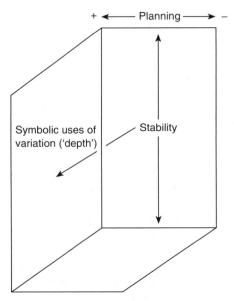

Figure 9.3:   An integrated model of language variation (from Preston 1989)

Preston raises the interesting possibility that learners will differ in the extent to which the variability of their systems is a product of the planning or the depth dimensions:

> Where there is no real community of learners and no previous accretion of symbolic depth, ... change will be more linguistically determined along the shallow, surface plane of the model proposed here.

Thus, classroom learners are more likely to manifest planning than social variability, although, as Preston is careful to point out, even these learners are likely to assign some symbolic value to developing forms.

Evaluation

This review of three variability theories demonstrates the need for models of considerable complexity if all the known sources of variability are to be accounted for. It is probably true to say that, as yet, there is no complete theory of interlanguage variation. Such a theory will need to explain (1) the cognitive processes involved in planning variability, (2) the nature of the form-function networks that learners construct at different stages of development, and (3) the systematic way in which learners use L2 knowledge to convey social meanings. Tarone's and my own theories are concerned almost entirely with (1), and hence their inclusion in a chapter dealing with cognitive accounts of L2 acquisition. My later work also considered (2). Preston's theory is the most comprehensive in that it accounts for both (1) and (3) and constitutes, therefore, a real attempt to integrate psycholinguistic and sociolinguistic perspectives. However, as presented in Preston (1989), it is not always very clear and does not appear to provide an explanation of (2). All three theories offer only partial explanations, therefore, although in this respect they probably do not differ from any other interlanguage theory.

Functionalist theories of second language acquisition

Functionalist theories of L2 acquisition share a number of concerns with variability theories. For instance, both are concerned not just with how linguistic knowledge is represented in the mind of the learner, but also with how this knowledge is used in discourse. Also, both types assume that syntax cannot be considered separately from semantics and pragmatics and, as such, are opposed to purely linguistic accounts of L2 acquisition.

According to Tomlin (1990):

> A general premise of FAs (functional approaches) is that the acquisition of a language arises from general circumstances of use and communicative interaction (1990: 161).

He distinguishes strong and weak functional views. In the former, language acquisition is determined solely by general learning mechanisms operating on the rich data provided by human interaction. In the latter, some linguistic knowledge is considered to be available from the outset, but the way this is manifested in specific languages must be discovered through participation in discourse.

In this section, we will consider a number of functional theories of L2 acquisition. We will begin examining the functional approach adopted by a number of researchers involved in the European Science Foundation Project in Second Language Acquisition by Adult Immigrants (for example, Perdue 1984 and 1991; Klein and Perdue 1989; Perdue and Klein 1992). We will then examine work informed by Givón's Functional-Typological Theory (for example, Sato 1988; Pfaff 1992). In both cases, the testing of the theories has led to detailed and painstaking description of L2 learners' productions in natural discourse, undertaken with a view to discovering the organizational principles that operate in learner-language. Thirdly, we will consider Bates and MacWhinney's Competition Model (for example, Bates and MacWhinney 1982 and 1987). This theory has afforded some very specific hypotheses, which have been tested experimentally.

The learner's four tasks

Klein (1986) characterizes the learner's task as that of overcoming four problems. These are described in Table 9.2. The learner faces these problems at one and the same time and must cope with them together. Thus, the analysis, synthetic, embedding, and matching problems are all interrelated and interdependent. Learners solve them by utilizing shared world knowledge, situational knowledge, and contextual information from the preceding discourse to help them understand input and produce output and, by so doing, they develop their interlanguages.

Learning a language involves mastering a number of fundamental functions of language—spatial and temporal reference, for example. The L1 learner has to learn both the functions themselves and the means for performing them. But in L2 acquisition, the learner already knows these functions and brings them to the input. Therefore, according to Klein (1991):

> It is these functions ... which drive the learner to break down parts of the input and to organize them into small subsystems, which is reorganized whenever a new piece from the flood of input is added, until eventually the target system is reached (or more or less approximated) (1991: 220).

In other words, the solution to the four problems lies in the learner's knowledge of functional meanings. For Klein, L2 acquisition is primarily functionally driven.

Problem	Description
Analysis	The learner has 'to segment the stream of acoustic signals into constituent units and to bring the latter into line with the parallel information on concurrent events which constitutes the situational context of the utterance' (1986: 59).
Synthesis	The learner has to try to put the sounds and words he has learnt together in order to produce and comprehend L2 utterances.
Embedding	The learner has to make utterances fit the context—situational and linguistic—in which they occur. This requires 'a sort of balance of linguistic and contextual information' (1986: 61).
Matching	'... the learner must continuously compare his current language variety with the target variety' (1986: 62).

Table 9.2:   The learner's four tasks in L2 acquisition (based on Klein 1986: 59–62)

A number of studies have demonstrated how L2 learners handle functions like temporal reference in the early stages. Klein (1986), for instance, describes the devices used by an Italian woman with very limited knowledge of German in telling a story about how her husband was involved in an industrial accident. The learner manifested almost no knowledge of German verb tenses and yet was able to convey successfully temporality by using techniques that relied on a small set of linguistic devices (for example, simple adverbials like 'dann' and 'morgen') and shared world knowledge. Perdue (1991) reports more generally on how the subjects studied in the European Science Foundation Project on Adult Second Language Acquisition handled spatial and temporal reference. The learners acquired a few simple words to express 'essential' reference and relations (for example, 'up/above' and 'left/-right'), they used transparent form-meaning relationships, they decomposed complex relations into simpler ones (for example, instead of 'between two chairs' they used circumlocutions like 'side of chair, side of other chair, middle'), and they relied on the inferencing capacities of their interlocutors. Perdue considers that learners who manifest such tendencies have access to only 'a "basic" learner language' (1991: 418), which they progress beyond in order to escape from 'the expressive constraints of a simple system' and 'to match the target language more closely' (1991: 419).

This idea of a 'basic variety' is explored further by Perdue and Klein (1992), in a study of two adult Italian learners of L2 English in London. Both learners began by producing utterances which were very simple, characterized by the use of strings of simple noun phrases and a limited number of adjectives and adverbials. They relied heavily on interlocutor scaffolding. Their utterances contained no case marking, few verbs, which were almost always in the base form, and hardly any copulas. One of the learners, Andrea, proceeded to 'grammaticalize' his speech over a period of about 20 months, whereas the other, Santo, maintained the 'basic variety' throughout. Grammaticalization took the form of the abandonment of a commonly used non-standard structure V + NP (as in 'have the one family' = 'there is/was a family) and the development of systematic verb morphology, case-markings for third-person pronouns, and target-like subordinate constructions. Perdue and Klein explain the differences in the development of the two learners in terms of the 'communicative style' they typically adopted in interactions with native speakers. Thus, whereas Santo tended to take charge of these interactions, Andrea generally avoided initiating topics, but was 'very receptive to native speakers' reformulations of his utterances' (1992: 270).

Language acquisition as syntactization

Like Klein, Givón (1979) also sees syntax as inextricably linked to discourse—it is 'a dependent, functionally motivated entity' in the sense that its formal properties reflect its communicative uses. He distinguishes two types of language, each with its own type of structures. There are the loose, paratactic structures found in informal/unplanned discourse, which constitute the 'pragmatic mode' (later referred to as the 'pre-grammatical mode' in Givón 1995). There are also the tight, 'grammaticalized' structures found in formal/planned discourse, which constitute the 'syntactic mode' (later called the 'grammatical mode'). An example of the former is the topic-comment structure of an utterance like:

Ice cream, I like it.

while an example of the latter is the subject-predicate structure of an utterance like:

I like ice cream.

Table 9.3 lists the main differences between the two types of language use. Givón argues that acquisition is characterized by *syntactization*, i.e. the gradual move from a pre-grammatical to a grammatical mode. However, adults retain access to the pre-grammatical mode which they employ when the conditions are appropriate. Givón also argues that others aspects of language—such as the historical evolution of languages and creolization—are also characterized by the same process of syntactization.

Pre-grammatical vs. grammatical discourse processing

Properties	Grammatical mode	Pre-grammatical mode
STRUCTURAL:		
a. Grammatical morphology	abundant	absent
b. Syntactic constructions	complex/embedded	simple/conjoined
c. Use of word-order	grammatical (subj/obj)	pragmatic (topic/comment)
d. Pauses	fluent	halting
FUNCTIONAL:		
e. Processing speed	fast	slow
f. Mental effort	effortless	laborious
g. Error rate	lower	higher
h. Context dependence	lower	higher
COGNITIVE:		
i. Processing mode	automated	attended
j. Acquisition	late	early
k. Evolution	late	early

Table 9.3:   Pre-grammatical v. grammatical discourse processing (from Givón 1995)

A number of studies have tested Givón's claims regarding syntactization (for example, Schumann 1987; Givón 1984; Sato 1988; Pfaff 1992; Ramat 1992). They have produced mixed results. For example, Sato's ten-month study of two child Vietnamese learners of English found little evidence of paratactic speech (non-propositional utterances, vertical constructions, and scaffolded utterances). In fact, both learners, contrary to the theory, encoded plenty of simple complete propositions from the start and were able to do so without the help of interlocutor scaffolding. However, there was some evidence of a shift from coordination to subordination in one of the learners, although simple juxtapositioning of propositions served as the main way of expressing logical relationships for both learners throughout the period of the study. Clearer evidence of the absence of syntactization was seen in the learners' failure to produce infinitival complements until near the end, and the almost complete absence of relative clauses and gerundive complements. Sato suggests that interaction may be insufficient to ensure full syntactization, and that encounters with written language may be crucial.

Somewhat more convincing evidence of syntactization comes from studies that have investigated the hypothesis that grammatical markers develop out of independent lexical items. Pfaff (1992) provides evidence for this in the acquisition of L2 German by pre-school and early school-age Turkish children in Berlin-Kreuzberg (the KITA Study). She found, for instance, that main verb use of 'sein' and 'haben' preceded the auxiliary use of the same verbs. Ramat (1992), in a study of the L2 acquisition of Italian by subjects of mixed language backgrounds, also provides support for this hypothesis. Adverbs preceded the use of inflected modal verbs as a device for conveying various meanings.

Givón has also identified a number of linguistic universals which are functional in nature. An example is the 'quantity universal', which states:

> More continuous, predictable, non-disruptive topics will be marked by less marking material; while less continuous, unpredictable/surprising, or disruptive topics will be marked by more marking material (1984: 126).

Pfaff's (1987a) study of Turkish adolescents' German interlanguage suggests that this principle operates in L2 acquisition. Using data from two elicited narratives, Pfaff was able to show that the protagonists in the stories were almost always indicated by a pronominal form ('less marking material'), whereas all the other participants were marked by article + noun ('more marking material'). However, Tomlin (1990) reports a study of advanced L2 learners that did not show any alternation in the use of pronominal and nominal structures in accordance with the quantity principle; the learners generally used nominal NPs throughout in a narrative task. Tomlin suggests that the learners preferred nominal structures 'as part of a communicative strategy to ensure coherent and complete understanding by a listener' (1990: 171).[6] The status of functional universals like the quantity principle in L2 acquisition is not yet clear.

Underlying both Klein's and Givón's positions is the assumption that learners will be functionally motivated to develop their interlanguages. That is, the drive to communicate more effectively leads learners to syntacticize. However, Sato and others (for example, Higgs and Clifford 1982) have cast doubts on whether communicative need by itself is sufficient to ensure high levels of interlanguage development.

The Competition Model

Like other functionalist models,[7] the *Competition Model* is a performance not a competence model. That is, it seeks to account for the kind of knowledge that underlies real-time processing in real-world language behaviour, although, as we will see, it has been investigated by means of experimental studies which elicited rather artificial language responses. Also like other functionalist models and unlike linguistic models associated with Universal Grammar, the Competition Model sees the human capacity for language learning as non-specific (i.e. as resulting from general cognitive mechanisms involved in other kinds of learning). It also resembles other functionalist models in that it is interactionist; that is, the learner's grammar is viewed as an emergent property resulting from the interaction between input and cognitive mechanisms relating to perceptual abilities, channel capacity, and memory.

Central to the model is the idea of form-function mappings. As Mac-Whinney, Bates, and Kligell (1984) put it:

> The forms of natural languages are created, governed, constrained, acquired and used in the service of communicative functions.

Any one form may realize a number of functions and, conversely, any one function can be realized through a number of forms. The learner's task is to discover the particular form–function mappings that characterize the target language. In this respect, the model is close to some variability theories (for example, Ellis 1985c; Huebner 1983).

Form–function mappings are characterized as being of varying 'strengths' in different languages. This is usually illustrated with reference to the function of 'agency', which has a number of possible formal exponents:

1 Word order: in the case of transitive constructions, the first noun mentioned in a clause is likely to function as the agent. For example, in the English sentence 'Mary kissed John', 'Mary' is the agent.
2 Agreement: the noun phrase which functions as agent may agree in number with the verb. Thus, in English, a singular noun phrase functioning as agent takes a singular verb form (for example, 'She likes ice-cream'), while a plural noun phrase takes a plural verb form (for example, 'They like ice-cream'). The object of the sentence has no effect on the verb form.
3 Case: the noun phrase functioning as agent may be morphologically marked in some way. For example, the agent is signalled in German by nominative case marking on the article, while the object is signalled by means of accusative case marking (for example, 'Der Mann ißt den Apfel' = 'The man is eating the apple').
4 Animacy: agents are normally animate, patients are normally inanimate.

Any one language is likely to utilize several devices for signalling the 'agent' of a sentence. English, for instance, uses all four, as illustrated in these sentences:

> Mary kissed John. (word order)
> Money they like. (agreement)
> She kissed him. (case)
> This book Mary likes a lot. (animacy)

However, as these examples also show, a language is likely to assign different weights to these devices in terms of the probability of their use in signalling a given function. English, for example, relies primarily on word order to encode agency, while Russian uses case marking and Japanese animacy. Like variability models, the Competition Model is probabilistic in nature.

The model take its name from the 'competition' that arises from the different devices or cues that signal a particular function. For example, in a sentence like 'that lecturer we like a lot' there is competition between 'lecturer' 'we' and 'lot' for the role of agent of the verb. 'Lot' rapidly loses out because, unlike 'lecturer' and 'we', it is inanimate, and because it follows rather than precedes the verb. The candidacy of 'lecturer' is promoted by its position in the sentence—it is the first noun—but, ultimately, this cue is not strong enough to overcome two other cues. 'We' is the strongest candidate for agent because it is nominative in case and because it agrees in number with the verb.

The task facing the L2 learner is to discover (1) which forms are used to realize which functions in the L2, and (2) what weights to attach to the use of individual forms in the performance of specific functions. This is what is meant by 'form–function mapping'. The input supplies the learner with cues of four broad types: word order, vocabulary, morphology, and intonation. The usefulness of a cue is determined by several factors: (1) 'cue reliability' (the extent to which a cue always maps the same form onto the same function), (2) 'cue availability' (how often the cue is available in the input) and (3) 'conflict validity' (whether a cue 'wins' or 'loses' when it appears in competitive environments). For example, if we consider the information available to the L2 learner regarding the role of word order in realizing agency in English, we can characterize this 'cue' as relatively reliable (the noun phrase preceding the verb is typically the agent) and readily available (the input is likely to supply plentiful examples of this mapping). Also, in English, word order tends to override other cues (except agreement). Thus, in a sentence like 'Mary bit the dog', 'Mary' is the agent, even though experience of the world might lead one to suspect that 'the dog' is the more likely agent.

There has also been some attempt to specify how learners use the information available from 'cues' to construct their language systems. McDonald (1986) has proposed a learning-on-error model, according to which the weights attached to specific form–function mappings are changed when the learner interprets an input cue incorrectly and is subsequently provided with feedback, a view of acquisition which, as we shall see later, accords with that of *Parallel Distributed Processing* (see page 403). McDonald suggests that this may account for the developmental shift noted in L1 acquisition from an initial dependence on cue reliability/availability to dependence on conflict validity. To begin with, children respond to those cues which are salient and easily detectable (such as word order), but once these have been established they turn their attention to sentences containing conflicting cues (for example, 'That person we all love', where there is conflict between the word order and agreement cues). Ultimately it is these sentences that help them to establish the dominance patterns of the cues. McDonald and Heilenman (1991) provide evidence from an experimental study of French/English bilinguals that supports such a view.

The Competition Model has informed a number of studies of L2 acquisition (for example, Harrington 1987; Gass 1987; Kilborn and Cooremann 1987; Kilborn and Ito 1989; McDonald and Heilenman 1991; Sasaki 1991). These studies take the form of sentence-interpretation experiments using bilingual subjects in a within-subjects, cross-language design. That is, speakers of different languages are asked to identify the function of different cues in both L1 and L2 sentences that have been designed to reflect both the coordination and competition of cues. For example, they may be asked to say which noun is the agent of an action in acceptable sentences like 'The boy is chopping the log' and in semantically unlikely sentences such as 'The logs are chopping the boy', where the animacy cue is in competition with the word order cue, but the agreement cue is in coordination. The studies then compare the responses of learners with different language backgrounds.

A good example of such a study is Harrington (1987). Harrington investigated the effects of three factors—word order, animacy and stress—on the processing strategies used by native speakers of English (the NL English group), native speakers of Japanese (the NL Japanese group), and Japanese speakers of English (the interlanguage (IL) group). There were twelve adult subjects in each group. They were asked to interpret 81 test sentences by stating which of two nouns in each sentence was the logical subject (i.e. agent). The sentences had been designed to incorporate the three factors systematically, either in competition or in coordination. The subjects, however, were not informed of this. Inevitably, some of the sentences were ungrammatical or unnatural, but Harrington argued that this was appropriate and that, in any case, information regarding the effects of converging and competing cues was 'extraordinarily difficult to obtain from natural speech' (1987: 360).

The analysis of the results was based on 'choice' (which noun each subject chose in each sentence) and 'latency' (the time it took each subject to make each choice). The results are extremely complex, reflecting a number of interactions between the subject and language variables. We will focus here on the results obtained for word order cue effects, which are summarized in Table 9.4. As expected, the NL English group interpreted the first noun in canonical NVN sentences and the second noun in the unnatural NNV and VNN sentences[8] as the agent. Also, as expected, the NL Japanese group demonstrated little sensitivity to word order as a signal of agency, exhibiting no more than a slight tendency to choose the first noun as the agent and no use at all of a 'second noun strategy'. In contrast to these results for the word order cue, the NL English showed less sensitivity to the animacy cue than the NL Japanese, although to complicate matters, a sub-group of the NL English did appear to be influenced strongly by this cue. The IL group were midway between the NL English and NL Japanese groups in their choice of agent in canonical NVN sentences, but, as predicted, behaved like the NL Japanese group in their interpretation of the unnatural NNV and VNN sentences. Harrington also produces results to indicate that even in the case of the NVN sentences, the IL group were responding more to the animacy than to the word order cue. He concludes that a word order strategy was evident but was 'only of limited strength' in the IL group. In contrast, there was clear evidence that animacy cues were of primary importance in the IL group's responses.

Group	Canonical sentences NVN	Unnatural sentences	
		NNV	VNN
NL English	81%	35%	33%
NL Japanese	59%	56%	54%
IL subjects	68%	59%	56%

Table 9.4:   Choice of first noun as agent in a sentence interpretation task (based on results reported in Harrington (1987))

The results of this study are encouraging for the Competition Model. They demonstrate that L2 learners are influenced by their L1 processing strategies, which they transfer when interpreting L2 sentences. Furthermore, the results suggest that the processing strategies utilized by L2 learners can be located somewhere on the continuum between the strategies used by native speakers of the two languages concerned. This suggests that the idea of a restructuring continuum may after all make some sense in the case of syntax, at least where sentence processing is concerned. Further evidence for this is available in Kilborn's (1987) study of German learners of L2 English, which shows that a group of advanced learners were much closer to a NL English group than were a group of novice learners where word order cues were concerned. It should be noted, however, that restructuring involves strategies rather than forms; it is not L2 forms that replace L1 forms, but rather L2 processing strategies.

There is also evidence to suggest that some interpretation strategies are more universal than others. Thus, Gass (1987) found that while English-speaking learners of L2 Italian made little use of their L1 syntax-based strategy, Italian-speaking learners of L2 English did transfer their lexical-semantic strategy (i.e. animacy cues). Further evidence of similar directionality effects in the transfer of L1 interpretation strategies comes from Sasaki's (1991) bi-directional study of the acquisition of English and Japanese. These results testify to the primacy of a semantics/pragmatics strategy and confirm the findings of other functionally-orientated models of L2 acquisition. The utilization of L1 interpretation strategies, therefore, depends on the universality of the strategy; the more universal a strategy is, the more it is likely to be transferred. Once again, then, we see evidence of constraints on transfer (see Chapter 8).

The strength of the Competition Model is that it allows researchers to test very precise hypotheses. In this respect it resembles UG-based theories (see Chapter 10). It also provides a convincing account of a number of aspects of

L2 acquisition which any theory must consider: the role of the L1, the effect of input and the gradual way in which native-like ability is acquired. There are, of course, other aspects which it does not address, at least at the moment. It is not clear, for instance, what kind of knowledge learners use in sentence interpretation, nor does the model have much to say about the cognitive mechanisms responsible for obtaining intake from input or for using L2 knowledge in production.

Probably the main weakness of the model is over-reliance on rather artificial interpretation tasks, a problem that is aggravated by the unnatural sentences that figure in such tasks. The justification for such a methodology is the Ecological Validity Hypothesis, according to which 'the processing of both grammatical and ungrammatical sentences proceed by reference to the same set of cues and processing patterns' (MacWhinney, Pleh, and Bates 1985: 199). But this has been queried by McLaughlin and Harrington (1989):

> ... it may be wise to question the 'ecological validity' of an experimental procedure in which subjects have to make decisions about sentences that are as deviant in English as: 'The apple is eating the man'. Perhaps subjects are not processing such sentences as they would in actual communicative situations, but are settling on a particular problem-solving strategy to get them through the many judgements of this nature they have to make (1989: 125).

It might be further argued that L2 acquisition takes place as a result of 'utterance processing' rather than 'sentence processing', the distinguishing feature being that utterances are contextualized whereas sentences are not. Utterance processing involves pragmatic procedures, which are ignored in the kind of sentence-processing tasks on which the Competition Model has relied.[9] However, as the quotation from McLaughlin and Harrington suggests, researchers are aware of the need to develop more natural, on-line ways of investigating input processing.

The Nativization Model and Operating Principles

Whereas the Competition Model was designed to account for sentence interpretation, *Operating Principles* have been formulated to explain why certain linguistic forms typically appear in learners' (L1 and L2) production before others. The idea of operating principles is not incompatible with the Competition Model, however, as they shed light on the general ideas of 'cue reliability' and 'cue availability'. They are based on the general assumption that those features that are easily attended to and easily processed will be the first to be learnt and thus to be used in production.

Operating principles in L2 acquisition have been investigated by Andersen. Andersen's earlier work (Andersen 1979; 1980; 1983b; 1984a) sought an explanation for how learners create and restructure their interlanguage systems as a product of participating in verbal interaction with more proficient speakers. It resulted in the 'Nativization Model', according to which L2 acquisition consists of two general processes, nativization and denativization. In the former, learners make the input conform to their own internalized view of what constitutes the L2 system. That is, they simplify the learning task by forming hypotheses based on knowledge that they already possess (L1 knowledge and knowledge of the world). In Andersen's terms, they attend to an 'internal norm'. The result is the kind of pidginization evident in early language acquisition and documented in Schumann's work (see Chapters 3 and 6). In denativization, learners accommodate to an 'external norm'; that is, they adjust their interlanguage systems to make them fit with the input, making use of inferencing strategies. Denativization is apparent in depidginization (the elaboration of a pidgin language which occurs through the gradual incorporation of forms from an external source). Subsequently, Andersen (1990) has recognized that nativization and denativization are not two separate 'forces' but aspects of the same overall process of acquisition. Andersen's later work is an attempt to develop the nativization model by further specifying the 'processes, cognitive operating principles, and communicative strategies' (1990: 48) that fit within it.

Andersen has been strongly influenced by Slobin's idea of operating principles. In a series of publications culminating in the two-volume publication *The Crosslinguistic Study of Language Acquisition* (1985a), Slobin has attempted to describe the universal principles that guide children in the process of L1 acquisition. These principles are conceived as the operating principles by which children extract and segment linguistic information in order to build a grammar of the language they are learning. According to Slobin (1973; 1985b), children possess a 'language making capacity' consisting of principles that enable them to perceive and segment items in the input (for example, 'Pay attention to stressed syllables in extracted speech units. Store such syllables separately and also in relation to the units in which they occur') and also principles that govern how they organize and store new information (for example, 'Keep track of the frequency of occurrence of every unit and pattern that you store'). In his 1985b paper, Slobin identifies a total of 40 such principles, a considerable increase on his earlier (1973) paper. Their investigation requires the painstaking analysis of production data from many unrelated languages, as this is the only way to separate out language-specific tendencies from universal principles.

Andersen points out that most of the operating principles he has identified in his own work can be related to Slobin's. However, he claims that his principles are not simply a translation to L2 learning, but rather 'macroprinciples', each one of which corresponds to a group of principles in Slobin's framework. The seven operating principles described in Table 9.5 evolved out of research that Andersen has conducted on the L2 acquisition of English and Spanish (for example, Andersen 1990).

Principle	Definition	Example
The one-to-one principle	'An interlanguage system should be constructed in such a way that an intended underlying meaning is expressed with one clear invariant surface form (or construction)' (Andersen 1984a: 79)	Clitic pronouns in French and Spanish are placed before the verb but in IL they are placed after the verb, like full NPs.
The multi-functionality principle	(a) Where there is clear evidence in the input that more than one form marks the meaning conveyed by only one form in the interlanguage, try to discover the distribution and additional meaning (if any) of the new form. (b) Where there is evidence in the input that an interlanguage form conveys only one of the meanings that the same form has in the input, try to discover the additional meanings of the form in the input.	Spanish learners of L2 English typically acquire a single negator, 'no', to begin with. However, the input supplies evidence of other negators, e.g. 'not' and 'don't', each with a different meaning.
Formal determinism principle	Pay closer attention to form-meaning relationships that are clearly and uniformly encoded in the input than to other form–function relationships.	Learners pay attention to negators other than 'no' in the input because the other forms are modelled clearly in the input such that their meanings are transparent.
Distributional bias principle	If both X and Y can occur in the same environments A and B, but a bias in the distribution of X and Y makes it appear that X only occurs in environment A and Y only occurs in environment B, when you acquire X and Y, restrict X to environment A and Y to B.	In Spanish, punctual verbs tend to occur in the preterite form, and state verbs in the imperfect form; L2 learners manifest this bias in the use of the two tenses.

Principle	Definition	Example
Relevance principle	If two or more functors apply to a content word, try to place them so that the more relevant the meaning of the functor is to the meaning of the content word, the closer it is placed to the content word. If you find that a notion is marked in several places, at first mark it only in the position closest to the relevant content word.	In the Spanish verb system, aspect is most relevant to the lexical item it is attached to (i.e. the verb), tense has a wider scope but is still closely related to the verb, and subject–verb agreement is least attached to the verb. L2 learners acquire aspect, tense, and agreement in this order.
Transfer to somewhere principle	A grammatical form or structure will occur consistently and frequently in IL as a result of transfer if, and only if: (1) natural acquisitional principles are consistent with the L1 structure, or (2) there already exists within the L2 input the potential for (mis-) generalization from the input to produce the same form or structure.	French learners of L2 English do not place pronouns before the verb even though this is possible in French because no model for such transfer is available in the input.
Relexification principle	When you cannot perceive the structural pattern of the L2, use your L1 with lexical items from the L2.	Japanese learners of L2 English have been observed to use English lexis in SOV sentence frames, but this may be short-lived because English provides no evidence of SOV word order.

Table 9.5:   Operating principles in L2 acquisition (summarized from Andersen 1990)

Operating principles have been criticized in both L1 and L2 acquisition research on a number of grounds. Dulay and Burt (1974d) and Larsen-Freeman (1975) have argued that they are difficult to test and are not mutually exclusive. Also, it is not clear how many principles are needed to explain acquisition. These criticisms, which were levelled at the earlier list (Slobin 1973), are still valid. Bowerman (1985) points out that Slobin only *lists* operating principles, but this is inadequate because we need to know how the various principles are related to each other and, importantly, what weight is to be attached to principles when they conflict. Andersen acknowledges these criticisms, but argues that they do not warrant rejecting the whole idea of operating principles. The solution is to work on them and refine them. However, as Pleh (1990) notes in her review of Slobin (1985a), there is an overriding difficulty—so far, there is no explanation of the principles themselves. Only when this is available will problems concerning the number and the form of the principles be resolvable.

The Multidimensional Model and processing operations

The Multidimensional Model resembles Andersen's work on operating principles in a number of respects. First, it is based on the painstaking analysis of naturally occurring learner speech. Second, it also sees the regularities in learner language as the product of cognitive processes that govern the linguistic operations learners are able to handle. However, the model constitutes a considerable advance on the idea of operating principles in that it relates the underlying cognitive processes to stages in the learner's development, explaining how one stage supersedes another. Also, the model provides an account of inter-learner variation.

The Multidimensional Model was developed by a group of researchers involved in the Zweitspracherwerb Italienischer und Spanischer Arbeiter (ZISA) project in the 1970s (see Clahsen, Meisel, and Pienemann 1983). This involved the longitudinal study of 12 adults and the cross-sectional study of 45 adults, the researchers arguing that cross-sectional studies only had validity if they were supported by longitudinal research. Subsequently, the model has been developed further as a result of studies of the naturalistic L2 acquisition of Australian English by Polish and Vietnamese immigrants (Johnston 1985) and also of L2 Japanese by (Yoshioka and Doi 1988). In addition, some of its claims have been tested in classroom studies investigating the effects of formal instruction on the acquisition of specific grammatical structures (for example, Pienemann 1984; 1989).

The model is in several respects more comprehensive than any of the other models so far considered, with the possible exception of Krashen's Monitor Theory. It makes the following general claims:

1 Learners manifest developmental sequences in the acquisition of a number of grammatical structures, such as word order and some grammatical morphemes.

2 Learners also display individual variation, both with regard to the extent to which they apply developmental rules and to the extent to which they acquire and use grammatical structures that are not developmentally constrained.

3 Developmental sequences reflect the systematic way in which learners overcome processing constraints. These constraints are of a general cognitive nature and govern production.

4 Individual learner variation reflects the overall orientation to the learning task, which in turn is the product of socio-psychological factors.

5 Formal instruction directed at developmental features will only be successful if learners have mastered the prerequisite processing operations
associated with the previous stage of acquisition. However, formal instruction directed at grammatical features subject to individual variation
faces no such constraints.

The account of the Multidimensional Model that follows will consider points
(1) to (4). Point (5) is considered in Chapter 14.

The claim that learners acquire a number of grammatical features in a clear
developmental sequence was based, initially, on the detailed study of German
word order rules by the ZISA researchers. The general pattern is described in
Chapter 3 (see Table 3.8). Subsequent work has demonstrated that similar
developmental patterns are evident in the acquisition of L2 English word order rules. More importantly, the claim that learners follow developmental sequences has also been extended to grammatical morphology, thus vastly
extending the scope of the model. Pienemann and Johnston (1988) distinguish 'local morphemes' and 'non-local morphemes' according to whether
the functional mapping performed by the morpheme occurs within a major
constituent or across constituents. For example, the plural -s and the regular
past tense -ed morphemes are seen as 'local' because they involve simple additions to the constituents to which they belong. However, 3rd person -s is
'non-local' because the function it performs (marking subject–verb agreement) involves the learner in relating two constituents, the subject noun
phrase and the verb. The extended sequence of acquisition of developmental
rules for English can be found in Table 3.9.

The ZISA researchers noted that within the defined stages of development,
there was considerable variation among learners (Meisel, Clahsen, and Pienemann 1981). This variation is of two kinds. First, learners differ in the extent
to which they apply a particular word order rule to different linguistic contexts. For example, the inversion rule in German applies in a number of contexts—after an interrogative pronoun, after a preposing adverbial, after the
topicalization of a direct object, and after a sentence-initial adverbial
clause—but when learners acquire this rule they do not invariably apply it to
all these contexts. Meisel, Clahsen, and Pienemann (1981: 126) comment:
'whereas some learners seem to acquire a rule perfectly before they move on
to the next learning task, others are less perfect in terms of the target language'. Second, learners vary in the extent to which they use *restrictive simplification* and *elaborative simplification*. This distinction works in much the
same way in learner language as it does in foreigner talk (see the discussion in
Chapter 6). Thus, restrictive simplification is designed to achieve 'optimal
results in communication' by 'reducing the grammar in a way that makes it
easy to handle' (Meisel 1980: 36). It is always evident in the early stages of acquisition. Elaborative simplification is 'a strategy that helps to complexify the
grammatical system' by formulating hypotheses that are 'approximations to

the actual rule' and often involve overextensions of a rule (op. cit.: 37). Not all learners engage in elaborative simplification.

The model therefore has two principal axes, the developmental and the variational, as shown in Figure 9.4. This allows for learners to be grouped both in terms of their stage of development and in terms of the kind of simplification they engage in. For example, Figure 9.4 shows two learners (A and B) at stage 5, two at stage 4 (C and D), and 2 others at stage 3 (E and F), reflecting their progress on the developmental axis. It also shows differences between the learners at each level. For example, learner B produces more standard-like language than learner A. Meisel, Clahsen, and Pienemann (1981) emphasize that progress on one axis or dimension is independent of progress on the other. It is theoretically possible, therefore, for a learner who practises elaborative simplification to use more target-like language overall than a learner who is 'developmentally' far more advanced. Learner F, for instance, is only at stage 3, but uses more standard-like constructions than Learner A, who is at stage 5.

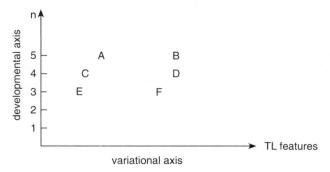

Figure 9.4:   The two axes of the Multidimensional Model

The identification of developmental patterns is of no value to theory-construction unless a principled explanation for them can be found. It is in this respect that the Multidimensional Model offers most to SLA research. It explains why learners pass through the stages of development they do, and also, on the basis of this, affords predictions regarding when other grammatical structures (those that have not yet been investigated) will be acquired. In other words, the model has both explanatory and predictive power.

The explanation rests on the idea of processing constraints. Clahsen (1984) has proposed that the sequence of acquisition of German word order results from 'reorderings and restructurings of various levels of underlying linguistic units' (1984: 221) and draws a direct comparison between his proposals and Slobin's operating principles. He identifies three language processing strategies, each one corresponding to the degree of psychological complexity involved in the production of a particular word order rule:

1 Canonical Order Strategy (COS)

No permutation or reordering of constituents in a structure occurs; utterances manifest a 'basic' order that reflects a direct mapping of meaning on to syntactic form. This strategy blocks the interruption of the underlying structure.

2 Initialization/Finalization Strategy (IFS)

No permutation involving the movement of an element from within a structure occurs, but movement of an initial element in a structure to final position and vice versa is possible.

3 Subordinate Clause Strategy (SCS)

No permutation of any element in a subordinate clause is possible, but movement of an element from within a main clause to another position in the clause is possible. Progress entails the removal of the processing 'blocks'. For example, learners who have acquired the verb separation rule and so can produce utterances like:

alle kinder muss die pause machen
(all the children must the pause make)

but have not yet acquired either inversion or verb-end (see Table 3.8 for examples) have overcome the constraint of the Canonical Word Order Strategy but not of the other two strategies. The three strategies are hierarchical in that SCS is not manifest until IFS is evident, which in turn cannot be employed until COS has been accessed. The acquisition of grammatical structures occurs as learners systematically overcome the constraints identified in these processing strategies. The strategies are themselves developmental, not in the sense that learners do not already 'know' them—they clearly do, as they are involved in L1 production—but in the sense that they can only be accessed in the L2 incrementally.

Johnston (1986) has described the general pattern of acquisition evident in L2 learners of English in Australia and identifies the nature of the processing operations involved at each of six stages of development, drawing on Clahsen's three strategies. The operations are summarized in Table 9.6 with examples from L2 English. It should be noted that the mastery of each processing operation is seen as making the acquisition of not one but several structures possible.

The Multidimensional Model also has a socio-psychological dimension that accounts for the simplification strategies employed by individual learners. This is described in terms of a continuum reflecting learners' orientations towards the learning task (Meisel, Clahsen, and Pienemann 1981). At one end is segregative orientation, which arises when there is a lack of interest

Stage	Processing operation	Linguistic realization
1	Production relies on non-linguistic processing devices. Learner has no knowledge of syntactic categories.	Undifferentiated lexical items; formulas such as 'I don't know' and 'I can't'.
2	Production of simple strings of elements based on meaning or information focus. Learner still has no knowledge of syntactic categories.	Canonical word order; intonation questions (e.g. 'You playing football?').
3	Learner is able to identify the beginning and end of a string to perform operations on an element in these positions e.g. learner can shift an element from beginning to end of string and vice versa. These operations are still pre-syntactic.	Adverb-preposing (e.g. 'Today I play football'); do-fronting (e.g. 'Do you play football?'); neg + V (e.g. 'No play football').
4	Learner is able to identify an element within a string and to move this element from the middle of the string to either the beginning or the end. This operation is again characterized as pre-syntactic.	Yes/No questions (e.g. 'Can you swim?'); pseudo-inversion (e.g. 'Where is my purse?').
5	Learner is now able to identify elements in a string as belonging to different syntactic categories. She is able to shift elements around inside the string.	*wh*-inversion (e.g. 'Where are you playing football?'); Internal neg. (e.g. 'He did not understand?').
6	Learner is now able to move elements out of one sub-string and attach it to another element. This stage is characterized by the ability of the learner to process across as well as inside strings.	Q-tags (e.g. 'You're playing football today, aren't you?'); V-complements (e.g. 'He asked me to play football?').

Source: Based on Johnston (1986); Pienemann, Johnston, and Brindley (1988)

Table 9.6:   Processing operations involved in the acquisition of grammatical rules

in contact with native speakers, discrimination on the part of native speakers, and a general lack of either instrumental or integrative motivation. At the other end is integrative orientation, which is evident in learners with either a strong desire to assimilate into the L2 culture or in those with no desire to acculturate but with a strong instrumental need to learn the L2. The socio-psychological dimension of the model echoes the social theories of L2 acquisition considered in Chapter 6. It explains the extent to which individual learners conform to target-language norms. The learner's orientation, however, has no effect on the general sequence of progression along the developmental axis.

As we have already noted, the Multidimensional Model is powerful not only because it provides a satisfactory explanation of observed development in learner-language, but because it also constitutes a predictive framework. The cognitive dimension afforded by the identification of underlying processing strategies and operations allows researchers to form hypotheses regarding which grammatical structures will be acquired at which general stage of development. The predictive framework has been applied to Japanese to test the validity of hypotheses relating to the acquisition of the particles 'wa', 'ga', and 'o' in a cross-sectional study. The results support the general prediction that the order of acquisition is wa > o > ga (Yoshioka and Doi 1988).[10] Pienemann and Johnston (1988) also report on the successful testing of predictions relating to a number of morphological and syntactical rules. The predictive power of the model is probably greater than that of any other model of L2 acquisition, with the possible exception of the Competition Model.

There are, however, several problems with the model. As Larsen-Freeman and Long (1991) note, there is no account of how or why learners overcome the processing constraints. Two other problems are the difficulty in identifying formulaic chunks of language and of establishing *a priori* which features are variational and, therefore, not subject to the constraints that govern developmental features. If a learner, supposedly at stage 2, produces an utterance like 'Where does he live?', which belongs to stage 5, to what extent does this falsify the theory? It is very easy to immunize the theory by claiming that such an utterance is a 'formula' and thus not subject to processing constraints. But unless there exists a clear method for identifying such formulas before the analysis proceeds, the theory runs the danger of becoming unfalsifiable. A similar argument can be made for variational features. Unless we are able to stipulate beforehand which features are variational and which developmental, it is easy to dismiss any feature that fails to conform to the predictive framework of the model on the grounds that it is variational. These are serious problems, for which Larsen-Freeman and Long advance no solutions.

Another problem concerns the operational definition of 'acquisition'. Whereas the original research on which the Multidimensional Model was based quantified all the features examined by indicating their overall proportion of suppliance in obligatory contexts (as in Meisel, Clahsen, and Pienemann 1981: 112), Pienemann and his co-workers have subsequently redefined acquisition in terms of 'onset' (i.e. the first appearance of a grammatical feature). Hulstijn (1987), while accepting that the study of 'onset' is legitimate in a model that emphasizes the importance of processing operations, nevertheless feels that much of the work lacks rigour because Pienemann 'does not set quantitative or qualitative criteria to be met by the learner's production, in order to be considered as evidence for the operation of a predicted processing strategy' (1987: 14). The problem of defining 'onset', of course, derives in part from the difficulty of identifying formulas and variational features.

Finally, we should note that the Multidimensional Model only provides an explanation of acquisition in terms of learner production. It tells us nothing about how learners come to comprehend grammatical structures, nor does it inform about how comprehension and production interact. In particular, the theory does not address how learners obtain intake from input and how this is then used to reconstruct internal grammars. It is in this respect that the theory is most limited.

Skill learning models of second language acquisition

The models and theories we have looked at so far have drawn extensively on constructs borrowed from cognitive psychology, but they have been specially designed to account for language learning (as opposed to some other kind of learning) and have taken 'language'—either the target language or learner language—as their starting point. The theories which we will consider in this section originate in cognitive psychology; they explain L2 acquisition in terms of general skill learning.

Anderson's Adaptive Control of Thought (ACT) Model

Anderson's *Adaptive Control of Thought (ACT) Model*[11] (Anderson 1976; 1980; 1983) rests on the distinction between *declarative* and *procedural knowledge*.[12] While admitting that the distinction between the two types of knowledge is not water-tight, Anderson (1976) characterizes the essential differences in the form of three assumptions:

1 Declarative knowledge seems to be possessed in an all-or-none manner, whereas procedural knowledge seems to be something that can be partially possessed.
2 One acquires declarative knowledge suddenly, by being told, whereas one acquires procedural knowledge gradually, by performing the skill.
3 One can communicate one's declarative knowledge verbally, but not one's procedural knowledge. (1976: 117)

Learning a language, like any other type of skill learning (for example, driving a car or playing tennis), involves the development of procedures that transform declarative knowledge into a form that makes for easy and efficient performance.

This transition of declarative to procedural knowledge takes place in three stages. In the declarative stage information is stored as facts for which there are no ready-made activation procedures. For example, we may be aware that 'drowned' consists of 'drown' and '-ed', and yet be unable to produce 'drowned' correctly in conversation. The second stage is the associative stage. Because it is difficult to use declarative knowledge, the learner tries to sort the information into more efficient production sets by means of 'composition' (collapsing several discrete productions into one), and 'proceduralization' (applying a general rule to a particular instance). For example, the learner may have learnt 'drowned' and 'saved' as two distinct items, but may come to realize that they can be represented more economically in a production set: 'If the goal is to generate a past tense verb, then add *-ed* to the verb'. This may then serve as a general procedure for generating past tense forms, including incorrect ones (such as 'goed'). Anderson (1983) notes that errors are particularly likely during the associative stage. In the autonomous stage, in which procedures become increasingly automated, the mind continues both to generalize productions and also to discriminate more narrowly the occasions when specific productions can be used. For example, the learner may modify the past tense production set (above) so that it applies to only a subset of verbs. At this stage the ability to verbalize knowledge of the skill can disappear entirely.

Anderson (1980 and 1983) discusses classroom L2 learning in the light of the ACT model. He sees the kind of knowledge taught to the classroom learner as different from adult L1 knowledge:

> We speak the learned language (i.e. the second language) by using general rule-following procedures applied to the rules we have learned, rather than speaking directly, as we do in our native language. Not surprisingly, applying this knowledge is a much slower and more painful process than applying the procedurally encoded knowledge of our own language.
> (1980: 224)

However, Anderson sees the differences between L1 and foreign language learning as merely a question of the stage reached. Whereas L1 learners almost invariably reach the autonomous stage, foreign language learners typically only reach the associative stage. Thus, although foreign language learners achieve a fair degree of proceduralization through practice, and can use L2 rules without awareness, they do not reach full autonomy.

The ACT model is enormously complex. A single communicative act, for instance, is likely to involve an elaborate sequence of interrelated 'production systems'. It is not possible to do justice to this complexity here. The central points to grasp are the theoretical claim that learning begins with declarative knowledge which slowly becomes proceduralized, and that the mechanism by which this takes place is *practice*.

McLaughlin's information processing model

The most detailed attempt to apply an information processing model to L2 acquisition can be found in the work of McLaughlin (McLaughlin 1978b; 1980; 1987; 1990a; McLaughlin, Rossman, and McLeod 1983). Although McLaughlin's ideas have developed somewhat over the years, it is possible to identify a number of central theoretical tenets related to (1) the idea of processing limitations and (2) the need for restructuring.

McLaughlin draws heavily on research in cognitive psychology into information processing (for example, Shiffrin and Schneider 1977). Learners are limited in how much information they are able to process by both the nature of the task and their own information-processing ability. They are not capable of attending to all the information available in the input. Some of it becomes the object of focused or selective attention, while other parts are attended to only peripherally. In order to maximize their information processing ability, learners routinize skills. Initially a skill may be available only through controlled processing, which McLaughlin, Rossman, and McLeod (1983) describe as follows:

> ... not a learned response, but a temporary activation of nodes in a sequence. This activation is under attentional control of the subject and, since attention is required, only one such sequence can normally be controlled at a time without interference (1983: 139).

In contrast, automatic processing 'involves the activation of certain nodes in memory every time the appropriate inputs are present'. Routinization, therefore, helps learners to reduce the burden on their information-processing capacity. It occurs when they have the opportunity to practise controlled processes. Routinization results in quantitative changes in interlanguage by making an increasing number of information chunks available for automatic processing.

Information-processing capacity is also extended in another way—through *restructuring*. This allows for qualitative changes in interlanguage. These changes relate to both the way knowledge is represented in the minds of learners and also the strategies they employ. Representational change involves a shift from exemplar-based to rule-based representation. McLaughlin (1990a: 118) gives the 'classic' example of past tense learning in English (the U-shaped learning pattern described on page 303). Another example of the general transition from exemplar-based to rule-based representation is the change from formulaic speech to rule analysis (see Chapter 3).[13] Restructuring is also facilitated by the flexible use of learning strategies. In a series of experiments, which are considered in Chapter 12, McLaughlin and his associates were able to show that 'expert' language learners display greater flexibility in restructuring rules, and are therefore able to avoid making certain types of error. McLaughlin (1990a) considers that practice is also important for restructuring.

McLaughlin's information processing model provides a useful general account of the language learning process. It is particularly helpful in that it helps to reconcile one of the problems we identified in the discussion of the explicit/implicit distinction. If explicit learning is characterized as involving focal attention and implicit learning as peripheral attention—a correlation that McLaughlin, Rossman, and McLeod (1983:142) actually make—and if this distinction is seen as distinct from the controlled/automatic distinction, then the nature of the interface between the different types of knowledge becomes clearer. It is possible to argue (Ellis 1993a) that whereas there is a clear interface on the controlled/automatic dimension (i.e. controlled knowledge can convert into automatic knowledge over time through practice), the interface between explicit and implicit knowledge is constrained by learnability factors (for example, the kind of strategies identified by Clahsen in the Multidimensional Model). In other words, automatizing knowledge does not lead to the conversion of explicit into implicit knowledge but only to the automatization of explicit or implicit knowledge. The continua intersect to produce different kinds of L2 knowledge, as shown in Figure 9.5.

	Controlled	Automatic
Explicit	**A** Rules and items that have been learnt formally through focal attention and that require controlled processing in performance.	**B** Rules and items that have been learnt formally through focal attention and that can be accessed rapidly and easily by means of automatic processes.
Implicit	**C** Rules and items that have been learnt implicitly through peripheral attention and that require controlled processing in performance.	**D** Rules and items that have been learnt implicitly through peripheral attention and that can be accessed rapidly and easily by means of automatic processes.

Figure 9.5:   L2 knowledge as intersecting continua

McLaughlin's discussion of restructuring suggests that a third dimension is needed to complete the model. The idea of progression from an exemplar-based to a rule-based representation cannot be easily equated with the conversion of explicit into implicit knowledge (or vice-versa). It is best treated as a separate dimension, relating most clearly to the way in which implicit knowledge changes qualitatively over time.

In some other respects the information-processing approach, as currently formulated, is rather limited. McLaughlin frequently talks of 'practice', for example, but never offers a clear definition. Does he mean 'opportunity to use a process under normal operating conditions' (i.e. in communication), or 'opportunity to practise specific rules and items in contrived drills and exercises'? If the latter is intended, the model runs up against the problem that several studies of formal instruction have shown that such practice does not always result in improved automatization or in restructuring (see Chapter 14). The model, in fact, struggles to account for why learners seem to acquire some rules and items before others. Also, the notion of restructuring provides only a very general account of the transitions that occur in interlanguage systems. It would not be possible on the basis of McLaughlin (1990a) to formulate precise hypotheses regarding which linguistic features are restructured when. Nor does the model give precise information about the factors that cause learners to restructure.

Summary

In this section we have examined a number of different theories and models of L2 acquisition that seek to explain how learners construct and organize their L2 knowledge. These theories vary in many respects but they are all 'cognitive' in nature in the sense that they view L2 acquisition as a mental process involving gradual mastery of items and structures through the application of general strategies of perception and production.

The framework for investigating L2 acquisition shown in Figure 9.1 suggests that a complete theory will need to account for three aspects of the acquisition process:

1 The relationship between input and knowledge (how learners attend to linguistic features in input and how they integrate this 'intake' into their L2 knowledge systems).
2 The representation of L2 knowledge (how L2 knowledge is organized in long-term storage, how it is influenced by L1 knowledge and how different types of knowledge, such as implicit and explicit, are related to each other).
3 The relationship between L2 knowledge and output (how L2 knowledge is used in production and how this relationship influences the way in which L2 knowledge is stored).

The theories discussed in this section tend to focus on just one or two of these three aspects. Table 9.7 provides a general summary of this section in relation to these three aspects.

Aspects of a theory of L2 acquisition	Theories
1 Relationship between input and L2 knowledge	Competition Model Operating Principles
2 Representation of L2 knowledge	
a Manner of representation	Functional theories Skill-building theories
b Role of the L1	Interlanguage Theory Competition Model
c Relationship between implicit and explicit knowledge	The Monitor Theory Bialystok's Model of Second Language Learning Schmidt's account of 'consciousness' and 'noticing'
3 Relationship between L2 knowledge and output	The Monitor Theory Variability theories Operating Principles Multidimensional Model

Table 9.7:   Theories of L2 acquisition in relation to general aspects of the acquisition process

Cognitive accounts of second language communication

In this section, we turn to theoretical accounts of the procedures that learners employ when using their L2 knowledge in communication. The focus shifts from how learners construct their L2 systems to how they use them in communication. Of course, as we have already seen and as Table 9.7 indicates, the distinction between 'acquisition of L2 knowledge' and 'use of L2 knowledge' is not clear-cut in cognitive theories, as a general assumption is that the way in which knowledge is stored reflects the way in which it is used. This is most evident in the skill-learning models of Anderson and McLaughlin, where the ideas of 'proceduralization' and 'automatization' relate very obviously to the idea of how knowledge is controlled in language use. Nevertheless, the distinction is valid, for, as Schmidt (1992: 359) has pointed out, a distinction can be drawn between 'procedural knowledge' (Anderson's concern) and 'procedural skill' ('the performance aspect of actually doing something in real time'). The focus of this section is on 'procedural skill' rather than 'procedural knowledge'.

To account for 'procedural skill' it is necessary to explain how learners make use of their existing L2 knowledge and also how they overcome the problems that result from insufficient L2 knowledge or inability to access L2 knowledge. To address these we will consider two aspects of L2 communication: (1) L2 speech planning, and (2) communication strategies.

Second language speech planning and the development of 'procedural skill'

L2 speech planning was considered briefly in Chapter 4 in relation to variability in learner language. Here we will focus more on how learners' ability to plan their speech changes over time (the developmental aspect), drawing on the work of a group of researchers at Kassel University, Germany (see Dechert, Möhle, and Raupach 1984). Their work is informed by Anderson's ACT model. Dechert (1984b: 216), for instance, notes that little attention has been paid in SLA research to 'procedural knowledge in language production' and argues that this is in need of special attention. It is clear, however, that he is more concerned with 'procedural skill' than 'procedural knowledge'. For Dechert and the other Kassel researchers, the study of speech planning phenomena serves as a means for examining the nature and extent of learners' procedural skill. Möhle and Raupach (1989) suggest that one way of distinguishing the application of declarative knowledge found in the associative stage of development (characteristic of many advanced L2 learners) from the full proceduralization evident in the autonomous stage (characteristic of native-speaker speech) is by examining speech planning phenomena.

These speech planning phenomena are of two basic kinds; temporal variables and hesitation phenomena. Table 9.8 summarizes the main variables, as

described in Wiese (1984). Both temporal variables and hesitation phenomena are on-line measures of speech and related to the idea of 'fluency'. They
have been derived from the earlier work of psycholinguists such as Goldman-
Eisler (1968) and Butterworth (1980b).

	Speech planning phenomena	Description
A	Temporal variables	Variables related to the rate of speaking.
	1 Speech rate	The number of syllables per second. This measure includes pause time.
	2 Articulation rate	The number of syllables per second of time of articulation. This measure excludes pause time.
	3 Pause length	The mean length of pauses above a stated threshold level (e.g. 0.20 seconds).
	4 Length of run	The mean number of syllables between pauses.
B	Hesitation phenomena	Variables relating to linguistic features that disturb the smooth flow of speech.
	1 Filled pauses	The use of phonetic devices such as 'uh' or 'mhm' to fill pauses.
	2 Repetitions	The unchanged re-occurrence of a sub-string of an utterance that has no syntactic/semantic function.
	3 Corrections	A change made to some part of the preceding utterance—from a single phoneme to a long sequence of text.

Table 9.8:   Speech planning phenomena (derived from Wiese 1984)

The basic methodology employed by the Kassel researchers is to record L2
learners performing an oral task such as telling a story in their L2 and their L1
and, in many cases to obtain a native-speaker performance of the same task.
The recorded speech is then carefully transcribed indicating such features as
pause length, intonation contours, vowel lengthening, fillers, drawls, and
false starts. These are then analysed using both qualitative methods (the detailed discussion of sections of a text) and quantitative ones (measuring
speech rate etc.). The overall aim of work on speech planning phenomena is
to describe the processes learners employ in the production of L2 speech. As
an example of this work we will consider Raupach's (1983) analysis of
formulas.

Through an analysis of the spontaneous productions of German students
of French from the Kassel corpus, Raupach shows that formulas function
both as 'fillers' and 'organizers'. For example, in the case of the former, the
learners resort to such expressions as 'je ne sais pas' and single words such as

'mais' and 'vraiment' to fill pauses and, in so doing, give themselves time for further planning activities. Organizers (for example, 'je crois que . . .' and 'on peut . . .') contribute to the development of ongoing speech by helping learners to establish a structure for phrases and sentences. These formulaic chunks provide learners with 'islands of reliability' that they can fall back on when they experience planning problems.

The study of speech planning phenomena can shed light on the nature of the development that learners undergo in acquiring procedural skill. As well as acquiring L2 knowledge, learners need to increase their control over that knowledge which has already been acquired (i.e. learn how to process this knowledge in unplanned as well as planned language use). Towell (1987) reports on a four-year long study of a British student's acquisition of L2 French, based on interview-type recordings made three times a year. In order to investigate the extent to which this learner's 'channel control' developed over time, Towell obtained measures of a number of temporal variables in approximately four minutes of speech elicited in the first and third years of the study when the learner was telling the same anecdote. Towell reports that the learner increased her speaking rate by 65 per cent, her pause/time ratio by 37 per cent, her articulation rate by 20 per cent, and the length of runs between pauses by 95 per cent. Also the average length of utterances increased considerably. Lennon (1989) also reports the advances in overall 'fluency' made by four advanced German learners of L2 English during a six-month residency in England. In this case 'fluency' was measured by means of native speakers' ratings of temporal variables.

One interesting possibility, discussed by Towell, is that the acquisition of 'knowledge' and 'control' (procedural skill) can proceed independently, with learners often opting for one or the other. This idea was supported by my study in Ellis (1990b). I examined the relationship between the development of 'control' (measured in terms of speech rate) and the development of 'knowledge' (measured in terms of the acquisition of word order rules and also by means of standard proficiency tests) in 39 adult classroom learners of L2 German. I found that the correlations between the measures of control and knowledge were very low, but that word order acquisition was significantly and negatively correlated with gains in speech rate. One interpretation of this result is that learners who opted to increase their store of L2 knowledge paid a price in terms of procedural skill and vice versa. Schmidt (1992) also considers the acquisition of knowledge and procedural skill as potentially proceeding separately. He gives as an extreme example a speaker of a pidginized interlanguage who can speak it very fluently.

The study of speech planning phenomena in relation to the development of L2 procedural skill is of obvious importance, but is also in its infancy. The work to date helps to shed light on the status of the learners' linguistic knowledge, for example by providing evidence of the use of formulaic chunks, and also, in longitudinal research, it helps to show in what ways learners develop their procedural skill. One question, identified by Schmidt (1992) as the key one, is the extent to which the development of procedural skill is dependent on learners learning how to produce specific items or exemplars—as in the case of formulas—or on learners learning how to perform abstract rules. It is premature to reach any conclusion on this but as Schmidt notes, 'there is ... little theoretical support from psychology for the common belief that the development of fluency in a second language is almost exclusively a matter of the increasingly skilful application of rules' (1992: 377).

Communication strategies

We now turn our attention to the second aspect of procedural skill: the communication strategies (CSs) that learners use to overcome the inadequacies of their interlanguage resources. CSs are used primarily to deal with lexical problems, such as when a learner who does not know the word for 'art gallery' refers to it as a 'picture place'. CSs can also be used to get around a grammatical problem, as when a learner deliberately elects to use 'ask' instead of 'make' because of uncertainty regarding which form of the infinitive (plain infinitive or 'to' + infinitive) to use with 'make'.

As a starting point, it is useful to distinguish two broad theoretical approaches to CSs. They can be viewed as discourse strategies that are evident in interactions involving learners, or they can be treated as cognitive processes involved in the use of the L2 in reception and production. If the first perspective is taken, the discussion of CSs belongs properly to the study of learner interaction (see Chapter 7). This is, in fact, how Larsen-Freeman and Long (1991) handle them. They treat them as devices of 'conversation maintenance'. In general, however, SLAR has treated CSs as cognitive processes and it is as a reflection of this that they are dealt with in this chapter.

The interactional approach

The study of CSs in an interactional approach began with Varadi (1980), in a paper that circulated for many years before its publication. Tarone (1977) also adopted an interactional approach. She defined CSs as involving 'a mutual attempt of two interlocutors to agree on a meaning in situations where requisite meaning structures do not seem to be shared' (Tarone 1981: 419). As such they differed from production strategies, which were defined as attempts to 'use one's linguistic system efficiently and clearly, with a minimum of effort'.

In her 1977 study, Tarone provided a typology of CSs, which is reproduced in Table 9.9. Nine subjects were asked to describe two simple drawings and a complex illustration in their L2 (English) and native language. The CSs described in Table 9.9 were derived from analysing transcripts of the learners' attempts to refer to a number of objects and events depicted. The strategies, therefore, were directly observable in the transcripts of the learners' productions. They are interactional—they reflect learners' attempts to make themselves understood to their interlocutors. Tarone's methodology has served a basis for subsequent studies of CSs, resulting in further typologies (see Tarone, Cohen, and Dumas (1976), Varadi (1980), and Paribakht (1985)).

Communication strategy	Description of strategy
1 Avoidance	
a Topic avoidance	Avoiding reference to a salient object for which learner does not have necessary vocabulary
b Message abandonment	The learner begins to refer to an object but gives up because it is too difficult
2 Paraphrase	
a Approximation	The learner uses an item known to be incorrect but which shares some semantic features in common with the correct item (e.g. 'worm' for 'silkworm')
b Word coinage	The learner makes up a new word (e.g. 'person worm' to describe a picture of an animated caterpillar)
c Circumlocution	The learner describes the characteristics of the object instead of using the appropriate TL item(s)
3 Conscious transfer	
a Literal translation	The learner translates word for word from the native language (e.g. 'He invites him to drink' in place of 'They toast one another')
b Language switch	The learner inserts words from another language (e.g. 'balon' for 'balloon'). NB Subsequently, Tarone (1981) refers to this as 'borrowing')
4 Appeal for assistance	The learner consults some authority—a native speaker, a dictionary
5 Mime	The learner uses a nonverbal device to refer to an object or event (e.g. clapping hands to indicate 'applause')

Table 9.9:   Tarone's (1977) typology of communication strategies

Research based on typologies, such as Tarone's, has focused on describing the strategies used by different learners and on identifying the factors that influence strategy choice (for example, the learners' level of L2 proficiency, the learners' personality, the learning situation, and the nature of the task used to elicit data). This research suffers from a number of problems, which have been thoroughly documented by Bialystok and Kellerman (1987), Bialystok (1990a), and Kellerman (1991). Bialystok notes that 'the criteria for assigning an utterance to a specific strategic category are sometimes vague, sometimes arbitrary and sometimes irrelevant' (1990a: 75) with the result

that the taxonomies are frequently not reliable. The taxonomies also lack validity in that they are not generalizable across tasks and, most important, they
are not psychologically plausible. Kellerman (1991: 146) points out that referring to 'an art gallery' as 'a picture-place' or as 'a place where you look at
pictures' clearly reflects the same underlying cognitive process. Therefore, to
code them separately as 'word coinage' and 'circumlocution', as happens in
Tarone's taxonomy, is misleading. He argues that it is not necessary to posit
different strategies simply because they have different linguistic realizations.
Finally, the taxonomies are not parsimonious. Categories tend to proliferate
like the branches of an enormous tree.

The psycholinguistic approach

The psycholinguistic approach is illustrated by the work of Færch and Kasper
(for example, Færch and Kasper 1980, 1983a, 1983b, and 1985). CSs are located within a general model of speech production, in which two phases are
identified: a planning phase and an execution phase. The aim of the planning
phase is to develop a plan which can then be executed to allow the speaker/
hearer to achieve communicative goals. In this phase 'the language user selects the rules and items which he considers most appropriate for establishing
a plan, the execution of which will lead to verbal behaviour which is expected
to satisfy the original goal' (1983a: 25). CSs are seen as part of the planning
process. They are called upon when learners experience some problem with
their initial plan which prevents them from executing it. One solution is
avoidance. This occurs when learners change their original communicative
goal by means of some kind of reduction strategy. The other solution is to
maintain the original goal by developing an alternative plan through the use
of an achievement strategy. The typology of CSs which Færch and Kasper
propose is based on this general distinction. Reduction strategies are further
subdivided into 'formal' (avoidance of L2 rules of which the learner is not certain) and 'functional' (avoidance of speech acts, topics, and modality markers). Achievement strategies are also divided into those that are
'compensatory' (replacement of an initial plan with a 'strategic' plan) and 'retrieval' (perseverance with the initial plan by, for example, searching for the
item(s) required).

The perspective afforded by this model is clearly psycholinguistic, although
many of the categories in their typology resemble those found in Tarone's.
For example, where Tarone has 'appeal for assistance', Færch and Kasper refer to 'co-operative strategies' involving 'direct' and 'indirect' appeal. Færch
and Kasper's typology is an advance on that of Tarone, however, in that their
psycholinguistic framework provides a basis for classifying the CSs into categories rather than just listing them. It locates the strategies they identify
within a theory of L2 production.

In the Færch and Kasper model CSs are seen as 'strategic plans', which contrast with 'production plans'. Strategic plans differ from production plans in two main respects: (1) problem-orientation and (2) consciousness. Learners employ CSs because they lack the L2 resources required to express an intended meaning (a problem in the planning phase) or they cannot gain access to them (a problem in the execution phase). In either case, there is a lack of balance between means and ends (Corder 1978c). CSs are, of course, not alone in being problem-orientated, as learning strategies can also be motivated by learners' recognition of gaps in their L2 knowledge. CSs differ from learning strategies in that the strategies are employed to meet a pressing communicative need—they are short-term rather than long-term solutions to a problem (Ellis 1985a: 181).

Færch and Kasper (1980) see consciousness as a *secondary* defining criterion of CSs. They recognize various problems in claiming that CSs are conscious and, in an attempt to deal with these, distinguish plans that are (1) always consciously employed, (2) never consciously employed, and (3) consciously employed by some but not all learners in some but not all situations. They suggest that CSs are plans belonging to (1) and (3), i.e. they 'are potentially conscious plans for solving what to an individual presents itself as a problem in reaching a particular communicative goal'.

Both the problematicity and the consciousness criteria have been criticized. Bialystok (1990a) argues that it is not clear how the distinction between 'production plans' (which are non-problematic) and 'strategic plans' (which are problematic) manifests itself in actual language processing. She notes that certain non-problematic instances of language use, such as giving definitions, will result in exactly the same kind of overt linguistic behaviour associated with CSs. For example, 'an instrument for grating cheese' might be considered as a circumlocution for 'cheese-grater' in one context, but as a straightforward definition of the object in another. Bialystok also criticizes Færch and Kasper's claim that CSs are potentially conscious on the grounds that there is no 'independent means' for deciding which plans fall into this category and that without this 'one is left to assume that *all* plans are potentially conscious' (1990a: 5).

At the purely descriptive level the identification of CSs is not necessarily problematic for as Bialystok notes, 'strategies ... should reliably produce forms of language that are different from those that one would expect to emanate from the autonomous processing system' (1990a: 19). Thus, they can be identified by comparing performance of the same task in the L1 and the L2, although few studies have done this. It is at the psycholinguistic level that definition of CSs becomes difficult. According to Bialystok, it can only be achieved if CSs are located within 'a coherent account of speech production' (1990a: 82). This, of course, is exactly what Færch and Kasper have tried to do but Bialystok, while approving of their attempt, considers it ultimately inadequate because the basic concepts of 'process,' 'plan', and 'strategy' are ill-defined and there is insufficient evidence to support the claim that planning and execution can be distinguished in the way Færch and Kasper do.

Bialystok's own solution to the problem of providing a psycholinguistic definition is to locate CSs within the theoretical framework that informs her whole work, i.e. the distinction between 'analysis' (or knowledge) and 'control'. She distinguishes 'knowledge-based' and 'control-based' CSs. The former involve the speaker in making some kind of adjustment to the content of the message by exploiting knowledge of the concept, for example by providing distinctive information about it, as in a definition or circumlocution. In a control-based strategy, the speaker holds the initial intention constant and manipulates the means of expression by integrating resources from outside the L2 in order to communicate it, as in the use of many L1-based strategies and mime. Bialystok emphasizes that both types of strategies need not be characterized by problematicity (gaps in knowledge or communication breakdown). Learners, like native speakers, select from their available options in order to communicate their intentions as precisely as they can within the constraints set up by particular tasks.

Bialystok's solution to the problem of finding a psycholinguistic definition is promising, as it enables CSs to be considered in relation to a general theory of language processing based on a distinction (knowledge v. control) that is firmly-grounded in cognitive psychology. Arguably, too, it provides a basis for overcoming the objections that have been levelled against much of the research into CSs.

The Nijmegen project

The most extensive study of CSs to date is the Nijmegen project, reported in a series of papers by Bongaerts, Kellerman, and Poulisse. The main study, which we will consider here was that of Poulisse (1990a; 1990b). Other studies (for example, Kellerman, Bongaerts, and Poulisse 1987; Kellerman, Amerlaan, Bongaerts, and Poulisse 1990) have made use of the same theoretical framework but with different materials or methods.

Poulisse's 1989 study, like the other studies, investigated lexical strategies only, seen as referential in nature (i.e. they involve attempts by speakers to encode messages that enable hearers to identify specific referents). The subjects consisted of three groups of 15 Dutch learners of L2 English with varied proficiency, as indicated by the number of years they had been studying English, school grades, teacher judgements, and cloze test scores. All the subjects were asked to perform four tasks in English: (1) a concrete picture description task involving everyday objects, the names of which the subjects were unlikely to know in English, (2) an abstract figure description task, (3) an oral interview, and (4) a story retelling task, where the subjects listened to a story in Dutch and retold it in English with the help of picture prompts. (2) was also performed in the learners' L1. (3) and (4) were video-recorded and played back to the subjects for their retrospective comments, which were audio-recorded and transcribed.

CSs were defined as 'strategies which a language user employs in order to achieve his intended meaning on becoming aware of problems arising during the planning phase of an utterance due to (his own) linguistic shortcomings' (Poulisse 1990a: 88). Few difficulties were encountered in the identification of CSs in the first two tasks, as the problems the learners would encounter had been predetermined through the design of the tasks. Tasks (3) and (4) presented greater difficulty, however, and to ensure reliability two independent judges were asked to identify CSs, and the retrospective comments of the learners were also used. Only 'clear cases' were finally included in the analysis.

One of the main contributions of this study is a simple and elegant taxonomy of CSs that the investigators claim has psychological plausibility (i.e. it reflects the nature of the mental processing involved in the production of CSs). This taxonomy is shown in Table 9.10. The taxonomy rests on two archistrategies, labelled 'conceptual' and 'linguistic' (or 'code'), which Kellerman (1991) describes as follows:

> Learners can either manipulate the concept so that it becomes expressible through their available linguistic (or mimetic) resources, or they can manipulate the language so as to come as close as possible to expressing their original intention.

These archistrategies can be further broken down, as shown in Table 9.10, and are eventually traceable to many of the CSs found in taxonomies such as Tarone's (1977). The distinctions between 'analytic' and 'holistic' and between 'transfer' and 'morphological creativity' constitute poles in a continuum of options rather than discrete options.

The Nijmegen typology highlights the commonalities that underlie what are discrete strategy types in Tarone's framework. It reveals, for instance, that word coinage, circumlocution, and approximation are 'conceptual' in nature, and that they all involve an 'analytic' process. It also distinguishes between types of non-verbal behaviour instead of lumping them together in a single category, 'mime'. Thus, 'ostensive definition' (pointing at an object) is seen as the non-verbal equivalent of a linguistic strategy, whereas 'mimetic gesture' (the modelling of some feature(s) of a referent through gesture, perhaps accompanied by imitative sounds) is 'conceptual' in nature.

The study examined the effects of proficiency and task on the learners' use of CSs and also considered whether there was any evidence that learners used CSs differently from native speakers. The main findings were as follows. The less proficient learners used more CSs than the more proficient, a function of their more limited control of L2 vocabulary. There was also some limited evidence of proficiency-related effects on the type of strategies used. For example, the more advanced learners made greater use of holistic strategies involving superordinates. However, there were very few proficiency-related

Archistrategies	Communication strategies
Conceptual	1 Analytic (circumlocution, description, and paraphrase)
	2 Holistic (the use of a superordinate, coordinate, or subordinate term)
Linguistic	1 Transfer (borrowing, foreignizing, and literal translation)
	2 Morphological creativity

Table 9.10:   The typology of communication strategies used in the Nijmegen Project (based on Poulisse 1990; Chapter 7)

differences in the ways in which the different strategies were realized. On the other hand, the nature of the task was found to have a marked effect on strategy selection. The subjects preferred elaborate analytic strategies in task (1), while in tasks (3) and (4) they made greater use of short holistic strategies and transfer strategies. Finally, the comparison of L1 and L2 referential behaviour failed to reveal any significant differences. The investigators have used this finding to challenge the 'uniqueness fallacy', (the claim that CSs are a distinctive second-language phenomenon), and to argue that L2 learners do not have to develop a special L2 strategic competence but instead can apply their L1 strategic competence.

An evaluation of communication strategy research

Clearly, the Nijmegen taxonomy is a great improvement on the earlier taxonomies in that it locates the description of CSs within a parsimonious cognitive framework. In general, though, work on CSs has been limited in scope. The research to date has concentrated almost exclusively on lexical problems and sheds no light on the CSs that learners use to cope with gaps in their grammatical knowledge. It is not clear whether the kinds of taxonomies that have been developed can cope with grammatical problems.

Furthermore, little has been discovered about the developmental nature of CSs in L2 production. Do learners simply use the strategic competence they have developed in relation to L1 production, or do they have to re-learn it for L2 use? Bialystok's (1983a) study suggests that there is a general switch from L1-based to L2-based strategies, but Poulisse (1990a) found little evidence of proficiency-related effects on strategy choice. This is an important issue for language pedagogy, as it bears on whether L2 learners need to be taught how to use CSs or can be expected to transfer them from their L1. Kellerman argues that 'there is no justification for providing training in compensatory strategies ... Teach the learners more language and let the strategies look after themselves' (1991: 158). But other researchers have felt that strategy training is desirable (for example, Færch and Kasper 1983a). At the moment, all that can be said is that there is insufficient evidence on which to base a decision.

The research to date has also made no attempt to investigate the relationship between the use of CSs and acquisition. There is only speculation. Corder (1978c) characterizes reduction strategies as 'risk-avoiding' and achievement strategies as 'risk-taking', and suggests that the latter rather than the former will contribute to successful language learning. Færch and Kasper (1980) express the same view, arguing that achievement behaviour encourages hypothesis formation, and also that risk is essential for automatization. Tarone (1980b), however, holds a different view, suggesting that CSs of any kind help learners to negotiate their way to the right target language forms. Also, CSs in general keep the channel open and thus secure more input for the learner. They are the means by which learners can act on Hatch's (1978b) advice never to give up. However, it could also be argued that CSs inhibit acquisition. Learners like Schmidt's (1983) Wes have been found to develop their strategic competence at the apparent expense of their linguistic competence. These conflicting views can only be resolved through careful research.

Summary

In this section we have considered two aspects of L2 production. We have found that where 'procedural skill' is concerned, there are clear differences between learners and native speakers, as evident in temporal variables and hesitation phenomena. Acquisition is characterized by a progressive control of L2 resources leading to greater fluency. Furthermore, there is some evidence to suggest that this development can occur independently of the development of L2 linguistic knowledge. In the case of communication strategies, the second aspect of L2 communication we have considered, the research has concentrated on identifying the strategies that learners use and developing taxonomies to account for them. The best taxonomy is that provided by the Nijmegen project. This characterizes the cognitive nature of CSs in terms of the distinction between 'conceptual' strategies, where learners engage in some manipulation of the concept that they are trying to convey, and 'linguistic' strategies, where learners resort to their L1 (or another L2) and to morphological creativity. Little is currently known, however, about whether CSs are developmental in nature, or of how their use affects L2 acquisition.

Parallel Distributed Processing and second language acquisition

The last account of L2 acquisition to be considered in this chapter is of a radically different nature. *Parallel Distributed Processing* (PDP) differs from other models in several respects but in particular in the way in which knowledge and learning are conceptualized. Knowledge is seen not as 'patterns' or 'rules', nor is there any distinction drawn between 'declarative' and 'procedural' knowledge. Instead, what learners 'know' is characterized as a labyrinth of interconnections between 'units' that do not correspond to any holistic concepts of the kind we normally recognize (for example, a real-life person or object or, where language is concerned, a word or grammatical feature). Performance (i.e. information processing) involves the activation of the requisite interconnections; learning arises when, as a result of experience, the strength of the connections (i.e. 'weights') between units is modified. PDP constitutes 'a unified model of cognition, straddling the traditional competence/performance distinction' (Plunkett 1988: 307).

Although the idea of 'parallel processing' is not a new one in psychology, the current interest in it has been stimulated by the recent work of Rumelhart, McClelland, and the PDP Research Group (see Rumelhart, McClelland, and the PDP Research Group 1986a and 1986b). This work entails the development of both a theory to explain information processing and learning, and various computer models that allow simulations of actual information processing or learning tasks to be run. The computer models function as tests of the theory. Both the theory and the models are extremely ambitious; as Schmidt (1988) notes, they aim 'to provide a mathematical model that captures the essence of both neural processing, on the one hand, and thought on the other' (1988: 55). They are also of great complexity, so no attempt will be made to explicate or illustrate them fully here. The main constructs that inform the theory will be considered, a brief account of one simulation of language learning will be provided, and some of the advantages and disadvantages of PDP as an account of L2 acquisition will be examined.

A good starting point for trying to understand PDP is an example of the kind of models of cognition that have been proposed. The one that follows is taken from McClelland, Rumelhart, and Hinton (1986). The problem addressed is 'How do we remember someone we know?' One possibility is that we construct separate memory boxes for each person we know, creating a kind of content index which we can consult when we want to recall a particular individual. One of the problems of such a theory is that we cannot easily locate the right entry in the index if some of the information we are using is faulty or incomplete. A second possibility—the one preferred by McClelland, Rumelhart, and Hinton—is that the information relating to a particular person is spread over a number of inter-connected units, such that the activation of one unit leads to the activation of all the other units, so making the total contents of the memory for this person available. In this case, the units consist of properties such as 'name', 'age', 'education', 'marital status', and 'occupation'. The instantiation of an individual person in memory may be activated by the person's name or by one or more of the other properties. The advantages of such a system are that it can successfully handle incomplete or even incorrect information and can also, because of the connections among units in the system, lead to 'spontaneous generalization' (for example, to the recognition that people who have professional occupations like 'lawyer' and 'doctor', represented by specific units in the system, also tend to be 'well-educated', represented by another connected unit).

The main properties of a PDP model are as follows:

1 Processing is carried out in parallel rather than serially. McClelland, Rumelhart, and Hinton (1986) point out that multiple constraints govern language processing, with semantic and syntactic factors constantly interacting without it being possible to say that one set is primary. They argue that if 'each word can help constrain the syntactic role, and even the identity, of every other word' (1986: 7), processing must take place not serially but simultaneously on different levels.

2 A PDP model consists of 'units' or 'nodes' connected in such a way that the activation of one unit can inhibit or excite others in varying degrees. The nature of these units varies, depending on what kind of behaviour is being modelled. In some cases the units stand for hypotheses about, for example, the syntactic roles of words in a sentence, while in other cases they stand for goals and actions, and in still others for aspects of things. Units have output values which they can pass on to other units in the system. Also, in many PDP models, the units are organized into different 'levels', such that any one unit excites or inhibits other units at both its own level and other levels. The resulting network is highly complex and is thought to mirror the neural structure of the brain.

3 Knowledge is viewed in terms of the microstructure rather than macrostructure of cognition, i.e. as connection strength rather than as generalized 'patterns' or 'rules'. As McClelland, Rumelhart, and Hinton put it: 'In these models, the patterns themselves are not stored. Rather, what is stored is *the connection strengths* between units that allow these patterns to be recreated' (1986: 31).

4 Processing is activated by 'input' which stimulates one or more units and, of course, their connections with other units. Thus, in computer simulations of PDP models, selected input in the form of 'training sets' is fed into the computer, often in successive runs. For example, MacWhinney (1989) tested a PDP model designed to learn German articles by feeding in 102 carefully selected nouns in different case contexts one hundred times.[14]

5 Learning is a by-product of information processing; as a result of responding to input, the association strengths among units are spontaneously modified. Learning consists of discovering the right connection strengths from the input. Interconnection strengths do not have to be built into the models by the researcher, but are derived through experience. The models, therefore, are 'dynamic, interactive and self-organizing systems' (McClelland, Rumelhart, and Hinton 1986: 42).

6 This process of adjusting connection strengths is governed by 'learning rules' such as the Hebb rule, which states: 'Adjust the strength of the

connection between units A and B in proportion to the product of their simultaneous activation' (op. cit.: 36). A number of complex learning rules have been identified.

7 PDP models can go beyond the input by means of 'spontaneous generalization'. The models can extract 'regularities' in the patterns of interconnections; these resemble higher order rules. However, PDP networks do not learn 'rules'; rather they learn to act as though they knew them.

8 PDP models display 'emergent properties'. That is, they represent learning as a gradual process involving a series of stages. As we will see, they behave like language learners in that they produce incorrect as well as target-like constructions. Importantly, these incorrect responses are generated by the network itself.

We will now consider Rumelhart and McClelland's (1986) simulation of past tense learning using a PDP model. This grammatical feature is of considerable interest to language researchers because, as we have seen, its natural acquisition typically involves U-shaped learning behaviour (for example, went—goed—wented—went). Overgeneralization errors, such as 'goed', have been held to provide strong evidence that learners must organize their linguistic knowledge into 'rules'. Given that PDP systems are constructed in such a way that no rules of this nature are represented, past tense learning provides a rigorous test of the ability of such systems to account for language learning.

The PDP system that Rumelhart and McClelland used to simulate past tense learning is too complex to describe here. In simple terms, it is equipped with (1) an encoding device that operates on the root form of verbs (for example, 'hope') and converts them into a set of context-sensitive phonological features (called Wickelfeatures); (2) a 'pattern associator' network that takes the output from (1) and computes the past tense form of the verbs, again in terms of Wickel features; and (3) a decoding device that converts the output of (2) into a normal set of phonological features. Large numbers of exemplars of both root and past tense verb forms were fed systematically into the model; they comprised the input. The pattern associator is also equipped to compare the output of the network with the target form. When the output matches the target, the model is doing the right thing and so none of the connection weights between the units in the pattern associator are adjusted, but when it does not match, adjustments to the weights are made.

One of the most interesting results obtained by the simulation was that the pattern observed in the L1 acquisition of past tense forms occurred. This was evident in similar learning curves for different classes of verb, similar stages of development, and the same errors. For example, the model generated the familiar U-shaped learning curve, and errors involving double past tense marking. Thus, for 'eat', 'ated' occurred later than errors involving overgeneralization ('eated'), a phenomenon also reported in L1 acquisition

(Kucczaj 1977). The model not only accounted for the major *known* features of acquisition, but also afforded a number of *predictions* regarding features not reported in the L1 acquisition literature, for example, that overgeneralization errors are more likely to occur in irregular verbs like 'come' whose past tense form does not involve any modification to the final phoneme of the base form. Rumelhart and McClelland argue that the simulation demonstrated that a 'reasonable account of the acquisition of past tense can be provided without recourse to the notion of "rule" as anything more than a *description* of the language' (1986: 267).

This conclusion is, of course, enormously challenging to mentalist theories of language learning, as it suggests that learning is environmentally driven and that learners need very little in the way of innate knowledge. Not surprisingly, therefore, it has been criticized by researchers working in the Chomskyan paradigm. Pinker and Prince (1989) observe that 'the fact that a computer model behaves intelligently without rules does not show that humans lack rules, any more than a wind-up mouse shows that real mice lack motor programs' (1989: 184). They also point out that Rumelhart and McClelland's simulation met with only limited success, as even after extensive training it achieved only 67 per cent accuracy in a test of the model's ability to generalize its knowledge to new verbs. In many cases, this test resulted in errors not attested in natural language acquisition (for example, 'typeded' for 'typed' and 'membled' for 'mailed'). Pinker and Prince suggest that such errors result precisely because the model has no representation of the 'root form of a verb'. They point out that many of the overgeneralizations that children make in L1 acquisition cannot be explained with reference to input frequency.[15] For Pinker and Prince, then, connectionist theories are 'revisionist' in a way that is 'not scientifically defensible' (1989: 198).

Connectionists have responded to these criticisms. They reject the claim that the theory underlying their work is 'revisionist' (i.e. behaviourist) in nature, pointing out that they are concerned with internal states and mental processes. PDP models do have an 'initial state', which is, in a sense, 'innate' and, as Gasser (1990) notes, connectionists are increasingly concerned with what it consists of. Gasser also points out that there are linguistic theories (for example, Langacker 1987) that are compatible with PDP models in that they emphasize the continuous nature of the differences between rules and exceptions. Similarly, Schmidt (1988) observes that PDP is good at dealing with variability and 'fuzzy concepts'. MacWhinney (1989) also finds that connectionism offers 'a powerful formal framework that correctly expresses the processing and learning claims of the Competition Model' (1987: 457). This is not surprising, perhaps, given that both PDP and the Competition Model share a number of features in common, such as the notions of 'network' and the 'weight' of cues or connections.

Gasser (1990) provides a balanced conclusion:

It is now clear that some form of connectionism will figure in a general model of human linguistic behavior. The only question is whether the role will be a minor one, relegated to low-level pattern matching tasks and the learning of exceptional behavior, or whether the connectionist account will supersede symbolic accounts, rendering them nothing more than approximations of the actual messy process (1990: 186).

The resolution to this question lies in further research into simulated language learning, including L2 learning, which to date has received little attention from PDP researchers.[16]

Conclusion

The theories that have been examined in this chapter afford a cognitive as opposed to a mentalist view of L2 acquisition. That is, they seek to explain how learners acquire an L2 in terms of cognitive processes of a general nature: 'strategies', 'operations', 'mappings', 'principles', 'learning rules', and the like. We have made a broad distinction between theories that address how L2 knowledge develops over time and theories that explain learners' 'procedural skill' (i.e. their ability to use their knowledge in communication). We have seen, though, that this distinction is not watertight, as many cognitive theories characterize the way in which L2 knowledge is represented in terms of how it is actually used. Indeed, it is characteristic of cognitive as opposed to linguistic theories that this distinction is blurred. In the case of one theory—Parallel Distributed Processing—it disappears altogether. One of the major issues in SLA research today is whether L2 knowledge is best characterized in terms of 'rules' which govern the behaviour of specific items—as claimed by many cognitive theories of L2 acquisition and the linguistic

theories to be examined in the following chapter—or whether it is best accounted for in terms of well-practised, discrete items stored either as self-contained units or as sets of inter-related features, as suggested by some of the approaches current in cognitive psychology, such as PDP.

It is not yet possible to construct a comprehensive cognitive theory of L2 acquisition, let alone an all-embracing theory that incorporates both a linguistic and a cognitive perspective. Nor is it easy to evaluate the different cognitive theories, for they differ in major ways with regard to (1) provenance, (2) scope, (3) the type of data they aim to account for, and (4) the precision of the hypotheses they advance. Theories like the Multidimensional Model have originated in work undertaken by L2 researchers, others were devised to account for L1 acquisition and were subsequently used in SLA research (for example, Slobin's operating principles) while still others are general cognitive theories applied to L2 acquisition (such as the skill-learning theories of Anderson and McLaughlin). We have seen that some theories focus on the way input is processed (for example, the Competition Model), some on the way L2 knowledge is represented (such as the Monitor Theory), while   others seek to account for L2 knowledge in relation to output (for example, the Multidimensional Model). Some theories have been constructed to account for naturalistic L2 data (for example, variability theories) while others are based on data elicited through experiments or simulations (such as the Competition Model and Parallel Distributed Processing). Finally, there are theories that afford very precise hypotheses that can be systematically tested (for example, The Competition Model and the Multidimensional Model) while others offer more general statements that provide only a broad-brush picture of how acquisition takes place (for example, theories based on the implicit/explicit distinction).

In Chapter 15 we will examine a number of criteria which have been used to evaluate theories, but it is unlikely that any one of the theories we have looked at here will win out over the others. The plethora of models and theories in L2 acquisition has often been noted, and in some cases regretted (for example, by Schouten 1979). It testifies to two general points. One is that SLA research is still a very new field of enquiry, scarcely more than twenty-five years old. The other is the enormous amount of interest which the study of L2 learning has generated.

Notes

1 Various alternative terms to 'interlanguage' have been used. Corder (1971a) refers to 'idiosyncratic dialects' and 'transitional competence', whereas Nemser (1971) uses 'approximative systems'. Although these terms have different shades of meaning, they all refer to the same general phenomenon. The term 'interlanguage' has stuck and will be the one used here.

2 Selinker (1972) has made it clear that fossilization applies to both non-target and target forms. Thus, it is evident not only when learners produce errors but also when they produce target-like utterances. In practice, however, fossilization has been used to refer to 'persistent errors' (Mukkatesh 1986; Major 1988).

3 Krashen's five hypotheses are: (1) the acquisition–learning hypothesis, (2) the natural order hypothesis, (3) the input hypothesis, (4) the monitor hypothesis, and (5) the affective filter hypothesis. In this chapter we focus on (1) and (4). Hypotheses (2), (3), and (5) are considered in Chapters 3, 6, and 11 respectively.

4 Schmidt (1990) speculates that parallel distributed processing models may provide an explanatory basis for implicit learning. That is, learners build up association strengths rather than 'rules' implicitly.

5 Krashen's position appears to have shifted somewhat over the years, as subsequent to the publication of Tarone's 1983 article he has accepted that variability can occur in unmonitored utterances as a result of what he

calls editing by 'feel' . He talks of 'inter-stage fluctuation' (Krashen 1985: 64–5).

6   Tomlin also reports that native speakers conformed to the quantity principle on the same task.

7   The Competition Model can also be seen as a connectionist theory and, as such, might belong to the section of this chapter dealing with Parallel Distributed Processing. However, given the centrality of form–function relationships to the model it is appropriate to consider it under 'functional theories'.

8   The choice of second noun in unnatural NNV and VNN sentences by native speakers of English has been noted in a number of previous studies and is considered to reflect the subjects' knowledge of the transformation which allows a direct object to take up an initial noun position (as in 'Mary John likes a lot') and which, as a consequence, moves the agent noun into the second noun position.

9   I am indebted to Widdowson for the observation that 'utterance' and 'sentence processing' do not involve the same processing procedures. Widdowson also points out that this failure to distinguish utterances and sentences was one of the reasons why earlier research on language processing based on transformational generative grammar proved to be such a dead-end.

10   Yoshioka and Doi (1988) report that 'the subjects who used *o* correctly at all also used *wa* correctly but the opposite direction is not necessarily the case' and also that 'the subjects who used *ga* correctly even once used *wa* and *o* correctly but the subjects who used *wa* and *o* correctly did not necessarily use *ga* correctly'. They point out, however, that a longitudinal study is needed to test the hypothesis properly.

11   Anderson's model has changed somewhat over the years. The 1983 version became known as ACT* (to be read 'ACT-star'). The distinction between declarative and procedural knowledge, however, is basic to all the ACT models.

12   Færch and Kasper (1985) also distinguish declarative and procedural knowledge. However, their definition of the distinction differs from Anderson's. For them procedural knowledge consists of procedures for using declarative knowledge (i.e. procedural skill) and it is not possible to talk of declarative knowledge transforming into procedural knowledge, as in Anderson's model.

13   McLaughlin's (1990a) account of 'restructuring' is not dissimilar to Bialystok's idea of 'analysis'. Exemplar-based representation corresponds to 'unanalysed knowledge' while rule-based representation corresponds to 'analysed knowledge'.

14   The selection of 'training sets' in PDP models for language is usually based on information regarding the typical frequency with which the

specific features or configurations of features that constitute the learning target occur in natural language use.

15 An additional criticism of PDP accounts of L2 acquisition (not made by Pinker and Prince) is that it is not clear how a PDP model can produce the 'restrictive simplification' evident in all early acquisition. How, for example, can a PDP model produce output consisting of copula-less sentences given an input that consists entirely of grammatical copula sentences?

16 Exceptions are Gasser's own exploratory study of transfer in L2 acquisition and Sokolik's (1990) attempt to illustrate the use of PDP modelling to explain the difference between child and adult L2 acquisition. It should also be noted that a language learning simulation, such as Rumelhart and McClelland's study of past tense learning, is neutral as to whether it involves L1 or L2 learning. In so far as these authors' point of comparison was studies of L1 acquisition it can be considered an L1 study. However, their results can also be compared to those obtained from L2 research. Obviously, though, a PDP model of L2 learning must in some way incorporate L1 knowledge into the initial state.

Further reading

An excellent account of some of the earlier theories considered in this chapter (Interlanguage Theory; Monitor Theory), and also of his own skill-building theory, can be found in
B. McLaughlin, *Theories of Second Language Acquisition* (Edward Arnold, 1987).
D. Larsen-Freeman and M. Long (eds.), *An Introduction to Second language Acquisition Research* (Chapter 7) (Longman, 1991) also provides an overview of many of these theories. Their account of the Multidimensional Model is particularly good.
The following are suggested readings for the individual theories:

1 Interlanguage theory

L. Selinker, M. Swain, and G. Dumas, 'The interlanguage hypothesis extended to children'. *Language Learning* (1975) 25: 139–91.

2 Theories based on the implicit/explicit distinction

S. Krashen, *Second Language Acquisition and Second Language Learning.* (Pergamon, 1981).
R. Schmidt, 'The role of consciousness in second language learning.' *Applied Linguistics* (1990) 11: 129–56.

3 Variability theory

E. Tarone, 'On the variability of interlanguage systems.' *Applied Linguistics* (1983) 4: 142–63.
R. Ellis, 'Sources of variability in interlanguage.' *Applied Linguistics* (1985) 6: 118–31.

4 Functional theories

The literature on functional theories tends to be technical and dense. *Studies in Second Language Acquisition*, Volume 14, is given over to 'Grammaticalization in second language acquisition'. Various L2 studies based on the Competition Model can be found in *Applied Psycholinguistics*, including Harrington (1987).

5 Operating principles

R. Andersen, 'Models, processes, principles and strategies: second language acquisition inside and outside the classroom' in B. VanPatten and J. Lee (eds.): *Second Language Acquisition – Foreign Language Learning* (Multilingual Matters, 1990).

6 The Multidimensional Model

J. Meisel, H. Clahsen, and M. Pienemann, 'On determining developmental stages in natural second language acquisition.' *Studies in Second Language Acquisition* (1981) 3: 109–35.
M. Pienemann and M. Johnston, 'An acquisition-based procedure for second language assessment.' *Australian Review of Applied Linguistics* (1986) 9: 92–122.

7 Skill-building models

J. Anderson, *Cognitive Psychology and its Implications* (Freeman, 1980).
B. McLaughlin, T. Rossman, and B. McLeod, 'Second language learning: an information-processing perspective'. *Language Learning* (1983) 33: 135–58.

8 Speech planning and temporal variables

H. Dechert, D. Möhle, and M. Raupach (eds.), *Second Language Productions* (Gunter Narr, 1984).
R. Schmidt, 'Psychological mechanisms underlying second language fluency.' *Studies in Second Language Acquisition* (1992) 14: 357–85.

9 Communication strategies

C. Færch and G. Kasper (eds.), *Strategies in Interlanguage Communication* (Longman, 1983).

E. Bialystok, *Communication Strategies: A Psychological Analysis of Second-Language Use* (Blackwell, 1990).

10 Parallel Distributed Processing

R. Schmidt, 'The potential of parallel distributed processing for S.L.A. theory and research.' *University of Hawaii Working Papers in ESL* (1988) 7: 55–66.

10 Linguistic universals and second language acquisition

Introduction

As we saw in the previous chapter, explanations of the internal mechanisms responsible for L2 acquisition can be divided into those that emphasize the general cognitive nature of acquisition and those that emphasize its specifically linguistic nature. The former discuss L2 acquisition in terms of 'processes', 'strategies', and 'operations', while the latter refer to 'linguistic rules', 'linguistic principles', and, increasingly, to 'linguistic universals'. Whereas cognitive theories look to psychology, linguistic theories look to linguistics.

It is customary to identify two broad approaches to the study of language, which, following Chomsky (1986a), can be called the *Externalized (E) Approach* and the *Internalized (I) Approach*. The former involves the collection of samples of a particular language or languages, which then serve as the data for developing a descriptive 'grammar'. It is concerned with 'behavior or the products of behavior' (Chomsky 1986a: 17), and the task of the linguist is to describe these. The I-Approach makes use of a native speaker's intuitions about what is grammatical and ungrammatical to investigate the abstract principles that shape the way the grammar of any particular language is represented in the mind of a speaker. The object of inquiry is 'the states of mind/ brain that enter into behavior' (op. cit.); that is, the knowledge system or grammar, generally referred to as *linguistic competence*, that underlies actual linguistic behaviour.

Chomsky (1988) notes that there has been a move away from an E-Approach to an I-Approach, as evident in the switch from the structural to the generative tradition in American linguistics. However, both approaches are extant in the study of linguistic universals. The study of *typological universals*, initiated by Greenberg (1966), has been continued by Hawkins (1983), Comrie (1984), and Croft (1990), among others. It involves the crosslinguistic comparison of a wide range of languages drawn from different language families in order to discover what features they have in common. In contrast, linguists working in the Chomskyan tradition seek to discover universals by the in-depth study of individual languages.[1] This results in the identification of the abstract principles that comprise *Universal Grammar* and that constrain the form of the grammar of any specific language.

The universals identified by the two approaches are very different. Typological universals are couched in the familiar language of grammatical descriptions (for example, 'all languages have nouns and verbs') and refer to specific linguistic properties. Universal Grammar consists of principles and parameters, which are described by means of highly abstract statements relating to general properties of language (for example, 'a language has the heads on the same side in all its phrases'—the phrase structure principle, which we will consider later). Such principles may be reflected in a whole series of rules in a particular language. The two approaches, although procedurally and conceptually very different, need not be seen as mutually exclusive, however. It is possible that at least some of the universals uncovered through typological comparison may have a basis in the abstract principles of Universal Grammar, while many generative linguists now seek to test the validity of the abstract principles they have uncovered by crosslinguistic comparisons. Also, many SLA researchers invoke both typological and UG arguments in constructing hypotheses. Nevertheless, it seems safer to examine each separately, as to do otherwise runs the risk of comparing apples and oranges.

Linguistic universals must be distinguished from other types of universals (see Selinker 1984). Cognitive theories also make claims about 'universals' (for example, processing universals), while, as we have seen, evidence exists to suggest that there are also developmental 'universals' (regularities in the order and sequence of L2 development). Linguistic universals may influence and, perhaps, help to explain processing and developmental universals, but they are distinct from them. Other factors of a cognitive nature, such as perception, memory, and retrieval, are also involved.

Interlanguage Theory: another perspective

In the last chapter we considered Interlanguage Theory as an example of a cognitive account of L2 acquisition. However, Interlanguage Theory has also informed linguistic approaches in SLA research, and so constitutes a useful starting point for this chapter.

According to Adjemian (1976), the *sine qua non* of the interlanguage hypothesis is that interlanguages are 'natural languages' and, therefore, subject to all the same constraints. A number of assumptions follow from this hypothesis: interlanguages consist of 'a set of linguistic rules which can generate novel utterances' (1976: 299); claims about the structure of interlanguages can be derived from grammatical theory; and, like natural languages, interlanguages can be idealized to make them amenable to linguistic analysis. Adjemian argues that the goal should be to describe and explain the nature of the learner's competence at different stages of development by analysing 'intuitional data' collected experimentally; the main focus should be 'the grammatical nature of a learner's IL' rather than 'strategies' (1976: 306). In this way, Adjemian put the case for a linguistic approach to the study of interlanguage.

The position which Adjemian's early paper outlined has subsequently been reaffirmed on numerous occasions. Eckman (1991: 24), for instance, invokes Adjemian in advancing what he calls the Interlanguage Structural Conformity Hypothesis, which states:

> The universal generalizations that hold for the primary languages also hold for interlanguages.

Eckman, like Adjemian, claims that interlanguages are languages and, further, that proposed linguistic universals are fully universal, in the sense that they apply to non-primary as well as primary languages. Eckman provides evidence from 11 adult Asian learners of English that universal phonological generalizations (for example, 'if a language has at least one final consonant sequence consisting of step + stop, it also has at least one final sequence consisting of fricative + stop', 1991: 24) also hold for interlanguages.

The purpose of this chapter is to explore to what extent 'the IL one is creating is susceptible to the force of several types of language universals' (Selinker 1992: 247). We will consider two broad types: typological universals, and those found in Universal Grammar.

Typological universals and second language acquisition

Linguistic typology and language universals

A typological approach to linguistic analysis involves a crosslinguistic comparison of specific features such as articles, word order or relative clause construction. It provides a basis for identifying both which features are rare in a particular language (for example, the use of inversion after initial adverbials in English[2]), and also which features are common. It is the latter that SLA research has focused on, although, as we saw in Chapter 8, there has also been some attention given to how L2 learners acquire rare features.

Various kinds of commonalities have been identified. There are a number of unrestricted or *absolute universals*, which are exemplified in all languages. For example, all languages have nouns and verbs and vowels and consonants. However, there are probably few such universals, universal tendencies being much more common. A specific feature may be found in a large number of languages, but be missing from some. For example, Dahl (1979) found that there is 'a universal tendency for Neg to have a definite position relative to the finite element' (1979: 91). ('Neg' here refers to the negator, for example, 'not' in English.) There was also a definite preference for the negator to take a preverbal rather than a postverbal position. As Comrie (1984) acknowledges, universal tendencies are problematic because they raise the question as to whether it is justifiable to talk of 'universals' when there are exceptions and also just how many exceptions can be tolerated. He argues, however, that the non-random distribution of alternative features in the worlds' languages is of significance.

Cutting across the distinction between absolute universals and universal tendencies is the distinction between implicational and non-implicational universals. Frequently, crosslinguistic comparisons demonstrate that there are connections between two or more features, such that the presence of one feature implies the presence of another or others. Implicational universals take the form of 'if/then' statements. These can be 'simple' or 'complex'. A simple implicational universal involves a connection between just two features. For example, Hawkins (1983) provides evidence to show that 'if a language has a noun before a demonstrative, then it has a noun before a relative clause' (1983: 84). A complex implicational universal involves a relationship between several features. Hawkins gives the following example: 'If a language is SOV, then if the adjective precedes the noun, then the genitive precedes the noun'. Implicational universals have been found to be particularly prevalent in the area of word order, as these examples show. The important point about both types of implicational universals is that they logically preclude at least one combination of features. For example, the example from Hawkins given above excludes the possibility that languages which have nouns before relative clauses will also have nouns before demonstratives—the implicature of the universal operates in one direction only.

Complex implicational universals sometimes take the form of a universal hierarchy. A hierarchy covers a chain of implicational universals, as in the *Noun Phrase Accessibility Hierarchy (AH)*, which we considered in Chapter 3 (see Table 3.7). This concerns the various functions of the pronoun in relative clauses. For example, the relative pronoun functions as the subject of its clause in this sentence:

1 I bought the puppy that made me laugh.

but as direct object of its clause in this sentence:

2 The puppy that I bought was a nuisance.

As we will shortly see, the function a relative pronoun performs in its clause is separate from the function of the relative clause in the sentence.

Comrie and Keenan's (1979) crosslinguistic study showed that languages varied in the noun phrases that were 'accessible' to relativization. It proposed the following hierarchy:

> subject < direct object < indirect object < oblique < genitive < object of comparative

Their study showed that this hierarchy reflected both the frequency of the different relative pronoun functions possible in the languages they investigated and also the presence and absence of specific functions in a single language.

For example, any language that permitted the indirect object to be relativized would also allow relativization of all the other noun phrase functions above it in the hierarchy (i.e. direct object and subject), but not below it (i.e. oblique, genitive, and object of comparative). The hierarchy was also found to be relevant for explaining the presence or absence of pronominal copies in a language. Thus, a pronominal copy (for example, '*The puppy that I bought *it* was a nuisance.') was most likely to occur with relative pronouns lower down the hierarchy than with those higher up.

The AH, as originally proposed by Comrie and Keenan, is problematic in a number of ways. Keenan (1975) points out that indirect object and oblique are indistinguishable in most languages (including English), as both are expressed as prepositional phrases, for example:

The official to whom Mary gave the present is sick.
The official to whom Mary spoke is sick.

Jones (1991a) argues that it is a mistake to include genitive in the hierarchy, as it has a separate and complete hierarchy of its own. He suggests that there are, in fact, two hierarchies, one for –Gen and the other for +Gen, as shown in Table 10.1. As we will see, this proposal is given support by the very mixed empirical results obtained for genitive, when this is viewed as part of a single hierarchy. Finally, object of comparison is problematic in English—a language that is supposed to manifest this function—because many native speakers do not accept that sentences with this function are grammatical.

Function	– Genitive	+ Genitive
Subject (SU)	The man who came ...	The man whose wife came ...
Direct object (DO)	The man (whom) I saw ...	The man whose wife I saw ...
Indirect object (IO)	The man (whom) I gave the book to ...	The man whose wife I gave the book to ...
Object of preposition (OP)	The man (whom) I looked at ...	The man whose wife I looked at ...
Object of comparative (OC)	The man (whom) I am bigger than ...	The man whose wife I am bigger than ...

Table 10.1:   The Accessibility Hierarchy for –Genitive and +Genitive (from Jones 1991a)

Relativization is not the only problem that learners face in acquiring relative clauses. There is also the question of where the relative clause occurs in the matrix sentence. Relative clauses can function as part of the direct object of the sentence, as in (1) above, or they can function as part of the subject of the sentence, as in (2). In (1) the relative clause is joined onto the main clause, while in (2) it is embedded in the main clause. As we saw in Chapter 3, whether the relative clause is joined onto or embedded in the main clause can affect L2 acquisition.

Of considerable importance for SLA research is the way markedness is handled in language typology. Whereas classical markedness, as defined by linguists in the Prague School of Linguistic Theory (for example, Trubetzkoy 1931), views features as either unmarked or marked (for example, in the pair of features 'a' and 'an', 'a' is unmarked and 'an' is marked), language typology sees markedness primarily as a relative phenomenon (i.e. one feature is more marked than another). Implicational universals presuppose a markedness relationship; if a language that has property X also has property Y, then Y is unmarked in relation to X. Hierarchies reflect degrees of markedness even more clearly. Thus, in the AH, the least marked function is that of subject and the most marked is that of object of comparative.

What, then, determines the level of markedness of specific linguistic features? Croft (1990) reviews Greenberg's (1966) early work on linguistic universals and identifies three main types of evidence:[3]

1 Structure: this concerns the presence or absence of a feature. For example, plural can be considered more marked than singular because it typically involves the addition of a morpheme.
2 Behaviour: this concerns whether one element is grammatically more 'versatile' than another—the more versatile it is, the more unmarked it is. Versatility is evident in both the number of inflections a specific grammatical category possesses (for example, singular 3rd person has three forms in English—'he', 'she', and 'it'—whereas plural third person has only one—'they') and in the number of syntactic contexts in which a specific grammatical element can occur (for example, more constructions occur with the active voice than with the passive voice).
3 Frequency: the unmarked value is likely to occur with greater frequency than the marked value, both in actual use (i.e. in actual texts) and also in the world's languages.

Croft considers that 'markedness is a fundamental concept, underlying much grammatical work in typology' (1990: 64).

To summarize, linguistic typology involves the crosslinguistic study of samples of the world's languages. It results in the identification of various types of universals: unrestricted universals, universal tendencies, implicational universals, and universal hierarchies. Also, it provides a principled basis for determining the degree of relative markedness of connected features.

Typologically motivated studies of second language acquisition

SLA research has used linguistic typology to seek answers to three main questions:

1 What influence do typological universals have on the order of acquisition of grammatical features?
2 What effect does markedness have on learning difficulty?
3 How does the typological status of grammatical features in the native and target languages affect L1 transfer?

We have already considered (3) in Chapter 8 (see pages 319–24), so we will focus our attention on (1) and (2) here.

The research based on linguistic typology has examined phonological features (for example, Eckman 1977, 1984, and 1991; Tarone 1980a) as well as grammatical features (for example, Levenston 1971; Hyltenstam 1977; Schmidt 1980; Rutherford 1983; Zobl 1989; Jones 1991b). No attempt will be made to provide a comprehensive review of this literature. Instead, selected studies will be considered as a way of examining the major theoretical issues.

Negative placement

Negative placement constitutes an example of a non-implicational universal tendency, with Dahl's (1979) survey showing a clear preference for preverbal over postverbal negative position in the world's languages. As we saw in Chapter 3, there is strong evidence that in the early stages of L2 acquisition learners opt for preverbal negation, even where the L1 manifests postverbal negation. If, on the basis of language typology, preverbal negation is considered unmarked in relation to postverbal negation, it would seem that learners acquire the unmarked form before the marked. Furthermore, as Wode (1984) notes, preverbal negation appears even when it is not present in either the target language or the learner's L1. This suggests that typological universals like negator + verb phrase may occur irrespective of the formal characteristics of the languages involved.

Jordens' (1980) re-analysis of Hyltenstam's (1977) data on the acquisition of the negative placement rule in Swedish by Turkish, Serbo-Croat, and Hamito-Semitic speakers lends support to a number of predictions based on typological markedness. Swedish is of particular interest because 'in main clauses the negation is placed after the finite verb, while in subordinate clauses it is placed immediately before the finite verb' (Hyltenstam 1977: 387). As such, it appears to contradict the 'universal tendency for Neg to have a definite position relative to the FE (finite element) of the sentence' (Dahl op. cit.: 91). Jordens argues that Hyltenstam's learners initially went for a negator + main verb ordering in both main and subordinate clauses:

> *han inte komme (he not comes)
> att han inte kommer (that he not comes)

The learners, therefore, appear to be behaving like other learners by opting initially for a negator in preverbal position (as reported in many studies of L2 negation) and also by placing the negator in a definite position. Jordens also points out that this position is initially determined not by the finite verb element (as this is not yet represented in the learners' interlanguage) but, more simply, by the main verb.[4]

Preposition stranding and pied piping

Preposition stranding and *pied piping* have been investigated by Mazurkewich (1984) and Bardovi-Harlig (1987). Preposition stranding is typologically rare and, therefore, might be expected to be acquired late. It is considered marked in relation to pied piping (see van Riemsdijk 1978 cited in Bardovi-Harlig 1987) on the grounds that any language that has preposition stranding also has pied piping, but not the reverse. Also, the relationship is considered to be implicational (i.e. languages that have preposition stranding also have pied piping). Both structures are found in *wh*-questions and relative clauses in English, as shown in these examples:

> With whom did Mary speak? (pied piping)
> The man with whom Mary spoke ... (pied piping)
> Who(m) did Mary speak with? (preposition stranding)
> The man who(m) Mary spoke with ... (preposition stranding).

Mazurkewich used a written question formation test to investigate the ease of acquisition of the two structures in *wh*-questions by French and Inuktitut speakers. The results indicated that the French speakers produced more instances of pied piping than preposition stranding, while the opposite was true for the Inuktitut speakers. In other words, the results were ambivalent, not lending clear support to the hypothesis that the unmarked structure would prove easier than the marked. One possible explanation for this could be L1 transfer; Inuktitut does not have prepositions and so, arguably, transfer is not an issue, whereas French has pied piping but not preposition stranding. The French learners may have transferred their L1 structure, therefore. However, this is not Mazurkewich's preferred explanation. She claims that the Inuktitut speakers were more advanced than the French speakers and, thus, more likely to have acquired the marked preposition stranding. She also argues that L1 transfer is not an adequate explanation of the French learners' results because the Quebec dialect, which they spoke, does manifest incidences of preposition stranding (for example, le boss que je travaille pour = the boss that I work for). Mazurkewich's arguments are dismissed by both Kellerman (1985b) and White (1986), both of whom consider that the transfer explanation is stronger.

Bardovi-Harlig's (1987) study indicates that the markedness hypothesis is, in fact, not tenable for pied piping/preposition stranding. This study used a similar linguistic manipulation task to Mazurkewich, but included items involving relative clauses as well as *wh*-questions. The subjects were 95 learners of English, divided into six proficiency levels. They had a variety of L1s, but in every case the L1 allowed only the unmarked pied piping. The results provided clear evidence that learners acquire preposition stranding before pied piping, contrary to the markedness hypothesis. Bardovi-Harlig also found that before learners attempt either rule, they omit the preposition entirely (a 'No-Prep strategy'), as in these examples:

Who did Mary give a book?
The man Mary baked a cake was Joe.

The order of acquisition, therefore, was (1) No-Prep, (2) preposition stranding, (3) pied piping. This order was evident in both *wh*-questions and relative clauses, although relative clauses, as the more difficult structure, were more likely to retain the 'simpler' forms (No-Prep and preposition stranding) than *wh*-questions. Bardovi-Harlig argues that the results indicate that the learners were not responding to linguistic factors (i.e. markedness) but to the availability of data in the input (i.e. salience). Thus, preposition stranding is acquired before pied piping because it is more frequent in the input. She suggests the following restatement of the markedness hypothesis: 'unmarked structures are acquired before marked structures, all things being equal' (1984: 402).

Relativization

Four major questions have figured in the research based on the Accessibility Hierarchy (AH): (1) does the AH account for avoidance behaviour? (2) does the AH explain the order of acquisition of relativizable NP positions? (3) does the AH explain the use of pronominal copies? and (4) does the AH explain the acquisition of the forms of different relativizers? In each case, the central issue is whether markedness factors, typologically determined, can be used to explain acquisitional phenomena.

Schachter's (1974) study of relative clauses, which we considered in Chapter 8, showed that learners of English whose L1 does not contain relative clauses or contains left-branching rather than right-branching clauses (for example, Japanese and Chinese) tend to avoid using relative clauses in their English production. Schachter did not investigate whether the extent of this avoidance was related to the function of the relative pronoun. However, Gass (1980: 138) did so. She used a sentence-joining task to elicit use of all the relative pronoun functions in the AH. She reported that her subjects (adult learners with mixed L1 backgrounds) tended to avoid relativizing on low positions in the AH by changing a part of one of the sentences in a sentence-joining task so as to make relativization in a higher position possible. For example the two sentences:

He saw the woman.
The man kissed the woman.

were intended to elicit the use of a relative pronoun functioning as direct object:

He saw the woman that the man kissed.

However, several learners contrived to use a subject relative pronoun, as in:

He saw the woman who was kissed by the man.

Akagawa (1990), however, found no support for the hypothesis that Japanese learners display more avoidance on lower positions than on higher positions in the AH. Thus, although there is clear evidence that differences between the L1 and L2 structure of relative clauses induce avoidance, to date there is only mixed evidence to show that the degree of avoidance corresponds to markedness.

There is much clearer evidence that markedness, as defined by the AH, influences the order of acquisition. Gass (1980) found strong support for the markedness hypothesis. Thus, fewest errors were evident in the subject position, with the most errors in the object of comparison position. However, Gass reported that the learners found the genitive function easier than the direct object function, contrary to predictions based on the AH, a point that will be commented on below.

Pavesi (1986), in a comparative study of instructed and naturalistic Italian learners of L2 English that used implicational scaling on elicited oral data, found that, in general, both groups of learners followed the order predicted by the AH. However, the pattern for indirect object and oblique and also for genitive and object of comparative was not always as expected. Learners varied with regard to which function in each pair they favoured, some preferring the unmarked before the marked member and others vice versa. Also, the genitive and object of comparison functions were almost entirely missing in the naturalistic group.

Further evidence in support of the markedness hypothesis can be found in Eckman, Bell, and Nelson (1988) for learners with mixed L1s, and Jones (1991b) for Japanese college students. In both studies, the accuracy order for the different pronoun functions on sentence-joining tasks conformed broadly to the AH, although, again, there were some discrepancies. Jones' study is of interest because he provides separate accuracy orders for genitive and non-genitive structures. He found that the subject function was considerably easier than the direct object and oblique positions (which were roughly equal) irrespective of whether the structure involved a genitive or not. Also, although non-genitive structures proved easier overall than genitive structures, accuracy levels on the genitive subject position were equivalent to those on non-genitive direct object and oblique positions. The importance of considering genitive and non-genitive structures separately is borne out by Hansen-Strain and Strain (1989), who found that the results for genitive in their study involving five different L1 groups on seven different tasks did not match the

AH. The learners performed much better than expected, possibly because they were only required to produce genitive subject structures.

Three studies have examined pronominal copies in relative clauses in terms of the AH. The studies by Gass (1979; 1980) and Hyltenstam (1984) have already been considered in Chapter 8. The conclusion was that markedness interacts with L1 transfer in the sense that although pronominal copy errors were more likely in the lower positions and less likely in the higher positions of the AH, the overall error frequency reflected whether or not pronominal copies occurred in the learners' L1. Gass felt that 'it is universal principles that play the leading role since they are dominant in assigning a relative order of difficulty' (1980: 140). A third study—Tarallo and Myhill (1983)—casts doubt on this conclusion, however. English L1 subjects were asked to judge the grammaticality of sentences containing pronominal copies in two right-branching languages (German and Portuguese) and two left-branching (Chinese and Japanese). Tarallo and Myhill reported that the learners of right-branching languages were most accurate in judgements of sentences involving the subject function, while those of left-branching languages were most accurate in judgements involving the direct object function. In other words, the learners of the right-branching languages conformed to the order predicted by the AH but those of left-branching languages did not. Tarallo and Myhill concluded that the crucial factor was the proximity of the relativized noun phrase (NP) site in the embedded sentence to the head of the relative clause. Thus, in English, the direct object function is more difficult than the subject function because the extraction site (shown by a _____) is further from the head NP (in italics) than is the case for subject function, for example:

The *puppy* that I bought _____ was a nuisance.
I bought the *puppy* that _____ made me laugh.

The opposite is the case in left-branching languages.

Finally, Hawkins (1989) examined the acquisition of the different forms of L2 French relativizers by three groups of adult English-speaking learners, who differed in their general level of proficiency. He found that the order of acquisition of the three relativizers, *qui*, *que*, and *dont*, conformed to the order predicted by the AH, but argued that this order could also be predicted on the basis of surface configurational factors. For example, *qui* could be expected to be acquired before *que*, which in turn would be acquired before *dont* because this order corresponds to the distance between the head and the extraction site, as shown in the following examples:

L'homme qui _____ connaît Pierre ... (The man who knows Pierre).
L'homme que Pierre connaît _____ ... (The man who Pierre knew).
Le visiteur dont j'avais oublié le nom _____ ... (The visitor whose name I had forgotten).

It is not possible, therefore, on the basis of these results, to decide between a 'relational view' (based on the AH) and 'a configurational view' (based on the surface relationships between grammatical elements). However, Hawkins went on to provide evidence to suggest that the configurational view is the right one, arguing, for example, that only this view can explain why the learners experienced greater difficulty with stylistically inverted relative clauses like:

L'homme que connaît Pierre ... (The man that Pierre knows ...)

than with relative clauses displaying the more conventional order. Such a conclusion may be premature, however, given that the difficulty with such stylistically inverted sentences may derive from L1-related factors (English does not permit subject–object inversion in relative clauses) rather than from configurational factors *per se*.

It is probably premature to reach firm conclusions regarding the effect of markedness, as represented by the accessibility hierarchy, on L2 acquisition. There is some evidence to show that linguistic markedness may have an effect on the extent to which learners avoid relative clauses, the order in which they acquire relative pronoun functions, and the extent to which learners make pronominal copy errors. The general finding is that acquisition is easier in the unmarked, higher positions and more difficult in the marked, lower positions of the hierarchy. There is, however, an alternative view advanced by Tarallo and Myhill (1983) and Hawkins (1989), namely that learners construct rules for relative clauses on the basis of the adjacency of categories in the surface configuration. According to this view, the difficulty that learners experience in learning relative clauses is not the product of the relative markedness of the relative pronoun functions, but a function of their capacity for processing sentences. We should also note that the L2 research suggests that there are problems with the AH, as formulated by Keenan and Comrie (1977). In particular, the fact that variable results have been found for genitive suggests that Jones' (1991a) proposal that there are in fact two hierarchies, one for genitive and the other for non-genitive, is right.

The role of typological universals in second language acquisition

What conclusions can we reach regarding the role of typological universals in L2 acquisition? The evidence from the studies of negation, preposition stranding/pied piping, and relativization which we have considered, indicates that the linguistic nature of the target structures may influence both the ease and the order of their acquisition. Learners seem to find it easier to acquire typologically unmarked structures than typologically marked structures. The assumption that underlies this research, namely that linguistic universals will affect interlanguages in the same way as they affect other languages, because ILs constitute natural languages, is supported.

It is clear, however, that typological markedness alone cannot account for L2 acquisition. Gass (1984) suggests that it constitutes not so much an 'absolute constraint' as an 'overall shaping factor'. Bardovi-Harlig's (1987) study of preposition stranding/pied piping shows that in some features at least, acquisition may not proceed in accordance with markedness. If a linguistically marked feature is strongly represented in the input learners are exposed to, then they will acquire this before a related unmarked feature that is only weakly represented. In other words, input frequency can over-ride the assumed difficulty of learning a marked feature. This raises a thorny question. Is it markedness *per se* or input frequency that is the real determinant of acquisition? In general, we can assume that unmarked features are likely to be frequent. Subject relative pronouns, for instance, occur more frequently than objective of comparison pronouns, and probably also more frequently than indirect object pronouns. The fact that learners acquire subject relative pronouns before object of comparison and indirect pronouns may therefore simply reflect input frequency. In order to decide whether it is markedness or input frequency that determines order of acquisition, it is therefore necessary to look at cases like preposition stranding/pied piping in English, where the two factors do not correlate. Bardovi-Harlig's finding that learners acquire the marked but frequent structure first is very damaging to the markedness hypothesis.

It would be premature, however, to dismiss markedness. Learners do not always respond to what is in the input, as the studies of negation show. The input shows learners of L2 English that negation in English follows the auxiliary verb and precedes the main verb, and yet learners almost invariably opt for preverbal negation in the initial stages. In this case, therefore, they appear to choose the unmarked form rather than the form supplied by the input. Again, however, the question arises as to whether the initial preference that learners show for preverbal negation reflects markedness or some other factor. For example, if learners 'simplify' the input by ignoring auxiliaries, English negation will appear to be preverbal. An explanation of early preverbal negation based on ease of processing is as likely, if not more so, than one based on typological markedness. According to the Multidimensional Model (see Chapter 9), for instance, preverbal negation occurs because learners have not yet removed the processing 'block' that prevents them inserting an element (the negator) into the middle of a string.

The underlying problem is to explain how typological universals affect acquisition. Two types of explanation are possible. One is that they affect learning *directly* because the learner has inbuilt grammatical knowledge that includes a theory of grammatical markedness. This is tantamount to suggesting that learners bring a knowledge of markedness relations, such as those represented in the AH, to the learning task, and thus are predisposed to expect unmarked grammatical features to be more likely than marked ones. This is the view that Hawkins (1989) considers and rejects, probably rightly.

The alternative view is that markedness relations are only *indirectly* related to language acquisition, and that to understand how they work it is necessary to uncover the factors that cause one linguistic feature to be more marked than another. This is the view taken by most L2 researchers. For example, Hyltenstam (1984) is careful to argue that the AH can only serve as a basis for making *predictions* about L2 acquisition and does not, in itself, provide *explanations*. There are reasons why some features are more common in the world's languages than others and it is these reasons that will explain acquisition.

What then are the factors that determine markedness? Gass and Ard (1984) identify a number of potential sources of language universals, which are summarized in Table 10.2. They acknowledge that their list is not exhaustive, and also that any one universal may have more than one source. 'There is a great deal of controversy with regard to the assignment of an origin to a particular universal' (1984: 35).

Source	Description
1 Physical basis	The universal reflects 'a physical fact, perhaps dependent on the way the world is, or … on the way the human body, especially the vocal and aural apparatus, is structured'.
2 Perceptual/ cognitive	The universal reflects 'factors in the human perceptual and cognitive apparatus and processing capabilities'. Such factors affect more than just language.
3 Language acquisition device	The universal reflects innate knowledge of language that a learner brings to the learning task.
4 Neurological basis of language acquisition	The universal reflects neurological predispositions towards the use of certain types of structure.
5 Historical change	Certain patterns may be missing from all languages because they cannot diachronically arise from the types of language extant.
6 Social interaction	Universals of interactive competence influence the universal nature of language.

Table 10.2:   Sources of linguistic universals (from Gass and Ard 1984: 35–38)

While Gass and Ard's attempt to uncover the factors that underlie universals is admirable, it does not take us very far in explaining acquisition. As they admit, their framework is programmatic.

Another difficulty of the typological perspective is that it places undue emphasis on syntactic, surface-level features. Rutherford (1982) has argued that linguistic universals should not be considered in isolation from discourse function, pointing out that 'one cannot hope to formulate meaningful generalizations about syntactic/discoursal order of acquisition by studying syntax alone' (1982: 103).

Gregg's (1989) verdict on typological universals is:

... typological generalizations are either uninteresting (no language has labiovelar stops) or interesting only in the questions they raise, not in the answers they provide (1989: 32).

Rutherford (1984b: 142) also feels that typological universals are of limited value—they offer little more than 'a collection of observations', albeit 'concerning a rather wide assortment of syntactic phenomena'. In so far as typological universals explain nothing, Gregg and Rutherford are right. Until it is possible to determine the precise source of specific universals, the typological approach will not be capable of explaining L2 acquisition. Typological universals still have a place in SLA research, however. They provide a basis for forming predictions about acquisition and are of value in what Hyltenstam refers to as 'the descriptive phase of research' (1990: 33).

Theorists like Gregg who dismiss typological universals out of hand are therefore overly harsh. However, an approach that concentrates on the nature of the abstract knowledge that determines the structure of any particular language is likely to be more revealing, for, as Lightbown and White (1987) point out, knowledge of universals and markedness might follow from this abstract knowledge and the properties of the human mind that give rise to it. We now turn to the Chomskyan view of linguistic universals and examine in what ways and to what extent this affords an explanation of L2 acquisition.

Universal Grammar and language acquisition

Whereas language typology is essentially data-driven and descriptive in nature, the approach that we will consider in this section is motivated by a powerful theory of language and a well-developed model of grammar. The theory is Universal Grammar (UG) and the model Government/Binding, as proposed by Chomsky (1976; 1981a; 1981b). We will focus attention on the theory. No attempt will be made to summarize the Government/Binding Model, although aspects of it will be considered by way of illustration.[5]

The Theory of Universal Grammar

One of the claims of L2 theorists working within a generative grammar framework is that any theory of L2 acquisition that is not based on an adequate theory of language will prove inadequate (Gregg 1989). The argument is that the Theory of Universal Grammar, as proposed by Chomsky, constitutes the best theory of grammar currently available, because it achieves both *descriptive* and *explanatory adequacy*. It follows that L2 acquisition research should be informed by this theory.

The terms 'descriptive' and 'explanatory adequacy' refer to two key ideas in the study of grammar. Speakers of a language manifest a 'steady state' of knowledge, which changes only in relatively insignificant ways (such as in vocabulary). To achieve descriptive adequacy, the linguist must provide a complete and explicit account of the steady state. To achieve explanatory adequacy, the linguist must account for how speakers arrive at the steady state from the initial state, given the nature of the linguistic data they are exposed to; that is, they must explain how children come to know their mother tongue. The Theory of UG, therefore, is both a description of language (more specifically, of grammar) and a theory of how knowledge of a language is acquired.

This section will address three questions:

1 What does UG consist of?
2 What role does UG play in L1 acquisition?
3 What should the domain of a theory of L2 acquisition be?

Readers should note that Chomsky himself has been concerned only with (1) and (2), and has had almost nothing to say about L2 acquisition.

Principles, parameters, and markedness

Chomsky defines UG as 'the system of principles, conditions and rules that are elements or properties of all human languages' (1976: 29). In other words, it comprises a set of linguistic universals. Subsequently, Chomsky (1981a) characterizes these universals as consisting of principles and parameters. The term 'principles' refers to highly abstract properties of grammar which apply to language in general and which, therefore, underlie the grammatical rules of all specific languages. Although the full range of principles will not be evident in all languages, there will be no language that contravenes any principle. The term 'parameters' refers to principles that vary in certain restricted ways from one language to another. That is, they take the form of a finite set of options which individual languages draw on and which define the variation possible between languages. Parameters have two or more 'settings', with different languages manifesting different settings. Chomsky (1988) likens parameters to the array of switches found in a switch box; the learner's task is to use experience to determine which position each switch must be in. The goal of generative grammar is to identify the principles and parameters that comprise UG and to specify which principles and which parameters are operative in specific languages.

An example of a principle is subjacency. This defines the restrictions that govern how far one phrase can be moved from 'deep' to 'surface' structure. Thus, questions like:

1 What did Randy think?
2 What did Randy think his brother had won?

are grammatical because they involve limited movement of the *wh*-element (i.e. 'what') from the deep structure object position:

Randy thought _____.
Randy thought his brother had won _____.

Sentences like the following, however, are ungrammatical:

3 *What did Randy wonder whether his brother would win?

because they involve movement of the *wh*-element from a 'remote' deep structure position:

Randy wondered whether his brother would win _____.

In the Government/Binding Model, movement is discussed very precisely in terms of the restrictions imposed by 'bounding nodes', which for English consist of noun phrase, embedded sentence, and sentence. According to Berwick and Weinberg (1984) 'movement may not cross more than one bounding node' at a time. Thus, sentences (1) and (2) above are grammatical because the *wh*-element does not cross more than one bounding node, whereas (3) is ungrammatical because it crosses two embedded sentence nodes. It should be noted, however, that what constitutes a bounding node is not itself universal and that languages vary in the extent to which movement is restricted. This is a point that will be illustrated later when we consider a number of L2 studies based on the subjacency principle.

An example of a parameter is 'pro-drop'. Languages vary according to whether they forbid the deletion of subject pronouns. English, for example, does not normally delete pronouns:[6]

*Is the President of the United States.

Spanish, on the other hand, permits null pronoun subjects:

Está el Presidente de los Estados Unidos.

The pro-drop parameter, therefore, 'determines whether the subject of a clause can be suppressed' (Chomsky 1988: 64). It has just two settings (other parameters may have multiple settings).

Parameters like pro-drop are of considerable interest to linguists, and, as we will see, also to SLA researchers, because they involve a number of linguistic features. Chomsky (1981a) has proposed that languages with null subjects, like Spanish and Italian, do not have expletives (for example, dummy 'it' and 'there' in English) and also permit variable word order, with the verb appearing both before and after the subject in sentences like:

Viene la chica (Is coming the girl).
La chica viene (The girl is coming).

In contrast, non-pro-drop languages like English have expletives and also manifest a fixed word order with the subject placed invariably before the verb in declarative sentences:

> *Is coming the girl.
> The girl is coming.

In addition Chomsky suggests that 'that'-trace effects occur in pro-drop languages but not in non-pro-drop:

> Chai hai detto che e venuto?
> *Who have you said that is come?
> (Examples from Gass 1989: 509)

Hyams (1983) has also claimed that non-pro-drop languages have a class of modal verbs, distinct from main verbs. Finally, Jaeggli and Hyams (1988) have proposed that null subjects only occur in languages with a uniform pattern of inflections (i.e. either all verbs are inflected, as in Spanish, or none, as in Japanese). These various grammatical properties—all entailed by the pro-drop parameter—constitute a cluster.[7]

UG also provides a basis for determining markedness. The degree of markedness depends on whether a feature is part of the 'core' or the 'periphery'. These notions have already been introduced in Chapter 8 (see Figure 8.1). The core features of a language are those that are governed by UG, while peripheral features are those that are not. Core features are considered unmarked because they require minimal evidence for acquisition, whereas peripheral features are considered marked because they require much more substantial evidence. The degree of markedness of a feature can also vary within the core, depending on the parameter setting involved. Parameter settings can be ordered according to how marked they are. Thus, for example, Hyams considers pro-drop to be unmarked in relation to non-pro-drop, with Spanish and Italian unmarked with respect to this parameter, and English marked. As White (1989a) points out, this view of markedness differs from that found in language typology because markedness is seen as internal to the learner, a consequence of the language faculty, rather than as something external, evident only in extant languages.

It is also possible to identify another rather different definition of markedness based on UG theory. Zobl (1983b) advances a notion of markedness based on the learner's *projection capacity*, as shown in Figure 10.1. As in the Theory of UG, markedness is understood in relation to the amount of primary linguistic evidence needed to acquire a given property. Zobl's Projection Model considers property z unmarked in relation to v, w, x, and y, on the grounds that the acquisition device does not require any actual experience of z in order to acquire it (i.e. z does not have to be attested in the input to which the learner is exposed). Instead, learners are able to infer the existence of z once they have discovered that certain other properties exist. Clusters of features—such as those associated with the pro-drop parameter—provide a basis for projection; evidence of one feature in a cluster may enable learners to acquire the other features associated with it, irrespective of whether they have experienced these features in the input. Markedness based on a projection model is also a learner-internal phenomenon.

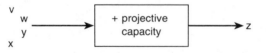

Figure 10.1:   A projection model of markedness (Zobl 1983b: 294)

Universal Grammar and first language acquisition

The Theory of Universal Grammar is intimately tied to a theory of L1 acquisition. Chomsky has consistently argued that UG principles are inherently impossible to learn, and that therefore, they must be innate. They make up the 'initial state', and as such provide the basis that enables a child to acquire a language. A child has access to a *language acquisition device* (LAD) that maps experience into the 'steady state', as shown in Figure 10.2.

Figure 10.2:   Chomsky's model of language acquisition (Chomsky 1981a)

Two key issues arise out of this model: (1) what is the nature of the child's 'experience' of the target language, and (2) what does the LAD consist of? The first question leads to a discussion of what has become known as the *poverty of the stimulus*, while the second involves an account of the language faculty.

The poverty of the stimulus

Generative theorists consider the experience which the young child has of the target language to be seriously impoverished in a number of ways. It was initially argued that input is degenerate (see Miller and Chomsky 1963; Chomsky 1965; McNeill 1966), in the sense that it contains ungrammaticalities and disfluencies which make it an inadequate source of information for language acquisition. The principal argument was that children would find it impossible to distinguish between what is grammatical and what is ungrammatical on the basis of such input. Subsequent research into caretaker talk, however, has demonstrated that simplified input of the kind most children experience in the early stages of acquisition is far less degenerate than was claimed (see Chapter 6).

The stimulus might be considered 'degenerate' in another way. Wexler and Culicover (1980) argued that the problem lies not in ungrammaticality but in the fact that the input is simplified, as this deprives children of the data they require to learn the more complex aspects of grammar. This view has since been endorsed by White (1989a) and Sharwood Smith (1986), among others. There are problems with this argument. First, the fact that the input is 'simplified' does not mean that children are deprived of data on all the grammatical features they have not yet learnt. Even simplified input may supply the child with some new information. Second, the caretaker research shows that input is only temporarily simplified; as the child's ability to understand grows, so the input becomes progressively more complex (see Wells 1985). The child, then, receives 'full' input in the course of time. The argument that children do not receive adequate input for acquisition because it is simplified does not seem to hold.

However, there are other more compelling reasons than 'degeneracy' for considering the input impoverished. Input seriously underdetermines the final grammar. The child will only be exposed to a subset of the total sentences possible in the target language and has no way of determining whether a given sentence is not heard because of coincidence (i.e. it just happens that the input to date has not provided evidence of it) or because it is not possible in the language. Furthermore, the input does not provide the child with the data needed to determine that certain constructions are not possible. White (1981) gives dative alternation as an example. English permits two constructions with many dative verbs, as in these examples:

Randy gave a present to Mary. (noun phrase (NP) + prepositional phrase (PP))
Randy gave Mary a present. (NP + NP)

However, other dative verbs permit only the NP + PP pattern:

Randy explained the problem to Mary.
*Randy explained Mary the problem.

Supposing the child works out that many verbs allow both patterns, how can the restriction on verbs like 'explain' be discovered? Again, positive evidence will not suffice, as the child has no way of knowing that, in time, sentences with NP + NP will not occur. White (1989a) and others argue strongly that underdetermination of this kind is the main problem with input.

One way in which this problem might be overcome is if the input provides the child with *negative evidence*. Logically, there are two kinds of evidence, positive and negative. Positive evidence comes from exposure to the speech of other speakers, but as we have seen, this is not adequate because it underdetermines the final grammar. It follows that if children are to learn on the basis of input alone they must receive negative evidence, i.e. be given feedback that shows them what is ungrammatical in their sentences. However, as we saw in Chapter 6, children do not typically receive direct negative feedback on the grammaticality of their utterances. If there is no negative feedback, how do children learn that sentences like:

*What did Randy wonder whether his brother would win?

are not possible sentences? The answer is, that with insufficient positive evidence and no negative evidence, they must rely on innate knowledge.

Another possible answer is that children act in accordance with *indirect negative evidence*. That is, they avoid certain kinds of errors because they never hear anyone produce them. The problem with this argument is that there is ample evidence to show that children do produce errors that they could never have heard in the input. Thus, as White points out 'we would need a theory which would explain why children notice the non-occurrence of some sentence types but not others' (1989a: 15). Such a theory would lead, in fact, to claims that children have innate knowledge that guides them in what to avoid. Thus, arguments based on indirect negative evidence cannot replace those based on innateness.

As White puts it, 'plausible theories of language acquisition must assume realistic input' (1990: 124). From the preceding arguments two points follow: (1) input alone cannot explain L1 acquisition, and (2) therefore the child must be equipped with knowledge that enables the deficiencies of the input to be overcome. We should note, however, that not all the arguments relating to insufficiency of input, in particular those concerning negative evidence, necessarily apply to L2 acquisition, a point we will take up later (see page 456).

The language faculty

The child overcomes input deficiencies with the help of the language faculty. This consists, in part, of UG, which assists the child in various ways. First, it ensures that relatively little evidence is needed for the child to determine that a given principle is operative in the target language or to decide which setting of a parameter is the right one. Second, it prevents children from constructing *wild grammars* (Goodluck 1986). That is, at no point does the child construct a rule that contravenes UG. In this way, the child does not have to unlearn certain types of errors, for which negative evidence would be necessary. Of course, children do produce errors in features like 3rd person *-s* (for example, 'Mommy like cake'), but these are 'benign' in the sense that they can be unlearned on the basis of positive evidence. Such structures involve language-specific properties and, therefore, are not governed by UG. 'Impossible errors' (errors that require negative evidence) do not need to occur precisely because they are prohibited by UG. In essence, then, a language is learnable because the child needs to entertain only a small subset of the hypotheses that are consistent with the input data. Without the constraints imposed by UG, L1 acquisition would be at best extremely slow and, in some respects, impossible.

There are two possibilities regarding the child's access to the contents of UG. One is that the entire contents are available from the start, as suggested by White (1981). The other is that they are subject to maturation, with different principles and parameters becoming accessible at different stages of acquisition, as proposed by Felix (1984).[8] The problem with the first alternative is that clearly children do not instantly arrive at the grammar of the target language. However, White argues that it can be assumed that there is an interaction between UG and the language parser (the mechanism responsible for processing input data), such that a certain principle is only triggered when the child is capable of perceiving the relevant input data. White's position is the one preferred by many generative theorists because it suggests that the developmental nature of L1 acquisition is the product of non-linguistic rather than linguistic factors, a point we will pick up later when we consider the domain of a theory of L2 acquisition.

Some theorists have suggested that the language faculty contains learning procedures or principles that are not properly part of UG but which operate in tandem with it to enable the child to eliminate or avoid errors. An example of such a principle is the Subset Principle (Berwick 1985). If learners construct a conservative grammar, Y, which generates a subset of the sentences generated by some other grammar, X (as shown in Figure 10.3), this grammar can subsequently be expanded on the basis of positive evidence. However, if learners began with a superset grammar, X, they would require negative evidence to narrow its scope in order to construct Y.[9] For example, if children initially construct a grammar that only allows NP + PP for dative verbs and thus only produce sentences like:

Randy explained the problem to Mary.

they can avoid making impossible errors, as in:

*Randy explained Mary the problem.

As a result they will require only positive evidence to discover that some verbs (like 'give') also permit NP + NP. In this way, they can overcome the limitations of the input—by avoiding, for example, the need for negative evidence.

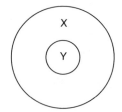

Figure 10.3:   The Subset Condition for two grammars (White 1989a: 145)

Chomsky views the language faculty as a mental organ, analogous to the liver or the heart. He sees it as ultimately related to physical aspects of the brain. Thus, 'in certain fundamental respects we do not really learn language; rather grammar grows in the mind' (1980a: 134). The language faculty is a child's biological inheritance.

The logical problem of language acquisition

To conclude this section, we will state the underlying problem which Chomsky's theory of language has been designed to address. The *logical problem of language acquisition* concerns how all children come to acquire with ease and complete success a rich and complex body of linguistic knowledge despite both their lack of cognitive sophistication and the poverty of the stimulus. The answer lies in the language faculty—the principles and parameters of UG, and learning procedures such as the Subset Principle.

The domain of a theory of second language acquisition

On the grounds that the same arguments used in support of UG and learning principles are also applicable to L2 acquisition, it is possible to specify in fairly narrow terms what it is that a theory of L2 acquisition needs to explain.

Grammatical competence

Essentially, the theory will need to account for the L2 learner's *grammatical competence*. That is, the theory should seek to account for 'knowledge' rather than 'behaviour' or *performance*). It should also focus on 'knowledge' rather than 'ability', and therefore need pay no attention to the variability inherent in learner language, as this is a reflection of learners' capacity to use their knowledge in communication. Finally, it should limit itself to explanations of the rules needed to account for the learner's *formal* knowledge of L2 grammar, and need not consider how form–function relationships are established.[10] 'Knowledge' here refers to knowledge that is implicit (unconscious and intuitive) rather than explicit (conscious and metalingual).

Generative theorists, including Chomsky, have acknowledged that it is possible to talk of *pragmatic competence* in the sense that speakers also internalize a set of rules that govern how language is used to construct discourse and to perform speech acts in socially appropriate ways. However, they typically exclude this too, not because an account of pragmatic competence is not needed, but because it is considered to be separate from grammatical competence and because it is still poorly understood. As Gregg (1989) puts it:

> ... in comparison with an attempt to construct a theory of acquisition in the domain of grammar, any attempt to construct a theory of acquisition in the domain of pragmatics or communication is going to be handicapped by the lack of a well-articulated formal characterization of the domain (1989: 24).

Pragmatic competence, therefore, is excluded on practical grounds.

The theory of L2 acquisition which generative theorists wish to see developed is one that focuses on knowledge of grammar, defined as syntax, phonology, and certain aspects of semantics. Such a theory is tenable if it is accepted that (1) grammar constitutes an autonomous area of language, and (2) the theory is modular in nature. These are seen as the essential characteristics of UG-based theories of L2 acquisition.

The autonomy of grammar

The claim that grammar constitutes an autonomous body of knowledge follows from the hypothesis that speakers possess a language faculty that is independent of other cognitive systems such as those responsible for perception, problem-solving or memorization. The evidence cited in support of this claim comes from the highly abstract, specific, and precise nature of the principles and parameters of UG. As Cook (1988) points out, 'to defeat the argument involves explaining how each and all of these principles could have been acquired from experience or from other faculties' (1988: 71). The generative argument is that no such explanation has been or can be given.

It has also been claimed that the language faculty exists independently of the mechanisms involved in using grammatical knowledge in performance. This has led Cook (1985) to distinguish 'acquisition' and 'development'. 'Development' refers to real-time learning of a language and is influenced by nonlinguistic factors such as *channel capacity*. 'Acquisition' is language learning unaffected by maturation, and is therefore dependent entirely on the learner's language faculty. Studies based on the analysis of performance data (for example, naturally occurring speech) only provide evidence of 'development'. In Chomsky's words, they are 'concerned with matters that may not properly belong to the language faculty' (1980a: 53) and provide evidence only of the 'fluttering notions of a fledgling before the organs of flight mature' (1981a: 35). It follows from such a view that to study 'acquisition' it is necessary to adopt a logical rather than an empirical approach, through a consideration of the relationship between the child's 'initial' and 'final state'.

According to Cook, therefore, 'acquisition' can only be examined in terms of 'an idealized "instantaneous" model in which time and experience play minimal roles' (1988: 81). For Cook, notions like 'order' and 'sequence', which, as we have seen, are the focus of much L2 research, have no clear place in such a model, as these are considered to reflect the learner's developing channel capacity rather than 'acquisition' itself. The view held by White (1981), that the entirety of UG is available to the child from the start and that 'development' is a reflex of improving perceptual abilities, also appears at first sight to exclude considerations of order and sequence. However, not all researchers working within a UG framework reject developmental data. As we noted earlier, Felix (1984) claims that 'the principles of Universal Grammar are themselves subject to an innately specified developmental process'—they emerge rather like teeth, in a pre-determined sequence. Also, a non-maturational view of UG, such as that preferred by White, still allows for a consideration of 'learning difficulty'. This is definable in terms of how a static language faculty responds to the available input, with unmarked features requiring less elaborate triggering experience than marked ones (see the section on markedness on pages 430–3). As Hyams (1991) points out, there are in fact two problems that need to be addressed: the 'logical problem', which 'treats acquisition as an instantaneous process', and the 'developmental problem', which recognizes that acquisition is non-instantaneous. As we will see, UG-oriented SLA research has addressed both problems.

Modularity

In claiming that grammar is autonomous, generative theorists recognize that other domains, such as perception and memory, are involved in language acquisition, and that these interact with the language module. In other words, a theory of how linguistic competence is acquired constitutes only one module in an overall theory of L2 acquisition. Furthermore, even within the language module itself, it may be necessary to identify various sub-domains, including UG, language learning procedures or principles, the domain responsible for the language specific learning needed to acquire peripheral grammatical features and vocabulary, and a language parser that analyses input (see Figure 10.4, from White 1989a). A complete theory, therefore, will have to explain how all the modules and sub-modules shown in Figure 10.4 interact.

We are a long way from being able to do this. The generative solution is to focus, narrowly and perhaps sensibly, on a specific domain. In so doing, generative theorists are at pains to acknowledge that the explanation they provide is only a partial one. The claim is only that 'UG plays a central and vital part in L2 learning, but there are many other parts' (Cook 1988: 189).

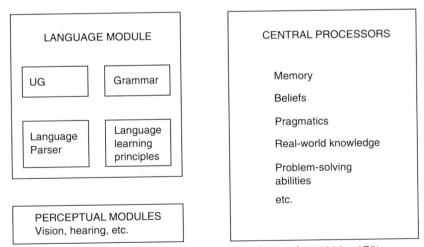

Figure 10.4:   Cognitive modularity (from White 1989a: 178)

Empirical studies of second language acquisition based on Universal Grammar

It was not until after the publication of Chomsky's *Lectures on Government and Binding* in 1981 that linguistic theory began to attract the serious attention of L2 researchers. Since then studies have proliferated. No attempt will be made to survey them in this chapter. Instead, representative studies that have examined the following key issues will be examined:

1 Do L2 learners have continued access to UG?
2 Do learners experience less difficulty with unmarked than with marked features of the L2?
3 Do L2 learners make use of the same learning principles as L1 learners?

Although a number of studies (for example, Hilles 1986; 1991) have studied learner language, much of UG-based SLA research has been directed at identifying learners' intuitions, and to achieve this has developed its own research methodology. It is appropriate to begin this section with a few comments about this.

The methodology of UG-based studies

Second language researchers basing their research on UG need to address several methodological issues (see White 1989a). One of these is how to ensure that the subjects have the requisite level of L2 proficiency to demonstrate whether or not a particular principle is operating in their interlanguage grammar. Many of the principles identified by UG grammarians involve complex sentences, and can therefore only be expected to manifest themselves in the later stages of development. White argues that it is essential to ensure that subjects are able to handle the necessary structures otherwise 'learners might violate a universal not because of the non-availability of UG, but because the structure in question is beyond their current capacity' (1989a: 61).

Another problem concerns the need to rule out the effects of the L1. If subjects act in accordance with UG, this might be because they have direct access to its contents or because they have indirect access through their L1. Thus, it is necessary to investigate learners with L1s that do not manifest the specific principle in question. Luckily this is possible, because not all UG principles operate in all languages. Subjacency, for example, does not operate in *wh*--questions in languages like Chinese, Japanese, and Korean (see page 443). Thus, if learners with these L1s follow this principle in an L2 like English, which does manifest it, this provides clear evidence that they are acting in accordance with UG constraints—providing it can be shown that they have not obtained knowledge of this principle through formal instruction.

In the case of studies of parameter setting, where the aim is to establish which setting out of those possible is reflected in the learner's interlanguage, bi-directional studies of the kind found profitable in language transfer studies (see Chapter 8) are needed. For example, the pro-drop parameter requires a study that investigates how English learners of L2 Spanish and Spanish learners of L2 English handle the relevant structural properties. Such studies are made even stronger if there are control groups where the L1 and L2 share the same parameter setting (for example, French and English). Only in this way is it possible to reach conclusions regarding the inter-related effects of transfer and markedness on acquisition.

Perhaps the most controversial methodological issue in UG-based studies concerns what kind of L2 data to collect. This is, of course, a problem for all L2 acquisition researchers but it is especially problematic in the case of UG-based research because of the need to obtain information about learners' competence rather than their ability to perform specific structures. There is also the difficulty of obtaining samples of language use that contain the kinds of complex structures needed to investigate most principles and parameters. For both these reasons, elicited data have been preferred.

White (1989a) mentions a number of methods for collecting data. These include the use of act-out tasks, picture identification tasks, sentence-joining tasks, and card-sorting tasks. However, the main method used to date is the grammaticality judgement task. This comes in several forms (see Ellis 1991b for an account of these), but always involves the learner in making some kind of metalingual assessment regarding the grammaticality of a mixed set of sentences, some grammatical and some ungrammatical. As White points out, the great advantage of this kind of task is that it forces subjects to consider sentences that are 'impossible' from a UG standpoint. Rejecting such sentences indicates that UG is alive, while accepting them shows that it is dead.

There are many problems with grammaticality judgements, however. Birdsong (1989) points out that they are not appropriate for learners with poor L2 literacy, and that differences in the metalinguistic skills of literate learners are also likely to affect responses. Furthermore, when learners reject sentences it is not always clear whether this is because of their grammatical properties or because of the difficulties that they experience in trying to parse them, a point taken up later. Birdsong also points out that often learners lack confidence and, therefore, are reluctant to commit themselves to a definite judgement, a point borne out in a study reported in Ellis (1991c). I tested different groups of Chinese and Japanese learners of English on two occasions, one week apart, using sentences with dative verbs (for example, 'show' and 'explain'), and found that the subjects frequently changed their judgements (up to 46 per cent of the time in one case). Variability in learners' judgements is therefore a major problem because it casts doubt on the reliability of the grammaticality judgement test.

Many of the problems that I and Birdsong raised may be overcome by better designed tests and by retesting to check reliability. However, in one other respect grammaticality judgements seem insuperably problematical. As Bialystok's (1979) study indicates, L2 learners make use of both implicit and explicit knowledge in reaching judgements. Indeed, the very nature of the grammaticality judgement task encourages the use of explicit knowledge. However, as was made clear in the previous section, UG is a theory of *implicit* linguistic knowledge. It might be argued that learners are not likely to have explicit knowledge relating to sentences that violate UG principles, but, as several studies have shown (for example, Seliger 1979; Sorace 1988), learners' explicit knowledge is often anomalous, with the result that their judgement of any sentence, including 'impossible' ones, may be uncertain and inconsistent. Unless some way can be found to ensure that learners do not use their explicit knowledge, it is not clear how the data obtained from such a task can be used to make claims about the role of UG in L2 acquisition.[11]

UG-based SLA research is typically experimental in nature: it involves control and experimental groups and elicited rather than naturally occurring language behaviour. This is because UG affords very precise hypotheses about the nature of L2 acquisition which lend themselves to an experimental treatment. Also, unlike much of the earlier research, where the primary goal was the description of learner language, UG-based research is explanatory in nature.

The availability of UG in second language acquisition; some empirical research

There has been extensive theoretical debate regarding the availability of UG in L2 acquisition. However, we will delay consideration of this until a later section (see page 453). Here we will examine what light empirical research has shed on this issue, focusing our attention on studies that have investigated the Subjacency Principle and the pro-drop parameter. (See page 430 in this chapter for a definition of subjacency, and White 1989a for an extensive review of the research.)

Subjacency

In an early study, Ritchie (1978b) investigated the 'right roof constraint', a principle that in more recent grammatical models falls under Subjacency. The right roof constraint limits the extent to which 'rightward movement' is possible, allowing sentences like:

A man in a car has just passed by.
A man has just passed by in a car.
That a man has just passed by in a car was not noticed.

but preventing sentences like:

*That a man has just passed by was not noticed in a car.

Ritchie investigated twenty adult Japanese graduate students at an American university and six native speakers by asking them to judge pairs of sentences, one of which conformed to the right roof constraint and the other of which did not. Japanese is a language with no rightward-movement rules. The majority of the subjects generally judged the sentences that violated the constraint to be 'less grammatical' than the sentences that did not (i.e. they performed significantly better than chance). However, there were some subjects whose judgements did violate the constraint. Ritchie's tentative conclusion was that the study provided 'preliminary support to the assumption ... that linguistic universals are intact in the adult' (1978b: 43).

Further evidence for adult learners' continued access to UG comes from a study by Bley-Vroman, Felix, and Ioup (1988). The subjects of this study were 92 advanced Korean learners of L2 English, most of whom had been living in the United States for several years, and as a result of which had had plenty of opportunity to learn naturalistically. Korean is not constrained by subjacency in *wh*-questions. The grammaticality judgement test required the subjects to indicate whether sentences were grammatical or ungrammatical, or whether they were not sure. The sentences, all of which involved *wh*-movement, were designed to test access to the Subjacency Principle. There were also a number of sentences which did not involve the principle and which were used as controls. The results showed a response bias (the learners manifested a tendency to reject sentences irrespective of whether they were grammatical or ungrammatical) and a reluctance to make use of the 'not sure' option. However, they also showed that the learners were not guessing at random; the typical response pattern resembled that of the native speakers. Bley-Vroman et al. conclude: 'Given these results, it is extremely difficult to maintain the hypothesis that Universal Grammar is inaccessible to adult learners' (1988: 26).

Further evidence for adult learners' continuing access to UG comes from a study by White, Travis, and Maclachlan (in press). This study looked at Malagasy learners of English, Malagasy being a language that permits subject extraction in *wh*-interrogatives where English does not. Thus, if the learners rejected sentences manifesting subject-extraction, this could not be explained by L1 transfer. Results from a grammaticality judgement test and a written elicited production task showed that nearly all the high-intermediate learners and half of the low-intermediate learners rejected Subjacency violations. White et al. argue that those subjects who accepted sentences that violated this UG principle did so only because they had not reached a stage of syntactical development for the Subjacency Principle to become active (i.e. they had not acquired *wh*-movement yet).

Whereas Ritchie's, Bley-Vroman et al.'s, and White et al.'s studies all support the 'UG is alive' position, Schachter's (1989) study indicates the opposite. Schachter chose as subjects learners whose L1 did not reflect subjacency in *wh*-questions (Korean), learners whose L1 provided only weak evidence of subjacency-based rules in *wh*-questions (Chinese), and learners whose L1 clearly manifests subjacency but not in *wh*-movement (Indonesian). In addition, there was a group of native speakers of English to act as controls. Schachter administered a grammaticality judgement test designed to assess whether the subjects had developed sufficient knowledge of the grammatical structures involved, in addition to the tests intended to show whether they violated the Subjacency Principle. The native speakers passed both the syntax and the subjacency tests. However, many of the learners passed only the syntax test—they exhibited knowledge of a syntactic construction without corresponding knowledge of the subjacency constraint. The behaviour of the learners was significantly different from that of the native speakers. There were also some differences among the different groups of learners but these were not significant. Thus, even if subjacency was instantiated in the learners' L1, it did not guarantee access to it in the L2. Schachter considers that the results constitute 'a serious challenge' to the claim that UG is available to adult L2 learners.

The picture is further complicated by uncertainty regarding the nature of learners' judgements when asked to judge the grammaticality of sentences like:

What did Bill think that the teacher had said?
*What did Sam believe the claim that Carol had bought?
(from Bley-Vroman et al. 1988: 8).

Bley-Vroman et al. note that the results they obtained may have reflected ease of parsing rather than UG effects. This hypothesis has been given support by a study by Schachter and Yip (1990). This produced clear evidence of processing effects in both native speakers' and learners' judgements of sentences involving *wh*-movement. Both sets of learners found it more difficult to make accurate judgements in sentences with three clauses than in sentences with a single clause. Schachter and Yip suggest that this is because subjects have to keep the *wh*-word in short-term memory until they discover the clause in which it fits. The subjects also performed much less accurately with sentences where the *wh*-extraction involved grammatical subjects than when it involved objects, irrespective of the number of clauses involved. In other words, both native speakers and learners treated grammatical extraction from object and subject positions differently. As this cannot be explained by reference to UG, it provides further evidence of processing factors at work. Schachter and Yip conclude that 'a number of earlier judgmental studies may need to be reexamined in terms of the possible effect of processing constraints', and that researchers need to be circumspect in accepting 'pure grammatical explanations'.[12]

A more recent study by Uziel (1993), however, suggests that learners' greater difficulty with subject extraction is explicable in terms of UG. Drawing on the grammatical arguments which Chomsky (1986b) presented in *Barriers* (a later framework than the *Government/Binding* model used in the earlier studies), Uziel hypothesized that subject-extraction would be rejected at a higher rate than object-extraction because it violates two principles (Subjacency and another), whereas object-extraction violates only Subjacency. He presents results from a small-scale study involving grammaticality judgements by 11 adult Italian and 10 adult Hebrew ESL learners that support this hypothesis. Uziel's study suggests that UG principles can help to explain why learners find some syntactic constructions more acceptable than others.

Given the problems that learners appear to experience with judging arcane sentences of the kind often found in the tests used in these studies, it is perhaps safer not to try to reach any conclusions regarding the availability or non-availability of UG.[13] Whether adult learners have access to the Subjacency Principle clearly requires further study directed at 'relative acceptability' rather than 'absolute obedience' to UG, as suggested by Uziel, and, ideally, involving data that are not drawn exclusively from grammaticality judgement tasks.

The pro-drop parameter

Another way of testing for the availability of UG is by investigating whether adult L2 learners are capable of resetting a parameter from the value found in their L1 to the value of the L2. If resetting does take place, this can be taken as evidence for the continued existence of UG. A second issue of considerable interest is whether learners reset all the features associated with a parameter (i.e. whether clustering effects are evident). We will focus here on studies based on the pro-drop parameter.

Two studies by White (1985; 1986) indicate that initially L2 learners opt for the L1 setting of the pro-drop parameter, but that as their proficiency increases they switch to the L2 setting. White also investigated whether pro-drop features cluster in interlanguage grammars. The subjects of the 1985 study were Spanish and French learners of L2 English, while the 1986 study also included two Italian learners. Spanish and Italian are pro-drop languages while French and English are non-pro-drop. The learners were asked to judge sentences, including some with missing pronoun subjects (both expletives, 'it' and 'there', and referential pronouns, such as 'he' and 'she'), some with ungrammatical subject–verb inversion, and some with a 'that' trace. White found clear evidence of differences in the performance of the Spanish and Italian learners compared to the French. They were more inclined to accept subjectless sentences. Also, of those subjects who demonstrated the necessary syntactical development, the Spanish learners were more likely to accept 'that'-trace than the French. However, there was no difference in their judgements of sentences with ungrammatical subject–verb inversion. The accuracy level of the learners' judgements improved in accordance with their overall proficiency. These results suggest the following conclusions: (1) L2 learners do not interact directly with L2 data but, instead, initially transfer the L1 setting of a parameter, (2) given time, learners succeed in resetting a parameter to the new L2 value, and (3) target-language features may cluster in interlanguage grammars, although not entirely as predicted by linguistic theory.[14]

Whereas White's research was based on grammaticality judgements and, in one of the studies, elicited question production, the studies to be considered next have all made use of more naturally occurring learner language. Given the doubts that exist regarding the reliability and validity of grammaticality judgement tasks, they provide an important alternative source of evidence.[15]

Hilles (1986; 1991) made use of the longitudinal data collected by Cancino et al. (1978) in their study of the naturalistic L2 acquisition of English negatives and auxiliaries, by Spanish speakers (see Chapter 3). In the 1986 study, Hilles looked at just one learner, Jorge, a 12-year-old Colombian. Hilles hypothesized that Jorge would begin with the L1 setting (pro-drop), and subsequently switch to the L2 setting (null pro-drop). She further hypothesized that this switch would co-occur with the emergence of auxiliary, and that it would be triggered by the acquisition of the expletives 'it' and 'there'. Her analysis supported these hypotheses, although Hilles was careful to point out that more evidence was needed before firm claims could be made.

The 1991 study focused on two of the features associated with the pro-drop parameter—the use of pronominal subjects and verb inflection—and sought to establish to what extent the two were correlated over time.[16] In this study, all six of Cancino et al's subjects (two children, two adolescents and two adults) were included, thus allowing Hilles to investigate to what extent age was a factor in the availability of UG. Three of the learners—the two children and one adolescent (Jorge)—manifested a strong correlation between the emergence of pronominal subjects and verb inflection, suggesting that their acquisition was guided by UG. Hilles argues that the developmental sequence these learners followed mirrored that found in L1 acquisition. L1 learners begin with null subjects and uniformly uninflected verbs, and subsequently switch to pronominal subjects once they realize that English is not uniform with regard to verb inflection (see Jaeggli and Hyams 1988). In contrast, the other adolescent and the two adults displayed no such correlation, indicating that they lacked access to UG.

A problem of Hilles' studies is that because there are no controls (i.e. subjects with non-pro-drop L1s like French), it is impossible to tell whether her Spanish subjects' early preference for the pro-drop setting is a true reflection of L1 acquisition or the result of L1 transfer. Lakshmanan's (1991) study, however, allows us to consider this question, at least in the case of children. Lakshmanan examined longitudinal data for three learners: Marta (one of the children in Cancino et al.'s study), Muriel (a French-speaking child studied by Gerbault 1978) and Uguisu (the Japanese child studied by Hakuta 1974). Whereas Spanish and Japanese can be considered pro-drop languages, French, like English, is non-pro-drop. The results support neither a 'transfer' nor a 'developmental' explanation, nor do they provide unequivocal evidence in favour of the clustering effect Hilles reported. Marta began by using null subjects, but these rapidly gave way to pronominal subjects. However, Marta never mastered English verb inflections in the period covered by the study. Muriel's use of null subjects was restricted to contexts involving 'it is' and, again, there appeared to be no relationship between her use of pronominal subjects and verb inflections. Uguisu did not employ any null subjects, but, contrary to the claims of the pro-drop parameter, treated English as morphologically uniform in the early stages. As Lakshmanan points out, these results are not readily explicable in terms of UG.[17]

Phinney's (1987) study also compared learners with different L1s, once again focusing on the presence and absence of subject pronouns and the verb inflectional system. In this case, however, the study was bidirectional in nature, comparing English-speaking learners of L2 Spanish and Spanish-speaking learners of L2 English. The data for this study came from written compositions. All the learners were fairly accurate in subject–verb agreement, but they differed in their use of subject pronouns. The L2 English learners omitted few referential pronouns but many expletive pronouns ('it' and 'there'), suggesting that they might have transferred the L1 value of the parameter. The L2 Spanish learners, however, provided no evidence of transfer, correctly omitting both referential and expletive pronouns. As White (1989a) points out, it is difficult to reach clear conclusions on the basis of this study as the two groups of subjects may not have been equivalent.

Overall, these studies provide no real support for a parameter-setting model of L2 acquisition. One general finding is that learners with pro-drop L1s tend to omit subject pronouns in the L2 to begin with and then later learn to include them (although Lakshmanan's study provides counter-evidence). But it is not clear that this requires a UG explanation; it is not necessary to invoke 'parameter-setting' to explain why L2 learners with pro-drop L1s produce sentences with no subject pronouns in the L2. Nor, on the basis of these studies, is it possible to conclude that UG works in child L2 acquisition but not in adult. Nor is there clear evidence of any clustering effect. White's and Hilles' studies suggest that there is some degree of clustering in the acquisition of the features hypothesized to be related to the prodrop parameter, although this does not always conform to the predictions of the linguistic models on which these studies were based. Other studies (Lakshmanan's and Phinney's), however, provide no evidence of clustering.

Markedness in UG and second language acquisition

We turn now to considering some of the empirical research that has examined the relationship between markedness and L2 acquisition. This research was based on the UG-based definitions of markedness considered earlier.

It will be recalled that in UG theory, 'core' rules are unmarked and 'peripheral' rules marked (see page 432). Mazurkewich (1984; 1985) investigated dative alternation, arguing that the NP + PP pattern is unmarked and the NP + NP pattern marked. One reason she gives is that the former is more productive than the latter (i.e. almost all dative verbs take NP + PP complements while only some take NP + NP). Another reason is that case assignment is transparent in the NP + PP pattern but is problematic in the NP + NP pattern. Mazurkewich considers the NP + PP complement to be a core rule and NP + NP a peripheral rule. She hypothesized that sentences like:

John baked a cake for Mary. (_____ NP + PP)

would be easier to acquire than sentences like:

John baked Mary a cake. (_____ NP + NP)

The subjects in Mazurkewich's (1984) study were 45 French-speaking high school and college students and 38 Inuktitut-speaking high school students. They were divided into beginner, intermediate, and advanced levels on the basis of scores on a cloze test. There was also a group of native-speaker controls. Judgements about sentences containing dative verbs with both the NP + PP and the NP + NP patterns were elicited from all the learners and the controls. Mazurkewich found that both the French and Inuktitut speakers judged the sentences with the unmarked NP + PP pattern more accurately than the sentences with marked NP + NP. She also found that the level of accuracy in the marked pattern increased with proficiency. Taken together, these results suggest that the learners acquired the unmarked structure first.

There have been several criticisms of Mazurkewich's research, however. Kellerman (1985b) points to a number of design flaws. White (1989a) notes that the French learners may have been influenced by their L1 (which permits only the NP + PP pattern) rather than by markedness, and she also notes that the results obtained for the Inuktitut speakers were very similar to those obtained for the native speakers. She argues, therefore, that the study does not provide any evidence for an acquisition sequence determined by markedness. Hawkins (1987) goes further, challenging Mazurkewich's notion of markedness. He points out that dative alternation is generally seen as a lexical property of verbs and that lexical properties belong to the periphery rather than the core. He argues that, according to current linguistic theory, dative alternation cannot be used as an example of the core/periphery distinction.

Hawkins' own study of dative alternation investigated ten adult French speakers spending a year at a British university. They were given a grammaticality judgement task similar to Mazurkewich's and a sentence construction task that required them to add a preposition ('to' or 'for') to any sentences they thought required them. Through a highly detailed analysis of the results, Hawkins provides evidence of a series of stages in the acquisition of dative alternation, reflecting the progressive introduction of syntactic features into the interlanguage grammar. To begin with, learners distinguish dative verbs according to whether they take a pronominal or a lexical object (for example,

'... give Mary it' v. '... give a present to Mary'). Later they introduce a distinction between 'to' and 'for' verbs (for example, 'give' and 'cook'), while later still they distinguish native and non-native verb forms (for example, 'give' and 'donate'). These stages were evident in individual dative verbs rather than across the board, suggesting that there was 'a progressive spread through the verbs of the learner's lexicon' (1987: 24). On the basis of these findings, Hawkins argues that it is misleading to isolate a single aspect of dative alternation, as Mazurkewich does, and raise it to the status of a UG-determined feature of L2 acquisition. His own preference is for a theory of markedness based on cognitive notions of 'learning complexity'.

There have been several other studies of the role of UG-derived markedness in L2 acquisition, but in just about every case they face similar criticisms to those levelled against Mazurkewich's research. The main problem rests in the twists and turns of linguistic theory. Noting this, Van Buren and Sharwood Smith (1985) ask 'when linguistics coughs, should second language acquisition catch pneumonia?' (1985: 21). They go on to answer this question by claiming that the theoretical foundations (i.e. Chomsky's Government/ Binding Theory) are sufficiently robust to warrant application in SLA research. This is not a view shared by all researchers however, (for example, Hawkins). Lack of consensus about the details of the theory is often evident, as, for instance, in the debate centring on Flynn's research on the head-final/ head-initial parameter (see Flynn 1987, Bley-Vroman and Chaudron 1990, and Flynn and Lust 1990). It is clearly premature to reach any conclusions as to whether markedness, as defined by the theory of UG, is a relevant factor in L2 acquisition.

Learning principles in second language acquisition

Earlier we noted that some theorists have posited the need for learning principles, such as the Subset Principle, to ensure that learners do not build grammars with rules that cannot be disconfirmed solely on the basis of positive evidence (see page 436).

White (1989b) investigated the L2 acquisition of adverb placement by adult French-speaking learners of English.[18] Whereas French allows adverbs to be positioned between the verb and the direct object:

Marie a mangé rapidement le diner.

English does not:

*Mary ate rapidly her dinner.

White argues that the Subset Principle should lead the learners to opt for a grammar that excluded adverb placement between verb and direct object (the conservative option). L1 transfer, on the other hand, would result in an L2 grammar that allowed this placement.

Three different data collection tasks were used: a paced grammaticality judgement test, an unpaced multiple choice grammaticality judgement test, and a preference task (where the subjects were asked to examine pairs of sentences and indicate which seemed 'better'). These tests were administered to the 43 learners and to a group of native-speaker controls. The results showed that the learners were much more likely to accept the ungrammatical sentences (i.e. those where the adverb was placed between verb and direct object) than the native speakers in the grammaticality judgement tests, and were much more likely to rate the grammatical and ungrammatical sentences as the same in the preference test. White concludes that these results support a transfer rather than a subset hypothesis.

This study and others (for example, Zobl 1988; Thomas 1989) indicate that the Subset Principle is non-operative in L2 acquisition. L2 learners appear to construct a superset grammar when such a grammar is suggested by their L1. This raises the question as to whether learners are subsequently able to readjust to a subset grammar. Evidence that they are able to reconstruct their grammars in this way would indicate that UG is still available to them (i.e. they have access to new, non-L1 parameter settings). Conversely, evidence that they cannot do so would suggest that they are stuck with the L1 settings of parameters because UG is not available. In essence, this takes us back to the same question we addressed when we considered parameter setting. Studies by Thomas (1989) and Hirakawa (1989) suggest that even though learners construct superset grammars, contrary to the Subset Principle, some, at least, ultimately arrive at the target-language setting.

How, then, do L2 learners move from a superset to a subset grammar? Logically, this is not possible on the basis of positive evidence. Indeed, the Subset Principle was set up to account for the impossibility of eliminating problematic errors by means of positive evidence. The French learner of L2 English can never be certain that sentences like:

> *Mary ate rapidly her dinner.

are not permitted. One possible solution to this conundrum, proposed by White (1989a), is that L2 learners make use of grammatical explanations and negative evidence (in the form of corrections of their errors) to help them establish what is grammatical and what is ungrammatical. In other words, L2 learners differ from L1 learners because they do not have access to learning principles like the Subset Principle, but they are able to overcome the difficulties that this gets them into by utilizing negative evidence not available to the L1 learner. Another possibility, of course, is that the Subset Principle is incorrect and the linguistic theory is wrong.

To sum up, the available research strongly suggests that L2 learners do not have access to learning principles like the Subset Principle. Consequently, they build a superset L2 grammar, often influenced by their L1. Subsequently, however, they restructure this grammar by restricting rule application, thus creating a subset grammar. It has been suggested by White that this requires negative evidence.

This position affords several testable hypotheses. One is that L1 learners will not make certain kinds of error (for example, placement of an adverb between verb and direct object) whereas L2 learners will. This hypothesis has received some support from studies which have investigated another UG principle (the Governing Category Parameter), which concerns what governs the relationship between pronouns and their antecedents (see, for example, Finer 1991). In L1 acquisition, children appear to conform to the narrowest value of this parameter, while in L2 acquisition, adults start off with the widest value if that is the setting in their L1. In other words, L1 acquisition conforms to the Subset Principle, whereas adult L2 acquisition does not. A second hypothesis is that L2 learners with no access to negative evidence (for example, naturalistic learners) will fail to eliminate superset errors. This has not been investigated. A third is that L2 learners who receive formal instruction will eliminate them. This has received support and will be considered further in Chapter 14.

Summary

This section has examined some of the L2 research based on the theory of UG. Much of this research has made use of grammaticality judgement tasks, which are problematic in a number of ways, in particular because we do not know whether they tap implicit or explicit knowledge. The research does not provide a clear answer as to whether UG is alive or dead in the L2 learner: studies of L2 learners' access to the Subjacency Principle and the pro-drop parameter have produced mixed and indeterminate results. Similarly, there is no clear evidence to support the hypothesis that learners acquire unmarked 'core' features before marked 'peripheral' features, at least in the case of dative alternation. Clearer results have been obtained where learning principles are concerned. L2 learners do not follow the Subset Principle, although some still do ultimately arrive at a correct target-language grammar, perhaps because they have access to negative evidence. Overall, although the studies considered in this section have afforded a number of insights into how learners handle formal grammatical properties, they have not provided clear answers to the key questions, partly because of methodological problems and partly because the details of the linguistic theory on which they have been based have been unstable.

Theoretical issues

We return now to address the main theoretical issues in UG accounts of L2 acquisition. Given the indeterminacy of the results of empirical research, it is not surprising to find quite contradictory views expressed. As Eubank (1991a) so aptly puts it, the current state of is one of 'point counterpoint'.

The logical problem of second language acquisition

A number of theorists have argued that the logical problem of language acquisition applies just as much to L2 acquisition as it does to L1 acquisition. Cook (1988), for instance, claims that like L1 learners, L2 learners possess knowledge of the L2 that they could not have acquired from the input and which must, therefore, have existed within their own minds. In other words, 'the poverty of the stimulus argument applies equally to L2 learning' (1988: 176). He also argues that imitation, grammatical explanation, correction and approval, social interaction, and dependence on other faculties cannot account for L2 acquisition any more than they can for L1 acquisition. For Cook, the essential difference between L1 and L2 acquisition is that L2 learners already know another language, which may serve as a alternative source to UG.

There are, however, several other significant differences between first and second language learners and it is these that theorists like Bley-Vroman (1989) and White (1989a) point to in arguing that the logical problem of language acquisition is somewhat different in the case of L2 acquisition. Bley-Vroman identifies a number of differences (see Table 3.10) and on the basis of these argues:

> The logical problem of foreign language acquisition becomes that of explaining the quite high level of competence that is clearly possible in some cases, while permitting the wide range of variation that is possible (1989: 49–50).

The question arises as to whether the solution to this logical problem, which is very different to that of L1 acquisition, necessitates an innate domain-specific acquisition system. Bley-Vroman's answer is a definite 'no', but, as we will see, other theorists have been more circumspect. White (1989a: 45), for instance, answers with a 'not sure', pointing out that the differences do not require the abandonment of UG-mediated L2 learning, while also noting that the arguments in favour of it are not clear-cut.

The differences discussed by Bley-Vroman are essentially quantitative in nature. But what if L2 acquisition can be shown to be qualitatively different to L1 acquisition? Schachter (1988) notes that even proficient L2 learners fail to acquire movement rules such as rules relating to topicalization and adverb placement.('Topicalization' refers to 'the use of various grammatical devices for placing the topic of a sentence in sentence initial position (e.g. "As for love, it is no substitute for money")'). Schachter argues that many learners achieve communicative fluency without complete grammatical mastery of the L2. Schachter queries whether any adult L2 learner is capable of achieving a mental state comparable to that achieved by a native speaker of the target language. In other words, she sees the L2 learner's grammatical competence as different in nature from that of the L1 learner. If this view of L2 acquisition is accepted, the logical problem becomes very different—it is that of explaining why L1 and L2 competences are qualitatively different.

In summary, there are different positions regarding the logical problem of L2 acquisition. One is that it is essentially the same as for L1 acquisition. Another is that it is different because L2 learners achieve variable success. A third is that it is different because L2 competence is qualitatively different from L1 competence. These positions lead to different views regarding the role of UG in L2 acquisition.

Access to UG in second language acquisition

A number of different views relating to the availability of UG in L2 acquisition can be distinguished: these are (1) the complete access view, (2) the no access view (sometimes referred to as 'the Fundamental Difference Hypothesis', (3) the partial access view, and (4) the dual access view. We will outline each position before attempting an evaluation of them.

The complete access view is evident in the *Parameter-setting Model* of Flynn (1984; 1987). Flynn argues that 'the essential faculty for language evidenced in L1 acquisition is also critically involved in L2 acquisition' (1987: 29). However, Flynn also acknowledges a crucial role for the L1. In cases where the L1 and L2 parameter settings are the same, learning is facilitated because 'these L2 learners are able to consult the structural configuration established for the L1 in the construction of the L2 grammar' (op. cit.: 30). Where the L1 and L2 parameter settings are different, the learner has to assign new values and, although this is not problematic according to Flynn, it does add to the learning burden. Flynn (1987) hypothesizes that where the L1 and L2 have identical settings, the pattern of acquisition of complex sentence structures (of the kind that UG principles typically address) will correspond to the later stages of L1 acquisition. She also hypothesizes that where the L1 and L2 have different settings, the pattern of acquisition will correspond to the early stages of L1 acquisition, as the learners need to first discover the relevant structural configuration in the L2.

Flynn's parameter-setting model rests on the assumption that adult L2 learners have access to the same language faculty as L1 learners.[19] As such it rejects the claim advanced by other theorists that age is a significant factor in L2 learning (see Chapter 13 for a detailed discussion of this issue). Flynn and Manuel (1991) explicitly address the age issue and conclude that 'it is impossible to argue for a monolithic critical period in L2 learning' (1991: 140). They present three arguments in favour of this position. First, like L1 learners, L2 learners possess grammatical knowledge that could not have been learnt purely on the basis of input. Second, L2 learners possess knowledge that is structure-dependent. Third, they exhibit the same infinite productivity of new sentences as L1 learners. In essence, Flynn and Manuel are asserting that the logical problems of L1 and L2 acquisition are the same.

It is possible, of course, that adult L2 learners may have continued access to UG, while the grammars that they build sometimes manifest properties that violate UG principles. White (forthcoming) refers to this as the 'different competence, same mechanisms' position, which might be considered a weaker version of the complete access position. White advances the argument that one reason why adult L2 learners may sometimes construct a grammar that is not in conformity with UG is because their L1 leads them to misanalyse the input—they do not so much transfer an L1 property as misinterpret the input in terms of expectancies based on their L1.

A number of theorists support a no-access view (for example, Clahsen and Muysken 1986; Meisel 1991). This position rests on two related claims. The first is that adult L2 acquisition is very different from L1 acquisition. The second is that this difference arises because whereas L1 learners make use of their language faculty, adult L2 learners resort to general learning strategies. Not surprisingly, advocates of the no-access position place considerable emphasis on identifying differences between L1 and adult L2 acquisition. Clahsen and Muysken (1986), for instance, compare the acquisitional sequences of German word order in L1 and L2 acquisition and find 'essential differences'. They argue that these reflect the existence of 'learning capacities specific to language' in the case of children and 'acquisition strategies which may be derived from principles of information processing and general problem solving strategies' (1986: 111) in the case of adults. In effect, Clahsen and Muysken are arguing that where L1 acquisition requires a linguistic theory, L2 acquisition requires a cognitive theory of the kind provided by the Multidimensional Model (see Chapter 9).

The partial-access position draws on the distinction between principles that have parameters and those that do not. Schachter (1988) raises the interesting possibility that learners may have access to linguistic principles but not to the full range of parametric variation. This view makes two assumptions. One is that adult learners will not manifest 'wild grammars' (i.e. they will not produce 'impossible errors') because they are constrained by UG principles. The other is that they will not be able to acquire the L2 values of parameters when these differ from the L1. Clahsen and Muysken (1989), in a later paper to that referred to above, also adopt this position, arguing that adult L2 grammars are constrained by those principles that hold for all languages (such as structure dependency) but do not have access to parametric options. In accordance with their earlier views, however, Clahsen and Muysken claim that learners are not necessarily stuck with L1 parameter values, as they can develop alternative hypotheses by means of general learning strategies. In some cases, this may result in similarities between L1 and L2 acquisition sequences.

Finally, Felix (1985) has advanced a dual access position. According to his

Competition Model (not to be confused by the model of the same name discussed in Chapter 9), adults have continued access to UG but also make use of 'a general problem solving module', which competes with the language-specific system. Felix claims that the problem-solving system is 'a fundamentally inadequate tool to process structures beyond a certain elementary level' (1985: 51) and that this accounts for why adults fail to attain native-speaker levels of competence. Thus, when learners reach the Piagetian stage of formal operations at the onset of puberty, they develop the ability to form hypotheses about abstract phenomena. They are now able to call on two distinct and, in Felix's view, autonomous cognitive systems to deal with abstract linguistic information. Adult learners are unable to suppress the operation of the problem-solving module. This 'interferes' with UG, which alone is capable of ensuring complete grammatical competence.

How can we evaluate these different positions? As we have already seen, it is doubtful whether the empirical studies of the kind considered in the previous section provide an adequate basis for evaluation. White (1990) claims that these studies 'at the very least . . . indicate that there is accessibility via the L1' (1990: 131) and thus supports a partial access position. However, before such a conclusion can be reached, it must be shown that the L1 effects evident in L2 acquisition are explicable *only* in terms of a UG framework and not in terms of some other cognitive framework. For example, the fact that L2 learners appear to make initial use of their L1 pro-drop setting does not constitute convincing evidence of L1-mediated access to UG, as it can be predicted on the basis of a more traditional model of language transfer. To be convincing, evidence is needed that L2 learners access the cluster of features entailed in the pro-drop parameter, but as we saw, such evidence is, at best, weak. The available research does not produce a clear answer.

We are left, therefore, with indirect evidence and theoretical arguments. Table 10.3 summarizes the different positions on UG access and indicates the main assumptions of each position. The assumption that there is no critical period for the acquisition of L2 syntax is perhaps the most questionable, as the available evidence on the age issue (considered in Chapter 11) indicates that adults rarely if ever achieve native-speaker levels of competence. This calls into question the 'complete access' position. The 'no access' and 'partial access' positions share two related assumptions, namely that there is a critical period beyond which full grammatical competence is unobtainable and that L2 is not the same as L1 acquisition. Both assumptions are tenable, although it does not follow that differences between L1 and L2 acquisition are the result of lost or diminished access to UG, as they may reflect other variables, such as general cognitive development and socio-affective factors. The 'no access' and 'partial access' positions are distinguished in terms of their assumptions regarding 'wild grammars'. This is clearly an aspect of acquisition that needs further study and it is probably premature to reach any firm conclusion. It is difficult, therefore, to choose between the 'no access' and 'partial access' positions. It is also difficult to evaluate the dual access position. The key assumption is that adults will manifest types of linguistic behaviour not seen in children. The problem here is that it is extremely difficult to demonstrate that differences are attributable to the operation of different learning systems, for, as Cook (1985) has pointed out, the enhanced channel capacity of the adult learner, evident in 'development', can mask similarities in 'acquisition'.

It is clear from this discussion that no verdict can be reached. White (1989a) claims there is a growing consensus in favour of the view that UG is available via the L1, but neither the empirical evidence currently available nor theoretical arguments provide uncontrovertible support. In particular, it is not yet clear that the L1 effects that have been identified require a UG explanation.

Position	Description	Main assumptions
Complete access	L1 provides learners with a 'quick' setting for the L2 parameter if the value is the same, otherwise, the L2 learner proceeds in same way as the L1 learner. L2 learners have full access to UG principles.	L2 learners will be able to attain full linguistic competence; there is no critical period blocking L2 acquisition.
No access (the Fundamental Difference Hypothesis)	L2 learners no longer have access to the principles and parameters of UG; general learning strategies replace UG.	L2 ≠ L1 acquisition; adults fail to achieve full linguistic competence; 'wild grammars' can occur.
Partial access (i.e. via L1)	L2 learners have full access to UG principles but can only access those parameters operative in their L1; they may be able to reset L1 parameters by means of general learning strategies.	L2 and L1 acquisition are the same in part; adults fail to achieve full linguistic competence; no 'wild grammars' are evident.
Dual access (the Competition Model)	L2 learners have access to UG but this is partly blocked by the use of general learning strategies.	L2 = L1 acquisition in part; adults fail to achieve full linguistic competence; adults manifest similar and different linguistic behaviour to children.

Table 10.3:   Alternative positions regarding access to UG in L2 acquisition

The role of negative evidence

A third issue of considerable theoretical importance is the role of negative evidence in L2 acquisition. We have already seen that this is typically not available to the L1 learner, whereas the adult L2 learner may have access to both corrective feedback and to explicit grammatical information. The general effect that these have on L2 acquisition is considered in Chapter 14. Here we will consider negative evidence in relation to UG.

Assuming for the moment that the provision of negative evidence is indeed beneficial to L2 learning, two theoretical positions are tenable. One is that negative evidence enables learners to acquire grammatical properties that would otherwise be lost because they do not have continued access to learning principles. This is the view that White (1991) adopts. She provides evidence to show that adverbial placement rules in L2 English, which are typically not acquired by learners whose L1 lacks them (see the earlier section relating to the Subset Principle, page 436), can be successfully learnt through formal instruction. The claim is that negative evidence triggers the resetting of a parameter to its L2 value.

The second position, associated with Schwartz (for example, Schwartz 1986 and Schwartz and Gubala-Ryzak 1992), is that UG can be activated only by means of positive evidence and that negative evidence, therefore, plays no role in UG-based acquisition. Schwartz acknowledges that negative evidence can result in the acquisition of grammatical knowledge, but argues that there is no mechanism that can 'translate' this knowledge into input of the type required by UG. In support of this position, Schwartz and Gubala-Ryzak reanalyse the data from White (1991) in order to argue that, while the learners were clearly successful in temporarily eliminating an incorrect adverbial placement rule, they achieved this without restructuring their interlanguage grammars. This is tantamount to claiming that negative evidence aids the development of explicit L2 knowledge, but not implicit (see Chapter 9).

Again, the resolution of this argument requires us to distinguish between the operation of UG and general learning strategies, which, as we have already noted, is no easy task. We might note, however, that if UG exists to enable children to acquire grammatical competence solely on the basis of positive evidence, as is generally accepted, it is hardly felicitous to propose that L2 learners can access parts of it with the help of negative evidence.

Universal Grammar and second language acquisition: an evaluation

Some researchers are strongly committed to a UG-based theory of L2 acquisition, while others are equally strongly opposed. We will begin this evaluation by considering some of the objections that have been levelled at the theory. These objections concern (1) the domain of the theory, (2) methodological issues, (3) the empirical research based on the theory, and (4) the principal tenets of the theory. We will conclude with a consideration of the theory's strengths.

The domain of the theory

Earlier, we saw that a UG-based theory of L2 acquisition is directed at explaining a fairly restricted phenomenon—that part of grammatical competence that is determined by an innately specified and abstract knowledge of grammatical principles. Much, therefore, is excluded. The theory does not address how learners acquire the 'skill' of using their grammatical knowledge, and it also ignores other aspects of competence—how learners develop their lexicon, how they construct form–meaning networks, and how they learn to perform speech acts appropriately, for example. Indeed, the theory does not even fully explain how 'grammar' is acquired, as it concerns itself only with those aspects of grammar that fall within the 'core'. In the eyes of some researchers, the theory is unconvincing because it fails to explain crucial aspects of language and language use.[20]

Methodological problems

A number of methodological problems have already been considered, for example, the over-reliance on grammaticality judgement tests and the relative lack of longitudinal studies (see page 441). A further problem concerns the definition of 'adult'. This is of considerable importance, as a UG-based theory of L2 acquisition is, in the main, a theory of adult language acquisition. Child L2 learners are assumed to have the same access to UG as L1 learners.[21] The key issue is whether adult L2 learners are also guided by UG. To examine this issue it is necessary to investigate learners who *started* to learn an L2 in adulthood, but many of the studies do not do this. It is also necessary to determine when 'adulthood' commences. As we will see in Chapter 11, the critical age for grammar appears to be fairly late, around 15 years. Few of the studies to date have examined learners who began their L2 learning after this age.

Methodological problems of these kinds do not in themselves pose major objections to the theory, however. The answer lies in better designed research, a point fully recognized by UG-oriented researchers.

The indeterminacy of the results obtained from empirical research

Given these methodological problems, it is, perhaps, not surprising to find that the empirical research has produced such indeterminate results. We examined studies directed at three issues—the availability of UG in adult L2 acquisition, the role of markedness, and learners' access to learning principles such as the Subset Principle. While the research did suggest that learners have at least partial access to UG, more specific conclusions were not possible. Again, this need not be seen as a serious defect, for as White (1989a) points out 'what we are witnessing here is developing theories being applied to a particular domain' (1989: 137). In such a case, indeterminacy can be expected.

Theoretical problems

Theoretical problems are evident in both the theory of language and the model of grammar that together inform L2 theory. As we have seen, the details of the model of grammar are constantly changing. How many settings does a particular parameter have? What does each setting consist of? Which grammatical features cluster within a parameter? Not surprisingly, such questions have produced a variety of answers as linguists explore the various possibilities. The continual revision of the model is problematic to L2 researchers, however, who may find themselves working with a model that becomes obsolete before they can complete their research.

A more serious problem, though, is that of falsifiability. How can we be sure, for instance, that learners are or are not behaving in accordance with UG? Learners' behaviour is not categorical, but variable, or as Hilles (1986: 234) calls it, 'fuzzy'. Can this be dismissed as performance variability, or does it reflect an indeterminate competence—'a period during which the parameters may waver between two values'? The central issue is what constitutes confirming and disconfirming evidence of hypotheses based on UG theory. Do learners demonstrate access to UG if they perform judgements correctly above the level of chance, or if they produce sentences providing evidence of parameter resetting just 5 per cent (or even 1 per cent) of the time? Conversely, do they demonstrate lack of access to UG if they perform judgements incorrectly above the level of chance or provide evidence in the sentences they produce of 'impossible errors'? Bley-Vroman et al. (1988) note:

> Universal Grammar, after all, is concerned with the notion of possible grammar. The consequences of UG are not merely statistical. Violations ... are not just ungrammatical 'more often than not'. They are ungrammatical—period (1988: 27).

And yet, most researchers have examined the 'statistical consequences'. One possible solution can be found in Uziel's (1993: 55) proposal that researchers abandon testing whether there is 'absolute obedience' to a given principle, and instead focus attention on the 'relative acceptability of certain syntactic constructions as it is predicted by the principles of UG'.

The falsifiability problem is evident in two other ways. It is generally accepted, even by UG theorists, that adult L2 learners can make use of faculties other than their language faculty to learn L2 rules. How, then, can we distinguish between UG-based and general cognitive learning? There is a pressing need for researchers to agree on empirically verifiable indicators of these two types of learning, so as to improve their ability to test UG-inspired hypotheses. Similarly, a number of researchers (for example, Bley-Vroman et al. 1988; Schachter and Yip 1990) have pointed out that the difficulties which many learners experience with sentences that violate UG principles may derive from problems with parsing rather than from their inability to access UG. Again, how can we distinguish these?

The validity of the 'logical problem of language acquisition', as stated by Chomsky and others, has also been challenged. Klein (1991), for example, disputes the existence of this problem on the grounds that (1) L1 acquisition is not instantaneous (it is 'a difficult and cumbersome process that extends over many years'), (2) it is an 'essentially accumulative process', and (3) 'it presupposes a vast amount of input' that obviates the need for a specific language faculty. On the basis of these claims (and others of a less controversial nature), Klein challenges the assumption that a theory of language acquisition needs to posit the existence of a special language faculty. He suggests that the assumption of such a faculty runs up against Occam's razor—the requirement that no theory should contain unnecessary principles. He comments:

> A theory that can do without the assumption of a specific 'language module' is much better than a theory which requires the assumption . . . If everything can be explained without an extra cognitive capacity, why assume it?

Hyams (1991) tackles each of Klein's claims head on. She points out: (1) that children are able to learn certain complex structures with 'remarkably little effort' (1991: 73), (2) that 'the assumption that acquisition is cumulative in no way eliminates the logical problem inherent in the instantaneous model' (1991: 76), and (3) that even if large amounts of input are required by the child (a point she doubts), this does not justify the claim that input is more than just a trigger of the language acquisition device.

It is difficult to evaluate the claims that children learn with little or considerable effort, as neither Klein nor Hyams explain what they mean by these epithets. The essential points are (2) and (3), however. Point (2) rests on evidence provided by linguists that certain syntactical constructions (like question formation in English) are not learnable on the basis of input alone. O'Grady (1991) and Parker (1989), however, have presented linguistic arguments to demonstrate that certain types of knowledge, such as those found in the Subjacency Principle and the pro-drop parameter, are not as 'abstract' as Chomsky and others have claimed, and can be accounted for in terms of input. O'Grady, for instance, provides an interesting, non-UG based explanation for pro-drop phenomena in the L1 and L2 acquisition of English. He suggests that initially learners are unable to distinguish between finite and non-finite verbs and thus are unable to distinguish between subject-taking and non-subject-taking verbs. He presents evidence to show that subjects emerge in the speech of L1 learners when they acquire tense. O'Grady's position is similar to Klein's, namely that 'there is an acquisition device that is especially well suited for the task of grammar instruction, but it does not include "UG" or any other inborn syntactic knowledge' (1991: 340). He argues that learners can make much fuller use of 'positive evidence' than Chomsky has allowed for. Although it is clearly premature to reject the linguistic arguments that have been advanced in support of an innate language faculty, it is equally clear that alternative arguments may become available.

It is also difficult to arrive at firm conclusions regarding (3). Hyams is obviously right to emphasize that the issue of quantity of input is irrelevant where its function is concerned. Irrespective of whether input is abundant or not, if it can be shown that input functions as a 'trigger', the UG position is supported. However, the evidence for a 'triggering' effect (for example, in the case of the pro-drop parameter) is mixed, and is sometimes confounded by alternative accounts of the relevant parameters. Hyams' other argument against the importance of input is that learners deprived of large amounts of input (for example, the children of deaf parents) show no delay in language development. However, this cannot be considered evidence in support of a specific language faculty. It demonstrates only that children have a remarkable capacity for language learning, which may be specifically linguistic or more generally cognitive in nature.

The Klein–Hyams debate mirrors an ongoing controversy in language acquisition research, namely whether it is necessary to posit a special language faculty. According to UG theory it is; according to the cognitive theories examined in the previous chapter it is not. At the moment, it is difficult to see whether the argument has been conclusively won one way or the other.

The strengths of a UG-based theory of second language acquisition

Despite the controversy surrounding the idea of a special language faculty, there is general acceptance that at least some aspects of language learning concern purely formal properties of language. It would follow that it is not always essential to investigate form–meaning relationships (see Foster 1990 for a development of this argument). UG provides a theoretical basis for an examination of the way L2 learners acquire purely formal properties of language.

UG-inspired SLA research enjoys one obvious advantage. In contrast to many of the cognitive theories of L2 acquisition we have considered in this chapter, UG theory affords very precise hypotheses about specific linguistic properties. Also, in contrast to many other theories, UG-based theory is very strictly defined, covering only part of the total phenomena which a comprehensive theory of L2 acquisition will need to account for. While in the eyes of some this constitutes a limitation, in the eyes of many it is an enormous strength, as it provides a means for delimiting the field of enquiry to manageable proportions. It is also possible that L2 research can contribute to the development of linguistic theory. UG-based theory affords a way of unifying the efforts of linguists and SLA acquisition researchers.

Conclusion

Any explanation of L2 acquisition must take account of what learners are try-ing to learn—language. The explanations considered in this chapter have sought to achieve this by drawing on the findings of two kinds of linguistic enquiry—the study of language typology and of Universal Grammar. We have seen that the former, which involves the crosslinguistic description of languages with a view to identifying universals, has afforded a number of insights into how learners acquire an L2 but is unable to provide an adequate explanation because the linguistic universals it has identified have no theoret-ical status. In contrast, we have seen that Universal Grammar offers a power-ful theoretical account of L2 acquisition, but, to date, lacks convincing empirical support for many of its specific hypotheses and also faces a number of methodological problems, although in this respect it is arguably in no worse shape than other theories.

We should also note that both approaches are directed at explaining only a subset of the total L2 phenomena that must be ultimately be accounted for. They have dealt exclusively with a limited set of grammatical phenomena. This is both a limitation and a strength of linguistic theories of L2 acquisition.

Notes

1 Chomsky writes: 'I have not hesitated to propose a general principle of linguistic structure on the basis of observations of a single language' (1980a: 48).
2 A limited number of adverbials (for example, 'never', 'hardly', 'scarcely') require subject–verb inversion in English when they occur sentence-initially. However, most adverbials do not. In contrast, all sentence-initial adverbials require inversion in German.
3 Croft identifies a fourth factor involved in markedness— 'neutral value' (for example, 'old' is used in both statements and in neutral questions re-ferring to someone's age)—but argues that this is of less importance in typological study.
4 Evidence for the claim that learners position the negator in relation to the 'main verb' rather than the 'finite element' can be found in the fact that initially learners produce sentences like:

> han kan inte komma (he can not come)

which are grammatically correct. It is counter-intuitive, however, to ar-gue that learners acquire correct negator position in verb phrases with an auxiliary before those consisting simply of main verbs. As Jordens points out it is more plausible to argue that negative placement is determined ini-tially by the learners' recognition of what constitutes the main verb. The early rule, negator + main verb, accounts for negator position in all sentences.

5 Cook (1988: 170) distinguishes a 'general level of the theory' (i.e. the Theory of Universal Grammar), which has changed little from its inception, from 'the most particular' (i.e. the Government/Binding Model), which changes almost from minute to minute.

6 It is, in fact, arguable whether English is a non-pro-drop language, as we saw in Chapter 6 when discussing the study by Gass and Lakshmanan (1991). This study showed that speakers of standard English regularly drop pronouns in the speech they address to learners. Also, certain dialects and registers of English permit the pronoun to be dropped.

7 Linguists do not always agree about what features cluster in a particular parameter or indeed whether parameters entail clustering. Thus, Chomsky and Hyams offer somewhat different accounts of the pro-drop parameter (see page 431), while Wexler and Mancini (1987) present an account of parameters that does not allow for clustering.

8 If Felix's proposal is correct, 'wild grammars' may be possible. That is, children may construct grammars that conform only with those principles of UG that are available to them at a given time and do not conform to those principles which have not yet matured.

9 There are, in fact, two different proposals regarding how children come to construct conservative grammars (see White 1989b: 139) for a discussion and further references). One concerns the Subset Principle, as described in the text. This is seen as extraneous to UG, part of a separate module of the language faculty. The other suggests that parameters are ordered according to markedness, such that children automatically opt for an unmarked before a marked parameter and by so doing avoid building grammars that cannot be subsequently disconfirmed. This proposal obviates the need for a separate Subset Principle, if it can also be shown that all subset problems are handled by means of parameters.

10 Generative descriptions focus on the formal properties of language on the basis that these can be separated from functional properties. The principles and parameters of UG, for example, relate exclusively to formal properties. Chomsky has argued consistently against the view that language should be viewed as a tool of communication, pointing out that it is often used for non-communicative purposes (such as thinking). His views contrast starkly with those of functional grammarians like Givón (1979) and Halliday (1978), who treat form and function as inseparably linked.

11 Measuring the time it takes for learners to make judgements may provide a way of determining what kind of knowledge they use. Bialystok's (1979) study indicated that learners first try to use their implicit knowledge, and only when this fails to provide them with a clear answer do they resort to explicit knowledge. Very few studies, however, have used timed judgements (see Cook 1990 for an exception).

12 Eubank (1987a) also argues that failure in parsing can account for the difficulties learners experience with pronominal reference in sentences like

'When *he* entered the office, the janitor questioned the man'. Eubank points out that 'any study that considers performance data must take into account multiple sources of variation' and must be prepared to consider 'multiple cognitive mechanisms' (1987a: 63). In other words, Eubank queries whether the results obtained from UG-inspired studies can be interpreted solely in terms of UG.

13 As is evident from this short survey of studies investigating the availability of the Subjacency Principle, the linguistic theory on which they are based has changed. In addition to the differences between the *Government/ Binding* and *Barriers* models, other problems arise. White (1989a), for example, cites Saito (1985) as arguing that Subjacency does exist in languages like Japanese. If this is the case, the assumption of several of the studies (for example, Ritchie and Bley-Vroman et al.) that Japanese and Korean learners do not have access to Subjacency in *wh*-questions via their L1 is not justified.

14 The data from White's question-formation task lent support to the results obtained from the grammaticality judgement task. The Spanish subjects were more likely to produce a 'that'-trace in *wh*-questions than the French, which White saw as further evidence of the influence of the L1 parameter setting.

15 Gass (1989) cites a study by Lakshmanan (1986) which used grammaticality judgements to investigate Spanish-, Arabic-, and Japanese-speaking learners of L2 English. This study also indicated that L2 learners make use of their L1 parameter setting but not with all its hypothesized properties.

16 Hilles' (1991) study also addressed a second question—whether the absence of pronominal subjects in the learners' early interlanguage was the result of the transfer of the L1 setting or the result of treating English as a topic-deleting language. The results were not conclusive, however.

17 Lakshmanan offers a number of interesting explanations for her findings. For instance, she suggests that Uguisu used subject pronouns from the start because English, unlike Japanese, does not permit null subjects of any kind. In other words, her hypothesis might have been 'If no null subjects, then no null pronouns'. This, of course, has nothing to do with UG.

18 White argues that adverb placement is related to a binary parameter of UG, the Adjacency Condition on Case Assignment, which requires that an NP with case must be next to its case assigner.

19 In the case of L2 acquisition, parameter setting is frequently 'parameter resetting'. It should be noted that the idea of 'parameter resetting' is not restricted to proponents of complete access. Theorists like White, who adopt the view that learners can only access UG via their L1, also allow for parameter resetting with the help of negative evidence.

20 What is deemed the 'crucial' domain of a theory depends on the purpose for which the theory is intended. This point is developed in Chapter 15.

21 The assumption that child L2 learners acquire grammar in the same way as L1 learners needs to be tested, of course. Some studies (such as Hilles 1991) have done so.

Further reading

There are two helpful overview articles on linguistic universals and L2 acquisition:

P. Lightbown and L. White, 'The influence of linguistic theories on language acquisition research: description and explanation.' *Language Learning* 37 (1988): 483–510.

S. Gass, 'Language universals and second-language acquisition.' *Language Learning* 39: (1986) 497–534.

A good starting point for reading about typological universals and second language acquisition is one of the general survey books on language typology such as

B. Comrie, *Language Universals and Linguistic Typology* (Basil Blackwell, 1981) or

W. Croft, *Typology and Universals* (Cambridge University Press, 1990).

The main book for the study of typological universals as they relate to L2 acquisition is

W. Rutherford (ed.): *Language Universals and Second Language Acquisition* (John Benjamins, 1984).

Interesting empirical studies based on typological universals include:

K. Hyltenstam, 'The use of typological markedness conditions as predictors in second language acquisition: the case of pronominal copies in relative clauses' in R. Andersen (ed.): *Second Languages: A Cross-linguistic Perspective* (Newbury House, 1984).

R. Hawkins, 'Do second language learners acquire restrictive relative clauses on the basis of relational or configurational information? The acquisition of French subject, direct object and genitive restrictive relative clauses by second language learners.' *Second Language Research* 5 (1989): 158–88.

A very readable account of Chomsky's ideas about language can be found in

V. Cook, *Chomsky's Universal Grammar* (Basil Blackwell, 1988).

L. White, *Universal Grammar and Second Language Acquisition* (John Benjamins, 1989) provides an excellent account of UG-based work in SLA research.

There are also a number of collections of papers dealing with UG and L2 acquisition, of which the following are perhaps the most significant:

S. Flynn and W. O'Neill (eds.): *Linguistic Theory in Second Language Acquisition* (Kluwer, 1988).

S. Gass and J. Schachter (eds.): *Linguistic Perspectives on Second Language Acquisition* (Cambridge University Press, 1989).

L. Eubank (ed.): *Point Counterpoint: Universal Grammar in the Second Language* (John Benjamins, 1991).

Journal articles on UG and L2 acquisition can be found in abundance, in particular in *Second Language Research* and *Language Learning*. It is difficult to pick out 'key' articles, but the following raise important issues:

L. White, 'The "pro-drop" parameter in adult second language acquisition.' *Language Learning* (1985) 35 : 47–61.

S. Felix, 'More evidence on competing cognitive systems.' *Second Language Research* (1984) 1: 47–72.

H. Clahsen and P. Muysken, 'The availability of Universal Grammar to adult and child learners – a study of the acquisition of German word order.' *Second Language Research* (1986) 2: 93–119.

J. Schachter, 'Second language acquisition and its relationship to Universal Grammar'. *Applied Linguistics* (1988) 9: 219–35.

R. Bley-Vroman, S. Felix, and G. Ioup, 'The accessibility of Universal Grammar in adult language learning.' *Second Language Research* (1988) 4: 1–32.

S. Uziel, 'Resetting Universal Grammar parameters: evidence from second language acquisition of Subjacency and the Empty Category Principle.' *Second Language Research* (1993) 9: 49–83.

PART FIVE

Explaining individual differences in second language acquisition

Introduction

The chapters in the previous section of the book treated second language (L2) acquisition as a phenomenon that has universal, structural properties, and advanced various explanations for them. The underlying assumption, based on the observed regularities in learner language described in Part Two, was that all learners analyse input and store information about the L2 in much the same way. However, it is also true that learners vary enormously in both the ways they set about learning an L2 and also in what they actually succeed in learning. The study of individual learner differences (IDs) comprises an important area of work in SLA research and contributes to theory development.

The study of IDs in SLA research seeks answers to four basic questions: (1) In what ways do language learners differ? (2) What effects do these differences have on learning outcomes? (3) How do learner differences affect the process of L2 acquisition? and (4) How do individual learner factors interact with instruction in determining learning outcomes? We will consider the first three questions in this part of the book. Chapter 11 will address questions (1) and (2). Here we will describe various kinds of individual differences relating to learners' beliefs, their affective states, and certain key general factors such as age, language aptitude, and motivation. These differences help us to understand why learners vary in how quickly they learn and why most learners fail to achieve native-speaker competence. Chapter 12 will focus on question (3) by addressing the learning strategies learners use to obtain and understand input, to retain new L2 information, and to regulate their own language learning. Answers to question (4) will be delayed until Chapter 14, when we consider the role of formal instruction in L2 acquisition.

We have already examined a number of factors that distinguish learners. In Chapter 6 we studied various social factors (in particular social class, sex, and ethnicity) and saw that these influence the extent and type of exposure to L2 input. These factors affected learners as *groups*—hence the label 'social'. In this section, we focus on factors that affect learners as *individuals* and that are psychological in nature. A full account of how learners differ with regard to how, how much, and how fast they learn a L2 will need to take account of both social and psychological factors, and how these interact.

11 Individual learner differences

Introduction

There is a veritable plethora of individual learner variables which researchers have identified as influencing learning outcomes. Table 11.1 lists the main variables mentioned in three surveys. It demonstrates the importance attached to individual differences (IDs) by different researchers, and also the different ways they classify them. The constructs referred to in Table 11.1 are often vague and overlap in indeterminate ways. This makes it difficult to synthesize the results of different studies, and even more difficult to arrive at a coherent overall picture.

Another problem, related to that of classifying learner variables, is the choice of terms for labelling the different factors. Often there is no clear distinction drawn in the use of terms like 'belief', 'attitude', 'state', and 'factor', while often it is not clear what terms likes 'learning style' and 'motivation' refer to. Further, as we will see in Chapter 12, the term 'strategy' has been used to refer to such an assortment of notions that it is in danger of becoming vacuous.

Despite these problems the study of IDs has attracted a lot of attention in SLA research, and has made considerable advances. As Table 11.1 shows, there are a number of dimensions of learner differences which are generally acknowledged (for example, age, aptitude, motivation, cognitive style, and learning strategies).

The chapter begins by attempting to define a number of central constructs and by outlining a framework for examining IDs. Next, it considers the main ways in which IDs have been studied. The bulk of the chapter is taken up with surveys of research which has investigated learners' beliefs about language learning, their affective states, and various general factors ('age', 'aptitude', 'learning style', 'motivation', and 'personality'). No attempt will be made, however, to examine all the dimensions of inter-learner variation listed in Table 11.1. This is because little is known about many of these dimensions and because the IDs mentioned above have been considered the ones of greatest importance for L2 acquisition.

Altman (1980)	Skehan (1989)	Larsen-Freeman and Long (1991)
1 Age	1 Language aptitude	1 Age
2 Sex	2 Motivation	2 Socio-psychological
3 Previous experience with language learning	3 Language learning strategies	factors a motivation
4 Proficiency in the native language	4 Cognitive and effective factors	b attitude
5 Personality factors	a extroversion/introversion	3 Personality a self-esteem
6 Language aptitude	b risk-taking	b extroversion
7 Attitudes and motivation	c intelligence	c anxiety
8 General intelligence (IQ)	d field independence	d risk-taking
9 Sense modality preference	e anxiety	e sensitivity to rejection
10 Sociological preference (e.g. learning with peers vs. learning with the teacher)		f empathy g inhibition h tolerance of ambiguity 4 Cognitive style a field independence/ dependence
11 Cognitive styles		b category width
12 Learner strategies		c reflexivity/impulsivity
		d aural/visual
		e analytic/gestalt
		5 Hemisphere specialization
		6 Learning strategies
		7 Other factors e.g. memory, sex

Table 11.1:   Factors listed as influencing individual learner differences in language learning in three surveys

A framework for investigating individual learner differences

The framework that will guide our examination of IDs is shown in Figure 11.1. Three sets of interrelating variables are identified. The first set consists of IDs, which are of three main types. Learners have been shown to have beliefs about language learning. Horwitz (1987a) and Wenden (1987a) have shown that learners have strong, pre-conceived ideas about such issues as the importance of language aptitude, the nature of language learning, and the strategies that are likely to work best. Second, learners have been shown to be strongly influenced by their *affective states* (see Bailey 1983). Some learners are fearful of starting to learn an L2, while some are confident. Some develop anxiety as a result of their competitive natures and their perceptions of whether they are progressing or not. Both learners' attitudes and their affective states are subject to change as a result of experience. Third, there are various general factors. These constitute major areas of influence on learning and can be ranged along a continuum according to how mutable they are. For example, language aptitude is generally considered a stable factor, not readily influenced by the environment (Carroll 1981), while certain types of motivation are likely to change as a result of the learner's learning experiences (see Berwick and Ross 1989; Crookes and Schmidt 1990). The general factors also vary according to the extent of the learners' control over them. For example, learners can do nothing about their age, but they may be able to change their learning style (Thomas and Harri-Augstein 1990). Clearly, beliefs, affective states, and general factors are interrelated. For example, learners' beliefs and their affective responses to learning situations may be influenced by personality variables. One of the goals of ID research is to identify the nature of these interrelationships.

The second set of variables consists of the different strategies that a learner employs to learn the L2. These will be considered in detail in the following chapter, together with studies of the 'good language learner'. The third set concerns language learning outcomes. These can be considered in terms of overall L2 proficiency, achievement with regard to L2 performance on a particular task, and rate of acquisition. Learning outcomes constitute the 'products' of the acquisitional process.

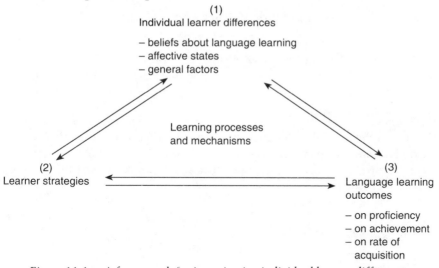

Figure 11.1: A framework for investigating individual learner differences

These three sets of factors are related in complex ways. ID research to date has concentrated on investigating the effects of different ID variables on learner proficiency, achievement, or rate of progress, measured in terms of performance on some kind of language test. There has also been little work done on the effect that learning outcomes can have on IDs. It is likely that the more mutable factors exist in a symbiotic relationship with achievement. For example, anxiety and motivation influence learning (positively or negatively), but perceived success or failure in learning will also have an effect on motivation. The strategies learners employ will be influenced by ID variables and may also have an effect on them, for instance, when successful use of a particular strategy leads to enhanced motivation or reduced anxiety. Finally, as we will see in Chapter 12, strategy choice can affect learning outcomes, which in turn can have an influence on strategy use (for example, certain strategies may only become available when learners have reached a threshold of L2 proficiency).

In the inner part of the triangle in Figure 11.1 are 'learning processes and mechanisms', so positioned because they are largely hidden. These account for how input becomes intake and how intake is integrated into the learner's interlanguage system; they were considered in Part Four of this book. The extent to which learning processes are influenced by IDs or by conscious use of learner strategies is a matter of some dispute. Seliger (1984) has claimed that IDs do not affect the 'deep' processing involved in L2 acquisition. To date, there has been little attempt to examine the relationship between IDs and the process of acquisition by examining whether different kinds of learners produce different kinds of errors or manifest different developmental patterns.

The methodology of individual difference research

Following Skehan (1989), it is possible to distinguish two general approaches to the study of IDs: (1) the *hierarchical* approach, and (2) the *concatenative* approach. These concern the relationship between theory and research.

The hierarchical approach

The hierarchical approach has as its starting point a theory that affords predictions about how particular IDs affect learning. These predictions generally take the form of specific hypotheses which can be tested empirically (i.e. they can be confirmed or disconfirmed by carrying out studies that have been specially designed to investigate them). As Skehan notes, however, this approach has been relatively little used in ID research because of the absence of a sufficiently detailed theory of IDs.

The concatenative approach

This is a research-then-theory approach. Its starting point is the identification of a general research question (such as 'To what extent does motivation account for L2 achievement?'). The next step is to collect data that can be used to identify various IDs (the independent variables), and perhaps also to obtain measures of L2 learning (the dependent variable). Various procedures are then used to investigate the nature of the relationships among the independent variables (for example, to see whether 'aptitude' is related to 'motivation') and also the relationship between the independent variable(s) and the dependent variable. Such research is typically correlational in nature; that is, it can demonstrate the existence of relationships but cannot easily determine what is cause and what is effect. Nevertheless, it can contribute to theory development. The concatenative approach has been widely used in SLA research, a good example being the study of motivation by Gardner and his associates (see Gardner 1985).

In addition to these two general approaches, it is possible to distinguish two general research traditions in ID research: (1) naturalistic research, and (2) confirmatory research. These traditions are evident in all branches of the social sciences. They concern the way subjects are chosen for study, the nature of the data that are collected, and how they are typically analysed.

Naturalistic research

In naturalistic research people are studied in real-life settings. There is no attempt to manipulate the learning context, nor are subjects randomly assigned to pre-determined groups. Naturalistic research also typically involves the collection of qualitative data.

The major method for collecting data in naturalistic research is the detailed observation of subjects and settings. However, this method has not been very successful in the study of IDs, as what learners do often does not reveal much about their psychological states and characteristics or the strategies they use to learn (see Rubin 1975 and Cohen 1984). However, methods involving introspection and retrospection have proved helpful. Diary studies have provided a wealth of information about IDs (see Fry 1988; Bailey 1991). In these, learners are asked to keep journals of their progress in learning an L2. The journals are then subjected to careful analysis in order to identify the significant variables and how they influenced learning. Learners can also be asked to *think aloud* as they perform typical language-learning tasks and the resulting protocols subjected to careful analysis, or they can be interviewed about their beliefs, attitudes, reactions, and strategies. It should be pointed out, though, that the validity and reliability of these kinds of self-report methods is not universally accepted. (See the papers in Færch and Kasper (1987) for a discussion of introspective methods.)

Another naturalistic method, widely accepted but little used in ID research, involves the collection and analysis of samples of learner language, an approach characteristic of the descriptive research in mainstream SLA research (see Part Two of this book). However, whereas the mainstream research has focused on identifying general features of learner language in order to establish universal processes of L2 acquisition, ID research has sought to identify differences in the learner language produced by individual learners. The general procedure consists of obtaining data from two or more learners performing the same or similar tasks, analysing the data in order to identify differences, and then trying to identify different 'performance styles' or 'task orientations'. Hatch's (1974) distinction between 'rule formers' and 'data gatherers' (see the section on *Learning styles* from page 499 onwards) was based on a series of studies of individual learners which employed product analysis.

Confirmatory research

In contrast to naturalistic enquiry, confirmatory research is interventionist in nature. That is, it seeks to control the learning environment and to manipulate key variables. This kind of research does not typically make use of intact groups of subjects, but rather assigns them to specific groups. Confirmatory research is often conducted by means of carefully designed experiments involving some kind of 'treatment'. Data are collected by asking learners to complete various kinds of tests. These afford numerical data which can be analysed statistically. A good example of this kind of research can be found in Gardner and MacIntyre's (1991) study of instrumental motivation. This study involved two groups of learners—an experimental and a control group—who received different treatments regarding how they were rewarded for performing a vocabulary learning task. The difference between the two groups was measured by reference to their scores on the vocabulary task. Confirmatory research can also be correlational in nature, using data collected from tests or closed-item questionnaires to establish whether predicted relationships occur. Hansen and Stansfield's (1981) study of the relationship between learners' cognitive styles and their performance on various tests of linguistic and communicative competence is an example of this kind of research.

ID research, then, can be characterized in terms of (1) the general approach, and (2) the research tradition, affording four main types, as shown in Figure 11.2. Concatenative research of both type B and type D has been the principal method of enquiry, but hierarchical research in the confirmatory tradition (type C) is gaining in popularity, as theories are developed. Hierarchical research that employs a naturalistic methodology (type A) is the least well-represented.

ID researchers are increasingly making use of more than one way of collecting information about learners in a single study. In this way they can obtain a 'rich' databank. For example, Abraham and Vann (1987) and I (Ellis (1989a) conducted case studies of individual learners involving a concatenative approach that included introspective, performance, and test data. Such research, which allows for triangulation (the use of diverse kinds of data as a means of achieving more accurate and reliable results), seems particularly promising in shedding light on the complex relationships that exist among ID variables.

We turn now to a survey of the research which has investigated IDs, beginning with an account of learners' beliefs about language learning.

	Hierarchical approach	Concatenative approach
Naturalistic tradition	A Theory-led studies that examine IDs in how learners learn and use the L2 in naturally occurring settings.	B Exploratory studies that examine IDs in the way learners learn and use the L2 in naturally occurring settings (e.g. Hatch's (1974) review of descriptive studies of L2 learners)
Confirmatory tradition	C Theory-led studies that examine IDs experimentally, i.e. by assigning learners to special groups and by manipulating their learning experiences (e.g. Gardner and MacIntyre's (1991) study of instrumental motivation).	D Correlational studies designed to investigate whether expected patterns of relation-ships involving IDs and L2 learning occur in specially selected groups of learners (e.g. Hansen and Stansfield's (1981) study of the relationship between different cognitve styles and L2 proficiency)

Figure 11.2: Types of ID research

Learners' beliefs about language learning

Language learners—especially adults—bring a variety of beliefs to the class-room. According to Hosenfeld (1978), students form 'mini theories' of L2 learning. There has been relatively little research into the nature of these theories and even less about how learners' beliefs affect language learning.

Wenden (1986a; 1987a) reports a study of 25 adults enrolled in a part-time advanced level class at an American university. She elicited their views about language learning in a semi-structured interview and then summarized them in terms of twelve explicit statements, grouped into three general categories. The first category is 'use of the language'. It includes beliefs relating to the im-portance of 'learning in a natural way'—practising, trying to think in the L2, and living and studying in an environment where the L2 is spoken. The se-cond category concerns beliefs relating to 'learning about the language'. Learners with beliefs in this category emphasized learning grammar and vocabulary, enrolling in a language class, receiving feedback on errors they made, and being mentally active. The third category is labelled 'importance of personal factors'. It includes beliefs about the feelings that facilitate or inhibit learning, self-concept, and aptitude for learning. Wenden found that her learners varied enormously in their beliefs, but that each learner seemed to have a preferred set of beliefs that belonged to one of the three categories.

Horwitz (1987a) used a questionnaire (The Beliefs about Language Learning Inventory) to elicit the beliefs of 32 intermediate level students of different ethnic backgrounds who were studying on an intensive university English program in the USA. Horwitz discusses the results in terms of five general areas. Most learners (81 per cent) felt that people were born with a special aptitude for learning foreign languages and were confident that they possessed such an aptitude themselves! They believed that some languages were more difficult than others, English being perceived as of average difficulty. Many of the students held restricted views about the nature of language learning, believing, for instance, that the best way to learn English was to spend most of their time memorizing vocabulary and grammar rules. With regard to culture, 94 per cent of the learners believed that it was necessary to know something about English-speaking cultures in order to speak English well. With regard to learning and communication strategies, the learners favoured the use of audio materials and overwhelmingly endorsed the need to repeat and practise. However, the learners varied in the extent to which they felt it necessary to avoid errors. Finally, most of the learners indicated that their main reason for learning English was to speak the language fluently. They were keen on developing friendships with Americans, but were also aware of the instrumental value of learning English.

Neither Wenden's nor Horwitz's study investigated the relationship between learners' beliefs and success in language learning. Little is currently known about this. Abraham and Vann (1987) found some evidence that beliefs might affect learning outcomes in a case study of two learners. Both learners believed that it was important to create situations for using English outside the classroom, to practise as much as possible, and to have errors corrected. Both also believed it important to participate actively in class. Gerardo, however, believed that paying conscious attention to grammar was important, while Pedro did not and expressed a strong dislike of meta-language. Also, Gerardo thought that it was important to persevere in communicating or understanding an idea, while Pedro considered topic abandonment the best strategy in some cases. Abraham and Vann characterize Gerardo's philosophy of language learning as 'broad' and Pedro's as 'narrow'. They suggest that this might have contributed to Gerardo's better TOEFL score (523 v. 473) at the end of a course of instruction. Pedro, however, did better on a test of spoken English, which might suggest that different views about language learning result in different kinds of success.

An interesting question is what determines learners' beliefs about language learning. Little, Singleton, and Silvius (1984, reported in Little and Singleton

1990) surveyed random samples of undergraduate and postgraduate students of foreign languages at Trinity College, Dublin. They found that 'past experience, both of education in general and of language learning in particular, played a major role in shaping attitudes to language learning' (1990: 14). For example, the students stated that they preferred to learn by production activities (repeating orally and writing) rather than through receptive activities involving listening and reading. Little and Singleton claim that this belief reflected the general nature of the instruction they had experienced. Learners' beliefs are also likely to be influenced by general factors such as personality and cognitive style, as Abraham and Vann's (1987: 97) model of L2 learning suggests. However, no studies have examined this relationship to date.

The study of learners' opinions about language learning constitutes an important area of enquiry, as it is reasonable to assume that their 'philosophy' dictates their approach to learning and choice of specific learning strategies. Future research will need to find ways of ensuring that learners' verbal reports of their beliefs reflect their actual beliefs, and of investigating what effects different 'philosophies' have on learning outcomes.

Learners' affective states

Learners, in particular classroom learners, react to the learning situations they find themselves in a variety of affective ways. For example, F. Schumann (Schumann and Schumann 1977) reports being unable to settle down to studying Farsi and Arabic (in Iran and Tunisia) until she had achieved order and comfort in her physical surroundings. Bailey (1980) discusses a 'classroom crisis' that occurred when her French teacher administered a test that the class considered unfair. One of the beginner learners of German that Ellis and Rathbone (1987) studied reported a period during which she was unable to learn any German because of a boyfriend problem. These and other studies testify to the complexity and dynamic nature of learners' affective states and the influence these have on their ability to concentrate on learning. Learners, it seems, need to feel secure and to be free of stress before they can focus on the learning task—the importance of which is directly acknowledged in humanistic approaches to language teaching (see Moskowitz 1978).

It is, of course, not easy to study the role that affective states play in L2 learning in a systematic manner, if only because they are so individualistic and changeable. Some of the best work has investigated one particular affective factor—anxiety.

Anxiety

A distinction can be made between *trait anxiety*, *state anxiety*, and *situation-specific anxiety*. Scovel (1978), drawing on work in general psychology, defines trait anxiety as 'a more permanent predisposition to be anxious'. It is perhaps best viewed as an aspect of personality. State anxiety can be defined as apprehension that is experienced at a particular moment in time as a response to a definite situation (Spielberger 1983). It is a combination of trait and situation-specific anxiety. This latter type consists of the anxiety which is aroused by a specific type of situation or event such as public speaking, examinations, or class participation.

The study of situational anxiety has received considerable attention in SLA research (see, for example, Horwitz and Young's (1991) collection of papers on anxiety in classroom settings) and will be our main concern here. It has been carried out concatenatively by means of correlational studies involving measures of anxiety and learning (Type D research) and through diary studies (Type B research). In both cases, the research indicates that learners frequently experience 'language anxiety', a type of situation-specific anxiety associated with attempts to learn an L2 and communicate in it.

One of the key questions the research has addressed is 'What causes state or situation anxiety?' The diary studies indicate that learners' competitive natures can act as a source of anxiety. Bailey (1983) analysed the diaries of 11 learners and found that they tended to become anxious when they compared themselves with other learners in the class and found themselves less proficient. She noted that as the learners perceived themselves becoming more proficient, and therefore better able to compete, their anxiety decreased. Bailey also identified other sources of anxiety, including tests and learners' perceived relationship with their teachers. Ellis and Rathbone (1987) reported that some of their diarists found teachers' questions threatening. For example, one of their subjects, Monique, commented:

> I was quite frightened when asked questions again. I don't know why; the teacher does not frighten me, but my mind is blocked when I'm asked questions. I fear lest I give the wrong answer and will discourage the teacher as well as be the laughing stock of the class maybe. Anyway, I felt really stupid and helpless in class (Ellis 1989a: 257).

However, other learners experienced no worries about using German in class. When anxiety does arise relating to the use of the L2, it seems to be restricted mainly to speaking and listening, reflecting learners' apprehension at having to communicate spontaneously in the L2 (Horwitz, Horwitz, and Cope 1986). Matsumoto's (1989) learner, M, for example, displayed little anxiety but when she did it was in connection with her perceived problems in listening to and speaking English. Learners can also experience anxiety as a result of fear or experience of 'losing oneself' in the target culture. As Oxford (1992) points out, this is closely related to the idea of 'culture shock'. She lists the affective states associated with this source of anxiety: 'emotional regression, panic, anger, self-pity, indecision, sadness, alienation, "reduced personality"...'.

These and other possible sources of anxiety in the foreign language class-room are reflected in the questionnaires which a number of researchers have devised to measure learner anxiety. Gardner and Smythe (1975) developed a French Class Anxiety Scale based on responses to a questionnaire, and in subsequent studies developed scales to tap English Use Anxiety and English Test Anxiety. Horwitz, Horwitz, and Cope (1986) developed a Foreign Language Classroom Anxiety Scale, based on conversations with beginner learners who identified themselves as anxious. This questionnaire consists of thirty-three items relating to three general sources of anxiety: (1) communication apprehension, (2) tests, and (3) fear of negative evaluation. Examples of the kinds of statements learners are asked to respond to on a five-point scale are:

I tremble when I know I am going to be called on in language class.
I keep thinking that other students are better at language than I am.
I get nervous when I don't understand every word the language teacher says.

MacIntyre and Gardner (1991b) have also developed an extensive set of scales (23 in all) to measure various forms of anxiety.

The second main question which researchers have addressed is 'What effect does anxiety have on learning?' MacIntyre and Gardner (1991b) point out that anxiety can be hypothesized to affect three stages of the learning process: input, processing, and output. However, most of the research to date has examined output and so little is known about the effects on input and the process of learning. In an early study, Chastain (1975) found that measures of anxiety in American university students were positively and significantly related to marks in Spanish, positively but not significantly related to marks in German, and negatively related to marks achieved by one group of audio-lingual French learners, but not related at all to marks in another 'regular' French group. Kleinmann (1978) provides evidence to show that Spanish- and Arabic-speaking learners of English who reported anxiety (i.e. responded positively to statements like 'Nervousness while using English helps me do better') were less likely to avoid complex grammatical structures such as infinitive complements and the passive voice than those students who reported no such anxiety.

Subsequent research has been based on models of language learning developed by Gardner, Clement, and their colleagues (for example, Gardner, Smythe, Clement, and Gliksman 1976; Clement and Kruidenier 1985). MacIntyre and Gardner (1991b) found that what they term 'language anxiety' (the anxiety specifically generated by attempts to learn the L2) was negatively and significantly correlated with L2 performance on a Digit Span test and on a French Categories test (which tested free recall of vocabulary items associated with specific semantic fields), whereas no such correlation was found between anxiety and these tests performed in the learners' L1 (English).

MacIntyre and Gardner (1991a), in a comprehensive review of these studies, conclude:

> Covering several measures of proficiency, in several different samples, and even in somewhat different conceptual frameworks, it has been shown that anxiety negatively affects performance in the second language. In some cases, anxiety provides some of the highest simple correlations of attitudes with achievement (1991a: 103).

It should be noted, however, that not all the studies in their review produced significant correlations between anxiety and achievement.

In fact, studies of learner anxiety have often produced even more mixed results. Horwitz (1986) reports sizeable negative correlations (around –0.5) between foreign language classroom anxiety and final grades achieved by American university students. Young (1986) found that measures of anxiety were correlated significantly with measures of oral proficiency in a group of prospective language teachers, but the relationship disappeared after controlling for ability, measured by means of other proficiency measures. Gardner, Moorcroft, and MacIntyre (1987) found a significant relationship between various measures of anxiety and scores on a word production task, but no relationship between the anxiety measures and free speech quality. Parkinson and Howell-Richardson (1990) failed to find a relationship between measures of anxiety, based on an analysis of fifty-one diaries kept by adult learners of L2 English in Scotland, and rate of improvement—a result they consider 'surprising'. Ely (1986a) found no relationship between anxiety and university learners' level of participation in class, but the study did show that those learners with a high level of discomfort were less likely to take risks in class.

There are several reasons for these mixed results. One is that the relationship between anxiety and achievement is probably not a simple linear one. Many of the above studies are premised on the assumption that learners with low anxiety will learn better. Krashen (1981: 23) suggests how this might come about:

> The student who feels at ease in the classroom and likes the teacher may seek out more intake by volunteering . . . and may be more accepting of the teacher as a source of input.

Scovel (1978), however, draws attention to Alpert and Haber's (1960) distinction between *facilitating* and *debilitating anxiety*. The former motivates learners to 'fight' the new learning task, prompting them to make extra efforts to overcome their feelings of anxiety, although Horwitz (1986) suggests that this may only occur in fairly simple learning tasks. The latter causes the learner to 'flee' the learning task in order to avoid the source of anxiety. Williams (1991) suggests that the distinction between these two types of anxiety may correspond to the intensity of the anxiety, with a low-anxiety state having a facilitating function and a high-anxiety state a debilitating effect. Also, the two kinds of anxiety may sometimes cancel each other out, resulting in no apparent effect on achievement.

What is needed is a model to account for the role that anxiety plays in language learning, such as that proposed by MacIntyre and Gardner (1991a) and summarized in Table 11.2. According to this model, the relationship between anxiety and learning is moderated by the learners' stage of development and by situation-specific learning experiences. The model also recognizes that poor performance can be the cause as well as the result of anxiety, a point also made by Skehan (1989).

Stage	Type of anxiety	Effect on learning
Beginner	Very little—restricted to state anxiety	None
Post-beginner	Situation anxiety develops if learner develops negative expectations based on bad learning experiences	Learner expects to be nervous and performs poorly
Later	Poor performance and continued bad learning experiences result in increased anxiety	Continued poor performance

Table 11.2:   *A model of the role of anxiety in language learning (based on MacIntyre and Gardner 1989a)*

There is sufficient evidence to show that anxiety is an important factor in L2 acquisition. Anxiety (its presence or absence) is best seen not as a necessary condition of successful L2 learning, but rather as a factor that contributes in differing degrees in different learners. The work done to date has gone only a limited way to determine the conditions under which anxiety will have an effect. It has also relied exclusively on self-report questionnaires rather than on the measurement of somatic responses (for example, galvanic skin response).[1]

The importance of learners' affective states

Learners' affective states are obviously of crucial importance in accounting for individual differences in learning outcomes. Whereas learners' beliefs about language learning are likely to be fairly stable, their affective states tend to be volatile, affecting not only overall progress but responses to particular learning activities on a day-by-day and even moment-by-moment basis. Studies in the naturalistic research tradition may prove most effective in exploring how these transitional states are brought about and what effect they have on learning.

General factors contributing to individual differences in second language learning

Learners' beliefs and affective states are likely to have a direct effect on L2 learning, but they themselves may be influenced by a number of general factors relating to learners' ability and desire to learn and the way they choose to go about learning. In this section we will examine in some detail the general factors that have received the most attention in SLA research.

Age

There is a widely-held lay belief that younger L2 learners generally do better than older learners. This is supported by the *critical period hypothesis*, according to which there is a fixed span of years during which language learning can take place naturally and effortlessly, and after which it is not possible to be completely successful. Penfield and Roberts (1959), for example, argued that the optimum period for language acquisition falls within the first ten years of life, when the brain retains its plasticity. Initially, this period was equated with the period taken for lateralization of the language function to the left side of the brain to be completed. Work on children and adults who had experienced brain injuries or operations indicated that damage to the left hemisphere caused few speech disorders and was rapidly repaired in the case of children but not adults (Lenneberg 1967). Although subsequent work (for example, Krashen 1973; Whitaker, Bub, and Leventer 1981) has challenged the precise age when lateralization takes place, resulting in doubts about the neurological basis of the critical period hypothesis, the age question has continued to attract the attention of researchers.

It continues to be controversial, however (see, for example, the papers by Flege (1987) and Patkowski (1990) in *Applied Linguistics*). The controversy centres on both whether there are significant differences in L2 learning according to age, and also on the theoretical explanations for those differences which researchers claim to have found.

One of the reasons for the lack of consensus on the age issue is undoubtedly the difficulty of comparing the results of studies that have employed very different methods. There are longitudinal studies based on groups of learners with the same starting time (for example, Snow and Hoefnagel-Höhle 1978) and also longitudinal studies based on groups of learners with different starting ages (for example, Burstall 1975). There are cross-sectional studies of groups of learners who differ with regard to both when individual learners began to learn the L2 and, inevitably, the number of years they have been learning it (for example, Oyama 1976). Finally, there are experimental studies, which have sought to investigate the effects of attempts to teach groups of learners varying in age-specific features of an L2 (for example, Neufeld 1978). The studies have also varied in how they have measured learning. In some cases, performance measures based on samples of planned or unplanned language use have been used. In others, the grammaticality judgements of learners of different ages have been examined (for example, Coppieters 1987), while in still others native speakers have been asked to rate the performance of mixed groups of learners and native speakers in terms of how 'native' their use of the language is (for example, Scovel 1981). It is perhaps not surprising that the results obtained by these studies fail to agree.

As Larsen-Freeman and Long (1991) point out, however, the age issue remains an important one for theory building in SLA research, for educational policy-making, and for language pedagogy. If it can be shown that older learners are different from younger learners, the claim that adults have continued access to Universal Grammar is called into question. If it can be shown that younger learners do better than older learners, the case for an early start in foreign language education is strengthened. If it can be shown that children learn in different ways to adults, language teachers will need to identify different approaches and techniques to suit the two kinds of learners.

In order to untangle the research results, it is helpful to consider a number of separate but related questions:

1 What effect does age have on the rate of L2 learning?
2 What effect does age have on learners' ability to achieve native-speaker levels of proficiency?
3 What effect does age have on learners' levels of L2 achievement (in those learners who do not reach native-speaker proficiency)?
4 What affect does age have on the processes of L2 learning?

It is also helpful to distinguish the effects of age according to learning context (in naturalistic as opposed to instructed situations). Finally, the effects of age on the learning of L2 pronunciation and L2 grammar need to be considered separately. Unfortunately, there has been very little research that has investigated other aspects of L2 learning.

The effects of age on rate of second language learning

In their review of the research that has addressed the age issue, Krashen, Long, and Scarcella (1979) conclude that (1) adults are superior to children in rate of acquisition, and (2) older children learn more rapidly than younger children. The study most often cited in support of these conclusions is Snow and Hoefnagel-Höhle (1978). This study investigated the naturalistic acquisition of Dutch by eight- to ten-year-old English-speaking children, twelve- to fifteen-year-old adolescents, and adults over a ten-month period. The learners' proficiency was measured on three separate occasions (after three months, six months, and at the end of the study). With regard to morphology and syntax the adolescents did best, followed by the adults, with the children last. However, there were only small differences in pronunciation, and the grammar differences diminished over time as the children began to catch up. Experimental studies have also shown that adults outperform children in the short term. For example, Olsen and Samuels (1973) found that American English-speaking adolescents and adults performed significantly better than children after ten 15–25 minute German pronunciation sessions. However, other studies suggest that, at least where pronunciation is concerned, adults do not always progress more rapidly than children. Cochrane (1980), for example, investigated the ability of 54 Japanese children and 24 adults to discriminate English /r/ and /l/. The average length of naturalistic exposure was calculated as 245 hours for the adults and 193 for the children (i.e. relatively little). The children outperformed the adults, although in a follow-up experiment in which the two groups were taught the phonemic distinction, the adults benefited while the children did not. The research gives general support to Krashen, Long and Scarcella's generalization that adults learn faster than children. It appears to be more applicable to grammar than pronunciation (where children seem to learn as rapidly, if not more rapidly, than adults), although in the case of formal learning situations adults seem to do better even in this area of learning. It is not yet clear at what point children start to catch up.

The effects of age on the acquisition of native-speaker proficiency

The controversy regarding the role of age is fiercest when it comes to considering the effects of age on the achievement of native-speaker levels of proficiency. This question is the crucial one for the critical period hypothesis. Neufeld's (1978) study is often cited by those seeking evidence to refute the hypothesis. In this study, 20 adult native speakers of English were given 18 hours of intensive instruction in the pronunciation of Chinese and Japanese. To test the 'nativeness' of their pronunciation, the learners were then given an imitation test and their utterances judged on a five-point scale (from 'unmistakably native' to 'heavily accented') by native speakers of the two languages. Nine and eight of the subjects were rated as 'native' for Japanese and Chinese respectively. This study suggests, therefore, that under the right conditions adults can achieve native ability in pronunciation—the area of language generally considered to be the most difficult for adults to acquire. Neufeld (1977; 1979) conducted other studies with similar results. However, his studies have been strongly criticized by supporters of the critical period hypothesis. Long (1990a), for instance, argues that Neufeld's subjects represented an 'elite', that the imitation test produced 'rehearsed' rather than natural data, and that the instructions given to the raters predisposed them to think that some of the subjects were native speakers. These criticisms—and those made by Patkowski (1990)—are legitimate, but they do not refute the essential claim that Neufeld seeks to make—namely that it is possible for adults to achieve native-speaker levels of proficiency in an L2. Clearly the study needs further replication.

Another frequently cited experimental study provides evidence to support the critical period hypothesis. Coppieters (1987) tested 21 highly proficient speakers of French, all of whom had begun learning as adults, and compared their performance on a grammaticality judgement task with that of 20 native speakers. Coppieters notes that it was not possible to distinguish the two groups by the mistakes they made, their choice of lexis, or grammatical constructions, and six of the subjects were also described as having no traces of a foreign accent. The results of the grammaticality judgement test, however, showed clear differences between the two groups, suggesting that despite the native-like performance of the learners in language production, their grammatical competence differed from that of native speakers.[2] Again, though, it is possible to raise methodological objections to this study. Coppieters did not include a group of learners who had started to learn L2 French as children, thus we cannot be sure that the results he obtained reflect age as opposed to some other factor. Also, as in the case of Neufeld's imitation test, doubts can be raised about whether grammaticality judgements constitute a valid means of measuring competence (see the discussion of grammaticality judgement tasks in Chapter 10). Birdsong (1992) identifies 'numerous procedural and methodological features of the Coppeters study that compromise its conclusions' (1992: 711).

Birdsong's own replication of this study casts serious doubts on the results Coppeters obtained. Birdsong administered a grammaticality judgement test to 20 English-speaking learners of L2 French, who were near-native in their oral ability, and to 20 native speakers of French. The study was motivated by Long's (1990a) challenge to researchers to investigate 'whether the very best learners actually have native-like competence' (1990a: 281). Contrary to Coppeters, Birdsong found no evidence of any dramatic differences in the judgements of the non-native speakers and native speakers. A number of the non-native spearkers performed in the same range as the native speakers on the grammaticality judgement test. Furthermore, Birdsong could find no evidence of marked differences between the two groups in the think-aloud data that he collected from the subjects as they performed their judgements. This study, then, suggests that at least some learners who start learning a L2 after puberty achieve a level of competence indistinguishable from that of native speakers.

Another way of investigating the claims of the Critical Period Hypothesis is to investigate whether learners who start learning an L2 as young children and enjoy favourable learning conditions succeed in reaching native levels of proficiency. Thompson's (1991) study of foreign accents in Russian immigrants in the United States addressed this question.[3] Thompson found that those learners who had arrived before they were ten years old had a more native-like English accent than those who came after this age—a finding that bears out the results of earlier studies reported in the next section. What is interesting about this study, though, is that two subjects who came to the US at the age of four years were still rated as having a 'slight accent', a result that Thompson considers 'a problem for the Critical Period Hypothesis' (1991: 199). Thompson speculates that these learners' failure to achieve native-speaker levels of pronunciation was because they had maintained a high level of speaking proficiency in Russian, and that this led to what Weinreich (1953) has called an 'interlingual' identification. Thompson's study is important because it suggests the need to consider age in relation to other factors, such as L1 maintenance, and that not all learners will wish to sound like native speakers.

Yet another way of assessing whether learners can achieve native-speaker levels in an L2 is to see whether they are able to recognize spoken or written 'accents' in the same way as native speakers. Scovel (1981) asked four groups of judges (adult native speakers, child native speakers, adult non-native speakers, and adult aphasics) to rate speech samples and written pieces produced by a mixture of native and non-native speakers. He found that even the most advanced non-native speakers achieved an accuracy rate of only 77 per cent, which was about the same as the child native speakers (73 per cent) but less than the adult native speakers (95 per cent) and even the aphasic native speakers (85 per cent). Like Coppieters' study, this study suggests that even very advanced learners lack some of the linguistic abilities of native speakers.

The experimental studies that have investigated the effects of age on the acquisition of native-speaker levels of proficiency have produced mixed results and, at this stage, the verdict must remain an open one. It is possible that under ideal circumstances learners who start after puberty can learn to produce speech and writing that cannot easily be distinguished from that of native speakers. Whether qualitative differences in competence still remain, as claimed by Coppieters, is still not clear, although Birdsong's carefully designed study would suggest that at least some learners achieve native-speaker levels of grammatical knowledge. Also, as Thompson's (1991) study shows, starting early is no guarantee that native-speaker abilities will be achieved, even in the most favourable learning situations.

The effects of age on learners' second language achievement

The majority of L2 learners fail to reach native-speaker levels of ability. It is also important to ask whether age effects are evident in such learners. Do learners who begin learning as children in general reach higher levels of L2 ability than those who start as adolescents or adults? This question has been addressed in research that has compared the level of proficiency reached by L2 learners who began as children with that of learners who began as adults. We do not know, of course, if these studies show the effects of age on these learners' ultimate level of attainment, as the assumption that they have reached their 'final state' (are fossilized) may not be justified.

A number of studies have investigated the relative effects of starting foreign language education in the primary school as opposed to the secondary school on the levels of attainment. For example, Burstall (1975) reports on a pilot scheme in England and Wales. She compared two groups of students with five years of instruction. One group had begun learning French at the age of 8, while the other had begun at the beginning of secondary school (11 years). She found that the older learners were 'consistently superior'. When both groups were compared at the age of 16, the secondary school starters out-performed the primary school starters on tests of speaking, reading, and writing and were inferior only on a test of listening. Harley (1986) investigated the levels of attainment of children in French bilingual programmes in Canada. She focused on the learners' acquisition of the French verb system, obtaining data from interviews, a story repetition task, and a translation task. She compared early and late immersion students after both had received 1,000 hours of instruction. Neither group had acquired full control of the verb system, but the older students demonstrated greater overall control. However, the early immersion group showed higher levels of attainment at the end of their schooling, a result that may reflect the additional number of years' instruction they had received rather than starting age. The results from these and other school-based studies (see Singleton (1989) for a review) is not supportive of the claim that children's level of attainment is greater than that of adolescents/adults. One possible explanation for this—advanced by Singleton—is that formal learning environments do not provide learners with the amount of exposure needed for the age advantage of young learners to emerge.

Studies of learners in naturalistic learning situations provide the most convincing evidence that younger is better and, therefore, some support for the Critical Period Hypothesis. We will examine some of the most frequently cited studies.

Learners who start as children achieve a more native-like accent than those who start as adolescents or adults. Oyama (1976) investigated 60 male immigrants who had entered the United States at ages ranging from 6 to 20 years and had been resident there for between 5 and 18 years. She asked two adult native speakers to judge the nativeness of the learners' accents in two 45-second extracts taken from performance on a reading-aloud task and a free-speech task. Oyama reports a very strong effect for 'age of arrival' but almost no effect for 'number of years' in the United States. She found that the youngest arrivals performed in the same range as native-speaker controls. Other studies which have investigated the effects of age on pronunciation (for example, Asher and Garcia 1969; Tahta, Wood, and Loewenthal 1981) support the younger-is-better position.

Similar results have been obtained for the acquisition of grammar. Patkowski's (1980; 1990) study of 67 educated immigrants to the United States found that learners who had entered the United States before the age of 15 were rated as more syntactically proficient than learners who had entered after 15. Furthermore, there was a marked difference in the distribution of the scores (based on native speakers' ratings on a five-point scale) for the two groups. The adult group's scores were evenly distributed, with the majority at midpoints on the rating scale. The child group's scores clustered at the high end of the rating scale, with 29 out of 33 achieving a rating of 4+ or 5. Patkowski also investigated the effects of number of years spent in the United States, amount of informal exposure to English, and amount of formal instruction. Only the amount of informal exposure had any significant effect, and even this was negligible in comparison with the age factor. Patowski's findings are confirmed by Johnson and Newport's (1989) study of 46 native Koreans and Chinese who had arrived in the United States between the ages of 3 and 39, half before the age of 15 and half after 17. The subjects were asked to judge the grammaticality of 276 spoken sentences, about half of which were grammatical. Overall the correlation between age at arrival and judgement scores was −0.77 (i.e. the older the learners were at arrival, the lower their scores). Far less variation was found in the scores of the 'child' group than in the adult group. Neither the number of years of exposure to English beyond five nor the amount of classroom instruction was related to the grammaticality judgement scores, and although an effect for 'identification with American culture' was found, this was much weaker than that for age.

In his summary of these and other studies, Singleton (1989) writes:

> Concerning the hypothesis that those who begin learning a second language in childhood in the long run generally achieve higher levels of proficiency than those who begin in later life, one can say that there is some good supportive evidence and that there is no actual counter evidence (1989: 137).

This is one of the few definite conclusions that Singleton feels able to reach in a comprehensive survey of age-related research. It is worthwhile noting, however, that this conclusion may not hold true for the acquisition of L2 literacy skills. Cummins and Nakajima (1987) examined the acquisition of reading and writing skills by 273 Japanese children in grades two to eight in Toronto. They found that the older the students were on arrival in Canada, the more likely they were to have strong L2 reading skills and, to a lesser extent, better L2 writing skills. The explanation Cummins and Nakajima offer is that the older learners benefited from prior literacy experience in Japanese (see the discussion of the Interdependency Principle in Chapter 6).

The effect of age on the process of second language acquisition

There have been few studies of the effects of age on the process of L2 acquisition. The morpheme studies (see Chapter 3) showed that the order of acquisition of a group of English morphemes was the same for children and adults (Bailey, Madden, and Krashen 1974; Fathman 1975). However, conclusions based on the morpheme studies are circumspect given their methodological problems. Studies which have investigated the sequence of acquisition in transitional structures such as negatives and interrogatives are not subject to the same methodological strictures, however. They show that adults go through the same stages of acquisition as children (for example, Cancino et al. 1978). Age, therefore, does not appear to affect the general developmental pattern.

By far the most detailed study of the effects of age on the acquisition process is Harley's (1986) investigation of early and late immersion programmes. Harley found remarkably similar patterns in the two groups' acquisition of the French verb phrase. For example, the two age groups generally made similar types of errors and both groups tended to use the relatively unmarked French verb forms more accurately than the marked forms. A few differences were noted but these were minor, and Harley did not feel that they constituted evidence of different mental processes, arguing instead that the differences reflected variations in the L2 input to which the learners were exposed.

Process differences may occur in L2 pronunciation, however. Riney (1990) reviewed literature relating to whether learners display a preference for an open syllable structure in early interlanguage. He argued that in the case of learners who began before the age of 12 years, no open syllable preference is evident (as Sato's (1987) study indicates), but in the case of learners beginning after 12 years there was, as in Tarone's (1980a) study. In data collected from Vietnamese learners of English, Riney was able to show that whereas age had no effect on the final deletion of consonants (one way of making a target-language closed syllable open), it did have a marked effect on epenthesis (the insertion of a vowel at the end of a closed syllable). Whereas the incidence of epenthesis in 10–12-year-old children was less than 5 per cent, in some adult learners it was over 30 per cent. Furthermore, epenthesis in adult learners did not significantly decline with increased exposure to English.

It is obviously premature to conclude that age has no effect on the process of acquisition. The research to date suggests that the effect may be a minimal one in the case of grammar, but possibly more significant in the case of pronunciation.

Some general conclusions

The research that has addressed the age issue is quite enormous. Not surprisingly, commentators have arrived at different conclusions, but despite this some common ground is emerging:

1 Adult learners have an initial advantage where rate of learning is concerned, particularly in grammar. They will eventually be overtaken by child learners who receive enough exposure to the L2. This is less likely

to happen in instructional than in naturalistic settings because the critical amount of exposure is usually not available in the former.

2 Only child learners are capable of acquiring a native accent in informal learning contexts. Long (1990a) puts the critical age at 6 years, but Scovel argues that there is no evidence to support this and argues for a pre-puberty start. Singleton (1989) points out that children will only acquire a native accent if they receive massive exposure to the L2. However, some children who receive this exposure still do not achieve a native-like accent, possibly because they strive to maintain active use of their L1. Adult learners may be able to acquire a native accent with the assistance of instruction, but further research is needed to substantiate this claim.

3 Children may be more likely to acquire a native grammatical competence. The critical period for grammar may be later than for pronunciation (around 15 years). Some adult learners, however, may succeed in acquiring native levels of grammatical accuracy in speech and writing and even full 'linguistic competence'.

4 Irrespective of whether native-speaker proficiency is achieved, children are more likely to reach higher levels of attainment in both pronunciation and grammar than adults.

5 The process of acquiring an L2 grammar is not substantially affected by age, but that of acquiring pronunciation may be.

Explaining the role of age in second language acquisition

These general conclusions provide substantial support for the existence of at least a sensitive period for L2 acquisition. The distinction between a 'critical' and a 'sensitive' period rests on whether completely successful acquisition is deemed to be only possible within a given span of a learner's life, or whether acquisition is just easier within this period. The conclusions also lend some support to Seliger's (1978) proposal that there may be multiple critical/sensitive periods for different aspects of language. The period during which a native accent is easily acquirable appears to end sooner than the period governing the acquisition of a native grammar.

A number of explanations have been advanced to account for the existence of a critical or sensitive period. These have been admirably reviewed in Singleton (1989) and Long (1990a), and are summarized in Table 11.3. Singleton points out the problems that exist with all the explanations and declines to come down in favour of one. One of the major points of controversy is whether the differences between child and adult learners are to be explained as primarily the result of environmental factors or of changes in the mental and neurological mechanisms responsible for language learning. Mühlhauser (1986), after an extensive study of the developmental stages of pidgin languages and their similarities to language acquisition, concludes that 'adults and children appear to behave very much in the same manner', which indicates that 'activation of certain linguistic developments is dependent on the presence of specific environmental factors, rather than on different cognitive abilities of children and adults' (1986: 265–6). Long, on the other hand, concludes that a neurological explanation is best and proposes the attractive-sounding 'mental muscle model', according to which 'the language-specific endowment remains intact throughout adult life, but access to it is impeded to varying degrees and progressively with age, unless the faculty is used and so kept plastic'. Such a view is compatible with studies of exceptional language learners (for example, Obler 1989), which demonstrate that some adult learners are capable of achieving native-speaker levels of competence. As Birdsong (1992) points out, the question then arises as to whether it is possible to maintain the Critical Period Hypothesis if many such learners are found.

One puzzle is why there is so little evidence of any differences in the process of L2 acquisition by child and adult learners. If adults substitute inductive cognitive learning strategies for the language acquisition device used by children, differences in the process of acquisition might be expected to occur. In the case of phonology, some clear process differences have been reported, suggesting that children and adults rely on different mechanisms. However, in the case of grammar no clear differences have been observed, suggesting that learners of all ages rely on the same learning mechanisms. Long's 'mental muscle model', therefore, may not provide a satisfactory explanation where L2 phonology is concerned, but seems to offer a convincing account of why child and adult learners do not differ in the process of acquiring an L2 grammar.

It is not necessary to posit neurological explanations to account for why older learners learn more rapidly. One possibility, which we considered in Chapter 6, is that older learners experience more negotiation of meaning and, therefore, better input. Another obvious possibility is that adolescents and adults possess more fully developed cognitive skills, which enable them to apply themselves studially to the task of learning a L2. This is likely to give them an initial advantage over children, but may not be sufficient to guarantee high levels of L2 proficiency. Most likely, the rate advantage enjoyed by adults is the result of a combination of factors.

To conclude, it is not yet possible to reach any definite decisions on such key issues as whether adults have continued access to a language-specific acquisition device such as Universal Grammar. One tentative conclusion suggested by the research is that the acquisition of phonology (which appears to be particularly sensitive to age) proceeds somewhat differently from the acquisition of grammar (which appears much less sensitive). This conclusion, it should be noted, accords with the conclusion we reached when considering the role of L1 transfer in L2 learning (see Chapter 8).

Type of explanation	Main arguments
1 Sensory acuity	The language learning capacity of adults is impaired by deterioration in their ability to perceive and segment sounds in an L2.
2 Neurological	There are changes in the neurological structure of the brain at certain ages which affects learners' abilities to acquire L2 pronunciation and grammar. Various accounts of the nature of these changes have been proposed to account for the 'loss of plasticity' that occurs with age (e.g. lateralization and cerebral maturation).
3 Affective-motivational factors	Child learners are more strongly motivated to communicate with native speakers and to integrate culturally. Also, child learners are less conscious and therefore suffer less from anxiety about communicating in an L2.
4 Cognitive factors	Adult learners rely on general, inductive learning abilities to learn an L2, while children use their language acquisition device.
5 Input	The language input received by children is superior to that received by adults. However, adults may experience more negotiation of meaning.
6 Storage of L2 information	Children store L1 and L2 information separately (i.e. become coordinate bilinguals); adults store L1 and L2 knowledge together (i.e. become compound bilinguals).

Table 11.3:   Explanations of the role of age in L2 acquisition

Language aptitude

In an article reviewing early aptitude research, Carroll (1981) defines general aptitude as 'capability of learning a task', which depends on 'some combination of more or less enduring characteristics of the learner'. In the case of language aptitude the capability involves a special propensity for learning an L2.

The general claim that language aptitude constitutes a relevant factor in L2 acquisition entails, in Carrol's view, a number of more specific claims. The first is that aptitude is separate from achievement. Carroll argues that they are conceptually distinct and also that they can be distinguished empirically (by demonstrating that there is no relationship between measures of aptitude and measures of proficiency at the beginning of a language programme, but that there is a relationship at the end of the programme). Second, aptitude must be shown to be separate from motivation. On this point, however, there is some disagreement, as Pimsleur (1966) treats motivation as an integral part of aptitude. Carroll argues that research by Lambert and Gardner (reviewed later in this chapter) has consistently shown that aptitude and motivation are separate factors. Third, aptitude must be seen as a stable factor, perhaps even innate. In support of this claim, Carroll refers to studies which show that learners' aptitude is difficult to alter through training. Fourth, aptitude is to be viewed not as a prerequisite for L2 acquisition (as all learners, irrespective of their aptitude, may achieve a reasonable level of proficiency), but as a capacity that enhances the rate and ease of learning. Aptitude tests, therefore, provide a prediction of rate of learning.

Finally, Carroll argues that aptitude must be found to be distinct from general intelligence. He refers again to research by Lambert and Gardner which has shown that aptitude and intelligence measurements are not related. There are doubts about this claim, however. Pimsleur considers intelligence an important part of aptitude. Oller and Perkins (1978) have also argued that verbal intelligence is a major factor as it is needed to answer tests of the kind used to measure aptitude and language proficiency and thus is a common factor to both. In contrast, although finding significant correlations between scores on a verbal intelligence test and a test of foreign language proficiency, Skehan (1990) argues that there are clear differences between them. Similarly, Obler (1989), in a study of one exceptional learner who had a record of 'picking up' languages with great rapidity and ease, concluded that 'generally superior cognitive functioning is not necessary for exceptional L2 acquisition' (1989: 153). We will return to the question of intelligence later.

The two main instruments used to measure aptitude were developed in the 1950s and 1960s. The Modern Language Aptitude Test (MLAT) (Carroll and Sapon 1959) was developed initially as a means of screening candidates for foreign language instruction at the Foreign Service Institute in the United States. It exists in various forms. There is a full form, a short form, and an MLAT-Elementary, which was designed for selecting, guiding, and placing children in the Foreign Language in the Elementary School (FLES) programme. Versions have also been developed for use with languages other than English—French, Italian, and Japanese. The Pimsleur Language Aptitude Battery (PLAB) (Pimsleur 1966) was developed as an alternative to MLAT and, in particular, with a view for use in the junior high school. It measures a very similar range of abilities to MLAT. Other less well-known aptitude tests include the Defence Language Aptitude Battery (Petersen and Al-Haik 1976). This tested learners' ability to learn an artificial language through auditory and visual materials. It was designed for use with learners at the higher ends of the ability range. The York Language Aptitude Test (Green 1975) tested the ability of learners to use analogy to produce forms in an unknown language (Swedish). MLAT and PLAB are the most commonly used in aptitude research.

Carroll (1965) identified four factors in language aptitude:

1 Phonemic coding ability (the ability to code foreign sounds in a way that they can be remembered later). This ability is seen as related to the ability to spell and to handle sound–symbol relationships.
2 Grammatical sensitivity (the ability to recognize the grammatical functions of words in sentences).
3 Inductive language learning ability (the ability to identify patterns of correspondence and relationships involving form and meaning).
4 Rote learning ability (the ability to form and remember associations between stimuli). This ability is hypothesized to be involved in vocabulary learning.

Somewhat surprisingly, however, Carroll and Sapon's MLAT does not include a separate measure of (3), inductive language learning ability, perhaps because this is very close to (2), grammatical sensitivity. The PLAB covers a similar range of characteristics, but has no test of verbal memory. Also, in this test a score is awarded for 'Grade point average in academic areas', as a measure of intelligence.

Aptitude research has adopted a concatenative approach. Measures of language aptitude are correlated with measures of language proficiency and achievement. The main aim of the research has been to establish to what extent it is possible to predict learning outcomes. A secondary aim has been to identify which specific aspects of aptitude individual learners are strongest in, so that matching forms of instruction can be provided (Wesche 1981). A general assumption of the research is that aptitude will only have an effect on learning outcomes if the learners are sufficiently motivated to learn (i.e. make the effort to use their intrinsic abilities).

A fairly strong relationship has been consistently found between language aptitude and learning. Carroll (1981) reports that the studies he carried out using the MLAT produced correlations between .40 and .60 with a variety of criterion measures (final course grades, objective foreign language attainment tests, and instructors' estimates of learners' language learning abilities). Gardner (1980), in a review of several studies of the effects of motivation and aptitude on the learning of French in schools throughout Canada, reports a median correlation for aptitude of .41. Pimsleur, Sundland, and MacIntyre (1966) emphasize the importance of sound discrimination, having found that 20 to 30 per cent of the children in their study were underachieving because of particular problems with this component of aptitude. With the exception of a study by Horwitz (1987b), and Skehan's recent work on aptitude, however, there has been little research since the 1970s.

Horwitz's study is interesting because it suggests that language aptitude is related to measures of both linguistic and communicative competence. It investigated 61 female high school students of French in the United States. Aptitude scores on MLAT correlated significantly with scores on a discrete-point written grammar test (0.41) and with scores on a series of oral tasks requiring relatively spontaneous language (0.40).

Skehan's research (1986a, 1986b, and 1990) has been directed at two general issues. One concerns the nature of the abilities which aptitude tests measure. The other is whether aptitude is best seen as a cumulative aggregation of abilities or as differentiated, thus affording more than one route to success.

In order to re-examine the nature of aptitude, Skehan used data from Wells' (1985) longitudinal study of the L1 acquisition of English by some sixty plus children in the Bristol area of England. He investigated (1) the relationship between measures of L1 development and standard measures of aptitude, (2) the relationship between measures of foreign language learning by the same children at 13 years of age and aptitude, and (3) the relationship between L1 development and foreign language achievement. A number of significant relationships involving measures of L1 development and aptitude were found. The highest correlations were between measures of fragile syntax (for example, auxiliary and pronoun systems) and analytic aspects of aptitude. Language aptitude was also strongly related to foreign language achievement. However, only test-based and lexical measures of L1 development were related to the measures of foreign language achievement, which were derived exclusively from tests. Skehan explains these results by arguing that the aptitude tests he used measured two main aspects: (1) an underlying language learning capacity, which is similar in L1 and L2 learning, and (2) an ability to handle decontextualized material, such as that found in formal language tests. This research constitutes an important extension of the earlier research because it shows that aptitude involves both the kind of abilities Carroll and Pimsleur had identified earlier and, additionally, the ability to deal with context-free language.

Skehan's research also helps to illuminate the question of whether intelligence is to be seen as part of aptitude (as Pimsleur and Oller claimed) or as distinct from it (as Carroll claimed). Here Cummins' (1983) distinction between basic interpersonal communication skills (BICS) and cognitive academic language proficiency (CALP) is relevant (see Chapter 6). The former consists of those skills required for oral fluency and the sociolinguistically appropriate use of a language. The latter concerns a dimension of language proficiency that is strongly related to overall cognitive and academic language skills and can be equated with the global language proficiency factor, which Oller and Perkins (1978: 413) have claimed accounts for 'the bulk of the reliable variance in a wide range of language proficiency measures' and is identical with the 'g' factor of intelligence. A number of studies support a connection between CALP and intelligence. Genesee (1976) found that intelligence was strongly related to the development of academic L2 French language skills (reading, grammar, and vocabulary) but was largely unrelated to ratings of oral productive ability. Ekstrand (1977) also found low-level correlations between intelligence and proficiency as measured on tests of listening comprehension and free oral production, but much higher correlations when proficiency was measured by tests of reading comprehension, dictation, and free writing. The underlying learning capacity which Skehan found can be hypothesized to relate to BICS, a claim that is supported by the strong relationship between aptitude and L1 acquisition (which takes place in the course of developing BICS). The ability to handle decontextualized language, however, suggests that aptitude is also related to CALP, and therefore also involves intelligence. So, in a sense, Carroll and Pimsleur were both right.

Skehan's research has also addressed another issue—the extent to which the effect of aptitude is to be viewed 'globally', as the aggregation of aptitude strengths in the different components, or differentially, with learners finding different routes to success in language learning depending on the nature of their aptitude. Skehan (1986a) reports a study in which he used cluster analysis to identify different kinds of learners who were studying colloquial Arabic in the Army School of Languages in Britain. The results were not entirely clear, but they suggested that whereas some learners were grammatically sensitive and demonstrated finely-tuned inductive language learning ability, others were strong on memory and 'chunk-learning'. This led Skehan (1989) to propose that there are two types of foreign language learners, analytic and memory-orientated. Both kinds can achieve a high level of success. Studying the differences in the type of aptitude that individual learners have serves as one way of investigating learning style (see the next section).

Research into language aptitude was popular in the 1960s and 1970s, but has largely gone into abeyance since. One reason for this is undoubtedly the strong link that existed between the models of aptitude developed during that time and the prevailing views of language (structuralist), language learning (behaviourist), and language teaching (audiolingual). As these views were challenged, so interest in aptitude declined. The research was restricted in that it only looked at learners in formal learning situations, and in general tended to use criterion measures of learning that reflected CALP rather than BICS. Despite these limitations, the early research provided convincing evidence that classroom learners' language aptitude has a major effect on their success in learning an L2. As Gardner and MacIntyre (1992) comment:

> Research makes it clear that in the long run language aptitude is probably the single best predictor of achievement in a second language (1992: 215).

Horwitz's and Skehan's studies have helped to reopen the research agenda. Skehan (1991) suggests three ways in which aptitude research might progress. First, there is a need to revise the basic model to take account of current theories of language and language learning. Second, the tests need to be revised to more strongly reflect the kind of abilities involved in BICS. Third, research needs to be conducted in a variety of learning contexts including informal ones.

In the light of Skehan's conclusions, it is interesting to note that Carroll himself is 'somewhat skeptical about the possibilities for greatly improving foreign language aptitude predictions beyond their present levels' (1990: 27). He specifically addresses the possibility of including tests of verbal fluency factors—which might be considered of importance in communicative language teaching—but dismisses them on the grounds that these had been explored in his early research and found not to make any significant contribution to prediction. However, Carroll does offer a number of suggestions for improving aptitude measures. The existing tests might be 'fine-tuned' (for example, by distinguishing auditory ability and phonemic coding ability). Some new tests might be developed (for example, memory tests that measure aspects of memory other than rote learning ability). He also suggests that other potentially useful abilities for language learning might be identified by examining the nature of the cognitive abilities needed to perform different kinds of language learning tasks.

There have, in fact, been almost no attempts to develop alternative language aptitude tests. One exception is Parry and Child's (1990) work on VORD, an aptitude test based on an artificial language that was initially developed in the early 1970s. The development consisted of incorporating a component designed to test language aptitude in a contextual framework by requiring subjects to apply general rules to particular segments of texts. However, in a small-scale study involving 36 adult subjects, many of whom were experienced language learners, Parry and Child found that MLAT was a better overall predictor of language-learning success than VORD. This study, then, bears out Carroll's skepticism about improving tests of language aptitude.

Learning styles

The second general factor we will consider is learning style. The idea of *learning style* comes from general psychology. It refers to the characteristic ways in which individuals orientate to problem-solving. Keefe (1979) defines learning style as:

> ... the characteristic cognitive, affective and physiological behaviours that serve as relatively stable indicators of how learners perceive, interact with and respond to the learning environment ... Learning style is a consistent way of functioning, that reflects underlying causes of behaviour.

Learning style, therefore, reflects 'the totality of psychological functioning' (Willing 1987). An individual's learning style is viewed as relatively fixed and not readily changed. However, Little and Singleton (1990) argue that it is possible to help adult learners to explore their own preferences and to shape their learning approach to suit the requirements of a particular learning task. It is this belief that underlies the idea of 'learner training' (Holec 1987).

A number of learning style distinctions have been made in cognitive psychology. Bruner, Goodnow, and Austin (1957) distinguished 'focusers' and 'scanners'. The former tackle a problem by concentrating on one feature at a time, in a step-by-step process, while the latter deal with several features at the same time and allow their ideas to crystallize slowly. Pask and Scott (1972) distinguished 'serialists' and 'holists', according to whether learners operate with simple hypotheses (consisting of a single proposition) or complex hypotheses (involving multiple propositions). Other distinctions, which seem to reflect personality as much as learning style differences, include 'impulsive' v. 'reflective' thinkers and 'divergent' v. 'convergent' thinkers. However, only the distinction between *field independence* (FI) and *field dependence* (FD) has attracted much attention in SLA research.

Field dependence/independence

This distinction is taken from the work of Witkin and associates. Witkin, Oltman, Raskin, and Karp (1971) provide the following description:

> In a field-dependent mode of perceiving, perception is strongly dominated by the overall organization of the surrounding field, and parts of the field are experienced as 'fused'. In a field-independent mode of perceiving, parts of the field are experienced as discrete from organized ground … 'field dependent' and 'field independent', like the designations 'tall' and 'short' are relative (1971: 4).

To investigate subjects' perception of a 'field' as 'fused' or as composed of 'discrete parts', a variety of tests of space-orientation (for example, the body-adjustment test, which measured subjects' perception of an upright position) were developed. Later, Witkin and his associates developed various pencil-and-paper tests that required subjects to locate a simple geometrical figure within a more complex design. Witkin claimed that they measured the same construct as the space orientation tests. The version most widely used in SLA research is the Group Embedded Figures Test (GEFT).[4] This provides a measure of the extent to which individuals are field independent but, as McLaughlin (1985) has pointed out, there is no separate measure of field dependency.

As a result of research with the GEFT conducted by Witkin and his associates, various claims regarding the relationship between FI/FD and other variables have been advanced (see Table 11.4). Precisely what the test measures, however, is a matter of some controversy. Griffiths and Sheen (1992) suggest that many of Witkin's claims are 'expansive'. They argue that it is not possible to extrapolate from visual–spatial abilities, which they claim the test measures, to other cognitive abilities or to personality dimensions. They suggest that the GEFT is a test of 'ability' rather than 'style', 'specifically in the visuo-spatial domain, but also related to general intelligence' (1992: 141). This is a view shared by Chapelle and Green (1992). They point to Witkin's later work (for example, Witkin and Goodenough 1981), which defined FI/FD as involving three major constructs: reliance on internal v. external referents, cognitive restructuring skills, and interpersonal competencies. However, they argue that the GEFT only measures 'cognitive restructuring ability'. They also suggest it constitutes a measure of one type of intelligence, 'fluid ability' (the ability that is independent of any body of content knowledge and that is involved in problem solving). The value of the L2 research based on the GEFT, then, would seem to lie more in the light it throws on aptitude, as Chapelle and Green's (1992) subsequent discussion demonstrates, than in illuminating the role of cognitive style. It is discussed in this section only because the bulk of L2 studies have treated the GEFT as a measure of style.

Another problem with the GEFT is that it may be culturally biased, favouring certain groups over others (see Willing 1987). Griffiths (1991b) reports marked differences in the scores obtained by nationals of different Asian countries (for example, 10 out of a maximum of 18 by Samoans as opposed to 15 plus for Japanese). Certainly, the characterization of FI and FD individuals, as shown in Table 11.4, is contentious.

Field independence	Field dependence
adolescents/adults	children
males	females
object-oriented jobs	people-oriented jobs
urban, technological societies	rural, agrarian societies
free social structures	rigid social structures
individualistic people	group-centred people

Table 11.4:   Variables associated with field in dependence and field dependence

There are now a considerable number of studies that have investigated the relationship between FI/FD and L2 learning (see Table 11.5). One hypothesis that has been investigated is that FI learners do better in formal language learning, while FD learners do better in informal language learning. However, with the exception of Abraham and Vann (1987), who studied only two learners, this hypothesis has not received support. In general, FI learners do better on measures of formal language learning (for example, discrete point tests)—see, for example, studies by Seliger (1977), Stansfield and Hansen (1983), Chapelle and Roberts (1986), and Carter (1988). But FI learners also do better on integrative tests and tests of communicative competence, designed to favour FD learners—see studies by Hansen (1984), Chapelle and Roberts (1986), and Carter (1988). Also, a number of studies (for example, Bialystok and Fröhlich (1978), Day (1984), and Ellis (1990b)) have failed to find a significant relationship between GEFT scores and measures of learning. Other studies comment on the weakness of the relationship. D'Anglejan and

Renaud (1985), for instance, report that FI explained less than 1 per cent of the variance in tests of all four language skills. Even some of the studies that report a relationship between FI and L2 achievement also comment that it loses significance once the effects of the learners' general scholastic ability have been statistically removed (for example, Hansen 1984). d'Anglejan and Renaud (1985) found a considerable overlap between FI/FD, as measured by the GEFT, and verbal intelligence, as measured by Raven's Progressive Matrices, a result that led them to question Witkin and Berry's (1975) insistence that the two cognitive traits were distinct and that reinforces the views expressed by Griffiths and Sheen (1992) and Chapelle and Green (1992) that GEFT is really an aptitude test.

Another hypothesis which has not received convincing support from the research carried out to date is that FD learners will interact more and seek out more contact with other users of the L2. Seliger (1977) found that FI learners interacted more in the classroom. He argues that this was because they were not reliant on the approval of others, and were therefore more prepared to take risks, but his results could also be interpreted as contradicting the hypothesis that FD learners will interact more. Day (1984) found no relationship whatsoever between FI/FD and participation. Carter (1988) reports that FI learners were more concerned with meaning than FD learners, which also works against the hypothesis.

Two studies have investigated learner–instruction matching. Abraham (1985) reports that FI learners did better with a deductive method of instruction, while FD learners benefited from being given examples. However, Carter (1988) found that FI learners did better than FD learners in both a formal and a functional language course. Again, then, there is no clear support for the hypothesis that FI learners gain from a form-focused, deductive approach and FD learners from a meaning-focused, inductive approach.

A number of studies have also considered the FI/FD distinction in relation to aptitude. Bialystok and Fröhlich (1978) report a general relationship between FI and aptitude (measured with MLAT). In Ellis 1990b I reported significant correlations of moderate strength (around .30) between aptitude measures of grammaticality sensitivity, word memory and sound discrimination, and FI. However, if it can be shown that the GEFT measures much the same thing as aptitude tests, its value becomes questionable. As Skehan (1991) points out, an advantage of aptitude tests is that they allow for learners with both alternative orientations to be identified (for example, analytic v. memory) and for learners with strong, combined orientations (for example, analytic and memory). H. Brown (1987) has also suggested that some learners may have 'flexible' cognitive styles, combining FI and FD modes of processing and adapting their approach to suit different learning tasks. However, the GEFT is based on the assumption that the less one is FI, the more one is FD, and so it cannot be used to investigate the presumed advantages of a flexible learning style.

Study	Subjects	Setting	Proficiency level	Measures of learning	Results
Tucker, Hamayan, and Genesee 1976	School learners of L2 French in Canada	Second language	Lower intermediate	Listening comprehension; reading comprehension; oral production task; achievement test of general language skills	FI/FD failed to correlate significantly with any of the learning measures except the achievement test.
Seliger 1977	Adult learners at university in USA	Second language	Upper intermediate	Frequency of interaction in the classroom; structure test; aural comprehension test; cloze test	FI correlated significantly with all measures of learning and with the measure of classroom interaction.
Naiman et al. 1978	School learners of L2 French in Canada	Second language	Intermediate and above, Grades 8, 10, and 12	Listening comprehension; imitation	FI correlated at 5% level with imitation and at the 1% level with comprehension.
Bialystok and Fröhlich 1978	31 learners of L2 French in Canada	Second language	Intermediate, Grades 9 and 10	Reading comprehension	No significant correlation between FI/FD and learning. FI significantly related to measure of aptitude (MLAT).
Hansen and Stansfield 1981	253 learners of L2 Spanish at university in USA	Foreign language	Beginners	6 measures of linguistic competence, communicative competence, and integrative competence	Significant correlations between FI and all 6 measures of learning at 5% or better; relationship weakened when scholastic ability partialled out.
Stansfield and Hansen 1983	250 learners of L2 Spanish at University in USA	Foreign language	Beginners	The students' written exam grade average the students' oral grade; cloze test	Modest relationship between all achievement measures and FI found. Correlation between FI and cloze scores highest (r = .43).
Abraham 1983	Adult ESL learners	Second language	High intermediate	Use of monitoring strategy in three language learning tasks	FI related to higher incidence of monitoring.

(continued overleaf)

Study	Subjects	Setting	Proficiency level	Measures of learning	Results
Hansen 1984	Adult learners of L2 English from different Pacific island cultures	Second language	Mixed levels	Cloze test	Significant relationships between FI and cloze performance found but there was considerable variation according to sub-group; also, effects of FI largely disappeared when scholastic attainment partialled out
Day 1984	25 adult learners of L2 English in Hawaii; divided into high and low input generators	Second language	Intermediate	Oral proficiency; (interview assessment of learners' grammatical, pragmatic and socio-linguistic competence; cloze test	No relationship found between GEFT scores and measures of learning or between GEFT scores and measures of participation in classroom interaction
Abraham 1985	61 15–19-year-old learners of L2 English; mixed language backgrounds; two treatments (deductive and examples)	Second language	High intermediate	Sentence-joining task testing participle structures	FI learners did better if they received deductive treatment and FD learners did better with examples
Chapelle and Roberts 1986	61 adult learners of L2 English (Japanese, Spanish and Arabic)	Second language	Intermediate	TOEFL test; MC grammar test; cloze test; dictation; oral test of communicative competence.	FI significantly related to all measures of learning at beginning and end of semester; relationship strongest with TEOFL scores; FD not related to measure of communicative competence
Abraham and Vann 1987	Two adult learners; of L2 English; L1 Spanish	Second language	Both intermediate; one high and one low proficiency	Michigan English Placement test; TOEFL; test of spoken English; performance on different lang. learning tasks	FI related to TOEFL; FD related to oral ability FI also related to greater variety of strategy use and to greater concern with correctness

Study	Subjects	Setting	Proficiency level	Measures of learning	Results
Bacon 1987	95 learners of L2 Spanish in supportive instructional group and 93 in non-supportive	Foreign language	Beginner	Oral interview used to measure quantity and quality of L2 production (using NS raters)	No relationship between GEFT scores and quantity/quality of L2 production—irrespective of treatment provided. FD learners attached more importance to speaking another language.
Carter 1988	72 learners of L2 Spanish taught in two courses—formal and more functional	Foreign language	Beginner/low intermediate	Regular written final examination; ACTEFL/ELTS Oral Proficiency interview; questionnaire about learners' views regarding utility of different learning strategies	FI related to both formal linguistic achievement and to functional language use; this relationship was evident in both formal and functional courses. FI students in both types of course considered focus on meaning more important than FD students.
Ellis 1990b	39 learners of L2 German; mixed L1s	Foreign language	Beginner	Measure of German acquisition; measure of spoken fluency; vocabulary test; grammar test; cloze test	Relationship between GEFT scores and all measures of learning very weak and non-significant

Table 11.5:   Survey of studies which have investigated the effect of cognitive style on L2 acquisition

To conclude, the research into FI/FD has shed little light on the relationship between cognitive style and L2 learning. Griffiths and Sheen (1992) are particularly dismissive of it, arguing that the research is seriously flawed by a failure to test hypotheses derivable from Witkin's theory, a failure to recognize that the GEFT measures ability rather than style, and a failure to acknowledge the rejection of Witkin's theory in mainstream psychology. They conclude that the FI/FD construct is 'a wasteland, bereft of meaningful hypotheses for L2 researchers' (1992: 145). Quite apart from these theoretical objections, the research itself has proved inconclusive; most of the studies have found either no relationship between FI and L2 achievement or only a very weak one. If FI/FD and the GEFT have a future in SLA research, it is probably in investigations of aptitude rather than of cognitive style. In this respect, as Chapelle (1992) points out in her response to Griffiths and Sheen, the research may still have some value.

Other approaches to investigating learning style in second language learners

Some of the other approaches for investigating learning style are more promising. A number of researchers have used survey techniques to collect data on learners' stated preferences. On the basis of such data, Reid (1987) distinguished four perceptual learning modalities:

1 visual learning (for example, reading and studying charts)
2 auditory learning (for example, listening to lectures or to audio tapes)
3 kinaesthetic learning (involving physical responses)
4 tactile learning (hands-on learning, as in building models).

He then administered a questionnaire to 1,388 students of varying language backgrounds to investigate their preferred modalities. This revealed that the learners' preferences often differed significantly from those of native speakers of American English. They showed a general preference for kinaesthetic and tactile learning styles (with the exception of the Japanese), and for individual as opposed to group learning. With regard to the latter, Reid comments: 'Every language background, including English, gave group work as a minor or negative preference'. Proficiency level was not related to learning style preference, but length of residence in the United States was—the longer the period, the more an auditory style was preferred, reflecting perhaps an adaptation to the prevailing demands of the American educational system.

In another survey, Willing (1987) investigated the learning styles of 517 adult ESL learners in Australia. Their responses to a 30-item questionnaire were analysed by means of factor analysis (a statistical procedure designed to discover if there were any combinations of items which afforded parallel responses). Willing identified two major dimensions of learning style. One was cognitive and corresponded closely to that of field independence/dependence.

The other was more affective in nature; it concerned how active learners were in the way they reported approaching L2 learning tasks. Skehan (1991) suggests that the second dimension reflects a personality as much as a learning style factor. Based on these two dimensions, Willing describes four general learning styles (summarized in Table 11.6). Willing's study is interesting, but it suffers from a number of methodological problems, which cast doubt on the results obtained. Willing's study did not include sufficient numbers of subjects to permit a statistically valid analysis of many of the nationalities it sampled. Also, the subjects were not equally distributed into the four learning styles. Perhaps the most serious reservation concerns the validity and reliability of the questionnaire Willing used.

General learning style	Main characteristics
1 Concrete learning style	Direct means of processing information; people-orientated; spontaneous; imaginative; emotional; dislikes routinized learning; prefers kinaesthetic modality.
2 Analytical learning style	Focuses on specific problems and proceeds by means of hypothetical–deductive reasoning; object-orientated; independent; dislikes failure; prefers logical, didactic presentation.
3 Communicative learning style	Fairly independent; highly adaptable and flexible; responsive to facts that do not fit; prefers social learning and a communicative approach; enjoys taking decisions.
4 Authority-orientated learning style	Reliant on other people; needs teacher's directions and explanations; likes a structured learning environment; intolerant of facts that do not fit; prefers a sequential progression; dislikes discovery learning.

Table 11.6:   Four learning styles used by adult ESL learners (based on Willing 1987)

Willing's questionnaire was also used (in a slightly adapted form) by Gieve (1991) in a study of the learning styles of 156 first-year female students at a Junior College in Japan. Gieve analysed the data using a variety of statistical procedures, the most revealing of which was cluster analysis (a procedure that groups people according to the similarity of their response profiles). Five clusters emerged, which can be identified as follows: (1) learners with instrumental motivation together with communicative orientation, (2) learners with no motivation, (3) learners interested in general intellectual development, (4) learners with a strong motivation but with no clear aims, and (5) learners with integrative motivation interested in living abroad. Most students fell into cluster (2). This analysis suggests that the strength and nature of learners' motivation works as a major dimension of learning style. Gieve also makes the interesting point that the students' responses reflected their environment at least as much as innate qualities, as shown by the fact that significant differences were found in learners' responses depending on whether the questionnaire was administered by a Japanese or native-speaker researcher! Again, then, doubts are raised as to whether the results obtained by the questionnaire can be considered reliable.

Further evidence of differences in learning styles comes from product analyses of learner language. Researching L1 acquisition, Nelson (1973) distinguishes 'referential' and 'expressive' learners. The former use language to name things while the latter prefer to use it to indicate feelings, needs, and social forms. Peters (1977) suggests that some learners are 'analytic' (i.e. are word-learners and progress incrementally through a recognizable sequence of stages of acquisition) and some are 'gestalt' (i.e. are sentence-learners who begin with whole sentences which are used to perform functions that are important to them). In SLA research, somewhat similar types of learners have been identified. Hatch (1974), for example, talks of 'rule-formers', who pay close attention to linguistic form, sort out the rules, and develop steadily, and 'data-gatherers', who show greater concern for communication and make extensive use of formulaic chunks. Krashen (1978) distinguishes 'monitor-over-users' and 'monitor-under-users', allowing also for 'optimal monitor users'. Dechert (1984a) compared the styles of two advanced learners in a narrative reproduction task. One was 'analytic' (manifesting long pauses at chunk boundaries, few corrections, and serial processing) while the other was 'synthetic' (manifesting shorter pauses throughout, more corrections, and episodic processing). The terms used to characterize the differences in language produced by different learners proliferate, but it is tempting to identify one general distinction that seems to underlie many of those mentioned above—the experiential, communicatively-orientated learner as opposed to the analytical, norm-orientated learner.

At the moment there are few general conclusions that can be drawn from the research on learning style. Learners clearly differ enormously in their preferred approach to L2 learning, but it is impossible to say which learning style works best. Quite possibly it is learners who display flexibility who are most successful, but there is no real evidence yet for such a conclusion. One of the major problems is that the concept of 'learning style' is ill-defined, apparently overlapping with other individual differences of both an affective and a cognitive nature. It is unlikely that much progress will be made until researchers know what it is they want to measure.

Motivation

Language teachers readily acknowledge the importance of learners' *motivation*, not infrequently explaining their own sense of failure with reference to their students' lack of motivation. SLA research also views motivation as a key factor in L2 learning. There have been differences, however, in the way in which teachers and researchers have typically conceptualized 'motivation' (see Crookes and Schmidt 1990).

In an attempt to characterize a non-theoretical view of motivation, Skehan (1989) puts forward four hypotheses:

1 The Intrinsic Hypothesis: motivation derives from an inherent interest in the learning tasks the learner is asked to perform.
2 The Resultative Hypothesis: learners who do well will persevere, those who do not do well will be discouraged and try less hard.
3 The Internal Cause Hypothesis: the learner brings to the learning situation a certain quantity of motivation as a given.
4 The Carrot and Stick Hypothesis: external influences and incentives will affect the strength of the learner's motivation.

These hypotheses have their correlates in the study of motivation in SLA research, but one of them, (3), has received the lion's share of researchers' attention. We will begin, therefore, by examining the research which has addressed this hypothesis.

Integrative motivation

According to Gardner's socio-educational model (which we examined in some detail in Chapter 6), an integrative orientation involves an interest in learning an L2 because of 'a sincere and personal interest in the people and culture represented by the other language group' (Lambert 1974: 98). It contrasts with an instrumental orientation, which concerns 'the practical value and advantages of learning a new language'. 'Orientation', however, is not the same as motivation, which is defined by Gardner as 'the combination of effort plus desire to achieve the goal of learning the language plus favourable attitudes towards learning the language' (1985: 10). Thus, whereas 'orientation' refers to the underlying reasons for studying an L2, 'motivation' refers to the directed effort individual learners make to learn the language. Over the years, Gardner has become increasingly critical of research that focuses narrowly on the role of orientation in L2 learning, arguing that the effects of learners' orientations are mediated by their motivation—that is, whereas orientation and L2 achievement are only indirectly related, motivation and achievement are directly related.

What, then, is '*integrative motivation*'? Crookes and Schmidt (1989) point out that the answer to this question is not entirely clear, as Gardner has provided different operational definitions of this concept in different studies. As we saw in Chapter 6, Gardner's research rests on the use of self-report questionnaires. Questions relating to a number of orientational and motivational variables are included, and learners' responses are factor-analysed in order to identify general factors. One of the factors that has consistently emerged from this procedure is 'integrative motivation'. Table 11.7 shows the variables that

Gardner and MacIntyre (1991) included in their composite measure of this factor. It should be noted that the variable 'integrative orientation' is included in this measure together with a number of other variables to do with the learners' attitudes, interest, and desire regarding the learning of French.

Variable	Questionnaire items	Example
Attitudes towards French Canadians	Five positively-worded and five negatively-worded items	'If Canada should lose the French culture of Quebec, it would indeed be a great loss'.
Interest in Foreign Languages	Five items expressing a positive interest and five a relative disinterest.	'I enjoy meeting and listening to people who speak other languages'.
Integrative orientation	Four items expressing the importance of learning French for integrative reasons.	'Studying French can be important because it allows people to participate more freely in the activities of other cultural groups'.
Attitudes towards the learning situation	Four items referring to French teachers in general and four referring to French courses—half positive and half negative.	'French courses offer an excellent opportunity for students to broaden their cultural and linguistic horizons'.
Desire to learn French	Three positive and three negative items.	'I wish I were fluent in French'.
Attitudes towards learning French	Three positive and three negative items.	'I would really like to learn French'.

Table 11.7:   An operational definition of 'integrative motivation' (based on Gardner and MacIntyre 1991)

A consistent correlation between integrative motivation and L2 achievement has been found in studies of anglophone Canadians learning French. In the earlier research (for example, Gardner and Lambert 1972), integrative orientation was seen as a more powerful predictor of achievement in formal learning situations than instrumental orientation. In later research, Gardner (1985) has continued to assert the importance of integrative motivation, although he now acknowledges that instrumental motivation can also lead to successful learning (see below). However, Gardner argues that whereas instrumental motivation emerges as a significant factor only in some studies, integrative motivation has been found to be invariably related to L2 achievement.

Learners can, of course, have both *integrative* and *instrumental motivation* (a possibility not clearly allowed for in the earlier work but acknowledged in the later). Muchnick and Wolfe (1982), for instance, found that measures of the integrative and instrumental motivation of 337 students of Spanish in high schools in the United States loaded on the same factor, suggesting that for these learners, it was impossible to separate the two kinds of motivation. Ely (1986b) investigated the types of motivation found in first-year university students of Spanish in the United States. He found evidence of both strong integrative and strong instrumental motivation. In this study, the two types emerged as separate factors, but they were both present in the same students.

In order to demonstrate the overall effect of motivation on L2 achievement, Gardner (1980; 1985) chooses to report the effects of a general measure of motivation (based on the Attitude Motivation Index, which includes variables relating to both integrative and instrumental motivation). A survey of seven different geographical areas in Canada revealed a median correlation of 0.37 between the AMI scores and French grades. Thus, general motivation (comprised primarily of measures of integrative motivation) accounts for approximately 14 per cent of the variance in achievement scores. According to Gardner, this constitutes a 'remarkably strong' relationship.

Some studies, however, have failed to find a positive relationship between integrative motivation and L2 achievement. For example, Oller, Baca, and Vigil (1977) report that Mexican women in California who rated Anglo people negatively were more successful in learning English than those who rated them positively. Oller and Perkins (1978) suggest that some learners may be motivated to excel because of negative attitudes towards the target language community. In this case negative feelings may lead to a desire to manipulate and overcome the people of the target language—a phenomenon which they refer to as *Machiavellian Motivation*. In other studies (for example, Chihara and Oller 1978) the relationship between measures of integrative motivation and achievement has been weak and insignificant. Gardner (1980) has defended the results of his own research vigorously, pointing out the sheer number of studies which have reported a significant effect for integrative motivation and also attacking the design of the self-report questionnaires used in the studies by Oller and associates.

There is something of a mismatch between the theoretical definition of motivation which Gardner provides and the operational construct that he has investigated. This is because self-report questionnaires do not provide any indication of the actual effort which learners put into their learning and which Gardner sees as a key dimension of motivation. However, a number of studies have tried to investigate 'effort' and a related concept, 'persistence', seeking to show that measures of motivation (and, in particular, integrative motivation) are related to the amount of effort and persistence that individual learners display in classroom contexts. The assumption here is that 'active' learners will achieve more than 'passive' learners.

One possible definition of an active learner is one who participates frequently in classroom interaction. In a series of studies inspired by Gardner's socio-educational model, Gliksman (for example, in Gliksman 1976; Gliksman, Gardner, and Smythe 1982) has provided evidence to show that students studying French in Canadian high schools receive directed teacher questions, volunteer answers, give correct answers, and receive positive re-inforcement according to the strength of their integrative motivation. The higher their integrative motivation, the more these classroom behaviours are evident. Naiman et al. (1978) found a similar relationship, although in this case 'effort' on the part of the learners was also associated with instrumental motivation. They were also able to show that a number of classroom behavi-ours associated with effort (such as hand-raising) were significantly related to L2 achievement. However, the relationship between learner participation in the classroom and L2 learning remains uncertain, as other studies have failed to find one or have even come up with a negative one (see Chapter 14).

There have also been a number of studies that have investigated the rela-tionships between motivation, persistence, and achievement. Clement, Smythe, and Gardner (1978) investigated what factors caused Canadian stu-dents in grades 9, 10, and 11 to drop out of a French programme. They found that motivation proved a more powerful predictor than language aptitude, classroom anxiety, or even L2 achievement. Ramage (1990) investigated the factors causing high school students of French and Spanish to drop out in the United states. Her most significant finding was that students who chose to continue their studies beyond the second year attached very low importance to fulfilling curriculum requirements, and instead reported an interest in the target-language cultures (which suggests an integrative motivation) and the desire to attain proficiency in all language skills. There were other factors that played a part, such as grades achieved in previous foreign language courses and when the students started to study (the early starters were more likely to continue). Ramage's study suggests, not surprisingly, that, although integra-tive motivation contributes to persistence in foreign language study, it is not the only factor.

Integrative motivation is not the only kind of internal motivation involved in L2 learning, as Clement and his co-workers' research demonstrates (see Clement and Kruidenier 1983 and 1985; Clement 1986; Kruidenier and Clement 1986). Clement (1986), for example, investigated 293 francophone students at the University of Ottawa, dividing them into a majority and mi-nority group, depending on whether francophones were in the majority or minority in their home areas. The subjects completed a questionnaire de-signed to produce measures of a variety of variables such as integrativeness, fear of assimilation, motivation (defined in terms of 'attitudes' and 'desire'), self-confidence, frequency of contact, and acculturation. English language ability was measured by means of an oral interview and a general proficiency test. One of the main findings of this study was that integrativeness was not related to language outcomes, nor was it influenced by the status of the learn-ers (i.e. whether they belonged to the majority or minority group). The best predictor of language proficiency proved to be self-confidence, a finding that held for both groups. Clement points out that many of Gardner's earlier studies had investigated school students and that the rather different results he obtained might reflect the greater maturity and autonomy of his (Clement's) subjects, who typically learned and used English on a day-to-day basis, mainly outside the classroom. Clement suggests that for such learners 'frequency of contact and the concomitant self-confidence might be more important in determining second language proficiency than socio-contextual or affective factors' (1986: 287).

Kruidenier and Clement (1986) also failed to find any evidence in support for Gardner's integrative orientation in another study of language learners in Quebec. Instead they found evidence of a number of different orientations (friendship, travel, knowledge, and instrumental) with different groups of learners revealing different dominant orientations, depending on their learning situation. For example, learners of a minority language like Spanish were more influenced by a travel orientation, whereas francophone learners of English were more influenced by a friendship orientation. One possibility raised by Dornyei (1990), however, is that these various orientations are all part of a general integrative orientation, with different groups of learners emphasizing different constituents of this.

To sum up, integrative motivation has been shown to be strongly related to L2 achievement. It combines with instrumental motivation to serve as a powerful predictor of success in formal contexts. Learners with integrative motivation are more active in class and are less likely to drop out. However, integrativeness is not always the main motivational factor in L2 learning; some learners, such as those living in bilingual areas, may be more influenced by other factors like self-confidence or friendship. There are also a number of limitations to the research paradigm that has been used to study integrative motivation (see Chapter 6). In particular, it takes no cognizance of the potential effect that learning experiences can have on learners' motivation, as opposed to the effect that motivation has on language learning.

Instrumental motivation

The Carrot and Stick Hypothesis sees external incentives and influences as determinants of learners' motivational strength. It has been investigated in SLA research through studies of instrumental motivation.

It is again useful to distinguish 'orientation' and 'motivation'. Gardner and MacIntyre (1991) measure the former by means of a self-report questionnaire in which learners respond to statements such as 'Studying French can be important because it is useful for one's career'. They equate 'instrumental motivation' with giving students a financial reward for performing a task successfully.

Much of the research has investigated the effects of an instrumental orientation (as opposed to motivation) on learning. The results have been variable, reflecting the situational/cultural context of learning. Thus, whereas instrumental motivation has been found to be only a weak predictor of foreign language achievement in several Canadian studies (see Gardner and Lambert 1972), it appears to be much more powerful in other contexts where learners have little or no interest in the target-language culture and few or no opportunities to interact with its members. For example, Gardner and Lambert (1972) found that a measure of instrumental orientation accounted for a significant proportion of the variance in Tagalog learners of L2 English in the Philippines. Similarly, Lukmani (1972) found that an instrumental orientation was more important than an integrative orientation in non-westernized female learners of L2 English in Bombay. The social situation helps to determine both what kind of orientation learners have and what kind is most important for language learning.

Surprisingly, there have been few studies which have investigated the direct effect of an instrumental motivation (i.e. the provision of some kind of incentive to learn). In a very early study, Dunkel (1948) (cited in Gardner and MacIntyre 1992) offered financial rewards to students learning Farsi and found that although this did not result in a significantly better performance on a grammar test, there was a tendency in this direction. Gardner and MacIntyre (1991) report a study in which 46 university psychology students were rewarded with $10 if they succeeded in a paired-associate (English-French) vocabulary task, while the same number were just told to do their best. The students offered the reward did significantly better. They also spent more time viewing the pairs of words, except on the sixth and last trial in the task, when the possibility of a reward no longer existed. This led Gardner and MacIntyre to claim that once any chance for receiving a reward is eliminated, learners may cease applying extra effort. They see this as a major disadvantage of instrumental motivation.

To sum up, learners with an instrumental reason for learning an L2 can be successful. In some 'second' as opposed to 'foreign' settings an instrumental orientation may be the most important one. Providing learners with incentives (such as money) may also aid learning by increasing the time learners spend studying, but the effects may cease as soon as the reward stops.

Resultative motivation

In the studies considered above, integrative and instrumental motivation were seen as causes of L2 achievement. However, the majority of studies were correlational in design and, as has often been pointed it, it is not possible to attribute direction in a correlational relationship. We do not know, therefore, whether motivation is to be seen as the cause or the result of success in L2 learning or both.

Gardner (1985) claims that motivation constitutes a causative variable, although he is also prepared to accept that some modification of learners' attitudes can arise as a result of positive learning experiences, particularly in courses of a short duration. Spolsky (1989) reviews a number studies (for example, Gardner, Smythe, and Brunet 1977; Gardner, Smythe, and Clement 1979) which suggest that 'while greater motivation and attitudes lead to better learning, the converse is not true' (1989: 153).

Other studies, however, suggest that learners' motivation is strongly affected by their achievement. Strong (1983; 1984) investigated motivation and English language attainment in Spanish-speaking kindergarten children and found that fluency in English preceded an inclination to associate with target-language groups. Savignon (1972) reported that students' desire to learn French increased with gains in French proficiency. Finally, a study by Hermann (1980) also suggested that it is success that contributes to motivation rather than vice-versa. Hermann advanced the 'Resultative Hypothesis', which claims that learners who do well are more likely to develop motivational intensity and to be active in the classroom.

The Resultative Hypothesis may be particularly applicable in contexts where learners have very low initial motivation. Berwick and Ross (1989) investigated 90 first-year Japanese university students majoring in international commerce and taking obligatory English classes. These students had a strong instrumental motivation to learn the English they needed to pass the university entrance examinations, but typically became demotivated once they were at university. Berwick and Ross found little evidence of any motivation on a pre-test administered at the beginning of the English course, but much more on a post-test given at the end. The students' motivation appeared to broaden as a result of the course with two new motivational factors, labelled 'support' and 'interest', emerging. This study provides clear evidence of 'an experiential dimension to learner's motivation'.

It is likely that the relationship between motivation and achievement is an interactive one. A high level of motivation does stimulate learning, but perceived success in achieving L2 goals can help to maintain existing motivation and even create new types. Conversely, a vicious circle of low motivation = low achievement = lower motivation can develop.

Motivation as intrinsic interest

The notion of intrinsic motivation is an old one in psychology. It was developed as an alternative to goal-directed theories of motivation that emphasize the role of extrinsic rewards and punishments. Keller (1984) (cited in Crookes and Schmidt 1989) identifies 'interest' as one of the main elements of motivation, defining it as a positive response to stimuli based on existing cognitive structures in such a way that learners' curiosity is aroused and sustained. It is this view that underlies discussions of motivation in language pedagogy. Crookes and Schmidt (1989: 16) observe that 'it is probably fair to say that teachers would describe a student as motivated if s/he becomes productively engaged on learning tasks, and sustains that engagement, without the need for continual encouragement or direction'. Teachers see it as their job to motivate students by engaging their interest in classroom activities.

One way in which intrinsic interest in L2 learning might be achieved is by providing opportunities for communication. McNamara (1973) has argued that 'the really important part of motivation lies in the act of communication'. Rossier (1975) also emphasizes the importance of a desire to communicate, arguing that without this an integrative motivation may not be effective. It is the need to get meanings across and the pleasure experienced when this is achieved that provides the motivation to learn an L2.

One possibility, supported by a strong pedagogic literature (see Holec 1980 and 1987; Dickinson 1987), is that interest is engendered if learners become self-directed (i.e. are able to determine their own learning objectives, choose their own ways of achieving these, and evaluate their own progress). Dickinson refers to a study by Bachman (1964) which indicated that involving learners in decision-making tended to lead to increased motivation and, thereby, to increased productivity. Gardner, Ginsberg, and Smythe (1976) compared the effects of two sorts of instructional programmes on 25 learners of French at Dalhousie University in Canada. One was very traditional—lockstep teaching with a heavy focus on grammatical accuracy—while the other was innovative, with individualized instruction and opportunity for free communication. The students who experienced the traditional programme indicated that they were more likely to withdraw and had a more negative view of their French teacher. Those who experienced the innovatory programme reported a greater desire to excel and a more positive attitude to learning French. Diary studies also provide evidence to suggest that self-direction is important to learners. For example, J. Schumann (Schumann and Schumann 1977) reports frustration with the instructional programme he was following because of his wish to maintain a personal language learning agenda. It is possible, however, that not all learners will benefit from opportunities for self-direction (see the earlier section on learning style).

Crookes and Schmidt (1989) suggest a number of other ways in which teachers seek to foster intrinsic motivation. They try to make sure that the learning tasks pose a reasonable challenge to the students—neither too difficult nor too easy. They provide opportunities for group work. They base tasks on their perceptions of learners' needs and wants and they try to provide for plenty of variety in classroom activities. Above all, perhaps, they try to ensure that motivation is engendered as a result of a good rapport with the learners. As Finocchiaro (1981) puts it:

> Motivation is the feeling nurtured primarily by the classroom teacher in the learning situation. The moment of truth—the enhancement of motivation—occurs when the teacher closes the classroom door, greets his students with a warm, welcoming smile, and proceeds to interact with various

individuals by making comments or asking questions which indicate personal concern.

However, there has been very little systematic research of the effects these various pedagogic procedures have on motivation.

The effect of motivation

Motivation in L2 learning constitutes one of the most fully researched areas of individual differences. The bulk of the research, however, has focused rather narrowly on integrative and instrumental motivation, relying almost exclusively on self-report questionnaires and correlational designs. Little work on motivation as intrinsic interest has taken place. Also, little attention has been paid to the effect of motivation on the process of learning (as opposed to the product). Crookes and Schmidt (1989) argue that research that links teachers' and learners' actions to persistence and effort in language learning would have a more 'real-world' impact. Skehan (1989; 1991) argues for more research on motivation in naturalistic as opposed to classroom settings.

Personality

In the eyes of many language teachers, the personality of their students constitutes a major factor contributing to success or failure in language learning. Griffiths (1991b), for example, conducted a survey of 98 teachers of ESL/EFL in England, Japan, and Oman in order to determine how important they rated personality and two other IDs. He reports a mean rating of 4 on a five-point scale—slightly higher than the rating for intelligence and just below that for memory. Learners also consider personality factors to be important. Of the 'good language learners' investigated by Naiman et al. (1978) 31 per cent believed that extroversion was helpful in acquiring oral skills. It is somewhat surprising, therefore, to find that the research that has investigated personality variables and L2 learning is so scanty and, in many ways, so unsatisfactory.

This research is broadly summarized in Table 11.8. A number of general observations arise from this summary. First, the personality variables constitute a very mixed bag. Some relate to well-established theories of personality (such as extroversion/introversion) but have been investigated without reference to the theory from which they have been drawn. Others are based only very loosely on constructs in general psychology (for example, risk-taking). Others entail an extension of a psychological construct to make it applicable to L2 learning (for example, Guiora's notion of a 'language ego').

A second observation, evident from the descriptions of the different dimensions of personality in Table 11.8, is that the variables are sometimes vague and overlap in ill-defined ways. The concepts of extroversion, empathy, and

Aspect	Description	Measuring instrument	Main studies	Main results
Extroversion/ introversion	Extroverts are sociable, risk-taking, lively, and active; introverts are quiet and prefer non-social activities.	Eysenck Personality Inventory (EPI)	Busch 1982; Strong 1983	Busch found a negative relationship with L2 proficiency; Strong found that extrovert children learnt faster.
Risk-taking	Risk-takers show less hesitancy, are more willing to use complex language, and are more tolerant of errors. They are less likely to rehearse before speaking.	Self-report questionnaire	Ely 1986a	Risk-taking positively related to voluntary classroom participation.
Tolerance of ambiguity	It entails an ability to deal with ambiguous new stimuli without frustration and without appeals to authority. It allows for indeterminate rather than rigid categorization.	Budners scale; MAT-60 (a self-report measure)	Naiman et al. 1978; Chapelle and Roberts 1986	Naiman et al. found tolerance of ambiguity was significantly related to listening comprehension scores but not to imitation test scores; Chapelle and Roberts found no relationship with proficiency measures.
Empathy	This concerns the ability to put oneself in the position of another person in order to understand him/her better. Empathy is seen as requiring a good understanding of oneself.	Hogan Empathy Scale; Micro-Momentary Expression test (measures perceptions of changes in facial expressions)	Naiman et al. 1978; Guiora et al. 1967	Naiman et al. found no relationship with proficiency; Guiora et al. report a positive correlation with proficiency—a result not clearly replicated in later studies.
Self-esteem	This refers to the degree to which individuals feel confident and believe themselves to be significant people. Self-esteem is manifested at different levels (global, situational, and task)	Self-report questionnaires	Heyde 1979; Gardner and Lambert 1972	Heyde found that self-esteem correlated positively with oral production; Gardner and Lambert failed to find a significant relationship.
Inhibition	The extent to which individuals build defences to protect their egos. People vary in how adaptive their 'language egos' are, i.e. how able they are to deal with the identity conflict involved in L2 learning.	Alcohol and valium administered in differing quantities to reduce inhibition.	Guiora et al. 1972 and 1980	Subjects given alcohol showed better pronunciation; valium had no effect.

Table 11.8:   Dimensions of personality and L2 learning

risk-taking would appear to be related, as would those of self-esteem and inhibition, but in what ways is not clear.

Third, the instruments which have been used to measure (or control) the personality variables are varied and, in some cases, of doubtful validity and reliability. Most of them consist of self-report questionnaires of different kinds (for example, the Eysenck Personality Inventory and the Hogan Empathy Scale). Some of them (such as the ones just mentioned) have been developed by psychologists and have been subjected to extensive testing. Others, however, have been devised specifically for use with L2 learners (such as Ely's and Gardner and Lambert's questionnaires), and it is not always clear that these instruments measure what they purport to measure. This is perhaps most true in the series of studies conducted by Guiora and associates.

In one set of studies (Guiora, Lane, and Bosworth 1967; Taylor, Guiora, Catford, and Lane 1969; Guiora et al. 1972) an instrument known as the Micro-Momentary Expression test was used to measure learners' empathy by having them identify when a woman in a film changed her facial expression. In the first of the studies a positive correlation between empathy (so measured) and accuracy of pronunciation by fourteen French teachers was reported. A subsequent study, however, found no such relationship, while a third study found a positive relationship for some languages and a negative one for others. In another set of studies (Guiora et al. 1972; Guiora, Acton, Erard, and Strickland 1980) learners were administered quantities of alcohol and valium in order to reduce their level of inhibition. Alcohol resulted in better pronunciation but valium did not—a result that has interesting possibilities for application in language teaching! However, as H. Brown (1987) has pointed out, even the positive results obtained for alcohol cannot be interpreted as showing that reduced inhibition facilitates L2 pronunciation, as it is possible that the effects of the alcohol were due to reduced muscular tension (a purely physical phenomenon). While not all the studies mentioned in Table 11.8 are of such doubtful validity as Guiora's, instrumentation is a general problem.

A fourth observation based on Table 11.8 is that the results obtained by different studies are inconsistent. Thus, whereas Naiman et al. (1978) found a positive relationship between tolerance of ambiguity and scores on a listening comprehension test, they failed to find any relationship with scores on an imitation test. Chapelle and Roberts (1986) also report low correlations between this personality factor and criterion measures of L2 proficiency. Similar inconsistencies can be observed in the main results for extroversion, empathy, and self-esteem. One explanation is that different instruments were used to measure the same personality variable, but this is not always the case (as can be seen in Naiman et al.'s results). The main problem is that there is often no theoretical basis for predicting which personality variables will be positively or negatively related to which aspects of L2 proficiency.

It is easy to take a rather bleak view of personality studies in SLA research. There follows a detailed discussion of the research that has examined one aspect of personality—extroversion/introversion—which shows that the study of personality does hold considerable promise.

Extroversion/introversion

The *extroversion/introversion* distinction refers to one of several dimensions or traits which together constitute an individual's personality (see Eysenck 1970; Cattell 1956). In Eysenck's theory, for example, there are three major dimensions—extroversion/introversion, neurotic/stable and psychotic/normal. In choosing to investigate the extroversion/introversion distinction, therefore, researchers are investigating only one aspect of learners' personality.[5]

Extroversion/introversion represents a continuum (i.e. individuals can be more or less extroverted), but it is possible to identify idealized types:

> Extraverts are sociable, like parties, have many friends and need excitement; they are sensation-seekers and risk-takers, like practical jokes and are lively and active. Conversely introverts are quiet, prefer reading to meeting people, have few but close friends and usually avoid excitement. (Eysenck and Chan 1982: 154)

The extent to which individuals verge towards one of these types is usually measured by analysing responses to self-report questions such as those in the Eysenck Personality Questionnaire.

There are two major hypotheses regarding the relationship between extroversion/introversion and L2 learning. The first—which has been the most widely researched—is that extroverted learners will do better in acquiring basic interpersonal communication skills (BICS). The rationale for this hypothesis is that sociability (an essential feature of extroversion) will result in more opportunities to practise, more input, and more success in communicating in the L2. The second hypothesis is that introverted learners will do better at developing cognitive academic language ability (CALP). The rationale for this hypothesis comes from studies which show that introverted learners typically enjoy more academic success, perhaps because they spend more time reading and writing (see Griffiths 1991b).

There is some support for the first hypothesis. Strong (1983) reviewed the results of 12 studies which had investigated extroversion or similar traits (sociability, empathy, outgoingness, and popularity). He shows that in the 8 studies where the criterion measure was 'natural communicative language' and which, therefore, provided an indication of BICS, 6 of them showed that extroversion was an advantage. Strong then reports his own study of 13 Spanish-speaking kindergarten children in which various dimensions of personality were investigated using both classroom observation and Coan and

Cattell's (1966) Early School Personality Questionnaire. Interestingly, he found that those measures derived from observation accounted for nearly all the statistically significant correlations with language measures based on the children's natural communicative language. The important variables were talkativeness, responsiveness, and gregariousness, all of which are behaviours associated with extroversion.

The second hypothesis has received less support. Strong's survey of studies that have investigated the effects of introversion on 'linguistic task language' reveals that less than half report a significant relationship. Busch (1982), in a study not included in Strong's survey, also failed to find a relationship. She used the Eysenck Personality Inventory to obtain measures of extroversion/introversion. Her subjects were adolescent and adult Japanese learners of English in Japan. The correlations between extroversion and scores on a four-part written proficiency test were non-significant (with one exception) and generally negative in the case of the adolescents, and non-significant but positive in the case of the adults. This study, then, also fails to lend much support to the hypothesis that introversion aids the development of academic language skills. Interestingly, Busch also failed to find a clear relationship between extroversion and scores on an oral interview test (presumably more representative of BICS). It is possible that extroversion/introversion has little to do with L2 learning in Japan because the classroom situation requires all learners to exhibit introverted-type behaviour out of respect for the teacher.

One profitable line of enquiry might be to investigate the relations between personality variables and the different kinds of behaviours that learners engage in. Ehrman (1990) examined the relationship between personality and choice of learning strategies in a study we will consider in the next chapter. Robson (1992) undertook a small-scale study of Japanese college students, measuring personality by means of the Yatabe/Guilford Personality Inventory, and obtaining measures of voluntary participation from oral English classes. His general finding was that learners who are extrovert and emotionally stable were more likely to engage in oral participation than introverts and neurotics. It does not follow, of course, that such learners will be more successful, as high levels of classroom participation may not enhance L2 learning.

To sum up, the evidence linking extroversion to the acquisition of BICS is fairly substantial, but there is no clear support for the claim that introversion benefits the acquisition of CALP. Furthermore, the effects of extroversion/introversion may be situation-dependent, evident in some learning contexts but not in others. Also, there is a suggestion (in Strong's research) that better results may be obtained when the measures of extroversion/introversion are based on observation than when they are based on self-report questionnaires. Finally, it should be noted that better results may be obtained if researchers explore specific interactions between personality measures such as extroversion/introversion and learners' performance under different instructional conditions, as suggested by Griffiths (1991b).

Summary

The following statements constitute a general summary of the research reviewed in the previous sections. Readers are also referred to the summary statements at the end of each section in this chapter.

1 Beliefs

Learners have been found to hold different beliefs about how an L2 is best learnt. These differences reflect their past learning experiences and general factors such as learning style and personality.

2 Affective state

Learners' affective states vary dynamically and have a significant impact on their ability to learn. Anxiety arising out of poor performance, communication apprehension, tests, and fear of negative evaluation is likely to have a debilitating effect on L2 learning, but it can also have a facilitative effect. How anxiety affects learning will depend on its strength and the situational context.

3 Age

Children generally enjoy an advantage over adults in L2 learning because of their age, particularly in pronunciation. However, this will only become evident after substantial exposure to the L2. In the short term, adults may learn faster. The evidence relating to the existence of a critical period for L2 acquisition, after which full competence is not possible, is mixed, with no definite conclusion possible. Children and adults manifest similar processes of learning.

4 Aptitude

Both quantitative and qualitative differences in language aptitude have been found. These relate to the development of both linguistic and communicative L2 abilities. Language aptitude involves both an underlying language learning capacity and a capacity to handle decontextualized language. Language aptitude has been found to be one of the best predictors of L2 learning.

5 Learning style

Learners manifest different learning styles (for example, analytical v. experiential) but it is not yet clear whether some styles result in faster and more learning than others. The distinction between field dependent and field independent, which has attracted considerable interest in SLA research, is best treated as a distinction of ability rather than style. In many studies, it does not emerge as a major factor in L2 learning.

6 Motivation

Strength of motivation serves as a powerful predictor of L2 achievement, but may itself by the result of previous learning experiences. Learners with either integrative or instrumental motivation, or a mixture of both, will manifest greater effort and perseverance in learning. Other internal sources of motivation, such as self-confidence, may be more important than either type of motivation in some contexts. Motivation can also take the form of intrinsic interest in specific learning activities and, as such, may be more easily influenced by teachers than goal-directed motivation.

7 Personality

The relationship between personality variables and L2 learning is not yet clear. There is some evidence to show that extroverted learners are advantaged in the development of the kind of language associated with basic interpersonal communication skills. Extroverted learners may also be more likely to participate actively in oral communication.

These individual differences produce variation in the rate of learning and the ultimate level of L2 attainment. Overall, there is little evidence to suggest that they have a marked effect on the internal processes that account for interlanguage development.

Conclusion

As Skehan (1991) has pointed out there is still no comprehensive theory of IDs in SLA research. A full theory will need to identify those IDs that are important for successful learning, indicate the relative contribution of particular IDs to learning, specify how IDs interrelate, account for their influence on the learner's choice of specific strategies, and account for the effect that learning outcomes can have on IDs. It will also have to make clear what effect (if any) IDs have on the process of L2 acquisition.

One way of viewing IDs is as conditions of learning (Spolsky 1989). In general, IDs constitute 'typical' and 'graded' rather than 'necessary' conditions. For example, learners do not have to have a high aptitude or a particular learning style or one type of personality in order to learn an L2. Rather, some learners do better than others because they satisfy the conditions for learning relating to these IDs to a greater extent. Some of the factors, however, might be viewed as necessary conditions. For example, it may be necessary for learners to start learning an L2 before puberty if they are to acquire a native pronunciation. Similarly, learners probably need at least a modicum of motivation to learn anything.

Research into IDs to date has told us little about the relative strength of different learner factors or how they interrelate. Gardner's research has shown that aptitude and motivation constitute separate factors, both accounting for a substantial amount of the variance in learners' L2 proficiency. These factors have explanatory power. However, the picture is less certain where many of the other factors (in particular learning style and personality) are concerned. This is largely because the various constructs that have been investigated have not been defined with sufficient rigour and have been poorly operationalized. These factors do not have much explanatory power at the moment.

Two views regarding the nature of the relationship between IDs and L2 learning are possible. According to the aggregate view, success is the result of the accumulative effect of facilitative IDS. For example, a child with low anxiety, high overall language aptitude, an inclination to be analytic, strong integrative motivation, and an outgoing personality could be considered likely to succeed. According to the alternative view, there are many ways to achieve success and it is not possible to draw up a single profile of the successful learner. This view of IDs has important implications for language instruction because it acknowledges the need to take account of learner–instruction interactions (i.e. to recognize that different learners can achieve the same level of success if the instruction matches their own preferred approach to learning). Learner–treatment interactions will be examined in Chapter 14.

As Skehan (1991) notes, ID research has been primarily concatenative in approach. It has been mainly concerned with scale and test construction and has employed statistical techniques to identify the interrelationships among the multiple influences on learning and their relationship to L2 achievement. This approach has a number of problems, not least the question of how best to measure ID and criterion variables. Although Skehan considers the 'fertility' of the concatenative approach 'far from exhausted' (1991: 292), he also argues for more studies that employ a naturalistic methodology. Such studies can shed light on the individuality of single learners and can also show the dynamic nature of the interaction between the more malleable aspects of individual difference (for example, anxiety and motivation) and learners' learning experiences. A further advantage of naturalistic studies is that they can provide measures of learning based on natural language use rather than on tests or ratings, a major need in ID research.

Notes

1 A study by Castagnaro (1992) has attempted to use physiological measures of learners' classroom anxiety and, interestingly, found sizeable and significant positive correlations between these measures and measures of anxiety obtained from anxiety questionnaires.

2 One of the interesting results obtained by Coppieters was that the differences between the native-speaker and non-native-speaker judgements were not uniform. Coppieters reports that divergence was less marked in constructions 'normally covered by the term UG' and more marked in 'functional' distinctions (for example, *passé composé* v. *imparfait*). This result, then, provides support for the claim that adult L2 learners have continued access to UG (see Chapter 10). It should be noted, however, that Birdsong's (1992) replication of Coppieter's study failed to find that native-speaker/ non-native-speaker divergences were explicable in terms of UG and non-UG constructions.

3 Ioup (1989) also investigated an L2 learner who began L2 learning as a child but still failed to acquire native-speaker ability despite very favourable learning conditions. However, in this case the learner did acquire a native accent, failing only to acquire certain grammatical and semantic distinctions. Ioup finds this surprising, commenting that 'one would assume that the ability to acquire the phonology would imply the ability to acquire syntax and semantics' (1989: 171). It is possible, however, that her subject's difficulty with grammar and semantics reflects the general difficulty she experienced where cognitive academic language ability (CALP) is concerned—a difficulty that many native speakers may also experience.

4 There is also the Embedded Figures Test (EFT) and the Child Embedded Figures Test (CEFT). Different versions of these tests also exist. One of the problems claimed by Griffiths and Sheen (1991) is the lack of equivalence of these different versions.

5 There are, in fact, several approaches to describing and investigating personality in the psychological literature. Whereas Eysenck's trait theory has been influential in Britain, factor analytic models (for example, Cattell 1956) have been popular in the United States. Robson (1993), in a review of these (and other) theories, claims that the traits of neuroticism and extroversion are the 'most unquestionably basic' in that they figure in all approaches.

Further reading

Surveys of individual differences in second language learners

Skehan's surveys of the research into individual differences are comprehensive, objective, and very readable:

P. Skehan, *Individual Differences in Second-Language Learning* (Edward Arnold, 1989).

P. Skehan, 'Individual differences in second language learning'. *Studies in Second Language Acquisition* (1991) 13: 275–98.

Another very readable but more subjective account of many of the particular individual differences discussed in this chapter can be found in:
H. D. Brown, *Principles of Language Learning and Teaching* (2nd Edition) (Prentice Hall, 1987).
A useful overview of quantitative research is:
R. Gardner, 'Second Language Learning in Adults: Correlates of Proficiency'. *Applied Language Learning* (1991) 2: 1–29.

Suggested readings for particular IDs

Beliefs

E. Horwitz, 'Surveying student beliefs about language learning' in A. Wenden and J. Rubin (eds.): *Learning Strategies in Language Learning* (Prentice Hall, 1987).

Affective factors (anxiety)

K. Bailey, 'Competitiveness and anxiety in adult second language learning: looking at and through the diary studies' in H. Seliger and M. Long (eds.): *Classroom Oriented Research in Second Language Acquisition* (Newbury House, 1983).
E. Horwitz and D. Young, *Language Learning Anxiety: From Theory and Research to Classroom Implications* (Prentice Hall, 1991).

Age

There are a number of excellent books dealing with the age issue:
D. Singleton, *Language Acquisition: The Age Factor* (Multilingual Matters, 1989).
T. Scovel, *A Time to Speak: a Psycholinguistic Inquiry into the Critical Period for Human Speech* (Newbury House, 1988).
B. Harley, *Age in Second Language Acquisition* (Multilingual Matters, 1986).
In addition, Long provides a thoughtful and provocative discussion of the Critical Period Hypothesis:
M. Long, 'Maturational constraints on language development'. *Studies in Second Language Acquisition* (1990) 12: 251–85.
There are many individual studies of the age issue. A recent very interesting one is
D. Birdsong, 'Ultimate attainment in second language acquisition'. *Language* (1992): 68: 706–55.

Aptitude

A number of important articles on language aptitude can be found in:
K. Diller (ed.), *Individual Differences and Universals in Language Aptitude*, (see in particular the articles by Carroll and Wesche) (Newbury House, 1981).
Also recommended is:
J. Carroll, 'Cognitive abilities in foreign language aptitude: then and now' in T. Parry and C. Stansfield (eds.): *Language Aptitude Reconsidered* (Prentice Hall Regents, 1990).

Learning style

A useful general account of learning styles, together with an account of one study, can be found in:
K. Willing, *Learning Styles in Adult Migrant Education* (Adult Migrant Education Resource Centre: National Curriculum Resource Centre, 1988).
Perhaps a good way into the wealth of literature on FI/FD in SLA research is Griffiths and Sheen's polemical critique:
R. Griffiths and R. Sheen, 'Disembedded figures in the landscape: a reappraisal of L2 research on field dependence-independence'. *Applied Linguistics* (1992) 13: 133–48.
C. Chapelle's response to it is in *Applied Linguistics* (1992) 13: 375–84.

Motivation

A good summary of Gardner's work and views on motivation can be found in:
R. Gardner, *Social Psychology and Second Language Learning: The Role of Attitudes and Motivation* (Edward Arnold 1985).
Numerous articles on motivation can be found in *Language Learning*, including the important:
G. Crookes and R. Schmidt, 'Motivation: reopening the research agenda'. *University of Hawaii Working Papers in ESL* (1989) 8: 217–56.

Personality

The literature is less impressive on personality, but Strong provides a useful survey of the early research together with an account of his own study:
M. Strong, 'Social styles and the second language acquisition of Spanish-speaking kindergartners'. *TESOL Quarterly* (1983) 17: 241–58.

12   Learning strategies

Introduction

In the last chapter we investigated individual differences by looking at the relationship between various learner factors and learning outcomes. However, little was said about the mechanisms that establish these relationships. In this chapter we will consider the mediating role of *learning strategies*. According to the model of L2 acquisition shown in Figure 12.1, individual learner differences (beliefs, affective states, general factors, and previous learning experiences) together with various situational factors (the target language being studied, whether the setting is formal or informal, the nature of the instruction, and the specific tasks learners are asked to perform) determine the learners' choice of learning strategies. These then influence two aspects of learning: the rate of acquisition and the ultimate level of achievement. The success that learners experience and their level of L2 proficiency can also affect their choice of strategies.

The study of learning strategies has seen an 'explosion of activity' in recent years (Skehan 1991: 285). In this chapter we will examine the main findings of this research. We will begin by considering a number of definitions of 'learning strategy' and then consider the main methods that have been used to investigate them. This will be followed by a discussion of various frameworks for classifying learning strategies. The next section will deal with the factors that influence learners' choice of strategies. The relationship between learning strategies and L2 learning is considered with reference to studies of the 'good language learner', cross-sectional studies that try to identify correlations between strategy use and L2 proficiency, and longitudinal studies of groups of learners. Finally, attempts to train learners to employ particular strategies will be considered.

Defining 'learning strategies'

The concept of 'strategy' is a somewhat fuzzy one, and, as we noted in the introduction to Part Four, not easy to tie down. There we settled for a general definition; a strategy consisted of mental or behavioural activity related to some specific stage in the overall process of language acquisition or language use. We will now examine a little more fully what a 'strategy' consists of in an attempt to arrive at a definition of 'learning strategy'.

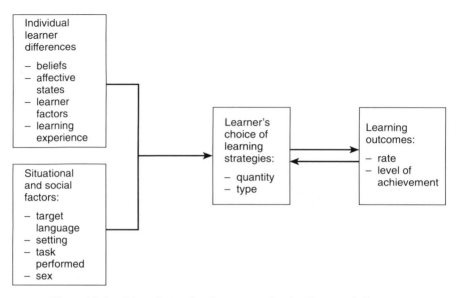

Figure 12.1:   The relationship between individual learner differences,
situational factors, learning strategies, and learning outcomes

A distinction is often made between three types of strategies: production, communication, and learning. Tarone (1980b: 419) considers the first two of these under the heading 'Strategies of language use'. A *production strategy* consists of 'an attempt to use one's linguistic system efficiently and clearly, with a minimum of effort'. Examples are simplification, rehearsal, and discourse planning. Communication strategies, which we examined in some detail in Chapter 9, consist of attempts to deal with problems of communication that have arisen in interaction. A language learning strategy is 'an attempt to develop linguistic and sociolinguistic competence in the target language'. Examples given by Tarone include memorization, initiation of conversation with native speakers, and inferencing. These distinctions are important, but as Tarone observes, they are not easily applied as they rest on learners' intentions which are often not clear or easy to establish. There is, for example, no easy way of telling whether a strategy is motivated by a desire to learn or a desire to communicate.

It is also useful to distinguish two types of learning strategy: language learning strategies and skill learning strategies. The former, as defined by Tarone, are concerned with the learners' attempts to master new linguistic and sociolinguistic information about the target language. The latter are concerned with the learners' attempts to become skilled listeners, speakers, readers, or writers. Writers, for instance, employ a variety of strategies for exploiting teachers' feedback on their written compositions (see Cohen 1987; 1991). Again, however, the distinction is not an easy one and the literature on learning strategies does not always distinguish clearly between these two

Source	Definition
Stern 1983	'In our view strategy is best reserved for general tendencies or overall characteristics of the approach employed by the language learner, leaving techniques as the term to refer to particular forms of observable learning behaviour.'
Weinstein and Mayer 1986	'Learning strategies are the behaviours and thoughts that a learner engages in during learning that are intended to influence the learner's encoding process.'
Chamot 1987	'Learning strategies are techniques, approaches or deliberate actions that students take in order to facilitate the learning, recall of both linguistic and content area information.'
Rubin 1987	'Learning strategies are strategies which contribute to the development of the language system which the learner constructs and affect learning directly.'
Oxford 1989	'Language learning strategies are behaviours or actions which learners use to make language learning more successful, self-directed and enjoyable.'

Table 12.1:   Definitions of learning strategies

types. Cohen (1990: 15), for instance, refers to learning strategies directed at the 'language skill' of 'vocabulary learning', although this is clearly an aspect of linguistic knowledge. The focus of this chapter will be on language learning strategies.

A sample of definitions of language learning strategies taken from the recent literature (see Table 12.1) reveals a number of problems. It is not clear whether they are to be perceived of as behavioural (and, therefore, observable) or as mental, or as both. Oxford (1989) appears to see them as essentially behavioural, whereas Weinstein and Mayer (1986) see them as both behavioural and mental.

A second problem concerns the precise nature of the behaviours that are to count as learning strategies. Here there is considerable uncertainty. Stern (1983) distinguishes 'strategies' and 'techniques'. The former are defined as general and more or less deliberate 'approaches' to learning (for example, 'an active task approach'), whereas the latter constitute observable forms of language learning behaviour evident in particular areas of language learning such as grammar (for example, 'inferring grammar rules from texts') and vocabulary (for example, 'using a dictionary when necessary'). Other researchers, however, have used the term 'strategy' to refer to the kind of behaviours Stern calls techniques.

A third problem is whether learning strategies are to be seen as conscious and intentional or as subconscious. Many of the definitions in Table 12.1 avoid addressing this issue, but Chamot (1987) refers to them as 'deliberate actions'. Seliger (1984) distinguishes 'strategies' and 'tactics'. He defines the former as 'basic abstract categories of processing by which information perceived in the outside world is organized and categorized into cognitive structures as part of a conceptual network' (1984: 4). In contrast, 'tactics' are variable and idiosyncratic learning activities, which learners use to organize a learning situation, respond to the learning environment, or cope with input and output demands. This distinction is helpful. It is clear that what Seliger refers to as 'strategies' was what we were focusing on in Chapter 9 when we examined various cognitive theories of L2 learning. What he calls 'tactics' is the focus of the present chapter. However, as we will shortly see, not all researchers make such a clear distinction between 'strategies' and 'tactics' on the basis of consciousness. Some consider that what starts out as a conscious 'tactic' may evolve into a subconscious 'strategy'. Also, useful as it might be to make a terminological distinction along the lines proposed by Seliger, L2 acquisition researchers have not done so, using the term 'strategy' to refer to both conscious and subconscious activities. We will follow suit in this chapter, although our focus will be on learning strategies as conscious or at least potentially conscious actions which learners employ intentionally (i.e. Seliger's 'tactics').

A fourth problem concerns whether learning strategies are seen as having a direct or an indirect effect on interlanguage development. Rubin (1987), somewhat controversially, asserts that the effect is a direct one. But other researchers, such as Seliger, consider it to be more indirect—strategy use provides learners with data, upon which the 'deep' subconscious processes can work.

Finally, there are differences in opinions about what motivates the use of learning strategies. All the definitions in Table 12.1 recognize that they are used in an effort to *learn* something about the L2, but Oxford (1989) also suggests that their use can have an affective purpose (i.e. to increase enjoyment).

Perhaps one of the best approaches to defining learning strategies is to try to list their main characteristics. The following list characterizes how the term 'strategies' has been used in the studies to be considered in this chapter:

1 Strategies refer to both general approaches and specific actions or techniques used to learn an L2.
2 Strategies are problem-orientated—the learner deploys a strategy to overcome some particular learning problem.
3 Learners are generally aware of the strategies they use and can identify what they consist of if they are asked to pay attention to what they are doing/thinking.
4 Strategies involve linguistic behaviour (such as requesting the name of an object) and non-linguistic (such as pointing at an object so as to be told its name).
5 Linguistic strategies can be performed in the L1 and in the L2.
6 Some strategies are behavioural while others are mental. Thus some strategies are directly observable, while others are not.

7 In the main, strategies contribute indirectly to learning by providing learners with data about the L2 which they can then process. However, some strategies may also contribute directly (for example, memorization strategies directed at specific lexical items or grammatical rules).
8 Strategy use varies considerably as a result of both the kind of task the learner is engaged in and individual learner preferences.

Definitions of learning strategies have tended to be *ad hoc* and atheoretical. However, O'Malley, Chamot, and Walker (1987) and O'Malley and Chamot (1990) have attempted to ground the study of learning strategies within the information-processing model of learning developed by Anderson (1980; 1983), which we considered briefly in Chapter 9. We noted that Anderson distinguishes three stages of skill-learning: (1) the cognitive stage, where the learner is involved in conscious activity resulting in declarative knowledge, (2) the associative stage, where the learner strengthens the connections among the various elements or components of the skill and constructs more efficient production sets, and (3) the automatic stage, where execution becomes more or less autonomous and subconscious. Anderson's theory provides for two interpretations of the term 'strategy'. One, favoured by Rabinowitz and Chi (1987, cited in O'Malley and Chamot 1990) is that strategies only occur in the early cognitive stage when they are conscious; they cease to be 'strategic' when they are performed automatically. The other view is that strategies occur in all three stages of development. They take the form of production sets (i.e. 'if ... then' statements). For example, the strategy of inferencing has this form:

> *If* the goal is to comprehend an oral or written text, and I am unable to identify a word's meaning, *then* I will try to infer the meaning from context.

Initially, such sets exist only in declarative form; they are conscious and can only be accessed through controlled processing. Gradually, they are proceduralized, until a point is reached where the learner is no longer conscious of employing them. This is the view that Chamot and O'Malley seem to hold. However, this difference in view may not be of much significance as strategies can only be effectively studied in the declarative stage of learning, when learners are able to verbalize them. For research purposes, therefore, strategies can be defined as production sets that exist as declarative knowledge and are used to solve some learning problem.

Methods used to investigate learning strategies

Attempts have been made to identify different learning strategies by observing learners performing a variety of tasks, usually in classroom settings. Some researchers have found this approach to be 'not very productive' (Rubin 1981), since it reveals nothing about the mental operations learners use and, frequently, classrooms afford little opportunity for learners to exercise behavioural strategies. Naiman et al. (1978) and Cohen and Aphek (1981) also comment on the failure of classroom observation to provide much information about learners' strategies. Chesterfield and Chesterfield (1985), however, were able to report on a number of strategies that young children used in a bilingual classroom. It may be, therefore, that observation works with young children, whose behaviour may serve as a good indicator of their mental activity, but not with adult learners, who often engage in internal processing not linked to actual behaviour.

A method that has been found to be more successful involves the use of structured interviews and questionnaires, both of which call for retrospective accounts of the strategies learners employ. A large number of studies have used these methods (for example, Naiman et al. 1978; Rubin 1981; Politzer and McGroarty 1985; Oxford 1985; Wenden 1986a; Chamot 1987). Interviews and questionnaires can require learners to report on the learning strategies they use in general or in relation to a specific activity. For example, Naiman et al. (1978: 108) asked fairly general questions about the techniques learners used for studying the sound system, grammar, vocabulary, and the four skills:

> Would you say that you have developed any language habits (gimmicks, tricks, ways and techniques) that you would find useful in learning a new language?
> 1) in learning the sound system
> e.g. reading aloud to yourself (in front of a mirror), repeating words silently to yourself after the teacher etc.

Wenden (1987a) conducted interviews in which she asked learners to comment on specific learning activities. She had them first complete a 'Grid of daily activities' and then asked them to 'recreate' each activity by describing it. Finally, she asked more specific questions relating to the strategies they used to express themselves, to understand what was said to them, and to think in the L2. Methods such as these have provided the most detailed information about learning strategies, although Rubin (1981) notes that learners vary greatly in their ability to describe their strategies and that most of the students she investigated needed to be tutored in self-reporting.

Diary studies serve as another way of collecting information on learning strategies by means of retrospective reports. As we saw in Chapter 11, the diary studies have been primarily used to shed light on the learners' affective states and how these influence learning. Some researchers, however, have used them to explore learning strategies (for example, Brown 1985; Parkinson and Howell-Richardson 1990).

Think-aloud tasks that require concurrent reporting have also been used profitably (for example, by Abraham and Vann 1987; Mangubhai 1991). These require learners to introspect on the strategies they employ while performing a particular task. In general, think-aloud tasks may tell us more about skill learning (such as translation) than language learning strategies (see articles in Færch and Kasper 1987), although Mangubhai's study of the reception strategies used by students when they responded to oral commands shows that they can also shed light on the use of learning strategies.

It is not always practical to use think-aloud tasks. Beginner learners will only be able describe the strategies they use in their L1, and this may interfere with the way in which they perform the learning task. Also, learners may vary in their ability to think aloud as they perform the task, with the result that the strategies uncovered by such research may reflect the learning activities of a rather special group of learners. There are, however, other ways in which learners can be induced to verbalize their strategies.

One way is to ask learners to work in pairs to discuss their solutions to particular tasks. Haastrup (1987) has used this technique to good effect in a study of lexical inferencing strategies used by Danish learners of English. She found that 'pair thinking aloud' provided 'rich and informative data' (1987: 202), although she points to the problem of 'enormous variability between protocols', suggesting that the learners' ability to verbalize their strategies was still an issue. Morren (1993) also used pair thinking aloud, but allowed his Japanese subjects to discuss in their L1, a procedure that worked well with these learners, who possessed little oral ability in English.

Many of the most successful studies have employed multiple data collection procedures (for example, retrospective accounts obtained through interviews together with introspective accounts of performance on specific tasks). As O'Malley and Chamot (1990: 95) point out, a disconcerting feature of this approach is that the strategies identified by each procedure often vary considerably.

Many of the earlier studies of learner strategies (for example, Naiman et al. 1978) were entirely exploratory, aiming at identifying and describing a broad range of strategies. More recent studies (for example, O'Malley 1987; Manghubai 1991) have tended to focus on the strategies used to learn while performing individual tasks.

Classifying learning strategies

Much of the earlier research (for example, Rubin 1975 and 1981; Wong-Fillmore 1976 and 1979; Stern 1975; Naiman et al. 1978) concentrated on compiling inventories of the learning strategies that learners were observed to use or reported using. Little attempt was made to classify the strategies into general categories. The strategies identified tended to reflect the type of learners under study, the setting, and the particular interests of the researchers.

Summarizing this early work, Skehan (1989) identifies three areas common to the different taxonomies. One is 'the learner's capacity to impose himself on the learning situation'. Naiman et al. refer to 'an active task approach', which is evident in such behaviours as seeking out and responding positively to learning opportunities and engaging in practice activities. 'Clarification/ verification', which Rubin (1981) puts at the top of her list of strategies, also belongs to this area. This strategy includes asking for examples of how to use a word or expression, putting words in a sentence to check understanding, looking up words in a dictionary, and paraphrasing a sentence to check understanding. Wong-Fillmore lists two strategies that fall into this area: 'get some expressions' and 'make the most of what you have got'.

The second general area concerns the learner's 'technical predispositions'. Examples are Naiman et al.'s 'realization of language as a system' (which involves making judicious use of crosslingual comparisons, analysing the target language, and making inferences about it), Rubin's 'guessing/inductive inferencing', and Wong-Fillmore's 'look for recurring parts in formulae'.

The third general area involves the learner's capacity to evaluate. For example, Naiman et al. and Rubin both refer to the importance of monitoring. This involves testing out guesses, correcting errors, and noting the sources of errors.

However, the early taxonomies differ in a number of ways, reflecting the particular subjects that the researchers worked with. Thus Rubin and Naiman et al., who elicited information from adults, emphasize the importance of learners reflecting on their own learning and of conscious analysis, while Wong-Fillmore, who studied 5–7-year-old Spanish-speaking children in play situations, emphasizes the social aspects of learning. For example, Rubin lists 'memorization' and 'deductive reasoning' among her strategies, while Wong-Fillmore identifies 'join a group' and 'count on your friends' as important. These differences also seem to reflect whether the setting is a formal or informal one, raising the possibility that the learning strategies involved in classroom and naturalistic acquisition may not be the same.

Subsequent descriptive studies have endeavoured to identify broad classes of learning strategies, under which large numbers of more specific strategies can be grouped. The work of O'Malley and Chamot (for example, O'Malley et al. 1985a and 1985b; O'Malley and Chamot 1990), Wenden (1991), and Oxford (1990) has made an important contribution to our knowledge of learning strategies.

In O'Malley and Chamot's framework (see Table 12.2, pages 537–8), three major types of strategy are distinguished, in accordance with the information-processing model, on which their research is based. *Cognitive strategies* refer to 'the steps or operations used in problem-solving that require direct analysis, transformation or synthesis of learning materials' (Rubin 1987). They have an operative or cognitive-processing function. Among the cognitive strategies listed by Chamot (1987) are 'repetition' (imitating a language model, either covertly or overtly), 'note-taking' (writing down information presented orally), and 'elaboration' (relating new concepts to other information in memory). Cognitive strategies such as these appear to be directly linked to the performance of particular learning tasks. *Metacognitive*

Learning Strategy	Description
Metacognitive	
Advance organizers	Making a general but comprehensive preview of the concept or principle in an anticipated learning activity.
Directed attention	Deciding in advance to attend in general to a learning task and to ignore irrelevant distractors.
Selective attention	Deciding in advance to attend to specific aspects of language input or situational details that will cue the retention of language input.
Self-management	Understanding the conditions that help one learn and arranging for the presence of those conditions.
Advance preparation	Planning for and rehearsing linguistic components necessary to carry out an upcoming language task.
Self-monitoring	Correcting one's speech for accuracy in pronunciation, grammar, vocabulary, or for appropriateness related to the setting or to the people who are present.
Delayed production	Consciously deciding to postpone speaking to learn initially through listening comprehension.
Self-evaluation	Checking the outcomes of one's own language learning against an internal measure of completeness and accuracy.
Cognitive	
Repetition	Imitating a language model, including overt practice and silent rehearsal.
Resourcing	Defining or expanding a definition of a word or concept through use of target language reference materials.
Directed physical response	Relating new information to physical actions, as with directives.
Translation	Using the first language as a base for understanding and/or producing the second language.
Grouping	Reordering or reclassifying and perhaps labelling the material to be learned based on common attributes.
Note-taking	Writing down the main idea, important points, outline, or summary of information presented orally or in writing.
Deduction	Consciously applying rules to produce or understand the second language.
Recombination	Constructing a meaningful sentence or larger language sequence by combining known elements in a new way.
Imagery	Relating new information to visual concepts in memory via familiar easily retrievable visualizations, phrases, or locations.
Auditory representation	Retention of the sound or similar sound for a word, phrase, or longer language sequence.

Learning Strategy	Description
Key word	Remembering a new word in the second language by (1) identifying a familiar word in the first language that sounds like or otherwise resembles the new word, and (2) generating easily recalled images of some relationship with the new word.
Contextualization	Placing a word or phrase in a meaningful language sequence.
Elaboration	Relating new information to other concepts in memory.
Transfer	Using previously acquired linguistic and/or conceptual knowledge to facilitate a new language learning task.
Inferencing	Using available information to guess meanings of new items, predict outcomes, or fill in missing information.
Social/affective Cooperation	Working with one or more peers to obtain feedback, pool information, or model a language activity.
Question for clarification	Asking a teacher or other native speaker for repetition, paraphrasing, explanation and/or examples.

Table 12.2:   O'Malley and Chamot's typology of learning strategies (Chamot 1987)

strategies make use of knowledge about cognitive processes and constitute an attempt to regulate language learning by means of planning, monitoring, and evaluating. They have an executive function. Examples given by Chamot are 'directed attention' (deciding in advance to pay attention to specific aspects of language input) and 'self-management' (displaying understanding of the conditions which help learning and trying to bring these about). Chamot gives examples from interviews with ESL learners of the kinds of behaviours that are representative of these strategies. Self-management, for instance, is evident in the following comments from learners:

> I sit in the front of the class so I can see the teacher's face clearly.

> It's a good idea to mix with non-Hispanics because you're forced to practise your English. If you talk with a Chinese who is also studying English you have to practise the language because it is the only way to communicate.

Social/affective strategies concern the ways in which learners elect to interact with other learners and native speakers. Chamot gives as examples 'co-operation' ('working with one or more peers to obtain feedback, pool information or model a language activity') and 'question for clarification' ('asking a teacher or other native speaker for repetition, paraphrase, explanation and/or examples').

Wenden's (1983) research examined the strategies that adult foreign language learners use in order to direct their own learning. Her focus, therefore, is on what O'Malley and Chamot call metacognitive strategies. She identifies three general categories of self-directing strategies: (1) knowing about language (relating to what language and language learning involves), (2) planning (relating to the what and how of language learning), and (3) self-evaluation (relating to progress in learning and the learner's response to the learning experience). Wenden found that adult learners pose questions relating to each category and then take decisions depending on the kind of answers they come up with. For example, in the planning category, learners might ask 'What should I learn and how?' and then go on to decide on linguistic objectives, resources, and use of resources. Wenden's framework was devised as a basis for learner training.

Perhaps the most comprehensive classification of learning strategies to date is that provided by Oxford. Oxford built on the earlier classifications with the aim of subsuming within her taxonomy virtually every strategy previously mentioned in the literature. The classification scheme she first came up with (Oxford 1985) was used as a basis for constructing a questionnaire on learning strategies. The Strategy Inventory for Language Learning (SILL) (Oxford 1986) contained items tapping sixty-four individual strategies divided into two main groups, primary strategies and support strategies (which correspond closely to O'Malley and Chamot's cognitive and metacognitive types). The inventory has undergone considerable revision since, as has the taxonomy of strategies.

In Oxford (1990) a new taxonomy is presented, the general framework of which is shown in Figure 12.2. A general distinction is drawn between direct and indirect strategies. The former consist of 'strategies that directly involve the target language' in the sense that they 'require mental processing of the language' (1990: 37), while the latter 'provide indirect support for language learning through focusing, planning, evaluating, seeking opportunities, controlling anxiety, increasing cooperation and empathy and other means' (1990: 151). The subcategories of direct and indirect strategies shown in Figure 12.2 have familiar labels. Each subcategory is broken down into two further levels. For example, one type of cognitive strategy is 'practising', which consists of five different kinds of behaviour (repeating, formally practising, recognizing and using formulas, recombining, and practising naturalistically). The scheme is marred by a failure to make a clear distinction between strategies directed at learning the L2 and those directed at using it. Thus, somewhat confusingly, 'compensation strategies' are classified as a direct type of 'learning strategy'. In this Oxford departs from other researchers, who treat compensation strategies as distinct from learning strategies (for example, Rubin 1987). However, the organization of specific strategies into a hierarchy of levels and the breadth of the taxonomy is impressive.

Considerable progress has been made in classifying learning strategies. From the early beginnings, when researchers did little more than list strategies, comprehensive, multi-levelled, and theoretically-motivated

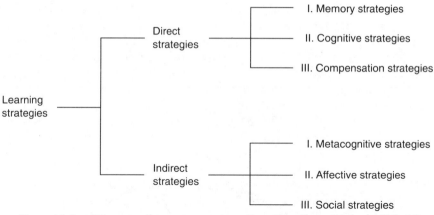

Figure 12.2:   Diagram of a strategy system: Overview (from Oxford 1990: 16)

taxonomies have been developed. The frameworks developed by O'Malley and Chamot, Wenden, and (in particular) Oxford, provide a basis for studying which strategies or combinations of strategies are effective in promoting learning (see the later section on 'Learning strategies and language learning', page 545). Problems still remain, however. The categories that have been established are 'high-inference' in nature, their identification often requiring considerable interpretation on the part of the researcher. The strategies listed as belonging to a single type frequently vary on a number of dimensions such as specificity (for example, 'repetition' is much more specific than 'self-management') and the extent to which they are observable (for example, 'question for clarification' constitutes an overt behaviour, while 'elaboration' does not). It is not yet clear whether the range of strategies available to the learner is finite or infinite in number. These problems are serious blocks to reliable research, but they are, perhaps, less important where learner training is concerned.

Factors affecting strategy choice

Learners have been found to vary considerably in both the overall frequency with which they employ strategies and also the particular types of strategies they use (O'Malley et al. 1985a; Chamot et al. 1987 and 1988; Ehrman 1990). A key question is whether this variation is systematically related to L2 proficiency and, more especially, to differential success in learning an L2—a question we take up in the next section. Here we consider the range of factors that have been found to affect strategy choice.

Individual learner differences

Chapter 11 considered individual learner differences in terms of (1) attitudes, (2) affective states, and (3) general factors. There has been little research into the effect that learners' affective states have on strategy choice, so we will focus here on how attitudes and general factors influence learners' use of learning strategies. We will also consider how learners' personal backgrounds affect strategy use.

Beliefs about language learning

Bialystok (1981b) found that Grade 10 and 12 learners of L2 French in Canada varied in the extent to which they believed that language learning involved formal as opposed to functional practice, and that this influenced their choice of strategies. Wenden (1987a) also found that learners who emphasized the importance of learning tended to use cognitive strategies that helped them to understand and remember specific items of language, while learners who emphasized the importance of using language employed few learning strategies, relying instead on communication strategies. Learners who stressed personal factors did not manifest any distinct pattern of strategy use.

Learner factors

Age emerges as a clear factor affecting the way strategies are used. Young children have been observed to employ strategies in a task-specific manner, while older children and adults make use of generalized strategies, which they employ more flexibly (see Brown et al. 1983, cited in O'Malley and Chamot 1990). Young children's strategies are often simple, while maturer learners' strategies are more complex and sophisticated. For example, Brown et al. found that 'rehearsal' for children consisted of rote repetition, while for adults it involved 'active, systematic and elaborative procedures'. Ehrman and Oxford (1989) also report adults using more sophisticated strategies. These differences may help to explain why older children and adults generally learn faster initially than young children (see Chapter 11, page 485) and also why this advantage is more evident in grammar and vocabulary, for which there are many learning strategies, rather than pronunciation, for which there are few. However, as we saw in Chapter 11, there are other explanations for age differences in rate of learning.

Aptitude does not appear to be strongly related to strategy use. Bialystok (1981b) found that aptitude was not as influential as learners' beliefs. However, it is possible that learners with enhanced decontextualized language skills (seen by Skehan (1989) as one aspect of aptitude) will be better able to talk about the strategies they use. Leino (1982) found that learners with high conceptual levels were better at describing their strategies than learners with low conceptual levels. It is possible, then, that learning strategies are related to that part of language aptitude shared with a general intelligence factor.

Oxford (1989) claims that 'it is likely that a strong relationship exists between the individual's use of learning strategies and the individual's learning style', but admits that little research has examined the relationship. The

descriptors that Willing (1987) provides of the four learning styles he identified in ESL learners in Australia (see Table 11.6, page 507) are suggestive of
the different learning strategies that might be associated with each style.

The strength of learners' motivation can be expected to have a causal effect
on the quantity of learning strategies they employ. Oxford and Nyikos
(1989), in a study of students of foreign languages in universities in the United
States, found that 'the degree of expressed motivation was the single most
powerful influence on the choice of language learning strategies' (1989: 294).
Highly motivated learners used more strategies relating to formal practice,
functional practice, general study, and conversation/input elicitation than
poorly motivated learners. The type of motivation may also influence strategy
choice. In the same study, Oxford and Nyikos reported that formal practice
and general study strategies were more popular than functional practice strategies, perhaps reflecting the students' strong instrumental goal of fulfilling
course requirements and obtaining good grades in a programme that stressed
analytical skills. However, in a different context an instrumental motivation
can result in a preference for more communication-orientated strategies, as
Ehrman's (1990) study of adult students at the US Foreign Service Institute
learning languages for career reasons showed. Politzer and McGroarty
(1985), in a study we will consider in detail in the next section, also make the
point that learners' goals are likely to determine strategy use. For example,
the strategy of asking the teacher how an expression is used may be seen as
relevant by the student concerned with developing communicative competence, but not by one concerned only with reading technical literature in the
L2. It does not follow, of course, that students will always be correct in their
assumptions about which learning strategies are best suited to their particular
goals (see Abraham and Vann's (1987) account of Pedro's inflexible use of
learning strategies).

It is intuitively appealing to hypothesize a close relationship between personality types and strategy choice. Erhman (1990) used the Myers-Briggs
Type Indicator to measure overall personality type with teachers and students
at the Foreign Service Institute. The general approach Ehrman takes is to suggest that each personality trait is associated with 'assets' and 'liabilities'
where language learning is concerned. For example, extroverts are credited
with a willingness to take risks (an asset) but with dependency on outside
stimulation and interaction (a liability). However, she offers little evidence in
support of such claims. The relationships between individual traits and reported strategy use were also puzzling in some cases. It is to be expected, perhaps, that extroverts should report greater use of affective and visualization
strategies, but other relationships noted by Ehrman are counter-intuitive. For
example, another finding was that introverts reported significantly greater
use of strategies that involved searching for and communicating meaning
than did extroverts, which is surprising given that extroverts have been found
to be generally more successful at acquiring basic interpersonal communica-

tion skills than introverts (see Chapter 11). Several of the other results reported by Ehrman and Oxford are also quixotic—for example, 'feeling-people' reported using general study strategies to a greater extent than 'thinkers'. Such results suggest that the measurements of personality and/or strategy use may not be reliable. If there are important links between personality and strategy choice, they remain to be demonstrated.

The learner's personal background

There is considerable evidence to support a link between learners' personal backgrounds and strategy use. Ehrman (1990) found that professional linguists reported using more strategies more frequently than untrained instructors and students. Also, students with at least five years of study reported using more functional practice strategies than students with four years or fewer. Chamot et al. (1987) also found that higher-level high school students of Spanish and Russian in the US reported using more strategies than did beginning-level students. However, O'Malley et al. (1985a), in a study of ESL high school students, found the opposite, although this may have been due to the fact that the interviews with the beginners were conducted in their mother tongues while those with the more advanced learners were carried out in the L2. The general superiority of more experienced language learners over less experienced is again evident in one of the few longitudinal studies of learning strategies. Chamot et al. (1988) found that novice high school learners of a FL were likely to panic when they realized they lacked procedural skills for solving a language problem, whereas expert learners (defined as those who had studied another FL previously) approached tasks calmly and were able to employ the strategies they had developed elsewhere. Nation and McLaughlin (1986) also provide evidence of the superiority of experienced language learners over inexperienced. They taught groups of monolingual, bilingual, and multilingual subjects an artificial language and found that the multilinguals did better on an implicit learning task, a result they explained by suggesting that multilinguals were more able to utilize learning strategies automatically.

Situational and social factors

Individual learner differences constitute one source of variation in the use of learning strategies. Another source is situational factors: the language being learnt, the setting in which learning takes place, and the tasks that the learner is asked to perform. Factors of a social nature, such as sex, have also been shown to influence strategy use (see Figure 12.1, page 530).

There is evidence to suggest that learning some languages results in greater strategy use than learning others. Chamot et al. (1987), in the study referred to above, found that FL students of Russian reported greater strategy use than students of Spanish. Politzer (1983) found that students of Spanish used fewer strategies than those of French and German. However, as Oxford (1989) points out, this may be because it is more able students who elect to study the languages less commonly taught in schools in the US.

A number of differences between the learning strategies used by learners in a classroom as opposed to those used in a more natural setting have been found. Studies of classroom learners suggest that social strategies are rare. Chamot et al. (1988), for example, noted that their classroom learners mentioned social and affective strategies infrequently, the only exception being 'questioning for clarification'. They suggest that the adult–student interview situation may have inhibited the occurrence of strategies such as 'co-operation' and 'self-talk'. It is likely, however, that in many classrooms the kind of interaction that takes place affords little opportunity for the use of social strategies (see Chapter 13). Wong-Fillmore (1976; 1979), however, reports extensive use of social strategies by young learners in a play situation.

There may also be differences in strategy use according to whether the classroom setting is a second or foreign language one. The FL students investigated by Chamot et al. (1987) claimed to use some strategies not mentioned by O'Malley et al.'s (1985a) ESL students (for example, rehearsal, translation, note-taking, substitution, and contextualization). The FL students also reported relying on cognitive strategies (in relation to metacognitive and socio-affective strategies) to a lesser extent than the ESL students.

It is likely, though, that it is not so much macro-differences (such as the FL/SL distinction) as micro-differences to do with the specific learning settings in classrooms that have the greater effect on strategy use. Evidence for this comes from the effect that task type has been found to have on strategy choice in the series of studies conducted by O'Malley and Chamot and their associates. O'Malley et al. (1985a) found that ESL learners reported using the highest frequency of strategies for vocabulary learning tasks and oral drills. The lowest frequencies were for listening comprehension, inferencing, making an oral presentation, and engaging in operational communication. Chamot et al. (1987) and Chamot et al. (1988) provide evidence to show that task type had a marked influence on learners' choice of both cognitive and metacognitive strategies. For example, vocabulary tasks led to the use of the cognitive strategies of 'resourcing' and 'elaboration' and the metacognitive strategies of 'self-monitoring' and 'self-evaluation', while listening tasks led to 'note-taking', 'elaboration', 'inferencing', and 'summarizing' as cognitive strategies, and to 'selective attention', 'self-monitoring', and 'problem-identification' as metacognitive strategies.

These studies suggest that learners' ability to use a broad range of strategies flexibly may depend crucially on the nature and range of the instructional tasks that they experience in the classroom. However, it may not always be possible to predict the kinds of strategies that an individual learner will employ in performing a particular task. Hosenfeld (1979) showed that one learner adapted a language drill to her own preferred approach by immediately seeking to apply the grammatical explanations provided by the task to an imagined communicative situation. Specific tasks may predispose learners to use particular strategies, but they cannot predetermine the actual strategies that will be used.

Less attention has been paid to the role of social factors such as socio-economic group, sex, and ethnicity on the use of learning strategies. However, Oxford and Nyikos' (1989) study found that sex had 'a profound choice on strategy choice' in their study of university students learning foreign languages. The results tend to bear out previous studies of male–female language differences (see Chapter 6). Thus, females used conversation input elicitation strategies more frequently than males, perhaps because they were more orientated towards social interaction. Ehrman (1990), in a study of teachers and students in the Foreign Services Institute, found that females reported greater overall use of strategies than males.

Factors in strategy use

To sum up, there is now evidence to suggest that a number of individual learner differences and situational factors are related to strategy use. Learners' beliefs about language learning, the learner factors of age and motivation, and personal background emerge as important factors. So far, however, there is only weak evidence to connect the learners' affective states, language aptitude, learning style, and personality to learning strategy use. In some cases it is possible to suggest what factors might contribute to superior strategy use (for example, older learners who are strongly motivated and who have previous experience of language learning are likely to use more strategies more frequently). In other cases, the factors result in different but not necessarily less successful strategic approaches to learning. Situational and social factors that have been found to be important are: the language being learnt, the learning setting, the type of learning tasks, and the learner's sex. The fact that learning strategies vary according to learning task suggests that it might be possible to change learners' strategic behaviour through training. Such intervention will only be viable, however, if information is available about the contribution that different strategies make to learning outcomes.

Learning strategies and language learning

Most of the studies that have investigated the relationship between learning strategies and language learning have been cross-sectional and correlational in nature. In one set of studies, the strategies that 'good language learners' reported using have been examined. In another set of studies, the relationships between strategy use (with regard to both frequency and type) and criterion measures of learning have been explored using statistical techniques. There have also been a number of interesting studies that focus on the strategies used to learn vocabulary. The majority of studies have examined adult L2 learners but there are also a few studies of the learning strategies used by children.

The 'good language learner' studies

The 'good language learner' studies include most of the early studies of learning strategies already referred to, together with some more recent ones (see Table 12.3). Two approaches have been followed. In one, successful learners are identified and interviewed and/or asked to complete a written questionnaire (for example, Naiman et al. 1978; Lennon 1989). In the other, comparisons of more and less successful learners are made (for example, Reiss 1985; Huang and Van Naersson 1985).

It is easy to overstate the commonalities in strategy use among good language learners. Stevick (1989), in a study of seven successful language learners, noted that they 'differ markedly with regard to what . . . they prefer to do and not to do' (1989: 128). He nevertheless thinks that it is possible to identify an 'overall pattern'.[1] This is what we will try to do.

There are, perhaps, five major aspects of successful language learning, as evidenced by the various studies summarized in Table 12.3: (1) a concern for language form, (2) a concern for communication (functional practice), (3) an active task approach, (4) an awareness of the learning process, and (5) a capacity to use strategies flexibly in accordance with task requirements.

Rubin's (1975) study listed 'attention to form' and 'monitoring one's own and other's speech' as key strategies. Naiman et al. (1978) include 'self-monitoring and critical sensitivity to language' as an important characteristic. They found that good language learners treat language as a system by making effective crosslingual comparisons, analysing the target language, and using reference books. Such learners also monitor their L2 performance and try to learn from their errors by asking for corrections when they think these are needed. Reiss (1985) found that 'monitoring' and 'attending to form' came out as the most common strategies used by learners whom teachers picked out as 'good'. Reiss comments that 'it is surprising that attending to meaning was of less importance than attending to form'. However, Huang and Van Naersson's (1985) study found no difference between high- and low-proficiency groups on two strategies that reflected attention to form ('formal practice' and 'monitoring'), although this may have reflected the fact that learners were asked to report on the strategies they used *outside* the classroom. Gillette (1987) also reports that her two successful learners did not pay much attention to learning conscious rules, although she notes that they used their errors as a tool for learning, suggesting, perhaps, that they did make efforts to attend to form. Overall, there is convincing evidence from the good language learner studies to show that paying attention to the formal

Study	Learners	Method	Results
Rubin 1975	Learners of mixed ages in classroom settings	Observation—Rubin emphasizes the importance of using a video camera	Following strategies discussed: 1 preparedness to guess 2 attempt to communicate (i.e. get the message across) 3 willingness to appear foolish 4 attention to form 5 practising (e.g. by initiating conversation) 6 monitoring own and others' speech 7 attending to meaning (e.g. by attending to context)
Naiman et al. 1978	1 34 graduate L2 learners—many multilingual 2 students of L2 French in grades 8, 10, and 12	1 interview questionnaire—semi-directed and directed parts 2 classroom observation schedule—not successful	Following general strategies identified: 1 Active task approach 2 Realization of language as a system 3 Realization of language as a means of communication and interaction 4 Management of affective demands 5 Monitoring L2 performance Each major strategy further divided into more specific sub-strategies. Also various 'techniques' identified, e.g. having contact with native speakers
Rubin 1981	Young adults in classroom settings	1 classroom observation schedule—not successful 2 observation of learner performance on specific lang. learning tasks 3 unstructured self-reports—learners varied in ability to report but many vague 4 directed self-report—focus on specific strategies	Strategies in these areas identified: 1 clarification/verification 2 monitoring 3 memorization 4 guessing/inductive inferencing 5 deductive reasoning 6 practice (i.e. learner practises on own)
Reiss 1983	College learners of L2 French/German—18 'A' and 18 'C'/'D' students compared	Questionnaire presenting 3 hypothetical learning situations	Characteristics of successful learners: 1 they are specific in their learning task 2 they constantly look for meaning 3 they seem to know themselves and to know how to internalize information Successful learners also gave more specific answers to questionnaire

(continued overleaf)

Study	Learners	Method	Results
Huang and Van Naersson 1985	20 high- and 20 low-proficiency Chinese learners of English in China	1 written questionnaire on use of formal practice, functional practice, and monitoring 2 in-depth interview	The main results were: 1 No significant differences between high- and low-proficiency learners with regard to formal practice and monitoring 2 Significant differences for some functional practice strategies: speaking L2 with others, thinking in English, and participation in oral group activities
Reiss 1985	College learners at elementary and intermediate levels—some identified as good lang. learners	1 general questionnaire about personality variables and learning strategies 2 strategies questionnaire listing 19 strategies from which students selected the ones they used most often	Strategies identified (in rank order): 1 monitoring 2 attention to form 3 attention to meaning Reiss argues that good lang. learner is 'active' in process of conscious lang. learning, but learner can be active by being a silent speaker' (i.e. practising silently while listening to others)
Gillette 1987	Two beginners of L2 Spanish/successful learners of L2 French	1 extensive classroom observation 2 classroom notes from one of the learners 3 attitude/motivation questionnaire (Lambert and Gardner) 4 interview 5 teachers' comments	Instrumental motivation; democratic, anti-authoritarian; high self-esteem or confident; tolerant of ambiguity; one learner risk-taker but other learner rarely volunteers in class; good at getting 'big picture' without worrying about details; aware of learning process; 'active thinking'; self-regulated; individualized approach to learning; focus on meaning rather than on conscious rules; errors seen as useful tool for learning
Lennon 1989	4 Germans learning L2 English in UK—advanced	1 written answers to general questionnaire 2 personal interview	Aware of progression, performance, and state of competence; switch modes of production; aware of gaps in their knowledge; stressed linguistic experimentation; concentrated on both communicating and learning (trading one off against other in different situations)

Table 12.3:   Studies of the good language learner

properties of the target language contributes to success—a view that seems to conflict with the claims of Krashen's (1985) Input Hypothesis (see Chapter 7).

Good language learners also attend to meaning. All the studies listed in Table 12.3 refer to the importance of this aspect of strategy use. Indeed, Huang and Van Naerssen found that 'functional practice' distinguished the more from the less successful learners in their study, whereas 'formal practice' and 'monitoring' did not. In most of the studies, however, the learners appeared to benefit from attending to both form and meaning. For example, Gerardo, the more successful learner in Abraham and Vann's (1987) study, paid attention to both, while Pedro, the less successful, paid attention only to meaning. Good language learners search for meaning in the L2 data they are exposed to and try to engage in real communication by seeking out opportunities for natural language use. Naiman et al. (1978) reported that the learners they studied emphasized fluency in the early stages, giving more attention to form later. Lennon's (1989) study of very advanced learners of L2 English showed that they were adept at alternating between a focus on learning the language and on communicating in it. The ability to switch to and fro in attending to meaning and form may be a crucial feature of successful language learning.

Good language learners show active involvement in language learning. They appreciate teachers who are systematic, logical, and clear, but prefer to treat them as 'informants' rather than to rely on them (Pickett 1978). They like to take charge of their own learning by identifying and pursuing goals and by trying to introduce new topics into a conversation. However, being 'active' does not necessarily mean engaging in language production. Reiss (1985) reported that many successful classroom learners were 'silent speakers' (i.e. they rehearsed and practised silently while listening to others)—a finding that will be picked up in Chapter 13 when considering a number of studies that indicate listening may be as important, if not more so, than oral participation in classroom language learning.

The fourth general characteristic of the good language learner—awareness of the learning process—suggests the importance of what O'Malley and Chamot have called 'metalingual strategies'. Successful learners are thoughtful and aware of themselves in relation to the learning process. They take conscious decisions and they follow their own preferred learning style. These are the learners who are able to talk effectively about their language learning because they have a well-developed metalanguage for doing so. Reiss (1983) found that students awarded 'A' grades by their teachers were able to give very specific accounts of how they would approach different learning tasks, while learners with lower grades were often vague and imprecise. For example, asked to comment on how they would set about learning a new task that had been explained in class, the 'A' students gave answers such as the following:

'Try to practise the new tense while speaking.
Look for similar endings to those already known.'

while 'B' students gave answers such as this:

'Keep going over it.
Study it until I understand.'

Good language learners also make use of metacognitive knowledge to help them assess their needs, evaluate progress, and give direction to their learning. Such awareness gives learners control over their own learning.

One of the most comprehensive studies of learner strategies to date, Chamot et al. (1988), provides evidence in support of the final general characteristic of good language learners—flexible and appropriate use of learning strategies. Chamot et al. investigated beginner, intermediate-, and advanced-level students of Spanish and Russian over four school semesters. The students were classified as 'effective' or 'ineffective' by their teachers. No clear pattern was evident in the strategies the learners used from one time to the next, although changes were evident in the performance of specific tasks over time. For example, the beginners more than doubled their use of strategies in a writing task and also showed a number of more qualitative changes in strategy use (for example, greater use of 'comprehension monitoring'). However, what set the 'effective' students apart was their use of a greater range of strategies and, in particular, their ability to choose strategies that were appropriate for particular tasks. The effective learners were also more purposeful in their approach, engaged in 'comprehension monitoring' to a greater extent than 'production monitoring' (involving attending to separate linguistic components), and made extensive use of their general knowledge as well as L2 linguistic knowledge.

Studying good language learners has proved a useful way of investigating how strategies affect language learning. It has afforded both generalized comment and fine illustrative detail. It is not clear, however, how much store should be set by the studies undertaken to date. They have focused mainly on classroom learners and the 'good' strategies that have been identified necessarily reflect the formal learning setting. The main methods of collecting data—learners' verbal reports—may give an advantage to the kind of learner who is able to talk about language learning easily and skilfully. This may be why 'metacognitive' strategies have been so strongly emphasized. Also, it is not clear whether the strategies that have been identified are the cause or the result of success. Despite these reservations, the good language learner studies have provided some of the richest insights into the kinds of behaviours associated with successful language learning. They constitute one of the most effective lines of enquiry in learning strategy research.

Correlational studies employing statistical procedures

A number of studies have sought to examine whether there are specific strategies that are statistically related to L2 proficiency. The results obtained by these studies are not always clear, but they lend some support to the main findings of the 'good language learner' studies.

In a series of studies, Bialystok explored the relationship between four strategies and L2 proficiency. Two concerned the learning resulting from communicating in an L2 ('functional practice' and 'inferencing'), and two concerned more conscious attempts to learn the L2 ('formal practice' and 'monitoring'). These studies were informed by Bialystok's Model of Second Language Learning, which was described in Chapter 9. In her main study, Bialystok (1981b) investigated students studying French in Grades 10 and 12 in Canada. She used a questionnaire to collect information on the students' reported use of the four strategies in both oral and written tasks. Proficiency was measured by means of oral and written tasks that required attention to meaning and to form. The results are not easy to interpret and in some respects are counter-intuitive. For example, Bialystok failed to find any relationship between inferencing and proficiency, although elsewhere a strong theoretical case for the importance of inferencing in L2 learning has been made out (see Carton 1971; Bialystok 1983a). Another result that seems a little odd is that only functional practice correlated significantly with proficiency in the Grade 10 students, whereas three strategies (functional practice, formal practice, and monitoring) were related to proficiency in the Grade 12. It is possible, of course, that this reflects a shift in strategy use as proficiency develops, but it is also possible that the data elicited by means of the questionnaire were not reliable.

If Bialystok's attempt to show a statistical relationship between strategy use and proficiency was only partly successful, Politzer and McGroarty's (1985) attempt was even less successful. This study focused on a much broader range of strategies, but once again made use of a questionnaire. Although considerable attempts were made to ensure the validity of this instrument by basing its contents on previous studies of good language learners, the generally unsatisfactory nature of the results obtained again suggests that 'reported strategy use' may not provide an accurate account of what learners actually do, a problem that Politzer and McGroarty acknowledge.

The study elicited information about the behaviours learners reported using in (1) study inside the classroom, (2) individual study, and (3) social interaction outside the classroom. The subjects in this study were 37 learners from two major ethnic groups (Hispanics and Asians) enrolled on an eight-week intensive ESL course at American universities. Learning gains were calculated from scores on three tests (a comprehension test, a discrete item test of linguistic competence, and a test of communicative ability), which were administered at the beginning and the end of the course. Very few statistically significant correlations were found. Social interaction strategies were related to gains in communicative ability, but no other relationships between the three general groups of strategies and the criterion measures were found. However, different clusters of strategies were found to be related to gains in different tests. For example, reported behaviours associated with active inquiry concerning language use (for example, 'asking teacher about an expression' and 'asking for confirmation of correctness') were correlated with gains in listening comprehension and communicative ability, while reported behaviours involving attention to form (such as 'keeping track of new vocabulary' and 'trying to use new words') were linked to gains in linguistic competence. Politzer and McGroarty argue that this was the most interesting finding. It points to a general weakness in much of the learning strategy research, namely that strategies have tended to be considered in isolation rather than in groups.

The final correlational study we will consider is in many ways the most interesting and the most insightful. Mangubhai (1991) studied the strategies used by five adult beginner learners of L2 Hindi who received four weeks of instruction by means of Total Physical Response (Asher 1977)—a method based mainly on the use of oral commands that students have to listen to and carry out. Information about the learning strategies they used came from concurrent think-aloud tasks, immediate retrospective reports, and discussions at the end of each instructional session. Three sets of strategies were identified, depending on whether the focus of the different behaviours was (1) on form, (2) on meaning, and (3) on memory (retrieval and storage). Achievement was measured by means of a test consisting of oral commands similar to those used in the instruction, a sentence repetition test and a listening comprehension test. On the basis of these tests, the learners were divided into two groups: Group A, consisting of three 'high' achievers and Group B of two 'low' achievers. Table 12.4 summarizes the main differences in strategy use in the two groups of learners. This shows that the 'high' achievers used more memory strategies, were more likely to direct their attention to chunks than to individual words, relied less on translation, and paid more attention to the form of the commands once they had extracted the meaning. The strength of Mangubhai's study is that it elicited information relating to strategy use in a variety of ways, making it possible to compare what learners reported doing retrospectively with what they reported doing during an actual language learning task.

These three studies—all of which investigated classroom language learners—afford only limited information about the relationship between learning strategies and L2 learning. Two of them (Bialystok's and Politzer and McGroarty's) have produced rather indeterminate results, perhaps because they relied on learners' reported use of strategies in a written questionnaire. Mangubhai's study overcame this limitation and also benefited from investigating complete beginners over a period of time, thus allowing us to

Group A		Group B	
1	Lesser focus on meaning relative to memory	1	Greater focus on meaning relative to memory
2	Greater focus on memory relative to meaning	2	Lesser focus on memory relative to meaning
3	Lesser focus on single words under meaning	3	Greater focus on single words under meaning
4	Less translation into English	4	More translation into English
5	More practising	5	Less practising

Table 12.4:   Differences in strategy use between high and low achievers in a four-week Hindi course (Mangubhai 1991: 282)

tentatively attribute a causal role to the strategies his learners employed. The results suggest that a learning approach that might be described as 'audio-lingual' in nature works well,[2] but this may simply reflect the ability of the successful learners to adapt to the particular learning task they were asked to perform. A study of five learners, of course, does not permit generalization. These three studies also investigated different sets of strategies, reflecting one of the main problems of strategy research, namely the lack of agreement regarding what strategies and what combinations of strategies should be studied. It is not possible to reach any general conclusion on the basis of them.

Studies of vocabulary-learning strategies

A number of specific strategies for learning vocabulary have been identified (see Nation 1990; Cohen 1990; Oxford 1990). A general distinction needs to be drawn between those strategies used to memorize isolated lexical items and those strategies used to learn new words from context. We will consider two studies, one longitudinal and the other experimental.

A study by Cohen and Aphek (1981) suggests that the use of mnemonic association aids vocabulary learning. It investigated seventeen English-speaking students (nine beginners, six intermediate, and two advanced) learning Hebrew over a 100-day period. Not surprisingly perhaps, the learners' main approach was simply to try to memorize the words they did not know. Most of the learners reported using associations of various kinds and Cohen and Aphek were able to identify eleven different types, involving the target language, the learners' L1, and extralinguistic signs. The general conclusion was that any attempt to form an association involving the target word aided retention. In contrast, the frequency with which the learners reported encountering the items outside the classroom had no effect on retention. Again, though, we should not note that what learners report experiencing and what they actually experience might not be the same. Another interesting finding of Cohen and Aphek's study was that there was an interaction between the learners' overall level of proficiency and the kind of task that worked best for vocabulary learning. Beginners found tasks that involved listing best, while the intermediate learners found tasks that involved contextualization more effective, suggesting that contextualization strategies work better for learners who already possess a fair level of L2 knowledge.

A study by Brown and Perry (1991) investigated the success of three vocabulary-learning strategies: (1) keyword, (2) semantic, and (3) keyword-semantic. The keyword strategy involves asking learners to form a visual association between the target word and some acoustically similar word they already know (the keyword). For example, to learn the Japanese word 'ski' (= 'like'), learners might use the keyword 'skiing' and imagine themselves enjoying skiing down a mountain slope. A semantic strategy involves some kind of attempt to integrate the target word into the learner's existing semantic systems, for example by identifying how a word relates to other known words. A keyword-semantic strategy involves a combination of (1) and (2). Brown and Perry hypothesized that strategies that involved greater 'depth of processing' (see Craik and Lockhart 1972) would result in better retention. Their prediction was that processing at the 'shallow' sensory level of the kind involved in the keyword strategy aids retention less than processing at the 'deep' semantic level. Processing that involves both shallow and deep levels was hypothesized to be more effective still. An experimental study of six intact upper-level classes at the English Language Institute of the American University of Cairo lent support to Brown and Perry's hypothesis; the class taught to use the semantic-keyword strategy retained significanctly more words, as measured by cued-recall and multiple choice tests, than the class taught the keyword strategy, while the results for the class taught the semantic strategy were intermediate.

The study of vocabulary-learning strategies is a promising area of enquiry. This is because it is possible to define the learning targets and strategies very precisely, and also to investigate strategies that have wide currency in the literature. Also, vocabulary-learning strategies lend themselves to experimental investigation, which O'Malley and Chamot (1990) suggest is now needed to develop the field of learning strategy research. Most important, perhaps, Brown and Perry's study shows that it is possible to locate vocabulary strategy research within a strong theoretical framework (i.e. depth-of-processing theory).

Studies of learning strategies used by children

The great majority of learning strategy studies have examined adolescents or adults. However, one or two studies have also looked at children. Perhaps the best known is Wong-Fillmore's (1976; 1979) nine-month study of five Mexican children learning English in the United States. Wong-Fillmore collected natural spoken data by pairing each learner with a native-speaking child in a play situation. Perhaps as a reflection of the way in which the data were collected, 'social strategies' are emphasized. One such strategy is 'Join a group and act as if you understand what is going on, even if you don't'. Linked to each social strategy is one or more cognitive strategies. For example, the cognitive strategy linked to the social strategy described above is 'Assume what people are saying is relevant to the situation at hand' and 'Guess'.

The strategies described by Wong-Fillmore are those employed successfully by children in the early stages of language learning. A study by Chesterfield and Chesterfield (1985) examined how children's learning strategies change as their knowledge of the L2 develops. The subjects in this study were fourteen Mexican-American children, eight of whom were studied at three different points during their first year of schooling. Data were collected through observations in bilingual classrooms. The strategies used by these children emerged in a distinct order. The ones to appear first were mainly receptive and self-contained (for example, 'repetition', 'memorization', and 'use of formulaic expressions'). Later strategies to emerge were those based on interpersonal interaction (for example, 'appeal for assistance' and 'requests for clarification'), while later still were those that reflect metacognitive knowledge (for example, 'monitoring'). Chesterfield and Chesterfield did not try to find out which strategies contributed most to language development.

Whereas the study of learning strategies in adults has relied largely on self-report data, that involving children has made use of observational data. This is reflected in the kinds of strategies identified (i.e. social and discourse strategies predominate). Studies of adults have emphasized cognitive and metacognitive strategies. What is not clear, then, is whether the differences in the kinds of strategies used by adult and child subjects is a reflection of their age or of the research methodology.

Relating learning strategies to second language development

Caution must be exercised in drawing conclusions from the research that has investigated the relationship between learning strategies and L2 development. Studies have varied enormously in the kind of learners studied, in the procedures used to obtain information about strategy use, and in the ways in which learning 'success' has been assessed. The following conclusions, therefore, are tentative:

1 The strategies that learners elect to use reflect their general stage of L2 development. For example, there is some evidence to suggest that strategies that relate to the functional use of language and that involve processing chunks of language precede those that involve close attention to form and single words. Metacognitive strategies are more evident in advanced learners.

2 Successful learners appear to use learning strategies more frequently and in qualitatively different ways than learners who are less successful. For

example, successful adult beginners seem more adept at the use of memory strategies.

3 Successful language learning involves attention to both form and meaning. Good language learners appear able to switch the focus of their attention while they are performing a task—even as beginners.

4 Different kinds of learning strategies may contribute to different aspects of L2 proficiency. Thus, strategies that involve formal practice may contribute to the development of linguistic competence, while strategies involving functional practice aid the development of communicative competence.

5 Learners need to employ strategies flexibly by selecting those strategies that are appropriate for performing a particular learning task.

6 Because of (5), metacognitive strategies involving goal identification, planning, monitoring, and evaluation assume considerable importance, at least for adults. However, many learners appear to under-utilize this type of strategy.

7 The more successful adult learners are better able to talk about the strategies they use.

8 The learning strategies used by children and adults may differ; social and interactional strategies may be more important with young learners.

These constitute very general conclusions and it might be argued that not enough is yet known about the relations between learning strategies and language learning to justify attempts to train learners to use particular strategies. In particular, not enough is known about what *combinations* of strategies are most effective. However, this has not prevented a number of attempts at strategy training.

Training learners in the use of learning strategies

There is now a wealth of material that has been developed to train learners to use effective language learning strategies: for example, Ellis and Sinclair 1989; Brown 1989; Oxford 1990; Wenden 1986b and 1991. Somewhat surprisingly, however, there have been few empirical studies that have attempted to evaluate the success of this training on L2 learners. We will briefly review the major studies and then identify a number of key issues in language learning strategy training.

One area in which strategy training may be particularly useful is in vocabulary acquisition. Bialystok (1983b) carried out two experiments to investigate a number of ways in which the ability of Grade 10 students of L2 French to inference the meanings of words in a continuous text could be improved. In one of the experiments, a fifteen-minute lesson on how to inference resulted in more effective overall comprehension of a written text than providing the learners with picture cues or letting the learners use a dictionary. However, dictionary use (but not picture cues) resulted in better scores on a vocabulary test than did the strategy training. In the second experiment the strategy training proved less effective in promoting either comprehension or vocabulary acquisition than the other two conditions.

Cohen and Aphek (1980) gave adult learners of L2 Hebrew a short training session in how to learn vocabulary through associations. The results indicated that forming associations helped in vocabulary recall tasks and that failure to employ an association often led to incorrect recall. Cohen and Aphek also reported that those students who were more proficient at the outset were also the most successful in using association in recall tasks, suggesting that training in forming associations might be most helpful for advanced rather than beginner learners.

A third study of the effects of strategy training on vocabulary learning failed to show significant results, but is interesting because it suggests the complexity of the issues involved. O'Malley et al. (1985b) studied the effects of two kinds of training on 75 intermediate-level ESL students of mixed ethnic backgrounds (Hispanic and Asian). One group received training in the use of 'imagery and grouping' (a cognitive strategy), while a second group received training in this strategy and also in 'self-evaluation' (a metalingual strategy). There was also a control group. Although no significant differences among the treatment groups were found, a detailed analysis of the results showed that while the Hispanic training groups outperformed the Hispanic control group, the reverse was the case for the Asian groups. Apparently the Asian students had resisted using the strategies during training, preferring to rely on rote memorization instead. This study shows that the learning styles of different cultural groups need to be taken into account in planning strategy training.[3]

The study by O'Malley et al. also investigated the effects of strategy training on the learners' performance on a listening and a speaking task. In the case of listening, the cognitive group was taught 'note-taking' and 'co-operation' (a social/affective strategy), while the metacognitive group was taught 'selective attention' in addition. In the case of the speaking task, one experimental group was taught how to use 'cooperation' (a social/affective strategy), while the other was taught both this strategy and 'functional planning' (a metacognitive strategy). In the speaking task, which required students to present a two-minute talk, the group taught functional planning outperformed the other experimental group which, in turn, outperformed the control group. No significant differences were found in the listening task used as a post-test.

Clearly, there are many issues that need sorting out before strategy training can be implemented effectively. First, more work is needed to discover what strategies and, in particular, what combinations of strategies should be taught. Second, ways have to be found of taking into account learners' own preferred learning strategies. Third, some learners may need convincing that strategy training is worth while. Wenden (1987b), for example, found that students in the American Language program at Columbia University responded negatively to a training component she included in their language course. As O'Malley and Chamot (1990) point out, the very learners that need strategy training are most likely to be the ones that reject it. Fourth, it is not clear whether learner training will work best when it exists as a separate strand in a language programme (as Wenden tried) or when it is fully integrated into the language teaching materials, as proposed by O'Malley and Chamot (1990) in their Cognitive Academic Learning Approach (CALLA). A fifth issue is when strategy training should be attempted. With beginners it will only be possible if undertaken in the L1. A final issue is whether learners should be made conscious of the strategies they are taught, or whether just providing practice opportunities is sufficient. As Skehan (1991) states, 'there is a lot to play for'.

Conclusion

The study of learning strategies holds considerable promise, both for language pedagogy and for explaining individual differences in L2 learning. It is probably true to say, however, that it is still in its infancy. For this reason, perhaps, discussions of learning strategies typically conclude with the problems that have surfaced and that need to be addressed before progress can be made.

There is no agreement about what constitutes a 'learning strategy'. There is no widely accepted theoretical basis for identifying and describing strategies, although O'Malley and Chamot have anchored their own work, with some success, in a cognitive theory of information processing, while Brown and Perry have shown how the study of vocabulary-learning strategies can be informed by depth-of-processing theory. The work done to date has been essentially descriptive, reflecting the corpora of data that different researchers have worked on. As a result, the nature of the strategies that have been identified varies enormously.

Despite this, considerable progress has been made in developing taxonomies of learning strategies. Where the early research listed, the later research classifies. O'Malley and Chamot's three-way distinction between cognitive, metacognitive, and social/affective strategies is useful and has been generally accepted. The classification of strategies within these general types remains more problematic, however.

A lot of the research has been based on the assumption that there are 'good' learning strategies. But this is questionable. The beneficial effect of strategies may be relative to the kinds of tasks they are deployed in. For example, some strategies may work in tasks aimed at the development of linguistic competence and others in tasks with more communicative objectives. Effective strategy use may consist of the flexible deployment of the right strategies in the right task, but little is currently known about this. It is also possible that different strategies are important for classroom and naturalistic language learning and for children as opposed to adults. Much of the research to date has studied the kind of analytic learning found in adult classroom learners.

The general assumption that effective strategy use involves frequent strategy use is also questionable. It is likely that it is not so much how often learners use strategies as when and with what purpose they use them. It is also likely that strategies will prove most helpful when they are deployed in clusters, but precisely what groupings work best is not known.

Implicit in much of the research is the assumption that strategies are causal (see Figure 12.1, page 530). But, as we have seen, a case can also be made out for treating them as the result of learning. Thus, advanced learners may employ certain strategies simply because they are advanced.

Much of the research has relied on learner self-reports, as with the exception of some studies of children, most researchers have found observation ineffective. Retrospection (through interviews, questionnaires, and diaries) and introspection (in concurrent think-aloud tasks) have provided rich information on learning strategies, but doubts remain about the reliability of such methods (see Seliger 1984). Also, there is always the danger that these methods conflate the strategies learners use with their ability to self-report.

Finally, nearly all the research has been cross-sectional in nature with the result that we know little about how learners develop the ability to deploy learning strategies over time or what effect their deployment has on L2 learning. More longitudinal case studies are sorely needed if solutions to the problems mentioned above are to be found.

Notes

1 Stevick's approach to describing the 'overall pattern' evident in his study of the seven successful learners is rather different from that adopted by other researchers. In fact he specifically avoids using the term 'strategy' on the grounds that this is not used consistently in the literature and is not yet part of 'the public vocabulary' (1989: 146). Instead, Stevick considers the 'overall pattern' in terms of the 'images', verbal and non-verbal, and the way these are locked into memory.

2 I am grateful to Peter Skehan for this observation. He notes that Mangubhai's successful learners were 'an audiolingual teacher's dream'.

3 The importance of taking cultural differences into account is also indicated by Politzer and McGroarty's (1985) study, where differences between the Hispanic and Asian subjects' reported strategy use were noted.

Further reading

There are now a number of full-length books dealing with learning strategies: A. Wenden and J. Rubin (eds.), *Learner Strategies in Language Learning* (Prentice Hall International, 1987).

J. O'Malley and A. Chamot, *Learning Strategies in Second Language Acquisition* (Cambridge University Press, 1990). This surveys the research to date and includes useful summaries of their own studies.

R. Oxford, *Language Learning Strategies: What Every Teacher Should Know* (Newbury House, 1990). This is a training manual for teachers. It contains a comprehensive list of strategies and the Strategy Inventory for Language Learning (a valuable diagnostic tool) is made available in an appendix.

For the reader who would like to read some of the original research reports, a number of the 'good language learner' studies are strongly recommended:

N. Naiman et al., *The Good language Learner* (Ontario Institute for Studies in Education, 1978). This is sometimes difficult to obtain, but is probably the single most important study of learning strategies.

M. Reiss, 'The Good Language Learner: another look'. *Canadian Modern Language Review* (1985) 41: 257–66.

A number of other studies are also worth reading. The following serve as examples of the kind of research that has been undertaken, although the results they obtained were not very conclusive.

R. Politzer and M. McGroarty, 'An exploratory study of learning behaviours and their relationship to gains in linguistic and communicative competence'. *TESOL Quarterly* (1985) 19: 103–23.

F. Mangubhai, 'The processing behaviours of adult second language learners and their relationship to second language proficiency'. *Applied Linguistics* (1991) 12: 268–98.

J. O'Malley et al., 'Learning strategy applications with students of English as a second language'. *TESOL Quarterly* (1985) 19: 285–96.

PART SIX

Classroom second language acquisition

Introduction

The previous sections of this book have been concerned with questions of general import to the study of second language acquisition. They have endeavoured to provide descriptions of how an L2 is acquired, and to explain the structural processes that account for its universal properties and the social and personal factors that account for variation in the rate and success of individual learners. Although some attention has been given to the impact that the acquisitional setting can have on outcomes (see Chapter 6), the primary concern has been to account for the regularities in acquisition evident across settings. Thus, no clear distinction has been drawn between the acquisition that takes place in untutored and tutored settings.

Much of the research that has been reported in the earlier sections, however, has involved classroom learners. This is particularly true of experimental or correlational studies (for example, studies based on the Competition Model or Gardner's research on motivation in Canada). One reason is that the large numbers of learners needed for such research are more accessible in *educational* than in *naturalistic* settings. However, this research has not been concerned with classroom L2 acquisition *per se*; rather it has used classroom learners to investigate questions of general significance to SLA research.

In this section, we focus our attention specifically on classroom L2 acquisition. In so doing, of course, we will revisit many of the general issues raised earlier in the book—for example, the role of interaction in shaping learning, the difference between implicit and explicit knowledge, the role of negative feedback, and the significance of acquisitional orders and sequences. In fact, the classroom constitutes an ideal setting for examining the key theoretical issues because it is possible to observe closely how input is made available to the learner and what kinds of output learners produce in specific classroom contexts. It is also possible to engineer what input learners are exposed to and what output they produce in order to investigate specific hypotheses about how learning takes place.

The reason for focusing on the classroom, however, is not merely to shed further light on how L2 acquisition takes place. It is also motivated by a desire to discover what classroom conditions are most likely to facilitate acquisition. In other words, it has a pedagogic purpose. However, this pedagogic purpose is not quite the same as that addressed in methodological handbooks for teachers, where the aim is to suggest specific techniques or activities that teachers can use. The research we will consider in this section invites us to consider pedagogy not in terms of 'techniques' or 'activities', but in terms of what kinds of classroom behaviours teachers need to engage in to promote learning—what questions to ask, when and how to correct learners' errors, how to instigate negotiation for meaning in a classroom, etc. Furthermore, whereas methodologists base their advice on what might be called 'sound pedagogy', accumulated from centuries of experience of language teaching, the pedagogical proposals drawn from L2 classroom acquisition research are informed by theoretical concepts drawn from SLA research. It is not intended, however, to suggest that such an approach to language pedagogy is the preferred one—a point that we will take up in the final chapter of this book.

It is possible to identify two major strands in classroom L2 acquisition research, corresponding to two ways of viewing the classroom. According to one view, what happens in the classroom provides opportunities for learning, which can be explored by examining the relationship between interaction—the means by which the opportunities are provided—and L2 learning. An alternative is to view the classroom as a place where attempts are made to intervene directly in the process of L2 learning—to ask, in other words, 'Do learners learn what they have been taught?'. Chapter 13 examines research belonging to the first strand, while Chapter 14 looks at the effects of direct intervention on learning.

13 Classroom interaction and second language acquisition

Introduction

The classroom affords the L2 researcher three different perspectives. The first perspective is that found in *comparative method studies*. These seek to compare the effect of different language teaching methods on L2 learning. Such studies are 'product'-based because they rely entirely on measurements of language learning and make no attempt to examine the instructional and learning 'processes' that take place inside the classroom.

A second perspective involves going inside the 'black box'[1] of the classroom itself. It views the classroom as a place where interactions of various kinds take place, affording learners opportunities to acquire the L2. Allwright (1984: 156) sees interaction as 'the fundamental fact of classroom pedagogy' because 'everything that happens in the classroom happens through a process of live person-to-person interaction'. This perspective has drawn heavily on the research and theories dealing with the relationship between input/interaction and L2 learning (see Chapter 7). It leads the researcher to observe and describe the interactional events that take place in a classroom in order to understand how learning opportunities are created. Ideally, it should also lead to attempts to demonstrate the effects of different types of interactional opportunity on L2 learning, but as we saw in Chapter 7, few studies have investigated this relationship directly.

The third perspective involves investigating the effects of formal instruction. In this case, instruction is viewed as an attempt to intervene directly in the language learning process by teaching specific properties of the L2. The question that is asked is 'Do learners actually learn what they are taught?' Researchers have been particularly interested in whether instruction directed at specific grammatical items and rules has any effect on interlanguage development. This chapter will consider research that has adopted the first two perspectives, and the following chapter will examine research relating to the third.

First of all, this chapter will consider some of the principal research methods that have been used to investigate the role of classroom interaction in language learning. It will then review a number of comparative method studies. The main part of the chapter is given over to a survey of research that has examined different aspects of classroom interaction: teacher talk, error treatment, teachers' questions, learner participation, task-based interaction, and small group work. Finally, consideration is given to the relationship between classroom interaction and L2 learning and, in particular, whether classroom environments are capable of providing the kinds of opportunities needed to develop full L2 competence.

A distinction can be drawn between 'classroom research' and 'classroom-orientated research' (see Nunan 1991: 249). The former consists of studies that have investigated learners inside actual classrooms, while the latter consists of studies conducted outside the classroom (for example, in some kind of experimental setting) but which have been motivated by issues of clear relevance to classroom L2 acquisition. This chapter will consider both types of research, but will try to make clear which is which.

Methods of researching learning in the second language classroom

A number of different research traditions in L2 classroom research can be identified. Chaudron (1988) describes four (see Table 13.1). The psychometric and interaction analysis traditions typically involve 'quantitative' and 'explanatory' research, while the discourse analysis and ethnographic traditions make use of more 'qualitative' and 'descriptive' methods.

Tradition	Typical issues	Methods
Psychometric	Language gain from different methods, materials, treatments.	Experimental method—pre- and post-tests with experimental and control groups.
Interaction analysis	Extent to which learner behaviour is a function of teacher-determined interaction.	Coding classroom interactions in terms of various observation systems and schedules.
Discourse analysis	Analysis of classroom discourse in linguistic terms.	Study classroom transcripts and assign utterances to pre-determined categories.
Ethnographic	Obtain insights into the classroom as a cultural system.	Naturalistic 'uncontolled' observation and description.

Table 13.1:   A summary of Chaudron's four research traditions in L2 classroom research (taken from Nunan 1990b: 23)

The psychometric tradition

The psychometric tradition is evident in the comparative method studies to be considered in the next section and in program–product comparisons of the kind used to evaluate different types of immersion programmes (see Swain and Lapkin 1982 for a review). The main problem with such studies is that without a process element to provide information about the actual events that take place inside the classroom, it is difficult to be certain that the method–program distinctions actually result in different classroom behaviours (see Long 1984). The psychometric approach is also evident in correlational studies that have examined the relationship between specific classroom behaviours (such as teachers' requests) and learning outcomes (for example, Politzer 1980; Politzer, Ramirez, and Lewis 1981). Chaudron (1988: 30) notes that these studies suffer from a failure to validate the categories used to measure instructional features, as well as from a failure to establish theoretical links between the processes observed and learning outcomes.

Interaction analysis

Interaction analysis involves the use of a form or schedule consisting of a set of categories for coding specific classroom behaviours. Long (1980b) refers to three different types of interaction analysis: in a category system each event is coded each time it occurs, in a sign system each event is recorded only once within a fixed time span, while in a rating scale an estimate of how frequently a specific type of event occurred is made after the period of observation. Initially, schedules were developed for content classrooms (see Flanders 1970 for an account of this early work), but these were rapidly adapted to the language classroom (for example, Moskowitz 1967). Frequently, the categories listed in a schedule reflected the researcher's assumptions about what behaviours were important and were not theoretically motivated. The Marburg schedule (Freudenstein 1977) included categories such as 'phases of instruction', assuming that the basic pattern of a lesson would follow the pattern 'warming up', 'presentation', 'learning', and 'using'. However, subsequent schedules (for example, Fanselow 1977a; Allwright 1980) have attempted to produce more comprehensive and method-neutral sets of categories, while some (for example, Allen, Fröhlich, and Spada 1984) have been based on a theoretical understanding of the nature of L2 acquisition.[2]

Long (1980b) lists twenty-two interaction analysis systems to which several more must now be added. This proliferation reflects differences in research foci. It makes comparison across studies extremely difficult. Also, because the behaviour of the teacher and the learners is often treated separately, information is lost about 'the sequential flow of classroom activities' (McLaughlin 1985: 149). Often interaction analysis runs the risk of producing disconnected tallies of behaviours that obscure the general picture, as there is no basis for deciding which *combinations* of features might be important. Interaction analysis depends on a number of assumptions—for example, that it is possible for an observer to 'read' the intentions of the teacher and students. Such assumptions can be questioned, thus casting doubt on the reliability and validity of the measurements. However, this is more of a problem with 'high inference' categories (for example, 'degree of teacher control exercised over materials') than with 'low inference' categories (for example, 'type of materials—text, audio or visual'), as Long (1980b) has pointed out.

Discourse analysis

Discourse analysis serves as a device for systematically describing the kinds of interactions that occur in language classrooms. Drawing on initial work on content classrooms by Bellack et al. (1966) and by the Birmingham school of linguists (Sinclair and Coulthard 1975; Coulthard and Montgomery 1981; Sinclair and Brazil 1982), discourse analysts give attention not only to the function of individual utterances but also to how these utterances combine to form larger discoursal units. They aim to account for the joint contributions of teacher and student and to describe all the data, avoiding the kind of 'rag bag' category found in many interaction analysis schedules.

McTear (1975) has shown how the Birmingham framework can be adapted to account for the discourse structure found in language lessons. Researchers at CRAPEL in the University of Nancy (e.g Gremmo, Holec, and Riley 1978; Riley 1985) have also made use of discourse analysis to show how 'natural' discourse is distorted in the language classroom as the result of the teacher's dominance. Other researchers (for example, Ellis 1980 and 1984a; Van Lier 1982 and 1988) have developed frameworks based on discourse analysis to characterize the different types of interaction that can occur in the L2 classroom. More commonly, researchers have used the techniques of discourse analysis to develop comprehensive accounts of specific areas of discourse. Chaudron (1977), for example, provides an analysis of teacher feedback, while Long and Sato (1983) offer a discourse-based analysis of teachers' questions. In the case of these latter studies, discourse categories have served as a basis for quantitative research, but, as Chaudron (1988) notes, much of the research within the discourse analysis tradition has been descriptive in nature, concentrating on the development of comprehensive analytical systems.

The ethnographic tradition

The ethnographic tradition involves the kind of detailed descriptive work advocated by Van Lier (1988). It emphasizes the importance of obtaining multiple perspectives through triangulation. Long (1980b) identifies a number of ethnographic approaches. Participant *ethnography* involves the researcher taking a regular part in the activities under study. Non-participant *ethnography* sets the researcher outside the classroom events being observed. It uses a variety of data collection techniques: note-taking, interviewing, questionnaires, ratings of personal opinions, and written documents (for example, teachers' handouts and students' homework). Constitutive ethnography (see Mehan 1979) aims to make explicit the way in which classroom participants succeed in creating and managing the events in which they take part by repeated viewings of videotaped lessons and by soliciting the re-actions of the participants to the events that took place. Microethnography, which focuses on 'particular cultural scenes in key institutional settings' (Erickson and Mohatt 1982, quoted in Mitchell 1985) works in a similar way to constitutive ethnography, but restricts the object of study to contexts of activity recognized as real by the participants (for example, 'getting ready for a break').

The ethnographic tradition has been particularly evident in research into bilingual classrooms (for example, Phillips 1972; Trueba, Guthrie, and Au 1981; Wong-Fillmore 1985; Cathcart 1986) and the diary studies discussed in Chapter 11. Gaies (1983a) gives three advantages of such research: (1) it can account for learners who do not participate actively in class, (2) it can provide insights into the conscious thought processes of participants, and (3) it helps to identify variables which have not previously been acknowledged. Disadvantages include the time-consuming nature of the work needed to collect data, the difficulty of generalizing results, and the danger of ignoring superordinate variables relating to the learners' social context.

These four traditions have produced a wealth of research into L2 class-room processes and products. It is to the results (and insights) which this re-search has provided that we now turn.

Comparative method studies

The aim of comparative method studies is to establish which of two or more methods or general approaches to language teaching is most effective in terms of the actual learning (the 'product') that is achieved after a given period of time. Many of the earlier studies were 'global' in nature, conducted over weeks, months, and even years. The later ones have tended to examine differ-ences resulting from shorter periods of exposure to different methods.

The 1960s were characterized by what Diller (1978) called 'the language teaching controversy'. This pitted the claims of rationalist approaches to lan-guage teaching against those of empiricists. Methods such as the traditional grammar–translation method and the cognitive–code method emphasized the provision of explicit knowledge through rule explanation and of learning simultaneously through all four skills, while so-called 'functional' methods such as audiolingualism and the oral approach emphasized inductive rule learning through listening and extensive oral practice. At the time, it seemed logical to investigate which method produced the better results.

In an early study, Scherer and Wertheimer (1964) compared the grammar–translation method and the audiolingual approach by following the progress of different groups of college-level students of L2 German taught by each method and tested at the end of the their first and second year of study. The results showed that students in the grammar–translation group did better in reading and writing while the students in the audiolingual group did better at listening and speaking. In other words, each method resulted in learning 'products' that reflected the instructional emphasis.

A subsequent large-scale study known as the Pennsylvania Project (Smith 1970) compared the effects of three methods on beginning and intermediate French and German classes at the high-school level. The three methods were (1) 'traditional' (i.e. grammar–translation), (2) 'functional skills' (essentially the audiolingual approach), and (3) 'functional skills plus grammar'. Student achievement in the four skills of listening comprehension, speaking, reading, and writing was evaluated at mid-year and at the end of the year using a battery of standardized tests. The results in general showed no significant differences between the three methods, except that the 'traditional' group was superior to the other two groups on two of the reading tests. After two years, the 'traditional' group again surpassed the 'functional skills' group in reading ability but did significantly worse on a test of oral mimicry. No differences were found in the students' performance on the other tests.

Hauptman (1970) compared the effects of instruction based on a 'structural' approach (where the grammatical structures were sequenced according to level of difficulty) and a 'situational' approach (consisting of dialogues arranged by situation). In this case the learners were third to sixth grade students of Japanese. In general, the situational group performed better than the structural group on situational test items, and did as well on structural test items; however, this difference was found to be significant only for high aptitude/high IQ students in the situational group. Design problems (such as the short length of the teaching programme—only three weeks—and the fact that one person did all the teaching) make it difficult to reach firm conclusions from this study.

In general, therefore, these studies failed to provide convincing evidence that one method was superior to another. One possible explanation, as suggested by Clark (1969) in his detailed discussion of the Pennsylvania Project, was that the distinctions between the different methods were not in fact clear. Clark comments:

> If ostensibly different teaching methods tend in the course of the experiment to resemble one another in terms of what actually goes on in the classroom, the likelihood of finding significant differences in student performance is accordingly reduced.

As Allwright (1988) has carefully documented, this led to the development of instruments for observing what actually takes place during the course of instruction (for example, Jarvis 1968) and a focus on describing language lessons at the level of technique rather than method (for example, Politzer 1970).

Comparative method studies were not abandoned, however. Asher and associates (for example, Asher, Kusudo, and de la Torre 1974; see Asher 1977 for a review) conducted a number of studies designed to compare the effects on learning of Total Physical Response (TPR), a method devised and promoted by Asher, and other methods, in particular the audiolingual approach. Asher claims that the results of these studies show that TPR results in greater short-term and long-term retention of new linguistic material and better understanding of novel utterances. He also suggests they indicate that learners are able to transfer the training in listening they received to other skills—speaking, reading, and writing. Furthermore, Asher reports that students taught by TPR were more likely to continue studying the foreign language and displayed more positive attitudes. Krashen (1982: 156) concludes his survey of Asher's studies by claiming that 'the TPR results are clear and consistent, and the magnitude of superiority of TPR is quite striking'. A number of caveats are in order, however. First, Asher had a vested interest in finding in favour of TPR; second, the period of instruction was relatively short—only 20 hours in some studies; third, only beginners were investigated. We do not know, therefore, whether the method is equally effective in the long term or with advanced learners. Nevertheless, the TPR studies stand out in comparative method studies as providing evidence that support the superiority of a particular method.

More recent discussions of language teaching methodology have emphasized the importance of providing opportunities for learners to communicate. The few studies that have investigated the effectiveness of communicative language teaching, however, have led to the same kind of indeterminate results found in the early global method studies. Palmer (1979) compared the effects of 'traditional' instruction and 'communicative' instruction involving extensive peer-communication based on language games. The subjects were Thai learners of English. No significant differences between the groups were found. One possible explanation for this unexpected finding, according to Krashen (1981), was that while teacher talk was in the target language in the traditional group, it was in the learners' L1 in the communicative class. Hammond (1988) compared groups of students in a Spanish program at two universities. Eight experimental groups were taught by means of the Natural Approach (Krashen and Terrell 1983) and 52 control groups were taught by means of the grammar–translation method, which emphasized the deductive learning of grammar. Although in general the experimental groups outperformed the control groups in both a mid-term and a final examination, many of the differences were not significant. This study did show, however, that students in a communicative classroom did no worse in learning grammar than those in a traditional program—a point we will take up in a later section.

The difficulties of conducting effective comparisons between 'communicative' and 'non-communicative' classrooms are also evident in a carefully planned study by Allen, Swain, Harley, and Cummins (1990). This was based on Stern's (1990) distinction between 'experiential' and 'analytic' teaching strategies (see Table 13.2). Allen et al. used an interaction analysis schedule (cailed the Communicative Orientation to Language Teaching, or COLT) to describe the teaching strategies used in eight grade 11 French classes in Toronto. The information provided by this was used to rank the classes according to how experiential/analytic they were. This study differs from the earlier ones, then, in that the comparison involved examining classrooms that varied in terms of the actual processes observed to take place (in other words, it had a process element). It was hypothesized that the analytic classes would perform better on the written and grammatical accuracy measures and that the experiential classes would do better on measures of sociolinguistic and discourse competence, but when pre- and post-test measures were compared, this was not found to be the case. There were a few statistically significant differences between the two most experiential and the two most analytic classes, but even in this comparison Allen et al. admit the results were 'somewhat disappointing'.

Experimental features	Analytic features
1 Substantive or motivated topic or theme (topics are not arbitrary or trivial).	1 Focus on aspects of L2, including phonology, grammar functions, discourse, sociolinguistics.
2 Students engage in purposeful activity (tasks or projects), not exercises.	2 Cognitive study of language items (rules and regularities are noted; items are made salient, and related to other items and systems.
3 Language use has characteristics of real talk (conversation) or uses any of the four skills as part of purposeful action.	3 Practice of rehearsal of language items or skill aspects.
4 Priority of meaning transfer and fluency of over linguistic error avoidance and accuracy.	4 Attention to accuracy and error avoidance.
5 Diversity of social interaction.	5 Diversity of social interaction desirable.

Table 13.2:   Experiential and analytic features in language pedagogy (from Stern 1990)

With the exception of the TPR studies, then, comparative method studies have failed to produce evidence that one method results in more successful learning than another. There are many reasons for this. As Lightbown (1990) notes in her discussion of Allen et al.'s study, one is that foreign language lessons of any type often result in relatively little progress. Another is that individual learners benefit from different types of instruction (a point taken up in the next chapter). A third reason is that language classes tend to offer very similar opportunities for learning irrespective of their methodological orientation. It is probably true to say that comparative method studies, even when conducted with due regard for classroom 'processes', afford little insight into how instructional events contribute to learning. 'Method' may not be the most appropriate unit for investigating the effect that language teaching has on L2 learning.

Aspects of classroom interaction

The perceived failure of the global method studies of the 1960s led to the development of an alternative approach to investigating classroom language learning. According to Gaies (1983a), *classroom process research* was based on three basic premises; a rejection of the notion that classrooms differ on a single variable such as 'method', an emphasis on describing instructional events as fully as possible as a way of generating (rather than testing) hypotheses, and the priority of direct observation of classroom lessons. Following work on content classrooms, the perceived goal was to discover and describe how teachers 'accomplish classroom lessons' (Mehan 1974). Classroom process research viewed language lessons as 'socially constructed events' and sought to understand how they took place. As Allwright (1983) notes, the research was 'illuminative' rather than hypothesis-testing.

Initially, the research was not informed by any underlying theory of L2 acquisition, but attention focused increasingly on examining instructional events in relation to the kinds of interactional theories discussed in Chapter 7. In particular, Long's claims about the value of interactionally modified input has supported a number of studies investigating the extent to which the negotiation of meaning occurs in different instructional contexts. Some of these studies continued to rely on the direct observation of actual classroom events, but others sought to manipulate instructional variables such as participant (as in studies of small group work) and task (as in studies of different types of pedagogic tasks) experimentally.

No attempt will be made here to follow the historical progression of classroom-orientated L2 research. Instead, we will begin with research that has considered the general nature of L2 classroom discourse, and then move on to examine studies that have investigated a number of different aspects of classroom interaction (for example, teacher talk and teachers' questions).

The nature of second language classroom discourse

Classroom discourse mediates between pedagogic decision-making and the outcomes of language instruction, as Figure 13.1 from Allwright and Bailey (1991) shows. Teachers plan their lessons by making selections with regard to what to teach (syllabus), how to teach (method), and perhaps also the nature of the social relationships they want to encourage (atmosphere). When acted on, their plans result in 'classroom interaction'. This is not planned in advance, but rather is 'co-produced' with the learners. In part, it will reflect the pedagogic decisions that have been taken, but it will also evolve as part of the process of accomplishing the lesson. The interaction provides learners with opportunities to encounter input or to practise the L2. It also creates in the learners a 'state of receptivity', defined as 'an active openness, a willingness to encounter the language and the culture' (op cit.: 23).

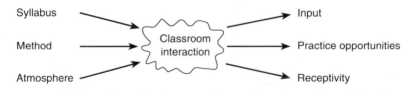

Figure 13.1:   The relationship between plans and outcomes (from Allwright and Bailey 1991: 25)

Our concern here is with the nature of classroom interaction. Although classroom interactions are not usually designed in advance of a lesson, they have been found to manifest distinct and fairly predictable characteristics. These will be considered in terms of (1) the structure and general characteristics of classroom discourse, (2) types of language use, (3) turn-taking, and (4) differences between classroom and naturalistic discourse.

Structure and general characteristics

Classroom discourse has an identifiable structure. Mehan (1979) distinguished three components in general subject lessons: (1) an opening phase, where the participants 'inform each other that they are, in fact, going to conduct a lesson as opposed to some other activity', (2) an instructional phase, where information is exchanged between teacher and students, and (3) a closing phase, where participants are reminded of what went on in the core of the lesson. However, language lessons often seem just to start and stop (i.e. they consist entirely of the instructional phase), perhaps because the content is 'language' itself.

In one of the best known accounts of classroom discourse, Sinclair and Coulthard (1975) develop a hierarchical model by identifying the following 'ranks' in the structure of a lesson: (1) lesson, (2) transaction, (3) exchange, (4) move, and (5) act. Overall, a 'lesson' has only a weakly defined structure, consisting of 'an unordered series of transactions'. A 'transaction' consists of a 'preliminary', one or more 'medial', and a 'terminal' exchanges. It is most easily identifiable by means of 'boundary exchanges', signalled by framing and focusing moves. The element of structure that is most clearly defined, however, is that of 'teaching exchange', which typically has three phases, involving an 'initiating' move, a 'responding' move, and a 'follow-up' move, as in this example:

T: Ask Anan what his name is? (initiating)
S: What's your name? (responding)
T: Good. (follow-up).

This exchange became known as 'IRF'. Each move is realized by means of various kinds of 'acts'—the smallest unit in the discourse system. For example, the follow-up move can be performed by means of an 'accept' (for example, 'yes'), an 'evaluate' (for example, 'good') or a 'comment' (for example, 'that's interesting').

This system was not developed to account for language lessons, but as McTear (1975) has shown, it fits remarkably well. Only small changes are necessary. For example, students in the L2 classroom often produce an additional response after the follow-up move in IRF exchanges:

T: What do you do every morning?
S: I clean my teeth.
T: You clean your teeth every morning.
S: I clean my teeth every morning.

The exchange structure is, therefore, IRF(R). It should be noted, however, that this structure is only likely to arise in classroom discourse which is teacher-controlled. Although IRF(R) exchanges tend to dominate, other kinds can also be found. Van Lier (1988) points out that it is easy to overstate the lack of flexibility evident in L2 classroom discourse. He found that although the discourse is often strictly controlled by the teacher, learners do sometimes initiate exchanges, and 'schismic talk' (talk that deviates from some predetermined plan) also occurs, at least in some classrooms.

A number of interaction analysis schedules have also attempted to account for the general characteristics of classroom discourse. Some of the most frequently cited are Fanselow (1977a), Allwright (1980) and Allen, Fröhlich and Spada (1984). The last mentioned was used in the comparison of experiential and analytic teaching approaches discussed in the previous section. We will focus on it here.

The Communicative Orientation in Language Teaching (COLT) (Allen, Fröhlich and Spada 1984) differs from the systems that preceded it in that it was not only informed by current theories of communicative competence and communicative language teaching but also by research into L1 and L2 acquisition.[3] The authors comment:

> The observational categories are designed (a) to capture significant features of verbal interaction in L2 classrooms and (b) to provide a means of comparing some aspects of classroom discourse with *natural* language as it is used outside the classroom (1984: 232).

The system is in two parts. The first part, 'A description of classroom activities', is designed for use in real-time coding. It consists of a set of general categories broken down into narrower sub-categories, in line with earlier systems. The main unit of analysis is 'activity type'; examples of the kinds of activities that might be identified are drill, translation, discussion, game and dialogue. Each activity is then described in terms of participant organization (whether whole class, group work, or individual work), content (the subject matter of the activities), student modality (the various skills involved in the activity), and materials (type, length, and source/purpose). This part, therefore, relies on pedagogic rather than interactional constructs. However, the second part, 'Communicative features', reflects a more discoursal perspective on the classroom. Coding is based on an audio recording of the classes observed. Seven communicative features are identified relating to use of the target language, whether and to what extent there is an information gap, sustained speech, whether the focus is on code or message, the way in which incorporation of preceding utterances takes place, discourse initiation, and the degree to which linguistic form is restricted. Table 13.3 illustrates Part Two of the system by comparing extracts from two lessons, one reflecting a 'stereotyped routine', and the other communication that is closer to natural language behaviour. Unlike other interaction analysis systems, COLT has been used quite extensively in classroom research (Spada 1987; Harley, Allen, Cummins, and Swain 1990). It has been successfully used to distinguish the types of interaction that occur in different L2 classrooms.

A   Analytical instruction

	Utterance	Communicative features
T:	What's the date today?	L2/pseudo-request/minimal speech
S_1:	April 15th	L2/predictable information/ultraminimal speech/limited form
T:	Good.	L2/comment/minimal speech
T:	What's the date today?	L2/pseudo-request/minimal speech
S_2:	April 15th.	L2/predictable information/ultraminimal speech/limited form
T:	Good.	L2/comment/minimal speech

B   Experiential instruction

	Utterance	Communicative features
T:	What did you do on the weekend?	L2/genuine request/minimal speech
S:	I went to see a movie.	L2/giving unpredictable information/minimal speech/ unrestricted form
T:	That's interesting. What did you see?	L2/comment/elaboration (genuine request for information)/ sustained speech
S:	E.T. I really liked it. He's so cute.	L2/giving unpredictable information/sustained speech/ unrestricted form
T:	Yes. I saw it too and really liked it. Did anyone else see it?	L2/comment/expansion/elaboration (genuine request for information)/sustained speech.

Table 13.3:   Interaction in analytical and experiential type lessons (from Allen, Fröhlich, and Spada, 1984)

The aim of interaction analysis systems such as COLT is to identify significant aspects of L2 classroom discourse and to develop specific categories that allow for quantification. By so doing they provide a basis for investigating which interactional features are important for language acquisition. However, as we noted earlier in this chapter, they have a number of drawbacks.

Types of language use

Other researchers have sought to describe classroom interaction by identifying the different types of language use or interaction found in L2 classrooms. We will now examine a number of such accounts.

Allwright (1980) provides what he calls 'a macro-analysis of language teaching and learning' by identifying three basic elements:

1 *Samples*, instances of the target language, in isolation or in use
2 *Guidance*, instances of communication concerning the nature of the target language
3 *Management activities*, aimed at ensuring the profitable occurrence of (1) and (2) (1980: 166).

These elements are not mutually exclusive, as instances of 'guidance' and 'management activities' automatically provide 'samples'. They are held to vary according to their relative proportion, their distribution between teacher and learner, their sequencing, and the language used (target or other).

Other accounts of types of classroom use distinguish between interaction where the focus is the code itself (a key feature of the language classroom) and interactions which centre on genuine meaning exchange. McTear (1975), for instance, identifies four types of language use based on this general distinction:

1 Mechanical (no exchange of meaning is involved)
2 Meaningful (meaning is contextualized but there is still no information conveyed)
3 Pseudo-communicative (i.e. new information is conveyed but in a manner that is unlikely in naturalistic discourse)
4 Real communication (i.e. spontaneous speech resulting from the exchange of opinions, jokes, classroom management, etc.).

Mechanical and meaningful language use involve a focus on the code, while real communication by definition entails genuine information exchange; pseudo-communicative lies somewhere in between.

The frameworks developed by myself and Van Lier are a little more complicated, as they involve two dimensions rather than one. In Ellis 1984a, I distinguished 'goal' (the overall purpose of an interaction) and 'address' (who talks to whom). Three goals were specified: (1) core goals, where the focus is on the language itself (medium), on some other content (message), or embedded in some ongoing activity such as model-making (activity); (2) framework goals associated with the organization and management of classroom events; and (3) social goals. I discussed interactional sequences taken from an ESL classroom in Britain to illustrate how the type of goal influences the discourse, and then speculated about the learning opportunities each type affords. I pointed out that interactional events with core goals are likely to restrict learners to a responding role, whereas framework and social goals provide opportunities for them to initiate discourse and to perform a wider range of language functions. Kaneko (1991) used this framework to examine the effect of language choice (target or the learners' L1) on learning. She found that the items that Japanese high school students reported learning in English lessons occurred most commonly in interactional events with core goals where there was an element of spontaneous language use.

In Van Lier's (1982; 1988) framework, there are four basic types of classroom interaction, according to whether the teacher controls the topic (i.e. what is talked about) and the activity (i.e. the way the topic is talked about). Type 1 occurs when the teacher controls neither topic nor activity, as in the small talk sometimes found at the beginning of a lesson or in private talk between students. In Type 2 the teacher controls the topic but not the activity; it occurs when the teacher makes an announcement, gives instructions, or delivers a lecture. Type 3 involves teacher control of both topic and activity, as when the teacher elicits responses in a language drill. In Type 4 the teacher controls the activity but not the topic, as in small-group work where the procedural rules are specified but the students are free to choose what to talk about. In a further development of this framework, Van Lier (1991) adds a third dimension: the function that the language serves. He follows Halliday (1973) in distinguishing three types of function: ideational (telling people facts or experiences), interpersonal (working on relationships with people), and textual (signalling connections and boundaries, clarifying, summarizing, etc.).

These broad frameworks have been developed through ethnographic studies of language classrooms and, as such, were not intended to serve as schemes for coding specific classroom behaviours. Often it is not clear what unit of classroom discourse they are intended to relate to—in Ellis (1984) I considered them in terms of interactional 'sequences', loosely defined as a unit of discourse with a unitary topic and purpose, while Van Lier illustrates his framework with reference to instructional activities. Their advantage is that they provide a tool for understanding classroom interaction and how it might affect learning. Their disadvantage is that they do not permit precise quantification, and thus cannot be easily used in experimental or correlational research that seeks to establish relationships between classroom processes and L2 learning statistically.

Turn-taking

Research which has specifically examined turn-taking in the L2 classroom has drawn extensively on ethnomethodological studies of naturally occurring conversations (for example, Sacks, Schegloff, and Jefferson 1974). These identified a number of rules that underlie speaker selection and change: only one speaker speaks at a time; a speaker can select the next speaker by nominating or by performing the first part of an adjacency pair (for example, asking a question that requires an answer); a speaker can alternatively allow the next speaker to self-select; and there is usually competition to take the next turn. Classroom researchers frequently highlight the differences between turn-taking in natural and classroom settings. McHoul (1978), for instance, has shown that classroom discourse is often organized so that there is a strict allocation of turns in order to cope with potential transition and distribution problems and that who speaks to whom at what time is firmly controlled. As a result there is less turn-by-turn negotiation and competition, and individual student initiatives are discouraged.

Turn-taking in language classrooms does not differ from that in general subject classrooms. Lörscher (1986) examined turn-taking in English lessons in different types of German secondary schools and found that turns were almost invariably allocated by the teacher, the right to speak returned to the teacher when a student turn was completed, and the teacher had the right to interrupt or stop a student turn. Lörscher argues that these rules are determined by the nature of the school as a public institution and by the teaching–learning process.

The most extensive discussion of turn-taking in the L2 classroom can be found in Van Lier (1988). In an attempt to identify participation in classroom discourse characterized by learner initiative, Van Lier identifies a number of turn-taking behaviours that he considers indicative of such initiative. Examples, under the headings provided by Van Lier, are:

Topic

The turn is off-stream (i.e. discontinuing), introduces something new, or denies/disputes a proposition in a previous turn.

Self-selection

Selection originates from the speaker.

Allocation

The turn selects one specific next speaker.

Sequence

The turn is independent of sequence.

Van Lier goes on to provide an example of how this system can be used to assign a 'participation index' for each of the participants in an interaction. He uses this type of analysis to challenge McHoul's claim that 'only teachers can direct speakership in any creative way' (1978: 188), pointing out that in his L2 classroom data many of the teacher's utterances were undirected and the learners frequently did self-select. He also notes that explicit turn-taking sanctions are rare in adult L2 classrooms and that there is a considerable degree of tolerance of unintelligibility. It would seem, therefore, that the rigid rules of turn-taking described by Lörscher are not always evident.

Studies of turn-taking in the L2 classroom make explicit comparisons between classroom and naturalistic discourse, the underlying assumption being that the former is less conducive to successful L2 acquisition than the latter. Van Lier offers an interesting explanation for why this might be the case. He suggests that if turn-taking is rigidly controlled, the learners have no need to attend carefully to classroom talk to identify potential transition points when they can take their turn. As a result, they lack 'an intrinsic motivation for listening' and so are robbed of input. However, to date there have been no studies investigating the effect of different types of turn-taking on acquisition.

The difference between classroom and naturalistic discourse

The discourse that results from trying to learn a language is different from that which results from trying to communicate. Edmondson (1985) draws on Labov's idea of the Observer's Paradox (see Chapter 4), to suggest that there is also 'the teacher's paradox', which states:

> We seek in the classroom to teach people how to talk when they are not being taught (1985: 162).

Thus, there is a tension between discourse that is appropriate to pedagogic goals and discourse that is appropriate to pedagogic settings. However, because the classroom affords opportunities to communicate as well as to learn, there are 'co-existing discourse worlds'. Kramsch (1985) suggests that the nature of classroom discourse will depend on the roles the participants adopt, the nature of the learning tasks, and the kind of knowledge that is targeted. Instructional discourse arises when the teacher and the students act out institutional roles, the tasks are concerned with the transmission and reception of information and are controlled by the teacher, and there is a focus on knowledge as a product and on accuracy. Natural discourse is characterized by more fluid roles established through interaction, tasks that encourage equal participation in the negotiation of meaning, and a focus on the interactional process itself and on fluency. One way in which the two worlds can be brought together is through communicating about learning itself, as suggested by Breen (1985).

However, although the potential exists for natural discourse to occur in the classroom, studies show that it seldom does. Pica and Long (1986) found that there was very little negotiation of meaning in elementary ESL classrooms in Philadelphia in comparison to native speaker–non-native speaker conversations outside the classroom, as evident in significantly fewer conversational adjustments by the teachers. Politzer, Ramirez, and Lewis (1981) report that 90 per cent of all student moves were responses, testifying to the limited nature of opportunities to participate that learners are afforded in classrooms—a point we will take up later. These and other studies (see Glahn and Holmen 1985; Kasper 1986) testify to the restricted nature of pedagogic discourse, although other studies, such as Enright (1984) show that there can be considerable variation between classrooms.

The teacher's control over the discourse is the main reason for the prevalence of pedagogic discourse. Researchers at CRAPEL (for example, Gremmo, Holec, and Riley 1977; 1978) have argued that in the classroom setting discourse rights are invested in the teacher. It is the teacher who has the right to participate in all exchanges, to initiate exchanges, to decide on the length of exchanges, to close exchanges, to include and exclude other participants, etc. When teachers elect to act as 'informants' or 'knowers' (Corder 1977b), they are likely to make full use of their rights, and as a consequence the learners are placed in a dependent position. As a result there is a preponderance of teacher acts over student acts (typically in a 2:1 ratio), because teachers open and close each exchange.

In the opinion of some, pedagogic discourse constitutes a 'falsification of behaviour' and a 'distortion' (Riley 1977), but other researchers see it as inevitable and even desirable (for example, Edmondson 1985). To date, there are more arguments than evidence, although as we will see in Chapter 14, formal instruction does appear to result in faster learning and higher levels of ultimate achievement.

Teacher talk

The bulk of L2 classroom research has focused on specific aspects of interaction, which we will now consider, beginning with teacher talk. Chaudron (1988: Chapter 3) provides a comprehensive survey of studies of teacher talk. His main conclusions are summarized in Table 13.4.

Feature	Main conclusions	Main studies
Amount of talk	In general, the research confirms the finding for L1 classrooms—namely, that the teacher takes up about two-thirds of the total talking time.	Legaretta 1977; Bialystok et al. 1978; Ramirez et al. 1986.
Functional distribution	There is considerable evidence of variability among teachers and programs, but the general picture is again one of teacher dominance in that teachers are likely to explain, question and command and learners to respond.	Shapiro 1979; Bialystok et al. 1978; Ramirez et al. 1986.
Rate of speech	Teachers, like native speakers in general, slow down their rate of speech when talking to learners in comparison to other native speakers and also do so to a greater extent with less proficient learners. However, there is considerable variability among teachers.	Henzl 1973; Dahl, 1981; Wesche and Ready 1985; Griffiths 1990 and 1991a.
Pauses	Teachers are likely to make use of longer pauses when talking to learners than to other native speakers.	Downes 1981; Hakansson 1986; Wesche and Ready 1985.
Phonology, intonation, articulation, stress	There have been few studies which have attempted to quantify these aspects of teacher talk, but teachers appear to speak more loudly and to make their speech more distinct when addressing L2 learners.	Henzl 1973 and 1979; Downes 1981; Mannon 1986.
Modifications in vocabulary	Several studies provide evidence of a lower type–token ratio and teachers also vary in accordance with the learners' proficiency level, but Wesche and Ready (1985) found no significant vocabulary modifications in university lectures to L2 learners.	Henzl 1979; Mizon 1981.
Modifications in syntax	There is a trend towards shorter utterances with less proficient learners, but some studies which use words per utterance as a measure report no modifications. The degree of subordination tends to be lower, but again results have been mixed. Teachers use fewer marked structures such as past tense. More declaratives and statements than questions are used in comparison to natural discourse. Ungrammatical teacher talk is rare.	Pica and Long 1986; Gaies 1977; Kleifgen 1985; Early 1985; Wesche and Ready 1985.
Modifications in discourse	There is some evidence that teachers use more self-repetitions with L2 learners, in particular when they are of low level proficiency.	Hamayan and Tucker 1980; Ellis 1985d.

Table 13.4:   Main features of teacher talk (summarized from Chaudron 1988: Chapter 3)

The research indicates that teachers modify their speech when addressing L2 learners in the classroom in a number of ways and also that they are sensitive to their learners' general proficiency level. Many of these modifications are the same as those found in foreigner talk, but some seem to reflect the special characteristics of classroom settings—in particular the need to maintain orderly communication. However, Chaudron does not consider teacher talk sufficiently different to justify calling it a distinct sociolinguistic register.

Tutor talk (the talk addressed by classroom learners to other, less proficient learners in the context of peer tutoring) has been studied by Flanigan (1991). She studied pairs of non-native speaker elementary school children, where the more linguistically competent child was asked to assist the less competent in how to use a computer in a graded reading and listening 'station'. She found that little negotiation of meaning took place, as the less proficient learners lacked the ability to respond. However, the more proficient children made use of the same discourse strategies as those observed in adult caretakers and teachers: repetitions, expansions, explanations, rephrased questions, and comprehension checks. Interestingly, the child non-native speaker tutors made no attempt to simplify their talk grammatically or lexically.

Teacher talk has attracted attention because of its potential effect on learners' comprehension, which has been hypothesized to be important for L2 acquisition (see Chapter 7). However, little is known about what constitutes optimal teacher talk. It is not even clear on what basis teachers make their modifications. Hakansson (1986) speculates that they may aim at some hypothetical average learner, in which case the input is not likely to be tuned very accurately to the level of many of the learners in some classrooms. This suggests that tutor talk may be more facilitative of acquisition than the teacher talk that occurs in lockstep teaching. Indeed, Flanigan hypothesizes that it may provide 'an optimum environment for successful language learning in the elementary school' (1991: 153).

Error treatment

There is now a considerable literature dealing with *error treatment* (see Hendrickson 1978; Chaudron 1987 and 1988; Allwright and Bailey 1991 for surveys of the literature). Much of this literature is taken up with addressing whether, when, and how errors should be corrected and who should correct them. There have been very few studies that have examined the effect of error treatment on acquisition. In this section we will attempt to clarify the main issues that have been identified in the research rather than provide a comprehensive survey.

The first issue is terminological in nature. A number of terms have been used to refer to the general area of error treatment; these are 'feedback', 'repair', and 'correction'. 'Feedback' serves as a general cover term for the information provided by listeners on the reception and comprehension of messages. As Vigil and Oller (1976) have pointed out, it is useful to distinguish 'cognitive' and 'affective' feedback; the former relates to actual understanding while the latter concerns the motivational support that interlocutors provide each other with during an interaction. 'Repair' is a somewhat narrower term used by ethnomethodologists such as Schegloff, Jefferson, and Sacks (1977) to refer to attempts to identify and remedy communication problems, including those that derive from linguistic errors. 'Correction' has a narrower meaning still, referring to attempts to deal specifically with linguistic errors; it constitutes an attempt to supply 'negative evidence' (see Chapter 10) in the form of feedback that draws the learners' attention to the errors they have made.

In an attempt to give greater precision to the term 'treatment', Chaudron (1977) distinguishes four types:

1 Treatment that results in learners' 'autonomous ability' to correct themselves on an item.
2 Treatment that results in the elicitation of a correct response from a learner.
3 Any reaction by the teacher that clearly transforms, disapprovingly refers to, or demands improvement.
4 Positive or negative reinforcement involving expressions of approval or disapproval.

Type (1) cannot be determined within the context of a single lesson as it requires evidence that the feedback has had some effect on acquisition. Type (4) is limiting because it restricts the object of enquiry to occasions when the teacher draws explicit attention to learner performance. Most studies have examined (2) and (3).

A second issue concerns learners' attitudes towards error treatment. Cathcart and Olsen (1976) found that ESL learners like to be corrected by their teachers and want more correction than they are usually provided with. Chenoweth et al. (1983) found that learners liked to be corrected not only during form-focused activities, but also when they were conversing with native speakers. This liking for correction contrasts with the warnings of Krashen (1982) that correction is both useless for 'acquisition' and dangerous in that it may lead to a negative affective response. Krashen may be partly right, though, as Cathcart and Olsen also report that when a teacher attempted to provide the kind of corrections the learners in their study said they liked, it led to communication which the class found undesirable.

Of considerable interest is the extent to which teachers should correct learners' errors. Here, there are widely diverging opinions, reflecting the different theoretical arguments about the need for negative feedback (see the section on 'Error evaluation' in Chapter 2). Irrespective of what teachers *should* do, there is the question of what they actually *do* do. Chaudron (1988) reviews a number of studies which have investigated this (Salica 1981;

Courchene 1980; Chaudron 1986; Fanselow 1977b; Lucas 1975). The main conclusions are that certain types of errors are much more likely to be treated than others: discourse, content, and lexical errors receive more attention than phonological or grammatical errors; that many errors are not treated at all; that the more often a particular type of error is made, the less likely the teacher is to treat it; and that there is considerable variation among teachers regarding how frequently error treatment takes place. Edmondson (1985) has also pointed out that teachers sometimes correct 'errors' that have not in fact been made!

Another issue concerns who performs the treatment. Studies of repair in naturally-occurring conversations have shown a preference for self-initiated and self-completed repair (see Chapter 7). In classroom contexts, where, as we have seen, discourse rights are unevenly invested in the teacher, other-initiated and other-completed repair can be expected. This is what Van Lier (1988) predominantly found. Other patterns of repair can also occur, however. Kasper (1985) found that in the language-centred phase of an English lesson in a Grade 10 Danish gymnasium, the trouble sources were identified by the teacher but they were repaired either by the learners responsible for them or by other learners. In the content phase of the same lesson, self-initiated and self-completed repair was evident, although the learners were inclined to appeal for assistance from the teacher. As Van Lier (1988: 211) points out, the type of repair work is likely to reflect the nature of the context which the teacher and learners have jointly created. Also, the teacher's personal teaching style may influence the type of repair work that occurs, as Nystrom's (1983) study of the correction styles of four teachers in bilingual classrooms demonstrates.

Probably the main finding of studies of error treatment is that it is an enormously complex process. This is evident in the elaborative decision-making systems that have been developed (Long 1977; Day et al. 1984; Chaudron 1977) and also in the extensive taxonomies of the various types of teachers' corrective reactions (Allwright 1975; Chaudron 1977; Van Lier 1988). Chaudron's system, for example, consists of a total of 31 'features' (corrective acts that are dependent on context) and 'types' (acts capable of standing independently). These descriptive frameworks provide a basis for examining teachers' preferences regarding types of error treatment. Studies have shown, for instance, that repetitions of various kinds are a common type of corrective feedback (Salica 1981; Nystrom 1983). The frameworks are indicative of the careful descriptive work that needs to be done before it is possible to set about investigating the effects of different kinds of error treatment on acquisition.

Further evidence of the complexity of the decision-making process during error treatment is the inconsistency and lack of precision that teachers manifest. Long (1977) notes that teachers often give more than one type of feedback simultaneously, and that many of their feedback moves go unnoticed by the students. Teachers are likely to use the same overt behaviour for more than one purpose. A teacher repetition can occur after a learner error and serve as a model for imitation, or it can function as a reinforcement of a correct response. Teachers often fail to indicate where or how an utterance is deviant. They respond positively even when the learners continue to make the error. They correct an error in one part of the lesson but ignore it in another. They may give up on the task of correction if learners do not seem able to cope. Nystrom (1983) sums it all up with this comment:

> teachers typically are unable to sort through the feedback options available to them and arrive at the most appropriate response.

According to some (for example, Allwright 1975), inconsistency is inevitable and even desirable, as it reflects the teacher's attempts to cater for individual differences among the learners, but according to others (for example, Long 1977), it is damaging. These differences in opinion reflect the relative emphasis given to 'cognitive' and 'affective' aspects of feedback.

Given the amount of research that has been devoted to error treatment, the lack of studies that have investigated its effect on acquisition is disappointing. Chaudron (1986) reports that only 39 per cent of the errors treated in the immersion classroom he studied resulted in successful student uptake (i.e. were eliminated in the next student utterance). This might suggest that error treatment is often not successful, but it is possible that by raising learners' consciousness it contributes to acquisition in the long run (see Chapter 14 for a discussion of the possible delayed effect of formal instruction). Ramirez and Stromquist (1979) report a positive correlation between the correction of grammatical errors and gains in linguistic proficiency, but this study did not examine the relationship between the correction and elimination of specific errors.

At the moment, therefore, opinions abound about what type of error treatment is best, but there is little empirical evidence on which to make an informed choice. Currently, two recommendations seem to find wide approval. One is that error treatment should be conducted in a manner that is compatible with general interlanguage development (for example, by only correcting errors that learners are ready to eliminate). The other is that self-repair is more conducive to acquisition than other-repair, as it is less likely to result in a negative affective response (Van Lier 1988). These recommendations await empirical support.

Teachers' questions

Teachers, whether in content classrooms or in language classrooms, typically ask a lot of questions. For example, in three hours of language-content teaching, Johnston (1990) observed a total of 522 questions of various types. Long and Sato (1983) observed a total of 938 questions in six elementary level ESL lessons. One reason for the prevalence of questioning is undoubtedly the control which it gives the teacher over the discourse. Thus, a question is likely to occupy the first part of the ubiquitous three-phase IRF exchange. Questions typically serve as devices for initiating discourse centred on medium-orientated goals, although they can also serve a variety of other functions.

Much of the work on questions has centred on developing taxonomies to describe the different types. In one of the earliest taxonomies, Barnes (1969; 1976) distinguished four types of questions he observed in secondary school classrooms in Britain: (1) Factual questions ('what?'), (2) Reasoning questions ('how?' and 'why?'), (3) Open questions that do not require any reasoning, and (4) Social questions (questions that influence student behaviour by means of control or appeal). Barnes made much of the distinction between two types of reasoning questions: those that are *closed* in that they are framed with only one acceptable answer in mind, and those that are *open* because they permit a number of different acceptable answers. Barnes also points out that many questions have the appearance of being open, but, in fact, when the teacher's response to a student's answer is examined, turn out to be closed; he calls these *pseudo-questions*.

Kearsley (1976) provides an extensive taxonomy of question types based on conversational data. Long and Sato (1983) made use of this framework in their study of ESL teachers' questions, but found it necessary to make a number of changes to include new categories to accommodate questions not accounted for by Kearsley's categories, and to eliminate other categories not exemplified in their classroom data. Their taxonomy can be found in Table 13.5. It centres on the distinction between echoic questions, which ask for the repetition of an utterance or confirmation that it has been properly understood, and epistemic questions which serve the purpose of acquiring information. The latter type include *referential* and *display questions*, which Long and Sato discuss in some detail. This distinction is similar but not identical to the open/closed distinction of Barnes. Referential questions are genuinely information-seeking, while display questions 'test' the learner by eliciting already known information, as in this example:

T: What's the capital of Peru?
S: Lima
T: Good.

Referential questions are likely to be open, while display questions are likely to be closed, but it is possible to conceive of closed referential questions and of open display questions.

Other taxonomies have focused on other aspects of teachers' questions. Koivukari (1987), for example, is concerned with depth of cognitive processing. Rote questions (those calling for the reproduction of content) are considered to operate at the surface level, while two kinds of 'comprehension' questions (those calling for the reproduction of content and those calling for the generation of new content) operate at progressively deeper levels.

Type	Sub-category	Example
1 Echoic	a comprehension checks	All right?; OK?; Does everyone understand 'polite'?
	b clarification requests	What do you mean?; I don't understand; What?
	c confirmation checks	S: Carefully T: Carefully?; Did you say 'he'?
2 Epistemic	a referential	Why didn't you do your homework?
	b display	What's the opposite of 'up' in English?
	c expressive	It's interesting the different pronunciations we have now, but isn't it?
	d rhetorical	Why did I do that? Because ...

Table 13.5:   A taxonomy of the functions of teachers' questions (from Long and Sato 1983; based on Kearsley 1976)

Hakansson and Lindberg (1988), in an analysis of questions in Swedish, distinguish questions according to form and cognitive level as well as their communicative value and orientation. There are three formal categories: nexus questions (questions that can be answered 'yes' or no'), alternative questions (that provide the responder with an alternative to select from), and x-questions (where there is an unknown element, as in *wh*-questions). At the cognitive level, questions are distinguished according to whether they relate to cognitive memory (i.e. they require some kind of reproduction of information), convergent thinking (i.e. they require the 'analysis and integration of given or remembered data within a tightly structured framework', 1988: 77) or divergent/evaluative thinking (i.e. they require data to be generated freely and independently). The categories relating to communicative value reflect the referential/display distinction, while those relating to communicative orientation concern whether the question is focused on the language itself (the medium) or on real-life topics (the message). This latter distinction is viewed as continuous rather than dichotomous. Hakansson and Lindberg's taxonomy is probably the most comprehensive yet devised for the language classroom.

Whereas there are few problems in assigning teachers' questions to formal categories, difficulties do arise with functional, communicative, or cognitive categories. These are 'high inference' and often call for substantial interpretative work on the part of the analyst. It is not always clear-cut, for example, whether a question is referential or display, as this example from White (1992) illustrates:

T: How long have you worn glasses? How long have you had your glasses?
S: I have worn these glasses for about six years.
T: Very good. Same glasses?

In one sense the teacher's question is referential as it concerns an area of the student's private life she has no knowledge of, but in another sense it can be considered display, as it is clearly designed to elicit a specific grammatical structure and was evaluated accordingly. This question suggests the need for an additional category, such as Barnes' (1969) 'pseudo-question'. But it can only be considered 'pseudo' if we know that the teacher *intended* the question to be of the display variety—something that we cannot be sure about, as teachers may ask a referential question only to treat the students' responses in the same manner as they would their responses to a display question. The above exchange is certainly an example of what McTear (1975) called 'pseudo-communication'. Its prevalence in many classrooms makes the coding of individual questions problematic to a degree not always recognized by researchers.

Studies of teachers' questions in the L2 classroom have focused on the frequency of the different types of questions, wait time (the length of time the teacher is prepared to wait for an answer), the nature of the learners' output when answering questions, the effect of the learners' level of proficiency on questioning, the possibility of training teachers to ask more 'communicative' questions, and the variation evident in teachers' questioning strategies. Much of the research has been informed by the assumption that L2 learning will be enhanced if the questions result in active learner participation and meaning negotiation.

Barnes (1969) found that the secondary school teachers he investigated showed a clear preference for closed reasoning-type questions. Open reasoning-type questions, where the teacher accepted a number of answers, were rare. Barnes argues that the teachers saw their role as 'more a matter of handing over ready-made material, whether facts or processes, than a matter of encouraging pupils to participate actively and to bring their own thoughts and recollections into the conversation' (1969: 23). Closed questions are indicative of a transmission style of education; Barnes argues in favour of a more interpretative style. Long and Sato (1983) adopt a similar position. They found that the ESL teachers in their study asked far more display than referential questions (476 as opposed to 128). This contrasts with native-speaker behaviour outside the classroom where referential questions predominate (999 as opposed to 2 display questions in the sample they studied). They conclude that 'ESL teachers continue to emphasize form over meaning, accuracy over communication' (1983: 283–4). Other studies (for example, White and Lightbown 1984; Early 1985; Ramirez et al. 1986; Johnston 1990; White 1992) also indicate that display/closed questions are more common than referential/open questions in the L2 classroom.[4]

Teachers also seem to prefer instant responses from their students. White and Lightbown (1984) found that the teachers in their study rarely gave enough time for students to formulate answers before repeating, rephrasing, or redirecting the question at another student. The shorter the wait time, however, the fewer and the shorter the student responses.

One way in which teachers' questions might affect L2 acquisition is in terms of the opportunities they provide for learner output. In Chapter 7 (page 282) we considered the *comprehensible output hypothesis*, according to which 'pushed output' helps learners to reconstruct their interlanguages. A key issue, therefore, is whether teachers' questions cater for such output. Brock (1986) found that responses to referential questions (mean length = 10 words) were significantly longer than responses to display questions (mean length = 4.23 words) in four advanced ESL classes at the University of Hawaii. Similar results have been obtained by Long and Crookes (1987), Nunan (1990a), and White (1992), suggesting that the findings are fairly robust. However, as White illustrates, it does not follow that *all* display questions produce short responses. It is obvious that 'there is no meaning left to negotiate' in exchanges such as the following:

T: What's this?
S: It's a cup.
T: Good.
(Long and Crookes 1987)

However, this is not the case in the following exchange based on a reading comprehension lesson:

T: Did anyone manage to find some reasons for this?
S: With the decline of religion there is no pressure on woman to get married.
(White 1992: 26)

In both cases, however, the exchange began with a display question. White argues that there is a need for a more delicate categorization of display questions to allow for the different types of student response evident in these two exchanges. Banbrook (1987) provides similar examples to show that referential questions can also elicit responses of varying lengths and complexity. It should also be noted that the length of the student's response to a question is only one of several possible measures of learner output. Of equal interest, perhaps, is the length of the sequence initiated by a question. In this respect, Long and Crookes (1987) report that display questions elicited more student turns than referential questions. Clearly, more work is needed to tease out the relationship between question type and learner output.

Very few studies have examined the relationship between teachers' choice of questions and the learners' proficiency level. In Ellis (1985d), I found no difference in the use a teacher made of open and closed questions with two learners over a nine month period, but I did find evidence to suggest that the cognitive complexity of the questions changed, with more questions requiring some form of comment as opposed to object identification evident at the end of the period. White (1992) found that one of his teachers used more referential questions with a high-level class and more display questions with a low level class, but the other teacher in this study followed the opposite pattern.

Given the indeterminate nature of the findings of many of the studies, it might seem premature to prescribe questioning strategies in teacher education. A number of studies, however, have investigated the effect of training teachers to ask specific types of questions. Brock (1986) and Long and Crookes (1987) found that instructors given training in the use of referential questions did respond by increasing the frequency of this type of question in their teaching. Koivukari (1987) found that training led to teachers using more 'deep' comprehension questions and fewer superficial rote questions, and was also able to demonstrate that an experimental group who benefited from this treatment showed improved comprehension scores.

Finally, several studies have pointed to the necessity of acknowledging individual variation in teachers' questioning strategies. White (1992), for instance, found very different patterns of questioning in his two teachers. Other studies by Long and Sato (1983), Long and Crookes (1987), Koivukari (1987), and Johnston (1990) also report extensive differences, although not all these researchers bothered to draw the reader's attention to them explicitly. Banbrook and Skehan (1990) provide illustrative evidence to argue that there is both intra- and inter-teacher variation. They identify three sources of intra-teacher variation: '(a) general teacher variation, (b) variation that takes place over the phases of the lesson and (c) variation in question asking . . . that is the consequence of the teaching tasks or activities engaged in' (1990: 150). They argue that although variation in teachers' questions is well attested, its parameters are not yet well understood.

These comments by Banbrook and Skehan lead us back to one of the central issues in L2 classroom research—the extent to which it should be 'qualitative' and descriptive as opposed to 'quantitative' and experimental. Many of the studies discussed above have belonged to the latter paradigm, but one might feel along with Van Lier (1988) that:

> the practice of questioning in L2 classrooms, pervasive though it is, has so far received only superficial treatment . . . An analysis must go beyond simple distinctions such as display and referential to carefully examine the purposes and the effects of questions, not only in terms of linguistic production, but also in terms of cognitive demands and interactive purpose (1988: 224).

It might also stretch to examining the questions asked by learners. Studies by Midorikawa (1990) and Robson (1992) suggest that, when learners are given the opportunity to ask questions, they automatically elect to use open, referential-type questions. Rost and Ross (1991) have shown that certain types of learner question (for example, 'forward inference' questions in which the learner asks a question using information that has already been established) facilitate comprehension and, also, that such questioning strategies are trainable.

Finally, more attention needs to be paid to the socio-cultural context of questioning strategies. Poole (1992), for example, has suggested that the use of display or closed questions in most of the classrooms that have been studied may reflect the caretaker practices evident in white, middle-class western society. Teachers from such a background ask questions because they provide a means by which an expert (the teacher) and a novice (the learner) can jointly construct a proposition across utterances and speakers. Poole suggests that this may be why such questions are so ubiquitous and why they are difficult to get rid of; teachers are being asked to reject a strategy that they feel to be culturally warranted. A corollary of this line of reasoning is that display questions may not be the norm in classrooms where the participants belong to a culture that does not utilize such caretaking practices.

Learner participation

Given that learners are often restricted to a responding role, it is not surprising to find that their opportunities for participating productively in the L2 classroom are constrained. If, as has been hypothesized, opportunities for using L2 resources are important for acquisition (see the account of the comprehensible output hypothesis in Chapter 7), then it would seem that learning may be inhibited in the classroom. The assumption that participation is important for learning also underlies several of the studies of motivation discussed in Chapter 11. We will consider participation here both from the point of view of both (1) quantity and (2) quality.

Quantity of participation

There is no clear evidence that the extent to which learners participate productively in the classroom affects their rate of development. Table 13.6 summarizes a number of correlational studies that have examined the relationship between amount of learner classroom participation and L2 achievement/proficiency. The results are mixed. Whereas studies by Seliger (1977),[5] Naiman et al. (1978), and Strong (1983; 1984) report positive correlations between various measures of learner participation and proficiency, Day (1984) (in a careful replication of Seliger's study) and to a large extent Ely (1986a) found no such relationships. Allwright (1980) also found that the learner who participated the most in the lesson he analysed was not among those who showed the greatest advances. As Chaudron (1988) and I (Ellis 1988b) have pointed out, correlational studies of learner participation are not easy to interpret, as there is no way of telling whether a 'participation causes learning' or 'proficiency causes participation' explanation is correct when a significant relationship is discovered. As we will see in Chapter 15,

Study	Subjects	Measures of participation	Measures of learning	Results
Seliger 1977	6 adults learning English	Amount of verbal interaction; any student speech act counted as interaction; initiations and responses scored separately.	Cloze test; structure test; aural comprehension test.	Total interaction scores correlated significantly with structure and aural comprehension tests; proportion of initiations correlated significantly with aural comprehension test.
Naiman et al. 1978	Learners of L2 French in Grades 8, 10, and 12 in schools in Canada	Various measures of classroom behaviour (e.g. student hand-raising, student complete/partial responses; student correct/incorrect responses.	Comprehension test; imitation test.	Hand-raising, complete responses, correct responses and no. of responses over 10 significantly related to both criterion measures. Negative correlations for incorrect/partially correct responses found.
Strong 1983/1984	13 kindergarten pupils in bilingual classrooms	Responses to utterances produced by others	Various measures of linguistic correctness, vocabulary and pronunciation based on classroom speech.	Children's responsiveness correlated significantly with proficiency measures.
Day 1984	26 adult learners of L2 English	Responses to teacher general solicits; self-initiated turns	Oral proficiency assessment of grammatical, pragmatic, and sociolinguistic competence; cloze test.	No significant relationships between measures of participation and criterion measures reported.
Ely 1986b	72 first year adult learners of L2 Spanish; half in first and half in second quarter.	Number of self-initiated utterances in Spanish, i.e. volunteering a question or a response.	Oral fluency in a story reproduction task; oral correctness (based on error count); written correctness.	Weak relationship between participation and oral correctness found for first quarter students; no other significant relationships found.

Table 13.6:   Classroom-based studies of learner participation

when studies investigating the effects of quantity of practice directed at specific grammatical structures are considered, there are grounds for believing that practice does not make perfect, suggesting that the preferred interpretation ought to be that proficiency causes participation. That is, the more proficient the learners are, the more they get to participate.

Quality of learner participation

While the amount of participation may not be a key factor in L2 acquisition, a stronger case can be made for the importance of high-quality participation, as we will see in the following sections that deal with tasks and small-group work. Swain's (1985) comprehensible output hypothesis claims that acquisition is promoted when there are opportunities for pushed output, not just any kind of output.

One of the factors that seems to determine the quality of learner participation in classroom settings is the degree of control the learners exercise over the discourse. Cathcart (1986) studied the different kinds of communicative acts performed by eight Spanish-speaking children in a variety of school settings (recess, seatwork, free play, ESL instruction, playhouse, interview and storytelling). She found that situations where the learner had control of the talk were characterized by a wide variety of communicative acts and syntactic structures, whereas the situations where the teacher had control seemed to produce single-word utterances, short phrases, and formulaic chunks. Other researchers have also found marked differences in the quality of learners' participation depending on the kind of activity they are involved in. House (1986), for instance, compared the performance of advanced German learners of L2 English in a role play situation, where they had considerable freedom, and a teacher-led discussion. She found that the learners confined themselves to an 'interactional core' in the discussion, failing to use 'discourse lubricants' such as topic introducers (for example, 'You know...') and various kinds of supportive and amplifying moves. In contrast, the role-play conversations sounded much more natural. In cases where participation is strictly controlled, there may be few opportunities for learners to practise communicative strategies (Rosing-Schow and Haastrup 1982, cited in Holmen 1985). This may be one reason why many foreign language learners reliant on the classroom fail to develop much strategic competence.

Interactions derived from controlled language practice such as pattern drills are likely to be characterized by strict teacher control. In Ellis (1988b), however, I emphasized that practice of this kind is still to be considered a 'social event involving personal investment on the part of the learner' (1988b: 34), and that some degree of negotiation is still involved. I identified a number of factors that may affect the nature of the interactions in practice sessions, for example whether the learners' responses are volunteered or nominated, the teacher's policy regarding the distribution of practice opportunities, and individual learner differences that affect the degree of anxiety experienced. Gaies (1983b) also argued that negotiation is evident in teacher-dominated lessons. He studied the kind of feedback that learners provide in tasks that required the teacher to describe graphic designs and found evidence of considerable variation among the learners. It is important, therefore, not to over-emphasize the restrictive nature of learner participation in teacher-controlled interaction.

Tasks and interaction

The study of 'tasks' has proved to be one of the most productive seams of L2 classroom research. It has been motivated in part by proposals for 'task-based syllabuses' (see Long 1985b; Prabhu 1987; Long and Crookes 1992). These attempt to specify the content to be taught in terms of a series of activities to be performed by the students, either with the teacher or in small group work. The term 'task' remains a somewhat vague one, however, as Crookes' (1986) very general definition illustrates:

> a piece of work or an activity, usually with a specified objective, under-taken as part of an educational course, or at work.

In practice it appears to refer to the idea of some kind of activity designed to engage the learner in using the language communicatively or reflectively in or-der to arrive at an outcome other than that of learning a specified feature of the L2.[6] A task, so defined, can be a real-world activity or a contrived, ped-agogic activity (Nunan 1989), as long as the *process* of completing the task corresponds to that found in discourse based on the exchange of information.

The main research goal has been to uncover how specific variables affect the interaction that occurs when learners attempt to perform a task. These variables can usefully be classified into those that relate to the task itself and those that relate to the participants performing the task. We will consider the former in this section, reserving the latter to the following section.

One of the main problems facing research into task variables is determining which variables to investigate. As Pica, Kanagy, and Falodun (forthcoming) point out, there are a vast number of social and cognitive parameters that may lead to variation in learner performance. They argue that there is a need for some kind of 'task framework' that can be used to classify and compare dif-ferent tasks. The one they provide is based on two general dimensions: (1) procedures for communicating the information—who holds the informa-tion, who conveys it, who requests it, who gives feedback on comprehension, the direction of the information flow, whether the information-exchange is required or optional and the degree of preciseness required; and (2) the task resolution—whether it is divergent or convergent. However, they also re-cognize that there are other dimensions that are potentially important, in-cluding the linguistic and cognitive requirements of the task and the sociolinguistic context in which the task is carried out. Attempts to classify task variables in this way are helpful, but we are a long way from developing a taxonomy that is both complete and psycholinguistically justified.

Equally important in the study of tasks is the choice of measures of interaction (the dependent variable). A number of studies have examined the quantity of interactional modifications found in the negotiation of meaning (see Chapter 7) on the grounds that these are important for comprehension, and thereby also for acquisition. One criticism that might be levelled at such studies is that they ignore important qualitative differences in the way meaning is negotiated (Ehrlich, Avery, and Yorio 1989; Newton 1991). A number of studies have also examined to what extent interlocutors provide feedback that non-native speakers then act on by incorporating corrected features into their own production. Other aspects of interaction which have been investigated include the number and size of turns, repair (and, more narrowly, self-corrections), speaking speed, reference (exophoric v. anaphoric), topic, instructional input, hypothesizing and procedural moves. However, most of these have been investigated in only one or two studies, making it difficult to reach any firm conclusions.

Table 13.7 summarizes the main studies that have investigated task variables. From this it can be seen that several studies have examined the effects on interaction of tasks that involve a one-way exchange of information as opposed to those that require a two-way exchange. Examples of the former include giving instructions and telling a personal story, while an example of the latter is types of communication games in which the participants each hold part of the information needed to complete the task. The essential difference lies in whether the exchange of information is optional or required. A number of studies (Long 1980a; Doughty and Pica 1986; Newton 1991) show that two-way tasks result in increased negotiation of meaning. Gass and Varonis (1985a), however, found no difference in the number of indicators of nonunderstanding (a measure of meaning negotiation) in the two types of tasks. They suggest that the distinction between one-way and two-way tasks is better seen as continuous rather than dichotomous, which 'makes comparison a complex process' (1985a: 159). However, Long (1989) considers the results of the research sufficiently robust to claim that 'two-way tasks produce more negotiation work and more useful negotiation work than one-way tasks' (1989: 13).

This is one of three conclusions regarding task-types that Long arrives at in his own survey of the research. The second is that 'planned tasks "stretch" interlanguages further and promote destabilization more than unplanned tasks' (1989: 14). This is supported by task-based studies of learner variability (see Chapter 4) which show that learners tend to produce more complex and more target-like language when they have time to plan their output. It should be noted, however, that it is not yet clear whether performing in planned tasks subsequently helps learners to perform better in unplanned tasks.

Study	Subjects	Task variables	Main results
Long 1980a	16 NS–NS and 16 NS–NNS dyads	One way vs two-way information gap tasks	Performance by NS–NNS dyads sigificantly different on two-way but not one-way tasks.
Tong-Fredericks 1984	NNS–NNS dyads	(1) Problem-solving task, (2) role play task (3) 'authentic interaction' task	Self-corrections more evident on (2) and (3) than on (1). More turns per minute on (1). No differences in speaking speed.
Gass and Varonis 1985a	9 NNSs in 3 dyads and 1 triad	One way vs two-way information gap tasks	No significant differences according to task found.
Crookes and Rulon 1985	15 NS–NNS dyads	(1) free conversation task, (2) closed/convergent task and (3) two-way information-gap task.	NS feedback following non-target-like usage more evident in (2) and (3). NNSs more likely to incorporate NS feedback in (2) than in (1).
Duff 1986	4 NNS dyads	Convergent vs divergent tasks	Longer turns and more negotiation of meaning in divergent tasks found.
Doughty and Pica 1986	NNS–NNS dyads	One way vs two-way information gap tasks	More negotiation of meaning found in two-way tasks.
Berwick 1990	12 NS–NNS dyads	(1) teaching vs non-teaching tasks, (2) social exchange vs problem-solving and (3) experiential vs expository.	More repair and negotiation of meaning found in non-teaching than in teaching tasks. Exophoric and anaphoric reference more evident in experiential and expository tasks respectively. Teaching/expository tasks were 'the most conservative discourse environment'.
Brown 1991	NNS dyads	(1) tight vs loose tasks, (2) open vs closed tasks and (3) procedural vs interpretative tasks	Procedural task did not result in instances of 'instructional input' or 'hypothesizing'. No other significant differences found.
Newton 1991	2 groups of ESL learners	(1) one-way vs two-way tasks, (2) medical topic vs zoo topic and (3) open vs closed tasks.	More negotiation found on tasks that were two-way/closed than on the one-way/open tasks. Also, the two-way/closed tasks led to a focus on language and task content while one-way/open tasks led to a focus on opinions and meaning.
Jones 1991	13 adolescent ESL learners	(1) role-play debate and (2) a crisis simulation—(2) being more open-ended than (1).	No difference between tasks for amount of talk and turn length but (2) led to more topic sequences.

Table 13.7: Studies investigating the effects of task-variables on L2 interaction

Long's third conclusion is that 'closed tasks produce more negotiation work and more useful negotiation work than open tasks' (1989: 16). An open task is one where the participants know there is no predetermined solution; examples include free conversation, debate, ranking activities, and suggesting preferred solutions to problems. A closed task requires the participants to reach a single, correct solution or one of a small, finite set of correct solutions; examples include identifying the differences between two pictures and identifying the perpetrator of a crime. Studies by Duff (1986) and Berwick (1990) lend support to Long's conclusion. Long claims that closed tasks result in more topic and language recycling, more feedback, more feedback incorporation, more rephrasing, and more precision. However, as F. Jones (1991) points out, more open-ended tasks may afford learners greater interactive freedom to practise conversational skills such as topic selection and change.

The work so far has helped to identify a number of task variables that affect participant performance, but it is probably premature to reach firm conclusions. In particular, it is still not clear which task variables are the most important ones, and even less clear what effect combining different sets of variables has. Also, little is known about how the performance elicited by different tasks affects acquisition (see Chapter 7). Thus, despite Long and Crookes' (1987) claim that 'it should be possible to build up a multidimensional classification, organizing tasks in terms of their potential for second language learning on the basis of psycholinguistically and psychologically-motivated dimensions', it is likely to be a long time before such a system becomes available.

Small-group work and interaction

Another area of L2 research of considerable pedagogic interest is interaction in small groups. Group work is often considered an essential feature of communicative language teaching (see Brumfit 1984). Long and Porter (1985) summarize the main pedagogical arguments in favour of it. It increases language practice opportunities, it improves the quality of student talk, it helps to individualize instruction, it promotes a positive affective climate, and it motivates learners to learn. In addition to these pedagogic arguments, a psycholinguistic justification has been advanced: group work provides the kind of input and opportunities for output that promote rapid L2 acquisition.

A number of studies have compared the interaction in teacher-centred lessons with that found in group work. Long, Adams, McLean, and Castanos (1976) report that students working in small groups produced a greater quantity of language and also better quality language than students in a teacher-fronted, lockstep classroom setting. Small-group work provided more opportunities for language production and greater variety of language use in initiating discussion, asking for clarification, interrupting, competing for the floor, and joking. Pica and Doughty (1985a), however, found no difference in the overall quantity of interactional adjustments in a one-way task performed in a lockstep setting and in small-group work, but when they replicated this study using a two-way task (Pica and Doughty 1985b), they did find significant differences. The overall results of these two studies are shown in Table 13.8. They indicate that there is an interaction between the participation pattern and the type of task. Thus, group-work only results in more negotiation of meaning if the task is of the required-information exchange type.

Task	Participation pattern			
	Teacher-fronted		Group	
	n	%	n	%
Optional information exchange	347	49	145	40
Required information exchange	385	45	400	66

% = % of T-units and fragments combined.

Table 13.8:   Comparison of modified conversational interaction generated by optional vs required information exchange tasks on teacher-fronted and group participation patterns (from Pica and Doughty 1988: 51)

As reported in Chapter 7, several other studies confirm the value of interlanguage talk as a source of opportunities for meaning negotiation (for example, Gass and Varonis 1985a and Porter 1986). Rulon and McCreary (1986) investigated the effect of participation pattern on the negotiation of content, defined as 'the process of spoken interaction whereby the content of a previously encountered passage (aural or written) is clarified to the satisfaction of both parties' (1986: 183). They found little difference between small-group and teacher-led discussions with regard to length of utterance, syntactic complexity, or interactional features, but they did find that significantly more negotiation of content occurred in the small-group discussions.

From these studies it seems reasonable to conclude that interaction between learners can provide the interactional conditions which have been hypothesized to facilitate acquisition more readily than can interaction involving teachers. However, a word of caution is in order. Both Pica and Doughty, and Porter, show, not surprisingly, that interlanguage talk is less grammatical than teacher talk. It is possible, therefore, as Plann (1977) has suggested, that exposure to incorrect peer input may lead to fossilization. However, two of Porter's findings give reason to believe that this may not be the case. She reports that when learners corrected each other's errors, they did so wrongly only 0.3 per cent of the time and also that only 3 per cent of the errors the learners produced could be attributed to repetition of a fellow-learner's error. In general, therefore, learners do not appear to be unduly disadvantaged by exposure to deviant input from other learners. In one respect, though, interlanguage talk may be inferior. Porter found that non-native speakers did not provide sociolinguistically appropriate input and suggests that learners may not be able to develop sociolinguistic competence from each other—a point that is taken up in the following section.

These studies were guided by Long's hypotheses regarding the importance of interactionally modified input. Bygate (1988), however, like Hatch (1978a), emphasizes the role of learner output in collaborative discourse construction. He suggests that group work facilitates acquisition by affording learners opportunities to build up utterances through the use of satellite units. These are words, phrases or clauses that constitute either moodless utterances that lack a finite verb or some kind of syntactically dependent unit, as in the following example:

S1: at the door
S2: yes in the same door I think
S3: besides the man who is leaving
S2: behind him.

Bygate found numerous examples of such units in the speech produced by learners working in small groups. He argues that the use of satellite units allows for flexibility in communication, allows the learner time to prepare messages, and allows messages to be built up collaboratively thus helping to extend learners' capabilities. However, as Bygate provides no comparable data from teacher-controlled lessons, it is not clear whether satellite units are a special feature of group work. Færch's (1985) examples of vertical constructions in interactions controlled by the teacher suggest that they might not be, although it is probable that they are at least more frequent in interlanguage talk.

Other studies of non-native speaker–non-native speaker interaction have focused on the participant variables that affect the quality of the talk. One variable that has been found to be important is sex (see Chapter 6). Another variable that has been investigated is the proficiency level of the learners. Porter (1986), in the same study referred to above, investigated the input and output in non-native speaker dyads of mixed proficiency levels. Not surprisingly, intermediate learners got more input and better quality input from advanced than from other intermediate learners. Conversely, advanced learners get more opportunity to practise when they are communicating with intermediate learners. Porter feels that mixed pairings offer something to both sets of learners. In a very careful study involving a task that required the resolution of a number of 'referential conflicts' (the subjects were given maps that differed in a number of ways), Yule and McDonald (1990) examined the effects of proficiency in mixed-level dyads, where in some interactions the sender of the information was of low proficiency and the receiver high proficiency (L>H) and in others the opposite (H>L). They found that the L>H interactions were at least twice as long as the H>L interactions. Furthermore, negotiated solutions to the referential problems were much more likely to take place in the L>H condition than in the H>L (a 67.5 per cent success rate as opposed to 17.5 per cent). Where mixed ability pairings are involved, therefore, success (and perhaps also acquisition) is more likely if the lower-level learner is in charge of the key information that has to be communicated.

To sum up, the research suggests that learners will benefit from interacting in small group work. They will have more opportunity to speak, to negotiate meaning and content, and to construct discourse collaboratively. This may help acquisition. They will also be exposed to more ungrammatical input. Whether this has an adverse effect is not yet clear. It is possible, however, that small group work does not aid the development of sociolinguistic competence. Less is known about the ideal composition of small groups, but studies suggest that mixed gender and mixed proficiency pairs may be optimal.

Summary

In this section we have considered a number of aspects of L2 classroom discourse. Given the diversity of classroom settings and the breadth of research now available, it is difficult to arrive at a general picture. The following statements constitute an attempt to do so, but should be treated circumspectly:

1 L2 classroom discourse often manifests a well-defined structure, consisting of IRF(R). Different types of language use are evident, reflecting in particular whether the focus of an interaction is on learning the L2 or communicating in it. L2 classroom discourse is likely to differ from natural discourse in a number of ways, including the rules and mechanisms for turn-taking.
2 Teachers adapt the way they talk to classroom learners in similar ways to foreigner talk. They also modify their language in accordance with the learners' proficiency level.
3 Error treatment constitutes an interactional event of considerable complexity. Teachers do not correct all their students' errors and they are often inconsistent in whether they correct and which errors they correct. Learners often fail to incorporate the teacher's corrections in their subsequent responses.
4 Teachers vary considerably in the number and the type of questions they ask. Several studies have shown that display/closed questions predominate over referential/open questions. The latter type may result in more meaning negotiation and more complex learner output.
5 Studies investigating the relationship between learner participation and L2 proficiency have produced inconsistent results. Both a 'participation causes proficiency' and a 'proficiency causes participation' explanation need to be considered, with the latter more likely.
6 The quantity and quality of interaction varies according to task. Although much work needs to be done to establish how specific task characteristics affect interaction, there is some preliminary evidence to suggest that tasks which require information exchange, allow learners to

plan their output, and have a limited number of possible outcomes result in interaction which facilitates acquisition.

7 Small-group work has been found to provide more opportunities for meaning negotiation than lockstep teaching, if the tasks are of the 're-quired-information exchange' type. The quality of interaction also appears to be enhanced if the learners comprising the pair/group are heterogenous with regard to sex and proficiency level. Group work may not be the best way to develop sociolinguistic competence.

It needs to be emphasized that the studies considered in this section have been descriptive in nature. They provide no direct evidence to show any link between particular aspects of classroom discourse and L2 learning. In many cases, however, they have been informed by theories of L2 acquisition, and it is on the basis of these that claims regarding the facilitative or debilitative effects of certain kinds of interaction have been based.

The relationship between classroom interaction and second language learning

We shall now consider the few studies that have investigated the relationship between classroom interaction and L2 learning. We will begin with studies that have examined whether successful L2 learning is possible in a favourable classroom environment and then move on to look at studies that have tried to establish direct links between features of interaction and learning.

Second language learning in the communicative classroom

A number of scholars have proposed that the most effective way of developing successful L2 competence in a classroom is to ensure that the learners have sufficient opportunities to participate in discourse directed at the exchange of information (see Krashen 1982; Swain 1985; Prabhu 1987). According to this view, the failure of many classroom learners derives from the lack of comprehensible input and/or comprehensible output. One way of investigating this claim is by studying to what extent a communicative classroom environment results in successful L2 learning.

There is now convincing evidence that learners can learn 'naturally' in a communicative classroom setting. We have already considered Hammond's (1988) study (see page 571). Terrell, Gomez, and Mariscal (1980) showed that elementary learners of L2 Spanish can successfully acquire various question forms simply as a result of being exposed to questions in the input. 74 per cent of 7th grade students' questions and 82 per cent of the 8th and 9th grade students' questions were correctly formed even though no explicit instruction had been provided. Prabhu (1987) developed a programme known as the Communicational Teaching Project (CTP), which had as its aim the development of linguistic competence through a task-based approach to language teaching. This project, which was conducted in a number of secondary schools in Bangalore and Madras with beginner learners of L2 English, was evaluated by Beretta and Davies (1985). Although not all the results showed an advantage for the project schools over the control schools, which were taught by means of the structural–oral–situational method, Davies and Beretta interpret the results as 'being, on the whole, positive' and conclude that 'they provide tentative support for the CTP'. Finally, Lightbown (1992) reports on an interesting project in New Brunswick, in which Canadian French children in grades 3–6 were taught English by listening to tapes and following the written text. Results at the end of the third year of the project showed that 'students in this program have succeeded in learning at least as much English as those whose learning had been guided by the teacher in a more traditional program' (1992: 362). They were as good even at speaking English. The program also resulted in very positive student attitudes. These studies, therefore, demonstrate that the communicative classroom is effective in promoting L2 acquisition. However, it should be noted that in all these studies the learners were at an elementary level.

Other studies suggest that communicative classrooms may not be so successful in promoting high levels of linguistic competence. Krashen (1982) has claimed that immersion classrooms have succeeded in developing very high levels of L2 proficiency, but there is growing evidence that they are not quite so successful as Krashen claims. Researchers have for some time recognized that immersion learners generally fail to acquire certain grammatical distinctions (see Chapter 7). Other studies also suggest there may be limitations on what can be achieved in communicative classrooms. Spada and Lightbown (1989) found that an intensive ESL course (5 hours a day for 5 months), which was taught by means of communicative methods emphasizing tasks leading to natural interaction, produced little evidence of syntactic development. For example, the students were only 50 per cent accurate in their use of plural -*s* and only 20 per cent in the case of V + -*ing*. My study of the requests produced by two classroom learners (Ellis 1992a) also suggests that the communicative classroom may not be well-suited to the achievement of sociolinguistic competence. I argue that classroom learners may experience interpersonal needs to perform speech acts such as requests, and also expressive needs that lead them to do so in a varied ways, but that they do not experience any sociolinguistic need to modify the way they perform requests in accordance with situational factors. This is because 'the classroom constitutes an environment where the interactants achieve great familiarity with each other, removing the need for the careful face-work that results in the use of indirect request-types and extensive modification' (1992a: 20).

One interpretation of the research on communicative classrooms is as follows:

1 Giving beginner learners opportunities for meaningful communication in the classroom helps to develop communicative abilities and also results in linguistic abilities no worse than those developed through more traditional, form-focused approaches.
2 Communicative classroom settings may not be sufficient to ensure the development of high levels of linguistic and sociolinguistic competence, although they may be very successful in developing fluency and effective discourse skills.

The fact that communicating in a language does not guarantee full target-language competence accords with the findings of other non-classroom studies (for example, Schmidt 1983) and with the arguments of Higgs and Clifford (1982) regarding the limitations of 'natural' learning. The problem, therefore, may not be the classroom *per se*, but in learners' general inability to utilize all the information available to them in the input.

The effect of interaction on acquisition

In Chapter 7 we considered a number of experimental studies that investigated whether providing learners with the opportunity to negotiate meaning led to interlanguage development. All of these studies were classroom studies (see Table 7.5). They suggested that negotiation and contextual support can aid the acquisition of vocabulary. However, no study to date has shown that comprehensible input enables learners to acquire grammatical features, although Nobuyoshi and Ellis (1993: Chapter 6) were able to provide limited support for the comprehensible output hypothesis.

In addition to these experimental studies, there have been a number of correlational studies which have looked for a relationship between various aspects of classroom interaction and either learner proficiency or learner output during instruction. A number of these have already been considered in this chapter (for example, those investigating the role of learner participation). Others were considered in Chapter 7. They have produced somewhat mixed results. Snow and Hoefnagel-Höhle (1982), for instance, found no significant relationships, whereas Ramirez and Stromquist (1979) and Mitchell, Parkinson, and Johnstone (1981) did find that some measures of interaction (in particular those relating to formal language work—for example, teacher's use of metalanguage, overt correction, and vocabulary explanation) were correlated with performance on language tests. One explanation for the mixed results can be found in McDonald, Stone, and Yates' (1977) study of 14 adult ESL classes in the United States. This showed that different types of classroom behaviours were related to different kinds of language proficiency. A structured teaching style involving teacher-directed practice activities or question-and-answer sequences was related to improved scores on tests of formal reading skills, while a more open teaching style characterized by free responses, games, and discussion was related to improved oral proficiency.

Correlational studies, however, provide only weak, uncertain evidence of the effects of interaction on learning.

Another approach has been to compare the L2 learning that takes place in classrooms that differ in a number of major ways. Wong-Fillmore (1982) distinguished two basic types of classroom organization in a longitudinal study of classroom ESL learners in a kindergarten setting: (1) teacher-directed classrooms, where interaction involved the teacher and the class, and (2) learner-centred organization, where interactions between teacher and individual students and between the learners themselves took place. The classrooms she investigated also differed with regard to the proportion of L2 learners and native English-speaking children in them. Wong-Fillmore found that these two factors interacted to influence L2 learning. Successful language learning occurred in classes that had a high proportion of L2 learners and were teacher-directed, and also in classes that were more mixed in composition (i.e. had more native English-speaking children) and an open organization. Conversely, much less learning took place in mixed, teacher-directed classes and open classes with large numbers of L2 learners. This study suggests that what is important is access to plentiful, well-formed input tailored to the level of the learner. In classrooms where the learners spend a lot of time talking to other learners (often in their L1) or where the instructional language is not properly adapted, little learning is likely. It should be noted, though, that Wong-Fillmore's (1982) study was based on a small number of classrooms, and also that no attempt was made to quantify either the interactional differences found in the classrooms or the learning gains.

It can be argued, however, that qualitative research of the kind carried out by Wong-Fillmore has contributed most to our understanding of what constitutes an 'acquisition-rich' classroom. In a subsequent paper (Wong-Fillmore 1985), she identifies a number of factors that detailed observations of some 60 classrooms have shown to work for language learning. These are grouped into two sets: (1) class organization and (2) characteristics of teacher talk. With regard to (1), she reports that 'the most successful classes for language learning were the ones that made the greatest use of teacher-directed activities' and, conversely, that 'classes that were open in their structure and those that made heavy use of individual work were among those found to be among the least successful for language learning' (1985: 24). This conclusion, which is similar to that of her earlier study, denies the advantages often claimed for small-group work (see the earlier section in this chapter). The features of teacher-directed interactions that Wong-Fillmore considers facilitative of acquisition include formal lessons with clearly marked boundaries, the use of 'lesson scripts' (i.e. regular formats), and well-established procedures for allocating turns. The important teacher-talk characteristics are a clear separation of languages (i.e. avoidance of translation), an emphasis on communication and comprehension by ensuring message redundancy, the avoidance of ungrammatical teacher-talk, the frequent use of patterns and routines, repetitiveness, tailoring questions to suit the learners' level of proficiency, and general richness of language. It is interesting to note that these include many of the features of foreigner talk which have been hypothesized to facilitate learning (see Chapter 7).

Qualitative research of the kind conducted by Wong-Fillmore provides a broad picture of how interaction in the classroom can affect L2 learning, but it does not shed any light on how specific linguistic features are learnt. This has been one of the goals of the Lancaster group led by Allwright. The method they have developed involves asking classroom learners to complete an 'uptake chart' by recording the items that they think they learnt during a particular lesson. The lesson is recorded and transcribed and the researcher then identifies where the uptaken items occurred during the lesson. This provides a means for exploring the interactional conditions that might have caused learners to uptake items. The main study to date is Slimani (1989). This indicated that neither learner participation nor negotiating meaning led to uptake. What seemed to have an effect was listening to other students. Items 'topicalized' by other students—rather than by the teacher—were most likely to figure as 'uptake'. However, it is not possible to generalize on the basis of this study, which examined only a few lessons in one setting. Also, little is known yet about the reliability and validity of 'uptake' as a measure of L2 learning.

Summary

In general, the research that has investigated the effects of interaction on L2 acquisition has been sparse and disappointing, and few conclusions are possible. There is some evidence to support the following:

1 Opportunities to negotiate meaning may help the acquisition of L2 vocabulary (Tanaka 1991; Yamazaki 1991).
2 Pushing learners to reformulate their utterances to make them more target-like may lead to greater grammatical accuracy in the long term (Nobuyoshi and Ellis 1993).
3 Teacher-controlled 'pedagogic discourse' may contribute to the acquisition of formal language skills, while learner-controlled 'natural discourse' may help the development of oral language skills (McDonald, Stone, and Yates 1977).
4 Learners need access to well-formed input that is tailored to their own level of understanding. This can be achieved in teacher-directed lessons with a clearly-defined structure and by well-adjusted teacher talk (Wong-Fillmore 1982; 1985).
5 Listening to other students in teacher-led lessons may be more important for learning than direct learner participation (Slimani 1989).

These 'insights' have been derived from studies employing very different research methods and they have been informed by widely varying theoretical perspectives. It is not surprising, therefore, that they do not fit neatly together into a sharply-defined, balanced picture.

Conclusion

It is easy to point to the weaknesses of L2 classroom research. Long (1990b) gives a number of reasons why the findings are not yet ready to be passed on to teachers: (1) the studies have generally been small-scale, (2) they have tended to be short-term with the result that little is known about the long-term effects of specific classroom behaviours, (3) the findings have tended to be partial or fragmented in that they have focused on isolated aspects of classroom life, and (4) many of the studies are methodologically flawed (i.e. the analyses have not been tested for reliability or for statistical significance). Long also criticizes 'the absence of theoretical motivation' in many studies, but this reflects his own preference for a 'theory then research' over a 'research then theory' approach, as shown in Long (1985a), and would not be accepted by some researchers, such as Van Lier.[7]

While it is necessary to recognize the weaknesses of the research to date, it is also important to acknowledge its achievements. These include (1) a general acceptance of the need to balance 'external' accounts of language pedagogy of the kind found in methodology handbooks with 'internal' accounts of what actually happens inside the classroom; (2) the availability of a substantial body of descriptive information about specific interactional behaviours (for example, error treatment and questions); (3) a developing understanding of how specific variables (for example, the learners' proficiency and the participation pattern) affect interaction; (4) the availability of a broad set of tools for examining classroom interaction that can be used not only for formal research purposes but also in teacher education and by teachers who wish to join in 'the research enterprise', as Allwright (1988: 257) puts it; and (5) some insights into how interaction shapes L2 learning.

In short, the work done so far has made a real contribution to improving language pedagogy but has contributed little to our understanding of how interaction affects acquisition. This is because, understandably given the short history of L2 classroom research, the bulk of the work has been descriptive rather than explanatory, hypothesis-forming rather than hypothesis-testing. It is not even clear yet how the relationship between interaction and acquisition can be effectively researched in the multi-participant setting of the typical classroom. This is so much more complex than the one-to-one participant settings studied in L1 and naturalistic L2 acquisition research. The methodologies that have been used to date (experimental, correlational, qualitative, and 'uptake' tracing) all have their limitations. Probably the future lies in careful longitudinal studies that focus on both specific classroom behaviours and individual learners, and which make use of both observational and introspective data.

Notes

1 The term 'black box' is often used to describe the learner's mind, or the internal mechanisms responsible for learning. It is used by Long (1980b) to refer to the classroom. As was the case with the learner's mind, little was known for a long time about what actually took place inside the 'black box' of the classroom.

2 What distinguishes these interaction analysis schedules from the earlier ones is the attempt to provide a comprehensive rather than selective account of classroom discourse. Not surprisingly, therefore, they require the analyst to work with recorded lessons rather than through observation of classroom events in real time.

3 Mitchell, Parkinson, and Johnstone (1981) describe another very comprehensive observational schedule which they used in a series of studies of foreign language classrooms in Scotland. Four basic dimensions were identified: (1) topic of discourse, (2) language activity, (3) pupil mode of involvement, and (4) class organization.

4 Chaudron (1988) cites one study (by Bialystok, Fröhlich, and Howard 1978) which showed teachers preferring general information questions, which Chaudron considers 'potentially referential'. However, general information questions can also be of the display/closed types. Johnston's (1990) study of content classrooms shows that this is in fact often the case. It is a mistake, therefore, to associate referential/open questions with information exchange and display/closed questions with a focus on language form.

5 As Chaudron (1988) points out, there are methodological problems with Seliger's study which make the results he obtained very questionable. For example, it is based on only six learners selected from a group of twelve learners, and misuses correlational statistics.

6 This does not accord with all definitions of 'task'. In some definitions (for example, Breen 1987) 'task' is seen as referring to form-oriented as well as meaning-oriented activities.

7 Long does in fact accept that *post hoc* interpretation of results has a place in L2 classroom research. What is disputable is his assertion that 'the lack of a theoretical motivation for studies greatly reduces the value of their findings' (1985a: 166).

Further Reading

There is now an enormous body of L2 classroom research.

M. Long, 'Bibliography of research on second language classroom processes and classroom second language acquisition.' *Technical Report No. 2,* Center for Second Language Classroom Research (University of Hawaii, 1985), provides a list of several hundred.

A number of full-length books provide summaries of the research. The most comprehensive, but perhaps not the most readable, is
C. Chaudron, *Second Language Classrooms* (Cambridge University Press, 1988).
L. Van Lier, *The Classroom and the Language Learner* (Longman (1988), provides an ethnographic perspective;
D. Allwright, *Observation in the Language Classroom* (Longman, 1988) provides an interesting account of the historical development of observational research;
D. Allwright and K. Bailey, *Focus on the Language Classroom* (Cambridge University Press, 1991) provides an accessible account of much of the research in a book designed to encourage teachers to become researchers.

There are also some useful collections of research papers:
H. Seliger and M. Long (eds.), *Classroom Oriented Research in Second Language Acquisition* (Newbury House, 1983).
R. Day (ed.), *Talking to Learn: Conversation in Second Language Acquisition*, (Newbury House, 1986).
G. Kasper (ed.), *Learning, Teaching and Communication in the Foreign Language Classroom*, (Aarhus University Press, 1986).

Key papers or chapters relating to the various topics covered in this chapter are:

1 Interaction analysis

D. Allwright, 'Turns, topics and tasks: patterns of participation in language learning and teaching' in D. Larsen-Freeman (ed.), *Discourse Analysis in Second Language Research* (Newbury House, 1980).
P. Allen, M. Fröhlich, and N. Spada, 'The communicative orientation of language teaching' in J. Handscombe, R Orem, and B. Taylor, (eds.), *On TESOL '83: The Question of Control* (TESOL, 1984).

2 Types of classroom interaction

R. Ellis, *Classroom Second Language Development*, Chapter 5 (Pergamon/ Prentice Hall International 1984).

3 Teacher talk

S. Gaies, 'The nature of linguistic input in formal second language learning: Linguistic and communicative strategies' in H. Brown, C. Yorio, and R. Crymes (eds.), *On TESOL '77* (TESOL, 1977).

4 Error treatment

M. Long, 'Teacher feedback on learner errors: mapping cognitions' in H. Brown, C. Yorio, and R. Crymes (eds.), *On TESOL '77* (TESOL 1977).

5 *Teacher's questions*

M. Long and C. Sato, 'Classroom foreigner talk discourse: Forms and functions of teachers' questions' in H. Seliger and M. Long (eds.), *Classroom Oriented Research in Second Language Acquisition*, Newbury House(1983).

6 *Learner participation*

R. Day, 'Student participation in the ESL classroom.' *Language Learning* (1984) 34:69-98.

7 *Task-based interaction*

S. Gass and E. Varonis, 'Task variation and non-native speaker/non-native speaker negotiation of meaning' in S. Gass and C. Madden (eds.), *Input in Second Language Acquisition* (Newbury House, 1985).

8 *Small-group work and interaction*

P. Porter, 'How learners talk to each other: Input and interaction in task-centred instruction' in R. Day (ed.), *Talking to Learn* (Newbury House, 1986).

9 *The effect of interaction on L2 acquisition*

R. Ellis, 'Learning to communicate in the classroom: a study of two learners' requests.' *Studies in Second Language Acquisition* (1992) 14: 1-23
L. Wong-Fillmore, 'When does teacher talk work as input?' in S. Gass and C. Madden (eds.), *Input in Second Language Acquisition*, (Newbury House, 1985).

14 Formal instruction and second language acquisition

Introduction

In previous surveys of the research that has investigated the effects of *formal instruction* (for example, Long 1983c and 1988; Ellis 1985a and 1990a; Larsen-Freeman and Long 1991), the term 'formal instruction' has been understood to refer to grammar teaching. This reflects both the importance which has been traditionally attached to grammar teaching in language pedagogy, and also the centrality of grammar in SLA research. The focus on grammar has had both a practical and a theoretical motivation. It has helped teachers to understand the factors that determine whether instruction is successful, and it has helped researchers to explore a number of issues of importance for theory building—in particular, the relationship between the linguistic environment and the learner's internal processing mechanisms.

It is useful to take a broader look at the role of formal instruction. To this end, it is helpful to identify a number of general areas of language pedagogy. Figure 14.1 distinguishes between formal instruction directed at cognitive goals, where the focus is on developing linguistic or communicative competence, and metacognitive goals, where the focus is on the use of effective learning strategies. Cognitive goals can be divided into two types, depending on whether the instruction is language-centred or learner-centred. In language-centred instruction, the goal is some aspect of phonology, lexis, grammar, or discourse, where all learners receive the same instruction. In learner-centred instruction, the instruction is still directed at some aspect of language, but an attempt is made to match the type of instruction to the learner, so that different learners are taught in different ways. Formal instruction directed at metacognitive goals is concerned with attempts to train learners to use effective learning strategies. Overall, then, this framework allows us to address the following three questions:

1 To what extent does instruction directed at teaching specific linguistic items or rules work? Do learners learn what they are taught?
2 Does *learner–instruction matching* result in improved language learning?
3 Does learner training enhance learners' ability to learn from formal instruction?

This chapter will seek answers to questions (1) and (2). Learner training has already been considered in Chapter 12.

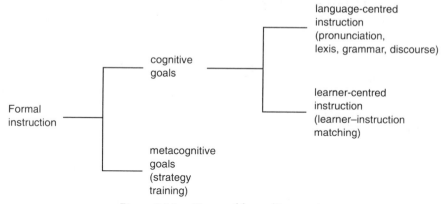

Figure 14.1:   Types of formal instruction

Language-centred instruction

In the previous chapter we considered whether learners were able to develop a native-like competence as a result of communicating in the L2. We saw that the favourable opportunities for communicating provided by immersion classrooms result in near-target levels of discourse and strategic competence, but do not appear to lead to high levels of sociolinguistic or grammatical competence. We considered a number of explanations for this finding, one of which was that fully successful classroom language learning requires formal instruction. It is important to ask, therefore, whether formal instruction does result in better learning. It is also important to ask whether some types of formal instruction work better than others.

The effects of formal instruction on second language learning

There is now a substantial body of research that has investigated whether formal instruction results in better L2 learning. This research is of four different kinds. One group of studies has sought to examine whether learners who receive formal instruction achieve higher levels of L2 proficiency than those who do not. A second group has considered the effects of formal instruction on the accuracy with which learners use specific linguistic items and rules. A third group has studied whether formal instruction affects the order or sequence of acquisition. A fourth group has investigated to what extent any effects for instruction are durable (i.e. whether the effects are short term or long term).

These studies have used a variety of research methods. Some researchers have sought to compare classroom learners with naturalistic learners. In such cases, the effects of instruction are demonstrated by showing that there are differences in the proficiency or in the sequence of acquisition of the two sets of learners. Such comparisons are not easy to interpret, given that any differences may be the result of general differences in the learning environments rather than of focusing on specific properties of the target language. Other researchers have designed experiments to study whether instruction directed at specific features results in their acquisition. These experiments provide clearer evidence, but they are subject to the problems that arise with this kind of research in educational settings, in particular the difficulty of controlling extraneous variables (for example, factors affecting the learners and the teacher as individuals).

Researchers have also measured learning outcomes in different ways. In some cases a formal language test has been used (for example, a multiple choice test or a grammaticality judgement test). In other studies, spontaneous language use has been elicited by some kind of communicative task and obligatory occasions for the use of specific features identified. As we shall see later, it is possible that formal instruction will show an effect in the case of tests but not in natural production—as is predicted by some theories of L2 acquisition such as Krashen's Input Hypothesis (see page 273).

This diversity in research methodology can be justified by the need to conceptualize the relationship between formal instruction and acquisition in different ways. Teachers use formal instruction because they want to develop learners' general proficiency, to improve the accuracy with which they use specific features, and to help them acquire new linguistic features. However, the diversity also makes it difficult to compare the results obtained by different studies and, therefore, to reach firm conclusions. For this reason, we will first consider each major area of research separately.

The effects of formal instruction on general language proficiency

All the studies reviewed in this section have considered learners' general proficiency, measured in a variety of ways. These studies did not investigate whether formal instruction affected learners' ability to perform specific linguistic features.

In one of the first reviews of the literature on formal instruction, Long (1983c) considered a total of eleven studies that had investigated whether learners who receive formal instruction achieve higher levels of proficiency than those who do not. He concluded that six of the studies (Carroll 1967; Chihara and Oller 1978; Briere 1978; Krashen, Seliger and Hartnett 1974; Krashen, Jones, Zelinksi, and Usprich 1978) lent support to formal instruction. Three studies (Upshur 1968; Mason 1971; and Fathman 1975) indicated that instruction did not help, while one study (Martin 1980) showed that exposure without formal instruction was beneficial. Long considered two other studies to be 'ambiguous cases' because, although they produced negative results for instruction, this was because they had been wrongly inter-preted. For example, Long points out that variables to do with instruction, socio-economic background, amount of exposure, and parental attitudes were conflated in Hale and Budar's (1970) study, with the result that it was impossible to determine which factors were responsible for the observed dif-ferences in proficiency level.

Long's general conclusion was that 'there is considerable evidence to indic-ate that SL instruction does make a difference' (1983c: 374). He claimed that the studies suggested that instruction was advantageous (1) for children as well as adults, (2) for both intermediate and advanced learners, (3) irrespect-ive of whether acquisition was measured by means of integrative or discrete-point tests, and (4) in acquisition-rich as well as acquisition-poor environ-ments.

A study published since Long's review lends support to these general con-clusions. Weslander and Stephany (1983) examined the effects of instruction on 577 children with limited English proficiency in grades 2 to 10 in public schools in Iowa. Students who received more instruction did better on the Bi-lingual Syntax Measure (Burt, Dulay, and Hernandez 1973—see Chapter 3). The effects were strongest at the lowest levels of proficiency in the first year of schooling and diminished in later years. Weslander and Stephany's results contrast with those obtained by Hale and Budar (1970). This study, which Long classified as 'ambiguous', found that learners who spent two to three periods each day in ESL classes 'were being more harmed than helped' (1983c: 297).

In general, then, these studies show an advantage for formal instruction over exposure. Long, in his original review, claimed that this conclusion was damaging to Krashen's position on formal instruction (namely, that instruc-tion does not contribute directly to 'acquisition' and should be limited to a few 'learnable' rules). Krashen (1985: 28–31) responded by arguing that the studies did not in fact show an advantage for formal instruction *per se*, but only that learning in a classroom was helpful for 'beginners', who found it dif-ficult to obtain the comprehensible input they needed in normal communica-tion outside the classroom. In this respect, it should be noted that Weslander and Stephany (1983) reported that it was the beginners who benefited most from formal instruction in their study. To protect himself against Long's con-clusion that the studies also showed formal instruction was advantageous for advanced learners, Krashen argued that the subjects in some of the studies had been wrongly classified as 'intermediate' and 'advanced'. In a response to this, Long (1988) pointed out that his other main conclusions (i.e. (1), (3), and (4) above) were also problematic for the Input Hypothesis and that the conclusion that Krashen himself had reached in an earlier paper was, in fact, the right one—'formal instruction is a more efficient way of learning English for adults than trying to learn it in the streets' (Krashen, Jones, Zelinski, and Usprich 1978: 260).

These studies—and Long's and Krashen's subsequent debate—are based on comparisons of the relative effects of formal instruction and exposure. However, many learners—including many of those in the studies Long reviewed—experienced both together. It is conceivable, therefore, that what works best is some form of combination of the two. This possibility has been examined directly in three other studies.

Savignon (1972), in a frequently cited study of communicative language teaching, compared the grammatical and communicative skills of three classes of learners of French as a foreign language who had received four hours of instruction per week. The experimental group, which was given an extra hour of communicative tasks, outperformed the other two groups on a number of 'communicative' measures, but not on 'linguistic' measures. This study, then, suggests that a combination of formal and informal instruction aids the development of communicative language skills in foreign language learners.

Spada (1986) sought to establish whether there was any interaction between type of contact and type of instruction. She investigated the effects of instruction and exposure on 48 intermediate-level adult learners enrolled in an intensive six-week ESL course at a Canadian university. Spada found that although type and amount of contact appeared to account for variation in some aspects of the learners' proficiency before the effects of instruction were considered, it did not account for differences in the learners' improvement during the course. Overall, instruction was more important than contact in accounting for differences in the learners' L2 proficiency. She also found evidence of an interaction between the type of instruction that different groups of learners received and commented:

> ... contact positively accounted for differences in learners' improvement on the grammar and writing tests when the instruction was more form-focused, and negatively accounted for differences on those measures when the instruction was less form-focused (1986: 97).

In other words, those learners who had access to both formal instruction and to exposure to English showed the greatest gains in proficiency. As Spada (1987: 133) commented, 'attention to both form and meaning works best' for L2 learners.

This conclusion is also given support by another study (Montgomery and Eisenstein 1985). This compared the gains in proficiency observed in a group of working-class Hispanic students who, in addition to regular ESL classes aimed primarily at improving grammatical accuracy, also enrolled in a special oral communication course, involving field trips to sites where they routinely needed to communicate in English, and a group of similar learners who experienced only the regular ESL classes. The two groups were compared for accent, grammar, vocabulary, fluency and comprehension. Both groups improved their rating from pre- to post-test, but the group who had experienced the oral communication programme showed greater gains in grammar and accent and were also more successful in passing the ESL course (86 per cent pass rate as opposed to 57 per cent). Montgomery and Eisenstein propose that 'a combination of form-oriented and meaning-oriented language teaching was more beneficial than form-oriented teaching alone' (1985: 329). It should be noted, however, that the group in the joint programme received more overall instruction and that it might have been the total amount of instruction, rather than the type that accounted for their advantage.

In general, then, there is support for the claim that formal instruction helps learners (both foreign and second) to develop greater L2 proficiency, particularly if it is linked with opportunities for natural exposure. Foreign learners appear to benefit by developing greater communicative skills, while second language learners benefit by developing greater linguistic accuracy. As I pointed out in Ellis 1990a, however, there are several reasons for exercising caution in interpreting the studies considered in this section.

First, many of the studies, like Montgomery and Eisenstein's, failed to control for overall amount of combined contact and instruction. Studies which show that learners who receive instruction and exposure do better than learners with just exposure are, by themselves, not very convincing, as this may simply reflect their greater overall contact. To counter this objection, Long (1983c) points out that whereas some studies showed that differences in amounts of instruction were related to differences in proficiency in learners with the same overall exposure, the reverse was not the case—differences in the amount of exposure had no effect on the proficiency of learners matched for amount of instruction. Long argues that these contrasting results enable us to be more confident in finding a positive effect for instruction in studies which failed to control for overall opportunities for learning. However, if such studies are removed on the grounds of this design flaw, the number of studies in Long's original review that unambiguously show that instruction helps is reduced to two.

Another problem is that the studies do not take account of individual differences in learners. Fathman (1978) found that the informal learners in her study varied in English oral proficiency much more than the formal learners, leading her to suggest that some were skilful at learning informally while others had difficulty. Similar points have been made about differences in the ability of formal learners (see the section on Language aptitude in Chapter 11, page 494). It is also possible that motivation functions as an important intervening variable. As Krashen, Jones, Zelinski and Usprich (1978) recognized, students who are more highly motivated to learn are more likely to enrol in classes. The positive effect found for instruction may simply reflect stronger motivation rather than the instruction itself.

Perhaps the most serious problem, however, is that many of the studies made no attempt to ascertain what took place in the name of 'instruction'. They simply equated formal instruction with the number of years spent in the classroom. As a result, we do not know for certain, whether the instruction was form-focused or communication-orientated. We cannot be sure whether the classroom learners did better than the naturalistic learners because of formal instruction or because of access to comprehensible input.

More convincing is the evidence provided by the three later studies, which suggest that learners progress most rapidly when they experience both formal instruction and communicative exposure. It should be noted that this accords with the findings of the 'good language learner' studies (see Chapter 12), which have indicated that successful learners pay attention to language form and also seek out opportunities for communicating in the L2. As we will see in a later section, it is possible that the long-term effectiveness of formal instruction is contingent on the availability of opportunities to communicate in the L2.

The studies referred to in this section are summarized in Table 14.1.

The effects of formal instruction on production accuracy

In this section we turn our attention to studies that have investigated the effects of formal instruction on learners' ability to produce specific linguistic features accurately. These studies constitute a much more powerful test of the general question 'Does formal instruction work?'

A number of studies have investigated whether grammar instruction defined as quantity of practice directed at specific grammatical features results in increased accuracy. In Ellis 1984c, for example, I found that three hours of instruction in *wh*-questions did not help a group of 13 child ESL learners to produce this structure more accurately in a game that was designed to elicit relatively spontaneous oral questions. However, some of the learners did improve substantially. I investigated whether this was related to the amount of practice which individual learners had received during the lessons, and found that those learners who improved the most had practised the least—further evidence that participation in classroom interaction may not be the secret to success (see Chapter 13, page 594). Long (1988) accounts for the failure of instruction to work in this study by suggesting that it was directed at a structure too far in advance of the learners' stage of development. He points out that *wh*-questions involve complex syntactical permutations which typically make them acquired late (see Chapter 3).

In a later study (Ellis 1992b), I found that differences in the accuracy with which adult beginners of L2 German performed the difficult 'verb-end' word order rule in communicative speech were not accountable for by differences in the amount of practice in this structure they had received over a six-month period. However, I did note that many of the classroom learners appeared to have achieved greater accuracy in the use of verb-end than the purely naturalistic learners studied in the ZISA project (see Meisel 1983). It is possible, then,

Study	Type of classroom	Subjects	Proficiency	Data	Results
Carroll 1967	Foreign language learning in United States (exposure abroad)	Adults—first language English	All proficiency levels	Integrative test	Both instruction and exposure help, but exposure helps most.
Chihara and Oller 1978	EFL in Japan	Adults—first language Japanese	All proficiency levels	1 Discrete point test 2 Integrative test	Instruction helps, but exposure does not.
Krashen, Seliger and Hartnett 1974	ESL in United States	Adults—mixed first languages	All proficiency levels	Discrete point test	Instruction helps, but exposure does not.
Briere 1978	Spanish as a second language in Mexico	Children—local Indian language is first language	Beginners	Discrete point test	Both instruction and exposure help, but instruction helps most.
Krashen and Seliger 1976	ESL in United States	Adults—mixed first languages	Intermediate and advanced	Integrative test	Instruction helps, but exposure does not.
Krashen et al. 1978	ESL United States	Adults—mixed first languages	All proficiency levels	1 Discrete point test 2 Integrative test	Both instruction and exposure help, but instruction helps most.
Hale and Budar 1970	ESL in United States	Adolescents—mixed first languages	All proficiency levels	1 Discrete point test 2 Integrative test	Exposure helps but instruction does not—results doubtful, however.
Fathman 1976	ESL in United States	Children—mixed first languages	All proficiency levels	Integrative test	Exposure helps but instruction does not—results doubtful, however.
Upshur 1968	ESL in United States	Adults—mixed first languages	Intermediate and advanced	Discrete point test	Instruction does not help.
Mason 1971	ESL in United States	Adults—mixed first languages	Intermediate and advanced	1 Discrete point test 2 Integrative test	Instruction does not help.
Fathman 1975	ESL in United States	Children—mixed first languages	All proficiency levels	Integrative test	Instruction does not help.

Study	Type of classroom	Subjects	Proficiency	Data	Results
Ellis 1984c	ESL in Britain	Children—mixed first languages	Post-beginner level	Spontaneous speech from picture task	Instruction had no overall effect on production of *wh-* questions—individual development not related to instructional opportunities.
Weslander and Stephany 1983	ESL in United States	Mixed children and adolescents—Grades 2 to 10	Mixed levels of proficiency	Bilingual Syntax Measure	Instruction helps—particularly at lower proficiency levels.
Ellis and Rathbone 1987	German as FL in UK	Adults in higher education	Complete and false beginners	1 Spontaneous speech task 2 Discrete point test	Learners who attended most showed greatest gain on 1 and 2.
Montgomery and Eisenstein 1985	ESL in United States	28 adult Hispanic ESL learners	Intermediate	Oral interview rated for accent, grammar, vocabulary, fluency and comprehension.	Learners receiving communicative and formal instruction improved more than learners receiving only form-focused instruction—particularly in accent and grammar.
Spada 1986	ESL in Canada	Adults in short intensive course	Intermediate	Various tests of communicative competence	Positive effect for formal instruction, but this most evident in learners who also had plenty of exposure.

Table 14.1: Empirical studies of the effects of formal instruction on general language proficiency (based on Long 1983c)

that the instruction did have some effect but that this effect was not readily explicable in terms of amount of practice.

Other studies, however, have produced results more supportive of formal instruction. Lightbown, Spada, and Wallace (1980) studied the effects of half-hour grammar lessons on the accuracy with which 175 French speaking school learners of English judged sentences to be grammatical. In this case the structures involved were morphological (plural -*s*, possessive -*s*, 3rd person singular -*s*, copula -*s*, auxiliary -*s*, and locative prepositions). With the exception of locative prepositions, all the structures had been previously taught. Overall scores improved by 11 per cent from pre- to post-test, a significant increase given the brevity of the instruction. A control group, which did not receive any instruction in these features, improved by only 3 per cent. Lightbown et al. (1980) emphasize, however, that the learners may not have acquired the functions of the various forms, in other words that acquisition was only partial. Pica (1983; 1985) also produces evidence to suggest that some grammatical features are performed more accurately if learners have access to formal instruction. She compared the accuracy with which three groups of learners (a natural group, a mixed group, and an instructed group) performed a number of grammatical morphemes in unplanned speech. The instructed learners performed plural -*s* more accurately than the naturalistic learners. However, they performed progressive -*ing* less accurately, while no difference between the groups was found for another feature (articles). Pica explains these interesting results by suggesting that instruction only aids the acquisition of features which are formally easy to acquire and which manifest transparent form–function relationships. This accords with the suggestion made above that the success of instruction may depend on the complexity of the target structure. Pica makes the additional point that instruction may be effective in inhibiting (although not preventing altogether) the use of ungrammatical but communicatively effective constructions found in pidgins.

Yet other studies have indicated that formal instruction has an effect on accuracy in planned but not in unplanned production. In both of my studies referred to above (Ellis 1984c and 1992b), acquisition was measured with reference to relatively unplanned language use (i.e. when the task did not encourage learners to attend consciously to the target structures). Schumann (1978a) also found that his learner (Alberto) did not improve the accuracy with which he spontaneously produced English negative structures after a period of instruction, but that he did show a significant improvement in an imitation test. Kadia (1988) studied the effects of 40 minutes of one-to-one instruction on a Chinese learner's acquisition of ditransitive (for example, 'I showed him the book') and phrasal verb constructions such as 'I called him up'. She concluded:

> . . . formal instruction seemed to have very little effect on spontaneous production, but it was beneficial for controlled performance (1988: 513).

Again, though, it should be noted that the structures that Schumann and Kadia investigated are complex and typically acquired late. In the Pica study, instructional effects were evident in unplanned language use when the target structure was easy to acquire.

Another intriguing possibility is that formal instruction may have a delayed effect. That is, its effects may become evident only some time after the instruction. Empirical evidence for such a hypothesis is limited and difficult to collect, but the hypothesis is compatible with a number of research findings. As we will shortly see, attempts to teach specific grammatical structures which learners are not yet developmentally ready to process may not prove successful. However, studies such as mine in Ellis 1989b and 1992b indicate that learners who receive such instruction may still do better than untutored learners, suggesting that they may have been able to make use of the information they received through instruction at a later time. A delayed effect hypothesis, then, is compatible with the general finding that instruction accelerates learning and results in higher proficiency levels (see previous section) even though learners may fail to immediately learn what they have been taught.

There is also some evidence to suggest that formal instruction can have a deleterious effect. Felix (1981), in a study of 34 children studying L2 English in their first year of a German high school, found that drilling in negatives involving the auxiliary 'doesn't' led to errors in declarative sentences such as the following:

Doesn't she eat apples.

Here, 'doesn't' has replaced the more normal 'no' as a pre-negator. Eubank (1987b) also found evidence of unique negative structures in the production of tutored adult L2 learners of German. In this case, the learners placed the negator at the end of the sentence, a phenomenon not attested in naturalistic L2 acquisition. He suggests that this arose when the learners resorted to an operating strategy (i.e. preserve the basic word order) in order to cope with the instructional demand that they compose in complete sentences. In other words, when asked to perform beyond their level, learners simplify and unusual errors occur. Lightbown (1983) showed that francophone learners over-learnt progressive *-ing* as a result of teaching. They overgeneralized it, using it in contexts that required the simple form of the verb, which they had used correctly prior to the instruction. Pica (1983) also found evidence that instruction can trigger the oversuppliance of a number of regular morphological features such as past tense *-ed* and progressive *-ing*. Weinert (1987) and VanPatten (1990) also provide evidence to suggest that instruction can impede acquisition of negatives in L2 German and clitic pronouns in L2 Spanish respectively. In all these studies the reason given for the failure of the formal instruction is that it distorts the input made available to the learner and thus prevents the normal processes of acquisition from operating smoothly.

Formal instruction can also impede acquisition in another way—by making learners too conservative. Felix and Weigl (1991) asked German high school students of L2 English to judge sentences such as the following:

1 That John will win the race everyone expects.
2 For him to pass the test would be a surprise.
3 Who did he see pictures of?

All of these sentences are 'marked' in some way: (1) and (2) do not follow canonical English word order and (3) displays prepositional stranding. The results showed that all the learners, irrespective of the number of years of instruction, tended to judge these grammatical sentences as ungrammatical. Felix and Weigl suggest that these marked structures are typically not taught and that the learners followed the strategy 'if it hasn't been taught, you better believe it's wrong'. In this case, then, formal instruction made learners 'overly cautious'. It should be noted, however, that Felix and Weigl do not report any comparative data for untutored learners.[1] This study is also flawed by the failure to include a control group of native speakers. It is not at all clear that native speakers would judge all the sentences above as grammatical.

The general picture which emerges from the studies we have examined so far is that formal instruction often does not work, particularly when acquisition is measured in relation to spontaneous speech. However, a number of other studies carried out in Canada suggest that grammar teaching can have positive effects on learning. These studies have examined the role of formal instruction in the context of communicative language teaching (i.e. when opportunities for communicating in the L2 are supplemented with grammar lessons). A feature of all the studies has been the provision of instruction that has been carefully planned, in accordance with current pedagogic views about what constitutes 'good' grammar teaching. A second feature is that the instruction has been extensive.

Harley (1989) devised a set of functional-grammar materials to teach French immersion students the distinction between *passé composé* and *imparfait*, which as we have seen is one of the features that is typically not acquired by immersion learners. She found that eight weeks of instruction resulted in significant improvement in the accuracy with which the two verb tenses were used in a written composition, in a rational cloze test and in an oral interview. The instructional effects were therefore evident in both planned and unplanned language use. However, a control group subsequently caught up with the experimental group. Harley suggests that this might have been because the control group also subsequently received formal instruction directed at this feature. The Harley study is encouraging for supporters of formal instruction.

Two other Canadian studies also support this view. White (1991) investigated the effects of instruction on adverb placement, examining whether it was successful in eliminating this error made by French learners of L2 English:

*John kissed often Mary (SVAO).

and in teaching these learners to use adverbs between subject and verb, a position not allowed in French:

*Jean souvent embrasse Marie (SAVO).

White argues that the latter structure is learnable through positive input (i.e. through input obtained from communicative exposure), but that avoidance of the adverb placement error requires negative evidence such as that provided by formal instruction. The learners were children in Grades 5 and 6 in an intensive ESL program. Two weeks of instruction in the use of frequency and manner adverbs was provided three months into the program. The instructed learners showed significantly greater gains in accuracy in a number of manipulative tasks (a grammaticality judgement task, a preference task and a sentence construction task) in comparison to control groups. These results held true for both use of SAVO and for avoidance of SVAO word order. White was also interested in whether the learners recognized that sentences of the kind:

John ran quickly to the end of the street (i.e. SVAPP)

were permitted in English even though they had not been taught this. However, the subjects did not learn that SVAPP was possible where SVAO was not, and White suggests that they made 'a conscious overgeneralization' to the effect that 'adverbs must not appear between the verb and something else'. This study indicates that the learners responded to instruction, but that they were unable to make fine distinctions (i.e. between SVAO and SVAPP) that they had not been taught.

The second study (White et al. 1991) studied the effects of instruction on question-formation (*wh-* and 'yes/no') on the same groups of learners as those used in the adverb study. Five hours of instruction over a two-week period were provided. Acquisition was measured by means of a cartoon task, a preference grammaticality judgement task, and an oral communication task. In comparison to a control group, the experimental group showed substantial gains in accuracy in all three tasks. The instructed learners in this case showed that they had learnt how to use inversion in questions.

The studies considered in this section are summarized in Table 14.2. What general conclusions can we come to on the basis of the research which has investigated the effects of formal instruction on accuracy? There is sufficient evidence to show that formal instruction can result in definite gains in accuracy. If the structure is 'simple' in the sense that it does not involve complex processing operations and is clearly related to a specific function, and if the formal instruction is extensive and well-planned, it is likely to work. However, if the instruction is directed at a difficult grammatical structure which is substantially beyond the learners' current interlanguage, it is likely that it will only lead to improved accuracy in planned language use, when learners can

Study	Type of classroom	Subjects	Proficiency	Data	Results
Schumann 1978b	ESL in the United States (one-to-one instruction)	One adult learner—L1 Spanish	Fossilized—i.e. no development taking place.	Spontaneous speech and imitation test	Instruction in negatives had no effect on spontaneous speech but led to improved performance in imitation test.
Lightbown et al. 1980	ESL in Canadian schools	Children and adolescents—grades 6, 8, and 10.	Mixed ability levels.	Grammaticality judgement test.	Instruction resulted in increased accuracy in grammaticality judgements in the short term. However, accuracy fell away in follow-up test 5 months later.
Felix 1981	German as a FL in secondary schools.	11-year-old children.	Complete beginners.	Recordings of classroom speech.	Similar errors in negatives, interrogatives, and pronouns as found in naturalistic learners.
Felix and Hahn 1985	German as a FL in secondary schools.	11-year-old children.	Complete beginners.	Recordings of classroom speech.	Analysis of pronoun errors indicates same processes as in naturalistic acquisition.
Lightbown 1983; 1987	ESL in schools in Canada.	Children in grades 6, 7, and 8.	Mainly lower-intermediate.	Spontaneous speech on a picture task.	V + *-ing* over-used by grade 6 children; replaced by simple verb form in grade 7. Progressive aux. followed similar pattern of development. Forms 'overlearnt' but natural processing takes over later. Effect of instruction delayed.
Pica 1983; 1985	EFL in Mexico/ESL in the United States.	6 adult EFL learners, 6 adult ESL learners, and 6 natural learners.	Mixed levels of ability.	Audiotaped conversations with researcher.	Instructed learners more accurate in some forms (e.g. plural -s), less accurate in others (e.g. V + *-ing*) and the same in others (e.g. articles).
Ellis 1984c	ESL in Britain.	13 children adolescents (10 to 15 yrs).	Mainly low-level ability.	Game designed to elicit unmonitored *wh*-interrogatives.	Instruction had no significant effect on accuracy of production of interrogatives for group as a whole, but individual learners showed marked gains.

Study	Type of classroom	Subjects	Proficiency	Data	Results
Weinert 1987	German as a FL in Scotland.	Students in forms 1 to 4 in secondary schools.	Complete beginners to low-intermediate.	Non-communicative classroom speech and communicative speech in a communication game.	Similar errors found in naturalistic acquisition. Instruction led to heavy reliance on formulas, blocking IL development.
Ellis and Rathbone 1987	German as FL in London.	Adults in higher education.	Complete and false beginners.	Spontaneous speech from information gap task.	Levels of attendance in Term 1 correlated significantly with word order accuracy at the end of Term 2.
Eubank 1987b	German as FL in the United States.	6 adult learners at university.	Beginners.	Oral description of pictures.	Learners manifested unique errors by placing negator at the end of a clause.
Kadia 1988	ESL in Canadian university.	One adult learner.	Fossilized, i.e. no development taking place.	Spontaneous speech substitution and grammaticality judgement tests.	Instruction had no effect on spontaneous production. Performance on grammaticality judgement test declined but that on substitution test improved.
Harley 1989	French as a FL in Canada.	319 grade 6 learners in immersion programmes.	Intermediate and upper intermediate.	Ratings based on written compositions; cloze test scores; error scores based on oral interview.	The instructed students better than control students on cloze and oral interview scores on immediate post-test. Gains maintained in follow-up test 3 months later.
VanPatten 1990	Spanish as a SL and as a FL in Puerto Rico and United States.	One 14-yr-old and one adult learner.	Intermediate and relative beginner.	Oral interviews supplying more or less spontaneous data.	Many similarities between the naturalistic and instructured learner, but the latter manifested some errors in the use of clitics not seen in the former (e.g. use of wrong person).
Felix and Weigl 1991	German as a FL in Germany.	77 learners aged from 12 to 17 yrs.	Beginner, intermediate, and advanced.	Grammatically judgement test.	Grammatically judgements influenced by L1 at beginner and intermediate levels; advanced learners reluctant to generalize beyond what they had been explicitly caught.

(continued overleaf)

Study	Type of classroom	Subjects	Proficiency	Data	Results
White et al. 1991	ESL in Canada.	82 grade 5 and 6 students	Post-beginner/low-intermediate.	Grammaticality judgement task, preference task, and card sorting task.	Instructed learners made fewer judgement errors and scored higher scores on card-sorting task than did control. However, gains largely disappeared in follow-up test administered 5 months later.
White et al. 1991	ESL in Canada.	56 grade 5 and 6 students.	Post-beginner/low-intermediate.	Grammaticality judgement task, preference task and oral production task.	Instructed learners performed better on all three tasks than controls. Gains maintained in follow-up test 6 months later.

Table 14.2:   Studies investigating the effects of instruction on accuracy

pay conscious attention to the structure. It will either have no effect on accuracy in unplanned language use or may result in idiosyncratic deviations as learners resort to alternative processing operations within the compass of their current abilities. It is possible, though, that in such cases learners may store some explicit representation of the feature, which may aid subsequent acquisition of the feature for use in unplanned discourse.

It is clear from these conclusions that one important factor determining whether formal instruction results in improved accuracy is the learner's stage of development. Instruction may lead to more accurate use of grammatical structures in communication providing a learner is able to process them. In other words, there are constraints on learners' ability to acquire grammatical structures and, if formal instruction is to be successful, it has to work in accordance with the internal processes that govern why some structures are acquired before others.

Formal instruction and the sequence of acquisition

In Chapter 3, we considered the evidence that supports a standard order of acquisition (for example, a 'natural' order based on the accuracy with which L2 learners perform a set of English morphemes) and a regular sequence of acquisition (for example, the acquisition of English negatives and interrogatives manifests stages of development involving 'transitional constructions' *en route* to the target-language constructions). It is of both theoretical interest to SLA researchers, and of practical importance for language pedagogy, to ask whether formal instruction can 'subvert' the natural order and also whether it can enable the learner to acquire target language constructions immediately and so avoid transitional constructions.

Do classroom learners (who are presumed to have received grammatical instruction) manifest a different accuracy/acquisition order from naturalistic learners? Table 14.3 summarizes the studies that have addressed this question. Studies by Fathman (1978) of EFL and ESL learners, by Makino (1980) of Japanese learners of English, and by Pica (1983) of Spanish learners failed to find any significant differences. Turner (1979) found that the accuracy/acquisition orders manifested by three 18-year-old Spanish learners of English enrolled in an intensive English language program correlated highly with each other but not with the order of instruction. Perkins and Larsen-Freeman (1975) found that the order obtained for twelve Venezuelan students at the beginning of a course of instruction did not differ significantly from that obtained at the end. These studies were used to claim the inviolability of the morpheme order. Sajavaara (1981b), in a study of adolescent EFL learners in Finland, and also Lightbown (1983), in the study referred to earlier, however, found differences between the instructed and natural morpheme orders and those produced by the learners who had received formal instruction.

Morpheme order studies:

Study	Type of classroom	Subjects	Proficiency	Data	Results
Perkins and Larsen-Freeman 1975	ESL in the United States.	12 Venezuelan students just arrived in the United States.	Intermediate.	Translation test and spontaneous speech on a picture description task.	Morpheme order in spontaneous data same as natural order and did not change as a result of instruction. Order on translation task did change, however.
Fathman 1978	EFL in Germany vs ESL in United States.	Adolescents in high school.	Mixed ability.	Oral production task.	Morpheme order for EFL and ESL learners were significantly correlated, but differences in types of errors found (e.g. EFL learners made more overgeneralization errors).
Turner 1979	Intensive ESL in the United States.	Three 18-yr-olds.	Beginners.	Spontaneous speech and grammar task.	Order of morpheme acquisition same as natural order and different from order of instruction. Effect of instruction evident in grammar test.
Makino 1980	EFL in Japan.	Students in grades 9 and 10 of high school.	Lower-intermediate.	Written data based on picture stimuli.	Order of morpheme acquisition same as natural order and different from order in textbooks.
Sajavaara 1981b	EFL in Finland.	Adolescents in high school.		Elicited speech.	Morpheme order differed from natural order—articles ranked lower.
Pica 1983	EFL in Mexico/ESL in USA.	6 adult EFL learners/6 adult ESL learners and 6 natural learners.	Mixed ability levels.	Audio-taped conversations with the researcher.	Morpheme order the same as natural order—but see Table 14.2.

Study	Type of classroom	Subjects	Proficiency	Data	Results
Order of acquisition in grammatical subsystem:					
Pavesi 1984; 1986	EFL in Italy; ESL in Scotland.	48 adolescents in high school; 38 Italian workers.	Mixed ability levels.	Oral data on relative clauses elicited by picture cues.	Instructed and untutored learners displayed same acquisition order, but the instructed learners showed greater quantitative development.
Sequence of acquisitions:					
Pienemann 1984	German as a SL in Germany.	10 children aged 7–9 yrs.	Mixed ability levels.	Oral interviews and hidden recordings.	Inversion rule acquired by one learner who was developmentally ready, but not acquired by another who was not ready; accuracy in copula increased initially but decreased some 9 months later; instruction in inversion caused learner who was not developmentally ready to abandon already acquired rule.
Pienemann 1987; 1989	German as a FL in Australia.	3 adult learners at university.	Complete beginners.	Oral interviews.	The learners acquired 'easy' word order rules when taught, but difficult rules (e.g. general order of acquisition) corresponded to natural order.
Ellis 1989	German as a FL in Britain.	39 adult learners in higher education.	Beginners and false beginners.	Spontaneous speech in information gap task.	Order of development of word order rules same as in naturalistic learners and different from instructional order; but instructed learners displayed greater development in the late-acquired verb-end rule.

(continued overleaf)

Study	Type of classroom	Subjects	Proficiency	Data	Results
'Projection' studies:					
Gass 1982	ESL in the United States.	Adults at university.	Intermediate.	Grammaticality and sentence-joining tasks.	Group that received instruction on marked relative pronoun function showed improvement on this function and on unmarked functions; group that received instruction on unmarked relative function showed improvement primarily on this function only.
Zobl 1985	ESL by French speakers in Canada.	Adults.	Low level.	Oral questions based on pictures, designed to elicit noun phrases with possessive adjectives.	One group that received instruction in human-possessed entities (= marked) generalized to non-human possessed entities (= unmarked) but reverse did not occur. Types of error also differed.
Eckman et al. 1988	ESL in the United States.	Adults in intensive university course.	Low intermediate and intermediate.	Sentence-joining task.	Generalization of learning occurred from marked to unmarked structures, but little took place in opposite direction.
Jones 1991a	EFL in Japan.	210 adult females at Japanese university.	Intermediate.	Sentence-joining task.	Teaching marked DO structure was more efficient than teaching unmarked S structure (i.e. more generalization occurred). However, no difference found for teaching relative pronoun as direct object and object of preposition.
Jones 1991b	EFL in Japan.	160 adult females at Japanese university.	Intermediate.	Oral production task based on pictures.	Similar results to Jones 1991a.
Comprehension studies:					
Buczowska and Weist 1991	EFL in Poland.	60 adult university students (+ 60 L1 learners).	Mixed ability levels.	Sentence-comprehension test based on pictures.	Instructed L2 learners manifested different sequence of acquisition to naturalistic learners (both L1 and L2). Differences facilitated rather than impeded acquisition process.

Table 14.3:   Studies investigating the effect of instruction on the course of L2 acquisition

It should also be noted that, even though no difference was found between the orders of instructed and naturalistic learners in most of the studies, there was evidence in some studies that specific morphemes were performed more accurately as a result of instruction (see, for example, Perkins and Larsen-Freeman and Pica, and the discussion in the previous section).

The results obtained by the morpheme studies can be considered, at best, only weak evidence that formal instruction has no effect on the developmental route. As we saw in Chapter 3, the methodology of the morpheme studies has been strongly criticized (Hatch 1978b) on a number of grounds. Also, the theoretical view of L2 acquisition which underlies these studies is extremely doubtful. Learners do not acquire the L2 grammar as a set of 'accumulated entities' (Rutherford 1988: 5) but rather work on a number of features simultaneously, gradually sorting out the form–meaning relationships which they encode, and on the way constructing a number of unique interim grammars in the manner described in Chapter 4. Finally, as we have already seen, morphological features such as those investigated in the morpheme studies can pose substantial learning problems and are often not acquired by even advanced L2 learners (see Bardovi-Harlig and Bofman 1989). The similarity in acquisition orders of instructed and naturalistic learners is perhaps best treated as further evidence of this.

A number of other studies that have focused on the order of acquisition in specific grammatical sub-systems also suggest that instruction is powerless to alter the general pattern of development. In Chapter 3 we saw that the functions of relative pronouns are acquired in a predictable order that reflects their typological status. Pavesi (1984; 1986) found this 'universal' order of acquisition in both a group of instructed EFL learners in an Italian high school and a group of waiters learning English naturalistically in Edinburgh, Scotland. Once again, however, this study found that the instructed group showed higher levels of acquisition, both in the sense that they had progressed further along the universal order and in the sense that the errors they manifested were less 'primitive' (for example, they used pronoun copies rather than noun copies).

More interesting, perhaps, is the research that has examined the effects of formal instruction on the *sequence* of acquisition of a number of syntactical features. Felix and Hahn (1985), in a study based on the same learners studied by Felix (1981), found that they acquired pronouns in an identical fashion to naturalistic learners. In this case, the instruction took the form of explanations and practice of each separate pronoun form in an incremental fashion. However, the learners did not master the pronouns one at a time but rather one feature at a time (i.e. gender was acquired first, followed in turn by person, number, and case). Felix and Hahn argue that the learners made use of 'instruction-independent learning strategies'.

Research on German word order rules has provided the clearest evidence that formal instruction is unable to affect acquisitional sequences. This work is based on studies of naturalistic learners which suggest there is a definite sequence of acquisition of word order rules (see Chapter 3). Pienemann (1984), in a frequently cited experimental study, showed that instruction in inversion was successful in the case of a learner who had reached the immediately preceding stage, but not in the case of another learner who was at a much earlier stage. Subsequent longitudinal studies of the classroom acquisition of German by university students in Australia (Pienemann 1986 and 1989) further demonstrated the immutability of the word order sequence and the failure of instruction to alter it. My study of 39 adult learners of L2 German in higher education in Britain (Ellis 1989b) also suggested that instruction is powerless to alter the sequence of acquisition of these word order rules. This study, as we have already noted, indicated that the instructed learners appeared to progress along the sequence at a much faster rate than naturalistic learners. Two cross-sectional studies (Daniel 1983 and Westmoreland 1983) also show that the sequence of acquisition for German word order rules is the same in instructed and naturalistic acquisition.

Research on word order rules in other languages has produced similar results. Thus, whereas in Ellis (1984c) I found that many of my learners failed to acquire inversion in *wh-* questions in L2 English, probably because they had not yet developed the necessary processing requisites, Brindley (1991) reports that instruction that was more carefully tailored to the learners' level did result in substantial acquisitional gains in English question formation. He found that the eight learners in his study produced considerably more questions after the instruction, and that they progressed through the stages in the order predicted by the Multidimensional Model. He notes, however, that even after 600 hours of instruction (not all of which was directed at questions), the learners were still using a relatively restricted range of question forms. Even with instruction the acquisition of complex rules takes time.

There is also the question of what happens if learners are given instruction in a structure before they are developmentally ready for it. Do they simply fail to learn it? Or does it have some other effect? A study by Pienemann (1987) suggests that premature instruction can have a deleterious effect by inducing avoidance behaviour. He provides evidence to show that three adult classroom learners of L2 German tended to avoid using the present perfect, preferring modal + verb structures because these gave them a greater chance of conforming to target-language norms, as the main verb consisted of the unmodified infinitive. According to Pienemann, the present perfect is acquired late, as a Stage 5 structure (see Chapter 9). Pienemann suggests that the avoidance was the result of being forced to produce this structure at an early stage. Pienemann's study, based on acquisition sequence, concurs with the studies referred to earlier, which provide evidence that formal instruction can inhibit the normal processes of acquisition.

Whereas in the case of the German word order rules, instruction only works if it follows the developmental sequence, the acquisition of relative pronoun functions appears to be accelerated if learners are taught the more marked, (i.e. typologically less frequent) functions first. Gass (1982) and Eckman, Bell, and Nelson (1988) conducted studies based on the Accessibility Hierarachy for relativization (see Chapters 3 and 10) and found that instruction directed at the object of preposition function (for example, 'This is the man who we spoke about') triggered acquisition of the less marked features (direct object and subject functions), as demonstrated in a written production task. The reverse, however did not occur to the same extent: for example, students taught the subject function did not show much gain on the object and object of preposition functions. Subsequent studies by A. Jones (1991b and 1992) replicated these results for Japanese college-level learners of English, and also showed that the predicted order was evident in oral as well as written production.[2] A study by Zobl (1985) also lends support to the triggering effect achieved by teaching marked structures. It provides evidence to suggest that learners who received instruction directed at the marked use of possessive pronouns (possessive + human entity, for example, 'his mother') improved in both this feature and in the unmarked use of possessive pronouns (possessive + inanimate entity, for example, 'her car'). However learners who received instruction in the unmarked feature did not show any improvement in the marked feature and, in one study, not in the unmarked feature either. These studies indicate that some structures may be hierarchically linked in such a way that learners are able to generalize knowledge of marked features to unmarked features but not vice versa.

There is some evidence to suggest that formal instruction directed at features that are not subject to developmental constraints can succeed irrespective of the stage the learner has reached. Pienemann (1984) found that learners at different stages of development who were taught German copula were able to perform this structure much more accurately. Other studies have also shown that the accuracy of 'simple' structures improves with instruction (see the previous section). Pienemann suggests that variational features (see Chapter 9), such as copula, are amenable to instruction.

It is also possible that developmental constraints on formal instruction do not occur when acquisition is considered in terms of comprehension, as opposed to production. Buczowska and Weist (1991) compared the acquisition of temporal locatives in English (indicators of past v. present and progressive v. aspect) by 60 classroom L2 learners, who differed in the total amount of instruction they had received, with that by 60 L1 learners, who were divided into five groups according to age. Comprehension data were collected by means of a sentence–picture matching test. The study found that the L2 learners did not follow the acquisitional route prototypical for the L1 learners. Neither did they follow the pattern of development of untutored L2 learners, as reported in studies based on learner production (for example, Meisel 1987 and Bhardwaj, Dietrich, and Noyan 1988). It is possible, therefore, that adults are capable of comprehending form–meaning distinctions which they cannot yet produce and that instruction can help them to achieve this. This is a point that we will take up later when we consider the effects of different kinds of formal instruction.

As we noted in Chapter 9, studies which demonstrate the existence of developmental patterns are interesting, but without a theory to *explain* them they will have limited applicability. This is one of the weaknesses of the morpheme studies. The Multidimensional Model proposed by Meisel, Clahsen, and Pienemann (1981) and subsequently developed by Pienemann and his associates in Australia, constitutes one the strongest theories of L2 acquisition currently available (see the account of this theory in Chapter 9). This theory predicts that instruction will only succeed in teaching a learner a new developmental structure if the learner is 'ready' to acquire it. On the basis of the theory, Pienemann (1985) advances what he calls the *teachability hypothesis*:

> The teachability hypothesis predicts that instruction can only promote language acquisition if the interlanguage is close to the point when the structure to be taught is acquired in the natural setting (so that sufficient processing prerequisites are developed) (1985: 37).

Pienemann goes on to discuss the relevance of this hypothesis to syllabus design, arguing that if grammar instruction directed at a developmental feature is to be effective, it must be timed to take place when the learner is ready for it.

The studies based on linguistic markedness also have a theoretical basis. Eckman (1977) has put forward the Markedness Differential Hypothesis, which makes predictions about the areas of difficulty a learner will experience on the basis of markedness relations between native- and target-language features (see Chapter 8). He claims, for instance that L2 learners will only experience difficulty with target-language features that differ from native-language features if they are more marked. Zobl (1983b) has argued that languages are enormously complex and cannot be acquired purely on the basis of input. Learners must possess a *projection capacity* which enables them to go beyond the information available to them in the input (see Chapter 10). Both Eckman and Zobl propose that acquisition along one parameter entails acquisition along another related parameter. This simplifies the learning task. The implication for formal instruction is that it may be most effective if it focuses on those marked grammatical properties which are able to trigger acquisition of associated unmarked properties. It should be noted, though, that teaching learners marked grammatical properties does not disturb the 'natural' order of acquisition, but rather hastens progress along it by enabling learners to acquire a number of features at the same time. Also, as Eckman points out, it is not possible to conclude on the basis of this theory that instruction will be most efficient if it focuses on marked properties. Spending a short period of time teaching each structure in the order in which it occurs on the hierarchy may work out as more effective than spending a longer period teaching a relatively marked feature.

It is not easy to reconcile the theoretical positions of the Multidimensional Model and the Projection Hypothesis.[3] In particular, it is not clear whether instruction should seek to follow the natural order of acquisition or should try to teach the more marked features in the hope that learners will generalize their new knowledge to implicated unmarked features.

Studies that have investigated the effects of formal instruction on the order and sequence of acquisition were summarized in Table 14.3. The following tentative conclusions attempt to reconcile the various findings:

1 Instructed learners manifest the same order of morpheme acquisition as naturalistic learners (for example, Fathman 1978).
2 Instructed learners also manifest the same order of acquisition of features comprising grammatical sub-systems such as relative pronoun functions as naturalistic learners (for example, Pavesi 1986).
3 Grammar instruction may prove powerless to alter the natural sequence of acquisition of developmental structures, as these are manifest in learner production (for example, Pienemann 1989).
4 Premature instruction may cause learners to avoid using structures and so may inhibit acquisition (for example, Pienemann 1987).
5 Grammar instruction can be effective in enabling learners to progress along the natural order more rapidly. One way in which this might be achieved is by teaching marked features within the sequence (for example, Eckman et al. 1988).
6 Grammatical features that are not subject to developmental constraints may be amenable to instruction (for example, Pienemann 1984).
7 Formal instruction may help learners to comprehend the meanings of grammatical structures, even if it does not enable them to use the structures in production (for example, Buczowska and Weist 1991).

Again, though, caution needs to be exercised. The notions of 'acquisition order' and 'sequence' remain controversial. Also, many of these conclusions are based on very limited research. There is a clear need to conduct more studies to investigate the effects of instruction on comprehension, for instance.

It is should also be noted that the research has been concerned with acquisition orders and sequences in relation to implicit knowledge. There is no evidence that explicit knowledge of grammatical rules is acquired in some fixed order or sequence. Indeed, it would seem that this is unlikely. Thus, formal instruction directed at such knowledge may not be subject to the kind of processing constraints which Pienemann has identified. If, then, the goal of grammar teaching is explicit knowledge rather than implicit knowledge, it may not be necessary to take account of the learner's stage of development. The teachability hypothesis, as formulated by Pienemann, therefore, may be of relevance only for grammar instruction that has implicit knowledge as its goal.

It is also not at all clear what practical use teachers can make of the research which has examined the effects of instruction on the order/sequence of acquisition. How can they ensure that grammar instruction is timed to match individual learners' stages of development? Clearly they would need information about which processing operations learners had already mastered. Pienemann, Johnston and Brindley (1988) outline a procedure which teachers can use to establish this, but the procedure is a complicated one calling for the accurate completion of an observation form in order to identify individual learners' developmental gaps. It is doubtful if most teachers will be able to use this with sufficient precision. To overcome this problem, and also to facilitate the analysis of L2 data for research purposes, Pienemann and his co-workers (see Pienemann 1992) have developed a software computer package called COALA. However, this package requires the data to be prepared manually before it can be analysed, and so may not be readily usable by teachers. Even if a reliable method of diagnosing learners' stages of development can be found, there is still the problem of how to cope instructionally with the inevitable variation in proficiency which exists within even a relatively homogeneous group of learners. In some teaching contexts (for example, those with access to computer technology), the necessary individualization might be possible, but in many, probably most, it would be impossible.

Problems also exist in applying the Projection Hypothesis. So far, the evidence for this hypothesis is restricted to a few structures. Attempts to extend it to other areas such as adverb position (White 1991) have not proved successful. It would seem that projection which is predicted to occur on the basis of markedness relations identified by linguistic theory does not always occur. In such cases, researchers tend to query the linguistic theory. It is possible, however, that it is the Projection Hypothesis itself that is faulty.

The durability of formal instruction

One possibility that we need to consider is that even in cases where instruction appears to have worked, the beneficial effects may be only temporary. The increased levels of accuracy that result from instruction may prove to be impermanent, or the acquisition of a new grammatical feature illusory. As time passes the effects may gradually atrophy and the learners return to similar levels of performance to those observed before the instruction. If this were to be the case, the utility of formal instruction would be severely limited.

A number of studies already referred to (see Tables 14.2 and 14.3) indicate that the effects of grammar instruction may not last. Lightbown et al. (1980) found that the overall scores of the learners they investigated dropped to a level approximately halfway between that of the pre-test and the immediate post-test in a follow-up test administered six months after the instruction.

Pienemann (1984) found that the gains which one learner made in the accurate use of the copula as a result of instruction began to disappear after as little as one week. White (1991) found that gains in the correct positioning of adverbs were largely lost five months after the instruction.

However, other studies have found that the effects of instruction are durable. Harley (1989), for example, retested her subjects three months after the instruction and found that the learners' improved ability to use French *imparfait* and *passé composé* as evident in an immediate post-test, had not only been maintained but extended even further. White et al. (1991) found that increased accuracy in the formation of questions evident in the same learners that White had investigated did not slip back to pre-instruction levels. In fact, the learners were still improving some six months later.

What explanation can be given for these mixed results? One possibility that seems very plausible is that advanced by Lightbown (1991a). She notes that whereas learners had few opportunities for either hearing or using adverbs once the period of instruction was over, the same was not true for questions. Questions occurred frequently in the classroom input. Also, the intensive ESL learners asked many questions themselves, and so were able to obtain continuous feedback on their ability to perform them accurately. Lightbown suggests:

> ... the findings of these experimental studies can be interpreted as showing that, when form-focused instruction is introduced in a way which is divorced from the communicative needs and activities of the students, only short-term effects are obtained.

In other words, for the effects of instruction to be lasting, learners need subsequent and possibly continuous access to communication that utilizes the features that have been taught.

Although this is an attractive explanation, it does not appear to account fully for the results of all the studies mentioned above. It is reasonable to assume, for instance, that the structures investigated by Lightbown et al. (1980)—various -*s* morphemes, copula 'be', and locative prepositions—and that investigated by Pienemann (1984)—copula 'be'—are frequent in classroom input and that opportunities for producing them were available to the learners. Yet the effects of instruction directed at these features tended to disappear. It would seem, then, that other factors are involved.

We can only speculate at what these factors might be. One possibility is the nature of the linguistic feature itself. Lightbown (1991a) noted that whereas questions are developmental, adverbs may be variational, in terms of the theoretical framework used by Pienemann (see the previous section).[4] Developmental features may be less susceptible to influence by input, but once acquired—through instruction or through communication—they constitute stable interlanguage rules. In contrast, the acquisition of variational features may be more amenable to input but such forms may continue to be unstable in the learner's interlanguage and so easily atrophy.

A second possibility, not incompatible with the one above, relates to the learner's perception of a grammatical feature. Features such as copula 'be' and -*s* morphemes are not very salient. Thus, although they occur frequently, they may not be easily perceived in continuous speech. These features may also not be seen as very important by learners. Whereas they contribute relatively little to successful communication, structures such as questions and the distinction between *passé composé* and *imparfait* may be considered more important for message conveyance. If learners are motivated primarily by communicative need, then they will probably retain only those features that they perceive to be important for communication, as suggested by Meisel, Clahsen, and Pienemann (1981) and by proponents of some functional theories of L2 acquisition (see Chapter 9). Only if learners are motivated to acquire native-speaker norms, as a result perhaps of a desire to become integrated into the target-language culture, or as a result of an instrumental need to pass an examination that places a premium on grammatical accuracy, will they retain features that from a purely communicative point of view are redundant. According to this view, the durability of instructional effects is closely linked to the nature of the learner's motivation. It should be noted that these explanations are subtly different from the one Lightbown has advanced. Whereas Lightbown emphasizes opportunity for hearing and using a structure, these explanations suggest that such opportunity constitutes a necessary but not sufficient condition to ensure retention of learnt grammar—the learner needs both to be able to perceive structures in the input and also requires a reason for remembering them.

It is clearly essential to establish whether the learning that results from instruction persists, and also what factors determine whether it does or not. This calls for an experimental research design that includes a delayed as well as an immediate post-test—a design increasingly favoured by L2 classroom researchers. To date, few definite conclusions are available but there is sufficient evidence to show that learners retain at least some of the grammatical structures they have been taught.

The effects of different types of formal instruction

The research that we have considered so far has attempted to answer the question 'Does formal instruction result in the acquisition of the features that have been taught?'. This research has viewed formal instruction generically as involving a focus on form and the provision of corrective feedback (see Krashen and Seliger 1975). In taking this view, researchers have been able to gain insight into the nature of the complex relationship between instruction and L2 learning, and also to shed light on the processes of acquisition. From the teacher's perspective, however, another question is of equal if not of greater importance—'What kind of formal instruction works best?' We will now consider some of the research that has tried to answer this question by focusing on a number of methodological options available to teachers.[5]

Focus on forms v. focus on form

An important distinction is that between a focus on forms and a focus on form (Long 1991). Focus on forms refers to instruction that seeks to isolate linguistic forms in order to teach and test them one at a time. It is found when language teaching is based on a structural syllabus. Focus on form involves 'alternating in some principled way between a focus on meaning and a focus on form' (Long 1991). It occurs when teachers follow a task-based syllabus, but focus learners' attention on specific linguistic properties in the course of carrying out communicative activities. Long argues that instruction built around a focus on forms is counter-productive, while that which allows for a focus on form results in faster learning and higher levels of proficiency.

A focus on form can be achieved in two principal ways. First, activities can be devised that require learners to communicate while also focusing their attention on specific formal properties. Second, teachers can elect to provide corrective feedback on learners' errors during the course of communication activities.

A good example of the first way is to be found in Doughty's (1991) study.[6] This compared the effects of 'meaning-oriented instruction' and 'rule-oriented instruction' on the acquisition of relative clauses by 20 intermediate-level ESL students from different language backgrounds. The materials consisted of computer-presented reading passages, specially written to contain examples of clauses where the direct object had been relativized. All the subjects skimmed the texts first. The meaning-orientated group received support in the form of lexical and semantic rephrasings and sentence clarification strategies. The rule-orientated group received instruction in the form of explicit rule statements and on-screen sentence manipulation. A control group simply read the text again. The results showed that the meaning-orientated group and the rule-orientated group both outperformed the control group in their ability to relativize. The meaning-orientated group, however, also demonstrated an advantage with regard to comprehension of the content of the text.

The role of corrective feedback in language acquisition has been extensively debated (see Schachter 1991) and, as discussed in Chapter 13, there has been a considerable body of research into the nature of teachers' corrections in language classrooms. However, there have been few studies that haveinvestigated what effect, if any, formal corrections have on language acquisition.

An investigation by Tomasello and Herron (1988; 1989) provides evidence that formal correction can have a real effect on acquisition. They compared the effects of two kinds of instruction directed at problematic constructions that lead to overgeneralization and transfer errors in beginner learners of L2 French.[7] In one treatment, the problems were explained and illustrated to the students. In the other, which Tomasello and Herron referred to as the 'down the garden path' treatment, the typical errors were induced and then corrected. The results of this study show that leading students down the garden path was the more effective. Two explanations for the results are offered. First, Tomasello and Herron suggest that the 'garden path' technique encourages learners to carry out a 'cognitive comparison' between their own deviant utterances and the correct target-language utterances. Second, they suggest this technique may increase motivation to learn by arousing curiosity regarding rules and their exceptions.

In Tomasello and Herron's treatment there was a focus on forms, but it can be argued that the 'garden path' option corresponds to a focus on form—the kind of grammar instruction that Long (1991) favours—in that the errors that were being corrected were of the kind that students would make naturally in communication.

Lightbown and Spada (1990) examined the effects of corrective feedback in the context of communicative language teaching—exactly what Long had in mind. This study investigated a number of classrooms which were part of an intensive communicative ESL programme in Quebec. Lightbown and Spada found that, although the teaching was mainly communicative in focus, some of the teachers paid more attention to the students' formal errors than others. They found that the learners who did receive error correction achieved greater accuracy in the production of some structures (for example, the use of the correct 'There is . . .' in place of the L1 induced error 'It has . . .') but not of others (for example, adjectival placement).

It is possible, of course, that a focus-on-forms approach could have achieved the same results (i.e. the avoidance or elimination of errors such as 'It has . . .'). However, Lightbown (1991a) points out that learners she investigated in an earlier study (Lightbown 1983; 1987) who had had hours of practice and drill with 'there is' shifted to 'have' as soon as they were taught it. She comments:

> In the 'successful' intensive programme class, the situations in which the teacher drew students' attention to their be/have error were precisely those situations in which the students knew what they wanted to say and the teacher's interventions made clear to them that there was a particular way to say it (Lightbown 1991b: 209).

These studies—together with the theoretical arguments relating to the need for negative evidence, which we considered in Chapter 10—suggest that corrective feedback, when it occurs in response to naturally-occurring errors or in the context of ongoing efforts to communicate, is helpful to L2 acquisition. Other studies, however, have found corrective feedback less effective.

Cohen, Larsen-Freeman, and Tarone (1991) refer to two studies in which most of the students failed to manifest any improvement. Rosenstein (1982) investigated the effects of correcting learners' 'public errors' (errors that they were told they were making) and their 'secret errors' (errors that they did not know about). He found that after repeated correction the success rate was only 50 per cent for public and 20 per cent for secret errors. The other study suggests the reason for these poor results. Alamari (1982) found that 20 per cent of the advanced adult learners of L2 Hebrew she studied reported not paying attention to the teacher's corrections and only 15 per cent said they wrote down the correction in their notebooks. In other words, correction of oral utterances may not be sufficiently attended to by learners.

Carroll, Swain, and Roberge (1992) investigated the effects of corrective feedback on the acquisition of two complex noun suffixes (*-age* and *-ment*) by intermediate and advanced learners of L2 French. The rules for both suffixes were explained to two groups of learners, but only the experimental group received feedback when they produced errors during practice sessions. The results suggested that the correction helped learners—especially the advanced learners—to retain the words actually taught, but that it did not help them to construct morphological generalizations (i.e. the learners in the experimental group did no better than those in the control group in using the two suffixes to form nouns from verbs they had not been taught). This study, then, also suggests that formal correction has a fairly limited effect on acquisition.

There are many possible reasons for these mixed results. One is that corrective feedback is only likely to result in rule acquisition if it occurs in conjunction with natural learning processes—when there is a focus on form rather than a focus on forms. Another possibility, however, as Schachter (1991) notes and as the Lightbown and Spada (1990) study suggests, is that the effectiveness of corrective feedback depends on the particular aspects of language being corrected. 'Teacher correction needs to be judicious' (Cohen, Larsen-Freeman, and Tarone 1991: 144). It is likely that both the conditions relating to the provision of teacher correction and the choice of feature to be corrected affect success.

A focus-on-form approach to language instruction is attractive as it provides a way of integrating 'fluency' and 'accuracy' work but it may be premature to reject a focus-on-forms approach. For one thing, Long's main objections are based on the difficulty of ensuring that instruction directed at *new* linguistic features works, while, as we have already seen, there is plenty of evidence to suggest that formal instruction can help learners improve the *accuracy* of features they have already learnt. The options that we will now consider all involve a focus on forms.

Implicit v. explicit instruction

Formal instruction can take the form of an implicit treatment, where learners are required to induce rules from examples given to them, or an explicit treatment, where learners are given a rule which they then practise using. This distinction underlies the 'language teaching controversy' (Diller 1978) of the 1960s and early 1970s, in which the claims of an empiricist approach (such as the audiolingual method) were pitted against those of a rationalist approach (such as the cognitive code method).[8] As we saw in Chapter 13, a number of comparative method studies (for example, Smith 1970) sought to establish which approach was most effective. The results were generally inconclusive, although the GUME project in Sweden (Von Elek and Oskarsson 1975; cited in Krashen 1982) did show some advantages for an explicit approach. There were no overall differences between implicit and explicit methods but the latter seemed to work better for adult and female adolescent learners of above average intelligence.

Other studies have focused on the effects of implicit and explicit instruction in individual lessons rather than in whole programmes. Seliger (1975) found that adult ESL learners in the United States retained knowledge of a rule better after it had been presented explicitly. However, Hammerley (1975) found that some grammatical structures were more amenable to a deductive approach, while others were better suited to an inductive approach. This finding is supported by psychological research on implicit and explicit learning. A series of studies conducted by Reber (Reber 1976; Reber et al. 1980), for instance, indicates that explicit instruction works when the material to be learnt is relatively 'simple', but not when it is 'complex'. The crucial factors are (1) the number of variables to be learnt and (2) the extent to which the critical features in the input are salient.

Other work in general psychology also points to another factor that may be important where the explicit presentation of rules is concerned—whether the rule is presented in isolation or in conjunction with examples (see Gick and Holyoak 1983). N. Ellis (1991) compared the effects of three kinds of instruction on adult university students' ability to learn the rules of soft mutation in Welsh. These rules require that initial consonants in Welsh nouns mutate (for example, /t/→/d/) in accordance with a complex set of contextual factors. Learners taught implicitly (i.e. given randomly ordered examples of mutating and non-mutating nouns in different contexts) showed very uncertain knowledge of the rules of soft mutation. Learners taught explicitly (i.e. given an account of the rules for soft mutation) developed a solid knowledge of the rules but could not always make accurate use of them when asked to judge correct and incorrect noun forms. Learners given a 'structured' treatment (i.e. rules and examples of how to apply them) did best. They learnt the rules and they were also successful in using them in judging the grammaticality of sentences.

Ellis notes that 'this group alone knows when novel phrases are ungrammatical'.

On balance, the available evidence indicates that an explicit presentation of rules supported by examples is the most effective way of presenting difficult new material.[9] However, the effectiveness of an implicit or explicit instructional treatment may depend on the type of linguistic material being learnt and the characteristics of the individual learner.

Practice v. 'consciousness-raising'

Traditionally, a focus-on-forms approach has involved giving learners the opportunity to practise. In Ellis 1991d, I identified a number of features of language practice from the teacher's perspective: (1) there is some attempt to isolate specific grammatical features, (2) learners are required to produce sentences containing the targeted structure, (3) they must do so repetitively, (4) they are expected to do so correctly, and (5) they receive corrective feedback. It follows from these features that learners will be aware that they are engaging in 'practice' and, also that they will be aware of what item or structure they are trying to learn. I go on to suggest that formal instruction might alternatively take the form of *consciousness raising*, which differs from practice primarily with regard to (2), (3) and (4).[10] That is, in consciousness-raising activities the learners are not expected to produce the target structure, only to understand it by formulating some kind of cognitive representation of how it works. Whereas practice is aimed at developing implicit knowledge of the rule, consciousness raising is directed only at explicit knowledge (i.e. there is no expectancy that learners will be able to use the rule in communicative output).

In Chapter 13 we examined a number of studies relating to the role of participation in classroom language learning and saw that the results were very mixed. Overall, there is no evidence to support the claim—which is central to those who advocate the need for practice—that participation results in learning. In this chapter, we have also reviewed a number of studies that suggest that the extent to which individual learners practise specific grammatical features is not related to the accuracy with which they subsequently perform them in communication. In Ellis 1991d, I note that these results are not encouraging for supporters of practice. One possible reason for the failure of practice is that learners are not yet ready to learn the features they are being taught (see the earlier discussion concerning the effects of instruction on the order and sequence of acquisition).

My advocacy of consciousness-raising as an alternative to practice is based on two main arguments. First, consciousness-raising need not involve production by the learner—at least not on the scale required by practice activities. Second, because consciousness raising is directed at explicit rather than implicit knowledge, it does not run up against the teachability hypothesis.

There is no evidence to suggest that the notions of order and sequence apply to explicit knowledge and thus there is no need to ensure that learners are 'ready' to learn an explicit rule.

The question that then arises is 'What is the use of explicit knowledge to the L2 learner?' Krashen (1977) provides one answer. What he terms 'learnt knowledge' can be used to monitor and thereby to improve the accuracy of communicative output. At least two other uses can be identified. As we saw in Chapter 9, when we considered the role of consciousness in L2 learning, learners who have explicit knowledge of target-language features may be more likely to notice these features in natural input. Also, the process of cognitively comparing what is present in the input with what is the current interlanguage rule is facilitated if learners have explicit knowledge. In these ways explicit knowledge may have an *indirect* effect on the development of implicit knowledge.

There is as yet no research that has directly investigated my claims in Ellis 1991d, although studies by Fotos and Ellis (1991) and Fotos (1993) provide indirect support. These showed that Japanese college students can form accurate representations of the rules for dative alternation, adverb placement and relative clauses as a result of carrying out consciousness-raising tasks that require them to construct explicit rules from structured input data. Also, because these tasks were constructed in accordance with information-gap principles, the learners were also given opportunities to communicate. 'Grammar' became the content that the learners 'negotiated' in order to achieve mutual understanding (see Rulon and McCreary's (1986) study of content negotiation referred to in Chapter 11).

In Fotos' (1993) study, 160 Japanese university EFL learners were asked to complete a number of consciousness-raising tasks directed at the three grammatical structures mentioned above in small groups. One week after completing each task, they were given a listening and a dictation exercise, the texts of which contained exemplars of the target structures under investigation. After completing these tasks, they were given the full texts in writing and asked to underline any 'special use of English' which they had noticed. The results showed that the learners who had undergone the consciousness raising reported noticing all three structures in the input to a significantly greater extent than learners in a control group. Fotos also reports that the gains in knowledge that resulted from the consciousness-raising tasks were maintained in a follow-up test administered two weeks afterwards. This result contrasts with the results in Fotos and Ellis (1991), where the subjects did not receive subsequent exposure in specially designed language activities and, possibly as a result, did not maintain the immediate gains in knowledge evident in the post-test. Fotos' research suggests that (1) consciousness raising directed at specific structures can result in subsequent noticing of these structures in input, and (2) this noticing may help retention of the structures.

Consciousness raising provides a logical way of avoiding many of the pedagogic problems that arise from the teachability hypothesis. It is not surprising, therefore, that it has received considerable attention in language pedagogy (see Rutherford 1988). It remains, however, relatively untested. Also, as I pointed out in Ellis 1991d, not all learners will be interested in or capable of inducing explicit representations of grammatical rules.

Interpretation v. practice

When we talk about the 'comprehension' of grammatical structures we can refer to two rather different notions. One sense refers to the idea of learners' conscious efforts to develop an explicit representation of a rule. A second sense refers to the learners' ability to identify the meaning(s) which can be realized by a particular grammatical structure—to the idea of developing an understanding of what Widdowson (1978) calls the 'signification' of grammatical forms. Whereas the first sense underlies the discussion of consciousness raising above, the second sense informs the idea of 'interpretation' tasks.

Interpretation involves (1) noticing the presence of a specific feature in the input, and (2) comprehending the meaning of the feature. In effect, it corresponds to the stage of input-processing referred to as intake in Chapter 9 (i.e. those features that are noticed in the input and taken into short-term and, possibly, medium-term memory, but which are not yet part of the learner's interlanguage system). One of the assumptions of formal instruction directed at interpretation is that it is psycholinguistically easier to manipulate the process of intake than it is to ensure that learners accommodate intake by undertaking the necessary restructuring of their interlanguage systems. Pienemann (1985) noted that developmental constraints only apply where learner production in communicative language use is involved. He comments: 'the input to the comprehension system does not need to be adjusted to the level of complexity of the production learning task since there are different types of processing procedures in the two systems' (1985: 53). Like consciousness-raising tasks, therefore, interpretation tasks serve as devices for avoiding the instructional problems associated with the teachability hypothesis.

Interpretation teaching typically requires learners to display their comprehension of input that has been carefully structured to contain examples of specific rules or items (Ellis 1993b). It involves, therefore, a comprehension-based approach to language teaching (Winitz 1981). Asher's (1977) Total Physical Response, for example, requires learners to demonstrate their understanding of commands, which have been constructed to teach specific lexical items or grammatical structures, by acting out their responses. We saw in Chapter 13 that Asher reports very favourable results for this method in comparison with practice-orientated methods such as audiolingualism, not only when achievement is measured in listening tests but also in speaking and discrete-item grammar tests.

VanPatten and Cadierno (1993) report an interesting study in which they compared the effects of two instructional treatments, one directed at manipulating learners' output to effect change in their developing interlanguage systems (i.e. practice), and the other aimed at changing the way the learners perceived and processed input (i.e. interpretation). Learners of Spanish at university level who received interpretation training relating to Spanish word order rules and the use of clitic pronouns performed better in comprehension tests than a group of similar learners who received production training. This result is not perhaps surprising, as it can be argued that the comprehension test favoured the interpretation group. However, this group also performed at the same level as the practice group in a production task that favoured the latter.

There are strong theoretical reasons—and some limited empirical evidence—to give support to a focus-on-forms approach based on interpretation. As with consciousness raising, the problems of ensuring that the instruction is made compatible with the way learners learn is achieved by delimiting the goal of the instruction.

Summary and conclusion

It is probably premature to reach any firm conclusions regarding what type of formal instruction works best, but the research that has been undertaken lends support to the following compatible hypotheses:

1 A focus-on-form approach that encourages learners to pay attention to the formal properties of language in the context of trying to communicate—either by means of meaning negotiation or by corrective feedback—may facilitate acquisition (for example, Lightbown and Spada 1990).

2 If a focus-on-forms approach is adopted, this is more likely to succeed if:
   – rules are presented explicitly and supported by examples (for example, N. Ellis 1991)
   – the instruction is aimed at developing explicit knowledge through consciousness-raising activities (for example, Fotos 1993).
   – the instruction is directed at enabling learners to establish form–meaning connections during comprehension (for example, VanPatten and Cadierno 1993).

3 In contrast, there is a growing consensus that instruction directed at promoting growth of learners' interlanguage systems (i.e. their implicit knowledge) through production-training is problematic (for example, Pienemann 1985).

It must be emphasized, however, that there is a need for much more research before the more traditional approaches to formal instruction (those based on the notion of practice) can be dismissed. As was shown in the previous section, there is evidence that these approaches can work for some target features. Also, practice may well serve as one of the ways in which learners can improve their accuracy over linguistic features they have already acquired. The main objections to practice as an instructional strategy lie in the problems of teaching new structures that are developmental in nature. This suggests that one solution to the teachability problem is to look out for those areas of the learner's interlanguage that are in the process of developing. As Hyltenstam points out, 'it is precisely in those areas where the learner exhibits variation that instruction should help the most' (1985: 128).

For practice to be of any real benefit, however, it may be necessary to ensure that it takes place 'under real operating conditions' (K. Johnson 1988) by providing opportunities for learners to produce the target structure in similar circumstances to those that prevail in normal communication. The difficulty of contriving communicative tasks where the use of the target structure in production is essential, however, provides a further reason for exploiting comprehension-based tasks more fully in formal instruction (see Loschky and Bley-Vroman 1990 for a very full discussion of communicative grammar tasks).

Learner–instruction matching

The search for the most efficient type of formal instruction has been motivated by the recognition that the process of L2 acquisition manifests certain structural properties that are universally present in language learners. However, as discussed in Chapters 11 and 12, learners also vary considerably in the way in which they set about trying to learn an L2. This suggests, as Nicholas (1985) has argued, that there is no unique 'best' path to ultimate communicative competence. Rather, learners will differ in the kind of instruction that they respond to best.

It is possible, therefore, that the optimal type of instruction will be that which matches the individual learner's preferred approach to learning. *Learner–instruction matching* can take place informally, as teachers make *ad hoc* adjustments in the nature of the demands they place on learners in the context of their day-by-day teaching. Arguably, this is the most effective way of accommodating individual differences (see Willing 1987). However, it is also possible to make a conscious attempt to ensure a good fit between the instruction and the learner by matching the learner's 'aptitude' to an appropriate teaching style. Educational research which has investigated the effects of such instruction is known as *Aptitude-Treatment-Interaction* (ATI) (Cronbach and Snow 1977).

A good example of ATI research is Pask and Scott's (1972) study. This investigated the ability of native speakers to perform classification tasks. The subjects were divided into 'serialists' and 'holists' (a distinction that corresponds loosely to that between field-independent and field-dependent). The learners were then placed into four groups in order to investigate the effects on learning when the instruction matched and failed to match their preferred learning style. The results were quite striking. The eight learners in the matched condition, irrespective of their learning style, all achieved higher scores than the eight learners in the complementary condition.

It should be noted, however, that not all ATI studies in general education have produced such clear results. Cronbach and Snow (1977) in their review of ATI research conclude that overall there is only weak support for matched instruction. Willing (1987) points out that there are many problems with ATI research. It is not clear, for instance, what dimension of individual difference is pivotal where instruction is concerned. Also, given that learners can differ on a number of factors (language aptitude, learning style, personality, etc.), matching based on a single factor may be ineffective. ATI research in general has focused on cognitive factors (in particular learning style) and has tended to ignore affective factors. Another problem is that many of the studies have failed to ascertain whether the intended 'treatment' was actually manifest in the instructional practices that occurred, as they lacked a 'classroom process' element—the same problem that we saw in the case of the comparative method studies. These methodological weaknesses also apply to research into ATI in L2 acquisition.

A number of experimental ATI studies are summarized in Table 14.4. Ideally, an ATI study needs to be factorial in order to account for two or more independent variables (see Hatch and Lazaraton 1991: 369ff). In such a design at least four groups of learners are needed to allow for both a matched and a complementary condition for each instructional treatment. However, relatively few of the studies in Table 14.4 are truly factorial. In many cases, only two groups were used and the interaction between treatment and individual differences was computed statistically after the event. This is a further weakness in the studies into L2 acquisition.

Four areas of individual difference have been investigated: (1) IQ, (2) expert v. novice learners (3) language aptitude, and (4) field-dependent/holistic v. field-independent/analytic learning styles. With regard to IQ, there is some evidence to suggest that learners with high levels of intelligence benefit from a highly structured instructional method, whereas learners with lower levels benefit from a less systematic approach (see Carrol and Spearritt 1967), although other studies cited in Skehan (1989) have produced the opposite results (for example, Maier and Jacob 1966). At the moment no conclusion is possible.

Good language learner studies (such as Naiman et al. 1978) have indicated that experience in learning an L2 is an important factor. Nation and McLaughlin's (1986) study compared 'novices' (i.e. monolingual and bilingual learners) and 'experts' (i.e. multilingual learners). They found that all the subjects, irrespective of their experience, benefited from a structured as opposed to a random presentation of stimuli relating to an artificial language.

Study	Subjects	Individual differences	Treatment	Results
Carroll and Spearritt 1967	12-year-old children	High v. non-high IQ.	Instruction in grammar rules of artificial language given in (1) ordered fashion and with error explanation and (2) random fashion and with no error explanation.	High-IQ students did better with (1) and non-high-IQ students did better with (2) in working through instruction booklet.
Wesche 1981	Adult learners of L2 French	High aptitude overall v. high-analytical ability but low phonetic coding ability.	Audio-visual inductive approach v. deductive, analytical approach.	Students in matched condition achieved higher scores and reported greater interest in learning French.
Hartnett 1985	34 adult learners of L2 Spanish.	Analytic v. holistic thinkers	Students were allowed to choose between classes taught by an inductive and deductive method.	Subjects choosing inductive method were holistic thinkers; those choosing deductive method were analytic. Subjects in matching method did better than those in unmatched.
Abraham 1985	Adult ESL learners	Field dependent v. field independent	Inductive v. deductive approach to teaching participle phrases.	No main effect for method evident, but interactional effect found—FI learners did better with deductive lesson and FD learners with inductive.
Nation and McLaughlin 1986	Three groups of learners; monolingual, bilingual, and multilingual.	'Expert' learners vs. 'novice' learners.	Stimuli based on artificial language varied according to whether the presentation was (1) implicit or explicit and (2) random or structured.	All learners did better with structured presentation (i.e. no effect for IDs evident). Expert learners did better on implicit task, but no difference on explicit task.
Bacon 1987	Adult beginner learners of L2 Spanish.	Field dependent v. field independent.	One group's efforts at speaking given verbal and non-verbal support; the other group's efforts not supported.	No effect for treatment or for ID evident; also no interaction found.
Carter 1988	72 beginner/low intermediate learners of L2 Spanish.	Field dependent v. field independent.	Learners taught using formal and more functional approaches.	Main effect found for cognitive style (i.e. FI learners did better) but no interactional effect evident.
Akagawa 1992	Intermediate Japanese EFL learners.	Field dependent v. field independent; high v. low language aptitude.	Inductive vs. deductive approach to teaching participle phrases.	No main effect for method found and no interactional effect where FI/FD or aptitude concerned.

Table 14.4: Experimental aptitude–treatment interaction studies

However, they found a strong interaction effect with the other learning condition they investigated, explicit v. implicit. Whereas the 'experts' performed equally well with both explicit and implicit instruction, the 'novices' were found to do much better in the explicit condition. In a subsequent study, Nayak, Hansen, Krueger, and McLaughlin (1987) investigated the interaction between experience and use of learning strategies under two conditions—memorization and looking for underlying rules. They found that the 'experts' used a greater variety of different strategies in the rule-discovery than in the memory condition, but that no such difference existed for the 'novices'. In reviewing these and other studies, McLaughlin (1990b: 170) suggests that the 'experts' may have developed 'greater plasticity in restructuring their internal representations of the rules governing linguistic input'.

It is also possible, as Eisenstein (1980) suggests, that it is not just the amount of experience, but also the type of learning experiences that individual learners have had, that influences the kind of instruction they prefer and benefit from most. Learners whose experience is restricted to a foreign language classroom where a premium is placed on formal grammar training may be encouraged to develop high levels of conformity and control, as these appear to be important for success in such environments (see Genesee 1978). Learners who have experienced a more communicative mode of instruction, such as that provided in immersion programmes, may develop somewhat different types of ability. It is possible, therefore, that there are different kinds of 'expert' learners.

The third factor investigated in ATI studies is language aptitude. Wesche's (1981) study of students of L2 French enrolled in courses designed for Canadian public service employees is probably the best ATI study in SLA research to date. Wesche started with the assumption that 'learning conditions which are optimal for one individual may be inappropriate for another' (1981: 125), and that aptitude tests could be used to identify the special abilities and weaknesses of individual learners. Two types of student were identified. Those in type A had a high overall score on the MLAT and PLAB tests (see Chapter 11). Those in type B manifested a high level of analytical ability but demonstrated problems with phonetic coding and listening. The two treatments consisted of (1) an audiovisual, inductive approach organized around the presentation of linguistic structures sequenced according to order of difficulty and (2) a more deductive, analytical approach, which taught oral and literacy skills together and provided explanations of grammatical points and of how to produce specific sounds. In an initial study, type A students were taught by approach (1), and type B students by approach (2). The results were encouraging. There were no significant differences in achievement between A and B students, suggesting that the matched condition led to equal achievement.

Wesche then used a standard ATI design, assigning students of both types to matched and complementary conditions. The results of an achievement test showed that students in the matched conditions gained higher scores. Also, when interviewed these students reported greater interest in foreign language study, more initiative in practising French outside the classroom, and less anxiety in class. In a partial replication of this study with Japanese college students, Akagawa (1992) failed to find any interaction between degree of aptitude (high v. low) and treatment (inductive v. deductive). However, Akagawa did not look at the effect of different types of aptitude.

The favoured individual difference variable in ATI studies in SLA research is learning style—in particular, field dependence/independence, which, as we saw in Chapter 11, has exerted considerable fascination for SLA researchers. In general, the results have not been very impressive.

Hartnett's (1985) study of learners studying L2 Spanish at university used a rather unusual method of determining learning style. She tested the lateral direction of the subjects' eye movements when thinking, arguing that right eye movements indicated the use of the left hemisphere of the brain and, therefore, analytic thinking, while left eye movements indicated right hemisphere activity and holistic thinking. The learners were given the choice of joining an inductive or a deductive programme. She hypothesized that those choosing the deductive method would be indicative of an analytic learning style, while those choosing the inductive method would have a holistic style, which proved to be the case. The study showed that, in general, the students knew their learning style and were able to opt for the method that suited it. Furthermore, the students who chose the instructional programme that matched their learning style outperformed those who did not on cloze and dictation tests.

Of the studies involving field dependence/independence, only Abraham's (1985) has produced a significant interaction effect; field-dependent learners performed better with an inductive treatment, while the field-independent ones did better with a deductive treatment. The other three studies (Bacon 1987; Carter 1988; Akagawa 1992) failed to find any significant interaction between FI/FD and treatment. Given the general doubts that surround this particular construct (see Chapter 11), further studies are probably not warranted.

Skehan (1989) reaches three conclusions based on his review of ATI research:

> ... first, that the completed condition-seeking research has been some of the most fascinating in applied linguistics; second, that there are many studies whose interpretation is not clear for research/design reasons; and third, that abysmally little research of this sort has actually been done.

While many might disagree with the first of these conclusions, there can be little controversy about the other two. There is limited evidence to suggest that some IDs (L2 learning experience and language aptitude) interact with the instructional approach (explicit/deductive v. implicit/inductive) to affect learning outcomes. This lends support to the common sense conviction that such interactions do occur. As Bialystok (1985) puts it, there needs to be a 'minimal congruity' between the learner's preferred learning strategies and the type of instruction for L2 acquisition to proceed efficiently. ATI research to date, however, has been restricted with regard to both the IDs and the instructional conditions that have been investigated. In particular, there is a need for research to examine how the instructional options discussed in the previous section affect different kinds of learner.

The role of formal instruction: some theoretical positions

Now that we have reviewed the substantial body of research that has examined the effects of formal instruction on L2 acquisition, we can try to evaluate a number of theoretical positions relating to its role.

One of the main issues in language pedagogy is what Stern (1983) calls 'the code–communication dilemma'. There are advocates of what Widdowson (1983) refers to as 'pure education . . . and its associated permissive pedagogy of non-intervention'. There are also those who argue that while instruction may not be necessary for L2 acquisition, it does help learners to acquire more quickly. Finally, there are a number of scholars who maintain that for some aspects of language at least, formal instruction is necessary.

The 'zero option'

The zero option advocates the abandonment of formal instruction. As a result of early work in L2 acquisition which provided evidence of a 'natural' route of development (see Chapter 3), a number of researchers (for example, Dulay and Burt 1973; Krashen 1982) and also educationalists (for example, Newmark 1966; Corder 1976; Terrell 1977; Prabhu 1987) have proposed that classroom language learning will proceed more effectively if language learners are allowed to construct their interlanguages 'naturally', in the same way as they would if they were learning grammar through the process of learning how to communicate. Prabhu (1987), for instance, has argued:

> . . . the development of competence in a second language requires not systematization of language inputs or maximization of planned practice, but rather the creation of conditions in which learners engage in an effort to cope with communication (1987: 1).

The Communicational Teaching Project in southern India, under Prabhu's leadership, sought to demonstrate that 'form can best be learned when the learner's attention is focused on meaning' (Beretta 1989: 233). It should be noted, however, that Prabhu does not actually claim that grammar cannot be learnt through formal instruction, only that learning it through communication is more effective.

In contrast, Krashen (1982) does argue that grammatical competence cannot be taught. His position, which might be referred to as a 'non-interface hypothesis',[11] is that 'learning' does not become 'acquisition' (see Chapter 9). Formal instruction, therefore, is rejected because it does not contribute to the development of the kind of implicit knowledge needed for normal communication. No matter how much the learner practises, explicit knowledge cannot be converted into implicit knowledge. Krashen does accept, however, that formal instruction can contribute to the learning of explicit knowledge,[12] although he sees this as a limited role because only rules that are formally simple and deal with meanings that are easy to explain can be 'learned'. Most rules have to be 'acquired'. Krashen also claims that explicit knowledge is of limited value because it can only be used in 'monitoring' when the learner is focused on form and has sufficient time.

The zero position, as advocated by Krashen and Prabhu, entails not only a rejection of planned intervention by means of the presentation and practice of different items and rules but also of unplanned intervention in the form of error correction. Krashen (1972: 74) refers to error correction as a 'serious mistake' and argues that it should be limited to rules that can be 'learned'. He claims that it puts students on the defensive and encourages them to avoid using difficult constructions. Also, it is likely to disrupt the all-important focus on communication. However, negative feedback in the form of communicative responses to learners' efforts to convey messages—of the kind found in caretaker and foreigner talk (see Chapter 7)—is permitted. Thus, although systematic correction is prohibited, incidental feedback is allowed. Beretta (1989), in research based on classrooms in the Communicational Teaching Project, has been able to demonstrate that such a distinction is pedagogically operational.

To what extent does the research reported in the previous sections lend support to the zero option? Some of it does. The finding that formal instruction only works where planned language use is concerned (see studies by Schumann 1978a and Kadia 1988) bears out Krashen's claim that formal instruction is only useful for monitoring. Also, studies which show that the 'natural' route of acquisition is impervious to formal instruction (for example, Pica 1983; Ellis 1989b) help to confirm the non-interface hypothesis. However, other findings suggest that the zero position is not tenable. A number of studies (for example, Harley 1989; White et al 1991) have shown that formal instruction helps to improve grammatical accuracy, even in unplanned language use, and that the gains that learners make can be durable. Other studies (for example, Pienemann 1984) suggest that formal instruction can result in new knowledge if the structure is variational and, in the case of developmental features, if the learner has already developed the prerequisite processing operations to acquire it. In short, there is substantial evidence that formal instruction works not just because it happens to supply comprehensible input for 'acquisition' but because, on at least some occasions, learners actually learn what they have been taught. It is not surprising that the zero option has been seriously challenged by a number of scholars (for example, Stevick 1980; Sharwood Smith 1981; Færch 1985).

Instruction as facilitation

The essential claim of the facilitative position is that although formal instruction is not necessary to acquire an L2, it helps learning, in particular by speeding up the process of 'natural' acquisition. There are, in fact, several different versions of the facilitative position. One is the *interface hypothesis*—the claim that by practising specific structures learners can 'control' them (i.e. that explicit knowledge gradually becomes implicit). The second is the *variability hypothesis*, according to which instruction can directly affect the learners ability to perform structures in some kinds of use but not in others. The third, associated in particular with Pienemann, is the *teachability hypothesis*. The fourth is that formal instruction helps to make the internalization of rules easier in the long term by helping learners to notice them. We can refer to this as the *selective attention hypothesis*.

The interface hypothesis

According to the interface hypothesis, instruction facilitates acquisition by (1) supplying the learner with conscious rules, and (2) providing practice to enable them to convert this conscious, 'controlled' knowledge into 'automatic' knowledge. Sharwood Smith (1981) builds on the work of Bialystok and McLaughlin (see Chapter 9) in order to develop a full interface model. He claims that 'it is quite clear and uncontroversial to say that most spontaneous performance is attained by dint of practice' (1981: 166). Stevick's (1980) 'Levertov Machine' also allows for 'learnt' knowledge to become 'acquired'. He suggests that 'acquired' knowledge is developed through communicating and is stored in tertiary memory. 'Learnt' knowledge relates to secondary or medium-term memory. In certain cases learners can make use of 'learnt' knowledge while they are communicating and, thereby, 'acquire' it.

The main problem with the interface hypothesis is that it does not give recognition to the difficulty of altering developmental sequences; learners do not 'acquire' structures they are not ready for, no matter how much they practise.

The variability hypothesis

The variability hypothesis differs from the interface hypothesis in one major respect: it claims that teaching learners new structures will affect their *careful style* but not their *vernacular style* (see Chapter 4 for an account of the stylistic continuum). Thus, its effects will be evident when learners are performing in planned language use but not in unplanned language use. In Ellis

1987c, I claim that the explanation for this lies in the relationship between different types of classroom interaction and the learner's variable inter-language system:

> Participation in the kind of planned discourse that results from teacher-directed language drills leads to the acquisition of target language norms in the learner's careful style .... Participation in the more freely-structured discourse that results from unfocused activities requires the performance of a greater range of speech acts and induces the negotiation of meanings required for the development of the vernacular style (1987c: 191–2).

In addition to the direct effect that formal instruction has on learners' careful styles, it can have an indirect effect on their vernacular styles. Tarone (1983) has suggested that there is movement along the stylistic continuum over time, while Dickerson (1974, cited in Tarone 1982) claims that the continued advancement in the careful style may have a 'pull effect' on the vernacular style. In other words, forms that enter a learner's interlanguage in the careful style will gradually become available for use in unplanned discourse.

The variability hypothesis can account for a number of the research findings. It explains why some researchers found instruction to affect planned but not unplanned language use. It explains why instruction is powerless to alter the 'natural' route of acquisition, as this is evident only in the learner's vernacular style. It also explains why instructed learners do better overall than untutored learners, as the former benefit from the 'pull effect' of a more developed careful style. In one respect, however, the variability hypothesis is unsatisfactory; it fails to account for why under certain conditions formal instruction can have a direct effect on learners' unplanned production.

The teachability hypothesis

The third version of the facilitative position—the teachability hypothesis—has already been considered briefly. It has a considerable history (see Nickel 1973; Bailey, Madden, and Krashen 1974; Valdman 1978) but by far the most detailed proposal has come from Pienemann (1985). His main proposals are:

1 Do not demand a learning process which is impossible at a given stage (i.e. order of teaching objectives to be in line with stages of acquisition).
2 But do *not* introduce deviant forms.
3 The general input may contain structures which were not introduced for production
(1985: 63).

The main difficulty arises with (1). Lightbown (1985a) has rightly pointed out that our knowledge of natural acquisition sequences is still too limited to make specific recommendations about how they should be related to teaching

sequences. Pienemann and his fellow researchers have subsequently attempted to overcome this problem by extending our knowledge of
acquisition sequences, by developing a broad theoretical framework with
predictive power (see the account of the Multidimensional Model in Chapter
9) and by devising means for diagnosing a learner's stage of acquisition. Nevertheless, as we noted earlier in this chapter, problems still remain. In particular, as Long (1985b) has observed, Pienemann's proposals rest on the
challengeable assumption that the best way to facilitate natural language development is through the presentation and practice of a series of discrete linguistic teaching points (i.e. a focus on forms).

The selective attention hypothesis

The fourth version of the facilitative position, the selective attention hypothesis, is that formal instruction acts as an aid to acquisition, not by actually
bringing about the internalization of new linguistic features, but rather by
providing the learner with 'hooks, points of access' (Lightbown 1985a). The
position is reflected in Sharwood Smith's Pedagogical Grammar Hypothesis
(see Sharwood Smith 1980, as cited in Rutherford and Sharwood Smith
1985):

> Instructional strategies which draw the attention of the learner to specific-
> ally structural regularities of the language, as distinct from message con-
> tent, will under certain conditions significantly increase the rate of
> acquisition over and above the rate expected from learners acquiring the
> language under natural circumstances where attention to form may be
> minimal and sporadic (1985: 275).

In other words, instruction does not enable learners to fully acquire what is
taught when it is taught, but prepares the way for its subsequent acquisition.
As Gass puts it, instruction 'triggers the initial stages in what eventually
results in grammar restructuring' (1991: 137). Instruction works by helping
learners to pay selective attention to form and form–meaning connections in
the input. It provides learners with tools that help them to recognize those
features in their interlanguages which are in need of modification.

Pedagogical rules constitute one type of tool for facilitating selective attention. The question arises as to whether learners are capable of learning such
rules (see the discussion of explicit knowledge in Chapter 9). A study by
Seliger (1979) suggests that the conscious rules that learners learn as a result
of instruction are often anomalous. Different learners ended up with different
versions of the same pedagogical rule (in this case the difference between 'a'
and 'an'). Sorace (1985), in a small-scale study of learners of L2 Italian, also
found that the learners reformulated the rules they had been taught and that,
as a result, the rules were clearly inadequate both as 'linguistic' and as 'pedagogic' rules. However, Sorace suggests that the ability to actually verbalize a
rule occurs only as the final stage of metalingual development, and thus

represents 'an advanced specialized form of it'.[13] It is possible, therefore, that the conscious rules learners develop are sufficient, even at an early stage, to act as 'acquisition facilitators' by focusing learners' attention on 'critical attributes of the real language concept that must be induced' (Seliger 1979: 368).

A second type of tool is the interpretation task—a device for helping learners to notice and comprehend features in the input. We considered a number of studies that suggest that such a tool is effective in promoting intake (for example, VanPatten and Cadierno 1993) and, ultimately, the restructuring required for interlanguage development (for example, Doughty 1991).

Overall, the research we have considered in this chapter lends considerable support to the facilitative position. We have seen that instruction appears to result in faster learning and higher levels of proficiency (Long 1983c). There is research to support each version of the position, but the selective attention hypothesis is probably the most tenable. Practice does work, but not always. In particular, practice may often fail to bring about any development in the learner's vernacular style. Teaching learners structures they are ready for, however, can result in 'full' acquisition and can cause learners to use the structures in a wide range of linguistic contexts, but there are practical problems in achieving this. Facilitating selective attention by devising instructional activities that equip learners with conscious rules, or that help them interpret the meanings of specific forms in the input, is both psycholinguistically feasible and possible in practical terms. Finally, we should note that formal instruction may prove most facilitative when it matches the learners' own preferred learning styles.

The necessity for instruction

There is little, if any, support for the claim that classroom learners must have formal instruction in order to learn the L2. Despite reservations regarding 'the permissive pedagogy of non-intervention', there is general recognition that much of the language learning that takes place in the classroom takes place 'naturally', as a result of learners processing input to which they are exposed. It is possible, however, that there are certain linguistic properties that cannot be acquired by L2 learners (especially adults) unless they receive instruction in them.

One occasion on which instruction may be necessary is when the learner is in danger of constructing an over-inclusive grammar. We saw in Chapter 10 that principles such as the Subset Principle may not operate effectively in L2 acquisition, with the result that certain types of 'problematic overgeneralization' occur. According to White (1991b), this is likely to arise when the learner's L1 is more general than the L2, as shown in Figure 14.2. Such a situation arises when francophone learners of L2 English attempt to insert an adverb between the verb and the direct object (for example, *John drank yesterday some coffee). White argues that this type of error cannot be eliminated purely on the basis of the positive evidence supplied by communicative input, because the learner could never be sure that such sentences were not possible. In such cases, negative evidence in the form of a grammar lesson or corrective feedback is required.[14]

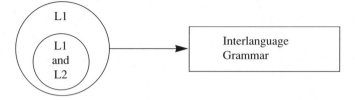

Figure 14.2:   Cases where L1 is more general than the L2 (from White 1991b: 195)

It has also been suggested that even 'benign overgeneralizations' (i.e. errors that can be eliminated on the basis of positive evidence) may require instruction. Rutherford (1989) suggests that learners may fail to expunge such errors on the basis of positive evidence because they have come to understand that language tolerates synonymy. Thus, noticing 'went' in the input may not be sufficient to eliminate 'goed', if the learner operates with the hypothesis that both forms are possible. It follows that learners need to have the fact that 'goed' and 'went' are not acceptable synonyms brought to their conscious attention.

In effect, these arguments bear upon the results of the research we considered in Chapter 13, which indicated that even under favourable conditions classroom learners fail to develop full L2 linguistic competence simply by communicating. It should be noted, however, that it does not follow that formal instruction is the answer. It is possible that many adult learners will fail to develop high levels of grammatical competence no matter what the instructional conditions. d'Anglejan, Painchaud, and Renaud (1986) conclude their study of the effects of intensive mixed instruction (teaching that combined form-focused work with more communicative activities) on adult immigrant learners of L2 French in Canada as follows:

> It is both disappointing yet challenging to discover that after 900 hours of formal instruction, the vast majority of the subjects have attained proficiency levels which at best can be described as minimal (1986: 199).

In other words, there may be limits to what is achievable through classroom learning for the simple reason that there are limits regarding what most learners are capable of achieving under any conditions. Certainly, White's (1991) finding that the beneficial effects of instruction on adverb placement wore off over time would lead to such a conclusion, as would Brindley's (1991) finding that even after intensive instruction the learners in his study showed relatively little development in interrogative forms. It is possible, however, that formal instruction may produce better results with learners who possess better literacy and metalinguistic skills (such as university learners) than the learners in these studies, but this still remains to be demonstrated.

Conclusion

This chapter has reviewed research and theoretical positions relating to the role of formal instruction on L2 acquisition. As we saw in Chapter 13, there are major weaknesses in the second language classroom research. These apply just as much to studies of formal instruction as to other kinds of classroom research. It is important, therefore, to exercise caution in reaching conclusions. The following, however, are compatible with the research findings to date:

1 Benefits of formal instruction

The case for formal instruction is strengthening and the case for the zero option is weakening. Formal instruction results in increased accuracy and accelerates progress through developmental sequences. Also, its effects are, at least in some cases, durable. Formal instruction is best seen as facilitating natural language development rather than offering an alternative mode of learning.

2 Constraints on formal instruction

There are constraints on whether formal instruction works and, if it does, on whether the effects are lasting. Factors such as the degree of markedness, form–function transparency, and the nature of the processing operations involved determine how difficult different structures are to teach. Also, the learner's stage of development affects whether the instruction is successful. Formal instruction combined with opportunities to experience the structures in communication appears to produce the best results. For some structures (for example, those where 'problematic overgeneralizations' occur), formal instruction may be necessary to ensure the target structure is learnt.

3 Types of formal instruction

It is not yet clear which kind of instruction works best but there is evidence to suggest that focusing learners' attention on forms, and the meanings they realize in the context of communicative activities, results in successful learning. There may also be a case for consciousness raising directed at helping learners to formulate explicit knowledge. Although practice activities directed at language production may help learners achieve greater control over structures they have already partially acquired, they may be less successful in enabling learners to acquire 'new' developmental features.

4 *Factors affecting formal instruction*

Although it may be possible to establish the general characteristics of effective formal instruction, allowance will probably also have to be made for variations in learners' learning style, although it is not yet clear what instructional and learner factors need to be taken into account to ensure an effective matching.

Finally, it is necessary to acknowledge the impossibility of teaching the total grammar of a language (see Krashen 1982). It follows that in order to achieve full competence, learners must rely primarily on positive input. The issue is, then, not whether instruction should provide access to language as used in the communicative exchange of meaning, but whether it should *also* seek to draw learners' attention to specific linguistic properties. The answer is 'yes'; this chapter has tried to show both why this needs to be done and also how.

Notes:

1 Felix and Weigl (1991) further suggest that formal instruction may result in factors that 'lead to the total elimination of any kind of UG control'. The results of their study gave a clear 'no' to the question of whether the subjects had access to Universal Grammar.

2 Jones (1992) queries whether the order found in the oral production task can be adequately explained by the Accessibility Hierarchy (AH). He suggests that although the distinction between DO and OP is clear to grammarians, his learners did not see it the same way. Their performance on the oral task indicated that they treated verbs with prepositional phrases (for example, 'working on the floor') as if they were VP + NP constructions, where the verb consisted of a two-word chunk 'working on'. This bears out the conclusion reached in Chapter 10, namely that the acquisition of relative pronoun functions is best explained in terms of processing difficulty rather than the AH.

3 'Sequence' theories and 'projection' theories are not necessarily contradictory. First, projection theories do not claim that input rich in marked features enables learners to learn 'out of sequence', but only that it will enable them to acquire a cluster of features simultaneously. Second, as Jones (1991b) has suggested, projection may only be applicable to the reactivation of items that have been learnt earlier but which have become dormant. It is noticeable that none of the projection studies have examined the effects of instruction on completely new grammatical structures.

4 Lightbown has subsequently reversed her view that adverbs may be variational (personal correspondence). She now thinks they are probably developmental.

5 It is not intended to suggest that these 'options' constitute 'approaches'. Any particular lesson may be made up by selecting from the range of options available.

6 Another example of how a focus on forms can be achieved is Nobuyoshi and Ellis' (1993) study (see Chapter 7).

7 Tomasello and Herron's studies have been criticized by Beck and Eubank (1991) on both theoretical and methodological grounds. Tomasello and Herron (1991) have defended themselves against these criticisms.

8 The effectiveness of an explicit instructional treatment is also demonstrated by Doughty's (1991) study, referred to in the previous section of this chapter. Doughty's rule-orientated group did just as well as her meaning-orientated group when it came to learning the target structure (that is, relativization).

9 The terms 'explicit' and 'implicit' are not to be equated with the terms 'analytic' and 'experiential' (see Chapter 13). The term 'formal instruction' can be equated with 'analytic' instruction; such instruction can be either 'explicit' or 'implicit'. It should be noted, however, that, rather confusingly, the term 'implicit' is sometimes used in connection with communicative language teaching (i.e. 'experiential' instruction) by other authors.

10 The term 'consciousness raising' has been widely used in SLA research by researchers interested in the role of formal instruction. It is frequently used to refer to any attempt to focus the learner's attention on a specific target structure, i.e. as a synonym for formal instruction (see Sharwood Smith's (1981) use of the term). In this sense, language practice activities also involve consciousness raising. In a later article, Sharwood Smith (1991) suggests a better term might be 'input enhancement'. He argues that we can only know what we do with input, not what effect our attempts have on the learner (i.e. whether the input actually raises consciousness). However, the term 'consciousness raising' is preferred in this chapter in acknowledgement of its wide currency. It is used with the narrow definition given in Ellis (1991d).

11 Krashen suggests that his Input Hypothesis constitutes a 'weaker-interface position' on the grounds that learner output produced with the help of 'learned' knowledge can serve as comprehensible input for the purposes of 'acquisition'. However, in so far as Krashen argues that 'learned' knowledge does not convert directly into 'acquired' knowledge, his position is tantamount to a strong non-interface position.

12 Krashen (1982) also recognizes a second use of formal instruction—it can serve as subject matter for 'language appreciation lessons'.

13 Sorace (1985: 244) identifies three stages in the development of conscious metalingual knowledge: subjects are (1) unable to identify errors in correct sentences, (2) able to identify and correct errors but not to state the grammatical rules concerned, and (3) are able to identify and correct errors, and also to state the grammatical rules.

14 It should be noted that White does not argue that formal instruction should be limited to 'problematic overgeneralizations'. She also argues that it can have a valuable facilitative effect when 'benign errors' occur.

Further Reading

There are a number of general surveys of the literature on the role of formal instruction in L2 acquisition, the most recent of which are:
M. Long, 'Instructed interlanguage development' in L. Beebe (ed.), *Issues in Second Language Acquisition* (Newbury House, 1988).
B. Harley, 'Effects of instruction on SLA: issues and evidence.' *Annual Review of Applied Linguistics* (1988) 9: 165–78.
R. Ellis, *Instructed Second Language Acquisition*, Chapter 6 (Blackwell, 1990).
D. Larsen-Freeman and M. Long (eds.), *An Introduction to Second Language Research*, Chapter 8 (Longman, 1991).

Perhaps the best way into what is now a very extensive literature is to read a selection of articles reporting empirical studies dealing with the various issues discussed in this chapter. The following are recommended as representative of the kind of research that has been carried out:

1 *The effects of instruction on general language proficiency*

S. Krashen, C. Jones, S. Zelinski, and C. Usprich, 'How important is instruction.' *English Language Teaching Journal* (1978) 32: 257–61.

2 *The effects of instruction on production accuracy*

P. Lightbown, 'Exploring relationships between developmental and instructional sequences' in H. Seliger and M. Long (eds.), *Classroom Oriented Research in Second Language Acquisition* (Newbury House 1983).

3 *The effects of instruction on the order/sequence of acquisition*

T. Pica, 'Adult acquisition of English as a second language under different conditions of exposure.' *Language Learning* (1983) 33: 465–97.
M. Pienemann, 'Psychological constraints on the teachability of languages.' *Studies in Second Language Acquisition* (1984) 6: 186–214.

4 *Instruction and 'projection'*

F. Eckman, L. Bell, and D. Nelson, 'On the generalization of relative clause instruction in the acquisition of English as a second language.' *Applied Linguistics* (1988) 9: 1-20.

5 The durability of instruction

L. White et al., 'Input enhancement and L2 question formation.' *Applied Linguistics* (1991) 12: 416–32.

6 Comprehension-based formal instruction

C. Doughty, 'Second language instruction does make a difference: Evidence from an empirical study of SL relativization.' *Studies in Second Language Acquisition* (1991) 13: 431–70.

7 Learner-instruction matching

M. Wesche, 'Language aptitude measures in streaming, matching students with methods and diagnosis of learning problems' in K. Diller (ed.), *Individual Differences and Universals in Language Learning Aptitude* (Newbury House 1981).

For more theoretical discussions of the role of formal instruction, the following provide a variety of perspectives:

S. Krashen, *Principles and Practice in Second Language Acquisition* (Pergamon 1982).

M. Sharwood Smith, 'Consciousness-raising and the second language learner.' *Applied Linguistics* (1981) 11:159-68.

M. Pienemann, 'Learnability and syllabus construction' in M. Pienemann and K. Hyltenstam, (eds.), *Modelling and Assessing Second Language Acquisition* (Newbury House 1985).

R. Ellis, 'Contextual variability in second language acquisition and the relevancy of language teaching' in R. Ellis (ed.), *Second Language Acquisition in Context* (Prentice Hall International 1987).

M. Long, 'Focus on form: a design feature in language teaching methodology' in K. de Bot, D. Coste, R. Ginsberg, and C. Kramsch (eds.), *Foreign Language Learning Research in Cross-cultural Perspective* (John Benjamins 1991).

PART SEVEN

Conclusion

Introduction

In this final section of the book it would be pleasing to demonstrate how all the separate lines of enquiry which we have pursued in the earlier sections come together to form a single, well-defined picture. However, this is not possible. The object of our enquiry—second language (L2) acquisition—is best seen as a complex, multi-faceted phenomenon—more like a many-sided prism than a neat picture with clearly identifiable objects. The images that the prism presents vary in accordance with the angle from which it is viewed and the light directed at it, with the result that, while they are in some way interrelated, they also afford different perspectives of the same entity. At this stage in second language acquisition research, it may be possible, as Long (1990c: 656ff) contends, to provide a list of 'well-established findings about learners, environments, and interlanguages'—indeed, this has been one of the goals of the preceding chapters—but it is not yet possible to arrive at a single, comprehensive theory to explain them. Therefore, none will be attempted.

Instead, we will consider the increasing tendency in SLA research to turn in on itself—to examine its own navel, so to speak—by addressing a number of epistemological issues of considerable importance to the whole enterprise. These issues concern the kind of data used in SLA research, theory construction, and the application of the findings of SLA research to other fields.

15 Data, theory, and applications in second language acquisition research

Introduction

In this chapter, we will address three questions:

1 What kinds of data are required to investigate L2 acquisition?
2 How should theory-building proceed in SLA research?
3 Can the results of SLA research be applied to other fields, in particular, language pedagogy,[1] and, if so, how?

These questions are, of course, interrelated. For example, the kind of data we collect to investigate L2 acquisition is likely to reflect our theoretical views. The applicability of SLA research to language pedagogy will depend on both the perceived relevance of the research (which, in turn, is likely to depend on the kind of data used), and the nature of the theory advanced to explain the results obtained. The nature of these interrelationships will become more apparent in the following sections.

The aim of this chapter is the same as preceding chapters: to provide an account of differing positions as objectively as possible. However, personal views always encroach on objectivity and in this chapter perhaps more so than the others. I have followed the procedure of describing alternative positions before offering my own views.

The issues discussed in this chapter relate to issues of wide epistemological concern. However, it is not my intention to embark on a full examination of them, although there is undoubtedly a need for such as examination. I have set myself a narrower goal; one that accords with the general aim of this book (i.e. to provide a balanced and, as far as possible, objective account of work undertaken in SLA). I shall seek only to identify the issues relating to data, theory, and pedagogical applications as these have been reflected in the SLA literature to date.

The choice of data in second language acquisition research

We have come up against the kinds of problems that SLA researchers face with regard to data at various points in this book: in Chapter 2, where we considered the data needed to examine learners' errors; in Chapter 4, where we noted that the descriptive 'facts' of learner-language vary according to the 'task' used to collect data; in Chapter 5, where we considered the merits of discourse completion questionnaires for investigating pragmatic features of learner language; in Chapter 10, where we examined some of the problems attendant on using data from grammaticality judgement tests; and in Chapters 12 and 13, where we saw the importance attached to the use of self-report data in the study of learner differences and learning strategies, but also noted the doubts that exist regarding the validity and reliability of such data. As in other social sciences, there is no agreement about what constitutes the 'right stuff' in SLA research.

We can distinguish three broad types of data in SLA research. First, there is what might be called 'language use data'—data that reflect learners' attempts to use the L2 in either comprehension or production.[2] This type of data can be further distinguished according to whether it constitutes some form of 'natural language use' (i.e. it occurs in the course of using the L2 in the kind of communication that learners engage in when they are not being studied) or 'elicited language use', where, following Corder (1976), we can identify two further categories: clinical elicitation (inducing the learner to produce data of any sort) and experimental elicitation (inducing the learner to produce data relating to the specific feature(s) in which the researcher is interested). The second major data type consists of learners' metalingual judgements, of the kind elicited by a grammaticality judgement test. The third type is self-report data, obtained through questionnaires, interviews and think-aloud tasks. These various types are shown in Figure 15.1.

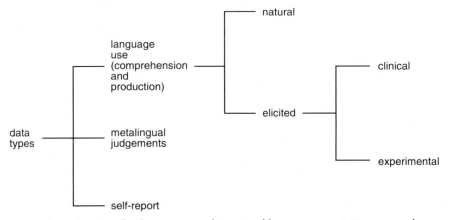

Figure 15.1:   The data types used in second language acquisition research

Different kinds of SLA research have tended to favour different data types. Thus, the early descriptive work that led to claims about 'order' and 'sequence' showed a clear preference for language use data—natural language use in the early case studies, and clinical and experimental elicitation in the cross-sectional studies (for example, the morpheme studies). The study of interlanguage pragmatics, however, has relied extensively on experimentally elicited data, using, for example, Discourse Completion Questionnaires, although some work has also been based on natural language use. In contrast, research based on 'strong' theories, such as Universal Grammar and the Competition Model, has relied heavily on learners' metalingual judgements. Research into individual differences has found language use data of limited value, and has turned to various kinds of self-report data. This, then, is the first, obvious point to be made: the type of data used closely reflects the research goals. We will now consider the pros and cons of each data type.

Natural language use

The main strength of natural language use is that it provides information about what learners actually *do* with the L2 when they try to use their L2 knowledge in communication (i.e. the data can be considered 'authentic'). For example, the importance of formulaic speech in L2 production is only evident in data reflecting natural language use. This kind of data shows the linguistic and pragmatic features of the L2 that learners typically employ in different situations.[3] It can be used to investigate to what extent and in what ways learners achieve procedural control over their knowledge. It can shed light on the socio-affective factors that influence language performance. In particular, it affords insight into the kinds of strategies that learners employ in constructing and using their interlanguage. In Labovian terms, natural language use shows us the learner's vernacular style, which some researchers consider to be 'basic' in the sense that it reflects the most normal way knowledge of language is utilized.

There are also several well-attested disadvantages of natural language use. The most obvious are that it is time-consuming and difficult to collect, and may not provide information relating to the specific features that are the target of the study, or not in sufficient amounts to make a quantitative analysis possible. It is no accident that early studies focused on negatives and interrogatives, as these structures occur frequently in natural language use. Other disadvantages also exist. As Beebe and Cummings (forthcoming) comment in a discussion of natural speech act data:

> ... many studies of natural speech have not given us scientifically collected speech samples that represent the speech of any identifiable group of speakers. They do not give us situational control, despite the fact that situation is known to be one of the most influential variables in speech act performance.

The significance of this criticism is that it comes from researchers, who by virtue of their chosen area of enquiry (interlanguage pragmatics) are disposed to look favourably on natural speech data. However, Beebe and Cummings find this type of data 'unsystematic'. In effect, they are challenging the value of natural language use and asserting the need for elicited language use so that variables that influence performance can be investigated systematically.

Elicited language use

The elicitation of language use provides researchers like Beebe and Cummings with the 'systematic data' they feel are necessary. Clinical elicitation has been accomplished by means of various kinds of spoken and written tasks. Data from written compositions, for example, have been used extensively in error analyses (see Chapter 2). Information-gap tasks of various kinds have been widely used to obtain samples of relatively spontaneous speech (for example, by Lightbown 1983; Ellis 1989b). Other devices that have figured in SLA research are oral interviews and role plays. Such instruments provide the researcher with ample data and also with greater 'situational control' over the data. However, the status of the data is uncertain, as we cannot know for sure what 'style' the data represent. Is the language produced in an information-gap task a true reflection of the learner's vernacular style? Also, one of the problems of natural language use—inadequate information relating to specific language features—may not be overcome.

It is the need for data on specific linguistic or pragmatic properties that provides the principal justification for experimental elicitation. Larsen-Freeman and Long (1991) list the various instruments that have been used to elicit experimental L2 data: reading aloud (subjects are asked to read words, sentences, or passages out loud), structured exercises (for example, transformation exercises, fill-in-the-blanks, and sentence combining), completion tasks (involving either discrete sentences or whole passages), imitation tasks (where learners are asked to imitate sentences read to them), translation, guided composition, and story-retelling. All these devices serve, like tests,[4] to provide the researcher with samples of learner language containing copious exemplars of the particular property that is the target of the investigation.

The key issue surrounding these experimental elicitation devices is the extent to which they supply valid data. We will examine this issue with reference to one device—the Discourse Completion Questionnaire—which has gained popularity in the study of interlanguage pragmatics. This device, which we discussed and illustrated in Chapter 5, provides learners with a situation designed to elicit a specific illocutionary act such as a request or apology, and asks them to write down what they would say. The usual way to establish the validity of the data collected by this instrument is by establishing to what extent they display the same features as natural speech data. Thus, Beebe and Cummings (forthcoming) compared refusals elicited by a Discourse Completion Questionnaire with those occurring more or less naturally in telephone conversations.[5] The results of their study suggest that there are both similarities and differences. They found that the elicited data produced shorter responses, fewer repetitions and turns, and, in particular, less remedial work (attempts to mitigate the force of a refusal). But they also noted that the elicited data provided an accurate picture of the different semantic formulas used to perform the illocutionary act. In the eyes of Beebe and Cummings this 'validated' the data. We should note, however, that concurrent validation of this kind requires the researcher to collect samples of natural language use in addition to the experimentally elicited data, which, often enough, has not been done. We might also note that not all researchers would accept that elicited data is 'valid', even if it can be shown to match natural language use.

Metalingual judgements

This is precisely the position adopted by some researchers who make use of learners' metalingual judgements. Asking learners to judge the grammaticality of sentences (as in much UG-inspired research) or asking them to identify which noun functions as the agent or subject in a sentence (as in research based on the Competition Model) taps into their metalingual knowledge. One justification for such tasks is that they provide evidence about what learners *know* as opposed to what they *do*, about competence rather than performance. Such a claim is probably not warranted, however. Metalingual judgements involve 'performance' just as much as natural language use, albeit of a different kind. There is no direct window into competence. Also, conversely, data taken from natural language can provide evidence of learners' competence, not just of their performance. In short, all data, from whatever source, can be used to investigate both competence and performance.[6] Metalingual judgement data do not have a privileged status, as is now generally recognized.

The great advantage of metalingual judgement tasks is that they enable researchers to investigate linguistic properties that would be otherwise very difficult (and perhaps impossible) to investigate. Language use data—natural or elicited—provide only information about the language that learners produce or comprehend in particular situations. They tell us nothing about the language learners do not use. Thus, we do not know whether the fact that learners fail to produce sentences such as:

*What did Randy wonder whether his brother would win?

is just because they have not got round to doing so or because their interlanguage grammars do not permit them to do so. Metalingual performance data can shed light on this issue.

There are obvious disadvantages, however (see Chapter 10). Birdsong (1989) has written at length on the 'logical problem of the data' collected by means of metalingual judgement tasks. The pitfalls include the difficulty of obtaining reliable judgements from illiterate bilinguals, response biases, the problem of determining exactly what it is that learners judge when they evaluate sentences, and the variability that arises from different learners' 'skill' in performing such tasks. Birdsong suggests ways in which these pitfalls can be overcome. Like others before him (for example, Arthur 1980; Chaudron 1983a), he also suggests that metalingual performance data take on validity when the results they provide converge with those obtained from other data sources, in particular language use. In fact, though, despite Chaudron's claim that 'metalinguistic judgements in NSs and NNSs tend to be validated by other measures of performance' (1983a: 371), there is plenty of evidence that they do not (see, for example, the studies of variability in learner language discussed in Chapter 4).

Self-report

The third major type of data in SLA research is self-report data. These have proved invaluable in exploring individual differences in learners and identifying the various learning strategies they employ (see Chapters 11 and 12). Self-report data have been obtained in various ways: by means of written questionnaires such as those used by Gardner and his associates to measure learners' attitudes and motivation (see Gardner 1985), by means of oral interviews of the kind used by Wenden to identify learners' beliefs about language learning (see Wenden 1987a), and by think-aloud tasks, performed either by individual learners or by pairs of learners and used to identify the nature of the problem-solving strategies learners employ in various language tasks (see the papers in Færch and Kasper 1987). Self-report data has proved invaluable in uncovering some of the affective and cognitive factors involved in L2 learning, factors that are not readily observable in language behaviour.

Again, though, there are problems. One concerns the extent to which learners are sufficiently aware of their affective states and cognitive processes to report on them. This is a problem of validity, but not a serious one, perhaps, as we can simply acknowledge that self-report data are limited in this respect and, therefore, like any other type of data, incomplete. Another problem is that 'subject's reports may derive more from what they think they should have been doing than what from what they actually were doing' (McLaughlin 1990c: 629). This is a problem of reliability, which might be overcome by comparing data collected from the same subjects using the same instrument on two separate occasions and establishing re-test reliability—a procedure which, regrettably, has been little used in SLA research.

The question of validity

Underlying this discussion of the pros and cons of the different types of data is the central problem of validity. What constitutes valid L2 data? One answer is that valid data are those that enable a researcher to infer underlying phenomena. The distinction between 'data' and 'phenomena' is made much of by Gregg (1993). Citing Bogen and Woodward (1988), Gregg emphasizes that theory construction is concerned with phenomena (i.e. some generalized aspect or event such as the melting point of lead) and not with data (i.e. particular observations such as the actual measurements of the temperature at which samples of lead melt). The question that arises, of course, is how 'phenomena' can be derived from 'data'. On this Gregg has nothing to say.

The answer customarily given is that data provide evidence of phenomena when the results they provide are consistent. To demonstrate consistency, it is necessary to show that the data are not just a reflection of the instrument used to collect them. This can be achieved by comparing the results obtained from one set of data with those obtained from another—ideally, some 'baseline' such as natural language use. We have seen recourse to this notion of concurrent validity in Beebe and Cumming's evaluation of data obtained by means of a Discourse Completion Questionnaire and in Birdsong's (and others') justification of metalingual judgement data. There is, however, a logical objection to such a procedure, of which Birdsong (1989) is fully aware:

> One must be aware that not all tasks, linguistic or metalinguistic, tap the same source of linguistic knowledge. Thus the results of one type of test may not be useful in proving the concurrent validity of another source (1989: 118).

In effect, Birdsong is acknowledging the position adopted by variabilists and, in fact, he explicitly refers to the work of one variabilist, Bialystok. Learners vary in the way they use their linguistic knowledge in accordance with a variety of linguistic, situational, and psycholinguistic factors (see Chapter 4). It is to be expected, therefore, that data collected from one source will not completely match those collected from another.

If data cannot be validated concurrently, where does this leave us? One possibility, advanced by the variabilists, is to argue that competence itself is variable, but this solution is not acceptable to many. Another solution is to acknowledge that different types of data will serve different purposes and shed light on different aspects of L2 acquisition—a view that is compatible with the analogue of the prism in the introduction to Part Seven of this book. The data needed to investigate the kinds of specific hypotheses derived from the Competition Model or UG theory are only readily available through experimental elicitation. The data needed to investigate the claims of the Multidimensional Model need to reflect natural language use. However, while admitting that 'good data' are, above all, relevant data, we also need to recognize the dangers of highly controlled data for, as Hatch, Shirai, and Fantuzzi (1990) have pointed out, they may mislead because the results they provide fail to generalize to other types of data. At the very least, then, researchers need to study whether consistency is present and, when it is not, acknowledge the problem and search for an explanation.

It follows that multiple data sources are needed. This is, in fact, what we find most researchers currently recommending and many actually practising. Good data, then, are data that are relevant to the particular descriptive or theoretical goals of the research and which are compared with other data. Good research is research that makes use of multiple sources of data, that gives recognition to the limitations of the data sources used, and, in Birdsong's words, recognizes that 'each method carries with it impediments to the translation of data to theory' (1989: 613).

The construction and role of theories in second language acquisition research

It would be a mistake to suggest that all SLA research is or should be directed at theory development. Gregg (1993) points out that much research in any field is usefully directed at measuring phenomena, constructing new instruments, or creating new phenomena. Nevertheless, many researchers are increasingly committed to providing an explanation of how an L2 is acquired. While much of the earlier work was primarily concerned with describing the object of enquiry (the language produced by L2 learners), subsequent research has been directed at developing theories to explain the wide range of phenomena that have been discovered and to predict new phenomena. In the 1980s, in particular, theories appeared at a startling rate. It is not surprising, therefore, that some L2 acquisition researchers have felt the need to ask a number of basic questions about theory-building in their discipline, drawing on recent work in the philosophy of human science (for example, Darden 1991 and Laudan 1990), which seeks an understanding of how research programs are actually conducted.[7] The main questions are as follows:

1 What approach to theory-building should SLA research adopt?
2 What should be the scope of a theory of L2 acquisition?
3 What form should a theory take?
4 How can different theories be evaluated?

Approaches to theory building in SLA research

Long (1985a) draws on the work of Reynolds (1971) to identify two broad approaches to theory building: the 'research-then-theory' approach and the 'theory-then-research' approach. He suggests that a research-then-theory approach involves the following four activities:

1 Select a phenomenon and list all its characteristics.
2 Measure all the characteristics in as many and as varied situations as possible.
3 Analyse the resulting data by looking for systematic patterns.
4 Formalize significant patterns as theoretical statements (the laws of nature).

This provides an accurate description of much of the early SLA research. The phenomenon under study was 'learner language', its characteristics (errors, developmental features, variability, etc.) were examined, and 'systematic patterns' were identified. This led to the formulation of a number of 'laws' in the form of generalizations about L2 acquisition (for example, 'in the early stages of development learners tend to simplify by omitting both grammatical functors and content words'). It would seem, though, that there is also the possibility of a fifth step, not mentioned by Reynolds or Long:

5 Gather together the 'theoretical statements' into an explicit theory expressed in axiomatic or causal process form.

This step is evident in the theories that came out of the descriptive work of the 1970s—for example, 'creative construction theory' or the 'variable competence model'. It constitutes an optional rather than a required step. In Gregg's (1993) view, it results in 'shallow theories' (i.e. theories that stick as closely as possible to what is observable and, therefore, do not address 'phenomena').

The research-then-theory approach is characterized by Reynolds (as in Long 1985a: 390) in terms of the following activities:

1 Develop an explicit theory in axiomatic or causal process form.
2 Derive a testable prediction from the theory.
3 Conduct research to test the prediction.
4 If the prediction is disconfirmed, modify the theory and test a new prediction (or abandon the theory altogether).
5 If the research findings confirm the prediction, test a new one.

It is clear, then, that what is the possible end point of a research-then-theory approach can serve as the starting point in a theory-then-research approach. This approach, however, also lends itself to the construction of 'deep theories' (i.e. theories that go beyond what has been observed by acknowledging the importance of those aspects of nature that cannot be observed). Importantly, such theories do more than just explain; they also allow for predictions to be formulated, tested, and modified. One possibility afforded by this approach is the adoption of a theory for step (1) from outside the realm of SLA research. This has increasingly happened: for example, the skill-building models adopted from cognitive psychology or the linguistic models taken from theoretical linguistics.

It is unnecessary and, indeed, unwise, to try to argue that one approach to theory building is superior to the other. Indeed, the two approaches can interlock in a cyclical endeavour. Long (1985a) rightly recognizes that both approaches have their strengths and weaknesses. He argues that researchers in the research-then-theory approach are less likely to be 'wrong' because their theoretical claims are based firmly on empirical evidence—always providing, of course, that their observations are valid and reliable—but the end result of their efforts may be 'limited' and perhaps ultimately 'irrelevant', and, in

Gregg's eyes, result in a 'shallow' theory. However, there would seem to be no reason why a 'shallow theory' should not develop into a 'deep theory' over time, as in fact often happens when theorists in this tradition go beyond the empirical evidence. Long argues that researchers in the theory-then-research tradition are able to offer an 'approximate answer' right away and also are more likely to bring about a paradigm shift, as it is this approach that is associated with 'scientific revolutions'. He recognizes, however, that they tend to resist abandoning their theories, preferring, if necessary, to modify or add parts to them in order to immunize them against disconfirming evidence.

These approaches reflect the two ways in which SLA research can proceed. Beretta (1991: 505) refers to them as 'bottom-up and top-down strategies'. He argues that the former requires researchers to seek plentiful data before they formulate any theory, and intimates that researchers should resist the temptation to formulate an explicit theory prematurely. According to Beretta, a top-down strategy requires the researcher to formulate a provisional theory immediately so that this can then guide enquiry. It is probably true to say that most L2 researchers accept that both strategies are legitimate and useful, although some, like Gregg (1989) have sufficient belief in one particular theory (Universal Grammar) to argue forcefully for a theory-first approach and against a data-led one. Beretta also notes that there are advantages in the advocacy of a 'tribal model' (a theory that it is aggressively promoted so that it stimulates others to explore and elaborate it). The problem with a theory-first strategy, of course, is that it requires a theory of sufficient strength to command allegiance, and it is this which, in the eyes of many researchers, is still lacking.

The scope of a theory of second language acquisition

Second language acquisition is an enormously complex phenomenon—so complex, perhaps, that it is not yet clear exactly what a theory of L2 acquisition needs to account for. One way of specifying the scope of such a theory might be to start by identifying the facts of L2 acquisition. This is the approach that Long (1990c) adopts. He lists what he calls the 'well-established findings' of SLA research (1990c: 656), and argues that these constitute 'the least that a second language acquisition theory needs to explain'. Such an approach makes obvious sense and, incidentally, provides a justification for such a book as this one, which has as one of its major goals a review of what has been discovered about L2 acquisition. Nevertheless, it also has problems. The first is that there is often no agreement about what constitutes the 'well-established findings'. While it is often possible to agree on broad generalizations (for example, 'age differences systematically affect how fast learners learn'), it is less easy to reach agreement on more specific statements (such as 'the "critical period" for the acquisition of a native-like phonology ends at the age of six'). Second, there is the question of deciding how many of the well-established findings a theory needs to account for. Long, for instance, states that 'a theory must account for at least *some* of the *major* accepted findings' (1990c: 660, my emphasis added), inviting questions as to what 'some' and 'major' mean, questions for which, not surprisingly, no answers are provided. It is probably true to say that, to date, there is no agreement in SLA research about what facts or how many facts need to be accounted for. This, above all, is why the field is characterized by a multiplicity of theories.

Three views regarding the scope of an L2 acquisition theory can be identified. One is that the field should strive towards a single, comprehensive theory, or at least seek to eliminate inferior theories. The second view is that a modular approach will work best, informed perhaps by an over-reaching framework that enables researchers to identify fairly specific domains in which to theorize. The third view is that multiple, overlapping theories are inevitable and even, perhaps, desirable.

Probably the most substantial attempt to construct a comprehensive theory is that of Spolsky (1988; 1989). This theory, which Spolsky refers to as a 'general theory', takes the form of a set of statements that describe the 'conditions' under which L2 learning can take place. As we saw in Chapter 11, these conditions are of various kinds—'necessary', 'typical', and 'graded'—depending on the nature of the relationship between a particular condition and a particular outcome. Because many of the conditions are of the 'typical' and 'graded' kind, Spolsky refers to his theory as a 'preference model'. The model contains a total of 74 statements of conditions, which Spolsky claims are 'the natural and logical conclusion of current research in second language learning' and 'a description of the state of the art' (1988: 384). In addition, Spolsky (1989: 28) provides a schematic outline of the different components of the model. This is important because it provides a basis for grouping the various conditions (for example, under such headings as 'social context', 'attitudes', and 'learning opportunities') and also because it indicates the nature of the relationship among the various components.

A comprehensive theory such as Spolsky's general theory is attractive to SLA research because it affords a basis for systematic enquiry. It provides a framework in which individual researchers can locate their specific lines of enquiry, it allows for specific predictions based on the conditions to be tested, and it provides a blueprint for investigating the whole of L2 acquisition (i.e. for determining which factors contribute to the universal and variant properties of L2 acquisition and to what extent they do so). In other words, it helps to shape the whole field and caters for research with both micro and macro goals. Such a comprehensive theory has a number of drawbacks, however. First—and perhaps most serious—the interrelationships among the different sets of statements (i.e. the components of the model) are underspecified, as to specify them fully would run the risk of producing a model of unwieldy complexity. Spolsky's theory is, in the final analysis, little more than a list of more or less unrelated statements, with all the limitations that this entails.

Second, there is the danger—acknowledged by Spolsky—that the statements will be pitched at such a high level of generality as to be of doubtful value. One wonders, for example, about the explanatory value of conditions such as the 'Attitude Condition', which blandly states that 'a learner's attitudes affect the development of motivation' (Spolsky 1989: 23). Finally, it is not clear how the whole theory can be falsified (although, as we will shortly see, the notion of 'falsification' is itself problematic). It may be possible to falsify the specific conditions, but how many conditions have to be shown to be false before the whole theory becomes untenable? Spolsky's general theory results in a 'messy, fuzzy, overlapping picture' (Hatch, Shirai, and Fantuzzi 1990: 711). Some researchers find this tolerable because of the importance they attach to forming a whole picture.

Many researchers, however, prefer a modular approach to theory building. A good example of such an approach is that found in White (1989a) and discussed in Chapter 10 (see Figure 10.4, page 439). The case for modularity can be made on both theoretical and procedural grounds. In the case of White and other researchers in the UG tradition, there are logical arguments for claiming the existence of a 'language module' that can be investigated independently of other domains (such as perceptual modules). UG researchers stake out a claim for the necessity of examining the language module separately from other modules. However, other researchers may choose to investigate a specific domain simply because it is procedurally convenient to do so. For example, Gardner's work on attitudes and motivation (see Chapters 6 and 11) has proceeded without reference to the existence of developmental universals in learner language, probably because the psychometric tradition, to which Gardner adheres, has employed data collected by means of tests and ratings, which do not readily afford a developmental perspective.

For a theory to be truly modular, it is necessary to specify (1) the domain covered by the theory, as narrowly as possible, and (2) the domains that are not covered by the theory, in broad outline. Many theories are modular in the very restricted sense that they tackle only part of the picture, but they neither state explicitly what domain they seek to explain, nor do they provide any indication of the domains not covered by the theory. UG-based theories, though, can legitimately call themselves 'modular' as they conform to both the above requirements.

One of the dangers of modularity is unwarranted reductionism (i.e. the domain of investigation is delimited over-narrowly and without theoretical justification). Another serious problem is atomism (i.e. the investigation of one domain takes place in total isolation from the study of other domains). An explanation may satisfactorily account for a delimited set of phenomena and yet be found wanting when these same phenomena are viewed as part of the complete picture. As Hatch, Shirai, and Fantuzzi put it, 'to make our research feasible, we try to limit our investigations to one area, but in so doing, we may advance explanations that are faulty' (1990: 702).[8] This led them to argue that 'partial theories are misleading'. Ultimately, therefore, a modular theory has to be tested in relation to the whole picture. It is valid in the extent to which its explanation of a single domain holds true when this domain is considered in relation to other domains.

Most theories of L2 acquisition are neither comprehensive nor truly modular. Rather they tackle a particular area or adopt a particular perspective (often derived from a parent discipline—cognitive psychology, social psychology, sociolinguistics, linguistics, neurolinguistics, education) without reference to other areas or perspectives. A multiplicity of theories is the result, as is amply demonstrated in this book (see Part Four in particular) and in other survey books. In Ellis 1985a I reviewed seven theories, McLaughlin (1987) considers five, while Larsen-Freeman and Long (1981) also examine five (although not the same five as McLaughlin). Furthermore, this theoretical pluralism shows no signs of abating, for as Spolsky has observed 'new theories do not generally succeed in replacing their predecessors, but continue to coexist with them uncomfortably' (1990: 609).

The question that arises is to what extent this multiplicity is to be viewed positively or negatively. Beretta (1991) notes that opinions differ considerably on this point. On the one hand there are the 'relativists' like Schumann (1983) who view SLA research as an 'art' rather than a 'science', and argue that 'in art perspectives are neither right or wrong; they are simply more or less appealing to various audiences' (1983: 66). On the other hand, there are those like Griffiths (1990), Long (1993), and, to a certain extent, Beretta himself, who see multiple theories as problematic for SLA research and consider the elimination of some theories in favour of others a necessary goal if the field is to advance. Long points out that whereas some theories can be seen as complementary, others are clearly oppositional. He gives examples of rival claims in choice of domain (for example, UG-based theories v. variabilist theories), within a single domain (for example, the conflicting arguments regarding the availability of UG in adult learners), and with regard to the specific variables considered important by mentalist, environmentalist and interactionist theories. He argues that where opposition exists, 'culling' needs to take place, pointing out that the history of science shows that successful sciences are those that are guided by a 'dominant theory'. Culling calls for the identification of assessment criteria. Before we turn to this issue, however, we will consider what *form* theories of L2 acquisition can take.

The form of a theory of second language acquisition

There has been far less discussion about the form that a theory of L2 acquisition should take. Crookes (1992) and Gregg (1993) distinguish 'property theories' and 'transition theories'. The former are concerned with providing accounts of static systems; they are 'ways of representing dispositions, competencies, or bodies of knowledge' (Crookes, 1992: 433). Such theories are useful in that they help to identify the states of L2 knowledge and the components of such states to be found in learners at different stages of their development. Much of the modelling of L2 knowledge found in UG-based theories of L2 acquisition is of this nature (see, for example, Figure 8.1 or, again, Figure 10.4). But there is general recognition that property theories in themselves cannot satisfactorily explain L2 acquisition. A transition theory that seeks to account for how changes in the state of a system take place is also needed. Crookes argues that an adequate theory must specify the 'mechanisms' that are responsible for such changes. Long (1990c: 654) defines 'mechanisms' as 'devices that specify how cognitive functions operate on input to move a grammar at Time 1 to its new representation at Time 2', although this probably needs to be broadened to include mechanisms of a more affective nature such as motivation. A satisfactory theory, then, must identify the mechanisms—cognitive and affective—responsible for acquisition.

How, then, should this be done? Crookes points out that traditionally theories have taken the form of a series of deductively related sentences, often utilizing a highly formalist language such as that provided by mathematics or logic. However, this kind of theory has never figured strongly in SLA research, which instead has preferred what Crookes calls 'a statement-picture complex' form. According to this, a theory consists of some kind of pictorial element (the 'model') and a supporting set of statements containing generalizations based on and supporting the model. The 'model' provides an iconic element and is likely to employ an analogy of some kind, which may or may not be explicitly acknowledged. For example, Crookes suggests that Krashen's Monitor Theory incorporates a ladder analogy (in the natural order hypothesis) and a learner-as-sponge analogy (in his account of how 'acquisition' takes place). Schumann (1983), with tongue only partly in cheek, discusses a number of pictorial models of L2 acquisition from the perspective of a 'curator of an exhibition of SLA art' (1983: 67) to make his point that theories need to be considered from an aesthetic point of view. The supporting statements, Crookes suggests, need to be clear and explicit, which can be achieved through the appropriate use of formalisms, although few L2 acquisition theories have attempted this.

Evaluating second language acquisition theories

Three approaches to theory evaluation can be identified. One consists of identifying a set of criteria that can be applied to all theories as a way of eliminating those that are unsatisfactory. This, according to Beretta (1991) and Long (1993), should be the goal of SLA research. The second approach is to abandon any attempt to evaluate theories on rational grounds, and to turn instead to aesthetic criteria. The third approach is to accept that theoretical pluralism is not just a temporary feature of an immature discipline, but is here to stay and to try to avoid the attendant problems of absolute relativism by evaluating theories in relation to their particular contexts and purposes. We will briefly consider these three approaches.

A number of criteria are traditionally invoked to evaluate theories. McLaughlin (1987; 1990c), for instance, mentions the following:

1 Norms of correspondence: the extent to which the theory fits the facts that it seeks to explain
2 Norms of coherence: the extent to which the theory fits the body of knowledge that has already been established and is consistent with other related theories
3 Practicality: the extent to which a theory is 'heuristically rich' in stimulating and guiding research (McLaughlin 1990c: 619)
4 Falsifiability: the extent to which the theory affords hypotheses that can be disconfirmed.

In particular, McLaughlin emphasizes the importance of falsifiability. However, this has recently come under attack. Beretta (1991) argues that it is problematic because of the impossibility of obtaining neutral, objective data with which to test theoretical claims and, also, because L2 acquisition theories tend to be formulated in such a way that they allow for *ad hoc* or auxiliary hypotheses as a way of immunizing initial hypotheses against disconfirming evidence. Schumann (1993) makes the same point when he points out that it is very difficult to test a hypothesis in isolation because every hypothesis is embedded in 'a network of auxiliary assumptions'. Thus, when the results fail to support the hypothesis, we cannot tell whether this is because the hypothesis is wrong or because one or more of the auxiliary hypotheses is wrong. He argues that 'falsification is ... extremely difficult, if not impossible to achieve' (1993: 296).

Long (1993), however, sees greater merit in falsifiability, although he also acknowledges the problems. He draws on Darden's (1991) work on how theory changes in genetics to suggest five sets of 'assessment strategies':

1 Criteria applicable before the empirical testing of a theory (for example, internal consistency)
2 Criteria for assessing the empirical adequacy of a theory (for example, explanatory adequacy and generality)
3 Criteria for assessing a theory's future potential (for example, fruitfulness)
4 Consistency with accepted theories in other fields
5 Metaphysical and methodological constraints (for example, experimental testability).

Long suggests that these criteria provide a basis for theory evaluation but he also accepts 'that there is no consensus on a universal set of criteria at present' (1993: 239).

Indeed, Beretta (1991) concludes his excellent discussion of the various evaluative criteria with the assertion that there are no foolproof, indispensable criteria available. However, he goes on to argue that SLA research must find ways of eliminating theories to achieve maturity, and advances the 'modest' notion that 'evidence' (in the form of data that fail to confirm a hypothesis or unsuccessful attempts to replicate findings) is capable of changing our views. In short, although it is not logically possible to falsify hypotheses, we must (and do) act as if it is. Long (1993) also suggests that we need to act as if a set of universally valid assessment criteria exists. He argues that different criteria may be important at different stages of theory development, and that the failure to identify a universal set of criteria may reflect a 'problem in the timing of their application, not conflicts in principle' (1993: 242). He goes on to suggest that criteria, like theories, should be subjected to empirical testing and adjusted when they are found to be 'false'. It would seem, though, that the same problems that exist with regard to demonstrating the falsifiability of theories are also likely to hold where assessment criteria are concerned.

There are other possible approaches to theory evaluation. Schumann has advanced two. Schumann (1983) makes much of the fact that scientists working in the physical sciences now acknowledge that there is no 'objective reality'. The recognition that 'we create the reality we study' leads to an acceptance of 'philosophical flexibility' (1983: 51) and to treating science as 'art'. Clearly, a very different set of criteria are called for if this perspective is adopted. Citing Kramer (1980), Schumann suggests that 'innovation', 'tone of voice', and 'metaphor' can be used to evaluate theories, and goes on to apply these criteria to a number of L2 acquisition theories. This approach to theory evaluation is attractive, not least because it may reflect what many of us covertly do when we consider theories, but ultimately it is unsatisfactory because it denies any role for rationality in theory development. Ultimately a theory is not 'good' because it is 'beautiful', but also because it 'makes sense'.

In a later article, Schumann (1993) suggests that theory development should be seen as a process of 'exploration'. This refers to 'efforts to expand, revise, alter, and ultimately to understand and assess the validity of the construct' (1993: 301). Schumann suggests that one way in which exploration can take place is by trying to understand a phenomenon at a different level of organization or in relation to another field. For example, socio-affective theories, which are the main focus of his own research (see Chapter 6), can be explored in terms of social/psychological factors and through neurological enquiry. Schumann sees a 'reductionist' approach that accommodates explanation at different levels as preferable to a 'closurist' approach of the kind favoured by Long.

Schumann's reductionism comes close to relativism (the belief that any theory is as good as another and that, therefore, culling is neither desirable nor possible). There is considerable resistance to such a position, however (see the papers by Beretta and Long referred to above). The problem is this: how   can we avoid relativism if there are no agreed criteria for choosing among theories? One answer might be to adopt the third approach—to evaluate theories in relation to the context in which they were developed and the purpose(s) they are intended to serve. A UG-based theory, for example, is to be understood in terms of the field of Chomskyan linguistics from which it was developed, and needs to be evaluated with regard to the contributions that it makes to this field. It would be entirely inappropriate to try to understand and evaluate such a theory from the point of view of a foreign language teacher. In contrast, the Variable Competence Model (Ellis 1984a) was designed to account for the kind of variable performance which I observed in my longitudinal study of three language learners in a London language unit. It would not be appropriate to evaluate such a theory in terms of the contributions it can make to linguistic theory. This perspective also allows for variation in the form that theories take; for example, whereas some theories will need to provide very precise statements couched in formalist language, others may be better served by statements of a more general nature.

An approach to evaluation that acknowledges that theories are contextually determined allows for an acceptance of complementarity without a commitment to absolute relativism, for it can still be argued that among theories constructed for the same purpose and context, one does a better job than another because it is more complete, fits the facts better, affords more interesting predictions, is more consistent with other theories, etc. Bialystok's Theory of L2 Learning (see Chapter 9), for example, might be considered a better theory than Krashen's Monitor Theory because it allows for an interface between explicit and implicit knowledge, for which there is empirical support (for example, Pienemann 1989). But theories designed to meet different purposes in different contexts will be allowed to co-exist.

We noted earlier that theories of L2 acquisition are great survivors. Theories in SLA research are not usually dismissed as a result of empirical study or powerful argumentation but, instead, tend to slip slowly and gently into oblivion. Thus, over the years, it is possible to detect a gradual waning of influence of some theories (such as the Contrastive Analysis Hypothesis or Monitor Theory), although many of their ideas live on and are incorporated into other models. This is a reflection, perhaps, of the general recognition that L2 acquisition is extremely complex, and therefore does not lend itself to a single explanation. Different explanations are seen as useful because they focus attention on different sides of the prism—to invoke again the image with which we began this section. The multiplicity of theories also reflects the fact that different theories appeal aesthetically to different people and, more crucially, that theories are developed in (and for) a particular context, and that the context shapes the content and form that a particular theory takes.

To sum up, we have seen that there is considerable disagreement among SLA scholars about theories. This is evident in the role of theory in SLA research, the scope of a theory, the form it should take, and how it should be evaluated. We can detect two poles, with many shades of opinion in between. At one pole there is 'a healthy and unusually polite acceptance of the possibility of pluralism in the answers proposed, a willingness to concede that different models might be needed for different aspects of the problem, an acceptance that different points of view might lead to different theories' (Spolsky 1990: 613). At the other there is the belief that research should follow the assumed methods of the hard sciences, with no room allowed for complementarity or personal preference (Griffiths 1990). At the moment the pluralists are winning out over the closurists. This is perhaps as it should be; those theories that are found useful by researchers and practitioners (such as teachers) for their varying purposes will continue to flourish.

The application of second language acquisition research to other fields of enquiry

On a number of occasions in the preceding chapters, we have noted that the study of L2 acquisition may be of value to other disciplines. One of the most obvious ways in which it can be of service is by providing a rich body of data that can be used to address theoretical issues of importance in the 'parent' disciplines. For example, the study of how L2 learners grammaticalize their interlanguages (see Chapter 9) can inform functional theories of grammar. Similarly, experimental studies designed to test UG-based hypotheses can be used to refine the model of grammar on which they are based. SLA research and linguistics enjoy a symbiotic relationship, for as Gass (1989) has put it:

> ... facts of second-language learners force us to look deeper into questions of language. Facts of language force us to consider them in the light of second language learners. Whether it is the chicken first or the egg first comes largely from one's major interest and not in anything inherent in the chicken or the egg (1989: 526).

We might note, though, that this symbiosis is not without its problems. It is not clear, for instance, what should give way—the 'facts of second-language learners' or the 'facts of language'—when the results of empirical studies of L2 learners are not in conformity with the predictions of linguistic theory.[9]

The main area of application, however, is probably L2 pedagogy. As Spolsky notes, 'we have a traditional concern to consider not just the explanatory power of a theory but also its relevance to second language pedagogy' (1990: 610). This is reflected in a series of articles over the years that have addressed the relationship between SLA research and second/foreign language teaching (for example, Tarone, Cohen, and Dumas 1976; Hatch 1978e; Corder 1980; Lightbown 1985; Widdowson 1990; Long 1990b; Nunan 1990b and 1991; Ellis 1993c). In these articles we can identify a number of different positions:

1 The results of SLA research cannot be safely applied to language pedagogy because they are too uncertain.

2 SLA research provides a basis for teacher 'education' but not for teacher 'training'. That is, it can help teachers develop reasonable expectations about what they can achieve in their teaching, but cannot be used to tell them how to teach.

3 SLA research provides information and actual data that can be used in the construction of tasks designed to raise teachers' awareness of the likely relationship between teaching/learning behaviours and L2 acquisition.

4 The results of SLA research (and, in particular of classroom-oriented research) provide 'hard evidence' which should be used to advise teachers about what techniques and procedures work best.

As we can see, these position range from a super-cautious 'don't apply' to a confident 'go ahead and apply'.

The cautious 'don't apply' position is evident in early articles by Tarone et al. (1976) and Hatch (1978e). Tarone et al. gave seven reasons why SLA research fails to provide the teacher with satisfactory guidelines. These included: it was restricted in scope, it had only just begun to investigate the cognitive processes and learning strategies involved in L2 acquisition, the contribution of individual variables such as personality and motivation had not been evaluated, the methodology for both the collection and analysis of data was still uncertain and few studies had been replicated. Tarone and her colleagues noted that the practices of teaching and research were very different, for whereas teachers had immediate needs they must meet, researchers could afford to follow a slow, bit-by-bit approach. Hatch (1978e) is similarly cautious. She notes that researchers have been over-ready to make applications for pedagogy, commenting: '... our field must be known for the incredible leaps in logic we make in applying our research findings to classroom teaching'.

One answer to the views expressed by Tarone et al. and Hatch would be to demonstrate that there have been considerable developments in SLA research, which now it make it possible to apply findings with greater confidence. It is true that much more is known about some issues (such as the nature of developmental sequences, language transfer, or learning strategies), but it is also true that many problems continue to exist, not least because of the data problems discussed earlier. Not surprisingly, then, doubts have continued about whether SLA research should serve as a basis for giving advice to teachers. Lightbown, for example, concludes that 'second-language acquisition research does not tell teachers *what* to teach, and what it says about *how* to teach they have already figured out' (1985: 182). However, Lightbown does find one role for SLA research. She suggests that a knowledge of the findings of SLA research will help teachers to have 'much more realistic expectations about what can be accomplished'. This is a fairly humble claim that might lead many teachers to ask whether it is really worthwhile going to all the time and effort of familiarizing teachers with the results of SLA research. The teacher's task can be made easier, however, by the provision of short, readable accounts of the main findings. A good example of such an account is Lightbown and Spada (1993).[10]

A somewhat stronger version of this second position can be found in Widdowson (1990). Whereas Lightbown feels that SLA research should not be applied to teaching because of its continuing limitations, Widdowson adopts a more fundamental position. He argues that the procedures involved in conducting research and in language teaching are not the same, thus making the direct application of theory and research to language pedagogy impossible. For Widdowson, theory and research involve 'an abstraction', whereas teaching takes place in concrete and varied contexts. It follows that 'application cannot simply model itself on the procedures of empirical research' (1990: 60). One conclusion from this line of argument might be that theory and research are of no use to the teacher. However, this is not the position Widdowson adopts. Instead, he argues that what is needed is an attempt to mediate between 'outsider research' and 'insider research' (i.e. actual teaching). This mediation requires 'teacher education' (rather than 'teacher training') and should take the form of discussion of 'issues of current pedagogic concern' (1990: 66), informed by 'generalities' and 'principles' supported by theory and research. By engaging in a 'process of pragmatic mediation', teachers can examine how their particular pedagogic problems can be addressed. This view of the relationship between theory/research and teaching, then, emphasizes the inevitability of variable solutions, as teachers seek to utilize the information available to them in terms of their own teaching context. It is a far cry from the fourth position discussed below.

The third position is, perhaps, best seen as an extension of the second. In Ellis 1993c, I argued that SLA research is a rich source of information and data which can be used to foster the processes that lie at the centre of teacher development (i.e. the formation of a language teaching ideology, the acquisition of techniques and procedures for action, and the evaluation of these through reflection). I suggested that one way of making practical use of SLA research is by developing activities to raise teachers' awareness about such issues as the relationship between the questions they ask and L2 learning. The research, then, provides teachers with ideas at different levels, which they can then test out in their own classrooms.

Other scholars have shown less reticence in advocating that teachers follow where the research leads. Corder (1980) sensibly points out that teachers cannot wait until researchers have got it right and that it is natural to expect them to go ahead and make use of the best information available. Long (1990b) is more forthright still. He argues that teaching and teacher training should be grounded in 'hard evidence about what works'. He claims that the teaching profession, like the medical profession, needs to be informed by specialized knowledge unknown to the lay person and to be guided by research information. He is critical of the ungrounded 'assertions and prescriptions' found in teaching manuals. Thus, although, like others, he is aware of the limitations of the research, he believes that there are sufficient studies affording reliable results to make it possible to transmit them to teachers in the form of information about what and how to teach.

It is clear that we have come a long way from the uncertainties of the 1970s. There is now greater confidence in SLA research and more conviction that its results can inform language pedagogy. However, not all researchers would agree with Long's views, not least because they feel that teacher development does not take place through being told what and how to teach but by exploring and reflecting on the options available to them. The positions adopted by Widdowson, Lightbown, and myself, therefore, seem more in accord with current views of teacher development (see Richards and Nunan 1990). Furthermore, some educationalists might feel that research undertaken by professional researchers will always be of limited value to language teachers and that a more worthwhile and exciting approach is action research, where teachers become researchers by identifying research questions important to them and seeking answers in their own classrooms (see Nunan 1990b).

Conclusion

In this chapter we have examined a number of issues that are of epistemological and philosophical importance to SLA research. We have restricted our discussion to those positions reflected in the SLA literature to date. In accordance with the main aim of this book, no attempt has been made to argue strongly in favour of particular positions, although my own views have necessarily intruded. The treatment of the issues has necessarily been somewhat limited, a reflection perhaps of where SLA research currently stands on them. It is, however, significant that SLA researchers have felt the need to discuss these issues in recent years—a sign of a field of enquiry coming of age.

It is probably true to say that SLA research, some twenty-five years after its inception as an identifiable field of enquiry, is characterized by facts, opinions, explanations, positions, and perspectives that frequently exist in an uneasy state of complementarity and opposition. This is not to suggest that progress has not been made—in broadening the overall scope of SLA research, in identifying the essential issues in need of investigation, in developing methods for studying them, and in collecting an enormous amount of information about them. Also, the discovery of competing and overlapping phenomena might be seen as evidence of the principal strength of SLA research—a willingness to explore a wide range of issues by means of alternative paradigms and methods. No doubt, over time, the pictures provided by the different sides of the prism will become clearer, but whether this will lead to a single, unifying account of L2 acquisition, as some believe is necessary, remains to be seen.

Notes

1 Van Lier has pointed out to me that consideration also needs to be given to applications in the other direction—for example, language pedagogy can serve as a source of theoretical and empirical knowledge about L2 acquisition. The applications of such fields as linguistics, sociolinguistics, cognitive and social psychology, and language pedagogy to SLA research have been considered throughout this book.

2 Although there has been a substantial amount of work that has examined the effect of input on comprehension, there have been few attempts to study how learners' abilities to comprehend develop, or how they differ from their abilities to produce (but see Berent 1985). One reason for this is that comprehension can take place by means of 'semantic processing', involving top-down processing, with the result that it is difficult to obtain data on learners' ability to understand specific linguistic features.

3 Natural language use is likely to display considerable variability. It is for this reason that it invites the kind of contextual analysis undertaken by variabilists and pragmatists.

4 Larsen-Freeman and Long (1991) argue that there is a difference between experimental elicitation tasks and tests, reflecting differences in purpose. Whereas tests measure target-language performance, tasks provide data about interlanguage language performance. This difference, of course, may exist for both the researcher/teacher and the learner or for one but not the other. Arguably, it is the learner's perspective that is crucial.

5 The telephone calls were not entirely 'natural' as they were undertaken by the researchers with the specific aim of obtaining data about refusals. However, they did have a communicative purpose and there is no reason to believe that the persons answering the call treated them as anything but authentic calls. The distinction between 'natural language use' and 'clinically elicited language use' is a fine one.

6 We might also note that the need for a distinction between 'competence' and 'performance' is not accepted by all SLA researchers (for example, researchers in the functionalist tradition discussed in Chapter 9).

7 Beretta (1993) points out that whereas earlier work in the philosophy of human science tended to be prescriptive in nature and, therefore, of limited value, more recent work has been directed at achieving an understanding of how actual research is conducted.

8 This is really a restatement of the data problem. One source of data may afford results that are not supported by other data sources. In particular, there may be differences between what data elicited experimentally and natural data show.

9 This is an obvious problem in UG-based SLA research. If L2 learners fail to provide evidence of access to a particular principle of UG, this might suggest (1) that they do not have access to UG or (2) the principle has been incorrectly formulated in linguistic theory.

10 Lightbown and Spada's book is about 'how languages are learned'. In accordance with Lightbown's earlier views concerning the role of SLA research in education (as opposed to training), this book is directed at helping teachers to 'evaluate proposed changes in classroom methodology'. It is to be used alongside 'the teacher's own experience' (1993: xiii).

Further reading

D. Johnson, *Approaches to Research in Second Language Learning* (Longman, 1992) provides a very readable account of different research paradigms that addresses many of the issues raised in this chapter.

An excellent description of the different data collection instruments can be found in D. Larsen-Freeman and M. Long, *An Introduction to Second Language Acquisition Research* (Chapter 2) (Longman, 1991).

Useful articles on theory in SLA research include:

M. Long, 'Input and second language acquisition theory' in S. Gass and C. Madden (eds.), *Input in Second Language Acquisition* (Newbury House, 1985).

Articles by B. Spolsky, B. McLaughlin, M. Long, and E. Hatch, Y. Shirai, and C. Fantuzzi in *TESOL Quarterly* 24: 4.

A. Beretta, 'Theory construction in SLA: complementarity and opposition'. *Studies in Second Language Acquisition* (1991) 13: 493–511.

Articles by M. Long, K. Gregg, and J. Schumann in *Applied Linguistics* 14: 3.

Three articles indicative of the range of opinions about the application of SLA research to language pedagogy are:

E. Hatch, 'Apply with caution.' *Studies in Second Language Acquisition* (1978) 2: 123–43.

P. Lightbown, 'Great expectations: second-language acquisition research and classroom teaching.' *Applied Linguistics* (1985) 6: 173–89.

M. Long, 'Second language classroom research and teacher education' in C. Brumfit and R. Mitchell (eds.), *Research in the Language Classroom* (Modern English Publications, 1990).

Glossary

absolute universals

See *typological universals*.

Accessibility Hierarchy (AH)

The Accessibility Hierarchy is a statement of the markedness of various relative pronoun functions (for example, subject, direct object). It lists these functions in an implicational ordering, such that a given function implies the existence of all other functions above it. The hierarchy is an example of a *typological universal* and has been widely used as a basis for SLA research.

Acculturation Model

This is a theory of L2 acquisition developed by Schumann (1978a). It treats L2 acquisition as one aspect of acculturation (the process by which the learner becomes adapted to a new culture). Various factors influence the social and psychological 'distance' of the learner from the target-language culture and thereby the rate and ultimate success of L2 acquisition. See also *social distance* and *psychological distance*.

'acquisition'

Krashen (1981) uses the term 'acquisition' to refer to the spontaneous and incidental process of rule internalization that results from natural language use, where the learner's attention is focused on meaning rather than form. It contrasts with *'learning'*.

Adaptive Control of Thought (ACT) Model

This is Anderson's (1980; 1983) model of skill learning. The model accounts for how learners' ability to perform a skill develops from a declarative stage, where information is stored as facts, to an autonomous stage, where information is stored as easily accessed procedures. The model views L2 acquisition as an example of skill-learning.

additional language

The term 'additional language' is preferred to 'second language' in some settings (for example, South Africa). This is because it suggests that the L2 will exist alongside the L1 and be of equal but not necessarily greater importance to the learner.

additive bilingualism

See *bilingualism.*

affective state

The learner's affective state is influenced by a number of factors, for example, anxiety, a desire to compete, whether learners feel they are progressing or not. It is hypothesized that it can influence the rate of L2 acquisition and the ultimate level of achievement.

analytical strategy

Peters (1977) found that some children seemed to analyse the input into parts. They manifested systematic development involving first a one-word and then a two-word stage, etc. Hatch (1974) refers to L2 learners who learn in this way as 'rule-formers'. See also *gestalt strategy.*

anomie

Anomie is experienced by L2 learners (usually in natural settings) who feel disconnected from the target social group and from their own speech group. Such learners feel insecure because they believe they do not belong to any social group.

anxiety

Anxiety is one of the affective factors that have been found to affect L2 acquisition. Different types of anxiety have been identified: (1) trait anxiety (a characteristic of a learner's personality), (2) state anxiety (apprehension that is experienced at a particular moment in response to a definite situation), and (3) situation-specific anxiety (the anxiety aroused by a particular type of situation). Anxiety may be both facilitating (i.e. it has a positive effect on L2 acquisition, or debilitating (i.e. it has a negative effect).

aptitude–treatment interaction (ATI)

See *learner–instruction matching.*

avoidance

Avoidance is said to take place when specific target-language features are under-represented in the learner's production in comparison to native-speaker production. Learners are likely to avoid structures they find difficult as a result of differences between their native language and the target language.

backsliding

L2 learners are likely to manifest correct target-language forms on some occasions but deviant forms on other occasions. When this happens they are said to 'backslide'. Backsliding involves the use of a rule belonging to an earlier stage of development. It can occur when learners are under some pressure, as, for instance, when they have to express difficult subject matter or are feeling anxious (Selinker 1972).

balanced bilingualism

See *bilingualism*.

Basic Interpersonal Communication Skills (BICS)

Cummins (1981) uses the term 'Basic Interpersonal Communication Skills' (BICS) to refer to the kind of L2 proficiency that learners require in order to engage effectively in face-to-face interaction. BICS involve the mastery of context-embedded uses of language in communicative tasks that are relatively undemanding.

behaviourist learning theory

Behaviourist learning theory is a general theory of learning (i.e. it applies to all kinds of learning). It views learning as the formation of habits. These are formed when the learner is confronted with specific stimuli which lead to responses, which are, in turn, reinforced by rewards or corrected. Behaviourist learning theory emphasizes environmental factors as opposed to internal, mental factors.

bilingualism

Bilingualism refers to the use of two languages by an individual or a speech community. There are various types of bilingualism. In the case of *additive bilingualism*, a speaker adds a second language without any loss of competence to the first language. This can lead to *balanced bilingualism*. In the case of *subtractive bilingualism*, the addition of a second language leads to gradual erosion of competence in the first language.

borrowing transfer

See *language transfer*.

capability

This is the term used by Tarone (1983) to refer to the learner's actual ability to use particular rules in language use. Tarone intends it to contrast with *competence*. As such, it seems very similar in meaning to L2 *proficiency*.

careful style

This is a term used by Labov (1970) to refer to the language forms evident in speech that has been consciously attended to and monitored. Such forms are used more frequently with higher-status interlocutors. A careful style is used in formal language tasks such as reading pairs of words or doing a grammar test. See also *vernacular style* and *stylistic continuum.*

caretaker talk

When adults (or older children) address young children, they typically modify their speech. These modifications are both formal (for example, the use of higher pitch or simple noun phrases) and interactional (for example, the use of expansions).

casual style

See *vernacular style.*

change from above

This refers to changes to the dialect spoken by a social group as a result of so-cial pressures. Speakers are aware of the change. The linguistic feature in-volved in the change can be stigmatized or prestigious. Preston (1989) sees 'change from above' as analogous to *monitoring* in L2 acquisition.

channel capacity

This refers to the language learner's ability to process utterances in compre-hension or production. It involves the ability to recover rules and items from memory and to use them easily and spontaneously. In the early stages of L2 acquisition, learners have limited channel capacity and slowly develop this at the same time as they acquire L2 knowledge.

classroom process research

The aim of classroom process research is to subject the teaching–learning be-haviours that occur in a classroom to careful observation with a view to describing as fully as possible what takes place. It views language lessons as 'socially constructed events' and seeks to understand how they take place.

closed question

A closed question is one that is framed with only one acceptable answer in mind (for example, 'What is the name of the day after Tuesday?')

code-switching

Code-switching is one kind of intra-speaker variation. It occurs when a speaker changes from one variety or language to another variety or language in accordance with situational or purely personal factors.

Cognitive Academic Language Proficiency (CALP)

Cummins (1981) uses the term 'Cognitive Academic Language Proficiency' (CALP) to refer to the kind of L2 proficiency required to engage effectively in academic study. In particular, CALP involves the ability to communicate messages that are precise and explicit in tasks that are context-reduced and cognitively demanding.

cognitive strategies

O'Malley and Chamot define cognitive strategies as learning strategies that 'operate directly on incoming information, manipulating it in ways that enhance learning' (1990: 44). They involve such operations as rehearsal, organizing information, and inferencing.

cognitive style

Some psychologists consider that individuals have characteristic ways of perceiving phenomena, conceptualizing, and recalling information. Various dimensions of cognitive style have been identified, including *field dependence* and *field independence*.

communicative competence

Communicative competence consists of the knowledge that users of a language have internalized to enable them to understand and produce messages in the language. Various models of communicative competence have been proposed, but most of them recognize that it entails both linguistic competence (for example, knowledge of grammatical rules) and pragmatic competence (for example, knowledge of what constitutes appropriate linguistic behaviour in a particular situation).

communication strategy

Communication strategies are employed when learners are faced with the task of communicating meanings for which they lack the requisite linguistic knowledge (for example, when they have to refer to some object without knowing the L2 word). Various typologies of learning strategies have been proposed.

comparative method studies

These are studies carried out to measure the different learning outcomes achieved by two different teaching methods. An example of such a study is the Pennsylvania Project (Smith 1970), which compared the cognitive-code and audiolingual methods.

Competence

This term refers to a language user's underlying knowledge of language, which is drawn on in actual *performance*. Theories of language vary in how they define competence. See also *linguistic competence, pragmatic competence*, and *proficiency*.

Competition Model

This is a functional model of language use and language acquisition, proposed initially by Bates and MacWhinney (1982). It views the task of language learning as that of discovering the particular form–function mappings that characterize the target language. These mappings are viewed as having varying 'strengths' in different languages. For example, in English, case is a relatively weak signal of agency, whereas in Russian, it is a strong signal.

comprehensible input

'Input' refers to language that learners are exposed to. Input that can be understood by a learner has been referred to as 'comprehensible input' (see Krashen 1981a). Input can be made comprehensible in various ways: through simplification, with the help of context, or by negotiating non- and misunderstanding. Some researchers (such as Krashen) consider comprehensible input a necessary condition for L2 acquisition.

comprehensible output hypothesis

'Output' is language produced by the learner. It can be comprehensible or incomprehensible to an interlocutor. Swain (1985) has proposed that when learners have to make efforts to ensure that their output is comprehensible (i.e. produce 'pushed output'), acquisition may be fostered.

concatenative research

In a concatenative approach to the study of individual learner differences, a general research question serves as a basis for collecting data which then are used to investigate the relationships among learner factors, and between these factors and L2 acquisition. Such research is typically correlational in nature.

consciousness raising

The term 'consciousness raising' is used by some researchers with much the same meaning as 'formal instruction' (i.e. an attempt to focus the learner's attention on the formal properties of the language). In Ellis 1991d, I use this term with a narrower meaning. I contrast 'consciousness raising' with 'practice', the former term referring to attempts to help learners understand a grammatical structure and learn it as explicit knowledge. An alternative term for consciousness- raising is 'intake enhancement' (Sharwood Smith 1991).

context

The 'context' of an utterance can mean two different things: (1) the situation in which an utterance is produced—this is the situational context; (2) the linguistic environment—the surrounding language—this is the linguistic context. Both types of context influence the choice of language forms, and therefore have an effect on output. See also *psycholinguistic context*.

contrastive analysis

Contrastive analysis is a set of procedures for comparing and contrasting the linguistic systems of two languages in order to identify their structural similarities and differences.

Contrastive Analysis Hypothesis

According to the Contrastive Analysis Hypothesis, L2 errors are the result of differences between the learner's L1 and the L2. The strong form of the hypothesis claims that these differences can be used to predict all errors that will occur. The weak form of the hypothesis claims that these differences can be used only to identify some out of the total errors that actually occur.

correction

See *feedback*.

creative construction

Dulay, Burt, and Krashen define 'creative construction' as 'the subconscious process by which language learners gradually organize the language they hear, according to the rules they construct to understand and generate sentences' (1982: 276).

creole

A creole is a pidgin language that has become the native language of a group of speakers. A creole is generally more linguistically complex than a pidgin language as a result of a process known as 'creolization'. This results in a 'creole continuum', made up of 'lects' (i.e. varieties) that vary in complexity depending on whether they are closest to a pidgin or the standard language. An example of an English-based creole is Jamaican Creole.

Critical Period Hypothesis

This states that there is a period (i.e. up to a certain age) during which learners can acquire an L2 easily and achieve native-speaker competence, but that after this period L2 acquisition becomes more difficult and is rarely entirely successful. Researchers differ over when this critical period comes to an end.

cross-linguistic influence

This is a term proposed by Sharwood Smith and Kellerman (1986: 1) to refer to 'such phenomena as "transfer", "interference", "avoidance", "borrowing" and L2-related aspects of language loss'. Whereas the term 'transfer' is closely associated with *behaviourist* learning theory, 'crosslinguistic influence' is theory-neutral.

debilitating anxiety

See *anxiety*.

declarative L2 knowledge

Declarative knowledge is characterized by Anderson (1983) as 'knowledge that'. In the case of language, it consists of factual information about the L2 that has not yet been integrated or automatized.

descriptive adequacy

An account of a language (i.e. a 'grammar') is considered to have 'descriptive adequacy' if it constitutes a complete and explicit description of the rules and items that comprise native-speaker competence. See also *explanatory adequacy*.

developmental feature

See *Multidimensional Model*.

developmental pattern

See *pattern of development*

developmental sequence

One of the main findings of L2 research is that learners pass through a series of identifiable stages in acquiring specific grammatical structures such as negatives, interrogatives, and relative clauses. To a large extent, although not entirely, these sequences are not affected by the learner's L1. See also *sequence of development*.

discourse completion questionnaire

A discourse completion questionnaire provides learners with a description of a situation designed to elicit a specific *illocutionary act* (for example, an apology) and then asks learners to write down what they would say in such a situation or asks them to select what they would say from choices provided. It is used to investigate learners' L2 *pragmatic competence*.

discourse management

When native speakers (or other L2 learners) are addressing L2 learners, they may seek to modify their speech interactionally in order to avoid communication problems. For example, they may restrict the kind of information they try to convey or use comprehension checks.

discourse repair

When native speakers (or other L2 learners) experience a communication problem with an L2 learner, they may seek to repair the breakdown (for example, by *negotiation of meaning*) or to repair a learner error through correction.

display question

A display question is one designed to test whether the addressee has knowledge of a particular fact or can use a particular linguistic item correctly (for example, 'What's the opposite of "up" in English?'). See also *closed question*.

educational settings

Whereas many researchers are happy to talk of 'foreign' (as opposed to 'second') language acquisition, others, including the author of this book, prefer to distinguish different types of language acquisition in terms of context or setting. A key distinction is between acquisition that takes place in 'educational settings' (such as schools) and that which takes place in 'natural settings' (such as the street or the work-place).

elaborative simplification

This is a term used by the ZISA researchers (for example, Meisel 1980) to refer to the simplification that occurs when learners are trying to complexify their *interlanguage* systems (for example, through the use of *overgeneralization*). It contrasts with *restrictive simplification*.

error

According to Corder (1967), an 'error' is a deviation in learner language which results from lack of knowledge of the correct rule. It contrasts with a *mistake*. An error can be overt (the deviation is apparent in the surface form of the utterance) or covert (the deviation is only evident when the learner's meaning intention is taken into account). Various frameworks for describing errors have been developed, including descriptive taxonomies, which focus on the observable surface features of errors, and surface strategy taxonomies, which reflect the way in which target language surface structure is altered by learners.

Error Analysis

Error Analysis involves a set of procedures for identifying, describing, and explaining errors in learner language (see Corder 1974). Error Analysis for pedagogical purposes has a long history but its use as a tool for investigating how learners learn a language is more recent (it began in the 1960s).

error evaluation

Error evaluation involves a set of criteria and procedures for evaluating the effect that different errors in learner language have on addressees, both native speakers and non-native speakers. Error evaluation results in an assessment of *error gravity*.

error gravity

Error gravity concerns the seriousness of an *error*. This can be determined with reference to such criteria as intelligibility, acceptability, and irritation (Khalil 1985).

error treatment

Error treatment concerns the way in which teachers (and other learners) respond to learners' errors. Error treatment is discussed in terms of whether errors should be corrected, when, how, and by whom.

ethnography

Ethnography makes use of procedures such as detailed observation, interviews, and questionnaires to collect data that are 'rich' and that afford multiple perspectives. It has been extensively used in the study of bilingual classrooms.

explanatory adequacy

An account of a language (i.e. a 'grammar') is considered to have 'explanatory adequacy' if it not only provides a complete and explicit description of native-speaker competence, but also provides an explanation for how this competence is achieved. That is, it must explain how children learn their mother tongue. The theory of *Universal Grammar* seeks to achieve explanatory adequacy.

- ## explicit L2 knowledge

Explicit L2 knowledge is that knowledge of rules and items that exist in an analysed form so that learners are able to report what they know. Explicit L2 knowledge is closely linked to *metalingual knowledge*. It contrasts with *implicit knowledge*.

externalized (E) approach

Chomsky (1986a) distinguishes an 'E-approach' and an 'I-approach' to language study. The former involves the collection of samples of a particular language or languages which are then used to develop a 'descriptive grammar'. See also *internalized (I) approach*.

extroversion/introversion

These terms describe the dimension of personality which has been most thoroughly investigated in SLA research. They reflect a continuum: at one end are learners who are sociable and risk-takers, while at the other end are learners who are quiet and avoid excitement.

facilitating anxiety

See *anxiety*.

feedback

In language acquisition, the term 'feedback' refers to information given to learners which they can use to revise their interlanguage. A distinction is often made between 'positive' and 'negative' feedback (sometimes referred to as 'negative evidence'); positive feedback refers to information that indicates a hypothesis is incorrect. A distinction is also made between 'on-record' and 'off-record' feedback (Day et al. 1984) depending on whether the feedback is direct (i.e. a correction) or indirect (for example, in the form of request for confirmation). On-record feedback supplies 'direct negative evidence', while off-record feedback supplies 'indirect negative feedback'.

field dependence/independence

Field dependence/independence constitutes one kind of *cognitive style*. Field-dependent learners are believed to operate holistically (i.e. they see the field as a whole), whereas field-independent learners operate analytically (i.e. they perceive the field in terms of its component parts). Although a number of L2 researchers have made use of this distinction to account for differences in learners, others dispute its usefulness.

foreigner talk

When native speakers address learners, they adjust their normal speech in order to facilitate understanding. These adjustments, which involve both language form and language function, constitute 'foreigner talk'. Foreigner talk has been hypothesized to aid L2 acquisition in a number of ways (for example, by making certain features more salient to the learner).

foreign language acquisition

A number of researchers distinguish 'foreign language acquisition' (for example, the learning of French in schools in the United States) and 'second language acquisition' (for example, the learning of English by speakers of other languages in the United States). Other researchers find this distinction problematic. See *educational settings*.

formal instruction

Formal instruction involves some attempt to focus learners' attention on specific properties of the L2 so that they will learn them. Different types of formal instruction can be distinguished, including inductive (where learners are provided with structured input designed to help them learn a rule or item) and deductive (where learners are given explicit information about a rule or item).

form–function analysis

In a form–function analysis, all instances of a specific linguistic form are identified in the data and the different meanings realized by this form are identified.

formulas/formulaic speech

Many learners, particularly in the early stages of L2 acquisition, acquire ready-made phrases like 'I don't know' and 'Can I have a _____?'. These are known as formulas. See also *routines* and *patterns*.

fossilization

Selinker (1972) noted that most L2 learners fail to reach target-language competence. That is, they stop learning while their internalized rule system contains rules different from those of the target system. This is referred to as 'fossilization'. It reflects the operation of various internal processes.

fragile features

Fragile features of language are those that are acquired late, often with effort, and only when there is access to adequate input. Examples of fragile features are plural and tense markings. Fragile features contrast with *resilient features*.

free variation

When a speaker uses two or more variants of a variable structure randomly (i.e. selects variants without reference to the linguistic or situational context), free variation occurs. In Ellis (1985c), I argued that free variation arises in learner language when learners acquire a new form side by side with a previously acquired form and use it to realize the same meaning.

frequency analysis

This is the method of analysing learner language that involves identifying the *variants* of a given structure and examining the frequency of occurrence of each variant. For example, a learner may make negative utterances using (1) 'no' + verb, (2) 'don't' + verb and (3) auxiliary + verb. A frequency analysis of the negative utterances produced by this learner would involve counting each occurrence of the three variants.

frequency hypothesis

The frequency hypothesis states that the order of development in L2 acquisition is determined by the frequency with which different linguistic items occur in the input.

functionalist model

Functionalist models of L2 acquisition view the task of learning a language as involving the construction of form–function networks. That is, learners have to discover which forms perform which meanings in the L2. These models recognize that learners are likely to construct idiosyncratic form-function networks (i.e. use forms to perform functions not performed by these forms in the target language). Functionalist models emphasize the role that communication plays in the acquisition process.

gestalt strategy

Peters (1977) found that some children in L1 acquisition remain silent for a long time and then suddenly begin producing full sentences. Hatch (1974) refers to this kind of L2 learner as a 'data-gatherer'. See also *analytical strategy* and *silent period*.

global error

Global errors are errors that affect overall sentence organization (for example, wrong word order). They are likely to have a marked effect on comprehension. See also *local error*.

good language learner

Researchers have investigated the individual learner factors that contribute to L2 learning by investigating what expert, successful L2 learners do in order to learn an L2. These studies are known as the 'good language learner studies'. One of the best known is Naiman et al. 1978.

gradual diffusion model

Gatbonton's (1978) gradual diffusion model identifies two broad phases in L2 acquisition: an 'acquisition phase', characterized by free variation, and a 'development phase' where free variation gives way to systematic variation and categorical language use. See also *variability hypothesis*.

grammatical competence

See *linguistic competence*.

grammaticality judgements

One way of obtaining data on what learners know about the L2 is by asking them to judge whether sentences are grammatically correct or incorrect. This method is favoured by some researchers because they believe it provides information about learners' institutions and thus caters for an *internalized (I) approach*.

grammaticalization

Some *functionalist models* of L2 acquisition consider that early L2 acquisition is characterized by the use of pragmatic strategies for conveying meanings that are conveyed grammatically by native speakers. Gradually, learners move from this pragmatic mode to a grammatical mode as they learn the grammatical properties of the L2.

hierarchical research

In the hierarchical approach to the study of *individual learner differences* (IDs), predictions based on a theory of IDs are made and then tested empirically. In fact, this approach has been little used as there is no generally accepted theory of IDs.

horizontal variation

This refers to the variation evident in learner language at a particular moment or stage in a learner's development. It contrasts with *vertical variation*.

hypercorrection

Some native speakers over-use a linguistic form which is associated with social prestige. For example, some speakers of British English may overextend a feature like /h/ to words such as 'hour', even though this word does not have this sound in the standard dialect. Preston (1989) has suggested that this process is analogous to *overgeneralization* in L2 acquisition.

hypocorrection

This consists of the retention of an old norm in the speech of the working class because it has covert prestige. Preston (1989) suggests this is analogous to *negative transfer* in L2 acquisition.

hypothesis-testing

According to one view of interlanguage development, learners form hypotheses about the structures of the target language and then 'test' these out on the evidence available from input, with the result that they either accept them or abandon them and form new hypotheses. This process is not necessarily a conscious one.

Ignorance Hypothesis

Newmark and Reibel (1968) argue that what is commonly referred to as 'interference' is in fact merely an attempt by the learner to fill gaps of knowledge by using previous knowledge.

illocutionary act

This term is taken from *speech act* theory (see Austin 1962). An utterance is seen as having not only propositional meaning (i.e. saying something about the world) but also functional meaning (i.e. doing something). An illocutionary act is the functional meaning performed by an utterance. Examples are 'requesting' and 'apologizing'. Searle (1969) has identified various 'conditions' that have to be met in order for a specific illocutionary act to be performed successfully. For example, for the act of 'giving an order' to be successfully performed, both speaker and hearer must recognize that the speaker is in a position of authority over the hearer.

immersion education programme

In immersion education programmes the L2 is not taught as a separate subject. Rather, it is taught by using it as the medium of instruction for teaching the content of other school subjects. Immersion education has been widely used in Canada.

implicational scaling

Implicational scaling is a technique used by sociolinguists and some SLA researchers to represent variation in L2 performance. It rests on the notion that the presence of one linguistic form in learner language occurs only if one or more forms are also present. Thus, one form 'implicates' other forms.

implicit L2 knowledge

Implicit knowledge of a language is knowledge that is intuitive and tacit. It cannot be directly reported. The knowledge that most speakers have of their L1 is implicit. The study of *linguistic competence* is the study of a speaker-hearer's implicit knowledge. See also *explicit L2 knowledge*.

impression management

Impression management concerns the way speakers make use of their linguistic resources in interaction to create social meanings favourable to themselves. For example, L2 learners may make deliberate use of primitive interlanguage forms to mitigate the force of threatening speech acts.

incorporation strategy

One way in which learners can construct an utterance is by borrowing a chunk from the previous utterance and extending it by adding an element at the beginning or end. See also *vertical constructions*.

indicator

An indicator is a *variable form* that is responsive to social factors such as social class, age, and gender. See also *marker*.

indirect negative evidence

See *feedback*.

individual learner differences (IDs)

The term 'individual learner differences' refers to the differences in how learners learn an L2, how fast they learn, and how successful they are. These differences include both general factors such as language learning aptitude and motivation, and specific learner strategies. The differences can be cognitive, affective, or social in nature.

induced error

Induced errors arise in learner language when learners are led to make errors that otherwise they would not make by the nature of the formal instruction they receive.

inner-directed learners

According to Saville-Troike (1988: 568), inner-directed learners 'approach language as an intrapersonal task, with a predominant focus on the language code'.

Input Hypothesis

The Input Hypothesis was advanced by Krashen (1982) to explain how 'acquisition' takes place. It states that 'we acquire ... only when we understand language that contains structure that is 'a little beyond where we are now' (1982: 21). Elsewhere Krashen has referred to the idea of input that is 'a little bit beyond' as 'i + 1'.

instructed language acquisition

This term refers to language acquisition that takes place as a result of attempts to teach the L2—either directly through formal instruction or indirectly by setting up the conditions that promote natural acquisition in the classroom.

instrumental motivation

See *motivation*.

intake

Intake is that portion of the input that learners notice and therefore take into temporary memory. Intake may subsequently be accommodated in the learner's interlanguage system (i.e. become part of long-term memory). However, not all intake is so accommodated.

integrative motivation

See *motivation*.

interactional act

An interactional act is an utterance considered in terms of its structural function in discourse, for example, whether it opens, closes, or continues a conversation.

interactional modification

Interactional modifications occur when some kind of communication problem arises and the participants engage in interactional work to overcome it. They take the form of discourse functions such as comprehension checks, requests for clarification, and requests for confirmation. See also *negotiation of meaning*.

interaction analysis

Interaction analysis is a research procedure used to carry out classroom observation. It involves the use of a system of categories to record and analyse the different ways in which teachers and students use language. Various types of system exist, for example: a category system for coding specific events every time they occur, a sign system for coding the events that occur within a predetermined period, and a rating system for estimating the frequency of specific events.

interactionist learning theory

Interactionist learning theory emphasizes the joint contributions of the linguistic environment and the learner's internal mechanisms in explaining language acquisition. Learning results from an interaction between the learner's mental abilities and the linguistic input. The term 'interactionist' can also be applied to theories that explain L2 acquisition in terms of social interaction—how communication between the learner and other speakers leads to L2 acquisition.

interdependency principle

Cummins (1981) formulated the 'interdependency principle' to refer to the idea that *cognitive academic language proficiency* (CALP) is common across languages, and can therefore easily be transferred from L1 use to L2 use by the learner. It explains why people who are literate in their L1 find fewer problems in developing CALP in an L2 than those who are not.

interface position

Theories of L2 acquisition that emphasize the distinctiveness of implicit and explicit knowledge can either maintain that these are completely separate, or that each knowledge type 'leaks', so that explicit knowledge can become implicit and vice-versa. This latter position is known as the 'interface position'. See also *skill-building hypothesis*.

interference

According to *behaviourist learning theory*, old habits get in the way of learning new habits. Thus, in L2 acquisition the patterns of the learner's mother tongue that are different from those of the L2 get in the way of the learning the L2. This is referred to as 'interference'. See also *language transfer*.

Inter-group Theory

This is a theory of L2 acquisition proposed by Giles and Byrne (1982). It characterizes L2 acquisition as 'long-term convergence' and explains it in terms of attitudes relating to relationship between the learner and the target-language community. See *Speech Accommodation Theory*.

interlanguage

Selinker (1972) coined the term 'interlanguage' to refer to the systematic knowledge of an L2 which is independent of both these learner's L1 and the target language. The term has come to be used with different but related meanings: (1) to refer to the series of interlocking systems which characterize acquisition, (2) to refer to the system that is observed at a single stage of development ('an interlanguage'), and (3) to refer to particular L1/L2 combinations (for example, L1 French/L2 English v. L1 Japanese/L2 English). Other terms that refer to the same basic idea are 'approximative system' (Nemser 1971) and 'transitional competence' (Corder 1967).

interlanguage talk

L2 learners often obtain input from other L2 learners. For many learners interlanguage talk may the primary source of input. In classroom contexts, interlanguage talk has been referred to as 'tutor talk' (Flanigan 1991).

internalized (I) approach

Chomsky distinguishes an externalized (E) approach and an internalized (I) approach to the study of language. The latter makes use of native-speaker intuitions about what is grammatical and ungrammatical in order to investigate the abstract principles that underlie particular grammars. Chomsky favours the I-approach. See also *externalized (E) approach*.

inter-speaker variation

In some communities, no speaker has access to all the varieties used by the community. Instead, one speaker may have access to one variety, another speaker to a second variety and so on. Inter-speaker variation contrasts with *intra-speaker variation*.

intralingual error

Intralingual errors are errors in learner language that reflect learners' transitional competence and which are the result of such learning processes as *overgeneralization*. An example might be '*They explained her what to do'.

intra-speaker variation

This refers to the variation in the use of specific linguistic features evident in the speech and writing produced by individual learners on any one occasion. This variation reflects linguistic, social, and psychological factors. See also *inter-speaker variation*.

L1=L2 hypothesis (or identity hypothesis)

According to the L1=L2 hypothesis, L2 acquisition is either identical or very similar to L1 acquisition. The similarity may be evident at the level of product (i.e. in the kind of language produced by the two kinds of learner) or process (i.e. the mechanisms responsible for acquisition). Views differ considerably on the validity of this hypothesis.

language acquisition device(LAD)

Mentalist theories of language acquisition emphasize the importance of the innate capacity of the language learner at the expense of environmental factors. Each learner is credited with a 'language acquisition device' (LAD), which directs the process of acquisition. This device contains information about the possible form that the grammar of any language can take. See *Universal Grammar*.

language learning aptitude

It has been hypothesized that people possess a special ability for learning an L2. This ability, known as 'language learning aptitude', is considered to be separate from the general ability to master academic skills, often referred to as 'intelligence'. Language learning aptitude is one of the general factors that characterize individual learner differences. Various tests have been designed to measure language learning aptitude, for example, the Modern Language Aptitude Test.

language transfer

Odlin (1989) gives this 'working definition' of 'transfer':

> Transfer is the influence resulting from similarities and differences between the target language and any other language that has been previously (and perhaps imperfectly) acquired (1989: 27).

'L1 transfer' occurs when the 'influence' results from the learner's mother tongue. Two types of transfer are commonly identified: borrowing transfer (where the L2 influences the L1) and substratum transfer (where the L1 influences the L2).

learner–instruction matching

Learner–instruction matching involves an attempt to ensure that the teaching style is suited to the learner. It is based on the assumption that learners have different learning styles and that they will learn most effectively if the instruction matches their particular learning style. Educational research based on learner–instruction matching is sometimes referred to as *aptitude–treatment interaction*.

learner strategy

Learner strategies are the behaviours or actions that learners engage in, in order to learn or use the L2. They are generally considered to be conscious— or, at least, potentially conscious—and, therefore, open to inspection. See also *cognitive* and *metacognitive strategies*.

'learning'

Krashen (1981) uses the term 'learning' to refer to the development of conscious knowledge of an L2 through formal study. It means that same as *explicit knowledge*.

learning strategy

A learning strategy is a device or procedure used by learners to develop their *interlanguages*. It is one type of *learner strategy*. Learning strategies account for how learners acquire and automatize L2 knowledge. They are also used to refer to how they develop specific skills. It is possible, therefore, to talk of both 'language learning strategies' and 'skill-learning strategies'. Learning strategies contrast with *communication* and *production strategies*, both of which account for how learners use rather than acquire L2 competence. See also *cognitive*, *metacognitive*, and *social/affective strategies*.

learning style

See *cognitive style*.

linguistic competence

Researchers who work within the theoretical framework developed by Chomsky consider it necessary to distinguish *competence* and *performance*. 'Competence' refers to what speaker-hearers know, and 'performance' to the use of this knowledge in communication. Linguistic competence refers to the knowledge of the items and rules that comprise the formal systems of a language. It can also be distinguished from *pragmatic competence*. See also *pragmatic competence* and *communicative competence*.

linguistic context

See *context*.

linguistic universals

See *typological universals* and *Universal Grammar*.

local errors

Local errors are errors that affect single elements in a sentence (for example, errors in the use of inflections or grammatical functors). They contrast with *global errors*.

logical problem of language acquisition

This is a term used by researchers in the Chomskyan tradition. It refers to the gap between what can logically be learnt from the available input and what actually is learnt. Input is considered to 'underdetermine' language acquisition. It is therefore necessary to posit the existence of innate knowledge of language to account for children's ability to achieve full linguistic competence.

Machiavellian motivation

See *motivation*.

markedness

Various definitions of linguistic markedness exist. The term refers to the idea that some linguistic structures are 'special' or 'less natural' or 'less basic' than others. For example, the use of 'break' in 'she broke my heart' can be considered marked in relation to the use of 'break' in 'she broke a cup'. SLA researchers are interested in markedness because it can help to account for patterns of attested L2 acquisition.

Markedness Differential Hypothesis

This is a hypothesis advanced by Eckman (1977). It makes use of 'markedness' to explain why some L1 forms are transferred while others are not. It claims that learners transfer target-language features that are less marked than equivalent features in their L1 but do not transfer those that are more marked.

marker

Some variable forms are both 'social' and 'stylistic'. That is, as well as manifesting variation according to social factors such as social class, they also manifest variation according to situational factors (for example, the addressee). See also *indicators*.

mentalist theories of language learning

Mentalist theories of language learning emphasize the learner's innate mental capacities for acquiring a language. Researchers in the Chomskyan tradition consider children (and possibly adults) to possess knowledge of abstract principles of language which serve as a basis for acquiring the rules of particular languages. Input is seen as a 'trigger' that activates these principles. See also *Universal Grammar* and *LAD*.

metacognitive strategy

Many L2 learners are able to think consciously about how they learn and how successfully they are learning. Metacognitive strategies involve planning learning, monitoring the process of learning, and evaluating how successful a particular strategy is.

metalingual knowledge

Metalingual knowledge is knowledge of the technical terminology needed to describe language. Metalingual knowledge enables L2 knowledge to become fully explicit.

mistake

According to Corder (1967), a 'mistake' is a deviation in learner language that occurs when learners fail to perform their competence. It is a lapse that reflects processing problems. A mistake contrasts with an *error*.

modality reduction

When L2 learners are under communicative pressure, they may omit grammatical features such as modal verbs and adverbials that are associated with the expression of modal meanings like possibility and tentativeness. This is known as 'modality reduction'.

monitoring

Both native speakers and learners typically try to correct any 'mistakes' they make. This is referred to as 'monitoring'. The learner can monitor vocabulary, grammar, phonology, or discourse. Krashen (1981) uses the term 'Monitoring' (with a capital 'M') to refer to the way learners use 'learned' knowledge to edit utterances generated by means of 'acquired' knowledge.

monolingualism

This refers to speakers or speech communities who know and use only one language—their L1. It can also be characterized as a failure to learn an L2 and may be associated with a strong ethnic identity and negative attitudes towards the target-language centre.

morpheme studies

In the 1970s a number of researchers (for example, Dulay and Burt) conducted studies of a group of English morphemes (for example, V + *ing*, *-ed*, 3rd person *-s*) with a view to determining their order of acquisition. These studies, which were both cross-sectional and longitudinal, were known as 'morpheme studies'.

motivation

In general terms, motivation refers to the effort which learners put into learning an L2 as a result of their need or desire to learn it. In one theory of motivation, Gardner and Lambert (1972) distinguish 'instrumental motivation', which occurs when a learner has a functional goal (such as to get a job or pass an examination), and 'integrative motivation', which occurs when a learner wishes to identify with the culture of the L2 group. Other types of motivation have also been identified, including (1) 'task motivation' or 'intrinsic motivation'—the interest that learners experience in performing different learning tasks, (2) 'Machiavellian motivation'—the desire to learn a language that stems from a wish to manipulate and overcome the people of the target language, and (3) resultative motivation—the motivation that results from success in learning the L2.

Multidimensional Model

Meisel, Clahsen, and Pienemann (1981) proposed a model of L2 acquisition in which a distinction is drawn between *developmental* and *variational features*. The former are acquired sequentially as certain processing strategies are mastered. The latter are acquired at any time (or not at all), depending on the learner's social and affective attitudes. The model has been elaborated by Johnston and Pienemann (1986).

multilingualism

This is the use of three or more languages by an individual or within a speech community. Frequently, multilingual people do not have equal control over all the languages they know and also use the languages for different purposes.

natural settings

A natural setting for L2 acquisition is one where the L2 is used normally for everyday communicative purposes (for example, in the street or the workplace). See also *educational settings*.

naturalistic language acquisition

This refers to language acquisition which takes place in *natural settings*. It contrasts with *instructed language acquisition*.

negative evidence

See *feedback*.

negative transfer

See *interference*.

negotiation of meaning

Communication involving L2 learners often leads to problems in understanding and breakdown. Frequently, one or more of the participants—the learner or the interlocutor—attempts to remedy this by engaging in interactional work to secure mutual understanding. This work is often called 'negotiation of meaning'. It is characterized by *interactional modifications* such as comprehension checks and requests for clarification. Interactionally modified discourse also occurs when there is 'negotiation of content', defined by Rulon and McCreary (1986) as the process by which previously encountered content is clarified.

non-interface position

Theories of L2 acquisition which emphasize the distinctiveness of explicit and implicit knowledge and which claim that one type of knowledge cannot be converted directly into the other type adopt a 'non-interface position'. See also *interface position*.

Noun Phrase Accessibility Hierarchy

See *Accessibility Hierarchy*.

obligatory occasion analysis

This involves identifying contexts that require the obligatory use of a specific grammatical feature in samples of learner language and calculating the accuracy with which the feature is actually supplied in these contexts (see Brown 1973). See also *target-like use analysis*.

Observer's Paradox

According to Labov (1970), good data require systematic observation but the act of trying to observe contaminates the data collected. He refers to this as the Observer's Paradox.

open question

An open question is one that has been framed with no particular answer in mind—a number of different answers are possible. Some questions have the appearance of being open, but are in fact closed; Barnes (1969) calls these 'pseudo-questions'.

Operating Principles

Slobin (1973) coined the term 'operating principles' to describe the various learning strategies employed by children during L1 acquisition. Examples include 'Pay attention to the ends of words' and 'Avoid exceptions'. Andersen (1984a; 1990) has shown how similar principles can be seen at work in L2 acquisition.

order of development

A number of studies of L2 acquisition (for example, the morpheme studies) have produced evidence to suggest that learners achieve mastery of grammatical features in a particular order irrespective of their L1 or their age. For example, Verb + *-ing* has been found to be mastered before Verb + *-ed*.

other-directed learner

According to Saville-Troike (1988: 568), other-directed learners 'approach language as an interpersonal, social task, with a predominant focus on the message they wish to convey'. See also *inner-directed learners*.

output hypothesis

See *comprehensible output hypothesis*.

overgeneralization

Language learners in both first and second language acquisition produce errors like 'comed'. These can be explained as extensions of some general rule to items not covered by this rule in the target language. Overgeneralization is one type of *over-use*.

over-use

Over-use involves the use of an L2 feature more frequently than the same feature is used by native speakers. It constitutes an 'over-indulgence' (Levenston 1971), which may be brought about by differences between the native and target languages. It may be reflected in errors (*overgeneralization*) or just a preference for one target-language form to the exclusion of other possible target forms.

Parallel Distributed Processing

This is theory of language use and acquisition developed by Rumelhart and McClelland. Whereas most theories view language as consisting of a set of rules and items, Parallel Distributed Processing models view it as complex network of interconnections between 'units' that do not correspond to any linguistic construct. Learners gradually learn networks with interconnections of the same 'strengths' as those in the networks of users of the target language.

parameter

This is a term used in Chomsky's theory of *Universal Grammar*. Some universal *principles* are 'parameterized': that is, they permit a finite set of options, which individual languages draw on and which thus define how languages differ. A language learner needs to discover which parameter settings apply in the target language. See also *principle* and *Parameter-setting Model*.

Parameter-setting Model

This is a theory of L2 acquisition proposed by Flynn (1984). It is based on the theory of *Universal Grammar* and assumes that adult L2 learners have continued access to this. Their task is to discover how each principle is realized in the L2 (i.e. what parameter settings are needed).

pattern of development

This term is used in this book to refer to the overall shape of L2 acquisition, from the initial stages to the final stages. It serves as a cover term, therefore, for both *order of development* and *sequence of development*.

patterns

Patterns are one type of *formulaic speech*. They are unanalysed units with one or more open slots, for example, 'Can I have a _____?'. See also *formulas* and *routines*.

performance

This term refers to the actual use of language in either comprehension or production. It contrasts with *competence*. See also *linguistic competence*.

pied piping

This is a term used in grammar. It refers to the proximity of two tied grammatical elements. For example, the preposition 'for' and the pronoun 'whom' are placed next to each other in the sentence: 'For whom did you get the present?'. Pied piping contrasts with *preposition stranding*.

planned discourse

Ochs (1979: 55) distinguishes 'discourse that lacks forethought and organizational preparation' (i.e. unplanned discourse) and 'discourse that has been thought out and organized prior to its expression' (i.e. planned discourse). See also *speech planning*.

positive transfer

According to *behaviourist* accounts of L2 acquisition, learners will have no difficulty in learning L2 patterns when these are the same as L1 patterns. Support for positive transfer occurs when it can be shown that learners acquire L2 features which are the same or similar to L1 features with little difficulty.

poverty of the stimulus

Researchers in the Chomskyan tradition view the input available to learners as an inadequate source of information for building a grammar. The stimulus can be considered impoverished on several grounds: (1) input is degenerate (for example, it contains ungrammatical sentences), (2) input underdetermines the grammar that needs to be constructed, and (3) the input to children does not typically contain *negative evidence*.

pragmalinguistic failure

This is a term used by Thomas (1983). It arises when a learner tries to perform the right speech act but uses the wrong linguistic means.

pragmatic competence

Pragmatic competence consists of the knowledge that speaker-hearers use in order to engage in communication, including how speech acts are successfully performed. Pragmatic competence is normally distinguished from linguistic competence. Both are seen as relating to 'knowledge', and are therefore distinct from actual performance.

pragmatics

Pragmatics is the study of how language is used in communication. Among other aspects of language use, it includes the study of *illocutionary acts*.

preposition stranding

In some languages, like English, a preposition does not always have to be proximate to the noun or pronoun to which it grammatically belongs, as in this sentence: 'Who did you get the present for?'. Preposition stranding contrasts with *pied piping*.

principle

This is a term used in Chomsky's theory of *Universal Grammar*. It refers to highly abstract properties of grammar which underlie the rules of specific languages. Principles are thought to constrain the form that grammatical rules can take. They constitute part of a child's innate knowledge of language.

private speech

Some L2 learners who go through a *silent period* engage in private conversations with themselves, thus, perhaps, preparing themselves for social speech later.

proactive inhibition

Proactive inhibition is the way in which previous learning prevents or inhibits the learning of new habits. L2 learners are hypothesized to experience difficulty in learning target-language forms that are different from first-language forms. See *interference* and *transfer*.

procedural knowledge

Two related but different uses of procedural knowledge can be found in SLA research. On the one hand, it is used in contrast to *declarative knowledge* to refer to knowledge that has become proceduralized so that it is available for automatic and unconscious use. On the other hand, it refers to knowledge of the various strategies that learners employ to make effective use of their L2 knowledge in communication (for example, *communication strategies*).

production strategy

Production strategies refer to the utilization of linguistic knowledge in communication. They differ from *communication strategies* in that they do not imply any communication problem and in that they are generally used without conscious awareness.

proficiency

L2 proficiency refers to a learner's skill in using the L2. It can be contrasted with the term 'competence'. Whereas, competence refers to the knowledge of the L2 a learner has internalized, proficiency refers to the learner's ability to use this knowledge in different tasks.

projection capacity

Zobl (1984) suggests that L2 learners (like L1 learners) have the ability to 'project' knowledge of one rule to enable them to acquire another, implicated rule, for which they have received no direct evidence in the input. Thus acquiring rule x automatically enables learners to acquire rule y, if x implicates y.

prototypically

This term is used by Kellerman (1977) to refer to perceptions that learners have regarding the structure of their own language. These perceptions lead them to treat some structures as transferable and others as non-transferable.

pseudo-question

See *open question.*

psycholinguistic context

This is a term used in this book to refer to the extent to which a particular context of use affords time for planning linguistic production and also whether it encourages or discourages monitoring of output.

psychological distance

A term used by Schumann (1978a) in his *Acculturation Model.* It refers to the distance between a learner and the target-language community resulting from various psychological factors such as language shock and rigidity of ego boundaries.

psychotypology

Kellerman (1978) has suggested that learners have perceptions regarding the distance between their L1 and the L2 they are trying to learn. These perceptions constitute their psychotypology.

recreation continuum

Corder (1978a) has suggested that one way of viewing the interlanguage continuum is as a recreation continuum. One possible starting point is 'some basic simple grammar', which is recalled from an early stage of L1 acquisition. Learners gradually comlexify this system.

reference group

L2 learners—particularly those in natural settings—often have a choice of language variety as the target model. Their choices are influenced by the particular social group or groups they wish to identify with.

referential question

A referential question is a question that is genuinely information-seeking (for example, 'Why didn't you do your homework?'). See also *open question* and *closed question.*

resilient features

Resilient linguistic features are those that are acquired relatively easily even when the only input available to the learner is deficient. Examples are word order rules. Resilient features contrast with *fragile features*.

restrictive simplification

Researchers in the ZISA project (for example, Meisel 1980) used the term 're-strictive simplification' to refer to learners' continued use of simplified structures such as the delection of function words, even though they have developed knowledge of corresponding non-simplified structures. It contrasts with *elaborative simplification*.

restructuring

This is a term used in information-processing theories of L2 acquisition to re-fer to the qualitative changes that take place in learners' *interlanguage* at certain stages of development (see McLaughlin 1990a). For example, learners may begin by representing past-tense forms as separate items and then shift to representing them by means of a general rule for past-tense formation.

restructuring continuum

Corder (1978a) suggested that one way of viewing the interlanguage continuum is as a restructuring continuum. The starting point is the learner's L1. The learner gradually replaces L1-based rules with L2-based rules.

routines

Routines are one type of *formulaic speech*. They are units that are totally unanalysed and which are learnt as wholes. A common routine is 'I don't know'. See also *formulaic speech* and *patterns*.

selective attention hypothesis

According to this hypothesis, formal instruction aids L2 acquisition not by actually causing new linguistic features to become part of the learner's *interlanguage*, but by providing the learner with 'hooks, points of access' (Lightbown 1985). In particular, it has been suggested that formal instruction initiates the process of acquiring a feature by helping learners to notice a new feature in the input.

semilingualism

In some contexts, when learners of an L2 develop negative attitudes towards both their own culture and that of the target language, semilingualism can result, i.e. the learners fail to develop full proficiency in either language. This idea is controversial, however.

sequence of development

This book distinguishes order and sequence of development. 'Sequence of development' refers to the stages of acquisition through which a learner passes in acquiring specific grammatical structures such as interrogatives, negatives, and relative clauses. See also *order of development*.

silent period

Some L2 learners, especially children, undergo an often lengthy period during which they do not try to speak in the L2. However, they may be learning the L2 through listening to others speak it and may also be engaging in *private speech*.

situational context

See *context*.

situation-specific anxiety

See *anxiety*.

skill-building hypothesis

According to Krashen (1989), the skill-building hypothesis states that rules are first learnt consciously and then gradually automatized through practice.

social/affective strategies

These are one type of *learning strategy*. They concern the ways in which learners elect to interact with other learners and native speakers (for example, 'asking a teacher for repetition'—Chamot 1987).

social distance

This is a term used by Schumann (1978a) to account for why some L2 learners learn very slowly or achieve low levels of proficiency. Various factors such as the size of the learner's L2 group and the learner's desire to acculturate influence the 'distance' between the learner and the target-language community.

Socio-educational Model of L2 Learning

This is a model of L2 learning developed by Gardner (1985). It posits that the social and cultural milieu in which learners grow up determines the attitudes and motivational orientation they hold towards the target language, its speakers, and its culture. These in turn influence learning outcomes.

sociolinguistic variables

A sociolinguistic variable is a linguistic feature that varies in accordance with factors such as age, sex, social class, and ethnic membership. For example, Labov (1972) illustrates how variation in /r/ in the speech of New Yorkers reflects the social class of a speaker.

sociopragmatic failure

This is a term used by Thomas (1983). It occurs when a learner performs the wrong *illocutionary act* for the situation and constitutes a deviation with regard to appropriateness of meaning. An example is a learner who apologizes where a native speaker would thank someone.

Speech Accommodation Theory

Speech Accommodation Theory is a social-psychological model of language use proposed by Giles to account for the dynamic nature of variation within the course of a conversation. Speakers can converge (i.e. make their speech similar to the style of their addressee) or diverge (i.e. make their speech different from the style of their addressee). In some situations speech maintenance occurs (i.e. speakers make no changes). Speech accommodation is motivated by the attitudes speakers hold towards their audience.

speech act

A speech act is an utterance that performs a locutionary and an illocutionary meaning in communication. For example, 'I like your dress' is a speech act concerning a proposition about a person's dress with the illocutionary force of a compliment.

speech planning

In some contexts of language use, speakers have the opportunity to plan their speech, while in others they have to use the language more spontaneously. Speech planning influences the choice of linguistic form. For example, L2 learners may use a target-language form in planned language use but an interlanguage form in unplanned language use. Speech planning is sometimes investigated by studying 'temporal variables' (for example, speech rate and pause length).

state anxiety

See *anxiety*.

structural and semantic simplification

Learner language produced by beginners is characteristically simpler than the target language, and in many respects resembles a pidgin language. Structural simplication is evident in the omission of grammatical functors. Semantic simplification is evident in the omission of propositional elements (for example, '*Hitting' instead of 'Kurt is hitting his sister').

style shifting

Both native speakers and L2 learners use different *variants* of a *variable form* depending on the degree of attention they pay to their speech (i.e. whether they are accessing their *vernacular* or *careful style*). Labov refers to these changes in speech as 'style shifting'.

stylistic continuum

Tarone (1983), drawing on the work of Labov, suggests that learners internalize different 'styles' of language, ranging from a *careful* to a *vernacular style*. The stylistic continuum accounts for *variability* in learner language.

submersion

The term submersion is used to refer to educational settings where L2 learners are required to learn in classrooms where most of the students are native speakers so that few input adjustments take place.

subtractive bilingualism

See *bilingualism*.

substratum transfer

See *language transfer*.

syntactization

See *grammaticalization*.

target-like use analysis

This is an extension of *obligatory occasion analysis*. It is designed to take into account the incorrect use of specific grammatical features in contexts that do not require them in the target language (for example, '*Mary and Peter likes travelling.'), as well as non-suppliance in contexts that require the feature (for example, '*Simon eat an apple every day.').

task-induced variation

This is a blanket term used to refer to the *variability* in language use evident when learners are asked to perform different tasks. Ultimately, it is traceable to other sources (such as *linguistic* and *situational contexts*).

teachability hypothesis

According to Pienemann (1985: 37) 'the teachability hypothesis predicts that instruction can only promote acquisition if the interlanguage is close to the point when the structure to be taught is acquired in the natural setting.' This hypothesis is derived from the *Multidimensional Model*.

teacher talk

Teachers address classroom language learners differently from the way they address other kinds of classroom learners. They make adjustments to both language form and language function in order to facilitate communication. These adjustments are referred to as 'teacher talk'. See also *foreigner talk*.

think-aloud tasks

These are tasks designed to collect introspective data on the strategies learners use. Learners are asked to perform a task (for example, completing a cloze test) and to concurrently report the thought processes they are using to accomplish the task.

trait anxiety

See *anxiety*.

transfer errors

These are errors in learner language that can be accounted for in terms of differences between the structures of the L1 and the L2. See *language transfer* and *proactive inhibition*.

transitional constructions

Dulay, Burt, and Krashen (1982) define transitional constructions as 'the interim language forms that learners use while they are still learning the grammar of a language'. For example, before learners master the rule for English negatives, they operate with interim rules (such as 'no' + verb).

tutor talk

See *interlanguage talk*.

typological universals

Typological universals are identified by examining a representative sample of natural languages in order to identify features that are common to all or most of these languages. Typological universals can be absolute (i.e. occur in all languages), tendencies (i.e. occur in a large number of, but not all, languages), or implicational (i.e. the presence of one feature implies the presence of another).

Universal Grammar

This is a term used by Chomsky to refer to the abstract knowledge of language which children bring to the task of learning their native language, and which constrains the shape of the particular grammar they are trying to learn. Universal Grammar consists of various *principles* which govern the form grammatical rules can take. Some of these principles are 'paramaterized' (i.e. are specified as consisting of two or more options). See also *principles* and *parameters*.

unplanned discourse

See *speech planning* and *planned discourse*.

usage

Widdowson (1978: 3) uses the term 'usage' to refer to 'that aspect of performance which makes evident the extent to which the language user demonstrates his knowledge of linguistic rules'. The term contrasts with *use*.

use

Widdowson (1978: 3) uses the term 'use' to refer to that aspect of performance which 'makes evident the extent to which the language user demonstrates his ability to use his knowledge of linguistic rules for effective communication'.

U-shaped behaviour

L2 learners have been observed to manifest a target-language form in their output at an early stage of development only to manifest an interlanguage form in its place at a later stage. Eventually the correct target-language form reappears (for example, 'came' becomes 'comed' and, later still, 'came' again). This pattern of development is known as 'U-shaped behaviour'.

variability hypothesis

This is a term used in this book to refer to the possibility that formal instruction may have an effect on the learner's *careful style* but is less likely to have an effect on the learner's *vernacular* style. See also *stylistic continuum*.

Variable Competence Model

A variable competence model seeks to account for the variability evident in learner language by positing that this reflects a competence that is itself variable (i.e. it contains variable rules or different styles). Tarone (1983) has proposed that the learner's competence comprises a *stylistic continuum*.

variable form

A variable form is a phonological, lexical, or grammatical feature that is realized linguistically in more than one way. The linguistic devices that realize a variable form are known as *variants*.

variants

A *variable form* has two or more variants, i.e. it can be realized by two or more linguistic structures. For example, English copula has two variants—contracted and full copula.

variational features

See *Multidimensional Model*.

vernacular style

This is a term used by Labov (1970) to refer to the language forms evident when speakers are communicating spontaneously and easily with interlocutors familiar to them. It contrasts with *careful style*, and for this reason is also sometimes referred to as 'casual style'. See also *stylistic continuum*.

vertical constructions

Vertical constructions are learner utterances which are formed by borrowing chunks from the preceding discourse and then adding to these from the learner's own resources. For example, a learner utterance like 'No come here' could be constructed by taking 'come here' from a previous utterance and adding 'no'. According to one view of L2 acquisition, vertical constructions are the precursors of horizontal constructions.

vertical variation

This refers to the differences in learner language evident from one time to another. It reflects the development that is taking place in the learner's *interlanguage*.

Wave Theory

This is a sociolinguistic theory developed by Bailey (1973) to account for linguistic change. It explains how old rules spread from one speech community to another and how new rules arise. It also accounts for how rules spread from one linguistic environment to another.

wild grammar

Goodluck (1986) has used the term 'wild grammar' to refer to a grammar that contains rules that contravene *Universal Grammar*. It is argued that children do not in fact construct wild grammars.

Bibliography

Aboud, F. and **R. Meade** (eds.). 1974. *Cultural Factors in Learning and Education*. Bellingham, Washington, 5th Western Washington Symposium on Learning.

Abbott, G. 1980. 'Toward a more rigorous analysis of foreign language errors'. *International Review of Applied Linguistics* 18: 121–34.

Abraham, R. 1983. 'Relationships between use of the strategy of monitoring and cognitive style'. *Studies in Second Language Acquisition* 6: 17–32.

Abraham, R. 1985. 'Field independence-dependence and the teaching of grammar'. *TESOL Quarterly* 20: 689–702.

Abraham, R. and **R. Vann.** 1987. 'Strategies of two language learners: a case study' in Wenden and Rubin (eds.) 1987.

Adams, K. and **D. Brinks** (eds.). 1990. *Perspectives on Official English: the Campaign for English as the Official Language of the USA*. Berlin: Mouton de Gruyter.

Adams, M. 1978. 'Methodology for examining second language acquisition' in Hatch (ed.) 1978.

Adamson, H. and **V. Regan.** 1991. 'The acquisition of community norms by Asian immigrants learning English as a second language: a preliminary study'. *Studies in Second Language Acquisition* 1:1–22.

Adger, C. 1987. 'Accommodating cultural differences in conversational style: a case study' in Lantolf and Labarca (eds.) 1987.

Adjemian, C. 1976. 'On the nature of interlanguage systems'. *Language Learning* 26: 297–320.

Africa, H. 1980. 'Language in education in a multilingual state'. Unpublished PhD thesis. University of Toronto: Ontario Institute for Studies in Education.

Akagawa, Y. 1990. 'Avoidance of relative clauses by Japanese high school students'. *JACET Kiyo* 21.

Akagawa, Y. 1992. 'A replication of Abraham's study in "Field Dependence and the Teaching of Grammar" '. Unpublished paper, Tokyo: Temple University Japan.

Alamari, M. 1982. 'Type and immediate effect of error correction for Hebrew second-language learners'. Jerusalem: School of Education, Hebrew University. Cited in Cohen et al. 1991.

Albrechtsen, D., B. Henriksen, and **C. Færch.** 1980. 'Native speaker reactions to learners' spoken interlanguage'. *Language Learning* 30: 365–96.

Allen, J. and **S. P. Corder** (eds.). 1974. *The Edinburgh Course in Applied Linguistics, Vol. 3*. London: Oxford University Press.

Allen, J., M. Fröhlich, and **N. Spada.** 1984. 'The communicative orientation of language teaching: an observation scheme' in Handscombe, Orem, and Taylor (eds.) 1984.

Allen, P., M. Swain, B. Harley, and **J. Cummins.** 1990. 'Aspects of classroom treatment: toward a more comprehensive view of second language education' in Harley et al. (eds.) 1990.

Allwright, D. 1988. *Observation in the Language Classroom*. London: Longman.

Allwright, D. and **K. Bailey.** 1991. *Focus on the Language Classroom: An Introduction to Classroom Research for Language Teachers*. Cambridge: Cambridge University Press.

Allwright, R. 1975a. 'Problems in the study of the language teacher's treatment of learner error' in Burt and Dulay (eds.) 1975.

Allwright, R. (ed.). 1975b. *Working Papers: Language Teaching Classroom Research*. University of Essex, Department of Language and Linguistics.

Allwright, R. 1980. 'Turns, topics and tasks: patterns of participation in language teaching and learning' in Larsen-Freeman (ed.) 1980.

Allwright, R. 1983. 'Classroom-centred research on language teaching and learning: a brief historical overview'. *TESOL Quarterly* 17: 191–204.

Allwright, R. 1984. 'The importance of interaction in classroom language learning'. *Applied Linguistics* 5:156–71.

Alpert, R. and **R. Haber.** 1960. 'Anxiety in academic achievement situations'. *Journal of Abnormal and Social Psychology* 61: 207–15.

Altis, J. (ed.). 1968. Report of the Nineteenth Annual Round Table Meeting on Linguistics and Language Studies. Georgetown University, Washington D.C.: Georgetown University Press.

Altman, H. 1980. 'Foreign language teaching: focus on the learner' in Altman and Vaughan James (eds.).

Altman, H. and **C. Vaughan James** (eds.). 1980. *Foreign Language Teaching: Meeting Individual Needs*. Oxford: Pergamon.

Andersen, R. (ed.). 1979a. *The Acquisition and Use of Spanish and English as First and Second Languages*. Washington D.C.: TESOL.

Andersen, R. 1979b. 'Expanding Schumann's Pidginization Hypothesis'. *Language Learning* 29: 105–19.

Andersen, R. 1980. 'The role of creolization in Schumann's Pidginization Hypothesis for second language acquisition' in Scarcella and Krashen (eds.) 1980.

Andersen, R. (ed.). 1981. *New Dimensions in Second Language Acquisition Research*. Rowley, Mass.: Newbury House.

Andersen, R. 1983a. 'Transfer to somewhere' in Gass and Selinker (eds.) 1983.

Andersen, R. 1983b. 'Introduction: a language acquisition interpretation of pidginization and creolization' in Andersen (ed.) 1983c.

Andersen, R. (ed.). 1983c. *Pidginization and Creolization as Language Acquisition*. Rowley, Mass.: Newbury House.

Andersen, R. 1984a. 'The One-to-One Principle of interlanguage construction'. *Language Learning* 34: 77–95.

Andersen, R. (ed.). 1984b. *Second Language: a Crosslinguistic Perspective*. Rowley, Mass.: Newbury House.

Andersen, R. 1990. 'Models, processes, principles and strategies: second language acquisition inside and outside of the classroom' in VanPatten and Lee (eds.) 1990.

Anderson, J. 1976. *Language, Memory, and Thought*. Hillsdale, N.J.: Lawrence Erlbaum.

Anderson, J. 1980. *Cognitive Psychology and its Implications*. San Francisco: Freeman. (2nd ed. 1985).

Anderson, J. 1983. *The Architecture of Cognition*. Cambridge, Mass.: Harvard University Press.

d'Anglejan, A. 1978. 'Language learning in and out of classrooms' in Richards (ed.) 1978.

d'Anglejan, A., G. Painchaud, and **C. Renaud.** 1986. 'Beyond the classroom: a study of communicative abilities in adult immigrants following intensive instruction'. *TESOL Quarterly* 20: 185–205.

d'Anglejan, A. and **C. Renaud.** 1985. 'Learner characteristics and second language acquisition: a multivariate study of adult immigrants and some thoughts on methodology'. *Language Learning* 35: 1–19.

Arabski, J. 1979. *Errors as indicators of the development of interlanguage*. Katowice: Universytet Slaski.

Arnaud, P. and **H. Bejoint** (eds.). 1992. *Vocabulary and Applied Linguistics*. Basingstoke: Macmillan.

Arthur, B. 1980. 'Guaging the boundaries of second language competence: a study of learner judgments'. *Language Learning* 30: 177–94.

Arthur, B., M. Weiner, J. Culver, L. Young, and **D. Thomas.** 1980. 'The register of impersonal discourse to foreigners: verbal adjustments to foreign accent' in Larsen-Freeman (ed.) 1980.

Asher, J. 1977. *Learning Another Language Through Actions: The Complete Teachers' Guidebook*. Los Gatos, Calif.: Sky Oaks Publications.

Asher, J. and **R. Garcia.** 1969. 'The optimal age to learn a foreign language'. *Modern Language Journal* 53: 334–41.

Asher, J., J. Kusudo, and **R. de la Torre.** 1974. 'Learning a second language through commands: the second field test'. *Modern Language Journal* 58: 24–32.

Aston, G. 1986. 'Trouble-shooting in interaction with learners: the more the merrier?' *Applied Linguistics* 7: 128–43.

Atkinson, M. 1986. 'Learnability' in Fletcher and Garman (eds.) 1986.

Au, S. 1988. 'A critical appraisal of Gardner's social-psychological theory of second language (L2) learning'. *Language Learning* 38: 75–100.

Austin, J. 1962. *How To Do Things With Words.* Oxford: Clarendon Press.

Bach, E. and **R. Harms** (eds.). 1968. *Universals of Linguistic Theory.* New York: Holt, Rinehart, and Winston.

Bachman, J. 1964. 'Motivation in a task situation as a function of ability and control over task'. *Journal of Abnormal and Social Psychology* 69: 272–81.

Bachman, L. 1990. *Fundamental Considerations in Language Testing.* Oxford: Oxford University Press.

Bacon, S. 1987. 'Differentiated cognitive style and oral performance' in VanPatten et al. (eds.) 1987.

Bacon, S. 1992. 'The relationship between gender, comprehension, processing strategies, and cognitive and affective response in second-language listening'. *Modern Language Journal* 76: 160–78.

Bacon, S. and **M. Finnemann.** 1992. 'Sex differences in self-reported beliefs about foreign-language learning and authentic oral and written input'. *Language Learning* 42: 471–95.

Bahns, J. and **H. Wode.** 1980. 'Form and function in L2 acquisition' in Felix (ed.) 1980a.

Bailey, C. 1973. *Variation and Linguistic Theory.* Washington D.C.: Center for Applied Linguistics.

Bailey, K. 1980. 'An introspective analysis of an individual's language learning experience' in Scarcella and Krashen (eds.) 1980.

Bailey, K. 1983. 'Competitiveness and anxiety in adult second language learning: looking at and through the diary studies' in Seliger and Long (eds.) 1983.

Bailey, K. 1991. 'Diary studies of classroom language learning: the doubting game and the believing game' in Sadtano (ed.) 1991.

Bailey, N. 1989. 'Theoretical implications of the acquisition of the English simple past and past progressive: putting together the pieces of the puzzle' in Gass et al. (eds.) 1989b.

Bailey, K., M. Long, and **S. Peak** (eds.). 1983. *Second Language Acquisition Studies.* Rowley, Mass: Newbury House.

Bailey, N., C. Madden, and **S. Krashen.** 1974. 'Is there a "natural sequence" in adult second language learning?' *Language Learning* 21: 235–43.

Baker, C. 1988. *Key Issues in Bilingualism and Bilingual Education.* Clevedon, Avon: Multilingual Matters.

Ball, P., H. Giles, and **M. Hewstone.** 1984. 'The intergroup theory of second language acquisition with catastrophic dimensions' in Tajfel (ed.) 1984.

Banbrook, L. 1987. 'Questions about questions: an inquiry into the study of teachers' questioning behaviour in ESL classrooms'. *TESOL Quarterly* 20: 47–59.

Banbrook, L. and **P. Skehan.** 1990. 'Classroom and display questions' in Brumfit and Mitchell (eds.) 1990.

Bardovi–Harlig, K. 1987. 'Markedness and salience in second language acquisition'. *Language Learning* 37: 385–407.

Bardovi-Harlig, K. and **T. Bofman.** 1989. 'Attainment of syntactic and morphological accuracy by advanced language learners'. *Studies in Second Language Acquisition* 11: 17–34.

Bardovi-Harlig, K. and **B. Hartford.** 1990. 'Congruence in native and nonnative conversations: status balance in the academic advising session'. *Language Learning* 40: 467–501.

Barnes, D. 1969. 'Language in the secondary classroom' in Barnes et al. (eds.) 1969.

Barnes, D. 1976. *From Communication to Curriculum*. Harmondsworth: Penguin.

Barnes, D., J. Britton, and M. Torbe (eds.). 1969. *Language, the Learner and the School*. Harmondsworth: Penguin.

Barnes, S., M. Guttfreund, D. Satterly, and G. Wells. 1983. 'Characteristics of adult speech which predict children's language development'. *Journal of Child Language* 10: 65–84.

Bates, E. and B. MacWhinney. 1982. 'Functionalist approaches to grammar' in Wanner and Gleitman (eds.) 1982.

Bates, E. and B. MacWhinney. 1987. 'Competition, variation and language learning' in MacWhinney (ed.) 1987.

Beck, M. and L. Eubank. 1991. 'Acquisition theory and experimental design: a critique of Tomasello and Herron'. *Studies in Second Language Acquisition* 13: 73–6.

Beebe, L. 1974. 'Socially conditioned variation in Bangkok Thai'. PhD dissertation, Ann Arbor: University of Michigan.

Beebe, L. 1977. 'The influence of the listener on code-switching'. *Language Learning* 27: 331–9.

Beebe, L. 1980. 'Sociolinguistic variation and style-shifting in second language acquisition'. *Language Learning* 30: 433–47.

Beebe, L. 1981. 'Social and situational factors affecting the communicative strategy of dialect code-switching'. *International Journal of Sociology of Language* 32: 139–49.

Beebe, L. 1982. 'Reservations about the Labovian paradigm of style shifting and its extension to the study of interlanguage'. Plenary paper presented at Los Angeles Second Language Research Forum.

Beebe, L. 1985. 'Input: Choosing the right stuff' in Gass and Madden (eds.) 1985.

Beebe, L. (ed.) 1988a. *Issues in Second Language Acquisition: Multiple Perspectives*. New York: Newbury House.

Beebe, L. 1988b. 'Five sociolinguistic approaches to second language acquisition' in Beebe (ed.) 1988a.

Beebe, L. and M. Cummings. 1985. 'Speech act performance: A function of the data collection procedure'. Paper presented at TESOL Convention, New York.

Beebe, L. and M. Cummings. (forthcoming). 'Natural speech act data vs. written questionnaire data: how data collection method affects speech act performance' in Neu and Gass (eds.).

Beebe, L. and H. Giles. 1984. 'Speech accommodation theories: a discussion in terms of second language acquisition'. *International Journal of the Sociology of Language* 46: 5–32.

Beebe, L. and T. Takahashi. 1989a. ' "Do you have a bag?" Social status and patterned variation in second language acquisition' in Gass et al. (eds.) 1989a.

Beebe, L. and T. Takahashi. 1989b. 'Sociolinguistic variation in face-threatening speech acts' in Eisenstein (ed.) 1989.

Beebe, L., T. Takahashi, and R. Uliss-Weltz. 1990. 'Pragmatic transfer in ESL refusals' in Scarcella et al. (eds.) 1990.

Beebe, L. and J. Zuengler. 1983. 'Accommodation theory: an explanation for style shifting in second language dialects' in Wolfson and Judd (eds.) 1983.

Bell, A. 1984. 'Language style as audience design'. *Language in Society* 13: 145–204.

Bell, R. 1974. 'Error analysis: a recent pseudoprocedure in applied linguistics'. *ITL Review of Applied Linguistics* 25–6: 35–9.

Bellack, A., A. Herbert, M. Kliebard, R. Hyman, and F. Smith. 1966. *The Language of the Classroom*. New York: Teachers College Press.

Bennet-Kastor, T. 1988. *Analyzing Children's Language: Methods and Theories*. Oxford: Blackwell.

Berent, G. 1985. 'Markedness considerations in the acquisition of conditional sentences'. *Language Learning* 35: 337–72.

Beretta, A. 1989. 'Attention to form or meaning? Error treatment in the Bangalore Project'. *TESOL Quarterly* 23: 283–303.

Beretta, A. 1991. 'Theory construction in SLA: complementarity and opposition'. *Studies in Second Language Acquisition* 13: 493–511.

Beretta, A. 1993. ' "As God said, and I think, rightly . . ." Perspectives on theory construction in SLA: an introduction'. *Applied Linguistics* 14: 221–24.

Beretta, A. and **A. Davies.** 1985. 'Evaluation of the Bangalore Project'. *English Language Teaching Journal* 39: 121–7.

Berko, J. 1958. 'The child's learning of English morphology'. *Word* 14: 150–77.

Berwick, R. 1985. *The Acquisition of Syntactic Knowledge*. Cambridge, Mass.: MIT Press.

Berwick, R. 1990. *Task Variation and Repair in English as a Foreign Language*. Kobe University of Commerce: Institute of Economic Research.

Berwick, R. and **S. Ross.** 1989. 'Motivation after matriculation: are Japanese learners of English still alive after examination hell'. *JALT* 11: 193–210.

Berwick, R. and **A. Weinberg.** 1984. *The Grammatical Basis of Linguistic Performance: Language Use and Acquisition*. Cambridge, Mass.: MIT Press.

Bhardwaj, M. 1986. 'Reference to space by a Punjabi acquirer of English'. Nijmegen: ESF Working paper.

Bhardwaj, M., R. Dietrich, and **C. Noyan.** 1988. 'Second language acquisition by adult immigrants: temporality'. *Final Report Volume 5*. Strasbourg, France: European Science Foundation.

Bhatia, T. and **W. Ritchie** (eds.). (forthcoming). *Handbook of Language Acquisition*. New York: Academic Press.

Bialystok, E. 1978. 'A theoretical model of second language learning'. *Language Learning* 28: 69–84.

Bialystok, E. 1979. 'Explicit and implicit judgements of L2 grammaticality'. *Language Learning* 29: 81–104.

Bialystok, E. 1981a. 'The role of linguistic knowledge in second language use'. *Studies in Second Language Acquisition* 4: 31–45.

Bialystok, E. 1981b. 'The role of conscious strategies in second language proficiency'. *Modern Language Journal* 65: 24–35.

Bialystok, E. 1982. 'On the relationship between knowing and using forms'. *Applied Linguistics* 3: 181–206.

Bialystok, E. 1983a. 'Some factors in the selection and implementation of communication strategies' in Færch and Kasper (eds.).

Bialystok, E. 1983b. 'Inferencing: testing the "hypothesis-testing" hypothesis' in Seliger and Long (eds.) 1983.

Bialystok, E. 1985. 'The compatibility of teaching and learning strategies'. *Applied Linguistics* 6: 155–262.

Bialystok, E. 1990a. *Communication Strategies: A Psychological Analysis of Second-Language Use*. Oxford: Basil Blackwell.

Bialystok, E. 1990b. 'The competence of processing: classifying theories of second language acquisition'. *TESOL Quarterly* 24: 635–48.

Bialystok, E. 1991. 'Achieving proficiency in a second language: a processing description' in Phillipson et al. (eds.) 1991.

Bialystok, E. and **M. Fröhlich.** 1978. 'Variables of classroom achievement in second language learning'. *Modern Language Journal* 62: 327–36.

Bialystok, E., M. Fröhlich, and **J. Howard.** 1978. 'The teaching and learning of French as a second language in two distinct learning settings'. Project report. Toronto: Modern Language Centre, Ontario Institute for Studies in Education.

Bialystok, E. and **E. Kellerman.** 1987. 'Communication strategies in the classroom' in Das (ed.) 1987b.

Bialystok, E. and **E. Ryan.** 1985. 'A metacognitive framework for the development of first and second language skills' in Forrest-Pressley et al. (eds.) 1985.

Bialystok, E. and **M. Sharwood Smith**. 1985. 'Interlanguage is not a state of mind: an evaluation of the construct for second language acquisition'. *Applied Linguistics* 6: 101–17.

Bickerton, D. 1975. *Dynamics of a Creole System*. Cambridge: Cambridge University Press.

Bickerton, D. 1981. 'Discussion of "Two perspectives on pidginization as second language acquisition" ' in Andersen (ed.) 1981.

Bickerton, D. and **T. Givón**. 1976. 'Pidginization and syntactic change: from SXV and VSX to SVX' in Stever et al. (eds). 1976.

Billmyer, K. 1990. ' "I really like your lifestyle": ESL learners learning how to compliment'. *Penn Working Papers in Educational Linguistics* 6: 31–48.

Bingaman, J. 1990. 'On the English Proficiency Act' in Adams and Brinks (eds.) 1990.

Birdsong, D. 1989. *Metalinguistic Performance and Interlanguage Competence*. New York: Springer.

Birdsong, D. 1992. 'Ultimate attainment in second language acquisition'. *Language* 68: 706–55.

Blatchford, C. and **J. Schachter** (eds.). 1978. *On TESOL '78: EFL Policies, Programs, Practices*. Washington D.C.: TESOL.

Blau, E. 1982. 'The effect of syntax on readability for ESL students in Puerto Rico'. *TESOL Quarterly* 16: 517–28.

Bley-Vroman, R. 1983. 'The comparative fallacy in interlanguage studies: the case of systematicity'. *Language Learning* 33: 1–17.

Bley-Vroman, R. 1988. 'The fundamental character of foreign language learning' in Rutherford and Sharwood Smith (eds.) 1988.

Bley-Vroman, R. 1989. 'The logical problem of second language learning' in Gass and Schachter (eds.) 1989.

Bley-Vroman, R. and **C. Chaudron**. 1990. 'Second language processing of subordinate clauses and anaphora—first language and universal influences: a review of Flynn's research'. *Language Learning* 40: 245–85.

Bley-Vroman, R., **S. Felix**, and **G. Ioup**. 1988. 'The accessibility of Universal Grammar in adult language learning'. *Second Language Research* 4: 1–32.

Bloom, L. 1970. *Language Development: Form and Function in Emerging Grammars*. Cambridge, Mass.: MIT Press.

Bloomfield, L. 1933. *Language*. New York: Holt, Rinehart, and Winston.

Blum-Kulka, S. 1991. 'Interlanguage pragmatics: The case of requests' in Phillipson et al. (eds.) 1991.

Blum-Kulka, S., **J. House**, and **G. Kasper** (eds.). 1989a. *Cross-cultural Pragmatics: Requests and Apologies*. Norwood, N.J.: Ablex.

Blum-Kulka, S., **J. House**, and **G. Kasper**. 1989b. 'Investigating cross-cultural pragmatics: an introductory overview' in S. Blum-Kulka et al. (eds.) 1989a.

Blum-Kulka, S. and **E. Olshtain**. 1984. 'Requests and apologies: a cross-cultural study of speech act realization patterns (CCSARP)'. *Applied Linguistics* 5: 196–213.

Blum-Kulka, S. and **E. Olshtain**. 1986. 'Too many words: length of utterances and pragmatic failure'. *Journal of Pragmatics* 8: 47–61.

Bodman, J. and **M. Eisenstein**. 1988. 'May God increase your bounty: the expression of gratitude in English by native and non-native speakers'. *Cross Currents* 15: 1–21.

Bogen, J. and **J. Woodward**. 1988. 'Saving the phenomena'. *Philosophical Review* 97: 303–52. Cited in Gregg 1993.

Bohn, O. 1986. 'Formulas, frame structures, and stereotypes in early syntactic development: some new evidence from L2 acquisition'. *Linguistics* 24: 185–202.

Bohn, O. and **J. Flege**. 1992. 'The production of new and similar vowels by adult German learners of English'. *Studies in Second Language Acquisition* 14: 131–58.

Bolte, H. and **W. Herrlitz** (eds.). 1985. *Kommunikation im Sprachunterricht*. Utrecht: Instituut 'Franzen', University of Utrecht.

Bonikowska, M. 1988. 'The choice of opting out'. *Applied Linguistics* 9: 169–81.

Born, W. (ed.). 1979. *The Foreign Language Learner in Today's Classroom Environment.* Montpelier, Vermont: Northeast Conference on the Teaching of Foreign Languages.

Bourhis, R. and **H. Giles.** 1977. 'The language of intergroup distinctiveness' in Giles (ed.) 1977.

Bowerman, M. 1985. 'What shapes children's grammar?' in Slobin (ed.) 1985a.

Boyle, J. 1987. 'Sex differences in listening vocabulary'. *Language Learning* 37: 273–84.

Braine, M. 1971. 'The acquisition of language in infant and child' in Reed (ed.) 1971.

Breen, M. 1985. 'The social context for language learning—a neglected situation?' *Studies in Second Language Acquisition* 7: 135–58.

Breen, M. 1987. 'Learner contributions to task design' in Candlin and Murphy (eds.) 1987.

Briere, E. 1978. 'Variables affecting native Mexican children's learning Spanish as a second language'. *Language Learning* 28: 159–74.

Brindley, G. 1991. 'Learnability in the ESL classroom: a pilot study'. Paper presented at RELC Regional Seminar on Language Acquisition and the Second/Foreign Language Classroom, Singapore.

Brock, C. 1986. 'The effects of referential questions on ESL classroom discourse'. *TESOL Quarterly* 20: 47–8.

Broeder, P., G. Extra, and **R. van Hout.** 1989. 'Vocabulary acquisition'. *AILA Review* 1989. Amsterdam: Free University Press.

Broen, P. 1972. 'The verbal environment of the language learning child'. *American Speech and Hearing Monographs*, No. 17.

Brooks, N. 1960. *Language and Language Learning.* New York: Harcourt Brace and World.

Brown A., J. Bransford, R. Ferrara, and **J. Campione.** 1983. 'Learning, remembering and understanding' in Flavell and Markman (eds.) 1983.

Brown, C. 1985. 'Requests for specific language input: differences between older and younger adult language learners' in Gass and Madden (eds.) 1985.

Brown, H. 1980. 'The optimal distance model of second language acquisition'. *TESOL Quarterly* 14: 157–64.

Brown, H. 1987. *Principles of Language Learning and Teaching* (2nd Ed.). Englewood Cliffs, N.J.: Prentice Hall.

Brown, H. 1989. *A Practical Guide to Language Learning.* New York: McGraw Hill.

Brown, H., C. Yorio, and **R. Crymes** (eds.). 1977. *On TESOL '77.* Washington D.C.: TESOL.

Brown, P. and **C. Fraser.** 1979. 'Speech as markers of situation' in Scherer and Giles (eds.) 1979.

Brown, P. and **S. Levinson.** 1978. 'Universals of language usage: politeness phenomena' in Goody (ed.) 1978.

Brown, R. 1968. 'The development of Wh-questions in children's speech'. *Journal of Verbal Learning and Language Behavior* 7: 279–90.

Brown, R. 1973. *A First Language: the Early Stages.* Cambridge, Mass.: Harvard University Press.

Brown, R. 1977. 'Introduction' in Snow and Ferguson (eds.) 1977.

Brown, R. 1987. 'A comparison of the comprehensibility of modified and unmodified reading materials for ESL'. *University of Hawaii Working Papers in ESL* 6: 49–79.

Brown, R. 1991. 'Group work, task difference, and second language acquisition'. *Applied Linguistics* 21: 1–12.

Brown, R. and **C. Hanlon.** 1970. 'Derivational complexity and order of acquisition in child speech' in Hayes (ed.) 1970.

Brown, T. and **F. Perry.** 1991. 'A comparison of three learning strategies for ESL vocabulary acquisition'. *TESOL Quarterly* 25: 655–70.

Brumfit, C. 1984. *Communicative Methodology in Language Teaching.* Cambridge: Cambridge University Press.

Brumfit, C. and **R. Carter** (eds.). 1986. *Literature and Language Teaching.* Oxford: Oxford University Press.

Brumfit, C. and **R. Mitchell** (eds.). 1990. 'Research in the Language Classroom'. *ELT Documents* 133: Modern English Publications.

Bruner, J., J. Goodnow, and **G. Austin.** 1957. *A Study of Thinking.* New York: Wiley and Sons.

Buczowska, E. and **R. Weist.** 1991. 'The effects of formal instruction on the second-language acquisition of temporal location'. *Language Learning* 41: 535–54.

Burmeister, R. and **P. Rounds** (eds.). 1990. *Variability in Second Language Acquisition: Proceedings of the Tenth Meeting of the Second Language Research Forum, Vol 1.* Eugene, Oregon: University of Oregon.

Burstall, C. 1975. 'Factors affecting foreign-language learning: a consideration of some relevant research findings'. *Language Teaching and Linguistics Abstracts* 8: 105–25.

Burstall, C. 1979. 'Primary French in the balance' in Pride (ed.) 1979.

Burt, M. 1975. 'Error analysis in the adult EFL classroom'. *TESOL Quarterly* 9: 53–63.

Burt, M. and **H. Dulay** (eds.). 1975. *On TESOL '75: New Directions in Second Language Learning, Teaching and Bilingual Education.* Washington D.C.: TESOL.

Burt, M., H. Dulay, and **M. Finnocchario** (eds.). 1977. *Viewpoints on English as a Second Language.* New York: Regents.

Burt, M., H. Dulay, and **E. Hernandez.** 1973. *Bilingual Syntax Measure.* New York: Harcourt Brace Jovanovich.

Burt, M. and **C. Kiparsky.** 1972. *The Gooficon: a Repair Manual for English.* Rowley, Mass.: Newbury House.

Busch, D. 1982. 'Introversion–extroversion and the EFL proficiency of Japanese students'. *Language Learning* 32: 109–32.

Bush, R., E. Galanter, and **R. Luce** (eds.). 1963. *Handbook of Mathematical Psychology, Vol II.* New York: Wiley and Sons.

Butterworth, B. (ed.). 1980a. *Language Production, Vol. 1.* New York: Academic Press.

Butterworth, B. 1980b. 'Some constraints on models of language production' in Butterworth (ed.) 1980a.

Butterworth, G. and **E. Hatch.** 1978. 'A Spanish-speaking adolescent's acquisition of English syntax' in Hatch (ed.) 1978a.

Bygate, M. 1988. 'Units of oral expression and language learning in small group interaction'. *Applied Linguistics* 9: 59–82.

Canale, M. 1983. 'From communicative competence to language pedagogy' in Richards and Schmidt (eds.) 1983.

Canale, M. and **M. Swain.** 1980. 'Theoretical bases of communicative approaches to second language teaching and testing'. *Applied Linguistics* 1: 1–47.

Cancino, H., E. Rosansky, and **J. Schumann.** 1978. 'The acquisition of English negatives and interrogatives by native Spanish speakers' in Hatch (ed.) 1978.

Candlin, C. and **D. Murphy** (eds.). 1987. *Lancaster Practical Papers in English Language Education: Vol 7. 'Language Learning Tasks'.* Englewood Cliffs, N.J.: Prentice Hall.

Carlisle, R. 1991. 'The influence of environment on vowel epenthesis in Spanish/English interphonology'. *Applied Linguistics* 12: 76–95.

Carrell, P. 1981. 'Relative difficulty of request forms in L1/L2 comprehension' in Hines and Rutherford (eds.) 1981.

Carrell, P. and **B. Konneker.** 1981. 'Politeness: comparing native and nonnative judgments'. *Language Learning* 31: 17–31.

Carroll, J. 1965. 'The prediction of success in foreign language training' in Glaser (ed.) 1965.

Carroll, J. 1967. 'Foreign language proficiency levels attained by language majors near graduation from college'. *Foreign Language Annals* 1: 131–51.

Carroll, J. 1969. 'Reaction to Brimer's article'. *Journal of Research and Development in Education* 9: 18–1.

Carroll, J. 1981. 'Twenty-five years of research on foreign language aptitude' in Diller (ed.) 1981.

Carroll, J. 1990. 'Cognitive abilities in foreign language aptitude: then and now' in Parry and Stansfield (eds.) 1990.

Carroll, J. and S. Sapon. 1959. *Modern Language Aptitude Test—Form A*. New York: The Psychological Corporation.

Carroll, J. and D. Spearritt. 1967. 'A study of "A Model of School Learning" '. Unpublished report, Graduate School of Education, Harvard University. Cited in Cronbach and Snow 1977.

Carroll, S., M. Swain, and **Y. Roberge.** 1992. 'The role of feedback in adult second language acquisition: error correction and morphological generalizations'. *Applied Psycholinguistics* 13: 173–98.

Carter, E. 1988. 'The relationship of field dependent/independent cognitive style to Spanish language achievement and proficiency: a preliminary report'. *Modern Language Journal* 72: 21–30.

Carton, A. 1971. 'Inferencing: a process in using and learning language' in Pimsleur and Quinn (eds.) 1971.

Castagnaro, P. 1992. 'Introduction of physiological measures in locating aversive stimulation related to second language learning among Japanese university students'. Unpublished manuscript, Tokyo: Temple University Japan.

Cathcart, R. 1986. 'Situational differences and the sampling of young children's school language' in Day (ed.) 1986.

Cathcart, R. and J. Olsen. 1976. 'Teachers' and students' preferences for correction of classroom errors' in Fanselow and Crymes (eds.) 1976.

Cattell, R. 1956. 'Personality and motivation theory based on structural measurement' in McCary (ed.) 1956.

Cazden, C. 1972. *Child Language and Education*. New York: Holt, Rinehart, and Winston.

Cazden, C., E. Cancino, E. Rosansky, and **J. Schumann.** 1975. *Second Language Acquisition in Children, Adolescents and Adults. Final Report*. Washington D.C.: National Institute of Education.

Cazden, C., V. John, and **D. Hymes** (eds.). 1972. *Functions of Language in the Classroom*. New York: Teachers' College Press.

Ceci, S. (ed.). 1987. *Handbook of Cognitive, Social and Neuropsychological Aspects of Learning Disabilities*. Hillsdale, N.J.: Lawrence Erlbaum.

Celce-Murcia, M. (ed.). 1985. *Beyond Basics: Issues and Research in TESOL*. Rowley, Mass.: Newbury House.

Cervantes, R. 1983. ' "Say it again Sam": the effect of repetition on dictation scores'. Term paper, ESL 70, University of Hawaii at Manoa. Cited in Chaudron 1988.

Chambers, J. and P. Trudgill. 1980. *Dialectology*. Cambridge: Cambridge University Press.

Chamot, A. 1978. 'Grammatical problems in learning English as a third language' in Hatch (ed.) 1978.

Chamot, A. 1979. 'Strategies in the acquisition of English structures by a child bilingual in Spanish and French' in Andersen (ed.) 1979a.

Chamot, A. 1987. 'The learning strategies of ESL students' in Wenden and Rubin (eds.) 1987.

Chamot, A., J. O'Malley, L. Kupper, and **M. Impink-Hernandez.** 1987. *A Study of Learning Strategies in Foreign Language Instruction: First year Report*. Rosslyn, Va.: Interstate Research Associates.

Chamot, A., L. Kupper, and **M. Impink-Hernandez.** 1988. *A Study of Learning Strategies in Foreign Language Instruction: Findings of the Longitudinal Study*. McLean, Va.: Interstate Research Associates.

Chapelle, C. 1992. 'Disembedding "Disembedded Figures in the Landscape ...": an appraisal of Griffiths and Sheen's "Reappraisal of L2 research on field dependence/independence" '. *Applied Linguistics* 13: 375–84.

Chapelle, C. and P. Green. 1992. 'Field independence/dependence in second language acquisition research'. *Language Learning* 42: 47–83.

Chapelle, C. and C. Roberts. 1986. 'Ambiguity tolerance and field independence as predictors of proficiency in English as a second language'. *Language Learning* 36: 27–45.

Chastain, K. 1975. 'Affective and ability factors in second language acquisition'. *Language Learning* 25: 153–61.

Chastain, K. 1981. 'Native-speaker evaluation of student composition errors'. *Modern Language Journal* 65: 288–94.

Chaudron, C. 1977. 'A descriptive model of discourse in the corrective treatment of learners' errors'. *Language Learning* 27: 29–46.

Chaudron, C. 1982. 'Vocabulary elaboration in teachers' speech to L2 learners'. *Studies in Second Language Acquisition* 4: 170–80.

Chaudron, C. 1983a. 'Research on metalinguistic judgements: a review of theory, methods and results'. *Language Learning* 33: 343–77.

Chaudron, C. 1983b. 'Foreigner talk in the classroom—an aid to learning?' in Seliger and Long (eds.) 1983.

Chaudron, C. 1985. 'A method for examining the input/intake distinction' in Gass and Madden (eds.) 1985.

Chaudron, C. 1986. 'Teachers' priorities in correcting learning errors in French immersion classes' in Day (ed.) 1986.

Chaudron, C. 1987. 'The role of error correction in second language teaching' in Das (ed.) 1987a.

Chaudron, C. 1988. *Second Language Classrooms: Research on Teaching and Learning*. Cambridge: Cambridge University Press.

Chaudron, C. and J. Richards. 1986. 'The effect of discourse markers on the comprehension of lectures'. *Applied Linguistics* 7: 113–27.

Chenoweth, A., R. Day, A. Chun, and S. Luppescu. 1983. 'Attitudes and preferences of nonnative speakers to corrective feedback'. *Studies in Second Language Acquisition* 6: 79–87.

Chesterfield R. and K. Chesterfield. 1985. 'Natural order in children's use of second language learning strategies'. *Applied Linguistics* 6: 45–59.

Chiang, D. 1980. 'Predictors of relative clause production' in Scarcella and Krashen (eds.) 1980.

Chick, K. 1985. 'The interactional accomplishment of discrimination in South Africa'. *Language in Society* 14: 299–326.

Chihara, T. and J. Oller. 1978. 'Attitudes and attained proficiency in EFL: a sociolinguistic study of adult Japanese speakers'. *Language Learning* 28: 55–68.

Chomsky, C. 1969. *The Acquisition of Syntax in Children from 5 to 10*. Cambridge, Mass.: MIT Press.

Chomsky, N. 1959. 'Review of "Verbal Behavior" by B. F. Skinner'. *Language* 35: 26–58.

Chomsky, N. 1965. *Aspects of the Theory of Syntax*. Cambridge, Mass.: MIT Press.

Chomsky, N. 1976. *Reflections on Language*. London: Temple Smith.

Chomsky, N. 1980a. *Rules and Representations*. New York: Columbia University Press.

Chomsky, N. 1980b. 'On cognitive structures and their development: a reply to Piaget' in Piatelli-Palmarini (ed.) 1980.

Chomsky, N. 1981a. 'Principles and parameters in syntactic theory' in Hornstein and Lightfoot (eds.) 1981.

Chomsky, N. 1981b. *Lectures on Government and Binding*. Dordrecht: Foris.

Chomsky, N. 1986a. *Knowledge of Language: its Nature, Origin and Use*. New York: Praeger.

Chomsky, N. 1986b. *Barriers*. Cambridge, Mass.: MIT Press.

Chomsky, N. 1988. *Language and Problems of Knowledge: the Nicaraguan Lectures*. Cambridge, Mass.: MIT Press.

Chun, A., R. Day, A. Chenoweth, and S. Luppescu. 1982. 'Errors, interaction, and correction: a study of non-native conversations'. *TESOL Quarterly* 16: 537–47.

Cicourel, A. et al. (eds.). 1974. *Language Use and School Performance*. New York: Academic Press.

Clahsen, H. 1980. 'Psycholinguistic aspects of L2 acquisition' in Felix (ed.) 1980a.

Clahsen, H. 1982. *Spracherwerb in der Kindheit: eine Untersuchung zur Entwicklung der Syntax bei Kleinkindern*. Tübingen: Gunter Narr.

Clahsen, H. 1984. 'The acquisition of German word order: a test case for cognitive approaches to L2 development' in Andersen (ed.) 1984b.

Clahsen, H. 1988. 'Critical phases of grammar development: a study of the acquisition of negation in children and adults' in Jordens and Lalleman (eds.) 1988.

Clahsen, H. 1990. 'The comparative study of first and second language development'. *Studies in Second Language Acquisition* 12: 135–54.

Clahsen, H., J. Meisel, and M. Pienemann. 1983. *Deutsch als Zweitsprache: der Spracherwerb ausländischer Arbeiter*. Gunter Narr: Tübingen.

Clahsen, H. and P. Muysken. 1986. 'The availability of universal grammar to adult and child learners—the study of the acquisition of German word order'. *Second Language Research* 2: 93–119.

Clahsen, H. and P. Muysken. 1989. 'The UG paradox in L2 acquisition'. *Second Language Research* 5: 1–29.

Clark, H. and E. Clark. 1977. *Psychology and Language: an Introduction to Psycholinguistics*. New York: Harcourt Brace Jovanovich.

Clark J. 1969. 'The Pennsylvania Project and the "Audio-Lingual vs. Traditional" question'. *Modern Language Journal* 53: 388–96.

Clark, R. 1974. 'Performing without competence'. *Journal of Child Language* 1: 1–10.

Clarke, M. and J. Hanscombe (eds.). 1983. *On TESOL '82*. Washington D.C.: TESOL.

Clement, R. 1980. 'Ethnicity, contact and communicative competence in a second language' in Giles et al. (eds.) 1980.

Clement, R. 1986. 'Second language proficiency and acculturation: an investigation of the effects of language status and individual characteristics'. *Journal of Language and Social Psychology* 5: 271–90.

Clement, R. and B. Kruidenier. 1983. 'Orientations in second language acquisition: 1. The effects of ethnicity, milieu and target language on their emergence'. *Language Learning* 33: 273–91.

Clement, R. and B. Kruidenier. 1985. 'Aptitude, attitude and motivation in second language proficiency: a test of Clement's model'. *Journal of Language and Social Psychology* 4: 21–38.

Clement, R., P. Smythe, and R. Gardner. 1978. 'Persistence in second language study: motivational considerations'. *Canadian Modern Language Review* 34: 688–94.

Clyne, M. (ed.) 1975. 'Foreigner Talk'. *International Journal of the Sociology of Language* 28.

Clyne, M. 1978. 'Some remarks on foreigner talk' in Dittmar et al. (eds.) 1978.

Coan, R. and R. Cattell. 1966. *Early School Personality Questionnaire*. Champaign, Illinois: Institute for Personality and Ability Testing.

Cochrane, R. 1980. 'The acquisition of /r/ and /l/ by Japanese children and adults learning English as a second language'. *Journal of Multilingual and Multicultural Development* 1: 331–60.

Cohen, A. 1984. 'Studying second-language learning strategies: how do we get the information?' *Applied Linguistics* 5: 101–12. Also in Wenden and Rubin (eds.) 1987.

Cohen, A. 1987. 'Student processing of feedback on their compositions' in Wenden and Rubin (eds.) 1987.

Cohen, A. 1990. *Language Learning: Insights for Learners, Teachers, and Researchers.* New York: Newbury House/Harper Row.

Cohen, A. 1991. 'Feedback on writing: the use of verbal report'. *Studies in Second Language Acquisition* 13: 133–59.

Cohen, A. and **E. Aphek.** 1980. 'Retention of second language vocabulary over time: investigating the role of mnemonic associations'. *System* 8: 221–35.

Cohen, A. and **E. Aphek.** 1981. 'Easifying second language learning'. *Studies in Second Language Acquisition* 3: 221–36.

Cohen, A., D. Larsen-Freeman, and **E. Tarone.** 1991. 'The contribution of SLA theories and research to language teaching' in Sadtano (ed.) 1991.

Cohen, A. and **E. Olshtain.** 1981. 'Developing a measure of sociocultural competence; the case of apology'. *Language Learning* 31: 113–34.

Cohen, A. and **M. Swain.** 1979. 'Bilingual education: the "immersion" model in the North American context' in Pride (ed.) 1979.

Cole, P. and **J. Morgan** (eds.). 1975. *Syntax and Semantics 3: Speech Acts.* New York: Academic Press.

Coleman, L. and **P. Kay.** 1981. 'Prototype semantics: the English word "lie" '. *Language* 55: 26–44.

Collier, V. 1992. 'The Canadian bilingual immersion debate: a synthesis of research findings'. *Studies in Second Language Acquisition* 14: 87–97.

Committee on Irish Language Attitudes Research (CILAR). 1975. 'Report of the Committee on Irish Language Attitudes Research'. Dublin: Government Stationery Office. Cited in Baker 1988.

Comrie, B. 1984. *Language Universals and Linguistic Typology.* Oxford: Basil Blackwell.

Comrie, B. and **E. Keenan.** 1979. 'Noun phrase accessibility revisited'. *Language* 55: 649–64.

Conrad, L. 1989. 'The effects of time-compressed speech on native and EFL listening comprehension'. *Studies in Second language Acquisition* 11: 1–16.

Cook, V. 1971. 'The analogy between first and second language learning' in Lugton (ed.) 1971.

Cook, V. 1973. 'The comparison of language development in native children and foreign adults'. *International Review of Applied Linguistics* 11: 13–28.

Cook, V. 1977. 'Cognitive processes in second language learning'. *International Review of Applied Linguistics* 15: 1–20.

Cook, V. 1985. 'Chomsky's universal grammar and second language learning'. *Applied Linguistics* 6: 2–18.

Cook, V. (ed.). 1986. *Experimental Approaches to Second Language Acquisition.* Oxford: Pergamon.

Cook, V. 1988. *Chomsky's Universal Grammar: an Introduction.* Oxford: Basil Blackwell.

Cook, V. 1989. 'Universal grammar theory and the classroom'. *System* 17: 169–82.

Cook, V. 1990. 'Timed comprehension of binding in advanced L2 learners of English'. *Language Learning* 40: 557–99.

Coppieters, R. 1987. 'Competence differences between native and near-native speakers'. *Language* 63: 544–73.

Corder, S. P. 1967. 'The significance of learners' errors'. *International Review of Applied Linguistics* 5: 161–9.

Corder, S. P. 1971a. 'Idiosyncractic dialects and error analysis'. *International Review of Applied Linguistics* 9: 149–59.

Corder, S. P. 1971b. 'Describing the language learner's language'. *CILT Reports and Papers,* No. 6. CILT.

Corder, S. P. 1973. 'The elicitation of interlanguage' in Svartvik (ed.) 1973a.

Corder, S. P. 1974. 'Error analysis' in Allen and Corder (eds.) 1974.

Corder, S. P. 1976. 'The study of interlanguage' in Proceedings of the Fourth International Conference of Applied Linguistics. Munich, Hochschulverlag. Also in Corder 1981a.

Corder, S. P. 1977a. ' "Simple codes" and the source of the learner's initial heuristic hypothesis'. *Studies in Second Language Acquisition* 1: 1–10.

Corder, S. P. 1977b. 'Language teaching and learning: a social encounter' in Brown et al. (eds.) 1977.

Corder, S. P. 1978a. 'Language-learner language' in Richards (ed.) 1978.

Corder, S. P. 1978b. 'Language distance and the magnitude of the learning task'. *Studies in Second Language Acquisition* 2: 27–36.

Corder, S. P. 1978c. 'Strategies of communication'. *AFinLa* 23. Also in Corder 1981a.

Corder, S. P. 1980. 'Second language acquisition research and the teaching of grammar'. *BAAL Newsletter* 10.

Corder, S. P. 1981a. *Error Analysis and Interlanguage*. Oxford: Oxford University Press.

Corder, S. P. 1981b. 'Formal simplicity and functional simplification' in Andersen (ed.) 1981.

Corder, S. P. 1983. 'A role for the mother tongue' in Gass and Selinker (eds.) 1983.

Corder, S. P. and H. Roulet (eds.). 1977. *Actes du V ème colloque de Linguistíque appliquée de Neuchâtel*. Geneva: Droz et Université de Neuchâtel.

Coulmas, F. (ed.). 1981. *Conversational Routines: Explorations in Standardized Communication Situations and Prepatterned Speech*. The Hague: Mouton.

Coulthard, M. 1985. *An Introduction to Discourse Analysis*. London: Longman.

Coulthard, M. and M. Montgomery (eds.). 1981. *Studies in Discourse Analysis*. Routledge, Kegan, and Paul.

Coupland, N., H. Giles, and J. Weimann (eds.). 1991. *Miscommunication and Problematic Talk*. Newbury Park: Sage Publications.

Courchêne, R. 1980. 'The error analysis hypothesis, the contrastive analysis hypothesis, and the correction or error in the second language classroom'. *TESL Talk* 11/2: 3–13 and 11/3: 1–29.

Courchêne, R., J. Glidden, J. St. John, and C. Therien (eds.). 1992. *Comprehension-based Second Language Teaching*. Ottowa: University of Ottawa Press.

Crago, M. 1992. 'Communicative interaction and second language acquisition: an Inuit example'. *TESOL Quarterly* 26: 487–505.

Craik, F. and R. Lockhart. 1972. 'Levels of processing: a framework for memory research'. *Journal of Verbal Learning and Verbal Behavior* 11: 671–84.

Croft, W. 1990. *Typology and Universals*. Cambridge: Cambridge University Press.

Cronbach, L. and R. Snow. 1977. *Aptitudes and Instructional Methods*. New York: Irvington.

Crookes, G. 1986. 'Task classification: a cross-disciplinary review'. *Technical report No. 4.* Honolulu: Center for Second Language Classroom Research, Social Science Research Institute, University of Hawaii.

Crookes, G. 1989. 'Planning and interlanguage variability'. *Studies in Second Language Acquisition* 11: 367–83.

Crookes, G. 1991. 'Second language speech production research: a methodologically oriented review'. *Studies in Second Language Acquisition* 13: 113–32.

Crookes, G. 1992. 'Theory format and SLA theory'. *Studies in Second Language Acquisition* 14: 425–49.

Crookes, G. and K. Rulon. 1985. 'Incorporation of corrective feedback in native speaker/nonnative speaker conversation'. *Technical report No. 3.* Honolulu: Center for Second Language Classroom Research, Social Science Research Institute, University of Hawaii.

Crookes, G. and R. Schmidt. 1989. 'Motivation: Reopening the research agenda'. *University of Hawaii Working Papers in ESL* 8: 217–56.

Cross, T. 1977. 'Mother's speech adjustments: the contribution of selected child listener variables' in Snow and Ferguson (eds.) 1977.

Cross, T. 1978. 'Mothers' speech and its association with rate of linguistic development in young children' in Waterson and Snow (eds.) 1978.

Crystal, D. 1976. *Child Language Learning and Linguistics: an Overview for the Teaching and Therapeutic Professions.* London: Edward Arnold.

Crystal, D. 1988. *The English Language.* Harmondsworth: Penguin.

Cummins, J. 1981. *Bilingualism and Minority Children.* Ontario: Ontario Institute for Studies in Education.

Cummins, J. 1983. 'Language proficiency and academic achievement' in Oller (ed.) 1983.

Cummins, J. 1984. *Bilingualism and Special Education: Issues in Assessment and Pedagogy.* Clevedon, Avon: Multilingual Matters.

Cummins, J. 1988. 'Second language acquisition within bilingual education programs' in Beebe (ed.) 1988a.

Cummins, J., B. Harley, M. Swain, and P. Allen. 1990. 'Social and individual factors in the development of bilingual proficiency' in Harley et al. (eds.) 1990.

Cummins, J. and K. Nakajima. 1987. 'Age of arrival, length of residence, and interdependence of literacy skills among Japanese immigrant students' in Harley et al. (eds.) 1987.

Cummins, J. and M. Swain. 1986. *Bilingualism in Education.* London: Longman.

Cummins, J., M. Swain, K. Nakajima, J. Handscombe, D. Green, and C. Tran. 1984. 'Linguistic interdependence among Japanese and Vietnamese immigrant students' in Rivera (ed.) 1984.

Dagut, M. and B. Laufer. 1985. 'Avoidance of phrasal verbs—a case for contrastive analysis'. *Studies in Second Language Acquisition* 7: 73–9.

Dahl, D. 1981. 'The role of experience in speech modifications for second language learners'. *Minnesota Papers in Linguistics and Philosophy of Language* 7: 78–93.

Dahl, O. 1979. 'Typology of sentence negation'. *Linguistics* 17: 79–106.

Dakin, J. 1973. *The Language Laboratory and Language Learning.* London: Longman.

Daniel, I. 1983. 'On first-year German foreign language learning: a comparison of language behavior in response to two instructional methods'. Unpublished PhD thesis, University of Southern California.

Danielewicz, J. 1984. 'The interaction between text and context: a study of how adults and children use spoken and written language in four contexts' in Pellegrini and Yawkey (eds.) 1984.

Danoff, M., G. Coles, D. McLaughlin, and D. Reynolds. 1978. 'Evaluation of the impact of ESEA Title VII Spanish/English bilingual education program: overview of study and findings'. Palo Alto, Calif.: American Institutes for Research.

Darden, L. 1991. *Theory Change in Science: Strategies from Mendalian Genetics.* New York: Oxford University Press. Cited in Long 1993.

Das, B. (ed.). 1987a. *Patterns of Classroom Interaction.* Singapore: SEAMEO Regional Language Centre.

Das, B. (ed.). 1987b. *Communication and Learning in the Classroom Community.* Singapore: SEAMEO Regional Language Centre.

Davies, A. 1989. 'Is international English an interlanguage?' *TESOL Quarterly* 23: 447–67.

Davies, A., C. Criper, and A. Howatt (eds.). 1984. *Interlanguage.* Edinburgh: Edinburgh University Press.

Davies, E. 1983. 'Error evaluation: the importance of viewpoint'. *English Language Teaching Journal* 37: 304–11.

Day, R. 1984. 'Student participation in the ESL classroom, or some imperfections of practice'. *Language Learning* 34: 69–102.

Day, R. 1985. 'The use of the target language in context and second language proficiency' in Gass and Madden (eds.) 1985.

Day, R. (ed.). 1986. *Talking to Learn: Conversation in Second Language Acquisition.* Rowley, Mass.: Newbury House.

Day, R., N. Chenoweth, A. Chun, and S. Luppescu. 1984. 'Corrective feedback in native-nonnative discourse'. *Language Learning* 34: 19–45.

de Beaugrande, R. and W. Dressler. 1981. *Introduction to Text Linguistics*. London: Longman.
de Bot, K. 1992. 'A bilingual production model: Levelt's "Speaking" model adapted'. *Applied Linguistics* 13: 1–24.
de Bot, K., D. Coste, R. Ginsberg, and C. Kramsch (eds.). 1991. *Foreign Language Research in Cross-cultural Perspectives*. Amsterdam: John Benjamins.
Decamp, D. 1971. 'Implicational scales and sociolinguistic theory'. *Linguistics* 17: 79–106.
Dechert, H. 1983. 'How a story is done in a second language' in Færch and Kasper (eds.) 1983a.
Dechert, H. 1984a. 'Individual variation in language' in Dechert et al. (eds.) 1984.
Dechert, H. 1984b. 'Second language production: six hypotheses' in Dechert et al. (eds.) 1984.
Dechert, H. (ed.). 1990. *Current Trends in European Second Language Acquisition Research*. Clevedon, Avon: Multilingual Matters.
Dechert, H., D. Möhle, and M. Raupach (eds.). 1984. *Second Language Productions*. Tübingen: Gunter Narr.
Dechert, H. and M. Raupach (eds.). 1989a. *Transfer in Language Production*. Norwood, N.J.: Ablex.
Dechert, H. and M. Raupach (eds.). 1989b. *Interlingual Processes*. Tübingen: Gunter Narr.
de Jong, J. and D. Stevenson (eds.). 1990. *Individualizing the Assessment of Language Liabilities*. Clevedon, Avon: Multilingual Matters.
Derwing, T. 1989. 'Information type and its relation to nonnative speaker comprehension'. *Language Learning* 39: 157–72.
de Villiers, J. and P. de Villiers. 1973. 'A cross-sectional study of the development of grammatical morphemes in child speech'. *Journal of Psycholinguistic Research* 1: 299–310.
Dickerson, L. 1974. 'Internal and external patterning of phonological variability in the speech of Japanese learners of English'. Unpublished PhD thesis, Urbana: University of Illinois.
Dickerson. L. 1975. 'The learner's interlanguage as a system of variable rules'. *TESOL Quarterly* 9:401–7.
Dickinson, L. 1987. *Self-instruction in Language Learning*. Cambridge: Cambridge University Press.
Diller, K. 1978. *The Language Teaching Controversy*. Rowley, Mass.: Newbury House.
Diller K. (ed.). 1981. *Individual Differences and Universals in Language Learning Aptitude*. Rowley, Mass.: Newbury House.
Dittmar, N. 1981. 'On the verbal organization of L2 tense marking in an elicited translation task by Spanish immigrants in Germany'. *Studies in Second Language Acquisition* 3: 136–64.
Dittmar, N. 1992. 'Grammaticalization in second language acquisition: Introduction'. *Studies in Second Language Acquisition* 14: 249–59.
Dittmar, N., H. Haberland, T. Skuttnab-Kangas, and U. Telman (eds.). 1978. Papers from the First Scandinavian–German Symposium on the Language of Immigrant Workers and their Children. Linguistgruppen, Roskilde Universiteits Center.
Dornyei, Z. 1990. 'Conceptualising motivation in foreign language learning'. *Language Learning* 40: 45–78.
Doughty, C. 1991. 'Second language instruction does make a difference: evidence from an empirical study on SL relativization'. *Studies in Second Language Acquisition* 13: 431–69.
Doughty, C. and T. Pica. 1986. ' "Information gap" tasks: do they facilitate second language acquisition?' *TESOL Quarterly* 20: 305–25.
Dowd, J., J. Zuengler, and D. Berkowitz. 1990. 'L2 social marking: research issues'. *Applied Linguistics* 11: 16–29.
Downes, N. 1981. 'Foreigner talk inside and outside the classroom'. Unpublished paper, Department of Linguistics, University of Pittsburgh. Cited in Chaudron 1988.
Duda, R. and P. Riley (eds.). 1990. *Learning Styles*. Nancy, France: University of Nancy.
Dudley-Evans, A. and T. Johns. 1981. 'A team teaching approach to lecture comprehension for overseas students' in ELT Documents Special: *The Teaching of Listening Comprehension*. London: The British Council.

Duff, P. 1986. 'Another look at interlanguage talk: taking task to task' in Day (ed.) 1986.

Dulay, H. and M. Burt. 1972. 'Goofing, an indicator of children's second language strategies'. *Language Learning* 22: 234–52.

Dulay, H. and M. Burt. 1973. 'Should we teach children syntax?' *Language Learning* 23: 245–58.

Dulay, H. and M. Burt. 1974a. 'You can't learn without goofing' in Richards (ed.) 1974.

Dulay, H. and M. Burt. 1974b. 'Errors and strategies in child second language acquisition'. *TESOL Quarterly* 8:129–36.

Dulay, H. and M. Burt. 1974c. 'Natural sequences in child second language acquisition'. *Language Learning* 24: 37–53.

Dulay, H. and M. Burt. 1974d. 'A new perspective on the creative construction processes in child second language acquisition'. *Language Learning* 24: 253–78.

Dulay, H. and M. Burt. 1975. 'Creative construction in second language learning and teaching' in Burt and Dulay (eds.) 1975.

Dulay, H. and M. Burt. 1977. 'Remarks on creativity in language acquisition' in Burt et al. (eds.) 1977.

Dulay, H. and M. Burt. 1980. 'On acquisition orders' in Felix (ed.) 1980a.

Dulay, H., M. Burt, and S. Krashen. 1982. *Language Two*. New York: Oxford University Press.

Dunkel, H. 1948. *Second Language Learning*. Boston: Ginn.

Duskova, L. 1969. 'On sources of errors in foreign language learning'. *International Review of Applied Linguistics* 7: 11–36.

Early, M. 1985. 'Input and interaction in content classrooms: foreigner talk and teacher talk in classroom discourse'. Unpublished PhD thesis, University of California at Los Angeles.

Eckman, F. 1977. 'Markedness and the contrastive analysis hypothesis'. *Language Learning* 27: 315–30.

Eckman, F. 1981. 'On the naturalness of interlanguage phonological rules'. *Language Learning* 31: 195–216.

Eckman, F. 1984. 'Universals, typologies and interlanguage' in Rutherford (ed.) 1984a.

Eckman, F. 1985. 'Some theoretical and pedagogical implications of the markedness differential hypothesis'. *Studies in Second Language Acquisition* 7: 289–307.

Eckman, F. 1991. 'The structural conformity hypothesis and the acquisition of consonant clusters in the interlanguage of ESL learners'. *Studies in Second Language Acquisition* 13: 23–41.

Eckman, F, L. Bell, and D. Nelson (eds.). 1984. *Universals of Second Language Acquisition*. Rowley, Mass.: Newbury House.

Eckman, F., L. Bell, and D. Nelson. 1988. 'On the generalization of relative clause instruction in the acquisition of English as a second language'. *Applied Linguistics* 9: 1–20.

Edelsky, C., B. Altwerger, F. Barkin, B. Flores, S. Hudleson, and K. Jilbert. 1983. 'Semilingualism and language deficit'. *Applied Linguistics* 5: 113–27.

Edmondson, W. 1985. 'Discourse worlds in the classroom and in foreign language'. *Studies in Second Language Acquisition* 7: 159–68.

Edmondson, W. and J. House. 1991. 'Do learners talk too much? The waffle phenomenon in interlanguage pragmatics' in Phillipson et al. (eds.) 1991.

Edwards, G. 1977. *Second language retention in the Canadian Public Service*. Ottowa: Public Service Commission of Canada.

Edwards, J. 1984. 'Irish: planning and preservation'. *Journal of Multilingual and Multicultural Development* 5: 267–75.

Ehrlich, S. P. Avery, and C. Yorio. 1989. 'Discourse structure and the negotiation of comprehensible input'. *Studies in Second Language Acquisition* 11: 397–414.

Ehrman, M. 1990. 'The role of personality type in adult language learning: an ongoing investigation' in Parry and Stansfield (eds.) 1990.

Ehrman, M. and R. Oxford. 1989. 'Effects of sex differences, career choice, and psychological type on adult language learning strategies'. *Modern Language Journal* 73: 1–13.

Eisenstein, M. 1980. 'Grammatical explanations in ESL: Teach the student, not the method'. *TESL Talk* 11: 3–13.

Eisenstein, M. 1982. 'A study of social variation in adult second language acquisition'. *Language Learning* 32: 367–92.

Eisenstein, M. 1983. 'Native reactions to non-native speech: a review of empirical research'. *Studies in Second Language Acquisition* 5: 160–76.

Eisenstein, M. (ed.). 1989. *The Dynamic Interlanguage: Empirical Studies in Second Language Variation*. New York: Plenum Press.

Eisenstein, M., N. Bailey, and C. Madden. 1982. 'It takes two: contrasting tasks and contrasting structures'. *TESOL Quarterly* 16: 381–93.

Eisenstein, M. and J. Bodman. 1986. ' "I very appreciate": expressions of gratitude by native and non-native speakers of American English'. *Applied Linguistics* 7: 167–85.

Eisenstein, M. and G. Verdi. 1985. 'The intelligibility of social dialects for working-class adult learners of English'. *Language Learning* 35: 287–98.

Ekstrand, L. 1977. 'Social and individual frame factors in L2 learning: comparative aspects' in Skuttnab-Kangas (ed.) 1977.

Ellis, G. and B. Sinclair. 1989. *Learning to Learn English: a Course in Learner Training*. Cambridge: Cambridge University Press.

Ellis, N. 1991. 'Rules and instances in foreign language learning: interactions of explicit and implicit knowledge'. Unpublished paper, Bangor: University College of North Wales.

Ellis, R. 1980. 'Classroom interaction and its relation to second language learning'. *RELC Journal* 11: 29–48.

Ellis, R. 1982. 'The origins of interlanguage'. *Applied Linguistics* 3: 207–23.

Ellis, R. 1984a. *Classroom Second Language Development*. Oxford: Pergamon.

Ellis, R. 1984b. 'Formulaic speech in early classroom second language development' in Handscombe et al. (eds.) 1984.

Ellis, R. 1984c. 'Can syntax be taught? A study of the effects of formal instruction on the acquisition of Wh-questions by children'. *Applied Linguistics* 5: 138–55.

Ellis, R. 1985a. *Understanding Second Language Acquisition*. Oxford: Oxford University Press.

Ellis, R. 1985b. 'The L2=L1 Hypothesis: a reconsideration'. *System* 13: 9–24.

Ellis, R. 1985c. 'Sources of variability in interlanguage'. *Applied Linguistics* 6: 118–31.

Ellis, R. 1985d. 'Teacher–pupil interaction in second language development' in Gass and Madden (eds.) 1985.

Ellis, R. (ed.). 1987a. *Second Language Acquisition in Context*. London: Prentice-Hall International.

Ellis, R. 1987b. 'Interlanguage variability in narrative discourse: style-shifting in the use of the past tense'. *Studies in Second Language Acquisition* 9: 1–20.

Ellis, R. 1987c. 'Contextual variability in second language acquisition and the relevancy of language teaching' in Ellis (ed.) 1987a.

Ellis, R. 1988a. 'The effects of linguistic environment on the second language acquisition of grammatical rules'. *Applied Linguistics* 9: 257–74.

Ellis, R. 1988b. 'The role of practice in classroom language learning'. *AILA Review* 5: 20–39.

Ellis, R. 1989a. 'Classroom learning styles and their effect on second language acquisition: a study of two learners'. *System* 17: 249–62.

Ellis, R. 1989b. 'Are classroom and naturalistic acquisition the same? A study of the classroom acquisition of German word order rules'. *Studies in Second Language Acquisition* 11: 305–28.

Ellis, R. 1989c. 'Sources of intra-learner variability in language use and their relationship to second language acquisition' in Gass et al. (eds.) 1989b.

Ellis, R. 1990a. *Instructed Second Language Acquisition*. Oxford: Blackwell.

Ellis, R. 1990b. 'Individual learning styles in classroom second language development' in de Jong and Stevenson (eds.) 1990.

Ellis, R. 1990c. 'A response to Gregg'. *Applied Linguistics* 11: 384–91.

Ellis, R. 1990d. 'Grammaticality judgements and learner variability' in Burmeister and Rounds (eds.) 1990.

Ellis, R. 1991a. 'The interaction hypothesis: a critical evaluation' in Sadtono (ed.) 1991.

Ellis, R. 1991c. 'Grammaticality judgments and second language acquisition'. *Studies in Second Language Acquisition* 13: 161–86.

Ellis, R. 1991d. 'Grammar teaching—practice or consciousness-raising' in R. Ellis. *Second Language Acquisition and Second Language Pedagogy*. Clevedon, Avon: Multilingual Matters.

Ellis, R. 1992a. 'Learning to communicate in the classroom'. *Studies in Second Language Acquisition* 14: 1–23.

Ellis, R. 1992b. 'On the relationship between formal practice and second language acquisition'. *Die Neueren Sprachen* 91: 131–47.

Ellis, R. 1993a. 'Second language acquisition and the structural syllabus'. *TESOL Quarterly* 27: 91–113.

Ellis, R. 1993b. 'Interpretation-based grammar teaching'. *System* 21: 69–78.

Ellis, R. 1993c. 'Second language acquisition research and teacher development: the case of teachers' questions'. Paper given at Second International Conference on Teacher Education in Second Language Teaching, City Polytechnic of Hong Kong.

Ellis, R. and M. Rathbone. 1987. *The Acquisition of German in a Classroom Context. Mimeograph*. London: Ealing College of Higher Education.

Ellis, R. and C. Roberts. 1987. 'Two approaches for investigating second language acquisition in context' in Ellis (ed.) 1987a.

Ellis, R. and G. Wells. 1980. 'Enabling factors in adult-child discourse'. *First Language* 1: 46–82.

Ely, C. 1986a. An analysis of discomfort, risktaking, sociability, and motivation in the L2 classroom'. *Language Learning* 36: 1–25.

Ely, C. 1986b. 'Language learning motivation: a descriptive and causal analysis'. *Modern Language Journal* 70: 28–35.

Enright, D. 1984. 'The organization of interaction in elementary classrooms' in Handscombe et al. (eds.) 1984.

Epstein, N. 1977. *Language, Ethnicity and the Schools*. Washington D.C.: Institute for Educational Leadership.

Erickson, F. and G. Mohatt. 1982. 'Cultural organization of participation structures in two classrooms of Indian students' in Spindler (ed.) 1982.

Erickson, F. and J. Schultz. 1982. *The Counselor as Gatekeeper: Social Interaction in Interviews*. New York: Academic Press.

Ervin-Tripp, S. 1974. 'Is second language learning like the first?' *TESOL Quarterly* 8: 111–27.

Ervin-Tripp, S., A. Strage, M. Lampert, and N. Bell. 1987. 'Understanding requests'. *Linguistics* 25: 107–43.

Eubank, L. 1987a. 'Parameters in L2 learning: Flynn revisited'. *Second Language Research* 5: 43–73.

Eubank, L. 1987b. 'The acquisition of German negation by formal language learners' in Van-Patten et al. (eds.) 1987.

Eubank, L. 1990. 'Linguistic theory and the acquisition of German negation' in VanPatten and Lee (eds.) 1990.

Eubank, L. 1991a. 'Introduction' in L. Eubank (ed.) 1991b.

Eubank, L. (ed.). 1991b. *Point Counterpoint: Universal Grammar in the Second Language*. Amsterdam: John Benjamins.

Eysenck, H. 1970. *The Structure of Human Personality*. London: Routledge, Kegan, and Paul.

Eysenck, S. and J. Chan. 1982. 'A comparative study of personality in adults and children: Hong Kong vs. England'. *Personality and Individual Differences* 3: 153–60.

Færch, C. 1980. 'Describing interlanguage through interaction: problems of systematicity and permeability'. *Working Papers on Bilingualism* 19: 59–78.

Færch, C. 1985. 'Meta talk in FL classroom discourse'. *Studies in Second Language Acquisition* 7: 184–99.

Færch, C. and **G. Kasper.** 1980. 'Processes and strategies in foreign language learning and communication'. *Interlanguage Studies Bulletin* 5: 47–118.

Færch, C. and **G. Kasper** (eds.). 1983a. *Strategies in Interlanguage Communication.* London: Longman.

Færch, C. and **G. Kasper.** 1983b. 'Plans and strategies in foreign language communication' C. Færch and G. Kasper (eds.) 1983a.

Færch, C. and **G. Kasper.** 1985. 'Procedural knowledge as a component of foreign language learners' communicative competence' in Bolte and Herrlitz (eds.) 1985.

Færch C. and **G. Kasper.** 1986a. 'The role of comprehension in second language acquisition'. *Applied Linguistics* 7:257–74.

Færch, C. and **G. Kasper.** 1986b. 'Cognitive dimensions of language transfer' in Kellerman and Sharwood Smith (eds.) 1986.

Færch, C. and **G. Kasper** (eds.). 1987. *Introspection in Second Language Research.* Clevedon, Avon: Multilingual Matters.

Færch, C. and **G. Kasper.** 1989. 'Internal and external modification in interlanguage request realization' in Blum-Kulka et al. (eds.) 1989a.

Fanselow, J. 1977a. 'Beyond "Rashomon"—conceptualizing and describing the teaching act'. *TESOL Quarterly* 10: 17–39.

Fanselow, J. 1977b. 'The treatment of error in oral work'. *Foreign Language Annals* 10: 583–93.

Fanselow, J. and **R. Crymes** (eds.). 1976. *On TESOL '76.* Washington D.C.: TESOL.

Fasold, R. 1984. 'Variation theory and language learning' in Trudgill (ed.) 1984.

Fasold, R. and **R. Shuy** (eds.). 1975. *Analyzing Variation in Language.* Washington D.C.: Georgetown University Press.

Fathman, A. 1975. 'Language background, age, and the order of acquisition of English structures' in Burt and Dulay (eds.) 1975.

Fathman, A. 1976. 'Variables affecting the successful learning of English as a second language'. *TESOL Quarterly* 10: 433–41.

Fathman, A. 1978. 'ESL and EFL learning: similar or dissimilar?' in Blatchford and Schachter (eds.) 1978.

Felix, S. 1978. 'Some differences between first and second language acquisition' in Waterson and Snow (eds.) 1978.

Felix, S. (ed.). 1980a. *Second Language Development: Trends and Issues.* Tübingen: Gunter Narr.

Felix, S. 1980b. 'Interference, interlanguage and related issues' in Felix (ed.) 1980a.

Felix, S. 1981. 'The effect of formal instruction on second language acquisition'. *Language Learning* 31: 87–112.

Felix, S. 1984. 'Maturational aspects of Universal Grammar' in Davies et al. (eds.) 1984.

Felix, S. 1985. 'More evidence on competing cognitive systems'. *Second Language Research* 1: 47–72.

Felix, S. and **A. Hahn.** 1985. 'Natural processes in classroom second-language learning'. *Applied Linguistics* 6: 223–38.

Felix, S. and **W. Weigl.** 1991. 'Universal grammar in the classroom: the effects of formal instruction on second language acquisition'. *Second Language Research* 7: 162–80.

Ferguson, C. 1971. 'Absence of copula and the notion of simplicity: a study of normal speech, baby talk, foreigner talk and pidgins' in Hymes (ed.) 1971b.

Ferguson, C. 1975. 'Towards a characterization of English foreigner talk'. *Anthropological Linguistics* 17: 1–14.

Ferguson, C. 1977. 'Baby talk as a simplified register' in Snow and Ferguson (eds.) 1977.

Ferguson, C. and **C. Debose.** 1977. 'Simplified registers, broken languages and pidginization' in Valdman (ed.) 1977.

Ferguson, C. and D. Slobin (eds.). 1973. *Studies of Child Language Development*. New York: Appleton-Century-Crofts.

Ferrier, L. 1978. 'Some observations of error in context' in Waterson and Snow (eds.) 1978.

Fiksdal, S. 1989. 'Framing uncomfortable moments in crosscultural gatekeeping interviews' in Gass et al. (eds.) 1989a.

Fillmore, C. 1968. 'The case for case' in Bach and Harms (eds.) 1968.

Filmore, C., D. Kempler and W. Wang (eds.). 1979. *Individual Differences in Language Ability and Language Behavior*. New York: Academic Press.

Fine, J. (ed.). 1988. *Second Language Discourse: a Textbook of Current Research*. Norwood, N.J.: Ablex.

Finer, D. 1991. 'Binding parameters in second language acquisition' in Eubank (ed.) 1991b.

Finocchiaro, M. 1981. 'Motivation: its crucial role in language learning' in Hines and Rutherford (eds.) 1981.

Fisher, J., M. Clarke, and J. Schachter (eds.) 1980. *On TESOL '80*. Washington D.C.: TESOL.

Fisherman, J., C. Ferguson, and J. Das (eds.). 1968. *Language Problems of Developing Nations*. New York: Wiley and Sons.

Fisiak, J. 1981a. 'Some introductory notes concerning contrastive linguistics' in Fisiak (ed.).

Fisiak, J. (ed.). 1981b. *Contrastive Linguistics and the Language Teacher*. Oxford: Pergamon.

Fischer, J. 1958. 'Social influences in the choice of a linguistic variant'. *Word* 14: 47–56.

Fishman, J., R. Cooper, and A. Conrad. 1977. *The Spread of English*. Rowley: Mass.: Newbury House.

Fishman, J., R. Cooper, and R. Ma (eds.). 1968. *Bilingualism in the Barrio*. New York: Yeshiva University.

Fitzpatrick, F. 1987. *The Open Door: The Bradford Bilingual Project*. Clevedon, Avon: Multilingual Matters.

Flanders, N. 1970. *Analyzing Teaching Behavior*. Reading, Mass.: Addison-Wesley.

Flanigan, B. 1991. 'Peer tutoring and second language acquisition in the elementary school'. *Applied Linguistics* 12: 141–58.

Flavell, J. and M. Markman (eds.). 1983. *Carmichael's Manual of Child Psychology: Vol 3*. New York: Wiley and Sons.

Flege, J. 1987. 'A critical period for learning to pronounce foreign languages'. *Applied Linguistics* 8: 162–77.

Fletcher, P. and M. Garman (eds.). 1986. *Language Acquisition* (2nd ed.). Cambridge: Cambridge University Press.

Flick, W. 1979. 'A multiple component approach to research in second language acquisition' in Andersen (ed.) 1979a.

Flick, W. 1980. 'Error types in adult English as a second language' in Ketterman and St. Clair (eds.) 1980.

Flores d'Arcais, G. and W. Levelt (eds.). 1970. *Advances in Psycholinguistics*. Amsterdam: North-Holland Publishing.

Flowerdew, J. 1992. 'Definitions in science lectures'. *Applied Linguistics* 13: 202–21.

Flynn, S. 1984. 'A universal in L2 acquisition based on a PBD typology' in Eckman et al. (eds.) 1984.

Flynn, S. 1987. *A parameter-setting model of L2 Acquisition*. Dordrecht: Reidel.

Flynn, S. and B. Lust. 1990. 'In defense of parameter-setting in L2 acquisition: a reply to Bley-Vroman and Chaudron '90'. *Language Learning* 40: 419–49.

Flynn, S. and S. Manuel. 1991. 'Age-dependent effects in language acquisition: an evaluation of the "critical period" hypothesis' in Eubank (ed.) 1991b.

Flynn, S. and W. O'Neill. (eds.). 1988. *Linguistic Theory in Second Language Acquisition*. Dordrecht: Kluwer.

Forrest-Pressley, D., G. Mackinnon and T. Waller (eds.). 1985. *Metacognition, Cognition, and Human Performance, Vol 1*. New York: Academic Press.

Foster, S. 1990. *The Communicative Competence of Young Children: a Modular Approach*. London: Longman.

Fotos, S. 1993. 'Consciousness-raising and noticing through focus on form: grammar task performance versus formal instruction'. *Applied Linguistics* 14: 4.

Fotos, S. and R. Ellis. 1991. 'Communicating about grammar: a task-based approach'. *TESOL Quarterly* 25: 605–28.

Fraser, B. 1981. 'On apologizing' in Coulmas (ed.) 1981.

Fraser, B. 1983. 'The domain of pragmatics' in Richards and Schmidt (eds.) 1983.

Fraser, B., E. Rintell, and J. Walters. 1980. 'An approach to conducting research on the acquisition of pragmatic competence in a second language' in Larsen-Freeman (ed.) 1980.

Fraser, C. and K. Scherer (eds.). 1982. *Social Psychological Dimensions of Language Behaviour*. Cambridge: Cambridge University Press.

Freed, B. 1980. 'Talking to foreigners vs. talking to children: similarities and differences' in Scarcella and Krashen (eds.) 1980.

Freed, B. 1981. 'Foreigner talk, baby talk, native talk'. *International Journal of the Sociology of Language* 28: 19–39.

Freed, B. 1990. 'Language learning in a study abroad context: the effects of interactive and noninteractive out-of-class contact on grammatical achievement and oral proficiency' in Proceedings of the Georgetown University Round Table on Languages and Linguistics 1990. Washington D.C.: Georgetown University.

French, F. 1949. *Common Errors in English*. London: Oxford University Press.

French, P. and M. McLure (eds.). 1981. *Adult–Child Conversation*. New York: St Martin's Press.

Freudenstein, R. 1977. 'Interaction in the foreign language classroom' in Burt et al. (eds.) 1977.

Fromkin, V. 1971. 'The non-anomalous nature of anomalous utterances'. *Language* 47: 27–52.

Fry, J. 1988. 'Diary studies in classroom SLA: problems and prospects'. *JALT Journal* 9: 158–67.

Fujimoto, D., J. Lubin, Y. Sasaki, and M. Long. 1986. 'The effect of linguistic and conversational adjustments on the comprehensibility of spoken second language discourse'. Unpublished manuscript, Department of ESL, University of Hawaii at Manoa. Cited in Larsen-Freeman and Long 1991.

Furrow, D., K. Nelson, and H. Benedict. 1979. 'Mothers' speech to children and syntactic development: some simple relationships'. *Journal of Child Language* 6: 423–42.

Gaies, S. 1977. 'The nature of linguistic input in formal second language learning: linguistic and communicative strategies' in Brown et al. (eds.) 1977.

Gaies, S. 1982. 'Native speaker-nonnative speaker interaction among academic peers'. *Studies in Second Language Acquisition* 5: 74–82.

Gaies, S. 1983a. 'The investigation of language classroom processes'. *TESOL Quarterly* 17: 205–18.

Gaies, S. 1983b. 'Learner feedback: an exploratory study of its role in the second language classroom' in Seliger and Long (eds.) 1983.

Gardner, R. 1979. 'Social psychological aspects of second language acquisition' in Giles and St. Clair (eds.) 1979.

Gardner, R. 1980. 'On the validity of affective variables in second language acquisition: conceptual, contextual, and statistical considerations'. *Language Learning* 30: 255–70.

Gardner, R. 1983. 'Learning another language: a true social psychological experiment'. *Journal of Language and Social Psychology* 2: 219–40.

Gardner, R. 1985. *Social Psychology and Second Language Learning: The Role of Attitude and Motivation*. London: Edward Arnold.

Gardner, R. 1988. 'The socio-educational model of second language learning: assumptions, findings and issues'. *Language Learning* 38: 101–26.

Gardner, R. 1991. 'Second-language learning in adults: correlates of proficiency'. *Applied Language Learning* 2: 1–28.

Gardner, R. and R. Clement. 1990. 'Social psychological perspectives on second language acquisition' in Giles and Robinson (eds.) 1990.

Gardner, R., R. Ginsberg, and P. Smythe. 1976. 'Attitudes and motivation in second language learning: course related changes'. *The Canadian Modern Language Review* 32: 243–66.

Gardner, R., R. Lalonde, and J. MacPherson. 1985. 'Social factors in second language attrition'. *Language Learning* 35: 519–40.

Gardner, R., R. Lalonde, and R. Pierson. 1983. 'The socio-educational model of second language acquisition: an investigation using LISREL causal modeling'. *Journal of Language and Social Psychology* 2: 1–15.

Gardner, R. and W. Lambert. 1959. 'Motivational variables in second language acquisition'. *Canadian Journal of Psychology* 13: 266–72.

Gardner, R. and W. Lambert. 1972. *Attitudes and Motivation in Second Language Learning.* Rowley, Mass.: Newbury House.

Gardner, R. and P. MacIntyre. 1991. 'An instrumental motivation in language study: who says it isn't effective?' *Studies in Second Language Acquisition* 13: 57–72.

Gardner, R. and P. MacIntyre. 1992. 'A student's contributions to second language learning. Part 1: Cognitive variables'. *Language Teaching* 25: 211–20.

Gardner, R., R. Moorcroft, and P. MacIntyre. 1987. 'The role of anxiety in second language performance of language dropouts'. *Research Bulletin* No 657. London, Ontario: The University of Western Ontario.

Gardner, R. and P. Smythe. 1975. 'Second language acquisition: a social psychological approach'. *Research Bulletin* No 332. Department of Psychology, University of Western Ontario. Cited in Gardner 1985.

Gardner, R., P. Smythe, and G. Brunet. 1977. 'Intensive second language study: effects on attitudes, motivation and French achievement'. *Language Learning* 27: 243–62.

Gardner, R., P. Smythe, and R. Clement. 1979. 'Intensive second language study in a bicultural milieu: an investigation of attitudes, motivation, and language proficiency'. *Language Learning* 29: 305–20.

Gardner, R., P. Smythe, R., Clement, and L. Gliksman. 1976. 'Second language learning: a social-psychological perspective'. *Canadian Modern Language Review* 32: 198–213.

Garnica, O. 1977. 'Some prosodic and paralinguistic features of speech to young children' in Snow and Ferguson (eds.) 1977.

Gaskill, W. 1980. 'Correction in native speaker – nonnative speaker conversation' in Larsen-Freeman (ed.) 1980.

Gass, S. 1979. 'Language transfer and universal grammatical relations'. *Language Learning* 29: 327–44.

Gass, S. 1980. 'An investigation of syntactic transfer in adult second language learners' in Scarcella and Krashen (eds.) 1980.

Gass, S. 1982. 'From theory to practice' in Hines and Rutherford (eds.) 1981.

Gass, S. 1983. 'Language transfer and universal grammatical relations' in Gass and Selinker (ed.) 1983.

Gass, S. 1984. 'A review of interlanguage syntax: language transfer and language universals'. *Language Learning* 34: 115–32.

Gass, S. 1987. 'The resolution of conflicts among competing systems: a bidirectional perspective'. *Applied Psycholinguistics* 8: 329–50.

Gass, S. 1988. 'Integrating research areas: a framework for second language studies'. *Applied Linguistics* 9: 198–217.

Gass, S. 1989. 'Language universals and second language acquisition'. *Language Learning* 39: 497–534.

Gass, S. 1990. 'Second and foreign language learning: same, different or none of the above?' in VanPatten and Lee (eds.) 1990.

Gass, S. 1991. 'Grammar instruction, selective attention, and learning' in Phillipson et al. (eds.) 1991.

Gass, S. and J. Ard. 1980. 'L2 data: their relevance for language universals'. *TESOL Quarterly* 16: 443–52.

Gass, S. and J. Ard. 1984. 'Second language acquisition and the ontology of language universals' in Rutherford (ed.) 1984a.

Gass, S. and G. Crookes (eds.). (forthcoming). *Task-based Learning in a Second Language.* Clevedon, Avon: Multilingual Matters.

Gass, S. and U. Lakshmanan. 1991. 'Accounting for interlanguage subject pronouns'. *Second Language Research* 7: 181–203.

Gass, S. and C. Madden (eds.). 1985. *Input in Second Language Acquisition.* Rowley, Mass.: Newbury House.

Gass, S., C. Madden, D. Preston, and L. Selinker (eds.). 1989a. *Variation in Second Language Acquisition Volume I: Sociolinguistic Issues.* Clevedon, Avon: Multilingual Matters.

Gass, S., C. Madden, D. Preston, and L. Selinker (eds.). 1989b. *Variation in Second Language Acquisition Volume II: Psycholinguistic Issues.* Clevedon, Avon: Multilingual Matters.

Gass, S. and J. Schachter (eds.). 1989. *Linguistic Perspectives on Second Language Acquisition.* Cambridge: Cambridge University Press.

Gass, S. and L. Selinker (eds.). 1983. *Language Transfer in Language Learning.* Rowley, Mass.: Newbury House.

Gass, S. and E. Varonis. 1985a. 'Task variation and nonnative/nonnative negotiation of meaning' in Gass and Madden (eds.) 1985.

Gass, S. and E. Varonis. 1985b. 'Variation in native speaker speech modification to non-native speakers'. *Studies in Second Language Acquisition* 7: 37–57.

Gass, S. and E. Varonis. 1986. 'Sex differences in NNS/NNS interactions' in Day (ed.) 1986.

Gass, S. and E. Varonis. 1991. 'Miscommunication in nonnative speaker discourse' in Coupland et al. (eds.) 1991.

Gasser, M. 1990. 'Connectionism and universals of second language acquisition'. *Studies in Second Language Acquisition* 12: 179–99.

Gatbonton, E. 1978. 'Patterned phonetic variability in second language speech: a gradual diffusion model'. *Canadian Modern Language Review* 34: 335–47.

Genesee, F. 1976. 'The role of intelligence in second language learning'. *Language Learning* 26: 267–80.

Genesee, F. 1978. 'Individual differences in second language learning'. *The Canadian Modern Language Review* 34: 490–504.

Genesee, F. 1984. 'French immersion programs' in Shapson and D'Oyley (eds.) 1984.

Genesee, F. 1987. *Learning Through Two Languages: Studies of Immersion and Bilingual Education.* Cambridge, Mass.: Newbury House.

George, H. 1972. *Common Errors in Language Learning: Insights from English.* Rowley, Mass.: Newbury House.

Gerbault, J. 1978. 'The acquisition of English by a five-year-old French speaker'. MA thesis, University of California at Los Angeles.

Gibbons, J. 1985. 'The silent period: an examination'. *Language Learning* 35: 255–67.

Gick, M. and K. Holyoak. 1983. 'Schema induction and analogical transfer'. *Cognitive Psychology* 15: 1–38.

Gieve, S. 1991. 'Goals and preferred language styles of Japanese English majors' in Proceedings of the Conference on Second Language Research in Japan. International University of Japan.

Giles, H. 1971. 'Our reactions to accent'. *New Society*, 14th October.

Giles, H. (ed.). 1977. *Language, Ethnicity and Intergroup Relations*. New York: Academic Press.

Giles, H. and J. Byrne. 1982. 'An intergroup approach to second language acquisition'. *Journal of Multicultural and Multilingual Development* 3: 17–40.

Giles, H. and P. Johnson. 1981. 'The role of language in ethnic group relations' in Turner and Giles (eds.) 1981.

Giles, H. and W. Robinson (eds.). 1990. *Handbook of Language and Social Psychology*. Chichester: John Wiley and Sons.

Giles, H., W. Robinson, and P. Smith (eds.). 1980. *Language: Social Psychological Perspectives*. Oxford: Pergamon Press.

Giles, H. and E. Ryan. 1982. 'Prolegomena for developing a social psychological theory of language attitudes' in Ryan and Giles (eds.) 1982.

Giles, H. and R. St. Clair (eds.). 1979. *Language and Social Psychology*. Oxford: Blackwell.

Gillette, B. 1987. 'Two successful language learners: an introspective report' in Færch and Kasper (eds.) 1987.

Gingras, R. (ed.). 1978. *Second Language Acquisition and Foreign Language Teaching*. Arlington, VA.: Center for Applied Linguistics.

Givón, T. 1979a. *On Understanding Grammar*. New York: Academic Press.

Givón, T. 1979b. *Syntax and Semantics, Vol 12: Discourse and Semantics*. New York: Academic Press.

Givón, T. 1984. 'Universals of discourse structure and second language acquisition' in Rutherford (ed.) 1984a.

Givón, T. 1995. *Functionalism and Grammar*. Amsterdam: J.Benjamins.

Glahn, E. and A. Holmen (eds.). 1985. *Learner Discourse*. Anglica et Americana 22. Copenhagen: University of Copenhagen.

Glaser, R. (ed.). 1965. *Training, Research, and Education*. New York: Wiley and Sons.

Gleason, J. and S. Weintraub. 1978. 'Input language and the acquisition of communicative competence' in Nelson (ed.) 1978.

Gleitman, L., E. Newport, and H. Gleitman. 1984. 'The current status of the motherese hypothesis'. *Journal of Child Language* 11: 43–79.

Gliksman, L. 1976. 'Second language acquisition: the effects of student attitudes on classroom behavior'. Unpublished MA thesis, University of Western Ontario.

Gliksman, L., R. Gardner, and P. Smythe. 1982. 'The role of integrative motivation on students' participation in the French classroom'. *Canadian Modern Language Review* 38: 625–47.

Godfrey, D. 1980. 'A discourse analysis of tense' in Larsen-Freeman (ed.) 1980.

Goldin-Meadow, S. 1982. 'The resilience of recursion: a study of a communication system developed without a conventional language model' in Wanner and Gleitman (eds.) 1982.

Goldman-Eisler, F. 1968. *Psycholinguistics: Experiments in Spontaneous Speech*. New York: Academic.

Goldstein, L. 1987. 'Standard English: the only target for nonnative speakers of English?' *TESOL Quarterly* 21: 417–36.

Goodluck, H. 1986. 'Language acquisition and linguistic theory' in Fletcher and Garman (eds.) 1986.

Goody, E. (ed.). 1978. *Questions and Politeness*. Cambridge: Cambridge University Press.

Grauberg, W. 1971. 'An error analysis in the German of first-year university students' in Perren and Trim (eds.) 1971.

Green, P. 1975. 'Aptitude testing: an ongoing experiment'. *Audio-Visual Language Journal* 12: 205–10.

Green, P. and K. Hecht. 1992. 'Implicit and explicit grammar: an empirical study'. *Applied Linguistics* 13: 168–84.

Greenberg, H. 1966. *Universals of Language* (2nd Ed.). Cambridge, Mass.: MIT Press.

Greenfield, P. and C. Dent. 1980. 'A developmental study of the communication of meaning: the role of uncertainty of information' in Nelson (ed.) 1980.

Gregg, K. 1984. 'Krashen's Monitor and Occam's Razor'. *Applied Linguistics* 5: 79–100.
Gregg, K. 1989. 'Second language acquisition theory: the case for a generative perspective' in Gass and Schachter (eds.) 1989.
Gregg, K. 1990. 'The variable competence model of second language acquisition and why it isn't'. *Applied Linguistics* 11: 364–83.
Gregg, K. 1993. 'Taking explanation seriously; or, let a couple of flowers bloom'. *Applied Linguistics* 14: 276–94.
Gremmo, M., H. Holec, and P. Riley. 1977. 'Interactional structure: the role of role'. Melanges Pedagogiques, University of Nancy: CRAPEL.
Gremmo, M., H. Holec, and P. Riley. 1978. 'Taking the initiative: some pedagogical applications of discourse analysis'. Melanges Pedagogiques, University of Nancy: CRAPEL.
Griffiths, R. 1990. 'Speech rate and NNS comprehension: a preliminary study in time-benefit analysis'. *Language Learning* 40: 311–36.
Griffiths, R. 1991a. 'Pausological research in an L2 context: a rationale and review of selected studies'. *Applied Linguistics* 12: 345–64.
Griffiths, R. 1991b. 'Personality and second-language learning: theory, research and practice' in Sadtano (ed.) 1991.
Griffiths, R. and R. Sheen. 1992. 'Disembedded figures in the landscape: a reappraisal of L2 research on field dependence/independence'. *Applied Linguistics* 13: 133–48.
Gudykunst, W. and S. Ting-Toomey. 1990. 'Ethnic identity, language and communication breakdowns' in Giles and Robinson (eds.) 1990.
Guiora, A., W. Acton, R. Erard, and F. Strickland. 1980. 'The effects of benzodiazepine (valium) on permeability of language ego boundaries'. *Language Learning* 30: 351–63.
Guiora, A., B. Beit-Hallahmi, R. Brannon, C. Dull, and T. Scovel. 1972. 'The effects of experimentally induced changes in ego states on pronunciation ability in a second language: an exploratory study'. *Comprehensive Psychiatry* 13: 421–8.
Guiora, A., H. Lane, and L. Bosworth. 1967. 'An explanation of some personality variables in authentic pronunciation in a second language' in Lane and Zale (eds.) 1967.
Gumperz, J. 1982a. *Discourse strategies*. Cambridge: Cambridge University Press.
Gumperz, J. (ed.). 1982b. *Language and Social Identity*. Cambridge: Cambridge University Press.
Gundel, J. and E. Tarone. 1983. 'Language transfer and the acquisition of pronominal anaphora' in Gass and Selinker (eds.) 1983.
Guy, G. 1988. 'Language and social class' in Neymeyer (ed.) 1988.

Haastrup, K. 1987. 'Using thinking aloud and retrospection to uncover learner's lexical inferencing procedures' in Færch and Kasper (eds.) 1987.
Hakansson, G. 1986. 'Quantitative studies of teacher talk' in Kasper (ed.) 1986.
Hakansson, G. and I. Lindberg. 1988. 'What's the question? Investigating second language classrooms' in Kasper (ed.) 1988.
Hakuta, K. 1974. 'A preliminary report on the development of grammatical morphemes in a Japanese girl learning English as a second language'. *Working Papers on Bilingualism* 3: 18–43.
Hakuta, K. 1976. 'A case study of a Japanese child learning English as a second language'. *Language Learning* 26: 321–51.
Hakuta, K. and E. Cancino. 1977. 'Trends in second language acquisition research'. *Harvard Educational Review* 47: 294–316.
Hale, T. and E. Budar. 1970. 'Are TESOL classes the only answer?' *Modern Language Journal* 54: 487–92.
Hall, B. and W. Gudykunst. 1986. 'The intergroup theory of second language ability'. *Journal of Language and Social Psychology* 5: 291–302.
Halliday, M. 1973. *Explorations in the Functions of Language*. London: Edward Arnold.

Halliday, M. 1978. *Language as a Social Semiotic*. London: Edward Arnold.

Hamayan, E. and **R. Tucker.** 1980. 'Language input in the bilingual classroom and its relations to second language achievement'. *TESOL Quarterly* 14: 453–68.

Hammarberg, B. 1973. 'The insufficiency of error analysis' in Svartvik (ed.) 1973a.

Hammarberg, B. 1979. 'On intralingual, interlingual and developmental solutions in inter-language' in Hyltenstam and Linnarud (eds.) 1979.

Hammerley, H. 1975. 'The deduction induction controversy'. *Modern Language Journal* 59: 15–18.

Hammerley, H. 1987. 'The immersion approach: litmus test of second language acquisition through classroom communication'. *Modern Language Journal* 71: 395–401.

Hammerley, H. 1989. *French Immersion: Myths and Reality*. Calgary, Alberta: Detselig Enterprises.

Hammond, R. 1988. 'Accuracy versus communicative competency: the acquisition of grammar in the second language classroom'. *Hispania* 71: 408–17.

Hanania, E. and **H. Gradman.** 1977. 'Acquisition of English structures: a case study of an adult native speaker of Arabic in an English-speaking environment'. *Language Learning* 27: 75–91.

Handscombe, J., R. Orem, and **B. Taylor** (eds.). 1984. *On TESOL '83: The Question of Control*. Washington D.C.: TESOL.

Hansen, J. and **C. Stansfield.** 1981. 'The relationship of field dependent–independent cognitive styles to foreign language achievement'. *Language Learning* 31: 349–67.

Hansen, L. 1984. 'Field dependence–independence and language testing: evidence from six Pacific island cultures'. *TESOL Quarterly* 18: 311–24.

Hansen-Strain, L. and **J. Strain.** 1989. 'Variation in the relative clause of Japanese learners'. *JALT Journal* 11: 211–37.

Harder, P. 1980. 'Discourse as self-expression—on the reduced personality of the second language learner'. *Applied Linguistics* 1: 262–70.

Harkness, S. 1977. 'Aspects of social environment and first language acquisition in rural Africa' in Snow and Ferguson (eds.) 1977.

Harley, B. 1986. *Age in Second Language Acquisition*. Clevedon, Avon: Multilingual Matters.

Harley, B. 1988. 'Accounting for patterns of lexical development in a classroom L2 environment'. Paper prepared for proceedings of Explaining Interlanguage Development Conference held in Melbourne, August 1987.

Harley, B. 1989. 'Functional grammar in French immersion: a classroom experiment'. *Applied Linguistics* 19: 331–59.

Harley, B., P. Allen, J. Cummins, and **M. Swain** (eds.). 1987. *The Development of Bilingual Proficiency: Final Report, Vol III: Social Context and Age*. Toronto: Modern Languages Center, IOSE.

Harley, B., P. Allen, J. Cummins, and **M. Swain** (eds.). 1990. *The Development of Second Language Proficiency*. Cambridge: Cambridge University Press.

Harley, B. and **M. Swain.** 1978. 'An analysis of the verb system by young learners of French'. *Interlanguage Studies Bulletin* 3: 35–79.

Harrington, M. 1987. 'Processing transfer: language-specific processing strategies as a source of interlanguage variation'. *Applied Psycholinguistics* 8: 351–77.

Hartnett, D. 1985. 'Cognitive style and second language learning' in Celce-Murcia (ed.) 1985.

Hatch, E. 1974. 'Second language learning—universals?' *Working Papers on Bilingualism* 3: 1–17.

Hatch, E. (ed.). 1978a. *Second Language Acquisition*. Rowley, Mass.: Newbury House.

Hatch, E. 1978b. 'Discourse analysis and second language acquisition' in Hatch (ed.) 1978a.

Hatch, E. 1978c. 'Discourse analysis, speech acts and second language acquisition' in Ritchie (ed.) 1978a.

Hatch, E. 1978d. 'Acquisition of syntax in a second language' in Richards (ed.) 1978.

Hatch, E. 1978e. 'Apply with caution'. *Studies in Second Language Acquisition* 2: 123–43.

Hatch, E. 1980. 'Second language acquisition—avoiding the question' in Felix (ed.) 1980a.

Hatch, E. 1983a. *Psycholinguistics: A Second Language Perspective*. Rowley, Mass.: Newbury House.

Hatch, E. 1983b. 'Simplified input and second language acquisition' in Andersen (ed.) 1983c.

Hatch, E. 1992. *Discourse and Language Education*. Cambridge: Cambridge University Press.

Hatch, E. and H. Farhady. 1982. *Research Design and Statistics for Applied Linguistics*. Rowley, Mass.: Newbury House.

Hatch, E. and A. Lazaraton. 1991. *The Research Manual: Design and Statistics for Applied Linguistics*. New York: Newbury House/Harper Collins.

Hatch, E. and M. Long. 1980. 'Discourse analysis, what's that?' in Larsen-Freeman (ed.) 1980.

Hatch, E., S. Peck, and J. Wagner-Gough. 1979. 'A look at process in child second language acquisition' in Ochs and Schieffelin (eds.) 1979.

Hatch, E., R. Shapira, and J. Wagner-Gough. 1978. 'Foreigner talk discourse'. *ITL Review of Applied Linguistics* 39/40: 39–60.

Hatch, E., Y. Shirai, and C. Fantuzzi. 1990. 'The need for an integrated theory: connecting modules'. *TESOL Quarterly* 24: 697–716.

Hatch, E. and J. Wagner-Gough. 1976. 'Explaining sequence and variation in second language acquisition'. *Language Learning, Special Issue* 4: 39–47.

Haugen, E. 1956. *Bilingualism in the Americas*. The American Dialect Society.

Hauptman, P. 1970. 'An experimental comparison of a structural approach and a situational approach to foreign language teaching'. Unpublished PhD thesis. Ann Arbor: University of Michigan.

Hawkins, B. 1985. 'Is the appropriate response always so appropriate?' in Gass and Madden (eds.) 1985.

Hawkins, J. 1983. *Word Order Universals*. New York: Academic Press.

Hawkins, R. 1987. 'Markedness and the acquisition of the English dative alternation by L2 learners'. *Second Language Research* 3: 20–55.

Hawkins, R. 1988. 'Comparing the effect of aural and written presentation of foreign language material on learners' memory for that material'. Unpublished paper, University of Sheffield.

Hawkins, R. 1989. 'Do second language learners acquire restrictive relative clauses on the basis of relational or configurational information? The acquisition of French subject, direct object and genitive restrictive relative clauses by second language learners'. *Second Language Research* 5: 158–88.

Hayes, J. (ed.). 1970. *Cognition and the Development of Language*. New York: Wiley and Sons.

Heath, S. 1983. *Ways with Words: Language, Life and Work in Communities and Classrooms*. Cambridge: Cambridge University Press.

Heidelberger Forschungsprojekt 'Pidgin Deutsch'. 1978. 'The acquisition of German syntax by foreign migrant workers' in Sankoff (ed.) 1978.

Hendrickson, J. 1978. 'Error correction in foreign language teaching: recent theory, research, and practice'. *Modern Language Journal* 62: 387–98.

Henning, C. (ed.). 1977. Proceedings of the Los Angeles Second Language Research Forum. University of California at Los Angeles.

Henzl, V. 1973. 'Linguistic register of foreign language instruction'. *Language Learning* 23: 207–27.

Henzl, V. 1979. 'Foreigner talk in the classroom'. *International Review of Applied Linguistics* 17: 159–65.

Herbert, R. 1989. 'The ethnography of compliments' in Oleksy (ed.) 1989.

Hermann, G. 1980. 'Attitudes and success in children's learning of English as a second language: the motivational vs. the resultative hypothesis'. *English Language Teaching Journal* 34: 247–54.

Heyde, A. 1979. 'The relationship between self-esteem and oral production of a second language'. Unpublished PhD thesis, Ann Arbor: University of Michigan. Cited in Larsen-Freeman and Long (eds.) 1991.

Higgs, T. (ed.). 1982. *Curriculum, Competence and the Foreign Language Teacher*. Skokie, Ilinois: National Textbook Company.

Higgs, T. and **R. Clifford.** 1982. 'The push toward communication' in Higgs (ed.) 1982.

Hilles, S. 1986. 'Interlanguage and the pro-drop parameter'. *Second Language Research* 2: 33–52.

Hilles, S. 1991. 'Access to Universal Grammar in second language acquisition' in Eubank (ed.) 1991b.

Hinde, R. (ed.). 1972. *Non-verbal Communication*. Cambridge: Cambridge University Press.

Hines, M. and **W. Rutherford** (eds.). 1981. *On TESOL '81*. Washington D.C.: TESOL.

Hirakawa, M. 1989. 'A study of the L2 acquisition of English reflexives'. *Second Language Research* 6: 60–85.

Hirvonen, T. 1985. 'Children's foreigner talk: peer talk in play context' in Gass and Madden (eds.) 1985.

Holec, H. 1980. 'Learner training: meeting needs in self-directed learning' in Altman and Vaughan James (eds.) 1980.

Holec, H. 1987. 'The learner as manager: managing learning or managing to learn?' in Wenden and Rubin (eds.) 1987.

Holmen, A. 1985. 'Analysis of some discourse areas in the PIF data and in classroom interaction' in Glahn and Holmen (eds.) 1985.

Holmes, J. 1986. 'Compliments and compliment responses in New Zealand English'. *Anthropological Linguistics* 28: 485–508.

Holmes, J. 1988. 'Paying compliments: a sex-preferential positive politeness strategy'. *Journal of Pragmatics* 12: 445–65.

Holobrow, N., F. Genesee, and **W. Lambert.** 1991. 'The effectiveness of a foreign language immersion program for children from different ethnic and social class backgrounds: Report 2'. *Applied Psycholinguistics* 12: 179–98.

Holobrow, N., W. Lambert, and **L. Sayegh.** 1984. 'Pairing script and dialogue: combinations that show promise for second language learning'. *Language Learning* 34: 59–76.

Hornstein, N. and **D. Lightfoot** (eds.). 1981. *Explanation in Linguistics: the Logical Problem of Language Acquisition*. London: Longman.

Horwitz, E. 1986. 'Preliminary evidence for the reliability and validity of a foreign language anxiety scale'. *TESOL Quarterly* 20: 559–62.

Horwitz, E. 1987a. 'Surveying student beliefs about language learning' in Wenden and Rubin (eds.) 1987.

Horwitz, E. 1987b. 'Linguistic and communicative competence: reassessing foreign language aptitude' in VanPatten et al. (eds.) 1987.

Horwitz, E., M. Horwitz, and **J. Cope.** 1986. 'Foreign language classroom anxiety'. *Modern Language Journal* 70; 125–32.

Horwitz, E. and **D. Young.** 1991. *Language Learning Anxiety: from Theory and Research to Classroom Implications*. Englewood Cliffs, N.J.: Prentice Hall.

Hosenfeld, C. 1978. 'Students' mini-theories of second language learning'. *Association Bulletin* 29: 2.

Hosenfeld, C. 1979. 'Cindy: a learner in today's foreign language classroom' in Born (ed.) 1979.

House, J. 1986. 'Learning to talk: talking to learn. An investigation of learner performance in two types of discourse' in Kasper (ed.) 1986.

House, J. and **G. Kasper.** 1987. 'Interlanguage pragmatics: requesting in a foreign language' in Lörscher and Schultze (eds.) 1987.

Huang, J. 1970. 'A Chinese child's acquisition of syntax'. Unpublished MA TESL thesis, University of California at Los Angeles.

Huang, J. and E. Hatch. 1978. 'A Chinese child's acquisition of English' in Hatch (ed.) 1978a.

Huang, X. and M. Van Naerssen. 1985. 'Learning strategies for oral communication'. *Applied Linguistics* 6: 287–307.

Huebner, T. 1979. 'Order-of-acquisition vs. dynamic paradigm: a comparison of method in interlanguage research'. *TESOL Quarterly* 13: 21–8.

Huebner, T. 1980. 'Creative construction and the case of the misguided pattern' in Fisher et al. (eds.) 1980.

Huebner, T. 1983. *A Longitudinal Analysis of the Acquisition of English*. Ann Arbor: Karoma Publishers.

Huebner, T. 1985. 'System and variability in interlanguage syntax'. *Language Learning* 35: 141–63.

Huebner, T. and C. Ferguson (eds.). 1991. *Crosscurrents in Second Language Acquisition and Linguistic Theories*. Amsterdam: John Benjamins.

Hughes, A. and C. Lascaratou. 1982. 'Competing criteria for error gravity'. *English Language Teaching Journal* 36: 175–82.

Hulstijn, J. 1987. 'Onset and development of grammatical features: two approaches to acquisition orders'. Paper given at Interlanguage Conference, Trobe University, Melbourne.

Hulstijn, J. 1989a. 'A cognitive view of interlanguage variability' in Eisenstein (ed.) 1989.

Hulstijn, J. 1989b. 'Implicit and incidental second language learning: experiments in the processing of natural and partly artificial input' in Dechert and Raupach (eds.) 1989b.

Hulstijn, J. 1990. 'A comparison between the information-processing and the analysis/control approaches to language learning'. *Applied Linguistics* 11: 30–45.

Hulstijn, J. and W. Hulstijn. 1984. 'Grammatical errors as a function of processing constraints and explicit knowledge'. *Language Learning* 34: 23–43.

Hulstijn, J. and E. Marchena. 1989. 'Avoidance: Grammatical or semantic causes'. *Studies in Second Language Acquisition* 11: 242–55.

Hyams, N. 1983. 'The acquisition of parameterized grammars'. Unpublished PhD thesis, City University of New York.

Hyams, N. 1991. 'Seven not-so-trivial trivia of language acquisition: comments on Wolfgang Klein' in Eubank (ed.) 1991b.

Hyltenstam, K. 1977. 'Implicational patterns in interlanguage syntax variation'. *Language Learning* 27: 383–411.

Hyltenstam, K. 1984. 'The use of typological markedness conditions as predictors in second language acquisition: the case of pronominal copies in relative clauses' in Andersen (ed.) 1984b.

Hyltenstam, K. 1985. 'L2 learners' variable output and language teaching' in Hyltenstam and Pienemann (eds.) 1985.

Hyltenstam, K. 1990. 'Typological markedness as a research tool in the study of second language acquisition' in Dechert (ed.) 1990.

Hyltenstam, K. and M. Linnarud (eds.). 1979. Interlanguage Workshop at the Fifth Scandinavian Conference of Linguistics.

Hyltenstam, K. and L. Obler (eds.). 1989. *Bilingualism Across the Lifespan: Aspects of Acquisition, Maturity and Loss*. Cambridge: Cambridge University Press.

Hyltenstam, K. and M. Pienemann (eds.). 1985. *Modelling and Assessing Second Language Acquisition*. Clevedon, Avon: Multilingual Matters.

Hymes, D. 1971a. *On Communicative Competence*. Philadelphia, P.A.: University of Pennsylvania Press.

Hymes, D. (ed.). 1971b. *Pidginization and Creolization of Languages*. Cambridge: Cambridge University Press.

Ioup, G. 1977. 'Interference versus structural complexity as a predictor of second language relative clause acquisition' in Henning (ed.) 1977.

Ioup, G. 1989. 'Immigrant children who have failed to acquire native English' in Gass et al. (eds.) 1989b.

Ioup, G. and S. Weinberger (eds.). 1987. *Interlanguage Phonology: the Acquisition of a Second Language Sound System*. Rowley, Mass.: Newbury House.

Issidorides, D. and J. Hulstijn. 1992. 'Comprehension of grammatically modified and nonmodified sentences by second language learners'. *Applied Psycholinguistics* 13: 147–71.

Itoh, H. and E. Hatch. 1978. 'Second language acquisition: a case study' in Hatch (ed.) 1978a.

Jackson, H. 1981. 'Contrastive analysis as a predictor of errors, with reference to Punjabi learners of English' in Fisiak (ed.) 1981b.

Jackson, K. and R. Whitnam. 1971. 'Evaluation of the Predictive Power of Contrastive Analyses of Japanese and English'. Final report; Contract No. CEC–0–70–5046 (–823), US Office of Health, Education and Welfare.

Jaeggli, O. and N. Hyams. 1988. 'Morphological uniformity and the setting of the null subject parameter' in *Proceedings of the Northeastern Linguistics Society* 18, University of Massachusetts at Amherst: Graduate Linguistics Students Association.

Jain, M. 1974. 'Error analysis: Source, cause and significance' in Richards (ed.) 1974.

Jakobovits, L. 1970. *Foreign Language Learning: a Psycholinguistic Analysis of the Issue*. Rowley, Mass.: Newbury House.

James, C. 1971. 'The exculpation of contrastive linguistics' in Nickel (ed.) 1971.

James, C. 1977. 'Judgments of error gravity'. *English Language Teaching Journal* 31: 116–24.

James, C. 1980. *Contrastive Analysis*. London: Longman.

James, C. 1990. 'Learner Language'. *Language Teaching Abstracts* 23: 205–13.

Janicki, K. 1985. *The Foreigner's Language: a Sociolinguistic Perspective*. Oxford: Pergamon.

Jarvis G. 1968. 'A behavioral observation system for classroom foreign language learning'. *Modern Language Journal* 52: 335–41.

Johansson, S. 1973. 'The identification and evaluation of errors in foreign languages: a functional approach' in Svartvik (ed.) 1973a.

Johnson, D. 1992. *Approaches to Research in Second Language Learning*. New York: Longman.

Johnson, K. 1988. 'Mistake correction'. *English Language Teaching Journal* 42: 89–96.

Johnson, L. and E. Newport. 1989. 'Critical period effects in second language learning: the influence of maturational state on the acquisition of English as a second language'. *Cognitive Psychology* 21: 60–99.

Johnson, P. 1981. 'Effects on reading comprehension of language complexity and cultural background of a text'. *TESOL Quarterly* 15: 169–81.

Johnston, M. 1985. 'Syntactic and morphological progressions in learner English'. Research report, Department of Immigration and Ethnic Affairs, Commonwealth of Australia.

Johnston, M. 1986. 'Second language acquisition research in the adult migrant education program' in Johnston and Pienemann.

Johnston, M. and M. Pienemann. 1986. *Second Language Acquisition: a Classroom Perspective*. New South Wales Migrant Education Service.

Johnston, S. 1990. 'Teacher questions in the academic language-content classroom'. Unpublished paper, Tokyo: Temple University Japan.

Jones, A. 1991a. 'Review of studies on the acquisition of relative clauses in English'. Unpublished paper, Tokyo: Temple University Japan.

Jones, A. 1991b. 'Learning to walk before you can run'. Unpublished paper, Tokyo: Temple University Japan.

Jones, A. 1992. 'Relatively speaking'. Unpublished paper, Temple University Tokyo.

Jones, F. 1991. 'Classroom riot: design features, language output and topic in simulations and other communicative free-stage activities'. *System* 19: 151–69.

Jordens, P. 1980. 'Interlanguage research: interpretation and explanation'. *Language Learning* 30: 195–207.

Jordens, P. 1988. 'The acquisition of word order in L2 Dutch and German' in Jordens and Lalleman (eds.) 1988.

Jordens, P. and **J. Halleman** (eds.). 1988. *Language Development*. Dordrecht: Foris.

Judd, E. 1978. 'Language policy and TESOL: socio-political factors and their influences on the profession' in Blatchford and Schachter (eds.) 1978.

Kachru, B. 1981. 'The pragmatics of non-native varieties of English' in Smith (ed.) 1981.

Kachru, B. 1982. *The Other Tongue: English Across Cultures*. Urbana Illinois: University of Illinois Press.

Kachru, B. 1986. *The Alchemy of English*. Oxford: Pergamon.

Kachru, B. 1989. 'Teaching World Englishes'. *Cross Currents* 16: 15–21.

Kadia, K. 1988. 'The effect of formal instruction on monitored and spontaneous naturalistic interlanguage performance'. *TESOL Quarterly* 22: 509–15.

Kamimoto, T., A. Shimura, and **E. Kellerman.** 1992. 'A second language classic reconsidered—the case of Schachter's avoidance'. *Second Language Research* 8: 231–77.

Kaneko, T. 1991. 'The role of the L1 in second language classrooms'. Unpublished EdD thesis. Tokyo: Temple University Japan.

Karmiloff-Smith, A. 1986. 'From metaprocess to conscious access: evidence from children's metalinguistic and repair data'. *Cognition* 28: 95–147.

Kasper, G. 1981. *Pragmatische Aspeckte in der Interimsprache*. Tübingen: Gunter Narr.

Kasper, G. 1984a. 'Pragmatic comprehension in learner-native speaker discourse'. *Language Learning* 34: 1–20.

Kasper, G. 1984b. 'Perspectives on language transfer'. *BAAL Newsletter* 24.

Kasper, G. 1985. 'Repair in foreign language teaching'. *Studies in Second Language Acquisition* 7: 200–15.

Kasper, G. (ed.). 1986. *Learning, Teaching and Communication in the Foreign Language Classroom*. Aarhus: Aarhus University Press.

Kasper, G. 1989. 'Variation in speech act realisation' in Phillipson et al. (eds.) 1991.

Kasper, G. 1990. 'Linguistic politeness: current research issues'. *Journal of Pragmatics* 14: 193–218.

Kasper, G. 1992. 'Pragmatic transfer'. *Second Language Research* 8: 203–31.

Kasper, G. (ed.). 1988. 'Classroom Research'. *AILA Review* 5: 73–88.

Kasper, G. and **M. Dahl.** 1991. 'Research methods in interlanguage pragmatics'. *Studies in Second Language Acquisition* 12: 215–47.

Kearsley, G. 1976. 'Questions and question-asking in verbal discourse: a cross-disciplinary review'. *Journal of Pyscholinguistic Research* 5: 355–75.

Keefe. J. 1979a. 'Learning style: an overview' in Keefe (ed.) 1979b.

Keefe, J. (ed.). 1979b. *Student Learning Styles: Diagnosing and Describing Programs*. Reston V.A.: National Secondary School Principals.

Keenan, E. 1974. 'Conversational competence in children'. *Journal of Child Language* 1: 163–83.

Keenan, E. 1975. 'Variation in universal grammar' in Fasold and Shuy (eds.) 1975.

Keenan, E. and **B. Comrie.** 1977. 'Noun phrase accessibility and universal grammar'. *Linguistic Inquiry* 8: 63–99.

Kelch, K. 1985. 'Modified input as an aid to comprehension'. *Studies in Second Language Acquisition* 7: 81–90.

Keller, J. 1984. 'Motivational design of instruction' in Reigeluth (ed.) 1984.

Kellerman, E. 1977. 'Towards a characterization of the strategies of transfer in second language learning'. *Interlanguage Studies Bulletin* 2: 58–145.

Kellerman, E. 1978. 'Giving learners a break: native language intuitions as a source of predictions about transferability'. *Working Papers on Bilingualism* 15: 59–92.

Kellerman, E. 1979. 'Transfer and non-transfer: where are we now?' *Studies in Second Language Acquisition* 2: 37–57.

Kellerman, E. 1983. 'Now you see it, now you don't' in Gass and Selinker (eds.) 1983.

Kellerman, E. 1985a. 'If at first you do succeed ...' in Gass and Madden (eds.) 1985.

Kellerman, E. 1985b. 'Dative alternation and the analysis of data: a reply to Mazurkewich'. *Language Learning* 35: 91–106.

Kellerman, E. 1986. 'An eye for an eye: crosslinguistic constraints on the development of the L2 lexicon' in Kellerman and Sharwood Smith (eds.) 1986.

Kellerman, E. 1987. *Aspects of transferability in second language acquisition. Chapter 1: Cross-linguistic influence: a review.* Unpublished manuscript, University of Nijmegen.

Kellerman, E. 1989. 'The imperfect conditional' in Hyltenstam and Obler (eds.) 1989.

Kellerman, E. 1991. 'Compensatory strategies in second language research: a critique, a revision, and some (non-) implications for the classroom' in Phillipson et al. (eds.) 1991.

Kellerman, E. 1992. 'Another look at an old classic; Schachter's avoidance'. Lecture notes, Tokyo: Temple University Japan.

Kellerman, E., A. Amerlaan, T. Bongaerts, and N. Poulisse. 1990. 'System and hierarchy in L2 compensatory strategies' in Scarcella et al. (eds.) 1990.

Kellerman, E., T. Bongaerts, and N. Poulisse. 1987. 'Strategy and system in L2 referential communication' in Ellis (ed.) 1987a.

Kellerman, E. and M. Sharwood Smith. (eds.). 1986. *Cross-linguistic Influence in Second Language Acquisition.* Oxford: Pergamon.

Kelley, P. 1982. 'Interlanguage, variation and social/psychological influences within a developmental stage'. Unpublished MA in TESL thesis, University of California at Los Angeles.

Ketterman, B. and R. St. Clair (eds.). 1980. *New Approaches to Language Acquisition.* Heidelberg: Julius Groos.

Khalil, A. 1985. 'Communicative error evaluations: native speakers' evaluation and interpretation of written errors of Arab EFL learners'. *TESOL Quarterly* 19: 225–351.

Kilborn, K. 1987. 'Sentence processing in a second language: seeking a performance definition of fluency'. Unpublished thesis, University of California, San Diego.

Kilborn, K. and A. Cooremann. 1987. 'Sentence interpretation strategies in adult Dutch-English bilinguals'. *Applied Psycholinguistics* 8: 415–31.

Kilborn, K. and T. Ito. 1989. 'Sentence processing strategies in adult bilinguals' in MacWhinney and Bates (eds.) 1989.

Kinsella, V. (ed.). 1982. *Surveys 1: Eight State-of-the-art Articles on Key Areas in Language Teaching.* Cambridge: Cambridge University Press.

Klaus, G. and M. Buhr (eds.). 1976. *Philosophisches Wörterbuch.* Leipzig: VEB Bibliographisches Institut. Cited in Færch and Kasper 1983.

Kleifgen, J. 1985. 'Skilled variation in a kindergarten teacher's use of foreigner talk' in Gass and Madden (eds.) 1985.

Klein, W. 1981. 'Some rules of regular ellipsis in German' in Klein and Levelt (eds.). 1981

Klein, W. 1986. *Second Language Acquisition.* Cambridge: Cambridge University Press.

Klein, W. 1990. 'A theory of language acquisition is not so easy'. *Studies in Second Language Acquisition* 12: 219–31.

Klein, W. 1991. 'Seven trivia of language acquisition.' in Eubank (ed.) 1991b.

Klein, W. and N. Dittmar. 1979. *Developing Grammars: the Acquisition of German Syntax by Foreign Workers.* Berlin: Springer.

Klein, W. and W. Levelt (eds.). 1981. *Crossing the Boundaries of Linguistics: Studies Presented to Manfred Bierswisch.* Dordrecht: Reidel.

Klein, W. and C. Perdue. 1989. 'The learner's problem in arranging words' in. MacWhinney and Bates (eds.) 1989.

Klein, W. and B. Rieck. 1982. 'Der Erwerb der Personalpronomina im ungesteuerten Spracherwerb'. *Zeitschrift fur Literaturwissenschaft und Linguistik* 45: 35–71. Cited in Klein 1986.

Kleinmann, H. 1978. 'The strategy of avoidance in adult second language acquisition' in Ritchie (ed.) 1978a.

Klima, E. and V. Bellugi. 1966. 'Syntactic regularities in the speech of children' in Lyons and Wales (eds.) 1966.

Koivukari, A. 1987. 'Question level and cognitive processing: pyscholinguistic dimensions of questions and answers'. *Applied Psycholinguistics* 8: 101–20.

Kramarae, C. 1990. 'Changing the complexion of gender in language research' in Giles and Robinson (eds.) 1990.

Kramer, A. 1980. 'The languages of linguistic theory: aesthetic dimensions of a scientific discipline'. Unpublished doctoral thesis, University of Michigan. Cited in Schumann 1983.

Kramsch, C. 1985. 'Classroom interaction and discourse options'. *Studies in Second Language Acquisition* 7: 169–83.

Kramsch, C. and S. McConnell-Ginet (eds.). 1992. *Text and Context: Cross-Disciplinary Perspectives on Language Study.* Lexington, Mass.: D. C. Heath and Company.

Krashen, S. 1973. 'Lateralization, language learning and the critical period: some new evidence'. *Language Learning* 23: 63–74.

Krashen, S. 1976. 'Formal and informal linguistic environments in language acquisition and language learning'. *TESOL Quarterly* 10: 157–68.

Krashen, S. 1977. 'Some issues relating to the Monitor Model' in H. Brown et al. (eds.) 1977.

Krashen, S. 1978. 'Individual variation in the use of the monitor' in Ritchie (ed.) 1978a.

Krashen, S. 1980. 'The theoretical and practical relevance of simple codes in second language acquisition' in Scarcella and Krashen (eds.) 1980.

Krashen, S. 1981. *Second Language Acquisition and Second Language Learning.* Oxford: Pergamon.

Krashen, S. 1982. *Principles and Practice in Second Language Acquisition.* Oxford: Pergamon.

Krashen, S. 1983. 'Newmark's ignorance hypothesis and current second language acquisition theory' in Gass and Selinker (eds.) 1983.

Krashen, S. 1985. *The Input Hypothesis: Issues and Implications.* London: Longman.

Krashen, S. 1989. 'We acquire vocabulary and spelling by reading: additional evidence for the input hypothesis'. *Modern Language Journal* 73: 440–64.

Krashen, S., J. Butler, R. Birnbaum, and J. Robertson. 1978. 'Two studies in language acquisition and language learning'. *ITL: Review of Applied Linguistics* 39/40: 73–92.

Krashen, S., C. Jones, S. Zelinksi, and C. Usprich. 1978. 'How important is instruction?' *English Language Teaching Journal* 32: 257–61.

Krashen, S., M. Long, and R. Scarcella. 1979. 'Age, rate and eventual attainment in second language acquisition'. *TESOL Quarterly* 13: 573–82. Reprinted in Krashen et al. (eds.) 1982.

Krashen, S., M. Long, and R. Scarcella (eds.). 1982. *Child–adult Differences in Second Language Acquisition.* Rowley, Mass.: Newbury House.

Krashen, S. and R. Scarcella. 1978. 'On routines and patterns in second language acquisition and performance'. *Language Learning* 28: 283–300.

Krashen, S. and H. Seliger. 1975. 'The essential characteristics of formal instruction'. *TESOL Quarterly* 9: 173–83.

Krashen, S. and H. Seliger. 1976. 'The role of formal and informal linguistic environments in adult second language learning'. *International Journal of Psycholinguistics* 3: 15–21.

Krashen, S., H. Seliger, and D. Hartnett. 1974. 'Two studies in second language learning'. *Kritikon Litterarum* 3: 220–8.

Krashen, S. and T. Terrell. 1983. *The Natural Approach: Language Acquisition in the Classroom.* Oxford: Pergamon.

Kruidenier, B. and R. Clement. 1986. 'The effect of context on the composition and role of orientations in second language acquisition'. Quebec: International Centre for Research on Bilingualism.

Kucczaj, S. 1977. 'Old and new forms, old and new meanings: the form–function hypothesis revisited'. Paper presented at the Society for Research in Child Development, New Orleans.

Kumpf, L. 1984. 'Temporal systems and universality in interlanguage: a case study' in Eckman et al. (eds.) 1984.

Labov, W. 1969a. 'Contraction, deletion, and inherent variability of the English copula'. *Language* 45: 715–52.

Labov, W. 1969b. 'The Logic of Non-standard English'. *Georgetown Monographs on Language and Linguistics* 22. Washington D.C.: Georgetown University, Center for Applied Linguistics.

Labov, W. 1970. 'The study of language in its social context'. *Studium Generale* 23: 30–87.

Labov, W. 1972. *Sociolinguistic Patterns*. Philadelphia, P.A.: University of Pennsylvania Press.

Labov, W. 1991. 'The intersection of sex and social class in the course of linguistic change'. *Language Variation and Linguistic Change* 2: 205–51.

Lado, R. 1957. *Linguistics Across Cultures: Applied Linguistics for Language Teachers*. Ann Arbor, Michigan: University of Michigan.

Lakshmanan, U. 1986. 'The role of parametric variation in adult second language acquisition: a study of the "pro-drop" parameter'. Papers in Applied Linguistics—Michigan 2: 97–117.

Lakshmanan, U. 1991. 'Morphological uniformity and null subjects in child second language acquisition' in Eubank (ed.) 1991b.

Lalonde, R. and R. Gardner. 1985. 'On the predictive validity of the Attitude/Motivation Test Battery'. *Journal of Multilingual and Multicultural Development* 6: 403–12.

Lambert, W. 1974. 'Culture and language as factors in learning and education' in F. Aboud and Meade (eds.) 1974.

Lambert, W. and G. Tucker. 1972. *The Bilingual Education of Children: the St. Lambert Experiment*. Rowley, Mass.: Newbury House.

Lambert, W., R. Hodgson, R. Gardner, and S. Fillenbaum. 1960. 'Evaluational reactions to spoken languages'. *Journal of Abnormal and Social Psychology* 60: 44–51.

Lane, H. and E. Zale (eds.). 1967. *Studies in Language and Language Behaviour, 4.*

Langacker, R. 1987. *Foundations of Cognitive Grammar*. Stanford, California: Stanford University Press.

Lange, D. 1979. 'Negation in natürlichen Englisch–Deutschen Zweitsprachenerwerb: eine Fallstudie'. *International Review of Applied Linguistics* 17: 331–48.

Lanoue, G. 1991. 'Language loss, language gain: cultural camouflage and social change among the Sekani of Northern British Columbia'. *Language in Society* 20: 87–115.

Lantolf, J. and A. Labarca (eds.). 1987. *Research in Second Language Learning: Focus on the Classroom*. Norwood, N.J.: Ablex.

Larsen-Freeman, D. 1975. 'The acquisition of grammatical morphemes by adult ESL students'. *TESOL Quarterly* 9: 409–30.

Larsen-Freeman, D. 1976a. 'Teacher speech as input to the ESL learner'. University of California. *Working Papers in TESL* 10: 45–9.

Larsen-Freeman, D. 1976b. 'An explanation for the morpheme acquisition order of second language learners'. *Language Learning* 26: 125–34.

Larsen-Freeman, D. 1978. 'An ESL index of development'. *TESOL Quarterly* 12: 439–48.

Larsen-Freeman, D. (ed.) 1980. *Discourse Analysis in Second Language Research*. Rowley, Mass.: Newbury House.

Larsen-Freeman, D. 1983. 'The importance of input in second language acquisition' in Andersen (ed.) 1983c.

Larsen-Freeman, D. 1991. 'Second language acquisition research: staking out the territory'. *TESOL Quarterly* 25: 315–50.

Larsen-Freeman, D. and M. Long. 1991. *An Introduction to Second Language Acquisition Research*. London: Longman.

Laudan, L. 1990. *Science and Relativism. Some Key Controversies in the Philosophy of Science.* Chicago: University of Chicago Press.

Leather, J. and **A. James.** 1991. 'The acquisition of second language speech'. *Studies in Second Language Acquisition* 13: 305–41.

Lee, W. 1957. 'The linguistic context of language learning'. *English Language Teaching Journal* 11: 77–85.

Lee, W. 1968. 'Thoughts on contrastive linguistics in the context of language teaching' in Alatis (ed.) 1968.

Leech, G. 1983. *Principles of Pragmatics.* London: Longman.

Legaretta, D. 1977. 'Language choice in bilingual classrooms'. *TESOL Quarterly* 11: 9–16.

Leino, A. 1982. 'Learning process in terms of styles and strategies'. *Research Bulletin* No. 59. Helsinki, Finland.

Lenneberg, E. 1967. *Biological Foundations of Language.* New York: Wiley and Sons.

Lennon, P. 1989. 'Introspection and intentionality in advanced second-language acquisition'. *Language Learning* 39: 375–95.

Lennon, P. 1991. 'Error: Some problems of definition, identification and distinction'. *Applied Linguistics* 12: 180–95.

Le Page, R. and **A. Tabouret-Keller.** 1985. *Acts of Identity: Creole-based Approaches to Language and Ethnicity.* Cambridge: Cambridge University Press.

Levelt, W. 1983. 'Monitoring and self-repair in speech'. *Cognition* 14: 41–104.

Levelt, W. 1989. *Speaking: From Intention to Articulation.* Cambridge: Cambridge University Press.

Levenston, E. 1971. 'Over-indulgence and under-representation: aspects of mother tongue interference' in Nickel (ed.) 1971.

Levenston, E. 1979. 'Second language lexical acquisition: issues and problems'. *Interlanguage Studies Bulletin* 4: 147–60.

Levinson, S. 1983. *Principles of Pragmatics.* Cambridge: Cambridge University Press.

Li, X. 1989. 'Effects of contextual cues on inferring and remembering meanings of new words'. *Applied Linguistics* 10: 402–13.

Liceras, J. 1985. 'The role of intake in the determination of learners' competence' in Gass and Madden (eds.) 1985.

Lightbown, P. 1980. 'The acquisition and use of questions by French L2 learners' in Felix (ed.) 1980a.

Lightbown, P. 1983. 'Exploring relationships between developmental and instructional sequences in L2 acquisition' in Seliger and Long (eds.) 1983.

Lightbown, P. 1984. 'The relationship between theory and method in second language acquisition research' in Davies et al. (eds.) 1984.

Lightbown, P. 1985a. 'Can language acquisition be altered by instruction?' in Hyltenstam and Pienemann (eds.) 1985.

Lightbown, P. 1985b. 'Great expectations: second-language acquisition research and classroom teaching'. *Applied Linguistics* 6: 173–89.

Lightbown, P. 1987. 'Classroom language as input to second language acquisition' in C. Pfaff (ed.) 1987b.

Lightbown, P. 1990. 'Process-product research on second language learning in classrooms' in Harley et al. (eds.) 1990.

Lightbown, P. 1991a. 'Getting quality input in the second/foreign language classroom' in Kramsch and McConnell-Ginet (eds.) 1991.

Lightbown, P. 1991b. 'What have we here? Some observations on the effect of instruction on L2 learning' in Phillipson et al. (eds.) 1991.

Lightbown, P. 1992. 'Can they do it themselves? A comprehension-based ESL course for young children' in Courchêne et al. (eds.) 1992.

Lightbown, P. and A. d'Anglejan. 1985. 'Some input considerations for word order in French L1 and L2 acquisition' in Gass and Madden (eds.) 1985.

Lightbown, P. and N. Spada. 1990. 'Focus-on-form and corrective feedback in communicative language teaching: effects on second language learning'. *Studies in Second Language Acquisition* 12: 429–48.

Lightbown, P. and N. Spada. 1993. *How Languages are Learned*. Oxford: Oxford University Press.

Lightbown, P., N. Spada, and R. Wallace. 1980. 'Some effects of instruction on child and adolescent ESL learners' in Scarcella and Krashen (eds.) 1980.

Lightbown, P. and L. White. 1987. 'The influence of linguistic theories on language acquisition research: description and explanation'. *Language Learning* 37: 483–510.

Little, D. and D. Singleton. 1990. 'Cognitive style and learning approach' in Duda and Riley (eds.) 1990.

Little, D., D. Singleton, and W. Silvius. 1984. *Learning Second Languages in Ireland: Experience, Attitudes and Needs*. Dublin: Trinity College, Centre for Language and Communication Studies. Cited in Little and Singleton 1990.

Lococo, V. 1976. 'A comparison of three methods for the collection of L2 data: free composition, translation and picture description'. *Working Papers on Bilingualism* 8: 59–86.

Long, M. 1977. 'Teacher feedback on learner error: mapping cognitions' in Brown et al. (eds.) 1977.

Long, M. 1980a. 'Input, interaction and second language acquisition'. Unpublished PhD thesis. University of California at Los Angeles.

Long, M. 1980b. 'Inside the "black box": methodological issues in classroom research on language learning'. *Language Learning* 30: 1–42.

Long, M. 1981a. 'Input, interaction and second language acquisition' in Winitz (ed.) 1981b.

Long, M. 1981b. 'Questions in foreigner talk discourse'. *Language Learning* 31: 135–57.

Long, M. 1983a. 'Native speaker/non-native speaker conversation and the negotiation of comprehensible input'. *Applied Linguistics* 4: 126–41.

Long, M. 1983b. 'Native speaker/non-native speaker conversation in the second language classroom' in Clarke and Handscombe (eds.) 1983.

Long, M. 1983c. 'Does second language instruction make a difference? A review of the research'. *TESOL Quarterly* 17: 359–82.

Long, M. 1984. 'Process and product in ESL program evaluation'. *TESOL Quarterly* 18: 409–25.

Long, M. 1985a. 'Input and second language acquisition theory' in Gass and Madden (eds.) 1985.

Long, M. 1985b. 'A role for instruction in second language acquisition: task-based language teaching' in Hyltenstam and Pienemann (eds.) 1985.

Long, M. 1985c. 'Bibliography of research on second language classroom processes and classroom second language acquisition'. *Technical Report* No. 2. Honolulu: Center for Second Language Classroom Research, Social Science Research Institute, University of Hawaii at Manoa.

Long, M. 1988. 'Instructed interlanguage development' in Beebe (ed.) 1988a.

Long, M. 1989. 'Task, group, and task-group interactions'. University of Hawaii *Working Papers in ESL* 8: 1–26.

Long, M. 1990a. 'Maturational constraints on language development'. *Studies in Second Language Acquisition* 12: 251–86.

Long, M. 1990b. 'Second language classroom research and teacher education' in Brumfit and Mitchell (eds.) 1990.

Long, M. 1990c. 'The least a second language acquisition theory needs to explain'. *TESOL Quarterly* 24: 649–66.

Long, M. 1991. 'Focus on form: a design feature in language teaching methodology' in de Bot et al. (eds.) 1991.

Long, M. 1993. 'Assessment strategies for SLA theories'. *Applied Linguistics* 14: 225–49.

Long, M., L. Adams, M. Mclean, and **F. Castanos.** 1976. 'Doing things with words: verbal interaction in lockstep and small group classroom situations' in Fanselow and Crymes (eds.) 1976.

Long, M. and **G. Crookes.** 1987. 'Intervention points in second language classroom processes' in Das (ed.) 1987a.

Long, M. and **G. Crookes.** 1992. 'Three approaches to task-based syllabus design'. *TESOL Quarterly* 26: 27–56.

Long, M., S. Ghambiar, V. Ghambiar, and **M. Nishimura.** 1982. 'Regularization in foreigner talk and interlanguage'. Paper presented at the 17th Annual TESOL Convention, Toronto, Canada.

Long, M. and **P. Porter.** 1985. 'Group work, interlanguage talk, and second language acquisition'. *TESOL Quarterly* 19: 207–28.

Long, M. and **C. Sato.** 1984. 'Methodological issues in interlanguage studies: An interactionist perspective' in Davies et al. (eds.) 1984.

Lörscher, W. 1986. 'Conversational structures in the foreign language classroom' in Kasper (ed.) 1986.

Lörscher, W. and **R. Schultze** (eds.). 1987. *Perspectives on Language in Performance.* Tübingen: Gunter Narr.

Loschky, L. 1989. 'The effects of negotiated interaction and premodified input on second language comprehension and retention'. Unpublished MA thesis. University of Hawaii.

Loschky, L. and **R. Bley-Vroman.** 1990. 'Creating structure-based communication tasks for second language development'. University of Hawaii *Working Papers in ESL* 9: 161–212.

Lott, D. 1983. 'Analysing and counteracting interference errors'. *English Language Teaching Journal* 37: 256–61.

Lowenberg, P. 1986. 'Non-native varieties of English: nativization, norms, and implications'. *Studies in Second Language Acquisition* 8: 1–18.

Lucas, E. 1975. 'Teachers' reacting moves following errors made by pupils in post-primary English as a second language classes in Israel'. MA thesis, School of Education, Tel Aviv University. Cited in Chaudron 1988a.

Ludwig, J. 1982. 'Native-speaker judgements of second-language learners' efforts at communication: a review'. *Modern Language Journal* 66: 274–83.

Ludwig, J. 1983. 'Attitudes and expectations: a profile of female and male students of college French, German and Spanish'. *The Modern Language Journal* 67: 216–27.

Lugton, R. (ed.). 1971. *Toward a Cognitive Approach to Second Language Acquisition.* Philadelphia, Penn.: Center for Curriculum Department.

Lujan, M., L. Minaya, and **D. Dankoff.** 1984. 'The universal consistency hypothesis and the prediction of word order acquisition stages in the speech of bilingual children'. *Language* 60: 343–71.

Lukmani, Y. 1972. 'Motivation to learn and language proficiency'. *Language Learning* 22: 261–73.

Lynch, A. 1988. 'Speaking up or talking down: foreign learners' reactions to teacher talk'. *English Language Teaching Journal* 42: 109–16.

Lyons, J. 1968. *Introduction to Theoretical Linguistics.* Cambridge: Cambridge University Press.

Lyons, J. 1972. 'Human language' in Hinde (ed.) 1972.

Lyons, J. and **R. Wales** (eds.). 1979. *Psycholinguistic Papers.* Edinburgh: Edinburgh University Press.

MacIntyre, P. and **R. Gardner.** 1991a. 'Methods and results in the study of foreign language anxiety: a review of the literature'. *Language Learning* 41: 25–57.

MacIntyre, P. and **R. Gardner.** 1991b. Language anxiety: its relationship to other anxieties and to processing in native and second languages. *Language Learning* 41: 513–34.

MacWhinney, B. (ed.). 1987. *Mechanisms of Language Acquisition*. Hillsdale, N.J.: Lawrence Erlbaum.

MacWhinney, B. 1989. 'Competition and connectionism' in MacWhinney and Bates (eds.).

MacWhinney, B. and **E. Bates** (eds.). 1989. *The Crosslinguistic Study of Sentence Processing*. Cambridge: Cambridge University Press.

MacWhinney. B., E. Bates, and **R. Kligell.** 1984. 'Cue validity and sentence interpretation in English, German and Italian'. *Journal of Verbal Learning and Verbal Behavior* 23: 127–50.

MacWhinney, B., C. Pleh, and **E. Bates.** 1985. 'The development of sentence interpretation in Hungarian'. *Cognitive Psychology* 17: 178–209.

Magnet, J. 1990. 'Canadian perspectives on official English' in Adams and Brink (eds.) 1990.

Maier, M. and **P. Jacob.** 1966. 'The effect of variations in self-instruction programs on instructional outcomes'. *Pyschological Reports* 18: 539–46.

Major, R. 1986. 'Paragoge and degree of foreign accent in Brazilian English'. *Second Language Research* 2: 53–71.

Major, R. 1987. 'A model for interlanguage pronunciation' in Ioup and Weinberger (eds.) 1987.

Major, J. 1988. 'Balancing form and function'. *International Review of Applied Linguistics* 26: 81–100.

Makino, T. 1980. 'Acquisition order of English morphemes by Japanese secondary school students'. *Journal of Hokkaido University Education* 30: 101–48.

Malouf, R. and **C. Dodd.** 1972. 'Role of exposure, imitation and expansion in the acquisition of an artificial grammatical rule'. *Developmental Psychology* 7: 195–203.

Maltz, D. and **R. Borker.** 1982. 'A cultural approach to male–female miscommunication' in Gumperz (ed.) 1982b.

Mangubhai, F. 1991. 'The processing behaviours of adult second language learners and their relationship to second language proficiency'. *Applied Linguistics* 12: 268–98.

Mannon, T. 1986. 'Teacher talk: a comparison of a teacher's speech to native and non-native speakers'. Unpublished MA TESL thesis, University of California at Los Angeles.

Maple, R. 1982. 'Social distance and the acquisition of English as a second language: a study of Spanish-speaking adult learners'. Unpublished doctoral thesis, University of Texas at Austin.

Martin, G. 1980. 'English language acquisition: the effects of living with an American family'. *TESOL Quarterly* 14: 388–90.

Mason, C. 1971. 'The relevance of intensive training in English as a foreign language for university students'. *Language Learning* 21: 197–204.

Mateene, K. and **J. Kalema** (eds.). 1980. 'Reconsideration of African linguistic policies'. *OAU/ BIL Publication* 3. Kampala: OAU Bureau of Languages.

Mateene, K., J. Kalema, and **B. Chomba** (eds.). 1985. 'Linguistic liberation and unity of Africa'. *OAU/BIL Publication* 6. Kampala: OAU Bureau of Languages

Matsumoto, K. 1989. 'Factors involved in the L2 learning process'. *JALT Journal* 11: 167–92.

Mazurkewich, I. 1985. 'Syntactic markedness and language acquisition'. *Studies in Second Language Acquisition* 7: 15–35.

Mazurkewich, I. 1984. 'The acquisition of dative alternation by second language learners and linguistic theory'. *Language Learning* 34: 91–109.

McCary, J. (ed.). 1956. *Psychology of Personality*. New York: Logos.

McClelland, J., D. Rumelhart, and **G. Hinton.** 1986. 'The appeal of parallel distributed processing' in Rumelhart et al. (eds.) 1986.

McClelland, J., D. Rumelhart, and the **PDP Research Group** (eds.). 1986. *Parallel Distributed Processing: Explorations in the Microstructure of Cognition, Vol. 2: Psychological and Biological Models.* Cambridge, Mass.: MIT Press.

McDonald, F., M. Stone, and **A. Yates.** 1977. 'The effects of classroom interaction patterns and student characteristics on the acquisition of proficiency in English as a second language'. Princeton, N.J.: Educational Testing Service.

McDonald, J. 1986. 'The development of sentence comprehension strategies in English and Dutch'. *Journal of Experimental Child Psychology* 41: 317–35.

McDonald, J. and **K. Heilenman.** 1991. 'Determinants of cue strength in adult first and second language speakers of French'. *Applied Psycholinguistics* 12: 313–48.

McHoul, A. 1978. 'The organization of turns at formal talk in the classroom'. *Language and Society* 7: 183–213.

McLaughlin, B. 1978a. *Second Language Acquisition in Childhood.* Hillsdale, N.J.: Lawrence Erlbaum.

McLaughlin, B. 1978b. 'The Monitor Model: some methodological considerations'. *Language Learning* 28: 309–32.

McLaughlin, B. 1980. 'Theory and research in second-language learning: an emerging paradigm'. *Language Learning* 30: 331–50.

McLaughlin, B. 1985. *Second Language Acquisition in Childhood, Vol. 2: School-age Children.* Hillsdale, N.J.: Lawrence Erlbaum.

McLaughlin, B. 1987. *Theories of Second Language Learning.* London: Edward Arnold.

McLaughlin, B. 1990a. 'Restructuring'. *Applied Linguistics* 11: 113–28.

McLaughlin, B. 1990b. 'The relationship between first and second languages: language proficiency and language aptitude' Harley et al. (eds.) 1990.

McLaughlin, B. 1990c. ' "Conscious" vs. "unconscious" learning'. *TESOL Quarterly* 24: 617–34.

McLaughlin, B. and **M. Harrington.** 1989. 'Second-language acquisition'. *Annual Review of Applied Linguistics* 10: 122–34.

McLaughlin, B., T. Rossman, and **B. McLeod.** 1983. 'Second language learning: an information-processing perspective'. *Language Learning* 33: 135–58.

McNamara, J. 1973. 'Nurseries, streets and classrooms: some comparisons and deductions'. *Modern Language Journal* 57: 250–55.

McNeill, D. 1966. 'Developmental psycholinguistics' in Smith and Miller (eds.) 1966.

McNeill, D. 1970. *The Acquisition of Language.* New York: Harper Row.

McTear, M. 1975. 'Structure and categories of foreign language teaching sequences' in Allwright (ed.) 1975b.

Meara, P. 1984. 'The study of lexis in interlanguage' in Davies et al. (eds.) 1984.

Meara, P. (ed.). 1986. *Spoken Language.* London: CILT.

Mehan, H. 1974. 'Accomplishing classroom lessons' in A. Cicourel et al. (eds.) 1974.

Mehan, H. 1979. *Learning Lessons: Social Organization in the Classroom.* Cambridge, Mass.: Harvard University Press.

Meisel, J. 1980. 'Linguistic simplification' in Felix (ed.) 1980a.

Meisel, J. 1983. 'Strategies of second language acquisition: more than one kind of simplification' in Andersen (ed.) 1983c.

Meisel, J. 1987. 'Reference to past events and actions in the development of natural second language acquisition' in Pfaff (ed.) 1987b.

Meisel, J. 1991. 'Principles of Universal Grammar and strategies of language learning: some similarities and differences between first and second language acquisition' in Eubank (ed.) 1991b.

Meisel, J., H. Clahsen, and **M. Pienemann.** 1981. 'On determining developmental stages in natural second language acquisition'. *Studies in Second Language Acquisition* 3: 109–35.

Midorikawa, H. 1990. 'An exploratory study of the relationship of teacher questions to learner output'. Unpublished paper, Tokyo: Temple University Japan.

Miller, G, and N. Chomsky. 1963. 'Finitary models of language users' in Bush et al. (eds.) 1963.

Milon, J. 1974. 'The development of negation in English by a second language learner'. *TESOL Quarterly* 8: 137–43.

Mitchell, R. 1985. 'Process research in second language classrooms'. *Language Teaching* 18: 330–52.

Mitchell, R., B. Parkinson, and R. Johnstone. 1981. 'The foreign language classroom: an observational study'. *Stirling Educational Monographs* No. 9. Stirling: Department of Education, University of Stirling.

Mizon, S. 1981. 'Teacher talk: a case study from the Bangalore/Madras communicational ELT project'. Unpublished MA thesis, University of Lancaster.

Möhle, D. and M. Raupach. 1989. 'Language transfer and procedural knowledge' in Dechert and Raupach (eds.) 1989a.

Montgomery, C. and M. Eisenstein. 1985. 'Real reality revisited: an experimental communicative course in ESL'. *TESOL Quarterly* 19: 317–33.

Moore, T. (ed.). 1973. *Cognitive Development and the Acquisition of Language*. New York: Academic Press.

Morren, B. 1993. 'Lexical inferencing procedures (K. Haastrup 1989)—a replication'. Unpublished paper, Tokyo: Temple University Japan.

Morris, R. (ed.). 1989. *Parallel Distributed Processing: Implications for Psychology and Neurobiology*. Oxford: Clarendon Press.

Morrison, D. and G. Low. 1983. 'Monitoring and the second language learner' in Richards and Schmidt (eds.) 1983.

Moskowitz, G. 1967. 'The Flint system: an observational tool for the foreign language classroom' in. Simon and Boyer (eds.) 1967.

Moskowitz, G. 1978. *Caring and Sharing in the Foreign Language Classroom*. Rowley, Mass.: Newbury House.

Muchnick, A. and D. Wolfe. 1982. 'Attitudes and motivations of American students of Spanish'. *Canadian Modern Language Review* 38: 262–81.

Mühlhauser, P. 1986. *Pidgin and Creole Linguistics*. Oxford: Basil Blackwell.

Mukkatesh, L. 1977. *Problematic areas in English syntax for Jordanian students*. University of Amman, Jordan.

Mukkatesh, L. 1986. 'Persistence in fossilization'. *International Review of Applied Linguistics* 24: 187–203.

Muysken, P. 1984. 'The Spanish that Quechua speakers learn' in Andersen (ed.) 1984b.

Myers, T. (ed.). 1979. *The Development of Conversation and Discourse*. Edinburgh: Edinburgh University Press.

Nagara, S. 1972. *Japanese Pidgin English in Hawaii: a Bilingual Description*. Honolulu: University Press of Hawaii.

Naiman, N., M. Fröhlich, H. Stern, and A. Todesco. 1978. *The Good Language Learner. Research in Education Series No 7*. Toronto: The Ontario Institute for Studies in Education.

Naro, A. 1983. 'Comments on "Simplified Input and Second Language Acquisition" ' in Andersen (ed.) 1983c.

Nation, P. 1990. *Teaching and Learning Vocabulary*. New York: Newbury House/Harper Row.

Nation, R. and B. McLaughlin. 1986. 'Experts and novices: an information-processing approach to the "good language learner" problem'. *Applied Pyscholinguistics* 7: 41–56.

Nattinger, J. and J. DeCarrico. 1992. *Lexical Phrases and Language Teaching*. Oxford: Oxford University Press.

Nayak, N., N. Hansen, N. Krueger, and **B. McLaughlin.** 1987. 'Language-learning strategies in monolingual and multilingual subjects'. Unpublished paper, Santa Cruz: University of California. Cited in McLaughlin 1990b.

Nelson, K. 1973. 'Structure and Strategy in Learning to Talk'. *Monographs of the Society for Research in Child Development 38.*

Nelson, K. 1977. 'Facilitating children's syntax acquisition'. *Developmental Psychology* 13: 101–7.

Nelson, K. (ed.). 1978. *Children's Language, Vol 1.* New York: Gardner's Press.

Nelson, K. (ed.). 1980. *Children's Language, Vol 2.* New York: Gardner's Press.

Nemser, W. 1971. 'Approximative systems of foreign language learners'. *International Review of Applied Linguistics* 9: 115–23.

Neu, J., and **S. Gass** (eds.). (forthcoming). *Speech Acts Across Cultures.* Berlin: Mouton de Gruyter.

Neufeld, G. 1977. 'Language learning ability in adults: a study on the acquisition of prosodic and articulatory features'. *Working Papers on Bilingualism* 12: 45–60.

Neufeld, G. 1978. 'On the acquisition of prosodic and articulatory features in adult language learning'. *Canadian Modern Language Review* 34: 163–74.

Neufeld, G. 1979. 'Toward a theory of language learning ability'. *Language Learning* 29: 227–41.

Newmark, L. 1966. 'How not to interfere in language learning'. *International Journal of American Linguistics* 32: 77–87.

Newmark, L. and **D. Reibel.** 1968. 'Necessity and sufficiency in language learning'. *International Review of Applied Linguistics in Language Teaching* 6: 145–64.

Newport, E. 1976. 'Motherese: the speech of mothers to young children'. Unpublished PhD thesis, University of Pennsylvania.

Newport, E., H. Gleitman, and **L. Gleitman.** 1977. ' "Mother, I'd rather do it myself": some effects and non-effects of maternal speech styles' in Snow and Ferguson (eds.) 1977.

Newton, J. 1991. 'Negotiation: negotiating what?' Paper given at SEAMEO Conference on Language Acquisition and the Second/Foreign Language Classroom, RELC, Singapore.

Neymeyer, F. (ed.). 1988. *Linguistics: The Cambridge Survey, Vol IV: The Socio-cultural Context.* Cambridge: Cambridge University Press.

Nicholas, H. 1985. 'Learner variation and the teachability hypothesis' in Hyltenstam and Pienemann (eds.) 1985.

Nicholas, H. 1986. 'The acquisition of language as the acquisition of variation'. *Australian Working Papers on Language Development* 1: 1–30.

Nickel, G. (ed.). 1971. *Papers in Contrastive Analysis.* Cambridge: Cambridge University Press.

Nickel, G. 1973. 'Aspects of error analysis and grading' in Svartvik (ed.) 1973a.

Nobuyoshi, J. and **R. Ellis.** 1993. 'Focused communication tasks'. *English Language Teaching Journal* 47:203–10.

Nunan, D. 1989. *Designing tasks for the communicative classroom.* Cambridge: Cambridge University Press.

Nunan, D. 1990a. 'The questions teachers ask'. *JALT Journal* 12: 187–202.

Nunan, D. 1990b. 'The teacher as researcher' in Brumfit and Mitchell (eds.) 1990.

Nunan, D. 1991. 'Methods in second language classroom-oriented research: a critical review'. *Studies in Second Language Acquisition* 13: 249–74.

Nyikos, M. 1990. 'Sex related differences in adult language learning: socialization and memory factors'. Modern Language Journal 3: 273–87.

Nystrom, N. 1983. 'Teacher-student interaction in bilingual classrooms: four approaches to error feedback' in Seliger and Long (eds.) 1983.

Obler, L. 1989. 'Exceptional second language learners' in Gass et al. (eds.) 1989b.

Ochs, E. 1979. 'Planned and unplanned discourse' in Givón (ed.) 1979b.

Ochs, E. 1982. 'Talking to children in Western Samoa'. *Language in Society* 11: 77–104.

Ochs, E. and **B. Schiefflin** (eds.). 1979. *Developmental Pragmatics*. New York: Academic Press.

Ochs, E. and **B. Schieffelin.** 1984. 'Language acquisition and socialization: three developmental stories and their implications' in Shweder and LeVine (eds.) 1984.

Odlin, T. 1989. *Language Transfer*. Cambridge: Cambridge University Press.

Odlin, T. 1990. 'Word-order transfer, metalinguistic awareness and constraints on foreign language learning' in VanPatten and Lee (eds.) 1990.

O'Grady, W. 1991. 'Language acquisition and the "pro-drop" phenomenon: a response to Hilles' in Eubank (ed.) 1991b.

Okamura-Bichard, F. 1985. 'Mother tongue maintenance and second language learning: a case of Japanese children'. *Language Learning* 35: 63–89.

Oleksy, W. (ed).) 1989. *Contrastive Pragmatics*. Amsterdam: John Benjamins.

Oller, J. 1977. 'Attitude variables in second language acquisition' in Burt et al. (eds.) 1977.

Oller, J. 1981. 'Research on the measurement of affective variables: some remaining questions' in Andersen (ed.) 1981.

Oller, J. (ed.). 1983. *Issues in Language Testing Research*. Rowley, Mass.: Newbury House.

Oller, J., L. Baca, and **A. Vigil.** 1977. 'Attitudes and attained proficiency in ESL: a sociolinguistic study of Mexican Americans in the Southwest'. *TESOL Quarterly* 11: 173–83.

Oller, J. and **K. Perkins.** 1978. 'Intelligence and language proficiency as sources of variance in self-reported affective variables'. *Language Learning* 28: 85–97.

Olsen, L. and **S. Samuels.** 1973. 'The relationship between age and accuracy of foreign language pronunciation'. *Journal of Educational Research* 66: 263–67. Reprinted in Krashen et al. (eds.) 1979.

Olshtain, E. 1983. 'Sociocultural competence and language transfer: the case of apologies' in Gass and Selinker (eds.) 1983.

Olshtain, E. 1989. 'Apologies across languages' in Blum-Kulka et al. (eds.) 1989b.

Olshtain, E. and **S. Blum-Kulka.** 1985. 'Degree of approximation: non-native reactions to native speech act behavior' in Gass and Madden (eds.) 1985.

Olshtain, E. and **A. Cohen.** 1983. 'Apology: a speech act set' in Wolfson and Judd (eds.) 1983.

Olshtain, E. and **A. Cohen.** 1989. 'Speech act behavior across languages' in Dechert and Raupach (eds.) 1989a.

Olshtain, E., E. Shohamy, J. Kemp, and **R. Chatow.** 1990. 'Factors predicting success in EFL among culturally different learners'. *Language Learning* 40: 23–44.

Olshtain, E. and **L. Weinbach.** 1985. 'Complaints: a study of speech act behavior among native and non-native speakers of Hebrew' in Verschuren and Bertucelli-Papi (eds.) 1985.

O'Malley, J. 1987. 'The effects of training in the use of learning strategies on acquiring English as a second language' in Wenden and Rubin (eds.) 1987.

O'Malley, J. and **A. Chamot.** 1990. *Learning Strategies in Second Language Acquisition*. Cambridge: Cambridge University Press.

O'Malley, J., A. Chamot, G. Stewner-Manzanaraes, L. Kupper, and **R. Russo.** 1985a. 'Learning strategies used by beginning and intermediate ESL students'. *Language Learning* 35: 21–46.

O'Malley, J., A. Chamot, G. Stewner-Manzanaraes, R. Russo, and **L. Kupper.** 1985b. 'Learning strategy applications with students of English as a second language'. *TESOL Quarterly* 19: 285–96.

O'Malley, J., A. Chamot, and **C. Walker.** 1987. 'Some applications of cognitive theory to second language acquisition'. *Studies in Second Language Acquisition* 9: 287–306.

Oxford, R. 1985. 'A new taxonomy of second language learning strategies'. Washington D.C.: ERIC Clearinghouse on Languages and Linguistics.

Oxford, R. 1986. 'Development of the strategy inventory for language learning'. Manuscript. Washington D.C.: Center for Applied Linguistics.

Oxford, R. 1989. 'Use of language learning strategies: a synthesis of studies with implications for teacher training'. *System* 17: 235–47.

Oxford, R. 1990. *Language Learning Strategies: What Every Teacher Should Know.* Rowley, Mass.: Newbury House.

Oxford, R. 1992. 'Who are our students? A synthesis of foreign and second language research on individual differences with implications for instructional practice'. *TESL Canada Journal* 9: 30–49.

Oxford, R. and **M. Nyikos.** 1989. 'Variables affecting choice of language learning strategies by university students'. *Modern Language Journal* 73: 291–300.

Oyama, S. 1976. 'A sensitive period in the acquisition of a non-native phonological system'. *Journal of Psycholinguistic Research* 5: 261–85.

Palmberg, R. (ed.). 1979. *Perception and Production of English: Papers on Interlanguage.* AFTIL Vol 6. Publications of the Dept. of English, Abo Akademi.

Palmer, A. 1979. 'Compartmentalized and integrated control: an assessment of some evidence for two kinds of competence and implications for the classroom'. *Language Learning* 29: 169–80.

Pankhurst, J., M. Sharwood Smith, and **P. Van Buren** (eds.). 1988. *Learnability and Second Languages: a Book of Readings.* Dordrecht: Foris.

Paribakht, T. 1985. 'Strategic competence and language proficiency'. *Applied Linguistics* 6: 132–46.

Parker, K. 1989. 'Learnability theory and the acquisition of syntax'. University of Hawaii. *Working Papers in ESL* 8: 49–78.

Parker, K. and **C. Chaudron.** 1987. 'The effects of linguistic simplifications and elaborative modifications on L2 comprehension'. University of Hawaii. *Working Papers in ESL* 6: 107–33.

Parkinson, B. and **C. Howell-Richardson.** 1990. 'Learner Diaries' in Brumfit and Mitchell (eds.) 1990.

Parry, T. and **J. Child.** 1990. 'Preliminary investigation of the relationship between VORD, MLAT and language proficiency' in Parry and Stansfield (eds.).

Parry, T. and **C. Stansfield.** (ed.). 1990. *Language Aptitude Reconsidered.* Englewood Cliffs, N.J.: Prentice Hall.

Pask, G. and **B. Scott.** 1972. 'Learning strategies and individual competence'. *International Journal of Man-Machine Studies* 4: 217–53.

Patkowski, M. 1980. 'The sensitive period for the acquisition of syntax in a second language'. *Language Learning* 30: 449–72.

Patkowski, M. 1990. 'Age and accent in a second language: a reply to James Emir Flege'. *Applied Linguistics* 11: 73–89.

Pavesi, M. 1984. 'The acquisition of relative clauses in a formal and informal context' in Singleton and Little (eds.) 1984.

Pavesi, M. 1986. 'Markedness, discoursal modes and relative clause formation in a formal and informal context'. *Studies in Second Language Acquisition* 8: 38–55.

Pawley, A. and **F. Syder.** 1983. 'Two puzzles for linguistic theory: nativelike selection and nativelike fluency' in Richards and Schmidt (eds.) 1983.

Peck, S. 1978. 'Child–child discourse in second language acquisition' in Hatch (ed.) 1978a.

Peck, S. 1980. 'Language play in child second language acquisition' in Larsen-Freeman (ed.) 1980.

Pelligrini, A. and **T. Yawkey** (eds.). 1984. *The Development of Oral and Written Language in Social Contexts.* Norwood, N.J.: Ablex.

Penfield, W. and **L. Roberts.** 1959. *Speech and Brain Mechanisms.* New York: Atheneum Press.

Perdue, C. 1984. *Second Language Acquisition by Adult Immigrants: a Field Manual.* Rowley, Mass.: Newbury House.

Perdue, C. 1991. 'Cross-linguistic comparisons: organizational principles in learner languages' in Huebner and Ferguson (eds.) 1991.

Perdue, C. and **W. Klein.** 1992. 'Why does the production of some learners not grammaticalize?' *Studies in Second Language Acquisition* 14: 259–72.

Perkins, K. and **D. Larsen-Freeman.** 1975. 'The effects of formal language instruction on the order of morpheme acquisition'. *Language Learning* 25: 237–43.

Perren, G. and **J. Trim** (eds.). 1971. *Applications of Linguistics.* Cambridge University Press.

Peters, A. 1977. 'Language learning strategies: does the whole equal the sum of the parts?' *Language* 53: 560–73. Also in Diller (ed.) 1981.

Petersen, C. and **A. Al-Haik.** 1976. 'The development of the Defense Language Aptitude Battery (DLAB)'. *Educational and Psychological Measurement* 36: 369–80.

Pfaff, C. 1987a. 'Functional approaches to interlanguage' in Pfaff (ed.).

Pfaff, C. (ed.). 1987b. *First and Second Language Acquisition Processes.* Cambridge, Mass.: Newbury House.

Pfaff, C. 1992. 'The issue of grammaticalization in early German second language'. *Studies in Second Language Acquisition* 14: 273–96.

Phillips, S. 1972. 'Participation structures and communicative competence: Warm Springs children in community and classroom' in Cazden et al. (eds.) 1972.

Phillipson, R., E. Kellerman, L. Selinker, M. Sharwood Smith, and **M. Swain** (eds.). 1991. *Foreign/Second Language Pedagogy Research.* Clevedon, Avon: Multilingual Matters.

Phinney, M. 1987. 'The pro-drop parameter in second language acquisition' in Roeper and Williams (eds.) 1987.

Piatelli-Palmarini, M. (ed.). 1980. *Language and Learning.* London: Routledge and Kegan Paul.

Pica, T. 1983. 'Adult acquisition of English as a second language under different conditions of exposure'. *Language Learning* 33: 465–97.

Pica, T. 1984. 'Methods of morpheme quantification: their effect on the interpretation of second language data'. *Studies in Second Language Acquisition* 6: 69–78.

Pica, T. 1985. 'The selective impact of instruction on second language acquisition'. *Applied Linguistics* 6: 214–22.

Pica, T. 1987. 'Second language acquisition, social interaction in the classroom'. *Applied Linguistics* 7: 1–25.

Pica, T. 1988. 'Interlanguage adjustments as an outcome of NS–NNS negotiated interaction'. *Language Learning* 38: 45–73.

Pica, T. 1991. 'Classroom interaction, participation and comprehension: redefining relationships'. *System* 19: 437–52.

Pica, T. 1992. 'The textual outcomes of native speaker–non-native speaker negotiation: what do they reveal about second language learning' in Kramsch and McConnell-Ginet (eds.) 1992.

Pica, T. and **C. Doughty.** 1985a. 'Input and interaction in the communicative language classroom: a comparison of teacher-fronted and group activities' in Gass and Madden (eds.) 1985.

Pica, T. and **C. Doughty.** 1985b. 'The role of group work in classroom second language acquisition'. *Studies in Second Language Acquisition* 7: 233–48.

Pica, T. and **C. Doughty.** 1988. 'Variations in classroom interaction as a function of participation pattern and task' in Fine (ed.) 1988.

Pica, T., L. Holliday, N. Lewis, D. Berducci, and **J. Newman.** 1991. 'Language learning through interaction: what role does gender play?' *Studies in Second Language Acquisition* 13: 343–76.

Pica, T., L. Holliday, N. Lewis, and **L. Morgenthaler.** 1989. 'Comprehensible output as an outcome of linguistic demands on the learner'. *Studies in Second Language Acquisition* 11: 63–90.

Pica, T., R. Kanagy, and **J. Falodun** (forthcoming). 'Choosing and using communication tasks for second language research and instruction' in. Gass and Crookes (eds.).

Pica, T. and **M. Long.** 1986. 'The linguistic and conversational performance of experienced and inexperienced teachers' in Day (ed.) 1986.

Pica, T., R. Young, and C. Doughty. 1987. 'The impact of interaction on comprehension'. *TESOL Quarterly* 21: 737–58.

Pickett, G. 1978. *The Foreign Language Learning Process*. London: The British Council.

Pienemann, M. 1980. 'The second language acquisition of immigrant children' in Felix (ed.) 1980a.

Pienemann, M. 1981. *Der Zweitsprachenerwerb ausländischer Arbeitskinder*. Bonn: Bouvier.

Pienemann, M. 1984. 'Psychological constraints on the teachability of languages'. *Studies in Second Language Acquisition* 6: 186–214.

Pienemann, M. 1985. 'Learnability and syllabus construction' in Hyltenstam and Pienemann (eds.) 1985.

Pienemann, M. 1986. 'Is language teachable? Psycholinguistic experiments and hypotheses'. *Australian Working Papers in Language Development* 1: 3.

Pienemann, M. 1987. 'Determining the influence of instruction on L2 speech processing'. *Australian Review of Applied Linguistics* 10: 83–113.

Pienemann, M. 1989. 'Is language teachable? Psycholinguistic experiments and hypotheses'. *Applied Linguistics* 10: 52–79.

Pienemann, M. 1992. 'COALA—A computational system for interlanguage analysis'. *Second Language Research* 8: 59–92.

Pienemann, M. and M. Johnston. 1986. 'An acquisition-based procedure for second language assessment'. *Australian Review of Applied Linguistics* 9: 92–122.

Pienemann, M. and M. Johnston. 1988. 'Processing constraints and learnability'. Unpublished manuscript, University of Sydney.

Pienemann, M., M. Johnston, and G. Brindley. 1988. 'Constructing an acquisition-based procedure for assessing second language acquisition'. *Studies in Second Language Acquisition* 10: 217–43.

Pimsleur, P. 1966. *Pimsleur Language Aptitude Battery (PLAB)*. New York: Harcourt Brace Jovanovich.

Pimsleur, P. and T. Quinn (eds.). 1971. *The Psychology of Second Language Learning*. Cambridge; Cambridge University Press.

Pimsleur, P., D. Sundland, and R. MacIntyre. 1966. *Underachievement in Foreign Language Learning*. Washington D.C.: Modern Language Association.

Pinker, S. and A. Prince. 1989. 'Rules and connections in human language' in Morris (ed.) 1989.

Plann, S. 1977. 'Acquiring a second language in an immersion situation' in H. Brown et al. (eds.) 1977.

Pleh, C. 1990. 'The search for universal operating principles in language acquisition'. *Studies in Second Language Acquisition* 12: 233–41.

Plunkett, K. 1988. 'Parallel distributed processing'. *Psyke and Logos* 9, 2: 307–36.

Politzer, R. 1970. 'Some reflections on "good" and "bad" language teaching behaviors'. *Language Learning* 20: 31–43.

Politzer, R. 1980. 'Requesting in elementary school classrooms'. *TESOL Quarterly* 14: 165–74.

Politzer, R. 1983. 'An exploratory study of self-reported language learning behaviors and their relation to achievement'. *Studies in Second Language Acquisition* 6: 54–67.

Politzer, R. and M. McGroarty. 1985. 'An exploratory study of learning behaviors and their relationship to gains in linguistic and communicative competence'. *TESOL Quarterly* 19:103–23.

Politzer, R. and A. Ramirez. 1973. 'An error analysis of the spoken English of Mexican-American pupils in a bilingual school and a monolingual school'. *Language Learning* 18: 35–53.

Politzer, R., A. Ramirez, and S. Lewis. 1981. 'Teaching standard English in the third grade: classroom functions of language'. *Language Learning* 31: 171–93.

Poole, D. 1992. 'Language socialization in the second language classroom'. *Language Learning* 42: 593–616.

Porter, J. 1977. 'A cross-sectional study of morpheme acquisition in first language learners'. *Language Learning* 27: 47–62.

Porter, P. 1986. 'How learners talk to each other: input and interaction in task-centred discussions' in Day (ed.) 1986.

Poulisse, N. 1990a. *The Use of Compensatory Strategies by Dutch Learners of English*. Enschede: Sneldruk.

Poulisse, N. 1990b. 'Variation in learners' use of communication strategies' in Duda and Riley (eds.) 1990.

Prabhu, N.S. 1987. *Second Language Pedagogy*. Oxford: Oxford University Press.

Prator, C. 1968. 'The British heresy in TESL' in Fishman et al. (eds.) 1968.

Preston, D. 1981. 'The ethnography of TESOL'. *TESOL Quarterly* 15: 105–16.

Preston, D. 1989. *Sociolinguistics and Second Language Acquisition*. Oxford: Blackwell.

Pride, J. (ed.). 1979. *Sociolinguistic Aspects of Language Learning and Teaching*. Oxford: Oxford University Press.

Purcell, E. and R. Suter. 1980. 'Predictors of pronunciation accuracy: a reexamination'. *Language Learning* 30: 271–87.

Quirk, R. 1982a. 'International communication and the concept of nuclear English' in Quirk (ed.).

Quirk, R. (ed.). 1982b. *Style and Communication in the English Language*. London: Edward Arnold.

Quirk, R. 1985. 'The English language in a global context' in Quirk and Widdowson (eds.).

Quirk, R. and H. Widdowson (eds.). 1985. *English in the World: Teaching and Learning the Language and Literatures*. Cambridge: Cambridge University Press.

Rabinowitz, M. and M. Chi. 1987. 'An interactive model of strategic processing' in Ceci (ed.) 1987.

Ramage, K. 1990. 'Motivational factors and persistence in foreign language study'. *Language Learning* 40: 189–219.

Ramat, A. 1992. 'Grammaticalization processes in the area of temporal and modal relations'. *Studies in Second Language Acquisition* 14: 297–322.

Ramirez, A. and N. Stromquist. 1979. 'ESL methodology and student language learning in bilingual elementary schools'. *TESOL Quarterly* 13: 145–58.

Ramirez, J., S. Yuen, D. Ramey, and B. Merino. 1986. 'First year report: longitudinal study of immersion programs for language minority children'. Arlington, V.A.: SRA Technologies.

Rampton, B. 1987. 'Stylistic variability and not speaking "normal" English: some post-Labovian approaches and their implications for the study of interlanguage' in Ellis (ed.) 1987a.

Raupach, M. 1983. 'Analysis and evaluation of communication strategies' in Færch and Kasper (eds.) 1983a.

Ravem, R. 1968. 'Language acquisition in a second language environment'. *International Review of Applied Linguistics* 6: 165–85.

Reber, A. 1976. 'Implicit learning of synthetic learners: the role of instructional set'. *Journal of Experimental Psychology, Human Learning and Memory* 2: 88–94.

Reber, A., S. Kassin, S. Lewis, and G. Cantor. 1980. 'On the relationship between implicit and explicit modes in the learning of a complex rule structure'. *Journal of Experimental Psychology, Human Learning and Memory* 6: 492–502.

Reed, C. (ed.). 1971. *The Learning of Language*. New York: Appleton-Century-Crofts.

Reid, J. 1987. 'The learning style preferences of ESL students'. *TESOL Quarterly* 21: 87–111.

Reigeluth, C. (ed.). 1984. *Instructional Design Theories and Models*. Hillsdale, N.J.: Lawrence Erlbaum. Cited in Crookes and Schmidt 1989.

Reiss, M. 1983. 'Helping the unsuccessful language learner'. *The Canadian Modern Language Review* 39: 257–66.

Reiss, M. 1985. 'The good language learner: another look'. *Canadian Modern Language Review* 41: 511–23.

Rescorla, L. and S. Okuda. 1987. 'Modular patterns in second language acquisition'. *Applied Psycholinguistics* 8: 281–308.

Reynolds, P. 1971. *A Primer in Theory Construction*. Indianapolis, Bobbs Merrill.

Richards, J. 1971a. 'Error analysis and second language strategies'. *Language Sciences* 17: 12–22.

Richards, J. 1971b. 'A non-contrastive approach to error analysis'. *English Language Teaching Journal* 25: 204–19.

Richards, J. (ed.). 1974. *Error Analysis*. London: Longman.

Richards, J. (ed.). 1978. *Understanding Second and Foreign Language Learning: Issues and Approaches*. Rowley, Mass.: Newbury House.

Richards, J. 1972. 'Social factors, interlanguage and language learning'. *Language Learning* 22: 159–88.

Richards, J. and D. Nunan (eds.). 1990. *Second Language Teacher Education*. Cambridge: Cambridge University Press.

Richards, J. and T. Rogers. 1986. *Approaches and Methods in Language Teaching*. Cambridge: Cambridge University Press.

Richards, J. and J. Schmidt (eds.). 1983. *Language and Communication*. London: Longman.

Riley, P. 1977. 'Discourse networks in classroom interaction: some problems in communicative language teaching'. Melanges Pedagogiques, University of Nancy: CRAPEL.

Riley, P. 1985. *Discourse and Learning*. London: Longman.

Riley, P. 1989. 'Well don't blame me! On the interpretation of pragmatic errors' in Oleksy (ed.) 1989.

Riney, T. 1990. 'Age and open syllable preference in interlanguage phonology' in Burmeister and Rounds (eds.) 1990.

Ringbom, H. 1986. 'Crosslinguistic influence and the foreign language learning process' in Kellerman and Sharwood Smith (eds.) 1986.

Ringbom, H. 1978. 'The influence of the mother tongue on the translation of lexical items'. *Interlanguage Studies Bulletin* 3: 80–101.

Ringbom, H. 1987. *The Role of the First Language in Foreign Language Learning*. Clevedon, Avon: Multilingual Matters.

Ringbom, H. 1992. 'On L1 transfer in L2 comprehension and L2 production'. *Language Learning* 42: 85–112.

Ringbom, H. and R. Palmberg (eds.). 1976. *Errors made by Finns and Swedish-speaking Finns in the Learning of English*. Abo, Finland: Dept. of English, Abo Akademi, ERIC Report ED 122628.

Rintell, E. 1981. 'Sociolinguistic variation and pragmatic ability: a look at learners'. *International Journal of the Sociology of Language* 27: 11–34.

Rintell, E. and C. Mitchell. 1989. 'Studying requests and apologies' in Blum-Kulka et al. (eds.) 1989a.

Ritchie, W. (ed.). 1978a. *Second Language Acquisition Research*. New York: Academic Press.

Ritchie, W. 1978b. 'The right roof constraint in adult-acquired language' in Ritchie (ed.).

Rivera, C. (ed.). 1984. *Communicative Competence Approaches to Language Proficiency Assessment: Research and Application*. Clevedon, Avon: Multilingual Matters.

Roberts, C. and M. Simonot. 1987. ' "This is my life": how language acquisition is interactionally accomplished' in Ellis (ed.) 1987a.

Robinett, B. and J. Schachter (eds.). 1983. *Second Language Learning: Contrastive Analysis, Error Analysis and Related Aspects*. Ann Arbor: The University of Michigan.

Robson, G. 1992. 'Individual learner differences and classroom participation: a pilot study'. Unpublished paper, Tokyo: Temple University Japan.

Robson, G. 1993. 'The effects of learner personality and anxiety on participation and the relationship between participation and proficiency'. Doctoral thesis proposal, Tokyo: Temple University Japan.

Rodriguez, R. 1982. *Hunger of Memory: the Education of Richard Rodriguez*. Boston: David R. Godine.

Roeper, T. and E. Williams (eds.). 1987. *Parameter Setting*. Dordrecht: Reidel.

Rogers, S. (ed.). 1976. *They Don't Speak Our Language*. London: Edward Arnold.

Romaine, S. 1984. *The Language of Children and Adolescents*. Oxford: Blackwell.

Rosansky, E. 1976. 'Methods and morphemes in second language acquisition'. *Language Learning* 26: 409–25.

Rosenstein, D. 1982. 'The efficiency of correcting recurrent errors among EFL students'. Beersheva, Israel: Department of English as a Foreign Language, Ben-Gurion University. Cited in Cohen et al. 1991.

Rosing-Schow, D. and K. Haastrup. 1982. 'The use of communication strategies in classroom and spontaneous discourse'. Unpublished manuscript, Department of English, University of Copenhagen. Cited in Holmen 1985.

Rossier, J. 1975. 'Extroversion–introversion as a significant variable in the learning of English as a second language'. Unpublished doctoral thesis, University of Southern California. *Dissertation Abstracts International* 36: 7308A–7309A.

Rost, M. 1990. *Listening in Language Learning*. London: Longman.

Rost, M. and S. Ross. 1991. 'Learner strategies in interaction: typology and teachability'. *Language Learning* 41: 235–73.

Rubin, J. 1975. 'What the "good language learner" can teach us'. *TESOL Quarterly* 9: 41–51.

Rubin, J. 1981. 'Study of cognitive processes in second language learning'. *Applied Linguistics* 11: 117–31.

Rubin, J. 1987. 'Learner strategies: theoretical assumptions, research history and typology' in Wenden and Rubin (eds.) 1987.

Rulon, K. and J. McCreary. 1986. 'Negotiation of content: teacher-fronted and small group interaction' in Day (ed.) 1986.

Rumelhart, D. and J. McClelland. 1986. 'On learning the past tenses of English verbs' in McClelland et al. (eds.) 1986.

Rumelhart, D., J. McClelland, and the PDP Research Group (eds.). 1986. *Parallel Distributed Processing: Explorations in the Microstructures of Cognition, Vol 2. Psychological and Biological Models*. Cambridge, Mass.: MIT Press.

Rutherford, W. 1982. 'Markedness in second language acquisition'. *Language Learning* 32: 85–108.

Rutherford, W. 1983. 'Language typology and language transfer' in Gass and Selinker (eds.) 1983.

Rutherford, W. (ed.). 1984a. *Typological Universals and Second Language Acquisition*. Amsterdam: John Benjamins.

Rutherford, W. 1984b. 'Description and explanation in interlanguage syntax: state of the art'. *Language Learning* 34: 127–55.

Rutherford, W. 1988. *Second Language Grammar: Learning and Teaching*. London: Longman.

Rutherford, W. 1989. 'Preemption and the learning of L2 grammars'. *Studies in Second Language Acquisition* 11: 441–57.

Rutherford, W. and M. Sharwood Smith. 1985. 'Consciousness raising and Universal Grammar'. *Applied Linguistics* 6: 274–82.

Rutherford, W. and M. Sharwood Smith (eds.). 1988. *Grammar and Second Language Teaching: A Book of Readings*. Rowley, Mass.: Newbury House.

Ryan, E. and H. Giles (eds.). 1982. *Attitudes Towards Language Variation*. London: Edward Arnold.

Sachs, J. 1977. 'The adaptive significance of linguistic input to prelinguistic infants' in Snow and Ferguson (eds.) 1977.

Sacks, H., E. Schegloff, and G. Jefferson. 1974. 'A simplest systematics for the organization of turn taking in conversation'. *Language* 50: 696–735.

Sadtano, E. (ed.). 1991. *Language Acquisition and the Second/Foreign Language Classroom*. Singapore: SEAMEO Regional Language Centre.

Saito, M. 1985. 'Some asymmetries in Japanese and their theoretical implications'. Unpublished doctoral thesis, Cambridge, Mass.: MIT Press.

Sajavaara, K. 1981a. 'Contrastive linguistics past and present and a communicative approach' in Fisiak (ed.) 1981b.

Sajavaara, K. 1981b. 'The nature of first language transfer: English as L2 in a foreign language setting'. Paper presented at the first European-North American Workshop in Second Language Acquisition Research. Lake Arrowhead, California.

Salica, C. 1981. 'Testing a model of corrective discourse'. Unpublished MA in TESL thesis. University of California at Los Angeles. Cited in Chaudron 1988.

Sankoff, D. (ed.). 1978. *Linguistic Variation: Model and Methods*. New York: Academic Press.

Santos, T. 1987. 'Markedness theory and error evaluation: an experimental study'. *Applied Linguistics* 8:207–18.

Sasaki, Y. 1991. 'English and Japanese interlanguage comprehension strategies: an analysis based on the competition model'. *Applied Psycholinguistics* 12: 47–73.

Sato, C. 1981. 'Ethnic styles in classroom discourse' in Hines and Rutherford (eds.) 1981.

Sato, C. 1984. 'Phonological processes in second language acquisition: another look at interlanguage syllable structure'. *Language Learning* 34: 43–57. Also in Ioup and Weinberger (eds.) 1987.

Sato, C. 1985. 'Task variation in interlanguage phonology' in Gass and Madden (eds.) 1985.

Sato, C. 1987. 'Phonological processes in second language acquisition: another look at interlanguage syllable structure' in Ioup and Weinberger (eds.) 1987.

Sato, C. 1988. 'Origins of complex syntax in interlanguage development'. *Studies in Second Language Acquisition* 10: 371–95.

Saunders, N. 1987. 'Morphophonemic variations in clusters in Japanese English'. *Language Learning* 37: 247–72.

Savignon, S. 1972. *Communicative Competence: an Experiment in Foreign Language Teaching*. Philadelphia: Center for Curriculum Development.

Saville-Troike, M. 1988. 'Private speech: evidence for second language learning strategies during the "silent period" '. *Journal of Child Language* 15: 567–90.

Savord, J-G. and L. Laforge (eds.). 1981. *Proceedings of the Fifth Conference of AILA*. Laval: University of Laval Press.

Scarcella, R. 1979. 'On speaking politely in a second language' in Yorio et al. (eds.) 1979.

Scarcella, R. 1983. 'Discourse accent in second language performance' in Gass and Selinker (eds.) 1983.

Scarcella, R., E. Andersen, and S. Krashen (eds.). 1990. *Developing Communicative Competence*. New York: Newbury House.

Scarcella, R. and C. Higa. 1981. 'Input, negotiation and age differences in second language acquisition'. *Language Learning* 31: 409–37.

Scarcella, R. and S. Krashen. (eds.). 1980. *Research in Second Language Acquisition*. Rowley, Mass.: Newbury House.

Schachter, J. 1974. 'An error in error analysis'. *Language Learning* 27: 205–14.

Schachter, J. 1983. 'A new account of language transfer' in Gass and Selinker (eds.) 1983.

Schachter, J. 1986a. 'In search of systematicity in interlanguage production'. *Studies in Second Language Acquisition* 8: 119–34.

Schachter, J. 1986b. 'Three approaches to the study of input'. *Language Learning* 36: 211–25.

Schachter, J. 1988. 'Second language acquisition and its relationship to Universal Grammar'. *Applied Linguistics* 9: 219–35.

Schachter, J. 1989. 'Testing a proposed universal' in Gass and Schachter (eds.) 1989.

Schachter, J. 1991. 'Corrective feedback in historical perspective'. *Second Language Research* 7: 89–102.

Schachter, J. and M. Celce-Murcia. 1977. 'Some reservations concerning error analysis'. *TESOL Quarterly* 11: 441–51.

Schachter, J. and W. Rutherford. 1979. 'Discourse function and language transfer'. *Working Papers on Bilingualism* 19: 3–12.

Schachter, J. and V. Yip. 1990. 'Grammaticality judgments: why does everyone object to subject extraction?' *Studies in Second Language Acquisition* 12: 379–92.

Schegloff, E., G. Jefferson, and H. Sacks. 1977. 'The preference for self-correction in the organization of repair in conversation'. *Language* 53: 361–82.

Scherer, A. and M. Wertheimer. 1964. *A Psycholinguistic Experiment in Foreign Language Teaching*. New York: McGraw Hill.

Scherer, K. and H. Giles (eds.). 1979. *Social Markers in Speech*. Cambridge: Cambridge University Press.

Schinke-Llano, L. 1990. 'Can foreign language learning be like second language acquisition? The curious case of immersion' in VanPatten and Lee (eds.) 1990.

Schmidt, M. 1980. 'Coordinate structures and language universals in interlanguage'. *Language Learning* 30: 397–416.

Schmidt, R. 1977. 'Sociolinguistic variation and language transfer in phonology'. *Working Papers on Bilingualism* 12: 79–95.

Schmidt, R. 1983. 'Interaction, acculturation and the acquisition of communication competence' in Wolfson and Judd (eds.) 1983.

Schmidt, R. 1988. 'The potential of parallel distributed processing for S.L.A. theory and research'. *University of Hawaii Working Papers in ESL* 7: 55–56.

Schmidt, R. 1990. 'The role of consciousness in second language learning'. *Applied Linguistics* 11: 129–58.

Schmidt, R. 1992. 'Psychological mechanisms underlying second language fluency'. *Studies in Second Language Acquisition* 14: 357–85.

Schmidt, R. and S. Frota. 1986. 'Developing basic conversational ability in a second language: a case-study of an adult learner' in Day (ed.) 1986.

Schouten, M. 1979. 'The missing data in second language learning research'. *Interlanguage Studies Bulletin* 4: 3–14.

Schumann, F. and J. Schumann. 1977. 'Diary of a language learner: an introspective study of second language learning' in H. Brown et al. (eds.) 1977.

Schumann, J. 1978a. 'The acculturation model for second language acquisition' in Gingras (ed.) 1978.

Schumann, J. 1978b. *The Pidginization Process: a Model for Second Language Acquisition*. Rowley, Mass.: Newbury House.

Schumann, J. 1978c. 'Social and psychological factors in second language acquisition' in Richards, (ed.) 1978.

Schumann, J. 1979. 'The acquisition of English negation by speakers of Spanish: a review of the literature' in Andersen (ed.) 1979a.

Schumann, J. 1980. 'The acquisition of English relative clauses by second language learners' in Scarcella and Krashen (eds.) 1980.

Schumann, J. 1983. 'Art and science in second language acquisition research'. *Language Learning Special Issue* 33: 49–75.

Schumann, J. 1986. 'Research on the acculturation model for second language acquisition'. *Journal of Multilingual and Multicultural Development* 7: 379–92.

Schumann, J. 1987. 'The expression of temporality in basilang speech'. *Studies in Second Language Acquisition* 9: 21–41.

Schumann, J. 1990. 'Extending the scope of the acculturation/pidginization model to include cognition'. *TESOL Quarterly* 24: 667–84.

Schumann, J. 1993. 'Some problems with falisification: an illustration from SLA research'. *Applied Linguistics* 14: 295–306.

Schumann, J. and N. Stenson. (eds.). 1974. *New Frontiers in Second Language Learning*. Rowley, Mass.: Newbury House.

Schwartz, B. 1986. 'The epistemological status of second language acquisition'. *Second Language Research* 2: 120–59.

Schwartz, B. and B. Gubala-Ryzak. 1992. 'Learnability and grammar reorganization in L2A: against negative evidence causing the unlearning of verb movement'. *Second Language Research* 8: 1–38.

Schwartz, J. 1980. 'The negotiation for meaning: repair in conversations between second language learners of English' in Larsen-Freeman (ed.) 1980.

Schwartz, R. and S. Camarata. 1985. 'Examining the relationship between input and language development: some statistical issues'. *Journal of Child Language* 12: 13–25.

Schweder, R. and R. LeVine (eds.). 1984. *Culture and its Acquisition*. New York: Academic Press.

Scollon, R. 1976. *Conversations with a One-year Old*. Honolulu: The University of Hawaii Press.

Scollon, R. and S. Scollon. 1983. 'Face in interethnic communication' in Richards and Schmidt (eds.) 1983.

Scovel, T. 1978. 'The effect of affect on foreign language learning: a review of the anxiety research'. *Language Learning* 28: 129–42.

Scovel, T. 1981. 'The recognition of foreign accents in English and its implications for psycholinguistic theories of language acquisition' in Savord and Laforge (eds.) 1981.

Scovel, T. 1988. *A Time to Speak: a Psycholinguistic Enquiry into the Critical Period for Human Speech*. Rowley, Mass.: Newbury House.

Scribner, S. and M. Cole. 1973. 'Cognitive consequences of formal and informal learning'. *Science* 182: 553–9.

Searle, J. 1969. *Speech Acts*. Cambridge: Cambridge University Press.

Searle, J. 1975. 'Indirect speech acts' in Cole and Morgan (eds.) 1975.

Searle, J. 1976. 'The classification of illocutionary acts'. *Language in Society* 5: 1–24.

Seliger, H. 1975. 'Inductive method and deductive method in language teaching: a re-examination'. *International Review of Applied Linguistics* 13: 1–18.

Seliger, H. 1977. 'Does practice make perfect? A study of the interaction patterns and L2 competence'. *Language Learning* 27: 263–78.

Seliger, H. 1978. 'Implications of a multiple critical periods hypothesis for second language learning' in Ritchie (ed.) 1978a.

Seliger, H. 1979. 'On the nature and function of language rules in language teaching'. *TESOL Quarterly* 13: 359–69.

Seliger, H. 1984. 'Processing universals in second language acquisition' in Eckman et al. (eds.) 1984.

Seliger, H. 1989. 'Semantic transfer constraints in foreign language speakers' reactions to acceptability' in Dechert and Raupach (eds.) 1989a.

Seliger, H. and M. Long (eds.). 1983. *Classroom-oriented Research in Second Language Acquisition*. Rowley, Mass.: Newbury House.

Selinker, L. 1969. 'Language transfer'. *General Linguistics* 9: 67–92.

Selinker, L. 1972. 'Interlanguage'. *International Review of Applied Linguistics* 10: 209–31.

Selinker, L. 1984. 'The current state of interlanguage studies: an attempted critical summary' in Davies et al. (eds.) 1984.

Selinker, L. 1992. *Rediscovering Interlanguage*. London: Longman.

Selinker, L. and D. Douglas. 1985. 'Wrestling with context in interlanguage theory'. *Applied Linguistics* 6: 190–204.

Selinker, L. and J. Lamendella. 1978. 'Two perspectives on fossilization in interlanguage learning'. *Interlanguage Studies Bulletin* 3: 143–91.

Selinker, L., M. Swain, and G. Dumas. 1975. 'The interlanguage hypothesis extended to children'. *Language Learning* 25: 139–91.

Shapiro, F. 1979. 'What do teachers actually *do* in language classrooms?' Paper presented at the 13th Annual TESOL Convention, Boston.

Shapson, S. and V. D'Oyley (eds.). 1984. *Bilingual and Multicultural Education: Canadian Perspectives*. Clevedon, Avon: Multilingual Matters.

Sharwood Smith, M. 1980. 'The competence–performance distinction in the theory of second language and the Pedagogical Grammar Hypothesis'. Paper presented at the Contrastive Linguistics Conference, Boszkowo. Cited in Rutherford and Sharwood Smith 1985.

Sharwood Smith, M. 1981. 'Consciousness-raising and the second language learner'. *Applied Linguistics* 2: 159–69.

Sharwood Smith, M. 1984. 'Discussant of "The study of lexis in interlanguage" by Paul Meara' in Davies et al. (eds.) 1984.

Sharwood Smith, M. 1985. 'From input to intake: on argumentation in second language acquisition' in Gass and Madden (eds.) 1985.

Sharwood Smith M. 1986. 'Comprehension vs. acquisition: two ways of processing input'. *Applied Linguistics* 7: 239–56.

Sharwood Smith, M. 1991. 'Speaking to many minds: on the relevance of different types of language information for the L2 learner'. *Second Language Research* 7: 118–32.

Sharwood Smith, M. and E. Kellerman. 1986. 'Crosslinguistic influence in second language acquisition: an introduction' in Kellerman and Sharwood Smith (eds.) 1986.

Shatz, M. 1978. 'On the development of communicative understanding: an early strategy for interpreting and responding to message'. *Journal of Cognitive Psychology* 10: 271–301.

Shatz, M. and R. Gelman. 1973. 'The development of communication skills: modifications in the speech of young children as a function of listener'. *Monographs of the Society for Research in Child Development* 38, no. 5.

Sheorey, R. 1986. 'Error perceptions of native-speaking and non-native speaking teachers of ESL'. *English Language Teaching Journal* 40: 306–12.

Shiffrin, R. and W. Schneider. 1977. 'Controlled and automatic human information processing: II. Perceptual learning, automatic attending and a general theory'. *Psychological Review* 84: 127–90.

Shimura, A. 1990. 'Why do the Japanese learners produce fewer relative clauses in English'. Unpublished term paper. ESL 750: University of Hawaii.

Simon, A. and E. Boyer (eds.). 1967. *Mirrors for behavior: an anthology of classroom observation instruments*. Philadelphia: Center for the Study of Teaching at Temple University.

Sinclair, J. and D. Brazil. 1982. *Teacher Talk*. Oxford: Oxford University Press.

Sinclair, J. and M. Coulthard. 1975. *Towards an Analysis of Discourse*. Oxford: Oxford University Press.

Sinclair-de-Zwart, H. 1973. 'Language acquisition and cognitive development' in Moore (ed.) 1973.

Singleton, D. 1987. 'Mother and other tongue influence on learner French: a case study'. *Studies in Second Language Acquisition* 9: 327–45.

Singleton, D. 1989. *Language Acquisition: the Age Factor*. Clevedon, Avon: Multilingual Matters.

Singleton, D. and **D. Little** (eds.). 1984. *Language Learning in Formal and Informal Contexts.* Dublin: IRAAL.

Sjoholm, K. 1976. 'A comparison of the test results in grammar and vocabulary between Finnish- and Swedish-speaking applicants for English' in Ringbom and Palmberg (eds.) 1976.

Sjoholm, K. 1979. 'Do Finns and Swedish-speaking Finns use different strategies in the learning of English as a foreign language?' in Palmberg (ed.) 1979.

Skehan, P. 1986a. 'Cluster analysis and the identification of learner types' in Cook (ed.) 1986.

Skehan, P. 1986b. 'Where does language aptitude come from?' in Meara (ed.) 1986.

Skehan, P. 1989. *Individual Differences in Second-language Learning.* London: Edward Arnold.

Skehan, P. 1990. 'The relationship between native and foreign language learning ability: educational and linguistic factors' in Dechert (ed.) 1990.

Skehan, P. 1991. 'Individual differences in second language learning'. *Studies in Second Language Acquisition* 13: 275–98.

Skinner, B. 1957. *Verbal Behavior.* New York: Appleton-Century-Crofts.

Skuttnab-Kangas, T. (ed.). 1977. Papers from the First Nordic Conference on Bilingualism. Helsingfors: Universitet.

Skuttnab-Kangas, T. 1986. 'Who wants to change what and why—conflicting paradigms in minority education research' in Spolsky (ed.) 1986.

Skuttnab-Kangas, T. 1988. 'Multilingualism and the education of minority children' in Skuttnab-Kangas and Cummins (eds.) 1988.

Skuttnab-Kangas, T. and **J. Cummins** (eds.). 1988. *Minority Education.* Clevedon, Avon: Multilingual Matters.

Slimani, A. 1989. 'The role of topicalization in classroom language learning'. *System* 17: 223–34.

Slobin, D. 1970. 'Universals of grammatical development in children' in Flores d'Arcais and Levelt (eds.) 1970.

Slobin, D. 1971. *Psycholinguistics.* Glenview, Illinois: Scott Foresman.

Slobin, D. 1973. 'Cognitive prerequisites for the development of grammar' in Ferguson and Slobin (eds.) 1973.

Slobin, D. (ed.). 1985a. *The Crosslinguistic Study of Language Acquisition, Vol. 2, Theoretical Issues.* Hillsdale, N.J.: Lawrence Erlbaum.

Slobin, D. 1985b. 'Cross-linguistic evidence for the language-making capacity' in Slobin (ed.).

Smith, D. 1972. 'Some implications for the social status of pidgin languages' in Smith and Shuy (eds.) 1972.

Smith, D. and **R. Shuy** (eds.). 1972. *Sociolinguistics in Cross-cultural Analysis.* Washington D.C.: Georgetown University Press.

Smith, F. and **G. Miller** (eds.). 1966. *The Genesis of Language: a Psycholinguistic Approach.* Cambridge, Mass.: MIT Press.

Smith, L. (ed.). 1981. *English for Cross-cultural Communication.* London: Macmillan.

Smith, L. 1983. *Readings in English as an International Language.* London: Pergamon.

Smith, P. 1970. 'A comparison of the audiolingual and cognitive approaches to foreign language instruction: the Pennsylvania Foreign Language Project'. Philadelphia: Center for Curriculum Development.

Snow, C. 1972. 'Mother's speech to children learning'. *Child Development* 43: 549–65.

Snow, C. 1976. 'The language of the mother-child relationship' in Rogers (ed.) 1976.

Snow, C. 1977. 'Mothers' speech research: from input to interaction' in Snow and Ferguson (eds.) 1977.

Snow, C. 1986. 'Conversations with Children' in Fletcher and Garman (eds.) 1986.

Snow, C. 1987. 'Beyond conversation: second language learners' acquisition of description and explanation' in Lantolf and Labarca (eds.) 1987.

Snow, C. and **C. Ferguson** (eds.). 1977. *Talking to Children: Language Input and Acquisition.* Cambridge: Cambridge University Press.

Snow, C. and **M. Hoefnagel-Höhle.** 1978. 'The critical age for language acquisition: evidence from second language learning'. *Child Development* 49: 1114–28.

Snow, C. and **M. Hoefnagel–Höhle.** 1982. 'School age second language learners' access to simplified linguistic input'. *Language Learning* 32: 411–30.

Sokolik, M. 1990. 'Learning without rules: PDP and a resolution of the adult language learning paradox'. *TESOL Quarterly* 24: 685–96.

Sorace, A. 1985. 'Metalinguistic knowledge and language use in acquisition-poor environments'. *Applied Linguistics* 6: 239–54.

Sorace, A. 1988. 'Linguistic intuitions in interlanguage development: the problem of indeterminacy' in Pankhurst et al. (eds.) 1988.

Spada, N. 1986. 'The interaction between types of content and type of instruction: some effects on the L2 proficiency of adult learners'. *Studies in Second Language Acquisition* 8: 181–99.

Spada, N. 1987. 'Relationships between instructional differences and learning outcomes: a process–product study of communicative language teaching'. *Applied Linguistics* 8: 137–61.

Spada, N. and **P. Lightbown.** 1989. 'Intensive ESL programmes in Quebec primary schools'. *TESL Canada* 7: 11–32.

Spielberger, C. 1983. *Manual for the State-Trait Anxiety Inventory (Form Y).* Palo Alto, Calif.: Consulting Psychologists Press.

Spindler, G. (ed.). 1982. *Doing the Ethnography of Schooling: Educational Ethnography in Action.* New York: CBS College Publishing. Cited in Mitchell 1985.

Spolsky, B. 1969. 'Attitudinal aspects of second language learning'. *Language Learning* 19: 271–85.

Spolsky, B. 1986a. 'Overcoming language barriers to education in a multilingual world' in Spolsky (ed.).

Spolsky, B. (ed.). 1986b. *Language and Education in Multilingual Settings.* Clevedon, Avon: Multilingual Matters.

Spolsky. B. 1988. 'Bridging the gap: a general theory of second language learning'. *TESOL Quarterly* 22: 377–96.

Spolsky, B. 1989. *Conditions for Second Language Learning.* Oxford: Oxford University Press.

Spolsky, B. 1990. 'Introduction to a colloquium: the scope and form of a theory of second language learning'. *TESOL Quarterly* 24: 609–16.

Sridhar, S. and **K. Sridhar.** 1986. 'Bridging the paradigm gap: second language acquisition theory and indigenized varieties of English'. *World Englishes* 5: 3–14.

Stansfield, C. and **L. Hansen.** 1983. 'Field-dependence-independence as a variable in second language cloze test performance'. *TESOL Quarterly* 17: 29–38.

Stauble, A. 1978. 'Decreolization: a model for second language development'. *Language Learning* 28: 29–54.

Stauble, A. 1984. 'A comparison of the Spanish-English and Japanese-English interlanguage continuum' in Andersen (ed.) 1984b.

Stenson, B. 1974. 'Induced errors' in Schumann and Stenson (eds.) 1974.

Stern, H. 1975. 'What can we learn from the good language learner?' *Canadian Modern Language Review* 31: 304–18.

Stern, H. 1983. *Fundamental Concepts of Language Teaching.* Oxford: Oxford University Press.

Stern, H. 1990. 'Analysis and experience as variables in second language pedagogy' in Harley et al. (eds.) 1990.

Stever, S., C. Walker, and **S. Mufwene** (eds.). 1976. *Papers from the Parasession on Diachronic Syntax.* Chicago: Chicago Linguistic Society.

Stevick, E. 1980. *Teaching Languages: a Way and Ways.* Rowley, Mass.: Newbury House.

Stevick, E. 1989. *Success with Foreign Languages.* New York: Prentice Hall.

Stockwell, R. and **J. Bowen.** 1965. *The Sounds of English and Spanish.* Chicago: Chicago University Press.

Stockwell, R., J. Bowen, and J. Martin. 1965. *The Grammatical Structures of English and Spanish*. Chicago: Chicago University Press.

Strevens, P. 1980. *Teaching English as an International Language*. Oxford: Pergamon.

Strong, M. 1983. 'Social styles and second language acquisition of Spanish-speaking kindergarteners'. *TESOL Quarterly* 17: 241–58.

Strong, M. 1984. 'Integrative motivation: cause or result of successful second language acquisition?' *Language Learning* 34: 1–14.

Sundquist, L. 1986. 'Lexical inferencing among Swedish- and Finnish-speaking primary-school pupils'. Unpublished Masters thesis. Abo Akademi University, Abo (Turku), Finland.

Svanes, B. 1988. 'Attitudes and "cultural distance" in second language acquisition'. *Applied Linguistics* 9: 357–71.

Svartvik, J. (ed.). 1973a. *Errata: Papers in Error Analysis*. Lund, Sweden: CWK Gleerup.

Svartvik, J. 1973b. 'Introduction' in Svartvik (ed.).

Swain, M. 1981. 'Target language use in the wider environment as a factor in its acquisition' in Andersen (ed.) 1981.

Swain, M. 1985. 'Communicative competence: some roles of comprehensible input and comprehensible output in its development' in Gass and Madden (eds.) 1985.

Swain, M. and J. Cummins. 1979. 'Bilingualism, cognitive functioning and education'. *Language Teaching and Abstracts* 4–18. Reprinted in Kinsella (ed.) 1982.

Swain, M. and S. Lapkin. 1982. *Evaluating Bilingual Education: a Canadian Case Study*. Clevedon, Avon: Multilingual Matters.

Swan, M. 1987. 'Non-systematic variability: a self-inflicted conundrum' in Ellis (ed.) 1987a.

Tahta, S., M. Wood, and K. Loewenthal. 1981. 'Age changes in the ability to replicate foreign pronunciation and intonation'. *Language and Speech* 24: 363–72.

Tajfel, H. (ed.). 1984. *The Social Dimension, Vol 2*. Cambridge, Cambridge University Press.

Takahashi, T. 1989. 'The influence of the listener on L2 speech' in Gass et al. (eds) 1989a.

Takahashi, T. and L. Beebe. 1987. 'The development of pragmatic competence by Japanese learners of English'. *JALT Journal* 8: 131–55.

Tanaka, N. 1988. 'Politeness: some problems for Japanese speakers of English'. *JALT Journal* 9: 81–102.

Tanaka, S. and S. Kawade. 1982. 'Politeness strategies and second language acquisition'. *Studies in Second Language Acquisition* 5: 18–33.

Tanaka, Y. 1991. 'Comprehension and L2 acquisition: the role of interaction'. Unpublished paper, Tokyo: Temple University Japan.

Tarallo, F. and J. Myhill. 1983. 'Interference and natural language in second language acquisition'. *Language Learning* 33: 55–76.

Tarone, E. 1977. 'Conscious communication strategies in interlanguage: a progress report' in H. Brown et al. (eds.) 1977.

Tarone, E. 1978. 'The phonology of interlanguage' in Richards (ed.) 1978.

Tarone, E. 1979. 'Interlanguage as chameleon'. *Language Learning* 29: 181–91.

Tarone, E. 1980a. 'Some influences on the syllable structure of interlanguage phonology'. *International Review of Applied Linguistics* 4: 143–63. Also in Ioup and Weinberger (eds.) 1987.

Tarone, E. 1980b. 'Communication strategies, foreigner talk, and repair in interlanguage'. *Language Learning* 30: 417–31.

Tarone, E. 1982. 'Systematicity and attention in interlanguage'. *Language Learning* 32: 69–82.

Tarone, E. 1983. 'On the variability of interlanguage systems'. *Applied Linguistics* 4: 143–63.

Tarone, E. 1985. 'Variability in interlanguage use: a study of style-shifting in morphology and syntax'. *Language Learning* 35: 373–403.

Tarone, E. 1988. *Variation in Interlanguage*. London: Edward Arnold.

Tarone, E. 1990. 'On variation in interlanguage: a response to Gregg'. *Applied Linguistics* 11: 392–400.

Tarone, E., A. Cohen, and G. Dumas. 1976. 'A closer look at some interlanguage terminology: a framework for communication strategies'. *Working Papers on Bilingualism* 9: 76–90.

Tarone, E. and B. Parrish. 1988. 'Task-related variation in interlanguage: the case of articles'. *Language Learning* 38: 21–44.

Tarone, E., M. Swain, and A. Fathman. 1976. 'Some limitations to the classroom applications of current second language acquisition research'. *TESOL Quarterly* 10: 19–31.

Taylor, B. 1975. 'The use of overgeneralization and transfer learning strategies by elementary and intermediate students of ESL'. *Language Learning* 25: 73–107.

Taylor, D. 1980. 'Ethnicity and language: a social psychological perspective' in Giles et al. (eds.) 1980.

Taylor, D. 1988. 'The meaning and use of the term "competence" in linguistics and applied linguistics'. *Applied Linguistics* 9: 148–68.

Taylor, G. 1986. 'Errors and explanations'. *Applied Linguistics* 7: 144–66.

Taylor, L., A. Guiora, J. Catford, and H. Lane. 1969. 'The role of personality variables in second language behavior'. *Comprehensive Psychiatry* 10: 463–74.

Terrell, T. 1977. 'A natural approach to second language acquisition and learning'. *Modern Language Journal* 61: 325–36.

Terrell, T. 1991. 'The role of grammar instruction in a communicative approach'. *Modern Language Journal* 75: 52–63.

Terrell, T., E. Gomez, and J. Mariscal. 1980. 'Can acquisition take place in the classrrom' in Scarcella and Krashen (eds.) 1980.

Thakerar, J., H. Giles, and J. Cheshire. 1982. 'Psychological and linguistic parameters of speech accommodation theory' in Fraser and Scherer (eds.) 1982.

Thomas, J. 1983. 'Cross-cultural pragmatic failure'. *Applied Linguistics* 4: 91–112.

Thomas, L. and E. Harri-Augstein. 1990. 'The technology of learning conversations: a constructive alternative to the mythology of learning styles' in Duda and Riley (eds.) 1990.

Thomas, M. 1989. 'The interpretation of English reflexive pronouns by non-native speakers'. *Studies in Second Language Acquisition* 11: 281–303.

Thomason, S. and T. Kaufman. 1988. *Language Contact, Creolization, and Genetic Linguistics.* Berkeley: University of California Press.

Thompson, E. 1991. 'Foreign accents revisited: the English pronunciation of Russian immigrants'. *Language Learning* 41: 177–204.

Thorndike, E. 1932. *The Fundamentals of Learning.* New York: Columbia Teachers College.

Tollefson, J. 1991. *Planning Language, Planning Inequality.* London: Longman.

Tomasello, M. and C. Herron. 1988. 'Down the garden path: Inducing and correcting overgeneralization errors in the foreign language classroom'. *Applied Psycholinguistics* 9: 237–46.

Tomasello, M. and C. Herron. 1989. 'Feedback for language transfer errors: the garden path technique'. *Studies in Second Language Acquisition* 11: 385–95.

Tomasello, M. and C. Herron. 1991. 'Experiments in the real world: a reply to Beck and Eubank'. *Studies in Second Language Acquisition* 13: 513–17.

Tomiyana, M. 1980. 'Grammatical errors and communication breakdown'. *TESOL Quarterly* 14: 71–9.

Tomlin, B. 1990. 'Functionalism in second language acquisition'. *Studies in Second Language Acquisition* 12: 155–77.

Tong-Fredericks, C. 1984. 'Types of oral communication activities and the language they generate: a comparison'. *System* 12: 133–34.

Tosi, A. 1984. *Immigration and Bilingual Education.* Oxford: Pergamon.

Towell, R. 1987. 'Variability and progress in the language development of advanced learners of a foreign language' in Ellis (ed.) 1987a.

Tran-Chi-Chau. 1975. 'Error analysis, contrastive analysis and students' perceptions: a study of difficulty in second language learning'. *International Review of Applied Linguistics* 13: 119–43.

Trueba, H., G. Guthrie, and K. Au (eds.). 1981. *Culture and the Bilingual Classroom: Studies in Classroom Ethnography.* Rowley, Mass.: Newbury House.

Trevise, A. and R. Porquier. 1986. 'Second language acquisition by adult immigrants: exemplified methodology'. *Studies in Second Language Acquisition* 8: 265–76.

Triandis, H. 1971. *Attitude and Attitude Change.* New York: Wiley and Sons.

Trubetzkoy, N. 1931. 'Die phonologischen Systeme'. *Travaux du Cercle Linguistique de Prague* 4: 96–116.

Trudgill, P. (ed.). 1984. *Applied Sociolinguistics.* London: Academic Press.

Tucker, G., E. Hamayan, and F. Genesee. 1976. 'Affective cognitive and social factors in second language acquisition'. *Canadian Modern Language Review* 32: 214–16.

Tucker, G., W. Lambert, and A. Rigault. 1977. *The French Speaker's Skill with Grammatical Gender: an Example of Rule-governed Behavior.* The Hague: Mouton.

Turner, D. 1979. 'The effect of instruction on second language learning and second language acquisition' in Andersen (ed.) 1979a.

Turner, J. and H. Giles (eds.). 1981. *Intergroup Behavior.* Chicago, Illinois: University of Chicago Press.

Upshur, J. 1968. 'Four experiments on the relation between foreign language teaching and learning'. *Language Learning* 18: 111–24.

Uziel, S. 1993. 'Resetting universal grammar parameters: evidence from second language acquisition of Subjacency and the Empty Category Principle'. *Second Language Research* 9: 49–83.

Valdman, A. (ed.). 1977. *Pidgin and Creole.* Indiana University Press.

Valdman, A. 1978. 'On the relevance of the pidginization–creolization model for second language learning'. *Studies in Second Language Acquisition* 1: 55–77.

Valdman, A. 1992. 'Authenticity, variation and communication in the foreign language classroom' in Kramsch and McConnell-Ginet (eds.) 1992.

Van Buren, P. and M. Sharwood Smith. 1985. 'The acquisition of preposition stranding by second language learners and parametric variation'. *Second Language Research* 1: 18–26.

Van Els, T., T. Bongaerts, G. Extra, C. Van Os, and A. Janssen-Van Dieten. 1984. *Applied Linguistics and the Learning and Teaching of Foreign Languages.* London: Edward Arnold.

Van Lier, L. 1982. 'Analysing interaction in second language classrooms'. Unpublished PhD thesis, Lancaster: University of Lancaster.

Van Lier, L. 1988. *The Classroom and the Language Learner.* London: Longman.

Van Lier, L. 1991. 'Inside the classroom: learning processes and teaching procedures'. *Applied Language Learning* 2: 29–69.

Van Naerssen, M. 1980. 'How similar are Spanish as a first and foreign language?' in Scarcella and Krashen (eds.) 1980.

Van Riemsdijk, H. 1978. *A Case Study in Syntactic Markedness.* Liss: Peter de Ridder Press.

Vander Brook, S., K. Schlue, and C. Campbell. 1980. 'Discourse and second language acquisition of Yes/No questions' in Larsen-Freeman (ed.) 1980.

Vann, R., D. Meyer, and F. Lorenz. 1984. 'Error gravity: a study of faculty opinion of ESL errors'. *TESOL Quarterly* 18: 427–40.

VanPatten, B. 1990. 'The acquisition of clitic pronouns in Spanish: Two case studies' in VanPatten and Lee (eds.) 1990.

VanPatten, B. and T. Cadierno. 1993. 'Explicit instruction and input processing'. *Studies in Second Language Acquisition* 15, 225–43.

VanPatten, B., T. Dvorak, and J. Lee (eds.). 1987. *Foreign Language Learning: A Research Perspective.* New York: Newbury House/Harper and Row.

VanPatten, B. and J. Lee. (eds.). 1990. *Second Language Acquisition—Foreign Language Learning.* Clevedon, Avon: Multilingual Matters.

Varadi, T. 1980. 'Strategies of target language learner communication: message adjustment'. *International Review of Applied Linguistics* 18: 59–71.

Varonis, E. and **S. Gass.** 1985. 'Non-native/non-native conversations: a model for negotiation of meaning'. *Applied Linguistics* 6: 71–90.

Verhoeven, L. 1991. 'Predicting minority children's bilingual proficiency: child, family and institutional factors'. *Language Learning* 41: 205–33.

Veronique, D. 1987. 'Reference to past events and actions in narratives in a second language: insights from North African workers' French' in Pfaff (ed.) 1987b.

Verschuren, J. and **M. Bertucelli-Papi** (eds.). 1985. *The Pragmatic Perspective.* Amsterdam: John Benjamins.

Vigil, F. and **J. Oller.** 1976. 'Rule fossilization: a tentative model'. *Language Learning* 26: 281–95.

Vincent, M. 1986. 'Simple text and reading text Part 1: some general issues' in Brumfit and Carter (eds.) 1986.

Vogel, T. and **J. Bahns.** 1989. 'Introducing the English progressive in the classroom: insights from second language acquisition research'. *System* 17: 183–94.

Von Elek, P. and **M. Oskarsson.** 1975. 'Comparative method experiments in foreign language teaching'. Department of Educational Research, Molndal (Gothenburg, Sweden): School of Education.

Wagner-Gough, J. 1975. 'Comparative studies in second language learning'. *CAL-ERIC/CLL Series on Language and Linguistics* 26.

Wagner-Gough, J. and **E. Hatch.** 1975. 'The importance of input data in second language acquisition studies'. *Language Learning* 25: 297–308.

Walter-Goldberg, B. 1982. 'A stranger in Portugal: a study of Portuguese foreigner talk'. Term Paper, Ed. 676, University of Pennsylvania. Cited in Larsen-Freeman and Long 1991.

Walters, J. 1979. 'The perception of deference in English and Spanish' in Yorio et al. (eds.) 1979.

Walters, J. 1980. 'Grammar, meaning and sociocultural appropriateness in second language acquisition'. *Canadian Journal of Psychology* 34: 337–45.

Wanner, E. and **L. Gleitman** (eds.). 1982. *Language Acquisition: the State of the Art.* New York: Cambridge University Press.

Wardhaugh, R. 1970. 'The Contrastive Analysis Hypothesis'. *TESOL Quarterly* 4: 123–30.

Waterson, N. and **C. Snow** (eds.). 1978. *The Development of Communication.* New York: Wiley and Sons.

Watson, J. 1924. *Behaviorism.* New York: Norton.

Weinert, R. 1987. 'Processes in classroom second language development: the acquisition of negation in German' in Ellis (ed.) 1987a.

Weinreich, U. 1953. *Languages in Contact.* The Hague: Mouton.

Weinstein, C. and **R. Mayer.** 1986. 'The teaching of learning strategies' in Wittrock (ed.) 1986.

Wells, G. 1980. 'Apprenticeship in meaning' in Nelson (ed.) 1980.

Wells, G. 1985. *Language Development in the Pre-school Years.* Cambridge: Cambridge University Press.

Wells, G. 1986a. *The Meaning Makers: Children Learning Language and Using Language to Learn.* London: Hodder and Stoughton.

Wells, G. 1986b. 'Variation in child language' in Fletcher and Garman (eds.) 1986.

Wells, G. and **M. Montgomery.** 1981. 'Adult–child interaction at home and at school' in French and McLure (eds.) 1981.

Wenden, A. 1983. 'Literature review: the process of intervention'. *Language Learning* 33: 103–21.

Wenden, A. 1986a. 'What do second language learners know about their language learning? A second look at retrospective accounts'. *Applied Linguistics* 7: 186–201.

Wenden, A. 1986b. 'Helping language learners think about learning'. *English Language Teaching Journal* 40: 3–12.

Wenden, A. 1987a. 'How to be a successful learner: insights and prescriptions from L2 learners' in Wenden and Rubin (eds.) 1987.

Wenden, A. 1987b. 'Incorporating learner training in the classroom' in Wenden and Rubin (eds.) 1987.

Wenden, A. 1991. *Learner Strategies for Learner Autonomy*. New York: Prentice Hall.

Wenden, A. and J. Rubin (eds.). 1987. *Learner Strategies in Language Learning*. Englewood Cliffs, N.J.: Prentice Hall.

Wenk, B. 1986. 'Crosslinguistic influence in second language phonology: speech rhythms' in E. Kellerman and Sharwood Smith (eds.) 1986.

Wesche, M. 1981. 'Language aptitude measures in streaming, matching students with methods, and diagnosis of learning problems' in Diller (ed.) 1981.

Wesche, M. and D. Ready. 1985. 'Foreigner talk in the university classroom' in Gass and Madden (eds.) 1985.

Weslander, D. and G. Stephany. 1983. 'Evaluation of English as a second language program for Southeast Asian students'. *TESOL Quarterly* 1983: 473–80.

Westmoreland, R. 1983. 'German acquisition by instructed adults'. Unpublished paper, Hawaii: University of Hawaii.

Wexler, K. and P. Culicover. 1980. *Formal Principles of Language Acquisition*. Cambridge, Mass.: MIT Press.

Wexler, K. and R. Mancini. 1987. 'Parameters and learnability in binding theory' in Roeper and Williams (eds.) 1987.

Whitaker, H., D. Bub, and S. Leventer. 1981. 'Neurolinguistic aspects of language acquisition and bilingualism'. *Annals of the New York Academy of Sciences* 379: 59–74.

White, L. 1977. 'Error-analysis and error-correction in adult learners of English as a second language'. *Working Papers on Bilingualism* 13: 42–58.

White, L. 1981. 'The responsibility of grammatical theory to acquisitional data' in Hornstein and Lightfoot (eds.) 1981.

White, L. 1985. 'The pro-drop parameter in adult second language acquisition'. *Language Learning* 35: 47–62.

White, L. 1986. 'Implications of parametric variation for adult second language acquisition: an investigation of the "pro-drop" parameter' in Cook (ed.) 1986.

White, L. 1987a. 'Against comprehensible input: the input hypothesis and the development of second language competence'. *Applied Linguistics* 8: 95–110.

White, L. 1987b. 'Markedness and second language acquisition: the question of transfer'. *Studies in Second Language Acquisition* 9: 261–86.

White, L. 1989a. *Universal Grammar and Second Language Acquisition*. Amsterdam: John Benjamins.

White, L. 1989b. 'The adjacency condition on case assignment: do learners observe the Subset Principle?' in Gass and Schachter (eds.) 1989.

White, L. 1990. 'Second language acquisition and universal grammar'. *Studies in Second Language Acquisition* 12: 121–33.

White, L. 1991a. 'Adverb placement in second language acquisition: some effects of positive and negative evidence in the classroom'. *Second Language Research* 7: 133–61.

White, L. 1991b. 'Argument structure in second language acquisition'. *French Language Studies* 1: 189–207.

White, L. (forthcoming). 'Universal grammar and second language acquisition: current trends and new directions' in Bhatia and Ritchie (eds.).

White, L. and P. Lightbown. 1984. 'Asking and answering in ESL classes'. *Canadian Modern Language Review* 40: 288–344.

White, L., N. Spada, P. Lightbown, and L. Ranta. 1991. 'Input enhancement and question formation'. *Applied Linguistics* 12: 416–32.

White, L., L. Travis, and A. Maclachlan. (in press). 'The acquisition of wh-question formation by Malagasy learners of English: evidence for Universal Grammar'. *Canadian Journal of Linguistics*.

White, M. 1992. 'Teachers' questions—form, function, and interaction: a study of two teachers'. Unpublished paper, Tokyo: Temple University Japan.

Widdowson, H. 1974. 'An approach to the teaching of scientific discourse'. *RELC Journal* 5.

Widdowson, H. 1977. 'Pidgin and babu' in Corder and Roulet (eds.) 1977.

Widdowson, H. 1978. *Teaching Language as Communication*. Oxford: Oxford University Press.

Widdowson, H. 1979a. 'The significance of simplification' in Widdowson 1979b.

Widdowson, H. 1979b. *Explorations in Applied Linguistics*. Oxford: Oxford University Press. Previously published in *Studies in Second Language Acquisition* 1.

Widdowson, H. 1979c. 'Rules and procedures in discourse analysis' in Myers (ed.) 1979.

Widdowson, H. 1983. *Learning Purpose and Language Use*. Oxford: Oxford University Press.

Widdowson, H. 1989. 'Knowledge of language and ability for use'. *Applied Linguistics* 10: 128–37.

Widdowson, H. 1990a. 'Pedagogic research and teacher education' in Widdowson 1990b.

Widdowson, H. 1990b. *Aspects of Language Teaching*. Oxford: Oxford University Press.

Wiese, R. 1984. 'Language production in foreign and native languages: same or different?' in Dechert et al. (eds.) 1984.

Wilkinson, L. (ed.). 1982. *Communicating in the Classroom*. New York: Academic Press.

Williams, J. 1989. 'Pronoun copies, pronominal anaphora and zero anaphora in second language production' in Gass et al. (eds.) 1989a.

Williams, J. 1990. 'Another look at yes/no questions: native speakers and non-native speakers'. *Applied Linguistics* 11: 159–82.

Williams, K. 1991. 'Anxiety and formal/foreign language learning'. *RELC Journal* 22: 19–28.

Willing, K. 1987. *Learning Styles and Adult Migrant Education*. Adelaide: National Curriculum Resource Centre.

Winitz, H. (ed.) 1981a. *The Comprehension Approach to Foreign Language Instruction*. Rowley, Mass.: Newbury House.

Winitz, H. (ed.). 1981b. *Native Language and Foreign Acquisition*. Annals of the New York Academy of Sciences, 379.

Witkin, H. and J. Berry. 1975. 'Psychological differentiation in cross-cultural perspective'. *Journal of Cross-Cultural Psychology* 6: 4–87.

Witkin, H. and D. Goodenough. 1981. 'Cognitive styles: essence and origins—field dependence and independence'. *Psychological Issues Monograph* 51.

Witkin, H., O. Oltman, E. Raskin, and S. Karp. 1971. *A Manual for the Embedded Figures Test*. Palo Alto, Calif.: Consulting Psychology Press.

Wittrock, M. (ed.). 1986. *Handbook of Research on Teaching*. (3rd Ed.). New York: Macmillan.

Wode, H. 1976. 'Developmental sequences in naturalistic L2 acquisition'. *Working Papers on Bilingualism* 11: 1–13.

Wode, H. 1977. 'The L2 acquisition of /r/'. *Phonetica* 34: 200–17.

Wode, H. 1978. 'The L1 vs. L2 acquisition of English negation'. *Working Papers on Bilingualism* 15: 37–57.

Wode, H. 1980. 'Phonology in L2 acquisition' in Felix (ed.) 1980a.

Wode, H. 1981. *Learning a Second Language 1: an Integrated View of Language Acquisition*. Tübingen: Gunter Narr.

Wode, H. 1984. 'Some theoretical implications of L2 acquisition research' in Davies et al. (eds.) 1984.

Wode, H., A. Rohde, F. Gassen, B. Weiss, M. Jekat, and P. Jung. 1992. 'L1, L2, L3: continuity vs. discontinuity in lexical acquisition' in Arnaud and Bejoint (eds.) 1992.

Wolfram, W. 1985. 'Variability in tense marking: a case for the obvious'. *Language Learning* 35: 229–53.

Wolfram. W. 1989. 'Systematic variability in second-language tense marking' in Eisenstein (ed.) 1989.

Wolfram, W. 1991. 'Interlanguage variation: a review article'. *Applied Linguistics* 12: 102–6.

Wolfson, N. 1976. 'Speech events and natural speech: some implications for sociolinguistic methodology'. *Language in Society* 5: 182–209.

Wolfson, N. 1983. 'Rules of speaking' in Richards and Schmidt (eds.) 1983.

Wolfson, N. 1989a. *Perspectives: Sociolinguistics and TESOL*. Rowley, Mass.: Newbury House.

Wolfson, N. 1989b. 'The social dynamics of native and nonnative variation in complimenting behavior' in Eisenstein (ed.) 1989.

Wolfson, N. and E. Judd (eds.). 1983. *Sociolinguistics and Second Language Acquisition*. Rowley, Mass.: Newbury House.

Wolfson, N., T. Marmor, and S. Jones. 1989. 'Problems in the comparison of speech acts across cultures' in Blum-Kulka et al. (eds.) 1989b.

Wong, H. 1934. 'The best English: a claim for the superiority of received standard English'. *Society for Pure English* 39: 603–21.

Wong-Fillmore, L. 1976. 'The second time around: cognitive and social strategies in second language acquisition'. Unpublished PhD thesis, Stanford University.

Wong-Fillmore, L. 1979. 'Individual differences in second language acquisition' in Fillmore et al. (eds.) 1979.

Wong-Fillmore, L. 1982. 'Instructional language as linguistic input: second language learning in classrooms' in Wilkinson (ed.) 1982.

Wong-Fillmore, L. 1985. 'When does teacher talk work as input?' in Gass and Madden (eds.) 1985.

Wong-Fillmore, L. 1992. 'Learning a language from learners' in Kramsch and McConnell-Ginet (eds.) 1992.

Wu, Z. 1981. 'Speech act—apology'. Los Angeles: ESL Section, Department of English, UCLA.

Yamazaki, A. 1991. 'The effect of interaction on second language comprehension and acquisition'. Unpublished paper, Tokyo: Temple University Japan.

Yorio, C., K. Perkin, and J. Schachter (eds.). 1979. *On TESOL '79*. Washington D.C.: TESOL.

Yoshida, M. 1978. 'The acquisition of English vocabulary by a Japanese-speaking child' in Hatch (ed.) 1978a.

Yoshioka, K. and T. Doi. 1988. 'Testing the Pienemann-Johnston model with Japanese: a speech-processing view of the acquisition of particles and word order'. Paper presented at the 8th Second Language Research Forum, Hawaii, University of Hawaii.

Young, D. 1986. 'The relationship between anxiety and foreign language oral proficiency ratings'. *Foreign Language Annals* 19: 439–45.

Young, R. 1988a. 'Variation and the interlanguage hypothesis'. *Studies in Second Language Acquisition* 10: 281–302.

Young, R. 1988b. 'Input and interaction'. *Annual Review of Applied Linguistics* 9: 122–34.

Young, R. 1989. 'Ends and means: methods for the study of interlanguage variation' in Gass et al. (eds.) 1989b.

Young, R. 1991. *Variation in Interlanguage Morphology*. New York: Peter Lang.

Young, R. 1993. 'Functional constraints on variation in interlanguage morphology'. *Applied Linguistics* 14: 76–97.

Young, R. and C. Doughty. 1987. 'Negotiation in context: a review of research' in Lantolf and Labarca (eds.) 1987.

Yule, G. and D. McDonald. 1990. 'Resolving referential conflicts in L2 interaction: the effect of proficiency and interactive role'. *Language Learning* 40: 539–56.

Zobl, H. 1980a. 'The formal and developmental selectivity of L1 influence on L2 acquisition'. *Language Learning* 30: 43–57.

Zobl, H. 1980b. 'Developmental and transfer errors: their common bases and (possibly) differential effects on subsequent learning'. *TESOL Quarterly* 14: 469–79.

Zobl, H. 1982. 'A direction for contrastive analsysis: the comparative study of developmental sequences'. *TESOL Quarterly* 16: 169–83.

Zobl, H. 1983a. 'Contact-induced language change, learner-language, and the potentials of a modified contrastive analysis' in Bailey et al. (eds.) 1983.

Zobl, H. 1983b. 'Markedness and the projection problem'. *Language Learning* 33: 293–313.

Zobl, H. 1984. 'Cross-language generalizations and the contrastive dimension of the interlanguage hypothesis' in Davies et al. (eds.) 1984.

Zobl, H. 1985. 'Grammars in search of input and intake' in Gass and Madden (eds.) 1985.

Zobl, H. 1986. 'Word order typology, lexical government, and the prediction of multiple, graded effects in L2 word order'. *Language Learning* 36: 159–83.

Zobl, H. 1988. 'Configurationality and the subset principle: the acquisition of "V" by Japanese learners of English' in Pankhurst et al. (eds.) 1988.

Zobl, H. 1989. 'Canonical typological structures and ergativity in English L2 acquisition' in Gass and Schachter (eds.) 1989.

Zuengler, J. 1989. 'Assessing an interactive paradigm: how accommodative should we be?' in Eisenstein (ed.) 1989.

Author index

Subject index

The Index covers the Introduction, Parts One to Seven, and the Glossary.

Entries are arranged in letter-by-letter alphabetical order, in which spaces between words are ignored; 'bilingualism' is therefore listed after 'bilingual classrooms' and before 'bilingual settings'.

References to chapter notes are indicated by page and note number, e.g. 'capacity 157n9'. Glossary references are indicated by 'g'.

distributional bias principle 380
divergence 128, 209–10, 525n2
divergent thinkers 500
domain
  discourse 149
  error analysis 70, 71n10
domains, universe of hypotheses 338
double-markings 172
downgrading
  apologies 175
  requests 167
downward convergence 128, 265
downward divergence 128, 265
drills, overdrilling 60
dual access view, UG 453, 455, 456
Dual Knowledge Paradigm 364
dual relevance of input 279
dynamic paradigm 125–7, 129–30, 133, 366

EA *see* error analysis
E-approach *see* externalized approach
Early School Personality Questionnaire 521
echoic functions, teachers' questions 588
Ecological Validity Hypothesis 378
editing by feel 409–10n5
educational contexts 222–8, 229
educational settings 25, 214–16, 700g
effective students, good language learners 550
effort 511, 512
EFT (Embedded Figures Test) 525n4
elaboration
  foreigner talk 254–5, 256
  interlanguage development 31
  strategy 536, 540
elaborative modifications 275
elaborative simplification 265, 383–4, 700g
elicitation 50, 670, 672–3
Embedded Figures Test 525n4
embedding 370
'embroidering' 259, 264
emergent properties, PDP 406
empathy 518, 519
encoding device, PDP 406
enrichment theory, bilingualism 223
environmental factors, relation to age 492–3
environments 125
epenthesis 112, 116n11, 253
epistemic functions, teachers' questions 588
epistemic sources of error 58
error analysis 18–20, 47–72, 139, 701g
error evaluation 48, 63–7, 701g

error gravity 66–7, 701g
errors 700–1g
  classification 61
  description 43–57
  evaluation 63–7
  explanation 57–63
  identification 50–4
  intralingual *see* intralingual errors
  negative transfer 301–2
  repair 262
error treatment 583–6, 701g
essential conditions, illocutionary acts 160
ethnic identity 207–10
ethnocentrism 199–200
ethnography 116n13, 164, 206, 566, 568–9, 701g
ethnolinguistic vitality 234
European Science Foundation Project in Second Language Acquisition by Adult Immigrants 98, 369, 370
exchanges, classroom discourse 574
execution phase 398
exemplar-based representation 410n13
expansions, promoting development 269
experience *see* language learning experience
experiential instruction 576
experiential teaching v. analytic teaching 571–2
experimental elicitation 50, 670, 672, 690n4
expert learners *see* good language learners
explanation, goal of SLA research 38
explanatory adequacy 429–30, 701–2g
explicit instruction 642–3, 661n9
explicit knowledge v. explicit knowledge 31, 349–50, 355–63, 441–2, 653, 702g
expressive learners v. referential learners 508
expressives, L1 acquisition 79
extent, error analysis 70, 71n10
external factors 16, 17, 24–8, 354
externalized approach 415, 702g
external modification 167, 172
external variation 127
extraction, markedness 320–1
extravergence 129
extrinsic motivation 36
extroversion/introversion 518, 520–2, 525n5, 702g
Eysenck Personality Inventory 519

face-threatening acts 167, 168, 174, 178
facilitating anxiety 482–3
facilitation